Sodbusting
to
Subdivision

With these verses from Ecclesiastes in mind; "1:4, One generation passeth away and another generation cometh: but the earth abideth forever. 1:9, The thing that hath been, it is that which shall be; and that which is done is that which shall be done: and there is no new thing under the sun," we present Sodbusting to Subdivision.

Copyright — 287517, Register 246
Standard Book No. 0-919213-86-3
Published by
De Winton & District Historical Committee
Box 42
De Winton, Alberta
Printed by
Friesen Printers
5720 Macleod Trail S.
Calgary, Alberta
Head Office: Altona, Manitoba

DEDICATION

The DeWinton and District Historical Society is proud to present this book in memory and in appreciation of early pioneers of the districts whose histories have been collected within this book. We hope their descendants will treasure the spirit of adventure, and the courage that they displayed and the hardships that they endured, in order that we should have a better future for ourselves and the generations that will follow.

"Homestead Kitchen"

By ELEANOR OLTEAN.

"Homestead Kitchen", painted in 1966, is my childhood memory of our farm kitchen of many years ago, while living in the country close to Midnapore, Alberta; where my parents engaged in mixed farming. During those years many happy hours were spent in this kitchen.

The painting depicts early morning in the fall of the year, with the breakfast sausages cooking before sunrise and a book still lying on the table from the previous evening's few leisurely moments.

The glow of a wood and coal stove hold memories of warmth and comfort for many. The sound of the crackling wood in the firebox, with its fragrance of burning green willow; the singing of a boiling kettle; the aroma of good home cooking and the ticking of the old kitchen clock all bring to mind a feeling of nostalgia.

Home baking of bread was a necessity. The large yellow ochre drum held over one hundred pounds of flour. The green container on the top of it stored the crusty fresh bread and was refilled every second or third day. The dish cupboard to the right was made of old packing cases. On the top of the cupboard the high tin held bolts, nails, etc. The red tin contained Old Virginia pipe tobacco, smoked by my father. Coal oil for the lamps was kept in the large jug and the same in the container with the long spout. The latter was used to bring a quick flame when lighting the fire in the cook stove, there was no danger of its contents becoming ignited.

The little bag hanging on the side of the cupboard held bits of string. The curtain always sagged for the string on which it hung never remained taught.

The Hudson Bay calendar was one of the largest and most scenic in those days and always helped to brighten a dreary kitchen wall, suffering from smoke, steam and drastic changes of temperature. A few hours away from home with no one to stoke the fires could drop the thermometer by thirty degrees, during cold weather.

Fly coils hung from all farm ceilings and usually had the best catch when hung in the warmth and the cooking aromas of the kitchen.

The floor was of rough boards and required frequent sweeping and scrubbing. The broom soon became worn and shapeless and always developed a point on one side of the bristles, which was very good for sweeping out the corners and the chips from around the wood box.

What a welcome of warmth the farm kitchen held when coming in from out-of-doors on a cold winter's day. Many long winter evenings were spent with us all seated around the kitchen stove in the dimness of lamp light, listening to stories read or told by my mother, who often gave up her limited leisure time to the enjoyment of her children.

Our Sodbusters

Olive Aldridge   Harry Bamford   Alex Blackwood   Ina Blackwood   Eben Bremner   Lloyd Fraser

Milt Grant   Bill Hamilton   Tom Hebson   Evelyn Herr   Forest Herr   Norman Hogge

Anne Jones   Idwal Jones   Iorwerth (Ed.) Jones   Otto Larson   Effie Leach   Les Marshall

Albert McKevitt   Jack Morash   Margaret Morash   Stella Nelubowich   Howard Norris   Laura Norris

George Riches   Pearl Riches   Grace Suitor   Jim Suitor   Walter Turnbull   Norman Waddell

The Sodbusters who were responsible for financial assistance through New Horizon Grant from the Federal Government.

FOREWORD—by M.M. (Bobby) Lee

In the not too distant past, most of us thought of history as being a record of uninteresting events that had happened a long time ago, in some far away place.

A few years ago, when some Canadian communities published the histories of their areas, it became evident that history is very interesting. Other districts began to realize, to their regret, that many important events in their areas had gone unrecorded. In order to salvage what they could of their lost heritage, they began to form committees, in their communities, to collect stories pertaining to their regions, and to prepare them for publication. Now, wherever you go, the prized possession of most people is a volume of the history of their own district.

The area south of Calgary holds many memories for me. My grandparents, George and Madeleine Hodgson, had passed through this region several times, in their Red River carts, before coming to settle here. In 1881, when my grandfather was hired to be farm instructor and interpreter on the Sarcee Indian Reserve, the family made their home on government land, at the Bow River, the present site of Burns' Ranch. In 1884 they moved to the Sarcee Indian Agency.

Shortly after his arrival at the Bow, my grandfather went in search of two of his horses that had strayed. He found them in Fish Creek Valley, grazing contentedly on the long prairie grass, amidst a great herd of buffalo.

He thought, "What a beautiful place. I would like to live here." And he did.

This was the very place that my parents bought in 1918, and where I was born and raised. In 1921 Grandpa and Grandma Hodgson came to live with us.

The Fish Creek Valley is the area that I know best. Many of us from that region attended Midnapore school, and fought our battles there. As we advanced to the higher grades, we were caught up in the craze of team sports. I think that all readers must remember those very important fast ball games that were held at De Winton, Red Deer Lake, Glenmore, and Midnapore schools. Every fall we looked forward to the school fairs at Red Deer Lake, where the students of the surrounding districts would congregate, to compete for prizes in the art, cooking and baking, handicrafts, livestock, vegetable, and grain classes, as well as in track and field.

During the depression years, residents of this area used to gather to view the exciting hockey and fast ball games that were held at De Winton, Westoe, Red Deer Lake, and Midnapore. Following World War II people congregated again at Red Deer Lake, during the time that the popular curling rink was in operation.

About three years ago the old-timers south of Calgary began to meet again—this time to undertake the biggest project of all times—to collect, and to prepare for publication, pictures and stories of the region, in an attempt to capture, and to preserve, a bygone era. Because of the persevering effort on the part of those who formed the history committees, all of us who have in any way been connected with that area shall have the pride of possessing a volume of the region just south of Calgary.

ACKNOWLEDGEMENTS

For the content of this publication we are indebted to many faithful people who worked tireless hours researching, gathering, typing, proofreading, compiling and assembling this book. The executive members of the De Winton and District Historical Society are as follows:

Jean Marshall: President
Ruth Lynch: Vice President
Anne Jones: Secretary
Virginia Jacobson and
Russell Martin: Treasurer
Les Marshall: Director
Eben Bremner: Director
Walter Turnbull: Director
Russell Martin: Director
Ernie Cole: Director
Walter Poffenroth: Director
Grace Suitor: Director
Harold Biswanger: Director
Albert McKevitt: Director

Photo committee: Harold Biswanger, Esther Jenkins, Dorothy Gerlitz, Ruth Hamilton, Albert McKevitt.

Sketches: Phylis Teskey, David Teskey, Olive Thompson. Animals, birds and flowers sketched in this book are or have been native to the area.

Maps: Harold Biswanger for research work. Cover by: Eleanor Oltean.

Brands: David Jenkins, Olive Thompson for researching and compiling.

Special recognition to Ina Blackwood and Effie Leach for work on Davisburg.

Typing, proofreading and photos: Sandra Neish, Dorothy Gerlitz, Ruth Lynch, Elsie Sharam, Betty Cole, Judith Adam, Grace Suitor, Lillian Irving, Doreen Powell, Esther Kwiat, Connie Hunt, Beverley Bews, Margaret Norris, Sharon Geddes, Sharon Hamilton, Reta Reynolds, Trisha Jones, David Jenkins, Provincial Archives, Edmonton; Glenbow-Alberta Institute, Georgeen Barrass; Canada Post Office; New Horizons Program, Department of Health and Welfare Canada, the De Winton Community Association Alberta Culture, Historical Resources Edmonton.

Memories are fond and dear, but facts we do forget. For any errors or omissions in this book we sincerely apologize.

TABLE OF CONTENTS

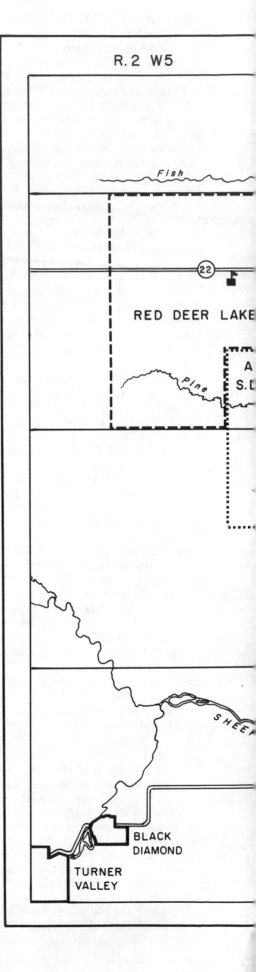

THE NINE SCHOOL DISTRICTS

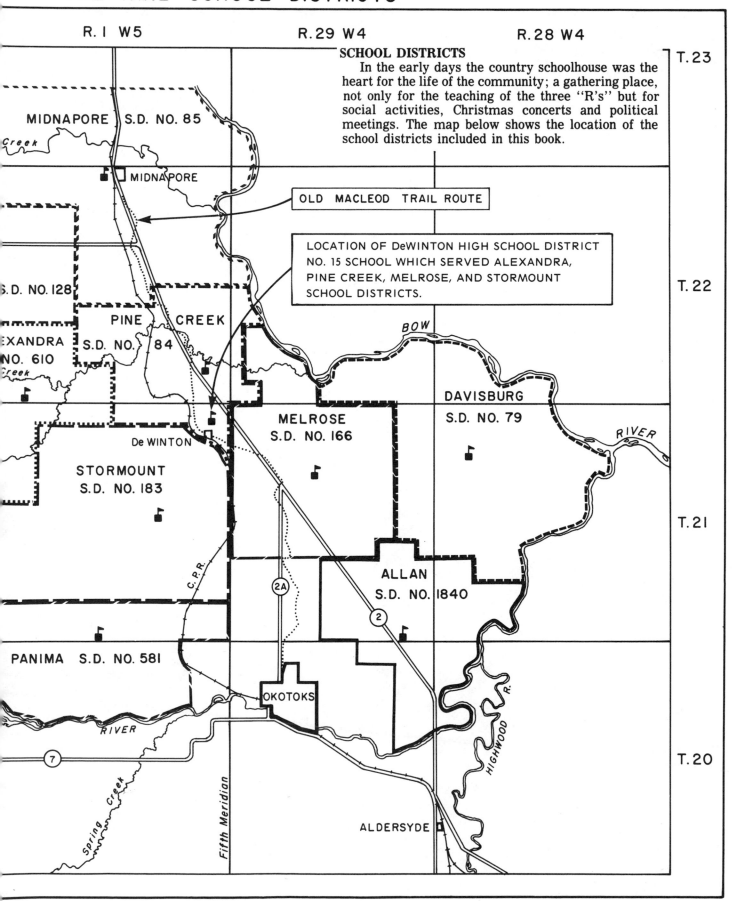

R. I W5   R. 29 W4   R. 28 W4

SCHOOL DISTRICTS

In the early days the country schoolhouse was the heart for the life of the community; a gathering place, not only for the teaching of the three "R's" but for social activities, Christmas concerts and political meetings. The map below shows the location of the school districts included in this book.

MIDNAPORE S.D. NO. 85

MIDNAPORE

OLD MACLEOD TRAIL ROUTE

LOCATION OF DeWINTON HIGH SCHOOL DISTRICT NO. 15 SCHOOL WHICH SERVED ALEXANDRA, PINE CREEK, MELROSE, AND STORMOUNT SCHOOL DISTRICTS.

S.D. NO. 128

PINE CREEK
S.D. NO. 84

XANDRA
NO. 610

BOW

DAVISBURG
S.D. NO. 79

RIVER

MELROSE
S.D. NO. 166

De WINTON

STORMOUNT
S.D. NO. 183

ALLAN
S.D. NO. 1840

C.P.R.

2A

2

PANIMA S.D. NO. 581

OKOTOKS

RIVER

7

HIGHWOOD R.

Fifth Meridian

Spring Creek

ALDERSYDE

T. 23

T. 22

T. 21

T. 20

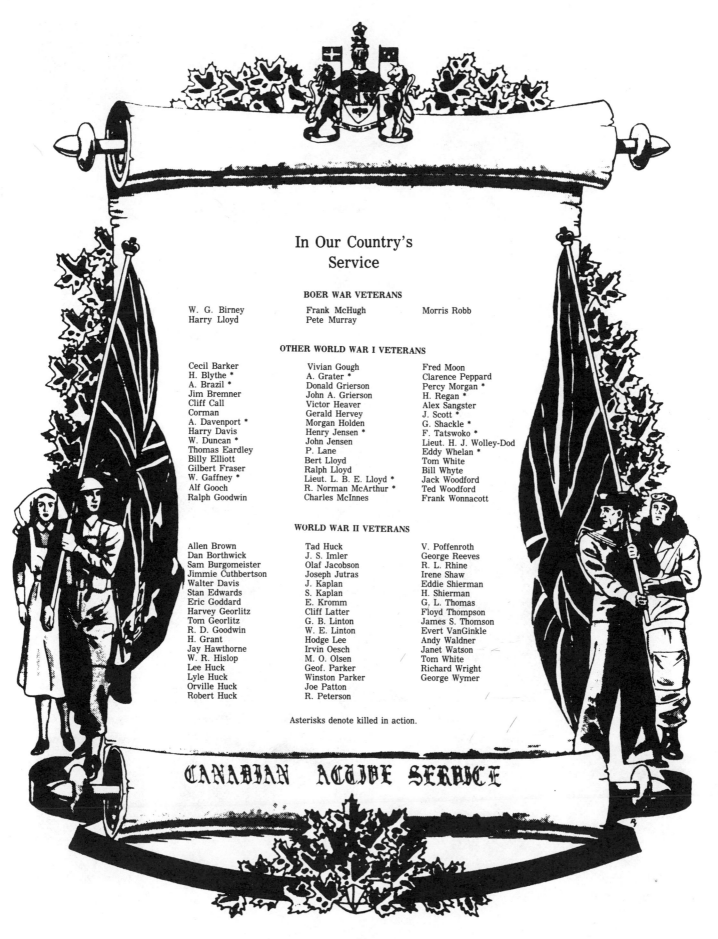

In Our Country's Service

BOER WAR VETERANS

W. G. Birney	Frank McHugh	Morris Robb
Harry Lloyd	Pete Murray	

OTHER WORLD WAR I VETERANS

Cecil Barker	Vivian Gough	Fred Moon
H. Blythe *	A. Grater *	Clarence Peppard
A. Brazil *	Donald Grierson	Percy Morgan *
Jim Bremner	John A. Grierson	H. Regan *
Cliff Call	Victor Heaver	Alex Sangster
Corman	Gerald Hervey	J. Scott *
A. Davenport *	Morgan Holden	G. Shackle *
Harry Davis	Henry Jensen *	F. Tatswoko *
W. Duncan *	John Jensen	Lieut. H. J. Wolley-Dod
Thomas Eardley	P. Lane	Eddy Whelan *
Billy Elliott	Bert Lloyd	Tom White
Gilbert Fraser	Ralph Lloyd	Bill Whyte
W. Gaffney *	Lieut. L. B. E. Lloyd *	Jack Woodford
Alf Gooch	R. Norman McArthur *	Ted Woodford
Ralph Goodwin	Charles McInnes	Frank Wonnacott

WORLD WAR II VETERANS

Allen Brown	Tad Huck	V. Poffenroth
Dan Borthwick	J. S. Imler	George Reeves
Sam Burgomeister	Olaf Jacobson	R. L. Rhine
Jimmie Cuthbertson	Joseph Jutras	Irene Shaw
Walter Davis	J. Kaplan	Eddie Shierman
Stan Edwards	S. Kaplan	H. Shierman
Eric Goddard	E. Kromm	G. L. Thomas
Harvey Georlitz	Cliff Latter	Floyd Thompson
Tom Georlitz	G. B. Linton	James S. Thomson
R. D. Goodwin	W. E. Linton	Evert VanGinkle
H. Grant	Hodge Lee	Andy Waldner
Jay Hawthorne	Irvin Oesch	Janet Watson
W. R. Hislop	M. O. Olsen	Tom White
Lee Huck	Geof. Parker	Richard Wright
Lyle Huck	Winston Parker	George Wymer
Orville Huck	Joe Patton	
Robert Huck	R. Peterson	

Asterisks denote killed in action.

CANADIAN ACTIVE SERVICE

**Boer
War**

Roderick MacRae

E. R. Mattless

**World
War
I**

Willie Cope

Russell Evans

Desmond Fitzgerald

William C. Gibbard

Henry H. Harper

Colonel H. C. A.
Harcourt Hervey

David Jamison

Stuart Jamison

Joe Johnson

Major and Mrs. Ralph Lloyd

Lt. J. A. Macdonald

Thomas McKevitt

Ervie Miller

Chas. Stockford

Will Turnbull

David Wylie

John William Butz

**World
War
II**

Bill Aldridge

Bill Anderson

| Robert Anderson | Angus Andrews | David Armstrong | Jack Armstrong | Allan W. Balderson |

| Bruce Balderson | Cecil Barker | Harry Barker | James Neil Blackwood | Jack Cameron |

| Wallace Cameron | Keith Carothers | Flying Officer Carr | James Carson | Melvin Christensen |

| Fred Cole | Tom Coulter | Boyd Cuthbertson | Larry Des Jardine | Robin Ecklin |

| Harold Fox | Dan Gerlitz | F. O. Campbell Gibbard R.C.A.F. | Douglas Gibbard | Sandy Giffen |

13

Harvey L. Gordanier 91 R.C.A. 30

Norman Graham

Harold Grant

James Hadden

Hugh Hamilton, Jr.

Ted Heaver

Vic Heaver

Jack Beatty, Henderson, H. Hervey

Jack Hogan

Harvey Hogge

Myfanwy Holden

Charles Hughes

Ross Hyde

Cecil Irving

Tom Irving

David Jamison

Arthur W. Jenkins

George Johnson

Graham Johnson

Ed. Kunder

Clifford Latter

Ted Lee

Walter Linn

Jim Macdonald

Don McKenzie

Daniel McNab

George McNab

Jack McNeill and Jack Ross

Joe Meehan

Richard Meehan and friend

Sergeant Dorothy Day R.C.A.F. and Pilot Officer Jack Miller, 1945.

Jack Miller

Fil Noel

L. to R. Bill Norrie, Bill Powell, Oliver Anderson, George Norrie

Harold Norris

Howard Norris

Lent Orton

Martin Poffenroth

Victor Poffenroth

Alfred Priest

Ron and Lyle Renard

William (Scotty) Rodger

Wilfred Sleno

Herb Stephenson   Jim Teeling   Walter Turnbull   Bill Wedderburn   John D. Wedderburn

John Wilson   Mary Wonnacott   R. to L. W. J. Norrie, Harry Anderson, Red Steele, George Norrie, Ted Allwarden, Archie Anderson, Jack Rudd, Bill Powell, Rudd's brother lost in air mission overseas.

Old Cars

John Currie's first car; L. to R. Etta (Forckel), Mabel (Wilson), Mrs. Currie, Wellie, Mr. Currie. (A 1910 Maxwell)

Alec S. Blackwood and his first car, 1916.

L. to R. Leta Shattuck, H. Banister, Mrs. Shattuck, Mr. Shattuck. 1914 Ford.

Cliff Suitor's car — Lucy (Adams) Davenport driving — 1923.

Frank Coyle's first car. Model T, 1924.

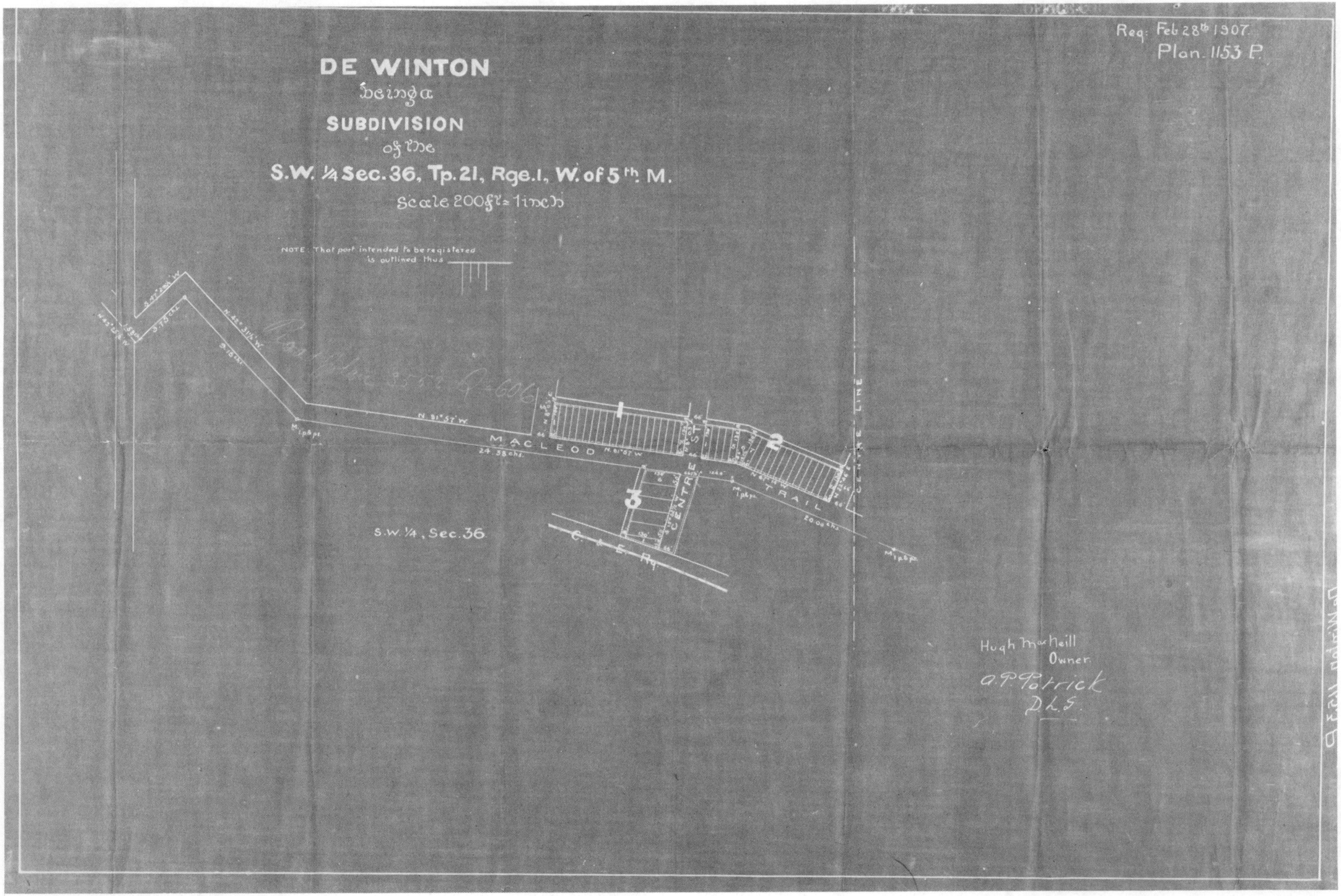

Reg: Feb 28th 1907
Plan 1153 P.

DE WINTON

being a

SUBDIVISION

of the

S.W. ¼ Sec. 36, Tp. 21, Rge. 1, W. of 5th M.

Scale 200 ft = 1 inch

NOTE: That part intended to be registered is outlined thus

Hugh Mitchell Owner
appatrick D.L.S.

CENTRE LINE

TRAIL

CENTRE ST.

MACLEOD ROAD

S.W. ¼ Sec. 36

1 2 3

De Winton

DE WINTON

De Winton came into being in 1892 with the arrival of the C.P.R. Colonel Francis De Winton (later Sr. Francis), Secretary to the Marquis of Lorne, Governor General of Canada, was the gentleman for whom it was named. The site was chosen because of the long hill to the north-west making it necessary to have a side track for sections of the longer trains that went through. Academy siding was established for the same reason and is still used as a side track although there is no other activity there.

In the beginning everything came by rail and travelling salesmen were in evidence most of the time. Stockyards appeared on the north side of the track just east of the station. Mr. Pashak had a store and a machine shed, there was a blacksmith shop and several houses. Grain and livestock were the main products shipped out and all grain was hauled with teams and shovelled by hand. When coal cars arrived they were emptied by hand as well and some men developed the art of shovelling to a high degree, being able to carry on for long periods of time without tiring. They claimed there was a real knack to it. All groceries came by rail and, of course, the mail. With the increased transient population it became necessary to find a place to feed and sometimes bed these people. Mrs. Willford, wife of the section foreman was the first one to offer meals and a limited boarding house. Soon the DeMings family started a stopping house "Minto House" which was the only other official stopping place ever in De Winton.

W. R. Macdonald had a vision of a large town being built on the site and acquired the surrounding land and had it surveyed into lots. Before the outbreak of W.W. I the peak of activity had been reached. There was a pool hall, livery stable, Anglican church, cabinet maker, blacksmith, store, dance hall and stopping house as well as several homes. The town never developed much beyond that point and soon began to shrink. The livery stable burned down as well as the blacksmith shop. The Anglican church was closed and the building became the new blacksmith shop. A garage flourished for a few years and died, the hall was closed and a new one erected, the cabinet maker left and, as cars became more prevalent, goods began to move on the roads rather than the rails. A high school to serve five school districts was in use for about 20 years and is now a part of the Community Centre.

Today the only business is a general store and a privately owned fertilizer operation. As a center of community activity De Winton still survives with the United church and the community center as the local gathering places.

The hamlet of De Winton lies within the borders of Pine Creek School District and the histories of the residents will be found under Pine Creek.

De Winton about 1906; machine shed, store, blacksmith shop, livery stable, Minto House.

De Winton 1914; Streeter Hall, Murray house, blacksmith shop, Willett house, store, Minto House, Anglican Church, Brinton house.

De Winton picnic — about 1918.

Tug-of-war. De Winton picnic about 1918.

Sack Race. De Winton picnic about 1918.

De Winton Garage about 1927

Minto House — about 1910.

Grandmother's Tea — De Winton 1938. Front row, l. to r.; Mona Macdonald, Reta Currie, Ruth Anderson, Doris Currie. 2nd row; Mrs. Frank Wonnacott, Mrs. J. Cole, Mrs. J. Hogge, Mrs. Patterson, Mrs. R. MacRae, Mrs. H. Banister, Mrs. Jack Dalzell, Mrs. C. Marshall, Mrs. E. Grant. 3rd row; ?, Mrs. Ed Hayes, Annie Everson, Mrs. W. Overand, Mrs. J. Carothers, Mrs. J. Martin, Mrs. T. McIvor. 4th row; Mrs. A. E. Fraser, Mrs. D. Herr, Audrey Sutherland, June Cole, Ella Hamilton, Dolly Dalzell, Mary Meehan, Margaret Goettler. 5th row; Mrs. Harold Grant, Mrs. Sid Mattock, ?, Cora Martin, Margaret Aggett, Mrs. Henry Poffenroth, Mrs. Alex Anderson. 6th row; Mrs. R. Brown, Lila Hillard, Agnes Martin, Eleanor Macdonald, Cynthia Bremner, Alison McNeill, Mrs. John Harrison, Mary Graham. Back row; Jean Marshall, Mrs. E. Currie, Mrs. G. Heaver, Mary Dick, Ruth Peppard, Mabel Wilson.

On the steps of the new De Winton Hall about 1919. L. to R.; Earl, Wenty, Goldy, ?, Travis, Paul, ?, (Brinton), Oneil twins, Don and Murray, Lucy Brinton.

De Winton General Store. Taken December, 1939.

Alberta's 60th anniversary 1965. l. to r. Margaret Norris, Sam Desjardine, Laura Norris, Cora Martin, Mel Martin, Howard Norris, Gordon Grant, Gilbert Young, Tom Dalzell.

De Winton U.F.W.A., 1933. Back row l. to r. Mary Dick, Claude Dalzell, Annie Everson, Bessie Heaver, Mrs. A. P. Bremner, Mrs. J. Sheepy, ?, Mrs. Shattuck, Dolly Dalzell, Cynthia Bremner, Middle; Maggie Jamison, Mrs. Andrews, Sarah Dalzell, Isabella Hamilton, Front; Marion Dalzell, holding Shirley Jamison, Jessie Dalzell, Mabel Wilson holding Andrew.

Local gathering at De Winton about 1953. Top row l. to r.; Mrs. A. Giffen, Mrs. C. Burkitt, Annie Everson, Mary Graham, Dolly Dalzell, Lois Knupp with Karen, Carrie Desjardine, Mary Dick, kneeling; Jennie Poffenroth, Louise ?, Ruby Graham, Annie Chernow, Muriel Heaver, Bertha King. Children; Larry Knupp, Joyce Heaver, Barry Poffenroth.

DE WINTON, SIR FRANCIS

De Winton was named after Major-General Sir Francis De Winton, G.C.M.G., C.B. (1835-1901), military secretary to the Marquis of Lorne, Governor General from 1878 to 1883. He organized the De Winton Ranch Company, also known as Brecon Ranch.

In Barneby's book, "Far West Life and Labour", he gives an account of his visit to this part of the country. He arrived in 1883 on a special train and after reaching the end of the steel, travelled, in company with Colonel Williams, to several farms and ranches south of Calgary.

The Bow crossing, by ferry, was situated east of the Glenn ranch near the confluence of the Bow and Fish Creek. Prices for the crossing were listed as: 1 horse; 100 cents: 2-150: Horse and rider; 50 cents: Cow or sheep; 25.

The De Winton Ranch was across the river and De Winton's two sons crossed in a small boat and took the visitors, one at a time, across to the ranch. Their house was described as being a 24' x 18' log house, earth floored. The ranch was six by five miles. It is not recorded just when the ranch was established nor how long it was in operation.

DE WINTON RURAL HIGH SCHOOL No. 15.

During the summer of 1930 it was decided that a high school was a necessity at De Winton to accommodate pupils from Melrose, Stormont, Alexandra and Pine Creek. These schools were required to make an annual contribution, depending on the number of pupils per district. It was necessary to have at least sixteen pupils to qualify for the government grant. Mr. Russell Evans was Secretary-Treasurer of the board from its beginning to closure.

While construction was being completed on the building, the first classes commenced in September at the "Minto House." Grade eight: Travis Brinton, Norman Graham, Jean Anderson. Grade nine: Jean McNeill, Reta Currie, Doris Currie, Lawrence Norris, Sheila McNeill, Alice Standish. Grade ten: Goldie Brinton, Margaret Wylie, Alma Merkle, Grace Murray, Muriel Grant. Grade eleven: Helen Dowling, Ralph Grant. In December of that year, teacher, Marjorie Winspear, moved, with her pupils, to the new high school. It boasted a science room, a library room and a tennis court where the present skating rink is located. A barn was necessary as some pupils rode horseback for many miles, probably those riding the farthest would be the Holden family. The teacher's salary was $1200.00 per year. Expenses would be higher for the first few years because of debentures, notes and interest charges.

De Winton High School 1932. Inez Irvine teacher. Back Row: L. to R. Muriel Grant, Max Demings, Murray Demings, Norman Graham, Travis Brinton, Reta Currie. Middle Row: L. to R. Doris Currie, Goldie Brinton, Frank Jacobs, Jean Anderson, Grace Murray. Front Row: L. to R. Inez Irvine, Jean McNeill, George Dunn, Leslie Norris, Sheila McNeill.

The following September, Inez Irving took over classes and stayed, for the one year. In September, 1932 Winnifred Fagan accepted the position of teacher and stayed on until June, 1936. During her years in De Winton, Miss Fagan boarded with the Eversons and took part in many community activities. It was customary for the teacher to keep the school tidy and also stoke up the coal furnace when necessary.

Gwen Barroll became teacher in the fall of 1936 and taught until June 1940. It is interesting to note that the class of '37 has held reunion every five years since that time with Miss Barroll, who lives in the U.S.A., attending all of them.

Elizabeth Sudre was the next and last teacher, commencing with the fall term, 1940 and continuing until the school was temporarily closed June, 1943, due to lack of students. During this time the W. B. Martin family occupied the building for approximately two years, after the De Winton store burned down in January, 1944.

Annual De Winton School Fair, 1937. L. to R. Jeanne Van Tighem, Louise Van Tighem, Allen Dick.

De Winton High School 1937-38. Front Row: Pat Marshall, Marion Dalzell, Jean Wylie, Alma Horricks, Ivadel Wylie, Barbara Carothers. Middle Row: Muriel Haddon, Kitty Harper, Martha Kromm, Margaret Hamilton, Elsie Giffen, Ruby Hart, Betty Pearson, Gwen Barrol. Back Row: Hugh Hamilton, Jack Ross, Myfanwy Holden, Les Gilmour, Jack Horricks, Howard Norris, Ted Heaver, Eddie Shierman.

De Winton High School. Back Row: Harold Schaber, Allan Dick, Jack Evans, Miss Sudre, Bob Martin, Wally Krom, Ron Martin. Middle Row: George Martin, Billy Watson, Shirley Jamison, Vera Evans, Jane Sangster, Catherine Norris, Jack Meehan. Front Row: Sheila Marshall, Hermina Nemeth, Lorena Fox, Lloyd Fox.

De Winton High School 1954. Back Row: L. to R. Mary Gorral, Doreen Marshall, Elaine Goddard, Virginia Graham, Miss Sudre, Marcel Van Tighem, LeRoy Rudd. Seated: Harvey Marshall, Robert Poffenroth.

Classes started again in September, 1946 with Miss Sudre as teacher and staying in the teacherage which had been located in the school yard. The final closing was in June, 1955 and the pupils were bused to Okotoks thereafter.

Foothills School Division sold the school building and 4.8 acres of grounds to the De Winton Community Association September 25, 1964 for the sum of $1,000.00

INEZ A. IRVINE (MRS. E. W. PRATER)

From 1931 to 1932, I taught the De Winton High School following Miss M. Winspear. It was through Mr. Kerslake, that I was accepted by the School Board. I was a school chum of Eva Kerslake and was her Bridesmaid in September 1931.

Mr. and Mrs. Jim Everson made my stay in their home very happy.

Nineteen pupils attended the school in grades eight to eleven. The school day started at 8.30 with Latin class and lasted until 3.30. After Christmas, the De Mings boys arrived from Lethbridge and I had classes in chemistry with them from 4.30 to 5.30.

We had a good turnout for our Hallowe'en party at the school with lots of fun.

For our Christmas concert we put on a three act play — "Mighty Like a Rose". The district had a drama club and put on several plays during the year.

My memories of De Winton are very happy.

MEMORIES OF DE WINTON HIGH SCHOOL — by Elizabeth M. (Sudre) Young

When I first came to De Winton the inspector assured me that the students were very ambitious. I found this to be true. They were very cooperative and made teaching very interesting.

There are some things about them that I remember:

Jean Wylie riding horseback a long distance to school in all kinds of weather.

Eleanor Jamison riding to school to do the caretaking of the school. She did a great deal of work in cerebral palsy here in Calgary in later years.

Anna Carothers and Russell Martin going to Calgary once a week to take Grade 12 Chemistry. The teacher took a great interest in their progress and looked forward to their coming each week. Anna became a successful nurse.

I remember two students of rather limited ability, who, through hard work and sheer perseverance, made their matriculation and went on to their chosen careers.

The young Colson boy who lived at the station, made first class honors in Grade 9.

I was touched when I went into the school, after it had been closed, to find a brooch that I had lost there. There was a message written on the board by some student saying they wished they were going back to the school again.

I feel that the people of the De Winton district can be proud of the children they sent to De Winton Rural High School and, for myself, I have many happy memories of the years I spent there.

ANGLICAN CHURCH SAINT PHILLIP AND SAINT JAMES

The Anglican Church, Saint Phillip and Saint James was built on three lots measuring 75' by 130', on part of SW¼ 36-21-1-W5 in 1900. It had a seating capacity of sixty persons. The value of the church was listed as $800.00 and it was free of debt by November 5, 1917. The value of the land was $75.00.

The church was moved into De Winton in 1910 and continued to be used as a place of worship until 1918 when it was purchased and moved to a new location to replace a blacksmith shop that had recently burned. Through the years it served in several capacities and a part of it is still in use as a private garage.

Moving the English Church to De Winton in 1910.

The first minister was Reverend Gervais Gale followed by Reverend Streeter in 1912 and Reverend Church in 1913. Reverend Grant was the last minister when the church was closed in 1917.

ST. ANDREW'S UNITED CHURCH — DeWINTON —
Researched and written by
I. Blackwood

A congregational meeting was held in Pine Creek School House on August 3, 1933 when the question of the erection of a new church was discussed. Some favored the old historic site, while others thought De Winton was the better location. At a meeting in 1934 a discussion was held concerning the amalgamation of Melrose, Pine Creek and De Winton and the results were agreed upon provided the church was built in De Winton.

One acre of the SW¼-36-21-W5 was donated by Mr. W. H. Cushing for the church. The excavation for the basement was begun on October 18, 1934 under the supervision of Mr. Stuart Jamison. The church was built by Mr. Alex Hislop and completed late that year. The first service in the new church was held January 6,

1935 and was conducted by Rev. Warwick Kelloway of Knox United Church in Calgary, assisted by the local minister, Rev. Percy Halstead.

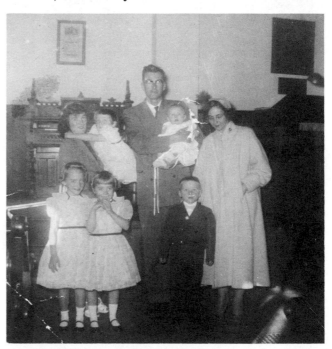

Christening of five eldest Hamilton children. Betty holding Joy, Rev. Bert Loree with Cameron, Jean Marshall. Front: Barbara, Patty and Richard (Buddy). De Winton United Church.

The first Board of Managers were R. Ness, A. T. Dalzell, A. Sangster, S. Jamison, F. Dick, S. Dalzell, A. Anderson, and H. Currie as secretary. It was also resolved that the name of the De Winton Church would be St. Andrew's United Church.

The first organists were Miss Jessie Dalzell, Mrs. Margaret Norris, Russell Martin, and Mrs. Ruth Lynch and Miss Lil Hart.

St. Andrews United Church, De Winton, 1973.

DE WINTON HALLS

The community of De Winton and district has always been very fortunate in having a building available as a center for social events, political, agricultural and sports meetings.

The first of these halls was built by the Pashak family about 1903, and was a General Store operated by the Pashaks, with a second story upstairs which was used as a hall for various meetings and events. Usually when a dance was to be held, it was a formal occasion, and invitations were sent out ahead of time, and also an invitation to come help clean the hall, scrub the floor, and decorate, also dance cards were handed out to the ladies, to be filled in by the men. After a few years, about 1908, the upstairs was used for living quarters and was no longer available, so it was necessary to look elsewhere for an entertainment centre.

First De Winton Hall about 1911.

During these years, one of the most popular forms of entertainment was play acting and concerts, and there were many in the district who were quite active and interested in the arts, as well as being quite accomplished as actors. One of these was the Anglican minister, Mr. Streeter, who helped organize and direct various plays, so it was decided to build a new hall. Not too much is known about the financing and arrangements in the building. One of the committees was comprised of the following: Miss M. Galvin, E. Currie, B. Currie, B. Duncan, D. Allan and J. McNeil. It was built about 1910. The hall was first known as the

The pleasure of the company
of

.... *Mr. & Mrs. L. M. Orton,* ....

is requested

at a

Ladies' Ball

to be held in De Winton Hall

Friday, February sixteenth

Nineteen hundred and seventeen

DANCING AT 9:00 P.M.   SUPPER AT 12:00

MUSIC BY GEBBIE BROS.

Streeter Hall, and was used quite extensively until 1918. The name later was changed to the Usher Hall, when Mr. Usher purchased the General Store and the property of the hall. After the De Winton Community Hall was built in 1918, it was used as a storeroom, a garage, also was used as an indoor skating rink, (which was never successful) and finally due to misuse and decay, was torn down in the 1940's to make room for the new De Winton Store on its site, after the old General Store burned down in 1944. The new De Winton Store is still quite active on the site.

DE WINTON COMMUNITY HALL

On April 20, 1918, a public meeting was held in Mr. Usher's Hall, De Winton, for the purpose of discussing the erection of a Community Hall. Mr. Angus McIntosh chaired the meeting and Jean Bremner was appointed secretary pro-tem. Mr. Usher had already generously donated two, clear title, lots on which to erect the hall and over six hundred and fifty dollars was already promised, it was decided to go ahead with the plans. Mr. Gray moved that four trustees be appointed to finance the building of the hall and Mr. Gallaugher seconded the motion. Mr. Usher, Mr. McIntosh, Mr. King and Mr. Ness became the trustees and Mrs. Gray, Mrs. Bremner, Mr. Brinton, Mr. Fred Dick, Mr. Cushing and Mr. Bryan were appointed as a building committee, with Jean Bremner as secretary. It was decided that a joint meeting of the two committees meet April 27 to discuss the matter further.

At the April 27 meeting a fifth trustee was appointed in the person of Mr. T. N. Martin, and the name of Mr. A. DeMings was added to the building committee. It was suggested the ladies of the Red Cross group be responsible for entertainment, to raise money, to pay off the debt but the following entertainment committee was appointed instead: J. R. McConnell, Mrs. Cushing, T. Dalzell, W. C. Currie, Miss Andrews, Miss Shattuck, Miss Gray and Barsby Martin. Mr. Brinton, chairman of the building committee, told of plans and estimates which he had procured. It was decided to get estimates on two sizes of buildings; 34' x 60' and 40' x 60' as well as estimates for putting in a cement foundation. Mr. Cushing and Mr. Bryan were appointed to be an advisory board to consult with the carpenter in the building of the hall. Mr. Hislop was to be asked to be in charge of the building.

By May 7, 1918, Mr. Brinton had not received any satisfactory information concerning estimates and it was decided to ask Mr. Hislop to make a list of all materials needed to construct a 40' x 60' square front building with a shingled roof and send to the T. Eaton Company at Winnipeg for quotations. Cement and bricks for the chimney were not to be included in the estimate.

A meeting held on May 21 produced much discussion about price estimates that had been submitted. One from T. Eaton for $1,590.91 and one from Prairie Builders for $1,586.87. The lower bid was agreed upon and the figures were to be turned over to Mr. McIntosh who would confer with the other trustees. Mr. King had resigned as trustee, owing to poor health and Mr. Andrews was made the new trustee. Owing to the fear of some of the trustees that the proposed square front would catch too much wind, it was decided that the front should have a jog in it and that the Prairie Builders should get the materials contract.

The trustees held a meeting on June 13 to make arrangements for a loan in order to pay for the materials when they arrived. Mr. Heaver was suggested as a sixth trustee but refused to act in that capacity. Mr. Usher offered the seats from the old hall at a price to be set by disinterested parties and also offered the stoves under the same conditions. Mr. Hislop was asked to value the said items. If $1,200.00 could not be raised from local residents a note was to be put through the Merchant's Bank at Okotoks. By June 15, the certificate of title for the land was available and the secretary was instructed to order 18 barrels of cement and to pay the Prairie Builders for 895 bricks that were already in De Winton. The bricks were to be paid for at the local price minus freight. Mr. Jim Dalzell was to assist Mr. Hislop with the building as two men could make better progress than one alone. As the building progressed, Mr. Wm. Kenney was asked to replace Mr. Jim Dalzell as a helper for Mr. Hislop as Mr. Dalzell was going to leave the district.

A total of $919.00 had been pledged by March 10, 1919, and a loan of $1,200.00 secured from the Merchant's Bank in Okotoks. By July of 1919, the work had progressed to the point where it was possible to have a dance on the rough floor. This effort yielded $12.88 — I wonder how they charged for it? The first dance in the hall brought in $38.65 but the opening entertainment, on September 27, brought in the grand sum of $221.75. There had been much discussion about the purchase of a piano and a committee of Mrs. Cushing, Miss Gray and Miss DeMings was given

authority to buy one, using their own discretion. The books show that the first payment for a piano was made September 17, 1918, $30.00. Each following payment was $12.00 with the final payment made September 24, 1920 for $61.19. One item appearing on the books states: 16 meals at Minto House at 40¢ — $6.40.

A schedule of fees was set up: $5.00 per monthly meeting for Red Cross or U.F.A. or Women's Institute, to be held in the kitchen. If the main hall was to be used an extra fee for the janitor and lighting was to be levied. Concerts or lectures, finishing by midnight, were to be $10.00, inclusive of janitor's fee. Dances, $15.00 plus janitor's fee, must be over at 3 a.m. A theatrical company would pay $25.00 and finish at midnight. Rent for the hall after an entertainment until 3 a.m. would be $5.00 plus janitor's fee and the consent of the trustees must be obtained. Mr. Rowland Ness was asked to audit the books.

Great plans for an autumn bazaar and dance were made in May of 1922. A committee of six was appointed, one from each of the six school districts within the area connected with the affairs of the hall: Mr. O'Neil for Pine Creek, Mr. Herr for Davisburg, Mrs. H. Currie for Melrose, Stuart Dalzell for Alexandra, Sam Hamilton for Stormont and Norman Anderson for Ballyhamage. These people were empowered to get whatever help they required. Circumstances must have prevented the bazaar and dance from being held when planned for returns of such an event are not shown until April 3, 1923 and the proceeds were $114.04. This must have been a satisfactory return for it was decided to appoint a new entertainment committee each year and put them in complete charge of some major effort.

The U.F.W.A. had a fence built around the property and there was cause for trouble when it was discovered that the young people were using the fence for tie posts for their horses, thus damaging the fence. Cedar posts had been supplied for tie posts and had never been put in. Throughout the years this little problem recurred at regular intervals and it was never completely resolved. Pete Murray's fence became involved in the hassle and, as late as 1935 the fence and the tie posts were objects of consideration in the annual minutes of the hall board. The fences were long gone and yard open to all types of traffic long before the hall burned down.

Through the years the ladies club did much to improve the hall supplying the money for ceiling the interior and adding a porch on the front, painting, repairing both inside and out, purchasing tables and chairs and kitchen supplies. The power of women was well demonstrated.

The hall was used for a great variety of functions from boxing matches to school clinics, from political meetings to wedding receptions, from machine demonstrations to concerts and from school fairs to box socials. Any and all ages were represented and with the help of competent hall committees it served the residents well.

Eleanor Gray (Macdonald) and Jean Bremner spearheaded the drive for funds. Jean Bremner was the secretary treasurer from 1918 to 1927, Jessie

Dalzell (Carothers) from 1927 to 1938. Mr. Hugh Hamilton, station agent, filled the vacancy pending appointment of a new secretary, Mr. Matthews, also a station agent, acted for a short time and then Melvin Martin held the position from 1939 to 1948, Ted Heaver served from 1948 to 1952 and Mr. C. L. Burkitt, another station agent, acted till 1954. Walter Poffenroth had the job from 1955 to 1965 when the hall board was disbanded prior to setting up a new type of management.

The De Winton Community Hall merged with the De Winton Community Association in 1965, and under its management was used quite extensively, as there were a greater amount of residents in the district, due to many people from the cities moving onto small acreages. The hall had just been completely renovated shortly before it was destroyed by fire on January 12, 1974, which was a severe blow to the district, however, due to the splendid cooperation of the community, plans were made immediately for the construction of a new hall. The Community Association continued to have their monthly dances, renting the Okotoks Elks Hall for these events.

De Winton Community Hall, January, 1974.

The first meeting held to plan for the building of a centre was held in the De Winton United Church basement, and was well attended by interested community residents. The De Winton High School building and grounds which was owned by the De Winton Community Association was the center of plans. Mr. Jim Burns was nominated as head of the building committee, and due to his considerable efforts, and donations, assisted by members of the board which consisted of Jim Airth, Don McDougall, Neville Cannon, Marion Martin, Ruth Lynch, Russel Martin and Kay Mills, the building of the new hall which adjoined the school building was begun at once. The building program would not have been possible, had it not been for the very generous donations of the community residents, the De Winton Riding Club, and a grant from the recreation board. Mention must be made of the donations of building supplies by various contractors and developers, in particular Bud Gustafson who supplied the building blocks used in construction, and other materials.

The hall was in a satisfactory stage of construction by November 2nd, 1974, to hold an auction sale, at which an abundance of articles, furniture, livestock

and everything you could think of was up for sale, this was all donated by district residents, and the services of Bob and Gary McLean who worked hard as auctioneers, to make this sale an outstanding success.

The opening of the hall which was named the De Winton Community Centre was held November 23rd, 1974, and was officially opened by the Honorable Clarence Copithorne, the Minister of Highways for Alberta, who presented a plaque to the Centre on behalf of the province of Alberta.

The Centre has been in a continuous stage of construction since then and by 1977, you could say was near completion, it has been used extensively by the community and is a source of much enjoyment by all, and has an interesting 5 year plan which it is hoped will contribute to a source of entertainment for all ages in the coming years.

It is to the credit of the Centre that at one of its early board meetings, a discussion was held with regards to the De Winton Historical Book, and with Mrs. Jean Marshall in attendance, who is the President of the Historical Society, it was decided to cooperate in the sponsoring of this project.

DeWINTON ELEVATORS

Prior to the rise of the elevators farmers hauled their grain to the railway platform where it was purchased by track buyers and loaded into box cars by hand. This involved a great deal of hard labor for the farmer.

Hauling grain to De Winton in pre-elevator days.

In the year 1923 a Winnipeg company, Hogg and Little, built the first elevator in DeWinton. This was for the purpose of seed handling and distributing. The project proved to be unsuccessful and the structure was sold to Parish and Heimbecker Grain Company who turned the operation into a grain elevator. Agents at the point over the years were Messrs. Ross Saunders, Pete Wilson, Wally Hurst, Jack Phillips, Harold Poffenroth and Winter Speer.

DeWinton was fast becoming a very productive grain producer and in the year 1925 Midland and Pacific Grain Corporation appeared on the scene and built a 30,000 bushel capacity elevator. This unit was powered by a 15 H.P., one cylinder engine and, before electricity came to the district, lighting was with the kerosene lamp. Agents for Midland and Pacific were: Herman Alverson, 1925-1930, H. James Everson, 1930-1954.

In 1954 United Grain Growers Grain Company

P and H elevator De Winton, Alberta.

purchased the two elevators from the respective owners and Jim Everson continued as agent of both units until his retirement in 1955. Mr. Ralph Stinn took over operations at this time and continued in this capacity until 1975 when the elevators were purchased by the present owner.

There was a Wheat Pool elevator in De Winton from September 1929 until May of 1936. This structure was torn down and Henry Poffenroth Junior bought the siding to cover his dairy barn. The rest of the building was dismantled and rebuilt in High River. Other statistics are under The Alberta Wheat Pool story.

**DE WINTON WOMEN'S INSTITUTE, 1916-1918 —
from the minute book.**

This Society was formed as an official branch of Alberta Women's Institute on June 16, 1916 when a meeting was held in the Demonstration train at the De Winton station. Miss Mary MacIsaac, Superintendant of Women's Institutes was in attendance to help with the organization. A slate of officers was installed with Mrs. E. A. Reid as President, Mrs. J. S. Latimer, Vice-President, Mrs. John McNeill, Secretary-Treasurer, three directors; Mrs. H. Usher, Mrs. Patrick Kelly, Mrs. A. S. Blackwood and two auditors; Mrs. W. R. Macdonald and Mrs. G. W. Gray. It was decided to have a meeting each month, held in the homes of the members in succession. Books were apparently available through the club as a librarian was appointed at the second meeting in the person of Mrs. A. DeMings. A program committee was also instated; Mrs. U. G. Campbell, Mrs. A. P. Bremner and Mrs. J. S. Latimer.

The meetings seemed to continue in an orderly fashion with papers on such subjects as 'Canning and Preserving Fruit', 'How We Benefit from Meeting Together!, 'Menu for a Christmas Dinner' and other helpful hints. By December 1916, there seemed to be some feeling that the ladies should forget about the type of meeting they were holding and work for the Red Cross. On February 8, 1917 it was unanimously

accepted that the group would work to aid the Red Cross. In June, Miss Pinkham was invited to attend the meeting and she gave an address on the work of the Red Cross Society in England and at home. She was successful in organizing a branch of the Red Cross in De Winton, to which the Institute would act as an Auxiliary. Three hundred and three dollars and twenty five cents was handed over to the Red Cross Branch, the proceeds of a mammoth bazaar. Eileen Evans was sent to the third annual convention of the Alberta Women's Institutes as the delegate for De Winton but the feeling that the Red Cross should have the complete attention of the group was quite evident and, as the same ladies were the main workers for each of the groups, it was difficult to separate the two. The annual meeting in December of 1917 decided in favour of continuing the Women's Institute "as the interest in the Red Cross Society, which has superseded the interest in the work of the Institute, ever since the organization of that society, in May, would diminish, when the need for the Red Cross work would be lessened by the cessation of the present 'Terrible War' which we hope will be in the year 1918.'' The meetings were continued but, September 1918 is the last meeting recorded so they must have decided to abandon the idea of continuing with the De Winton Branch.

One of the activities in which they were involved was to pay the school children for gopher tails and the total paid out was $26.44 which, at 1¢ per tail, amounted to an output of considerable energy on the part of the school children.

The members included; Mrs. A. W. Browne, Miss I. Fraser, Mrs. Harry Usher, Mrs. Angus McIntosh, Mrs. E. A. Reid, Mrs. G. Gray, Mrs. W. R. Macdonald, Mrs. John McNiell, Mrs. A. DeMings, Mrs. John H. Evans, Miss Eileen Evans, Mrs. Booth, Miss Mary Dalzell, Mrs. Herb Currie, Miss Marjorie Marshall, Mrs. Chas. Vader, Mrs. Campbell, Mrs. A. P. Bremner, Mrs. Stuckey, Mrs. Wm. Mencke, Mrs. E. H. Young, Mrs. A. S. Blackwood, Mrs. W. Bartlam, Miss Jean Bremner, Mrs. Harry Cushing, Mrs. G. Bailie, Mrs. J. S. Latimer, Mrs. A. Paxton, Mrs. John Harrison, Miss Myrtle DeMings, Miss Ethel Bremner, Miss Marjorie Macdonald, Miss Aggie Gray Mrs. S. J. H. Dyer.

The annual dues were 25¢ and a plant for a sick member cost 75¢. To hire the Gibbe brothers for musical services was $8.00 and eight gallons of ice cream, plus expense was $8.35. Music supplied at one dance was only $5.00 and two tins of milk, 30¢. Two dozen Nevada silver spoons, bought for a bazaar were $1.75 and eight dozen paper plates, for the same event, were 40¢. Times and prices have surely changed!! But, Guess what? the June, 1917 meeting included a paper on 'The legal status of women in Alberta!

THE CANADIAN RED CROSS LADIES' WORLD WAR ONE

When the call went out for help from the women of the nation during the First Great War, the ladies of the De Winton and adjoining districts responded with typical western generosity. A Red Cross Club was formed, officers elected and the ladies went to work with a will. Socks, mitts and other knitted wear came from the knitting needles of the group in great quan-

De Winton Red Cross about 1917; Bottom Row, l. to r. Edna Currie, Mary Dick, Jean Bremner, ?, ?, Mrs. Jack Dalzell, Mrs. H. Currie, Mrs. A. Blackwood, Mrs. T. Dalzell, ?, ?, ?, Mrs. Gallagher, Eleanor Gray, Eileen Evans, ?, ?, Top row; ?, ?, ?, Etta Currie, ?, ?, Mrs. Jack Evans, Mrs. Bartlam, ?, Margaret Hamilton. De Mings club house.

tities. Food was donated along with cash contributions and their efforts were recognized by a personal thank you from the Calgary Headquarters. The official name of the group was De Winton — Davisburg Red Cross.

Davisburg, Melrose and Pine Creek school districts put on concerts, dances, picnics and bazaars to augment the funds that were collected. The provincial branch as well as the French and British branches were aided by the efforts of the local group.

Mrs. A. S. Blackwood is credited with doing an enormous amount of work. Turning out quantities of sewing as well as redoing some of the garments that had been improperly finished. Many hours of her time went into this volunteer work and we bear tribute to her endeavor. One member should not be singled out for commendation as each did what they could for the cause. The boys that served in action were appreciative of the parcels sent to them as each one was a reminder of home and the ones that stayed behind.

De WINTON RED CROSS W. W. 2 — by B. Heaver

The De Winton Ladies' Community Club, President, B. G. Heaver, was disbanded in the Fall of 1939 to become a branch of the Calgary Red Cross Society. Mrs. C. Peppard was elected President, Mrs. Heaver was Vice President and Organizer, and Mrs. J. McNeill, Secretary-Treasurer. Mr. and Mrs. Eben Bremner kindly offered "the old Bremner house" for our meetings and workshop. Mrs. Stuart Jamison took

charge of the sewing group, Mrs. Alex Anderson, knitting and Mrs. Tom Dalzell, quiltmaking.

Our branch received many compliments from Mrs. Mason, President of the Calgary Branch for the quality and quantity of our donations. In 1942, a Junior group of high school students was organized and did excellent work of toys and knitted garments for refugee children.

A Comforts Fund was organized to send parcels of candies and cigarettes to our local soldiers on active duty and grateful letters were received from Walter Turnbull, the late Bill Anderson, David Jamison and others. Funds for these activities were raised by sponsoring dances in the old De Winton Hall, which were well attended.

A pageant, "The Temple of Fame," was performed by our members before a crowded hall audience. Mrs. Peppard narrated as the various characters of past history, wearing gowns of the period, such as Queen Victoria, Florence Nightingale, Jenny Lind, Joan of Arc and many others, appeared on stage. The Crown was finally won by the "Mother," beautifully portrayed by Mrs. Fred Dick, holding the hands of two of her children. The pageant was such a success that we were invited to repeat it in the Okotoks United Church Hall.

Later, at the request of the Red Cross Society, blood donor clinics were organized at De Winton, the R.A.F. Station and Okotoks.

At the end of the war, the group returned to the original Women's Community Club.

Annual Report of De Winton-Davisburg Red Cross

The following is the report of the De Winton-Davisburg Red Cross branch for the year ending Sept. 30

Receipts

Cash on hand	$ 242 19
Subscriptions paid in	624 75
Proceeds of chicken pool	85 31
Proceeds of bazaar	235 84
Proceeds of Davisburg concert	101 00
Proceeds of Davisburg dance	44 30
Proceeds of Melrose School bazaar	22 50
Proceeds of picnic	88 80
Raised by Pine Creek Sunday School	15 00
Proceeds of Royal Crown Soap wrappers	4 39
Donations	59 75
One life member	25 00
Thirteen active members	26 00
Nine associates	9 00
Badge pins	2 00
Wool sold	1 40
Total	**$1587 23**

Expenditure

Red Cross supplies	$ 807 52
Express on Red Cross supplies	5 60
Donations to Provincial office for general fund	323 50
Donation for British Red Cross	85 31
To Christmas Stocking fund	25 00
Stamps and post cards	2 50
Coal	2 98
Certificate framed	1 40
Expenses of bazaar	49 31
Express on Red Cross literature	25
Picnic expenses	33 05
Advertisement	50
	$1336 92
Cash on hand	250 31
Total	**$1587 23**

The following donations were also sent to Provincial Branch: four feather pillows, vegetables, eggs and Christmas cake.

MRS H. CURRIE,
Secy. Treas,

Raised for French Red Cross

The following is the result of the De Winton-Davisburg Red Cross Branch's effort for the French Red Cross:

Chickens

Mrs Poffenroth	6
" Marshall	6
" Warrack	6
" Hughes	5
" Davis	8
" Tyndal	1
" Gallangher	2
" J. Dalzell	4
" H. Currie	4
" Anderson	2
" Brinton	1
" McNeill	2
" Ness	3
" Hoffman	2
" Bremner	6
" Cushing	2
" Beustead	1
" Hamilton	2
" J. Davis	2
J. Harrison	1
Mrs Jacobs	3
" Reid	2
" De Mings	2
" Usher	2
" A. Currie	4
" Bartlam	2
" Kenny	3
" Gerlitz	1
" Ripp	2
D. McNeil	1
Mrs Kromm	1
Mr. Hughes	5
Mrs F. Davis	8

Money

Mrs Bryan	$ 2 00
" Kelly	2 00
Thos. Kelly	1 00
Mrs Gray	5 00
Wm. King	2 00
Mrs Westover	2 00
" Carslake	2 00
Robt. Currie	1 00
W. Currie	3 40
G. Sangster	2 80
Mrs T. Martin	2 00
" J. Andrews	1 00
" Wm. Stewart	5 00
Fred Durwin	2 00
Mrs Robt. Riddell	1 00
" A. S. Blackwood	10 00
A. Herr	2 00
Mrs J. R. McConnell	1 00
Mrs E. Grant	1 00
" E. Young	1 00
Miss Annie Ewing	1 00
Mr. Heaver & Sons	5 00
D. McIntosh	1 00
Mrs R. Clark	1 00
Mis A. Patterson	1 00
" Osington	2 00
Mrs Carlton	5 00
F. Blackwell	1 00
Total amount realized	$143.33

MRS H. CURRIE,
Secy.-Treas.

DE WINTON LADIES SEWING CIRCLE

In the late forties some of the local men began meeting on a regular basis during the winter months to play poker, taking turns hosting the games.

Some of the wives, possibly in self-defense, decided to get together on these poker nights and organized a sewing club. From this beginning of about half a dozen ladies, the original sewing circle has continued and grown over 25 years. The sewing circle, surprisingly enough, was authentic and the amount of crocheting, knitting, needlepoint, petit point, quilting and just plain mending and sewing accomplished over the years was impressive.

The ladies of the De Winton Sewing Circle have been meeting regularly, every second Wednesday, at each other's homes, which just goes to show that even a group of women can continue an association and stick together over the years.

DE WINTON MEMORIES — by Doris Jenkins (Daughter of Ed. and Frances Currie)

My dad homesteaded in the Sunnynook area from 1910 to 1925. During this time he met Frances Russell and they were married November 10, 1915. I was born November 10, 1916. My earliest memories seem to be mosquitoes in the summer and dreadful blizzards in the winter, with hard drifts that lasted all winter. There were good times however, when Mom and Dad, Uncle Pete and Aunt Mabel Wilson would set out for house parties in a big bob-sleigh. Russell and Isabelle Wilson and myself were put in blankets, on straw, in the bottom of the sleigh, to keep warm.

1925 saw us moving to De Winton to the Currie Home Farm where Mom, Dad and I lived with my grandparents, Mr. and Mrs. John Currie, for two years. Sunday family dinner seemed to be the highlight of the week.

I started school at Melrose, the same school my dad attended, after Easter, 1925. Mom had taught me the basics to grade three. I must have had a good teacher as I was able to pass to grade four at the end of June. At first I walked but later was given a gentle pony, named 'Sam'.

April, 1927 saw us move to our own quarter section that had belonged to Grandpa, John Currie. The location being NW¼-33-21-29-W4. Our first crop was completely hailed out by one of four storms in ten days. The last storm flooded a good crop of hay down to the Bow River as well. We were living in an old shack and a granary attached for the summer but Dad realized a more permanent home was required. Having no crop, his finances were very limited so, we built the basic four room structure and we were able to keep warm and dry. The finishing came much later.

I finished grade eight in Melrose in 1930. The previous Fall we had a big Hallowe'en party which involved numerous hours of practicing. Our parents were invited and admission was 25¢ and a can of Campbell's soup. For treats, we made various kinds of chocolates and for a trick, I dipped some silver-skin onions as well. The money raised was used to buy more soup and cocoa for hot lunches.

Our first class at De Winton High School was held at Mr. De Ming's house until the new school was completed. Marjorie Winspear was our teacher.

The Old Community Hall was the main centre for dances, bridal showers, Christmas concerts and school fairs. The Christmas concerts were a joint effort of entertainment with the complete schools of Melrose, Pine Creek, Stormount and Alexandra participating. There were always two, big, beautiful Christmas trees, one on each side of the stage. Usually by courtesy of Stuart Jamison.

The School Fairs were again a joint effort with all

the above mentioned schools taking part. Seeds were given out in the spring with a manual outlining all the aspects of exhibits. School penmanship and art work were shown along with cooking, sewing, vegetable and flower displays. The boys had their animals and vegetables too.

The 'Sod Busters' softball team provided many good Sunday games and entertainment for young and old.

In 1941, I married Arthur Jenkins from Okotoks district so De Winton was no longer my home but we made many trips back to visit Mom and Dad while they were on the farm.

Art and I farmed a year in Okotoks district at which time our first son, Gordon Arthur, was born January 16, 1942. The farm was sold so we moved to High River where Art joined the Air Force and worked at the High River No. 5 EFTS, during World War 2.

December, 1946, saw us move to Kimberly, B.C. and now, thirty years later, we are still here. Our second son, Harvey James, was born April 7, 1947, shortly after our arrival to the mountains.

Gordon lives in Edmonton and Harvey in Sherwood Park. We have three grandsons.

Dad and Mom sold the farm and moved to Kimberly in 1958. Mom passed away August 20, 1966 and, at the time of writing, my dad, Ed. Currie, is in the Dr. Green Memorial Home in Cranbrook, nearing his 89th birthday.

Art retired, June, 1976, having worked for the City of Kimberly since January, 1955. Prior to working for the city, he worked for several service stations.

Nostalgia, with mixed emotions is mine when we drive past the old home farm and see all the new homes sitting in close proximity on it and the surrounding farms. It is hard to find old, well remembered, land marks any more but this is what makes memories so greatly cherished.

MEMORIES OF DE WINTON — by Mrs. H. M. Horricks

It was the year of 1936 that we left the Springbank, West Calgary appointment and moved to De Winton. We found the manse was situated about four miles from De Winton, so the children had to go that far to school. That fall, Mr. MacDonald gave us the use of his house, which was about a mile or so from Pine Creek School.

The circuit was composed of three preaching places; De Winton, Davisburg and Red Deer Lake. Davisburg did not rally round the church. There was only one person came out the first Sunday, but the next week we had an increase of 100% . . . we had two! Ser-

vices were abandoned, but Mr. Horricks visited the school once a week, weather permitting, giving a kind of Sunday School. A story given by me, songs and hymns, and a short talk.

The following spring, the manse was moved to De Winton, which was quite an event. It was a large house to move, but stood the journey very well. This made living more convenient, with the church and a store, run by W. B. Martin, close by. The store was later burned down.

Ruth, our youngest daughter, attended the Pine Creek School. She comments; "Mr. Tom Dalzell used to transport the De Winton children to Pine Creek School in the back of his truck — this was always an exciting ride." She later left to attend school at McEwan, west of Nanton, where her sister was a teacher. This was principally for company, as Hazel was batching in a teacherage. Jack and Alma attended at De Winton High School, where Miss Gwen Barroll was the teacher.

Mr. Alex Currie, Mr. Herb Currie, Mr. Alex Sangster and Mr. Tom Dalzell were members of the church board and Miss Jessie Dalzell was the organist. We had a choir of young people that was appreciated. During our time the Sangsters moved to Grand Forks, B.C. and we missed them. The work at Red Deer Lake was quite good. There were many fine people there.

I can remember a very bad dust storm while we were on the MacDonald place. It came in from the west, where a field was in summer-fallow and the roads were gravelled. The dirt sifted into everything. Supper had to be postponed as there was no way to keep the food clean and the house was a mess with silt thick on everything. When the wind died down, I had to take the bedding out and hang it on the line. I had just finished when I saw another storm coming from the north, with the soil drifting just as badly, so I had to hurry in again and wait to clean up when the storm had ceased.

Mr. Bob Smith kept the Post Office and also kept our clocks and watches working.

We left De Winton in the summer of 1940 for Memorial Church in Medicine Hat and Gordon Memorial in Red Cliff.

Mr. Horricks died here in Calgary in 1968. Ruth and I share a house in Calgary and she teaches at Western Canada High School. J. T. (Jack) is the minister of the United Church at Chilliwack, B.C. Alma lives in Sydney, Australia, has a daughter married in Suva, Fiji, and a son who just finished a two year scholarship at Oxford, and he is flying as co-pilot before getting his captaincy. Alma also has a daughter in Australia. I have a granddaughter in Hong Kong and Lawrence lives in Bedford, England.

SNOWY OWL

LARGE WHITE OWL — WITHOUT EAR TUFTS

P.T.

SHAGGY MANE MUSHROOM

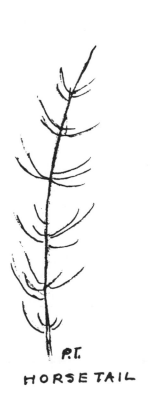

P.T.

HORSETAIL

CATTAILS

ALEXANDRA S.D. NO. 610

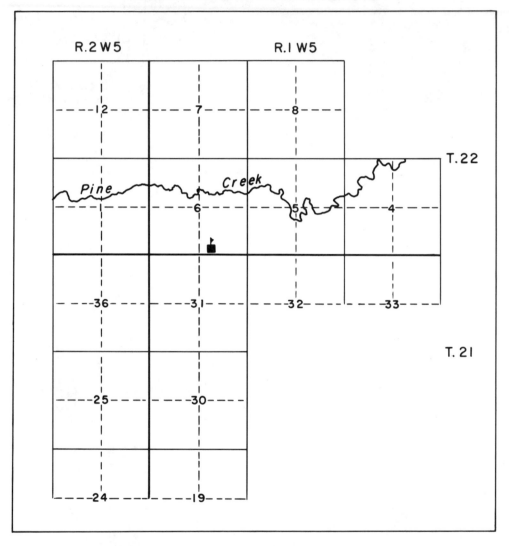

Alexandra School District

ALEXANDRA SCHOOL No. 610 — by Margaret Sheepy

Alexandra School opened in 1902. The first teacher was Miss McWilliams and the trustees were Jack Dalzell, George Wonacott and Mr. Turnbull. Some of the first pupils were Hartie Wonacott, 10½ years old, Bert Wonacott, 9 years, Mary and Lena Dalzell, Mary Kaiser, Ella Fitzgerald, the Copp girls and Phillips!

The following are the teachers up to 1921: Miss Hey, Miss I. McLean, Miss Jean Strople, Miss Crawford, Miss Clendenon, Miss H. Hoare, Mr. Davis and Miss Anna McKevitt.

Miss McLean stayed at her parents' home as it was only a quarter mile south west from the school. The other teachers boarded at Mrs. Jack Dalzell's, Turnbull's and Miss Maggie Wylie's. They either walked, or rode in the buggy or sleigh with the pupils. The pupils delighted in frightening the teachers by driving over bumps or drifts of snow, trying to throw them out.

Discipline of the pupils was hard for the teachers. Many of the boys were grown up. One day one of the fathers decided he would teach them discipline. He came to school with a quirt, called his own son first

and used it on him, then on the rest of the boys. He drove away in his buggy, called on the parents of the boys, and when they got home, they all got another licking.

Vera Marshall started teaching at Alexandra in 1920. She taught grade nine to some of the pupils of the previous year.

Following are the teachers from 1920-1929: Miss L. Dalzell, Miss I. Heagle, Miss Warren, Miss F. Brasso, Miss J. Williams, Miss Ethel Ewing and Miss K. Tedford.

Mrs. J. Dalzell and Mrs. J. Wylie boarded the teachers except for L. Dalzell and V. Marshall, whose homes were in the district.

A pupil would light the fire and sweep the floor for ten cents per day. Inspector Buchanan would visit the school once or twice a year to make sure the teacher and pupils were doing satisfactory work. The average enrollment was twenty-eight to thirty-one pupils, and the classes ranged from grades one to eight.

Alexandra School teacher and pupils would prepare a Christmas concert each year. Practicing would start after November 11th. Parents, friends and Santa would come. Pupils exchanged gifts and parents remembered the teacher with a gift, and supplied lunch.

De Winton had a large Christmas party in the hall, and Alexandra School would pick out the best of their programme to repeat at De Winton. Each district was given a certain amount of time for their programme. Stuart Jamison supplied the Christmas tree. Jack Wylie would take his family and friends in a sleigh. The horses would have lots of bells, and it was a real thrill to get home after midnight.

Alexandra School always had a picnic the last day of school. If it rained, it was held in the school. Otherwise it was held in Jack Wylie's field. Russell Evans would bring ice-cream from Calgary, which was a great treat. Everyone joined in the races and the fathers had a baseball game.

School fairs started about 1924. Students would enter school work, cooking, sewing, vegetables, grain, poultry and livestock. The highest point winner, boy and girl, would get a week's short course at Claresholm. When that school closed, the programme was carried on at Olds. Alexandra was represented a few times. The fair was held at De Winton hall and all the other districts took part.

Alexandra School — 1926. Back Row: Albert Poffenroth, Dan Poffenroth, Dan Kromm, Victor Poffenroth, Hugh Wylie, Gordon Poffenroth, Alex Shierman, Ed Kromm, Moore Pearson, Harry Shierman, Middle Row: — Joan Pearson, Eleanor Pearson, Margaret Wylie, Katherine Pearson, Lilly Krom, Florence Poffenroth, Hilda Krom, Rachel Goerlitz, Emma Kromm, Pauline Kromm, Katherine Wylie. Front Row: — Mary Wylie, Hilda Shierman, Bessie Wylie, Clara Poffenroth.

Alexandra School No. 610. About 1928. 1st row at back: Alma Girletz, Katherine Pearson, Alison Wylie, Lily Krom, Pauline Kromm. 2nd row: Lena Girletz, Eleanor Pearson, Joan Pearson, Emma Krom, Margaret Wylie, Catherine Wylie. 3rd row: Rachel Gerlitz, Hilda Kromm, Bessie Wylie, Hilda Shierman, Dan Poffenroth. 4th row: Alex McNab, Jack Ramsay, Victor Poffenroth, Dan Kromm, George   , Hughie Wylie, Alex Shierman, Donald Ramsay, Ronald Girletz, Charlie Ramsay, Jimmy McNab, Moore Pearson.

Alexandra School — 1945. Back Row: — Lenore Poffenroth, Ronnie Shierman, Harvey Goerlitz, Phyllis Shierman, Middle Row: — Stanley Poffenroth, Theresa Ruscak, Patsy Krom, Leonard Wylie, Front Row: — Paul Poffenroth, Andy Ruscak, Mary Ruscak, Norman Shierman, Betty Goerlitz, Vernon Poffenroth.

A new well was drilled and the horse barn was rebuilt. Russell Evans was the Secretary-Treasurer and the trustees were Jack Wylie, George Pearson and Morgan Holden.

The teachers from 1930-1956 were Miss D. Cooper, Miss I. McCallum, Miss M. Pickens, Mr. L. McConkie, Miss J. Mortez, Miss L. Baillie, Miss M. Bishop, Miss B. Athey, Mrs. Nicolson, Miss L. Middleton, Mrs. M. Hogan, Miss M. O'Neil and Miss L. McQuaid.

Miss Winnie Rogers was the last teacher. During this period Alexandra had obtained a teacherage and the windows were all moved to the west side for better lighting. The school closed in 1956.

Some of the families that went to Alexandra School were Dalzells, Fitzgerald, Copp, Phillips, Kaiser, Wilkins, Georlitz, Krom, Shierman, Poffenroth, Wonacott, Pearson, Bottomley and Wylie.

RECOLLECTIONS — by Desmond Holden

I remember, as a kid, some of the controversy about which way Red Deer Lake (Lloyd Lake) would drain if it ever got to the point of overflowing. Some of the oldtimers, at the time, felt that it would go to the north east through, what was then, Ralph Lloyd's and Jack Beatty's, and join the little creek in Joe McConkey's. However, in the late forties or early fifties had the water level risen another six inches, it would have run through the north east corner of our place (Holden's) and through Bill White's north west corner to Pine Creek.

The first I remember of Alexandra school, the foundation had fallen away to such a point that one (if small enough) could crawl under most of the building.

The first teacher in my day was Miss Daisy Cooper, city born and raised, and not too well versed in the stoking of the old Waterman Waterbury heater. For some time we used the coal from the old "OV" mine near Priddis, a coal, which was as much oil as coal, guaranteed to burn out grates in record time, or even melt the whole stove, if given the chance. Miss Cooper, in all innocence, would cover the whole fire bed with an even layer of this slack type coal. Given five to ten minutes of time for some of the oil to evaporate from the coal, there then would be a, not too slight, explosion. Both the main and ash doors would fly open and the stove pipe, which ran from the south east corner of the building to the north center where the bracket type chimney hung, would separate in at least three pieces, some of which would hit the desks, kids or what have you, before hitting the floor. For the next little while it would 'snow' ashes and soot, to say nothing of the thick yellow smoke that loaded the air. The next problem was to climb up on desks or what-ever, (we didn't have the modern convenience of a step-ladder) and put the pipes together again. Now, most of the pipes were made before they thought of crimping the ends, to make them fit easier, so you often trimmed a bit of skin off of your fingers in the process. There was more than once when our feet got so cold from resting them on the floor that we would go and run around outside to get the circulation going again.

When we were quite young, Dad bought us a donkey to ride to school. This was fine but the horses belonging to the other families would not go within a city block of her so, either they went in the barn or she did. One sunny day 'Jenny', the donkey, was tied to the plank fence around the pump. As the other horses were in the barn, the yard gate was left open. Seven of Jack Wylie's prize Clyesdales came in for a visit. As Jenny was hidden behind the fence they got to within a few feet of her before she came around and greeted them with a trumpeting "hee haw". At the first note they took flight and, I'm sure, they set a record time for the half mile, for Clyesdales, at least. I heard later that Mr. Wylie was quite puzzled at their puffing and heaving since there was no sign of anything biting at their heels.

In the late forties it was decided that the old Alexandra school was beyond repair and the Ballyhamage school was moved to the site and put on a foundation. As soon as practical, the old one was disposed of, I understand Hartie Wonacott took it apart for the lumber. Some of us felt the school should have been set half a mile east near the gas line but that was out-voted. However, shortly after this the school bussing system was started and the small schools were eliminated.

The Fordville school was moved to Midnapore and used as a portable, beside the main school; then as the school population changed it became a Scout hall, and when all the Midnapore kids began to be bussed to Calgary, once more it was vacant.

For some time we had been looking for one of the old Waterman Waterbury heaters for our cabin but without success. We hoped to buy the one out of the school. After some chasing around we found it was possible to have the heater but the Calgary School Board would rather we took the building too. Not being in the market for such a large undertaking, I passed the word to my brother, Arthur, who had asked me to look out for a building for him to take apart to move. He was quite happy to have the building material for a project he was working on. The Fordville school building is now a brooder house for hogs.

MR. AND MRS. ROBERT BOTTOMLEY — by Roberta Scott

Mother and Dad arrived at Section 8-22-1 west of the 5th in 1922 at ages 48 and 50 respectively at a time when most older people were working their way off the farms to an "easy and comfortable" life in the city.

Mother had grown up in a musical family in the pretty little town of Preston, Minn. Dad came from a productive farming community near Winnebago, Minn. They met and married in Fairmont where Mother had gone to teach music and Dad was County Superintendent of schools.

By 1907 the urge to come to Canada had struck. The time between then and 1916 was spent in Gadsby, Alberta where I was born. During those years Dad taught school on a permit, proved up on a homestead, raised cattle, worked for the Crown Lumber Co., acted as Justice of the Peace and did rather well as a real estate agent. An elderly friend who recently told me all this didn't say what he did with his spare time. According to Mother there also was a good deal of social activity. She loved the little town where everyone was young and full of pep with their futures before them.

The next six years were spent in Calgary where Dad had a partnership in a grocery store. Mother was dangerously ill with the flu, and I started school in the Little Elbow Park Cottage School.

Somewhere along the line my Father had edited a small town newspaper so maybe by 1922 after all his varied activities he was ready to move at his own pace back to the land. Mother I'm sure had some reservations.

Farming is farming and everybody had their ups and downs, but once in a while something happened which was of benefit or interest to the community as a whole.

Back, l. to r. Bob, Roberta and Mrs. Bottomley with friends, 1930.

In 1925 at a really wet period of the year, the pipe line from Turner Valley to Calgary went the full mile along the west side of the property and caused a lot of excitement. Years later another line went across the SE quarter and didn't cause a stir. Done with modern machinery it wasn't half as much fun as watching horses, wagons, crews of men and mud.

There was another flurry of excitement when Hudsons' Bay Oil and Gas Co. drilled the Twin Dome well on the property. It brought the old farm to life for a while, but just for a while.

In 1934 we watched the great Johnny Longden ride Peach Stone to victory in the Alberta Derby. Though she belonged to T. R. Stone she was foaled and raised on the farm so we felt we had a stake in her future.

The land was used one or two years by the Alberta Fish and Game Association for the purpose of stocking the country with pheasants. The birds settled in very quickly and the project was extremely successful.

For what it's worth, my teaching days began in the Little Alexandra School No. 610 in the thirties. Taking my Easter practice teaching there I was suddenly fully employed for a time while Miss Cooper recovered from an illness. The key word was "busy" as the little school was bulging with children from grades one to eight. Looking back, discipline was no problem, even with such congestion, which speaks very well for the parents and children. Evidently they were all out to help a young teacher.

Both my parents were well over the three score and ten mark by 1955. They were in reasonably good health and very interested in everything. Life had been good to them.

JOHN AND SARAH (JAMISON) DALZELL — by Marjorie Coulter

John Dalzell was born in Stratford, Ontario in 1866. In 1885 he came west, the year after the Rebellion, to Manitoba. The following year he came to Alberta and settled in the Calgary and De Winton districts and resided there till he died in December 1925. He is buried in Pine Creek Cemetery.

He married Sarah Jamison, who was born in Dorchester, Ontario and came with her family in 1886 to the De Winton district. There she met John Dalzell and they were married in 1895, in the Pine Creek Church.

They took their first homestead six miles west of De Winton and were there for several years. Then they sold it and moved about two miles farther north. While they were on the first homestead, they had two children, both girls, Mary and Lena. After moving to the second home, they had three more children, Stuart, Marjorie and Gordon. Gordon was drowned in the creek below the house in 1911, and is buried in Pine Creek Cemetery.

Mary married Fred Dick and lived in the De Winton district until 1971 when they moved to Calgary. A few months later, Fred took sick and died in February 1972. He is also buried in Pine Creek Cemetery. Mary still lives in Calgary.

Lena married Jim Montgomery from Blackie. They lived on a farm near Blackie until Jim died in 1971. Lena now lives in Blackie.

Stuart never married. He farmed the home place for a long while, and then sold out and moved to Calgary, where he passed away in 1975.

Sarah stayed on the farm with her son, Stuart, after John's death. In time she bcame too ill to stay on the farm and had to enter a nursing home in Calgary, where she passed away in September, 1963, at the age of 89. She too is buried in Pine Creek Cemetery.

Mary and Fred had three children, Ivan, Lois and Alan. Lena and Jim had four, Alvin, Betty, John and Jimmy. Marjorie and Tom Coulter have one daughter, Evie.

Four Generations — Mrs. Jack Dalzell, Grandma Jamison, Mary Dick, Ivan Dick.

Jack and Sarah Dalzell.

R. M. FITZGERALD — by Walter Turnbull

About 1897 the Fitzgeralds moved on to the S½ 5-22-1-W5. They were tenants. Their first names are not known but there was a son Desmond, who went to the first world war, and a daughter, Nina, perhaps other children. They were good neighbours and popular in the community. Mr. Fitzgerald was always referred to by the nickname "Fitz" and was a great friend of Jack Dalzell and Will Turnbull.

Tragedy struck the family when Fitz passed away at home in 1913. In those days there were no hearses to make rural calls and Jack Dalzell and Will Turnbull were the ones responsible for transporting the body to the undertaking parlour in Calgary. Unfortunately they had only their saddle horses, Will's Twinkle and Jack's "Star" to use as a team to hitch to the democrat. They had never been driven before and, with the body wrapped in a blanket, they set out on their trip. The horses were almost impossible to hold and they had quite a ride until they got them settled down, quite some way along the road to town. Mrs. Fitzgerald had been taken to stay with Mrs. Turnbull and they were watching out the window and saw a team of horses pulling a wagon, quite sedately, down the road and Mrs. Fitzgerald mentioned how carefully they were driving, thinking it was Jack and Will. It turned out to be a farmer from further down the road taking meat to Calgary. Jack and Will had been worried that they would be seen tearing along with the team all but out of control so they were pleased to hear that their neighbour and his quiet team had been mistaken for them. After the horses had settled down, Jack and Will were hailed by Johnny Hamilton, who always rode a beautiful horse, and he told them he had heard that Fitz has passed away that day. When Johnny found out what they were carrying he got his horse turned around and galloped off in the other direction. They got into the city with no further trouble and

Archie Bremner and Bob Fitzsimmons about 1922.

stopped in front of A. M. Shaver's funeral parlour. Jack stayed with the team and Will went into the office to tell the undertaker that he had a neighbour out in front.

The undertaker was horrified and said "Man! don't leave him out in front where people can see, get him around to the back!" The democrat was driven around to the back and the body duly delivered. Jack remarked, "Be Jayzuz, I hope his Missis didn't see us tearin' down the road!"

Mrs. Fitzgerald and the children left the farm just after WW1 broke out and it is not known what happened to them after that.

ROBERT FITZSIMMONS

"Bob" Fitzsimmons homesteaded the NW¼-32-21-1-W5 prior to 1885, patent 34559. He acted as cook while transporting supplies for the Riel Rebellion. In 1903 he moved to the Hesketh district near Drumheller. He is remembered as a kindly, helpful person. Leonard Wylie is the present owner of the place.

ADAM GEORLITZ — by Tom Georlitz

Adam Georlitz came to Canada in 1901. He worked for the C.P.R. until he took up a homestead. In 1903 he married Katherine Stang and, in 1905, they took up a homestead west of De Winton, 20-21-1-W5. They built a log house and later added more rooms to it. The place was mostly trees which they cleared, a few at a time, breaking with horses and walking plow. On this land they grew a little grain, sown by hand, and potatoes which they peddled in Calgary. The trip to Calgary was made with horse and wagon and took them from daylight till dark.

They had five children: Myself, Tom, Mary, John, Jacob and Rachael. After only fifteen years of married life my mother passed away. Two years of the fifteen were spent in bed, sick. My father was left with a young family, ranging in age from thirteen down to two years, to manage as best he could. I can remember my sister, Mary, baking bread at a very early age.

We all attended Alexandra School. If I can remember correctly, my first teacher was Miss Hey. She married Charlie Brown who was a school trustee at the time.

In 1931, my father came to live in Calgary and the farm was taken over by my brother, John. He married Jean Battle and they had three children, Betty, Doreen and Allen all of whom attended Alexandra School.

The log house was replaced with a new one and electricity installed. John passed away in 1958 and Jean sold the farm to Mrs. McQuarrie.

Father passed away in 1973 at the age of ninety-nine.

CONRAD, "JIMMY" AND ANNA MARIE (KROM) GIRLETZ — by Ron Girletz

My father, Conrad, known as "Jimmy" to all his friends and neighbours, and my mother, Anna Marie, were married in Russia in 1893. Following their marrige they immigrated to Eastern Canada in 1898, and moved on to Calgary the same year. Upon arriving in Calgary, Dad worked for the C.P.R.

About 1916 the Jimmy Conrad and Anna Marie Girletz family. Back row: Amy, Katy, Dave, Tillie. Front Row: Ronald, Father, Elma, Mother, Lena.

In 1901, he went homesteading on the N½-19-21-1-W5, being located 4½ miles S.W. of De Winton. In 1911, he sold the original homestead and moved back to Calgary. In 1914, he bought another farm from T. Copp, 3½ miles west of De Winton, E½-32-21-1-W5 and farmed this land until retiring to Calgary in 1935, when his son, Ronald, took over farming.

Conrad and Anna Marie Girletz had five daughters and two sons. The eldest, Katherine, "Katy", married Henry Stang, they have three daughters and two sons, Henry, now deceased; Anna Marie "Amy", married John Poffenroth, they have five sons and two daughters they farmed west of De Winton are both deceased, their sons, Edward and Harvey, still farm west of De Winton. Matilda, "Tillie", married Con Poffenroth, a brother of John, they have one daughter and three sons. Tillie and Con farmed west of De Winton and their sons Robert and David also farmed in the De Winton area. Con, now deceased. David Girletz married Anna Wathen of Okotoks. They have three sons and two daughters and are still actively farming

Conrad and Anna Marie Girletz, 50th Wedding Anniversary, 1943.

at Balzac. Alma, Sam Lesback, farm east of Red Deer, Alberta, they had two sons and one daughter, son, Alvin, deceased. Paulena "Lena", married Mark Rassmussen, they have one son and one daughter, all living in Calgary. I, Ronald, married Pauline Goodman, we have one daughter, Dixie (Simpson), and three grandchildren Debbie, Wendy and Robbie. We live on SE¼-5-22-1-W5 and enjoy our small farm operation.

My sisters, brother, daughter and myself all attended Alexandra School.

JOHN GOERLITZ — by F. Befus

In 1899 John came, with his family, from Saratov, Russia. He lived in Calgary the first few years and, about 1903, he moved to the Alexandra district. The early years in Canada were hard ones. He lost several children and his wife, Maria, in 1903, with diphtheria. He was left with a teen-age daughter, Jessie, (who stayed in Calgary and worked until her marriage to John Leinweber), and a two year old son, Frederick.

After living on the "Reid Place" for a while, John located three miles west on S.W.¼-25-21-2-W5. This land had been homesteaded by Mr. and Mrs. Phillip Konchuh and later became known as the "Norman Anderson Place". John and Phillip worked together until Phillip moved to Beiseker.

John married Christina and they worked hard and grew as much as they could. As early as 1907 John was helping new arrivals from Russia by taking them wagon loads of vegetables. Christina was handy with a brush and helped people kalsomine homes. They took their turn in holding Saturday church meetings in their home which many in the district attended.

Later John took a homestead, on S.E.¼-36-21-2-W5,

The John Goerlitz family. l. Harvey and Frances; r. John and Mrs. Goerlitz.

on a hill. A good spring was found and a log house built. In later years this house was moved closer to the road and another room added. The moving was done with wagons. John's father passed away here while working in the potato patch.

After Fred was married; John moved to Calgary and built several houses on the hillside in Bridgeland. He was 89 when he passed away, October, 1957.

Fred attended Alexandra School and, in 1923, married Mary Elizabeth Kromm. He took over his father's farm on the hill. The water supply wasn't always good but the panoramic view was. To them were born two children, Frances and Harvey.

Fred was plagued with bad health for 10 years and passed away in 1948 at the age of 47 years. No matter how badly he felt, he always had time to visit with people.

In 1948, Frances married Wilfred Befus. They lived in Calgary for nine years, farmed for fifteen years, fourteen miles west of Didsbury and are now living in Calgary again.

Harvey stayed on the farm and helped his mother until her death in 1967. In 1968 he married Shirley Taylor and they remain on the home place.

JAMES AND JEAN HARRISON — as told to Dot Gerlitz

Jimmy Harrison came out from Scotland in 1911 to join his brother John, who had emigrated to Canada in the early 1900's. He came over in the same boat as some of the Wylie family, and also Allison Scott. He landed in Montreal and came west to his brother

Jim Harrison and Pete Goerlitz — 1934.

John's farm at De Winton. John was engaged in farming and also road building, so Jimmy ran a road grader with eight horses for many years, building the district roads.

In the early days they hauled their grain to Calgary, taking two days for the round trip, but if the roads were good they loaded the grain the night before, and took off early in the morning and were able to return the same day.

In 1944 Jim married Jean Strople, who had been a schoolteacher at Consort and Alexandra. Mrs. Harrison had been born in Nova Scotia and had taught school for many years in the west.

When John Harrison died, Jimmy inherited a half section of land from him and he also leased the "Reid" place which belonged to Mrs. John Harrison. They stayed on the farm for six years, selling it in 1950. They retired to Calgary where Jimmy took ill and passed away in 1953.

He enjoyed life and liked nothing better then getting together with the boys, "to chew the fat." Mrs. Harrison is still active and resides in Calgary.

JOHN AND JESSIE (BOOTH) HARRISON — by Dot Gerlitz

John Harrison emigrated to Canada from Scotland in the early 1900s and came west to DeWinton, buying land from the Ancelles, NW¼ 28-21-1-W5. In 1913 he married Miss Jessie Booth, a registered nurse, who had taken her training in Milwaukee. Miss Booth had two sisters in the DeWinton district, Mrs. Reid and Miss Phoebe Booth, Mrs. Reid was married to a farmer in the area, Ernie Reid, and Phoebe, the other sister was a school teacher, also a very talented artist, painting many beautiful pictures. John Harrison was busy with mixed farming and road building. He kept eight teams of horses, using two teams of four alternately, the dirt was moved with fresnos, complete with the Johnson bar. His brother, James, came out

Jack Harrison.

from Scotland in 1911 and helped John with the road building, running the grader for him.

Mr. and Mrs. Harrison had an extended visit to the Old Country and while over there they went to see all the places of great historical interest in London. While going over the Mansion House it came to the ears of the Lord Mayor, that there were visitors there from Okotoks, Alberta. He sent for them and was greatly pleased to find that they knew his niece, Mrs. E. H. Robinson and he was most interested in hearing about her and her family, also about the west in general. Before leaving, the Lord Mayor presented them with souvenir copies of the London Times for themselves and also for Mrs. Robinson. They also stopped off in Ottawa and visited the Parliament Buildings, where G. Coate, M. P. showed them around so they had a very enjoyable holiday.

Mr. Harrison began to suffer from poor health and about 1937 they moved into Calgary to the Underwood Block for the winter. They moved back to the farm for the summer and Mr. Harrison passed away about 1938.

Jimmy Harrison looked after the farm after John's death, and then Mrs. Harrison sold her quarter section and moved into Calgary to live. She made two more trips to England and while there stayed with her sister, Mrs. Reid, who had returned there to live.

Mrs. Harrison is now ninety-five years old and is in the Cedars Villa Nursing Home in Calgary.

THE HOLDENS — by Mrs. K. A. Holden

We met, Morgan and I, when his mother, Mrs. Holden, came into the depot to keep her four year old son from either getting on the track or taking a ride on the train and my mother was getting my push cart from the luggage van (I was a year old), we were going to our new home in the country. Farnsfield was the name of the village. While we were youngsters Morgan and I went to the same parties and dancing classes. When he was sixteen he came out to his brother in Saskatchewan, near Lloydminster, where he had taken up a homestead. From there he roamed the country doing all sorts of jobs.

When World War I broke out he joined the 31st Battalion, went overseas was in France ten months, was wounded, had risen to Lieutenant while in the trenches. After his sick leave he spent the remainder of the war in charge on the machine gun school in Bramshott. He received the Military O.B.E. I was a V.A.D. cook in the local hospital, cycling to duty each morning and finishing at 3:00 p.m., four days a week.

The story that began on the depot platform took another step at the altar of Farnsfield church when we were married in 1921. Morgan had taken up his soldier settlement land, south of Oyen, near the Saskatchewan border. I had never ridden horseback in England, my father did not buy me a horse, he thought I should break my neck so, now was my chance! Morgan gave me a mare for a wedding present but she had a habit of bucking so he saddled his "grey" and said "go up the pasture and see what you can do about riding while I do the milking." I did and, let me add, I rode in all the local races a month later. Peggy, the mare he gave me, had a light mouth, it was only heavy hands that made her buck, I was no cowboy, she liked me.

After four years of drought on the prairies, we decided to try some other part of the country. Friends offered to look after the children so, with our old Ford and a tent that went over it and down to the ground on the other side, we set off. Camp grounds were, to put it mildly, primitive. There was one on the island, near the zoo, two store fireplaces for cooking served the whole campground. If there were others I never found them. The baker and the milkman came round in the morning, shouting their wares, you stuck your head out of the tent and yelled back, if you wanted something. We saw scores of farms. This one, south of Red Deer Lake, was not on the market, we had missed the Harvey Poffenroth place, by a day, and the agent said he thought this one might be coming on the market because, it did not look as if the lady that owned it would be able to pay her mortgage. He suggested, as she had walked off one place, known as the Harrison place, that we should look at it, then, we could come and see this one, on the pretext of asking her about the other. It worked! She invited us to tea. I can see her now, standing between the curtains, in the doorway of the sitting room, "Peter", five foot nothing, very stout, red hair cut short, brown suit, an English china cup and saucer in each hand and, looking at me, she remarked — "The bally cows have eaten the filthy stink-weed and the milk is putrid, can you drink your tea without it?" It appeared that Peter was on her best behaviour that afternoon, her language ladylike, it could be otherwise.

When we bought the place next spring there was a little round hole in the sitting room window glass. The story? Peter was a pretty good mechanic and the neighbours loved to put her tractor out of action to hear her 'basic English' (acquired in the army) SO, Peter put the tractor in front of the sitting room window and sat, with her 22, to catch the culprit. A fellow, on his way to the Sparrow ranch, lost his way and went past the tractor. Pete let drive. The next morning the air was blue, the bullet had blown a hole in the gas tank — Goodbye gas! "Oh I could write a book on Peter and we had a most entertaining afternoon." One day someone bet her she dare not drive her tractor (it had lugged wheels) up to the Palliser and leave it parked in front so, of course, she did!

In 1925 we bought this place, it was a gift from my father who believed in seeing his family enjoy things while he was alive, not wait till he was dead and then it might be too late for the things they had wanted. There had been no crops through the dry years at Oyen.

The first year the road came through, it was a bought road, over the hills west, and all the farmers, except the Holdens (who were newcomers), had a say in where the road went. And "where did it go?" right through the middle of all the filthy corrals and took a loading chute in its stride. It came within a few feet of the log house we used as a bunk house. This is how it happened — the man on the east side said he was not going to have the road in one place and the phone poles in another, the man on the other side had a jog put in the road because he had a hay crop and the road jogged back at the next half mile. If the whole road could have been built a few hundred feet south, there would have been no jogs, no hill and no coulee at Holden's for everyone to get stuck in that first, very wet, summer.

Morgan moved up here and, with the help of a man, put in the crop while I finished packing at our old place. Our hired man was the man who was to become famous as a landscape painter, Roland Gissing. At this time he was drawing mostly cowboy scenes being an admirer of Russel. He painted me a picture of this house and front yard, I think it was the first he ever did, and, as it is signed, and dated, is very valuable to me and, compared to the lovely views he painted late, this is 'very primitive'.

I was known as a jack-of-all-trades in a day when women were only just beginning to drive cars, I went one better and drove our McCormick-Deering tractor, "Mac", and ploughing nearly drove me nuts. The man who brought the tractor out burned the brake out, the plough had a trip on it so that if it hit a stone it came unhitched. Well! it could smell a pebble half a yard away and off it went. I would back up to it, get off, lift the heavy ploughshank and hook, Mac had moved back an inch on the slope, so it would not hook up, — try again! Well I beat it in the end by tying a rope on the plough, lifting the shank, backing and dropping it in but, that thing was heavy and I had to sit sideways so, once or twice, my foot slipped and the plough got a good wallop. But it's all in a lifetime. For awhile I combined tractor and housework but that was too much so, I was given the choice, should we get a man to do the outside work or, get a girl for housework and milking and I should go on helping Morgan? I chose the latter, he and I could work perfectly as a team, so why not go on with it that way?

Then we had a cyclone, to add to the excitement, a black funnel came out of the west, my husband saw it coming and rushed out to help our man to unhook the horses, there was a terrific wind, lumps of hail, all jagged in shape, and, of course, thunder and lightning. The wind was so strong it blew some of the shingles off the back porch roof, through the kitchen window and, this is hard to believe but it's true, the wind swept across the kitchen and the dish towels, hanging over the stove at the far end of my twenty foot kitchen, got damp. We took the children into the sitting-room and the radio lit up with a blue flame, shrieked like a banshee, and that was its swan song. Later on we went to survey the damage. We had lost our crop but not our buildings. The storm had twisted trees, lifted buildings into the air and thrown them down in bits. We lost only two trees near the house and a few shingles but the Sparrow ranch lost a very large barn and a row of granaries looked as if they had been playing hop scotch and were left with sore feet. Everything that could roll did roll, even round granaries. There wasn't a pole left on the De Winton road but, in one place, a buggy had run down into the ditch and a roof from some building had, very kindly, landed over it, covering it nicely. The Sparrow barn was in bits, scattered over a large area and a small building stood there, all serene, with its roof still sticking out in a long peak where it had been attached to the barn.

I remember what fun the school fairs were when they were held in the De Winton hall, in addition to seeds and flowers, there were classes for livestock.

One time, a couple of pigs, the Wylie children were taking, got out of their wagon and our clan tried to capture them but, these pigs eluded their captors and never went to the fair.

The Millarville races, our first visit there — between here and the race course there were fourteen gates to open, the kind made with wire and a few posts that I always called affectionate because, as soon as I open one, it falls into my arms, all tangled up, and takes a long time to get straightened out. In our model T we set out, I was, of course, the gate opener as I was not fond of driving that ornery car. We arrived and had a wonderful time till before the last race rain began to fall in businesslike style. Everyone started for home and we soon found out why. Once that steep bank, from the creek to the road, got wet, it was too slippery for the cars to get up under their own steam and it meant man power pushing. We made it O.K. then my fun began, trying to get those gates worked just ahead of the storm. That is when I counted fourteen gates, we just got into our yard when the heavens opened and we sat in the old car till it slowed down a bit.

I learned to drive in England, in a car with gears, and, somehow, I never made friends with that model T. Anyone who ever drove one will remember the joy of lifting the cushion off the driver's seat and poking a stick in to see how much gas was left in the tank. And the joy of cranking, with the spark lever down, and rushing round to put it up before the engine died. If you left it the wrong way before you cranked, and the engine fired, you got a kick which might break an arm. 'Old Lizzie', as we called her, once died down with me in the east subway after I had taken a sample of barley to the malting company. There I was with the wretch sitting squarely in the middle of the street car tracks and the engine needing cranking. There was an old man collecting manure in a wheel-barrow, I waved the crank at him and he came over and cranked for me, we got her going just in time, a street car was clanging at my rear. I actually got home with no more trouble. Sometimes I forgot whether I was driving Old Lizzie or Mac, the tractor. I came home with plough shares from town and took them out to the field, left them there with my husband and later I took over the tractor for a couple of hours. When I started to drive the car home I gave the wheel such a heave that I went straight into the ditch. I got onto the road and did the same thing into the other ditch; I forgot it did not take all my strengh, like old Mac, and by this time I was so scared that I went all the way home in low gear.

My family used to ride a good old pony, called Bob, we bought from Mr. Patterson, he was a treasure, then, as they grew older, they had other ponies and finally, took our hunters to school. I must not forget 'Jenny', the famous donkey. She was quite a character. One of the side shows sold four donkeys and we bought one, a little Mexican ass. Morgan brought her home in our horse trailer with a horse blanket covering her, except for her enormous, furry ears. Mr. Hugh Wylie was coming along the road, near his home, and almost at his gate, he had a wagon and a team of Clydesdales, the two men were going to exchange greetings but Jenny beat them to it by greeting the horses in Mexican. They simply left, that very minute, on the dead run, luckily they didn't take the gate post with them and stopped at the barn, feeling that home was the place to be with creatures like that around. The children used to ride her to school and she was taught to pull the buggy. The girl who was helping me, at the time, made a pet of Jenny and used to keep apple peelings for her. Jenny would come to the back gate and bray, Ethel would go out and give them to her. When we had a gang of threshers here all the cow pokes tried to ride Jenny and were pitched off on the manure heap or rubbed off on trees. One of them, seeing Ethel laughing, challenged her to ride. Jenny behaved like a lady and there were some very surprised fellows. Jack Wylie's prize Clydesdales could have been Canadian Derby winners on the day Jenny greeted them when they came to investigate the school yard.

I remember, years ago before we all got lazy with T.V., we had a form of entertainment called a surprise party. A few friends agreed to give one of their neighbours a party by finding out if the family would be home on a certain evening, the guests would arrive, all the ladies with cakes and sandwiches and someone with a fiddle or other kind of musical instrument. This was great fun. The last one we had was really a failure, for these reasons, we did not know about it, we had done a big wash, it was winter, the girl and I had not lit the sitting room fire, everyone was going to bed early, the kitchen was adorned with sheets and other small things, hung up to dry and we were sitting in the middle of the room when several people arrived. Down came the washing in a hurry and we lit the fire in the sitting room and moved the rug for dancing. To cut a long story short, in addition to the dozen friends who usually came, there were twenty or more from the south, who did not know that the ladies brought lunch, so arrived empty handed. We had to hurry up and cut a pile of sandwiches for all the extra guests. I can't call the evening a success, for one thing I didn't know some of the people well enough to carry the thing off with a laugh and the house was cold, the food scarce and there was no doubt, IT WAS A SURPRISE PARTY!!!

We used to enjoy the concerts at Alexandra. The school was small and we were packed in like sardines but, that seemed to add to our enjoyment for we knew our neighbours' children and liked to see and hear them do their songs and recite. The applause was terrific! Then, Santa and the gifts and, finally, coffee and sandwiches and, "Ooh! those cakes!"

Cooking for the threshing gang was, for me, one of life's nightmares. On the prairies, each threshing outfit had a cookcar with its own cook, the farmer provided fresh vegetables and the farmer's wife, very often, helped a little but, if she had a big family to look after, she was not expected to do any cooking for the threshers, her man ate with them. When I came up here and found I had to be cook and bottle washer, for a troop of hungry men, it reminded me of war days when I was part-time, V.A.D. cook, in a hospital. How those men could eat! I had an Irish girl working for me one year, with a brogue you could cut with a knife, she watched to see that everyone had enough to eat and I saw her offer pie to one fellow who refused it. She came to me and remarked, (if only I could give the accent) "and did you see Mr. So-and-So refuse the pie I was offerin' him? Well and would you believe he had three plates of stew, two pieces of pie and three cups of tea? Him so thin and NEVER A BULGE SHOWIN'?" I have thought of that so many times when I have seen a lean person with an enormous appetite.

I have called my husband, Morgan, because, before we came to live here, no one called him by his old army name, Tiny, but, in Calgary, among his friends, he became Tiny Holden again. His chest began to bother him and he could not stand the dust of land work. I suppose those months in Flander's mud were beginning to take their toll so, he bred a couple of race horses and, before you could say, Jack Robinson, we were touring the country, Calgary, Edmonton, Regina, Winnipeg and Vancouver. I saw Calgary on Stampede week, if I was lucky. A girl who used to work for me kept house for the family when we only went to Edmonton, then, the girls were old enough to take care of themselves. I simply made a home for us, I did not look after the horses but, if anyone thinks it is an easy life, let them try it. Up before five a.m., if you have horses running, you never get to bed before eleven, meals at all hours and, when you try to snatch some rest, along come the paper boys etcetera. The trophies in the sitting room prove it was worthwhile and Tiny simply loved it. I tagged along in his shadow as "Tiny Holden's wife."

Now it is 1977 so perhaps I had better bring the family story up to date. Myfanwy and Stanley live in Grande Prairie, their son, Fred, with his wife, Wendy, and three small children, live in Australia where Fred joined the Airforce and is in radio. Their daughter, Kay, is married, lives just outside Grande Prairie and teaches. Their second daughter, Arlene, is a nurse in the hospital there. Desmond and Arthur both live in Calgary, south west. Desmond and Ada have five; Joyce; married, Kevin is working, Elaine graduates from high school this summer and Linda and Morgan are still in school. Arthur and Helen have two daughters; Joan is married and Pat is working. Beatrice decided to stay single and she and I live at the old homestead, where her hobby is raising a little herd of cattle and mine is flowers so we don't get in each others hair, giving unwanted advice. I know very little about cattle and she knows less about flowers!

The Holden Family — Arthur, Myfanwy, Mrs. Holden, Beatrice, Desmond, F. M. Holden (Tiny).

Our land description is SW¼ 12-22-2-W5, where the buildings are and W½ 1-22-2-W5. I have a guide and Brownie camp as a memorial to my late husband, known as the Tiny Holden camp, it is located in the south end and very popular both winter and summer being near enough to Calgary for parents to bring the girls out on Friday evening and fetch them back Sunday, late afternoon.

I am very lucky to have very nice daughters-in-law and son-in-law and we all have a good time together. It is great being a granny, all the fun and none of the responsibility.

I am happy and hope to spend the rest of my life right here!

PHILIP KONSCHUH — by Katie Shierman — Granddaughter

My grandparents, Mr. and Mrs. Philip Konschuh came to Canada in 1901 from Saratov, Russia. They lived in Calgary for about four years before moving to the Alexandra district where they purchased the SW ¼-25-21-2-W5 from the C.P.R. They built a house from logs and clay and lived there for a few years. They said they settled in this area because they liked the good spring water.

There were nine children in the Konschuh family: Mary, John, Henry, Margaret, Katherine, Adam, Jake, Pete and Dave. Jake and Pete attended Alexandra School.

A few years later they sold the farm to John Goerlitz and moved to Beiseker, Alberta, then to Maple Creek, Saskatchewan, then back to Cluny, Alberta. They then retired to Calgary.

My grandfather told me that once when they were driving home from Calgary across country on the dusty trails, wild cattle suddenly surrounded the buggy. He used the buggy whip on the horses and they squeezed through an opening, narrowly getting away from the wild cattle.

MR. AND MRS. ADAM KROM

Mr. and Mrs. Adam Krom emigrated to Canada from Saratov Russia in 1898. It took them five to six weeks by C.P.R., to get to Calgary. They were met by the Poffenroth and Kaiser families at the station.

Mr. Krom's first job was digging post-holes for the city at 10¢ a hole. In 1900 he worked for Pat Burns on his ranch and later was employed by the Brewery for 10¢ per hour, ten hours a day. In 1903 De Winton was graced by the Krom family, now increased to three, with the birth of a baby girl, Mary, born in 1899. Back to Calgary in 1905 where he worked for the C.P.R. In 1906 they moved back to De Winton, to the same farm where the family grew to nine, three boys and four girls; Mary, Henry (Dick), Dave, Sophie, Fred, Tillie and Hilda. All attended Alexandra School.

Mr. and Mrs. Krom retired to Calgary in 1928 and son, Henry, farmed the family farm. Dave farmed five miles southwest of De Winton and daughter Mary, Mrs. Poffenroth, farmed 1½ miles north of De Winton.

Mr. Krom lived to the ripe old age of ninety years.

JOHN AND MARY KROMM — by Phyllis Dick — Granddaughter

John Kromm came to Canada in 1905 from Saratov, Russia and settled in Calgary, Alberta. He worked for the Calgary Brewery for ten years before moving to the Alexandra District in 1918 to farm.

He married Mary Konschuh and their children were: Mary, (deceased) who married Fred Goerlitz (deceased) of the Alexandra District. They had two children, Frances and Harvey; Amelia, who married John Schaber and now living in Calgary. They had three children, Gladys, Harold and Marjorie; Katie, who married Henry Shierman of the Alexandra District. They had four children, Phyllis, Ronald, Norman and Garry; Jessie, who married Humphrey Hemus of the Black Diamond District. They had three children, Cyril, Margaret, and Donald; Rienold who married Mary Mockett (deceased). They had five children, Hazel (deceased), William (Bill), Sharon, Allen and Meryle. Rienold is remarried and now lives at Red Deer, Alberta; and Albert (bachelor) of the home place.

Standing l. to r. Dave Konschuh, Lydia and Adam Konschuh and family, Mrs. Jake Konschuh, Mrs. Philip Konschuh, Amelia Kromm, Mrs. John Kromm, Rienold Kromm, Mr. John Kromm. Driver, Jake Kromm.

Standing left to right: Amelia, Katie, Mrs. John Kromm, Rienold, Mr. John Kromm and Jessie. Mary and Albert are missing.

The children did not attend school when they lived in the Alexandra District because it was too far away. Later when the family purchased the NE ¼-9-21-1-W5, the children went to Stormont School.

Seven Day Adventist church services were held every Saturday on a rotating basis in five or six different homes in the area. The services were usually conducted by the men because there was not a regular minister. The families attending church would stay for lunch and sometimes supper. During the seasons when the horses were being used for farmwork, the families walked to the services so the horses could have a day off to rest.

Mrs. Kromm passed away in 1926. Mr. Kromm retired to Calgary, Alberta in 1947 and died in 1955.

Farming, the church and raising a family were their only interests in life.

MR. AND MRS. CONRAD KROMM

In the spring of 1913 Mr. and Mrs. Conrad Kromm settled on SW¼ 32-21-1-W5 which they had bought in 1909. In 1929 they bought SE¼ 31, SW¼ 31, NW¼-30-21-1-W5. They lived on the farm from 1913 to 1943 when they retired to Calgary. There were nine children: Mary (deceased), Betty (deceased), Pauline (deceased) was married to Ross Sinclair of Vancouver; Philip, married Marie Miller, lives in Calgary, has two boys, two girls and two grandsons; Emma (Mrs. Gordon Stancer), Calgary, one son, one daughter, two granddaughters, one grandson; Daniel, married Lillias Baillie, lives in Calgary; Edward, Calgary, married Elsie Lienwebber has one son; Martha (Mrs. Bert Lee), Calgary; Louise (Mrs. Fred Knittel), Bradner, B.C., one son.

Daniel took over the farm in 1943 and farmed it until 1958 and moved into Calgary in 1959, where he works for Canadian Western Natural Gas Co. and Lil works for the Calgary School Board. Their family: Dianne (Mrs. Bertrum Kniss), Calgary, one son, one daughter; Anita (Mrs. Christian Nieslens), Prince

George, B.C., three daughters; Richard, at home, Lorne married Anita Sprenger, Calgary, one son and ?; Jane (Mrs. Robert Ford) Norma, at home.

JOSEPH AND VERNA MILLS

In April, 1930 Joseph and Verna Mills moved from Calgary to the Conrad Shierman quarter, west of De Winton, with five children; Elfleda, Irene, Billy, Harold and Ernest. Our furniture was sent to the De Winton Railway Siding.

Three teams went to pick up the furniture, Billy, eleven years old and Harold, eight, had their first experience driving horses. The road was quite new and rather heavy at that time of year. There was an experienced driver leading the way, two boys and Joe behind them to keep looking after them and, needless to say, Mother had two frightened sisters at home waiting for them.

The children started school after Easter Holidays at Alexandra School and, very quickly, learned to drive the buggy and ride horses to school.

In 1932 we bought the SW¼ 36-21-2-W5 where we had very nice neighbours, Robert Eliott, on the west, F. M. Holden Family, north, Fred and Mary Goerletz and family, east, Norman and Mrs. Anderson, south and Mr. and Mrs. Dave Wylie on the south west. Our first neighbours and, all in all, very wonderful families. We all enjoyed our work and home on the farm and soon had a dozen or more cows and horses and, close to a hundred sheep. The children grew up so fast and made wonderful friends, both at school and after. All three boys were farmers.

Billy went overseas at the country's call for men, after more than five years overseas, he was on his way home on furlough, on the high seas, when the Armistice was signed. He bought a farm west of the home place and farmed successfully.

Elfelda married Joseph J. Roberts and they went to Buck Lake and farmed.

Irene married Cecil Baxter of Aylmer, Ontario, later, being widowed, she moved west again with her two children.

Ernest went east to Aylmer to visit Irene, met and married Erie Berdan of Springfield, Ontario, moved west again after a few years and farmed at Buck Lake until his death, November 3, 1973.

Harold married Margaret McKevitt of the Red Deer Lake District and is living on the F. M. Holden ranch.

Billy married Jean Kunder of Red Deer Lake, they sold their farm and are living in Bluffton, Alberta.

MR. AND MRS. GEORGE A. PEARSON

Mr. Pearson bought the E½ and NW¼ 7-22-1-W5 in 1913. He was a trustee on the Alexandra school board and the children: Randolph, Eleanor, Kay, Betty, Moore and Joan (Wooten), attended Alexandra school. Several of them also attended De Winton high school.

During their residence in the area they raised sheep, about 200 in a flock, and Clydesdale horses. They remained in the district until the early '60's.

THE POFFENROTHS

In the spring of 1914, cousins John and Conrad

Poffenroth and their families, moved to the De Winton area with one cow, a dozen chickens, a team of horses and a walking plough each. The location of this farm was N.½-19-21-1-W5th, and there was fifty-five acres broke.

They stayed together for a year and then in 1915, John bought the farm and Conrad went back to Calgary. In 1917, they moved back to another farm in De Winton where Dalzells and Wylies were neighbours.

In the fall of 1922 they moved back to Calgary again. The Marshalls, Grahams and Andersons were their neighbours when they returned to the De Winton area in 1924. By now, Conrad and Annie had six children. They were Victor, Amy, Walter, Florence, Albert, Gordon, and Roy their last child was born that year of 1924.

Conrad and his family moved to our present location — N.½ 20-21-1-W5 in 1927. During that spring, Victor worked for his neighbour, John Poffenroth, on the farm that the families had moved to thirteen years before.

Conrad and his family were living in a granary at the time, while the house was being built. Victor came home during the Easter week-end and asked his brothers and sisters if the granary was cold. They told him it was so cold that the Easter eggs froze.

Victor claims the weather was beautiful for about six weeks during the spring of 1928. He worked for H. Graham and broke up land. The weather changed abruptly in June, and it rained every day for a month, making work impossible.

In 1931, Conrad and his family moved to Keoma, leaving Victor to farm by himself for a year.

The Victor Poffenroth Family, 1952 — Victor, Clara, Stanley, Ervan, Esther, Marilyn.

Wedding bells were in the offing, and in 1932 Victor married Clara Geier of Keoma. During the following years they had four children; Stanley, Ervan, Esther and Marilyn. Victor bought another quarter from Mr. McNiell, S.W.¼-28-21-1-W5th and they continued to live on the farm for twenty-nine years.

When Ervan married Shirley Jensen in 1961, Victor and Clara moved to Calgary. With Ervan now farming,

this made the third generation of Poffenroths to live on the same half section.

Stanley got married the following year, and he and his wife Betty and three children live in Calgary.

Esther and her husband, Merle Allen, also live in Calgary, and operate a store.

Marilyn and Robert Jones of Okotoks are married, and living in Wabamun with one son.

Ervan and Shirley have four children.

Clara passed away suddenly in the spring of 1966 leaving Victor a widower for six years. He then married Lily Benner (nee Kromm) in 1972. They reside in Calgary.

GEORGE AND JOHN POFFENROTH — by Edward Poffenroth

This is the story of my father, John, and my grandfather, George, Poffenroth as told to me by my aunt, my father's sister, Mary (Poffenroth) Weitz.

My Grandfather, George Poffenroth, was born in Saratov, Russia and first settled in the Idaho, Washington area of the North-Western United States along with other relatives and friends. In the late 1880s his wife, Mother, three brothers and sister, came to the Calgary area for an unknown number of years. Still undecided where to settle permanently, the family returned to Moscow, Idaho, where my father, John, was born. In 1894, when my father was only six weeks old, the family returned to Calgary. After a long journey by covered wagon, Grandfather's brother, Pete, settled near Wetaskiwin, Alberta, Henry and Chris, in the De Winton area and Grandfather, homesteaded in the Alexandra area, SE¼ 1-22-2-W5, which most people will remember as the Russell Evans farm.

Aunt Mary was born in 1896 and remembered much about her childhood years in the Alexandra District. The family lived in a three room log house. Their days were filled with work to provide a living. With little land broken for growing grain, they were mainly dependent upon their farm animals for their livelihood. They had five or six milk cows which, for the lack of a barn, had to be milked outside in a corral, whatever the weather. Even though they did not own a cream separator, one of the girls' chores was to churn butter for sale in Calgary.

The chickens, being more fortunate than the cows, lived in a chicken house topped with a sod roof. There were also ducks and pigs to be cared for. The weekly trip to Calgary to sell butter, eggs and whatever farm animals were available, was a long journey with horse and buggy. Dad talked about crossing Fish Creek, near Midnapore, when the creek was high from melting snow in the spring. The water was so deep the horses had to swim and the wagon box had to be fastened to the running gear to keep it from floating away.

The family's food consisted mainly of what was raised on the farm. Pork was salted to keep it from spoiling, saskatoons, rhubarb and apples were the common fruits. Fruits and vegetables were usually made into jam or pickles in order to keep them. These were stored in wooden pails.

When Dad was nine years old, the Alexandra School was built. Dad and Aunt Mary were amongst the first children to attend the school. It was there, at school, that Dad and Aunt Mary first learned to speak English. My Aunt's most vivid memory of the school was that the desks were nailed to the floor.

There was some grain grown on the farm. The fields were laboriously tilled with a walking plow. The seeding was done by broadcasting the seed by hand. When the grain was cut with a binder, Aunt Mary's job was to sit on the middle horse and prevent the horses from eating the grain. Three horses were used to run the threshing machine. The bundles were loaded on a rack and brought to the machine where the men cut the strings and fed the threshing machine by hand. Chris Poffenroth and Grandfather, owned a threshing machine together, and with their combined equipment and energy, managed to harvest their own grain. Later steam outfits were used.

Grandmother was fortunate enough to have a sewing machine. Aunt Mary learned to operate it before Grandmother but only because she practiced when she should have been churning butter. She chuckled with laughter when she admitted that she had made her younger sister do the churning.

The family highlight of the week was the Sunday gathering, at one home, for church and Sunday School. Conrad Girletz, my maternal Grandfather, was the layman who usually took charge of the service. Before the service they usually had Sunday dinner together. The host family provided the meal which usually consisted of such things as fruit soup, barley soup, meat and potatoes and a special home-made bread baked in a large square pan and topped with eggs. The men were first to sit to eat the meal, followed by the children and, last of all, the women. Aunt Mary considered this custom to be a particularly friendly arrangement as each person could visit with those that had common interests. Before departing, arrangements were made regarding their next place of meeting and everyone returned home to their regular duties until the following Sunday.

Eventually, the family moved to Calgary and, in 1905, bought the Elbow View Hotel in, what is now, the Mission District. This building was later renovated to accommodate stores and apartments and was demolished in the summer of 1976.

Dad enjoyed telling tales of his experiences as the taxi driver or 'buggy driver' from the C.P.R. Station to the hotel. During the years of prohibition the hotel was sold and Grandfather and Grandmother retired to the Riverside District.

My most vivid memory of my grandparents was their thankfulness that they were far away from the strife and civil war in Russia.

Dad married Marie Wills in 1913 and returned to the Alexandra District to farm the N½ 19-21-1-W5. When he commenced farming his resources were meagre but, with his determination and willingness to work hard, he proved to be a successful farmer.

Marie passed away in 1918, a victim of influenza. Dad's parents returned to the farm to live with him and help him care for his two small sons, Victor and Dan. In 1919 he was remarried to Anna Marie (Amy) Girletz (1901-1972). They later moved to the SW¼ 7-22-1-W5 where their son, Harvey now lives. They retired to Calgary in 1952 where they were both able to enjoy a more leisurely way of life.

Dad might be remembered as one to make "a hard bargain" but I remember him as a man that would keep that bargain whether it was to his advantage or not and, it didn't have to be on paper.

Mother was the wit of the family, always being thoughtful and kind to others and doing her bit to bring laughter and cheer to those around her.

Seven children: (1) Victor, married Hilda Shierman and now residing in High River, three children, Vernon, Arlene and Evelyn, ten grandchildren. (2) Dan, married Elsie Shierman and now residing in Kelowna, B.C., three children, Mary, Darlene and Kenneth, three grandchildren. Victor and Dan were sons of John and Marie. (3) Clara, married Bert Jacobson and now residing in Kelowna, B.C. (4) Edward, married Mary Bishop and now farming in the Red Deer Lake area, four children Larry, Garry, Keith and Carol, four grandchildren. (5) Harvey, married Victoria Collett and now farming near Red Deer Lake, five children, Corrine, Rhonda, Brian (deceased), Joan, Kevin, one grandchild. (6) Lenora, married Peter Antooshkin and now residing in Redlands, California, two children, Linda and Becky, one grandchild. (7) Paul, married Sandra Thirston and now residing in Calgary, four children, Cheryl, Karen (deceased), Matthew and Tracy.

HARVEY POFFENROTH — by V. Poffenroth

Harvey was born June 8, 1927 — son of John and Amy Poffenroth.

He attended Alexandra School. He farmed with his father on the home place — S.W. 7-22-15.

In 1951 he married Victoria Collett of Calgary. They had five children; Corinne, Rhonda, Brian, Joan and Kevin. Brian was killed in a motor cycle accident in 1970. Corinne is now Mrs. Brian Lynch. They have one son, Jesse. Rhonda married Graham Cannon from Okotoks and they have two children, Joel and Jody.

Harvey bought the home place from his father in 1962 and entered into the feedlot business — gradually expanding each year to feed up to 1000 head.

In 1968 he bought the Russell Evans farm which was the original homestead of his grandfather.

In 1975 he decided to go into the slaughter business, processing his own beef, selling sides and also custom killing. It is known as Red Deer Lake Meat Processing and opened its doors November 23, 1975.

VICTOR AND HILDA POFFENROTH — by Hilda Poffenroth

Victor is a native son, born in Calgary and brought by his parents to the farm eight miles west of De Winton, N½-19-21-1-W5.

It is very hilly country and they lived on this place until 1927 when his Dad, John Poffenroth, bought the Fletcher place about ten miles southwest of Midnapore. Victor left school to help with the farming, as they farmed both places.

I (Hilda Shierman) was born in Calgary and grew up in the same district; we both went to Alexandra School. We rode horses through deep snow and cold weather to a school that had a very poor heating system. Often we would have to sit with our coats and mitts on to do our lessons. The teacher then usually boarded at a neighbor's place. Our first teacher was Lena Dalzell, now Mrs. Jim Montgomery of Blackie.

In 1937 Victor and I were married and lived on the "old home place." In 1948 we built a new house and moved out of the 50-year-old, cold, log house. We did most of the building ourselves as $1.50 per hour for a carpenter seemed much too high. We certainly enjoyed our new house, but the old log house still holds many memories, like the children playing on the couch all day as the floor was too cold, and shovelling snow out of the kitchen after each blizzard, or trying to peel frozen vegetables — just little things like that. The children still love to reminisce.

In 1951 we got power and thought that nothing much nicer than that could happen. Just to switch on a light was wonderful. In June 1951 we had a freak snow storm that took our power out for almost two weeks. Some of the power poles were lifted right out of the ground.

We farmed in the De Winton district for twenty-two years, then in 1959 we sold the farm and bought a section in the High River district, ten miles west of town, known as the Sellers place. We lived there until 1968, then sold out and moved to town.

Our son Vernon farmed the George McIntosh place from 1962 to 1965.

We have three children, Vernon, Arlene and Evelyn. They also went to Alexandra School, making three generations of the family to attend the same school. They also rode on horseback and it hadn't been improved much over the years. They did dig a basement and put in a furnace, and there was quite a change of teachers.

The girls were bussed into Okotoks for high school. They enjoyed this but at times they would think about what some children missed by not riding a horse.

Vernon and his wife now live in Calgary and have four children — Wesley, Wanda, and twins, Trista and Terry.

Arlene and Winston Edwards lived in Okotoks for about eleven years, then moved to Salmon Arm, B.C. They have four children: Gary, Mark, and twins, Lynn and Lora.

Evelyn and Rubin started out in Calgary, but as Rubin works for a bank, they have been transferred from place to place, the last transfer being from Peace River to San Francisco. They now live in Concord, California, and have two children, Darren and Debra.

Twice we were able to take five generation pictures — Arlene and Gary first, then Vernon and Wesley with myself, my father, Adam Shierman, and grandmother, Mrs. Adam Shierman, Sr.

ANDREW AND ANNA RUSCAK

Andy and Anna Ruscak and their three children, two girls and a boy, moved to Midnapore in November of 1942 from a small irrigation district of Tilley, Alberta. They moved the cattle, horses, machinery and household things themselves on a one and a half ton truck except for a load of horses which a friend helped bring. Then we slowly settled in, the house was so cold

we had a pile of snow in one corner of the living room, the water had to be hauled from a spring quite a way from the house. There was no power so we used kerosene lamps, used a radio which used batteries. We kept the milk, butter and cream in a big container in the well to keep it cool.

The children went to Alexandra School about one and a half miles south east. The school was a very old building with a big stove at one end and stove pipes going from one end to the other of the school. It used to get so cold in there we had to bring our desks around the stove to keep warm. Andy Ruscak used to go to the school board and say, "you better do something about that school," so they asked him to be a trustee but he said, "Gee, my English isn't so good, get somebody else." They said, "you know what you are talking about," so he became a trustee. Then he fought for a better school and we did get one with a basement and a furnace which was a lot better.

We mostly travelled by truck but went to school on horseback. We finally got a power line in 1948, I think, and we were able to get a fridge, freezer, radio and even a T.V. in 1953. It was so nice just to push a switch and have light in the house. We got our first car in about 1950.

For farming at first we had a lug tractor, used horses for the binder, harrowing, cutting grass, stacking and hauling hay. Then years later, we used a rubber tire tractor, changed from threshing machines to swather and combine and also used the tractor more for haying.

JAMES SCOTT — by M. Sheepy

James Scott was born in Scotland in 1884 and was a saddle master. He raised a family of twelve children. His only surviving child, William Scott, celebrated his 90th birthday, November 8, 1976, at Brantford, Ontario. After the death of his second wife he came to De Winton Alberta to visit his daughter and son-in-law, Mr. and Mrs. John McNeill, and another son-in-law, Jack Wylie. After a short stay in Alberta he took sick and passed away in 1921 at the age of 77 years. Interment was in Pine Creek Cemetery.

JOSEPH AND JESSIE (DAZELL) SHEEPY — by R. J. Sheepy

Joseph Sheepy was born February 15, 1865, at Paisley, Ontario, son of Joseph and Anne Sheepy who had come from England. He had two brothers and two sisters.

In 1884, at the age of nineteen, he came to Alberta and worked on the railroad at Kicking Horse Pass, helping to put the railway through to Vancouver.

At the time of his passing, Mr. Sheepy owned a section of land which he began to accumulate when he bought the S.W.¼-21-22-1-W5 from the C.P.R. in 1885. He later acquired the S.E.¼ of the same section which was in School District 85 (Midnapore) as well as the S½-15-22-1-W5 in Pine Creek School District 84.

February 9, 1898 he married Jessie Dalzell, one of ten children of John and Isabella Dalzell who had come from Scotland. Jessie was born on September 11, 1874 and came from Stratford, Ontario to keep house for her brother, Jack, before her marriage.

Mr. and Mrs. R. J. Sheepy wedding picture Feb. 9, 1898.

A two-roomed house was built on S.W.½-21-22-1-W5 and, in 1907, three more rooms were added. This house is still standing (1976). Lightning struck the house in the summer of 1931 causing extensive damage and again a few years later causing minor damage. In 1927 it was hit by a cyclone which tore part of the roof off.

Porcupine Creek flows through this place and, in the late 1800's and early 1900's, pioneers, with buggies and wagons, travelled the ridge past the house on their way to Calgary. 14th Street, as it is now known, was all bog.

Mr. Sheepy gave his help and support to get a school for Midnapore. He was a school trustee, road councillor and travelled around the country by horse and buggy. He was one of the first to make a donation for the De Winton Hall, 1918.

Mr. and Mrs. Sheepy and family belonged to the Presbyterian Church at Pine Creek and attended regularly. Mrs. Sheepy was a member of the Women's Missionary Society of Pine Creek Church, and active worker for the Lacombe Home in Midnapore and the Wood's Christian Home for Orphan and Needy Children, Calgary.

Mr. Sheepy loved music so the family had a piano in the early 1900's. Many get togethers were held around the piano. He had one of the first phones installed and news of births, deaths, new families arriving and other messages were relayed from that phone.

Horses were another of his interests and he raised a number of colts. He owned "Gold Seal" a prize winning stallion at the Calgary Exhibition.

There were four children in the family; John Reginald (deceased 1972) was married to Blanche Moon, had one son, Cecil, of Calgary. William Thomas (deceased 1966) was married to Alice Green, had one daughter, Pat (Foster). Anne Isabelle, married John Hamilton (deceased 1973), has two sons, Jim and Jack. Robert Joseph, married Margaret Wylie has one daughter, Lila May, Calgary.

Robert Sheepy owns the S.W.¼-21-22-1-W5, the original land bought by his father.

Joseph Sheepy died suddenly, January 26, 1919 and Jessie died February 17, 1935.

ADAM SHIERMAN — by Hilda Poffenroth

Adam Shierman came from Russia at the age of five years with his parents. They settled for a time in Calgary. They later moved to a farm about twelve miles west of De Winton where Adam grew up with his brothers and sisters.

Education wasn't as important then as it is now. The Alexandra School was the only school then and that is where he went for what little education he got. He had to stay home and help with the farm a lot of the time that he should have been in school.

In 1913 he married Elizabeth Fisher of Calgary. They lived with his parents for a few years and then took over the farm.

In 1929 he bought the S½-33-21-1-W5, which didn't have buildings or fences. He developed it himself, still farming with horses. He bought his first tractor in 1941 and his first car was a Model T Ford.

In 1943 he left the farm and went to Calgary where he worked for the C.P.R. in the Ogden Shops until his retirement in 1960. The farm was sold in 1960.

Mr. Shierman lived out his life in Calgary, and passed away in January 1974 at the age of 78. His wife Elizabeth passed away in February 1939 at the age of 45.

They had five children, four of them still living (1975): Alexander in Calgary, Hilda in High River, and Harry and Edward in Calgary.

ADAM AND CATHERINE SHIERMAN — by Elaine Taylor

Adam and Catherine Shierman came to Canada in 1900 from Saratov, Russia. They were 31 and 28 years of age at the time.

There were seven children in their family and Henry, a nephew whom they brought from Russia with them. Their children were: Adam, born in Russia in 1895 (deceased), married Elizabeth Fisher. They had four children, Alex, Hilda, Harry and Edward. All the other children were born in Calgary, Alberta. They were: Katherine (Katie) born in 1900, married Philip Befus. They had five children, Edward, Sam, Ivan, Eugene and Caroline; Mary, born in 1902 (deceased) married Charlie Kimmel (deceased). They had three children, Walter, Harold and Wilfred (deceased), remarried Fred Tetreau; Dave, born in 1904, married Molly Schultz (deceased). They had four children, Helen, Donald, Audrey and Ruby (deceased), remarried Kay Begley; Henry, born in 1906, married

Mr. and Mrs. Adam Shierman.

born in 1912, married Margaret Tisher. They had one child, David. He remarried Josephine Dougherty and they had two children, Kathy and Sharon also a stepdaughter Carol.

Adam Shierman worked at the Calgary Brewery for a few years before renting land in the Alexandra District. In 1908 they purchased the SE¼-25-21-2-W5 from the Hudson's Bay Co. but by 1914 there was not enough land for the entire family on the quarter section so they bought the NE¼-30-21-1-W5 from Henry Kromm who quit farming and joined the army. The eldest son, Adam, remained on the first quarter for several years. From 1932 to 1934 Henry and family farmed it.

Both farms were raw land without buildings. Log houses were built at each place, of spruce trees hauled on the sleigh from Priddis during the winter. The houses were built by Mrs. Shierman and son Adam placing and stacking the logs on the ground and Mr. Shierman pulling them into place by rope. The cracks were filled with chinking made by the younger members of the family. Lumber was used on the roof. The other buildings were constructed of rails tied with wire, and they had straw roofs.

They homesteaded the NE¼-22-21-2-W5 although they never lived on it. As many as 40 or 50 horses were kept there at one time.

Church was a very important part of their life. They held weekly services Sunday in homes of about six families of the Lutheran denomination, primarily. Only rarely did a minister lead their worship. At the home where the service was held, everyone stayed for a meal which consisted of fruit or barley soup.

Mr. Shierman liked coyote hounds and had one which delivered dead coyotes on the step many mornings. Mr. Shierman did the landwork and Mrs. Shierman and the children did the chores.

Katherine (Katie) Kromm. They had four children, Phyllis, Ronald, Norman and Garry; Johanna, born in 1908, married Conrad Geier. They had five children, Melvin, Floyd, Howard, Leonard and Doris; Peter,

Mrs. Catherine Shierman seated in the centre with some of her great-grandchildren celebrating her 87th birthday at a family picnic.

Mr. and Mrs. Shierman retired to Calgary in 1928. Adam Shierman passed away in 1944 at the age of 74. Catherine Shierman died in 1969 at the age of 97. She had 27 grandchildren, 75 great-grandchildren and 14 great-great-grandchildren.

HENRY AND KATIE SHIERMAN — Cattle brand 2V Right Hip — by Pat Shierman

Henry and Katie Shierman were both born and raised in the Alexandra and Stormont School District west of De Winton, Alberta, and have spent their entire lives farming in this area.

Henry and Katie Shierman (nee Kromm) were married in Calgary on June 26, 1929 and took up residence on the family farm. The farm was rented from Henry's father until 1934 when they purchased the home quarter (NE 30-21-1-W5) and an adjoining quarter (NE 29-21-1-W5). In later years two additional quarters were purchased to complete the section and also farm land was leased. This land was home for Henry and Katie's four children, Phyllis, Ronald, Norman and Garry. While the children were growing up the farming was a family effort. Beef cattle and grain were raised but the primary income was the Dairy business.

When Phyllis became of age to attend High School, she left the farm and roomed and boarded in Calgary with her aunt (Katie Befus) and her Grandmother, while attending Western Canada High School. Ronnie and Norman's interests were the farming and dairy business in partnerships with their Dad. Garry continued his studies at Okotoks High School while living at home. He was President of the Okotoks High School Students Union in 1961-1962. Upon completion of his grade twelve at Okotoks he received 6 Proficiency Awards for his school subjects. He also received a $300.00 bursary from the Royal Caledonian Curling Club.

Ronnie married Evelyn Mossfeldt in 1951 and they have two children, Terry-Lynn and Donald. Terry married Bruno Poulsen and live in Calgary. Donald is at home.

Phyllis married David Nagloren in 1952 and they have three children, Kenneth, Janet and Cathi. Kenneth married Birtha Poulsen (Bruno's sister),

they have two children, Dennis and David and live in Calgary. Janet married Gerry Oster, a farmer at Hussar, Alberta. Cathi is with her parents in Calgary attending school.

Norman married Patsy Murphy in 1962.

Garry married Mary Sinclair in 1965 and they have a son Wayne.

Henry and Katie have now retired, but still reside on the family farm with Norman and Pat, and Ronnie and Evelyn as close neighbours. Phyllis and husband Alan Dick reside in Calgary, and Garry and wife Ethel make Pinawa, Manitoba their home.

Since Henry and Katie's retirement, traveling, camping, fishing and hunting are their interests of which they do a lot. They also keep busy in their yard growing and maintaining the lawn, garden, trees, shrubs and flowers.

THE SPARROW RANCH — Winnie Gilbert.

South west of Midnapore, about twelve miles into the hills, there are two sections of land known as the Sparrow ranch. This land was purchased by Mr. Herbert Gilbert in 1928 from T. M. Little, and sold to O'Connors in 1949. Listening to the reminiscing of the four sons, Elmore, Loyal, Stan and Morris, life was far from dull in that district.

The year before they took over the ranch, a tornado struck through the valley, completely demolishing a large dairy barn, and a garage with a car in it. Windows with the glass still intact, were found as far east as the Russel Evans place, and bits and pieces were ploughed up years later, where planks had been driven into the ground.

The original log house, believed to be the John Hamilton homestead, used as the bunk house, outlived the second larger log house. It was destroyed by fire on Christmas day in 1930. The boys still talk of the keepsakes they lost, not to mention the turkey.

Blocked roads were a problem back in the hills and as the mail route, run by Pop Ward, went twice a week, these roads had to be kept open. Before the municipality had a plough out, the Gilberts fashioned their own snow plough with two V shaped planks, and pulled it with six head of horses, or when possible they would drive the lug tractor up and down the roads to break trail to Midnapore. One hole was so bad in wet weather, the boys would fill it with posts. Needless to say, there is a bridge at that spot today.

The telephone line ended at the Sparrow ranch, so all the neighbors west of there came to use the phone. Like all rural districts of that period, it was very sociable. Bridge parties and other neighborhood get-togethers, were held at Maclins, Kierans, Pattersons, Latters, Griffiths, and Gilberts. Red Deer Lake and Priddis dances were also a highlight. The fellows still laugh about some of those escapades, like the night they emptied home brew beer into a jug to take to the dance, not realizing till they passed it around later, that it contained formaldehyde at one time.

At threshing time the neighbors helped each other. Gilberts first had a steam outfit, later threshed with a tractor, but it required large crews of men and horses to keep things going. Mrs. Gilbert was a good cook, and was called upon to feed up to twenty men in

Back row, L. to R.: Phyllis Dick, Carolyn, Kenneth and Scott Kimmel, Pamela (Carolyn's sister), Lydia Kimmel, Barbara Kimmel. Front row, L. to R.: Cathi Nagloren, Henry Shierman, Jeff, Ethel, Garry and Wayne Shierman, and Katie Shierman.

harvest time. Cooks were up at four in the morning to prepare breakfast while men tended and fed their horses. No dish washers in those days, so the noon day meal was being prepared while doing breakfast dishes. Following the big noon meal came the lunch which was taken out to the field to the men, dozens of fresh buns, or doughnuts, and pots of coffee. Supper was another large meal. By the time those dishes were finished, it would be ten o'clock, every one dropped exhausted into bed for tomorrow would be more of the same.

The Gilberts raised a lot of hogs, marketing around seven to eight hundred feeder pigs a year, but when the large hog house burned, this business was dealt a serious blow. Loyal tells how they fought to get the pigs out during the blaze, but the animals fought just as hard to go back in and a lot were lost.

Hunters were always a problem in that area in the fall. Mr. Gilbert used to spend a great deal of time on his saddle horse patrolling, like all farmers and ranchers, he resented the intrusion of thoughtless folk who didn't bother to get permission to hunt.

Nearly all the farmers milked cows and shipped cream at that time. Loyal Gilbert bought the cream route from Ivor Brain in 1936, married a Nanton girl, Winnie, and carried on the business of picking up the cream. The five gallon cans are now prized as antiques. Each housewife would entrust their grocery list and other shopping to Loyal. Most of the purchases were made at Williams Brothers who then dealt in groceries and hardware. The steamed and sterilized cream cans were returned to the farmers, together with their orders the same afternoon.

Eventually Loyal sold his route to Andy Templeton, and went farming at Nanton. He took over Gilbert Brothers real estate business upon the death of his father in 1963 but to keep his hand in farming, had land at Chestermere Lake until 1974. Loyal, his wife and son Dan live in Calgary.

Elmore, the eldest, joined the army and was posted east to Ottawa. He married Margaret there, and came back after the war, living for a short time at the ranch, later working at Lincoln Park until retiring. He has a son and daughter.

Stan and Bert Griffith were always working with electrical equipment, and built a neighborhood fence phone between Griffiths, Maclins and Latters. The phones worked fine providing the gates were kept closed. When the war came along, Stan joined the air force, was a navigator and upon his return to Calgary, became engineer for CJCJ working with Don McKay, then transferred to CFAC where he eventually became chief engineer, and retired in 1974.

Morris was in the airforce too, married Peggy, who was also in the forces. They have five children, all living in Calgary.

Jean Gilbert never lived at the Sparrow ranch but loved to spend weekends riding and visiting her brothers. She became an accomplished musician, winning gold medals in both violin and piano, and won scholarships to the Royal Academy in London, where she became pianist for Sadlers Wells Ballet Company. She now lives in Maryland.

As a prairie-raised girl, coming to the Midnapore district as Loyal's bride, I thought it was picturesque,

the abundance of cold clear spring water, the deep rich black soil, where Mrs. Gilbert and I could grow fantastic flowers and house plants. I remember picking saskatoons, or taking long walks in the warm summer afternoons, the friendly visits with the neighbors, the political arguments put forth by my father-in-law. If you were in favor of Social Credit, Mr. Gilbert argued against it, if he found you were anti Wm. Aberhart, he was for him. You learned both sides of the question that way. The Midnapore and Red Deer Lake districts hold pleasant memories for all of us. — Winnie

JAMES WILLIAM TURNBULL

Jim Turnbull was born in 1906. He worked for the Alberta Government in the Department of Highways and boarded with the Jim Dalzells in De Winton. In 1936 he started work in the Turner Valley Oilfields and continued this type of work in various points until 1951 when he moved to oil rigs in Saskatchewan, and then to northern B.C. He retired in 1956 and married. He and his wife, Grace, bought a hotel in Bromhead, Saskatchewan and he remained there until his death in 1962. His wife continued to run the business and passed away in 1967.

Jim Turnbull.

WILLIAM AND MARY (WISHART) TURNBULL —
by Walter Turnbull

J. W. "Will" Turnbull came to the De Winton Area in 1901 and bought Sam Ray's farm the same year, N½ 4 and SW¼ 9-22-1-W5. In 1904 he returned to Ireland and married Mary Wishart, my mother. My brother, Jim, was born in 1906, I was born in 1908 and my sister, Winnie in 1912. Will Turnbull played the piano at all the dances in De Winton for years. He also played the organ in the Anglican Church Saint Phillip's and Saint James. Winnie was christened in this church by Reverend Bennett. Father owned the organ.

In the fall of 1915, he joined the army, the 89th, and went overseas in 1916. In September, 1916 Mother took all three of us to England. We went over on a boat called the "Casandra" and there were only twenty-five passengers on board with twenty-seven stewards to look after us. The rest of the ship was filled with three hundred and fifty horses being shipped for the artillery and the cavalry. We returned on the "Scandanavian". Quite a voyage!! Most of the people were seasick and

Mrs. Turnbull and Winnie, 1914.

Will Turnbull, 1895.

Jim, Walter and Winnie Turnbull, 1913.

it was up to the mothers to keep things clean. I can still smell that ship!

Dad was killed in France, May 3, 1917. We lived in Calgary from October 1917 until spring of 1919 when Mother took a job of housekeeping on the farm that is now Haysboro. In October, 1921 we returned to Calgary and in November, 1922 Mother married Robert H. Collins and we returned to the farm at De Winton. In about 1911 a man by the name of Mr. Green turned the first pheasants out on our farm. The first, I believe, to be turned out in Alberta.

Jim worked on the oil rigs until 1953 when he bought the hotel in Bromhead, Saskatchewan. He died in 1962.

Mother died in 1951 and I took over the farm and still live on it. I never married because the girl I wanted wouldn't marry me and I still can't see getting married for the sake of being married.

Winnie married John Hogan in 1935. They had two sons Johnnie, married and living in Calgary and Terry, married and living in Minnesota. John Hogan died in 1965 and Winnie lives in Calgary.

Robert Collins died in 1974.

WILLIAM AND AGNES (OSWALD) WHYTE—submitted by Walter Turnbull

A confirmed bachelor, Bill Whyte farmed the SW¼ 36-21-1-W5 and 240 acres of NE½ 12-22-1-W5 which he purchased early in 1900 and farmed until his death in 1942.

As many people are, he was inclined to overindulge at the bar and sometimes cause concern to some of his neighbors. He had Barney McKevitt working for him when Barney was still in his teens. One time he had gone into Calgary and when he was ready to come home he phoned Barney to meet him at the Midnapore station. Barney saddled two horses and set out to pick him up. Deep in his cups and with a spare bottle in his hand, Bill got off of the train, handed the bottle to Barney while he got onto his horse and they proceeded home. Bill asked for the bottle so he could have a drink but Barney refused telling him to wait until he got home and, having the faster horse, Barney galloped off ahead. Bill was so mad at this turn of events that he fired Barney. Being alone now it became a problem to get away to town on his own but he devised a way whereby he would hitch up a team and drive to the station then turn the team around and tie up the lines, give the horses a slap and send them off home alone. The John Poffenroth family lived close by and when they would see the team coming with no passenger one of the boys would go out and catch them, tie them in the barn, feed them and look after the chores until Bill returned, sometimes for three or four days at a time. He was well liked in the area and always remained a Scottish gentleman.

In 1931, at the age of 62, Bill decided that the single life was no longer for him and he married Agnes Oswald "Ossie", a long time employee of the D.N.R. in Calgary, with whom he had attended school back in Scotland.

Ossie was of the Christian Science persuasion. One day when she was cooking for threshers and making preserves at the same time, she managed to scald her hand very badly with the syrup from the preserves. Being very busy, she called a lady of similar faith, a Mrs. Birney of Calgary, and told her what had happened, Mrs. Birney assured her that she would look after things from her end. Bill swore that Ossie went to bed that night and slept comfortably till morning.

Bill raised Aberdeen Angus cattle and, I believe, Clydesdale horses. He served overseas with the Canadian Army but no one can remember with which unit. Following his passing Ossie went to live in Winnipeg.

GEORGE AND EMILY (POWER) WONACOTT — by Bert Wonacott

George Wonacott was a member of the R.N.W.M.P. and came west with the second detachment. In July, 1891 he married Maria Emily Power in Pine Creek Presbyterian church with Reverend George Jacques performing the ceremony.

George Wonacott, N.W.M.P. Dress. 1890.

They had a family of six children; Hartnell Robert, 1892, George Albert, 1893, Grace Ivadell, 1896, Ruth Annetta, 1898, and Francis Edward, 1901, Gladys Jean Emily, 1906.

They homesteaded NE¼-6-22-1-W5 homestead No. 33318. He farmed in the district all of his life and passed away March 25, 1912. His wife died November 24, 1942.

The children all attended Alexandra school and lived in the district until they were grown. Many house parties were held in the Wonacott house, Mrs. Wonacott was an excellent pianist and supplied the dance music at these gatherings until she injured one of her hands and was unable to play. The family took part in the community activities and cared about the welfare of their neighbors.

Bertie (George Albert) is the only surviving member of the family. He lived on the home place until April of 1944 when he moved to the NW¼-5-22-1-W5 where he is still living. Frank married Bertha Standish, had one daughter, worked in the trucking business in Calgary both he and Bertha are deceased. Grace married Jack Wylie, her story is elsewhere in the book. Ruth married Jim Ross, had two sons, Jack and Gregor. Jack lives west of Didsbury. Gladys married Charlie Taylor, had one daughter, they lived in the district for a while and retired to Vancouver where Gladys died recently. Hartnell never married and lived in the district all of his life and farmed SE¼-6-22-1-W5.

DAVID LAIDLAW WYLIE — by Cecelia Taylor

David Wylie came to Canada from Lanark, Scotland soon after the turn of the century to join his older brothers, Hugh and Jack who were already farming in the De Winton area.

He worked for Burns Ranches, Midnapore; McInnes Ranch, Midnapore and John Dalzell, De Winton and in Calgary he did general hauling including coal and gravel.

In World War I he saw action in France in the 43rd Battalion as a lieutenant colonel. When he returned to Canada he purchased the NE¼-26-21-2-W5 and half of the NW¼-25-21-2-W5 through the Soldier Settlement Board. In 1928, he married Emily Fendall.

"The Well Dressed Cowboy". David Wylie, 1920.

Mr. and Mrs. George Wonacott, Hartley, Bert, Frank, Ruth, Grace and Gladys.

A keen horse enthusiast, he took great pleasure in raising and breaking Clydesdales having as many as 25 head at one time. One of his teams was exported to Scotland.

David Wylie served in the Veterans' Guard in various locations during World War II and played the drums in their band. Upon his discharge, he received the Canadian Volunteer Service Medal.

He passed away in May, 1948 at 59 years of age. His widow, Emily, sold the farm and retired to a house near her daughter and son-in-law, Cecilia and Bill Taylor. She died at 86 years of age in 1969.

JOHN COSSAR WYLIE — by Margaret Sheepy

John Cossar Wylie was born in Peebles, Scotland, August 6th, 1879. He came to Chatham, Ontario in 1902 and then came west in 1904 and settled on the N.E.¼ 31-21-1-W5th in 1913.

In 1911 he married Margaret Forrest Scott from Lanark, Scotland, in Pine Creek Church. Mrs. Wylie died in 1915 leaving two daughters. Alison, (Mrs. Norman Waddell), who died in 1953, leaving two children and Margaret (Mrs. R. Sheepy), Calgary, who has one daughter.

Jack married Grace Ivadell Wonacott of Midnapore in 1921. Their children: Jean (Mrs. Gegolick), Edmonton, has three children, Ivadell (Mrs. Befus), deceased 1973, leaving four children; Annabelle (Mrs. Krom), Calgary, two children; Ruth (Mrs. Krom), Calgary, four children, Leonard Wylie, living on the home place, two children; Evelyn Wylie, deceased 1937, Arnold Cossar Wylie, unmarried and living in Calgary.

Jack Wylie and first place team at Calgary. Exhibition and Stampede, 1928.

Jack was an active member of the community. He was chairman of the Alexandra School Board for a number of years, and also served on the Board of Pine Creek Church. He was a breeder and exhibitor of purebred Clydesdale horses.

To make life easier, gas from Turner Valley was installed in the house in the late 1920's. Jack Wylie's became the stopover house, between Turner Valley and Calgary, for the Gas Company and Royalite line walkers.

One of the few wind-mills in the district was on the Wylie farm. However, the water supply was very low, so in the winter, he had to haul water for his stock from a spring one-half a mile from the house. This was a daily chore when cattle had to be kept in the barn during the winter months.

Jack's parents, Mr. and Mrs. Hugh Wylie Sr., settled on the adjoining quarter west.

Jack was killed in an accident while driving a team on a bundle rack September 24th, 1946. Grace passed away January 4th, 1954.

HUGH WYLIE SR. AND JR.

It was the early part of the year 1904 that Hugh Wylie Sr. resigned from the Caledonian Railway and prepared to leave his native Scotland for Canada. Arriving in Woodstock, Ontario, he spent the rest of the year and part of the next one working here before venturing farther west to Alberta in 1905. He homesteaded in the De Winton district for a number of years with his brother John Wylie, before buying his own place which is known as N.E.¼ 5-22-1 -W5, and where he farmed until he passed away, suddenly, in January, 1941.

Hugh returned to Scotland in the latter part of the year 1912, where he married Sarah Anne Steele in 1913. He then brought his bride back to Alberta, and to their home where they resided for over twenty-five years. In 1944 Mrs. Wylie went to live in Calgary after leasing the farm which she sold before 1949. She had been very active in church work until she became ill in the early '50s and was forced to sell her home in Calgary and move to Edmonton. Here Mrs. Wylie lived with her daughter, Cathie, and her husband until she passed away in December 1955.

Hugh and Sarah had four children: one son, Hugh, and three daughters, Catherine (Cathie), Elizabeth (Bessie), and Mary. Hugh Jr. left the farm in 1944 to go into the Army which he had joined in 1940 before his father had passed away. When Hugh returned to Calgary after the war was over he resigned from the army and took up the plumbing trade. Hugh still resides in Calgary with his wife, Ruby (Gibson), formerly of Hanna, Alberta, and their family; one son, Robert (who is finishing University), and two daughters; Sandra, (Mrs. James Vincent), and Pamela (still a student).

Cathie also makes her home in Calgary, returning in 1961, after living in Edmonton approximately twelve years. It was in 1949 that Imperial Oil transferred the Coles to Edmonton where Cathie's husband, Peard, was killed in a car accident in 1953. They had four of a family: one son, Keith (Geologist), and three daughters, AnnaMae (Mrs. Gordon Johnson), Patricia (Mrs. Ken Martin), and Marifaith (Comptometer Operator), all of Calgary.

Bessie, and her husband, Harold Phillips made Edmonton their home after their marriage. Nine years later Bessie passed away in 1950. They had twin sons; Harold (Plumber in Richmond, B.C.), and Hugh (Schoolteacher in Edmonton).

Mary (Registered Nurse) went as a medical Missionary to Nigeria, West Africa, in 1952 where she was in charge of the out-patient clinic for a number of years. Mary is now in charge of the Egbe Hospital besides various other duties.

Hugh Wylie Sr. on horse, Margaret "Scott" Wylie and husband Jack Wylie.

MR. AND MRS. HUGH WYLIE SENIOR — by M. Sheepy

Hugh Wylie was born at Lanark, Scotland, 1858 and married Catherine Cossar of Peebles, Scotland, born 1856. They had six children; Hugh, 1877, Jack, 1879, James, 1884, Margaret Wylie, 1887, David, 1889 and Margaret (Jamison — Wereley), 1892.

Mr. and Mrs. Wylie came to Midnapore Alberta in 1911 and settled on a farm one mile west of Midnapore. After a two year stay in the Midnapore district they moved to Crossfield. During this time their son's (Jack) wife, Margaret Scott, died, leaving an infant daughter, Margaret (Sheepy). Mr. and Mrs. Wylie raised Margaret even though they were well on in years.

After a four year stay in Crossfield they moved back to the De Winton district and farmed a quarter section joining their son, Jack's, farm. They were both members of the Pine Creek Church. Mr. Wylie was very punctual in all his work. Mrs. Wylie was kind and gentle and loved children.

Mrs. Wylie died on April 4, 1935, aged 79 and Mr. Wylie died June 2, 1934 at age 76. Both are buried in Pine Creek Cemetery, De Winton.

Others Who Lived in the Alexandra District but Sent no History

Ancelle: French people lived on NW¼ 28-21-1-W5 and sold to J. Harrison about 1913.

Brazil: Brothers, Arthur and Bert with their sister rented NW¼ 22-21-1-W5 from Mr. Laybourne. Returned to England just after WW1 broke out.

Hemmingway: Built on W½ 7-22-1-W5 before WW1.

Laybourne, Algernon: English gentleman bachelor, salesman for English enamelware. Rented to Brazil before WW1, returned to England where he married. Later came back to Canada and lived in Victoria, B.C.

Phillips: Benjamin and Ida, two sons, Adrian and (?). Rented SW¼ 4-22-1-W5 from a Vancouver lawyer, W. D. Davis. Appeared on the Pine Creek Tax Roll in 1897, before Alexandra School District was formed.

Pitchford and Wooding: Lived on the S½ 8-22-1-W5 from about 1905-1908 and sold to DeLermy (?) who sold to Bottomley in about 1922.

Ramsay: Mr. and Mrs. John, had sons attending Alexandra School when they rented the Bill Whyte place in the 1920's. The Whyte place was later sold to Ruscak.

Ray: Stanley Samuel, owned the N½ 4 and SW¼ 9-22-1-W5, had two children in school and one under school age in 1897. Sold to W. Turnbull in 1901. Mentioned in Rev. Dyke's notes.

Dust storm in the 1930s.

Farm Work

C. Patton and gas tractor, 1912.

Les Marshall age 15, taken 1917.

W. H. Jenkins breaking sod in 1926 with an IHC 45 H. P. one cylinder tractor.

Walter Linn with Eben Bremner's nine horse team on a three bottom plow, 1927.

Plowing match 1939. Owner, Fred Davis; Driver, Harry Tucker.

Plowing. Maltman Shaw running engine. Unidentified fireman partly obscure view of Maltman. Hugh Shaw on the plow.

Graham Johnson wooden beam breaking plough.

Hauling grain out of Davisburg in 1925 for Herr Bros. Forest on lead, Fred Maxwell second, Alex Blackwood, Bill Herr then Cliff Herr in rear. Taken at sun up in the fall.

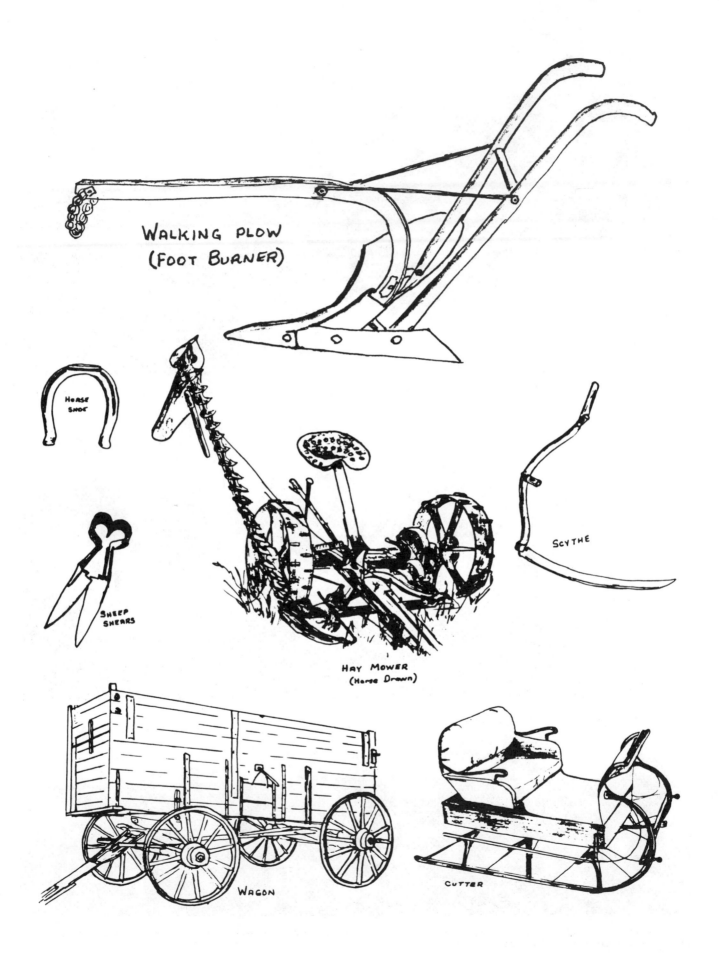

WALKING PLOW
(FOOT BURNER)

HORSE SHOE

SHEEP SHEARS

HAY MOWER
(Horse Drawn)

SCYTHE

WAGON

CUTTER

NIGHT HAWK
DISTINGUISHING WHITE
WING SPOTS

FLICKER
LARGE BROWN
BOBBING FLIGHT

KINGBIRD
: INSECT EATER

—RED

HAIRY WOODPECKER.
RED SPOT ON HEAD
LARGE BILL

CHICK-A-DEE
BLACK CAP
LIGHT BREAST

BANK SWALLOW
Brown above
white below

CATBIRD
Slate Gray Black cap
chestnut patch on
underside of tail

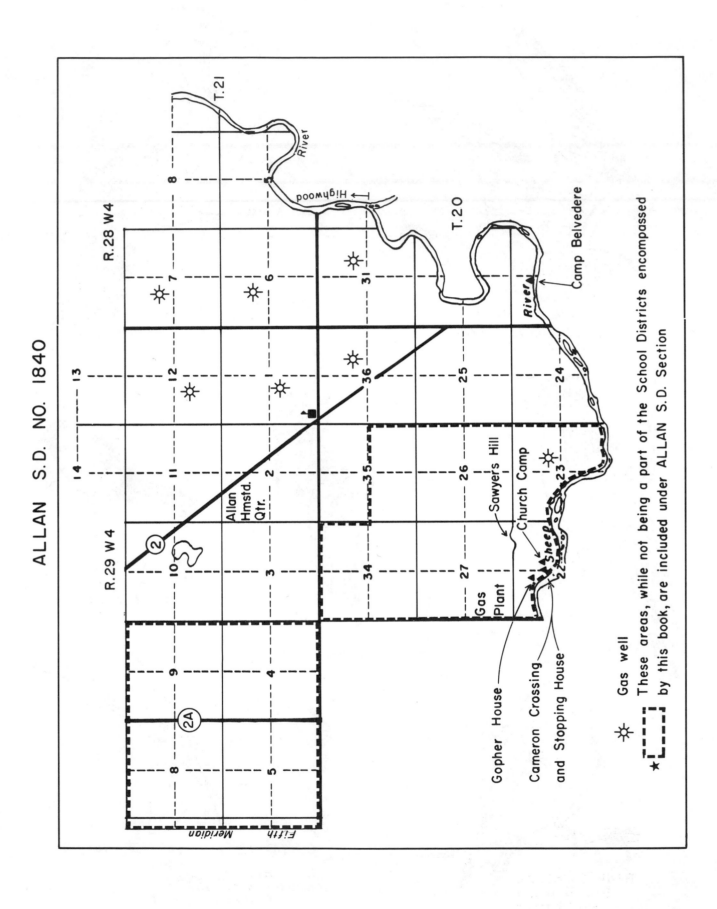

ALLAN S.D. NO. 1840

R.29 W4 R.28 W4

T.21

River

Highwood ←

T.20

River

Camp Belvedere

Allan Hmstd. Qtr.

Sawyer's Hill

Church Camp

Sheep

Gas Plant

Fifth Meridian

Gopher House

Cameron Crossing and Stopping House

☼ Gas well

★ ▪ These areas, while not being a part of the School Districts encompassed
by this book, are included under ALLAN S.D. Section

62

Allan School District

THE ALLAN SCHOOL DISTRICT

The distances to school facilities for many families living northeasterly from Okotoks to Davisburg were too great to permit regular class attendance. Hence a meeting was held at the home of A. Forckel on June 5th, 1908, to determine if there was adequate support for the formation of a further school district. Alex N. Allan was selected as chairman of that meeting. It was decided to proceed with a new school district and Frank Barker (the Elder), one of the early residents in the area offered the school site on the SW¼ 1-21-29-W4. Fittingly the school assumed its name in honor of the first chairman and oldest resident, Mr. Allan, who had arrived from Quebec in 1885 and homesteaded on the NW¼ 2-21-29-W4.

A contract was let to build the school and outbuildings and classes commenced October 28th, 1908, under the tutelage of Miss Ethel Andrews.

The area originally ascribed to the Allan School District No. 1840 comprised about fourteen square miles. From time to time portions of Section 35-20-29-W4 were removed from the Okotoks School District and added to the Allan School District as dictated by the choice of the taxpayer for schooling facilities. Likewise the SW¼ 13 and SE¼ 14 in Township 21-29-W4 fluctuated between the Allan and Davisburg School Districts.

The Allan School closed to classes in 1943 after thirty-five years' service and thereafter the pupils were transported to Okotoks by school bus. The school building was subsequently incorporated into the Sallenbach farmstead. It has been moved slightly from its original location and now serves as a garage and shop.

From its pioneer beginning in the late 1800's and the quarter section homesteads, there have been a few major changes to the Allan School District beyond those common to most other rural areas. The discovery of commercial sulphurous natural gas by Shell in May, 1951, a mile north of the District's north boundary, brought about further development drilling and six productive wells within the original boundaries. A gas plant was built by Texas Gulf Sulphur Company on the eastern edge of Okotoks and production commenced from these wells in June, 1959. The re-routing of Highway No. 2 to by-pass Okotoks introduced a four lane highway diagonally through the Allan School District in Aug. 1955. This new facility made the area much more accessible and was a major factor in fostering the subdivision of certain of its farmlands into small parcels. The combination of these and other circumstances has greatly altered the appearance of the district, particularly since World War II. Perhaps those who chose the name of this book "Sodbusting to Subdivision" had the Allan School District in mind at that time.

ALLAN SCHOOL DISTRICT NO. 1840 — by J. H. Jenkins

On June 5, 1908, a meeting was advertised for the purpose of taking a vote to see if a school district be formed. The meeting was held at A. Forckel's residence. Persons present were R. Children, A. Forckel, W. R. Smith, Frank Barker, J. A. Shields, H. E. Frear and F. P. Coyle.

A. N. Allan was elected chairman of the meeting and R. Children was elected secretary at a salary of $25 a year. It was agreed to form a school district. A. Forckel, A. N. Allan and F. Barker were elected as trustees for the Allan School District No. 1840. The school was named by the Department of Education, Edmonton, after Mr. A. N. Allan as he was the oldest resident at that time.

The board decided to visit the site being donated by Mr. Frank Barker. 1½ acres SW ¼ 1-21-29 W4.

July 10, 1908 the first meeting of the board of trustees was held at A. Forckel's residence. A. Forckel was made chairman of the board. August 29, 1908, R. Children was elected assessor of the district at a fee of $10 a year. The rate of 6¢ per acre was set for this year's taxes. The Canadian National Investment Company offer for debentures, at par, was accepted. Tenders were put out for the construction of the school. September 21, 1908, Mr. D. R. McDonald's tender of $770 for the erection of the school, was accepted. Mr. McDonald to furnish all materials and have it completed by October 31, 1908.

The district purchased the following: 2 desks no. 12, 3 desks no. 11, 3 desks no. 10, 2 desks no. 9. Chairs, table, Globe No. 404, maps, numeral frame, dictionary, Christies erasers 1 dozen, chalk 4 boxes, bell, thermometer. These articles were ordered from the Christie Catalogue.

October 14, 1908 Mr. D. R. McDonald & Shorts tender, for shed and outbuilding, was accepted at a cost of $170. Mr. Lazert proposed to dig the well and furnish the lumber for cribbing the same at $16 per foot up to 25 feet and $20 per foot if it is to exceed 25 feet.

October 28, 1908 Miss Ethel Andrews taught for the first month. Miss Agnes Creighton's application for teacher at a salary of $600 per year was accepted and her duties to begin November 16, 1908. Miss Creighton rode a horse, side saddle, from her parents farm now known as Ben Schmitke dairy farm west of the Big Rock to the Allan School, a distance of 14½ miles, every day except in the winter when she stayed at the W. R. Smith farm.

E. L. Christie's bill of $130 was paid as well as the D. R. McDonald's bill of $8 for grading around the school. Accounts with W. J. Thompson $18.10, Okotoks Review $1.80, Okotoks Furniture Store $6.10 and A. Forckel $14.10 were paid. The property of the district was insured for $1000 with Calgary Insurance Company, E. A. Hayes as agent. $100 was borrowed for 1 month.

November 28, 1908 a meeting was held in the school house. The school hours were set to open at 9:30 a.m. close at noon open at 1 p.m. and close at 3:30 p.m. The contractors bill for $940 was paid for the completion of the school and out buildings. December 15, 1908, $50 was paid to Mr. Coyle for the construction of a fence around the 1½ acres. Mr. Lazert was paid $36 for digging a water well. It was moved that the secretary have a pump put in the well but the cost not to exceed $20. $8.10 was paid to M. McHardy for coal.

The annual meeting opened at 10 a.m. January 9, 1909. A. Forckel chairman, R. Children secretary, other persons present were H. E. Frear, Henry Brice, J. A. Shields, F. P. Coyle, A. N. Allan and F. Barker.

January 9, 1909 first meeting of the Board of Trustees, A. Forckel Chairman R. Children secretary. Other trustees present F. Barker, A. N. Allan. F. Barker was elected chairman for the next year A. Forckel named secretary. Taxes were increased to 6½¢ per acre for the coming year.

March 12, 1909 $125 was borrowed from the Union Bank of Canada at not more than 8% per annum for 4 to 6 months. The small accounts were paid F. Barker fuel $1, F. Barker caretaking $5. September 30, 1909 the trustees paid the Union Bank of Canada $127 and then borrowed $100 for 2 months at 8% per annum.

Tina Allan in front of Allan School, 1913.

November 25, 1909 Miss Agnes Creighton was rehired at $600 for the year 1910.

January 8, 1910 the Board of Trustees agreed the secretary-treasurer and assessor A. Forckel be paid $40 for the coming year and 6½¢ per acre for taxes for the coming year. March 25, 1910, $200 at 8% per annum was borrowed from the Union Bank of Canada. October 29, 1910, $10.63 was paid for the renewal of the fire insurance policy. A $2 contribution to cover expenses and benefit Sailors. The Rt. Hon. Lord Strathcona's Nelson Shield, will be accepted. November 25, 1910, Miss Agnes Creighton was rehired for January 3, 1911, to March 13, 1911, (for 3 months) at $600 per year and Miss Muriel Mahon be engaged for the balance of the year at the same salary.

March 27, 1914 Miss Edna Myrtle Saunders, who held a second class certificate of qualification, be engaged as teacher at $60 per month for 3 months beginning April 1, 1914.

January 9, 1915, the Allan School District paid the Davisburg School District No. 79 $4.80 for the attendance of two, T. H. Haslam boys for 3 months. The secretary was to inquire to the Minister of Education concerning the Allan School District No. 1840 sending children to Okotoks School District. January 15 the taxes were 3¢ per acre with 10% rebate if paid before July 1, 1915. The windows and door of the school were ordered boarded up.

March 17, 1916 Mr. Aldridge applied for an allowance, in money, to convey his two children to and from Okotoks School. The board agreed to pay $50 to Mr. Aldridge for the year 1916. On March 19, 1917, the board refused to pay any further allowance for conveying children back and forth to school.

January 12, 1918, the rate of taxes was 5¢ per acre for the year and 10% rebate on all taxes paid before July 1, 1918. The district was to provide board and lodging and pay all school fees due to the Okotoks School for the education of the children of school age in the district, to begin attendance at the Okotoks School the first week in April 1918. W. H. Jenkins was to find suitable lodging at Okotoks for the children.

August 20, 1918, the Allan School was reopened and Miss Marie W. Mitchell was hired as teacher at $840 per year her duties to commence September 2, 1918. December 16, 1918 Miss Marie W. Mitchell resigned and Miss Laura Ethel May Riches was hired at $900 per year her duties to start January 6, 1919. The salary of the teacher shall be paid every 3 months at $75 per month and this includes the janitor work to be done to the school room.

December 22, 1919 Miss Laura Riches was engaged as teacher for another year at $1000 per year. On June 10, 1920 the secretary's salary was increased to $50 per year. Mrs. P. S. Idington being the secretary at this time. The tax rate for the coming year was to be 12½¢ per acre. July 14, 1920 Miss Laura Riches asked for a salary increase from $1000 to $1200 for the year 1921. On October 29, 1920 the board offered Miss Riches $1100 which she refused. The board was firm in its decision and Miss Riches was to let the Board know her decision not later than December 7, 1920.

On January 8, 1921, the board agreed to pay Miss Riches $1150 per year. The rate of taxation was 13½¢

SCHOOL  CENSUS

The following is a complete list, alphabetically arranged, surnames preceding, of all the children within the bounds of _____ *Allan* _____ S. D. No. *1840* who had attained the age of six years and who had not attained the age of fifteen years by January 1st, 1925.

NAME OF CHILD	DATE OF BIRTH			Distance from School or Van Route	FULL NAME OF PARENT OR GUARDIAN	ADDRESS
	Day	Month	Year			
Aldredge William	31	Mar	1911	½ mile	J Aldridge	Okotoks
Aldridge Phyllis	20	Oct	1913	½ m	J Aldridge	"
Gordanier	11	Mar	1918	1 m	W H Jenkins	Okotoks
Howrey Edwin	9	Aug	1912	2½ M	Zau Howrey	Okotoks
Howrey Dahl	22	Jan	1914	2½ M	" "	Okotoks
Jenkins Arthur	27	June	1911	2 m	J H Jenkins	Okotoks
Jenkins Edward	7	Oct	1915	2 m	J H Jenkins	Okotoks
Nichols Leon	4	April	1918		M Nichols	Okotoks

per acre. August 3, 1921, tenders were received on painting and decorating the exterior and interior of the school from the following: Mr. Coleman $124, Mr. Visser $143, Mr. Jones $120. The contract was given to Mr. Coleman.

On January 14, 1922, Miss Riches was engaged for the year at a salary of $1200 per year. December 4, 1922, W. H. Jenkins took over the secretary duties from Mrs. P. S. Idington at $50 per year.

December 28, 1923, Miss Riches was hired at a salary of $1000 for the coming year. The tax rate was 7½ mills for the coming year. On December 11, 1924 the board accepted Miss Laura Riches resignation. Miss N. B. Sinclair was engaged as teacher at a salary of $900 per year. The board agreed to pay Herbert Jenkins $3 per month to look after the fire at the school.

December 5, 1925, Miss N. B. Sinclair's resignation was accepted and on December 13, 1925 Miss Foster was hired as teacher at $900 per year but she did not

Art and Herb Jenkins on Molly going to Allan School.

accept the position Miss Garrison was engaged as teacher for the coming year at $900.

April 9, 1927, it was decided to purchase an organ for $12. On June 17, 1927, Miss Garrison resigned and Miss MacGougan was hired at $900 per year. January 14, 1928, W. H. Jenkins was paid $50 per year for being secretary-treasurer and Mr. G. C. S. Paterson $5 per year as auditor. The rate of taxation was to be 6½ mills and a 5% rebate if paid before June 15, 1928. July 6, 1928 Miss MacGougan resigned and Miss Metcalf was hired as teacher at $900 per year. A contract for cleaning and repainting inside of the school house for $65 was approved.

On January 12, 1929 the teacher's salary was to be increased $20 per year for sweeping the School floor. April 17, 1929, Miss Metcalf resigned and Miss Riches was hired to finish the year, from May 15 to June 30, at the same salary but on condition that she be paid $1000 for the next year. June 23, 1931 Miss Riches resigned and Mr. Malcolm E. MacGougan was hired at $850 per year. The secretary-treasurer's salary was reduced from $50 to $35.

June 23, 1933 M. MacGougan's salary was reduced to $840 M. B. Ardiel was a student teacher under the leadership of M. MacGougan. June 20, 1934 M. MacGougan was reengaged at the same salary and $3 was allowed for a picnic at the end of the term. June 26, 1935 it was agreed to plow the school grounds and plant some trees. The trees to be ordered from Indian Head. Ash and Carrigana were ordered.

January 18, 1935, the board sent $2 to the Alberta School Trustees Association as membership fee. February 29, 1936, $250 was spent for alteration, addition to School House and new floor. Miss Eileen Rushworth was engaged as teacher at $800 per year. It was agreed to purchase a piano at not more than $100, the board paying $25 and the teacher to raise the balance.

May 25, 1937 Miss Rushworth's salary was increased to $840 for the year. August 5, 1937 Miss Rushworth resigned and on August 10, Miss Scarr was hired as teacher at $800 per year. July 18, 1938 Miss Scarr resigned and Miss Tewkbury was engaged at $840 per year. June 6, 1939 Miss Tewkbury was transferred as the parents of students thought the discipline was not what it should be. June 30, the board hired Miss Elsie Kraft. Miss Eileen Christensen was the last teacher at the Allan School. The School closed in 1941 and the Allan School District joined the Okotoks School District.

Allan School, last class, 1943. Back; l. to r.: Lloyd Stinson, Warren Barker, Eileen Christensen (teacher), Betty Barker, Evelyn Forckel. Middle: Bob Nixon, Connie Herr, Doug Stinson. Front: Albert Herr, Chris Larsen, Douglas Larsen.

Parent's meeting at Allan School closing, 1943. L. to R. Back: Mrs. Walter Wilde, Willis Barker, Len Nixon. Middle: Olive Aldridge, Mrs. Willis Barker, Mr. Otto Larsen. Front: Mrs. Doug Herr, Mrs. David Stinson, Mrs. Forrest Herr, Mrs. Lillian Aldridge, Mrs. Otto Larsen.

Sunday afternoon service at Allan School. Back row: Eddy Apps, Frank Priest, Jack Armstrong, Bill Aldridge, Art Jenkins, Herb Jenkins. Front row: Joyce Whiting, Merle Armstrong, Muriel Priest, Phyllis Aldridge, Hilda Ward, Olive Aldridge, Fred Gordanier.

ALLAN SCHOOL — by Effie Leach

In 1913 I was teaching at Allan School, which was then comparatively new. It was pleasantly situated with a grand view of the Rockies, while the native poplars grew in and around the school yard. Mr. Forckel Sr. was the Secretary-Treasurer. In those days the teacher went to the Secretary's home to collect the pay cheque. I believe my wages were $720.00 per year of 210 or 212 actual teaching days. The first couple of months I stayed at the home of Mr. and Mrs. Frank Barker, but when spring came I rode horseback from home, a distance of four and a half miles.

Allan School No. 1840, 1910. Vera Johnson in middle with Anna Barker and Tina Allan.

After sixty some years, it is a bit difficult to recall some details. I know the enrollment was small and most of the youngsters rode their ponies bareback. Anna and Cecil Barker came through the fields. Lettie and Tina Allan rode double with Tina at the helm. There were two Haslam boys, Milton and Charlie. Etta and Jessie Eberly drove in a buggy. Etta was a young lady, older than I was, and already engaged to William Morrison, who was preparing for the ministry. She studied by herself and I tried to help her with her difficulties. Bobby Forckel was quite a big boy, always gentle and kind. I recalled that when he was just a little lad, he and Johnny came to Davisburg School, where I also had spent my first school years. At that time, probably around 1906, the Forckels were recent arrivals in Canada, the children speaking French. The English language was a bit of a problem for young Bobby. Our beloved teacher (and we all did love her), Miss Ethel Roach, had come from Montreal and spoke French fluently, which, I am sure made life more pleasant for the young man. I cannot remember the names of any other pupils.

MEMORIES OF ALLAN S.D. NO. 1840 1939-40-41 by Elsie (Kraft) Colliton

I came to the Okotoks district in the fall of 1939 to teach the Allan School (north and east of town). The trustees at that time were Mr. James Coombe and Mr. Willis Barker. Mr. George Wilson was superintendent.

Allan School was typical of the "ungraded" country schools of that time. There were about 25 pupils in most all grades through 1 - 12. It was one of the few schools to have a telephone and a radio! The older boys took turns bringing drinking water in a cream can every day or so. Most of the children rode horseback or came in a horse-drawn buggy.

Since there was not a lamp of any kind (even a kerosene one was considered a fire hazard), school in winter months did not begin until 9:30 in the morning. Many winter days were dull and stormy and the lack of adequate light was a problem.

The school was heated by a large black potbellied stove, placed near the back of the room. What trials that stove caused me! I never did acquire the knack of banking it before leaving at night. So, in the morning, if I were lucky, by building the fire an hour before the children came, the building would be reasonably warm when school began. Some mornings though, it obstinately refused to burn and we would put in a chilly morning. When warm weather came we had the habit of stuffing waste paper in the unused stove. Then came the day we lit a match to all this. Frightened by the roar of the flames and the suffocating smoke, everyone scurried out to the school-yard. A passing motorist, seeing black smoke billowing from all the windows and doors and flames erupting from the chimney rushed to our aid. He thought there must have been an explosion! Luckily nothing caught fire except the soot in the pipes. Needless to say, I was much relieved when an older pupil (Lloyd Stinson) later agreed to build the fires and do the care-taking. (The allowance for this was $6 per month.)

Some of the Allan pupils were:
The Cecil Barker children (3)
The Wilde boys (2)
Lloyd and Doug Stinson
Doris and Donnie McLeod
Bruce, Bob and Jim Miller
Muriel and Billie Coultry
Dorothy, Marnie and Johnny Fraser
Connie and Albert Herr
Chris and Henry Larsen and Mabel Walters (their Mother's sister)
Betty and Warren Barker
Gordon Ward

The families in the district, whether they had children in school or not were very interested in all school activities. Any time we had an entertainment (usually to raise funds for children's Christmas treats) everyone attended and helped. On such occasions all desks had to be moved outside to make room for the visitors.

When I first came to Okotoks I boarded with the George Riches family. I enjoyed my stay in their hospitable home. (Doug was a pre-schooler then). Following this, I boarded with the Jesse Aldridge family. Since my mode of transportation was via bicycle it seemed a real advantage to be closer to school. Mr. Aldridge spent many hours recounting to me how he had adapted his horticultural methods (learned in England as a youth), to successfully withstand the rigours of our Alberta climate. His beautiful gardens and shrubbery bore mute evidence of his success.

No reminiscences of Allan school would be complete without a tribute to Mr. Willis Barker. Mr. Barker was serving both on the local school board and was also a member of the first divisional board of the new school division (Foothills No. 38.) Many of the parents were disgruntled by, what they considered, a transfer of school authority to High River. Mr. Barker in his quiet conciliating way did much to smoothe over troubled waters. Besides this what practical aid he offered us! Whether it be to mend the fence, replace a broken window, haul a load of coal or bring books and supplies from High River, he could always be counted upon.

(After leaving Okotoks, I taught several years in Coutts and Warner and Medicine Hat. In 1945, I married Tom Colliton, a farmer, of the Coutts district. We lived at Coutts until 1949 when we moved to a farm near Blackie. Here we raise grain and Charolais cattle. Our family of three include: — Irene, the eldest who will graduate in Medicine from the University of Alberta this spring; Karen, now Mrs. Eldon Maronda of Lomond and Patrick. a Grade 10 student in Senator Riley, High River.

M. E. MacGOUGAN

Nearly a half century ago, the school was little changed from the day it was first opened in 1908. In the main, there were two windows on each side, two blackboards, a tiny library, a pump organ, original desks and a wood and coal burning stove. Outside, on the acre of land, was a pump, privies, a coal bin and the stable. All, except for the pump organ, were operative. The organ had been completely eaten out by field mice.

In my memory, about a dozen families were represented by approximately twenty pupils in Grades 1 to 8. Fine youngsters they were, and all (or most all) were anxious to learn. All time was not taken up with learning. We played games inside and out, caught weasels by hand, oiled the school floor by "skating" on Dust Bane with our boots and had Christmas Concerts in which the chorus was trained by a tone-deaf teacher. (It was some thirty years later he learned that he was tone-deaf.)

Those were the days before roads as we know them now. Snow, mud, dirt and dust were expected and accepted, and many times only by horse or by foot could one reach the school. I well remember coming

upon a Hungarian Partridge hen with her chicks on the road. Alarmed, the chicks hid in the horse's hoof prints previously in the mud.

I have many lasting memories of the families in the district. One funny incident occurred at the home of the late James Coombe who was Chairman of the School Board at the time. Mr. Coombe had invited four of us, all bachelors (Ben Bishop, George Woodford, Herb Jenkins and me), for a noon dinner one beautiful Sunday in mid-winter. A Chinook had hit the area and we had shirtsleeve temperatures. Our host had prepared a fine turkey dinner and we all anticipated stuffing ourselves. However, when the ex-Regimental Sgt. Major of the C.M.R.'s drew the razor sharp knife across the breast of the bird and the knife "bounced", he promptly threw the turkey out the open door into the snow. No one uttered a word. Not the least perturbed our host cooked steak.

Margaret Morris and Olive Aldrich at the Allan school pump late 1930's.

MEMORIES OF ALLAN SCHOOL — by Ethel (Andrews) Oneil

When Alberta was a young province, the opening of any school was an important event, and also a sign of progress. So it was with the Allan School. I believe seven children (school age), living in the district was necessary.

Enterprising parents proceeded to have the new school ready by September 1st, 1908, this accomplished, a teacher must be found. At that time most of our teachers were from Eastern Canada. However, Alberta was training some of their own. July 1st, 1908, a class of Grade XI students graduated at Okotoks, under the efficient and capable Mr. Skinner. From this class came Agnes Creighton (Mrs. Jack Lineham) and myself Ethel Andrews (Mrs. Hillyerd Oneil). Miss Creighton applied for the Allan School and was accepted to teach on a permit. However, in the meantime, Miss Creighton's application to attend Calgary Normal School was accepted. Now I, Ethel Andrews, came into the story. Having been a High

School chum of Miss Creighton's, she asked me to substitute for her (on a permit), for the four months she would be at Normal. How delighted I was!! (A childhood dream was becoming a reality.)

No boarding place could be found, so I rode side saddle on a pony called Dick, owned by my sister Laura (Mrs. Howard Norris), a distance of approximately six miles from my home (Mr. and Mrs. Wm. Andrews) farm in the Melrose District.

September and October were glorious months, lovely sunshine, ripening the fields of grain along the way. Red lilies, wild roses and many other flowers grew in abundance, now they almost have disappeared. Getting up at 6 A.M. was a minor detail.

In this area winter usually came in November and December, and certainly didn't fail to do so that year. Deep, deep snow and ever lowering temperatures. Pupils and myself never failed to be present at 9 A.M. A very dear, elderly couple (Mr. and Mrs. Henry Brice) sometimes (during very cold days) insisted I stay with them. Mr. Brice always saddled my pony and cared for him and Mrs. Brice packed a lovely lunch for me, which was always frozen, when arriving at the school. I also remember visiting at Mr. and Mrs. Forckel's.

Now, after writing so much, I have come to the most important part, (the children). I can just recall six, Harry, Cecil and Anna Barker, Lettie and Tena Allen and Robert Forckel. They were all so good, I hated to leave them and let Miss Creighton take over. I believe they also had to come to school on horseback.

I went to Normal in 1909, and taught in various schools till 1914 when I changed my name to Mrs. Hillyerd Oneil.

Wages were another minor detail. I have forgotten the exact figure, however, on leaving Normal, we all signed a paper saying we would not teach for less than $50 a month, that meant $600 per year.

Mrs. Ethel (Andrews) Oneil
Age 87.

JESSE AND LILLIAN ALDRIDGE — by Olive Aldridge and Phyllis Teskey

Jesse Aldridge was born May 20th, 1868, in Bishops Cleeve, Gloucestershire, England.

Lillian Slack was born January 22nd, 1871, in Ontario, and moved to England as a small girl. She married Jesse Aldridge in 1892, and returned to Canada with their five children in 1913, the year after the Titanic went down.

Their children are Lillian, born June 1896, Gwenneth, born November 12th, 1898, Edward, born March 4th, 1902, Olive, born January 29th, 1905, and Bill, born March 31st, 1911.

Mr. and Mrs. Aldridge and family journeyed across the country by train to Salmon Arm, B.C., where their sixth child, Phyllis, was born October 20th, 1913. They lived with a millionaire friend from England, George Radcliff, who owned an orchard. Mr. Aldridge did odd jobs around the country, and also worked in a lumber mill, but the heat was so terrible that he caught enteric fever and had to leave. Mrs. Aldridge worked part-time in Monta Bellow Hotel. They remained at Salmon Arm for one year.

First log barn on the Aldridge farm and Starlight. (Rained a day outside and a week inside).

Mr. Aldridge left for Alberta to find a farm and later sent for his family to join him on a C.P.R. farm at Kirkcaldy, south of Vulcan. Seeing no future here after a year, Mr. Aldridge gave up his down payment and moved to the Smith farm, called Woodland Ranch, northeast of Okotoks in the Allan School district and renting this farm in 1915 — N.E. ¼ S2 T21 R29 W4th. The Allan school was closed, so the children had to go to Okotoks School.

Two years later in 1917, they moved to the Big Rock district to the S.W. ¼ S20 T20 R1 W5th and rented a farm from Andy Price. They remained here two years. It was at this farm that Mr. Aldridge received a letter from his brother in England with the address "Mr. Jesse Aldridge, Big Rock, near Okotoks, near High River, near Black Diamond, North West Territories, Canada". Black Diamond Post Office sent it back to Okotoks and he finally received it.

The Big Rock School was also closed, so the children had to board in Okotoks to go to school.

Their next move was to the S½ of S2 T21 R29 W4th. This raw bush and tree — covered land which they purchased from Mr. Robert Shields, was four miles north-east of Okotoks in the Allan School District again. The school was now open. This land is still owned by Olive and Bill Aldridge.

After years of blood, sweat and tears, the land was finally cleared by Mr. and Mrs. Aldridge and son Edward. At first, horses were used for breaking, and later a Titan tractor, and then an Eagle tractor was used before the land was finally broke. This farm became one of the outstanding farms in the area.

Mrs. Aldridge, a hard-working woman, was always ready with a friendly cup of tea for any neighbour or friend who happened to drop in. In her early days in the district, she worked in the Alberta Hotel in Okotoks, and would bring home much needed left over food.

Mr. Aldridge was an old English gardener, and had a great love for his garden, flowers, birds and trees. He grew fruit trees of all kinds, small fruits and even peanuts. "If you can't grow it here, I am going to try", he would say, and was many times successful. He took many prizes at Okotoks fair with garden produce, flowers, fruit and livestock. Much of this produce was traded in Beattie's store, and later in Wentworth's General store, for necessary items.

Olive Aldridge received the Provincial Award for a

collection of weeds and an essay on weed control. Our father's method of weed control was to have his children go abreast through the whole crop, walking between the rows so as not to trample the grain, and carrying a bag over our shoulder to collect the weeds. These were carried off the field and later burned.

Mr. Aldridge bought his first car in the early 1920's at an auction sale of John MacDonald's. Olive took off from school on horse back through the brush to the sale, and saw her father standing by an old touring sedan Model T Ford, and immediately turned back toward school, meeting her brother and sister on the trail, and told them of this wonderful car their father had bought.

Mr. and Mrs. Aldridge celebrated their 50th wedding anniversary in August, 1942. Lillian died August 11, 1948 and Jesse, April, 1949.

Mr. and Mrs. J. Aldridge, 50th Wedding Anniversary.

Jesse Aldridge Family, L. to R. Olive, Gwynneth, Phyllis, Lillian, Edward, William and Mr. and Mrs. Aldridge.

Lillian married Ernest Biswanger from Calgary. They have six children. Merton, DeWinton, Harold, DeWinton, Reta, Three Hills, Olive, DeWinton, Joan, DeWinton, and Marilyn, Calgary.

(More about this family under Harold Biswanger).

Gwenneth married Douglas Ward, Okotoks. They have three children, Hilda, Armstrong, B.C., Allan, Okotoks and Gordon, Calgary.

(More about this family under D. Ward).

Edward never married. He was a farmer and in later years, worked in Big Horn Forest Reserve cutting timber, living in a tent. He also worked on many farms in Alberta and Saskatchewan and cooked for seismograph crew in the north country. He also worked as a chore man on wells in the McKenzie Delta for two years. Ed finished his High School by correspondence in his late sixties in Edmonton. Edward died on a farm west of Red Deer July 31, 1975, while looking after a very large garden and lawns at age 73.

Olive, a rancher, never married. She owns land north of Turner Valley at Whiskey Row corner N.W.¼ 18-20-2-W5th and also at Millarville being the S½ 1-21-3-W5th and part of the home place at Okotoks S.E.¼ 2-21-29-W4th and is in partnership with Victor Williamson of Okotoks. She grows a large garden and takes a few trips to far places like England, Australia, Yukon and Alaska.

William never married. He was in the Air Force during W.W.2 stationed at High River. He is now an accountant with an electrical firm in Calgary and lives on the home place S.W.¼ 2-21-29-W4th at Okotoks and helps look after their garden and green houses.

Phyllis married Ben Teskey January 28th, 1939 and lived on a farm west of Okotoks for one year. They later moved to Black Diamond where Ben worked in the oil fields. After working a few years, he purchased the Big Horn Lumber Company, operating in the forest reserve. Later, he moved the sawmills to Black Diamond and sawed there for a few years. Ben died in September, 1972. They have three children.

Dennis was born October 28th, 1939 and he operates Sheep River Electric, Turner Valley. He married Barbara Newby in Turner Valley, June 30th, 1962 and they live one mile north of Turner Valley. They have three children: Laureen, born June 23rd, 1963, Daryl, born August 8th, 1964 and Diana, born October 28th, 1967.

David was born November 19th, 1940 and married Joyce Jensen of Drumheller August 10th, 1963. David teaches in Calgary and lives at Millarville. Joyce is a nurse. They have two children: Karen Marie, born June 20th, 1967 and Mark, born December 6th, 1975 in Townsville, Australia while David spent two years teaching there.

Sharon was born October 19th, 1942 and married Dick Willcock of Turner Valley and they now live at Lloydminster. Dick is in the oil well servicing business. Sharon is a bookkeeper at a feed lot operation. They have four children: Kathryn, born January 27th, 1960; Richard, born April 14th, 1961, Sheryl, born April 14th, 1963 and Janet, born June 5th, 1964.

ALEX N. ALLAN 1861-1938 — by Mrs. Robert E. Grisdale

Alex N. Allan worked his way west from Aubrey, Quebec, south of Montreal and arrived at Calgary in 1885. Soon after his arrival he was employed by John Glenn, a well known rancher, at Fish Creek. He took out a homestead 4½ miles N.E. of Okotoks. He later bought a quarter section of C.P.R. land directly west of his homestead. Dan McDonald and Alex Smith were his closest neighbors, at one time even "baching" together.

On the morning of February 22, 1890, Janet Lang arrived in Calgary coming by train from Riverfield, Quebec. On the afternoon of the same day she and Alex Allan were married by the Rev. Herdman. The newlyweds travelled by horse and sleigh to the homestead, arriving there about supper time where Dan McDonald had prepared the wedding feast.

Like most farmers at that time, Alex grew oats, some of which he sold to the mounted police in Fort Macleod. The delivery of the grain entailed a weeks journey by horse and wagon. As the farm became established he raised beef cattle and Clyde horses. His registered brand for both cattle and horses was "66". Located on the left front shoulder on horses and left hip on cattle.

Alex Allan was well known for his fiddle playing and was often called upon to play at local dances. During the winters of 1896 and 1897 he travelled to Sandon, B.C. and worked in the Ruth Silver Mines.

Mr. and Mrs. Alex N. Allan.

The Allans had four children. A daughter Isabel and a son Melville, both passed away in infancy. A second daughter, Elizabeth "Lettie", married Harvey Outhet, who farmed near the Allan homestead. Christena M. completed the family. She married Robert E. Grisdale and they in turn had two children Margaret M. and Allan R. Margaret and her husband, Leslie Blight, have two children, Barry and Carolyn. Allan and his wife, Monica Scott, also have two children Margaret and Janet.

In 1908 A. N. Allan, A. Forckel and F. Barker were instrumental in establishing the Allan School District. This school was located on the F. Barker farm. It is our understanding that the name "Allan" was given the school district because A. N. Allan had resided longest in the district.

Alex Allan passed away in 1938, five years later, in 1943, Janet Allan sold the home place to F. M. Ballard and the other quarter to Ervie Miller. After selling the farm Janet Allan spent her remaining years with her family. Janet Allan passed away in 1951.

The Allans were members of the Southern Alberta Pioneers and also belonged to the Okotoks Country Club for many years.

DAVID ARMSTRONG — by Muriel Armstrong

Mr. and Mrs. David Armstrong moved to the Allan District from Didsbury in 1926. They had a large family and Ethel, the eldest had married Louis Diehl and was living in Invermere, B.C. at that time. They later moved to Edmonton where Lou died. She now lives with her sisters in Calgary. Ray was next and Olive, the third, had married Dave McEwen at Didsbury and passed away a few months after the family moved to Okotoks. Olive followed by William (Bill), Clara, Stella, Joe, Muriel and Jack.

Mr. Armstrong passed away while visiting his son Bill at Innisfail in 1942. Ray then sold the farm and moved to Innisfail. After the death of his son, Dave, in Italy in 1944, he and Bill moved to California where he married Elizabeth Brown. She passed away in Calgary in 1967 and Ray himself in 1975.

Bill married Irene Barker of Balzac, Alberta and retired in Calgary.

Clara married Cecil Barker who farmed a few miles from the Armstrongs. Some years later they moved to Sylvan Lake where they lived until Cecil's death in 1971. Clara lives at Strathmore, Alberta.

Joe married Leta Shattuck of the Davisburg district and after farming there for many years moved to Calgary.

Jack served four years in the Navy during World War 2 and returned to live in Okotoks for many years. He now resides in Spirit River, Alberta.

Stella and Muriel moved to Calgary with their mother who passed away on 1961. They still reside in that city.

THE BALDERSON FAMILY *

Edmond Balderson, born at Dalton in Furness, Lancashire, England, February 3, 1857, came to the U.S.A. in 1883, married Laura Luthera Vawter in 1887. Farmed at Lucas County Iowa, U.S.A. for 26 years, raising family, Gladstone Vawter, Aurthur Edmond, William Bruce, Blanche Elizabeth and Forrest Fell. The family settled on 18-6-21-W4 north of Magrath in 1909. William Bruce Balderson married Chlora Ida Stuart daughter of Albert William Stuart and Flora Roena (Caldwell) Stuart of Rising Sun, Iowa in 1916. They returned to, and eventually purchased, the original farmstead, where they farmed until 1946. Their children Gladys Margaret, Bruce Stuart, and Allan William were born and raised there.

Bruce and Chlora retired and moved with their

Allan and Pat Balderson's house 1955. Back row: Bruce Stuart, Dorothy, Donna, Pat, Blain, Allan William, Front row: Valerie, Bruce, Brent, Betty, Brian Balderson.

daughter, Gladys, to Calgary where Gladys teaches music and school. In 1954 they moved to their new home on Elma Street West Okotoks and lived there until they died, William Bruce in 1973 and Chlora Ida in 1975.

In 1947 the three quarters listed below were purchased. William Bruce and Chlora Ida bought the "Ed Bradshaw Place" from Stanley and Marie Horsky, wanting to keep their hand in the farming game. Although they never lived on the property father worked with his sons farming for several years and Allan William and Patricia Lenore lived in the house, which still stands, we still call it honeymoon lodge (located on the present Joe Driscoll acreage).

This quarter is very hilly and picturesque, bisected by coulees and a road. The story has it that the year Ed Bradshaw died his neighbours rallied around with some ten binders to cut his crop. They worked all day long and none ever saw any of the others. I believe it was inevitable that it would be one of the first farms to be subdivided in this area. Dudley Batchelor (now Stan Johnathon's) and Roland Gissing (Willow Croft) 1954 and 1955.

Bruce Stuart and Dorothy Dean (Anderson) Balderson bought the Gordon Giffin place. Stuart qualified for the V.L.A. loan because of his years of service with the R.C.A. overseas. They farmed and raised their family, Valerie, Brent Jay (deceased) Donna and Deana. These years were not the greatest for farming. They sold out in 1953 and Bruce Stuart bought grain for the National elevators at Okotoks, Gage and Hines Creek, in the Peace River country, and for Ellison at Picture Butte and Lethbridge. He died at home in Lethbridge in 1976. Dorothy and her family and grandchildren live in Lethbridge and area. The Maurice Davis family live in the renovated house on the Okotoks farmstead.

Allan William bought the "Kidd quarter", qualified for V.L.A. loan due to service in the R.C.A.F. He married Patricia Lenore Kauffman in Okotoks in 1948. Patricia is the only daughter of Paul Russel Kauffman, born North Manchester, Indiana and Lillian B. (Anderson) Kauffman, born in Blue Grass, Minnesota. The Kauffman's came to Arrowwood and Cluny from Kalispell, Montana, where Patricia was born, and then moved to Okotoks in 1936. The 3 children; Paul Jr.,

Patricia and Jimmie, attended school in Okotoks. Paul Russel Kauffman was town policeman for several years and moved to England after his military service in the war. Lillian lives in Colton, Oregon, U.S.A. near the rest of her family.

Allan William and Patricia Lenora Balderson farmed and raised their family: Brian Allan, Betty Anne, Bruce Paul and Blain William.

We have always thought it coincidental that farming weather conditions seemed to deteriorate in the area soon after our start at farming here, and never really believed that our neighbors seriously considered collecting a purse of money to assist us in locating elsewhere.

Brian and wife, Annie (McGundy) and Greg live in Destruction Bay, Yukon, on the shores of beautiful Kluane Lake. Brian works for the Ministry of Transport as a radio operator. Annie is a native of the Yukon and her father and mother live in White Horse.

Betty Anne and her husband, Dr. Rudy Boonstra live in Vancouver, B.C. and work at the University there. The Boonstra family emigrated from Holland after the war and Mother and Father and some members of the family live in Calgary.

Bruce Paul and wife, Johanna, live in their new home in Calgary. Bruce works for Canadian Linen and Johanna for the Royal Bank. Johanna's folks are of Ukrainian Origin and the Pidperyhora's are well known in Elfros, Saskatchewan.

Blain William lives in Banff, Alberta and cooks at the Banff Springs Hotel.

Pat and Al still live at the farmstead buildings they built and have retained 40 acres. Allan takes care of the acreage and rentals and Pat sews period costumes, at home, for Heritage Park.

Portions of the old Macleod Trail, which were in evidence on this quarter as late as 1950, have been farmed out, but another land mark, a large sandstone, buffalo rubbing, rock is being preserved jointly by the Neuss and Banks families. A commanding view of 180 miles of the Rocky Mountains and a panoramic view of the west country are possible from the high land on this quarter.

S.E. of 5-21-29-W4 — Drappo, Cassidy, Tindle, Gordon Giffin, Bruce Stuart Balderson.

S.W. of 5-21-29-W4 — Drappo, Cassidy, Tindle, Ed Bradshaw, Stan Horsky, William Bruce Balderson.

N.W. of 4-21-29-W4 — Isreal K. Blair (Minister, Doctor, and Okotoks districts first school teacher), W. B. Saunders, Reverend Kidd, Clarence C. Cameron (tenant) Allan William Balderson.

MARSHALL BALLARD — by Carol Fisher

Marshall Ballard was born in Uxbridge, Ontario on April 22, 1889. He came west in 1909 and after working for a few weeks he took up a homestead in the Bingville district north of Suffield, Alberta. He built this homestead into a ranch encompassing 10,000 acres including lease land. In 1931 he married Connie Welch of Suffield and they resided on the ranch until 1941 when their land was taken over by the government for war use. After living in Suffield for two years they purchased the Allan homestead at Okotoks NW¼ 2-21-29-W4.

Mr. and Mrs. Ballard and their children Bob and Carol arrived in the Allan district in April 1943. They arrived by train with only their suitcases because a ban on the highway prevented them from bringing their truckload of furnishings any farther than Brooks. Mrs. Allan generously supplied them with dishes and some furnishings until they could move their truck.

The first year Marshall put the crop in with horses but by the second spring had acquired a tractor. He rented the farm of Mrs. Joe Hogge for two years and then rented the half section of Mr. and Mrs. Renard. Threshing was done by the threshing outfits that moved through the district every fall. In 1948 Marshall bought a threshing machine in partnership with Harry Barker.

The Allan School closed the year the Ballards moved to the district so Bob and Carol attended school in Okotoks. Mr. Ballard actively farmed until 1963 when they moved into Okotoks. Bob and his wife Irene with their family took up residence on the home quarter and Bob farmed and worked in Okotoks. Four years later the farm was sold to Mr. and Mrs. Chester Flanders.

Marshall Ballard died November 4, 1972, at the age of 83. Mrs. Connie Ballard moved to High River in 1976.

Carol married Evert Fisher who farms in the Cayley District. They have 3 boys Deen, Greg and Bradley.

Bob married Irene Sager of Fort Qu'Appelle Saskatchewan. They have 2 children Colleen and Bruce who attended the Okotoks School. Colleen works in Calgary and Bruce attends Composite School in Claresholm, Alberta.

FRANK BARKER FAMILY — by Anna Trenholm and Mrs. Cecil Barker

On October 21, 1906, Frank and Hannah Barker arrived from Carman, Manitoba and settled six miles northeast of Okotoks. Frank and his three older sons, Willis, Earl and Harry travelled by cattle car with the animals, while Hannah, with the youngest children, Cecil and Anna, made their way by passenger train.

Frank purchased his farm 1-21-29 W4 from G. P. Smith in 1905. At that time only 27 acres were under cultivation, but the whole section was eventually broken. Initially, the farm buildings consisted of a house, machine shed, chicken house and barn. In 1915, Frank built a new large barn which remained a landmark to anyone driving on the High River road.

One acre in the S.W. corner of the Barker farm was donated by Frank, in 1909, for the erection of, what became, the Allan School, named after Tina Grisdale's father, Alex Allan. The school was opened the same year under trustees A. Forckel and A. N. Allan, but was closed at the beginning of World War I due to a drop in enrollment. The children were transferred to Okotoks with the Barker children travelling by buggy during the spring and fall, and by cutter in the winter.

In 1916, Frank and Hannah bought their first car, a Ford, which was most unique in that it ran out of water and oil after having travelled only one-half mile! The headlights were approximately 2 candle power! They travelled to Banff in 1917 and became stuck in the mud

1917 Willis, Anna and Cecil Barker and Uncle John. This is the day Cecil left for the war.

on the Cochrane Hill. Anna helped to push them out. Their troubles had only begun! The spindle broke at Exshaw and parts had to be awaited for from Calgary. The journey took two days, Okotoks to Banff, and one day on the return trip. What a trip. Frank used to go to McPherson Mine by wagon train for coal: that would make a two day trip. When he wanted to market his produce — butter and dressed pigs and chickens — in Calgary he would leave home at 5:00 AM and spend the night at the Burns Ranch on Anderson Road, and return home the second day.

Before moving off the home place in the "20's", Harry and Cecil purchased a Rumely Engine and Core Separator for threshing.

Harry married Marjorie Martin and bought a farm eight miles west of Okotoks where they resided for a few years before moving to the Laycock's place, one mile west of Okotoks. He farmed here until 1938 and due to serious illness of his wife moved to Vancouver where she died in 1939. Harry returned to the Allan District and farmed there until his death in 1958. Harry served with the "78 Battery" in World War 1, returning home in 1918. He also served in World War 2 as a Guard.

Cecil married Clara Armstrong and purchased a

L. to R. Eugene Goettler (top), Margaret Goettler, Mrs. Barker and Harry Barker — 1930.

Mr. and Mrs. Frank Barker, 1933.

farm one mile south of the home place where they raised their six children. In the early 1940's they moved to Sylvan Lake where they purchased a farm. Cecil served in World War 1, returning home in 1919.

Willis married Pearl Geham in 1927 and took over the home place. They raised their children, Warren and Betty there, prior to their moving to Edmonton in 1947 where Betty attended University and Warren went into radio work. Betty is now married and living in England, and Warren is news editor for CKNW in Vancouver.

Frank and Hannah retired to Okotoks in 1927 and celebrated their Golden Wedding Anniversary six years later. They purchased a home and drilled a well which provided them with soft water. A number of their neighbours came over to 'borrow' water with which to wash their hair.

Frank passed away in 1939 and Hannah, six years later. Earl, the eldest son, died at age 20. Harry died in the Colonel Belcher Hospital in 1959, and Willis passed away in Edmonton in 1968. Cecil died in Red Deer Hospital in 1971.

Anna born at Carman in 1900, is the last surviving member of the family. She worked in the telephone office in Okotoks until she moved, in 1925, to Detroit. At the peak of the oil boom, she returned to Turner Valley when the telephone office opened. In 1931 she married Henry Trenholm a steam engineer. They resided in Turner Valley until 1943 when they moved to Okotoks with their two children, Norma and Morley. Henry continued to work in the oil fields until his death in 1950. Anna continued to work in Okotoks until she moved to Calgary in 1960 where she operated the Acadia sub post office. At age 77 she still works five

days a week in the sub post office, does all her own housework, and all her own gardening. She is a real going concern. Anna is an avid supporter of the Centennial Hockey Team and the Calgary Stampeder Football Club. She's looking forward to a good year for the Stamps 1977!

PEARL AND WILLIS BARKER — by Pearl Barker

Willis Roy Barker was the oldest of the five children of Frank and Hannah Barker. The family moved from Carman, Manitoba to the farm northeast of Okotoks (purchased from Mr. Smith) in the fall of 1906, S½ 1-21-29 W4. That first winter was a very severe one and a shock as a balmier climate had been expected in southern Alberta.

Willis returned to Manitoba to take the degree course in Agriculture at Manitoba Agricultural College in Winnipeg. His brothers, Harry and Cecil, served in World War 1, but the effects of three bouts of rheumatic fever on his heart confined Willis to the family farm. After his marriage to Pearl Gehman in December, 1926, his parents retired to Okotoks and he and Pearl took over the farm.

She was the oldest of the family of Samuel and Loretta Gehman, who moved west from Galt in Waterloo County, Ontario in 1903 to the farm which they had bought, south of Okotoks, in the Maple Leaf District. Pearl taught piano for many years in Calgary, Okotoks, Gleichen, Arrowood and Blackie.

Her family loyally supported the Methodist Church there. Frank Barker took part in the act of Union of the Okotoks churches to form the United Church there in 1917, eight years before the national union took place. Willis and Pearl were very active in this church all their lives in the district, he as a steward, an elder, Sunday school teacher and choir member, she as choir member, organist, or choir leader.

Willis was a member of the Alberta Wheat Pool from its inception in 1924 and for many years was a director. He was also a member of the United Farmers of Alberta. He specialized in the growing of registered seed wheat which was in demand throughout the province. He was a long time member of the school board of the Allan School district, the school being located on what had been the southwest corner of the Barker farm section. When the Foothills School Division No. 38 was formed in December, 1938, Willis was one of the original five trustees and faithfully visited the schools in his area until shortly before he and Pearl retired to Edmonton in November 1947, as their daughter, Betty, had started to attend University of Alberta there. Betty quit teaching when she married and moved to Kent, England. Son, Warren, began his radio career with station C.J.C.A. In Edmonton. Warren has been news director of radio station C.K.N.W. New Westminster B.C. for many years.

Willis died on January 24, 1968 at the age of 78, Pearl still resides in Edmonton.

HAROLD BISWANGER

My grandfather, George Biswanger, born in Nova Scotia, was a sea captain on the Atlantic. His ancestors came to Canada from Germany about 1650.

My grandmother, Lidia Matilda Biswanger, was

born in Nova Scotia. She was a Rogers, whose ancestors were the Sir Roland Rogers and they came to Canada about 1590. They settled on a land grant in Nova Scotia, given to him by King Charles 2nd of England. Rogers was given all the land he could walk around in a week. This land is now the Annapolis Valley, but it was lost when he died with no direct heirs.

George and Lidia had nine children. Steven, William, Freeman and Benjamin came west by train in 1903 to Alberta, and took up land in Innisfail, Bingley and Rocky Mountain House country. Daughters, Mrs. Josephine Williams and Mrs. Jewell Ramer also came west at this time. Mr. and Mrs. George Biswanger and sons Ernest and James, and daughter, Christine, came west to Alberta in 1904. They settled in and around Red Deer.

Ernest was born in Spring Hill, Nova Scotia on July 31, 1888. He came to Calgary about 1907 from Red Deer, at the age of 18. He worked in a dry goods store in 1st Street West and 7th Avenue. Josie moved to Calgary and ran a boarding house and Dad lived with her. Later, Dad boarded with Mr. and Mrs. John McGinnis on 17th Avenue West. Ernest started painting in 1911. He went to the Calgary Industrial Exhibition (now Calgary Exhibition and Stampede) and asked the manager, Mr. E. L. Richardson for a job. He said "I will give you one building to paint and if we like it, you will be hired for more." He continued to paint there as part of his long painting and decorating businesss in Calgary, till he semi-retired in 1957. He also worked painting a great many of the country grain elevators in Alberta. He had many customers in and around Calgary, and built nearly a dozen houses there, and remodeled a number of others.

His brothers up north were great hunters and fishermen and Dad went with them to hunt and fish whenever he could get away. My uncle Steve lived mainly on wild meat, so sometimes his game was shot out of season. The game wardens suspected him, but he always hid his meat in a dummy "out house" and he was never caught.

Ernest was hanging paper for Dr. Peter John Healy, dentist, around 1920, where he met Miss Lillian Aldridge, who was keeping house for Dr. Healy. The courtship started and on September 7th, 1922, Ernest and Lillian were married.

Mother was the daughter of Mr. and Mrs. J. Aldridge of Okotoks. Mother had kept house for different people before she was married. The Walter Renard family of Okotoks, and the Police detachment in Okotoks with William Naylor, officer in charge. She moved with them to Innisfail, but later came back to Okotoks and worked for Court Wagerman, who lived west of Okotoks where Lars Willumsen is now. This was during the first World War and because he was German, feelings ran pretty high. She was told by her friends and neighbours that a lot of bad things would happen to her, but she ignored them all, for he was one of the finest persons she ever knew.

Lillian recalls one incident in Okotoks while working for Mr. Saunders. Mary Daggett who was about sixteen years old at the time, had a saddle horse pastured in a field near the house, and it fell into an old abandoned well, with only his nose sticking out of the water. The whole town turned out to help, and discussed the idea of digging a hole beside the well, but they decided it would take too long. They sent to High River for a derrick to lift the horse out, but had to go further south for one, and they finally got the horse out for Mary, who was a very relieved young girl.

Ernest and Lillian have six children. Merton, born June 20th, 1925, Harold, born January 3rd, 1928, Reta, born February 13th, 1929, Olive, born November 18th, 1930, Joan (Nonie), November 5th, 1932 and Marilyn, July 25th, 1935.

Merton married May Boyd, Nova Scotia, July 7th, 1945, while in the Navy during the second World War. He was a painter and decorator for many years, taking over the family business, working mainly for the Calgary Exhibition and Stampede. He later took the position of Grounds Superintendent. They have one boy, Richard, who works for a dry walling company.

Harold Leslie, born in Calgary, started out in lower Sunalta district. In 1934, he moved to the Bankview district and went to Bankview School, Mount Royal, Sunalta and Western Canada High School.

I worked with Dad from the age of 12 or 13 on weekends, doing painting and carpentry work. I helped in the building of five houses and remodeling of several others while going to school. One house we built across the road from where we lived, I dug the basement by hand when in Grade 9 and was paid $100.00, which was the going price at that time for a machine to do it. It was in winter with the ground frozen in heavy clay. I had to light fires every night using old street paving blocks soaked in tar. The down town area of Calgary was originally paved with these. I covered the fire with sheets of metal to keep the heat down. Next day after school I would dig out the soft dirt and wheel it out of the hole with a steel wheeled wheel barrow on planks to a cut bank about two hundred feet away and dump it. This took about three months, just in time to start building cement forms in the spring.

I spent a lot of time in summer holidays at Grandfather Aldridge's farm, and I always wanted to have a farm. Three years after finishing school, I bought the S.E.¼ of S27 T21 R3 W5th, from Ed. Blair of Millarville in 1951. I was in the process of buying two quarters in partnership with a life long school chum, Albert Vanner, but foot and mouth disease in cattle came that year, so money was very hard to borrow to buy land. I bought the quarter myself. In 1957, I pastured cattle and helped farm the land on the farm that Albert Vanner bought from Jack Barlow in Ballyhamage School district, being the S.E.¼ of S22, and the N.E.¼ S15 T21 R2 W5th. He sold that in 1959 and bought three-quarters from Mrs. Ethel Macleod south of Okotoks — the N½ of S15 and the S.E.¼ of S15 T20 R29 W4th. I pastured cattle there. In the spring of 1961 he sold the farm and bought three quarters of a section at Raven, and moved there.

After cutting, peeling and treating poplars, I fenced the quarter at Millarville. I sold it in 1953 and bought a quarter (N.W.¼ S6 T21 R28 W4th) of clear farm land seven miles north-east of Okotoks from Millicent Sandeman. Times were hard, so I went back to working at my trades, first with my brother at Calgary Ex-

Harold Biswanger on top of Big Rock, 1959.

hibition and Stampede and then in the Millarville, Priddis, Red Deer Lake districts assisting in the construction of the Priddis skating rink on a voluntary basis. I was also a member of the Millarville Racing and Agriculture Association, was Concession Director for twelve years, and three years on the main board as Development Director.

In 1962 my brother and I bought the S.E.¼ of S24 T21 R1 W5th from Eric Goddard. This was pasture and hay land. Mert built a house here in 1965 and still lives there.

I married Mrs. Jean Standish December 19th, 1964 and moved to her farm at Millarville. The marriage didn't work out, so I moved back to my DeWinton farm in the fall of 1965. I started building up the farm and am still working out. I am a member of the DeWinton Historical Society.

Reta married Don Reynolds May 20th, 1950 and they farm at Three Hills. They have four children. Bill, born August 30th, 1951, married Brenda Richardson February 23rd, 1974. He teaches at Grand Cache, Alberta. Michael, born March 9th, 1953, married Karen Webb October 23rd, 1976. He farms and works part-time in the oil fields. Ross, born April 5th, 1956, married Joanne Hummel December 4th, 1976, and he is a butcher at Caroline. Kathleen, born March 26, 1961, is going to school.

Olive married Bruce Thompson August 8th, 1952, who is a fireman at the sulphur plant in Rocky Mountain House. Olive lives with brother Merton at DeWinton. They have three children. Lyle, born May 23rd, 1953, died October 8th, 1974. Douglas, born October 10th, 1955, is an electrician living at Rocky Mountain House. Patricia, born April 18th, 1958, married Dale Scarlett, and they live in Innisfail.

Joan married John Petrashuyk February 7th, 1953 and they operate the hotel in Longview. They have three children. John Jr., born November 5th, 1953, is a barber in B.C. Terry, born June 16th, 1955, is a barmaid in Calgary. Leigh, born December 26th, 1958, is in school and Jamie, born October 24th, 1971, is in kindergarten.

Marilyn married Donald Miller September 10th, 1955. He works for Calgary Power in Calgary, and they have four children. Debra, born August 12th, 1956, married Gregory Paschke September 6th, 1975, and they live in Calgary. Dale, born September 25th, 1958, Martin, born March 17th, 1967, and Tammy, born December 13th, 1970, all go to school in Calgary.

Ernest died April 17th, 1957 at the age of 69 years. Lillian has three great-grandchildren, Daniel Paschke, born January 27th, 1976, Angela Scarlett, born January 31st, 1976 and Jennifer Reynolds, born February 5th, 1976. She lives at the Sarcee Auxiliary Hospital, Calgary.

JOHN "JACK" AND EMMA BOLTON — by Harold Biswanger

John Dew Bolton was born in Guelph, Ontario in 1873 and moved with his parents and five brothers, a sister and a cousin in 1889 to Calgary where they stayed that winter. Mr. James Bolton the father hauled lumber to their homestead located five miles east of Okotoks and one mile north of Aldersyde on the south banks of the Sheep Creek. NW¼ 30-20-29-W4.

In the spring when the house was finished they all moved in and the men started to break up the land for planting. In 1892 three of the boys moved to homesteads in the Gladys Ridge district they were Amos, Arthur and Edward. Shortly after in the early 1890's Jack took out a homestead a mile and a half north of Sheep Creek. This was NW¼ 30-21-28-W4 and in 1895 he married a neighbor girl Emma Rowles.

In 1909 he bought the Grand Central Hotel in Okotoks. Two years later in 1911 he traded the hotel for a farm near Trochu which consisted of five quarters and at that time was valued at $3,200.

They had two sons and one daughter. Mrs. Bolton died March 1927 and Jack Bolton died May 28, 1947. Reference from Trochu History Book and Leaves of the Medicine Tree.

THE CAMERON FAMILY HISTORY — by Mrs. Virtue *

Kenneth Cameron was born in 1841 in Beauly, Inverness, Scotland. He married Elizabeth Carstairs of Edinburgh, Scotland. She was born in 1844. After they both come to Canada. They settled in Paisley, Bruce County, Ontario. Where their seven children were born. From there they moved to Woodside, Manitoba. In 1880 Kenneth Cameron with a friend Alex McRae, decided to move west ahead of the railroad, find a suitable location and have his wife and children come later by train. So they left Manitoba one spring morning their wagon piled high with provisions, and several teams of oxen to pull the load, they travelled all summer along prairie trails and streams in September they reached Sheep Creek Crossing. A snow storm hit, so they had to make camp. Their oxen drifted away with the storm, Cameron and McRae stranded on foot decided to take out squatter's rights on the banks of the Sheep River. When surveyed, these places became their homesteads, and later on they got pre-emptions making a half section for each. Kenneth Cameron's land was on the west side of the old Macleod Trail and Alex McRae's on the east. There

McRae built his house. It was later occupied by Louis Flauret.

Cameron's family came out soon as the railroad was complete to Calgary. Soon after they arrived their second oldest daughter Anne married Alex McRae. Both these men homesteaded where the present town site is now.

Kenneth Cameron operated the stopping house in Okotoks at the foot of the big hill, where many years later the highway would pass. Travellers and freighters by-passed MacMillan's in favor of Cameron's stopping house. The reason was plain to see. The Camerons had five unmarried daughters.

Kenneth farmed the quarter on which the Okotoks Cemetery is located, as it was part of the homestead. Cameron Coulee which is southwest of Okotoks was also named after them. Cameron Crossing which is one half mile east of Okotoks town limits and one half mile south was another place named after them.

Kenneth Cameron had two sons and five daughters: Elizabeth (Mrs. John McRae); Anne (Mrs. Alex McRae); John (Jack) married (Emma Wilson); Mary (Mrs. Joe Wathen); Marion (Mrs. Norman McInnis); Robert never married; Bella (Mrs. James Bews); Kenneth passed away Jan. 14, 1893. He was 52 years old. His wife Elizabeth passed away Jan. 13, 1898. She was 54 years old.

Their son-in-law Alex McRae, made the caskets for both Mr. and Mrs. Kenneth Cameron when they died. The women relatives covered the wood with black cloth on the outside and white cloth on the inside for the lining.

There was a minister by the name of Angus Robertson who held church service at the Cameron Stopping House when he went by.

Their son, Jack Cameron, born in 1864 married Emma Wilson and took out a homestead south of his father's. On S.E. 20-20-29-W4. It is now the Jim Tucker place.

They had eleven children. Ethel born in 1892 married (Ernie Tillitson), had five children three boys and two girls (Reginald James, Loftus, Youel, Erial, Eunice,). Her husband passed away and she now resides in a home in Lacombe, Alberta.

Mary Elizabeth (Mamie) as she was better known born in 1893 married (Harry Henderson) eldest son of Richard (Dick) Henderson in 1912. They had two boys, Donald, who lives in Calgary. Thomas (Bud) who lives in Kamloops, B.C. and six girls: Helen (deceased); Audrey (Calgary); Emma (Turner Valley); Kathleen (Hardisty); Rita (B.C.); Beulah (Maple Ridge, B.C.); Kenneth Cameron Jr. born 1895 (whereabouts unknown); Clara born in 1897 married (Sam Virtue). They had two boys and three girls. Dorothy married, lives in Kamloops, B.C.; Samuel Lorne (Jim) Virtue, married, lives in Devon, Alta. Hilda (Billie), married, lives in Kamloops, B.C. Evelyn Joyce, married, resided in Kamloops, B.C. until her untimely death on April 6th, 1977.

Gordon Virtue resides on the old Cameron property

Left to right Kenneth Cameron, Emma and Jack Cameron, Robert Cameron on crutches, Kenneth and Elizabeth Cameron and Minister in doorway, rest unknown.

east of Okotoks. Albert J. Cameron born in 1898 at the time Albert was born they were still on the homestead. Albert married (Isabelle Chalmers) had one son Ralph who, with his wife, Anne, now lives in Calgary. Albert Cameron passed away in 1971, his wife in 1975; Donald, born in 1902, who now, with his wife, Dora, resides in White Rock, B.C. Charlie born in 1904 (whereabouts unknown); Isabelle born in 1906 (deceased); Beatrice born in 1908 moved to the States with a family by the name of Thomas that looked after her and her brother Robert. There she married Wesley Ramey. She has two daughters: Beatrice and her husband reside in Grand Rapids, Mich.; Earl Cameron born in 1910 married Anne Cook from Craigmyle (now deceased); had one son and now lives in Surrey, B.C. Robert born in 1913 (whereabouts unknown).

Jack Cameron was well known for calling at square dances. He called at local dances and was very good at it. When there was a dance he was going to be calling he would wind up the old gramophone and get all the family to square dance, they all learned very young how to dance, the girls were very good dancers I was told.

Jack and Emma Cameron owned and operated a butcher shop in a small metal covered building with a lean-to on the back located east of the old Wentworth Store. One day in 1894 or 1895 while Jack and Emma Cameron were working, they had taken their second eldest daughter with them as they were busy so they put the little girl on the counter where they could keep an eye on her. There were always Indians in the area at that time. The Indians came in to the store, picked up the little girl and headed south across the tracks, Mamie screamed in fright, the parents saw what was happening and took chase, the Indians dropped the little girl on the south side of the railroad tracks, then ran and hid in the bushes, Mamie was rescued by her parents. As far as we know that's where the story ends. In the early 1900's Emma Cameron purchased a parcel of land PTN NW 22-20-29 W4. There they built a two storey house they moved into in 1905, the younger children were born there. The first school they went to was on the old McIntyre place it was moved to Okotoks and used as a school, later it was the Hurst house. By 1912 two of the daughters had married. In 1912 Albert Cameron had met two little friends at school who had just moved here from England, Tom and Bob Grisdale, so he invited them down to his home to play with him and his brothers and sisters one Saturday and see the pigs, cows, chickens, well they went out to gather eggs as Bob recalls they had never seen so many eggs, then Clara cooked dinner.

In late 1912 Jack's brother, Robert, who had homesteaded southwest of the Tucker farm, was staying with Joe Wathen. He took sick and came over to stay at Jack and Emma Cameron's place, east of Okotoks where he died in January of 1913 of a ruptured appendix.

In February of 1913 Emma Cameron passed away so the small children were taken in by different families. Charlie, Isabelle, Earl, went with Ernie Stevenson south of Craigmyle. Beatrice and Robert, with a Thomas family who later moved to the States. Donald went to stay with a fellow by the name of Jack

Carter. Clara went to stay with her sister, Ethel, but only stayed a very short time then came back to Okotoks.

Later Jack Cameron met a lady by the name of Elsie, who worked for Saunders, they were married and went to work at an Indian School as caretakers. They had three children, two girls (Margaret and Primrose); and a boy, David. Elsie left and went to the coast. The girls reside in Duncan, B.C.

In 1925 Jack Cameron was on the road crew with Charlie Gratama, Bob Dunkle, E. Miller, Sam Johnson, that worked on the Sawyer hill and the road north, Sam Johnson drove a team and Jack worked the fresno that scooped up the dirt.

In later years a lady by the name of Mrs. Carby kept house for Jack Cameron. Times were hard in those days and she had three children so, by looking after his house and a big vegetable garden, along with chickens, she was able to feed her own family.

Well Jack lived there for years. He had a pinto pony called Peanuts that he drove hitched to a buggy.

Late in the fall of 1951 Jack Cameron went to stay with his daughter, Clara Virtue, in Turner Valley, came back and stayed on the home place for the summer then in the fall went to live at the Eventide Home for Men, in Gleichen, Alta. Mr. C. Halstead drove him there. He passed away there on Feb. 14, 1954.

Jack Cameron got all his teeth pulled and the day he got his set of "store teeth" he was driving home with old Peanuts. As he passed the town dump he sneezed so hard, his teeth flew out and landed in the dump. He hunted for hours but never found them. A $50.00 loss! So he went back to the dentist and had another set made.

One day in 1925 while the road gang were working on Sawyers' hill east of Okotoks, a lady by the name of Mrs. Dunkley who lived north of Sawyers hill, came by on her way back from her grocery shopping in town, when she got to the slaughter house she stopped to water her horse. Phil Tesky, who was also on the road gang and quite a gentleman, saw that her horse started acting up so went over to see if he could be of some assistance in getting the horse and buggy to the top of the hill. Mrs. Dunkley got out of the buggy and Phil Tesky got in, well the horse got scared and took a few jumps, tipped the buggy over and run away, Phil Tesky was nowhere to be found, so the crew caught the horse and fixed the buggy as best they could, got Mrs. Dunkley on her way home, then they went looking for Phil, all of a sudden he appeared on the road just covered from head to foot with flour which Mrs. Dunkley had purchased early in the day. In the runaway the bag had ripped and the contents covered Phil Tesky. The road crew all had a good laugh at the "Good Samaritan."

Albert Cameron told me that when they lived in the two storey house east of Okotoks in the 1900's every time there was a snow storm before they got out of bed in the morning they used to give the covers a flip so as to get the snow off that had blown in during the night.

FURTHER TO JACK CAMERON*
Gordon Virtue, son of Clara Cameron and Sam Vir-

tue, with his wife, Evelyn Peters, moved onto the old homestead land of his grandfather in 1959. They built a garage from the lumber taken from the old Cameron house and dug a well by hand. They started to build a new home in 1967 and finally finished it in 1976. They have three children: Gordon Jr. 1958, Pamela, 1959, and Lorne James, 1964. Thus an old family continues in the district.

THE CAMERONS, THOMAS AND ELIZABETH (SAUNDERS) — by Wallace Cameron *

Among the early settlers of the Okotoks district was Thomas Cameron, who was born May 20, 1846; and died at Okotoks, January 9, 1940, in his 94th year.

He was of Highland Scottish descent, his parents having emigrated from Glasgow, Scotland, in 1840, and settling in Grey County, Ontario. Thomas Cameron was the youngest of a family of five, having three older brothers: Joseph, Daniel, and Peter, and an adopted sister, Mary. Thomas spent the early part of his adult life in the lumber business, specifically logging, at a place known as The Portage, located between Lake Simcoe and Lake Couchiching, in Ontario. He became superintendent of the lumber company and was so employed for a number of years.

In October of 1870, he married Elizabeth Saunders, daughter of Mr. and Mrs. G. W. Saunders, St. Vincent Township, Ontario. The former's father was Major G.W. Saunders, United Empire Loyalist from the State of Vermont, and the latter was the descendant of an old Dutch family that had settled on Manhattan Island. The marriage resulted in the birth of two sons: Clarence and Lionel, who were later to acquire an adopted sister, Dorothy.

The children were raised and received their schooling, for the most part, in and around The Portage. The elder son, Clarence, however, supplemented his education by two years of military college at Kingston, Ontario.

The two boys came West in the middle 1890's; Clarence first, followed two years later by Lionel. They were employed as riders on the P. Burns Cattle Ranch for some time after having come West; finally settling on homesteads near a place known as "The Big Hill" in the Longview district, west of High River. (S½-Sec. 6-19-1-W5th.)

That was in 1902, the same year that they were joined in the West by their parents and sister, Dorothy, who filed their homestead in what is now known as Big Rock district. After "proving up" their homesteads at Longview, Clarence and Lionel, through a business deal with Mr. Henry Brockelbank, acquired quarter sections in the Big Rock district, not far from their father's homestead.

In the year 1910, the family moved to Saskatchewan where they farmed near Keystown until 1920, when they moved back to the Okotoks district.

Clarence Cameron, unlike his younger brother who married Evelyn Saunders in 1911, remained a bachelor during his entire life. Lionel's marriage resulted in a family of two boys: Kenneth and Wallace; and three girls: Alma, Norma, and Marion.

The elder boy, Kenneth, left the family farm in 1936, and, after working on a farm in the Blackie

Lionel and Evelyn Cameron — 1945.

district for four years, joined the staff of Standen's Ltd., spring manufacturers, in Calgary. There he remained employed until his death 35 years later, on February 2, 1975. He was survived by his wife, Eileen, whom he married in 1946; and a son, Dale.

The second brother, Wallace, is at present living in Calgary, and is employed by the Alberta Government. He and his wife, Ruth, have three sons: Tom, Malcolm, and Terry; and a daughter, Yvonne. Tom and his wife, Edith, have presented them with two grandsons, Robert, and Richard.

Lionel and Evelyn's eldest daughter, Alma, is at present living in the Okotoks district with her husband, Norman Hogge, the son of another prominent pioneer family whose history will appear elsewhere in this book.

The youngest daughter, Marion, married Russell Martin, also the son of a very old and well-known pioneer family whose history is also recorded elsewhere on these pages.

The middle daughter, Norma, was married in 1945 to Paul Laverty who is presently employed in the embossing business in Calgary. Their marriage resulted in a family of four children; two sons: Brian and Allan, residing in Indiana and Ontario respectively; and two daughters: Carol and Dawne, who live in Calgary. They presently have four grandchildren: Earl, Juanita, David, and Paul.

Thomas Cameron and the elder son, Clarence,

farmed north of Okotoks until the death of the former in 1940; and the latter in 1948. Lionel and his family lived on an adjoining quarter (SW¼ 4-21-29-W4th) until 1953 when the farm was sold and they moved to Calgary. Lionel was predeceased by his wife, Evelyn, in July, 1960; and passed away four years later in May, 1964.

Clarence and Lionel loved to relate interesting and worth-while stories concerning incidents that had occurred during their lifetime. It was told, for example, that while "proving up" their homesteads, the brothers lived alone in a little cabin with their dog. The fact that they left the cabin door open at night became quite advantageous to the dog, as it had acquired the habit of going out in the night to tease the coyotes in the area. On several occasions Lionel was amused to hear their dog come racing home with the coyotes in "hot" pursuit. Sometimes, in order to escape from them, the dog would come through that open door travelling at such a speed as to skid completely across the floor, and even bump against the far wall. A muffled snicker from Clarence's bunk indicated that he, too, was aware of the situation.

The pioneer history of the Camerons, as well as other families in the district, is, of a certainty, impressive; as facts and events pertaining to it are remembered through succeeding generations.

JOHN AND EMMA CHILDREN — by Roy Austin *

In the late 1890's John and Emma Children migrated from Sussex, Wisconsin, to homestead in the Okotoks area. They were accompanied by their sons and daughters, Cora, Ina, Lillian, Myrtis, Raymond and Stanley. The homestead was situated adjacent to the present sulphur plant east of town and was known for many years as the Johnson farm, 26-20-29 W4.

L. to R. Stanley, Lillian, Raymond, Emma Children, Cora, Myrtis between parents, John Children, Ina.

One son, Raymond, took another homestead a mile east of this and resided there for several years 25-20-29 W4.

While living here the Allan School district was formed in 1908 and he was the first secretary for the School District. During the period John Children

resided on his homestead, they also took up property in the Turner Valley area to run cattle in the summer. Little did John Children realize that this would be gas and oil producing property.

In late 1910 they disposed of all properties and moved to the city of Calgary, residing on 17 Avenue S.E. adjoining the Exhibition grounds and the property is still in the hands of a grandson.

Emma Children died in 1919 and John Children died in 1930. All of the sons and daughters are deceased and only grandsons and grandaughters are surviving.

Raymond Children disposed of his properties and took up another homestead in the Youngstown area, then located in other areas, Peace River and Calgary. Stanley Children also took up a homestead in the Scotfield area adjoining Youngstown, then moved to the Blackie area, then to Calgary where he died in 1927.

The daughters were all married — Ina to Jacob Stier and they resided in the Blackie area. Lillian to Frank Burns and they resided in the City of Spokane, Washington, Cora to Mel Folger and they resided in Okotoks and Calgary. Myrtis to John Austin and they resided in the City of Calgary.

Grandsons and grandaughters are — of the Stier family; Earl (deceased), Jack, Milo, Ernest (Pat) and James, residing in the Blackie, De Winton and Castlgar, B.C. areas. Of the Burns family, Valerie, Dorothy and Francis, all residing in the State of Washington. Of the Folger family, Delbert who resides in the City of Calgary in the family home. Of the Austin family, Roy who resides in the City of Calgary.

Raymond Children had one son, Vernon, who resides in the Seattle, Washington area. Stanley Children never married.

Del Folger on horse, Stan Children.

M. C. CHRISTENSEN FAMILY — by Mrs. M. C. Christensen

Melvin came to the Allan district in 1952 to work for his brother-in-law Walter Wilde (on the Cecil Barker place). S31-20-28-W4

Melvin was born and raised at Carseland on the farm his dad, Jens Martin Christensen, and mother,

Anna Mikkilson, came to from Iowa in 1910. Youngest brother, Harry, still farms the home place. Eleven brothers and sisters. Two brothers and one sister deceased. Others all married and living in Alberta.

My mother and dad, Archie Stewart and Margaret Foreman, came to homestead at Cessford, Alberta from Galt (Kirkwall) Ontario in 1910. In 1925 they moved to Dalemead to the farm which is now the home of the new Cominco Plant.

I received my schooling in Newton School, a rural school grades 1 to 8 then on to Dalemead Rural High School. There were eight brothers and sisters. Two older brothers deceased others are married and living in Alberta.

In 1938 my parents moved to Lyalta and I went to Little Chicago (Royalties now) in the oilfields where I worked in the Post Office. In 1940 I was working in the Carseland Hotel, met Melvin and we were married in October 1941. In December 1942 he joined the Armed Forces and went overseas the next summer with the Army Service Corps. He received his discharge on February 13, 1946.

Basic training was at Currie Barracks, Calgary and advanced training at Red Deer. He went overseas in 1943 and was stationed at Aldershot. A month after D Day he went to France with the Royal Canadian Army Service Corps. While in Continental Europe he contracted Diphtheria and was sent back to England in 1945.

He served in England, France, Belgium and Holland and received the Canadian Volunteer Medal star and the defence Medal.

He was then employed by Western Irrigation as drag line operator, later moved onto the headquarters at Carseland as ditch rider.

In 1952 we moved to the Allan district. We had good neighbors such as: Herb and Esther Jenkins, Harold Biswanger, Tom and Mercedes McMullin, Doug and Rusha Herr, Albert and Lucy Sevigny, Bob and Laura Sallenbach all of whom played a great part in making our move a happy one.

Branding bees were held when all the men worked together going from one farm to the next till all the cattle were done. In harvest time or seeding, whoever was finished first moved their outfits on to the next neighbors to give a helping hand.

Melvin Christiansen family: L. to R. Gordon, Doug, Kay, Melvin, Kevin and Ron.

Card games and surprise parties were our entertainment all year round. No one was ever too busy to come to a surprise party. These were happy times!

In 1967 we sold out and bought a home in the town of Okotoks on the hill where we now reside.

Our four sons Gordon, Ronnie, Douglas and Kevin received their education at Okotoks School. Gordon married Gail Lee from Swift Current Sask. They have two daughters Tracy and Kelly. Ronnie married Joan (Cookie) Foote from Calgary and they have two children Kari and Bryan. They all live in Okotoks.

We belong to the Royal Canadian Legion and Auxiliary and are members of the Okotoks Curling Club.

EDWARD CLANCY*

Ed came from Ontario and bought the SE¼ 27-20-29-W4 at the foot of the Sawyers Hill 1½ miles east of Okotoks. He was a bachelor all his life. He sold his land to John Bosgra in 1955 as the pollen from the blossoms bothered his asthma. He moved back east to his sister in 1955 and died that same year.

WILLIAM HENRY "BILLY" AND EMMA ANN COLE — by Harold Biswanger

Billy Cole and his wife, Emma Ann, took up a homestead four miles north east of Okotoks on the NE¼ 35-20-29-W4 in the early 90's acquiring the title in 1897, after coming from Grimsby, Ontario. They moved back to North Grimsby, county of Lincoln, Ontario in his 80's prior to selling in the spring of 1929 to Douglas Ward.

Billy was not one to set the world on fire and being in hard times did some pretty strange things. Like making all his fields very small so that the horses, as they were in very poor shape from lack of good feed, could see the other end of the field real close at hand, or they would not work to plow, or seed. He also had an alarm clock at one end of the field so when it went off he could hear it no matter where he was in the field, so he could go in for meals.

In the dryer years he put up buck brush in stacks to help feed his horses and cattle in the winter. They milked several cows and made very good butter from which they got some of their income by selling it in Okotoks.

He also had a lean-to kitchen on his house which he was always moving to a different side of the main house, and fastening it on again. The neighbor's children also discovered a bed in the bush, about one quarter mile from the house, made of poplar poles and a tarpaulin for a roof with books and papers to read, as a hideaway from his wife. He vowed vengeance on the children if they told anybody.

When going to visit the Aldridges he always carried a hand saw for protection against their dog as it did not like him. He would keep the sharp side of the saw between him and the dog.

He built his out house on a platform with a walk way out over a spring runway so when the spring run off and the heavy rains came it would wash everything clean.

He would take stock molasses in jars to the Aldridge children for birthday presents, but one had built up pressure and it blew the lid off and it hit the ceiling.

Billy also ate gophers and would pickle them in salt brine like pork for the winter.

Emma gave Hilda Ward a toy parasol wrapped in about six boxes one inside the other for her fourth birthday. She also made her a very lovely dress.

JAMES COOMBE — by Mrs. T. Sandeman

After the Boer War, James Coombe came to Canada from Devon England, settling in Airdrie, Alberta in 1904, homesteading and establishing his own business. He was a member of the town council and an officer in the 15 Light Horse Reserve. August 1914 he joined the 12 CMR for overseas which was later transferred to the Fort Garry Horse. In 1919 he took a position with the Dominion Government as a supervisor with the Soldier Settlement Board in the district from Bassano to Empress, Alberta.

In 1924 he purchased his farm from Mr. and Mrs. P. S. Idington where he lived until his death in 1944. Land description was NW¼ 6-21-28-W4.

Jim Coombe.

Mr. Coombe had two daughters, Millicent, Mrs. T. Sandeman, of Okotoks and Marjorie, Mrs. A. W. Bishop, of Redding, California.

THE COULTRY'S — by Harold and Cecil Coultry

In the early 1900's approximately 1904, the Coultry's, William Charles and his wife, Cora Lillian, and one year old daughter, Willa Vivian, left from Winnipeg and Indian Head then moved to Halkirk for a short time before moving to Calgary.

Mr. Coultry, in partnership with the late Billy Stokes, operated the old Empire Hotel on 9th Avenue. Mr. Coultry was also active in real estate and horse racing.

One son, George Harold Balfour, was born in Calgary, April 15, 1907. Another daughter, Muriel Donalda, was born October 2, 1908.

Leaving Calgary they settled in the Stavely district, also operating the local hotel. Mrs. Coultry returned home to Indian Head where another son was added to the family, William Spearman Cecil, born January 30, 1913.

Selling out their hotel business they moved to High River living in town and farming in the Longview country till 1917, then moving on to Okotoks. They bought the Hamilton farm four miles east of Okotoks, farmstead SE¼ 30-20-28-W4. Mr. Coultry farmed here till his death on September 26, 1937.

William Charles and Cora Lillian Coultry Family. L. to R. Willa (Mrs. R. A. Quinton) Cecil, Dad (died 1937 at 65 years of age) Harold, Donalda.

Mrs. Coultry. Bridge on irrigation ditch on farm 1927.

Crossing Sheep River north of Dwight Barretts place, 1954. No. 2 highway put in a bridge.

Mrs. Coultry passed away nine years later on August 25, 1946. Their son, Harold, continued to farm and lived on NW¼ 24-20-29-W4 until war was declared. He joined the Air Force and, on his discharge, joined the staff of Bird Construction where he retired. Harold married February 24, 1926 to Joyce Howery another old timer of the Allan district. They are now living in Kamloops, B.C. and have three children; Muriel, Jack and Bill. All three went to the Allan school and Okotoks school. The two Coultry boys are in construction in Calgary and Muriel also lives in Calgary. Their parents celebrated their 50 wedding anniversary in Calgary February 26, 1976.

Donalda (Dony) married V. W. Ohlsen of Turner Valley (old timers in that district) on January 25, 1933. They also have three children, two boys and one girl.

Willa married July 17, 1922 to a local boy Robert A. Quinton they have one son. Willa passed away in 1972.

Cecil Williams married Rosemary (Frankie) Victor of Alix, Alberta April 29, 1939. Cecil and Frankie are still living in the district. They have three children in their family. Sharon Lee, Noreen Gaye (Registered Nurse) and Wayne Allan (Lawyer in Calgary). Sharon is still single and living in Calgary.

Noreen Gaye married November 11, 1967 to Ken Culas of Powell River, B.C.

Wayne married February 21, 1976 to Huguette Forest of Souris, Manitoba they also live in Calgary.

Harold, Willa and Donalda all received their early schooling at the little Allan school. Cecil started school in Okotoks, later they all attended school there.

Willa, in her younger days, was active in flying. She was taught by the late Captain McCall (McCall airfield in Calgary was named in his honour). He landed his aeroplane in the field on the hill near Okotoks school. He came to have dinner most Sundays at the Coultry's. They lived in what is now Charles Tuckers house in Okotoks.

Cecil ran a trap line along the river west on the Sheep River past Okotoks and on west to Black Diamond. On his trap line he practiced his running for competition.

Leaving their home in Okotoks on a very cold night, well bundled up against the cold, he started running out to the farm (as he ran everywhere he went). Along near the Sawyer Hill he came upon a herd of cattle and spooked them and they turned about and ran east. He found out they were their own cattle that had broken out of their own pasture.

Cecil has been active in the district for 60 years,

still driving a School Bus for a private school (Strathcona-Tweedsmuir). He has also been active in sports all his life. Long distance running, participating in the local Herald Road Races in Calgary for a number of years. He was a hockey referee, enjoyed fishing and trap shooting, making the All Canadian Trap team in Canada in 1961 (one of the ten best shooters in Canada).

Cecil, at 64, drives on an average of 225 miles per day and still has time to go two miles training his new hunting dog.

The Coultry farm was a very active camp ground, people coming for miles around to camp out on weekends. The camp was known quite well as Camp Belvedere.

There is a little joke in the Bob Edwards Eye Opener book about a man trying to sell John Hamilton a wind broken horse and he was trotting him around for John's inspection. He stroked the horses back and drew attention to his lovely coat. His coats alright said John but I don't like his pants.

This incident took place at the Allan School when Malcolm MacGougan was teacher. Mac asked his students to explain a collision; an example being two bodies coming together. Bob Miller answered "Twin calves".

Cecil belongs to the Okotoks Elks and Okotoks curling club. His wife Frankie to the Royal Purple and Okotoks curling club.

AN ALBERTA FAMILY SHOWS THE WAY
Mr. and Mrs. Coultry, Okotoks, Transform Ordinary Farm Premises into a Beauty Spot — How It Is Done

Those who hold the opinion that tree planting, flower growing and allied ventures are more or less a waste of time would do well to visit the Coultry family, four miles east of Okotoks. In the short space of five years their farm has become one of the most beautiful in the entire district, and each season they reap a greater harvest of satisfaction and contentment; the farm has become a home. In bringing about this change the Coultrys have been assisted by two agencies — an ideal and a willingness to do the necessary work. These, they say, are all that are required to obtain results equal to their own on the average farm.

The first trees, some 1,500 in number, were planted five years ago and consisted of Russian poplars, Manitoba maples and caraganas, all of these being furnished by the Government Forestry Station, Indian Head. Balm of Gilead and native poplar trees were also secured from the creek banks and transplanted. All of the trees were put out in rows, four feet being allowed each way, on land that had been thoroughly summer fallowed the preceding year. At the time the cuttings were inserted into the ground by the use of a spade they were well watered and the earth was thoroughly tramped. Had there been a plentiful supply of moisture in the ground at the time of planting, Mrs. Coultry states she would not have resorted to the use of the water pail, particularly since the ground had been in fallow, but the growth made by the cuttings during a subsequent dry spell fully justified this procedure.

From the time the plantation was set out in May until late in August cultivation was carefully done. A one-horse cultivator and the hand hoe were the implements employed, and these were almost in constant use. The entire belt was fenced to keep out stock.

During the past five years the original plantation has been increased by the addition of some 7,000 trees of the varieties already named as well as some Jack pines, spruce and Western poplar. Given the same care shown in the first planting, these have all thrived and the result is most pleasing. The accompanying picture gives but a meagre idea of the transformation of this farm; to really appreciate its beauty it is necessary that one visit the premises. Nor is the work completed; Mrs. Coultry has further plans for this year, among which are the erection of a Chinese pergola and grape arbors.

The lawn comprises about an acre, and was sown early last spring. The previous year the land selected had been used for potatoes, and as a result of the constant cultivation required to keep it clean from weeds, the land was in an excellent state of tilth.

Before seeding, a duckfoot cultivator was used with the feet thrust as deep as possible; this was followed by the harrows used lengthwise and crosswise to the field several times. All lumps were broken down and stones removed. The surface was then carefully levelled with a float. A calm day was selected for the sowing, and one hundred pounds of seed was used, the area being lightly raked following the sowing and then left. Almost immediately rain fell and the seed was packed into the earth firmly. Several heavy downfalls resulted in quick germination and artificial watering was not required.

When the grass had developed to the stage where it was showing nicely a heavy packer was used, and the result of this was seen later in the season in a smooth surface and a uniform growth. The first mowing was accomplished on July 2 and throughout the season the grass grew at a surprising rate.

Those with little experience with flowers would marvel at the variety to be found on the Coultry farm. They include several varieties of roses, peonies, irises, lilacs, tulips, dahlias, gladioli, foxgloves, phlox, Sweet Williams, asters, delphiniums, gypsophila, hollyhocks, platycodons, poppies, carnations, golden glow, blanket-flowers, red-hot-pokers, aquilegias, campanulas, bluebells, forget-me-nots, lychnis and many others. These were all purchased from one of the local nurseries and as a result of careful attention have flourished. It would be difficult to pick out any one variety and say it has done best; all the perennials have made an excellent showing.

Last year Mrs. Coultry added a large number of annuals. The season was late and in order to avoid disappointment these were purchased from a Calgary greenhouse and planted out, only a few being grown from seed. Marigolds, pinks, cosmos, nasturtiums, nemesia, daisies, stocks, antirrhinums, scabiosa, salpiglossis, zinnias, verbenas, petunias, geraniums, sweet peas, candytuft, lobelias and a host of other varieties gave excellent results.

In addition to these, pansies, candytuft and sweet peas were grown from seed, and although fear was expressed at the time of planting, the ideal growth conditions of last season resulted in all of these developing rapidly and making a wonderful showing long before the frost clipped them off.

As would be expected, the flowers were grown in soil which varied considerably in the cultivation given it. Some of the plants went into virgin soil, while in other cases the land had been in use for other purposes a number of years. In the case of the latter a dressing of barnyard manure was given before it was dug, but apart from this no difference was made in the manner in which it was handled. The hole was dug as deeply as possible and the surface raked until all lumps were broken down and the ground level. In the case of the dahlias a heavy mulch of leaves and grass rakings was used to help retain the moisture.

Also on this farm is a very fine assortment of shrubs, lilacs, mock oranges, hydrangeas, snowballs, honeysuckles, golden elders and many varieties of the spirea. By allowing plenty of room between the plants for development, thoroughly cultivating between the plants and rows, and ensuring an adequate supply of water, they have been made to thrive and each year sees them more vigorous than the last.

The efforts of this family do not stop with flowers, trees and shrubs. Their garden is a source of revelation. The range of plants grown here is wide, and includes many small fruits as well as the commoner vegetables. Last year the pride of the garden was a monster pumpkin which at maturity weighed thirty pounds. Marrows weighing up to eighteen pounds were also harvested, as well as an excellent crop of cucumbers.

About 1,000 raspberry bushes of the Sunbeam and Flaming Giant varieties have been planted out and are commencing to give excellent yields. There are also several hundred black and red currant bushes well established. Mrs. Coultry prefers the Victoria variety of the former and the Perfection in the latter. During the past year or two a start has also been made with six different varieties of plums, three of cherries, three of apples and two of crabs. Grapes are also being tried out, a number of vines of the Beta variety having been planted.

Asked as to the essentials in the cultivation of small fruits. Mrs. Coultry gave it as her opinion that adequate cultivation, a study of the pruning operation, and straw protection during the winter months, are the main requirements. A fine showing is made in his garden by Victoria rhubarb. In winter a light covering of litter is place over the plants and up to date no trouble has been experienced in bringing them through the winter. Egyptian perennial onions have given like results under similar treatment.

It must not be supposed that these results have been attained without an expenditure of much thought and energy. One instance of the trouble they go to is in connection with the water supply. As yet no pipe system has been laid down and it is necessary to haul all the water for the garden from Sheep Creek. This is accomplished by means of a tank with a force pump and hose attached, and twice a week during the very hot weather the entire premises are given a thorough soaking. According to Mrs. Coultry energy is the limiting factor in this work; anyone who so desires can have such grounds and gardens if willing to do the work. She holds the opinion that small, well attended grounds offer greater returns than extensive ones and at the same time keep the cost down to a moderate figure.

As a profitable sideline, Mr. and Mrs. Coultry have found turkey raising very satisfactory. Last year they hatched seventy-five Bronze turkeys, the majority of these being brought out under Buff Orpington hens, a few under hen turkeys. The Buffs are preferred on account of their gentleness. The turkeys received no food until they were forty-eight hours old, at which time they were given oystershell, ground very fine on a dry board. For the first few days they were fed sparingly on hard-boiled eggs chopped fine and mixed with bread crumbs. When the youngsters were two weeks old a small quantity of shorts was added to their ration, and gradually the eggs and crumbs were discontinued altogether until finally the food consisted of shorts alone. The birds were protected from rains until they were six weeks of age and had developed their characteristic red heads, and from this time on they were given free range. Four weeks before killing time the turkeys were fed boiled wheat three times daily, but were still allowed to range about.

FRANK P. AND NELLIE MAY (GARDNER) COYLE — by L. Card

In the spring of 1905, two brothers from Walla Walla, Washington, Frank P. and Sidney Coyle, came to the Allan District to take up homestead land. Their half section was about five miles east and north of Okotoks. The Forckel family lived north of them as did the Barker family across the road from the Forckels. The land was worked and some buildings erected on the property. Frank remained there but Sidney returned to Walla Walla after a couple of years.

In June of 1907 Frank Coyle married Nellie May Gardner of Cayley. She had come to Canada early in 1902 with her father and seven brothers who all took homesteads in the Cayley area. She was working in High River when Frank met her and after their marriage they lived on his homestead till 1918. To this union four daughters were born, the first was still-born. The other three were Lillian May (Mrs. S. B. Card) of Calgary. Frances Merium (Mrs. N. McLean) of Islington, Ontario. Nellie Irene (Mrs. H. Forrest) of Port Coquitlam, B.C.

There was no school open in the district when Lillian was school age and Calgary was chosen as the

Nellie May Gardner and Frank Payne Coyle. Wedding day June 26, 1907.

place to move. The farm was sold to Mr. McDougall, he had a large family so the Allan School was opened shortly after. Mr. McDougall was unable to succeed on the land and it was reclaimed by Frank and in turn sold to Cecil Barker who had to let it go for repossession several years later. Mr. Walter Wilde was the next purchaser and was successful there for a number of years. I understand that presently it is in possession of the Morrisroe family.

Frank, Nellie and Lillian Coyle. Taken at Calgary fair, 1911.

Frank purchased a section of land in the Dog Pound area after moving to Calgary in the spring of 1918 and carried on a successful mixed farming operation, supporting his family who lived in Calgary where the girls attended Connaught Public and Central High Schools. The Dog Pound property was sold to Pete Sullivan, Coyle's hired man, who continued successfully for some time. Mr. Coyle then supervised a smaller tract of land in the Shepard area for a number of years and finally retired from his successful farming operations at 85 years of age.

He lived to be 96½ years old and passed away in May, 1965. Mrs. Coyle passed away in Febraury 1975 at 92 years of age.

BOYD CUTHBERTSON — NW¼ 9-21-29-W4 ★

My wife and I, and two young sons, Barry and Robert moved here from our 5 acres south of Calgary, in 1952, and therefore can make no "old-timer" claims. Not so for our house which was a turn-of-the-century homestead. Taxes in the area were paid here to the original first farmer and M.D. Secretary, a Mr. Hayes. It was a very derelict looking farmstead and our old friend of many years, Eva Reid of the Albertan, told us later that when she saw the house and yard, she went home and cried. We hauled junk and burned and tidied for days, the owner prior to us being an elderly widower in poor health. As a former manager of Ford's farm machinery division in Alberta, I loyally bought a new little Ford tractor and a 7' cultivator. We now have 75' of cultivating capacity. I inherited a model "D" John Deere, on steel lugs, with a crankshaft so flat I put a big block of stone over the crankcase so that if the connecting rods came through they would not hit me, and tied a rope from the clutch to my waist so that when breaking land, my bucked-off torso would stop the outfit. The seat on those old things was away out behind. Operator safety and comfort was a minor consideration in the old days of tractor design. However, one old "D" could out-pull two Ford-Fergusons of the same rated horsepower. Later, I was to buy two of them on rubber tires and for $1750 total cost — tandem, with a homemade hitch — Okotoks and De Winton's first four-wheel drive and I farmed with them on an expanding scale for 5 years,

Ray, Robert, Barry and Boyd Cuthbertson, 1959.

sold them and built a much more sophisticated rig, leased more land, and finally, to "store-bought" four-wheel drives, first Versatile and then a mighty John Deere, at a mighty price, and more land under lease.

But, to retract a bit. As I mentioned, our place is historic, not us. Perhaps we were, though, to our old time neighbors . . . certainly we imported some culture shock . . . some of them told me we were wasting our time planting the trees that grow today on our farmstead . . . "trees wouldn't grow here." "Nor wheat either." Thus forewarned, we took special care to summerfallow for two years. I often see city newcomers planting trees in sod or weedy ground — surely doomed to arboreal mediocrity.

Inside the old house, we tore out partitions, boarded up windows, cut in new ones, got 17 doors down to 7. My wife painted the house, and not white. Everybody was shocked — white was the only really permissable color, and comments on our basic colonial red were so frequently disparaging, we threw in a few other color shockers for the traditionalists. "Why" asked my wife, "have a white house when the country is covered with snow half the year?" (Born in the Emerald Isle, she detests snow!)

When we settled here, I thought we could buy another quarter section or two nearby, as time went on. Not to be. City pressure on land values and low farm-gate produce prices soon made land buying unrelated to agriculture. So, we sub-divided and expanded by leasing properties and growing grains. Lots of hard work, but lots of time for travel, too. Time also for community work in our day — but, over to the young ones now?

This is our little resume, and I conclude with the reflection that the work ethic is still viable in today's search for a new value system. Nil Sine Labore. Nothing without labor. One more comment on our community cultural direction I shall make for posterity. Why all the old emphasis on curling, physical recreation and horses? The cowboy ethic is well preserved, sometimes, I too often think, in our alcohol-dispensing institutions, and we are not prissy in this area . . . why not a Life Centre for the performing arts, serving as an ecumenical church as well? An Okotoks-De Winton country cathedral cum auditorium? I am sure this area has the resources and will for such a project. The concept of sharing the same physical edifice should be quite compatible with maintaining the Christian ethic.

I thank the initiators for creating this historical record, and my opportunity to tell a little of the past, in our farming operation . . . but where do we go from here? Anyone interested in a modern steam tractor against the days ahead when the energy crisis hits its biggest user, Agriculture? I have done some homework here. Any young farmer — or old one interested in pushing some local research on Fall barley? Most of our food production attitudes are of a rather red neck bias and change is essential. Anyone interested in the need of this community for a cultural centre, solving the churches' perennial problems whilst leaving denominational preferences purely private, come talk to me about making some new history for a new era.

JOHN DASHWOOD AND THE GOPHER HOUSE

There was a young Englishman, named Jack Dashwood, who was interested in purchasing a certain stopping house, owned by a Mr. MacMillan. He hung around one day to see how business was going, and noticed that the place seemed very busy. Cowboys and teamsters dropped in for their mail and something to eat, and in the evening there would be a card game and they would have a few drinks. After each order of drinks, the men would hand the proprietor, MacMillan a two or a five dollar bill. MacMillan would say, "Here's your change, mister." The man would reply, "That's fine, Mac. keep the change." The prospective buyer looked on in amazement and surprise at the way they gave their money away. This was a business he could not afford to pass up, so that night he bought the place for cash.

In the months to follow, business came to a virtual standstill. He must find a way to attract customers, or face starvation!

One day while sitting on the porch, watching the gophers popping in and our of their burrows, an idea came to him. The next day, he dug a hole large enough for his body to fit in, then he covered it.

He then advertised a show called "Gopher Jack", and had the gall to charge five dollars a person! When it came time for the show, everybody was surprised to see the bewhiskered Dashwood bob up and down in the hole several times, and then had the nerve to come out among the spectators. For some unknown reason, the cowboys took it as a big joke, and for the time he remained there, he was called, "Gopher Jack", and the house was referred to as the "Gopher House" for many years after.

In 1923, the stopping house was purchased by Lionel Cameron, and moved to his farm, four miles northwest. His own house had burned down, and he needed a home.

Jack Patterson agreed to move the house to the farm for Mr. Cameron, but most people said it would be very difficult to get it up Sawyer Hill, and it would have to stay on the hill overnight. The engine did stop on the hill because of excess water, but Jack let some of the water off, and away it went.

In the meantime, Johnny Forckel was coming down the hill and found the road blocked, so he went back to warn others that they couldn't pass. Later that week, the Camerons had a house to live in.

CECIL R. DUNCAN

My name is Cecil Duncan. I farmed ¾ section south of Davisburg School. My neighbors were Bryces, Doug Herr, Jenkins and Forckels. My mother and I bought the farm from Ray Armstrong in 1944 and farmed there until 1948. (five years).

I was born on a ranch near Dubois, Wyoming, one of four children. Two boys and two girls. When I was seven my parents went back to Scotland so that their children could get a better education.

We came out to Canada in 1923 and Dad bought the Bar C ranch on the Ghost River north-west of Cochrane. He died in 1934 and we sold the ranch in 1936. We farmed at Airdrie for eight years. When my brother Jack got married we sold that farm and my

mother and I bought the farm near Okotoks N½ & SE¼ 7-21-28-W4. My mother died in 1951.

I am living in Calgary. I was retired almost five years ago but, being in excellent health, I have found plenty of work to do since. I am married and have one daughter, who is married and has one son. Also five step-children all married with children. We have fifteen grandchildren.

My sister, Margaret, and brother, Jack, are both married, retired, and living in Calgary. My youngest sister died in 1928 at age 17.

MR. AND MRS. JAMES EBERLY

James Eberly was born near Pittsburgh, Pennsylvania, 1856. He left home in the early seventies and travelled to Nebraska, then on into Montana. In the spring of 1883, with two companions, he treked north from Helena with pack horse and wagons. Coming to Sheep Creek, he picked a location near a spring, and "squatted".

When the survey was made, he found that he was on C.P.R. land, so he took a quarter just to the south, across the road allowance. There he farmed for many years, using oxen for power during the '80's. Land location NW¼ 34-20-29 W4.

In 1890 he married Mary McMillan. Mary had been born in Glengarry County, Ontario, 1857. In 1878 she worked in Boston as a seamstress, but wishing to see the world, she moved to Oregon, then to San Francisco, and on to Arizona. When her father died, she returned to Ontario. In 1887 she sailed to England for the Victoria Jubilee. When she returned in 1888, she came to Alberta, and was employed as a seamstress in Calgary.

The Eberlys lived on the homestead, and raised good horses and cattle. James joined the I.O.O.F. in 1893, and was a member for twenty-three years. He was a faithful Elder in the Presbyterian Church at Okotoks, until his death in 1916. Mrs. Eberly died in 1942.

Two daughters survive, Etta, Mrs. William Morrison (Rev. Morrison) and Miss Jessie Eberly, both of Gleichen. Taken from "Leaves From The Medicine Tree".

The Morrisons were married in 1919 and William returned to University graduating in 1925 when he was

Mr. and Mrs. Wm. Hagerman and Mr. Eberly in car. Mrs. Eberly took the picture. September 1929.

the first minister to be ordained into the United Church of Canada in Saskatchewan. His ordination took place in Abbey, Saskatchewan. He continued preaching throughout Southern Alberta; Blackie, 1931: Peace River, 1941; Airdrie, 1946: Gliechen, 1957: Carmangay, 1962, Medicine Hat. Mrs. Eberly died in 1966 and he, in 1970.

There were three children; James, Ian and Gwen. Both boys are atomic scientists and have worked their whole adult lives in the Chalk River Atomic Plant. They have lived in Deep River, Ontario which is the resident town for plant employees. Gwen is married to Victor Brosz, Professor of Art at U. of C. Calgary.

William and Etta had twelve grandchildren.

CYRUS AND VIRGINIA (LEE) EBERLEY — by Mary Bailey

Cyrus Eberley and his wife, Virginia Lee, Family: Anna, Paul, Vyron A., Katie, Fern and Samuel R. arrived at Okotoks April, 1907 and settled on the farm next to James Eberley. In 1912 they moved to Calgary and the farm was sold a few years later. In 1924 Mr. and Mrs. Eberley with Lee and Sam, moved to Ontario, California and Vyron remained to work in the Merchant's Bank in Okotoks. He married Fern Harold, daughter of Mrs. Hagerman, and they later moved to Detroit. It was during his employment at the bank, it was rumored that he slept upstairs at the bank to act as night watchman, that the bank was robbed. The robbery was never solved but the strong box was found, still containing stolen papers, on the bank of the Elbow river, some years later.

Paul Eberley married a Miss Rosalind, whose folk lived on the Hagerman farm, in the mid-twenties.

Cyrus died in 1941, Virginia and daughter, Lee, in 1965, Sam in 1968 and Vyron in 1966. Katie lives in Parksville, B.C. and Paul in Edmonton.

WILLIAM FORAN — by Mrs. Gaunce ★

William Foran was born near Ottawa, Ontario in the early 1870's. As a young man he worked in the lumbering industry. He married Sarah Taylor at Parry Sound, where they lived for some years where five children were born. Pearl (Mrs. Sam Johnson) Lucy (Mrs. Wm. Ward), Ellwood, who died in Winnipeg in 1970, Pauline (Mrs. Jack Warwick), Adelaide (Mrs. Ervie Miller-Gaunce).

He later moved to Airdrie, Alberta in 1904 where Jessie (Mrs. Chas. Stewart), and Lillian (Mrs. Wm. Sawchuck) were born. He ranched at the Buttes for a few years then moved to Okotoks just outside of town. PT. NW¼ S22-T20-R29-W4. Here Fred was born and still lives at Okotoks. Mr. Foran again went into the lumbering business with the Lineham Lumber Co. They had lumber camps in the Big Horn Reserve. The logs were cut in the winter and driven down the Sheep River to the mill pond and saw mill at Okotoks, when the river was in flood in the spring. When the Saw Mill was dismantled and moved to High River, he worked for the town for awhile then joined the Dominion Forestry Department and was Forest Ranger at the Big Horn for some years.

He retired at the death of his wife, and moved to

New Westminster in British Columbia where he died at the age of 84.

He married again in New Westminster to another woman with the same name, Sarah Taylor. I met her once, a very nice woman too, she survived him a few years. It is too bad each of us don't keep a diary. It would help a lot when things like this book come up. You had better start writing your memoirs.

FORCKEL FAMILY

Father (Alexandre), Mother (Alice) and sons John H. and Robert L. came to Okotoks from Brussels, Belgium, in the fall of 1904. Prior to their arrival, eldest son, Charles F., a graduate of agricultural schools in Belgium and England, had preceded them in the spring of 1904 and purchased for the family the farm of Joe Bryce on secs. 5, 6 and 8, Tp. 21 Rge. 28 W4th M., northeast of Okotoks.

The large house on the farm was built the next year to accommodate the family and the considerable quantity of furnishing which had accompanied them from Belgium.

Forckel family at E.P. Ranch 1926. L. to R. Robert L., John H., Mother (Alice), Charles F., and Father (Alexandre).

Always of great interest to the district community were the antique furniture and clocks displayed in the house, the clocks being a legacy of Father Alexandre's early profession as a clockmaker and repairer.

The Forckels were successful and well known farmers of the Okotoks-De Winton area. Always active in district and community affairs, the family were also enthusiastic members of the Okotoks Country Club and great supporters of the Masons and Eastern Star.

Charles Forckel, in addition to farming, had a great interest in gardening. This was perhaps a reflection of his earlier horticultural training, and each year he had a fine display of flowers and vegetables in the several gardens he kept near the houses.

Son John was a prime mover in the formation of the Okotoks-De Winton Rural Electrification Association in the late 1940's and early 1950's. The Association was a co-operative of local farmers formed to provide electric power to all farms in the area.

Johnny Forckel and Mother.

Back row: Left to right: Johnny, Charlie Forckel and Mr.
Forckel Sr. Front row: Left to right: Mrs. Idington and ?

In their farming activities, the Forckels were always seeking better farming methods and improvements, and in the early 1900's were in the forefront in pioneering the usage of the new fangled gasoline powered farm machines.

Son John married Ette E. Currie of De Winton in June 1925. A bungalow was built near the large home for him and his bride. They had one daughter Evelyn M. (now Mrs. Eric Atkinson of Calgary). Son Robert married Mrs. Agnes McNeil of Okotoks in December 1950.

The Forckels farmed continuously from 1904 to 1955 when the farm was sold to Joe Sevigny and then later sold to L. C. Morrisroe. John and his family moved to Calgary and later to Victoria where he lived until his death in 1966. Son Robert moved to Okotoks where he lived until his death in 1961. Mother Alice died in 1929, Father Alexandre in 1934 and son Charles in 1943.

ALEXANDER E. AND ETHEL ALBERTA (HERR) FRASER — by Marilyn Rugg

Alexander Fraser was born December 11, 1900 in the Stormont district. Ethel Alberta Herr was born October 9, 1902 in the De Winton district. She married Alexander January 20, 1928. They lived on the Todd farm N.W.¼-11-21-29-W4 until 1932 then moved to the Shepard district. They returned to the second Todd farm (S.E.¼-14-21-29-W4) in the early spring of 1936.

Their 3 children Dorothy, John and Marilyn attended Allan school until the family moved to the Olds, Innis Lake district in 1942. They moved to a farm bordering Olds in 1945. They resided there until Ethel's death May 16, 1963. Alex passed away March 1975. They are both buried in the Olds Cemetery. Dorothy Bell farms at Carstairs. John Fraser and Marilyn (Rugg) both reside in Calgary.

Alex and Ethel Fraser. Back row: Marilyn Rugg, John Fraser and Dorothy Bell.

Alex's father came west to Winnipeg at the age of 14 with an uncle. With his uncle's assistance he got a team and wagon and started hauling freight. Eventually he hauled freight from Winnipeg to Edmonton for the soldiers during the Riel Rebellion. He then went south and worked on the C.P.R., building sidings, until the railway was finished. Alex's mother and father then built a house and barn in the locale of 2nd St. East and 7th Ave., Calgary. There was prairie up to the river at that time. Mr. Fraser was hauling freight from as far south as Macleod to as far north as Athabasca Landing. They moved to the De Winton area in 1893 to raise cattle.

Alex's mother, Emma, had always worked as a children's nurse. She had little knowledge of cooking but learned to bake her own bread. As she was London born and raised she was terrified of cattle. When Mr. Fraser did not get home before dark she had to go out on the unfenced prairie and hunt for the milk cows. At that time the ladies wore skirts down to the ground and the prairie wool was tall and hard to walk in. She would return very tired. She would then have to tie the cows in the barn which took all the nerve she had.

THE ROBERT FRASER FAMILY — submitted by F. Herr

Robert Fraser was born in Pictou County, Nova Scotia in 1857. He married Mary Anne Horner, born in Shawville, Quebec, in 1871. Mr. Fraser had taught school in the East and also for a few years in California and B.C., later working for the Federal Government in Ottawa in the Immigration Department until his retirement in 1931. Mrs. Fraser was one of the Horner family, several of whom were in the Government services, two of them being Dr. Hugh Horner, M.L.A. in Edmonton, and his brother Jack, M.P. from Pollockville, Alberta, Crowfoot riding.

After Mr. Fraser's retirement, they came west with their grown family of two sons and one daughter in the spring of 1933, buying the north half of Section 10, 21-29-W4th from Ed. Hayes, who had been the original owner of this farm, acquired by land script for his services in the Riel Rebellion of 1885, or by homestead.

Later the same year, their married daughter, Beryl, and her husband, Ray Harnett, came west by car, making their home with the Frasers. As Ray was a salesman, he was on the road most of the time. While they lived here, their first child, Janice, was born in 1935.

The Frasers farmed with horses during their years on the farm, raised a few chickens, turkeys and pigs, but as the depression of the 30's was at its peak during these years, farming wasn't a very rewarding occupation.

After Mr. Fraser's death in 1936, the family moved back to Ottawa. Elmer was the last to leave the farm, shipping a carload of machinery and a few head of livestock from Okotoks in late December of '36, riding in rail car, putting in a terribly cold trip through the Great Lakes region of Ontario. The property here was sold to Sam Vinge, and later to Mrs. W. Lang. In 1952, the new section of No. 2 Highway cut through the east quarter. Now this half section has been subdivided into small holdings with several families living on it.

The Fraser family were: **Elmer** born in Ottawa in 1904, farming in the Winchester district after returning to Ontario in 1936. September 1939, he joined the Canadian Army, going overseas in January 1940. In 1943 he landed in Palermo, Sicily, then to the Italian mainland, getting as far north as Ravenna. In February 1945, his unit entered France at Marseille, and went up through France, Belgium and Holland. When the war was over in May, 1945, he went to England on leave and was married to Marion Dixon of Manchester, whom he had met in 1942. Marion was in the Land Army during the war, helping on farms and timber crops. Elmer returned to Ottawa in May 1946 and after being demobilized, he was employed by the Statistics Canada in Ottawa (Federal Gov't.) until his retirement in 1969. He now works part time as a Security Guard at the Government Buildings in Ottawa. They have three children — Guy of Windsor, John of Toronto and Sara of Toronto, all university graduates. Elmer and Marion still live in Ottawa.

Beryl (1905-65) married Ray Harnett, living in Ottawa and Toronto. She had taught school until her marriage. They had three children — Janice, born at Okotoks, now teaches school in Toronto. Richard, an accountant at Peterborough, Ont. married with one son Christopher Robin. David, a teacher in Cochrane, Ontario, married with one son, Timothy Allan. Beryl died in 1965, buried in Toronto, after being almost totally paralyzed for nine years, the result of a car accident. She was always bright and cheerful even during her long stay in the hospital where she was confined to her bed or a wheel chair. Ray now resides in Montreal.

Aubrey, born in Ottawa in 1908, died in 1975. After returning to Ottawa in 1936, was employed at Winchester and Ottawa until joining the Army in September, 1939. As he was an accountant, he was soon put in the office doing paper work in connection with recruiting etc. Following an operation, he was discharged on medical grounds. He was later employed in a munitions plant, finishing as an accountant in the construction industry, where he remained for twenty years. He was married to Charlotte Horner from McCord, Saskatchewan, also a civil servant with the Federal Government. They had two sons — Brian, a printer in Ottawa, married with one son Teddy, and Robert in the Navy, stationed in Halifax. Aubrey died suddenly in December 1975. Charlotte resides in Ottawa.

Emma Sheila, the youngest of the Robert Fraser family, was a nurse. She married Robert Durant and they lived in Winchester, Ontario for some time. Sheila made a trip west in 1961 visiting in the district for some time. She returned to Ottawa where she passed away in 1968, buried at Shawville, Quebec. There were no chilren. Robert now lives at Unionville, Ontario.

Mr. Fraser Sr. died while on the farm at Okotoks in 1936, buried in New Westminster, B.C. Mrs. Fraser died in Ottawa in December, 1954, buried at Shawville, Quebec.

HARRY GALLAGHER — by J. H. Jenkins

When I first knew Mr. and Mrs. Gallagher they lived on the Worden place. They were raised in Ontario and after they came west they worked for P. S. Idington. They also lived in the old house on Bob Shields place, now owned by Doug Herr. From there they went to work for C. G. Barker. Then he rented the farm from Jack McDonald, 36-20-29-W4, and did very well there. Later on he gave up farming and moved to Okotoks and was in real estate and insurance.

The next move was to Irricana where they ran a restaurant and confectionary for some time. His later years were spent looking after apartments, for two years, in Calgary and long after retirement age, working for the Calgary City Parks Dept.

His first wife, Carrie, died in 1939 or 40 and he remarried Annie ?, from Ontario, in 1958 and she passed away in 1975.

Harry was a real sportsman; he liked baseball, football, hockey, curling and was an avid bowler. It was after he had moved into the Bow Valley Lodge that he passed away from a heart attack suffered while lawn bowling. This was in 1973. Mrs. Gallagher spent the last few years of her life in the auxiliary hospital (Crossbow) I believe.

The Gallaghers had an adopted daughter, Lois, but little is known about her.

GARBUTT FAMILY — by Mrs. Fern Garbutt

Grandparents Mr. and Mrs. Joseph H. Garbutt moved west from Bradford, Ontario in spring of 1909.

They settled on a half section about 2½ miles NE of Nanton with a family of eight: five sons and three daughters (three deceased children were left in the East one son and two daughters). The children were grown up so worked for others in the area.

Allon H. Garbutt the eldest son was married in Bradford, Ontario June 6, 1906 and moved west with the rest of the family. He farmed and raised cattle at Nanton. Allon and wife Ida, had son, Joseph Gilbert, July 18, 1910. Two years later 1912 he went homesteading to Kevin, Montana, U.S.A. May 13, 1913 a daughter Evelyn was born. In 1915 he moved back to Nanton, selling their homestead to oil companies who began to drill for oil. He bought another farm in the Nanton district and lived there through the 30's, when son Gilbert started to farm for himself. In 1936, Dec. 5, Gilbert was married to Fern Greighton of Nanton.

Five children were born there to Fern & Gilbert, Vera 1939, Verna 1940, John 1942, Robert 1944, Bev 1946.

Father Allon sold the Nanton farm in 1948 and bought the C. Duncan farm at Okotoks, so Gilbert and Fern moved there seven and a half miles N.E. of Okotoks. Allon and wife retired to Calgary. Allon Garbutt died in 1953, and Ida Garbutt in 1951.

Gilbert farmed at Okotoks N½ & SE¼ 7-21-28-W4 until 1955 then sold the farm and moved to Okotoks for a short while. Two children were born here Sandra 1953 and Norman 1954.

In spring of 1955 he moved to Hanna, Alberta, until 1958 was salesman for Watkins Co. After this he was

Garbutt Family 1971. Back: Debbie, Bev, Robert, Verna, Norman, Vera, John, Sandra, Florence, Front: Kenny, Fern, Gilbert, James.

Gilbert and Fern Garbutt's 25th wedding anniversary.

salesman for Fuller Brush up until 1975. Gilbert passed away Dec. 1975.

Four more children were born in Hanna, Deborah 1958, Florence 1960, James 1961 and Kenneth 1965.

Four children and Fern Garbutt still remain at Hanna. Florence, James and Kenneth still in school.

Deborah married Charles Acerley in 1975 and has a five month old son, they live at Hanna.

Vera married in 1959 to Darwin Feldberg and has two sons and a daughter and lives at Wetaskiwin, Alberta.

Beverley married 1964 to James Trottier and has a son and a daughter and lives at Adanac, Sask.

Robert married 1965 to Jane CeCrea, Hanna, Alberta and has two sons and one daughter and lives in Calgary.

John married in 1966 to Winnifred Hughes of Bangor, Sask. They have two sons and live in Calgary.

Sandra married in 1970 to Fredrick Charlton and has two daughters. They live in Tilley, Alberta.

Norman married 1975 to Shelly Betker, Yorkton, Sask. and lives in Calgary.

The three boys are in the dry cleaning business in Calgary.

Verna Garbutt is to marry on July 2, 1977 to Kenneth Brown of Nanaimo, B.C. They will live at Duncan, B.C.

MR. AND MRS. WILLIAM GIBBARD

Bill and Elfleda Gibbard were farming at Richmound, Saskatchewan, until October 1926. The wheat in that spring blew out, and flax seeded later suffered from drought, so Bill and Dave Stinson drove to the Davisburg district to visit Bob Riddell. They looked over the land as far as Olds, but saw nothing more attractive than the Okotoks — Davisburg area.

Bill decided to move, and bought the S.W.¼ of 13-21-29 from John Todd, the deal including Mineral Rights. Dave decided to hang on in Saskatchewan a few years longer.

Two freight cars were allotted by government for moving effects, including twelve horses, two cows, farm machinery, two steel granaries put in cars at Hilda, Alberta, nine miles west of Richmound. Two local boys agreed to look after the shipment. Bill drove the Ford Model T and Fleda and the twins took the trip from Medicine Hat by train.

Todd's offered one of their homes until May 1927 when Bill made over two wooden granaries into a comfortable home. We rented the adjoining quarter from Worden. Then when the '30's came and wheat dropped to twenty cents a bushel, Bill gave up renting and Dave Stinson left the dry belt in 1933 and rented the Worden quarter, until World War 2 recovery enabled him to live in Okotoks.

When the west flank of Turner Valley came into production in 1936, a boom resulted, giving Bill a Customs Office job in Okotoks. In ten years, truck traffic replaced rail, and he was transferred to Calgary. Later, he sold his farm with out Mineral Rights to Doug Thompson.

The Gibbard children — Margaret and Campbell, twins, were born in 1923 at Richmound, Saskatchewan, and Douglas in 1931 at Okotoks. All attended the Allan School and High School in Okotoks.

Margaret graduated as a Commercial Dietitian at University of British Columbia and is now in charge of food services at University of Alberta.

Campbell joined the R.C.A.F. in 1941 and did two tours of duty as a pilot in Egypt and the Middle East on Beaufighters, and in Scotland on Mosquitoes. He returned safely to graduate from the University of Alberta with a degree in Electrical Engineering. Married with five children, living in Edmonton, he has made his career with A.G.T. since 1950.

Douglas joined the Canadian Navy in 1948, training in electronics of Submarines. He is married, has two children, and lives in Victoria, B.C.

Bill and Elfleda Gibbard, Golden Wedding, Oct. 25, 1972.

Bill and Elfleda attended the reunion of World I flyers in London, England, in 1972 with one hundred other fliers and their ladies. The highlight of the trip was the reception of the group by Queen Elizabeth and Prince Philip at Buckingham Palace.

The Gibbards now make their home at 1611 Summit Street S.W., Calgary.

F. R. GORDANIER

I came to the Allan School District as a child following the death of my mother, the former Jessie Lucas, in 1922 to live with Mr. and Mrs. W. H. Jenkins. My father, Fred Gordanier, came from Brantford, Ontario and married my mother in 1911. He died May 12, 1932 at the age of 48.

My mother was the daughter of George Lucas, who, at that time, lived in the area of Saint Andrews Heights, where the Foothills Hospital now stands.

There were three of us children, all of whom were born in Edmonton. My sister is now Mrs. A. E. Beavers of Calgary, and my brother, Harvey, died overseas in 1945.

I went to the Allan School from 1925 to 1935, then finished my schooling in Okotoks.

In 1947 I married the former Joan Light, who came with her parents from London, England, in 1924.

We have four children, Diane Neathway, Maureen Gordanier both of Calgary and my sons, Kenneth and Robert. We also have a granddaughter, Jo-Laine Neathway.

Mr. W. H. Jenkins was my mother's cousin. When I came to live with my uncle (W. H. Jenkins) on the farm, the surrounding country was still fairly heavily bushed with willows and poplars, and most farmers were clearing their land.

Mr. Jenkins would hire Indians to clear the land. The Indians would come in and pitch their tents by a slough and then go to work. They came to buy eggs from us and my uncle held the opinion that they were honest hard working people. At night I could see the glow of their cooking fires through the bush and the fragrance of burning brush would be in the night air.

I remember one day when Herb Jenkins and my uncle came in for dinner from burning brush in our west field. At that time there was not a road allowance between our place and Forest Herr's farm, just a trail through the bush. During the noon hour a slight breeze came up and the fire from one of the piles of brush started burning towards Forest Herr's land. After dinner they saw what was happening and spent the rest of the afternoon getting the fire under control.

Another time my uncle hired two white men to cut brush, and we came home from Calgary one afternoon, and these men had broken into our house and had stolen silverware, belonging to Auntie Gladys, many other items were also missing. They were never caught by the police. These men buried some of the silverware where their tent had been and many years later I was plowing in that same field and the plow turned up a few pieces of the silverware.

My uncle was an ardent curler. I can still see him, "in my mind", heading across the fields to the nearest open road to Okotoks with a team of horses pulling a sulky plow. He would plow a furrow in the snow to the open road and back home again, leaving two furrows wide enough for the wheels of the car. Other farmers would take a team and sleigh to go to Okotoks to curl, or to some other social function.

I remember one winter's night, Herb and Arthur Jenkins and I rode saddle horse to Okotoks to see Chautauqua (an actor group) which had come to town. It was a long cold ride both ways although it was fortunate that there was a livery barn in town for the horses to stay in.

In 1947, I rented a quarter section of land from Mrs. W. E. Worden, who was living in Cranbrook, B.C. When she passed away her daughter, Mrs. John D. Adams, rerented the farm to me. The farm location was NW¼ 13-21-29-W4. I rented the quarter for over twenty years. Mrs. Adams decided to sell and now most of it is broken up into small holdings. Mrs. John D. Adams passed away March 4, 1976.

JOHN AND HARRY GREENFIELD — information from E. Leach

John Greenfield and his brother, Harry took over their homesteads about 1905 or 1906. Harry sold his land to Albert Herr Sr., S½-24-21-29-W4 and Mr. Todd bought John Greenfield's farm, S½-14-21-29-W4.

John was married and had a daughter, Annie. While the family lived in the district the Baptists often held their church services in the Greenfield home. When they left the district John donated money for the bell in the Baptist Church in Okotoks.

After he sold the homestead the family returned to Ontario and Annie graduated from the Guelph School of Agriculture.

ROBERT HAMILTON — by Ethel Morrison

Robert, George, John, Sam and Jim Hamilton left their home in New Brunswick in the early 1880's. They came by ship around the Horn up the west coast to British Columbia and later on to Alberta.

John better known as "Johnny" Hamilton had been driving a stage coach on the old Cariboo Trail before coming to Alberta. He was a good judge of horses. He owned a livery stable business in Calgary and dealt in horses all his life.

Robert had a ranch on the Sheep River four miles east of what is now called Okotoks. Land location was SE¼ 30-20-28-W4. Robert later married Mrs. James Colvin in Calgary in 1886 and they moved to the ranch. Mrs. Hamilton (nee Colvin) had two children from her first marriage (Harry and Ethel). Mrs. Hamilton and two children moved to Alberta from Ontario with her mother Mrs. Edward Fisk in 1883.

Mr. Hamilton owned a large number of cattle and horses. His brand was small circle on the right shoulder on horses and large circle on right hip on cattle. Around 1900 settlers were coming in and buying our pasture land and purchasing horses and cattle from us.

Later my step father decided to build a house in Okotoks so we did not have so far to go to school as there were three more boys and three more girls in the family. Later, this home became the Lineham house. Later, my brother Harry went to live with a man by the name of Jack Meehan and went to the Melrose school. I, Ethel went to Calgary and lived with my aunt and went to school there. When I finished school I worked in the Telephone office.

We drove to Calgary with horse and democrat to get extra provisions as we had no cars in those days up to about 1900.

We were living in Okotoks known at that time as ''Dewdney'' when my step father, Bob Hamilton, died in 1902.

My own father, James Colvin, came from Edinburgh, Scotland. He attended Edinburgh University where my grandfatner taught. He was very cross and strict so my father left home and came to Canada. He got work with the C.P.R. keeping books of all materials used to build the railway from Winnipeg to Calgary.

My mother Mrs. Robert Hamilton died in 1915.

I, Ethel Colvin was married in 1906, in our house in town, to Mr. James Morrison, who worked for the Gas Company. We moved into the house that Charles Tucker now owns.

EDWIN ALBERTA HAYES — by Marjorie L. Hayes, March 8, 1976 *

Edwin Alberta Hayes was born in Sussex, New Brunswick (1862) and came west to Winnipeg on March 20, 1882. During the summer he worked on construction for the C.P.R. near Kenora, Ontario and spent the winter in a logging camp at the Lake of the Woods. In the spring of 1883 he came to Maple Creek, Saskatchewan, which was the end of the line. During the next year he cooked at construction camps along the line as far as Golden. In the winter of 1884, Ed went to what is now the town of Leduc, where he opened a Stopping Place and in the spring he went to Calgary, where he joined the Steele Scouts. This was known as the North West Territories area.

The following is a story relating to the Steele Scouts.

The Steele Scouts reached Frog Lake just after a massacre. They had travelled 200 miles from Edmonton where they found bodies covered with flour from the Hudson Bay Company Trading Post. They buried the dead and continued on to the battle of Loon Lake. The following winter, it was reported that the Indians went back to the ruins at Frog Lake and dug up the flour rations for food. While in the Steele Scouts, the men never saluted an Officer. Major Sam Steele, was transferred from the R.N.W.M.P. detachment at Fort Steele, B.C. to Calgary to recruit men to curb the uprising.

When the Scouts reached the Red Deer River on their way to Edmonton, the Major dismounted, stripped and jumped into the river which had a thin coating of ice. The men were not about to follow and said: ''The Major must be a damned fool Englishman''.

Upon discharge from the Steele Scouts, Ed took script land from Queen Victoria, in lieu of three hundred dollars pay. The homestead was located three miles north and one and one-half miles east of Okotoks. In 1904 Ed was appointed Provincial Auditor and then Secretary-Treasurer of Sheep Creek Municipality, which office he held for forty years. He

Edwin Alberta Hayes — 1940.

was awarded the Coronation Medal in 1937 in recognition of his long service. George Hoadley was on the first Council which was formed for road improvements.

As Provincial Auditor in the newly formed Government of Alberta, he covered the country down to the American border and north to Red Deer, with his big brown trotting horse, which pulled a sulky. The sorrel's name was Rattler and soon was replaced by the horseless carriage. Those were the days when you drove your team with a load of barley to the market at Fort Macleod, where you received forty cents a bushel for the barley.

And those were the days when the Okotoks Agriculture Society would hold the annual fair one mile east of the town. Ed was the Secretary for many years and would show his chickens, and sometimes he was asked to judge the butter. On one occasion he was criticized for not awarding the prize to Mrs. ? and in reply and very seriously said "the hairs in her butter were not arranged as straight as the winner's butter."

It was his pleasure to relate stories of the early days, of the pioneers who were part of the development of the West and the legal land description of the settlers with whom he came in contact. One of his favorite stories was when he was cooking for the railway construction crew in the mountains. This particular gang were Italians who drank tea in great amounts. The only way to satisfy them was to make it in large copper boilers and boil it, but they still drank just as much. They would make their own macaroni, rolling it out every evening for the next day's meal. Many little glittering pieces of personal property were lost to the pack rats.

One hundred pounds of flour for fifty Italians did not last very long and it was at this time he learned the skill of making hotcakes and hot biscuits. His technique was not to measure anything, just pour it into the bowl, stir, bake and serve.

The first Mrs. Hayes was Adelia Ellen Crockett

(Thorpe from Seattle) who had a Halfway house on the old Andy Giffen farm. She died in 1925 and he remarried in 1926 to me, Marjorie L. Mossop, daughter of Frank and Ethel Mossop from Crossfield.

I graduated as a nurse from the Calgary General Hospital, class of 1924. The daughter of the first marriage, Mary Ellen, attended Melrose School and Okotoks School. She married Syd. H. Mattock and is now living in Calgary. Frank and Doris Hayes (Patterson) live at Millarville and Ralph lives in Calgary.

Edwin Hayes came west with the railway, found adventure, went prospecting for the Lost Lemon Mine, cooked and farmed from '85 to the 1900's and planted and reaped his last vegetable garden on the hill at Okotoks in 1948, the year of his passing.

BAYARD LEVERETT HAYES *

B. L. "Boyd" Hayes (1867-1956) came to the Okotoks district in 1887 from Sussex, New Brunswick. He homesteaded about two miles north of Okotoks. In 1896 he married Jane Lang (1870-1941) who had come west from Quebec in 1895. Later they purchased a farm about three and one half miles north of Okotoks where they continued farming (N.E. 8-21-29 W4M).

They had one son Melville Orin (1897-1961), who farmed with his father much of his life. He lived in Calgary for a number of years around 1920, during which time he worked in and later operated a small store. In his later years he farmed alone.

They had one daughter, Alice Mary (1900-1961) who lived in the Okotoks district most of her life, except for nine years in Calgary from 1913 to 1922. In 1928 she married William Henry Cope (1895-1952). They farmed about three miles north-west of Okotoks.

They had two sons, Barry and Bob.

THE DOUG HERRS — by Doug and Rusha

Doug Herr was born and raised in the Davisburg district. He was the youngest of the family of Albert and Blanche Herr. He received his public school education at Davisburg school starting in the year 1919. His first teacher was a native Indian female. Doug should surely go on record as being the youngest pallbearer ever. He acted as one of the pallbearers at a chum's funeral at the age of eleven. The school chum was David Riddle.

Doug took his high school grades in Okotoks, then took a business course at Garbutt's College in Calgary. Jobs were hard to come by in those days so he came home and worked on the farm with his brothers. In 1935 he married Rusha Carr (nee Campbell). Rusha was born at Fort Macleod, daughter of Ronald and Maude Campbell who travelled by covered wagon with their two sons, John and Neil, from Wise River, Montana. They later settled on a farm eleven miles southwest of Okotoks. Rusha took her public school grades at Skye Glen. In 1917-18 she attended Claresholm Agricultural College. In 1935 Doug and Rusha moved to a farm in the Allan School District. We are members of the United Church of Okotoks and have always taken an active part in the community affairs until we had to slow down for health reasons. Doug acted as director in the U.F.A., the telephone Company and the Okotoks De Winton Rural Elec-

Doug and Rusha Herr April 12th, 1935.

trification Association of which he is a charter member. Rusha was Sec'y-Treasurer of the R.E.A. for eighteen years, Past Matron of the Evening Star Chapter, a life member of the Royal Purple Lodge, a member of the W.A. of the Okotoks United Church and a charter member of the U.F.W.A. In the 41 years that we have been here we have been hailed out eight times, the worst one being in 1951. We had 57 panes of glass to replace after that. We are still living on the same farm, have a comfortable home and enjoy the company of good friends and neighbors.

ZEANOUS AND EDITH HOWERY — by Alvie Tillotson

Zeanous was born in 1873 in Oshkosh, Wisconsin, U.S.A. Edith was born in 1879 in Princeton, Missouri, U.S.A.

The Howerys came to Canada in 1924 from North Dakota. They rented the Armstrong farm 7 miles north east of Okotoks. SE¼ 7-21-29-W4 where some of the children went to the Allan School. The children are: Prudence, born Spencer, South Dakota 1897, she married Edward A. J. McLeod of Okotoks, she died May 18, 1968. Wesley Elmer married Alice Bice in Hanna. Harold married Rose Letke in Hanna, Joyce married Harold Coultry in Okotoks and later moved to Calgary, now retired in Kamloops, B.C. Edwin married Margaret Wartin of Edmonton. Dale never married, died 1973. Rex born 1904 farmed around Okotoks and Turner Valley district, he never married, died 1932.

They farmed this place for three years then moved to west of Okotoks to the Donald Gray farm SW¼ 4-21-1-W5 and farmed here for three years, then moved to what was called "The Old Lady Spencer Farm" east on highway from Okotoks and lived in a stone house NE¼ 14-20-29-W4. Later they moved to Okotoks.

Zeanous died in High River May 10, 1950 and Edith died in Calgary May 27, 1960.

MARVIN AND MARIE (PLEW) INDERGAARD — by Marie Indergaard *

The Marvin Indergaard family bought the farm at Okotoks on December 6, 1948, and moved there from Duchess, Alberta on January 16, 1949.

Marvin Indergaard, one of seven children, was born in Hatten, North Dakota, U.S.A. and came with his parents to the Cessford, Alberta area in 1917. On April 3, 1923 his family moved to Duchess where they farmed.

Marie Indergaard was born in Oklahoma City, Oklahoma, U.S.A. Her father, Grover M. Plew, started the first Aerial Photography for the United States Government in Washington, D.C., of which he was "The Chief" until his retirement in 1962. his ideas and hard work initiated the International Weather Data Processing Centre in Washington, D.C. It is presently referred to as the Environmental Sciences Services Administration or ESSA. He passed away in 1974 at the age of 87.

Marie came with her mother and stepfather to Duchess in April of 1923, from Pine Lake, Alberta where they resided for three years, having left Ennis, Montana in 1919, for Oklahoma; Oklahoma to Calgary in 1920, so to Pine Lake.

Marvin and Marie were married in the United Church in Duchess on December 8, 1935, and their daughter Mavis Marie was born in April 1939, and their eldest son Marvin Errol was born in March 1943. Marvin farmed in the Estevan Irrigation District until he bought the farm in Okotoks and the family moved on the Arthur Leigh farm, former Wm. Johnson farm, one mile east of Okotoks. It was one of the loveliest places they have ever had. SW¼ 27-20-29-W4. They raised R.O.P. Light Sussex chickens, coming second

for Canada in production and livability. Hatching as well as selling hatching eggs, chickens, baby chicks, some pigs and some cattle.

After coming from an area where one had cistern water and stock ponds it was wonderful to have spring water in the well and a flowing spring for the cattle. Natural gas was installed in September of 1952, having had rural electricity in for the incubators since 1950. Many good picnics were spent with neighbours in the area west of Okotoks, as well as many good evenings spent with U.F.A. and U.F.W.A. members of Okotoks and general district.

In April 1954 a second son was born, Kevin Carl, he is now returning to us in Calgary for four more years of University at the U. of C. after being supervisor in the Respiratory Department of the U. of A. in Edmonton for three years: so in 1977 we will have two grandsons, Allan and Todd Schaber, and Kevin at University.

Mavis married Harold Schaber of De Winton, Alberta in 1957, they have seven children, Allan, Todd, Curt, Lorraine, Karen, John and Krista-Anne.

Errol completed high school in Calgary and has been with the Calgary City Police for eleven and one half years. In 1964 he married Chere Gale Taylor, they have three children Allen, Roxanne and Candace. They all live near us. Chere has a Ceramic School and Business.

We were always very interested in the roads and mines on the hill where we lived. During the time we lived there one gentleman came along and said he had moved his family in early years up one of those roads on his way to homestead in The Berry Creek area. Some of his family returned and live in the area again, of course they returned by motor ways instead of by covered wagon.

When Marie delivered grain to the National Elevator in the fall of 1949, by way of tractor (Ford Ferguson and trailer), she heard a gentleman from S. W. Okotoks say: "First time I ever saw a woman deliver grain to an elevator." Not sure how elevator agent replied. Was I the first? I know I wasn't the last.

J. H. JENKINS — written by J. H. Jenkins (Herb)

J. H. Jenkins was born in 1882 in Monmouthshire, England. His father died when he was ten years old. He had to go to school and work to help support his mother and sisters. Later on he worked for his uncle who was a cattle dealer. They travelled to many Fairs showing livestock.

He came to Calgary in 1903 with his mother, Elizabeth Jenkins, and his youngest sister, now Mrs. Kate Logan, of Vancouver B.C. age 92. His other sister, Margaret, had three sons and came to Calgary in 1910. Her husband Tom Williams was a brother to Mrs. (Gladys) W. H. Jenkins.

W. H. Jenkins was the oldest of the family. He went to Kansas U.S.A. in 1899, then to Calgary in 1901. He worked on the construction of the Banff Springs Hotel and at Elko B.C. for the C.P.R. Later he homesteaded near Madden, Alberta. From there he moved to Calgary and worked for Stewards Lumber Company. In 1908 he went back to England. My mother, Mrs. J. H. Jenkins, came with him upon his return to Calgary.

Back row: Florence and Milt Munkholm and Marvin Indergaard. Front row: Gordon Munkholm, Mary Munkholm, Mavis Indergaard, Errol Indergaard.

In 1911 Gladys Williams came to Calgary and became Mrs. W. H. Jenkins.

My mother, (Edith), came to Calgary, July 1908 from Monmouthshire England where she was employed as a School Teacher. She married J. H. Jenkins in St. Stephens Anglican Church, Calgary in August 1908. They lived on 10 Ave. and 8 St., west of the subway, in Calgary. The Indians used to camp nearby and they used to come and look in the windows and sometimes walk through the house just to look at things. Mother made friends with some of them. Although I was very young at the time I can still remember seeing their Tee Pees and horses. Later Dad built a house in the Mount Royal district 23 Ave. West and lived there until we came to the farm in 1915. Mother (Edith) passed away in 1964.

Dad (J. H. Jenkins) worked for the C.P.R. bridge crew at Shepard and Strathmore. He often told us about unloading frozen cattle out of cattle cars after the big storm of 1907. It was so wet and cold that some of his friends who came over to this country with him died of typhoid at Shepard. His mother made him quit that job shortly afterwards.

While they lived in Calgary, Dad teamed lumber and coal for Stewards Lumber Co. He also had teams working in the building of the Calgary subways. He hauled sand and gravel for the City Hall and Holy Cross Hospital in their constructions. He later had his own business excavating basements and doing sidewalk cement work.

In 1913 they went back to England with their two sons Herbert and Arthur. They thought they would stay in England but when they got there and found things were no better there and, with the talk of war, they decided to come back to Calgary.

The old house of J. H. Jenkins in 1915.

1920 foot races l. to r. Bill and Harry Williams, Herb and Art Jenkins and Frank Davis.

L. to R., Back: Gladys Jenkins, Elizabeth Jenkins, Mrs. J. H. (Edith) Jenkins. Front:, Herbert, Arthur, and J. H. Jenkins. 1914. On the way to Priddis.

50th Wedding Anniversary of Mr. and Mrs. J. H. Jenkins.

In 1914 they bought a Model T Ford car in which they made many trips to Priddis to visit the Hunt family who were relatives. They made these trips by horse and buggy before they got the car.

Mrs. George Lucas, an aunt to the Jenkins Brothers, lived at St. Andrews Heights. Mr. and Mrs. George Lucas were Grandparents to Fred Gordanier.

J. H. Jenkins and W. H. Jenkins decided to try farming and bought the S½ of 12-21-29-W4, in the spring of 1915, and went under the name of Jenkins Brothers. This farm was owned by Jack and Bob Shields. At first we were called "The people with the car." Our neighbours were Frank Barker, A. Forckel, Jack Macdonald, Hugh Patterson, Coyle Brothers and Judge Idington of the Supreme Court of Canada, and his son Pete Idington.

In 1915 a third son was born to Mr. and Mrs. J. H. Jenkins (Edward), he passed away in 1973.

Senior Citizens Award to J. H. Jenkins.

The entertainment in those days was house parties, card games, dancing, hockey and ball games. It was then that the Country Club was formed.

The ladies knitted socks and wrapped parcels for the Red Cross during the First World War.

Dad belonged to the Oddfellows, Masons and loved to curl. Mother and Dad were both members of the Eastern Star, Country Club and St. Peters Church Okotoks. J. H. Jenkins passed away in 1962.

Dad bought his first tractor in the spring of 1921, it was a 10-20 Titan and it was this tractor that broke his leg in the fall of 1921 when the belt flew off the saw as we were sawing wood, this leg bothered him for the rest of his life. My brother, Arthur, was badly burnt in 1937 by a gas barrel blowing up when we were threshing on a very hot afternoon. He almost lost his life. We were using the high power Turner Valley Naptha gas at the time. We used to go to Turner Valley and buy this gas ourselves.

The Allan School was closed in 1918 so Arthur and I (Herb) had to go to school at Okotoks for a short time. We stayed there all week with Mr. and Mrs. Albert Barker. We came home for the weekends. September 1918 the Allan School was reopened. The students were the McDonalds, Coultrys, Aldridges, Jenkins and McDougalls.

After Arthur and I finished school we stayed home to help Dad as he was suffering with his leg. We did odd jobs and rented more farm land.

Arthur married Doris Currie in 1941. They farmed the McDonald place for one year then moved to High River. Arthur worked at the Airport for two years and then was in the army until his discharge in 1945. After the war he took up auto body work and opened his own business in Kimberly, B.C. Later he sold it and went to work for the City Public Works as a mechanic. July 1976 he plans to retire. They have two sons Gordon and Harvey both married and living in Edmonton. They also have three grandsons.

I stayed home and worked the farm and did custom work as well. I also did the trouble shooting for the Allan Mutual Telephone Company from the time it started until Walter Mosier took it over. I was also a director for the Company up to the time it was sold to A.G.T. My wages were 30¢ an hour, for the time I was out on call, and I had to supply my own transportation. Later on it rose to a dollar an hour. I thoroughly enjoyed this work. The hardest part was when a storm blew the lines down, but the telephone subscribers always rallied to the call for help.

The first threshers to thresh our crops were Calvin Imler, and Jack Patterson with the steam outfits. I helped to fire Jack's engine one afternoon, as the fireman had hurt his back. Boy was that thing hungry! We were also threshed by the Forckel Brothers. Barker Brothers and Armstrong Brothers. In 1930 Dad bought a thresher and we used it until 1941, when Arthur and I bought a combine.

In 1945 I bought a half section of land from the Forckel Brothers S½-8-21-29-W4. I now own the home place as well. In 1945 I married Esther Jones of Forest Lawn. Esther was born in Wrexham, North Wales and came to Canada in 1930 with her parents. She has seven brothers and three sisters.

I was in the Second Battalion Calgary Highlanders for a short time and in the local Militia. I was let out owing to ear trouble.

We have a daughter Eleanor Kemppainen of Calgary. They have a daughter Karen Ann and a son Curtis James.

David, our eldest son, is now running the farm and Richard, our youngest son, is working in Calgary. All three children went to school in Okotoks.

Our youngest daughter, Mary Elizabeth, passed away at the age of 18 months.

Richard, David, Eleanor, Herb and Esther Jenkins.

MR. W. H. JENKINS — by Fred R. Gordanier

Mr. William Henry Jenkins came from Monmouthshire, England to Kansas in 1899 and in 1901 he came to Calgary. I was always fascinated by stories that he told about the early days in Calgary.

He spoke of the Indians racing their ponies down eighth avenue on occasions and of the wooden sidewalks; when one could sink down to their ankles after a heavy rain; when a man could ride east to the Saskatchewan border, without seeing a line fence. He spoke of Paddy Nolan, "the lawyer" and of Bob Edwards, "Editor of the Eye Opener", and other men who helped to make up the history of Calgary.

Mr. Jenkins or "Bill", as his friends and neighbours called him, worked for a short while on one of the Patrick Burns Ranches; then on the construction of the first Banff Springs Hotel, which was partly destroyed by fire later; from there he worked at Elko, B.C. for the railroad, for a short period of time.

Mr. Jenkins and his partner, Arthur Apps, went homesteading in the Harmattan District. He gave up the homestead and returned to Calgary to work for Stewart's Lumber Yard.

In 1912 he married Gladys Williams of Monmouthshire, England and then in 1915, he and his brother J. H. Jenkins, went into partnership and bought a farm in the Allan School district. Later they dissolved this partnership and Bill Jenkins lived on the SW¼ 12-21-29-W4 and his brother on SE¼ 12-21-29-W4.

Mr. Jenkins and his wife were very active in community affairs. She belonged to the Order of Eastern Star and they were active in forming the Country Club in 1917. At first the musicians for this dance club were composed of local talent. Mr. Jenkins was active in the Masonic Lodge and was also auditor for the Allan School Mutual Telephones. In 1918 he became a trustee on the Allan School Board, in 1926 he became Secretary Treasurer until the school joined the "Big Unit" in Okotoks in 1941.

Mr. Jenkins passed away on January 28, 1973 at the age of 95 years and his wife, Gladys, predeceased him on December 25, 1969 at the age of 89.

MR. AND MRS. CHARLES WILLIAM JOHNSON — by Mrs. C. W. Johnson *

Will was born and educated in Neenah, Wisconsin, where he was office manager for Valvoline Oil Co. before coming to Alberta in 1914, where he farmed north of Langdon.

Doris was born in Oregon and came to Calgary with her family in 1909. Her father farmed north of Calgary also.

She and Will met in 1915 and were married in 1917, and farmed north of Langdon for six years. They had one daughter, named Myrrel.

In 1923 they bought a farm twenty miles from Wetaskiwin, where they lived for three years and then moved to Okotoks where Will managed and worked on a dairy farm west of town for three years. He heard of

L. to R. Mrs. Gladys Jenkins, Mrs. Idington, Mrs. Jenkins Sr., Mrs. Frank Barker, Mrs. North, Mrs. J. H. Jenkins.

Mr. and Mrs. W. H. Jenkins, 50th Wedding Anniversary, Jan. 29, 1962.

Mr. and Mrs. C. W. Johnson in 1917.

a good half section farm for rent north east of Okotoks SE¼ 34-20-29-W4, SW¼ 35-20-29-W4 and went to see the owner, Mrs. Alice Hagerman. She and her husband lived on the farm, which was formerly owned by some people named Smith. Mrs. Hagerman agreed to rent the farm to Will for one third of the crop per year, for the rent. We rented it from her until her death. She had one daughter Mrs. Fern Eberly who inherited the farm, and we continued to rent the farm from her until 1945 when we bought it.

In those days it was the custom to name a farm and Mrs. Hagerman had named that farm "Cozy Nook", but we never referred to it by that name.

We lived there until 1958. By that time Will had developed arthritis in his left hip, which made farming very painful for him.

We sold the farm in 1958 to Mr. and Mrs. Tom Jones. While living on the farm our daughter Myrrel attended Allan School, then went to High School in Okotoks where she graduated, then she went to business college in Calgary, and subsequently worked as a private secretary in an insurance office in Calgary. She married Bob Wilson (son of old timers in Okotoks) in 1941. He passed away suddenly of a heart attack in 1964. They had four children all of whom live in Calgary. Three of them are married, and Rick the oldest boy has four children, so I have four grandchildren and four great-grandchildren.

While living on the farm Will was active in lodge work in Okotoks, and he belonged to the Masonic Lodge and the Knights of Pythias. I belonged to the Eastern Star Lodge and still do.

After selling the farm we bought a home in Calgary and Will was bookkeeper for an oil company for several years.

My mother who is an invalid, lived with us for many years. She is now living in a nursing home and is 103 years old, and carries on a good sensible conversation in spite of her years.

W. H. JOHNSON — by Bess Johnson

Nels and Mary Johnson came up from Oregon to Okotoks in the spring of 1909; twelve strong. With a family of six girls: Christina, (Mrs. H. Best), Hilda, (Mrs. A. A. Davidson), Lobina, (Mrs. J. Vaughn), Verna, (Mrs. C. R. Wickson), Ione, (Mrs. M. H. Witters), Alva, (who died young, unmarried), and four sons Joseph, Henry, William, and Leone.

Fine wholesome people with blooming Scandinavian complexions. Nels and Mary were both born in Sweden, and came to the United States on that ship, of Atlantic Cable fame, the "Great Eastern". They married and lived successively in Iowa, Idaho and Oregon. The family were born in the various States in which they lived.

Nels was a merchant, hotelkeeper and farmer. He was also rather an adventurer at heart and only the responsibility of having a large family kept him off the "Trail of 98".

Nels bought the three quarter sections in the Allan District later known as Caravelle Ranches. Every acre of which is arable but which is now being developed for subdivision. Additional land was leased and at one time five hundred head of cattle were run

Mary and Nels Johnson.

Will Johnson's sisters and mother; Christine, Verna, Hilda, Lobania, Iona, with mother Mary.

for Pat Burns, and a horse kept available for him when he came to the farm.

Being of school age the two youngest of the family, Iona and Leone, attended Allan School for several terms.

The older girls worked in Calgary until their marriages when they moved to various parts of Canada and the United States. The sons worked on the farm with their father until Joe and Leone enlisted in World War I and Henry and Will began farming on their own. As "Johnson Brothers" Will and Henry ran a big steam threshing outfit in this district. With a crew of about twenty there was a cook car and bunk car which travelled from farm to farm with the outfit. The old cook car is still in existence.

Will sometimes mentions (when dinner is late) a cook who worked for them for eight years, and never served a late meal nor a poor one. Friends who recall working with them, on the thresher speak of having a full course turkey dinner on U.S. Thanksgiving Day.

Horses were used on the farm, sometimes twelve to a hitch, until the first tractor was purchased in 1911.

Henry married Margaret Teskey and raised a fine family of four sons and one daughter. Eleanor, now Mrs. Elmer O'Connor who lives in Australia. The sons are George of Victoria, James in Edmonton and Donald and Douglas in Okotoks.

Henry died in 1936, Margaret is still living in Okotoks and until recently taught a class in kindergarten.

Joe and Leone returned from overseas with injuries. Joe moved to Kinsella, married and had one daughter, who is now Mrs. Ralph Patterson. Both he and Leone died some years ago.

All the family is gone now except Verna, who lives in Victoria, and Will who still lives in Okotoks, having been a member of this community for sixty-seven years.

True, he built two houses on Rideau Rd. in Calgary and lived in each of them, but he still farmed in this district, and as he says he always considered Calgary a suburb of Okotoks.

Will was born in Britt, Iowa, which is the exact center of the United States. According to his wife, this is why he is so well balanced.

He began his career at fourteen, as a freighter, driving a four horse team out of Leurston, Idaho, usually making the trip in one day and returning the next. He worked on his father's farm in Oregon and still has the Bronze Medal, which he won at the "Leurs and Clark Centennial Exposition" in 1905, at Portland, Oregon, for corn raised by himself.

In 1916 Will took over the home farm and brand which is still registered in his name. That year he lost his first wheat crop by hail, but sold off some cattle and kept going. Next year a bumper crop paid off the mortgage, and he was on his way.

During the years he has owned several other farms, one, the property on which the sulphur plant now stands.

He retired in 1946 and built the house on Elma St. W. where he now lives in Okotoks.

Will Johnson with first wife and son Graham.

In 1918 Will married Ellen Graham. Their one son, Graham, was born in 1920. Returning from four years overseas during World War II Graham married Evelyn Patterson of the well known local family. They make their home in Okotoks when not travelling. Graham and Evelyn are the parents of Gale and Peter. Gale is married to Robin Cauvin and they have a son and daughter. They live in Okotoks.

After getting his B.Sc. degree and an extensive period of travel, Peter is doing social service work in Calgary.

With a background of so many years in this community, Will has a wealth of recollections. It is hard to choose those most outstanding, so many have been mentioned at other times.

As an example of the helpful attitude, characteristic of this community, when a clothing store burned some years ago, Will backed his truck up to the door, and willing hands formed a chain to load the stock into the truck so that all was saved.

Will is a charter member of the "Okotoks Senior Country Club" and was a member of the "Country Club" of former years, which was also a going concern. In those days dances and card parties formed the entertainment with music by Alec Gibbie, Roy McConnell or Neil Dorsey, on the violin and Mrs. Cushing and others playing piano.

Since 1922 Will has been a Member of Corinthian Masonic Lodge, and received his Fifty Year Jewel in 1972.

He has attended what is now the United Church in Okotoks longer than any other member and was for some years on the Church Board.

He also served as chairman of the Okotoks School Board for some time. Always interested in sports, Will is the oldest fan of the Okotoks Oilers. He played in the first curling game in the present arena, when Ted Robinson as Mayor, threw the first stone. He has a number of Curling prizes including the "52-53" "MacMillan Cup" trophy.

He still drives his car and received the Alberta Motor Association Quarter Century Award in 1970.

He helped organize the Alberta Wheat Pool in this district when it was formed.

Will's 90th birthday was celebrated in January 1976 with an Open House at the Senior Citizens Centre, Okotoks, when about one hundred and fifty friends called to extend their good wishes. Cards from two hundred were received.

George, James, Margaret, Douglas, Eleanor, Donald.

Will has married four times. Whether by coincidence or design, all his wives have been Nova Scotians.

His first wife Ellen Graham, died in 1939. In 1943

Will married Hazel Kinney, who died in 1948. Never one to yield to adversity, Will married her sister Bertha Fulmer, in 1950, who died in 1966.

Determined not to let life beat him, in 1967, Will married Elizabeth Thompson, a family friend, and they are living "Happily Ever After".

WILLIAM LANG — by Florence Robina May Munkholm (nee Lang) *

My Dad, William Lang came from Quebec in the year 1889. He bought the NW¼ 27-20-29-W4 from the C.P.R. It was on this quarter section the home was built. He also bought at the same time the SW¼ 34-20-29-W4.

Mother, Mary Abbott, came west from Quebec in the year 1891. She came west to marry Dad, William Lang, the marriage having been previously arranged. Upon her arrival they were married at his sister's home, Mrs. Alex Allan, October 5th, 1891.

The first born was a little girl who lived for just a short time. Then a son was born, Charles Wilfred Lang. Then a third child, a son William Albert Lang. Two more sons were born but both passed away shortly after birth. Then I was born, Florence Robina May Lang.

I have recollections of stories being told of Mother in the early days being very nervous of the Indians. An Indian came to the door one day to see my dad. Mother was so frightened, that the Indian told my dad that his wife trembled like leaves on a tree.

Dad farmed the half section and raised his family. All three of us children went to school in Okotoks. Mother passed away 18th of December 1922 and Dad passed away in the month of March 1944.

Charles Wilfred stayed on the farm and worked with his Dad until the year 1924, when he rented a farm and started farming on his own. He bought the SE¼ 4-21-29-W4 and later bought the NE¼ 4-21-29-W4. He married Laura Riches in 1939. They adopted one son, James. They made their home on the NE.¼ 4 until his death in 1971.

William Albert went through to become a school teacher. He taught at Barnwell and Maple Leaf schools. He enlisted for active service during the first World War. However, he never saw action, but had arrived in England before the war ended. When he came back from the war he went to university to further his education. Upon completing his courses and obtaining his degrees, he went to work for the Research Department for the Government of Alberta. He worked in this department until he retired. William Albert married Jessie Wilson from Edmonton in the year 1926. They have one son Donald, who is now a doctor at Kimberly, B.C.

I met my husband, Milton Munkholm, when he came to work for my cousins, Mr. and Mrs. William Cope. We were married in Calgary and came to live on the home farm with Dad for a short time. My husband, Milton Munkholm, then went to work at Royalties and Black Diamond. The oil industry was very active in that area at that time. We lived there until 1945, at this time we returned to Dad's farm and have resided there since. We have three children, William James, Mary Evelyn and Gordon Earl. William James

L. to R. William Lang, Mrs. A. Allan, Mrs. Boyd Hayes, Florence Munkholm, Lettie Outhet, Albert Lang, Alice Cope, Melville Hayes, Willie Cope. Front: Bobby Cope, Barry Cope and Jim Munkholm.

married Ardath Bly and lives at Creston, British Columbia. They have six children. Mary Evelyn married Robert Strang and are now living in Ottawa. They have two children. Gordon Earl married Eleanor Schmidt and is now living at Fort Saskatchewan. They have three children.

OTTO LARSEN

Otto Larsen was born March 14, 1906 in Denmark. He grew up on a farm and attended a small school there. At the age of fifteen he joined the Merchant Marines and spent 3½ years at sea. After this time he served time in the Danish Navy for a period of ten months. In 1927 work was hard to find and the pay very small. He learned that Canada was a land with golden opportunities and decided to emigrate to this country. He arrived in Halifax, March 12, 1927 at the age of 21. He travelled to Winnipeg by train which took 4½ days. The immigrants, of which there were 28, rode in a car toward the rear. For meals they would have to walk through quite a number of cars to get to the dining room. As they passed through these numerous cars on the way to the dining room, near the front of the train the smell of garlic was so strong that much of the appetite was lost along the way.

He spent one year in Manitoba and one year in Saskatchewan working long hours on farms. From Saskatchewan he went to Nelson, B.C. in 1930. Work was almost impossible to find there and he decided to come to Calgary. He arrived at the C.P.R. station during a downpour of rain. He was welcomed by a complete stranger who told him that he had come to the best place in Canada. He decided to buy a farm in partnership with Andy Christensen. Today Tom Hebson lives on that farm.

Things did not go well on that farm as they had to sell their first crop at 19¢ a bushel. After paying their bills from the proceeds of the crop, they were so broke that they had to make socks from old sheets. His partner asked him to go back and get three dollars from a bill he had paid so he could buy a pair of low rubbers for the winter. Other payments came due and they could not meet them so they had to leave the farm.

He then rented the farm on which he is still living

today. This farm is located on the S½ 10-21-29-W4. He rented this land for a period of 17 years after which time he bought it. After purchasing the land he started clearing willow bush of which he cleared 92 acres by hand with the use of an axe. He had some help from a hired man who was paid $5 a month by the Government and if he stayed for the winter the Government paid an additional bonus of $2.50 per month.

In 1933 he married Ivy Walters of Calgary and they raised four boys who attended the Allan School. Chris manages a ranch in Midale, Saskatchewan and Johnny lives in Cranbrook, B.C. and is a salesman for a welding equipment company, Henry farms the home place, and Douglas is a welder at the Tar Sands.

Doug Larsen having his pants sewn with them still on.

Larsen family. L. to R. Douglas, Chris, Otto, Ivy, John and Henry.

One day a number of friends came to visit and having no butter in the house and usually buying butter but milking cows and shipping cream we put some cream in an eight gallon can and hung it in a beef sling for churning. We took turns swinging it till the butter was made for supper.

John Larsen as a baby of 1½ years for several days was not hungry, we had a dog that had some pups and found to our surprise that John was helping himself along with puppies, with no after effects at all.

MR. AND MRS. ALBERT LEWIS — written by Edna Saunders

Both Mr. and Mrs. Lewis were born in Ontario. Mrs. Lewis (Margaret Cairns) moved to Gladstone, Manitoba, in 1878, and Albert (Ab) in 1894. They were married in 1898 and farmed near MacGregor, where their only child, Edna, was born.

In 1906 they moved to Kamloops, B.C. and lived there until 1915, and then moved to Okotoks, Alberta. There they visited with very good friends, the John Mundells, in the Big Rock district, and later moved into town.

They lived there until 1921, when Ab went as a foreman on Pat Burns 44 Ranch, west of Claresholm.

In 1930 they moved back to Okotoks and farmed in the Big Rock district NW¼ 21-20-1-W5 and in 1934 they moved to a farm North and East of Okotoks SE¼ 4-21-29-W4. There Mr. Lewis died in 1944. Mrs. Lewis then went to live with her daughter, Edna Saunders, in North Vancouver, B.C.

Mrs. Lewis died in 1956. Mr. and Mrs. Lewis are both interred in the cemetery at Okotoks.

E. R. MATTLESS — by E. R. Mattless

Here beginneth the life history of a low born farm boy. I was born on Saturday the 15 day of November 1884 at 4 o'clock in the morning on a farm near a village named Clenchwarton in the County of Norfolk in England. They tell me it was a cold foggy day and I think I have been in a fog ever since, for I seem to of got nowhere.

I can't remember much about being born being so young. My first memories are of starting school at 4 years of age, quite old, as the usual age for starting was 3 at that time, but as I had to walk two miles each way they kept me home another year. My memories of my first day at school were of getting into a fight. It came about this way. Being a young boy among five sisters I was somewhat of a pet and they adorned me with a bead necklace of which I was very proud. As was to be expected it was at once picked upon and one of the boys had nerve enough to snatch at it and broke it, the scrap was on. It ended up he with a bloody nose and I with the school Masters strap where it hurt most. That was a beginning.

My next recollection is of my mother finding livestock in my hair, and me under severe questioning where it came from. I had been sitting between 2 girls and I got orders I was not to sit there any more. The next morning at school I was told to go to my place by the teacher. I said my mother says I am not to sit with them lousy Morthers (Broad English for girls) with the usual result. From then on it was the usual daily drudges.

I must say I had 2 brothers but the youngest one was twenty years older than I. They at one end and I at the other of a family of twelve. I next remember us moving to Long Sutton (Lincolnshire) where we stayed a year and then returned to Clench Warton. Our next move was to Hillington in upper Norfolk, where my father worked as dairyman for several years. At that time I would be about seven years old and there I resumed my education. Our school consisted of one large room about twenty-four by twenty. It was divided into two parts one for the younger and one for the older children. There were eight classes or standards as they were then called. I must have been a pretty good student as I never failed a subject during my school career which was not very long, as by the time I was eleven years old I had passed the seventh standard and decided to leave school.

My parents didn't want me to but I decided I'd had enough. The fact was I had reached a class where I was having a pretty rough time. My father said if I would not go to school I would have to go to work. I chose work and got a job at the magnificent wage of twelve cents a day. I stayed at that a bit over a year and decided I'd had enough of it. So I got a job as Copper Hole Jack, in Canadian that means being chore boy to everybody, for the sum of thirty six cents a week, and my board and room. I stayed at that for a year and decided I needed a change so I got a job on a purebred Shorthorn dairy farm, where I stayed until I was about 14 years and a half, at much better wages. Then I decided I must try my wings, so I got a job as undergroom at a hunting lodge, at a place near Lincoln where I stayed nearly a year. After that I got a job as groom and gardener at a village near South Lincolnshire where I stayed a full year. Being then sixteen and a half years old I decided I ought to learn a trade, so I interviewed the village blacksmith, as my oldest brother was a blacksmith I thought I would be one too. He agreed to take me as an apprentice till I was twenty one years old. My parents objected but I had my way so they said if I was determined to be a smith they would have me legally bound so that I could not change my mind. So I put in four and one half years at real hard work eleven hours a day, six days a week.

The morning of my twenty first birthday I had a telegram from my brother that there was a job waiting for me in a little village near Grantham. So I started in right away running a country shop for a widow lady, I stayed there over 2 years.

Then I decided to come to Canada to join my younger brother who had been in this country for twenty years. I arrived in April 1908 and started looking for a job. The first one I got was in a carriage building shop at Toronto but the hands treated me too much as a green Englishman so I quit.

The next job I got was this way, I went into a General Blacksmith shop and asked one of the men where I would find the boss, he said that Big Fellow there, so I walked over to him and asked him how the chances were for a job. He looked me up and down then said you're English aren't you. I said yes. He said "we don't think much of Englishmen." I said "why" he said, "they are not up to their job." There were several horses being shod at the time, so I said, "do you consider those on to their job." He said "this is one of the best shops in the City". I said "well, where I come from they would be fired for doing work like that." Then he said to one fellow, "lend this fellow your apron, he is going to show us how a horse should

be shod." So I went to work and did it up brown. He looked at the job and said, "By God you can shoe, come in, in the morning."

I worked there for two years then decided to come west. That was in 1910. I came out on the spring excursion at a cost of ten dollars. I got as far as Calgary. Calgary at that time was not as big as it is now four or five blocks north or south of the C.P.R. Depot and you were in the country. Where the Chinook Shopping Centre is now, was a race track and south of that was Hays dairy farm. I did not stay in the city many days. There were many Employment Agencies on ninth avenue "Some phony". But I struck an honest one and got a job at Hardisty in a blacksmith shop at three fifty a day, which was considered good at that time. (Some what different to-day). I worked for a Norwegian for a month or two then I bought the business from him. I stayed at that about three years or so and then sold it.

During the winter of 1913 and 1914 I contacted a rather bad attack of rheumatic fever and did nothing but lay in bed and groan, but in the spring I was able to be up and around though not able to do much. That August the First World War broke out and I, like a lot more young fools, wanted to join the Army, but they would not have me, they said my heart was weak. So I hung around till fall and the Mounties were calling for recruits. So a Mountie with whom I was friendly said "why don't you join them". So I decided I'd try and me being a shoeing smith they took me on, though I had to sign an agreement that if anything happened to me they would not be responsible for me. I signed on for a year and I must say I enjoyed the experience.

E. R. Mattless N.W.M.P.

At the end of my service I tried the Army again and they took me on like a shot. I joined the Royal Canadian Dragoons in Toronto, and when I reported at the Orderly Room the O.C. said we have been expecting you. We have a letter from the police saying you are a first class shoeing smith. I would like you to join our staff of smiths. I declined, saying "I wanted to go overseas," knowing if I joined the staff I'd be stuck there. The O.C. said "I'll make a bargain with you. If you will help us out I promise you shall go out on the next draft." So I went to the forge and I had been there about a month when I was sent to the orderly room. The O.C. said I promised you should go out on the first draft, I had no idea it would be this soon but if you still want to go you shall. So from me joining up and being in England was just six weeks.

In England I ran into the same problem, but I said "no, I wanted to go to the front", so they put me in the riding school to learn to ride, which I considered an insult having passed through the hands of Toufy Griffin in the Police. I stood it for a while then I said to my troop officer, "I guess, Sir I'll be going down to the forge." He said "I'm glad. You know they would of kept you in the riding school for the duration." I had not been at the forge long when promotion came my way and I became one of the comparatively few sergeants confirmed in their ranks. This went on over a year and I began to get restless. In the meantime I had married my old sweetheart, I had been in love with for about nine years. After my return from our honeymoon I contacted the black and german measles and nearly died but eventually recovered. Then I started agitating to get to France. But got turned down time after time, so I worked a transfer to the Lord Strathcona Horse R.C., about the worst deal I ever made.

However I got to France. My first trip in the line was at Passchendaele with mud to your neck. We did not stay there long and from then on we were all over the place. Wherever there was a hole we were sent to plug it. This went on for about a year and then I contacted what they called trench fever and was out of commission for about three months. Then back to the regiment for the rest of the war: which ended as we were moving up to Mon's where it all began. We moved back to a village in Belgium. I forget the name of the place but had not been there long when an order came through that any ex-mounties who wished to return to the force would be returned to England, forthwith. Of course a lot of us took advantage of it. The trouble when we got to England was to find an excuse for not joining, "however" I managed to get out of it and have kicked myself ever since. It would have saved me years of grief which I will relate as briefly as possible.

I managed to pull a string or two and got back to Canada in April 1919. Then our troubles began. When we joined the Army we were told we would be taken care of when we returned. "we were" I should smile, when we looked for a job we were told they couldn't fire the man who had helped them out while we were having a good time fighting. "However" the Soldier Settlement Board would lend us enough to set up farming if we could pass certain tests. I being raised on a farm had no difficulty (worse luck).

I filed on a homestead at Hardisty in 1913. The first thing I had to turn this over to the board; they discovered I had acquired a few head of cattle and wanted those. I told them they could go where it was warm, so they bought me a C.P.R. quarter section and tools absolutely necessary to get started, but we had to mortgage everything we owned and pay interest on the loan. We had barely got started when the bottom fell out of everything. I sold a carload of stock for little more than I had paid for one cow. From then on it was a struggle for existence.

Hail, frost, drought and low prices, five cents a dozen for eggs and ten cents a pound for butter and at one time the Government gave us one and a half cents a pound for cattle to help us out. They were going to

Mr. and Mrs. Mattless, 60th Wedding Anniversary.

process them and we were going to get the balance. That was over fifty years ago and it is still coming. I was not in on that deal as I had lost my faith in Governments. But I had ten or a dozen cows I wanted to get rid of so I decided to let them go for the cent and a half. But when I got them to the stockyards I came across one of Burn's and Co. buyers. He said "what are you going to do with them" I said "the Government is giving a cent and a half a pound for them." He said "I'll give you two cents" I said "you've bought them." My name was mud for sometime with the neighbors, but after a while decided I was crazy like a fox so I was forgiven.

This went on for some years, I won't say we lived but we existed. I took on a bunch of cattle on shares for Bill Graburn of Calgary, which helped somewhat. Then the hungry thirties struck and nearly put us out of business and with worry and one thing and another an old war injury returned on me and for three years I was partially out of commission. I applied to the Government for relief but got mixed up in red tape so it came to nothing. My local doctor advised me to go to a specialist in Edmonton so I did. He diagnosed it as a brain damage and said I would be worse before I was better but it would not kill me. So I had to grin and bear it. Eventually I decided to sell out.

Bill Graburn decided to sell the herd of grade cattle and go in for purebred Shorthorns. He decided to buy a place near Okotoks SE½ 30-20-28-W4 and I undertook to start it for him. Which I did for a bit over a year and then decided I'd had enough so we bought a little cottage in Okotoks and I got a job with the Calgary Farm Machinery Company. I stayed there for five years then decided to retire.

This happened over twenty years ago and I have lived happy ever since, bar the usual upsets.

There you have a brief history of a life struggle of nearly 93 years. You asked for it, there it is.

J. A. McDonald family, Flo, Harold, Velma, Lu, Grandpa, Ted, Annie, Mother, Tom and Doug. Taken in front of farm home.

PAT AND WINNIFRED McCARTHY

Pat and Winnifred McCarthy moved onto the Gilbert Garbutt farm in March 1955. This was the former Armstrong place. They had one wee baby, Patrick Joseph, and had been farming the old Mydland place on the Longview Road six miles west of High River.

Pat was an Irishman from County Cork who had come to Canada in search of adventure and had worked near Nobleford for a short time before moving to the Twin Butte area south of Pincher Creek.

Winnifred had been raised in the Crowsnest Pass and had taught school in numerous places in Alberta. However, she had a married sister in Twin Butte and that is how the two met.

Pat and Winnifred spent seven years in the district and were blessed with two little girls, first Mary Anne and then Sheila Maureen.

Pat was a very busy man in those days. He milked cows, fed pigs, raised his own feed and even had a few chickens and started a beef herd.

When hail ruined the crops Winnifred returned to teaching and had numerous exciting experiences on stormy days.

When the farm was sold in 1963 the McCarthys moved to Forest Lawn until Winnifred completed the year teaching and then up to Camrose area where they still reside.

Young Pat is now married and has one daughter, Kara Marie. Mary Anne is taking nurses training at the Misericordia Hospital in Edmonton. Sheila is in Grade 11 and hopes to be a nurse also.

Pat rented the Okotoks farm from Winnifred's father J. J. McIntyre of Calgary. John Joseph and Mary Anne McIntyre were both raised in Glace Bay, N.S. and had come west when they were married. J.J. as he was commonly known had spent his adult life in the coal mining industry. In 1920 he moved to Bellevue and later in 1935 to Coleman where they raised a family of nine children.

They retired to Calgary in 1952 and purchased the farm as an interest for his retirement years. A few years ago they moved to Pincher Creek. Mr. McIntyre passed away in 1973 at the age of eighty-six. Mrs. McIntyre is still living in Pincher Creek and in fairly good health.

DAN AND KATHERINE McDONALD

Dan came from Glengarry, Quebec in the early 1900's. He bought land two and a half miles northeast of Okotoks S½ 10-21-29-W4. He bached for many years but later married. As a bachelor he was known as "Mr. Freeze Out" for he had a very poor house which was cold in the winter. Dan died while he was in the area. Katherine, his wife, moved back east some years after Dan's death and died Feb. 8, 1957.

In 1908 Dan took the contract for the erection of the Allan School for $770 and he was to supply all materials. Also later on he took the contract to build the barn and out buildings.

JOHN A. AND ISABELL McDONALD

John was a nephew of J. J. McDonald. He was born in New Glasgow, Eaden Lake, Nova Scotia and moved to the west coast in 1906. He worked as a carpenter in Nanaimo and Victoria, later moving to Fernie where he married Isabell Letcher in 1914, who was from Spring Hill, Nova Scotia, then moving to Edmonton. In 1915 he moved to J. J. McDonald's ranch at Okotoks and operated it along with a cousin, Frank McIntosh, from the Tongue Creek Ranch. His nephew, Jackie McDermid, and his wife's sister Lu Lu Letcher lived with them and because the Allan School was closed they went to Okotoks School until the Allan School reopened about 1918.

John McDonald belonged to the Masonic Lodge in Okotoks. John and Isabell had six children, two girls and four boys. Tom Alexander born Oct. 1916, Mary Jane died at age of six months, John Douglas born July 1920. Ruth Emma born July 1924 at Fernie, B.C., Robert Edward born at Eureka, Montana May 1928, Hubert Anderson born April 1930.

J. A. McDonald sold out in 1922 along with the Estate of J. J. McDonald and bought a ranch at Roosville, B.C. in the spring of 1923 which he operated along with son, John Douglas, until his death in 1971. Isabell still resides at Roosville, B.C.

Jack and Belle McDonald, Doug and Tom.

J. J. McDONALD

J. J. McDonald came west to Alberta in the early 1900's from Nova Scotia. He bought a ranch 6 miles northeast of Okotoks 36-20-29-W4 where he built a two-storey house. He remained a bachelor all his life but had nephews around him most of the time. He also

Tom and Doug McDonald and Herb Letcher.

owned a ranch on Tongue Creek south of Okotoks, his nephews, Don and Frank McIntosh, lived with him on this ranch.

J. J. McDonald was well known for his ability to

Annie McDermid and her uncle, J. J. McDonald.

make Nova Scotia biscuits and all visitors to his home sampled them along with a cup of tea.

J. J. McDonald died from the flu in 1919 and was buried in the Okotoks Cemetery.

TOM McKAY ★
Tom lived in Okotoks but owned the SE¼ 27-20-29-W4 where he raised hogs and ran a slaughterhouse. Tom also owned a butcher shop in Okotoks.

THOMAS McMULLIN — by Harold Biswanger
Tom, as I knew him, was born at Price, Carbon County, Utah. Tom was a mule skinner in his early adult life, freighting to and from mines at Kellog, Idaho. He drove a twelve mule hitch and was known as "Mule Mullen". He also knew about handling dynamite and how to use it. He used to show me how to blow rocks on my farm. Tom told me that when he was hauling dynamite to the mines he would always sit on a box of caps so if it ever blew up he would be killed and not just crippled.

He was in the U.S. army during World War I. He was also involved in the chasing out of New Mexico of Francisco "Pancho" Villa, the Mexican bandit who used to raid the southern states, in 1916.

In 1928 he came to Canada with his wife, Mercedes, whom he married at Kellog, Idaho, settling at Granum and farming there for ten years. Their daughter, Patricia Fay, died at Granum in 1930. He then moved to Diamond City and farmed there for ten years. In 1948 he moved to E½ 1-21-29-W4 located six miles north east of Okotoks which he bought from Paul Sallenbach, whose wife was Tom's niece.

Tom's son, Thomas Roy McMullin, died in 1949 on a fishing trip to Gorge Creek, west of Turner Valley.

Tom, Mercedes and Roy McMullin.

Tom raised purebred cattle and quarter horses. In later years he added NE¼ 36-20-29-W4 which he purchased from Mrs. Indergaard. The oil company drilled a well on this property during the wet years of the early 50's. They had to plank a road to the well but this still did not hold up so, being an old time teamster, Tom hauled the men and supplies to the well with horse and wagon.

I remember one incident with a horse, on his farm, that he had borrowed from Olive Aldridge. He could not find the horse one day so he set out to find it on horse back. He found it in a very narrow draw, stuck solid in mud, its head about four feet below the top of the draw. Many neighbors, including myself, tried to rescue it using tractors and man power but in vain. Looking towards the road we saw Ivor Renn's winch truck coming down the road so we waved him in. Hooking the winch to the horses neck we were able to pull him out. I swear the horse's neck stretched two feet. A sorry looking mess he was but he had no harmful after effects.

Tom belonged to the Cutting Horse Association and also belonged to the Church of Jesus Christ of Latter Day Saints. Mercedes belonged to the farm ladies club. Tom and Mercedes played cards, on many cold winter nights, with their neighbors. I also remember some very good New Year's Eve parties we had at their home.

Tom and Mercedes retired in 1961 and moved to Spokane, Washington, U.S.A. and bought a home at 7510 east Baldwin Ave.

Mercedes died in 1965 and Tom in 1969 in Spokane, Washington. Both are buried in Union Cemetery in Calgary with both children.

ERVIE HENRY MILLER — by Robert Alexander Miller

Ervie Henry Miller came to Alberta from Clifford, Ontario in 1909 with a survey company, surveying southern Alberta. After two years he came to Okotoks and worked for Mr. D. McIntyre until the outbreak of World War I. He enlisted and spent four years overseas with the engineers, driving horses. On his return he bought the quarter section 3-21-29-W4 through the Soldier Settlement Board. He farmed this quarter and later extended his holdings to one-half section.

In 1921 he married Mary Adelaide Foran. Addie was the daughter of William and Sarah Foran. She was born in Ontario and came to Okotoks with her parents in 1908. They lived one half mile east of town. She went to school in Okotoks and then worked in the telephone office there till she married.

Ervie was an ardent horse fan and was noted for his excellent horses. In those days all work was done by horse power. He freighted with six-horse teams to the oilfields before the trucks took over. The first snow fall always found Ervie with his matched team and sleigh, with sleigh bells ringing, on his way to town. Before he got to Beattie's store, the sleigh would be full of children out for the first sleigh ride of the season.

Ervie had a model T Ford. He went to town one night and was arrested by the provincial police for not having a tail light and was fined $5.00 and costs. The policeman was Joe Miller who later ran the hotel in Okotoks. The next night Ervie came into town on horseback with a tin can with a candle in it and stopped Joe on the street. He backed his horse up to him and said, "How do you like this tail light Miller?" The next morning the whole town was laughing about it.

Ervie died in 1946 from heart trouble. He left his widow now Mrs. Ken Gaunce of Calgary and five children.

John Duncan, better known as Jack, served in the Canadian Armed Forces for five years during World War 2. He was the equipment manager for the Okotoks Oilers hockey team from 1946-1955. In 1945 he married Dorothy Day from Salmon Arm, B.C. They farmed the SE ¼ 4-21-29-W4 from 1945 to 1960 when they moved to Markerville, Alberta and are now farming there. They have two children. Janice is a graudate in Pharmacy. She is married to Terrance Long and they live in Edmonton. They have one child Sarah. Jeffery is married to Mary Ann Page of Delburne and is farming with his dad at Markerville.

James Ervie is a C.P.R. engineer in Calgary. In 1945 he married Marjory Lumsden, from Hanna. They have three boys all living in Calgary. Ross is a machinist working for the C.P.R. Garth is a heavy industrial worker and David is studying engineering at the University of Calgary.

Sylvia Edna trained as a nurse at Holy Cross Hospital in Calgary. In 1951 she married John Rothenberger, of Winnipeg. Sylvia is now head nurse of the Lutheran Hospital of Winnipeg. They have two children, Christine is married to Glenn Stieben and lives in Thompson, Manitoba. Their two daughters are Sharon and Sandra. Curtis is attending school in Winnipeg.

Robert (Bob) Alexander Miller bought the E ½-35-20-29-W4, from W. H. Johnson in 1948. He is still farming this land and lives on the NE ¼. In 1950 he married Pauline Nielson from Standard, Alberta. They have four children. Ervie is an agricultural pilot and flying instructor for a local air service. Brian is married to Debora Ashmore from Aldersyde, they live on and farm the home place. Linda is a graduate in sewing and the study of fabrics from Olds College and is now working in Calgary. Dennis is still attending High School in Okotoks.

Bob played hockey for the Okotoks Oilers from 1945 to 1952. His two sons Ervie and Brian are playing for this team now. Bob coached the Davisburg Wheat Kings hockey team for two years around 1952.

Allan Bruce farmed his dad's farm from 1947 to 1974. Although he never built a home of his own he was one of the best cement mixers while helping build foundations for four or five neighbours homes. In those days cement mixing was done by hand. He played goal for the Okotoks Oilers from 1945 to 1955. Bruce passed away in 1975.

IKE AND (NIECE MARGARET) MORRIS — by Harold Biswanger*

Ike and Margaret Morris were born in Wales and came to Canada and settled on a farm in the Innisfail district before 1928. In 1928 they moved to and rented a farm two miles east of Okotoks known as the Cope farm 26-20-29 W4. They rented this farm for 30 years growing mostly grain, milking a few cows to sell cream and raised a few chickens.

What I remember most about them was that they used to visit my grandparents, Mr. and Mrs. J. Aldridge, and my Aunt Olive. I would be at the farm during the summer holidays. My brother and I would be sleeping in the bunk house and along about ten or eleven o'clock would be awakened to have cantaloupe and ice cream. This happened many times over several years and during the thirties this was quite a treat.

Another thing I remember was that Aunt Olive and Margaret Morris were good friends and Olive would go to visit Margaret on horse back. One day along about nightfall Olive tied the reins up on the horse and sent it home as she was going to ride home with the Morris's. Part way back to the Aldridges and at night, the horse jumped out of the ditch just as Ike was coming along and he hit it and killed it. That was a very tragic night.

Following is a story told to me by Dorothy Gerlitz:

"In 1945 I, Dorothy (McCulloch) Gerlitz, was not married and was a nurse. I was called out to "special" Margaret Morris who was suffering from a heart ailment. It was my first journey to the country and my first visit to a farm. It was in September during harvest so there was a great deal of activity taking place. I spent around ten days with Margaret and her Uncle Ike. Ike unfortunately had the misfortune of getting a barley beard in his eye and I had to take him to the doctor in Okotoks to have it removed. He was in considerable pain but he managed to give me directions on how to operate his car as I had never driven a car before. This was quite an adventure. We arrived at the doctor's and safely back home again. Ike was suffering with considerable pain from his eye and before it healed I had to deliver cream to the creamery in Okotoks. Ike recovered and off I went back to the city with a somewhat rudimentary education on farm life. Both patients were considerably improved."

Lyle Renard, Ike Morris, Jack Phillips in about 1937. Combine 1934.

During the thirties Ike purchased one of the first, of the smaller type, combines in the Okotoks area. Jack Phillips worked for Ike for many years and joined the Armed Forces in 1939. After the war he went back to New Zealand.

John Smitindorf also worked for Ike for several years and boarded with him in the winter and in the spring then put himself out for hire in the spring. He is now working for Jim Tucker south of Okotoks.

Margaret died in the spring of 1950. Ike sold out in 1958 and went back to Wales for a visit and then came back and lived in Calgary until his death in 1960.

LEONARD NIXON — by J. H. Jenkins

Mr. and Mrs. Nixon came to the Allan district in 1930-31 from Calgary. The farm location N½ 30-20-29-W4 and N.E. ½ 25-20-29-W4.

Leonard worked for the John Deere Company in Calgary. His parents lived in Manitoba. He loved sports and did a lot of curling. He also had a tennis court on his farm and we had some great games on it. At first he farmed with horses then he went to a tractor and combine.

Leonard and Myrtle Nixon had three children. Lillian now lives in Penticton, B.C. Bernice in Provost, Alberta and Robert Nixon in Calgary.

They sold the farm and moved to Okotoks then to Calgary. In Calgary they ran a confectionery store on 12 Avenue across from the Belcher Hospital. Later they retired and moved to Penticton, B.C.

Len is in poor health now and is in a rest home just out of Kelowna, B.C. Myrtle is also in this rest home. Both will be 80 years old this spring 1977.

Mrs. Outhet and Mrs. Lang extreme left, Mrs. Aldridge and three children Phyllis, Bill and Olive, also Florence Lang. Mr. Smith, Mr. Aldridge, Mr. Lang, Ed Aldridge, on Smith farm later occupied by the Aldridge family and later owned by Harvey Outhet.

GRACE AND HARVIE ROBERT OUTHET — written by Phyllis Teskey

Harvie was born February 6, 1882 at Lacole, Quebec. He moved to the Smith farm, N.E. ¼ 2-21-29-W4 in 1916, north east of Okotoks, after the Aldridge family left it to go to farm in the Big Rock area. He was a good neighbor, kind, interested in community affairs and had a great fondness for children, a world of good humor, and a keen interest in photography.

He told of being a cook in his early years on a road construction gang. At the start he had no experience whatsoever and, as they were a long way from town and had no one else, they had to keep him on. By the time they arrived back to town he had greatly improved and they kept him on. He became a very good cook.

He had a love for all animals and at one time had a pet badger.

His wife, Grace, passed away in 1939 and later he married Miss Lettie Allan. They retired in 1960 and resided in Aldersyde for several years. Lettie died in 1964 and Harvie died later in the Medicine Tree Manor in High River in March 1966.

Harvey Outhet.

THE PATTERSONS — by Bernice (Patterson) Barrett

In 1899 Alex Patterson, son Jack, brothers Gilbert, Hugh and wife, sister Susan and his mother, Mrs. John Patterson Sr. came from Quebec to take up homesteads on quarters around where Dinton Hall now stands. Mrs. Patterson sometimes acted as nurse or midwife. Mrs. Alex Patterson was able to travel to the prairies in 1900 after recovering from surgery.

Coal was hauled from McPherson's Mine at Black Diamond, about forty miles and fording the river to get to Okotoks could be very dangerous in high water.

The Pattersons lived there until 1905 when Alex and Hugh built the Grand Central Hotel and Livery Stable in Okotoks. Alexander drove Dr. Ardiel, one of the first boarders, all over the country, day or night to attend the sick. He sometimes provided transportation for the undertaker, John Wilson. They brought the body of Tucker Peach from his farm on the Bow River to Okotoks. Mr. Peach had been murdered some weeks earlier.

Around 1910 Alex and his wife, Jemima and Jack bought a farm west of Okotoks NE¼ 34-20-1-5W5 now owned by Allan Macdonald. They raised cattle and horses. Mr. and Mrs. D. J. Moore (Rawhide) were friends and neighbors. Frank Moore went to school in Okotoks and drowned in Sheep Creek. Jack owned a steam powered well drilling outfit. He sold it later and went to Fort Macleod to work in the power house where he started his training in steam engineering. He took correspondence courses also and got his papers later.

Mr. and Mrs. Hugh Patterson, son Leslie and Mrs. John Patterson bought 30-20-28-W4 and were there from about 1914-20. Mrs. John Patterson died there. Hugh bought part of NE ¼ 29-20-29-W4 above Okotoks hill where they lived until he died in 1931. His wife and son died in 1962.

Alex and his wife were in partnership with Hugh a

110

Jack Patterson's cook car outfit: l to r: Vera Andrews Gillespie, Mrs. Ted Cole, Margaret Raycraft, Mrs. Jack Patterson.

few years. Jack's first wife died in 1915, in Okotoks, leaving a baby daughter, Bernice who was raised by his parents.

The fall of 1917 Alex rented a farm 6 miles N.E. of Okotoks, NW 22-21-29-W4 from Joe Hogge. Melrose school was not far away. The next year Jack and Edith Learmonth and twin daughters, Edythe and Edytha moved from Ontario to go into partnership. Mrs. Learmonth and Mrs. Patterson were sisters. During this time the dreaded influenza struck the country. Hardly anyone escaped and many people died. Everyone in the family but Mrs. Learmonth fell ill and she had to do chores and cook until someone was able to work again. People wore masks to town.

The family milked 14 cows, churned the cream and sold butter to customers in Okotoks. There was a large barrel churn with a foot pedal. The barrel turned over and over. The lid was clamped down but there was a plug which was taken out periodically to relieve the pressure. One day Jack Learmonth was churning vigorously and thinking of other things, when suddenly the plug blew out and a stream of cream hit the walls, floor and everything in its path including the absent minded churner.

They raised cattle, chickens, grain but the purebred Clydesdales were Alex's pride and joy. The collie dog rounded up the turkeys when they strayed and protected them from coyotes. Learmonths went back to Ontario about 1922.

After four years, the Pattersons bought the Squire Place, North of Okotoks SW ¼ 33-20-29-W4 where they lived until 1927 when Alex was forced to sell due to a heart condition. He died at Okotoks in his home there in 1937. Mrs. Patterson lived with Jack and his second wife Vera until her death in 1953.

Jack worked in a power house in Okotoks, in sawmills and oil wells. He was an engineer at the Royalite plant in Turner Valley from about 1936-50. Around 1923 he bought a large Case steam engine and separator

along with tank wagon, cook bar and bunk house. For many falls he threshed around the district, and also broke up brushland with the big plows. The big engine was sometimes used to move houses. One was a very heavy old house known as the "Gopher House" from early days. It was east of Okotoks and was hauled up the hill to the Lionel Cameron farm. Jack's wife Vera cooked for the threshers until their young daughters kept her busy at home in Okotoks. After retiring from the Royalite plant Jack opened a plumbing business which he had for a few years. He was active in Lodges, Council and community until his death in 1970. Vera passed away in 1976. She was active in the Senior Country Club and busy with her ceramics.

CHARLIE PATTERSON

Charlie homesteaded at the junction of the Sheep and Highwood Rivers NE 31-20-28-W4. It is not known what year he homesteaded but there was evidence that his house was built in 1887 and was built with square nails as were most buildings at that time.

He grew oats and hauled them to Fort Macleod for the Mounties. The journey taking weeks by team and wagon, as there were no bridges so had to ford all rivers which could be very dangerous if there happened to be a heavy rain in the foothills and the rivers were high. Charlie and other homesteaders mined a poor soft grade of coal from the west side of the Highwood River to heat their homes.

Charlie Patterson had a son called George and in later years he was Postmaster in Okotoks.

Walter Wilde in later years on this farm found coal in his well above the river bank, and the fine coal eventually sealed the well off and it went dry.

THOMAS N. T. PRIEST — by Al Priest

I shall start this with the beginning of as much as I can remember of my Dad's journey through life.

He was born in 1882 in an area of London, England

111

called Clapham Common and grew up along with two brothers within the sound of Bow Bells. At age fifteen he fibbed about his age saying he was older and became a member of a British Expedition force to Africa where he was part of the military force Britain sent to battle the Boer's (as the Dutch people were then known). It was a case of jealousy and ill will between the Dutch settlers and British subjects over the discovery of gold. Dad had served approximately three years by the time he returned to England. Upon his return he could not settle and decided to join the migration of British subjects to the new land of Canada — arriving in 1902.

He was sent to a farm in Manitoba where he worked for a whole year for no financial remuneration. Deciding that was not for him and hearing stories of great opportunity further west he headed for Calgary — at that time in the throes of large scale land schemes. He worked in and around Calgary mostly for ranchers such as the S.L. Ranch west of what is now Cochrane and also a stint on the Pat Burns Ranches.

In 1907 he went back to England and in 1908 married his one time school girl friend Margaret Howey. They rented a farm at Chipstead Surrey, England and that is where Alfred (myself) was born in 1909. Before I was a year old Dad decided he had to get back to Calgary, Canada and so they set sail for the great new land. My

Mrs. Tom Priest.

birthday was on boardship. Arriving in Calgary after a long and tedious colonial express trip (as they were then known).

Mother and Dad settled into a house on Sixth Ave. and Fifth St. which was on the outskirts at that time. Mother took in boarders to make ends meet while Dad bought a team of horses and went to work on the new Hudson's Bay store. That was when they excavated the basement for the present site of the Hudson's Bay. When that job was finished Dad, who still had farming in his blood, rented a farm in the Fresh Fiely district this is known as part of Conrich.

He had many ups and downs for the next few years, prairie fires, and hail storms wiping out the crops and so, in 1915, he found a farm to rent in the Black Diamond area. To get there he must move all his possessions by team and wagon, as for his stock they must be herded by day and bedded by night. In those days a scarcity of funds for hired help it remained for a plan of self help and so Alfred, who was only seven years old, was delegated to drive the stock, horses, cows, and calves from fifteen miles north east of Calgary to fifty miles south west of Calgary to a place called the Creamery. This place is still called this today.

My recollection is hazy of this trip but I do remember Dad coming to find me and of us getting to the stockyards very late at night. Dad had the stock corralled and we stayed in the old Stockyards Hotel overnight. The next morning Dad spent some time getting me on the road out of Calgary and for the next three or four days it was travel by day and find a friendly place to stop for the night. Anyway Dad finally got everything gathered together and proceeded to farm. Mother even milked the cows even though she was terrified of them. About this time Dad came down with a cold and asked Mother if there was any medicine in the cupboard. Before Mother could answer Dad had taken a bottle from the shelf and drank some of it. He became violently sick and Mother called Dr. Ardiel in Okotoks. Fortunately a phone had been installed the week before. He asked Mother to read the label on the bottle and almost died from shock when she did. He said Tom has taken enough poison to kill six horses. Then he started barking orders over the phone for Mother to follow. It was a touchy situation for many hours but finally Dad responded and was able to get around again.

After a year at this place Dad rented another farm from Willard Thompson north and east of Black Diamond. It was while we were here that the great 1918 flu epidemic hit. Mother was one of those resourceful people who left nothing to chance and every day she scrubbed the house with what was then known as "stock dip" or creoline. It smelt awful but was highly disinfectant and so our family escaped the flu. People were dying everywhere but we children never even got the sniffles.

In 1919 Dad rented the Chapman place on Gladys Ridge and that was where we were living when that disastrous blizzard of May 1919 hit. Thousands of head of cattle were lost and even a few humans lost their lives. I remember Dad had gone to Mazeppa for coal. The blizzard began before he got back and after several hours Mother was frantic with worry, but at last Dad found his way back but NO COAL! Those few days were terrible, we even had snow in the house. It was while we were there that Dad acquired his first car.

In 1920 Dad moved us all into Okotoks. That was the year the town decided to do something about the river floods. Along with co-operation from the C.P.R. who brought in a train load of mountain rock from Frank Slide the townspeople, including Dad, unloaded all the cars and piled the rock on the river bank. About this time I started to work, I was twelve.

Then Dad rented the Spencer place half way between Aldersyde and Okotoks, he decided I should go back to school and so I went to Maple Leaf School. Dad did not stay here long and rented the Stockton place which was across the road. While there the Alberta Government decided to gravel the roads. They awarded the contract to Foster and Foster Contractors and purchased two acres of ground from Dad for $100 for gravel. They spent three months gravelling the road between Okotoks and Aldersyde, then gave Dad the job of maintaining this section of road in between periods of farming.

In 1922 Dad rented the Rowles place across the Sheep River and in 1924 bought the Johnson place from William Johnson Sec. 25-20-29-W4. He sold that in 1928 to William McLeod and moved into Calgary in the Mission District. While in Calgary he leased the service station on Centre St. and 4th Ave. from Texaco but only kept it for a short time. Then in 1929 he bought the Carstairs Hotel, he was there for two years and bought the Max Schell Farm at Madden. He farmed that until 1947 when he bought the General store at Dalemead, it was while there that Mother died. Dad could not settle after that and came to Calgary where he joined the Corps of Commissionaires until he retired and lived with me until he died in 1968. A FINER OR MORE HONEST MAN THAN HE — NEVER LIVED.

During the time Dad was living on the Willard Thompson place he was elected Trustee of the Black Diamond School Board and as such was instrumental in resolving many problems that education faced in those impoverished times. Our family also provided a familiar family haven for the local teachers of that time, one of whom I well remember by the name of Miss Vogel, and another of the name of Miss Potter. They too were living in our home at the time of the flu epidemic and like our family did not get the flu.

Dad became a Mason while in Okotoks and was quite active along with Mr. Hessel the druggist, Mr. Pamment, the west end grocer, Mr. Jack Wilson the local Ford dealer, Mr. Metcalfe. The Millinery Store and many others including the owner of the Willingdon Hotel who previously was an A.P.P. officer. When Dad moved to Carstairs he became very active in the local chapter of the Blue Lodge and was Worshipful Master, in later years he attended the Corinthian Lodge in North Calgary.

After Mother died Dad was very lonely. He never lost faith that someday he would be re-united in God's realm and lived his life accordingly. While in the Commissionaires he served on the entrance gates at Banff for three years and also served at the Imperial Office in Calgary for some time.

This is just a brief summary of my fathers life as I remember it.

RENARD, WALTER L. 1876 - 1959 *

Born at Lone Rock, Wisconsin, later moving to Larimore, North Dakota; married Adeline Collins. His first trip to Alberta was in 1898; he came back in 1900 to stay. In 1903 he homesteaded N.E. ¼ 17-20-3-W5, entering in 1910 and patenting it in 1915. He also bought a ¾ section S½ 27-NE¼ 27-20-29-W4, 2 miles east of Okotoks town, which was bought from the C.P.R. He also had other land in the area and for a time occupied Charles Lusk's place. The cattle were grazed in the hills in the summer, west of Turner Valley and taken to land he owned near the town of Okotoks in the winter. The cattle brand was K6 left rib and the horses K6 right shoulder.

W. J. Renard.

Thomas Priest (father), Frank (son), Dave (grandson) and great-grandson.

Mom Renard and cat.

Renard family. L. to R. Bill, Lyle, Marjorie, Babe (Vance), Ralph, Ron, wife of one of the boys.

The Renards ranched at Pocket Ranch and farmed at Okotoks until 1917, then lived in Okotoks town for several years. Mr. Renard died in 1959 aged 83 and Mrs. Renard a few years later. The Renards had a family of seven, two girls, Neva and Margie and five boys, Bill, Lyle, Vance (Babe) and twins Ronnie and Ralph. The children attended Plainview School at Kew and the Okotoks Schools.

The two daughters live in the United States. Bill makes his home in Calgary, Lyle and Ralph in Bellingham, Washington. Ronnie lost his life while serving with the U.S. Armed Forces during World War II.

Babe, who married Cora Tosh; daughter of William Simpson Tosh of Okotoks; and son, Ron, reside on original quarter. They also have a daughter Jackie who resides in Turner Valley.

Walter Renard was the first man to gravel the streets of Okotoks. They also had teams of horses which freighted every other day to Black Diamond Turner Valley District.

THE RICHES FAMILY — by George Riches

James L. and Jannet Riches and their two children Laura and George came to the district from Sherbrooke, Quebec in 1916.

They bought the Eberley farm. Mr. James Eberley was one of the early settlers to this district, coming here in about 1883. He homesteaded the NW 34-20-29-W4 and bought S½-3-21-29-W4 from the C.P.R. Mr.

Eberley died in the spring of 1916, so his wife and daughters, Etta, (Mrs. W. Morrison) and Jessie had the farm for sale. The sale bills were already posted for the stock and implements. When my father and uncle, Wm. Andrews of Melrose, came to look at the farm they had to do some fast thinking if my dad was to buy the stock or land. The stock was well bred Shorthorn cattle, branded 1Z and 2Z for the horses.

Dad saw the spring of water, abundance of hay and noted that it was only three miles from town, and he was sold on the farm. He bought most of the cattle, as beef was the main source of livelihood in the district at the time.

This part of the west was fairly familiar to Father as he was out here in 1911 for a visit.

Mother had never been out west but had three brothers, William, Angus, Osborne, and a sister Edith (Mrs. Wm. Wannop) who all had homesteaded in the Parkland district. She also had two uncles, William and Tom Andrews, in the De Winton district. She had heard of the west from letters and when her brothers and sister came back east for visits.

When we arrived one morning in early July we had a chilly reception as the night before the only twenty-five acres of oats dad had planted for the year had been pounded into the ground by a hail storm. Mom's impression of the west was just as chilly as the air that morning, and it was quite awhile before she changed her mind.

Father was a dairy farmer in the east and a breeder of Holstein cattle. He brought two cows and four young stock as well as two horses in the car of settlers' effects. This was the start of his Holstein herd here in the west.

The Allan school was closed in 1916 due to lack of children, so Laura and I went to the Okotoks school. Later Laura got her teachers degree at the Normal School in Calgary. She first taught in the Hobart school in the Nanton district. She came back to teach in the Allan school when it was reopened, as more children were in the area again. She also taught in the Raymond district.

In 1939 Laura married Wilfred Lang and they farmed in the district until his death in 1971. Wilfred's parents were early residents of the district.

I went to school until 1919, there were many other things to occupy our minds in the high school that year. There were only two pupils who passed in the room of three grades 9, 10, and 11. In the fall most students were passed on recommendation. I preferred the open air rather than books so I went into the farming business with Father and Mother.

The following years were not all rosy, there were dry years and low prices.

I remember our first harvest in 1917. The fields were not as large then and we had no granaries in the field so it took as many grain teams as there were bundle teams. We also needed an extra man or two to scoop the grain from the wagons into the granaries. Generally one or two of the neighbors hauled a few loads of grain to the elevators to help pay the threshing bill. By 1920 we had bins in the field, perhaps not so handy in the winter, but much better in harvest time.

Our Holstein herd had also increased in size by 1920,

so Mother decided she should start making butter again, which she had done for years in the east. Soon we had a good butter and egg trade in town. I delivered them every Saturday morning. I believe when I finished delivering butter and eggs I should have gone into politics. It was almost impossible not to have a bit of off flavor in the butter at certain times of the year; in the spring there was the grass and later in the year it was the weed flavor. We always had to have a reason or just play dumb, it was good political training. Before too long we had more butter than we had customers and it was too much for Mother, so we started shipping to the creamery.

In the spring of 1929 Father and Mother decided to build a much needed new house. It was complete in November, and the first Saturday in December we moved into the new house. Our joy was short lived, for on Sunday morning when dad was leading the bull to water, he was attacked and killed.

Mother died in May of 1932. They both lived long enough to build and accomplish their dream of an established home and farm in the west.

Pearl Hogge and I were married January the 16th, 1934. We have one son, Douglas and four grandchildren. Douglas and family now live in Victoria, while Pearl and I are still on the farm.

DOMINION OF CANADA

NATIONAL REGISTRATION REGULATIONS, 1940

REGISTRATION CERTIFICATE

This certificate must always be carried upon the person of the registrant.

Electoral District No. 214 *Calgary East* (Name)

Polling Division No. 65 *Davisburg* (Name if any)

THIS IS TO CERTIFY THAT

Pearl Jane Riches

residing at *Okotoks*

Alt. was duly registered under the above-mentioned Regulations this 2? day of *Aug* 1940.

J. G. Norris

Deputy Registrar.

Signature of Registrant — *Pearl Jane Riches*

Before concluding these notes I would like to try and tell how the wives and mothers helped in those early days. Along with the family to care for there were always one or more hired men during the spring and summer, quite often you did his washing, ironing, and sometimes mending.

Then in the harvest in the early years, there were binder men and stookers, at least three for a spell of two weeks to a month depending on the weather. Even if the weather was wet, there were always meals to get, as we ate whether we were harvesting or not.

Then as the gas tractor became popular so did the smaller threshing outfits. About every fourth farmer owned an outfit.

Even if you had help in the house, you were up at 4:30 or 5 a.m. getting breakfast as the men were in the field at 6:30 or 7 a.m., when we expected straw to be going out on that straw pile.

Along with three meals you served, there was also coffee and a bit of a snack at 10:00 a.m. and at 3:30 p.m. Supper was always after 7:00 p.m. There was no such thing as sliced bacon or convenience mixes in those days, so you and your helper put in a 16 hour day during threshing. No wonder everyone was happy with the modern combine.

THOMAS ROWLES AND SON ANDREW
W½ 24-20-29-W4

Among the early settlers, who found homes for themselves, in the North-West was Thomas Rowles (Old Daddy Rowles). He came from the County of Wellington, Ontario, in 1882, and homesteaded two miles east of Okotoks. The family arrived the following year, May 24th, coming through the United States by way of St. Paul to Winnipeg and then on to Maple Creek. From there the trip was made by ox cart. All of which was quite a journey for a woman and twelve children.

In the following years the children settled in the Gladys Ridge and Okotoks districts. The only two living at present are Mrs. George Hoadley in Edmonton and Mrs. Charles Wakeford in Okotoks, but many of the fifth generation carry on the name and some still live in this district.

Son Andrew was born in Hollin, Ontario, February 5, 1869. Though only sixteen years of age at the time, Andrew drove a supply wagon between Calgary and Edmonton during the Riel Rebellion. Later he joined Major Ferry's company, a part of the 65th Regiment of Montreal. He only got as far as Batoche when the Rebellion ended.

Andrew worked for Billy Cochrane at the CC until late 1886. In 1888 he bought the Tillotson place across Sheep Creek where he farmed for several years. He also teamed on the "C and E" Railway grade during construction. Later he moved into Okotoks where he engaged in the livery and draying business. It is thought his was the first dray in town. In 1900 Andrew went into the hotel business with his father, running the Alberta Hotel then owned by John Lineham. In 1903 he and his father built the Royal Hotel. In 1891 Andrew married Sara Willis. They had one daughter, Mrs. Wallace Hurst, of Okotoks.

There were twelve children in the Thomas Rowles family: Andrew, Kansas, William, Lucinda (Mrs. Tom Rowles), Ella (Mrs. Greenwood), Maria (Mrs. O'Connor), Henry, Wesley, Emma (Mrs. Jack Bolton), Bertha (Mrs. Chas. Wakeford), Lily (Mrs. G. Hoadley), and Ida (Mrs. Noah Wakeford).

Taken from "Leaves from the Medicine Tree".

OTTO SALLENBACH

My wife, Ivy, and I and five of our seven children came from Rosemary, Alberta to the Allan School District in the fall of 1948. We bought the farm by the Sheep River being part of the north ½ of 30-20-28-W4. Located four miles east and half mile north of Okotoks.

Betty, the oldest, and Lloyd stayed in Rosemary. Shirley, Marlene, Ted, Howard and Beverly went to school in Okotoks.

Now going back a few years, my wife and I lived on a farm three miles east of Brant, Alberta, right after

Otto Sallenbach family: front row: Marlene, Shirley, Ivy, Beverly, Betty. Back row: Howard, Ted, Otto, Lloyd.

we were married. After a few years we moved to Three Hills, Alberta, to work in a garage. Later we moved to Calgary and in the spring of 1943 we went to Rosemary, where I owned and operated a used machine business until 1948.

Betty is married, has five children and is now living in California with her husband.

Lloyd is married, had four children and is living in Calgary operating a milk truck business.

Shirley is married has six children and lives in Raymond, Alberta, her husband is the principal of a school.

Marlene is married has five children and lives in Calgary, her husband owns and operates a children's shoe business.

Ted is married has four children and lives at Langley, B.C. and is Vice-President of a large American Finance Co.

Howard went to B.Y.U. at Provo, Utah, U.S.A. has his Master's Degree in Engineering and lives in Midland, Texas. He has two children.

Beverly is married has two children and lives at Kirkland, Washington, U.S.A. Her husband is with the Government Telephone Co.

My wife and I bought a home in Cardston in Oct. 1975. At Okotoks we had a grain and cattle farm.

ROBERT AND LAURA SALLENBACH — by Laura Bennett and Marian Wakeford

In 1904 a bearded gent by the name of Robert Sallenbach Sr. with his wife, Bertha, and five small children started up homesteading three miles east of Brant and three miles north of Ensign. They had immigrated to Canada from Zurich, Switzerland the year before. They knew very little English so their native tongue was spoken around home. They set up to build their farmstead near a small creek on the south side of their land. It was here that they increased their family to eighteen, twelve of them lived, among those who died in infancy were two sets of twins.

He was a very religious man and never failed to go to church no matter what the weather. He attended Frankburg Church. He was a hard driving man and

work came before schooling so the older children suffered from lack of education. To make ends meet he drove steam engines for other people for he was a locomotive engineer in Switzerland for fourteen years.

They slowly built a few buildings and planted a few trees and dug an artesian well which is still flowing to this day. He built a large turreted house similar to houses in the old country but the inside was never finished. As time went on the older children married and moved away to start families of their own.

In 1924 he sold a half section to J. J. Burk whose daughter married the oldest Sallenbach boy, Jacob, who in turn built a home here and lived for some time. Mr. and Mrs. Sallenbach moved to Cardston about this time taking four of the youngest children with them and these children had the benefit of a better education than the rest of the family.

They celebrated their golden wedding anniversary in 1942. Mrs. Sallenbach died in 1947 at age 75 and Mr. Sallenbach in 1956 at the age of 86.

After moving to Cardston some of the children took turns farming the remaining half section and a quarter on an adjoining section. During the 30's the half section was finally lost to creditors and all the sons moved away to greener pastures.

Robert Jr. was born May 20, 1906. While living in Cardston he met Laura Brown and they were married Jan. 5, 1927. He worked on a farm after his marriage then he moved to Ensign on his father's farm. Robert Jr. who must have had more stamina than the others stayed and built a two room house and some out buildings on the other quarter and moved his family in. Some years later he built two more rooms onto the house as the family had grown to eight. Times were very hard and money scarce and crops poor. He went to work as a section hand for the railway. So with help of friends and neighbors who came to the rescue many times we, with many others, got by. But putting up the struggle for some twenty years we eventually lost the land to creditors through no fault of our own. We gave up and moved to greener pastures.

In 1927 arriving at Ensign as a bride I looked around at the scenery as such and said "I'll never stay here." Well the story is I did.

The children are Leon, born Nov. 1, 1927, he married Lavern Irving at Barnwall Nov. 3, 1947, they live in Lethbridge. Lavone born July 9, 1929 married

Mrs. L. Sallenbach.   Mr. Bob Sallenbach.

The Bob Sallenbach family: Left to right back row: Grant, Gordon, Norma, Leon, Lavone. Front row: Marion, Audrey, Evelyn.

Kenney Pilling at Cardston Aug. 8, 1947, they live in Lethbridge. Norma born Oct. 9, 1931 married Fred Roth April 8, 1948 at Lethbridge, they live at Coalhurst. Marian was born Feb. 25, 1932 and married Fay Wakeford in Okotoks Nov. 17, 1950, they live in High River. Evelyn was born May 10, 1933 she married Lyle Sproule in Lethbridge Jan. 1951, they still live in Lethbridge. Audrey was born Sept. 9, 1934 and married Henry Wallace in Okotoks Aug. 23, 1955, they live in Calgary. Grant was born Aug. 14, 1935 and married Edith Ironside from Black Diamond Aug. 5, 1961, they live in Medicine Hat. Gordon was born Aug. 23, 1936 and married Donna Lawton from Ninette, Manitoba Dec. 11, 1965 and they live at Ft. Churchill, Manitoba.

Those greener pastures were at Okotoks. In 1946 we rented the Frank Bagshaw farm south west of Okotoks NW¼ 1-20-1-W5 for one year then moved to Paul Sallenbach's farm N½ 36-20-29-W4 working this land till 1949. We then moved one mile east to the Forckel farm in 1950 S½ 6 - NE¼ 6 - N½ - 5 - Part of SW½ of 5-21-28 W4 and renting this land until 1954. This farm was sold to Albert Sevigny. We then moved to Paul Sallenbach's second farm W½ 1-21-29-W4 across the road from the first farm, this farm was the sight of the old Allan School and the school was now remodeled into a farm shop and garage. We farmed this half section and another quarter a mile south owned by Paul SW¼ 36-20-29 W4. We left here in 1963 and bought a house in Okotoks. Robert was working out on a farm at the time of his death in an auto accident Feb. 3, 1965.

Laura remarried in 1974 to a childhood beau, Mr. Bert Bennett, now living at Delta B.C.

SHIELDS FAMILY HISTORY — by Evelyn Shields Cameron

Two brothers, Jack and Bob Shields, came west to the Davisburg district, taking adjoining homesteads in 1892. My Aunt Agnes Shields came west a few years later to marry her cousin, Bob Shields, bringing her mother, (my grandmother) to live with them. They retired in 1907 making their home in Okotoks.

Jack Shields married Elizabeth McLeod of Okotoks, and were the first couple married in the little Presbyterian Church (now torn down) in Okotoks. They had four children.

My parents, John and Grace Shields, were pioneers in the Sandstone Valley. My father worked for an uncle of mine, A. Serviss, who owned a small brick yard a few miles from the large sandstone brick yards.

In 1908, my parents, my sister, Mildred, and I spent a year on my Uncle Bob's farm, the Doctor thinking a year away from the brick dust would be beneficial to a lung condition of my father's.

I began my schooling at the Allan School. The teacher was Agnes Creighton, who later married Jack Lineham of Okotoks. The families I remember were the Allans, Herrs and Barkers.

JOHN ANDREW SHIELDS — written by (Bessie Shields) E. Bourque

John Andrew Shields arrived in the Okotoks district at age 18 in 1883. He was born in Lake Field, Ontario in 1865 (June).

He married Elizabeth, the youngest daughter of Sara and Alexander McLeod of Okotoks who had come from Meaford, Ontario to settle South of Okotoks.

He homesteaded in the Allan district, the quarter adjacent to the J. Aldridge land. His brother Bob Shields several years later (1886) homesteaded the Aldridge place.

Mr. and Mrs. John Shields, Mildred and Evelyn. About 1904.

Bob Shields and his wife Agnes died many years ago without issue.

John and Elizabeth lived on the homestead in the log house until 1911. From stories we've heard their lives were happy and interesting, but must have been hard. Trips to Calgary, Burns mine, Bar U Ranch, even to Okotoks with a team and wagon, or buggy or sleigh must surely have necessitated many hot bricks and blankets in the winter.

Elizabeth's health failed, and in 1911 they built a house in the West end of Okotoks and a grocery store and warehouse on the property where the Telephone office now stands. Elizabeth died in their home in Okotoks on February 4, 1912 age 36 years.

The store and warehouse burned in 1913. However John Shields was a much too generous and kindly person to have successfully operated a grocery business.

From that time on he devoted his life to his children, installing in them pride and initiation and religion. His example was above reproach. He died January 13, 1941 at his home in Okotoks age 76 years.

John and Elizabeth had five children: Geo. McLeod Shields, Cayley, deceased, Veteran, World War I. Five sons and one daughter. John E. A. Shields, Grand Prairie, deceased, Veteran, World War I, three sons and two daughters. Cecil Gordon Shields, died age 3 years, buried in the Davisburg church yard. Clarence W. Shields, Grand Prairie, deceased, three sons and one daughter. Elizabeth Helen Shields wife of George Bourque, Edmonton, two daughters, Mrs. D. M. Simmons and Mrs. A. B. Ages.

There were seventeen grandchildren, fifteen of whom are living, five are veterans of the second World War and the Korean War. At the last count there are 57 great-grandchildren and six great-great-grandchildren.

Some were scamps, none were tramps. Several are making names for themselves in music, art, education, business and farming. Gary Shields has the old original brand at his farm in Cayley.

John Shields and Elizabeth McLeod, truly did make their contribution to Alberta and Western Canada.

GEORGE PACEY SMITH — by Mrs. A. S. Towle

Mr. George Pacey Smith was born in Kentore, Ontario June 27, 1869. He was an early - day haberdashery proprietor in Woodstock and Ingersoll, Ontario. He married Margret Lowery, daughter of H. P. Lowery of Napanee, Ontario, who worked at building furniture for Gibbard's Furniture Co., in Napanee. Mr. Smith and Mrs. Smith had a little boy Harry and a little girl Hazel, both born while they lived at Napanee, Ontario.

In June 1899 he accompanied (Libbie) Eilizabeth Jane McMurray to Calgary to meet Wm. C. Bryce who had sent for her to come. He also at that time, June 17, stood up with Mr. Bryce while Reverend Herdman's wife Mrs. Herdman stood up with Libbie McMurray. George Smith was Libbie's first cousin.

Mr. Smith at this time did not have the best of health as he was inside too much and the doctor told him, he had to be out more in the fresh air. He must have fell in love on this trip up here with Alberta as he returned with his family in 1901 and bought the whole section 1-21-29-W4. seven miles from Okotoks and one mile south of the farm that Mr. and Mrs. Bryce owned 18-21-28-W4. Wm. C. Bryce also built the Smith's a house on their farm. It still stands today.

Mr. and Mrs. Smith's youngest daughter, Ruberta, was born in this house in 1905. She is now Mrs. A. S. Towle and she and her husband are now retired, also she is now the only one of the family alive.

G. Pacey and Margaret Smith, top Hazel Mildred (Smith) Fox, Harry Earnest, Ruberta Elizabeth (Smith) Towle.

Mr. Smith sold out the farm in 1907 and moved out to the Coast where he went into the shingle mill business. In 1916 he sold out his business and decided to go back farming, buying a farm at Jardine where he farmed until 1930. Then he sold out and retired and moved to Maxwell Crescent, Milner, B.C. where he lived until he passed away in his 88th year.

He was a constant member of the Langley branch of the Old Age Pensioners Organization and an elder and member of the board of Milner United Church.

Mr. Smith had the misfortune, when a young boy, to fall off the roof of a building on to a scythe which was lying on the ground. He cut his knee on it. This gave him blood poison and he nearly lost his leg. This however left him with a bad limp and fortunately his leg.

Mr. Smith was also executor of his cousin Libbie's husband, Wm. Bryce's will.

CLARENCE STAGER

I was born on December 11, 1910 at Calgary, the oldest son of Morris and Alice Stager. All of my early years were spent in the Red Cross School District near Vulcan and like most other boys at that time I went to school, rode horses and followed father's footsteps giving a "helping hand". I'm afraid often being more "in the road" than anything else but mostly the days passed quickly.

There are a few things I remember quite clearly. Dad had a runaway with a drill. His seed grain was in a bin out in the field and he was filling the drill from the bin. One of the Dexter boys rode up, the horses spooked and all six of them took off across the field with the drill. This happened while Dad was in the bin. You can well imagine the condition of the drill and harness when they were caught — they were at the farthest end of the field.

The other incident is my falling off a horse and breaking my arm.

After Dad's death, I farmed the Gordon place for a number of years until, in 1940, a move was made to a farm at Okotoks S½-13-21-29-W4. In the fall of 1949, I decided to go farther north and acquired land at Dapp, north of Edmonton, possibly sixty or so miles.

I was having considerable trouble with a skin allergy so after a lot of hard work, clearing, etc. I held a sale in the fall of 1958 spending the winter around Vancouver. The skin allergy cleared up so I again wanted to farm. In the spring of 1959, I settled at Enderby, B.C. and went into the dairy business. This was sold and I bought just a few acres in the same district. In the fall of 1967, I sold this too. That fall, a camper truck became my home and I did some traveling. I took in Expo at Montreal and then went farther East to Newfoundland, then on down the east coast of the U.S.A. I spent the winter in the southern States arriving back in Canada in late March of 1968. In July of that year, I took off to the north and travelled with my camper all through Yukon and Alaska. It was my first trip to the far north and I thoroughly enjoyed my holiday.

Since returning, I bought a house on First Avenue in East Vancouver and live here at the present time.

In August 1973 I took off for a month tour of the South Pacific. I visited Fiji, New Zealand and Australia. In October 1974 I married Ruby Sarah (Blackemore) Pritchell 88 Melbourne St., Abermain, N.S.W., Australia.

My mother was Alice Irving, daughter of John Irving, who had come from Cardinal, Ontario in 1888 and settled at Davisburg. Mother and her brother and sisters rode to Calgary which was 25 miles away. Mother rode side saddle on a small buckskin pony that her dad got from an Indian tribe for a dead cow. The fresher the cow was, the better the horse was, so he only got a cayuse. He was named Claude and lived to be 34 years old.

As a small child Mother remembers the Indians coming into the house without saying a word, just to squat by the wall. Her mother, Mrs. Irving, just went on with her work. They had a large 2 to 3 gallon jug in which they made vinegar. She kept the jug out of sight as the Indians thought it was fire water.

I keep thinking of things that happened that Mother and Dad had told us about. When I was born in Calgary I was quite sickly and Grandma Irving insisted that Mother would nurse me but she thought otherwise. She went out and bought bottles and nipples and prepared to take me to the farm at Vulcan. The closest train service was at High River or Gleichen, so arrangements were made and Dad met her at High River with the team and sleigh in which he had put a stove to keep them warm during the thirty miles home. I did quite well on cow's milk. Dad saved it from one cow. This cow raised the six children in the family. I can remember the day they sold her. Even if she was getting old we hated to see her go.

STARKE FAMILY *

William Wilson Starke, the seventh child in a family of eight, was born in 1902 in the state of Washington.

Bill and his family moved to their homestead thirteen miles south east of Coronation in the spring of 1910.

On March 17, 1926 Bill married Mary Louise Stone, the only child of Agnes and Stephen Stone who had come from Syracuse, New York, in 1918 to homestead at Whatcheer, Alberta. Whatcheer was a settlement eighteen miles south of Coronation.

Bill and Louise had five children, Wallace, Lola, Raymond, Ralph, and Bob. The only ones really known to this district are Wallace and Ralph.

Bill was known as a dealer almost from day one, along with farming and also running a store and post office at Spondin in the earlier days, then he went on to having his own commission business in Calgary from 1945 to 1952. Bill then went into horse ranching east of Spondin, he stayed living in Calgary and drove back and forth, so, after three years he sold his horse ranch to buy two quarter sections in the Okotoks district.

In 1955 Bill bought the N.E. ¼ 9-21-29-W4 known at that time as the Hawthorne quarter. Wallace and his family moved on to this quarter doing the farming and a bit of trucking as well. Wallace was no newcomer to the district as he had run the Aldersyde Corner Service Station for six years. Wally had five children Judy, David, Larry, Bonnie, and Kenny. The older children started school in Okotoks before moving to Cayley in 1961.

In 1958 Bill bought the S.E. ¼ 5-21-29-W4 known as the Gordon Giffen quarter. Ralph and his family moved onto this quarter, farming it together with his Dad.

Bill was one of the pioneers of sub-division in this district as in 1959 he sub-divided the Giffen quarter into acreages and started selling them. Peris Jones was one of the first to buy one of these acreages and he is still living on this land.

In 1961 Bill sold the Hawthorne quarter to Charlie Gordon, it was sold as a full quarter section.

Bill and Louise Starke, 1976.

119

Shortly after Bill came to the district in 1955 he saw the need for a feeder's association, so he got together with a few others like Jock Noble, Jack Meston and many others who were interested and the Okotoks Feeder's Association was formed. Bill was put in as supervisor and held that position for twenty years until this association was dissolved in 1976.

Bill and Louise still reside at 628 — 75 Avenue S.W. Calgary.

HERB STEPHENSON FAMILY — by Herb Stephenson

Herb was born on his grandfather's farm six miles east of High River, and was raised on a farm six miles south of High River, attending school at Last Chance, Highview, Cayley, and Vancouver. He enlisted with the Calgary Highlanders and went overseas with this regiment in 1940. In England he met and married Billie Searle. Returning from overseas with a daughter, Terry, and son Dave, they settled in the East Longview district before moving on to the farm near Davisburg — land location S.W. 14-21-28-W4 in 1950.

The farm was known as the "Todd" place, although it was homesteaded by a man named Greenfield in 1885, and the main part of the house was built of log in 1886. When Herb was putting a cement block chimney up the outside of the house and cut a place through the eves to the well, he found old newspapers and a Deering machine catalogue dated 1880. These were so old and brittle they went to ashes when handled.

A daughter Paula, and a son Dan, were born during the time the family lived on the farm. At that time the roads were still dirt roads and practically impossible to travel on when it rained as those were wet years. During the summer of 1950 there was a bad hailstorm, and many houses in the district lost windows, crops and gardens were ruined. The family had been on a picnic to Millarville with Doris and Forest Herr, and upon returning to Forest Herr's place we had to borrow a team and wagon to travel home as the roads were so muddy that no car could travel on them.

Terry took nurse's training at the Holy Cross Hospital, and later married Dr. Gary Carter, a veterinarian in the district. They took up residence on the old "Todd" farm and still live there. They have two sons, Jay and Kyle.

Dave rode bulls at the rodeos and did quite well, but gave this up upon joining the R.C.M.P. He married Terry Alsip who lived in the De Winton area after coming to the west from Winnipeg. They are now stationed in Sturgis, Sask. They have three children, Tammy, Rod, and Clay.

Paula took Early Childhood Education at Grant McEwan College in Edmonton, and is presently working at the college in that area.

Dan is attending University in Calgary, and he and his dad are still raising shorthorns on the 40 acres west of the old farm.

Herb is presently Postmaster in the Okotoks Post Office and has been working in that capacity since 1958, while Billie commutes to Calgary daily working as a secretary.

MR. AND MRS. DAVE STINSON — by Muriel Stinson

David Thomas Stinson, born in North Dakota May 15th, 1888, came to Saskatchewan and homesteaded at Buffalo Head in 1911.

Edna Marian Mooney, born June 22, 1900, of London, Ontario, married David Stinson in 1922, and they lived on his homestead at Old Buffalo Head, a town which is no more, because when the railroad came through, Hilda, the closest town and Post Office, became prominent.

In 1931, due to illness, the family moved to Richmond for three years, and they left the drought area in 1934. There being absolutely no money in that country, anyone able to, left then. Stinsons had three children then: Kathleen — nine years, Lloyd — six years and Douglas — two and a half years of age.

The Stinsons had a little advantage in that when things got hard, Mrs. Stinson taught school. When opportunity came to rent one quarter section in the Okotoks district, they took advantage of it. They lived on the Worden place between Cliff Herrs and the Gibbards. All welcomed the sight of plenty of green grass and trees after the dried grass of the prairies. During the time they lived there, they had wonderful neighbours; the children rode horseback three miles to Allan School. In 1946 they moved into the town of Okotoks, and lived there until 1951 when they moved to Calgary.

After the children grew up, Kay took Bible School and nurses training, married Dick Goss and served as a missionary in Ethiopia. Lloyd graduated from Bible School and served as a missionary in Ethiopia where he married Muriel Bouck. Doug married Ruth Williams and took over the Williams farm near Vulcan. Kay and Dick live with their children in Washington and Doug and Lloyd and families live in Calgary.

Dave Stinson passed away October 20th, 1973. Edna Stinson lives at the Southwood Nursing Home, 211 Heritage Drive S.E., Calgary.

MIKE AND ANNA SOVC (SHOLTS) — by Harold Biswanger

Mike was born in Czechoslovakia December 26, 1891. They had one daughter who stayed in Czechoslovakia. Mike came to Canada in 1928 and worked in construction in Ontario with a friend, Joe Murrin, who later farmed a half mile north of Okotoks.

Mike moved to Tilley in 1929 and took a quarter section of irrigated land as did Joe Murrin.

Mike sent for his wife, Anna, in Czechoslovakia in 1930 to join him. He later increased his land to a half section, then sold out in 1948, and moved to the Okotoks area. He was located 3½ miles east of town in Allan school district, and farmed a half section, S½ 25-T20-R29-W4

George Karman, a neighbor from Tilley, also moved to a farm 4 miles south of Okotoks. George did some harvesting for Mike in later years.

Mike made a regular supply of fruit whiskey for himself and would often treat his friends and neighbors to some. Bill Crupechuck, who rented land north of Mike and worked for Joe Murrin later moved to British Columbia and sent well ripened fruit back by rail for Mike to brew. The fruit would often be dripping out of the crates and the station agent wondered what he was going to use messed up fruit for.

Mike and Anna did not believe in banking money and often hid it in places around the farm. One day when George Karman was working for Mike his truck broke down and Mike told him to push it into the garage and light a fire in the heater to warm up the garage as the weather was turning cold. As George was stuffing paper in the heater to start the fire he felt a glass jar, and pulled it out to find it full of money. He called to Mike, who said he had forgotten all about it and was glad George had noticed it for when they counted it out there was $4,800 in the jar.

Another time George and his family were visiting with Mike and Anna and one of the girls came running to mother with a $100.00 bill, that she had found in the front yard. They all went to see and found the dog shaking and dragging an old purse around and scattering bills all over the place. After gathering them all up they had $6,000.00. Anna had hid the old purse under the front steps and the dog had found it.

One very cold day in the winter of 1958 when it was 15 below with a stiff breeze blowing, I had been to the doctor's with my bad back and was driving home when the gas line froze so I stopped and tried to fix it near Mike's gate. I crawled under the truck and disconnected the gas line and blew through it but the connector came off the tank through the truck floor so I stuck my finger in the hole while I tried to blow the line out. Gas leaked down my arm and soaked my shoulder and chest. After getting it back together it still would not start and as I was nearly frozen with the gas soaked clothes I walked to Mike's farm a little over a quarter a mile away. I had always heard that because Anna could not speak English you could not get in her house if Mike was not there. I knocked at the door and started to walk in and she passed me coming out, shouting for Mike as I was trying to explain.

Mike came in and immediately set chairs around the pot bellied stove in the front room and started to hang my gas soaked clothes on the chairs. I said "Mike they're soaked in gas." He said "Oh my Gosh" and instantly took them off the chairs.

Anna came in with whiskey and sandwiches. I phoned my neighbor Pat McCarthy to go to my home and get me some clothes and come and tow my truck home.

Mike and Anna sold out in 1962 and rented a house in Okotoks and later bought a house. They went back to Czechoslovakia for three months then lived in Okotoks until Mike died in 1968, at the age of 77. Anna now lives in a nursing home in Calgary.

MR. AND MRS. TODD — by Dwight Barrett (nephew)
Mrs. Laura (Barrett) Todd born at Warren, Illinois, October 14, 1876. Moved with the Barrett family to Elmwood, Nebraska. She passed away at Platsmouth, Nebraska August 26, 1943. Interment, West Lawn Cemetery, Omaha.

Mr. John Payne Todd born at Omaha, Nebraska January 8, 1870 passed away near Platsmouth, Nebraska October 18, 1948. Interment, West Lawn Cemetery, Omaha.

Mr. and Mrs. Todd came from Nebraska to

Todd house on Greenfield farm bought in 1910.

Okotoks, Alberta in 1910 with Mrs. Todd's brothers Ray Barrett who farmed for 2 years south of Okotoks and Lynn Barrett of Aldersyde who lived there until his passing in 1962. Ray and family returned to the U.S.A. in 1913.

Mr. and Mrs. Todd had an auction sale in 1928 and stayed for sometime with Mr. and Mrs. Barrett at Aldersyde, where Mr. Todd did the gardening and some light chores. They lived in Calgary and Long Beach, California before returning to Nebraska about 1940. Mr. Todd had several relations in and around Platsmouth, Nebraska.

Laura and John Todd.

121

Mr. Todd owned E½ 17-21-29-W4, S½ 14-21-29-W4, SW¼ 13-21-29-W4, NW¼ 11-21-29-W4, this land was purchased in 1910 from John Greenfield who had homesteaded it in the 1880's.

NE¼ 11-21-29-W4, school land rented by Todd's and sold by the Government to L. W. Barrett at public auction sale November 13, 1928. Given to granddaughter Betty Jean (Barrett) Hemus by will in 1962.

The SE¼ 17-21-29-W4 was sold to Mr. and Mrs. Alex Hislop about 1940. Mr. Hislop sold it to Mr. and Mrs. Dave Lewis and now owned by Tom Hebson who purchased it at the Dave Lewis Auction Sale.

The NE¼ 17-21-29-W4 was rented out for some years and acquired by Betty Jean (Barrett) Hemus in 1950 and sold to Dave Lewis, this was sold by the Lewis Estate and is now subdivided.

The SE¼ 14-21-29-W4 was rented out after Mr. and Mrs. Todd retired until 1950 when it was sold by the Todd Estate Executors to Mr. Herb Stephenson. Mr. and Mrs. Todd lived on the NW¼ 11-21-29-W4 for some years before selling to Forest Herr.

The SW¼ 13-21-29W4 was sold to Mr. Gibbard.

MR. AND MRS. HENRY TYNDALL AND FAMILY —
written by Ethel A. Korth (Granddaughter) *

My grandparents and four of their seven children resided in the Allan School District of the De Winton area between 1918 and 1926.

My grandfather, Henry Tyndall, was born in Wicklow County, Ireland, October 25, 1860, the son of William Peter Tyndall and Martha Alice Johnson. In 1870 the family emigrated to America and settled in Minnesota.

My grandmother, Nellie Viola Reid, was born December 29, 1870 at Austin, Minnesota, the eldest of three children of William Reid and Sarah Nokes.

Henry (a blacksmith by trade) and Nellie (a school teacher of English ancestry) were married August 22, 1890 and moved to Canada in 1902 with their children Grace Maude, Henry Eugene, William Peter, Alice Martha, Leander Isaac and Howard Gavin. They homesteaded near Cudworth, Saskatchewan where Lloyd Herbert, (died at two years of age) and Sarah Ethel, were born.

Homesteading had its trials and tribulations. Henry Tyndall was in ill health much of the time and much of the workload was passed to his young sons. William, (Bill) served in the army during World War I. Though Nellie had her family to care for she still had time to help any in need and was remembered as "an angel of mercy" by many of the community.

In April, 1918, with their unmarried children, they moved to the Allan School District near Okotoks. Their new home was the former Joe Cassidy place at 8-21-29-W4. Though Grandpa's health continued to fail, he took great pride in his cattle and horses. Grandpa relied on Lea, (until his death in the 1918 flu epidemic) and Gavin, to carry on with the farming and care of his cattle. Gavin laughingly recalls bartering with James (Scotty) Vert for a colt. His anticipated saddle horse ended up as a bucking horse and was soon traded to Copes for "Betty", a horse that quickly became the family favorite.

Intervening years had seen Alice return to

Mr. and Mrs. Henry Tyndall, daughter, Ethel.

Saskatchewan to marry Ed Billesberger and she died at Cudworth in 1930. Bill returned from the war to spend a short stay with the family before also returning to Cudworth where he married Ida Lee and resided for a time before returning to Alberta. The oldest son, Gene, had preceded the family to Alberta and settled at Stavely where he married Carrie Parks. My parents had also decided to move to Alberta and settled a few miles away from Grandpa's farm on the old Hedley place. (see KORTH family account)

The trading centre for the Tyndall family was Okotoks, and Ethel rode there to attend school until the family moved to Calgary in 1926.

Grandpa Tyndall died at the family home in Calgary September 23, 1926 and is buried in the Okotoks Cemetery where Lea was also buried. Grandma continued to live in Calgary with her daughter Ethel until her death February 16, 1936. She is also buried in the family plot at Okotoks.

Gavin delivered mail from Penhold to Pine Lake from 1928 to 1932 and married Florence Henderson of Penhold. They resided in Calgary where Gavin was a lather for near forty years. He and his wife now live in retirement at their home on Bowness Road in Calgary. They have three children: Beverly (Mrs. Lonnie Anderson) and Gail (Mrs. Julius Lister) both of

Calgary, and Don of Vancouver, three granddaughters and two grandsons.

Ethel, the only other member of the immediate family still living, married Jerry Williams of Calgary. They have lived in England, Prince Rupert, and now reside at Duncan, British Columbia. They have a daughter Sharon (Mrs. Bob Colyn) and two grandsons.

My mother, Grace, married Jake Korth and prior to her death in 1970 resided in Lethbridge. She is survived by three sons, five daughters, fifteen grandchildren and fourteen great-grandchildren.

Gene and his wife, Carrie, farmed near Rimbey until his death June 28, 1966. A son, Howard, resides on the farm with his family of three daughters.

Bill and his wife Ida returned to Alberta where Bill worked in construction as a plasterer in Calgary and surrounding area until his death June 9, 1947. A daughter Jewel (Mrs. John Dicks) and a son, Basil, live in Toronto, and Violet (Mrs. Paul Lintereur) lives in Rhode Island.

ALLAN WARD

In 1949 when my dad and mother retired from farming and moved to Calgary, I took over the farm. (NE¼ 34-20-29-W4) the place where I was born and raised, to continue on with farming. It was in 1949 that I married Marion Williamson. In the years following, we had two children, a son Larry, and a daughter Doris. During my school years, my sister Hilda, brother Gordon and I attended the Allan School for a few years, and then later going to the Okotoks School.

One incident that I recall whilst attending the Allan School, was the time when the class was on a "nature study" trip, collecting bird's eggs. Jim Miller was elected to climb the tree in which there was a magpie's nest. Our teacher, Mr. MacGougan, surrounded by his students, was catching the eggs in his hat as Jim dropped them down. All went well, until teacher was looking down to the ground where an egg had fallen, and just at that time Jim dropped another egg — ker plunk! right down the neck of the teacher. Everyone, but the teacher, thought it was quite a joke.

Another incident during a "nature study" trip, was the time when the teacher tried to prove to the students that one would not get "scented up" by a skunk if the tail of said animal was kept down. Thus, while the students probed a skunk from a culvert, Mr.

MacGougan, who at the other end was armed with a long stick in order to keep the tail down. Well, evidently the scheme didn't work as teacher had to stand on a chair on the outside of the school, near a window to conduct the lessons.

THE WARDS — by Gordon Ward

The home quarter NE¼ 34-20-29-W4 was homesteaded by John McKinnon who acquired title in 1888. He sold to John William Sharer of Clovis, California, for $800 in 1904. He in turn sold to John Russell in 1907, who never resided on the land and who died May 16, 1917 in Pardeeville, Wisconsin, bequeathing the land to his wife, Sarah, and son, Kemper, of Cambria, Wisconsin. Douglas Ward purchased the land from the Russells for $3,500 in 1918.

Douglas Ward was born in Ditcheat, Somerset, England on July 14, 1892, the second last of the nineteen children of Christopher and Sarah Ward. Is it any wonder that they didn't give him a second name at baptism? Disgruntled with his job as a chauffeur, he immigrated to Canada in 1913 to Turner Valley area and worked at various farming and ranching jobs until his acquisition of the home quarter. He attempted to enlist in the Canadian Army during World War I but was refused on the basis that he had already lost his father and four brothers in that conflict.

Wedding bells rang for Doug and Gwynneth Kathleen Aldridge on May 20, 1918. Gwen was the second oldest of the six children of Jessie and Lillian Aldridge and was born in Cheltenham, Gloucestershire, England, November 12, 1898. The Aldridge family immigrated to Canada in the spring of 1913, first settling in Salmon Arm, B. C. After a year they moved to Alberta and spent about one year at Kirkaldy, 2 years at the Smith farm east of Okotoks and 2 years at Big Rock before establishing permanent residence on the "home quarter" SW¼ 2-21-29-W4, which corners on the Ward home quarter.

In 1929 Doug and Gwen purchased the NE¼ 35-20-29-W4 from William Henry Cole. Both of the Wards' quarters of land were essentially all dense bush and poplar land. The home quarter was cleared and broken solely by man and horse power but Patterson's steamer helped with the Cole quarter.

Like most farms in the area, the Ward farm was a mixed farming operation and as the great drought of the 1930's did not cause a complete crop failure, food was generally ample. However, hail storms in the middle and late '30s were very severe, particularly the one in 1935 which completely destroyed all grain crops. Hail storms in the subsequent years left some grain crop, and the salvage of some feed to augment the usually prolific hay crop for the livestock. Memories of the prolonged diet of "suet pudding" during those difficult times will remain forever.

One person who worked on the Ward farm will ever be fondly remembered by them, the neighbours and his many friends in the Okotoks area. Albert Elsdon, born in Durham, England in 1900, was with the Ward family almost continuously for the period 1934 through 1939. During those days of high unemployment, the Provincial Government paid $5 per month toward any farmer keeping a worker on the farm during the winter

Allan Ward and first prize Beef Club calf 1935-36.

months, provided said farmer gave him food and lodging in exchange for doing winter chores. In the fall of 1939, Albert enlisted with the Canadian Army and went overseas with the 49th Regiment at the end of the year. He spent the balance of the war years overseas, returning to Edmonton to work for the Provincial Government. He retired in 1965 and he and his wife, Vi, continue to reside in Edmonton.

Mechanization came to the Ward farm in 1941 with the purchase of their first tractor and a combine, one of the early combines in the area. It was a great crop that year but it was completely flattened by early wet snows. As swathing was not the practice at that time, the harvest was a very long, tedious "one-way" operation.

During his years on the farm Doug Ward was very active in community affairs, politics, the Masonic Lodge, school boards, St. Peters Anglican Church, the Okotoks High River Band and particularly in curling, being one of the founders of the most popular Farmers Bonspiel. He had a brief career as a golfer at Bowness Golf and Country Club. It was there that he discovered the expense of scoring a hole-in-one. The custom then was not merely to buy a round for the house, but to continue doing so until closing time.

Doug and Gwen retired to Calgary in the spring of 1949 where they were very active with flower gardening, winning several prizes in civic competition. In 1956 they moved to Royal Oak (Victoria) where Gwen resides in good health and very active with gardening. Doug's ashes rest at Royal Oak Burial Park since his death January 12, 1967.

The Wards raised three children, Hilda Kathleen born in 1920, Allan Maurice born in 1923 and Gordon

Douglas born in 1929. Hilda married Eric Russell Williamson in 1941 at Armstrong, B.C., where the Williamson family had moved to from the NW¼ 33-20-29-W4 in 1938. Hilda and Eric bought a farm there and have been dairying ever since. They have six children. Frederick, born in 1943, married Bonnie Morrison of Vancouver in 1967, and they reside in Armstrong with their three children. Fred has his own construction firm, Williamson Construction. The second son, Eric, born in 1945, married Barbara Naumann of Tilkerod, Germany, in 1971. They live in Armstrong with their two girls and where Eric owns Williamson Plumbing. David was born in 1950 and married Barbara Reidlinger of Calgary in 1969. David works for Riverside Lumber at Enderby, but lives in Armstrong with Barbara and their two children. June, born in 1951, married R.C.M.P. Corporal Beverly Dodd, a native of Olds. They presently live in Kelowna with their two children. Two more sons, Stephen, born in 1959 and Robert, born in 1961, live at home, Stephen working for his brother Eric and Robert attending school. Eric and Hilda and all of their children have been most active organizers and participants in 4-H affairs.

Allan continues to farm the old Ward property and the details concerning his wife Marion and their children appear elsewhere in this book.

Gordon, who holds the Allan School record for most strappings in one day (13, courtesy of Mac McGougan) married Dorothy Vern Gasper of Hanna in 1951. They have except for brief assignments in Regina and Edmonton, lived contiunuously in Calgary, where Gordon has worked in oil and gas exploration and since 1965, as President of a small exploration and producing company, Discovery Minerals Ltd. They have three children. Bryan, born in 1952, is presently interning at Victoria Hospital in London, Ontario. He married Barbara Burnworth of Calgary in 1976. Susan, born in 1955 is an animal health tecnhnologist and works for a Calgary veterinary clinic. Joanne, born in 1959, is in Grade 12 at Henry Wise Wood and aiming at a career in journalism.

A. H. AND MARY (CAMERON) WATHEN *

Alfred Herbert Wathen was born near London,

Mrs. Ward, Hilda and Doug Ward.

Mrs. Joe Alfred Wathen (Mary Cameron) and her daughter Minnie Bell taken 1910.

124

Alfred Wathen N.W.M.P.

Mr. and Mrs. John D. Wedderburn, wedding picture, 1943.

England in 1863. As a young man he came to Toronto. There he joined The North West Mounted Police. Took his training at Regina and Fort Macleod and was stationed at Okotoks from 1885 to 1890. He married Mary Cameron the daughter of Kenneth Cameron in 1890. Seen service in the North West Rebellion, after his service he received a silver medal from Queen Victoria. He took up land south of Okotoks S.E. 35-twp. 19-r1-w5 mer. his brand was +6 right ribs on cattle and left hip on horses. His brand was registered in 1897.

They had nine children, (Minie born 1893 deceased); (Herb born 1894 was in 137 Battalion in the first world war for a period of four years now deceased); Elizabeth born 1895 deceased); William born 1898 now lives in High River); (Harry born in 1900 now lives in Okotoks); (Annie Mrs. D. Gerlitz Balzac); (Robert born 1906); (Jane born 1914 deceased); (Rose born 1916 deceased).

They farmed until his retirement in 1928 when he moved to Okotoks. His wife died in 1920. She was 45 years old. He died in 1943 age 80 years.

MR. AND MRS. JOHN D. WEDDERBURN — by Mrs. J. (Pat) Wedderburn *

We moved here in November 1945, after John received his discharge from the Royal Canadian Air Force.

I was born and raised in Okotoks, the youngest child of Mr. and Mrs. Harold Banister, pioneers in Davisburg and written about in another part of this book. For many years I was organist in the Okotoks United Church.

John grew up at East Longview, and moved with his parents Mr. and Mrs. Dave Wedderburn, to a farm one mile north of Okotoks in 1938. His grandfather, Frank Watt, helped build the first steel bridge at Davisburg, also Christ Church in Millarville.

John was in the Militia in Okotoks in 1941 and joined the R.C.A.F. as an aero-engine mechanic in June 1942. He was in the Air Force for three and a half years, fourteen months of that time being spent in Iceland, and the rest of it in Nova Scotia.

We were married in July 1943 and have two children. Marie, the oldest, who taught school for a few years at Eckville, is now living at Bonnyville and teaching six miles away at Fort Kent. David, who married Maureen Zeran from Finch, Ontario, in July 1974, now works and lives in Calgary.

Our first few years here, we had to fight bad roads both in summer and in winter. In summer it was bogged down in mud as there was no gravel on it, in winter we were often stranded for several days, or even weeks, as there was no school bus coming on our road at that time so the snow plow didn't come very often.

I remember one time in particular when there was to be a big carnival at the arena in Okotoks which we were anxious to attend. John and Tom Hebson shovelled all day long so we could get out. By the time they had finished they were really too tired to go. As it happened it was a good thing we stayed home as in the evening there was a blizzard and the road was blocked again. In fact many country people were stranded in Okotoks after the carnival. The pictures show what our road looked like before and after the snow plow came following a bad storm in March 1951.

When Marie was a baby I remember we couldn't get out any way, except with a team of horses, for a few weeks. We got our groceries and canned milk for her formula from Mel Heyes who had a little store at his house just off the highway at the end of our road. Also John's father would bring the feed for the livestock up the highway, and John would meet him at the end of the road with wagon and team, where they would have to shovel the feed down the truck to the wagon.

For several years John was president of the Allan Mutual Telephone Company until it was taken over by A.G.T.

Our land location is NW ¼ 8-21-29-W4 and PTN NE 7-21-29-W4. For many years the buildings on our farm were at the south end and since there was no road out to the highway, the residents had to go through Mr. and Mrs. Jim Hogge's (Lorne's) yard to get to the highway.

Some former owners of our farm were John Arnold (1901-1904) (taken from Tales and Trails) Cassidy, Tyndall, Gross, Art Anderson, Broman (who moved the buildings up to where we live) and Herbig.

On our place is a Dominion of Canada Geological Stone which was placed there, I believe, in 1928, and shows that this is a "height of land". Many times we have surveyors come to take readings from that stone. The altitude there is 3,835.5 feet above sea level.

WALTER & VAL WILDE

After spending the first ten years of our married life working as a couple in the Carseland district we managed to make a small down payment on a section of land in the Okotoks-Davisburg district, formerly owned by Frank Coyle and farmed by Cecil Barker. We moved there in the spring of 1941 and started farming operations with very little equipment and less money, but with a certain amount of good luck, hard work and the help and co-operation of many good neighbors, we managed to struggle through the first few years and found it possible to afford such extravagances as a power washing machine and a tractor driven mower. We were on our way enjoying life in a friendly and sociable neighborhood.

In 1959 we rented the land to Melvin Christensen and went into a partnership on the livestock. The arrangement worked very well until we sold the farm in 1966.

We then bought a house in High River where we are enjoying an interesting retirement.

MR. AND MRS. FRANK WILLIAMS — written by George Riches

Mr. and Mrs. Frank Williams came here from Kansas in 1912. They bought the north-west quarter 3-21-29-W4, previously owned by Sirus Eberley.

They were real westerners, always ready and willing to help in the district in any way. Mr. Williams worked with his brother, who was a veterinarian, in Kansas. Veterinarians were few and far between in those days so Mr. Williams' help and advice were very much appreciated. He brought some of his equipment with him, so he did anything from filing horses teeth to prescribing a cure for bloat in cattle or colic in horses.

At the time the road allowance was not opened to their place so they went through our yard. This was nice for us, as we always got each other's mail and this meant a visit as well. I remember when Mr. Williams would bring the mail he would also bring the latest news from town. If he had been in Harry Barnes and Mrs. Kerans store the news was always much more up to date and witty than that published in any newspaper.

The Williamses assisted in organizing the country club in 1915 as the house parties were getting too big for the houses, so a hall had to be rented in town. The first hall rented was over the Richie and Allan Hardware, which was on the corner where the Royal Bank is now. This hall burned in the winter of 1917. The club then rented the hall in the Lineham block. Mr. and Mrs. Williams always had a joke to tell and had a way of keeping the parties in a jovial mood, they could always see the funny side of life.

Mrs. Williams' three brothers, Larry, Wendle, and Percy Riley, came here shortly after they did. Wendle worked for a time in the Merchants Bank. He later went farming with his two brothers at Rockyford.

In the fall of 1920 the Williams sold their farm to Ervie Miller. They moved to the house at the foot of Sawyer's Hill, known as the Johnson house. Mr. Williams was employed by the municipality for the next two years. In 1922 they moved to Calgary but returned to Okotoks in 1931.

Mr. Williams died in 1935 leaving Mrs. Williams and a daughter Kay who finished her schooling in Okotoks. Mrs. Williams died in 1943. Kay then moved to Calgary where she met and married E. A. Hagel and later moved to Conrad, Montana.

JARVIS WORDEN

Jarvis Worden, the great-great-grandfather of Helen Worden Adams came from Westchester, N.Y. to Saint John, N.B. in May 1783 with the United Empire Loyalists.

Mrs. Adams' father, Winslow Ernest Worden, came out from Saint John to Calgary in 1884 at the age of sixteen. He and his brother, Hiram Worden, owned a grocery and confectionery business on 8th Avenue and 1st Street East (Stephen Avenue) from 1887 to 1897. He wrote considerable history of the early days in Calgary, but nothing about buying the farm in the Allan School district.

However, the original title on NW ¼ 13-21-29-W4 was in the name of Winslow Ernest Worden and bears the following:

"I ceritify that the within instrument is duly entered and registered in the Land Titles office for the South Alberta Land Registration District of Calgary in the N.W.T. at 10:05 o'clock A.M. on the 9th day of April A.D. 1898, Horace Harvey, Registrar.

It is not known whether he ever worked the farm but a year or so later he moved to Slocan City, B.C. where he established a warehouse and transfer business, and then to Cranbrook, B.C. where he lived the rest of his life.

ROBERT (BOB) YOUNG

Bob was a big husky Eastern Canadian who took up a homestead and pre-emption along the north and south sides of Sheep River being E½ S24-T20-R29 W4, 3½ miles east of Okotoks in 1883. He was a good farmer growing mostly oats and selling them to ranchers along the Little Bow.

He was a bachelor and a heavy drinker. One winter evening in '98, after drinking in town, he headed for home, but never made it. He was out on the open prairie all night in the bitter cold. The next morning when he knocked on a neighbors door, his hands were so frozen that it sounded as if someone was pounding on the door with a rock. Both hands had to be amputated above the wrists. Later, he was fitted with hooks and he continued farming. At mealtime he would unscrew the hooks and screw a knife and fork into the socket so he could eat. Albert Smith was visiting Bob one time when a work mare crowded Bob against the barn door. He threw his arm back and somehow one of the hooks got caught in the mares lip. It looked like a bad mix-up for a few moments but the hooks pulled loose avoiding serious injury for Bob. In later years he rented the farm, but continued to live on the farm alone.

One very cold and blizzardy day about 40 below zero, Cecil and Harold Coultry were driving home in a cutter when they dimly noticed something on the fence on the Cope place. They continued on, then suddenly realizing what it was, and turned back to find Bob hanging over the barbed wire fence and singing aloud nearly frozen to death. They took him home. For several days when Cecil called to see Bob, he would find him with his leg in the oven trying to get warm. Cecil used to have to repair the panel on Bob's door. Bob continually would lose his key in the snow when trying to unlock his door with his hooks. In desperation he would pull the panel off his door to gain entry into his house. Cecil ran a trap line along the river and would pass his house each day.

It seemed strange to find Bob in town on a Wednesday, as his day was Thursday in town. It was later found that he was making out his will at the lawyer's office. It was on this Wednesday in January of 1936, Bob now an old man of 76, fate took its toll. After having his drinks, Bob ordered a load of coal and picked up his groceries and started for home. Someone in town picked him up and took him to his farm gate which was a quarter of a mile from his house. Next day the dray man, Hugh Patterson delivered the coal and found his groceries and key laying in the snow but no Bob in the house. A search party was organized by Constable Green, Joe Miller, later the operator of the Willingdon Hotel, Frank McKay and D. Fleiger and neighbors. It was nearly 30 below zero with drifting snow. Cecil, on his way home from his trap line, came across these men and helped in the search for Bob. Following the fence line, Cecil found his hook in the snow and tracks going out on an overhanging snow ledge at the river. He found where Bob had fallen through the snow to a junk pile at the river bank and found Bob in an old car body. On Friday Bob was taken to Dwight Barretts home, fighting and thrashing all the way there. He was very badly frozen and died a short time later. Cecil said years before that Bob had told him he always wanted to freeze to death. A nephew from Vancouver attended the funeral.

Others who have lived in the Allan district but have no histories.

Mr. and Mrs. Best SE¼ 30-21-28 W4.

Mr. Joe Brice SW¼ 6-21-28 W4. This land was homesteaded by Joe Brice in 1883, he sold out to Mr. and Mrs. A. Forckel.

Mr. Carrol SE¼ 30-21-28 W4. Mr. Carrol homesteaded this land in 1883 and sold out to Mr. Robert Hamilton. This land was known for many years as the Old Man Carrol place.

Mr. Dan Davis NE¼ 12-21-29 W4. Dan worked at the Sandstone Brick Mill and farmed with his brother Fred at Millarville then later purchased land at Cochrane.

Bouquet Davis NE¼ 22-20-29 W4. He owned this land but never farmed it, Henry Johnson rented it. Bouquet was an American and lived in Okotoks. He got his nick name Bouquet because he was always dressed up and wore a flower in his lapel. Bill Johnson was executor for his estate and later purchased this land.

Mr. and Mrs. Bert Frear SE¼ 7-21-28 W4.

William Graburn SE¼ 30-21-28 W4.

Mr. and Mrs. William Hagerman SW ¼ 35-20-28 W4. They sold out about 1926 to C. W. Johnson and moved to the U.S.A. Their daughter married Vern Eberly.

Judge Idington SE¼ 7-21-28 W4. He was a Supreme Court Judge.

P. S. Idington NW¼ 6-21-28 W4. He sold out in 1926 and moved to Vinland, Ontario.

Mr. Lee NW¼ 5-21-28 W4.

Mr. McCracken NW¼ 30-20-28 W4. Son James went to the Allan School he later became a Doctor and now is in Oregon.

Mr. A. McDougal and Co. NW¼ 31-20-28 W4. He moved from here to a farm near Frank Lake and later moved back to the States.

M. McKay NW¼ 30-21-28 W4. Came here from Victoria, B.C.

Herb Neil NW 22-20-29 W4. He worked for the Department of Highways, his widow lives in Calgary.

Mr. and Mrs. John Russel NE¼ 34-20-29 W4. Because he had a very small house he had the bed raised to the ceiling on pulleys for the day. Sold out in 1918 to D. Ward.

Mr. E. E. Saunders NW¼ 11-21-29 W4. Sold to J. P. Todd.

Mr. Securson SE¼ 12-21-28 W4.

W. R. Smith NE¼ 2-21-29 W4. Sold land about 1917.

Mr. Whittler NE¼ 2-21-29 W4.

Mr. P. P. Woodbridge NW¼ 6-21-28 W4. He was on the first Board of Directors of Alberta Farmers Co-operative Elevator Co. This Company amalgamated in 1917 with Grain Growers Grain Co. to form United Grain Growers. He also was secretary of United Farmers of Alberta in 1913 taking over from Mr. E. J. Fream.

Unwin & Baldwin SE¼ 7-21-28 W4. Baldwin worked for the Bar U Ranch.

PRAIRIE CROCUS

By Olive Thompson
Come neighbor, take a walk with me
Just a short way out from town
We'll find a narrow country lane
And pick rose-hips by the pound

The value of the rose-hip
Is known by one and all
So bring your pail along with me
Together, we'll have a ball

Just quiet conversation
And listening to the birds
Or we can think our very own thoughts
Not say a single word.

As we walk back to town again
Our worries will have ceased
Life will seem like roses
We'll know an inner peace

SANDSTONE VALLEY TRAIN — by Olive Thompson
The freight train thundering through the valley,
(the rhythm of its wheels on rail)
tells us we can count on it,
through snow and sleet or stormy gale.

"Count on me — count on me — I'll not let you down,
my power is great — I'm determined and strong"
You can have faith in whatever you do,
if you listen to the freight train's song.

Your Pioneer Friend S.H.S.
I would rather have one little Rose
From the garden of a friend
Then to have the choicest flowers
When my stay on Earth must end.

I would rather have a loving smile,
from the friends I know are true
Than tears shed round my Casket
When this world I've bid adieu
Bring me all the flowers today
Whether pink, or white, or red
I'd rather have one blossom now
Than a truck load when I'm Dead.

(Written for Lillian Biswanger on her 80th birthday)
(Lillian is the eldest daughter of Jesse Aldridge) — by
Olive Thompson
Thank you Mom for your 80 years
It gives us the pleasure to wish you good cheer
A smile on your face is all that we need
To know that your party is worth it, indeed.

Now that your children are grown and away
You have time to reflect on many a day.
To help you along, I'll add a few phrases,
From a kid's point of view, here are a few phases.

Those years of depression you'd not want returned,
Though it did teach us values, we may never have
learned.

Mert shining the floors for Christmas day,
He'd make the breakfast and keep us at bay
Until the chanting he could stand no more,
When the porridge was ready, he'd open the door.
The kitchen all cleaned before we could see
The presents that lay under the Christmas tree.

From your cut-glass bowl on the dining-room table,
Sprang rainbow reflections, that were quite like a
fable.

The kettle Dad boiled to thaw the old car,
On a cold winter morning, so it could go far.

Or maybe the smell of the paste he'd concoct,
At the stove he'd be stirring it, in an old pot.

The basement that Harold dug all by hand,
Or scrubbing Nonie's feet, to get out the sand.

The Sunday morning beans that simmered all night
long,
Dad's tea had to steep, or there'd be a song.

Mert's horses he kept in the garage at the back,
 till a neighbor decided "that's enough of that"

When you said, and I quote, "I've a bone to pick with
you"
Without any doubt, we were in trouble we knew.

The worry our toes would attract a wee mouse
When we knelt for our prayers, by the bed, in the old
house.

Uncle Steve's chewing tobacco, you'd scrub off the
walk,
His teeth in the cupboard, We'd swear they could talk.

Marilyn sucking her thumb with her finger curled o'er,
And bumping the chair till she'd nearly tip over.

Playing bear with Dad's old coat,
And Harold's little wind-up boat.

Reta, running barefoot in the snow,
So she wouldn't call me chicken, away I would go.

You darning the socks, and straining your eyes,
The piles of ironing, and your apple pies.

Saskatoon picking and trips to the farm,
The cod-liver oil to keep us from harm.

Going out after dark, throwing rocks at the bats,
Games at the mail box, and playing jacks.

I must add another I never forgot,
Harold shaking the pepper, and then breathing a lot.

These little reflections are just a small part
Of the memories that are dear to our hearts.

May your days be happy and full of good cheer,
OUR LOVE AND BEST WISHES, MOTHER DEAR.

AS TOLD TO ME — by Harold Biswanger
Being an Englishman Mr. Aldridge did not
pronounce his "h" properly. And as the story goes the
teacher was riding past the Aldridge farm to the Allan
School when a car came along and scared the horses.
Mr. Aldridge said to the family that he had to go out
and hold the teacher's "arse".

Laura Riches, Allan School teacher, asked her
students what kind of flowers they had for the school
fair from seed given to them in the spring. Muriel
Priest snapped her fingers first and answered
"Cauliflower".

Tom Aldridge did some work in the construction of
the new Railway Station in Okotoks, as a load counter
of the gravel loads brought in by teamsters. Tom
asked Ben Teskey while emptying the gravel, "Is
there any gold in this gravel?" Ben answered, "The

only gold you're going to get is from the money you get from this job."

Man making a purchase of nails in a hardware store, asked for a pound of each kind of nails and had them put in the same bag saying that he would sort them out when he got home. He handed the store owner a script "Social Credit Money" but the store owner refused to take it. The man said "I guess we can't do business", and walked out chuckling to himself.

Olive and Phyllis Aldridge and Gwenneth Ward and children went for a picnic north of Bert Jenkin's farm with horse and buggy, and Olive had her saddle horse. They tied their horses to the fence and went into the bush and spread out a blanket in a clearing, putting out all the food on it. After a while they heard what sounded like a bull bellowing and coming through the bush. Quickly gathering up the blanket and food and the children they ran for the horses. Olive could not find her saddle, but she found it soon, on a skinned, bloated and maggot infested carcass of a horse. The stench was unbearable while getting the saddle off. After putting the saddle in the buggy they saw and heard Bill Herr and Alex Blackwood laughing their heads off in the brush.

During a Hallowe'en night trick a number of boys worked very hard taking a buggy apart and putting the parts on a barn roof and reassembling it. Watching this all the time the owner came out when it was all assembled and made them take it all down and reassemble it.

Jimmy Lang sold Granddad Aldridge a gentle milk cow that stamped his hat into the ground. The cow was so miserable and mean he could not have it around, so took it back and turned it back into Jimmy Lang's field, but never got his money back.

Mac MacGougan, on Fridays, would have the children wash his car so he could go courting Marion McGilvery that evening. He would let the children out early that day.

Phyllis Aldridge used to come early to light the fires in the school heater before school started. Percy Davis would come in when no one was watching and close the dampers on the heater, when the teacher came the school was full of smoke. Phyllis would get in trouble and the children would get extra time outside to play until the smoke was cleared out.

Percy Davis climbed up the edge of the outside door of the school and slid back down. He caught his upper jaw on the door latch. The teacher seeing white objects flying about thought he lost his buttons off his shirt but it was his front teeth.

Telephone operator in a small town was asked by an inspector why her fire extinguisher was always empty, she answered "She did not know why". But one day the inspector walked into the telephone operator's office unannounced, and found the operator cooling a beer with the CO_2 from the fire extinguisher.

Gordon Griffen, living and farming a piece of land that was very prone to frost, would plant one potato plant in the field where he planted his grain. If it froze then good-bye grain crop.

Andy Griffen raised turkeys for show. With a show coming up in Calgary he asked Gordon and son Sandy to catch and crate his prize turkeys. Chasing them around the yard they seized one by the tail feathers and pulled them out. Not knowing what to do and fearing the consequences they caught the escape artist again and crated it with the feathers. They loaded it on the truck and took off for the show. After unloading the crates in Calgary Andy took the turkey out of the crate and said: "What happened to my prize turkey's tail feathers?"

On a nature study trip to a slough on the Barker farm the teacher pointed to rabbit droppings along the edge of the water. "O! children come look at the frogs eggs".

I REMEMBER — by Olive Aldridge

The threshers came in the afternoon with a huge steam engine, water wagon and twelve bundle racks, some spike pitchers and field pitchers and about twenty-five horses and nearly as many men. My Dad used to say the horses would eat all the bundles before they were threshed, especially if it rained. My Mother told me to go hitch the horse, as she had to go to town to get more food. Just before, she had baked a large batch of bread and set it on the table to cool. She had also cooked a large pot of potatoes and another of cabbage, so they would be ready when we got home. When we got home, Dad's pet cow had pushed the kitchen door open and entered the house. She ate all the bread and pushed both pots of vegetables off the stove. Two pigs followed her in, and they ate the potatoes and cabbage and turned over the swill pail. As I chased the cow out with a stick, she backed into the stove and knocked over the stove pipe, and soot went all over everything. The cow and pigs took off for further pastures with me in hot pursuit. My poor Mother cried, but then she cleaned up the mess and set about preparing more food. The men didn't get a banquet that night — baking powder biscuits, salt pork and garden produce. It was lucky we had a very large garden.

In 1915, the Allan School was closed because of lack of pupils, so my brother Ed and I had to walk to Okotoks School. It was a very long way. We walked through the bush across Shields' half section. The coyotes would follow us and peek out of the bush at us as we passed by. We walked winter and summer, blizzard and rain a distance of about six miles. One spring the floods were awful, and all the sloughs were full. Ed and I were going through Lang's field. We thought we could cross the slough by climbing on the fence and walking on the wire. Half-way across, the wire broke, and we fell in the water. We did not go home, but went on to school and sat in wet clothes.

On the Smith farm in 1915, we had a field that came up thick with wild oats. My Dad, not knowing about wild oats, thought the field had been planted, so he left it. It rained a lot that summer, so we had plenty of green feed. A neighbour came along and told him to cut it before it was ripe, this being a good way to clean up a field. He piled a lot on top of a shed to keep the snow out. Sixteen years later, a neighbour, Harvey Outhet, (now the owner of the land), became very short of feed. He took the top off this building and fed it to his cows. It was better than nothing, and some of it was still green.

Our Dad supplied meat and vegetables to the C.N.R. camp that was located on the south side of Sheep River at Bob Young's crossing, close to where the traffic bridge is now, on No. 2 Highway. It was a perilous crossing. Dad thought he could cross the river with a wagon and horses when the water was high. I had to go with him to help, as I always had to help him with everything. We started across the river, and the horses couldn't hold against the current, so we were swept away down the stream. We finally struck a gravel bar and were able to make it to the other side. Our dog disappeared down stream. When we came back across, one of the camp men rode a team of mules across after putting a tow line on our wagon. The mules were good at pulling, and we went back alright. Our dog arrived home the next day.

In the early thirties, feed was very scarce, and each town had straw come in by train. This was sold to the farmers, and a lot of them would fight to get a share.

My Dad got some seed potatoes from Mr. Allan back in 1920. These were Bove potatoes, an early pink variety. Approximately sixty years later, we are still growing these, and I doubt if they can be obtained from any other source.

Raymond Van Tighem holding hail stones from July 1951 storm.

Alex Currie doing washing — early 1900's.

Joe Mangan — Where did all the Prairie Chickens go?

Lionel Lynch, Alf and Walter Poffenroth moving cattle the hard way.

Milking time.

Farm Work

Will Johnson spreading manure.

Living high. L. to R. Jeff Jeffery, Bob Hamilton (son), Bobbie Hamilton, Nena and Dale Jeffery.

Ted Allwarden going out to drill.

Clara Jamison (Sunderland) milking cow.

Drilling a water well at Suitor's.

Hauling river water with a barrel at Suitor's.

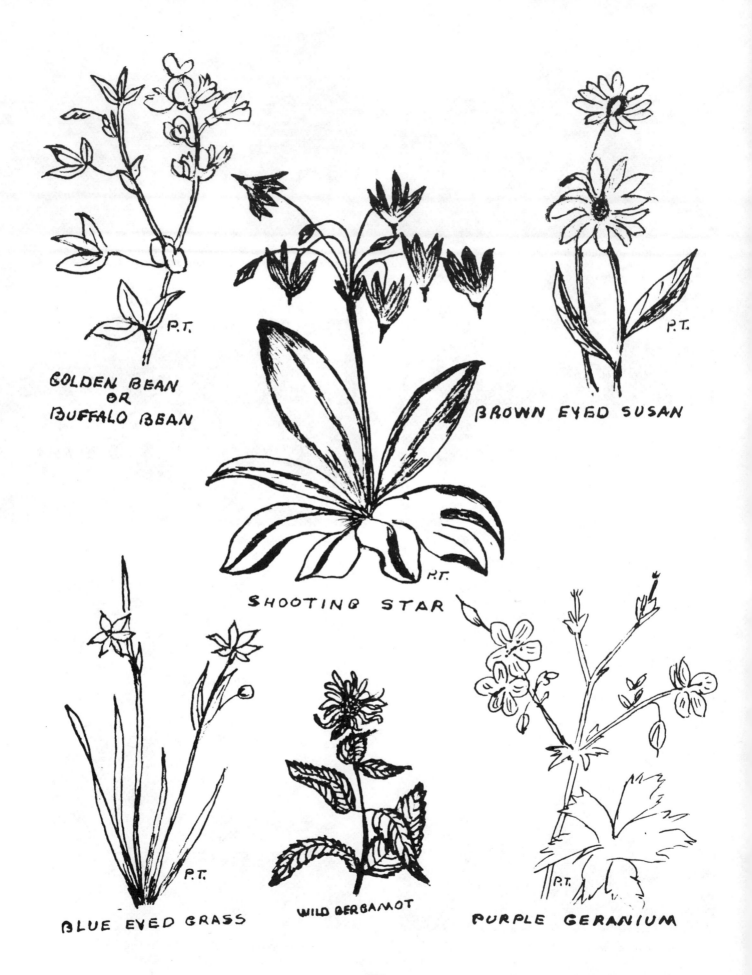

GOLDEN BEAN
OR
BUFFALO BEAN

BROWN EYED SUSAN

SHOOTING STAR

BLUE EYED GRASS

WILD BERGAMOT

PURPLE GERANIUM

EVENING GROSBEAK
Thick greenish-yellow bill
male- large areas of yellow
+brown, black + white
female - grey

AMERICAN
GOLDFINCH
Black + yellow

MEADOW LARK

BLACK V ON
YELLOW BREAST

MOUNTAIN BLUEBIRD

MALE- ALL blue
Female- grey-brown
blue wings-tail.

ROBIN
DARK GRAY BACK
REDDISH ORANGE
BREAST

HERMIT THRUSH
COLOR- BROWN
FINE SINGERS

BALTIMORE
ORIOLE

MALE - ORANGE + BLACK
FEMALE - DULL YELLOW-ORANGE + BLACK

133

DAVISBURG   S.D.   NO. 79

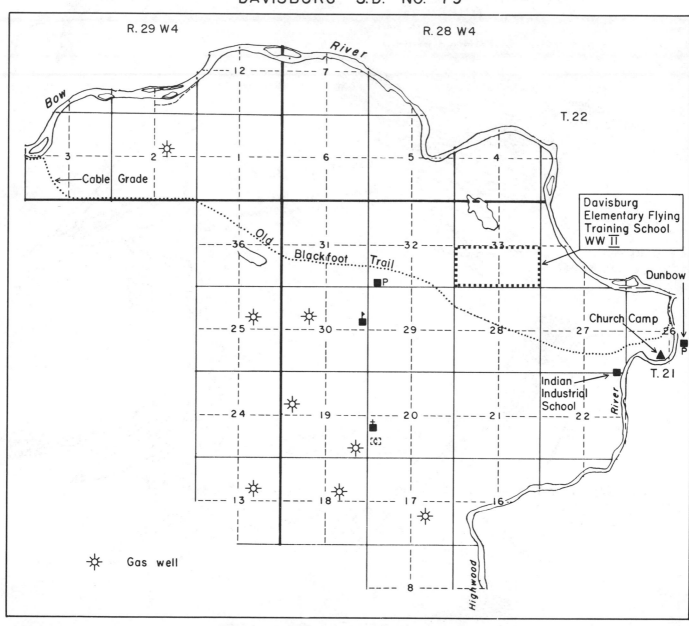

R. 29 W4

R. 28 W4

River

Bow

T. 22

12   7

3   2   1   6   5   4

Cable Grade

Davisburg
Elementary Flying
Training School
WW II

Old

36   31   32   33

Blackfoot   Trail

Dunbow

■P

Church Camp

25   30   29   28   27   26

▲

P

Indian
Industrial
School

T. 21

River

24   19   20   21   22

☼   ‡
      [C]

☼   13   18   17   16

☼

☼   Gas well

Highwood

8

134

Davisburg School District

DAVISBURG SCHOOL DISTRICT NO. 79 — by I. Blackwood

Davisburg School District was bounded on the north by the Bow River and on the east by the Highwood River. It extended two miles west and about two miles south of the present school site. It was first named Glenbeg in honor of the Begg family who lived in the "Glen." It was later changed to Davisburg after D. W. Davis, the first member of the Canadian House of Commons from Alberta.

The school was built in 1888 and was located on the NE¼-29-21-28-W4 and later moved to the NE¼-30 in 1897. In 1908 it was again moved, this time to the SE¼-30 and a new school was built. The old school was used as a stable.

A teacherage was built in 1913 and in 1914 it was attached to the school. This was later used as a kitchen.

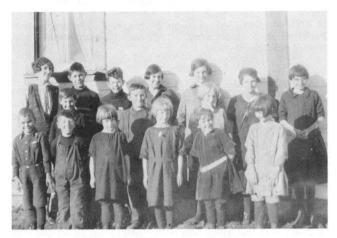

Davisburg School, 1925. Teacher, Mrs. Cannon. Back: Sheridan Hughes, Doug Herr, Laura Andrews, Stella Bryce, Leta Shattuck, Leta Stewart, Middle: Jim Davis,   , May Tucker. Front: Angus Andrews, Donald James,   , Violet Tucker, Lillian Davis, Kathleen Bryce.

Davisburg School No. 79.

The first inspector was I. A. Blair who wrote in his report of October 23, 1888 that he "visited the school today and was glad to be able to report favorably on the work of the teacher, Miss McArthur. The results are seen not less in the advance of the pupils in their studies, but in the organization of the school, looking to future advance. The district is to be congratulated on the establishment of their school under such promising indications."

The first teachers were Miss M. B. McArthur (1888) and Miss Maxfield. In his report on Miss Maxfield, Mr. Blair said, "In point of regularity of attendance, this is the banner school of my district — on the occasion of each of my visits the whole number of pupils were present."

The first pupils were: Alice Andrews, Jenny

Davisburg School 1932 Top Row: (Student teacher) Angus Andrews, Digby Hughes, Ross Hyde, Bruce Hyde, Teacher — Vera Gillespie. 2nd Row: — Kathleen Bryce, Nancy, Ralph, and Ethel Hyde, Cynthia Call. Third Row: — Lillian Davis, Donnie Hyde, Bobbie Ralph, Trixie Ralph.

Andy Magyer, Pat McHugh, Bobby Herr, Don Sutherland, Roger Blackwood, Larry Herr, Martin Henriksen. 1950. Davisburg School.

Banister, Eva Banister, Daisy Banister, Ida Banister, and Victor Banister.

Local girls who taught at Davisburg were: Effie Blackwood (Mrs. Chester Leach), Vera Andrews (Mrs. T. A. Gillespie), and Eva Herr (Mrs. D. H. Beattie). Two teachers who married and stayed in the district were Aggie Gray (Mrs. Barsby Martin) and Edith Crawford (Mrs. Bob Riddle).

The school continued in use until 1953 when the children went to Okotoks School by bus. Mr. Orla Hansen was our first bus driver and continued as such until 1963.

The buildings and land were sold to the community and have served as a social centre since, the school being used as a community hall. The barn which was formerly the school was sold to S. A. Hughes and moved away. A curling rink was built on the property and many a pleasant evening has been spent there.

Children from several families outside the district attended Davisburg School when there was no school closer to their homes. Some of these were the Merriam, Streeter, Quinn, Riddle, Dan Davis, Bartlam, Haslam, and Forckel families.

During the war years when the De Winton Airport was in operation, the maintenance personnel lived on the base and their children came to the Davisburg School. These were the Dirsten, McIntosh, Davis, Cuthbert, Brown, Juke, Park, Howard, and Nelson families.

DUNBOW (ST. JOSEPH'S) INDIAN INDUSTRIAL SCHOOL RESEARCHED AND WRITTEN — by Virginia Klatzel

As early as 1872 a recommendation was made to Father Lacombe that residential schools be established for young Indian children. The best way to persuade the Indian tribes to lead a peaceful and settled life would be to train them to engage in an industry.

Father Lacombe realized that such residential schools were possible only through financing by the Federal Government. When he was in Ottawa during the winter of 1883-84 he arranged through meetings with Sir John A. McDonald that three residential schools be built; one Protestant at Battleford and two Catholic schools; one at Qu'Appelle and one at Dunbow. Dunbow was in the Davisburg district, on the Highwood River near its' confluence with the Bow River. The Government agreed to erect the building, pay the principal a fair salary and make a per capita grant towards the maintenance of the pupils. The idea was to bring the very young children and teach them English and trades along with other schooling so that they might fit into the community of Europeans that now controlled the country.

With the help of the Oblate Fathers Order and the Federal Government, Father Lacombe chose the site and was responsible for building and organizing the school. The lumber with which to build the first part of the school was floated down the Bow River from Calgary to the mouth of the Highwood, and from there hauled with teams to the building site. Bricks were hauled by teams from Calgary. The site was on six sections of land where crops, gardens and stock could be raised, serving to make the school both self-sufficient and to give training in agriculture to the Indians.

On completion of the school, Father Lacombe rode out among the Bloods and Piegans asking the parents to send boys to the school. Father Legal and Jean L'Heureux did likewise at Blackfoot Crossing. The Indian parents refused to give up their young children. The school did however open October 17, 1884, with a staff of two lay brothers, three Grey Nuns; Sr. Delphine Guenette, Sr. Victoire LeMay and Sr. Victoire Thiffault, and Father Lacombe as principal. There were twenty pupils, all boys ranging in age from fifteen to seventeen. These boys were from the Blackfoot reserve and had been willingly sent by the parents as they were troublesome to the parents at home. They were also troublesome to the Oblate Fathers. They were strangers to any form of discipline. They had lived in Indian lodges, slept on buffalo robes, worn beads and buckskin and long hair, and lived on a diet of game, fish and berries. The routines of a boarding school were absurd to them. They refused to bathe, or have their hair cut, and indulged in riotous frolics which were damaging to the buildings and the nerves of the school staff. Father Lacombe said of his pupils during the first months of the school's opening; "They were about as much at home as wildcats in a beaver lodge. You open the door, look inside,

Indian boys from Dunbow School early 1920. Fishing with Harry Lusk.

and see Hell''. Father Lacombe was once called North for business, and in his absence only three pupils remained at the school. The older boys were very difficult to be trained to the ways of a school.

Gradually the Blackfoot parents allowed younger children, boys and girls to attend the school. They could see the value of the training that was given at the school and the care provided by the Grey Nuns. Younger children adhered to discipline and were quicker to profit by education than the older boys had been. The school had been planned to educate the children from the surrounding tribes, chiefly the Blackfoot people, but later some Crees from the North were taken in. The Crees did so well that they had an effect upon the Blackfoot, who could not be out done by their ancient enemies, so began to make better progress themselves.

Eventually the school had an enrollment of between 130-150 pupils. Complete high school was offered, as well as excellent training in a trade for the boys and home economics for the girls. The program of the public schools was followed as closely as possible and the students spent a half-day in the classroom and a half-day in industrial work. For the boys the main work was on the farm with its' various areas of stock raising (cattle, pigs, horses and poultry). These boys also became proficient in blacksmithing, shoemaking, and carpentering from the school's shops. As the boys became efficient and reliable they would be sent to a neighboring farm to gain further experience and knowledge in a white man's way of living and working. The kitchen, sewing room and laundry provided the girls with experience. More teachers were gradually added to the staff. Soon the school had an excellent band and choir, under the direction of Mr. W. Scollen, who it is recorded, was paid a large sum of twenty-five dollars a month.

It was under the direction of Father Naessens that the school had its greatest days. He organized first-rate hockey and football teams; teams which more than once defeated top rated teams of non-Indians. The school band and choir performed at the Calgary and Edmonton Exhibitions as well as the Territorial Exhibition in Regina. In Regina the band was awarded the first prize, and medals were presented by Lord Aberdeen, Governor General of Canada. The

Dunbow (St. Joseph's) Indian Industrial School, run by Sisters of Charity, Priest and Brothers burned down April 1954. Picture by courtesy of Glenbow — Alberta Institute, Calgary, Alberta.

Dunbow Industrial Indian School — run by Sisters of Charity, Priests and Brothers. Burned down in April 1954.

girls had a mandolin band. The Davisburg public often attended concerts given by these bands at the school's band stand. The farm also won prizes at shows with its pedigreed cattle and horses.

In September 1887, Dunbow had an unexpected visit by the Blackfoot runner Deer Foot, who was escaping from custody of the N.W.M.P. He had been confined by police in Calgary as a result of a raid on the home of William Thompson, near High River. During the raid Tucker Peach, the hired man, was shot in the arm by Deer Foot, while Thompson was attacked with an axe. In the escape, Deer Foot out ran the police to Dunbow although he was hampered by a ball and chain. The ball and chain was hidden under the Indian runner's blanket and few at the school knew that he was escaping. An instructor provided Deer Foot with lunch, and without anyone knowing, a nephew slipped a file to the escaper. Deer Foot left and a short time later two policemen arrived in hot pursuit on lathered horses. Upon enquiring for the escaped Indian, someone pointed Deer Foot out climbing a hill not far distant. The police gave chase but Deer Foot made good his escape and lived for sometime in Montana. The following summer Indian children on a picnic found the ball and chain in trees; it remained around the school for sometime but eventually disappeared.

The government gradually began to erect residential and day schools on the reserves, therefore, it became more and more difficult for Dunbow to obtain pupils. Parents naturally preferred to have their children nearer home. Industrial schools did an excellent job, an informant says "Their graduates stood head and shoulders above the graduates of any other school". After thirty-eight years of successful operation the school was closed March 28, 1922.

Dunbow was the first Indian Industrial school to be built in Alberta and the first large attempt to help Indian children to meet the problems of civilization and to enable the Government to begin to carry out the educational terms of Treaty No. 7.

The closed school was under the custodianship of Fred Davis until 1925 at which time Frank McHugh began farming the land, and in the spring of 1928 took up residence there.

In 1936 several of the buildings were dismantled and the lumber was used for the construction of buildings in the Turner Valley area during the oil boom years. The chapel bell was installed on the Catholic Church at Black Diamond. The large brick residence used by the girls was destroyed by fire in April 1954.

The correct name of the school was St. Joseph's Industrial School but it was most commonly known as Dunbow. The name "Dunbow" is thought to be derived from dune, a hill, on the east side of the Highwood River at the confluence of the Bow River, thus Dunbow.

Principals of the school were:
1884-   Rev. Albert Lacombe
1884-1891 Rev. E. Claude
1891-1907 Rev. A. Naessens
1907-1912 Rev. J. Riou
1912-1918 Rev. E. Nordmann
1918-1922 Rev. A. Demers

Brother Tom Morkin worked at Dunbow for twenty-

five years as farm manager. When Dunbow closed he went to Stand-off where he began developing a farm from the bald prairie. With the help of some of his old pupils from Dunbow a successful farm was established. Credit must be given to: Glenbow-Alberta Institute, Calgary, for the use of this picture of Dunbow in 1897. Sources of information: M. B. Byrne, From The Buffalo To The Cross; Katherine Hughes, Father Lacombe, Black Robe Voyageur; F. W. Anderson, Frontier Guide, Calgary to Medicine Hat; Fran Fraser, Newspaper clipping, Calgary Herald; Glenbow Archives, Calgary, Alberta.

DAVISBURG CHURCH AND CEMETERY — Researched and written by I. Blackwood

Davisburg Church was started about September 1889 on land donated by Herb Starkey which was a portion of the SW¼-20-21-28-W4. The work was done by volunteer labour and the church was finished before the end of the year. The first ministers were Rev. A. J. Matheson and Rev. J. A. Hellyer. The property was registered at the land titles office in Calgary in 1893 in ownership of David Thorburn, Morris Stewart and John Irving, who were the original trustees of the church. At first our church was part of the mission congregation of Sheep River, High River and Davisburg.

Rev. and Mrs. J. A. Matheson, Donald, Ursie and Kenneth Bertran.

For many years the churches of Red Deer Lake, Pine Creek, Melrose, and Davisburg were part of the Calgary Presbytery. For several summers we had student ministers. We contributed to the building and up-keep of the manse along with the Melrose and Pine Creek (later De Winton) congregations. We were

Davisburg United Church.

moved to the High River Presbytery and had services conducted by the minister stationed in Okotoks. In May 1958 we were told our church would close. When the building began to look dilapidated, the windows were boarded up and it was given a coat of paint. So, though not in use, it still stands tidy and bright — a land mark for miles around.

Many of our pioneers with their children and grandchildren are buried in the Davisburg Cemetery. It has been well cared for, with trimmed lawn and flowering shrubs. In 1965 a large fieldstone was placed in the yard with a plaque which reads: "To the memory of the pioneers of the Davisburg district." A steel link chain fence was erected around the church and graveyard in 1974.

Miss Ida Banister and three of the Blackwood girls, Bertha, Daisy and Effie, played the organ for church. During the four years that Bertha played, Billie Banister led the singing. Miss Olive Shattuck played the organ for many years. Mrs. George Sutherland was organist when the church was closed.

For about five years, 1911 to 1916, Mrs. Leah McConnell held Sunday School classes in her home. Miss Elaine McConnell played the organ. Children from both Melrose and Davisburg attended.

GRAVEYARDS OF DAVISBURG

Davisburg has three graveyards. One is the orthodox graveyard, next to the church. In it are buried many of the original settlers. Those who are being buried there in present times are grandchildren and great-grandchildren of the pioneers of our district. It is a neat, well-kept place with its lawn and flowering shrubs. A large field stone with a plaque bearing the words "To the memory of the pioneers of the Davisburg district" was erected in 1965. In 1974, through the generosity of one of our old-time families, a steel link chain fence was built around the church property.

An Indian graveyard is close to the bank of the Highwood River, at the site of the old Dunbow School. In 1975, the Department of Culture, Youth and Recreation granted us a sizeable amount of money to build a steel fence around it to protect it from roaming cattle.

The other, a little different, is known as the Buffalo Boneyard, and is found on the steep banks of the Bow River, on land that was originally settled on by Mr. A.

E. Banister, Sr. Strata of buffalo bones, along with strata of earth and clay, have been found along this cliff. The stratification leads one to believe that it was one of many buffalo jumps in the province.

Years ago, Mr. Steve Williams hauled these bones to De Winton by truck, to be hauled away by train. Car loads of them were sent out to De Winton.

Partly from notes by Miss E. G. Luxton at the Glenbow Foundation — the rest by Ina Blackwood

THE NORTH WEST MOUNTED POLICE IN DAVISBURG

A North West Mounted Police detachment was established at Dunbow, near the confluence of the Bow and Highwood Rivers from 1884-1895. The first man stationed there was Sergeant Todd. Another one was Sergeant Ralph Kendall, who later wrote police stories and was with the Calgary City Police in 1910. From the late 1880's a number of detachments were established in "E" division in this area. Generally, these consisted of one man — either a constable or non-commissioned officer, with one horse. Accommodation for these men was rented from various settlers.

The routine patrols to the settlements were carried out as frequently as possible, considering the men available. Each homesteader was visited on line of patrol. Any complaints were recorded and often settled on the spot, with the policeman acting unofficially to settle differences which had arisen between neighbours. Cattle and horses on range were inspected for signs of disease; unfamiliar brands noted, as well as the conditions of the crops and haylands. The policeman on patrol became familiar to the settlers and was aware of his circumstances. The presence of any strangers was investigated. Another duty of the man on detachment was to fight fires which were quite common — and persecution of whoever was guilty of starting them.

According to stories told by my mother, Sarah Irving Flett, one of the highlights of their pioneer life were the nights the Mounted Policeman, while on duty, spent at the home of her father, John A. Irving. Effie Blackwood Leach remembers that the policeman was allowed twenty-five cents a meal to eat at their home, and Alex Blackwood remembering Joe Miller, Alberta Provincial Policeman, on his black horse when he patrolled this country. Joe Miller later owned the Alberta and Willingdon Hotels in Okotoks.

Mr. A. S. Blackwood became Justice of the Peace in 1899 and the Blackwood children recall when court cases were heard in their living room. One amusing tale they tell is of two neighbours (who were known for their drinking habits), being marched up the road on foot, with two Mounties behind them on horseback. After being fined by Mr. Blackwood, they returned home on foot, and the police continued on their way.

Compiled by Ina G. Blackwood from notes in "The Leaves of the Medicine Tree", and from information received from Heritage Resource Development.

BERRY AND SHEARS FORT

In February, 1875, the North West Mounted Police received word of illicit traders operating in the

Highwood country. Captain Crozier, assisted by the half-breed guide and interpreter, Jerry Potts, led a detachment north, and made a number of arrests. Among them was Edward L. Smith from the Berry and Shears Fort at the confluence of the Bow and Highwood Rivers. As reported by Sergeant W. D. Antrobus "The men cleared out, and the hay and fort had been burned by the Indians."

The story of the arduous trip of the police from Macleod to the Highwood River in mid-winter is reproduced in the book "Jerry Potts" by Philip Long, from the diary of Sergeant Antrobus.

The fort was on land later owned by Mr. and Mrs. Ernie Irving. The stone foundation was still in place to give the general size of the building.

THE DAVISBURG BRIDGE — by I. Blackwood

One of the first steel bridges to be built in the Northwest Territories was the one across the Highwood River at what was known as Thompson's Crossing. It was built about 2¼ miles up river from the junction of the Highwood and Bow Rivers, which was the southeast portion of Davisburg. The bridge was first requested in 1890 and was built under contract in 1891 but was washed out in 1897. The two span steel bridge was constructed in 1898. The piers were reconstructed in 1903, 1921 and 1933.

The approaches to the bridge from either side were down long winding "river hills" which were often impassable in wet or winter weather. When it was found necessary to build a new bridge in 1963 the roads were straightened and the level of it is fifty feet above the water.

The old bridge was taken away in April 1964 and is presently at Heritage Park in Calgary.

Original Davisburg Bridge. L. to R. Olive Shattuck, Lucy Adams, Harry Bussy, Janie Adams, unknown, Maude King with baby, unknown, Bert King.

THE DAVISBURG ORANGEMAN'S HALL — by I. Blackwood

Although the hall was called Davisburg, it was outside the limits of the Davisburg district as it is known today. It was on 14-21-29-W4 on land owned by John Greenfield. It was used for lodge meetings, church meetings, dances, etc. It was referred to in records of the Davisburg Church in 1891. Early settlers such as Mrs. Robert Maxwell, Mr. David Suitor, Mr. George Carleton, and Mr. Albert Herr belonged to the Orangeman's Lodge. In later years the lodge meetings were held in Okotoks. The original Davisburg Lodge building remained for many years and at last served as a blacksmith shop for Mr. John Todd.

THE AIRPORT — by E. Leach

Due to the need for fliers in the Second World War, a chain of air training schools was scheduled from north to south in the Province of Alberta. The Federal Government was in charge but I am not aware of the financial arrangements with participating countries.

The land for No. 31 Elementary Flying Training School, De Winton, was acquired in the Davisburg district from Mr. James McK. Andrews and Mr. William Stewart. Both of these gentlemen had homesteaded here in the 1880s and were reluctant to sell. However the land was expropriated in 1940 and construction began in early 1941.

The school was opened that fall with trainees from many countries. Royal Air Force personnel were in charge and I believe the station was run wholly by R.A.F. men.

Under the Davisburg Bridge.

Moving Davisburg bridge, 1964.

However, in the summer of 1942 it became civilian operated, the staff coming mainly from a private flying club stationed at Malton, Ontario. It was still called No. 31 E.F.T.S. (R.A.F.) at Christmas 1942, but somewhere along the line it became the Malton Flying Training School with the motto "We teach the world to fly." Trainees did, indeed, come from many countries — Britain, Australia, New Zealand, Poland, France, and numerous other European countries. In the Christmas 1942 edition of **The Gremlin**, the station's newspaper, Squadron Leader Watts said that pupils had come from nearly twenty free nations. As time went on, more participated no doubt.

As soon as the place became civilian operated, the call went out for additional help. Men and women were required for various work — firemen, truck drivers, maintenance men, engineers, parachute packers, time keepers, cooks, canteen workers, janitors, guards, etc. Many of us were glad indeed of the opportunity to earn some money, a commodity which was a bit scarce at that time. Local help was given the preference, with De Winton and Okotoks also contributing. Many people came from Calgary.

Some of these commuted back and forth daily; others lived on the station, while some married couples had trailers or shacks outside the main compound, their children going to Davisburg school.

This was indeed a busy place with a bus making several trips a day to and from Calgary. Mr. E. Hanson operated the Bluebird Transportation Company, receiving at first the large sum of 70¢ for the round trip ticket. He found this far from adequate and after months of negotiating with the powers that be, he was allowed to charge $1.00.

Some of the local people that worked there were David and Kay Stinson, Merle Armstrong, Howard Norris, George Meehan, Martin and Georgina Davis, Cynthia and Bernice Call, Grace Suitor, Bertha Maconnachie, Kay Richardson, Ole and Eleata Hansen, Kay Noel, Tom Gillespie, Effie Leach, and Marion Davenport.

George Sutherland supplied the station with coal, hauling it from De Winton summer and winter.

From the De Winton area came Mrs. Everson, Ruth Anderson, Ruth Kerr, Mrs. Carothers, Sr., Barbara, Anna and Joe Carothers, Barsby and Madelyn Martin, and Scotty (A. W.) Lorimer, a veteran of the 1914-1918 war.

Several came daily from Okotoks. Sorry I can't list these names, for memory plays strange tricks. If names of some local people have been missed, our apologies; it was the best we could do.

Personally, I enjoyed the two years I was there in the office of "Works and Buildings" which was the maintenance part of the station. We were all well-treated, supplied with uniforms and overcoats, and well paid (at least we then thought we were). I feel we gave the company good service doing our bit to put fliers in the air and, incidentally, a bit to help win the war.

The airport was closed in the fall of 1944. We were each given the chance of a ride in one of the little training planes. The buildings were dismantled and the land reserved for veterans of W.W. II.

Bill (Scotty) Rodger and Jim Blackwood bought the land from the Government. The runways were later used by a glider club and the field is now designated as the South Calgary Airport.

NOTES ABOUT DAVISBURG

Mr. A. S. Blackwood won silver medals for the best dairy bull at the Calgary Fair in 1906 again in 1907.

Horses from Davisburg were sold to the Federal Government for use in the Boer war. One, formerly owned by Miss Sarah Irving was seen dead on the battle field. It was recognized by Jappy Rodgers when he saw Miss Irving's brand on it.

Notes of Interest from "Leaves of the Medicine Tree".

1890 — John Irving of Davisburg sowed a small acreage to wheat, although broadcast by hand from a wagon and then harrowed, it was a successful crop of good quality.

A. E. Banister of Davisburg started growing 'New Century' oats. 'Early Egyptian' was another variety of white oats introduced at this time. A variety of black oats was grown for several years after this. In 1937 Jack Shields still had a sample of black oats from his first crop in Alberta grown in 1886. Robert Burke of Davisburg brought in the first seed drill. It was a hoe-press seeder of VanBrunt make.

1887 — Jim Andrews of Davisburg purchased a Massey Harris binder.

FURTHER NOTES ON THE NAMING OF DAVISBURG

As we did not have a post-office here, it was decided to change the name of the district from Glenbeg to Davisburg, in honour of Mr. D. W. Davis, first member of Parliament for Macleod from 1888 to 1896. He had come from Montana to the Cypress Hills in the 1860's as a free trader with the Indians. After the establishment of the police at Fort Macleod, he became general manager for the I. G. Baker and Company, of their trading posts at Fort Macleod and Calgary. He married Miss L. Grier, the first teacher in an organized school district in the 1890's.

WILLIAM ADAMS

Born April 17, 1836 at Northampton, England; Died October 4, 1906 at Davisburg, Alberta.

William Adams — 1900.

Little is known about William Adams, except that he spent some years in the U.S.A., living in Buffalo, New York. He also farmed in Iowa before coming to Canada to settle in the Davisburg area.

MARY JANE BIRCHILL ADAMS

Born in Lissaphooca, Bandon, County Cork, Ireland around 1872; Died at Davisburg, Alberta around 1926.

At the age of twenty, Mary Jane Birchill left her home and family in Ireland to live in America. It is believed that she lived in Iowa for five years, and there she married William Adams. When their farm in Iowa was hit by a tornado, they salvaged what they could and headed for Canada.

Arriving in Calgary, just before 1900, they found mud and water everywhere, with even a lake in front of the C.P.R. station. They reported that a horse had stumbled and was submerged to its neck in this lake.

The William Adams' were able to buy out three homesteaders in the Davisburg area — Johnny and Tommy Thompson and a Mr. Cuff. Tommy had had an argument with an Indian — some reported a shooting — so he thought it best to leave. Tommy Thompson's place is still known as the "Devil's Hollow", which is owned by Jane McHugh. On the Tommy Thompson Homestead was a house and a log barn (16-21-28-W.4th) by what is now known as the Davisburg Bridge on the Highwood River. There wasn't any bridge there then: first there was a ferry, next a wooden bridge which was soon washed away with the high water.

Then the first steel bridge ever built in Alberta was placed right in front of the house. This bridge now is in Heritage Park in Calgary.

The new Adams ranch was named Kingsthorpe Ranch, and for the next five years Mary Jane was never off the ranch. During these years, two little daughters were born in the house that still stands close to the Highwood River. The girls were named Mary Jane Birchill Adams, and Susan Elizabeth Lucille Adams. Mary Jane later married Frank McHugh, and Lucy married Jim Davenport.

As this territory was on the edge of the Blackfoot Reserve with the Dunbow Indian School only two miles away, Indians were always in and around the Adams' doorstep. After her husband's death in 1906 Mary Jane Adams was so terrified of the Indians that she listed her ranch for sale. A buyer by the name of George Carleton came along to buy it, but instead married the widow and settled there. Mrs. Carleton unfortunately spent many of her last years as an invalid until her death there at the farm by the river.

GEORGE ANDREWS AND NORMAN CHESTER ANDREWS — by George Andrews

George Andrews and his unmarried son Norman came from Inverness in Megantic County, Quebec to the district in the early 20s, purchasing SE-30-21-28-W4 as a going concern from the Patterson brothers. This farm was once the location of a post office for the district. With the farm, seventeen horses were acquired and each of the older grandsons received a colt. The machinery consisted of an unusable small drill and a walking plow, with which the Pattersons plowed with three horses.

They brought a carload of household effects, two horses and a cow. These were prize animals in the East but fell far short of western standards. Included in the shipment was a large box of maple sugar, which darkened but lasted for years.

George was over 70 years of age when he came West and never really became adjusted to the West. When the wind blew and there were severe dust storms, he ranted about the "infernal West." He enjoyed listening to Aberhart on the radio prior to the advent of Aberhart's adoption of Social Credit, and while he still listened, it was no longer a pleasure. Although blind during the last several years of his life, he mustered strength to go and vote in several elections to uphold his bitter opposition to Social Credit.

SE ¼-30 was later owned by Osborne Andrews and presently by Angus Andrews, a grandson of George, and is farmed by Larry Herr.

In 1935 George received an autographed photograph from R. B. Bennett for life-time support of the Conservative Party. During his 90th year, he gave away his great-niece, Leta Shattuck (Mrs. J. Armstrong), in marriage in the Davisburg church.

Prior to 1910, George Andrew's daughter Eva was a teacher at Melrose School.

George died in 1938 at the age of 95, and Norman, in 1950.

MR. AND MRS. JAMES McKENZIE ANDREWS — by Vera Gillespie

Mr. Andrews came to the N.W.T. from Inverness (Quebec) in 1884, with his father - Thomas Henry Andrews. They hired saddle horses and rode south from Calgary to High River. Then they chose what they considered to be the most desirable land, which was eight miles east of De Winton.

They returned to Quebec to report to friends and relatives. It would be a wonderful life in a wonderful country. They were really enthusiastic about the opportunities in the West. So the following spring, 1885, a Colony Car brought the Andrews family, some relatives and friends to Calgary. In the train were implements, household effects, oxen, horses and cattle. The Andrews family and their three children Jim, Emma and Alice, settled on W½32-21-28-W.4th. Jim Andrews filed on his own land which included; E½32-21-28-W4th; E½29-21-28-W4; Sec.33-21-28-W.4; N½17-21-28-W.4.

At this period only diamonds and coal were reserved by the Crown. The oil and gas rights belonged to the homesteader. The oil and gas rights were later put on separate titles and are presently held by Tom and Vera Gillespie.

In 1940 the S½-33-21-28 W.4 was expropriated by the Federal Government and became the De Winton Elementary Flying Training School. Many thousands of United Kingdom boys learned to fly at this airport.

Mr. Andrews priced the land at fifty dollars per acre. The Government offered Twenty-five. The war had ended before the Government paid for the land.

In 1895 Mr. Andrews married Elizabeth Ann Martin who had come West from Streetville close to Toronto. The Martins settled near Aldersyde on the Sheep

Raising windmill at Jim Andrews' farm; 1904.

River. Elizabeth Martin completed her education in Calgary to become one of the first teachers in De Winton.

Mr. Andrews had a great deal of success as a farmer and rancher, raising purebred Clydesdales, Shorthorns, hogs, Oxford sheep and registered grain.

The couple were keenly interested in community life, particularly the Church and the School. The original name of the school was Glenberg and it was situated on E½-29-21-28 W.4. The school was moved twice as the centre of population shifted westerly. The name was changed to Davisburg No. 79 to honour Rider Davis, who was the area's first elected representative to Parliament. Unfortunately the early records have been destroyed. The school is closed and it is now a community centre with a curling rink added.

Mr. and Mrs. Andrews worked out the original plan for the mail route which covered Melrose, Davisburg and Gladys ridge. The mail was delivered three times a week from De Winton.

The pioneers of the area co-operated to build the school and the Davisburg Church, which was completed in 1893. These homesteaders raised their children to respect the church, value an education and accept responsibility. Many excellent teachers taught at Davisburg. One of the finest being Miss Effie Blackwood who had brothers and sisters attending classes. She had grades I through VIII. She was strict but fair. In school she was "Miss Blackwood." Out of school she was Effie to all her students.

In 1914 to 1917 Mr. Andrews was forced to retire to Calgary due to a series of heart attacks. Mr. and Mrs. Frank Tucker rented the farm on a share basis for three years.

Mrs. Andrews sold her land at Aldersyde and invested the money in Calgary properties. In 1940 Mr. and Mrs. Andrews built a bungalow and sheds on 75 acres southwest of the main farm buildings when their only daughter, Vera, and her husband came from Turner Valley to run the De Winton farm. The small parcel of land was later sold to Mr. and Mrs. Paul Groeneveld.

The necessary utilities came slowly. The telephones were installed in 1911. During the "Hungry Thirties" all but a very few were removed as the farmers could not pay for them. The second R.E.A. in Alberta was hooked up in Davisburg in 1951. Natural gas reached the area in fall of 1972. Mrs. Vera Gillespie was active in the development of the R.E.A., the gas and the formation of the Calgary Co-Operative Association Limited, which was a rural development originally.

The land homesteaded by Mr. and Mrs. Andrews has been sold to developers. Mr. and Mrs. Andrews remember having fifteen Indians in the kitchen. "We didn't know what they wanted, but we kept our wits about us enough to put on the kettle and find them something to eat." We discovered later that they had been given permission by the R.N.W.M.P. to remove the carcass of a steer. They went away quite calmly after their coffee break.

OSBORNE GEORGE ANDREWS AND ETHEL ANDREWS — by George Andrews

Osborne came to the Territories at the turn of the century from Inverness, Megantic County, Quebec. He worked for some time for Pat Burns, later operating a livery barn at Carmangay for his brother-in-law, Will Wannop. Then for some years he successfully farmed in the Vulcan district. He returned to Quebec to marry Ethel in 1909. Part of the honeymoon was by buckboard, in winter, from Parkland to Carmangay, approximately forty miles.

In 1918 he purchased from his uncle, Tom Andrews, the W ½-29 and the E ½-31-21-28-W4 in the Davisburg district. The move was necessary as his children, Laura and George, were of school age and the schools in the Vulcan area were inaccessible. The location was close to a school and kitty-corner to 79 acres, selected as a townsite, on a railroad loop from Aldersyde to connect with the C.P.R. line to Calgary. Although the grade was completed, no rails were ever laid.

In 1919 he and his brothers put up around 200 acres of prairie wool hay. His brother Angus shipped some cattle from Parkland for wintering and the balance of the hay was sold to a ready market, due to the tough winter of 1919-20, at around $40.00 per ton and to distances of up to 40 miles. Osborne would tell farmers not to come back as no more hay was available for sale, but in a few days some would return with four-horse teams and he did not have the heart to send them home with empty racks.

The first few years were difficult ones. The farm was stocked with heifer calves, some of which were held for two years and sold for less than purchase price. The farm, situated close to the confluence of the Bow and Highwood Rivers, was subject to hail and some damage was suffered the first seven years. However, the storms usually struck early in July and feed and some grain were harvested, although of low grade. In hopes of having a weed-free farm, the entire family was recruited to pull wagon loads of stinkweed.

When they first came, there were no grain elevators at De Winton and grain was hauled eleven miles to Okotoks or loaded in carloads over the platform at De Winton. When a car was loaded it was necessary to enlist the help of neighbors.

Cattle were marketed by driving them over the Blackfoot Trail to Calgary. The Blackfoot Trail cut through the east half of section 31. During winter sometimes they were driven to De Winton and shipped by rail. Osborne kept a good herd of Shorthorn cattle, and steers were marketed at two or three years of age directly from the grass. Even during the Depression, his cattle sold readily at near top prevailing prices. (Cattle brand listed with other brands.)

Ethel made butter from the milk of six to eight cows. As there were no refrigerating facilities, this was often done very early in the morning. The butter boxes were wrapped in wet canvas, taken to De Winton by buggy along with the eggs, and shipped to the Calgary market.

For some years the threshing was done by the Dunbow Industrial School. The crew consisted of ten racks, two men to a rack, and brother Tom and brother John. Feeding them their noon meal presented a problem as they had healthy appetites. Mrs. Frank Tucker usually assisted. Later threshermen with smaller outfits were the James brothers, Bob Riddle, and Alex Blackwood.

A disastrous fire during the Depression, in which the barn and combined implement shed and all contents were destroyed, nearly crippled them.

A son, Angus, assisted for several years in the operation of the farm, during which time they also rented the SE ¼-30. The home place was sold after Angus left the farm and they moved to the east half of 31 where Osborne, at the age of 68, was injured in the building of a house. Thinking he could no longer farm, this half was sold to Sher Hughes and they moved to the SE ¼-30, which they purchased and is still owned by Angus.

Osborne served a term as trustee of Davisburg School District No. 79, was on the church board and secretary-treasurer of the church for a long period.

He was a handyman and did most of his carpentry work, shoe repairing, harness repairing, including making replacement parts, butchering and curing meats. He was much in demand for treatment of sick animals. Some of his concoctions were enough to kill a horse but, surprisingly, most of them recovered.

They retired to Calgary but Osborne continued to spend the summers on the farm until shortly before his death. Ethel died in 1954 and Osborne in 1963.

Their children are: Laura, now Mrs. C. Laverne Wenger, who lives in Calgary and has two children, Larry in Australia and Irene at home; George, who married Isabel Smith, is retired and living in Olds after over 41 years' service with the Bank of Montreal. They have three children. Rodney was rector of St. Peter's Church in Okotoks for seven years and now lives in Red Deer. Margaret, married to Rev. Thomas Forgrave, lives in Sherwood Park, and Gwendolyn is now Mrs. Robert Moggey of Olds. Angus, who was born in the district and attended high school at De Winton, married Audree Aukland and is branch manager of Manufacturers Life Insurance, stationed in Edmonton. His children are Gay and Lorraine.

All the children received their public school education at Davisburg School No.79. Laura was janitor of the school for a while and received 15¢ per school day and an additional 10¢ per day when a fire was necessary.

THOMAS H. ANDREWS — by Olive La Berge

Thomas H. Andrews came West in 1884 from Inverness, Quebec and spent two weeks exploring around Calgary, looking for good rich land with lots of water, and finally filing on a homestead in what is now the Davisburg district.

He could see the wonderful prospects ahead for himself and his family and also for many of his neighbors in Inverness. Mrs. Andrews finally consented to the venture, then with the help of the family, spent the remainder of the winter making quilts and preparing the necessities for their future home in Alberta.

Spring of 1884 arrived and plenty of maple sugar and syrup was made. By this time a colony had been formed and named after Colonel Barwass. Making up the colony were Mr. and Mrs. T. H. Andrews and their three children, Emma, Jim and Alice, and several of their neighbors.

They brought with them what were called "settlers' effects," making up most of their train load. This was a long journey which took about two weeks. Finally they got a glimpse of the Rocky Mountains; then it was not long before they arrived in Calgary in July of 1885. They rested for a couple of days, assembling their wagons and buggies and unloading all their possessions off the railway cars. The third day they started south to the homestead site. That, too, was quite a trip, by ox team and horses, bringing cattle and chickens and not forgetting the dog.

They immediately started preparing for winter. Mr. Andrews started to build a sod shack, which was their home for the first winter. Then he built a log house which is still standing today. This house was later covered with siding and more living quarters were added as the years went on. So, whoever dismantles the old homestead will find the remains of some of the old original logs that came from Quebec.

Mr. and Mrs. Andrews farmed for many years,

Mr. and Mrs. T. H. Andrews homestead — 1885.

buying more land and raising many good Clydesdale horses. His horse brand was 19 on the right shoulder and the cattle brand was 19 on the right hip.

In 1909 they retired, moving to Calgary where Mrs. Andrews (nee Flora McKenzie) of Inverness, Quebec, died June 30, 1911, and Thomas Andrews died March 2, 1931. Both are buried in Union Cemetery in Calgary.

Their younger daughter Alice married Charlie E. Shattuck.

THE ANGEL FAMILY — by B. Angel

Murral, Bessie and Betty Angel arrived in the Davisburg district in April of 1938 and stayed two years, till April, 1940. We moved to Davisburg from the Table Butte district, near Stavely, Alberta. Our farm was located on N.W.¼-31-28-W.4, across the road, to the south of the Morasch farm. We purchased it from Mr. P. B. Ralph and sold it to Louis and Alice Sather.

JOE AND LETA (SHATTUCK) ARMSTRONG — by L. Armstrong

As a young man, in 1926, Joe arrived with his parents, Mr. and Mr. David Armstrong, from Didsbury, to farm in the Allan district.

On October 6, 1933, he was married to Leta Shattuck, youngest daughter of oldtimers, Alice and Charles Shattuck. The wedding took place in Davisburg United Church, where, forty years

previously, Leta's parents had been married on May 24, 1893.

Leta was born and raised in the Davisburg district, taking her schooling at Davisburg School. She then entered the Southern Alberta Institute of Technology in Calgary to take a millinery course.

After their marriage Leta and Joe farmed the S½-25-21-29-W4 until moving to Willow Park, in Calgary, in 1964. Joe was then employed by the Alberta Department of Highways until retiring in 1974.

The Armstrongs had two children, Margaret and Ralph. Ralph was married to Sharon Dick of De Winton in 1963. They continued to farm the home place until it was sold in 1971. Then Sharon, Ralph and family moved north to a farm at Rimbey. Marg resides in Calgary. There are three grandchildren, Debbie, Cody and Leanne.

Since retirement in 1974, the Armstrongs have spent the summers trailering and fishing in Alberta and B.C. and the winters, reliving the stories about "the big one that got away".

BANISTER, ALBERT EDWARD AND HELEN MARY — written by their granddaughter Audrey Banister Bolin

In 1884, Albert Edward Banister, veterinary surgeon, sailed from Bridport, England, for Canada, bringing with him his four oldest sons — Bertram, Albert, William and Harold. Left behind, were his

145

wife, Helen Mary and their eight children. Their boat, S.S. Sardinia, docked at Quebec ten days later. They then took the train to Owen Sound, the boat to Port Arthur, the train to Winnipeg and then on to Calgary. The population of the city was then under one thousand, and the nearest bank in Winnipeg.

They arrived in Calgary on a festive day and were awed by the sight of five or six hundred Indians coming down the Blackfoot Trail (now ninth avenue). Their black hair hung in long thick braids; they wore only breech cloths and were painted in brilliant colors of red and yellow, and bedecked in a gorgeous array of colored feathers. Arranging themselves in several circles, they performed a real Indian pow-wow to the beat of the tom-tom. This entertainment kept up as long as the white settlers extended gifts of tea or tobacco.

When the excitement died down, my grandfather was able to find temporary shelter, a tiny shack, one board thick with a mud floor, which he rented for twenty dollars a month. Here they lived until a homestead was located.

Mr. Banister was advised by Sam Livingstone, the self-styled "American Explorer", that thirty miles down the Bow River, at the Big Bend, was the finest land to be found anywhere. After several days of searching, the land at the Big Bend was selected — 500 acres of C.P.R. 5-22-28-W4. Later, a half section which constituted homestead and pre-emption was applied for nearby.

First, a mud-roofed log house built by a French Canadian who understood his work, and here Mr. Banister and his sons lived while the "Grotto" was being built. Strangely enough, they didn't seem to feel the cold too badly at first. The boys used to break ice in the river and go swimming. Brrrrr! Eleven year old Harold was supposed to be the cook but neighbors were all very good at helping the bachelors. Mrs. Tom Andrews used to mend for the boys.

In 1885, word was received that the Blackfoot Indians were on the war-path. As conditions worsened, white settlers were provided with guns and ammunition. The boys had a bad fright once when their father was unavoidably delayed in town. An excited rider came galloping by to tell them that the Indians were massacring all the white settlers along the road. The boys had visions of their father coming home to find four mangled corpses. Determined not to die without a struggle, they made preparations for an attack they felt sure would come after dark. Not satisfied with making sure their guns were loaded, they put into effect another scheme. After securely barricading the outside door of their home, they opened the cellar trap door and securely tied mowing machine blades together down below. Their plan was that the Indians would burst into the house, fall into the blades, and while attempting to extricate themselves, the boys would shoot them from above. Needless to say it was a sleepless night for the foursome. When their father arrived home next morning, he told them there had been no real danger. The neighbor had panicked unnecessarily and spread the alarm. Later, after the Blackfoot Treaty had been signed, Indians would

sometimes ride into the yard bearing placards which read, "FRIENDS OF WHITES".

With everyone helping, the Grotto was finished in 1887. The carpenter, Joe Phipps, was very skillful. Walls on the second floor were plastered, and on the ground floor Douglas fir was used. Built on the side of the hill, one could walk from the upstairs to outdoors and be on level ground. Much of their lumber was sawed with a pit-saw from logs washed down the river in floods.

The Grotto and its five occupants were ready and eager to welcome Mrs. Banister, her six daughters, Emmeline, Jennie, Florence, Margaret (Daisy), Eva and Ida, and two more sons, Victor (twin to Daisy), and Stephen, born the month after his father sailed for Canada. The oldest daughter, Fanny, joined them three years later. She would like to have stayed in London but could not bear to be parted from her family any longer. This family of thirteen was destined to be together only once.

The Grotto was purchased by Mr. Magee in 1907 and Mr. and Mrs. Banister with their youngest daughter, Ida, moved to Victoria, B.C. Mrs. Banister died there in 1909, and her husband in 1914. Their bodies lie in Ross Bay Cemetery.

Here in brief is what happened to the thirteen Banisters:

FANNY Helen — born 1864 — married the Reverend J. A. Matheson, a Presbyterian missionary in Davisburg from 1890 to 1895, and later in Ontario and Quebec. They had three children; Donald, 1895-1913, (unmarried); Ursula, 1900, married to Judge Grant, and now residing in Mississauga, Ontario; Kenneth, 1908-1929 (unmarried). FANNY died in 1936 in Calgary, the result of an accident while visiting her sister, Emmeline (Mrs. W. R. Hull).

EMMELINE — Born 1866. In speaking of those early days and the happy social events, she said, "Looking back, it seems like every day was a picnic". She was first married to Jack Ellis. He became a victim of T.B. and though his wife took him to Arizona for his health, he only lived a few years after their marriage. After his death, Emmeline went to England to visit an uncle in England. She remained there at her uncle's request until he died. Returning to Calgary after ten years of widowhood, she married William Roper Hull who died in 1925. She lived till 1953.

BERTRAM Turner — born 1868. He was unmarried and died as the result of a shooting accident. He is buried in Davisburg Cemetery.

ALBERT Edward — born 1869. He married Agnes Burns, daughter of Thomas Burns (at one time treasurer for the City of Calgary). They moved to Victoria, B.C. There were two children from the marriage, Thomas, retired from Victoria Police Force, and Margaret (Rita). The mother died when Rita was small and she later came to live with her Aunt Emmeline Hull until her marriage to the Reverend F. C. Vaughan Birch. Rita died in Sydney, B.C. in 1968, Albert served overseas in World War I.

WILLIAM (Billy) — Born 1870 — married Amelia Mills (Millie) Brown who taught at the Davisburg School. Their first child, Albert, died in infancy and is buried in Davisburg. Son, Franklin, received the

O.B.E. for his service as head chaplain of the first Canadian contingent overseas from 1939 to 1945. Their other son, Weston farmed with his father at Campbellcroft, Ontario, till Billie's death in 1968 and still resides in that area. Their only daughter, Emmeline, is married to Dr. Harold Hedley, recently retired as Superintendent of County Schools, Oxford, and they reside in Woodstock, Ontario.

HAROLD — Born 1872. He homesteaded in the Davisburg district south and east of the Grotto. Part of the original home still stands on the land now owned by Jack Morasch. In 1903 he married Laura Bryce, and six of their nine children were born in Davisburg. Additions were added to the house as the family expanded. Bertram, born 1904, and married Katherine Mercer who taught in Okotoks and he died in Taber in 1949. Mary was born in 1905 and died of diphtheria when nineteen months old. She is buried in Davisburg. Stanley (Chick), born 1906, married Hazel Robison of Turner Valley, and died in Calgary 1966. Dallas, born 1908, married William Wright and resides in Miami, Florida. Audrey, born 1910, married first to George Sutherland (See Sutherland, De Winton) who died in 1951 and is now married to Gus Bolin. George (Straw), born 1911, married Dorothy Knupp, High River, and they live in Edmonton. John (Jack) born 1914, married Dora Priestly, Calgary and now lives there. Ronald — 1917, married Inez Thorson, Okotoks and they live in Nassau and Virginia. Ida Patricia (Pat) — 1920, married to John Wedderburn and they farm north of Okotoks.

Mr. and Mrs. Harold Banister.

HAROLD sold his Davisburg farm and moved to Okotoks in 1913. He and his wife both served their terms as president of Southern Alberta Pioneer and Old Timer's Association. At the time of his death in 1934, Mr. Banister was mayor of Okotoks. Mrs. Banister died in 1946.

JENNIE — Born 1874 and died in Kamloops, B.C. 1953. She was married to Arthur Winterbottom, and they had a family of five. Their oldest son, Sydney, was killed in France, 1917. Helen (Coles) and Keith live in Vancouver. Joan (Kellman) died there in 1969. John, the youngest son had his surname changed to Winton after his mother's death. It is interesting to note here that my Aunt Jennie used to be most indignant if anyone made fun of her married name, and

John as a young man enjoyed quoting the following limerick: There was a young fellow of Tyre Who constantly sat on the fire; When asked if 't was hot, He replied, "It is not, For I'm John Winterbottom, Esquire".

FLORENCE — Born 1897 and married Charles Edwards. They had one daughter, Dorothy, but separated when she was a child. Dorothy (Hilliard) lives in Victoria, B.C. Florrie died in Kelowna — 1957.

MARGARET (Daisy) — Born 1897 — Married Charles Robert Brown and they farmed in the Shepard district later moving to Victoria, B.C. Returning to Alberta, they farmed in Big Valley area. (Their grandson, Ronnie Brown still farms this land). Daisy died in 1926 and was survived by her four children: Winnifred Tipper who died in 1975; Gordon, who with his wife Frances died in the plane crash at Tokyo, Japan Airport in 1966, returning home from a visit to their daughter in Australia. A son Victor died in the thirties. The lone survivor now is Margaret (Edwards) of Calgary.

VICTOR (twin to Daisy) — 1876 to 1961. Married Kitty Cooper in Victoria and lived there till the time of their deaths. Their only daughter, Mary (unmarried) still lives there.

Adelina EVA — 1880 to 1953. Married to Guy Pownall in Davisburg, 1898, and they also moved west. Their daughter Norah (Hughes) and son George live in Victoria. A daughter, Adeline died at the age of thirteen; a son David lives in Vancouver.

Aunt Eva and Aunt Ida used to tell the story of a sickly calf that was given to them as no one thought the animal would live. Through the girls' tender loving care, it survived and they sold it. The money they got for it was the first either had ever had. They were allowed to go to Calgary for the first time, to spend it, and they bought presents for every member of the family, that trip was the highlight of their young lives.

IDA Harriet Isabel — 1882-1968. She used to play the organ for the services in Davisburg Church and received a gift of money in appreciation when she moved with her parents to Victoria. With it she bought a sterling silver dresser set which she willed to her namesake, Ida (Pat) Wedderburn.

Ida stayed with her father till his death in 1914. She then trained as a nurse in the hope of being able to go overseas. However, at thirty-two, she was over the age of acceptance in Canada so continued her training in Spokane, Washington. With her limited schooling she found the course very difficult. She spent many years with her sister Emmeline in Calgary after the death of W. R. Hull in 1925, and did not marry till 1932. She used to say she was the hope of all spinsters. Her husband, John Turner, lived only a few years.

STEPHEN (Steno) — 1884-1961. He married Ida Miller at Macleod in 1874 and they took up a homestead at Nose Hills, west of Coronation in 1907. (He and Harold are the only sons of A. E. Banister to remain in Alberta.)

Due to ill health, Steno's wife moved to Vancouver with their two daughters, Ida (Birdie) and Kate, but he stayed in Coronation till he died. He spent a number of winters in Calgary with his sister, Emmeline Hull, and served a year as president of Southern Alberta Pioneer and Old Timer's Association in Calgary. His wife died in Vancouver in 1958 and his daughters still live there. Kate, a graduate of St. Paul's Hospital there, has recently retired as a Public Health nurse.

There are no survivors of the original thirteen children of Mr. and Mrs. A. E. Banister but their many children and grandchildren are living proof that the one "N" Banisters is a name not soon to die out.

My thanks to my sister Dallas Wright who was far-sighted enough to record many of our father's memoirs while he was still alive, and to my late Aunt Millie for the story of the GROTTO.

J. W. BARTLAM — by Mayme Martin

My father, J. W. Bartlam, came down to the Davisburg District in May of 1915 and lived on the Worden ¼ just south of Herr's and north of the John Todd place. Mother, my brother Gerald and I, came out August 5th, 1915, from Toronto, where we had gone in July, 1914, for me to undergo surgery. We lived on this land until March 1st, 1917, when Dad rented the L. M. Orton place, east of De Winton.

We attended Davisburg School and an English girl, Miss Livingston, was the first teacher, later we had Miss Aggie Gray (Mrs. Barsby Martin).

We were very green kids, never having driven a horse, and, I'm sure, afforded folks many a good laugh, to us, real tragedies, but eventually we learned.

When we moved in 1917 we attended Melrose School and our first teacher was Miss Doris Parrot, who is still alive and, I believe, lives in Calgary. Our next teacher was Miss Lockhart, a girl from Nova Scotia, she was followed by Rev. Clark.

When we first lived in Davisburg we attended church, then the Methodist, and also Sunday-School, at the home of one of the finest people, Mrs. McConnell. She was a Baptist and supplied the lesson books and S.S. papers out of her own pocket. Many a Sunday there would be so many people there, we'd sit on the floor and the stair steps.

After we moved to the Orton Place we attended church and S.S. at Pine Creek. During the summer there were services occasionally in the Melrose Schoolhouse, one evening a month. One evening when Rev. Clark was praying, all heads were bowed, all at once he stopped and of course we all looked up. A little child had crawled up and was clasping his leg firmly. Needless to say he was startled and the child looked so cute and said "Da Da Da."

We had good times in the Melrose School with Spelling Bees and good Christmas concerts. Edna Currie and I were always tied as the top Spellers. My brother was an excellent elocutionist and went to all the concerts around, reciting.

The ministers as I remember them were; Rev. Campbell who later was in Saskatoon, Rev. Clarke, the Clarkes had three children, Robert, Ruth and I don't remember the name of the youngest one. Then came a student minister from Ontario, Mr. Ellis. He had two children, Eden and Bobby. He was followed by a Mr. Treffry with wife and son Joey. That is all I can recall.

My Dad and Mother were quite community minded folk and belonged to the U.F.A. and the U.F.W.A., in fact, Mother was the president for a couple of years. They took in the dances at De Winton and after the community hall was built in 1920 they were active workers in it.

In 1920 my Dad bought a small ranch at Millarville but we did not move on to it until 1924. My Dad passed away quite suddenly in 1944 and Mother in 1956. They were buried in the Anglican Cemetery at Midnapore.

I went to High School in Calgary and Gerald went to Okotoks, later he went to Normal School in Calgary and after teaching for a few years moved to the States. He is retired now and lives in Bloomfield Hills, Michigan. His son, Bill, is married and has two children. I have a daughter, Gwen, (Mrs. N. E. Cohoe) who is living in Calgary and has two boys and three girls. My other daughter, Pat, went to the States in 1946 and passed away May 9, 1967. I now live in Strathmore where we have lived for the past 23 years. My husband passed away July 7, 1973.

In 1917 Mrs. George Gray formed a C.G.I.T. Group and the members were; Eleanor Gray, Vera and June Marshall, Mary and Lena Dalzell, Edna Currie, Georgina Warrack and myself. We were the first country C.G.I.T. Group in Alberta and were cheered at the First Baptist Church at a conference in 1919.

In 1918 Vera Marshall came home from teaching and started a girls' basketball team and Georgina Warrack was the outstanding player. We played in a yard in De Winton (the house belonged to De Mings, the Post Master). We played on Wednesday and Saturday evenings and quite thought that we were at least destined to be worthy opponents of any team in Western Canada.

THE BLACKWOOD FAMILY — by Effie Leach

My father, Alexander Scott Blackwood, was born in Kilmarnock, Ayrshire, Scotland in 1863. As a young man he left home for the life of a sailor on a sailing vessel bound first for the tropics and later to Seattle where he left the ship, having tired of salt-pork, hardtack and a restricted and far from glamourous life. He went to British Columbia and joined a construction gang of the C.P.R., working through the mountains. In the fall of 1884 he went back to Scotland to visit his parents, returning to Canada in the spring of 1885, just in time to get into the Northwest Rebellion. He was a scout and was wounded in the hip, for which he received the magnificent pension of $7.50 per year.

He was entitled to 320 acres of Crown land on which he did homestead duties, receiving the "Letters Patent" for same in 1891. This was a grant for taking part in the Northwest Rebellion of 1885. It was several years later that he discovered he was entitled to a regular homestead as well, but by that time all the land in that area had been taken.

He took active part in the forming of the school district, which was No. 79, and in building the Presbyterian Church, which still stands, a memorial to the pioneers in the 1880s.

Times were hard, money was scarce, and at one

time the half section of land was for sale at one dollar per acre. However, there was only one prospective buyer and he wanted a stack of prairie hay thrown in, so the deal was off.

Alex Blackwood and Isabella Brodie were married and moved to Vancouver where Father worked in a sugar refinery. They then moved to an acreage on the Shuswap Lake near Sicamous. It is interesting to note that there is a Blackwood Creek in this area. Ina and Alex investigated and found the remains of old buildings and believe it to be the place where our parents lived before I was born. They returned to Davisburg in the fall of 1894.

My mother, Isabella Brodie, was born of Scottish parentage in 1865 at Inverness, Megantic County, Quebec, and was orphaned as a young child. She was one of a group who came to Calgary in 1885. She later went by stagecoach, along with her brother-in-law and sister, Mr. and Mrs. William Andrews, to Pincher Creek where they all worked for Colonel J. F. Macleod. Afterwards she worked in the Brett Sanitarium at Banff.

In 1899, Father was appointed a Justice of the Peace for the Northwest Territories. Many a court case was held in the dining room of our house, where justice was dispensed with mercy and the doors shut securely to keep out curious eyes and little listening ears.

The Blackwoods 1950. Back row: Alex, Nellie, Edna, Jim. Front row: Effie, Jean, Bertha, Daisy.

Mrs. Alex S. Blackwood and son, Jim, 1927.

Father died in 1927 and Mother in 1950. Both are buried in the Davisburg Cemetery.

There were seven daughters and two sons in the family. Bertha, the eldest, married Archie Maconnachie and made her home in Bowden and Lacombe. She came back to Davisburg and worked at the De Winton Airport. Later she moved to Calgary where she lived for many years. Presently she makes her home at Sylvan Lake with sister Jean Palmer.

Daisy went to the United States as a young woman and married George Bently in Seattle. She has one son Harold and a daughter Lorraine (Mrs. Vernon Davis).

Effie was married to Chester Leach in 1928. See the Leach Family story.

Isabella Maple died in infancy and is buried at Davisburg.

Jean, after teaching school for several years, was married to Charlie Palmer. They tried fruit farming near Salmon Arm, B.C., eventually moving back to Alberta. They owned and operated the Sylvan Lake Dairy for many years. Charlie is now dead and Jean lives in Sylvan Lake. There were three daughters: Jean (Mrs. Ken Jensen) in Vancouver has two daughters; Barbara (Mrs. Jim Craig) in Calgary has one son and one daughter; and Shirley passed away at the age of fourteen.

Nellie, the sixth girl of the family, married Jack Crookes and spent her married life first in rural Alberta and later in the oil fields at Black Diamond and Turner Valley where Jack worked. They have one son Douglas who, at time of writing, is in England working for an oil exploration company. He is married to Vi Hokansen and they have three children, Ellen, Susan and Eric. Jack Crookes died in 1951 and Nellie worked for Howard Norris, Jr. at Canadian Linens for many years. Nellie married Bill Hahn, who has now passed on. She is presently a patient in Blunt's Nursing Home in Calgary.

Jim, the first of the boys, married Dolly Bruce. His story appears elsewhere.

Alex H. is married to Ina Flett. They live on the original Blackwood farm. (See story elsewhere.)

Edna, another schoolteacher, married Leland McGarvey and spent her married life on a farm near Ponoka. Edna died in 1951, leaving three children. They are Donna (Mrs. Bud Merrill) of Ponoka who has five children, Aurla (Mrs. Tom Johnston), and Carol (Mrs. Tony Nicollette), both of Vancouver, B.C.

We were a busy, happy family and never felt we were deprived of anything. Our parents gave us love and understanding and we all, as a family, appreciate the good principles we were taught. We look back with pride, gratitude and admiration for the honesty and integrity of our parents. I have so often thought of the tribute which Auntie Kate Andrews paid our father at the time of his death: "Justice and honour at any cost."

ALEXANDER HENRY BLACKWOOD — by I. Blackwood

Alex Blackwood is the younger son of Alexander Scott Blackwood and Isabella Brodie Blackwood, early pioneers of the Davisburg district. Alex was born April 14, 1906 on the farm where he still resides. This is the N½-24-21-29-W4.

On November 6, 1935 he married Ina Flett of Calgary, daughter of Andrew and Sarah Flett, and granddaughter of another pioneer family, John and Sarah Irving. They had three children, Rodger, Norma and Muriel. Ina graduated from the Calgary Normal School in 1929 and taught school at Gladys and Ensign.

Rodger married Jean Porter and they live on the original Blackwood home place. His son Scott makes the fourth generation to live there. He also has four step-children: Linda, Robert, Bradley, and Stephen Porter.

Norma married Ronald Lock, grandson of Mr. and Mrs. Frank Tucker, old-timers of the district. They live at Nanton and have five children — Michael, Gary, Brent, Carla, and Dana.

Muriel married Wayne Stordahl of Bawlf and they live in Edmonton.

In 1973, Alex and Ina bought a small acreage at Mara, B.C., where they spend their summers.

Our cattle brand is OIL on the left rib. This had been Alex's father's horse brand. Rodger has the brand which belonged to his grandmother Irving.

JAMES NEIL BLACKWOOD — by Dolly Blackwood

James Neil Blackwood was born October 24, 1903 at Davisburg. He drove trucks for James and Reimer for many years. On April 16, 1942 he joined the Canadian Active Army and served in Canada and the United Kingdom. He was discharged June 24, 1944. After the war he farmed in the Davisburg district until retiring to Okotoks in 1966.

On October 4, 1966 he married Dorothy Bruce and they remained in Okotoks until Jim passed away March 22, 1973. Dolly still lives in Okotoks.

BRYCE, HENRY AND MARY ANN — by Audrey (Banister) Bolin

Henry and Mary Ann Bryce were born in Ireland, and farmed near Port Hope, Ontario, before coming to the Allan district, N.W.¼ 6-21-28-W5. This was later farmed by James Coombes. Two infant sons were buried in Ontario and they brought with them their only child, eleven year old, Laura Beatrice.

Being an only child and raised by very strict elderly parents who didn't believe in either cards or dancing, Laura was often very lonely and used to wish fervently for a sister. I can picture the good times she enjoyed visiting the Grotto, the home of the large Banister family of whom she was to become a member by marrying Harold in 1903. Laura used to ride to the schoolhouse which was later moved to Okotoks and became the home of Mr. and Mrs. Andrew Rowles. They were to be her neighbors when she and her hus-

band moved into the house previously occupied by her parents, Mr. and Mrs. Bryce.

The wedding of Laura and Harold Banister took place in the Davisburg Church and was performed by the Reverend James Shortt. who many years later became the moderator of the Presbyterian Church of Canada. They were to raise a family of eight. Their first daughter, Mary Beatrice, died of dyphtheria when only nineteen months old and is buried in Davisburg cemetery. (See Banister re other members of the family.)

Mr. and Mrs. Bryce later moved to Okotoks where Mrs. Bryce died in 1910 at the age of sixty-seven. In 1913, Laura and Harold and their five children moved in with the ageing Mr. Bryce, who died in 1914 at 82. The three youngest children were born in this house.

Laura, a widow for twelve years, lived to see her family all married, and she became a grandmother many times over before her death in 1946 at 67.

P.S. For the records, it should be noted that the original spelling was BRICE. It was unofficially changed to BRYCE because Laura thought it a prettier way of spelling the name.

One son was named Stanley BRYCE (Chick).

JOSEPH LORNE AND THELMA IVY (MILLER) BRYCE — by Ken Bryce

My father, Joseph Lorne McMurray Bryce, was born in the farm home that my grandfather built in Davisburg, N.W.T. (as the address was known then). The address is now R.R. No. 1, De Winton, Alberta, Mrs. Thomas Andrews, who acted as mid-wife through the district in those days, and Dr. Welsh were present at my father's birth. Mrs. Andrews lived about four miles from my grandparents' home. My father was born on February 21, 1903.

When he was old enough to go to school, my grandfather took him to school on his saddle horse and then went on to do carpenter work around the neighbourhood. He would then bring him home when school was out in the afternoon. Father took all the education offered at the Davisburg school. This included receiving his grade eight diploma. After this he stayed home and farmed with my grandfather.

On December 27, 1932 he met my mother, Thelma Ivy Miller, who was born at Wolseley, Saskatchewan on April 23, 1908. She was living with her parents in Calgary at the time. They were married at the Pro Cathedral in Calgary on February 27, 1935. They lived on the farm and while they were there two children were born; Madeline, April 16, 1936 and I, Kenneth (Ken), July 17, 1941. My father received an offer from Rulon Rich to help him in the flour milling business in Okotoks so we, the family of four, moved to Okotoks, and bought a home there. The flour milling business did not last too long so Father got a mechanic's license. Then, with Grandfather's (Wm. C. Bryce) help, he was able to get his steam engineer's license.

In 1960 my parents and I decided to return to the farm in Davisburg. We bought a house in Aldersyde and moved it out to the farm. Things went wrong for us. Mother did not seem well and we just could not find out what was wrong. Dr. Cramer from High River came to see her and figured she had arthritis but when

Joseph Bryce's family: front L. to R. Joe, Thelma. Standing, L. to R. Madeline and Kenneth.

they took her to Calgary cancer was diagnosed. To make matters worse Father's diabetes flared up and he too landed in the hospital, shortly after Mother, in bad condition. When Father arrived home from hospital, he and I bought a house in Aldersyde to have more comfort for Mother, as it was more modern. Mother made it home for Christmas then returned to the hospital and passed away on January 12, 1967.

My father and I decided we would continue to live in Aldersyde and operate the farm in Davisburg. It was also more convenient for me to live in Aldersyde because when I completed my grade twelve at Okotoks High School, I also got my second class steam engineer papers and I have worked at the Okotoks Gas and Sulphur Recovery Plant for the past fifteen years. I am also shift foreman at the plant.

After my mother passed away, my father never had the best of health. Due to diabetes his feet always bothered him. He passed away very suddenly on March 9, 1974.

Madeline took approximately three years of schooling, attending the same Davisburg School as her father, and, when we moved to Okotoks, she took the balance of her education there. She then worked in the Jenkin's Groceteria at High River. It was while working there that she met Floyd Harley Swartz of High River whom she later married. They later moved to Blackie, Alberta where Harley was manager at the Pioneer Elevator. Madeline bought and ran a store there. In 1965 they moved to Edmonton where Harley works for Edmonton Power in the Clover Bar Generating Station. They have two little girls, Cori and Hayley.

WILLIAM CHARLES AND ELIZABETH (McMURRAY) BRYCE — by Stella Nelubowich

In the fall of 1898 my father, William Bryce, sold his farm near Kintore, Ontario and took the train from Thamesford, Ontario for Calgary, Alberta. He arrived in Calgary November 4, 1898 at 4 a.m. The population of Calgary was only 5,000 at that time. Mrs. William Lineham directed him to the Alberta Hotel where he stayed for a few days. Then went to Okotoks where he secured a job with John Lineham's Lumber Camp, up in the mountains. The winter was very cold up there and when the thermometer showed 50 degrees below zero, the men refused to go to work. Then one day the thermometer disappeared, where it went no one knows.

One Sunday afternoon, a wandering group of Indians called on the men in the camp when they were sitting around resting. Father admired the moccasins one of the Indians was wearing. The Indian immediately unlaced them and took them off, offering them to Father for 50¢. Father always said they were the best bargain he ever got for 50¢. To his surprise, the Indian fellow still had another pair on his feet for sale. How many more pair he had on was not known.

Father left his job in the bush about March 20 and got a job with Joe Brice, a rancher, who lived six miles NE of Okotoks. One day he sent Father to the Dunbow School and on the way he passed a farm that looked good to him. When he returned Joe Brice agreed that the farm was a good one and offered to loan Father a horse to go and get a better look at it. After riding over it he liked it better than ever so he was told to give 'Toby', the saddle horse, a good feed of oats and then go right to Calgary and buy the farm from J. G. VanWart as there were three other fellows after it Father left as soon as the horse had eaten and met with Mr. VanWart and bought the farm that same day. It was situated two miles north of Joe Brice's ranch, 18-21-28-W4.

After he had acquired the farm, he wrote to his childhood sweetheart, Elizabeth (Libbie) McMurray, who lived, a mile north of Kintore, Ontario, with her mother, on a farm. Mother arrived in Calgary June 15, 1899 and they were married June 17, 1899 by the Presbyterian minister, Reverand Herdman, at the manse. George T. Smith, Mother's first cousin, who came west with her, was their only relative in the west, saw them married. They stayed in Calgary for a few days and then came out to Okotoks on the old C. & E. Railroad. The rails were laid on ties which were lying on the prairie, with no road bed, and they had a real rough ride. Henry Brice met them at Okotoks and took them home for dinner and then they went home to the farm, Father had just bought.

The house that Mother came to was a lot different than the one she came from in the east. Just one room, built out of packing boxes. The cellar was a hole dug in the ground and it was full of water within one foot of the floor. Father went down to John Lineham's Mill and got mill ends to build on three more rooms. In later years, a kitchen and utility room were added on.

George Smith bought 1-21-29-W4, across the road from Joe Brice, my father built his house which is still standing today and is occupied by the James Scott family. George was married and had two daughters.

Father also homesteaded 12 miles straight north of Blackie, one mile south of the Pine Canyon School. I believe Ronnie Bird bought this quarter section in about 1947 or 1948.

Stella Bryce, holding a prairie chicken large threshing operation in background, 1914.

Mother and Father told us that the railroad from Calgary to Okotoks was built through a large slough, north of De Winton, on the Anderson place. It was dry when the railroad went through but later filled up with water. When the train was nearing the slough, the fireman would build up a good head of steam and, when they reached the slough the passengers had to get off. They put all the speed possible on the train and made a fast run across the water. When they reached the other side all the wet material had to be removed from the fire-box, a new fire built and a new head of steam built up. By the time the engine was ready to continue, the passengers had walked around the water to where the train was. The conductor would shout "All Aboard!" and away they would go, to Okotoks and all points south. When the trains returned from the south to Calgary they had to go through the same thing again.

Father got his cattle brand the same year he was married. When his horse brand accidentally ran out, a new one was taken out and the original cattle brand and the new horse brand are still in the family. These brands are shown elsewhere in the book.

Before coming west, Father served four years apprenticeship as a farmer, in Ontario, and used to be at all the big barn raising bees for miles around where he lived. When he came west he did a lot of building for people in the area to make extra money for himself to get started farming. He would take Joseph Lorne to school on his saddle horse and carry his tools along to do his carpenter work. Buggies were scarce in those days and most everyone travelled by saddle horse. In later years they bought a cart and it broke down, dropping them and Joseph at the horse's heels. Mother tried to throw Joseph clear but an umbrella handle caught his leg and nearly broke it. That is when they bought a buggy.

Mother was very fond of the country and she loved the view of the mountains. The Indians were her worst fear. One day, when Father was away, a band of roving Indians arrived at their little one room house. They rode around the little house, peeking in the windows and calling out "white squaw, white Squaw" and frightening her so badly, she hid in the bed.

Not long after my parents came, Mr. Thomas Andrews fenced the section of land across the road, east of their home, thus shutting off the Indian trails. The Indians just came across once, on this section, and came up against the barb-wire fence at a spot in front of the house and they were puzzled how to cope with the barbs on the Manitoba gate which Mr. Andrews had left. They wrapped their blankets around the barbs but still could not cope with the White Man's fence. They came and asked Father to help them. He went down and opened the gate for them and let them through. There was very little fenced land in those days. People just travelled straight across the prairie to Okotoks, cutting off many miles.

Father was winter feeding steers and Mother loved to ride horseback so, every morning she would go back to a large slough and chop a hole through the ice then she would come back and chase the steers to the hole to drink. One morning she decided it was a waste of time so she took the cattle down on the first trip. When she got down off her horse to chop the hole, she happened to look up and, to her horror, saw a stampede of cattle coming straight for her! They were not used to seeing anyone on foot. Fortunately, she jumped on her horse, just in time, and she had to chase the cattle away and go back to cut the hole in the ice. This was an experience that she never forgot.

Father said the winter of 1906-1907 was a memorable one. One morning as he and Mother were going to Calgary they saw a herd of Pat Burn's cattle standing in a field. Coming back home they noticed the cattle were still standing in the same place. Thinking this rather strange, he gave the reins to Mother to hold and went to investigate. The cattle were frozen stiff, standing on their feet. Even so, they said the good winters outnumbered the bad ones.

Also a licenced steam engineer, Father owned and ran his own threshing outfit. It was the first such outfit in the Davisburg district and, to my knowledge, the only one. He found out that it was not a paying proposition and sold it. However, he did a lot of threshing and broke up a lot of prairie land with it before he sold. He

William Bryce Family — 1949: l. to r.: Stella, Joe, Kay. Front Row: Mr. and Mrs. William Bryce.

also got William Allen to run the farm for him and went to run the steam engine at Canmore, where they took out the cement.

Mother and Father raised three children; one son, Joseph Lorne and two daughters Estella (Stella) Nelubowich and Kathleen (Kay) Noel.

In 1949, my parents retired and went back to Kintore, Ontario, but, they were lonesome for their home and the prairies so, came back after four months. In 1952, they decided once again to venture out and went to Victoria B.C., on Vancouver Island, but it had no appeal for them. They wanted to spend their last days in their home, on this side of the mountains so, they returned home.

Mother passed away July 12, 1957 and Father on February 17, 1961. Both are buried in Okotoks cemetery.

CLIFF CALL

Cliff Call came to Canada in 1906 from Bristol, England. He married Ruth Luff, also from England. Following is Mr. Call's history.

We left Pollockville (40 miles south of Hanna) in 1925 and took up residence on the McKid farm in Davisburg, Sec. 20, T.21 R.28 West of the 4th. We resided there until 1949, when we moved to our present location in Calgary.

We had three daughters; Cynthia (now Mrs. Eric Goddard, of Calgary) was born in the dry belt, Pollockville. The twins, Audrey and Bernice, were born on the McKid farm during the night of a December blizzard and four foot snowdrifts. Bernice (now Mrs. Jamison) lives in Edmonton and Audrey lives here with me.

My brother Bert, joined me in Pollockville and in 1914 my parents came out from England. Whilst they were on the Atlantic, the first war broke out, and they never went back. My father died in Pollockville district, and in 1926, Bert and my mother also came to the Davisburg district. My youngest brother, George, came with my parents and served in the second war in the navy. He was on the "Fraser", which was torpedoed in the Bay of Biscay. He escaped, was rescued and taken to England, but died there of injuries received.

I served in the first war in the 50th Battalion, and returned from service in July 1919.

Mr. and Mrs. Eric Goddard entertained friends in honour of her father's 90th birthday on February 19th, 1977. Lynn Goddard and Audrey Call served lunch.

On the following Thursday, February 24th, 1977, friends called on Mrs. Fred Davis in honour of her 88th birthday. Lilian Irving and Dorothy Davis served lunch.

Those attending the above birthday parties included many residents and former residents of Davisburg. These were Effie Leach and her daughter, Mary Esposito, Grace Suitor, Lilian Irving, Doris and Forest Herr, Ina and Alex Blackwood, Rusha and Douglas Herr, Olive and Ernie La Berge, Una and Bill Rodger, Stella Nelubowich, Marion Woodward, Virginia Klatzel, Laura and Laverne Wenger, Ilah Suitor, Elaine Lelek, and May and Ralph Stinn from De Winton.

MR. AND MRS. J. E. (TED) CAMPBELL — by Virginia Jacobson

The summer of 1944 Ted Campbell set out from their farm in the Reid Hill district east of Vulcan in search of greener pastures. The past years in this district had been quite dry, so Ted was anxious to move some place where he could grow some good hay for his cattle and have some better crops. His attention had been drawn to the NW¼-31-21-28-4 in the Davisburg Community and owned by Louis and Alice Sather. The deal was made to purchase and Oct. 6, 1944 Ted and Selma moved to their new home after living in the Reid Hill district since their marriage in 1913. Selma was terribly homesick at first for her old home and the place where they had brought up a family of seven daughters but it wasn't long before they had gotten acquainted with many of the good neighbors. One community event which was enjoyed by all was the summer community evening picnics held down at the Highwood River. Many good social times and visits were had there.

The family included: Viola, now living in Calgary, Vivian (Mrs. F. L. Booth) at Vulcan, Virginia (Mrs. Olaf Jacobson) at High River, Jean (Mrs. W. C. Bittorf) at Calgary, Louise, (Mrs. R. H. Sheldrake) at Lethbridge, Edna (Mrs. J. W. Palmer) at Blackfalds, and Lorraine (Mrs. D. R. Beard) at Carseland. Lorraine was the youngest and only daughter at home at the time of the move to Davisburg. She attended Davisburg School later going to Calgary to further her education. When she was home she met up with the young man, Raymond Beard, who was working for Jack Morasch and they were married in June 1949. They now reside at Carseland, Alta.

Virginia came to live with her parents at this time as her husband, Olaf Jacobson, was serving overseas in the Army. She worked along with her father on the farm also renting Effie Leach's farm. The hay crop was good that year and Ted was most pleased to have good feed for his cattle which were his pride and joy.

50th Wedding Anniversary of Mr. and Mrs. J. E. (Ted) Campbell, Feb. 26, 1963, at Davisburg Hall.

Selma enjoyed her good gardens and was able to preserve many vegetables for winter use. The power came to the farms in 1949 and this was a great benefit, now there were electric lights in the home and barns. The lamps and barn lantern were set on the shelf. An addition was built onto the house in 1953 to accommodate a bathroom and garage. Later a new well was drilled to make the water supply more plentiful.

Ted and Selma celebrated their 50th wedding anniversary, February 26, 1963 with a banquet for family and friends, in the Davisburg Hall followed by open house at home the next day.

Ted and Selma enjoyed their years in Davisburg both keeping active until Dec. 4, 1967 when Ted was stricken with a stroke and passed away in High River Hospital Jan. 3, 1968. Selma lived until March 8, 1970 when she passed away in Calgary. They are now at rest in the Mountain View Memorial Gardens Calgary.

GEORGE MONTGOMERY CARLETON

Born in Vermont, U.S.A. in 1857; died at Calgary in 1935.

George Carleton was born in Vermont, educated there and graduated from Randolph State College with a teacher's certificate. During the Gold Rush in the 1890's, he went to Alaska for gold and adventure, and travelled over the White Pass on foot. There were seven in this party, including one woman. All except the woman got scurvy; one man died. They found no gold but suffered many hardships.

On his return from Alaska, George stopped off in the North West Territories to start ranching in the Three Hills area. In 1910, he married Mary Jane Adams and moved to her ranch in Davisburg and lived there until his death. One daughter was born in this marriage — Lucy Annette Carleton — but she died at eight months.

See Adam's story.

FRANCIS CASEY — by Ted Casey

Mr. Francis George Casey came from England in 1892 to Manitoba and worked for two years at $5 a month. He took a homestead at Wapella, Saskatchewan in June 1894. The nearest railroad was 40 miles away. About this time Mr. Casey drove his team of oxen the 40 miles to meet his bride-to-be Miss Effie Watson, who had come from England. Mr. and Mrs. Casey lived in a crude shack, built of rough lumber. In winter the snow drifted in through the cracks. When Mrs. Casey got papers from England she pasted them on the wall to keep the snow out. She tried to smooth the rough boards on the floor with rough rock. Mrs. Casey had never lived on a farm before coming to Canada. The 40 mile trip to town took Mr. Casey five days for the return trip by oxen. Mrs. Casey once tried for two hours to milk their one cow. The cow finally tired of the procedure and not being corraled or tied up just walked away and laid down. A bachelor neighbour came along and finished the milking.

Around 1902 they sold the homestead and moved to Tantallon, where he built a store at the head of the railroad which ran northwest of Regina. As the railroad progressed the Caseys moved their store also. They traded with the Indians, selling supplies to them in exchange for seneca root, beaded work and wood. Mr. Casey drove to Regina with team and buggy for store supplies. He found that his share in the business was diminishing and the profits were not adequate for a growing family of four boys (they lost their first child, Violet, when on the homestead).

Joe recalls his father starting off to town with sacks of wheat (then 25 cents a bushel). Each time a hill loomed up Mr. Casey would unload part of the load and the oxen would haul the remaining load up and over the hill. Here he would unload and go back for the remaining part of the load. The trip was a long tedious one.

In 1906 the Francis Caseys moved to Olds. They bought the George Litten homestead on SE 10-33-3-W5 where they lived until 1917. They brought the store supplies that had been left on their hands, carefully packed and stacked the boxes beside the house as the house was not large enough to store them inside. Ironically their supplies went up in smoke when their house was burned. A frantic effort was made to build a new home.

Mrs. Casey had been a trained dressmaker in the old country and stated that if she had known what kind of climate she was coming into, she would have brought more clothes. She made many of her own clothes and for the children when they were small.

In 1917 they moved to De Winton. They remained there until 1922 when they moved to Calgary. From then on they spent some time at Calgary, Vancouver and Olds.

Mr. Joe Casey came back to the Waterside district. He married Miss Tillie Rice in 1924. They make their home on SW¼ 23-33-3-W5. Their daughter Evelyn married John Rosehill.

George Casey established his home on the homestead of Tom Ryley. He married Rose Ware of Eagle Hill. They have two sons and still reside on the same quarter.

TED CASEY — by Ted Casey

Mr. and Mrs. F. G. Casey and four boys, George, Joe, Ted, and Harry, the youngest, moved in March 1917, from west of Olds, Alberta to the Sheffield Estate, seven miles east of De Winton on the old Blackfoot Trail that left Calgary and followed the Bow River flats part of the way and then climbed the bank and angled through ours and many other farms to the Dunbow Industrial School on the Highwood River.

The two older boys, George and Joe, with a couple of neighbours from Olds, drove tbe fifty head of horses, as a loose herd, by-passing Calgary on the eastern outskirts and followed the Blackfoot Trail. We farmed about a section, half of it was west about a mile. A quarter was horse pasture and bordered the Bow River on the north. We used 24 head of horses for work in six and four horse teams. In harvest time, with the long days, we changed teams during the day so the horses had time to feed and rest. Each man used eight or more horses each day. The rest of the herd provided replacements.

Horses were cheap those days, with one exception. Dad bought a registered Clydesdale stallion for $1,-000.00 which was a lot of money in those days. We only had him a couple of years when he got sick and I had to

154

do away with him along with others that had to be put out of their misery, a job I didn't much like.

Harry and I (Ted) went to Davisburg School. We had a wonderful teacher, Miss Gray was her name, and somehow she managed to pass me to the next grade with honors.

World War I was going on then, George, being of age, was called up during the summer and that meant that I couldn't go back to school in the fall, instead I had to run the binder and haul bundles for threshing. For a couple of years we had a Stanley-Jones thresher which was hand fed and my job was to fork the straw away from the carrier behind the machine. It was a very dusty job as there was quite a bit of smut in the grain. It sure gave me some bad nose bleeds.

The last years Jim Martin and sons did the threshing with a steam engine, a Garrscot, and an Altman Taylor separator, with a 48" cylinder. They had fourteen bundle racks and teams.

From 1917 to 1922 were dry years, sometimes we cut wheat, with binders, that was eight to twelve inches high and some of it went only five bushels to the acre. We also had some good crops and hauled the grain to Okotoks or De Winton with a four horse team and wagon.

We moved to Calgary in February 1922 with two hay racks and our household effects. We got up at 4 a.m., made breakfast, then let the stove cool, that didn't take long as it was 25 degrees below zero. We left at 5 a.m. and got to Calgary at 10:30 p.m., via the Macleod Trail.

Harry and I and our wives went back to De Winton in 1972. We stopped at the school house and church where we attended about 55 years ago. They were still the same except the school is now a community hall and in the church yard are many of the friends and neighbours we knew.

Ted Casey married Violet Sande, daughter of Mr. and Mrs. Sam Sande of Eagle Hill. They have three children and live at Squamish, B.C.

Harry Casey married Margaret Williams of Clive and they live in Calgary. They have three children.

After a long active life in Canada, and witnessing the birth of Saskatchewan and Alberta, Mr. Francis George Casey passed away on April 18, 1958. Mrs. Casey reached the age of 97, passing away on August 30, 1964.

Mrs. Joe Casey cares for a wonderful garden and she has many exhibits of flowers and vegetables at the Olds Fair each year.

MR. AND MRS. EDWIN COLE — by Mrs. Eva Clarke

Edwin, or Ted, Cole came from Wales to Davisburg in 1911 with his parents, Mr. and Mrs. George Cole, brother William, sisters Mrs. Harriet Burn and son Tom, and Mrs. Eliza Ann Wymer and sons George and Charlie. They settled on the former Tom Andrews' farm. The others eventually moved away, leaving Ted. His fiancee, Miss Eva Hook, came from England and they were married in Calgary on April 3, 1921.

Mrs. Cole had a certificate in midwifery from Nottingham. She assisted Dr. Ardiel of Okotoks at the births of several Davisburg babies, namely, the Call twins, Bernice and Audrey, the McHugh twins,

Mr. and Mrs. Edwin (Ted) Cole.

Virginia and Douglas, Marion Davenport, and Walter Davis.

Ted died in 1947 and Mrs. Cole sold the place to Alfred Hendricksen. She made her home for a short time with Mrs. Fred Davis in Okotoks, then returned to England and married Mr. Tom Clarke. She is now widowed again and makes her home in Newport, Wales.

THE JOHN COPE FAMILY — by R. Cole

As far as is known, Thomas Cope came to Canada, from Lincolnshire, England, in the late 1800's. He returned to England in 1909 for a visit with his brother, John who had also been in Canada and had returned to England. He and his wife, Betsy Ann, with their family of two sons, William Henry and John Thomas, two daughters, Sarah Ann and Nellie, immigrated to Canada and settled in the Davisburg District, SE¼-28-21-28-W4, in April, 1910. The present owners of this parcel of land are Lil and Ernie Irving. John and his family remained here until the following July when they sold out to Fred and Lillian Davis of Sandstone, Alberta. They then settled on Sec. 26-20-29-W4, east of Okotoks, from where John and Nellie rode horseback to Okotoks School.

In 1918 the family moved to Sec. 1-21-1-W5 and this parcel of land still remains in the Cope family.

John was very interested in horses and was a prominent figure at the local auction sales. Betsy Ann was a dedicated member of the Saint Peter's Anglican Church, Okotoks.

John passed away in 1931, Sarah Ann in 1942, John Thomas in 1945, William Henry in 1952 and Betsy Ann in 1958. Nellie resides in Okotoks.

GERAINT AND LILLIAN CLIFFORD — by Lillian Clifford

We came to the Melvin Martin place near De Winton, from our farm at Vulcan in 1927. As we were unable to obtain more land in Davisburg, we stayed only till 1929.

My husband Geraint passed away in May, 1964. Elsie (Mrs. Jim Fetherston), our eldest child, has five children and lives in Victoria, B.C. Ross, our only son, served in the Navy all through the last war and presently lives with his wife and daughter in Toronto, Ontario. Our youngest daughter, May, passed away in 1936 and I, Lillian, am living in Calgary.

CUFFE BROTHERS — by Mrs. J. Bell

Arthur and George Cuffe were young single fellows like so many of our early western settlers. They had arrived before Alberta became a province in 1905. They were sons of a well to do London doctor, so they had all the advantages that money provides. Their education had taught them all the niceties of elegant living but they were not prepared for the rigors of the new west.

George was the younger of the two. He homesteaded in the Buffalo Hills, roughly forty miles east of High River. After proving up he sold out and moved to Busby, Alberta where he spent the rest of his life. He never married. His horse brand was a maple leaf.

Arthur had studied architecture, art, languages and also medicine. At 18 he had signed on as ship's cook to see more of the world. One of the crew's favorite desserts was plum duff (suet pudding) which Arthur often made. One day he couldn't find his pudding cloth. It just seemed to have vanished. He'd already wasted too much time and he'd be in hot water himself with the captain if mess wasn't ready on time. He found a nice new red neckerchief in his duffle bag and he dumped his pudding mixture onto it, then popped it into the kettle of boiling water. In those days dyes were not fast like today. As the pudding merrily danced in the kettle the dye ran. The pudding was sickly red when served. the captain gave the cook a severe reprimand for the plum duff which Arthur long remembered.

He also served in the 17th Lancers seeing service in India, I believe. The army training left a lasting impression and he always looked like he was on parade when astride a horse. Even his horse was always military groomed.

He homesteaded in the Davisburg district on the S.E.¼ 20-21-28 W4M in 1896. He often told incidents that had occurred when he worked for the Andrews, McBrides and Irvings. He could plow his two acres a day with a team and walking plow and was proud of his straight furrows.

While visiting his brother in the Buffalo Hills he met Edith Goldthorpe, the daughter of an English emigrant homestead family. They were married in Gleichen in 1909. After several years spent working for several farmers, they moved to Gladys Ridge where they bought land. Arthur's early life had left him with a wander lust. He farmed at Eastway, Lake McGregor and in 1932 he homesteaded again at Breton (Leduc oilfield area). He erected some log buildings but passed away in 1933.

JAMES LAWRENCE DAVENPORT

Jim was born on April 19, 1886, at Milwaukee, Wisconsin, and died at Davisburg on May 3, 1952. His parents died when he was very young, and he was raised by an aunt until he left home at the age of fourteen. His travels took him through the States westward to Oregon where he worked in lumber camps. He also worked at many odd jobs and finally obtained his First Class Steam Engineer's papers. This led him to Alberta where he worked on the Noble township near Taber and also in Lethbridge. He worked on the high-level bridge at Lethbridge and also planted trees in the townsite. His work with the steam engines led him around the country until he arrived in the Davisburg area. There he met and married Lucille Adams and farmed the home place for twenty-five years. He also worked on the first Twin Dome oil well by the Highwood River, at 16-21-8 W2 4th. During his years in Davisburg he was a fine neighbor and friend, being both the "thresher man" and the telephone lineman. He was a fine example of a good and loving husband and father, being a faithful man of temperate habits.

SUSAN ELIZABETH LUCILLE (ADAMS) DAVENPORT

The younger daughter of Mary Jane and William Adams was born at the Kingsthorpe Ranch on the Highwood River. She remembers missing a great deal of school at the Davisburg Schoolhouse and working at the farm home because of her mother's ill health. She recalls standing on a chair to knead bread when she was only eight years old. Her mother, at that time Mrs. George Carleton, spent about fifteen or more years in a wheelchair until her death in 1926.

Lucy recalls good times also and often mentions riding by horseback to dances in High River, Okotoks, De Winton or any other centre, and wonders how they must have smelled after riding to and from dances twenty miles away.

Lucy didn't get very far away from home, for she worked within the district both maintaining the farm and cooking on the "cook cars" for threshing crews. She married James Davenport who had arrived in the district with the big steam engines then in use for threshing operations. Between Lucy and Jim, many harvest crews were employed and fed; and between seasons the Davenports created a beautiful home by the river. They were famous for the Sundays at the farm with ball games, weiner roasts, skating parties or whatever fun people enjoyed in the depression years. During the Second World War, Lucy and Jim frequently had British airmen from the De Winton Airport — No. 31 E.F.T.S. — in as house guests on their days off duty and training. The Davenport home was "home away from home" for many, many people.

Nestled in a cozy area under the hills around the farmhouse was a fertile piece of ground Lucy and Jim cultivated for their garden. For years they marketed onions and potatoes, and created beauty with an abundance of flowers. Lucy's favorite became the gladioli, which she cared for by the thousands and finally was able to market them. During the latter part of the 1930's and '40's, the annual "Strawberry Tea" became a social highlight in the Davisburg district. The community club served a delightful lunch of strawberry shortcake and tea to the many visitors who came to enjoy the flowers and companionship on the Davenport's lawn.

The happy combination of working, living, farming with the mixed variety of cows, pigs, grain, a horse and a dog continued from about 1926 until Jim's death in 1952. During the War, Jim and Fred Davis fed pigs with the garbage from the De Winton Airport, and it happily resulted that Jim and Lucy were able to pay off the mortgage on their farm with the "pig money" in 1946.

Rural electrification inspired extensive renovations on the house around 1950. While these alterations were being done, Jim took ill and did not see the results of their planning. During the '50's, Lucy continued her gardening and feeding cattle alone. Paul and Tony Groeneveld farmed the crop land for a few years until around 1958 when tenants took over the whole farm and Lucy moved into Calgary.

In October, 1960, Lucy remarried. She is now Mrs. Cecil Goff. Cecil's home is in Palm Springs, California, so Lucy spends most of her time in Canada and vacations in the winters in Palm Springs. Her heart is still on the farm in Davisburg, but her body and time are busy and active with her daughter and four grandchildren and generally getting the most out of life.

MARIAN LUCILLE DAVENPORT

Jim and Lucy had one daughter, Marian, born in 1927. Her earliest playmates were her cousins, Jack, Virginia and Douglas McHugh, as well as other young people from Calgary who spent their holidays during the depression on the farm. This meant a saving to their parents who could not afford to feed extra mouths, as they thought. Like other children in the district, Marian rode her horse to the Davisburg School — the same school as her mother had attended. Her first teacher and idol was Miss Vera Andrews, whose friendship Marian still values highly. Very earliest memories of school involve being 'spoiled rotten' by the big kids in the school — Lilian Davis, and Bruce and Ross Hyde. Marian experienced intense rivalry with Don Hyde for highest marks, and this must have been worth while because they both ended up going to Calgary to Central Collegiate Institute and the University of Alberta in Edmonton. During country school days, Marian's best friends were Audrey and Bernice Call and Betty Angel. Other teachers at Davisburg after Vera Andrews were Miss Helen Webb from Calgary, Miss Ferne McKeague from High River and Miss Olga Anderson from Kathryn, Alberta. Even though these teachers taught all grades from one to nine, they provided good training which probably cannot be improved on today with specialized teaching and gadgets.

For high school, Marian and the others who continued had to go to a larger centre, so by luck Marian chose Central in Calgary and boarded with friends in Victoria Park. Then she attended Mount Royal College, then boarding with friends in Killarney. She intended to take the secretarial course, but another stroke of luck intervened and she found herself taking first year of a university course for teaching. In spite of her father's need of her help on the farm, she continued to attend university in Edmonton until she graduated with her degrees in Arts and Education in 1947.

Marian's holidays were always spent as close to the farm as possible, and for two summers she worked at the De Winton Airport — one year in the Canteen, serving coffee, doughnuts and milk shakes to the airmen, and the second year as a timekeeper of the student flights in their training. She also worked one summer in the office of the U.F.A. in Calgary for experience. Her mother still says it was the onion crop that put Marian through University.

When she was twenty, Marian started her teaching career, first at St. Hilda's School for Girls in Calgary where she was paid ninety-nine dollars a month and her room and board. Her second year of teaching took her to the Lethbridge Collegiate Institute where she continued her career until 1952. Meanwhile, in December of 1950, she was married to Hans William Reich, but continued teaching at the L.C.I. until Easter before her first child was born. Just a month later, her father died.

Marian and Hans farmed on the Cameron Ranch area twenty miles from Taber and forty miles from Lethbridge on two sections of dry land. They had four children — James Paul, born August 27, 1952; Susan Lynne, born June 21, 1954 (Lucy and Jim's wedding anniversary); Donna Jean, born September 5, 1956; and lastly, David Walter, born February 18, 1959.

The Reich family left farming on the Cameron in 1968 to try their luck in urban living, moving back to Lethbridge. Then in the fall of 1959, they moved to Calgary where they all still live. Marian and Hans were divorced in 1964; she remarried in 1967 and now goes by the name of Woodward. That was not a successful family arrangement, so since 1969, Marian and her family have lived in relative bachelorhood.

Careerwise, Marian went back to teaching high school in 1960: ten years at Henry Wise Wood High School and the last six at Central Memorial High.

Jim Reich lives at his grandmother's house on the farm, and commutes to work at the Calgary Herald. His training at S. A. I. T. qualifies him for work on their new computer print system.

Susan Reich (Eaton) is married, living in Calgary, working at Woodward's Department Store while her husband, John, is a truck salesman at Maclin Ford.

Donna and David Reich are currently attending high school in Calgary. David's hobby of racing dirt track motorcycles keeps him busy; Donna has her horse.

At the present time that ambition of the whole Davenport — Reich family is to settle down at the old Kingsthorpe Ranch homestead and try to recapture the good life close to the land.

FRED AND LILIAN DAVIS — by Mrs. Lilian Davis

My husband, Frederick Davis, was born on November 3rd, 1882 in Othery, Somerset, England. He came to Sandstone, Alberta, just west of Okotoks in 1909. His sister, Mrs. Frank Tucker, was living there at that time.

I was born in Netherstowey, near Bridgewater, Somerset, England in 1889. I came to Canada in 1910 and stayed with Mrs. Tucker at Sandstone. On the trip over, I was eleven days at sea and one week on the train. I stayed with Mrs. Tucker while her husband Frank, and Fred were on a homestead at Youngstown.

Fred Davis when he came to Canada, 1909.

Lilian Davis, 1910.

In August 1910, we were married by St. Peter's Anglican minister. We were married twice the same day. Being new to the country, we didn't know we had to have a licence. The minister went through the service and asked for the licence so we had to go to Okotoks for it, and the service was done over again. The minister said "Nobody can say you aren't married now".

We lived in a tent at Sandstone the first winter. My husband worked at the brick yard there. Then we had two rooms in the Manager's house. In 1912 we lived in a little house up the hill from Sandstone on a farm of Ma Huckvales. My son Martin was born there. In 1913 we bought the farm at Davisburg.

In the winter we had a party every week. Each neighbour took turns and we all had a lovely time. We danced to radio old time music. We travelled in wagons, sleighs, buggies etc., going home early in the morning.

In 1915 my son Jim was born and in 1919 my daughter Lilian was born. We moved to Okotoks in 1944 from the farm as Fred was in ill health, leaving my daughter Lilian and her husband, Ernie, on the farm. Fred died in May 1945 and I have lived here in Okotoks until now.

July 1, 1972 taken at Leslieville, Alta. Four generations. Jim, Les, Grandma Davis. Les holding Treen.

JIM DAVIS

I was brought into the world by Dr. Ardiel, May 1915, in the house at the home farm where my sister, Mrs. Lil Irving lives. I went to Davisburg school, riding horseback at first with my brother, Martin. When Lil started school, we took the buggy. I helped with the farm work at home, worked for some neighbours, and did some work for the municipality, such as putting in culverts and filling holes in the road with horses and slip.

We had quite a bit of entertainment, dances and card parties at the school house, Country Club dances in Okotoks, house parties for birthdays and anniversaries. Dad didn't like to miss the hockey game Saturday night on the radio. In summer, quite a few of us would meet at the river and go swimming. In winter, we'd skate or play hockey.

In the spring of 1941, I went to work for Clyde Lester of Keoma. I stayed with Mr. Lester until work was finished in the fall. Then I came home and worked at the DeWinton airport for a while. While working for Mr. Lester, I met my wife. Dorothy and I were married in April, 1942. We rented land from my brother, Martin three miles east of Okotoks on the Rohl place. There was no drinking water on this place, so it had to be hauled. We owned a car, a cow and some chickens.

We used Dad Davis' machinery after he was finished, so our seeding and summerfallow was late. We borrowed horses, rake and rack, and Dorothy and I put the hay up by hand. We got Herb Jenkins to combine the crop. I worked part-time in the summer for Mr. Graburn. Both Dorothy and I worked for Ike Morris in harvest time.

Dad Davis gave us a cow, let us milk another, so we shipped cream, taking it to Okotoks. Things were hard as the crop had to be split three ways. This place was sold, so we had to move in the spring. Our first son was born while we still lived there. We moved in May 1943 to the Hadden place six miles north-east of Okotoks. We rented this for a year from Mrs. Weiner of Delacour. Dad Davis helped us get some second-hand machinery and a couple more cows. Ted Cole let us have the cream from three heifers, provided we trained them to milk. We pastured Mrs. Weiner's cattle and also some horses of Hamilton's of De Winton. Dorothy and I went to a few dances at the Country Club in Okotoks.

In April 1944 we moved east of Strathmore. It was here the rest of our family was born — two more sons and two daughters. Dad died in May 1945, so we didn't have him with his wisdom to help make decisions. We went into more milk cows, were hailed out three times in six years, and I couldn't stand the grain dust. In November 1950, we moved north-west of Millarville where no grain is grown and started ranching as well as milking cows. Our family grew up here, taking their schooling at Millarville and Black Diamond.

Don married Margaret McKay of Midnapore. They have three girls, Deanna, Debbie and Donna. They are renting land at Leslieville, Alta.

Leslie married Louise McKay, Margaret's sister. They have rented their farm at Leslieville and moved to Vulcan where Les has the Imperial Oil Agency. They have two children, Treena and Kenny.

Reta married Bill Dubie; they live in Calgary and have three children, Terry, Sandy and Edward.

Gene married Shirley Racj; lives in Calgary, works for Atomic Transport and has one son, James.

Brenda married Bob Smyth from Ninga, Manitoba. She is a hairdresser in Calgary and they live in a trailer court there.

We have had good years and bad years, but experience is the best teacher and Dorothy and I are still farming.

MARTIN DAVIS

Born on a farm west of Okotoks in 1912, he was brought into the world, as were many others at that time, by Doctor Ardiel. He took his schooling at Davisburg, then took a mechanics course at Calgary. He married Georgina Hurst in 1937. They have two sons and a daughter.

Douglas married Kathy Beattie and they had six children, but one died. Now he is married to Lynda, and when she added her girl, it made a nice family of two boys and four girls. They live in Calgary.

Wallace married Sylvia Carr, daughter of Doug Carr, and they live in Calgary and have two sons.

Joan married Owen Rowlfe. They have a son and daughter and live in Olds.

Martin lived most of his married life in Okotoks, turning his hand to truck driving, working with large machinery, and farming. Now they reside on a farm west of Olds. Georgina works at Sundre Hospital while Martin looks after their farm.

WILLIAM ELLIOTT — by Grace Suitor

William Elliott arrived in Canada, from England, in 1911, as a teen-ager and worked for George Grant for a year before returning to England. He came back and worked for James Suitor Sr. until he entered the 10th Battalion in 1914. He went overseas that same year and was severely wounded from shrapnel, having seventy-two wounds. When he got out of hospital in 1919, he returned to the Davisburg district and rented the Davis farm while they were in England, and the Suitor farm, while they went to the coast for Mrs. Suitor's health.

He was greatly interested in radio, and obtained parts from other countries to build a radio. The neighbours would often phone to hear the news or perhaps a new song over the open line.

In 1923 he went to Coutts with the Immigration Department and served as a Customs Officer at various points along the Canada-U.S. border, until retiring with his wife at Victoria, B.C. in 1955. While at Coutts, he obtained news of the Davisburg district from Jim Blackwood, when he made the border crossing, hauling oil from Sunburst, Montana, driving for Bob James.

RUSSELL AND DORIS GRENEK

Russell and Doris Grenek with their family, Irma, Florence, and Larry came from Dalroy to the Davisburg district, purchasing the Chester Leach farm in 1951. We resided here until 1953, selling out to Arthur and Gladys Petts, and moving to the Gladys Ridge District.

We contined farming there until Doris passed away in 1971, and I Russell, later retired to High River.

THE HASLEM'S

There was two brothers Samuel and Steven Haslem and their families who came west in 1901 from Prince Edward Island.

Samuel and Steven were both carpenters by trade and owned Haslem Construction Company in Calgary which they started in 1904. Steven also owned a saw mill and lumber yard. They built a number of houses from 1905 until 1914. Hard times hit two or three years just before the war so in 1914 they decided to trade a house which they built on Elbow Drive for the equity that Metcalfs held on a farm in Davisburg 7-21-28 W4, Pete Idington held a mortage on this farm for the balance.

The Metcalfs moved into the house on Elbow Drive. Mr. Metcalf lost his life in this house when he fell downstairs into the basement, and broke his neck.

Haslems did not have enough land in this farm so tried to buy the NW¼ of this same section 7 then changed their minds and bought a larger farm up north of Calgary, near Sunnyslope, which is east of Didsbury.

Mr. and Mrs. Samuel Haslem had two children, Emma and Hensly, they both still live in Calgary. Mr. and Mrs. Steven Haslem had two boys in their family, Charlie and Milton.

The three boys Hensly, Charlie and Milton, along with Joseph Bryce, rode to Davisburg school on horse back. They also rode to Sunday School over at Roy McConnel's. Not too long after the Haslems moved to Sunnyslope, Milton got appendicitis which caused his death at an early age.

Charlie moved to B.C., in later years, and had a dairy, buying milk and cream from the dairy farmers. He passed away a number of years ago.

The Haslems also had a nephew who used to come down from north of Calgary to help them on the farm, his name was Ches McKay. The Post Office then was at Patersons, two brothers, remittance men from England. They lived about two miles straight north of Wm. Bryce.

Ches rode over to Wm. Bryce on a big heavy horse in the fall of the year about 1913 or 1914 hoping one of the Bryces had picked up the mail. The Bryces were milking the cows, so Ches said if he had a little better horse he would ride on down to get the mail, and Mr. Bryce gave him his horse to ride. As he rode up the road there was about 7 head of stray horses eating in the church yard, they heard hoof beats on the frozen ground and ran ahead of them. "Bubs", the horse, took chase after them with the bit in his teeth, Ches just had to hang on. He did manage to get Bubs in Paterson's gate. The Patersons had just got their remittance money so had lots of good cheer and a new gramophone.

When Ches went in they locked the door behind him and made him stay and enjoy the evening until 2 a.m. when they let him go home. By then Bubs was quite cold so gave Ches another swift ride home. When he got to the Bryce place he was white as a sheet and never did forget that ride for the mail.

ALFRED AND PAT HENRIKSEN — by Pat Henriksen

In May of 1948, we moved from Harmatton to the Davisburg District, to the farm on the W½-32-21-28-4, with our family. We have three boys, Martin, Richard and Wayne. Our daughter, Marilyn was born while we were at Davisburg.

After farming here for 25 years, we sold in 1973 and retired to 46 — Hallbrook Drive, S. W., Calgary.

Martin is married and lives in New Holland, U.S.A., and he has two children.

Richard is married with two children and lives in Calgary.

Wayne lives in Calgary.

Marilyn is married with one child, and lives in Rockyford.

THE HERR FAMILY

Albert was born at Chatham, Ontario in 1871. He was the only one of his family to come to the West. After working in Manitoba for five years, he arrived in Calgary in 1897, working for John Greenfield for a few years and on haying crews on Mosquito Creek for Sexsmith and McDougal. In 1899, he bought the south half of Sec. 24 TP. 21 R29 W4th and the same spring

Albert and Blanche Herr, 1900.

married Blanche Irving, whose family had come from Cardinal, Ontario in 1888. This farm is now occupied by Robert Herr, a grandson, and has been in the family for over 75 years.

Another grandson, Lawrence Herr, is on Sec. 19, Twp. 21, R28, settled by the John Irvings in 1887.

Blanche played the organ at the Davisburg Church for many years. Albert was a councillor on the M.D. of Sheep Creek for 10 years before it was amalgamated into the Foothills M.D. No.31. He was also a trustee for the Davisburg School No.79 for nearly thirty years. They had a family of three daughters and six sons, some of the family still farming in the district.

Albert Herr and sons, 1923. Cliff, Harold, Forest, Bill, Doug, Mr. Herr.

Blanche died in 1918, Albert in 1936, both buried at Davisburg. Their family is as follows:

Clifford married Mary Stewart of Gladys Ridge, whose family came to Calgary before the C.P.R. in 1883. They have one daughter and one son, and were on the original half section 24 where Robert still farms. **Florence**, after teaching school for a few years, married Keith Jobson, living in Halifax and Ottawa, and now of Victoria. They have three sons.

Robert married Sharon Ross of Okotoks. They have two sons and one daughter, Andrew (Drew), Paul and Melissa, and they live in Davisburg on the old home place. Cliff died in 1956, buried in Davisburg. Mary lives in Calgary.

William (Bill) Herr married Evelyn Kadey, R.N., of Okotoks, farming on Sec. 19 Tp. 21 R29, the original Irving land settled in 1887.

Lawrence farms the home place.

Marguerite, their daughter, married Gordon Dixson, farming at Claresholm.

Bill died in 1968, buried in Davisburg. Evelyn lives on the farm with Lawrence.

Ethel married Alex Fraser of DeWinton. They farmed at Shepard and Davisburg, moving to Olds in 1942 where they farmed until retiring to live in Olds in the '60's. They have one son and two daughters.

Dorothy married Harold Bell of Olds, now living west of Carstairs. They have one daughter and three sons.

160

Marilyn married Harold Rugg. They have two sons and one daughter, living in Calgary.

John married Francis Burke of Didsbury. They have one son and four daughters and live in Calgary.

Ethel died in 1963, Alex in 1975, buried in Olds.

Forest married Doris Lock of Okotoks, farming on Sec. 11 TP. 21 R28 W4th. They have four children.

Forest and Doris Herr.

Constance (Connie) married David Hunt of Endiang, farming on Sec. 26 Tp. 21 R29 that the Hunts bought in the late '40's. They raise purebred Herefords. They have three sons and one daughter, Danny, Peter, Christopher and Celia. Connie worked for a law firm in Calgary for a few years prior to her marriage.

Albert married Ann Sutherland, grand daughter of the Banisters who settled in Davisburg in 1884. After farming the Sutherland place for a few years, they moved back to farm the home place. He also runs the P & H elevator in Okotoks. They have three sons and one daughter, Bert, Harold, Ben and Audra.

Beverly after finishing school in Okotoks, worked in a Real Estate office in Calgary for a few years. Married Lawrence Bews of Longview. They have three sons, Troy, Tim and Tony and they live on Sec. 11 Tp. 21 R 29. Lawrence works in the oil industry, putting in some time in Iran and the Arctic, presently working in Calgary.

Gordon, after finishing school and two years at University in Calgary, joined the Calgary City Police Force. Married Judy Robins of this district — they lived at Millarville where Judy taught school for a few years. After five years in the Police force, Gordon

thought he would rather farm and handle livestock than pound the beat, so now is working for the Hunts doing what he likes best. They keep a few cattle and horses and have some land near St. Paul where they hope to live soon. They have one son, Cody, and one daughter, Joni-Lee.

Marjorie Herr, born 1906, died 1913, buried in Davisburg.

Eva, after finishing school in Davisburg and Okotoks, went to Normal School in Calgary, taught school for a few years before her marriage to Douglas Beattie of Okotoks. They farmed in the Big Rock district west of Okotoks, where their family of two were born.

Ralph married Betty Gerlitz of Okotoks, farming with his parents until his death in 1969. They have one daughter, Dianne, now Mrs. Bruce Foran, they have one son and live in Okotoks. Betty lives in Calgary.

Donna took her schooling in Okotoks, then trained for her R.N. at the Calgary General Hospital. Married Peter Berger of Parkland, and farmed there for a few years before moving to Lethbridge where Pete is a welder and Donna does part-time nursing. They have one son and two daughters. Eva died in 1965, Douglas in 1971.

Harold married Alice Watt of Vulcan and after farming for a few years in Davisburg moved to Vancouver in 1936 where he died the same year. They have one daughter, Wanda, now Mrs. Philip Pedneault. They have three children and live near Campbell River. Alice still lives in Vancouver.

Douglas married Jerusha Carr of Okotoks farming on Sec. 12 Tp. 21 R29. They have no children.

Melvin, the youngest of the family, born in 1916, died July 1917. Buried in Davisburg.

Herr Family, 1950: Forest, Bill, Ethel, Eva, Cliff, Douglas.

CLIFFORD AND MARY MARGARET (STEWART) HERR

Clifford Herr and Mary Margaret Stewart were united in marriage on July 12, 1932 at the home of Mary's parents. Mary was the second daughter of Mr. and Mrs. Alex Stewart of Gladys Ridge, who were early pioneers of the Davisburg and Gladys districts, coming to the area in 1882. Mary was a school teacher in the High River area before her marriage.

Cliff and Mary lived at the Todd place which is the home of Dr. Gary Carter, for four years, before moving to the Herr farm.

On June 19, 1935 they had a daughter, Florence, who was married to Keith Jobson on July 20, 1963. They have three boys; Tom, John and David. They are presently living in Victoria, B.C.

Robert was born on January 28, 1942 and married Sharon Ross on August 15, 1964. They have two boys and a girl; Andrew, Paul and Melissa. The family is presently living on the original Herr farm.

Cliff was a trustee of the Davisburg school and also a member of the Davisburg United Church Board. Mary was involved with Home and School as well as the Jolly Time Club.

Cliff died suddenly while fixing fence on June 18, 1956. Mary is in the Chinook Nursing Home in Calgary, in good health.

MR. AND MRS. HAROLD HERR — by Alice Herr

Harold Noah Herr was born in the Davisburg district and lived most of his life there. In 1932 he married Alice Watt, who had come to live in the district the year before. They moved to Vancouver in 1935, where Harold passed away in 1936. He was survived by his wife, who still lives in Vancouver, a son, Gordon Orval, living in Ontario, and a daughter, Wanda Lee, living on Vancouver Island. Orval has three daughters and Wanda has two daughters and a son.

MR. AND MRS. WILLIAM HERR — by Mrs. Evelyn Herr

William Herr was born at Davisburg, the second son of Mr. and Mrs. Albert Herr, on January 6, 1901. He farmed in this district all his life, first with his father, then on his own place, 19-21-28-W4.

On August 28, 1935 he married Evelyn Kadey of Okotoks, who had graduated from the Calgary General Hospital School of Nursing in 1925. They had two children, Lawrence Donald, born March 16, 1937, and Marguerite Jean, born December 28, 1938. Marguerite is married to Gordon Dixson and lives at Claresholm.

Bill Herr had his father's brand (⊢E R) and Lawrence now has this brand, as well as L.R. Marguerite's brand is M.H.

CHARLES AND MIRIAM (HYNDSEN) HUGHES — by Sheridan Hughes

Charles Hughes was a graduate of Epsom College and was then bound over for five years as an apprentice in a business office. When his contract expired he left for California and from 1895 he farmed reclaimed land in the San Joaquin Valley. Because of an outbreak of malaria he left to find a healthier climate and arrived in Alberta in 1903. He bought land, known as the Elkton Ranch, from Mr. Lee for $15.00 per acre. Mr. Troughton had been renting this land. Mr. Hughes lived here until his death in 1954.

Due to land conditions it was necessary to break the north end with horses but a steam engine was used to break the south end. He grew mostly oats and barley as the land was not suited to wheat. He never had a complete crop failure in all his years of farming. He raised cattle and always had good horses.

About the turn of the century, Miriam Hyndsen and two older sisters arrived in Alberta. Miriam was a qualified governess and had been tutor to the children of the Royal Family of Germany, then the House of Hohenzollern, and she continued her chosen career in this country. She was tutor to the Campbell and Peake children and spent some time visiting the Wyndham family in Okotoks. It was here she met Charles Hughes and in 1910 she became his wife.

Mr. Charles Hughes.   Mrs. Miriam Hughes — 1910.

I, Sheridan, was their first child and also the first baby born in the Scottish Nursing Home in Calgary. It was run by Miss Lena Blackwood, an aunt of Alex and Jim Blackwood. Digby, my brother was also born in Calgary. I was christened in the Anglican Church after it was moved to De Winton. Reverend W. Bennett Church was the Rector.

My mother taught me at home for my first few years of schooling. The five mile ride to Davisburg on a pony was too far for a small boy alone. In 1922, when I was eleven, I started to school, riding a saddle horse. I went to Okotoks for my high school education, boarding for a while with the Hislop family. Mother passed away in 1926 and the following year my father had Mr. Hislop build a house in Okotoks. We rented the farm and both boys went to school in Okotoks.

In 1929 we returned to the farm and in 1947 we bought a half section of land from Osborne Andrews and continued to farm until 1960. In 1965 this land was subdivided. In 1960 I moved to my present location and established "Fawndale Farms". Digby still owns Elkton Ranch but lives in a beautiful home in the Willow Park district in Calgary.

As a small boy of eight I remember a steady stream of taxis bringing men to file on claims along the creek where gold was supposedly discovered. It was in December of 1919 and a very cold year. The ground had been frozen since October, and the claim filers had difficulty getting their stakes to stay in the ground. I also recall, in 1927, when the now famous cyclone went through, the top of a 1917 car was ripped off and all the trees along the river valley were blown down. These trees were used as fuel in the '30s when times were so hard. Our granaries were also ruined by being literally bumped along the ground until they disintegrated.

My mother and her sisters used to take part in the plays put on in the "Old Streeter Hall." They were very Gala Affairs and well attended by the district residents.

I have a son, Christopher Shawn, and a daughter, Laureen Lee, and I spend most of my time taking them to horse shows and practises and caring for their horses.

DELBERT LEWIS HYDE AND MARY McPHAIL HYDE — by Ross Hyde

Delbert Lewis Hyde and Mary McPhail were married at Lang, Saskatchewan in 1908. They homesteaded at Sceptre, Saskatchewan and farmed there until 1929. In March 1930 they moved to the Davisburg district. In 1948 they retired and moved to Calgary.

The family consisted of six children — girls Maxine, Ethel and Beryl, and boys Bruce, Don and Ross. All except Maxine attended Davisburg School and, like most children of the time, rode saddle horses to school.

Maxine married Donald McKenzie who farmed in the district for a while. Bruce married Nan Cameron and they farmed the home place for a time after the elder Hydes' retirement. Ross married Audrey Nelson of Calgary, Beryl married George Woodward of Calgary, and Don married Kathleen Kruckshanks of Edmonton. Bruce, Ross and Beryl are presently living in Calgary; Maxine is at Sidney, B.C., and Don and family are in New York. Delbert, Mary, and Ethel are deceased.

The Hyde farm was located on the Bow River about seven miles east of the Weigh Scales and directly north of the De Winton airfield. The farm consisted of approximately 1,200 acres with about half cultivated and the rest in pasture. Del Hyde raised purebred Shorthorn cattle and Clydesdale horses. Sheep and hogs were also raised, so it was truly a mixed farm. The Hyde brand was D-H.

Mr. and Mrs. Earl James occupied the land prior to the Hydes. From information available to the author, people by the name of Martin were there before James and before them were Banisters. The Banisters were probably the ones who homesteaded the land. When Mr. and Mrs. Hyde sold out in 1958, they sold to Fred Mannix who, I believe, still owns it.

MEMORIES OF CARLETON IMPEY

Left Calgary by car with the family and "Snooky" the cat in the fall of 1915. Bumper crop that year and all granaries full but threshing stopped on account of snow storm just before we arrived. Bob Riddle was threshing for us with a 10-20 Titan and a 20 inch separator which had to be hand fed and had no blower. Straw had to be carried away by hay sweep. As the granaries were full I had to haul grain from the separator to the barn three-quarters of a mile away. Some job for a soft city guy!

During winter we had quite a few house parties and of course the odd dance at De Winton and Okotoks.

Elwin Jackman and I used to ride saddle to Okotoks, eleven miles, for a dance when no car was available, dance 'til 3 a.m. and sleep in the saddle coming home.

Had pick-up ball and hockey teams — used to play the Indians at the Dunbow School Industrial Farm east of us, at the junction of the Bow and Highwood Rivers. Played ball at Okotoks, Black Diamond, Midnapore, and on Marshall's farm west of De Winton (Billy Hamilton catcher and I pitched). Used to put on a boxing match at Pete Murray's blacksmith shop when the telephone gang was around that part of the country.

Dick Meehan, Jack Jamison and I bought a threshing outfit at Blackie in 1923, complete with cook car, bunk house, and tank wagon. Open fall that year and we paid for the outfit; however, we made the mistake of bringing it to our district in 1925 and lost money.

When the Dunbow School was closed I bought their big Hart Parr outfit with plows and broke up new sod for Billie Bryce, Gordon Heaver, and a section of land for Pa Carleton adjoining us. Always going to make big money but never did.

During WW I, we had two barn dances at our place, proceeds going to the Red Cross, with a five piece orchestra from Calgary and about three hundred people at each dance.

Our family went to Davisburg School and the Meehans to Melrose. Aggie Martin was teaching at Davisburg when Harry (Impey) and, I believe, Alex Blackwood were caught tickling the girls with grass while they were in the "biffy." She told me about it and gave an extra good whaling.

Billie Bryce was feeding about twenty steers for market one time and had to go into Calgary for a couple of days so we got his son Joe to drive them down to our corrals and we spent Sunday riding about fifty pounds of beef off each animal — Joe got Hell when the "Old Man" got home.

There was a gold rush on Snake Creek one early spring. The roads were a mess and people were coming out from Calgary and surrounding districts to stake claims. They came on foot, by car and bicycle, and horseback. Evidently, Blackwoods had sold some geese and when they were cleaned a few gold nuggets showed up and that started the stampede. A shaft was dug just inside Blackwood's line fence on the creek but it wasn't a paying proposition. I staked claims for the family.

The farm bought a Hart Parr 30 and a Waterloo separator in the '20s and when we finished threshing our place Jim Brown and I would rent it for $25.00 a day and thresh around our district. Pitched a tent for the crew and paid the farmer 30¢ per meal.

Elwin Jackman and I used to haul grain to Okotoks, eleven miles, before De Winton had an elevator. In the winter we would probably walk about eight out of the eleven miles in order to keep warm. Had a tank each and four horses and hauled about 100 bushels of wheat each load. When the snow came we used the "bobs" and had to rough lock going down the hills. Later we hauled to De Winton 7½ miles away when the new elevator was built.

I left the farm in the spring of 1925 for Calgary.

The above was written by Carleton Impey, the eldest son of Mr. and Mrs. Irvine Impey. He married Katie Meehan and they live in Winnipeg.

Other members of the family were Harry, who lived in Edmonton (deceased, 1975), Ross in Vancouver, and Ruby, the only daughter who lived, in Vancouver (but died in 1974).

ERNIE AND LILIAN (DAVIS) IRVING — by Lilian Irving

I was born on April 11th, 1919 in the same house we live in today. I was the third child born to Fred and Lilian Davis. I was their last — who could blame them, after the likes of me, who would risk another! I look back now, and I'm sure no one had as many kicks under the table as I received during my growing up. Mother always made sure I was sitting next to her at the table, and when I got that certain look, she seemed to know I was going to say what was on my mind. What was on my mind, I'm sure, proved quite embarrassing, time after time.

I was born on a farm where the animals received first and foremost consideration. Dad raised Clydesdale horses, and the ribbons they won testified to their quality. Later, he switched to Percherons. He also had an eye for good cattle and had some purebred Herefords at one time. We milked up to twelve cows and had range cows as well. We also had pigs, and Mum's department was the chickens and turkeys. I learned to love farming and especially the animals that go with it. It is, in my opinion, the only way of life.

We had lots of good times while growing up. In the winter there were house parties, skating on the river, and sleigh riding on the hills. There were dances at the school and the Okotoks Country Club. In the summer, there was baseball, riding and swimming in the river. Although quite young at the time, I remember going to Riddel's place (Chuck Groeneveld lives there now) to one of the get-togethers and coming home it was so dark "Uncle" Jimmy Suitor walked ahead of the teams with a lantern to light the way up the hill. At that time the hill coming out of there was right on the edge of the river. As a child I don't believe I ever came up there without closing my eyes till over the top, especially if we were in the car and the hill was slippery.

When the Riddel's were leaving the district, I was to present the gift to them. Before leaving for the party, I was having supper at Suitor's. The table was all set for supper when Jim and his cousin Lyle came in from chores. Jim grabbed me and threw me in the air. My feet hit the stove pipes (of which there were quite a few) and down they came. Well — soot all over! I remember standing in a corner wishing I could disappear, but Grace laughed and Uncle Jim winked at me and I thought I was safe. Poor Mrs. Suitor was cleaning soot off dishes and table.

We have had a lot of good neighbours down through the years. A good neighbour you can count on is a treasure whose worth can never be estimated in dollars and cents but how they are missed when no longer there.

My Dad was apt to play the odd joke on us, especially on April 1st. One time we had a new man just out from Scotland. His name was Bill and he had a bad habit of leaving the corral gate open. On April 1st, Dad met Bill at the door saying, "Bill, you left the gate open and the bull is going up the road". Bill took off like a rocket. Dad yelled "April Fool, Bill", but he didn't know what that meant, so kept running. Presently he came back scratching his head and said he couldn't see the bull. He never forgot to watch for April Fool's Day after that.

My husband Ernie was born in the Vulcan district just east of the corner store. He was the fourth child of Austin and Jenny Irving. I met him at a dance when he came up here to work for his cousins, the Herr boys. Ernie rode behind the chuckwagons at the Calgary Stampede, first with Eben Bremner, and then with the Goettler wagon.

We were married June 16th, 1942, and farmed here with Mother and Dad until they moved to Okotoks in 1944. During the war years, Ernie and Dad hauled the swill from the De Winton R.A.F. training airport north of us, cooked it and fed it to pigs, and I mean pigs. There were so many at times they seemed to be coming out of our ears. Jim Davenport also hauled to his place at the same time.

Our daughter, Theresa, was born in Calgary July 19th, 1945. Our son John, was born January 21st, 1949. My two brothers, myself, Theresa and John, were brought into the world by Dr. Ardiel from Okotoks.

Theresa and John both inherited the love of riding and horses, as well as Theresa's two boys, Wesley and Donald. They have a home with many gymkhana trophies on display.

Theresa married Wayne Berglund, son of Mr. and Mrs. William Berglund of Calgary, who now live on an acreage east of us. Theresa and Wayne live just north of the Davisburg school on an acreage they rent.

John married Marg Price and they live in Calgary.

Ernie and I rented the home place from Mom and Dad and managed to buy some school land. We have now sold all but the quarter we live on. Here I hope to stay. We are supposed to be retired, but I have never seen a retired housewife, have you?

THE JOHN AND SARAH IRVING FAMILY OF DAVISBURG

John Irving was born at Cardinal, Ontario, died in 1930 at Nanaimo, B.C. Married in 1874 in Cardinal, Ontario to Sarah Howell Hunter, born in 1851, died 1931, Calgary, Alta.

John came west on first excursion train to Calgary in 1887 and took up land in the Davisburg district on Sec. 19 Tp. 21 R28 W4thM, where Lawrence Herr and his mother still live. In the fall of 1888, Sarah came with the family of seven, ranging in age from thirteen down to the youngest of less than one year old. It took a week to make the trip west by train at that time as trains were much slower than today and didn't have dining and sleeping accommodation in the colonist cars of that time. The Macleod Calgary line of the C.P.R. was not built till the early '90's so all travel in the area was by teams and saddle horse. John helped build the Davisburg Church and was one of the first church board members. The Irving children all attended the Davisburg school, one of the schools in the territories being No. 79. The family were Blanche,

John A. Irving Family: Blanche (Herr), Sarah (Flett), John, Edwin, Austin, Alice (Stager) Percy, Nellie.

livestock. In 1904 the Irvings sold their land in Davisburg and moved to Calgary. Later, John and his two eldest sons, Ed and Austin took homesteads in the Arrowwood area twelve miles north of where Vulcan is now, on Sec. 2 Tp. 19 R24 W4th in 1905. The Austin Irvings later acquired the three homesteads, farming there till the '30's where the family were all raised, going to school at the Union Jack School, the nearest towns there then were Gleichen or High River, as the Aldersyde Kipp line of the C.P.R. wasn't built until 1911. Wm. Burgess farms this land now. The McBride family took over the Davisburg place when the Irvings left in 1904 selling out in 1913 also moving to Calgary. Two of the sons, Henry and Archie had taken homesteads near the Irvings at Vulcan. In 1914 a railroad grade was put through the old Irving place in Davisburg, all done by mule and horsepower, using dump wagons and elevating graders. There was a siding graded there for a proposed townsite but when war broke out in 1914 the construction stopped and the railroad was never completed. In 1926 the old Irving place was bought by the Herr brothers, now occupied by Lawrence Herr, nearly 90 years after being settled by the John Irvings in 1887. After three generations of the Irvings attending school in Davisburg, the school was closed, all the pupils being taken to Okotoks now by bus.

The John and Sarah Irving family were:

Blanche married Albert Herr. They had a family of three daughters and six sons and are mentioned in this book under the Herr family.

John and **James Henry** born in 1877 and 1878 both

Sarah, John, Edwin, Austin, Alice and Percy. Ellen, the youngest of the family and the only one born in the west, born in 1891, died in 1893, buried in Davisburg cemetery.

Two other sons of the Irvings died in Cardinal and buried there before the family came West. As most of this area at that time was virgin prairie, there wasn't much grain grown and most of it was used for feeding

Allie Irving Stager and Percy Irving in front of John A. Irving home in Davisburg.

died in the early 1880's and are buried at Cardinal, Ontario.

Sarah married Andrew Flett in 1909, died in 1953, buried in Davisburg. They had two daughters, Mrs. Alex (Ina) Blackwood of Davisburg and Mrs. Wm. (Una) Rodger of Okotoks.

John Irving born in 1882, died in 1895 the result of a run-away accident coming home from church service.

Edwin Irving born in Cardinal, Ontario 1884, married Rachel Cole in 1906. After living in Calgary and Vulcan they moved to Vancouver where Ed died in 1923. They had one son Thomas Edwin who died in 1927 at 19 years of age, and one daughter, Alice May who married Louis Head, living in Vancouver. They had no family.

Thomas Austin Irving born in Cardinal, Ontario in 1886. Married Jennie McMullen in 1909, farmed north of Vulcan on Sec. 2 Tp. 19 R24 W4th where the Irvings had homesteaded in 1904. They raised a family of six sons and five daughters. Austin was killed in a threshing accident in 1932. Jennie died in 1973 in Okotoks, both buried in Vulcan. Their family are:

George L. married Alice Standish of DeWinton farming north of DeWinton until moving to Sundre in 1951, farming there till 1973 when they sold out and moved into Olds. They have three daughters. **Francis Jean** Hart living in Hinton — they have one daughter. **Shirley Lorraine** Kubik living in Olds — they have one son and one daughter. **Betty Louise** Rose — living in Sundre. They have one son and two daughters.

Marjorie Irving married Robert Fisher of Vulcan where Bob farmed and Marjorie taught school. They later moved to the Turner Valley oil fields for a few years before moving to a farm east of Didsbury where she continued teaching until retiring in the middle '70's. They have two sons **Austin** married Betty Snell. They have two daughters and one son and farm with Bob in that area. **Norman** married Norma Turner. He is with the oil industry putting in some time in the North Sea as a driller, now living in Calgary. They have one son and one daughter.

Doris Irving married Lloyd Brown of Vulcan, living at Mossleigh for several years now retired and living in Okotoks. They have a family of four. **Edna** married Loring Piehl. They have two daughters and one son and live in Okotoks. **Ronald** now deceased. **Robert** employed in the Okotoks area and **Gordon** in Australia where he teaches school.

Ernest Irving married Lillian Davis of Davisburg farming in Davisburg district ever since they were married. They have one son and one daughter. **Teresa** married Wayne Bergland — they have two sons and live in Davisburg. **John** married Mary Price, living in Calgary. Ernie uses the JA1 cattle brand used by his grandfather before 1900. **Thomas Lyle** Irving married Eva Vanatta of Milo. They live in Okotoks where Tom has been with the road maintenance of the M.D. of Foothills for several years. They have one daughter **Karen** married Gary Livingstone — they have one daughter. Tom and Eva have five sons, **Dale, Austin, Donald, William** and **Ronnie** all living in Okotoks.

Mary Irving married Charlie McNiven. After farming in the Vulcan and Herronton districts for a few years they moved to Creston, B.C. where Charlie runs a grain elevator and feed mill. They have three children — **Edwin** married Joyce Hollihan — they have one daughter and live in Wynndel, B.C. **Elizabeth** married Gerald Brownell — they have one daughter and two sons and live in Creston, B.C. **Evelyn** married Douglas Anderson — they have one son and two daughters and live in Edmonton.

L. to R. Mr. and Mrs. Andrew Flett 1st and 2nd row. (nee Sara Irving) Mr. and Mrs. Albert Herr 1st and 2nd row (nee Blanche Irving). Grandma and Grandpa Irving center front row. Back row: 3rd and 4th left Jennie and Austin Irving, 5th and 6th from left Rachel and Ed Irving, right back row: Percy Irving, Alice Irving and Ethel Andrew 5 and 6 in front row: Herr and Ed Irving children in front row.

Cecil Irving married Audrey Lind, living at Midnapore for a few years before moving to west of Sundre where Audrey teaches school and Cecil operates heavy construction equipment and raises a few cattle. They have three sons — **Lee** works on a seismograph outfit, **Barry** and **Daniel** go to school. Their only daughter **Jennifer Anne** died in childhood. Cecil was overseas in World War 2 and was severely wounded twice while serving his country in Italy.

David Irving married Connie Hutton. They lived in Blackie for several years where David was employed by the M.D. of Foothills on road maintenance. They have two daughters — **Faye** married Darwin Williams, farming at Arrowwood — they have two daughters. **Darlene** married Brian Sweet. They live in Calgary and have two daughters.

Harry Irving, the youngest of the Irving boys, lives in Okotoks. He operates heavy road machinery and gravel crushers. He is not married.

Lorna Irving Orton, married Lent Orton of Okotoks where Lent was employed by the Dep't. of Highways. Their daughter **Donna** is a trained nurse, now Mrs. George Wilcox. They live in Fort St. John, B.C. and have one son. Lorna died in 1972. Lent lives in Calgary, still with the Dep't. of Highways.

Shirley May Irving, the youngest of the Irving family, died at Okotoks in 1944, buried at Vulcan.

Alice Irving Stager, born in Cardinal, Ontario, married Morris Stager in 1910. They farmed north of Vulcan on land they bought as all the homestead land had been filed on. Their place was on Sec. 25 Tp. 18 R24. They had two girls and four sons. Morris died in 1930, Alice died in 1951, both buried at Vulcan. Their family was:

Clarence, their eldest, farmed at Vulcan for a few years, then north east of Okotoks before moving to Dapp in 1950, farming west of town till moving to Enderby, B.C. In 1967 he sold his farm there, retiring to Vancouver and travelled to the World Fair in Montreal in 1967. Then south around the U.S.A., then to the Yukon and later to Australia where he met and later married an Australian girl, Ruby Pritchell of Abermain N.S.W. They now live in Vancouver where Clarence keeps busy driving taxi.

Viola Stager Fisher married Munden (Bud) Fisher from the Vulcan district. They started their married life at Cochrane raising cattle for a few years, later moving to the Turner Valley oilfields, then to Edmonton when the oil activity moved north. They put in a few years in Trinidad, B.W.I. with the oil industry coming back to Edmonton in 1960. They had a family of three girls and two boys. **Hazel** married Allan Burrell — they have one daughter. **Francis** married Ronald Clark — they have two daughters and one son. **Morris** was in the South Pacific from 1962-65, now assistant dean at the Lutheran College at Camrose. **Marlin** is still at home in Edmonton. **Lynne** their third daughter died when they lived at Crossfield. Bud died in 1966, buried in Edmonton, Viola still residing in Edmonton.

Aubrey Stager died at 20 years of age, buried at Vulcan.

Ralph Stager born at Vulcan married Donna Plourd of Carmangay in 1943, farmed at Vulcan till moving to Creston, B.C. in 1950, farming there for twenty-five years, now retired and living in Creston. They have two sons and two daughters. **Judith Anne** married Roderick Kingsmith and lives at Rocky Mountain House, they have two sons. **Gordon** married Marie Beattie, they have one daughter, live in Cranbrook, B.C. **Norman Louis** living at home in Creston working in the butcher trade. **Irene Alice** still attending school in Creston.

Florence Stager married Donald Sherman. They live in Vancouver where Donald is employed in the taxi business. They have two daughters.

Ivan Morris Stager took his schooling at Red Cross and Vulcan, going overseas with the Canadian Army seeing active duty in Italy, farming at Vulcan for a few years after the war. He married Lois Sawyer and they have two sons. They later sold the farm and now live in Calgary where Ivan is employed in the trucking business.

Percy Harold Irving, born at Cardinal, Ontario in 1888 the youngest son of John and Sarah Irving, coming west the same year with the family to Davisburg where he took his schooling. He moved to Calgary in 1906 where he learned the harness and saddlery trade. Percy started the first harness and furniture store in Vulcan a year after the Aldersyde Lethbridge section of the C.P.R. was built in 1911. His store burned to the ground in 1915. The Vulcan area was just being settled up so there was a big demand for both harness and furniture. He rebuilt after the fire, the building still in use on Main Street, Vulcan. A few years later he moved to west of Olds where he farmed until 1928 when he moved back to Calgary where he worked in the house construction business until his retirement. In the early thirties he married Fay Potts. They had a family of three girls and two boys. The family were:

Gwendolyne Fay married Arthur Hanna in 1952 — they have two sons and one daughter.

Patricia May married Frederick Neubaker in 1954 — they have one son and twin daughters.

Lavina Jennett married David Baskell in 1960 — they have two daughters and one son. Dave was a grandson of Charlie Lehr, oldtime round-up cook on the Bar U ranch in the late '90's. He was considered the best in the West at that time. All Percy's daughters live in Calgary.

Harold Alfred Irving born in Calgary in 1941 died in 1963, buried in Davisburg. Another son, **Lyndon** Percy died in infancy. Percy died in Calgary in 1954, buried in Davisburg. Fay still lives in Calgary.

Ellen Irving, the only one of John and Sarah Irving's family born in the West in 1891, died in 1893, buried in Davisburg.

IRVING — by Dallas Wright

"There were accidents, though, even in those days. The Davisburg Church was a popular gathering place for Sunday morning services. One such Sunday in September, 1895 it was the scene of one of the district's tragedies. Service was over, "visits" had been exchanged, and democrats, buggies and saddle horses were starting homeward. Something happened to frighten the team belonging to a family named Irving, and they bolted, careening down the hill. The minister's conveyance was involved and Mrs. Stewart (then Martha Suitor), remembers the runaway democrat ripping the wheel off the vehicle in which she and her brother were driving with their mother. They were thrown out, uninjured, her mother left clinging to the side. The pole on the runaway democrat finally dropped from the harness and stuck in the ground upending the vehicle and pitching its 14 year old driver, Johnny Irving, to the ground. He had stayed with the team after making sure that his brothers and sisters had jumped to safety. He died ten days later from injuries suffered in the accident, leaving a profoundly shocked neighborhood.''

MR. AND MRS. OLAF JACOBSON — by Virginia Jacobson

Olaf arrived in the Davisburg district December 19, 1945 upon his return from World War II joining Virginia, who was with her parents Ted and Selma Campbell. The spring of 1946 Olaf and Virginia moved onto the Effie Leach farm. During their stay there Olaf raised grain, chickens, hogs and cattle. Glen Alan arrived in the home on May 22, 1947. He took his place very well and a brother Lloyd Earl was born May 7, 1949, a playmate for Glen Alan. Now Olaf had two helpers, so Karen Virginia arrived September 17, 1950, as every Mother needs a daughter.

The spring of 1951 the Leach farm was sold to Russell Grenek so the Jacobson's moved up on the Campbell farm where Olaf engaged in a more extensive hog operation and leasing more farm land to complete his farming.

Life was more interesting for Glen Alan, Lloyd and Karen as their friends were now just across the road, George and Doug Morasch. The boys being very close in ages, all had many a happy fun time together over the years of growing up. Karen had Muriel Blackwood as her close friend as they were the same age. February 1961, the Jacobsons moved into their ''New Moon'' mobile home on the farm. Glen Alan, Lloyd and Karen all attended the Okotoks School and were privileged to have the same bus driver, Olie Hansen, all during their school years to Okotoks. Glen Alan went to S.A.I.T. in 1965 and took one year of Petroleum Technology and from there went into the oil-field work. Lloyd left school in 1964 and worked at different jobs until he established himself in the oil-field as well as a heavy-duty truck driver.

Karen took her Grade 12 at Crescent Heights High School in Calgary and a semester at Business College. In 1968 she married George Karman of Okotoks and they now live in Calgary. They have two boys, Gregory Todd and Gary Craig.

Olaf continued farming until the fall of 1972 when most of the land he had leased had been subdivided into 20 acre parcels and the Campbell farm was to be sold. The Slagter family now live in the Campbell home and two more homes have been added on the previous ¼ section. A whole new look to the Davisburg Community has developed, quite different from when we arrived in 1944.

Olaf, Virginia and family have some good memories of their life in Davisburg. Olaf enjoyed his farming and took part in the community activities, curling and community association. Virginia also enjoyed her many good times in the Jolly Time Club, Community Association, curling and when the family was in school she took an active interest in the Okotoks Home and School Association.

Olaf and Virginia celebrated their 25th Anniversary November 24, 1965, a very enjoyable celebration was had with family and friends in the De Winton Hall.

Mr. and Mrs. Olaf Jacobson and family, Glen Alan, Lloyd and Karen. 25th anniversary Nov. 24, 1965, at De Winton Hall.

Upon completion of farming Olaf and Virginia took up residence at the Ten-Jay Ranch on Pine Creek, October 1972 where Olaf is enjoying the cattle and a much easier life. September 25, 1975 we lost Glen Alan suddenly and he now rests beside his Grandpa and Grandma Campbell at Mountain View Memorial Gardens. Lloyd married Kathleen Copley at Okotoks and they have a son Cody Glen.

Upon completion of four years on the Ten-Jay Ranch we retired to the town to High River.

THE JAMES FAMILY— by Don James

The James family came from Illinois to a farm near Cochrane in June 1921. In 1922, they moved to the Grotto. Their land consisted of the E½ S. 6, all of sections four and five lying south of the Bow River and all of S. 3 lying south and west of the Bow, all in 22-28-W4th. They remained there for seven and one-half years, raising grain and cattle.

The farm was purchased by Dr. Robert L. James of Blue Island, Illinois on June 25th, 1920 from Arthur B.

Earle and Florence James, 1928.

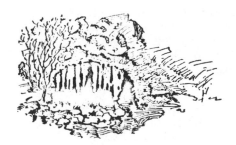

Grotto Stock Farms

De WINTON
ALBERTA, CANADA

BRAND $\overline{37}$

HEREFORD CATTLE
DUROC-JERSEY SWINE

February 10,1923.

Muir, who had purchased it the year before from Thomas N. Martin.

In 1922, a company known as the Grotto Stock Farms was formed by Dr. James and his sons, Earle and Robert.

Earle and his wife Florence moved here from Cochrane and were joined by Robert, who lived on the farm until 1926 or 1927, when he moved to Calgary and went into the trucking business.

According to the records, many people from the area worked at the Grotto. Earl Brinton, E. L. Jackman, F. W. Stoddard, are three of the names in the wage book.

Earle and Florence were part of a group called the Davisburg Orchestra. It ranged from two to five pieces, and from 1924 to 1928, played at such places as De Winton Hall, Blackwood's Granary, Okotoks Hall, Black Diamond Hall and Davisburg School.

l. to r.: Dr. R. L. James, Edna (Mrs. R. A. James), Robert A. James. Jessie, (Mrs. R. L. James), Earl James, Florence James, Front Row: Kathryn, Betty, Donald — 1928.

In September 1929, Florence returned to Illinois because of poor health, and the Grotto was sold to a family by the name of Hyde. Earle left Canada in January of 1930 and returned to Illinois.

Robert, Earle and Florence are deceased, but Earle's three children, Donald, Betty and Kathryn are living in Illinois.

OLIVE AND ERNIE LaBERGE

I, Olive, the daughter of Mr. and Mrs. Chas. Shattuck, was born in the Davisburg district November 27th, 1894, receiving my education in the home school at Davisburg, afterwards attending Mount Royal College in Calgary. When finished, I returned to the farm, where I spent most of my life, following in the footsteps of my parents.

Some of the experiences I shall never forget. Preferring to work outside, it was not long before I could turn my hand to most anything, as many of my old pals can tell you. This was always a great pleasure for me, but when Mother became ill, we had to move to Calgary. She rented the farm, and after her death, I became heir to the West half of 30-21-28-W4, being the old homestead. I also maintained the family brand L2.

At this point, I rented the farm to my nephew, Thomas King, who lived there with his family for many years.

Taking an active part in the community was always a pleasure for me, and I was organist at the Davisburg Church for years. One evening I was honoured by the congregation, who presented me with a beautiful walnut sewing cabinet, which I cherish to this day. I was also president of the High River Old Timers' Association, and served many years on the executive of the Southern Alberta Pioneers' and Old Timers' Association, Calgary.

May 1st, 1952, I married Ernest LaBerge, who was born in Huntingdon, Quebec, in 1893. He had read about the great opportunities in Western Canada, and decided that was the place to go. He came to Bindloss, Alberta, at the age of 18, and filed on a homestead in that district. After farming for a few years, he decided to sell the farm and equipment, then came to Blackie, Alberta, where he worked among the farmers for three years. He later settled in Calgary, where he was employed with some of the well-known plastering contractors.

We are now retired and live in our own home in Meadow Lark Park, Calgary, Alberta.

THE LEACH FAMILY — by E. Leach

Chester Leach came from near Sarnia, Ontario, working on farms in Saskatchewan and Alberta. For three winters, centering around 1912, he was in the Lineham Lumber Camps up the Highwood. Cliff and Bert Call also worked there. Life was primitive, with plenty of food but no luxuries. Each man did his own laundry in the creek, woollen underwear and all leaving it on the bushes to dry by sun or frost. Medication was looked after by the cook who, once a week, secretly added some epsoms salts to the soup or

169

tea. One spring Chester walked on the ice down the Highwood to High River, a distance of some sixty miles.

He homesteaded near Hanna where the only good crop was in 1917. After successive very dry years he and his wife Jessie abandoned the homestead and bought a one-half section of land in the Davisburg district in 1922. Some years later a machine salesman who must have been a bit of a gambler, traded a horse-drawn seed-drill for the deed of the Hanna homestead.

Jessie died in 1924. Chester and Effie Blackwood were married in 1928 and have one daughter, Mary Belle (Mrs. Peter Esposito), who is a public health nurse in Calgary.

Chester and Mary Leach — 1932.

I went to the old Davisburg school with my two older sisters. We rode Indian ponies to school and did not have saddles. Daisy and I went to high school in Calgary. I taught school for many years in rural Alberta, including a three-year stint at Davisburg. There I had all the grades, including the entrance to High School class, an enrollment of 36 pupils and a fine big salary of $1,300 a year. Please note: a year, not a month! Later, after a business course at Garbutt's Business College, I worked for Imperial Oil in Calgary.

After Chester's death Mary and I lived alone on the farm, but I did put in two years at the airport. We moved to Calgary in the fall of 1944. I worked at the U.F.A. Co-op for eighteen years.

I would like to mention here that our old Davisburg home, which was known as the old Worden place, was first homesteaded by a certain Mr. Thompson in the 1880s. He was unable to make a living there and rode horseback to Calgary to get assistance from the

Mounties. Application was made to Ottawa, but then, as now, the Government moved slowly. When Mr. Thompson went to Calgary a second time, the Mounties took him in. He died the next morning, a victim of starvation.

EUGENE MAGYAR

I arrived in the Davisburg district with Dad and Mother and other members of the family in the spring of 1945 from the Tilley, Alberta district.

I graduated from Brooks High School in 1944 and spent two years at the Provincial Institute of Technology and Arts: 1945-1947, graduating in Industrial Electricity.

I worked for the telephone company from 1948-1951 and was stationed in Innisfail and Red Deer.

From 1951 to 1963 I farmed with dad on W½-29-21-28 West of the 4th. This land was across from the present Davisburg hall. I married Emma Klingspohn in 1964, and have no children.

Present address is R.R. 1, De Winton, Alberta. I was born in Dorobanti, Roumania in 1924 and immigrated to Canada in 1930.

MR. AND MRS. STEVE MAGYAR — by Eugene Magyar

Mr. Steve Magyar immigrated to Canada from Roumania in 1927. His wife, Rosalia and four children followed in 1930 and they settled on a farm near Tilley, Alberta. In the spring of 1945 the family moved to the Davisburg district and settled on the farm formerly owned by Osborne Andrews, the W½ 29-21-28 W4th, across from the Davisburg School.

The following year, 1946, their son William, and wife Ethel followed, living firstly with the family, and then on the Dr. L. S. Mackid place, N.W.¼ 20-21-28 W4th, which Mr. Steve Magyar purchased.

Both Mr. and Mrs. Magyar passed away in 1963, Rosalia in June and Steve in October.

Their children and places of residence are as follows: Mr. and Mrs. William Magyar have been farming in the Elnora district since 1956; Mr. and Mrs. Eugene Magyar live on his parent's farm home in Davisburg; Mr. and Mrs. Norman Leischner (Rose) reside in Kelowna, B.C.; Mr. and Mrs. Gordon Leischner (Ethel) in Calgary; Mr. and Mrs. Steve Magyar Jr., in Okotoks; Mr. and Mrs. Frank Bernard (Rosalie) in Venezuela, South America; Mr. and Mrs. Joe Merkl (Margaret) farm in the Brooks area and Mr. and Mrs. Andrew Magyar farm in the Davisburg area near the Davisburg United Church.

JAMES MARTIN FAMILY — by Lila Hillard

Our family moved to the Davisburg district in the spring of 1913. Our farm was the former Banister place. There were six in the family.

Melvin, who married Cora Andrews. Barsby married Agnes Gray, who taught school at Davisburg. Sadie worked for a law firm for forty years. Clarence drove trucks for James Bros. Lila trained as a nurse at Vancouver General Hospital, married Tom Hillard. Ena took up stenography and worked at the stock yards before marrying Everett Rogers.

My mother died in 1922 and Dad stayed on the farm a few years longer.

Clarence Martin, Ernest Martin, Edwin Jackman, Carleton Impey, (Seated) Lila Martin, Ena Martin, Ruby Impey.

We had many happy days on the farm. The work was all done with horses and the grain was hauled to De Winton with four or six horse teams. My Dad and Uncle Tom had a threshing outfit and did the threshing for other farmers. They would hire young men from the East to work for harvest. This was quite a thrill for the young gals of the district.

I remember well the flu epidemic of 1918. I was going to High School in Calgary and brought the flu home. We were all down except Barsby. It really kept him busy nursing us, and doing the chores as well. We evidently had a case of crabapples which he stewed up and served every meal. They must have been good medicine, as we all recovered. I went to look after the Shattucks when they all came down with the flu and Sadie went to look after the Meehans.

THOMAS N. AND ELIZABETH MARTIN — by Polly Ritchie

In the spring of 1913 we moved from a farm north of Calgary to a farm in the Davisburg district, known as the "Grotto" because of the location of the house. It was quite old and built backing into a hill. From the upstairs a ramp ran up to the upper flat and from the main floor, steps descended to the lower farmyard. The farm included two sections of land. To the northeast and southeast it was bounded by the Bow River. On the west was the farm of James Martin and to the South, the Coles and J. Andrews.

One thing that might be of interest was the very large deposit of buffalo bones in the river bank and on the flat at the southeast corner. A man by the name of Mr. Aeillo of Calgary, contracted to dig and haul them

out by truck. He brought in a crew of men to do the work. First they had to build a road by hand down the steep river hill, then dig, load and move the bones out. From De Winton they were shipped to the sugar refinery.

The family lived in the district for seven years. There were four children in the family, Roy, Mac., Ernest and Polly.

DONALD AND ELIZABETH (ZEGGIL) McBRIDE

Donald McBride and Elizabeth Zeggil were married April 5, 1880 and Donald came west in 1890 from Singhampton, Ontario. The family followed in 1892. Their homestead was NE¼-20-21-28-W4. and they remained until 1912 or 1913.

There were thirteen children in this family: George Henry married Mary Hislop in Calgary in 1915, both are deceased, children: Isabel, Florence, Christina (Christie). Catherine (Katie) married Howard Stewart at Davisburg in 1903 with Reverend Shortt officiating, both are deceased, children: Harry, Marjory (deceased), Morris, Eva, Florence, Donald, Mary, Muriel, Clare, Ken. Isabella (Bella) married James Crawford in 1904, both are deceased, children: Jimmie, Isabel, Bill (deceased), Margaret, Jean and Fred. Emma Ann married Robert Sherradon at Davisburg in 1913, they had no family and both are deceased. Archie married Ruby McCullough at Irricana in 1914, Archie, deceased, Ruby lives in Sherwood Park, Alberta, children: George, Helen, Pearle (deceased), Bob, Bill and Betty. Margaret (Maggie) married John Sutcliffe at Nelson, B.C. in 1916, both deceased, children: Major (deceased), Frank, Margaret, Betty, Catherine, Jim and Bob. Mary Agnes married Donald Melvin McPhail at Calgary in 1917, Melvin, deceased and Agnes presently married to Robert Stevens, lives at Sidney, B.C. no children. Sarah married John Blenkensopp at Calgary in 1919, John, deceased, Sarah lives in Victoria, B.C., children: John, Ethel and Dorothy. Christina

McBride family taken at Davisburg 1906. Donald McBride (father), Elizabeth McBride (mother), Grandma Isabella Zeggil with Ethel on her knees, Henry McBride, Archie, Maggie, Katie, Bella, Ann, William, Fred, Christina, Sadie, Agnes, Bessie.

(Christie) married Harry McClain in Los Angeles in 1923, both are deceased, one son Dale. Fred, never married, deceased. William (Bill), bachelor, living in Mayfair Nursing Home, Calgary. Ethel (Essie) married Carl Nelson in Calgary, 1922, Carl deceased, Essie lives in Drumheller, children: Carol and Monna. Evelyn, deceased in infancy.

FRANK BOWES McHUGH FAMILY — by Virginia Klatzel (McHugh)

John Joseph McHugh was born in Ottawa in 1853. His father had come from Ireland and cleared timber on what is now Parliament Hill. John J. (J.J. as he was most commonly called) came from Ottawa to the West in 1874 as Inspector of the Indian Department, N.W.T. and later was Inspector of the Interior. He had boated up the Saskatchewan River to Edmonton where he started a government farm that would be used to teach Indians farming techniques. He was also Inspector of Indian Reserves until that position was abolished in 1884. As Inspector of the Interior he was the first land agent in Assiniboia.

In 1883 J.J. and his brother Tom located the McHugh Brothers' Ranch near Gleichen. Three years later another brother Felix came West to join his rancher brothers. Livestock for the ranch was shipped from Eastern Canada. The McHugh brothers were the first to bring purebred Clydesdale horses and Shorthorn cattle into Alberta in 1884. The McHughs also owned the first saddle horse that was shipped over the Rocky Mountains and back by rail in 1889.

On April 30, 1884, J.J. married Frances Elizabeth Bowes of Kingston, Ontario in Ottawa. Father Albert Lacombe assisted at the ceremony. Frank was born in Moosomin, Saskatchewan, March 4, 1885. He was the eldest of eleven children. Frank and his sister

Frank McHugh and Mrs. J. J. McHugh.

Kathleen were the only children to reach adulthood. At the age of three, Frank and his family moved to Calgary. He received his education in Calgary, Winnipeg and Montreal and spent the summers on the McHugh Ranch. After his schooling, Frank worked on the ranch until 1905. He then went into the teamsters business in Calgary and hauled sand and gravel for

The McHugh family in front of the barn at the Dunbow Industrial School — 1939.

many of Calgary's buildings, and Calgary Brewery, and much of the pavement of the streets from 1908-1913. The excavation of the Isis theatre, Knox United Church and Underwood Block were also supervised by him.

Frank was an ardent sportsman, excelling in hockey, football and polo. He played inside wing for the Calgary Tigers' Football teams of the 1907-1912 era. At 247 pounds he was the heaviest man playing football in the West. In hockey he played defence for St. Mary's Hockey Club. It was from this position that he gained the nickname of "Bull" for his strength and skating ability. It was a name that he disliked but it remained with him. Frank played polo for the Calgary Polo team as well as the High River team. The teams played in the United States and Western Canada, winning many championships.

For a period during World War I, Frank served as a transport Sergeant and later an Officer, having charge of the movement of troops and supplies to Sarcee Camp.

In 1915, Frank began farming in the Gladys Ridge district. His sister Kathleen married Charles Beeching in 1921. They farmed in the De Winton area until moving to Vancouver and later Victoria. In 1926, Frank married Mary Jane Adams of the Davisburg district. They moved to Dunbow in 1928 from their Gladys Ridge farm. The couple had four children; Francis (Jack), Virginia, Douglas, and Patrick. The children all attended Davisburg School. Jack later attended S.A.I.T. and operated a Royalite Service Station in Calgary before returning to farm on the family farm in the late 1950's. He married Eva Jones from Fort Resolution, N.W.T., and has four children. They reside in Calgary. Virginia attended high school in Calgary. Following teacher training at the Universities of Alberta and Calgary she taught school at Cluny, Forest Lawn and Calgary. She married Stephen Klatzel from Scott, Saskatchewan. They have three daughters and reside in Calgary. Douglas also attended high school in Calgary and has remained farming. He married Betty Stewart and has two sons. Pat has been a rodeo contestant for a number of years, and has won many championships. He lives in the Davisburg district. Frank passed away on November 15, 1957. Mary Jane continues to live at Dunbow where she keeps busy with her many interests and hobbies.

WILLIAM MOODIE

William (Bill) Moodie was born in Glenerul, Argylshire, Scotland on September 5th, 1867. He came to Millarville district in 1895, where he homesteaded for seven years. Returning briefly to Scotland, he married Margaret Laurie Kay in 1901. Mr. Moodie owned 531 acres of land in the Davisburg district close to De Winton, Alberta, known as "Riverside Farm," being the E½ of 1 and part of E½ of 12-22-29-W4th. His farm was noted for his Shorthorn cattle and thoroughbred and Clydesdale horses, several of which were distinguished with medals. Several were won in 1905 and 1906. One medal was won in 1905 for "Best Light Draught Stallion." Another was for the "Birks Medal for Champion Light Female" in 1906. In addi-

tion to these honors, Mr. Moodie was President of the Alberta Horse Breeders Association for many years.

Having lost his first wife in 1904, Bill married Agnes Gertwood Kay in 1906. Two sons by his first wife died in 1922 and 1926. Their names were Tom and Bill Moodie. They had one son, Duncan, born in 1908, by his second wife.

Mr. Moodie passed away at his farm home in 1947 and is buried in Union Cemetery in Calgary. His wife passed away in 1962. His son, Duncan, and wife Eva, now residing in Calgary, carried on with the family farm until it was sold in 1958.

GEORGE AND MARY MORASCH — told by Jack Morasch

My parents came from Russia in 1910, settling in Calgary with a family of seven children. In 1927 my father, George Morasch, and mother, Mary, bought the farm W½ 6-22-28 and part of Section 7 and Section 8 from Harold Banister. We moved to the farm in April 1928. My brother, George, and myself bached on the farm for two years before our parents moved out.

Mr. and Mrs. George Morasch — 1942.

Brother George passed away in 1943. My parents now had a retirement home in Calgary and spent most of their time there. Dad lived until 1947 and Mother until 1958.

I married Margaret Mons of Calgary in 1946. We have two sons, George and Douglas. Douglas is married to Mary Ann and they have a son, Clinton.

We still reside on the same place after selling all but the 40 acres which makes a nice place to retire.

THE NASH FAMILY — by Stan. Nash

Thomas Nash was born in 1868 in Birkhamstead, County of Hartfordshire, England. After working four years in Australia, he returned to England on a ship that took ten weeks to make the voyage. He arrived to find the family preparing to emigrate to Canada, so he

Mr. and Mrs. Tom Nash with Tommy, Jennie and Bert taken in 1902.

joined his father, John Nash, brothers Charles and Herbert and sister, Louisa, in the new venture. They landed in St. John, New Brunswick in April, 1893, after an arduous journey, and entrained for Calgary by C.P.R.

John Nash bought 160 acres in the Davisburg district where a home was established on the N.E. ¼ 28-21-28 W.4th. The horse and cattle brands are shown elsewhere in the book. Stan Nash still has the original cattle brand.

While helping thresh their crops, John Nash was fatally injured and was buried in the Davisburg cemetery on November 6th, 1897.

Charles, after working for Fred James and Finleys, took a homestead in 1898 on the N.W. ¼ 20-20-27-W4th, the same quarter the Gladys Ridge store was located on some years later. Charles never married. He lived on his farm until he sold it in October, 1944 and retired to Calgary where he died in 1954.

Herbert married Tillie Margrave, sister of Mrs. Tom Nash. They resided in Calgary. Herbert was a tailor and Tillie a dressmaker. They are both buried in Gladys Cemetery. The Gladys Anglican Cemetery is on the Tom Nash farm, S.E. 30-20-27-W4th.

Louisa married Herbert Wilson who came from Middlesex, England. They homesteaded S.E.¼ 30-20-27-W4th but lived on Section 5, south of a bend in the Highwood River and called it Sprucedale.

Tom worked on farms of McBride and Irving and one winter in Lineham's lumber camp to provide money to buy land of his own on Gladys Ridge. This was the original Chas. Wakeford homestead S.E.¼ 30-20-27-W4th. Miss Clara Margrave, a boyhood sweetheart of Tom's, made the long journey, alone, to Calgary where their marriage took place on April 23rd, 1898. They moved that fall to Gladys Ridge.

The Nash children, Tommy, Jennie, Bert, Sadie, Doris and Stanley, were all born after Tom and Clara moved to Gladys Ridge. Tommy died of scarlet fever while very young. Jennie married Jack Wilson, a school teacher from England. Jack taught in the Okotoks High School during the years 1943 to 1955. Sadie married Ed. Clozie and lives in Pincher Creek. Bert remained a bachelor and passed away in 1961 at the age of 58. Doris married Russell Grenek and they lived most of their lives around Gladys Ridge but did live at Davisburg during the years 1951 and 1952, on the farm of Chester and Effie Leach. Doris passed away in October, 1971. Stan married Isabel Peterson of Gladys Ridge where they still reside.

ADAM AND ESTELLA (BRYCE) NELUBOWICH — by E. Nelubowich

I was born April 12, 1911 in East Nissouri, Oxford County, Ontario one mile north of Kintore. At the age of three months Mother brought me to Alberta. She had gone down to visit her grandparents and both had passed away before she came back home. She also had my brother, Joseph Lorne with her who was Alberta raised and eight years old. Sister, Kay, was born August 15, 1919.

Mr. and Mrs. Tom Nash, Doris, Jennie, Bert, Sadie and Stan.

Stella and Adam Nelubowich.

174

I remember the terrible time we had with the flu epidemic in the winter of 1918. Mother, Joe and myself all had it at the same time. Father had to nurse all of us and do the chores as well but fortunately never came down with it. Dr. Ardiel had to be called out from Okotoks.

I stayed on in the family home after my parents passed away. I always enjoyed the outdoors and wanted to see things grow so became a farmerette — owning my own farm and equipment and having my own quota book.

On November 24, 1962 I married Adam Nelubowich. He and his father, Joseph, bought the E½ and NW¼-7-21-28-W4 in the spring of that year. They previously farmed near Robsart, Saskatchewan. We had less than seven years together and he passed away, suddenly, October 21, 1969.

FELIX (FIL) AND KAY (BRYCE) NOEL — by Kay Noel

Fil was born in Beauvallon, Alberta in 1916. His family moved to the St. Paul district in 1926. He was one of a family of thirteen and had to leave home at an early age to work and provide for himself. In the fall of 1935 he went to work for Wm. Bryce where he met Kay Bryce, youngest of a family of three. In the coming years he returned to the area for the harvest season and worked for the Forckel Brothers. He married Kay, at Midnapore, in October, 1939, planning to build a house that fall on a quarter section he had purchased in the St. Paul area.

Kay's parents were very sceptical of this venture. They felt that Kay and Fil were moving way back 'in the sticks'. Having pioneered themselves, they could see nothing but hardships ahead for the young couple in the north. They offered Fil a seventh crop share of the next year's crop if he did the seeding, summer-fallow and harvesting. This looked much better than building a house in the late fall and starting out on their own so, the deal was accepted. The lumber for the house was sold as it was too much of a risk to leave it piled and the money was also needed to pay for a hired man for seeding and harvesting, the following year.

Everything progressed well for the spring and summer. The year appeared to be a good one. Louis, the eldest child, in a family of six, was born in the end of September of that year. The crop was cut and stooked but the weather failed to co-operate. There was rain and then snow. The crop didn't really get dry enough for threshing. Alex Blackwood had the one and only threshing outfit in the country and having completed threshing for all the other farmers on his list he decided that our crop had to be done so he could finish for the year and get his outfit put away for the winter. The first grain was very tough and not acceptable for sale in the elevators. After a few days the grain had dried enough to be accepted but the share for Fil's work had already gone through wet. Bryces refused any part of this for it would heat and spoil before long. Needless to say, this was the end of the agreement made the previous year. Some of the wet grain was dealt away for weaner pigs to which the remainder of

the grain was fed. By the time spring came other plans had been made for the future.

The Second World War had commenced in the fall of 1939 and by the spring of 1941 work was not easy to get. There were still unfinished, feeder pigs and it appeared best to get a small acreage on which to finish the pigs and for Fil to get work. This proved to be unsuccessful and the pigs were sold and Fil joined the Army, March 6, 1941. He was given two weeks to get his affairs in order and report for duty. Since he was a married man with a family it was understood that he would train and remain in Canada for at least a year. A shock came Sunday morning, (after reporting for duty, midnight, Friday) after Church Parade, the Army Service Corps boys were sorted and he found himself among those transferred to the Calgary Tank Regiment, confined to barracks and shipped to Camp Borden on Monday night's train. They embarked for England July 1, and the next year was spent training for battle, as a radio operator, for the tanks. This regiment was among those sent to France for the Dieppe Raid August 19, 1942. Fil was taken prisoner of war there but Kay was notified that he was on the missing list, and later, that he was missing and presumed dead. Shortly after this message was received from the Government, a message of condolence came from the Padre of the Tank Regiment. It was not until November that Kay received a form letter, direct from Fil, stating that he was well and a prisoner of war. The Red Cross announced him as a P.O.W. in mid December and the Government, in January. He spent the first eleven months at Stalag VIII B and was one of a group sent to a dairy farm at Stalag 11 D, near Stetin. After milking cows for the Germans until the war was over, it was no wonder that he had no desire to ever milk cows again or eat margarine on his bread.

In February, 1945, the Germans decided that the war was not progressing favorably for them and took the prisoners on a lengthy march, criss-crossing the country, not knowing exactly what to do with them. The war ended in May of that year and he was sent back to England, by plane. He had a short stay in hospital and set sail for Canada, July 1, 1945, four years to the day from the time he sailed for England. He received his discharge from the Army in the late summer and harvest time was again spent working for the Forckel brothers.

By this time the method of harvesting had changed from stooking and driving horses on a bundle rack, to combine harvesting. His job that fall was much easier, driving a truck and hauling grain from the combine and unloading with a machine. When harvest was completed, Fil and Kay decided to look around for a farm and take a V.L.A. Settlement. It was difficult to make a choice and after looking at a place east of Red Deer they found that they would have to apply from the Red Deer office as it was not in the Calgary District.

It was at this time that Bryces approached Fil with an offer to rent three quarters of a section from them on a regular rent basis of one half share with their share delivered to the elevator. Fil was to pay all the land tax and have part of the house to live in. The offer was accepted.

Kay had worked, packing parachutes at the De Winton Air Port, during the war and had saved enough money for the purchase of a Massey-Harris tractor. The old machinery was purchased from the Bryces. It was a beautiful fall and preparations for next year's crop were started with Fil working in the fields when it was too damp to combine and Kay running the tractor when he was harvesting. This resulted in the most land possible being made ready for the crop next spring. By the time harvest was completed Fil was questioning his 'internal fortitude' as to whether or not to offer to purchase the E½ 8-21-28-W4, raw unbroken land, from the Forckel brothers. He didn't have a hope that they would sell cultivated land. Finally, one stormy morning, when he figured the brothers would be home, he went over and broached the subject to John. No agreement was reached at that time but shortly after we had the offer accepted but for the north half of the section, which was all cultivated. This was surely too good to be true. The north west quarter was already pretty well under cultivation and with the N½ it would make a good little farm.

It was at this time that the Veteran's Land Settlement was commenced. Cash was needed to go along with the Government loan for the purchase. The amount needed would equal the part which was to be free, to buy the machinery plus the amount spent for the purchase of a new tractor. It was after a great amount of frustration and worry that we learned there were a few good hearted and understanding people in the world. There were gratuities coming in the spring but that would be too far away. The tractor was taken back and parked in the Massey Harris shop and the money returned for the farm purchase. By spring, Fil had the money to reclaim the tractor and he was away on his farming venture with three quarters, rented from Bryces and the half section bought from the Forckell brothers. Kay and Fil lived in a part of the Bryce home until the fall of 1949. By this time there were three children; Louis, born in 1940, Maurice born in 1946 and Darline, born in 1949.

In the spring of that year Bryces decided that the renting was going OK and they would move back east. The change there had been so great since they came out west, fifty years before, that 'home' now could only be west and they were back in October.

Fil and Kay decided that their family was getting a little too much for Grandma and Grandpa and it was only right that if they chose to remain in their own house they should have a little peace and quiet. Fil had purchased lumber from the De Winton Air Port to build a house on his own farm. It was too late in the fall to build so a small house, on an acre of land, was purchased in Forest Lawn (now a part of Calgary). There was an advantage in living here, close to doctors, as Darline had been born with a blood tumor and if she should fall and rupture it she could bleed too much before getting medical help. Fil had hired a young couple, John and Ruth Peters, to help with the farming because Kay was no longer able to help outside as she had been doing. He built a little two room house for them on the half section. This was his first building experience, other than granaries, and a few things, such as a 7' instead of an 8' ceiling didn't work out too well. However, the young couple were quite

happy as they were among the displaced persons brought to Canada after the war. John could speak only German. Ruth's parents had had a store in the States and had gone for a visit to Lithuania and when war broke out they were not allowed to return. Ruth had taken English at school so they managed. They were a dependable, hard working couple and although it meant that Fil had to travel back and forth to Calgary, all went well. Wages were increasing and the limit was reached in 1951. In the fall of that year, with the help of Dr. Worrel, a dependable surgeon was found and Darline underwent a successful operation, in Toronto. A neighbor, in Forest Lawn, got together with others and gathered a gift of money to help with travelling expenses. In so doing, Mayor McKay's interest had been attracted and, as in many other cases of infant surgery, he raised enough money from the citizens of Calgary to pay the doctors, hospital and all other expenses. Words will never express the thanks and gratitude to all those people who helped us through that tragic time.

When Kay and Darline arrived back from the east, the little house was empty as Ruth and John had accepted a job in the Taber area, at higher wages. Darline's improvement was so great that it was decided that she could return to the farm to live. Louis had been sent to the boarding school at the Lacombe Home because the trip east was expected to last for much more that the six weeks that it took. Lydia was born that spring and even though Louis was away at school and staying with his grandparents on weekends, something had to be done. Fil had tried to build during the summer and the excavation was made. The weather would not co-operate and, each time we tried to pour cement, it rained. Fall arrived and still no house so Kay and the children were moved back to Forest Lawn.

The next spring Bryces decided to try a year at the Coast and, if they liked it there, to remain. We moved back to their house and Fil farmed alone that spring. Bryces didn't like the Coast and were back home in six weeks. When spring work was finished Fil, with the help of his Dad, jacked up the two room house and put in a cement flooring. Two bedrooms were added upstairs and an extra area for a bedroom and living room was added to the east side. This part was to be used for a garage when a house was built. Hail storms, together with wheat quotas, made it impossible to ever build a house.

During the mid-fifties, farming was cut down to the half section as the Bryces thought that the half and half agreement was too good a deal for Fil and Kay. and they had a better offer from Les Reid. Fil and Kay found that the taxes were already over the usual farm rental agreements and told the Bryces they had better accept the good offer. Strange though it may seem, Bryces realized less from 'the good deal' than they had, in previous years, with Kay and Fil.

It did strike a little hard to pay for machinery, bought to farm 1¼ sections, from the income from a half section. By doing custom work, feeding cattle, purchased through the Feeder's association, and milking a few cows, all went well.

In 1962, the Veterans of Dieppe decided to make a

20th Anniversary trip back to France and Fil made up his mind that he and Kay would go even if it meant selling the last cow to do it. That spring, an all out attempt was made to have the best crop ever. Commercial fertilizer was used for extra insurance for a good crop. The crop came up and looked good, for a while, but rain failed to come in enough quantity to dissolve the fertilizer. We had the trip regardless and it was an experience to remember. It lasted only two weeks and the time passed very quickly but the country was so green and the flowers so beautiful, in the cemetery in Dieppe, we enjoyed it all. We had a quick trip to parts of England and as far north as Dundee and Edinburgh, Scotland. In the lower altitude, Kay felt so much better than in the high altitude of Calgary that they decided, someday, they would move to a lower altitude.

The next year proved to be a good one, no hail, plenty of rain, which dissolved fertilizer from the previous year, resulting in a really good crop. This was the last of nineteen years of farming and the home they had planned for the N½ 8-21-28-W4.

In the spring an auction sale was held and Fil and Kay moved to a country store they had purchased, south of Salmon Arm, B.C., at Silver Creek. Louis, the eldest of the children, had married Grace Walls, after joining the Air Force. They have three girls and live in Armstrong, B.C. Darline and Lydia married brothers Maurice and Claude Labre. Darline and Maurice have a boy and a girl and live in a trailer home in Davisburg, near Kay's sister, Stella. Lydia and Claude have a boy and a girl and live in Calgary. Ronald married Sheryl Fraser, from Calgary, has two boys and lives in Salmon Arm. Vivianne, the youngest, is with her parents and working in Salmon Arm. The country store was sold and Fil has been working in the Real Estate Field since 1970 and makes his home in Salmon Arm.

TUCKER PEACH — by Ina Blackwood

Little is known of the early life of Tucker Peach but, it is believed he came from a well to do, English family in Lancastershire. He settled in Davisburg, near the mouth of the Highwood, in the mid-eighties. He moved to Gladys, taking out a homestead in 1889 on 20-21-27-W4 and, in 1907, he obtained the NE¼ 7-21-27-W4. He travelled widely over Southern Alberta shearing sheep and was well liked by everyone. It was believed that he carried a large sum of money, in a money belt, on his person.

Early in 1910 he disappeared and a report was circulated that he had sold his land, and horses, to Mr. T. M. Robertson and returned to England. However, in June, a headless body was found in the Bow, near his place, and, in November, a skull was found near the same place, it was positively identified as being that of Tucker Peach.

An investigation was conducted by the R.C.M.P. which resulted in the arrest of Robertson and Jack Fisk. A trial was held in Okotoks and both men were found guilty. Robertson received life imprisonment and Fisk was hanged in Calgary.

W. H. AND UNA RODGER — by Una Rodger

William Henry (Scotty) came from Lumphanon,

Aberdeenshire, Scotland, in 1929. He worked for the City of Calgary, in the Okotoks area, and in the Government Bridge Department. He served in the 1st Canadian Medium Artillery Regiment in W.W. II.

In 1946 he married Una Flett, younger daughter of Andrew and Sarah (Irving) Flett of Calgary, a 1940 graduate of the Holy Cross Hospital.

In 1947 they settled in the old De Winton Airport where they resided until retiring to Okotoks in 1972.

LOUIS AND ALICE SATHER — by Alice Reid

Louis Sather worked for A.G.T. in Bassano, Gleichen and Lethbridge retiring after 35 years. His pension amounted to $44.40 a month. We purchased the N.W.¼-31-21-28-4 in Davisburg the spring of 1939 where we took on the new duties of farming, milking cows, raising chickens, a few pigs and of course a garden which was our pride and joy. Our son Bob was home with us at this time and the fall of 1939 he went to Edmonton to University, training as a Chemical Engineer. He now works for Cominco at Vancouver. He married Freda Mason at Edmonton and they have three children, Donald, Karen and Nancy. Karen is married and has a son Byron.

We found the Davisburg community the most friendly place we have ever lived. The fall of 1944 we sold out to J. E. (Ted) Campbell from Vulcan and Louis and I moved to Calgary. Louis passed away in Calgary September 1950.

In 1953 I married Les Reid who had worked on the Alice Shattuck farm from 1935 until 1950. We later bought a farm east and south of High River where we farmed for 16 years, retiring to the town of High River in 1970.

CHARLIE E. SHATTUCK — by Olive La Berge

Charlie was born in Chardon, Ohio, U.S.A., October 6, 1862. He came West in the early 1890s. The first winter in the West was spent living with a very great friend by the name of Alex Stewart. Then he filed on a homestead known as SW ¼-30-21-28-W4. It was not long before he purchased more land at the price of $4.00 per acre, where he and his wife farmed for many years.

Mr. Shattuck took great pride in his cattle and horses and, like many other farmers, had just about everything they needed. His cattle brand was L2 on the right hip and the horse brand was L2 on the right shoulder.

Mr. Shattuck died March 14, 1919.

Mrs. Shattuck carried on with the farm for many years and was a very successful businesswoman. Ill health came her way and she had to move to Calgary where she also had a home. She passed away August 7, 1950. Both Mr. and Mrs. Shattuck are buried in the Davisburg Cemetery.

The Shattuck Homestead — 1893.

Mr. and Mrs. Charles Shattuck — Leta, Maude and Olive.

"Two Sweeties", Olive and Maude Shattuck about 1901.

Mrs. Shattuck and Olive, 1931.

Mr. and Mrs. Shattuck had three daughters, all born on the farm at Davisburg. Olive, the eldest, was born November 27, 1894. She retained the old homestead for many years and also the L2 brand, finally selling the farm and retiring to live in Calgary. Olive married Ernest M. La Berge on May 1, 1952. He was born in Huntington, Quebec in 1893. After reading about the great opportunities in Western Canada, he decided that was the place to go, coming to Bindloss, Alberta. At the age of 18 years, he filed on a homestead in that district and farmed for a few years. He decided to sell his farm and equipment and move further west, coming to Blackie, Alberta at the harvest time. He worked among the farmers for three years and then moved to Calgary.

Maude married Bert King and had three sons. She passed away in 1953. Leta married Joe Armstrong and lives in Calgary.

HERBERT T. AND GEORGIE (FLETCHER) SHEFFIELD — by Ted Sheffield

My father was in the real estate business in Calgary and prospered during the boom of 1911-12. When it collapsed he decided to try farming on a property he had acquired near De Winton, although he had never farmed before. I had been born in Calgary in 1912 so there were three of us—my father, my mother and me. I must have been very young when we went to the farm located on NE¼-25-21-29-W4.

Father worked the land until about 1916 when he developed a hernia and went to Calgary for an operation. A few days after the operation he suffered a blood clot and died. My mother stuck it out on the farm for some months, perhaps till sometime in 1917, and then moved back to Calgary. Whether the land was sold or repossessed, I do not know.

I remember Mother telling me about hauling grain in the cold weather and having hot stones at her feet to keep from freezing them. The grain was hauled to De Winton and loaded directly on to box cars, there was no elevator then.

I was sent to Nova Scotia to live with my Mother's widowed mother in Great Village. There I started school, but two years later (1919), returned to Calgary with my Grandmother. Soon after we set up in the little bungalow at 1728-13th Avenue W. My mother had got a job as an Accountant with the Canadian Chautauquas and worked there until ill health forced her to stop about 1930. I went east to Montreal in 1934, married there in 1938, served in the RCN, spent some time in Ottawa Headquarters, then to New York for a year 1946-47. We returned to Ottawa in 1947, moved to Toronto in 1966. I'll retire from the University of Toronto next year and we plan to return to Ottawa. We have two children, a girl in Toronto and a boy in Hamilton, and there are two grandchildren.

THE STARKEY FAMILY — by Evelyn Herr

Samuel Starkey and his sons, Herbert, Henry and Richard, homesteaded on Sec. 20-21-28-W4th in 1885 and the S.W. ¼ S.30 in 1890. Samuel Starkey was a Dominion Land Surveyor, and a descendant of United Empire Loyalists, who went to New Brunswick at the close of the Revolutionary War. His sons were often his crew when he surveyed in Alberta and Saskatchewan (then the North-West Territories. Richard left for Pennsylvania to earn degrees in dentistry and medicine and practiced in Washington and Idaho, having a post office in Idaho named Starkey in his honour.

Herbert and his wife had five children born in Davisburg, then Glenbeg district, and he gave a portion of his land for the church and cemetery.

An excerpt from Herbert Starkey's diary of 1885, sent in by his daughter, Ina Starkey Hunter follows:

Excerpt from writing by Herbert M. Starkey 1862-1951: "Fall 1885 —

I had bought some cattle and had to build sheds and cut hay, of which there was an abundance. We had bought a wagon, a mowing machine and a hay rake.

We soon got up plenty of hay as there was hay everywhere of the very finest quality. That was our first crop and it was excellent. The wheat went 45 bushels to the acre and oats 70 bushels of very heavy quality of 52 lbs. measured bushel. I had two acres in potatoes which were a very heavy yield, and which I sold in the field at three cents per pound, which was the best price I ever saw for potatoes in Alberta.

The winter comes early and we always got ready for snow and cold weather. We were expecting an addition to our family. We had a nurse staying with us, a Mrs. Adams. Her husband had a homestead on High River about three miles above Sheep Creek. They had only arrived a short time before, from Adamsville, Quebec, and had not got their house ready for occupancy, so it was very satisfactory for both of us.

The eventful day arrived, and on the night of October 27th, 1885, our eldest boy was born. He was a big baby and we named him Chauncey Lamont after Chauncey Cushing of Boston, and Lamont Thorne, my wife's half brother. Mrs. Adams stayed with us for several weeks, and was one of our closest friends as long as we stayed in Alberta.

They always got a shipment of maple syrup and buckwheat flour every fall and were very generous with both. They always stayed at our place on their way to Calgary and when I was hauling coal from upper High River, I would stop at their place if it was too late to make home the same night.

The following winter, I helped Henry get his house and stable up and get out fencing. The winter passed very quickly as we were very busy. The spring found us ready to go to work, and get in a good crop. Our cattle had come through the winter fine, and the calf crop was 100%. Things were looking prosperous and new settlers were coming in.''

EXCERPTS FROM THE WRITINGS OF HERBERT M. STARKEY

About the middle of June 1884, my brother Henry and I reached the SW¼-20-21-28-W4 where we permanently set up our tent, after driving from Moose Jaw.

We were the first settlers to make their home in what was later known as Davisburg, after D. W. Davis, the first member of the Canadian House of Commons from Alberta. It was Thomas Andrews, when he applied for a post office, who named the settlement after our own Member of Parliament.

About 1887 the people decided to build a church and all agreed that my place was the central location and asked if I would give two acres. Of course I was only too glad to do so. The Presbyterian Mission Board gave the grant for it and the balance was raised among the people. That winter I took the contract for doing the work, which was a small job as the inside was plain lumber.

Morris Stewart and family settled early on section 28 (to the best of my memory). Two grown sons, William and Alexander, both had taken up land. A girl, Cassie, married J. Hogge who had a homestead to the west and was a fine young man. The Stewarts were from the Province of Quebec originally but had been living west of Calgary along the line of the railroad.

The northern half of section 19 was bought by John Irving who built a frame house and took up residence. He had several girls — Blanche, the eldest, and Sarah, next. A boy John died before I left and was the second to be buried in the little cemetery by the church.

A footnote written by his daughter, Ina Hunter, goes on to say:

The reason my uncle and father drove from Moose Jaw was that the year before they had worked with their father, Samuel M. Starkey, a Dominion land surveyor, on a survey in Saskatchewan. Expecting to have a contract again in 1884, the equipment, horses, carts, etc., had been left in Moose Jaw. A friend, Mr. J. G. Van Wart of Calgary, had taken a claim a few miles from section 20 but had told my father of the good land on 20, which is why they came directly from Moose Jaw. My mother and father were married in Calgary in November 1884, one of the first white couples to be married there.

MORRIS AND ALEX STEWART — by Jim Stewart

Morris Stewart came from Aberdeen, Scotland and settled in Quebec where he farmed.

In 1882 he, his wife Agnes and children; Alex, Annie, Will and Catherine came west. After working on the C.P.R. for three years Morris homesteaded in the Davisburg district, filing on land that has been known as the Davis Place and later the Irving Place; S.21-21-28-W4, on April 16, 1885. During that time four sons, Harry, Donald, Howard and Colin and a daughter Isobel were born.

In 1906 Morris sold this land and bought 50 acres of S.16-21-28-W4, from Billie Adams on the south side of the river. He lived there till he died on Xmas Day in 1907 at the age of 77, his wife predeceased him in May of that year.

Alex and Will took up homesteads at the same time. Alex, on land on the Bow River a few miles north of his father's place, S.W.¼-34-21-28-W4 and Will's ¼ was on the Blackfoot Trail. Alex worked, at times, at the Indian Industrial School, Bob Begg's ranch on the Bow and put up hay for W. R. Hull and Mr. Thompson on the old Carleton Place. He also ran some cattle and horses, brands shown elsewhere in the book.

Alex married Martha Suitor in 1896, sold his homestead and lived on the south side of the Highwood River, just at the crossing, on land owned by Capt. Thorburn. Their first child, Ida, was born there. (She later married Dr. M. Burke of Blackie and is now deceased.) In 1899 Alex and family took up land on Gladys Ridge where Mary, (Mrs. Cliff Herr) now of Calgary, Jim, Nell, (Mrs. Ner Clarke of Lethbridge), George (deceased at two months), were born. Edith, living in High River and Hattie, deceased, were born in High River.

Alex and Martha farmed on "The Ridge" until 1956 when they retired to High River.

Jim continued farming the home place until 1964 when he and his wife Helen moved down on the Highwood to live on land her father, Bert Wilder, homesteaded in 1890.

WILLIAM MORRIS AND MARY ELIZABETH (DIMMA) STEWART — by Eleata Stewart

My Dad was one of a family of thirteen, which included step-brothers and step-sisters. He was born in Quebec, Quebec of Scottish parents. This family came west in 1883 with the C.P. Railway. They arrived at Canmore, Alta. and he became a water-boy for the C.P.R. at the age of 17. One day, while walking from Canmore to Banff, he discovered sulphur fumes coming out of the mountain. He told his bosses about it and they apparently got the credit. Being very reserved and shy at 17, he didn't realize what the outcome would be. Years later the Banff Springs Hotel was built near this location.

By 1899 he had acquired a homestead quarter in the Davisburg area for the sum of $3.00 per acre, plus two other quarters. His parents lived on the next quarter and they ran the post-office for many years.

My mother was Mary Elizabeth Dimma, born in Barry, Ontario and raised at Orillia, Ontario, prior to coming to Calgary, as a girl of 18, to help run a candy store for a couple always referred to as "Aunt and Uncle". One year later she married my Dad, June 12, 1899, and started her homestead life with him.

They had five children, four girls and one boy (deceased at fifteen months). I was the youngest.

Dad and Mother went for miles to help in time of need. There were no such things as funeral homes and undertakers and, when someone died, Dad would dress them in their last attire and Mother would fix or curl the hair and put on the make-up prior to taking them to their last resting place which was usually a rural community church yard. One time when they were moving a body from a residence, on a canvas stretcher, there was quite a gathering including "Cappy" Smart, an old timer with the Calgary Fire Department. They had all been into the "Sauce" and they managed to upset the stretcher while moving it to the democrat. They never seem to forget these stories of the "Wild West" and, as a child, I can remember hearing many such tales over and over again, when friends arrived for their weekly chicken dinner. Mother would coax the chickens with bread crumbs and have a broom stick handy. They would still be quivering, in the frying pan, minutes later.

Dad's hobbies were butchering for himself and surrounding neighbours. He loved to trap wild animals such as coyotes, mink and weasels. He drayed for the Indian Dunbow School. Brought all their supplies from Calgary. When an epidemic of flu broke out Mother and Dad did all the delivering of food, medicine and whiskey. They were among the few that didn't contact the bug. Nearly all the nursing staff (nuns) and the Fathers were down with it. Someone would always leave a drink of whiskey on a fence post near where they unloaded the supplies and Dad always said that was what kept them from coming down with the flu.

There was only one time when Dad had to stay away all night. It was at Wolley-Dod's place. A blizzard came up and the horses were unable to breathe. Dad did all the baking of bread and cakes for the school when their bake shop burned down and for a period of time while they rebuilt the shop.

My mother was crippled with arthritis for 25 years

Mr. and Mrs. William Morris Stewart and daughters Hazel, Lucille, Martha and Eleata — 1923.

and, as a child, I can remember her having difficulty getting around and she spent most of her later years in a wheelchair. At 12 years of age I had the responsibility of looking after her plus attending school and taking music lessons.

In 1939 I married and returned to the farm after spending a year and a half at Turner Valley. We moved our home to the farm and both of us worked, during the war, for De Winton Airport E.F.T.S. My husband on a flight line, driving a gas truck and yours truly booking out aircraft from "B Flight". The government expropriated our land north of the Blackfoot Trail (260 acres) and this left very little for agricultural purposes. This was in May, 1941.

My parents' pleasures were playing "500" with their neighbours at different homes throughout the community and, come Friday nights, they would travel with a crowd, to school houses for miles around. There was always a "Fiddler" in the crowd and with heated bricks and lots of blankets for warmth, they would pile twelve or fifteen people into a sleigh. With the bells on the horses' harness ringing and the people singing, they could be heard for miles when the temperature registered well below zero. They would dance from dark till daylight before returning home.

Dad was an avid swimmer and saved many an Indian boy from drowning off the "Big Rock". They would go fishing and slip off into whirlpools.

I can never recall Dad missing a Calgary Stampede "Parade Morning". He used to enjoy riding with his buddies, in the parade, in his later years and attended the annual dance at the Palliser Hotel for many years.

The homestead log house is still standing on this property at Davisburg. It has been converted to a barn. I started sub-dividing one of the quarters in 1967. Our daughter and son-in-law, Heather and Brian Jeffery reside on one of the twenty acre sub-divisions. They have been there since 1973.

Mother died on September 4, 1946 and Dad on December 1, 1946.

FURTHER TO WM. AND MARY STEWART — by Hazel Lancaster

Dad took up a homestead just east of De Winton in the Davisburg area in 1885. He homesteaded the NW¼

28-21-28-W4 and the SW¼ 28-21-28-W4 and pre-empted in 1885. In 1901 he homesteaded the SE¼ 28-21-28-W4.

Our grandfather Stewart homesteaded just a mile east, on the property now owned by Ernie Irving.

Dad went into the sheep business in later years and every day, after school, one of us four girls had to herd the sheep. This was on open prairie as four barb wires was nothing for sheep to go under. The pasture with sheep fence was just for night and during the day when Dad was busy on the land or gone for supplies. We also had the same job on week ends and we all got our fill of sheep herding. What a happy day for us when the sheep fence was put in!!

I, Hazel, was born in Grandma Dimma's house in Calgary which was located on Fifth Avenue just east of the Macleod Trail. Most of my schooling was in Davisburg and I finished in Okotoks High School.

In those early days Dad always kept a hired man. In the spring of 1923 Dad hired Wilbert Lancaster of Calgary and in the fall of 1923 "Bert" and I started to go together. My mother didn't approve so my dad got me a job working at the De Winton Post Office and restaurant owned by Mrs. Demings and operated by her daughter and son-in-law, Mr. and Mrs. Steve Williams. At that time Steve Williams drove the mail route, Pete Murray was the blacksmith and a steady customer at dinner time. He sure knew how to shoe horses. Barsby Martin operated the De Winton store.

Wilbert and I were married in 1925 and lived in Calgary for a year when Wilbert went to work for Royalite Oil at Turner Valley. When the big lay-off came in 1929 we started looking for a farm and finally settled on the NW¼ 32-22-3-W5 in 1930.

We had two children; our son passed away from a ruptured appendix in 1931; our daughter, Eileen (Mrs. R. McKenzie) lives in Alaska and has three children; Douglas in Wyoming, Sandra in Seattle, Callen in Alaska.

My sister, Lucille, was born in 1906 and had her share of milking cows, herding sheep and killing fowl. She married Harry Davis, raised a large family and now resides in Medicine Hat. Harry passed away in the Belcher Hospital, Calgary, February, 1976, at the age of 86 after a prolonged stay.

Martha was born in 1909, shared the work with the rest of us. Married Dave Henderson of Calgary (deceased), had two sons; Allan, a bachelor and Gordie who lives in B.C. with his wife and family. A daughter, Gloria, lives in Nova Scotia, has three children. Martha lives in B.C.

Wilbert and I celebrated our 50th wedding anniversary in 1975 and still reside at Priddis.

SUTHERLAND, GEORGE W. AND AUDREY A. (BANISTER) — by A. Bolin

In the spring of 1940, George Sutherland and his wife, the former Audrey Banister (daughter of Harold) moved from De Winton to Davisburg with their two children, Audrey Ann and Donald George. They rented part of section 7-22-28-W4 owned by Laura Banister and bought it from the estate after her death in 1946. Their son Robert Bruce was born in 1944.

George was well known in athletic circles. At the time of his death in 1951 at the age of forty-eight, he still held the Canadian championship for the best all round athlete. (see Sutherland, De Winton)

Ann married Albert Herr in 1957 and lived on the farm for many years before moving near Albert's parents, Forest and Doris Herr, north of Okotoks. They have three sons, Bert, Harold and Ben, and one daughter, Audra.

Donald now resides on part of the home place, all but sixty acres being sold in 1973.

Bruce, now a pilot in the Armed Forces and stationed at Trenton, Ontario is married to Eltie Schjodt formerly of Penticton, B.C. and they have one daughter, Paige.

Audrey, the former Mrs. George Sutherland married Gus Bolin in 1961 and they reside in Calgary.

THE SUITOR FAMILY — by Grace Suitor

David Suitor, born in 1830, came from County Antrim in Ireland, with his parents while still a small boy. They came in a sailing ship and took six weeks to make the trip. When he grew up, he farmed at Leeds, Quebec, and married Mary McKeage, who was of United Empire Loyalist ancestry. They had a family of thirteen children, five of whom died in infancy of diphtheria. When two of the grown boys, Jack and William, came west in 1889, David accompanied them. He was so enthused with the country that he returned to Quebec and brought out the rest of the family. They came to N.W.¼ 22-21-28 W.4, buying both quarters from James A. McKenzie and T. McKenzie. Jack left to take land in Gladys Ridge and David took over his quarter. He also bought some land from Edward Quinn, that was on the north side of the Highwood River.

His family consisted of David Jr., a blacksmith who started the Calgary Iron Works in Calgary; Robert, a carpenter who became an alderman in early Calgary; William and Jack who farmed at Gladys Ridge; and James, who took over the home place. The girls were Jane (Finley) of High River, Maggie (Maxwell) of Melrose district, Elizabeth (Wark) and Martha (Stewart) both of Gladys. David was a big man, proud of his strength, and delighted in later years to show his grandson how he could still lift one hundred pounds on his little finger straight out from the shoulder. He was an ardent Orangeman, but he had the greatest admiration for the work of Father Naissins and the Sisters at the Dunbow School. They and most of the people in the district attended band concerts, ball and hockey games at the Dunbow School. The Indian boys caught fish in the Highwood River and would sell them to the farmers. One could also buy loaves of bread from the cook, and in an emergency, one of the Sisters was a very good doctor. David died in 1916 and Mary in 1925, and they are buried in the Anglican Cemetery at Gladys Ridge.

James A., who was nine years of age at the time of moving west, attended school at Davisburg (then named Glenbeg) when the school was on east ½ Section 29-21-28-W4. When Jack left, his house was rented to Mr. and Mrs. Magee. Mr. Magee taught carpentry to the Indian boys at Dunbow School. Violet Bolton

Violet Suitor and James Suitor, Sept. 1938.

David and Mary Suitor, 1897.

stayed with the Magees and attended school. One day when carrying water from the barrels which had been brought up from the river on a stoneboat, Jim Suitor took the pails and carried the water to the house. Violet thanked him and said, "I'll dance at your wedding for that." About six years later she did, for she married him. Jim belonged to the Masons in Okotoks. He delighted in good driving and saddle horses and brought home many prizes from fairs and horse shows. He died in 1940, Violet in 1961 and they are buried in Davisburg Cemetery. Their son, James A. Jr., was born in 1903 and about the time he was grown, farming changed from using horses for work in the fields, to tractors. He bought the first rubber tired tractor in 1935, and the tractor company provided steel wheels as well as the wheels for tires, as the rubber tired tractors had not been proven in this area.

The depression of the 1930's was felt in this area, but perhaps not as severely as in Saskatchewan. Many ways were learned to do without money. Entertainment consisted of swimming and skating parties at the river, house parties dancing to the music on the radio or gramophone, with occasionally live music for a party at the schoolhouse. Taxes were often paid by working on the roads at twenty-five cents an hour. In the 40's, with more rainfall and slightly better prices for grain and cream, some improvements were made. Water was piped in to the house (the trenches for pipe being dug with a shovel) and with a pressure tank in the basement and a water front in the coal and wood cook stove, the windmill supplying the power to pump the water; hot and cold water was on tap. An electric bulb in each room, fed from batteries which were charged by a wind charger, replaced the coal oil and gasoline lamps. With high power coming to the farm in 1950, these were thankfully eliminated. Natural gas came to the farm in 1974.

James A. Jr. married Grace Welch of Okotoks in 1928, and their two children, Donald born 1933 and Marilyn born 1937, were raised on the farm and attended school at Davisburg, as their father and grandfather had done, riding the three and one-half miles to school. They furthered their education at Okotoks and Mount Royal College in Calgary. Donald

L. to R.: Ernie Irving, Jim Suitor, Jim Quinn — 1945.

earned his degree in Geological Engineering at Oklahoma University and was a Professional Engineer. He married Ilah Goddard of the De Winton district in 1956, and had four children, David, Donna, Darrell and Rhonda.

Marilyn married Flores Groeneveld of Blackie in 1958 and had two children, Toni Lynn and Glenn. Marilyn died in 1968 and Donald in 1975 and they are buried in the Davisburg Cemetery.

David and Darrell live on the farm and go to Okotoks School by bus. This makes five generations that have lived on the farm, each one as attracted to, and loving the farm as David did in the beginning.

FRANK TUCKER

Frank Tucker was born in Somerset, England, and came to Canada in the spring of 1902. He worked for Tom Andrews in Davisburg. In the spring of 1905, he returned to England to bring his bride, Beatrice Davis, to Canada. He worked for Tom Andrews, G. P. Smith, and the Lineham Ranch.

The two oldest children, James and Bessie were born on the Lineham Ranch. He then moved to Sandstone, where he was engaged at the brick factory until 1912.

Moving back to Davisburg, he again worked for Tom Andrews for a short time, until he obtained the McBride farm (later Bill and Evelyn Herr's farm), and farmed for himself. The rest of the family, Clifford, Ethel, Charles, May, Violet and Harry, was born on this farm.

In 1928, he bought the Lineham Ranch west of Okotoks, where he farmed for many years.

Bessie passed away in 1935, and Frank retired in 1941.

Jim married Florence McLeod. Their daughter Margaret married George Floer, and son Robert married Carol Going.

Clifford married Jean McIntyre. They had a family of seven. Valance married Marlene Kerr; Bessie (Mrs. Doug Spence); Joyce (Mrs. Stewart Schmidt); Ernest married Kathy Going; Judy (Mrs. George Yazlovasky); Donald died in 1970. Clifford died in 1968.

Ethel has made her home in and around Okotoks.

Charles married Ida Puzzi; family of two — Valerie (Mrs. Graham Allen) and Betty-Jean (Mrs. Ralph Turney).

May married George Lock — their family of two — Marian (Mrs. Keith Taylor) and Ronald married Norma Blackwood.

Violet married Leonard Wallace — their family of seven — Vernon, Marlin, twins Lois and Louise, Douglas, twins Danny and Sharon.

Harry married Peggy Skeet — family of three boys — David married Donna Hakin, Terry married Wendy Cram, Daryl at home.

Most of the family reside around Okotoks, Violet in Kamloops and Harry in Calgary.

MR. JOHN GEROW VAN WART

Mr. Van Wart was born in 1838 in Woodstock, New Brunswick, the son of Gerow and Martha Van Wart. His forebears came from Holland and settled in Brooklyn, New York, and at the time of Independence moved to Woodstock, New Brunswick, as United Empire Loyalists.

After a brief period in public school Mr. Van Wart journeyed around the Horn in California with the gold seekers of 1859. He returned to New Brunswick in 1859 and after remaining there a short time set out again, this time for British Columbia, from where he sailed to South America, crossing the Isthmus, he journeyed to Panama and sailed back to Victoria. Going to the mainland of British Columbia he journeyed into the country via the old Caribou trail. The province was such a wilderness the time of his first visit that the Governor's house was yet a log hut built within the walls of a fence to keep the Indians at a safe distance.

After a brief visit back to New Brunswick, another gold rush in Montana led him into that wild country where he made some money at placer mining and returning again to New Brunswick he opened a general merchandise store. At this time he married Martha Jane Jones. He stayed in the merchandising business in Woodstock until 1883 at which time he travelled to Swift Current where he and his partner bought a prairie schooner and with several pioneers travelled to Calgary, arriving there the same year.

When he arrived in Calgary, he set up a general merchandising store in a tent east of the Elbow River. This was one of the first stores in Calgary. He stayed in this location for approximately fifteen years. He then opened a feed store, with Irvin Anderson from New Brunswick as a partner, just east of the old Queen's Hotel. He stayed in this business until his retirement except for three years when he lived on a farm at Davisburg S½ 18-21-28-W4, with his wife and youngest daughter, Alberta. His son, John, farmed the north half of the south half of section 18, but this life did not appeal to him so he moved to Spokane, Washington, where he took up fruit farming.

Mr. Van Wart was one of the participants who went through all the hardships in the Alaskan country when the gold strike occurred in 1900.

Mr. Van Wart's wife and four children Edythe, Maybelle, John and Alberta followed him by train to Calgary, arriving here on May 24th, 1884. Their home was a small bungalow on 8th Avenue S.E., but they later moved to 1036 — 8th Avenue S.E. and this house is still standing and occupied. His children attended school in Calgary where there were 13 pupils.

Mr. Van Wart never took any active part in politics but was a staunch Liberal. He was a member of the first Parks Board and was one of the first handful of men who organized and established the first Baptist Church of Calgary.

At the time of his death in 1920 he was survived by his second wife, Drucilla, and by his four children — Mrs. J. C. (Edythe) Linton, Mrs. J. T. (Maybelle) McDonald, Mr. John Van Wart and Mrs. G. T. C. (Alberta) Robinson. He had sixteen grandchildren eight of whom are still living. These are Miss Anna Linton of Lethbridge, Mrs. J. A. Taylor (nee Helen Robinson) of Surrey, B.C., Mrs. F. B. Singleton (nee Doreen Robinson) of Calgary Mrs. W. E. Moore (nee Martha Robinson) of Victoria, B.C., Mr. John Robinson of Edmonton, Mrs. J. T. McIntyre (nee Jean McDonald of Calgary) and Mr. Gerow McDonald of

Vancouver, B.C. There are also 17 great-grandchildren, 26 great-great-grandchildren and 4 great-great-great-g...ndchildren, all descendents of Mr. Van Wart.

GEORGE AND DORA (GIBSON) WYMER — by Ina Blackwood

George Wymer was born in Wales in 1904. He came to live in Davisburg in 1909, along with his mother (who later became Mrs. Tom Hosegood) his brother Charlie, his grandparents Mr. and Mrs. G. T. I. Cole. They made their home with their uncle, Ted Cole.

George moved to Simon's Valley where he married Dora Gibson. He drove a milk truck before joining an Edmonton Regiment at the beginning of World War Two and served overseas for five years. He was with the Commandos at Spitzbergen, Norway, and all through Sicily, where he was wounded.

After the war, George and Dora and their eldest son Bill, lived at Davisburg for a few years before moving to Britannia Beach, B.C. where George worked in the copper mines. Later the family moved to New Denver, B.C. There they bought a butcher shop and locker plant which Dora ran while George worked in the logging business.

George died in 1972 and was buried in the Field of Honour in New Denver. Dora died in 1974 and is also buried in New Denver.

They had three sons; Bill, of Chilliwack, B.C., Rob, Fraser Lake, B.C., and Rick, of Cranbrook.

Others that Homesteaded in the Davisburg district but have no histories.

George Barclay: 1884, SE¼ 30-21-28-W4.
L. Armstrong: 1885, SE¼ 30-21-28-W4.
George Davidson: 1891, NE¼ 36-22-29-W4.
Henry Greenfield: SW¼ 24-21-29-W4.
William Greenfield: SE¼ 24-21-29-W4.
Neil McBride: 1893, SW¼ 30-21-28-W4.
C. C. Marshall: 1883, NW¼ 30-21-28-W4.
C. C. Marshall: 1886, NE¼ 30-21-28-W4.
McKenzie P.: 1889, SW¼ 30-21-28-W4.
J. A. and Tom McKenzie, brothers of Mrs. Tom Andrews: 1885, NW and SW¼ 22-21-28-W4.
Tom McKenzie built the United Church manse.
John Thompson: 1885, N½ 16-21-28-W4.
Tommy Thompson: S½ 17-21-28-W4.
Mrs. Caroline Thompson: 1891, 16-21-28-W4.
William Thompson: 1891, portion SW¼ 16-21-28-W4.
Thompson who starved to death: NE¼ 25-22-29-W4.
N. G. Worden: SE¼ 36-22-29-W4.
Others who lived in the district later.
Lemerman: 1914, N80-SE¼ 27-21-28-W4.
John and Charlie Patterson: brothers: SE¼ 30-21-28-W4.
John Mortimer: NW¼ 20-21-28-W4.
William Wakeford: NW¼ 20-21-28-W4.
T. B. Ralph: NW¼ 31-21-28-W4.
Gossel: NW¼ 31-21-28-W4.
Wheatly: NW¼ 31-21-28-W4.
Tom Magee: carpenter for Dunbow School.

From Calgary Weekly Herald and Alberta Livestock Journal for December 4th, 1889

The people of High River were rated for their hospitality, but none more so than those of Davisburg.

On Friday evening of last week, the district gave an oyster supper to commemorate the opening of the comfortable new Presbyterian Church just erected at the fair "burg". It was enough to make all the old bachelors in the neighborhood smile to see the number and beauty of young ladies who turned out on that occasion.

Davisburg seems to be filled with true religion, for all denominations vied with each other in making the night's entertainment a success, and judging from the crowded church and the pleasure manifested, their efforts were not in vain.

About one hundred sat down to a delicious oyster supper and the good cheer for which the district is famed when all were satisfied and the groaning board had been cleared, the new pastor, Rev. Mr. Munro, introduced the literary part of the program in some appropriate remarks, and during the continuance enlivened the audience from a never-failing supply of anecdotes. The singing, especially of the choir, was especially good, Miss Mansfield (the teacher) presiding at the organ.

From Calgary Herald

A special display featuring the Canadian soldier from 1785 to 1952 has been opened at the Glenbow-Alberta Institute. A part of the display will be Glenbow's only North-West Rebellion Medal awarded to a soldier wounded in action. The rebellion medal was presented to A. S. Blackwood (of Davisburg) in 1885. He was a member of the Winnipeg Rifles 90th Battalion.

From Calgary Weekly Herald February 21st, 1886

A hockey match was played at the Dunbow Industrial School on Saturday last between Okotoks and the School team, resulting in a victory for the latter.

A very pleasant evening was spent on Thursday last when the youth and beauty of Davisburg gathered at the home of Mr. J. A. Irving. Dancing and other games were indulged in until an early hour, when the guests took their departure with many thanks to the host and hostess for their kind hospitality.

From Calgary Herald about 1938

Seeded down for the year and rain clouds rolling in from the west, three De Winton farmers tarried long enough to see the rain come pelting down and then headed for Edmonton and the capital city's Highland Gathering. They did very well, thank you, picking up a dozen prizes in the eighteen events contested.

The trio, Alex Blackwood, William Rodger and George Sutherland, specialize in weight events, and bid fair to becoming a dominating combination in Alberta and possibly Canadian track and field.

Led by Sutherland, they placed one, two and three in the caber. George also won the 56 and 28 pound weight events with Blackwood placing third in both. Rodger won the shot put from Sutherland and also placed third in the discus. Sutherland's specialty — the hammer throw — was an easy mark for the athlete who has won trips to British Empire Games in London

and Australia, with his throws of the iron ball at the end of a cable.

From the scrapbook of Ina Blackwood

THE DAVISBURG AGRICULTURAL FAIR — by Grace Suitor

The Davisburg Agricultural Fair was held on the flat of NW¼ 15-21-28-W4, and north of the Highwood River, on Suitor land, purchased from Mr. Ed. Quinn. The hills around formed a natural grandstand from which the races on the surveyed half mile track could be viewed.

The Fair consisted of the showing and judging of vegetables and grains grown on the district farms, also sewing and baking. It was greatly anticipated and widely attended, Indians and settlers joining in the foot and horse races. The Indian Boys' Band, from Dunbow School, provided the music for these occasions and marched from Dunbow School, up the hill and down to the valley where the Fair was held, playing marching music all the way, thrilling the spectators, as the music reverberated from the hills. Everyone came on horseback, buggy or wagon; the horses were tied in the shade of the trees and spectators brought their lunches to eat near the river.

We have been unable to determine when the first fair was held but when Okotoks formed an Agricultural Society and Fair, Davisburg dropped their Fair and joined in with Okotoks. The race track was still visible in the 1940s when James Suitor Junior, broke up the area.

DAVISBURG RANCHERS' SOCIETY — 1888
Committee
> President — A. E. Banister Sr., Esq.
> Vice-President — Wm. Thompson Esq.
> Secretary — Robert A. Begg Esq.
> Treasurer — John Vanwart Esq.

Members
> Mr. A. E. Banister Sr.
> Mr. Wm. Thompson
> Mr. R. A. Begg
> Mr. John Vanwart
> Mr. J. J. Vanwart
> Mr. L. I. Rose
> Mr. T. Andrews
> Mr. Wm. Stewart
> Mr. B. Banister
> Mr. Herbert A. Starkey
> Mr. A. I. Tucker-Peach
> Mr. A. E. Banister Jr.
> Mr. C. Dennehy
> Mr. E. C. Picard
> Mr. J. J. Springer
> Mr. Henry Starkey
> Mr. Wm. Banister
> Mr. Henry Rowles
> Mr. George Wilmot Embury

Rules and Regulations

1. The president, vice-president, secretary and treasurer will be elected annually, and the accounts shall be produced by the treasurer and audited. The annual meeting shall be held on the Thursday before the full of the moon.

2. Members subscriptions shall be done annually and shall be paid at the October meeting.

3. The subscription shall be fifty cents and shall be paid at the time of forming the society.

4. At the October meeting, it shall be decided what steps shall be taken with regard to disposal of surplus funds, or in case of a deficiency, what means shall be adopted to raise any funds.

Excerpts from the Minute Book

On Wednesday, December 16th, 1888, a meeting was held for ranchers and farmers in the vicinity of High River. The name "Davisburg Ranchers' Society" was chosen.

January 9th, 1889.

Decided to hold meetings on the first and third Thursday. Mr. A. E. Banister read a very interesting paper on Blackleg.

January 17th, 1889.

An interesting paper was read on fattening and feeding of stock of different breeds. Polled Angus was approved to be the best stock for the country, both for breeders and butcher.

February 8th, 1889.

During this meeting, a discussion centred on the advisability of erecting a certain place where to burn all cattle dying of Blackleg in this district. It was also advised by Mr. Rushton and agreed by everyone that dead bodies of such cattle be carried to a burning place by wagon, and not to have them on the ground, thus preventing any possibility of infection.

Mr. Banister read a paper on the different breeds of thoroughbred cattle.

A creamery was also talked of, and of whether it would pay or not in this district.

February 22nd, 1889.

Mr. Wm. Thompson read a paper on the origin, prevention and cure of Blackleg.

March 15th, 1889.

Mr. Springer read a valuable paper on the different breeds of cattle. It was proposed by President Banister and carried that the secretary be asked to have Mr. Springer's paper published in the Tribune. Songs were sung by the members of the Society. The meeting closed by singing "God Save the Queen."

From the minute book of the Davisburg Ranchers' Society at Glenbow.

Researched by I. Blackwood.

ENTERTAINMENT IN DAVISBURG — by Ina Blackwood

Much of the entertainment for the early settlers of Davisburg was provided by the Indian pupils of the Father Lacombe Industrial School which was located on the west bank of the Highwood River, near where it emptied into the Bow. One of the highlights of the year was the Christmas Concert which was given at the school. The Indian Boys' Band was a proficient one and band concerts were also held. Their hockey team played against teams from Calgary and Okotoks as well as local ones. The children were taught by the priests and nuns.

An event of much interest each week was attending services at Davisburg Presbyterian Church. Picnics

Davisburg Ball Team. Front: L. to R. George Wymer, Harry Impey, Ross Impey. Back row: L. to R. Cliff Tucker, Max Streeter, Alex Blackwood, Jim Tucker, Percy Streeter, Harold Herr. Taken about 1919.

were well patronized, many being held on farm of J. A. Irving.

Horse racing took place at the race track on Suitors' Flat, near the Highwood. The women competed in the culinary arts and butter making.

All through the years there was fun to be had at the dances, held at the school house and, when a new barn was built, a barn dance was usually held. Most of the larger barns in the district were built by John Norris.

In 1944, during the time Miss Kay Van Amburg was the teacher, a Home and School Association was formed. This was the first one roomed school in Alberta to form one.

During the Second World War years, card parties were held, in the homes, to raise money to send treats to our boys in the armed forces.

The Jolly Time Club held meetings, for many years, when women and pre-school children met in the homes for a visit and a cup of tea.

In the 1940's money was scarce so we made do with cheap entertainment. One evening a week we would gather at the Beaverhead, on the Highwood, for a duck in the river and an exchange of stories around a camp-

L. to R.: Mr. and Mrs. Willoughby, Alec Blackwood, Mrs. Alec (Bella) Blackwood, William Andrews, Mrs. May (Paling) Brodie, Mrs. William (Kate) Andrews, Ernest Paling, Caroline (Paling) Hope, (Mrs. Jos. Hope). Marina Laura Paling, Richard Paling.

Picnic in Bryce's Grove: Ed Irving, Mr. Frier. Standing: Art Irving, Harry Outhet, P. H. Irving, Allie Irving, Mrs. Daggett, Tony Kefler, Jim Thorburn, Jack Shields, Mrs. Thorburn, Mr. and Mrs. George Smith, Jennie Ingles, Ivy Smith, Mrs. J. Shields, Sadie Irving, Flo Thorburn, Gertie Frier, Mr. and Mrs. Bob Shields. Seated: Mr. and Mrs. J. A. Irving, Mr. and Mrs. Brice, Mrs. Frier, Daisy Kefler.

fire. Everyone took their children, even the toddlers, and babies in baskets. A sandwich and a cup of coffee, brewed from river water, in a lard pail, over an open fire, climaxed the evening. Was there ever anything more delicous than that coffee, after you had skimmed off the ashes and twigs?

For many years hockey games were played on the Highwood River every Sunday with Davisburg playing

Playing hockey L. to R. back row: Joe Armstrong, Herb Jenkins, Bill Armstrong, Ray Armstrong. Front row: L. to R. Joe Bryce, Art Jenkins.

against those from Gladys. There was no need for goal posts when a pair of overshoes served the purpose. Rolled up newspapers or magazines made good shin pads. Dick Streit, the goalie for Gladys, used sweat pads to protect his shins! There were no referees and sometimes, there would be a hundred spectators. The players from Gladys were usually called the "Dutchmen". In after years, John Groeneveld used to say, "Blackwood, we should have used pitch forks instead of hockey sticks!" There were no picked teams, anyone and everyone played. Among the first players were; Jim Suitor, Jim Quinn, Fred Maxwell, Forest Herr, Frank Merriam, Alex Blackwood, Jim Blackwood, Doug Herr, Bill Herr, Frank McHugh, "Genty" Woolridge goalie. Later, other players were; "Scotty" Rodger, Doug McHugh, George Sutherland, Jack Morasch, "Fat" Morasch, Ernie Irving, Ian Gordon, Phil Petaski, Hans Hoff, Bruce Hyde, Ross Hyde, Joe Armstrong, Angus Andrews and Dick Streit, goalie.

Skating parties were also held on the river or at Bill Herr's slough. In the 1950's, Davisburg boys entered a hockey team, in the bush league, and they were known as the "Wheat Kings."

In December, 1954, the old Davisburg Schoolhouse,

barn and land were purchased from the newly formed Foothills School Division for $250.00 and the Davisburg Community Association was formed early the next year. The old school continued to be the centre of entertainment for the district until a new hall was built and opened, with a New Year's Eve dance, on December 31, 1976.

Plans were begun in March, 1956 to build a skating rink and curling rink, with work starting in the fall. The curling rink is still used every winter, when the weather co-operates, with many a happy hour being spent there.

A BACHELOR'S CHRISTMAS — by Mrs. J. Bell

Christmas was recalled by many a lonely bachelor in his homestead shack. Some wallowed in despair while others did something about it.

The Cuffe brothers, Arthur and George, decided to invite a few of the neighboring bachelors to a bang up dinner. They would have plum pudding with flaming brandy sauce. For vegetables they would have their home grown potatoes, turnips and carrots. They had seen nice round, fat turkeys in a butcher shop, so they decided to buy one. They wouldn't have fine china, gleaming crystal, polished silver or snowy linen they had in England. Their enamel plates and cups, cheap cutlery and an oilcloth table cover would have to do.

The turkey was to be the piece de resistance. They had asked the butcher to clean it, so he'd cut off the head and feet. The boys thought cleaned meant thoroughly cleaned, so they popped it in the oven. As it started roasting the smell wasn't very appetizing, but they had never been allowed in the "cooks" domain at home, so they weren't too upset.

The guests arrived, the table was set and waiting, and all eagerly awaited the feast. Arthur with knife poised, made a deep gash in the golden brown turkey. It wasn't until then he realized what he had mistakenly thought was stuffing was the turkey's innards. It had turned into a meatless Christmas feast.

A DEVIL OF A TIME IN DEVIL'S HOLLOW — W. E. Thomson

One of the lesser known stories of the Davisburg history is the shooting incident involving Tucker Peach and Deerfoot. This story comes from a number of different sources and each one a little different so this account may not be completely accurate.

According to Frank W. Anderson's book, Calgary to Medicine Hat* not all of the Blackfoot Indians were happy with Crowfoot when he signed Treaty No. 7 in September 1877 and one of the most unhappy was Deerfoot the famous Indian runner. This is the same Deerfoot that the Calgary freeway was named after. For a time Deerfoot was a messenger for the R.N.W.M.P. and one time was reported to have run from Fort Macleod to Calgary and back in three days.

In the August 20, 1938, Calgary Herald Thomas Clarke tells of the railway reaching Calgary in September 1883. About two weeks after the rails crossed the Elbow the first passenger train arrived carrying some C.P.R. officials and a number of passengers. To celebrate the occasion a big sports day was held with horse races, bronc riding and foot races in which Deerfoot took part. He easily won the one mile and three mile events. Deerfoot was a lean, lanky built man well over six feet tall and as thin as a crane. For racing he wore only a loin cloth about the size of a handkerchief, held in place by an aging leather thong tied around his middle. The races were run on a half mile track so the runners were always in plain sight of the spectators. In the five mile races Deerfoot was competing against a member of the Mounted police, at the beginning the Indian had a fair lead but half way through he began to tire and the two were running neck and neck. About 200 yards from the finish the policeman was ahead by a few feet when Deerfoot put on an extra burst of speed, more than the G-string could stand. Thirty yards behind the Mountie, Deerfoot finished the race in his birthday suit much to the consternation of a group of young ladies at the finish line, and much to the disappointment of the large number of Indians present. Soon after Deerfoot toured eastern Canada and the United States winning many high honors.

One story is that in one of these contests he was to race a white man and some fairly large bets were made on the outcome of the race. Because the white man ran with shoes on and Deerfoot ran in his bare feet, somone decided to make sure he won the bet by dropping broken glass on the race track. Because of that painful experience Deerfoot became an outlaw which the rest of this story seems to bear out.

About a mile north-west of John "Little Man" Thompson's place by the Davisburg bridge is the Devil's Hollow where his brother William Thompson lived. On the Wednesday before August 26, 1887 (according to the Calgary Herald of that date) Thompson and his hired man Tucker Peach were haying some distance from home when they received word that their house was open. On arriving home they found the house had been ransacked by Indians and some of their belongings stolen.

In Harold Banisters account of the event (As I Remember by Dallas Banister Wright) Thompson followed the travois tracks across the river and down the Bow to just above the Tucker Peach place which would make it quite close to the Will Janes homestead, where he found the Indians camped. On entering the tepee he recognized his own belongings and those of other settlers. While trying to retrieve his possessions, Thompson lost his temper and shot one of the Indians in the knee. The others hid in the long grass and a number of shots were exchanged. Frightened of running out of ammunition, Thompson took after one of the Indians on foot, chasing him round and round a large willow. Suddenly Thompson reversed direction, met the Indian and shot him through the chest then threw him over the river bank. The Calgary Herald account says Thompson shot the Indian who was rushing at Tucker Peach with an axe. This is the same as the Anderson story which gives this fatally wounded Indian's name as Trembling Man.

---

* Frontier Publishing Ltd. Book 24.
In addition to the sources of information given above our thanks to Patricia Banister Wedderburn, Ina Blackwood, Angus McKinnon and the Glenbow Archives.

As Thompson and Tucker Peach were leaving with their belongings, Deerfoot rode up behind and fired a shot wounding Tucker Peach in the arm. Thompson took Tucker Peach to the Dunbow Indian School to have the wound dressed and went on by himself to the "Grotto" as the Banister place was called. After hearing the whole story Mr. Banister urged him to go to Calgary and turn himself over to the N.W.M.P., which he did. The Indians went back to Blackfoot Crossing where Trembling Man died a few days later. The third Indian, presumably the one wounded in the knee returned to Calgary with Magnus Begg, the Indian agent.

On September 2nd, 1887, Colonel Herchmer of the N.W.M.P. called on Chief Crowfoot at the Blackfoot reserve requesting the surrender of Deerfoot. By this time Thompson was out on bail. Chief Crowfoot refused since the white man who had killed an Indian was free why should an Indian who had only wounded a white man be put in jail. With the kind of diplomacy the Mounted Police found so necessary to develop, Colonel Herchmer explained, as best he could, the law regarding self defence and bail. Deerfoot was turned over to the police and taken to Calgary to stand trial. After a lengthy trial before Major-General T. B. Strange, Thompson was acquitted and Deerfoot was sentenced to sixty days hard labor.

Although restrained by an iron ball chained to his ankle, Deerfoot escaped a few days later. That story is told in the history of the Dunbow Indian School elsewhere in this volume.

William Thompson left the country a year or two later and his brother "Little Man" Thompson sold out to Mr. Adams during the 1890's. A Caroline Thompson also filed on a homestead in that area in the 1880's but there is no record of what relation she was to John and William Thompson.

Tucker Peach lived for some time in his cabin by the Bow River. In the summer he toured the country shearing sheep, occasionally venturing as far afield as Maple Creek. In the winter he would walk across the river ice to the LK ranch about a mile east of his cabin where he would entertain ?? the McKinnon family with his atrocious singing. Some of the songs were never heard before or since so it is assumed they were his own creations. His talents as a composer were about equal to his singing ability. He homesteaded what was later known as the George Alexander place, and is now part of Meri-Bow Farm, north of Gladys. This is where he was living at the time of his tragic death in 1910.

The Calgary Herald report of August 26, 1887 ended with this comment: "The general opinion is the Indians got less than they deserved, and Thompson would have been justified in dropping a few more of the thieving rascals." If this really was the general opinion rather that of a few newsmen it would seem General Strange gave Deerfoot a very light sentence. Two things must be born in mind, this was very shortly after the Riel Rebellion and General Strange's ranch was quite close to the Blackfoot reserve. Maybe the General was just living up to his name — T. Bland Strange.

ACROSS THE DAVISBURG BRIDGE — W. E. Thomson

When the first homesteaders came to Gladys Ridge, Davisburg, was their community centre. It was there that they got their mail and attended church services. After they had harvested a crop of grain they took it to the Dunbow Indian School to be ground. Will and Fred Janes, John and Thomas Thomson and their families, and J. H. Connell were all part of the Davisburg community when they first settled on the Ridge. Prior to 1891 they crossed the Highwood river on a cable ferry operated by Alex Stewart. The first wooden bridge was built in 1891 and was washed away in the spring flood of 1897. When those early pioneers made their once a year trip to Calgary (two days each way) they followed the old Blackfoot Trail, not to be confused with freeway bearing the same name plagiarised by city planners. The old Blackfoot Trail ran from the Dunbow school up the valley past Billy Stewart's (brother of Alex) place to Cable's hill, where the old C.N. grade swings away from the river. From Cable's hill the trail followed the river valley past the old Burns ranch (now part of Fish Creek Park) to Calgary.

Charlie Yuen was the Chinese cook at the Burns ranch but hardly a typical Chinese of that era as he was at least six feet tall. Most of what he cooked was home grown, not just the beef from the ranch but the vegetables from his enormous garden. He is also credited with being the inventor of the "lazy-susan" type ranch dining table. Many a traveller along the old Blackfooot trail enjoyed both his hospitality and his culinary craftmanship, an art he had mastered completely. I recall as a small boy accompanying my father and grandfather on a visit to Charlie. The table was loaded with the most delicious smelling pies but Charlie was in something less than a good mood. His supplies at that time were sent out directly from the Burns packing plant and someone had made the mistake of sending him some rancid butter. True to the tradition of the old west he didn't fool around with bureaucracy, he immediately phoned Pat Burns and voiced his complaints loud and clear. Needless to say the mistake was corrected post-haste.

While hospitality was both a necessity and a tradition in the pioneer years, the Charlie Yuen type was not necessarily universal. In later years the trail changed and followed close to what is now the DeWinton airport road from Cable's Hill to the Macleod trail. One year my grandfather, John V. Thomson, was returning from Calgary feeling extremely fortunate because what he had sold had brought one whole dollar more than what he had had to buy. When he reached what was later the site of the Pine Creek school one of his horses lay down in the track, exhausted. He managed to get to the nearest homestead and asked to stay for the night. He was grudgingly given a place to sleep on the floor and a bowl of oatmeal the next morning. When he offered to pay his host said the charge was a dollar, although twenty-five cents would have been excessive in those years. It must have been a very traumatic experience because half a century later travelling by car he always breathed easier when we got by the place where his horse laid down.

During the 1890's the Davisburg fair was held on the river flats about a half a mile east of Little Man Thompson's (Lucy Davenport's place). Records of what years the fair was held seem to be lost but according to L. McKinnon's diary one very successful fair, which he attended, was held September 30, 1896. Along with this fair there were horse races and for this reason it is believed fairs had been held in previous years. About this time one fair was so successful that the promoters, Charlie Shattuck, Tom Andrews and Harold Bannister persuaded the prize-winners to send their exhibits on to the North-West Territorial fair in Regina (also known in those days as Pile of Bones). Among the exhibits that went to Regina were some of Davie Thorburn's Clydesdales and a tub of butter made by my grandmother, Mrs. John V. Thomson. The butter won first prize which was one of those triangular wooden gadgets with a fluted roller, known as a butter worker.

On June first, 1897, Thomas Thomson and Elizabeth Willoughby who had recently arrived from Walkerton, Ontario were married. However, the bride's trunks and other belongings did not arrive until some time later. Towards the end of June, Thomas Thomson went back to Calgary to pick up the shipment, on the way home he found the high water flowing over the deck of the Davisburg bridge. He left his team and wagon on the north side of the river and walked across the bridge to see if it was safe to drive the team across. Just as he got to the south end of the bridge the timbers gave away and the bridge washed down the river. He walked the remaining eight miles home and it was not until three weeks later that they got the team, wagon and trunks home. In that shipment was a sewing machine which their daughter, Mrs. Mary Humphrey of High River still uses.

People born in the 1850's and 1860's rarely had a middle name for this reason John "Little Man" Thompson and my grandfather John Thomson (spelled the dry way — no p) were always getting their mail mixed up so my grandfather put the first letter of my grandmother's maiden name (Verth) in the middle of his name and so became John V. Thomson.

Fred and Will Janes arrived about 1887 and pitched their tent beside a big slough on Fred's homestead. The first night they were there a blizzard came up so they named the place Blizzard Lake, the name you will still find on the maps today. Will's homestead was on the river bank about two miles farther north. Although both families left the district during the first world war the lilacs and rhubarb Will Janes planted around his house are still flourishing. Fred Janes moved to Courtenay on Vancouver Island and Will Janes to Santa Ana, California. During the 1930's Mrs. Will Janes became an invalid and Mr. Janes younger sister, Mrs. Morton, moved in to take over duties of cook, housekeeper and especially chauffeur. She continued to drive around southern California for many years but when she reached her ninetieth birthday in the early 1960's she decided she was to old to drive in downtown Los Angeles.

After the old wooden bridge went out in 1897 a new steel one was built which lasted until 1964. Charlie Shack who became a legend when he built Christ

The second Davisburg Bridge 1897-1964.

Lawrence A. Fowler on the bridge he helped build.

Church at Millarville with its vertical logs, was the contractor that built the second Davisburg bridge. One of his chief assistants was Lawrence Fowler who later homesteaded about three miles east of Aldersyde.

By the time the steel bridge was completed there was a post office and school at Gladys and it had become a community in its own right. But Davisburg was still the original landing place for many settlers that came down the Blackfoot trail. Sam and Joe Suitor, who were identical twins each spent a year in

Davisburg before taking up homesteads at Gladys. Sam and his wife spent their first year with James Suitor, a cousin, while Joe and his family stayed with the Maxwells. The Nash's first homestead was near Tom Andrews where they lived until their father was killed in a threshing accident. When they farmed at Gladys, Tom Nash owned the land on the south-west quarter of the Gladys intersection, the north-west quarter where the old Anglican church and cemetery were and the north-east quarter where the school was and the hall and United Church still are. Charlie Nash had the south-east quarter where the Gladys store was located. Louise Nash lived with her father and brothers in Davisburg for a while before she married H. H. Wilson. They lived for a while on the Highwood river flats across from the Andy Wakeford (formerly Jim Joyce) place before buying the Gladys store which they sold to Roy Peckham about 1919, About a year later the old store burned down and the original school was moved across the road to become the store.

Captain Arthur Cuff homesteaded across from the Davisburg church. He sold out to the Adams and lived for a time with H. H. Wilson on the Highwood flats. About 1915 he moved to Gladys where he farmed the quarter across the corner from the micro-wave tower until 1920. From 1920 to 1930 he lived at Milo, then moved to Warburg where he died in 1931. His wife remarried and continued to live at Warburg until her death in 1975.

In 1902 two lads from England, Percy Bird and his 16 year old brother Richmond (Dick) came to Davisburg. Dick's first job was herding sheep for the Adams. From 1902 to 1909 he worked for Davie Thorburn. During the spring floods logs from the Lineham saw mill in Okotoks would break loose and float down the river. One of Dick Bird's jobs was to ride into the river and rope these maverick logs. In many a corral along the Highwood were logs bearing the Lineham brand.

After leaving Thorburns, Dick Bird homesteaded on Section 2-21-27-W4, six miles northeast of Gladys. He served as councillor for a total of twenty years in the old M.D. of Dinton. He died at Cremona in 1971 at the age of 85.

THE GOLD RUSH — Researched and written by E. Leach

Some years ago there was a fine spring and creek in the coulee just west of the Blackwood home with a nice grove of poplars and willows on the hillside. This was a delightful place for children to play in summer, while in winter the pond above the dam gave us an outdoor skating rink.

The geese and ducks made use of the pond in summer and herein lies a story. What a job it was preparing the birds for market! As this was done in the late fall or winter, probably for Christmas trade, the weather was cold so the work was completed, in our house at least, in the kitchen. The down from the geese was particularly frustrating. How it could get into everything only those who have had experience would know. Every bit was saved for down comforters — our share of the operation. Our birds were sold at Beale's

Meat Market which, if memory serves me right, was located on Second Street East in Calgary.

In the fall of 1919 a customer found a few bits of pure gold in the gizzard of a certain goose he had bought at the market. (Girls please note, birds were not drawn in those days before purchase!) The customer contacted Mr. Sidney Beale as to where the bird had been purchased. When spring came, as it eventually did, the hunt was on to do a bit of prospecting. At first there was a great deal of secrecy until the Calgary men staked their claims on the Blackwood creek. Then it was open to the public.

My father, Alec S. Blackwood, and all the Blackwood family over 18 years of age staked claims with hopes of wealth on Snake Creek. The neighbors were notified and advised to get into the game, but as the date was the first of April, many thought it only an April Fool joke. These claims were registered in Calgary, the fee being five dollars. The records at the Department of Mines and Minerals were destroyed by fire in 1962 so it has not been possible to verify the dates, but as far as we can recall the gold rush was in the spring of 1920.

The Calgary promoters had some sort of equipment in the creek. The workers camped and did their cooking in a granary provided by Father. Why bother about a little rent when we were all going to be millionaires?

Excitement ran high for a while. Although a few traces of gold were found, the venture proved futile. Just another dream gone West!

Later, prospecting for gas and oil in the Davisburg area presented a rosier picture, but that is a different story.

The Glenbow-Alberta Institute in Calgary has more technical information which was printed in a Calgary newspaper in April, 1920.

THE BEEF RING — by Lilian Irving

The Beef Ring was formed to help keep fresh beef on the table in times when deep freezers were unheard of. My Dad was the butcher. Each member supplied a beef as his turn came up. Dad butchered it and each member received his share. You got a different cut each time till you had received every piece on the carcass. It was a good idea as it provided fresh beef each week. However, as in every group of people, there were the ones who had to have a good roast, as they were having company for dinner, or didn't like stew. Then there were the ones who didn't have anything to butcher when it was their turn.

As there had to be enough in the group to take a whole carcass each week, it meant there had to be quite a few members, usually around twenty.

Somewhere around the farm, the remains of the chopping block Dad used, can be seen. Mum can't recall how long the ring lasted, or who all the members were after all this time, but some of the members were Wm. Stewart, Jim Suitor, Edward Cole, Mortimors on the McKid farm.

REMINISCENCES I REMEMBER WHEN — by Effie Leach

Dr. Lafferty made monthly or semi-monthly trips

from Calgary to Dunbow Industrial School to look after the medical needs of the Indians. In summer he used horse and buggy, and in winter, horse and cutter. He was paid by the Federal Government.

Farmers hauled coal from a small mine at Black Diamond. The coal was soft and dirty, rapidly disintegrating, but created good heat in spite of the soot which accumulated in the stove pipes. The men took enough lunch to do them several days, as they often had to wait for the coal to be mined.

The Royal North West Mounted Police patrolled the country side. They listened to grievances, kept law and order, and were always treated with respect. They rode beautiful saddle horses which were always well groomed. The scarlet-coated guardians of the law were always a welcome sight. Their pay, depending on rank, was about a dollar a day and keep.

One of our early ministers was the Rev. James Shortt of the Presbyterian faith. He lived at Pine Creek, preaching three times every Sunday; Davisburg at 11 a.m., Pine Creek in the afternoon and I believe Red Deer Lake and Melrose had evening services on alternate Sundays.

At one point we had no minister. The Anglican minister came from De Winton holding services in the school house. There was a certain protocol to be respected.

In later years again there was a time when we were without services in our church. Mrs. McConnell Sr., who was a devout Baptist, had Sunday School classes in her own home. All the children and young people attended and we had a wonderful time. In order not to over-step, Mrs. McConnell used the Sunday School papers of our established church.

What wonderful times we had gathering wild berries. Saskatoons, chokecherries, strawberries, raspberries, gooseberries and even black currants were available. We always took a picnic lunch with us.

Yes, we did go to the Okotoks Fair, and later to the Calgary Exhibition. When Calgary had fire-works we were not left out. We just ran to the top of the hill west of our home and enjoyed the display - NO CHARGE.

In earlier times if a doctor was needed from Okotoks, or if some message had to go through, someone rode to Mr. Ed. Hayes' farm just north of Okotoks. He had a phone connection with Okotoks. When we got the rural phone in 1911, one of the construction crews camped at Alex Blackwoods' present home. No problem keeping fresh meat. It was pulled up to the top of a telephone post away from the flies.

The old fashioned pot-bellied stove in the school room was not too wonderful. In winter, children huddled around it the first hour or so. When the long pipes fell down, or when the stove exploded, there was surely a mess.

I remember when the teacher was an authorative person in the school. Teacher, by law, was responsible for the children from the time they left their own gates in the morning till they returned there after school. I don't know when the law was changed, but it was in effect when I started teaching in 1911. No wonder the teacher was held in awe!

One time there were weird cries and calls coming from the grove of poplars at the top of our hill. We kids, riding home, were sure someone was being murdered. It was only a Canadian lynx which had wandered down from the mountains and was later shot by our Dad. To this day we older ones speak of the Lynx trees.

The Indians roamed from place to place with all their possessions on travois or on horses. They were ill-clad and always hungry, calling at various farms for food. Tea was always a special request. I always knew they wanted to carry me off, so usually found refuge under the bed!

The surveyors left their markings at the corners of certain sections. These were four holes, each one about two feet square with an iron peg in the middle. It was a criminal offence to disturb the markings. All have now disappeared and no one went to jail.

The yearly school concerts were the social events of the year. Santa always managed to get through the drifts.

Following the business meetings at the church annual gathering, there was always a fine concert, after which a great lunch was served by the ladies.

Who can ever forget the Box Socials? ——— or the picnics held on May 24th?

There were lots of hardships no doubt, but lots of good times too. I really do not think country people ever forget to be neighbourly.

RECOLLECTIONS OF GROWING UP IN DAVISBURG — by Stella Nelubowich

Somewhere along in the year of about 1927 I think it was, I went out to get the cows one Sunday morning to milk them early. The cows were laying down near the road allowance fence. On the road allowance sat a car, a Plymouth sedan with a livery license on it and all the doors were open on it. I got off my horse, climbed through the fence, and closed the doors. I also thought it strange that this car was there. I brought home the milk cows and we milked them. I just could not get this car out of my mind so after breakfast I went back and checked and the car was still there, so I came back and got Lorne. We both rode back. When he looked in the car the switch was still turned on and he shut it off. He then measured the gas and there was just a bit under the gallon in it. The battery was very low so he took the crank and turned the motor over and it went right off. Then he said, "Come on Stella, let's go for a ride," and I said, "No, as we might get in trouble," so he said he wanted to check it out to see what was wrong with it so finally I went. It ran good so he took it back where we got it. He got out and so did I. He then pulled up the seat and a bullet rolled down from somewhere with one side of the end blunted off on it. You should have seen how fast Lorne moved then. He pushed the front cushion down in place, shut the door, and we jumped on our horses and phoned the R.C.M.P. They came right out; it was the car they had been hunting for all morning. They tracked it down on the back road for a mile and a half, then would go through the fields on a road Herr's had built for their own use. At this gate the Police lost track of the car. The car was down in a draw which was only visible for less than a minute, east of them, on the blind road. They could not cross this valley as it was hummicky and a steep hill covered with trees. I call this Echo Valley, and others call it Killer Coulee, there is a creek in here which flows most of every summer. (There is a road across this now, put in I think in 1960 or 61 by Devon-Palmer Oils at a cost of $50,000.)

There were two men and a young boy in his early teens who hired this taxi car driven by Mr. Midwinter to take them somewhere. When he had driven them down No. 2 highway to where those feed lots were south of Midnapore (there was summerfallow there then), they stopped him driving, they shot him and robbed him of $28, then threw him out in the summer-fallow and took off. He was still alive and crawled out onto the side of the road where someone found him and took him back to Calgary and hospital. He died shortly after.

After about a year or more these two men who shot Midwinter were picked up down in the States living in a cave on the river bank. I think it was in Montana. One of them turned King's Evidence so was not hung; the other one was. At the time of the trial the boy was in a boat out on the ocean. He would have hung also if the authorities got him, but being on the ocean saved him. He never knew they were going to shoot Midwinter and cried when he was shot. The two men in the murder both testified that the boy had no part in the murder. They also said they thought the car was out of gasoline when they abandoned it and they holed up in a grain bin until night and then went south on foot to get past the sentries on the other side of this before-mentioned valley. What they had in mind was to cross the Davisburg Bridge, then go south on the side roads so as to keep off the main roads. They missed the road to the bridge and turned down this side road behind us here.

One night when we were coming home from Calgary (I was maybe 6 or 7 years old at this time) a sudden rain and very severe electrical storm came up when we were out from Calgary a ways. Mother and Father thought we would be killed as the lightning danced down the reins. It also ran around the spokes of the wheels. I never saw anything like it since. Dad got cover as quick as possible at the Pine Creek Church. We got our horses and groceries under the driving shed which they had at the church. Lucky for us the church door was not locked so we got shelter inside. That church burned a few years later. It was sure a good thing it did not burn that night with the electrical storm

Years ago, it must have been before my time, Mother and Dad said every Sunday morning after church was in, these big rough guys who did not live too far away would come in with their spurs on and walk right up to the front pew of the Davisburg Church with their spurs jangling on the floor. There was so much racket that the minister would have to stop preaching until they sat down.

I have also heard Mother and Dad tell of a severe hail storm that came. The hail stones came through the north windows of the church and bounced in the middle of the floor and took all the south windows out as well.

Back in the '20s when we had Prohibition, some funny things went on. My folks used to see big locomotive type cars sneak down east on this road allowance which runs down to the Highwood River about a short mile and a quarter from our corner. I figure my folks must have wondered a little too much about it and had mentioned it to someone who was in maybe on the Big Deal. As my father and Lorne were outside one night, one of these big cars came up, stopped at the corner and swept the yards with a very powerful search light. They must have caught Dad and Lorne in the beam as they never used that road allowance again for whatever they were doing. My folks figured they were bootlegging the booze in a boat across the river somehow, then carrying it up the hill and loading it in their cars. The bridge was downstream just a ways from there but it was generally dangerous as this was where the Police would try to catch them.

In 1928 I begged my father to let me help him to chase some fat cattle to Calgary. In those days there were no trucks hauling livestock like now. At first he did not want me to go, then he finally consented. We left real early in the morning with two saddle horses and our lunches. We took them (about ten head) up the Bow Valley Road, or the Blackfoot Trail as it was commonly called then. We took them west to the Macleod Trail on the last road before we came to Fish Creek to take them over the steel bridge there. Just as we had them going onto the bridge, three or four boys leaned over the side of the bridge to have a look at them, then away they stampeded in every direction. We had a big time getting them rounded up, and found them everywhere, even in Joe Fachini's garden laying down. His son Mario, ran the service station there. It was quite late when we got them into the stockyards and we could not get them to go near the bridge after that so we had to make them ford Fish Creek, which took more time.

Then Dad and I decided to go up and stay the night with my grandmother and aunts. As we were on our way up we came face to face with a street car. The conductor had just let somebody off, then he took a look at Dad and me, blew his whistle toot-toot, and my saddle horse, June, whirled on one hind foot and was gone. Dad tried to catch her, but she ducked him. I finally got her under control and got her to go past the street car. Thank goodness that crazy conductor had enough sense to sit there until we got by.

The Hungry Thirties I will never forget, especially the dust storms we had. One of these came up in the middle of the afternoon, about 3 p.m. My father came in with an 8-horse team. I was trying to help him in this terrible dust storm and it was so dark in the stable the turkey gobbler was going to roost for the night and he ran into me. Even the hens went to bed when these storms hit.

I can also remember my father hauling all our coal from McPherson's Coal Mine at Black Diamond, with four horses on a grain tank, to keep us warm in the winter. It was stream coal and very gassy. He would get a good wood fire going then pour a little water on the coal in the pail and mix the water in it, then put a few shovels full in on the fire. The fire seemed to die down as though maybe it was going out, then all at once the stove seemed to almost jump off the floor and the lids would fly in the air as it exploded. Mother was none too happy, as she always had white curtains and they had to be washed often. We burnt this coal for many years, especially during the hungry thirties, because it was cheap. After the thirties, Mother would not let Dad get any more so we burnt wood in the summer and had Drumheller coal hauled in with truck for the winter.

Just prior to the 1914-1918 war the C.N.R. built a railroad grade from Calgary that came through Davisburg. It passed through section 7-21-28-W4 just in front of my parents' home and went on through to Aldersyde. The steel was also laid for about seven miles out from Calgary. Before they could finish it an order was passed in Parliament not allowing two railroads to operate within seven miles of each other. The C.P.R., going from Okotoks to De Winton and the C.N.R. going through Davisburg were within about six miles of each other, therefore the C.N.R. was shut down.

A couple of incidents happened in the building of this railroad grade. When they were building it through Bill Herr's slough, which was done with four mules on what they call a fresno, one of the mules in one of the four mule teams became very baulky and laid down in the water. There was no way they could persuade him to get up and he drowned. So off came the harness and the next fresno load was dumped on top of him burying him there.

During this time a bad storm came up and a man was standing in the entrance of a tent watching the storm. I believe the tent was located somewhere behind the Davisburg church. The tent was struck by a bolt of lightning that killed the man instantly.

There was a townsite of 80 acres reserved here for quite a few years but it was let go back to the original ¼ section of land. I do not know if any money changed hands in the transaction.

Pat Burns built and used a grain elevator on the steel that was laid out on this grade. The old grade is still visible from the Gulf Station near Aldersyde, back through here into Davisburg and on to Calgary.

In the 1930's an oil well was drilled on the west side of the Highwood river, southwest of the old Davisburg bridge. The land belonged to Davenports, I believe, and the well was called Twin Dome No. 1. de Foras and Hagerman drilled to somewhere around 15,000 feet then shut down the well and burned quite a good sized flare, probably about fifteen feet high. Chunks of oil could be seen floating out on the sludge from the well when they were drilling. It was a wooden derrick of the old pounded type method. After the flare was burned for a while it was shut off and never started again even though a lot of shares were sold.

Another oil well was drilled about 1938, this time just on the east side of the river on R. Riddle's land, not too far from the river bank. This was Twin Dome No. 2. They hit anthracite coal, a seam that could be 400-600 feet in depth. This seam runs in a slant and comes out on top of the ground at Cluny.

My father had a water well drilled on E½ 18-21-28-W4 which was also drilled through coal.

In 1949 a large block of cement was placed over the control head at Dome No. 2 as people were in the habit of turning on control valves and letting the oil run out.

During the hungry thirties there was a real shortage of feed. In one of those years a rancher brought 300 head of beautiful Hereford cows to Bob Young's farm, situated east of Okotoks and one and a half miles west of No. 2 highway. The snow came and, not having enough feed, the cows all died. Early in the spring people came out here and asked if we knew where the dead cattle were located. They skinned the animals for $1.00 a hide to get a little money to live on.

THE STRAWBERRY ROAN — by George Andrews

Even into the '20s, farmers usually left their doors unlocked. However, it was unwise to leave your gates open as you might wake up on a wintery morning to find a herd of up to fifty horses munching on the stacks of oat bundles or hay. The horses might belong miles away.

However, the Strawberry Roan was a lone maverick and wandered the roads in the Davisburg and Melrose districts over about a four mile radius for several years. He especially liked a triangular area by a small creek. He was a chunky little horse and appeared to be docile, have no owner, and have a disdain for fences.

Periodically the older boys of the district — the Herr brothers, Jim Suitor, and Fred Maxwell — would round up the Strawberry Roan for Sunday afternoon riding enjoyment (?).

MY CHRISTMAS — by Chris Hunt

I was sitting in English,
Dreaming one day,
About our cows on Christmas,
And feeding the hay.

It gets kind of boring,
Day after day,
Loading the wagon up,
And hauling it away.

But the cows have to eat,
And so do we,
That's where we get our food,
My family and me.

The cows on the range,
They have no worry,
But us in the farmyard,
We have to hurry.

I do the barn chores
Like to calves to tie up,
And clean pens and milk cows,
Then the milk to take up.

Mom does the separating,
Dad feeds the feedlot,
My sister sleeps and does nothing,
While everyone else does lots.

But this Christmas is special,
Like every other one,
And nobody opens presents,
Until all the work is done.

I really like Christmas
Especially on the farm,
From feeding the cows in the field,
To the "opening the presents" charm.

Oh Sunny Alberta, I love you so
in any direction, Where ever I go
Your Sunshine and blue skies
plains that I may roam
I love you Alberta, My Home Sweet Home.

Cattle on the range,
and wheat fields like gold
proud folks enjoy you
both young and old.
Sod Adobes and slough Water too

That was the best most folk
could do.
We thank the Lord for his blessings too.

Alberta, Alberta
We're so proud of you
Who knows better, then Guess Who?

Oh, our horses are of a nature race
Starvation and Blizzards
stares them in the face.
They do not leave, they only stay
like their brave masters, too poor to getaway.

Fashions

Lillian May Coyle, 1912.

Kate Young kept house for Kings.

Lillian and Frances Coyle, 1916.

Rain or Shine. Mary Ann Adams 1882.

195

Mary Jane Adams with daughters, Jane and Lucy, Mabel Hornibrook (seated). 1905.

Ida Banister in nurses' uniform, 1914.

"Proud Grandparents", Mr. and Mrs. Henry Bryce and Bert Banister about 1907.

Albert Edward (21) and Helen Mary (Weston) (19), Banister, 1864.

196

Alex Blackwood about 1908.

"Divided Riding Skirt" Effie Blackwood (Leach), 1919.

The Flett Sisters, Una Rodger and Ina Blackwood, 1934.

"Sunday Best" Ethel and Bill Herr, 1921.

197

Daughters of Mr. and Mrs. W. J. Andrews. L. to R. Laura, Cora and Ethel.

L. to R. Mabel and Emma Currie and Ethel Andrews. 1910, a well hatted trio.

Idwal Jones, 1907.

"Ready for Company". Francis and Leonard Pashak.

"Friends", Marion Dalzell and Helen Brinton, 1924.

198

"Maxi-Skirt" Clara Jamison, 1915.

Anyone for a ride? Vera Marshall, 1920. Note the angora saddle bag covers.

"A Visit to the Photographers". June, Vera, Marjorie and Les Marshall. 1909.

"Feathers were The Thing". Mr. and Mrs. Pete Murray, 1913.

Bathing Beauties. Vera Marshall, Donnie and Marie Cameron, 1920.

Donald Sutherland in native costume, 1930's.

Henry and Katherine Poffenroth, 1905.

Margaret, Bill, Cecilia and Sam Hamilton.

Isabella Hamilton on the farm at De Winton — 1920.

Hey Look us over! ?, George Sutherland, Bill Hamilton about 1920.

Frank Marshall — 1899.

"Wedding Finery". Jim and Lena Montgomery. 19?.

PORCUPINE

SQUIRREL

COYOTE

JACK RABBIT

BISON

BADGER

"FIELD MOUSE"

"CHIPMUNK"

SANDPIPER
SHOREBIRD

FRANKLIN GULL

COMMON SNIPE
Brown + white
white streaks
on crown

KINGFISHER
Blueish bird
Ragged Crest

GREAT BLUE
HERON

Blue grey
whitish head.

CURLEW
BUFFY-UNSTRIPED HEAD
HABITAT- PRAIRIE
OPEN AREA NEAR WATER.

MELROSE S.D. NO. 166

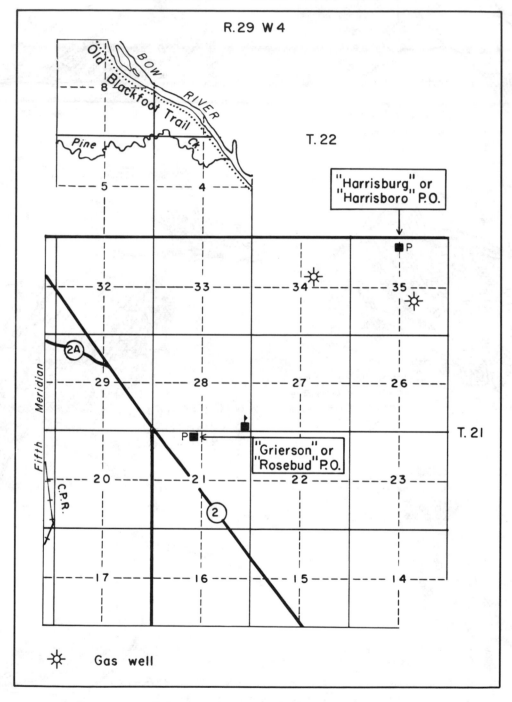

R.29 W4

T. 22

T. 21

"Harrisburg" or
"Harrisboro" P.O.

"Grierson" or
"Rosebud" P.O.

☼   Gas well

Melrose School District

MELROSE SCHOOL — by David J. Hunt

Formation

School District No. 166 of the North West Territories, was granted a Proclamation February 10th, 1890. This was the result of a meeting called at the home of John Currie on December 16th, 1889. The chairman of this founding meeting was Hugh B. Ingram, the secretary, J. E. Finnacy. The board members elected were Thomas Banbury, William Andrews and John Currie. The name, "Melrose", came from Scotland with the Currie family from the district south of Edinburgh.

First By-law

The first by-law of the district was drawn up at a board meeting held at James Grierson's home on February 18th, 1890. This by-law authorized the borrowing of up to $600.00 at not over 8% interest per annum, to be paid back in ten equal annual instalments.

This loan would really get the board members started with the business of obtaining an education for the district children. The district to the east had been formed several years earlier in 1887, and some of the children were travelling to that school, but more settlers were moving into the district yearly, and it was most evident that a school had to be built to look after their needs.

The men on the board who passed this memorable by-law were T. Banbury, chairman, John Currie and W. J. Andrews.

School Site

The history of the school district is quite clear and easy to reconstruct, thanks to people like the Maxwell family and the Martins, who had the foresight to hang on to the old records.

These records, including Minute Books, Assessment Rolls, letters and agreements, have been loaned to me for the purpose of this history, and include the original title for the school site, which is reproduced in the book. The location was the S.E.¼ of Section 28, Township 21, Range 29, West of the 4th meridian, containing one-half acre, and is described in chains and links.

A letter from the Department of the Interior, Ottawa, dated June 27th, 1890, granted the board permission to acquire the site on the S.E. 28-21-29-W4th, from Mr. W. Andrews, who held a pre-emption entry on the land, at the rate of $2.50 per acre, plus $10.00 Patent

Melrose School — 1903. 1st. Row: Etta Currie, Maggie Bristow, Cora Andrews, Donald Grierson, Pat Kenney, Jack Grierson. 2nd. Row: Mabel Currie, Laura Andrews, Mary Ann Bristow, Sarah Kenney, Ethel Andrews. 3rd. Row: Wellie Currie, Roy Maxwell, Harold Draper. Teacher — Eva Andrews.

fee. The letter from Ottawa is written in very beautiful longhand.

In 1935 the board moved to purchase an additional one-half acre to add to the school grounds for $25.00 from Mr. Peppard, but the purchase never did take place.

The title was registered in the South Alberta Land Registration District of the North West Territories on June 15th, 1892. Mr. J. A. McMillan, D.L.S. was employed to define (survey) the one-half acre school site.

Building

The specifications for the school building also had to be approved by the Department of Education in Regina, and this was done in a letter dated March 21st, 1890. The building was to measure 20' x 28' with a stone foundation, best quality lumber to be used, with a brick chimney.

P. O. Address_____   _____ *Registrar.*

P. O. Address_____   _____ *Registrar.*

P. O. Address_____   _____ *Registrar.*

P. O. Address_____   _____ *Registrar.*

P. O. Address_____   _____ *Registrar.*

CERTIFICATE OF OWNERSHIP.

The Melrose School District

Nº 166. of The North West Territories

Pt. S.E. ¼. 28. 21. 29. W. 4th M.

½ Acre.

Dated the 15th *day of* June *A.D.* 1892.

Register O.   *Folio* 88.—

Certificate of Ownership.

South Alberta — Land Registration District.

This is to Certify that The Melrose School District numbered 166, of the North West Territories

is now the owner of an estate in fee simple

of and in A portion of the South East quarter of Section Twenty-eight, in the Twenty-first Township in the Twenty-ninth Range West of the Fourth Meridian, in the Provisional District of Alberta, in the North West Territories, in the Dominion of Canada, which may be Particularly described as follows, that is to say:— Beginning at a point on the most Southerly boundary of the said quarter-section Twelve chains measured in a Westerly direction from the South East angle of the said quarter section; Thence Northerly and perpendicular to the said most Southerly boundary Two Chains and Twenty-three and six-tenths links; Thence in a Westerly direction and parallel to the said most Southerly boundary Two chains and Twenty-three and six-tenths links; Thence in a Southerly direction and perpendicular to the said most Southerly boundary Two chains and Twenty-three and six-tenths links; more or less to the said most Southerly boundary; Thence in an Easterly direction along the said most Southerly boundary Two chains and Six-tenths links more or less to the place of beginning, containing by admeasurement One-half of an acre, more or less, reserving unto Her Majesty, Her Successors and Assigns all mines and minerals which may be found to exist within, upon or under such lands, together with full power to work the same, and for this purpose to enter upon, and use and occupy the said lands or so much thereof and to such an extent as may be necessary for the effectual working of the said minerals, or the mines, pits, seams and veins containing the same.

subject to the encumbrances, liens and interests notified by memorial underwritten or endorsed hereon, or which may hereafter be recorded in the Register of Title.

In Witness Whereof I have hereunto subscribed my name and affixed my seal this Fifteenth day of June A.D. 1892.

P. O. Address Pine Creek. N. W. T.

J. A. McLean Registrar,
South Alberta Land Registration District

DATE OF INSTRUMENT.	PARTIES TO INSTRUMENT.	NATURE OR PARTICULARS OF INSTRUMENT.	NUMBER IN DAY BOOK.

P. O. Address, _____ Registrar. _____

[OVER]

The agreement to build the school was between the board and William E. McLeod on April 28th. It called for the construction of the school house and two outhouses for the magnificent sum of $145.00. Bricks at the time cost the board $1.50 per hundred.

George Bremner was hired to draw all the material from Calgary, including lumber, shingles, doors, windows, nails, paper, bricks and other material for the price of $47.00.

The Board of Education advised the district that they did not supply furniture for the school. This letter was sent to James Grierson, who was secretary at that time.

Outhouses didn't stand up

On February 5th, 1891, it was resolved to have two new outhouses built, to replace those destroyed by the wind, and that a competent builder be employed at not more than $2.00 per day, to do the job. Also that Thos. Banbury and W. Andrews be appointed to superintend and see that the work is done in a proper manner. The board was unable to hire carpenters at this rate, and after calling for tenders, finally hired James Grierson to do the job at $2.50 per day.

Assessment

An assessor for the district was appointed on March 31st, 1890 in the person of Neil W. Brodie. W. Andrews was a brother-in-law, and Mrs. A. Blackwood, Sr., was a sister to Mr. Brodie. The assessment for the year lists: Cattle, 284 head; Cows and two year old steers at $34.00 per head; Two year olds at $20.00 per head; Yearlings at $13.00 per head; Hogs numbered 19 and 2 litters; Horses — 110.

Land valued at $4.25 per acre with about 8,000 to 9,000 acres taxable.

With the C.P.R. syndicate owning 1,920 acres, and a total of 2,987 acres not taxable. The taxes collected in 1890 totalled $28.80 with the books showing a balance of cash on hand of $187.00.

Melrose School — 1917. Kate Kenney, Edna Currie, Agnes Meehan, Mamie Bartlam, Mary Meehan, Marjorie Tyson, Bob Clark, Gordon Grant, George Meehan, Norman Kenney, Maizie Meehan, Ethel Kenney. Teacher: Edna Lockhart.

Melrose School — 1917 or 18. 1st. Row: Fred Maxwell, Gordon Grant, Harry Lemmerman, George Meehan. 2nd. Row: Buster Lemmerman, Mary Meehan, Maizie Meehan, Ruth Meehan. 3rd. Row: Earl Grant, Helen Lemmerman, Lola Grant, Katie Meehan, Agnes Meehan, Mark Kenney. 4th Row: Arthur Maxwell, May Grant, Annie Ewing.

Melrose School — 1909. 1st Row: Isabel Bristow, Bessie Grierson, May Grant, Mark Kenney, George Meehan, Arthur Maxwell. 2nd Row: Clive Simpson, Katie Meehan, Ruby Grant, Lola Grant, Dunc Kenney, Dick Meehan, Frank Bristow, Gilbert Young. 3rd Row: Maggie Bristow, Etta Currie, Cora Andrews, Dave Grierson.

Taken at Melrose School 1919. Back row: George Meehan, Harold Grant, Norman Kenney, Gordon Grant, Gerald Bartlam, George McNab, Robert Clard, Edna Currie, Maizie Meeham, Mayme Bartlam. Front row: Marorie Tyson, Ruth Meehan, May Meehan, Agnes Meehan, Ethel Kenney, Kate Kenney.

In 1891, the taxes paid had gone up to $65.97. The government grant came to $64.33, but the total disbursements amounted to $289.64.

A listing of the first ratepayers of the Melrose district follows, along with their legal location, all in Township 21, Range 29 West of the 4th.

Peter Machay	Section 31
John Somerville	Section 32
H. B. Ingram	Section 32
W. E. Ingram	Section 32
J. S. Ingram	Section 33
R. C. Thomas	Section 33
John Owens	Section 34
Bryce Wright	Section 34 and 35
J. S. Lee	Section 26
Hudson Bay Co.	Section 26
P. Turner-Bone	Section 27
W. J. Andrews	Section 28
H. P. Griffin	Section 28
A. R. Griffin	Section 28
John Currie	Section 20
James Grierson	Section 20
J. A. Grierson	Section 21
James Wright	Section 21
Joseph Hogge	Section 21 and 22
James Hogge	Section 22
John Meehan	Section 22
Frank Percy	Section 22

In 1911 it was moved by board members H. Currie and E. Grant that the rate of tax be set at six cents per acre. In 1914, the rate was increased to eight cents, in 1919 ten cents per acre, and in 1921, taxes were set at twelve cents per acre, reflecting the creeping inflation of the times. An interesting insight into the constant struggle for revenues to cover costs of operating the school in those days, is reflected by a motion put forward at the meeting held January 7th, 1919, which asked of the Board of Education, permission to assess the hired men of the district for taxation purposes.

At an annual meeting held in the year 1922, it was moved by H. Norris that all untaxed land lying between Okotoks School District, Allan School District, Davisburg School District and Pine Creek School District, be taken into the Melrose School Division and taxed for school purposes. This would indicate that the districts were formed on a piece-meal basis, and attempts to have all lands included in school districts would be desirable. No doubt the need for a larger tax base was also a motive for this move by the ratepayers.

Government grants in the year 1892 were based on 70% of the teachers salary, $360.00 per year, and $25.00 per pupil, paid on a monthly basis. In 1919 the financial statement showed total receipts of $1,295.25 and payments of $1,050.37.

Tax Arrears

By 1896, unpaid taxes were becoming a thorn in the side of the Board of Trustees. The secretary was instructed to send letters to the tardy taxpayers threatening legal action. In April, 1897, the Board decided to possess and sell a stack of hay on the N.W. 28-21-29 owned by Hans Clark, to recover the amount of $2.96 in unpaid taxes. Also, one bay mare belonging to Robert Forrester, to recover his taxes owing.

Melrose School, June 1926. Top, Ralph Grant. Second Row: L. to R. Sandy Giffen, Reta Currie, Muriel Grant, Doris Currie, Lawrence Norris. Bottom Row. L. to R. Leslie Norris, Elsie Giffen, Jessie Giffen, Harold and Gordon Norris, Fred Wonnacott.

In 1900 the S.E. 32-21-29 was to be sold in order to collect the taxes owing against the land.

Non-Resident Pupils

Those pupils attending Melrose from outside the boundaries of the district were assessed a charge in lieu of taxes, which was paid directly to the teacher. In 1899, this charge amounted to two and one-half cents per day per family. In later years this was raised to seventy-five cents per pupil per month.

Board Members and Secretaries

The first members of the board have been noted earlier in this history, but it is interesting to note some of the later "early day" pioneers, who guided and attended and taught in the Melrose school.

The first secretary was Mr. Hugh Ingram. Another early secretary was James Grierson, who lived very near the school site. Some readers may remember the Grierson hill and post office located just east of the junction of highways 2 and 2A. There is a very good spring at the base of this hill, just south of the road on Martin's land, and no doubt Mr. Grierson chose this location because of the good water supply.

The next secretaries included E. H. Young, James E. Frinnacy, D. J. Simpson and Robert Maxwell, who was appointed in 1911. Mr. Maxwell held this position until 1928 when Mr. S. M. Martin took over, and he continued until the amalgamation of school districts in 1955.

The last class was held in the school during June, 1955.

The board membership varied only a little in the early years. Between 1911 and 1922 the stalwarts on the board included E. Grant, H. Currie, W. J. Andrews, A. J. Currie and Robert Maxwell.

Early Chairman Asked to Resign

The duties of the board were taken seriously as noted by a motion at the annual meeting on January 2nd, 1890. The Chairman of the board, William J. Andrews was asked to resign because of neglect of duties. Mr. E. J. Whelan was elected to the board in 1899. H. G. Norris was made a board member in January of 1924.

Melrose School 1932. Teacher, Miss Evelyn Shaw — 1930-34. Back row: Jessie Giffen, Elsie Giffen, Hedley Halstead, Percidel Halstead, Harold Norris. Second row: Gordon Norris, Ted Heaver, Howard Norris, Vic Heaver, Les Gilmour. Front row: Eva Heaver, Phyllis Brown, Mary Wonnacott, Catharine McConnell, Russell Martin.

First Woman Nominated

There were three nominations to fill one vacancy on the school board June 11th, 1930. They were A. Giffen, Thos. Young and Mrs. H. G. Norris. The vote was a three way tie, so the Chairman decided by voting Mr. Young to the Board of Trustees. Mr. Young lived on the quarter west of the school site, and for many years, this was known as Young's corner. Later on the Carson Kennels were also on this site. R. G. Dafoe was a board member for several years in the mid thirties until moving out of the school district.

J. R. McConnell was elected to the Board in 1933 and Mr. E. Grant resigned in this year.

No attempt has been made to list all of the people who helped guide the school district through its half century of educating the young, and to the many I have missed, apologies are certainly in order. Time and space are the limiting factors.

Teachers

Hiring and keeping teachers was one of the main problems to be solved by the Board of Trustees in early-day rural schools.

Teachers whom the board could afford to pay only a rather meagre salary, were usually female, young and single. Much interest was generated among the young blades of the district when a new "school marm" was hired. They passed through the district on a fairly regular basis.

The first teacher was Emma M. Andrews for the school year of 1890 at the rate of $40.00 per month for approximately six months. The teacher must have a place to board nearby, as transportation must have been a problem, especially during bad weather. The W. J. Andrews family provided board and room for many of the early teachers at the school, and later the S. M. Martin family also filled this post.

During the early years, no attempt was made to keep the school open during the bitter winter months. The meeting of November 21, 1890, saw a motion passed that the school be closed on December 9th for at least six months, and no further expense be incurred to the ratepayers. In 1910, it remained open all through the winter, and continued on a full school year of nine months.

Calgary Tribune-Herald

The Calgary weekly Tribune was used mainly by the school board to advertise for teachers, and the necessary ads were inserted quite regularly. In 1898, the Tribune took on the new and present name of The Calgary Herald, as evidenced by the Minute Book.

Miss Eva B. Andrews was engaged to teach in 1902, at $45.00 per month. There was always a big turnover of teachers nearly every year, and sometimes twice yearly. Wages in 1911 were $60.00 per month.

By 1922 the wage had gone up to $1,000.00 per year, plus $2.00 per month for cleaning the school if they wanted the work.

Edna Blackwood was appointed as teacher in 1929.

Melrose School, 1936-37. L. to R. Catherine McConnell, Vic Heaver, Mary Wonnacott, Russell Martin, Les Gilmour, Anna Carothers, Ted Heaver, Eva Heaver.

Melrose School — 1954 Last class. Front: Raymond Kenney, George Nigel, Donovan Martin, Glen Kenney, Donald Heichert, Tommy Linn, Ron Jones, Bob Airth. 2nd row: Margaret Cushon, Nina Pennock, Donna Hagerman, Sandra Gerlitz, Marlene Kenny. 3rd row: Melba Hagerman, Betty Nigel, Doreen Ruud, George Cushon. Top: Glenda Hagerman, Martha Nigel.

Miss Shaw's resignation was accepted in January 1934 after nearly four years as teacher. Salaries had dropped from $1,000.00 per year in 1929 to $800.00 in 1934, reflecting the depression. Miss Wonnacot was engaged at $700.00 per year to fill the vacancy.

Bad Boys

May 10th, 1929 the trustees moved that Miss Crawford be notified to send home Harry Meehan for rough conduct in the playground, and that all fighting at school must stop.

Daily Register

In July of 1899, the daily register showed: Teacher — Hazel Magee; Students — Edith Currie, Edward Currie, John McNeill, Geo. O. Moss, Laura Andrews, Wellie Currie, Hazel Ingram, Ernest Hogge, Barty Brown, Alfred Brown. The two Brown boys were cousins of the Meehans. They were both killed while working for the railroad. An older brother, Charlie, was also killed accidently while working for the C.N.R. in Edmonton.

In June 1905, the year Alberta became a province, the daily roll showed: Teacher — Eva B. Andrews; Students — Ethel Andrews, Annie Greenfield, Roy Maxwell, Laura Andrews, Nellie Currie, Donald Grierson, Ettie Currie, Mabel Currie, Mary Bristow, Ernest Hogge, John Grierson, Cora Andrews, Dalton Bristow, Maggie Bristow, Sarah Kenney, Gilbert Young, Dave Grierson, Ruby Grant, Richard Meehan, Duncan Kenney.

District Sidelights — Honourable J. A. Lougheed, Landholder

An appeal by J. A. Lougheed on the assessment of the N.E. 20-21-29 on the grounds that it was too high, was rejected by the Court of Revision on April 4th, 1896.

Again in 1899, Hon. J. A. Lougheed appealed the assessment on the West half of 14-21-29, on the same grounds, but again the appeal was denied.

Dunbow and the Postal Service

In 1897, the principal of Dunbow School, located near the confluence of the Highwood into the Bow river, was Rev. Father Maesseus. A letter to Melrose school ended up at Dunbow, and Father Maesseus forwarded it on. This letter contains post office stamps of Ottawa, Calgary, Rosebud, Dunbow and De Winton, all in the year 1897.

Section 27 was given to Mr. Turner-Bone for services, surveying for the C.P.R. The C.P.R. was assigned uneven numbered sections by the government of Canada.

Mr. Meehan homesteaded in 1887.

Typhoid fever moved into the district during 1898, that dread disease that took so many lives in the early days of the prairies. The Melrose Board of Trustees reacted by asking any families contracting the malady to keep their children out of school until a doctor verified that the attack had passed. This was done in preference to closing the school.

Mr. R. C. Thomas, an early district resident, may be remembered as having operated the Wales Hotel in Calgary during the 1940's and early '50's.

School District Succumbs to Amalgamation

In 1934, the School District of Melrose No. 166, set the path for its own destruction as a separate entity. At this time, the board sent a requisition for the sum needed to operate the school for the coming year, to the M.D. of Sheep Creek No. 190, rather than collect their own taxes. This led to the amalgamation of this district into the Foothills School Division No. 38 in 1946.

The last minutes on record end at February 6th, 1946.

MELROSE CHURCH — Researched and written by I. Blackwood

A meeting of the congregation was held in the school on January 17, 1900 for the purpose of organizing the congregation and appointing a board of managers. The meeting was conducted by the student missionary, W. Simons. The board of managers elected were George Headley, D. J. Simpson, and Robert Maxwell. The district was to be the area of the school district with two additional miles added to the south boundary, making it the township line between townships 20 and 21.

James A. Grierson and Alex Currie were appointed auditors for the year.

The Board was instructed to negotiate with the Davisburg and Pine Creek Boards in 1901 to get their share of daylight services, suggesting seventeen services as a fair share. On these conditions it was decided to give Rev. Wm. Simon a call and they agreed to pay $125 annually towards his stipend.

In 1905 the Board was increased to five members, with Herb Currie and Luke Draper being added. Herb Currie was elected secretary.

At the annual meeting of 1905 Melrose agreed to support Davisburg and Pine Creek in building a manse. Later in the same year, Herb Currie was elected to the Manse Board for Melrose.

In February 1922 the Melrose congregation indicated that they were willing to have the manse moved to De Winton provided there was no expense attached. While Rev. Percy Halstead was minister in 1934, the congregations of Melrose and De Winton were united.

JIMMIE AND DOROTHY AIRTH

Jimmie, second son of Mr. and Mrs. Robert M. Airth, was born in Johannesburg, South Africa. His father was a mining contractor in the gold mines, but due to ill health was advised to go to either Australia or Canada. He chose the latter and homesteaded in the Hutton district north of Brooks, near the Red Deer River, one of the driest areas of Alberta. His illness soon took his life, leaving his widow and two sons, Andrew and James.

Jimmie spent his boyhood days along the Red Deer river, getting his education in one room schools. Later, he and Andy started farming in the Duchess area. They moved to Brooks when the Eastern Irrigation District was formed, and bought part of the Duke of Sutherland's estate. Their mother came to join them there. This is where he met Dorothy Alberts, who had immigrated to the Millicent Flats with her parents from Ainsworth, Nebraska; the place of her birth. They were married on February 14, 1943 and moved to Madden, near Crossfield; where they lived for three years. Every year the crops were hailed. While there, Robert, their first son was born. They moved to Bowness where Jimmie opened a real estate office. While there, Ian, their second son made his presence known.

They moved to the Orton farm, just east of De Winton in the spring of 1949 when Ian was just two weeks old. They moved into the old house, part of which had been built by Jim Ingram when he homesteaded here in the 1880's. Jimmie was acquainted with the Ingram family in the Brooks area. At De Winton there was no power, no plumbing, no washing machine and no natural gas. The cold winter winds didn't go around the house but straight through it. They moved their beds into the room farthest from the direction of the wind. Heroes are made — not born.

Jim Ingram had a log boring machine with which he made wooden pumps and pipes for his neighbors. One of the originals is still on the farm.

The Airth's moved into their present home in 1951 which is located at NE 29-21-29 W4M. The cattle brand is the walking 'A' on the left rib, and from there the name of the present company was derived.

Bob started his schooling at Melrose and when it was closed, both he and Ian went to Okotoks. Later they both graduated from Olds Agricultural and Vocational College. Ian married Donna Powlesland and they ranch at Cochrane and have one son, Howard. Bob is taking over the farm operation here at De Winton. Dorothy and Jimmie will do some more travelling before the wheel chairs take over.

THE ANDREWS FAMILY — by Ethel (Andrews) Oneil

Norman George (my twin brother) and myself were born on Rock View farm NE 28-21-29 W of 4 on May 20, 1890, and registered by W. J. Benard, the then registrar, in Calgary, N.W.T.

Unfortunately Norman died in June, 1891.

In May, 1892, sister Laura (Mrs. H. G. Norris) was born, and on September 1st, 1896 Grandmother Ingram brought along sister Cora (Mrs. S. M. Martin) in a carpet bag!, or, so we were told!

As a growing child, I remember every one was terrified of fires that swept over the prairies. Settlers ploughed the fire guards to protect their homes. I remember my father walking and broadcasting grain from a leather apron, in the fall cutting it with a scythe and finally threshing on a flailing board. Progress came fast, soon binders were used.

Long ago, a creamery was built on my father's homestead, and managed by Mr. Hugh Ingram. Later this building was used for an ice house. The ice was cut by Mr. Kenney and my father from the Bow River, and was hauled home in sleighs.

In the very early days, bachelors were plentiful and young ladies scarce, so dances were almost nil. However, after much persuasion, my parents agreed to hold a dance in their home (providing everything but the girls). Mr. W. Stewart and Mr. K. Rowles brought their girls (who later became their wives) from Calgary, on horseback. Mr. Charlie Shattuck provided the music.

Water was scarce on the homestead. Below the rocks and on the road allowance, a never failing well was dug and used till 1900, when all the buildings were moved to the quarter south of the homestead. It was here where a creek ran through headed by a spring, on a quarter later owned by Mr. James Grierson.

In early 1890, a school was built on land donated by my father, and named "Melrose" by Mr. John Currie. At the age of six, I started at this school and walked across the homestead usually with Dinah, William and Spearman Kenney and Fred Bates. Once we found and tried to catch a family of baby skunks! Enough said! School days commenced March 1st. and ended October 31st. Then three months to forget what we had learned.

In 1905, under the tuition of Miss Day, I passed my "entrance exam" and on to Okotoks High where Mr. Skinner ably taught grade IX, X, XI and XII, without assistance.

In the fall of 1908, I opened the Allan School, on a permit, holding said school for my high school chum, Agg Creighton, from Tongue Creek, while she went to Normal for four months.

I rode seven miles from home as there was no boarding place. In 1909, I attended Calgary Normal where only three Western Canada students attended; the remainder came from Eastern Canada, and a few from England. For a pastime, we used to skate at Sherman's rink on 17th. Avenue E.

Now a new life began, as far as finances was concerned. Fifty dollars per month was top wages. In 1910 I taught at Stormont School, in 1911 at Panima, in 1912 Oneil school at Crossfield, and in 1913 I applied and taught at Melrose, where I first started school! I was the third Andrews girl to teach at Melrose. First, Emma, daughter of Tom Andrews, second, Eva, daughter of George Andrews.

In September, 1914, I was married to Hillyerd M. Oneil, of Crossfield, and happily became a farmer's wife and eventually the mother of five boys; W. Lorne, Norman H., Murray G., Donavon M. and Stanley. Stanley passed away as an infant.

Hillyerd and Ethel Oneil, 1962.

In May, 1920, we bought the De Winton store and stayed till 1922. Melvin Martin helped in the store.

In 1939, the Second World War broke out, and in January, 1940, Norman, Murray and Don joined the R.C.A.F. Norman was a rigger, Murray a bombardier, and Donavon a pilot. In 1944, Murray (then a navigator) was shot down over Berlin and never found.

Lorne and Norman now farm west of Airdrie. Lorne married Fern Whitney of Stavely and Norman married Mabel Pole of Airdrie. Both girls were daughters of real old timers.

After the war, Don became controller for C.N.R. in telecommunications and is stationed at Toronto. He married Dorothy Robb, daughter of Dr. Robb in Winnipeg.

From the farm we moved to Calgary, then to Winnipeg and Toronto for a short time; eventually back to Calgary in 1948, where we lived till my husband died in August, 1970.

Strange to say, I was born on Rock View farm, and now, 1976, I live at Rocky View Lodge in Crossfield.

I have four grandsons, four granddaughters, and one great-granddaughter.

WILLIAM AND CATHERINE ANDREWS

William J. Andrews was born in Inverness, Quebec in 1853. He married Catherine Brodie who was born in Inverness on April 6, 1854. The wedding took place at Inverness on July 12, 1878. They came west from Quebec to Alberta in 1885. Mrs. Andrews recalled their adventure in this way . . .

"Although we came here in a colonist car, we made the trip very comfortably and had a fine time. There were thirteen of us came together — Johnny George, Tom McKenzie, Mr. and Mrs. Tom Andrews and three children, Mrs. Marshall and her son Evert, Jimmy Hogge, my husband, myself, and my sister, now Mrs. Blackwood".

"Our car was fitted up as a regular dwelling in which we cooked and slept, as well as lived and ate. It was a mixed train with two cars of our cattle coming just next. This made things very convenient, for every night and morning one of the men could go out in the next car, milk the cows and bring back a pail of nice fresh milk. We left Asbestos Mine in Quebec on June 23, 1885, and landed in Calgary on July 5".

A daughter, Cora Martin, wrote . . . "They brought all their belongings with them, lumber to build a house somewhere, also oxen. Our father wanted to farm, but being short of money our mother went to work at the Royal Hotel".

Of this period Mrs. Andrews says . . . "The railway people were very good to us. When we arrived in Calgary they sidetracked our car and allowed us to continue living in it until we could make other arrangements. The reason we settled here was because Tom Andrews had been out the year before and liked the country between Calgary and Okotoks; and when we saw it we were sure that we could not have made a better choice".

"The Northwest Rebellion was going on when we left home and I was scared stiff of Indians but when we arrived in Calgary we found to our relief that the trouble was over. I recall that the old Royal Hotel was full of Steele's Scouts who had just come back from the north".

Mr. and Mrs. Andrews worked for Colonel Macleod for a time — Mrs. Andrews as cook and her sister, Isabella Brodie, as nursemaid. William Andrews was groomsman for the family.

As soon as they could, they moved to their homestead east of De Winton (NE 28-21-29-W4) where William Andrews had built a small house with a lean to for the livestock (an ox, two hens and a rooster).

Mrs. Cora Martin wrote . . . "The first night on the homestead a fire was started on the Bow River. Our father had a fire-guard so he ran one and a half miles to Joe Hogge's, to warn him of the fire as he had lumber piled up for a home and no fire-guard. They got busy with the plow and the fire went by".

Mrs. Andrews related that in 1888, after she and her husband were settled on their homestead, she had a frightening experience. One afternoon when she was all alone in the house with the doors on both the north and the south wide open, she happened to look out and there were a number of Indians coming up to the north door. In an instant without taking time to even close the doors, she dashed out the south door and never stopped running until she reached the home of Jim Hogge where she gasped, "The Indians are coming!" However, on returning home she found that though the Indians were beggars, they were not thieves — nothing had been disturbed; the house had not even been entered. The Indians had waited around outside in hope of seeing someone from whom they could beg. Failing that, they had slipped away without touching a thing.

"After I got used to the Indians", Mrs. Andrews said, "I often gave them something to eat. At first I would set the table for them, but when I found they always carried away all that was put on the table I stopped".

Although their first home had a magnificent view of the surrounding countryside, they were near an outcropping of rocks on the northern edge of their land, so therefore getting water was a problem. They carried water from a spring over a mile to the south. In time a well was dug and the young couple acquired horses, cattle and poultry. A few years later Mr. Andrews purchased the quarter to the south, a fine piece of land on which there was a stream and the flowing spring from which they had taken their water at first. In 1900 they moved their house from its site near the rocks to a pleasant spot near the spring. (NE¼ 21-21-29-W4). The kitchen and living room were moved in two parts. When they moved the kitchen, the fire was burning in the stove. A space was left between the two parts when they were settled on their new site. The space between was boarded up and used for storing grain at first. Later it became the dining room and the upstairs was finished as bedrooms. The Andrews had a home to be proud of which is still in use — the home of Mr. and Mrs. George Martin.

By this time the Andrews had three daughters; Ethel (Mrs. Hillyerd Oneil, born in 1890), Laura, (Mrs. Howard Norris, born in 1892), and Cora (Mrs. Melvin Martin, born in 1896). A son, Ethel's twin, Norman, lived only thirteen months. Mrs. Martin died in 1975.

Mr. Andrews' brother, Hugh, had bought the Grierson property, a quarter directly west of the Andrews' where the Grierson Post Office had been. When Hugh Andrews decided to go back to Quebec, he sold his quarter to his brother. The log barn was moved near the house and William Andrews hauled logs with oxen from Priddis to build a new barn in which no nails were used.

Mrs. Laura Norris recalls with amusement that, "Papa and Uncle Hugh hauled coal from west of Black Diamond one fall. They wore heavy Stanfield underwear and itched and itched. When they discovered they were covered with lice they had to stay in the bunk house!"

William Andrews Family — 1900. Catherine Andrews, Ethel, William. Seated — Cora, Laura.

The Andrews home was a very busy one. The spacious home became the boarding place for teachers and ministers. Catherine Andrews, with the help of her daughters, worked very hard cooking, cleaning, sewing, canning, and making soap. She was always knitting when she sat down, and sometimes traded a pair of mitts for a fish which the Kenney boys would bring to her. She also had a contest with her neighbor, Mrs. John Currie to see who could knit socks faster.

Mrs. Andrews provided a vital service in the community — that of midwife to families in the district. She attended alone the births at the Maxwells, the Grants, the Blackwoods, the Kenneys, the Griersons, and the Robinsons. She assisted Dr. Ardiel of Okotoks at the Whiting's and Dr. Stockton at the Holmes; Grandma Ingram attended Mrs. Andrews when her own children were born.

It is recalled that Mr. S. Kenney, in a great rush to have Mrs. Andrews attend his wife, transported her on an apple box mounted on a stone-boat with his horse galloping at top speed!

William Andrews raised Aberdeen Angus cattle and Clydesdale horses as well as grain. In 1890 he donated land from his original homestead for a school. He served as a trustee for Melrose School District No.166, for many years.

William Andrews died in 1924 at the age of 70.

Catherine Andrews lived with her daughter, Cora Martin, until her death in her 91st year in 1945.

BARNEY AND LILLIAN ASSMUS AND BILL AND DOREEN HEICHERT

Barney and Lillian Assmus, their daughter Doreen, husband, Bill Heichert, and two sons, Donald and Douglas, arrived from Swift Current, Saskatchewan in April of 1953, to make their home on the old Wonnacott place on the banks of the Bow River. The farm was purchased from the Boehlke brothers who had been the previous owners. Donald Heichert took grade one of his schooling at the Melrose School. The following year the little school was closed and the children were bussed to Okotoks School.

Four years were spent on this farm in the De Winton area and then it was sold to Pat and Merle Steir and to Merle's father and mother, Mr. and Mrs. Bert Robinson. Barney and Lil Assmus moved to the city of Calgary to retire, where they still live. Bill and Doreen and sons moved to the city too where Bill went back to work for Safeway Stores. After four years in the city farm life called once again and in the spring of 1961 the Heicherts purchased a small cattle ranch at Alix, Alberta, thirty miles east of Lacombe. They established themselves in the purebred Polled Hereford cattle business, and are still actively engaged in raising purebred stock. Both boys have left the farm and are married. Don lives in Edmonton and works for C.B.C. and Doug is in Calgary working as a chef in the restaurant industry.

We look back with fond memories of our few years at De Winton, and all the fine friends we made; friendships that encompass the years. One vivid memory is of the Pony Club led by Nan Graham, where many summer Sundays were spent by the children and adults, riding and picnicking.

DAVID AND ANNIE (ZEGGIL) BRISTOW — by Isabel Peterson

My dad, David Bristow, was born in Gray County, Ontario on September 12, 1865 and Mother, Annie Zeggil was born October 20, 1866, also in Gray County. They were married in 1887. In the spring of 1900 Dad, Mother and six children: David, Fred, Mary, Dalton, Margaret and Danny, and all their settler's effects, came west to Okotoks. Mother had a sister, Mrs. Dan McBride, living here. I believe they settled in the Davisburg district. They bought their farm, the Frank Meehan place, later buying the Alingham farm, I think the land description was NE¼ 14-21-29-W4 and E½ (80 acres) N.E.¼ 15-21-29-W4, S.E. ½ 22-21-29-W4.

Four more children were born in this home: Isabel, Frank, James and Nellie. Sad to say, one small son, Danny, passed away here, as the result of an accident, and is buried in Davisburg Cemetery. The children went to the Melrose school.

The boys were getting older and wanted land of their own. They heard of all open land, with lots of free range and good water, across the North Saskatchewan River, with the railway coming through the next year. Ironically enough, the railway came through eighteen years later.

In the spring of 1910 the family again picked up and moved to the Frog Lake District. Dad, David, Fred and Dalton were able to homestead on land, farming a block. The cost of filing on a quarter section was $10.00. The Frog Lake Indian Reserve bordered their place to the east. All machinery, household effects, 40 head of horses, (I don't remember any cattle but we may have had a milk cow), were loaded on box cars and came, by rail, to Kitscoty, forty-two miles from the homestead. While Dad and the older boys got the stuff unloaded and moved, Mother and the younger children lived above the Hardware Store in Kitscoty.

There was a ferry across the North Saskatchewan River at Lea Park, 20 miles north of Kitscoty. The Frog Creek had to be forded and, beyond the creek, there was no trail. They just had to pick open spots in the bush to travel the five miles to the homestead.

The family lived in a tent the first summer. While buildings were put up and corrals made for the horses and, of course, hay had to be put up for the livestock. Several of the horses died that first year from swamp fever.

Some points of interest might be that Mother was the first white woman to come to the district after the Rebellion of 1885 and Mary was the first bride, being married in 1912. Dad had the first threshing machine in the country, a steam powered outfit, a J.I. Case, and did work all over, even south of the Saskatchewan River. Kitscoty was our trading place, there was a post office at Lea Park and our closest doctor was in Kitscoty.

My brother, Dalton, went to the War in March, 1916 and was killed on August 9, 1918. There was no school, as yet, in the district so, in 1912, Mother and the school age children moved to a rented farm, south of the river and the children went to Elgin School till 1914. By this time the school had been built on the south east corner of Dad's homestead.

Frank has retired from farming but still lives on the original homestead.

He kept up the cattle brand and the horse brand, originally registered to David Bristow of De Winton, Alberta. He still has the original irons, made by a blacksmith in De Winton. Now his grandson, Kurt George, has taken over the registration of these brands.

Frank recalls that, before we left the south, there was an outbreak of mange in the cattle and the cure was to dip the cattle in a sulphur solution. Apparently the Bristows had a creek or spring in their barn yard just right for the dip so, proper pens were built and cattle were brought from all around the country to be treated here. No doubt there were lots of thrills, spills and cattle chasing, probably an exciting time in the life of a small boy. This cattle treatment was a Government sponsored project.

There are still four of the Bristow family living: Frank and Jim, in the Frog Lake District and Mary Bowtell and Isabel Peterson in Edmonton, Alberta.

NEIL AND MAY (CHAPLIN PALING) BRODIE — by Neil Stanley Brodie

As a young man Neil came west where he worked in a saw mill on a C.P.R. section crew, in the early 1880's. He was an ox team driver, taking supplies from Swift Current to Battleford during the Riel Rebellion and was taken prisoner on May 14, 1885, a few miles south of Battleford, by Poundmaker. He remained a prisoner until Poundmaker's surrender, which he witnessed. In 1883 he had a farm near Swift Current.

In the late 1880's, Neil was a cowboy on John Turner's ranch. Later he homesteaded a farm near De Winton SW¼-4-22-29-W4 where he remained until 1906 and then became a carpenter, painter and builder in Calgary. He was a game guardian from 1900 to 1916. From Calgary, he moved to a farm, just south of Cereal, in 1910. Mother, my sister, Eva, and I moved there in 1911. He was the country butcher in those early days and I helped him when I grew older. He also helped build the new local school No. 3204 and it was named Neilville. He helped the new settlers build their new homes. The farm was located on 7-27-6-W4.

My mother, May, (nee Paling), did a great deal of knitting of socks and sweaters during World War I as well as helping her neighbours with cooking, canning of vegetables and fruits and doing much work in her own garden.

Neil Brodie and May C. Paling, were married in 1895. My sister, Eva, and I joined them while they lived near De Winton. My mother passed away while visiting her nieces, Hilda Payne and Gladys Green, of Lousana, June 19, 1949. She is buried at Lousana. Dad died on August 7, 1935 and is buried at Cereal.

They were survived by a daughter, Eva, (Melville) deceased January 10, 1962 and a son Neil of Cereal. Eva leaves a son, Gordon, and three grandchildren.

THE NEIL BRODIE FAMILY — E. Leach

Following participation in the North West Rebellion of 1885 Neil Brodie homesteaded in the Melrose district. His location was just east of the present Victor Heaver home. He was a good practical carpenter and soon had a neat set of buildings which were always kept well painted. Even the dog had a painted kennel. Neil was a man of many trades and capabilities, whatever he did was well done, really professional. He was a good and kindly neighbour and helped many a less practical new homesteader over the hump of a stranger in a new land. Money, of course was scarce in the 1880's and 1890's. Pay seldom entered into a deal. However, the Melrose School records show, that when tenders were called for building a fence around the school, Neil Brodie was given the contract and was paid the sum of twelve dollars. That was in 1890. That same year he was given the job of assessing the property for school taxes.

Mrs. W. J. Andrews (Aunt Kate), and Mrs. Alec. S. Blackwood (my mother), were sisters of Uncle Neil, all had come from Inverness, Megantic County, Quebec.

May Brodie had come, as a child, from England, with her parents, brothers and one sister — the Paling family. Carrie, the sister, later became Mrs. Joe Hope of Red Deer Lake. Auntie May was a gentle little soul who never raised her voice in anger. I don't believe she ever said an unkind thing in her life. When we were children and became a bit naughty, (as even old-time children did) she would quietly threaten "I'll see your nose above your chin," which always calmed us down. We had visions of our faces undergoing a grotesque change. We must have been exceptionally dumb!

All we nieces and nephews loved Auntie May dear-

Neil and May Brodie. Eva and Neil Jr. about 1906 or 1907.

ly. It was indeed a great day when the Brodies came to visit. Auntie May always played games with us while the more staid relatives merely visited or played cards, such as 'Lost Heir' or 'Whist'.

Christmas and New Year's Day were gala occasions, with the relatives meeting at the various homes in turn. When the Andrews and the Blackwood families went to Uncle Neil's place the Paling and Hope families were there too and what a lovely time we had! We went for dinner and stayed for supper, as the custom was. How all the adults and children got into that small house remains a mystery. One year a terrible blizzard came up while we were there. To even think about going home was plain suicide. The horses had already been comfortably stabled, of course, so all the guests stayed all night and had breakfast too before going home!

There were not any children in the Brodie household for a few years so we children had extra attention from Auntie May and Uncle Neil. Finally Eva May and Neil Stanley made their appearances. Shortly after, the farm was sold and the family moved to Calgary. Their first home, which Uncle Neil built himself, was on Fourth Street S.W., about 21st Avenue. Later they moved to another new home, away out on the prairie, 510-25 Avenue S.W. It was near the famous Blue Rock Hotel, not far from the Mission Bridge.

There is already a short account of the Brodie family in the book but it was felt that there should be a few items about their life in the Melrose district and it has been my pleasure to recall some of the happy times we had long ago with the Neil Brodie family.

JAMES AND CATHERINE (KENNEY) BROWN — by James Brown

At the age of sixteen I came from Southampton, England to Edmonton. I was to have met my father there, but James Brown Senior was nowhere to be found. I left a message at his boarding house as to where I was going. I set out for a farm at Ardrossan, twenty-two miles east of Edmonton, and a job of cutting bush for fifteen dollars a month.

Three months later Father found me and we returned to Edmonton. Walking being the conventional mode of transport, the two of us set off on foot for Nestow and jobs in a logging camp. The first day Jim Senior hurt his hand and we were forced to walk back to Edmonton where Dad was laid up for over three months.

Two men and I, in search of employment, started out from Edmonton on the long walk to Collington. This was January, and with only twenty-five cents in my pocket, outdoor sleeping quarters, cold but uncrowded, were all that were to be had. Upon arriving in Collington we found there were no jobs. One fellow went on to Athabasca but the other fellow and I returned to Edmonton. By now it was spring and I found work shoveling gravel for thirty cents an hour on the Williamson Block on Jasper Avenue. I was in the money!

For five dollars an acre Dad and I went to Lacombe to cut, pile and burn bush. Before the job was finished Dad went on to a job bricklaying on a mainstreet Lacombe store. I completed the bush job and went to help Dad.

In the meantime we had filed blind on homesteads at Maloy, thirty miles north of St. Paul. We both went there when we finished in Lacombe, only to find solid poplar covering our land. We began improvements on the homestead but in the summer it was necessary to come to Calgary to make some money. We spent that fall stooking at Blackie then we returned to the homestead for our six months residency. That spring

The Brown family. Left to right back row: Kate, Phyllis, Jim, Buster Charlie and Jessie.

Dad remained at Maloy and I went to a mill near Edmonton to cut poplar for ammunition boxes for the war. I worked for a time driving a team there.

That summer I took a job on the grain elevators for A. J. Voss. My brother Ted joined us that year.

I soon found that winter work was in the bush and I even traveled into British Columbia swamping for loggers. In the fall I worked stooking or threshing from Morrin to Retlaw to Blackie. Finally I decided to do some serious farming. A fellow told me to call in the spring. He planned to go to Venezuela and I could rent his place. I was in a coffee shop trying to make the call about renting when I overheard two fellows talking. They were discussing their need of a tractor operator so I approached them and asked for the job. This was the position that brought me to work for Mr. Impey of De Winton who rented land from Dr. L. S. MacKid.

This position also gave me my first encounter with my wife-to-be, Catherine Kenney. I had gone to haul oats for Spearman Kenney when I spotted Catherine, with her head out of the upstairs window, making googlie eyes at me. While working at the elevator in De Winton I spotted her again. I called to her in her buggy and she took off at a dead run. This reaction of course requires an explanation. I had a rather dark complexion and dark hair. Kate mistook me for an Indian and she was frightened to death of Indians in those days. After I caught up with her and clarified the situation a four year courtship ensued and I saw no reason why we shouldn't marry and so we did on November 12, 1924.

Voss told me that working on elevators was no job for a married man and consequently he rented me his farm near Okotoks. We were there two years and accumulated horses, machinery, and Phyllis Catherine.

We then bought a quarter section on the Macleod Trail north of Okotoks. Benjamin James (Buster) was born while we were there.

On the morning of April 12, 1927 the stove blew up in our house. Kate jumped out of the window with baby Buster, saving only herself, her night dress and the baby for future use. I had been lighting the stove when the accident happened and my leg was badly burned. Phyllis was visiting her Grannie and Grampa Kenney the day of the fire.

When I was well again we renovated a granary and added a lean-to for a temporary home. Dad and I began work on the brick house that stands on the property today. Later we rented the upper storey of a huge brick house in Okotoks for two or three months. We then went to Charlie Hughes' farm on the Bow River for a little more than a year. Charles Edward was born during this time. In 1930 we moved back to our makeshift home on our own land. Jessie was born. Phyllis began school at Melrose; the same school her mother had attended.

I was still working on the brick house. In the beginning I bought more than enough bricks to build the house for forty dollars, and began building as I could afford the lime for mortar; usually three dollars worth at a time. It took over four years to complete the job and neighbors told me that I must be bringing the bricks home in my lunchkit. In September 1931 we moved into our house.

While living on Macleod Trail we had a well witched. We dug down by hand, thirty-three feet, and made a brick cribbing four feet in diameter only to have a nicely cribbed dry hole. Our next resort was nine sticks of dynamite; but still we got no water. We had no money but we were able to get a well driller to come in and dig and case fifty feet deeper to the water in exchange for a Rumely tractor. It was a success for us but the well driller didn't fare so well. While taking his tractor home down the steep grade of the Okotoks hill, the governor came loose and the tractor raced to a total wreck.

In December of 1931 we left the brick house and our farm and rented it out. We lived in Turner Valley while I worked plastering and bricklaying. In 1946 we sold the place on Macleod Trail and bought the Bradfield Ranch at Priddis. When we sold there in 1956 we moved to Turner Valley where we still live.

James Brown Senior lived with us most of the time until he passed away in 1947.

Phyllis married Mike Zuk and together they operated the Black Diamond Hardware Store. Buster is married to Patricia Stevens and he is a welding inspector presently working near Red Deer. Charlie married Ruby Feddema and works for Western Decalta in Turner Valley. Jessie is married to Thomas Adams and they farm at Priddis. Kate and I have twenty-two grandchildren and eight great-grandchildren.

THE BURKE FAMILY — by George I. Burke

Edward and Ellen Burke, with their family of six, settled out of Calgary, coming from Essex County, Ontario in 1899, to Claresholm. Eliza, (Mrs. Draper) with her husband, had a grocery store on 17th Avenue for many years; Maggie (Mrs. Jack Grant) of Turner Valley, George moved to Butte, and the Klondike, dying in South America, a well-known hotel man. Albert and his wife Edith, raised a family of four sons and four daughters. They had a dairy farm just outside the city limits. The youngest daughter, Effie, married Dr. Shipley, and still lives in Vancouver. Bob had a homestead in the Davisburg area. He died at High River in 1940, where he was operating the hotel. The Burkes celebrated their 60th wedding anniversary in 1921.

HISTORY OF THE EDWARD BURKE FAMILY, MELROSE DISTRICT 1889-1894 — by G. R. Rintoul, Great-Grandson

The Edward Burke family emigrated to Western Canada in the fall of 1889 having previously applied for, and received land from the Canadian Pacific Railway. The land consisted of the N½ and S.E. ¼ 25-21-29 W4th. and N. ½ 23-21-29 W4th. totalling 800 acres. Under the C.P.R. contract 4320 & 4321, for a price of $3.00/acre.

As you may know the C.P.R. received, from the Canadian Government, so many sections per township as further incentive to build the Trans-Canada Railroad.

The area was known as Davisburg in those days, however the children attended the Melrose school, including my Grandfather Albert Edward Burke one of Edward Burke's children.

George H. Burke son of Edward Burke.

The family who came west to this consisted of:
Edward Burke — Father
Ellen Burke (nee Murdock) — Mother
Eliza Emily Burke — Daughter
George Henry Burke — Son
Robert Cephas Burke — Son
Albert Edward Burke — Son
Margaret Anna Burke — Daughter
Effie Jane Burke — Daughter
Of these children the following married local Davisburg (Melrose) or closely located families or settled for a time in the area.

George Burke to "Kit" Ingram, July 1895, who settled for a time in the Melrose area. George subsequently followed the Gold Trail to the Klondike and died in Punta Arenas, Chile, looking for gold in 1906.

Robert Cephas Burke took over the "family" farm when his father took out a further homestead in the Porcupine Hills. This is the person who sold the farm and buildings to the Maxwell family — Fred Maxwell lived up to his recent death in the original house that my Great-Grandfather built in 1889-90. It is reported that Robert or "Rob", as he was known, brought the first seed drill into the Davisburg (Melrose) area. Robert Burke subsequently managed the St. George Hotel in High River, the Auditorium Hotel in Nanton and the Queens Hotel in Calgary. Robert died in 1940 at High River.

Margaret Anna married John Alexander Grant in

Edward Burke farm buildings.

May or June 1893 in the Burke home at Davisburg (Melrose) district, they subsequently farmed near the Big Rock.

Albert Edward Burke (my grandfather) moved to Porcupine Hills with his father, Edward Burke, and took out his own homestead. A creek was named after him at that location. He married Edith Louise Jordan of Chatham, Ontario, in 1900 at the Anglican Church of the Redeemer in Calgary. He subsequently farmed near Vernon, B.C., sold real estate in Victoria and farmed in Calgary. He died in 1951 at Calgary.

The other children's lives followed various paths as follows:

Eliza married Luke Draper in 1880 and subsequently opened up the first store and house on 17th Avenue between 1st Street West and 2nd Street West in Calgary. Both died at Calgary and the store still stands next to Jaques Funeral Home.

Effie married Dr. Earle Everard Shepley on December 28, 1909, at Church of the Redeemer. Dr. Shepley was instrumental in developing cobalt treatments for cancer while at the University of Saskatchewan, Saskatoon, and subsequently died of complications due to radiation burns. Effie is still living at Vancouver, B.C. and is the only living member of the original Burke family who homesteaded in the Davisburg (Melrose) area.

At my urging, Effie (Burke) Shepley, a few years ago, wrote a complete story of her life as it was when they came West. Please follow and read as you will at your pleasure "To The Time They Left For the Porcupine Hills At Lyndon, Alta." etc.

Edward and Ellen Burke. Homesteaders in Davisburg (Melrose) area. Golden Wedding anniversary.

3

Q'ns 5. My mother, Ellen Murdock, was born Jan. 21st 1842 at her father's home south of Cardinal, Ontario. She died at the St. George Hotel in High River, Alberta - the morning of Dec. 26th 1931. Brother Rob was manager there at the time. I had the privilege of caring for her for most of the time of her illness - over two months. It was hard to see her go - even though she was almost ninety.

Q'n 6. Father and mother came west from Grenville County, Ont. in the autumn of 1889, to the Davisburg district of Alberta - where father had bought a farm, which proved a bad investment. In those days there were many hail-storms - and the beautiful fields of grain would be ruined.

Our place was located less than a mile east of the Melrose School, and a very short distance from the Currie Post Office, to the west - Later on I went to school at Melrose. It was such a lovely walk, with many wild flowers and birds' nests along the way. - It must have been a summer-school, as I never went there in winter. Father eventually bought me a lovely Pony called Daisy. After that I frequently rode to school. - Father was the first trustee of Melrose School.

One of the earliest things I can remember of that country home; was of the Indians coming in large numbers; all riding; some with travoys behind their horses; bedding and supplies would be roped on the travoys. The Indian women usually had a papoose strapped to her shoulders - Thus, they would come to our

house, wanting something to eat. Mother would always give them food of some kind. In the summer she would feed them outside; they seldom came in the winter. I was afraid of them; when I saw them coming, I would run and hide in the down stair bed-room - under the bed; out of sight, until they were gone.

There was a stream, which ran thro' the south side of Fathers land; and a well treed hill beside the stream. Here, the Draper girls and I often played when they came out for summer holidays. Sometimes we would find saskatoons and raspberries on that hill.

I doubt if I was more than four, when one day as Father came in the house - Mother cried out, "Oh! Edward! whatever has happened to you?" Father's right hand was dripping with blood. - the little finger was torn off and the third finger badly mangled. He had been leading a steer, out to the drinking trough, when suddenly the gate, thro' which they had just passed - slammed shut - frightening the animal, - and causing him to bolt.

Father was taken immediately to the Calgary General Hospital for surgery. Weeks later he returned home, with an iodoform dressing on his badly damaged hand. To this day, when I smell iodoform - I think of Father's dreadful experience.

The winters could be quite cold in the Davisburg area. One time on Father's return from Calgary, his fall and whiskers were covered with heavy frost - and his nose was frozen. On such nights, a number of lanterns were

placed in the cellar, near the vegetables, to keep them from freezing.

We frequently drove over to the little English Church at Pine Creek for Sunday service. The clergy would often drive me home, and many times they stayed over night at our place - I so well recall my mother teaching me my earliest prayers and hymns; my first stories of God; and of His Blessed Son - our Lord Jesus Christ giving His Life upon The Cross; to cleanse us from our sins, if we would but believe in Him and trust Him - These I have never forgotten, - nor how truly I was blest.

The years at Davisburg were happy ones for me - my parents - sister "Maggie" - and brothers, Rob and Albert were all very kind to me. Sometimes Mother and I would go looking for strawberries, and if we found enough she would make me a pie to take to school. I certainly thought that was just right. When she was baking, I was right by the table, watching everything she did. If cookies were being made she would say, "Now you go outside and get me a pan of chips for the fire - and I'll give you a cookie with a raisin in the centre." I would be off, and back like a shot, with the chips; then triumphantly - eat my cookie, carefully leaving the raisin for the last -

Maggie and Jack Grant were married in May or June 1893 - at our family home. There was a big party and dance after; many people - all having a good time.

The autumn of 1893 I was taken by my parents

to attend school in Calgary. I felt heart broken leaving home. The bright spot was staying with my sister Eliza, her husband and family. They were all very kind, and eventually, I became as one of them. Each summer I would return home for the holidays and then back to the Drapers, for school in September.

Q'n 9 My parents, I believe, knew most of the people in the Davisburg area. At nearby Pine Creek lived the Watson family; among the first we knew well. They kept a lodging place - Another family, the Curries had the Currie Post Office - just a little west of the Melrose School. Others were - the Joe Hoggs and the Jim Hoggs; a very large Ingram family; the Bustons during and Blackwoods; a Dora Proctor and a Charlie Shattuck - Also there was a Bannister family. They had a son Harold. A daughter of the Bannisters, married W.R. Hull as rancher with large holdings in southern Alberta. In 1904 they had a very fine home in Calgary - which I believe later became The Ranchmen's Club.

Friends of ours were the Andrews. Also there was a Glanville family with whom we used to visit. They had a son Ernie - about my age. Across the road to the west and a bit south lived Jack Meighen - and his uncle, Frank Piercey a little south of him.

A telephone directory might help you. There are likely survivors.

Q'n 10. Rob went to work in the Butte Montana mines about 1892. There was a terrible explosion in the mines, while he was there. Fortunately, he was off shift at the time. I well remember how alarmed our family was until they heard he was safe.

Edward Burke died in Calgary, May 1926.
Ellen Burke died in High River at the age of 90 on December 29, 1931.
Edward Burke was a member of the Orange Lodge and his and Ellen's names are inscribed on the archway dedicated to the Old Timers on July 9, 1967, at the location of the Southern Alberta Pioneers' and Old Timer Association Headquarters.

The Burkes lived to celebrate their Diamond Wedding Anniversary.

ALEXANDER AND MARTHA SANGSTER

Alexander Sangster came from Scotland to Alberta in the early 1900's and worked in the De Winton district.

At the outbreak of war in 1914, he enlisted in the 12th Canadian Mounted Regiment in Calgary, as many others did from the De Winton area.

In 1916 he was wounded in the 2nd Battle of Ypres.

On his discharge from the army and return to Canada in 1920, he bought a quarter section of land a mile east of the Macleod Trail, on the road to Davisburg and also rented the adjoining Jakes quarter.

In 1922 he married Martha Ham, whose parents had recently bought the Snowden summer home and land in the Bow Valley at the foot of the Cable Grade.

There were three daughters, the eldest died in infancy, and Jane and Sue.

In 1947 the family moved to B.C. and bought a market garden property near Grand Forks; several years later retiring to the town, where Alex had been a devoted worker in the United Church until his death.

Jane became a teacher and after a year in Calgary, moved to Prince George where later she married and lived.

Sue married a U.S.A. army officer whose Regiment trained in Grand Forks, and later lived in the U.S.A.

Mrs. Sangster survived her husband for several years.

Jane and Sue attended Melrose School for several years. Mr. Sangster served on the board of De Winton United Church from 1935 until they left the district.

JOSEPH WEIRICH CAROTHERS

Joseph Weirich Carothers homesteaded in the Carseland area in the early 1900's. He and his wife, the former Mary Helen Read, were from Pottawattamie County, Iowa. They settled in the De Winton area in 1935, one-half mile southeast of De Winton (Frac. Sec. 19-21-29-W4th.)

Joe Carothers was a great one to reminisce and entertain the family on many a wintry evening with stories of the early days: of hauling grain to Gleichen across the Blackfoot Indian Reservation; of freighting oil well equipment to Turner Valley from the railway at Okotoks and bringing back black coal; of some of the ferry crossings of the Bow River during high water.

Helen Carothers' children and grandchildren were influenced by her personality and dedicated spirit. Also they were proud of the fact that she was top student and Valedictorian of her Normal School graduating class. Her friends and family alike knew her as one who was always alert and interested in the furthering of knowledge.

Six of their seven children made their home on the farm. Jim and Anna rode horseback to Melrose School and later attended De Winton Rural High School, as did Chrissy and Barbara.

Joe Sr. passed away in March 1940. Helen Carothers and her family carried on farming until 1955 when she sold the farm and retired to Calgary. Here she lived until her death in August 1965.

There were three sons and four daughters in the Carothers family, Joe, the eldest, and Jim, the youngest, have a farm at Bluffton, Alberta. Joe married Doris McBain McIntosh and has one daughter.

Keith married Jessie Dalzell and had one son and one daughter. He served overseas during World War II and was employed with the Canadian Western Natural Gas Company Limited until his death in a gas line explosion in 1964.

Virginia married Lawrence Watrin and farms west

Joseph and Helen Carothers Family — 1942. l. to r.: James Bruce, Barbara, Chrissy, Helen (Read), Joe (Jr.), Virginia, Keith, (holding Virginia's son, Duane), and Anna.

of High River. They have three sons and one daughter, all now married. Collectively they have provided their parents with fourteen grandchildren.

Chrissy married Allan Smith who farms east of High River. They have one son and one daughter. Chrissy has been involved extensively with 4H Clothing Club and with the Foothills District 4H Council.

Barbara, widowed in 1952, was married to Dr. Douglas Knight. She has worked in the business world in Calgary and maintained her home and raised her two sons alone since then.

Anna Gertrude, a registered nurse, married Richard Harder and lives in Calgary. They have one daughter and two sons.

James Bruce married Margaret Wilkinson and has three daughters and one son.

Of the eighteen grandchildren, it is interesting to note that there are only two boys to carry on the family name; Ronald, son of Keith, now living in Inuvik, N.W.T., and Wade, son of Jim, at Bluffton, Alberta.

EMMA CRONIE (nee CURRIE)

Married to Thcmas Cronie December 28th, 1910 and was a resident of Calgary until her death at the age of ninety-three, June 30th, 1972. Mrs. Cronie was a Life Member of the Southern Alberta Pioneer and Old Timers Association.

She was predeceased by her husband Thomas, February 10th, 1959. They had five children:

John James Cronie - now a resident of Penticton, B.C.

Thomas **Albert** Cronie - a resident of Trail, B.C.

William Archibald Cronie - deceased February 4th, 1930.

Etta Jane Edwards - of High River, Alberta.

Susan **Jean** Paschal - of Calgary, Alberta.

ALEXANDER CURRIE — by Lillian Armstrong

Alex lived on his farm east of De Winton until about 1946, when he moved to Okotoks. Later he moved to Calgary where he lived 'till the time of his death, December 24, 1961, at the age of 85.

In July of 1913, he married Jane (Jean) Stark, who predeceased him in December, 1936. They had one daughter, Margaret (Reta), who married Norman Cushon. They had two children, George and Margaret. Reta died January 15, 1965.

In 1948 Alex married Beatrice Quinton and they lived in Calgary.

For many years Alex served as school trustee and councillor for his district.

He had one of the first local, large threshing machines and steam powered tractor. He bought it in 1908. For the first few years the farmers stacked the grain sheaves and Alex threshed at the stacks. Later he threshed the stooks in the grain fields. This required more men, so he had a bunk-house where the men slept, and a cook car where the meals were cooked and eaten. In the early 1920s he sold his steam engine and what was his second threshing machine, to Jack Patterson.

Mr. and Mrs. A. J. Currie.

EDWARD CURRIE — by Lillian Armstrong

Ed and Bob went homesteading in 1910 and proved up their claim three years later when they took up residence. Their first post office was Flowerdale. Ed had a half section of land and Bob had a quarter section and a pre-emption quarter.

Ed and Frances Belle Russell were married

Mr. and Mrs. Ed Currie 50th Wedding Anniversary, Nov. 10, 1965. Four generations, seated Frances Currie, holding great-grandson Cameron Jenkins, Ed Currie on right, standing on left Gordon Jenkins (grandson) and Doris Jenkins (daughter).

November 10, 1915. Doris was their only child. They remained on the homestead until April, 1925 when they moved to De Winton where Doris started school. Her mother had taught her at home to this date, and going to school from April to June, she passed into grade four.

On the homestead, crops were seldom rewarding and the winters were long and bitterly cold. Doris remembers going to house parties when very young. Usually Uncle Pete (Wilson) and Aunt Mabel and family Russell and Isabel, went too. The kids were "bedded down" in blankets, on straw, in the bottom of the sleigh. Doris usually held a partially baked potato in her hands to keep them warm.

In 1958 Ed and Frances went to Kimberley, B.C. In 1965, they celebrated their Golden Wedding Anniversary. Frances died in 1966.

ETTA E. CURRIE

Etta E. Currie was born at De Winton, the daughter of John and Jane Currie, and the youngest of twelve brothers and sisters. She was educated at Melrose school and lived on the farm with her parents until her marriage to John H. Forckel of Okotoks in June 1925, when she went to live on the Forckel farm. She had one daughter, Evelyn M. (now Mrs. Eric Atkinson of Calgary) and lived on the Okotoks farm until moving to Calgary in 1948. She moved to Victoria in 1957 and returned to Calgary in 1969 where she presently resides.

As a young woman and after her marriage, she was always an enthusiastic member of the Okotoks Country Club. She is also an active member of the United Church, the Southern Alberta Pioneers' and Their Descendants, and the Daughters of the Nile, Victoria, B.C.

HERBERT CURRIE — by Lillian Armstrong

Herb. took out his homestead in 1887, and he lived on that farm until the spring of 1945 when he retired and moved to Calgary.

He married Maria Jamison and they were both faithful workers in the United Church.

Mr. and Mrs. Herb Currie, their golden wedding, June 20, 1950.

Maria died October 16th, 1957 and Herb died April 21, 1958 at the age of 88.

Their daughter, Edna, was drowned in 1923, in the Red Deer River near Buffalo, at the age of 19. She had taught school in that district the previous year.

MR. AND MRS. JOHN CURRIE — by Lillian Armstrong

In 1886, Mr. Currie and his eldest son, Herbert, came from Ulverton, Quebec, and located in the Davisburg district. Returning east in July of the same year, they brought out Mrs. Currie and the other eight children. They drove from Calgary to their sod-roofed house in a double wagon, and the children recall the fun of walking up the Cable Hill, for the new life in the west was a thrilling experience for them.

Mr. and Mrs. John Currie about 1886.

The hailstorm of 1886 destroyed their first crop, but after that Mr. Currie never had a complete crop failure.

The family lived in Davisburg for a year then moved to their homestead near De Winton.

Mr. Currie was post-master for several years of the Rosebud and later the Grierson post offices. The post office was in his residence. The mail was brought by stage-coach.

Mr. Currie was founder of the Melrose school

Mr. and Mrs. John Currie's 50th Wedding Anniversary. Back Row: L. to R. Pete Wilson, E. McDowell, T. Cronie, Jim Hogge and John, Mrs. Ed Currie and Doris, Mrs. H. Currie, Edna Currie, Myrtle Dalzell, Rob Dalzell, Mrs. A. Currie, W. C. Currie and Bob Currie. Next Row: Mrs. P. Wilson, Mrs. E. McDowell and Jane, Mrs. T. Cronie and Willie, Mrs. J. Hogge and Lillian, Ed Currie, H. Currie, Mrs. J. Currie, Mr. J. Currie, Etta Forckel (nee) Currie, Mrs. R. Dalzell, A. Currie and Reta, Mrs. R. Pinchbeck and Gilda. Bottom Row: Ab Cronie standing, John Cronie, Lorne Hogge, Norman Hogge, Ernest McDowell, Colin Dalzell, Bob McDowell, Bert Hogge, Bertha Dalzell, Pearl Hogge, Edith McDowell.

district. He was the first trustee elected at the first school meeting of the district held in his home.

Mrs. Currie was the daughter of Mr. and Mrs. George Richmond of Ulverton, Quebec. Before emigrating to Canada, Mr. Richmond served 25 years in the British Army. He had the honour of being one of Queen Victoria's body guards at the time of her coronation.

Mr. and Mrs. Currie had sixteen children - twelve of whom survived them. Mary and Bella died as children in the East and Alice and John died out West. Their surviving children were: - Herbert, Robert, Annie (Mrs. Robert Dalzell), Emma (Mrs. Thomas Cronie), Alexander, Lillie (Mrs. James Hogge), Jennie (Mrs. Everette McDowell), Edith (Mrs. Robert Pinchbeck), Edward, Wellington, Mabel (Mrs. Peter Wilson), Etta (Mrs. John Forkel).

On November 13, 1927, Mr. and Mrs. Currie celebrated their 60th wedding anniversary. About 45 guests sat down to tables for supper and more invited guests came later for the evening at De Winton Hall. Their twelve children were present as well as twenty-seven grandchildren and two great-grandchildren. Neil Dorsey supplied the music for dancing.

Mr. and Mrs. Currie had been married for sixty-four years when Mr. Currie died February 27, 1932, Mrs. Currie died two months later on April 18.

They had one of the first cars in the district, a Maxwell, it had no doors or top and had acetylene or carbide lights.

They also had one of the first radios that had a loud speaker. It had a large horn that sat on top of the radio. It was bought about 1923 and was a R.C.A. Radiola-Superheterodyne-Second Harmonica. It was battery operated and used one large "A" battery two 45 volt batteries and a small 22.5 "C" battery. There was a note on the chassis stating that it was distributed for experimental and entertainment purposes according to terms enclosed.

When they came from Quebec they brought a large wall clock, with weights, that had to be wound up every night. It was made by Wm. Gilbert Clock Co. Ltd. Conn. U.S.A., and was warranted if well used. It still keeps good time if wound regularly.

Another interesting article was a stereoscope. Other heirlooms included an ink bottle that was six inches high and made of heavy pottery, which was inherited from Mr. Currie's father, the first English child born in the "Citadel" at Quebec City. They also brought a music-box with them. The records were small, round, flat metal discs.

A few fond memories of the grandchildren included sitting on the settee in the parlour and looking at the stereoscope pictures; carefully walking around the spittoon that was beside Grampa's large leather chair; sitting at their large dining-room table for a Sunday dinner and watching to see how much food Grampa and Uncle Wellie could feed their large black cat before Grandma saw them and threw a nearby cushion at the cat! or sitting on the steps of the enclosed stairway with the cousins and trying to be quiet so that the adults could hear the music to dance to. At times the steps were occupied from top to bottom.

ROBERT CURRIE — by Lillian Armstrong

Bob lived with his parents until about 1900 when he moved to Pleasant Valley, south east of Lacombe. In 1910 he took out a homestead at Flowerdale, near Sunnynook which is about 100 miles east of Calgary. While he lived there he often played his violin or mouth organ for the dances and he called the square dances.

For a while he spent the winters with his relatives near De Winton and returned to his farm in the spring. Then in 1934, he moved back to live with his brother Wellie, where he stayed until his death, March 21, 1962, at the age of 90.

WELLINGTON CURRIE — by Lillian Armstrong

"Wellie" lived on the home place until he had to go to High River, due to ill health. He died September 26th, 1966, at the age of seventy-four.

He was the driver of the first Currie cars: Maxwell, Briscoe, King and Nash. He played the violin and his sister, Etta, played the piano for many parties and dances that were held in their home in the early days.

These items were copied from his 1914 diary: Sold a carload of barley for $265.80; Bought pair of overalls for $1.35; 1 pair shoes $1.75; 1 pair socks 50¢, 1 sheet $1.25; 1 hat $1.50; 2 pair boots $8.25; 1 pair gloves 60¢; 1 overcoat $10.00; 1 pair gloves $1.15; 1 lariat rope $1.85.

NORMAN CUSHON — by Margaret Barry (Cushon)

Norman Cushon first came to the De Winton area in 1937, when he worked for Wellie Currie during the harvest season and then worked for Alex Currie during the winter.

In 1940 Norman married Alex Currie's daughter, Reta. After they were married, they went to Oxbow, Saskatchewan to farm. In 1946 at the request of Mom's father, Alex Currie, they returned to assume the responsibility of operating and purchasing the farm which was located on the North ½ of 27-21-29-W4M.

Dad and Mom had two children George, born in Oxbow and myself (Margaret), born in Calgary. We started school at Melrose and graduated from Okotoks High School.

George attended the University of Alberta in Edmonton and graduated in 1968 with a Bachelor of Science in Chemical Engineering. Since graduation he has been working for Shell Canada, first in Vancouver, B.C. and now in Toronto, Ontario. He married Rita Synyshyn of Myrnam, Alberta in June, 1968. They have two children Bradley and Laura.

I also attended the University of Alberta in Edmonton and graduated in 1970 with a Bachelor of Science in Nursing, majoring in Public Health. I worked in hospitals following graduation, mostly at the Charles Camsell Hospital in Edmonton. I married Peter Barry of Edmonton, in 1972 and we have one son, Scott.

Mom passed away in 1965.

Dad sold the farm in 1969 and is now retired and living in Summerland, B.C. He married Mary Gilbert in 1976.

LUKE AND ELIZA DRAPER — by Mrs. Ella Coggan

In the spring of 1901, Luke Draper and his wife Eliza (daughter of Edward and Ellen Burke), rented a farm in the De Winton area, from Turner-Bone for a period of approximately three years. This farm was located on S.E. 34-21-29 W4M.

The family consisted of Luke and Eliza and their six children: Clara, Ella, Harold, Raymond, Irma and Stanley. Their nearest neighbours were Mr. and Mrs. Symons. Mr. Symons was the Presbyterian Minister.

Soon after the arrival of the Draper family in the De Winton area, the family was struck with dysentry. One night Raymond Draper became quite ill. Mrs. Draper turned him upside down, attempting somehow to ease his pain, but to no avail. In the morning, Mr. Draper with the help of neighbours, carried the living room sofa, with Raymond lying on it, onto the democrat down to the station at De Winton. The train arrived in Calgary and the sick boy was taken instantly to the hospital. An emergency operation was performed, but it was too late, his appendix had burst. At the age of eight years and eleven months, Raymond was buried in the Union Cemetery at Calgary. After this event, Mrs. Draper worried a great deal about being so far from a doctor.

While on the farm, work started early. At five o'clock, Clara and Ella would be out doing the milking. The girls each milked seven cows, twice a day. The only sounds they heard were the singing of the meadowlarks. It was so peaceful. The milk was put through the separator and then it was time for the girls to feed the chickens.

It was necessary to haul the water for cooking and drinking. As the well was quite a distance from the house the water was put in a barrel on a stoneboat drawn by a horse. The flat irons were heated on the kitchen range.

As Ella Coggan (nee Draper), relates "When it was necessary, we swept the carpets with a broom. In the spring, the carpets were taken up and hung over the clothes-line, and given a good beating to remove the dust. We owned a hand-operated washing machine which helped a lot. After we washed our lace curtains, we put them on a wooden frame, called a curtain stretcher. When dry, they were ready to hang up again."

"During grain threshing the neighbours got together and went from farm to farm until the work was finished. We would bake for several days ahead before the threshing 'bee' arrived."

"We didn't have very much in the way of entertainment except for reading, playing games and enjoying good sing-songs around the organ, which my sister Clara played. She also played the organ for the services at the Presbyterian Church, whenever we could get there. The church was called The Melrose Presbyterian Church."

As there were no telephones, the family was quite isolated during the winter months. Their only transportation was a one horse buggy, wagon and cutter.

Mr. and Mrs. Draper attended Reverend G. E. Gale's Anglican church in De Winton.

The Draper family returned to Calgary in May, 1904.

DANIEL ALBERT AND DOROTHY (McCULLOCH) GERLITZ — by Dot Gerlitz

Danny, the second youngest son of Adam and Mary Goerlitz was born on February 14, 1914. He worked hard at an early age, as each family member had chores to do to make a living off the farm. He was especially good with the horses and was driving teams at the age of six.

The Gerlitz children all rode horseback to and from school and at times Danny would rather have been home ploughing the fields than spending his days in the classroom. His sister Millie recalls him leaving the school before classes were dismissed, a red headed boy disappearing on his pony over the hill to home, to harness his horses for work in the fields. Before leaving for school, he had cows to milk so he had to be up at an early hour. The Gerlitz children spoke German at home and it wasn't until they attended school that they were taught their English.

Danny recalls having his tonsils out at the age of twelve. A hospital was set up in the De Winton Community Hall, with cots placed along the walls separated by bed sheets hung between them. With a huge tub for discarded tonsils, the Doctor set to work. The cost was $15.00 per child. Danny ran the binder till noon on the day of his operation, went to De Winton in the buggy, had his tonsils out and after returned home the same way.

Saturdays were always spent at one of the Seventh Day Adventist homes in the community. All day Saturday was spent listening to sermons and singing hymns and it was hard to keep the younger children still. Many excuses were made for permission to be absent for a short time! Dan's brother Peter played the saxophone and his sister Elizabeth played the organ and Rose the piano.

Danny and Millie were blessed with bright red hair and freckles. They were teased so much about their freckles that at one time after hearing that rubbing chicken manure on the freckles was a sure cure for their disappearance, they tried the treatment but with no results. Finally an ad was read in a magazine advertisement for "Double Strength Othene" a sure cure for freckles. Millie and Danny pooled their nickels and sent for a jar. They could hardly wait till it arrived by mail. But alas, it also was no cure, so they had to live with their freckles!

Christmas was a religious time and no gifts were exchanged. One Christmas when Danny was about ten, the younger ones gathered up 15 cents between them, and on Christmas morning Danny was elected to ride his horse to the De Winton Store to buy some nuts. The store was run by Barsby Martin, a kindly storekeeper and a favorite in the district. Danny hopped off his horse and banged at the door, as the store was closed for Christmas Day. There was no answer, so he banged again and a dime he was holding in his hand, rolled under the crack at the bottom of the door and into the store, and then there was a banging that would awaken the dead! Barsby came to the door and gave Danny the biggest bag of nuts he could carry, so he rode home happy with his Christmas errand accomplished.

When Danny was twelve years old he and his brother Peter went to work for Mr. John Harrison who was a road builder. Dan who was in charge of the fresno had to have the horses fed, harnessed and ready to go at 4 a.m. They built many of the district roads, some of them to Okotoks.

Danny was very interested in playing ball, and was instrumental in organizing many of the local teams. There was a great deal of rivalry amongst the neighboring towns, so the games usually had a good crowd of spectators.

At one time he took up selling Fuller Brushes and another time delivered bread with a horse and wagon. He thought this was harder than farming!

In 1945 he married Dorothy McCulloch, a graduate of the General Hospital School of Nursing, who was working at the Turner Valley Hospital at the time.

They stayed at her parents home in Calgary for three years, operating his farm and bulk fuel business from there. In 1949 they purchased a small home in Longview which they moved to De Winton. In the meantime, Danny had purchased the White Rose Service Station on the highway at De Winton and the house was moved next to this.

Danny and Dot were kept busy with farming, bulk gasoline deliveries, trucking and a service station to run. The days never seemed long enough. In 1948 the service station was sold to Morgan Kenny. At this time Danny and Dot had two children Sandra Lynne and Douglas Neil. Sandra started her schooling at Melrose and when it closed she and Doug rode their ponies to Pine Creek School, both finishing their education in Okotoks. Both Sandra and Doug were members of the Pine Creek Pony Club and were kept active participating in various local horse shows and gymkhanas. Doug married Bonnie Lynne Walkeden from Calgary. They have two children Travis Lane and Amy Joanne. They make their home in Calgary where Doug is active in the overhead door business. Sandra married David Neish from Aldersyde in 1971. They live on the same location as Danny and Dot. Sandra keeps busy at her job with an oil company in Calgary.

Dan Gerlitz family: L. to R.: John, Dot, Doug, Bonnie, Danny and Sandra.

In 1954 the government decided to widen the south highway. As the road was due to run through the front room of their home, they purchased thirty acres directly south of them from Frank Harmatta. On October 31st. they had the house moved to its new location on the S.E. 29-21-29-W4M where they have lived since. A new home was built here in 1975 and they are enjoying their life in it.

A second son Daniel (John) was born on May 12, 1956. He completed his education in Okotoks. John was a member of the 4 H Beef Club and also an avid sports fan. He is kept active reporting the Oiler hockey games to the local newspapers. John married Diana Brown from Okotoks in August, 1977. Their home is on

226

his grandfather's original homestead on N.E. 28-21-1 W5M. John keeps busy with his work on the farm.

Danny has been active in forming the original pony chuckwagon association and has been associated with it since its inception in 1952. At press time it appears that he may never retire from this sport! He also drove the Sicks Lethbridge Brewery Stagecoach for the fourteen years that it was operating in all the small parades. It was also entered in several Grey Cup Parades and the Expo Parade in Montreal.

Danny and his family enjoy their country lifestyle and although things have undergone a great change in the past years, their lives have been and continue to be packed full and running over with new places and new adventures.

Many of the readers might wonder at the difference in the spelling of Danny's surname. His spelling of Gerlitz was taken from his original birth certificate which he has used since.

ANDREW GIFFEN FAMILY — by Elsie Sharam
Arrival date: December 1924
Land location: W½ Sec. 16-21-29, W 4th.

Andrew and Annie Giffen, their son Sandy (Andrew James), their daughters, Elsie (Agnes Elizabeth) and Jessie Marie, after trailing the livestock from Orion, Alberta, settled on their farm three miles north of Okotoks, which they bought from Dick Meehan. This farm had a log house which was "The Halfway House" mentioned in Ralph Connor's book "Patrol Of the Sundance Trail."

Times were very hard, especially that first winter. There was no hay or grain for the stock. Ed Hayes gave Dad a stack of straw to tide him over, however the straw was not nutritious enough for such a hard winter and the stock did not have time to get acclimatized and adjusted before the hard winter set in. Nearly every morning there would be some animals dead. Somehow we got through the winter and we were all very glad when spring came.

The first time that we went to school Dad took us with a team and sleigh to Melrose school. I believe Beth Robinson was the teacher. Sandy often speaks of the time when Mr. Barrett, the minister who lived on a small parcel of land on the western edge of the Alex Currie farm, would drive by the school on a rainy day, try the hill by the school but fail to make it up. The teacher would send Sandy and a couple of other boys to push him up the hill. The boys would push him almost to the top, then pull him back down again. This would happen about three times and poor Mr. Barrett would decide it wasn't his day to go to town, however the boys would assure him that next time he would make it, and sure enough he would.

Work horses eventually were replaced by tractors. Dad's first tractor was a "Titan", he ran a threshing outfit in the area and often Mother did the cooking. Threshing time was exciting for us especially when Dad and Mother stocked the cook car in preparation for the threshing run. Sandy, Jessie and I had to do the chores while our parents were away threshing.

Mother stayed with Mrs. Dick Spackman when Mary was born. Mrs. Spackman looked after many mothers with babies in those days. While Mother was

Andrew and Annie Giffen 1944.

away we youngsters had the flu. I can remember being awake many nights and seeing the coal oil lamp burning all night.

As youngsters we had lots of good, simple fun. Jessie and I had our fun with horses, often riding many miles from home. Sandy was more interested in cars, tractors and machines.

On February 8th, 1935, at age fifteen, Jessie was killed on the highway while riding home from school. A high school dance had been planned for that night in De Winton. The dance went on as planned, but with no enthusiasm. The leader of the orchestra asked what was wrong with the crowd as usually everyone had a good time. After someone told him what had happened, he said. "Well what are we doing here? Let's go home". Those were sad days for us all.

Early in September everyone prepared for the school fair. Cooking, vegetables, school work, and animals were all part of the fair. What a fine time!

The second world war came and Sandy enlisted. While at Manning Pool in Toronto he met and married Arline Flynn. They have five children. Ronald is married and lives in Nelson, B.C., Kay lives in Calgary. Holly lives in Edmonton, and Terry and her husband, Terry McPhilamey, live in Cranbrook, B.C.

Sandy and Arline and their youngest daughter, Linden, live in Dawson Creek, B.C. from where Sandy farms in the Blueberry Mountain area of the Peace River country.

For many years Dad was president of the Okotoks Agricultural Society. This organization sponsored several plowing matches, some of the machine companies would loan tractors and plows for some of the participants. Our family was always well represented in these competitions. Mary entered the competition one year and won her class.

As years went by Dad became very interested in the production of pedigreed seed. He eventually became one of the best seed growers, specializing in barley, and in 1952, won the Robertson Associate Award, in recognition of his work for the seed industry in Canada. The seed inspectors liked coming to inspect Dad's grain because of the warm hospitality and Mother's delicious pie.

For a number of years Sandy farmed with his father, and also farmed the Squires place just north of Okotoks. He gave that up and moved to Dawson Creek B.C. where he operated a tractor parts business for a number of years, however he has sold his business and has gone back to farming.

Mary married Gordon Macaulay of Calgary, they both teach school in Calgary and live in Springbank. They had five children, Gordon, Laura, Heather, Margaret and Andrew.

Margaret was killed in a tractor accident in 1972, near C.F.C.N. at age 15. Elsie married Fred Sharam and lives in the Okotoks area.

Andrew died in May 1969, after a brief illness, at the age of 82. He tilled the soil until the year before he died.

The farm was sold to Alex Dietz in 1970.

Annie died in January 1976, at the age of 90. She lost her eyesight in 1968, and resided at Southwood nursing home, Calgary, for seven years previous to her death.

GORDON GIFFEN by Mary L. Macaulay

I remember Gordon Giffen from the time I was a very little girl. He had a special place in the family because he was a 'relative' (something quite rare for comparative newcomers to a district to have in the early thirties.) Gordon was Dad's second cousin and owned his own farm, SE¼ 5-21-29-W4, about two miles closer to Okotoks than we were.

I remember him at first as a frequent visitor whose quick movements, endless war stories, interest in politics, humorous stories, colorful language and rather rustic appearance all made him different from everyone else.

When I was about four years old Gordon was our hired man. He worked hard, talked long and, of course, called my dad "Andy" all the time. Beside that he helped to make my life a little more fun because he let me tag along when he walked over to the barn, a quarter mile away and even let me ride on top of a load of hay on the hay rack. He would sometimes play hide-and-seek with me which probably accounts for one of his life's bad moments. He was working on the pole for a horse drawn plough which happened to be situated behind a building. As he was working to sharpen the pole with a double bitted axe I crept around the corner to say "BOO" and scare him. I scared him alright because I caught the backswing of the axe across the tip of my nose, almost severing the tip. I imagine it was a very bloody, frightening sight. He took me up and carried me in to the house where Miss Gant, a trained nurse who was caring for Mother while she had rheumatic fever, bound the nose together.

Gordon helped off and on many time during his years as a bachelor. Not so often after he married and brought his bride to a new house he had built on his farm.

Gordon was a good worker but, more than anything, he liked to talk. He had seen many things in the first world war, some or which he would like to have forgotten. Stupidity and injustice upset him and he could wax eloquent about government bungling.

THE GRANT FAMILY — by Milton Grant and Gordon Grant

Ebenezer (known as "Ab") Grant came from the Ottawa Valley to De Winton on December 2, 1902 and rented the SW¼-34-21-29-W4. Ab married Bertha Robinson of Poltimore, Quebec in 1897 before coming West. He bought one-quarter section of 33-21-29-W4 for $6.00 per acre in 1903. He and his uncle Tom then went to Mossleigh and homesteaded the N½-2-21-2 in 1905. Then Ab came back to De Winton and bought one-quarter section of 34-21-29-W4 for $9.00 per acre in 1909. Then he bought the other quarter of 33-21-29 the same year.

They had a family of five boys and four girls; Ruby, May, Lola and Milton were born in the East. Gordon, Earl, Harold, Ralph and Muriel were born out West.

May, Lola, and Bertha Grant.

Ab did his farming with horses for a good many years, then he got modern and bought a tractor in 1920. He still used his horses for a good many jobs. Their life was very busy, bringing up their children and giving them a good education. They all attended the little school up the road, 1½ miles from home (Melrose School). A sight the "old-timers" will remember is Ab coming down the road with his shiny horse and buggy. Ab passed away in August 1949 and Bertha passed away in March 1960. They had thirteen grandchildren.

Ruby taught school for a time at Olds and Mossleigh, married Chauncey Coy, and passed away in 1959. May, now Mrs. N. Westergard, lives in Edmonton. Lola, now Mrs. L. Tyner, lives in Victoria. Earl died in 1919. Harold was in the army for five years. He married Jean White of Cochrane and farmed there until his death in 1962. Ralph married Julianna (June). He was in the army for several years and is now retired in Calgary. Gordon farmed for a while at Peace River and De Winton. He later went into the "Dude Ranching" business in the Cochrane and Bragg Creek areas. Muriel married Robin Echlin, ranched in the Cochrane area and now manages the Dude Ranch at Bragg Creek. Milton started farming the homestead at Mossleigh in 1917. He married Emma Cope in 1926 and farmed there until 1962. He then sold out and came back to De Winton where he is still farming the home place with his daughter Sharon and her husband George Naegeli. Milton is very active in the community. He belongs to the De Winton Community Club and is a director and active participant in the De Winton Riding Club with his four grandchildren.

GEORGE AND DESDEMONA GRAY — by Eleanor Macdonald

I hestitate to write in this book of early settlers of the De Winton District for we are not really considered Old Timers, however, I still look back upon my childhood days there with pleasure and gratitude.

My father, George Gray, came to Canada and fell in love with the country and the area and purchased S.W.¼-5-22-29-W4 and N.½-32-22-29-W4, from Mr. Whelan, who, I beleive, had homesteaded it. My father and his brother, Charlie, owned a prosperous shoe store in Galesburg, Illinois, which they sold. Charlie went to California and George came to Canada. Alberta was then still called the North-West-Territories.

The family came early in the spring of 1903 on an immigrant train. The family, furniture, farm, implements, cows, horses, and sheep all riding the same train. I remember that it was very cold but there was a sturdy two roomed building on the N.E.¼ into which we soon settled, with as much furniture as would fit. The remainder sat out in packing cases for over a year, even our precious piano, which took several trips, by stoneboat, to concerts in the school houses etc. This piano is still in use in our family. It has served four generations and is in fine condition. It is used daily by our grandson.

My father was no farmer except at heart. However, he learned much from books and more from experience. He enjoyed every minute of it. He was a truly "happy man" and soon became known, far and wide, as "Daddy Gray".

We called our farm "The Grange" and, in the spring of the following year, the house was moved to the S.W.¼-5-22-29-W4. A large barn was built, also, two separate rooms which, in our dreams, were to be granaries when we built our house — "SOMEDAY". Now we could unpack more of our things and make a comfortable home which my mother always called "The Shacks".

My mother had been a school teacher and had little experience with farm life but she soon learned to

Mr. and Mrs. G. W. Gray, 1916.

make butter and bread and cheese and to raise chickens and to work in the garden. She was most interested in all community work, especially in the Church and Missionary Society. She taught in the Sunday School and, in our little Pine Creek Church, she organized one of the very first C.G.I.T. Groups in Canada.

When the Community Hall was to be built, she took a very active part in fund raising by putting on concerts and plays, with the wonderful help of the whole Community.

My older sisters, Mary and Edith, both went to Pine Creek School until they were ready for High School. They both attended Sacred Heart Convent in Calgary. Mary specialized in music and became an accomplished musician. In 1909, she married Robert Porter Rogers of Clayton, New York. Mary and Rob had six children, three girls and three boys. The two oldest were born in Canada before the family left to take up permanent residence in Detroit Mich. Mary passed away in 1966 and Rob, two years earlier.

Edith finished her teacher training but, after a long illness, died at the age of nineteen. She was the first of our family to be buried in Pine Creek Cemetery.

My two older sisters were almost ready to leave Pine Creek School before I started. I think we drove to school together for a year or so. When I was on my own, I usually rode horseback but, when I was made official "Water Bearer", I drove with a tank of water on the back of the buggy.

229

I have many happy memories of Pine Creek. Though I seldom see friends that were made there, they are still warmly remembered. The wild games that we played, running miles through the woods, over streams, up and down hills and "Hares and Hounds" at noon hour. The boys were usually the "Hares" and always led us a merry chase. Our lunches were eaten under the boughs of the huge, "Big Tree". In spring the boys would shinny far up into the branches and bring back a treasure of spruce gum to us. Beautiful secret spots in the woods, a very special one, we called Violet Vale, where Vera and I used to find the biggest, bluest violets in the world. We thought it was our own secret but I hope generations of other children have found it and loved it as we did. There was baseball, Anti-I-Over, Fox and Geese, and I wonder where we got the energy and where it has gone now?

Vera and I were able to take our grade nine at Pine Creek but had to go to Calgary for our High School. We completed that at Crescent Heights. On looking back on those happy days I wonder at the freedom we had and the fact that I cannot remember one ugly word or action and I wish we could give our children and grandchildren that same joy and peace that we knew.

As I grew older, I was able to take on some of my mother's duties, at home as well as in the community. I took a Sunday School class and played the organ in the Pine Creek Church (very badly), from the time that I was big enough for my feet to reach the pedals. Many times my fingers ached with the Week's accumulated cold, which I industriously pumped out on the organ keys. Bobby Pratt, a great old Scot Presenter, helped by beating time, with vigour, and led the singing with a fine, strong voice. I remember some Sundays when the service was held around the big coal heater, it was too cold to leave it. I loved that little church and it was here, in 1919, that I was married to John A. Macdonald and here too, our first two babies were baptized.

My parents were both in poor health after the war, at the time of my marriage, and so were glad to sell the home quarter to my husband and to rent him the other half. Here we lived for another seven years and then Jack went to work for the Soldier Settlement Board. For many years we intended to return but the depression caught us and we never made it except for short periods of time. During the period from 1927-1947, the farm was rented out and in 1947, we sold it.

My father passed away in 1922 and my mother in 1941. They are both laid to rest in Pine Creek Cemetery.

JAMES GRIERSON — compiled by Mrs. Jean Grierson and Mrs. Norma Grierson Malin — May, 1976

The Grierson family of Pine Creek, Alberta, find their origins in Scotland. James Grierson was born in the year 1820, at or near Edinburgh, Scotland. In common with many other Scotsmen, his ancestry can be traced to King Alpin of Scotland. His father and also his grand-father were officers in the Royal Navy. His father was a Lieutenant on H.M.S. Victory in 1810. This ship carried a crew of eight hundred men and had been the flag-ship of Lord Horatio Nelson.

The obituary of James Grierson published in the January, 1903 issue of the Calgary Herald states he was the second son of Lieutenant John Grierson of The Royal Navy.

In June, 1822, James Grierson, not yet two years old, found himself, with his parents, brothers and sisters living in March township, Carlton County, Upper Canada. This place was about twenty-five miles from where the city of Ottawa now stands. At this date, adjoining Torbolton township, was being surveyed and divided into lots. In 1825, the family had chosen 800 acres of land in Torbolton township (this land was granted to Lieutenant John Grierson for his service in the Royal Navy) and the family had erected a temporary two storey log home, which now is being preserved by the Trefoil Guild. Here James Grierson received his education in a private log school built and financed by his father and the two or three neighboring families. The public school system had not yet been introduced. In 1833, this area was mapped by Lieutenant John Grierson, R.N. This map is preserved in the Public Archives of Canada and shows the names of land owners and road allowances, not yet built. At this date, the Ottawa River served as their highway. Lieutenant John Grierson was appointed the first superintendent of highways for this area.

In December, 1843, James Grierson took a bride, Elizabeth, the daughter of Captain Alexander MacMillan of adjoining Fitzroy township. She was born in Canada. During the following years, this marriage was blessed with twelve children. James Grierson and his wife knew the heart break of losing children to the dreaded ravages of unchecked contagious disease, only seven children survived.

During these passing years James Grierson was a busy man. He assisted in the family square timber business. He made many journeys, dangerous and exhausting, down the Ottawa and St. Lawrence rivers with long cribs of square timber, to be loaded on ships at Quebec City. This timber was used for ship building in Scotland or England. It has been said that some of these cribs of timber, composed of many rafts joined together were sometimes one-half mile long. Some historians have placed their value at ten to fifteen thousand dollars. It is said that after going through the rapids encountered in the Ottawa River near Montreal, the rafts had to be rebuilt. On the return journey home they bought merchandise to supply the settlers needs. In those days it was a major calamity to lose a darning needle, since it could be months before a new needle could be obtained.

Time brought changes. The price of square timber declined. In the summer of 1870 a huge forest fire swept through Carlton and Lanark Counties, destroying timber, homes and livestock, and in some places the land, exposing barren rock. Since misfortunes never occur singly, there was also a depression.

During some of this time James Grierson served as a justice of the peace. The 1863 Walling map of Torbolton township shows the letters of J.P. after his name.

James Grierson found himself with a grown family of four sons, James O., William, David and Alexander and three daughters, Annie, Mary and Jessie. They all wanted the opportunity to create their own homes. The future appeared dim in depressed Torbolton township. The railroad to the west was being built and the government was attracting people to this new land by putting up posters and advertisements, painting glowing pictures of the golden opportunities in the west.

In August of 1883, the Grierson family came west, to what was then the Northwest Territories. It is not known how they came, possibly by wagon train or on the newly completed railroad, which had been opened to Calgary in the same year. One can only surmise the hardships they must have endured coming to a frontier land in the fall of the year, with no home to go to and no provisions for the winter stored up from the previous summer. One wonders about the Indian tribes that were prevalent in this area at the time, as it was just six years after the Custer massacre and many surviving Indians came to Canada to escape retribution from United States Troops.

In 1884, some of the Grierson family were living in the Pine Creek and De Winton area of Alberta, according to the obituary of a son, James O. A. Grierson. At this date, James Grierson was now sixty-four years of age. The family somehow survived the dreadful winter of 1886. No information survives to tell us of the losses they probably endured that winter, as did all cattlemen.

We know very little of their life at this time. James Grierson was active in the Presbyterian Church at Pine Creek. His son William registered cattle brand 3ky for the years 1901 and 1903. His daughter Annie (Mrs. George Hedley) made a record of the births and deaths of her children on the inside cover of an Okotoks post office manual. This sad record showed that four of her children died on different days during the month of June, 1886. His daughter Jessie married Johnston Stevenson, and they lived on a homestead at Airdrie, Alberta, where they also operated one of the first half way houses between Calgary and Edmonton. Here probably many weary travellers found rest for a night during the Klondike gold rush of 1898. His daughter Mary married Hugh S. McLeod, a Calgary hotel owner and businessman. Her son Major Wm. McLeod, served in World War I. Her daughter Jessie was Queen of the Calgary Winter Carnival in 1925. James Orion Alexander Grierson was the only son to marry and raise a family. He married Miss Isabelle Galloway in 1892. They had sons Donald, John, David, Hugh and Robert, also one daughter Bessie who later married Ross Robinson.

James O. A. Grierson moved with his family to Lacombe in 1910. He took up farming in the district and was active in community affairs, serving on the school board as secretary-treasurer of the Elkhorn school district, councillor for the municipal district of Fertile Valley and was also a member of the Lacombe and District Old-Timers Association. Today only one of James O. A. Grierson's children survives him, Hugh Allan Grierson who resides with his wife Pearl in the town of Ponoka. His other children (with the exception of Donald who never married) raised families, most of them still are living in the Province of Alberta.

Several of James Grierson's descendants defended their country in World Wars I and II. John and Donald served in World War I and Hugh in World War II, also

his grandson Major James William (Bill) McLeod, son of Mary Grierson McLeod.

The name of James and his brother John Grierson have been family names for many generations before him and since and still survive today in 1976, in the names of his great-grandchildren's families. He passed away in January, 1903, at De Winton, at the home of his son William. He was buried at Pine Creek cemetery, located approximately six miles south of Calgary on highway No. 2. He was a true pioneer of Canada, breaking new ground as a child and man in Torbolton township, near Ottawa, then in his later years at Pine Creek, Alberta.

JAMES O. A. AND ISOBEL (GALLOWAY) GRIERSON — by Mrs. David Grierson

Mr. James Grierson was born in Tarboton, Ontario, April 28th, 1857 and lived there until he was a young man. In 1884 he came to Alberta and settled in the Okotoks district. In 1892 he married Isobel Galloway of Brandon, Manitoba. Mrs. Grierson was born in Aurora, Ontario, November 4th, 1876. To this union, six children were born; Donald James, May 22nd, 1893, died May 10th, 1955. Donald served overseas in the First World War.

John Andrew born September 26th, 1895. John served overseas in W.W. 1 in the 21st Reserve Battalion of Alberta, from May 1918 to June 1919. Part of this time was spent in England. He married Sadie

Mr. J. A. O. Grierson about 1940.

Mrs. J. A. O. Grierson, 1940.

Madden October 1st, 1929. There were seven children; Allen, Mildred, Norma, Annie, James, John and Milton, and these seven have a total of eighteen children. John Sr. died February 15th, 1939 in the Lacombe Hospital. Sadie is living at Chilliwack, B.C.

David Alexander, born January 7th, 1899, married February 15th, 1927 to Edna Patterson. They have two girls, Joy and Mae. Joy has three girls and Mae has one boy. David died of a heart attack September 10th, 1972 at the home of his daughter, Joy, southwest of Leduc. Edna is living in Wetaskiwin, Alta.

Bessie was born in 1905 and in 1922 married Ross Robinson. They had six children; Kathleen, John, Margaret, Patricia, William and Lorraine. John is deceased, William not married, Kathleen no children, and the others have a total of eight children.

The Jim Grierson family, Jack, Dave, Donald, back Hugh and Bessie, Front.

Hugh Allen born January 30th, 1906. Married to Pearl Douglas September 1st, 1958 and they are living in Ponoka, Alta.

Robert was born February 7th, 1910, married Vivian Morrow June 10th, 1946 and had three children,

Robert, Vera and Hazel. They have one child each. Robert Sr. passed away February 3rd, 1955.

Mr. Grierson used to run the Grierson Post Office about four miles south east of De Winton. There is also a hill called the "Grierson Hill" down near Melrose School. He was also Treasurer of the Melrose School District and a councillor in the M.D. of Sheep Creek.

In 1910 he and his family moved to the Elkhorn district near Lacombe, where he lived till he passed away May 9th, 1942, at the ripe old age of 85. He was predeceased by his wife March 25th, 1940.

FURTHER TO JAMES O. A. GRIERSON — by Laura Norris

Mr. Grierson was a real old-timer in this district. When he came to this part of the country he bought a quarter-section of land located at N.W.21-21-29-W4M. He built a small house at the bottom of a hill and had a spring just a few yards from his house — just a shallow well but real good water which is still in use and to my knowledge has never gone dry. To a good many people this hill is still called the Grierson Hill.

In the minutes of the first Melrose School book in 1889, the people decided they needed a school near by. In 1890 another meeting was called. They decided to build a school and call it Melrose School District No. 166. Mr. Grierson was nominated the first secretary which position he held for some years, so he must have been here before that date. His father and mother lived not far from him for a short while.

He had three sisters. Mrs. George Hedley lived on a farm southwest of her brother. Their daughter married Mr. McLennan and lived across the road from her mother. While here they had two children. Hugh and Annie.

Old-timers will remember the old Grand Central Hotel on Ninth Avenue in Calgary. It was owned and operated by another sister of Jim Grierson and her husband, Mr. and Mrs. Hugh McLeod (Mary). The other sister, Jessie, was here a few times. She married Mr. Stevenson and I never saw her again.

In far off Brandon, Manitoba, a young lady called Isabell Galloway decided to come to Calgary to find work and perhaps make a fortune. She found work in Mr. McLeod's hotel. Here she met Jim Grierson. They were married and came to live in Melrose district.

Mr. Grierson also had three brothers: Bill, Dave and Alexander. All remained bachelors. Bill lived near De Winton and after a good many years passed away. Dave bought the place the McLennans lived on and lived there until he passed away. Jim was the only one of the men to get married and raise a family. The Griersons had five boys and one girl; Donald, Jack, Dave, Bessie, Bob and Hughie.

In the early days, the King's mail was carried from De Winton to Gladys Ridge by horses and a buggy of some sort, which did not keep the driver warm in the winter. More Post Offices were set up and Mr. Grierson's home was chosen for the Melrose district. This Post Office was given the name "Grierson", and the family ran the post office until they sold the farm and went north, which was a long time ago.

At this time Father, Mother and myself and two sisters, Ethel and Cora lived about a mile north of the

Mr. and Mrs. Jack Grierson and family in 1937.

Griersons. Then our home was moved on to the quarter-section just east of theirs, which our parents (Mr. and Mrs. W. J. Andrews) had bought, so we had only a five minute walk from the Post Office and the Grierson home. We all took our public school education at Melrose School. All the Grierson children were born on their Melrose farm, and later they moved north of Ponoka.

Mrs. Grierson, not liking the north, came back with her daughter. When Dave Sr. passed away, she looked after the farm, milked the cows, had a big garden and lots of flowers. She passed away very suddenly while living in the district.

In 1926 or 27, Jack worked for my husband, Howard Norris, in the summer. At that time he and his wife Sadie and their two children, stayed with his mother.

Dave married Edna Patterson, a Calgary girl. Bessie married Ross Robinson and lived in Calgary. She passed away a very young woman, leaving six children; one a small baby, who her cousin, Annie, kept and looked after. Donald was like his mother, always thin, but able to work and make a good living. Jack was like his Father, strong and healthy. Hugh and Bob were too young when they left here, for me to know very well. The boys' cousin, Norma (Jack's daughter) wrote that Hugh was the only one still living and was still up north.

THE HAGERMAN FAMILY — by W. E. (Bill) and Muriel Hagerman

Mr. and Mrs. J. F. Hagerman (my parents) moved to De Winton in 1942 to the Melrose district, although they still retained their residence in Calgary. While here Dad operated a Holstein dairy located on the SW¼ 28-21-29-W4M. Subsequently, he sold the dairy in 1947 to myself.

I (Bill) also bought an acre of land located on the NW¼ 21-21-29-W4M from Mr. Mel Martin in 1946 and built a service station here that summer. Mr. John

Norris constructed the entire building from material obtained at the De Winton Airport. In 1948, I sold this business to Mr. Les Pennock.

When Muriel and myself moved to De Winton, our family consisted of Glenda, Miss Calgary of 1961; and Melba, a former Western Airlines' stewardess and executive secretary. Glenda Rowe is presently an executive secretary in Vancouver and Melba Davidson is a bookkeeper for her husband's chain of seven restaurants in Portland, Oregon, U.S.A. While living in De Winton, Donna and Carrol arrived. Donna is a University of Calgary graduate and City of Calgary policewoman. Carrol, now Mrs. Dunkley, is a physical education teacher at a Grande Prairie high school. Her husband Gord also teaches physical education at the college in Grande Prairie.

Just when everyone thought we were trying to start our own girls' basketball team, we had twin boys, Brian and Brent. I will inform everyone how this happened. The wife wished for a boy and I wished for a boy. We both received our wishes, simple as that. Brian and Brent still live with us. Brian is in the Faculty of Commerce at the University of Calgary and Brent has switched from that route to major in Journalism at Mount Royal College.

We moved from De Winton to Calgary in 1961, where we live on the west edge of the city and still operate a riding academy.

While living in De Winton, we had many interesting experiences, like importing an Indian boy to obtain the required number of pupils to keep Melrose School open. However, I do not wish to be guilty of monopolizing more than my share of this book. I considered it a privilege, while living in De Winton, to be surrounded by wonderful people. One small observation: we invariably all had one common denominator — agriculture. I also enjoyed the friendship and association as a member of the different organizations in De Winton, Okotoks, Melrose and Davisburg.

MR. AND MRS. C. HAM — by J. McGOUGAN

There was ten acres between the Bow and the old railroad grade purchased by C. C. Snowden of "Sliptivity" fame on which he built a summer home. This was the home of Mr. and Mrs. C. Ham when we, the Wonnacotts, moved to Strathpine. Mr. Ham was a C.P.R. employee who used to walk to the Macleod Trail to catch a ride to and from work and walk home. Their daughter, Martha, a stenographer in a large American city, home one year for a vacation, met and married, Alex Sangster, a veteran of the first world war and a confirmed bachelor. His property in the valley and on top was between us and Heaver's. They had two daughters (Jane and Sue). After Alex died, Vic Heaver bought the property and Martha and the girls moved to Grand Forks, B.C. Martha died while Mother was still alive. I haven't kept in touch since.

THE HAWTHORNE FAMILY

Billie or Will Hawthorne came from Ontario to Manitoba, where he homesteaded and farmed with oxen. Later, he moved to Winnipeg to work for the T. Eaton Co.

In 1916, with his wife, May, and three children,

Ethel, Ingram and Jay, he came to Okotoks and hauled freight to the new Turner Valley Oil fields, first with horses and later with trucks.

During the 1920's, the Hawthornes farmed east of Okotoks on Gladys Ridge.

Billie took pride in good horses and harness, and he raised and fitted teams, which were in demand at that time in Eastern Canada.

The Hawthornes moved to land north of Okotoks, and in the early thirties, built a house and farm buildings.

May died and Billie's health failed, and he died in 1942.

Ingram took over the farm in 1943, and spent many years clearing and breaking the land. He took a great interest in, and collected many Indian arrow heads and stone tools that turned up, as he cleared the land.

It is rather wry to note that to-day, the land that took so long to clear and break, is once more growing trees...this time to provide shade trees for Calgary homes.

Ingram now lives in Lethbridge.

Jay spent the war years overseas in the Canadian Army. He then farmed for a number of years in the Olds area. For the past 15 years, he has operated hardware stores at Milk River and Claresholm.

THE HEAVER FAMILY — by Ted Heaver

William Brown Heaver and his two sons, Gordon and Victor (birth and death details given below) arrived in Calgary from England July, 1909. They settled on the NE¼ of Section 5-22-29-W4th Meridian in the De Winton area. Total farm was made up of Section 8 (that portion south of the Bow River) and three quarters of Section 5 adjoining Section 8.

William Brown Heaver was born in 1867 and died in 1929 in England. W. G. S. (Gordon) Heaver was born in 1887 and died in 1951 in Calgary. H. V. (Victor) Heaver was born in 1889 and died in 1967 in Calgary.

Family of W. G. S. (Gordon) Heaver as follows: W. G. S. (Gordon) Heaver married Bessie G. Pitchford in Calgary in 1922 and resided at De Winton. Mrs. Bessie G. Heaver is presently residing in her Calgary residence in very good health. They had two sons and one daughter, as follows: W. E. (Ted) Heaver, born 1923; married Muriel C. McLellan 1949; now residing at 404 Wilverside Way, Calgary. They had two children: Joyce (Mr. and Mrs. Dave Woolridge) residing on a farm at High River with one son, Craig,

William Brown Heaver, about 1916.

Back Row: — Will Pitchford, 3rd Row: — Mrs. A. Wooding, Mrs. G. Heaver, Victor Heaver, Mrs. W. Heaver, Gordon Heaver. 2nd Row: — Tim Snell, W. Heaver, Arthur Wooding, Mrs. W. Pitchford. Front Row; — Pete Wooding, Janet Pitchford, (Early 20's).

and Ronald G. Heaver residing in Calgary. The second son, Victor N. Heaver, was born in 1924 and married Joyce Harvey in 1957 and now reside at De Winton and operate the farm there. Daughter, Eva Mary Heaver was born in 1926 and married W. L. Templeton. Mr. and Mrs. Templeton now reside at 620 Britannia Drive, Calgary with two daughters; Sally Marie, born 1966, and Ida Sue, born in 1967.

Previous to the Heaver family settling at De Winton, the farm first homesteaded by Joe Moss (approximately 1885) who remained there until 1900. He then moved to Mossleigh, and we understand that town was named after him. Joe Moss sold the De Winton farm to people named "Troutons" who in turn sold to my grandfather, father and uncle in 1909.

THOMAS WILLIAM AND WINNIE (PEGLER) HEBSON — by T. W. Hebson

I was born in Penrith, Cumberland, England in 1906. I have one brother and three sisters, who still live there. I emigrated to Canada on the ship "Montcalm", in the spring of 1927, arriving in Quebec after about ten days from sailing date. I boarded a train, along with many others, and headed west to Alberta. When the train stopped at Killam, I got off and inquired about farm jobs. I immediately got one, working for Mr. Gibb. He did mixed farming and also had a herd of purebred Angus Cattle. Mr. Gibb showed some of his cattle at the summer shows, at which time, his son, Ken, and I, had the job of showing and looking after them. I worked at this place for eighteen months, then went to De Winton, working for Mr. R. Ness, who ran a dairy farm. After I left there, I worked for Mr. F. Dick and later for Mr. J. Cole, in 1929. This was dairy and mixed farming. When working there, I met my future wife, Winnifred Pegler, the eldest daughter of Mr. and Mrs. P. Pegler. She was born and raised at Sandstone, and had most of her schooling at Panima School. I left Coles in 1932, and then I decided to look for a place of my own. There was a quarter section of land for sale, belonging to Mrs. Isabel Grierson, which was just a few miles away. This was N.W.¼-17-21-29-W4 and was situated between De Winton and Okotoks. I decided to buy this and put a down payment on it and moved on in the spring of 1933. There was only a one room shack, 14 by 20 feet, and several log and straw buildings on the place. The land was covered mostly with willow bush and some poplars, with only a few acres of broken land. It was bordered on the west by a big coulee and the main line of the C.P.R. I went to farm sales to purchase horses, cattle and machinery to start my farming operation. There was no drinking water here so it had to be carried from the neighbours. My neighbours, at that time, were; Mrs. Isabel Grierson, James (Scotty) Vert, Jim Beattie, Bob Nicholson, the Joe Blains, Boyd Hayes, A. Giffen, Herb Currie, John and Norma Adams and Tommy Young. By spring of 1934, I decided that I had enough of batching, Winnie took pity on me and we were married, in the Anglican Church, in Okotoks, April 2, 1934.

Tom and Winnie Hebson wedding April 2, 1934.

The next few years were busy ones for us. We had our shack remodelled, building on a couple of rooms etc., getting more brush cut to clear land for breaking. The willow bush made good fence posts and also firewood for our two stoves. Jim Beattie and Tommy Young helped to saw this wood, using Tommy's old Waterloo tractor. I also had a well drilled. We milked quite a few cows and also had a lot of pigs and poultry. I started raising purebred Hampshire sheep in 1937, when I got three head of sheep, in payment, for shearing Mr. Frank Wonnacott's sheep. I used hand shears and got about 5¢ to 10¢ a head for shearing sheep in the 1930's and 1940's. I started exhibiting sheep in the Calgary Fall Show and Sale, in 1938, and showed sheep for many years in exhibitions from Toronto to Vancouver and was fortunate in winning many ribbons and trophies. I also raised purebred Shorthorn cattle. In 1940, my neighbour, Mrs. Grierson, died and I bought her land which was adjacent to mine. I was farming with horses till 1945 when I bought my first tractor. By then I was doing custom farming besides my own. I was gradually getting more buildings to replace the old, log ones. Our family was growing by this time and we needed a bigger and better house. We purchased one from Turner Valley, in 1949, and had it moved to the present location. It was a lot bigger and quite modern.

During the years in the 1950's, we were hailed out many times, but had enough feed for our stock, which carried us through. We got Calgary power in 1956, replacing the 32 volt plant, which we had since 1951. We started using propane in our stove and furnace in 1955 and continued till natural gas was installed in this district, about 1965. This was a welcome change for us as now we had electric power, gas and water in our house.

T. W. Hebson family. From back, L. to R. Bill Jackson, Bill Hebson, Linda, Bob, Pat, Dorothy, Tom, Winnie, Joan, George Jackson, Kathy Hebson, Heather Jackson, Karen Hebson, Susan and Ryan Hebson. 1976.

We have raised four children; Bill, born in 1937, Dorothy, born in 1940, Bob, born in 1943 and Linda, born in 1952. They have all been active in 4-H activities, Okotoks 4-H Beef Club, and Foothills 4-H Sheep Club. They have each won 4-H trips, trophies, etc. and, throughout the years, each has held executive positions in these clubs. The two girls each had a flock of purebred Southdown sheep, which they showed at exhibitions during some of their years at home. Bill started to school at Melrose then to Okotoks and, for several years, rode horseback to Stormount, three miles away. Dorothy and Bob rode horseback to Stormount and, when this school closed, they went, by bus, to Okotoks. Linda went to Okotoks.

Bill married Patricia Downard, a Calgary girl, in 1960. They live on the former "Dave Lewis" farm, known as "Hillside Farm", three miles north of Okotoks. They have two daughters, Karen and Kathy.

Dorothy was a school teacher at the Priddis School and in 1962, she was married to William B. Jackson of Millarville. They live four miles north of the Millarville Race Track. They have a son, George and a daughter, Heather.

Bob married Joan Britton, also a Calgary girl, in 1965. They live in Calgary and have two children; a son, Bryan and a daughter, Susan.

Linda lives and works in Calgary, is very fond of the outdoors, enjoys horseback riding and likes animals.

We have had a busy, full life with some good times, and some, not so good, such as hail storms that finished our crops and garden. We always planted a big garden. Then there were the many times that we had to protect our home from the grass fires, started by the C.P.R. trains. We used to enjoy the De Winton Community Picnics and the neighbourhood card parties. We have had an active part in community affairs. I have been on the executive committees, beginning in 1942, on the Okotoks 4-H Beef Club, in the organization of the Foothills Sheep Club, in 1952, and on the Alberta Sheep Breeders', Millarville and Okotoks Agricultural Societies, the Calgary Stampede Board and St. Peter's Church.

We have sold all our cattle and sheep and part of our land. My last year of showing sheep was in 1973. I am now retired and hope to be able to stay on the farm for a few more years. I am still active in the 4-H Sheep Club, Agricultural Society etc. We both take an interest in the community affairs. We took a trip back to England in 1969 to see my folks but wouldn't want to live there now. There has been a lot of changes around here since I came in 1933, however, I have never regretted coming to Canada.

EDWARD WILLIAM HEBSON

I was born in a nursing home in Okotoks, in 1937, and was raised on my parents' farm, north of Okotoks, with my sisters, Dorothy and Linda and brother, Bob. I attended Melrose School with neighbours Carolyn and Leonard Rosicki when the teacher was Miss Helen Kennaugh (now Mrs. Ed. Jones, a neighbour). The school kids hauled water, by bucket, from nearby Martin farm. I then went to Okotoks School for two years and remember Mrs. Rhine and Miss MacKay as teachers. For the next five years, my sister, Dorothy, and brother, Bob, and I, went to Stormount School on horseback, opening and shutting numerous gates through the Eric Goddard, Bill Heater, Jack Dafoe and Singh farms. I remember that in the ninth grade the Stormount baseball team was the best in the area. I was the catcher. I then attended Okotoks School again but, this time, travelled by school bus. During this time I was active in both Sheep and Beef Clubs.

I worked for a time in the Banff National Park during the construction of the Transcontinental Highway. In 1957, in partnership with P. B. Milligan, we constructed and operated the Okotoks Feed Mill. In 1959 I sold my interest in the Feed Mill and went to work in the Swan Hills Oil Fields. In June, 1960, I married Patricia Downard and lived in Calgary, working for Barber Machinery. Also, I leased land and farmed in the Okotoks area. In 1964, I bought the Dave Lewis Place and have enjoyed farming and raising Shorthorn and Limousin cattle.

I have two daughters. Karen, born in 1963 and Kathy, born in 1965. They attend Okotoks Junior High School. The new Percy Pegler Elementary School, opened in 1976, was named after their great-grandfather. They have taken active parts in the Foothills 4H Sheep Club, The Okotoks Beef Club, Brownies, Girl Guides and the Okotoks School Band.

There have been many changes over the past few years and, looking out our windows at night, one sees many, many, sub-division yard-lights twinkling.

THE HISTORY OF A FARM ON 26-21-29 W4th — by David J. Hunt
BRYCE WRIGHT

Snake Creek meanders through Sections 26 and 35, running from the south and heading for the Bow. It takes a loop into Section 36 and just before cutting back into 35, the old Blackfoot Trail crosses it on its way to Calgary. Near the centre of 26, which was Hudson's Bay land, Bryce Wright located a farm about 1901 or 1902. Mr. Wright had homesteaded on the South East of Section 34 just to the west, but decided to move. This was probably because of the location of a good spring of fresh water along Snake Creek in the North East of 26-21-29 W4th. Alex Currie lived on the South East of Section 34 before he was married.

The West half of this section was still held by the Hudson's Bay Co., but in 1903, Mr. Maxwell bought the South West of 36-21-29 and in 1904, Bryce Wright acquired the North West quarter.

Mr. Wright was a cousin of John Turner and Peter Turner-Bone, and they had all immigrated from Scotland late in the 19th century. He had married one of the Anderson girls from Sheep Creek and then promptly had Mr. Minue build them a house just above the clearwater spring. This house still stands on the site, with some additions and modifications.

Bryce Wright had a glass eye, and enjoyed the odd nip from time to time, as did his cousins from Scotland, but this in no way hindered him from raising registered Shorthorns and Clydesdale horses. He also grazed sheep, which tended to stray from time to time, causing consternation to his neighbours. It has been purported that Mr. Wright came to Canada with about $90,000.00, so his holdings were significant. Roy Maxwell worked for Mr. Wright part-time, doing general farm work. On one occasion, Roy was asked to deliver a large Clydesdale stallion to John Turner's near Calgary, and not to raise a hair of sweat. The stud had been in the barn for some time, and was full of life. Mr. Wright suggested that Roy lead the animal the fourteen or fifteen miles on foot, but this request was refused, in favor of leading him with a saddle horse, which he did. Roy didn't get any dinner that day at Turner's, for he was quite late, trying to keep the horse from over-exerting.

Mr. Maxwell also did some plowing for Mr. Wright, supplying his own team and plow for the rate of $2.50 per acre. This was for stubble — the going rate for sod was $4.00 to $4.50 per acre. Dunc MacIntosh broke 90 acres on the South East of 26 with a fourteen inch Verity walking plow, pulled by four horses hitched two and two. The plow cost $14.00.

AILSA CRAIG

Bryce Wright called his place "Ailsa Craig Farm" in those days. Bill Durno, the venerable deacon of auctioneers, spent some of his first years in Canada on this farm. He had known Mr. Wright in the old country. John and Robert Turner, cousins of Mr. Wright, who had located just south of Calgary, were brothers. They built two large houses on the east side of the Macleod Trail, fairly close together.

It seems there was a falling out between them or their wives. A large fence was built between the houses and it was quite noticeable that all the window blinds were kept drawn on that side of the house facing the other. John Turner ran for the Alberta legislature against George Hoadley in one election, but was defeated. Bryce Wright sold the place in the spring of 1913.

THE SANGSTERS

Alex and George Sangster were brothers and they had come to Alberta from B.C. They took over this farm after Mr. Wright, and continued to raise Shorthorns until they sold to Charlie Beeching about 1918.

CHARLIE BEECHING

The farm, during the early years, contained three-quarters of Section 26 and the south half of 35. Harold Banister owned the North East of 35 earlier on, but this was later added to the farm also. Charlie Beeching was married to Frank McHugh's sister, Kathleen. They spent the summer months living on the farm, but also kept a home in Calgary. Mr. Beeching had come from the Chilcotin district of British Columbia. Fred McCall and Charlie flew together on occasion. McCall would land his plane on the McNeill quarter to the north and pick up Charlie.

HUNTER STOCK FARM

Very little is known about the period when Mr. Hunter owned the place. It was a time when ownership seemed to change regularly and the owners didn't operate the farm themselves, but had hired help on the place. Mr. Hunter moved to the Bahamas.

BROWNLEE

Mr. Brownlee acquired the farm in about 1938. He was the owner of Bruce Robinson Electric in Calgary, and never did live on the farm. During his ownership, a watering system from the springs was developed. Over a half-mile of one inch pipe was laid to bring water from a spring south of the buildings, down through the garden and corrals, to supplement the spring below the house. Sam Burgomaster worked on the place until he went to the war in 1942.

ERNIE HERBIG

Mr. Herbig bought the 940 acre farm in 1946, and raised registered Herefords. The Herbigs were from the High River area, and during their three year tenancy, had quite a bit of remodelling done on the house.

THE HUNTS

Harold Hunt had retired from the ranch at Endiang in 1943, and bought a house in Calgary. Florence and their youngest son, David, who was attending school in Calgary, saw little of their husband and dad, because he was frequently back out at the ranch. He found the inactivity of retirement hard to take, so in the spring of 1949, he bought the De Winton farm that had been changing hands so often, and came out of his very short retirement.

It was operated under the name of H. Hunt and Son until Harold's death in 1957. David had married Connie Herr in 1955, and they and their family, Danny, Peter, Chris and Celia, continue to operate the farm.

The history of a farm on 26-21-29-4. David Huut, De Winton. Present Owner.

Registered Herefords under the herd name "Ribstone", and commercial beef have been raised on the land since the Hunt's acquired it. The holdings have grown somewhat and now consist of over 1700 acres. The business was incorporated in 1972, and is now Ribstone Cattle Co. Ltd.

Having been located in the middle of the section, this farm had over one-half mile of private road across the fields, and another half-mile of road allowance that wasn't much better. As Bill Durno said to my Father after we had bought it, "It's a fine farm, Harold, but it's one Hell of a road into it."

MR. AND MRS. JAMES ALEXANDER HOGGE

Mr. Hogge came to Calgary in 1885 from Inverness, Quebec, and worked for a few years in construction work. He homesteaded in the Melrose district, (at that time it was called the Rosebud district). He returned to Calgary the following year, when he helped in the construction of the Langevin bridge. Later he bought a farm south-west of Okotoks.

In 1901 he bought the following land: S.E. ¼ 8-21-29-W4, N.E. ½ 5-21-29-W4, and farmed there until the time of his death, August 2, 1950 at the age of 83. He was well known in the district as a breeder of Clydesdale draft horses, and had won many prizes and gold medals at the Calgary Exhibitions and Okotoks Fairs.

In the early days in Okotoks, he had been director of the Okotoks Society. He was one of the first trustees of the Okotoks School board and held that position until the 1920's.

On March 4, 1903, he married Lillie Orilla Currie. They had seven children: Pearl (Mrs. George Riches), Lorne, of Okotoks, Norman of Okotoks, Albert (Bert) of Edmonton, twins — John who died March 15, 1931 and Lillian Armstrong, and Harvey of Edmonton.

Mrs. Hogge came to the district in 1886 with her parents Mr. and Mrs. John Currie. She died February 5, 1958 at the age of 78.

When we were small, she sewed all of our clothes, including our coats. How well we remember the smell of her freshly baked bread, ten or twelve loaves were baked once or twice a week. All of our butter was churned. Every summer 250-300 quarts of fruit were preserved, as well as many quarts of meat, jam, jelly and pickles. How well we remember helping to turn the hand powered washing machine. Ten or fifteen minutes seemed like such a long time to wash one load of clothes.

Pearl stayed with Grandma and Grandpa Currie and went to the Melrose school, for grade one, and then went to the Okotoks school. At that time school was not held during the winter months at the Melrose school. One of the highlights of her year at the Melrose school was having a ride to school one day in Dr. Murray's new car. It was the first car in the district.

Pearl and George's history is written in the Allan school district.

Norman married Alma Cameron. They farmed at Dinton during the years 1935-1938. They lived near Big Rock from 1939-1945. They farmed near De Winton on Sec. 20-21-29-W4. In 1945 they moved near Okotoks and bought S.W.¼ 9-21-29-W4.

Norman and Alma have three children: Harold, Lawrence and Kathleen.

Harold is a trucker and lives in Black Diamond. He and Leona have three boys, Norman, Eugene and Randy.

Lawrence lives in Saskatoon and works as a technician at the National Research Institute. He and Neva have one son, Jason.

Kathleen lives at home.

Bert married Eileen Geeson, they moved from Okotoks to Calgary in the spring of 1943, when he began to work for Imperial Oil. They moved to Edmonton in 1947. Bert and Eileen have three children, Donna, who is a doctor and presently living in Montreal, but plans to move to Toronto shortly. Lorraine is a nurse, she lives in Edmonton, and is married. Ron is taking an architectural course at the University in Winnipeg.

Eileen's father, Rev. Geeson was the United Church minister for the Okotoks and De Winton district during the 1940's. He came to Alberta from Grantham, England, in 1907, he graduated from St. Stephen's College and was ordained into the Methodist ministry in 1916. He was president of the United Church Conference in 1947-48. He died in 1970 at the age of 87 years. Eileen's mother, Bertha Allen became a school teacher and her first school was in the town of Frank, Alberta. Bertha Allen came from Ontario with her parents as a baby in 1892. The farm her father owned was a big one in Strathcona, and they have named that section of Edmonton where their farm once was Allendale. She died in 1962 at the age of 70.

Lillian has lived in the Okotoks district, except for ten years (1948-1958) when she was on the staff of the Prairie Bible Institute, at Three Hills. She was married and has one daughter, Joan, who is married to Les Herron. They live in Okotoks, and have three children, Lisa, John and Judy.

When Harvey was of school age, he joined us in going to school in the horse and buggy. Later he went by saddle horse, a bicycle and then a motor-cycle. He finished grade 12 in 1939. During the winter of 1939-40 he went to the Calgary "Tech" in the Dominion Provincial Youth Training Program. He joined the R.C.A.F. in May 1940. He did duty as a Wireless Instructor at Montreal, Winnipeg and Calgary Wireless Training Schools of the "Commonwealth Air Training Program." He was discharged in October 1945, and went to University of Alberta from 1946-50 for a degree in Chemical Engineering. He has worked for the Alberta Government since 1950.

He married Dorothy Stagg, and they have six children. Jim, who works for Campbell's Furniture, in Calgary, Phyllis, married Fred Polidano and lives in Trail, B.C. Susan, married Dr. Chris Godfrey and lives in Calgary. Tom, Bob and Greg live in Edmonton.

JOSEPH HOGGE — 1858-1945 — written by Elenor Wass

Born in Inverness, Quebec, he came to Calgary in 1884. He joined the C.P.R. building bridges in the mountain passes between Calgary and Revelstoke, British Columbia.

In 1887, he moved to the Melrose district where he took out his homestead. He raised registered cattle and Clydesdale horses.

In 1892 he married Catherine Stewart, daughter of Mr. and Mrs. Morris Stewart. In 1901 the Hogges rented their farm and moved to Okotoks, where Mr. Hogge and Mr. Riddell operated a store. Later, they returned to the farm for the summers, and lived in town during the winter. After many years they sold the house in town and lived year round on the farm. Mr. Hogge died at his home at the age of 87 in 1945.

Mr. and Mrs. James A. Hogge 33rd wedding anniversary.

Mrs. Hogge's family (the Stewarts) came from Montreal to Winnipeg early in 1882. From the spring to the fall they traveled by oxen beside the construction crews on the railroad, where her father and brothers worked. Arriving in Swift Current in the fall, the C.P.R. crews returned to Winnipeg for the winter, but Mr. and Mrs. Stewart and their nine children remained at Swift Current. They were the only people there for the winter, which was a very cold one. Mrs. Hogge would tell of covering the tents with buffalo hides to try and keep them warm.

In the spring of 1883 they went on by ox cart to Canmore, where Mr. Stewart ran a hostelry for the British soldiers. In 1885 they moved to the Davisburg district. Mrs. Hogge was President of the Calgary Pioneers and Old Timers in 1954.

After Joe Hogge died, Mrs. Hogge and her daughter-in-law, Lillian, sold the farm and moved to Okotoks.

Mrs. Hogge was born March 9, 1873 and died July 8, 1966 at the age of 93.

Catherine, Ernest and Joseph Hogge taken 1893.

The Hogges had one son Ernest Joseph Hogge, born in 1893 and died in 1941. Ernest was born on the farm in Melrose. He was a druggist in Blairmore from 1916 to 1918, and in Delbourne from 1918 to 1924. From 1924 to 1932 he lived in Seattle and Vancouver. From 1932 to 1940 he and his wife operated a grocery store and ice cream parlor in Okotoks. Then due to poor health, they moved to the farm to live with his parents. Ernest died in 1941 at the age of 47.

Mrs. Hogge was the former Lillian Podger, whose father came to Calgary in 1886 to work at McLaren's Flour Mills. After a few years they moved to Florida, later coming to Okotoks where Mr. Podger operated the local flour mill. From there they moved to Van-

couver where both Mr. and Mrs. Podger died. They had four girls Rietta, Lillian, Muriel and Dorothy, and one son Victor, who was wounded in the First World War and had to have his leg amputated.

After Mrs. Hogge Sr. and Lillian sold the farm and returned to Okotoks, Lillian clerked in the Drug Store for many years. In 1966 Lillian sold her home in Okotoks and moved to Calgary to live with her daughter.

Ernest and Lillian had one daughter, Elenor, who married Don Campbell. They had one son Darryl. Don was killed in a car accident. Later Elenor married John Wass, they now live in Calgary.

THE INGRAM FAMILY — by George I. Burke

Oliver Ingram and Sarah Somerville were married in 1842 in the Ottawa Valley and had a farm home at Portage du Fort, where six sons and six daughters grew up. Two daughters remained in the east. Two sons and one daughter came west, and the men worked on the C.P.R. construction into the mountians.

In Febraury, 1888, the family, with the four youngest, came west and took up land a half mile north of the De Winton C.P.R. depot, now owned by Jas. Airth. There are many tales of the trials they put up with. On some of their travels to Calgary they would return to find the streams in flood, and it would be necessary to turn back to Calgary, or put up at some farm.

James and John had the farm to look after, as Grandpa was poorly before they left the east. Jim and a helper dug a well, hit a flowing spring, but it was with difficulty the man at the bottom got out, and the tools are still down there.

A milk house was built over the well. The water flowed through the trough to cool the milk and then found its way out to water the stock, and make its own little creek. They bored logs to make wooden pumps, to be sold and installed.

During the days of construction of the railway, Calgary to Macleod, large quantities of farm produce were sold to the camps. It was all horse travel and life was what you made of it. Dances meant going many miles, dancing all night, going home tomorrow in the daylight. The early settlers were a friendly lot and all pitched in, giving their help where needed.

Matilda married and lived in Manitoba before returning to Calgary for many years. She (Mrs. Livingstone) went to Seattle in 1918 where she died in 1959. Catherine, my mother (Mrs. Burke) married George Burke of the area, and they set up home in Butte, Montana, where I was born. My dad went to the Klondike in 1897, a year ahead of the big rush. Part of that time we spent with the Burke family west of Claresholm, and at De Winton, where my sister Sadie was born. Mother suffered a painful injury (facial) and it was necessary to go to Montreal for an operation. Then we lived in Detroit, Michigan for seven years, returning to Nanton, which was home till Mother died in 1944.

James and John, with Grandma, took up land east of Parkland, on Mosquito Creek, operating the ranch under the XW and EP brands. They also had butcher shops at Okotoks, Cayley, Stavely and Nanton. Uncle

Oliver was the meat cutter. Jim had a hotel at Cayley also. The severe winter of 1906-07 took its toll, but the ranching was carried on until 1910. With homesteaders taking up the range, they sold the cattle, broke up the land and since then, it has been farmed by the Hunter family.

Jim moved to the new town of Brooks, built some business properties, and with two Nanton men, built the Brooks Hotel, and continued in business through the ups and downs of the town. When the Province went dry in 1916, other businesses pulled out, a store was started in the hotel bar, later to become a thriving general store, and still operated by a grandson.

Jim married Katie Ferguson, daughter of a homesteader family near Vulcan, having come west from Collingwood, Ontario. Their family consisted of Douglas, Edna (Mrs. J. Wilkie), Oliver and Jimmy. The last three live at Brooks, and Katherine (Mrs. Berry) in Calgary. Doug was drowned and is buried with his parents in Brooks. Grandpa and Grandma were put to rest in the Pine Creek Cemetery. Uncle Oliver and Mother are in the Nanton Cemetery.

Through the years, I recall meeting many of the oldtimers, friends of mother's. Angus McIntosh, at a Sunday School picnic at De Winton and where Mr. Wilford gave the kids rides on his C.P.R. handcar; the packrats carrying off Mr. McIntosh's small wares from his tent home, later found when cutting fence posts, thereby solving a mystery; Jack Smith with his fancy buggy; the Curries, Bremners, Cardiffs, Blackwoods, Jamisons, Andrews, Hogges and Donald Gray.

Thomas made the trip to Winnipeg, on to Brandon, and then to his homestead at Griswold, Manitoba, which was home until his death in 1932. He never married.

John went into the real estate business in Calgary, after the ranch was sold, and then had a very active part in the Brooks store. He also was a bachelor, dying in 1959 at age 86, in Calgary.

Mother took an active part in the Old Timers Ladies affairs, and it amazed me the way she got about the city to visit her shut-in friends and neighbours of the old days.

It is regrettable that this approach to a historical writing had been delayed for so long, as a great deal of the material has been lost to us.

FRED B. AND ANNE (REEVE) JACQUES — by Roger Dickson

Mr. Fred B. Jacques was born in Flesherton, Ontario in 1865. He came west at an early age and obtained a homestead in partnership with his brothers: NW¼ 4-22-29-W4. This homestead bordered on the Bow River and was held by the Jacques family for many years. In the early days the Blackfoot Trail ran through this property. The property was leased to a Mr. Sangster for the period 1929-1933. Records indicate that Mr. Jacques' share of the rental for one year was nine dollars ($9.00).

At one period in young Fred Jacques' life he was freighting during the Riel Rebellion. He did return to Eastern Canada where he took up the watchmaking trade. He returned west and operated a shop in Calgary in the early days. In 1889 he left Calgary and moved to the Okanagan country. Mr. Jacques resided in Vernon, B.C. with his wife, Anne, and their three children; Edna, Hazel and George. This information is provided by a grandson, Roger J. Dickson who, with his family, now resides two miles south of the original homestead.

ANNIE WINNIFRED JONES (NEE COPITHORNE)

I was born a twin, one boy and one girl, and the second daughter of Mr. and Mrs. Richard Copithorne, at the C L Ranch in Jumping Pound, on the 3rd day of October 1906. It must have been an eventful day because there was already two boys and one girl in the family. I was left to believe, as I grew up, that we were a "bit much" at that time. However, my uncle, John Copithorne, did present the twins with a lovely baby carriage as a gift. It must have taken some of the load off the dear folks that had to attend us. There were two more boys born to the family, Arthur James and Clarence. Arthur was killed by a horse when he was learning to ride at five years of age. Clarence, who is the baby of the family, is fourteen years younger than I am. Robert Percy is the eldest member of the family and Margaret Jane next and then George William. George passed away when he was 56 years of age.

L. to R. Richard Francis and Winnifred Annie Copithorne — 1907.

My twin brother Frank and myself had many happy times together as we grew up. We loved to get into mischief. Of course, this brought us many chastisings and spankings too. It seemed that we liked to play with matches and on several occasions we got good fires going, but luckily the only real damage done was one day we set fire to a stack of hay in the sheep corral. It was a Monday morning and Mother came to our rescue with pails of wash water. However, it did burn the stack and the feed racks before Mother managed to get it out. I remember very well that day, as I had pleaded with Frank, not to set the fire. "It will get away," I said. "Oh, no," said Frank, "there is a nice big snow drift there. We will get it out O.K." That snow bank was too little too late once the fire got started.

We loved to play cowboys. Frank would always want to be Clem Gardner and so I had to be Dick. Dick, of course, was short for Richard, our Dad. Clem was a daring cowboy with a rope, bucking horses, etc., and Dick was not quite so daring. I don't ever remember getting to play Clem in any of our little games.

When we started school we had to ride three miles on horseback. We had many experiences to and from school to the top of Little Signal Hill, as we called the first hill. Mr. Bateman's cows were all sleeping peacefully in our path. Frank, who had a very smart pony, was in the lead. He saw a cow in the way and thought his horse would jump it and carry on with the race. However, the cow started to get up just as Ginger, his pony, started to jump. Horse, cow and Frank were all in a heap. Poor Frank, he was badly shaken up. We lifted him back on to his horse and he rode the three miles home, crying all the way. He was in bed about two weeks after that, recovering from broken ribs and bruises. I don't know to this day how he escaped with his life from that episode.

Father bought eight acres of land with a home, at Gordon Head, on Vancouver Island, in the year 1913. He moved his family there in 1914, to go to school and to live. Uncle John was already established in Victoria at that time as the owner of "The Sunbeam Dairy," a flourishing business. However, none of us transplanted very well and after one year he brought us all back to the ranch in September 1915. We missed our ponies and the way of life on the ranch, so our move to a small farm for one year was more or less a disaster.

Mother was taken from us in the spring of 1923, leaving Clarence, a little boy of two years and four months old. My sister, Margaret was twenty-one and I was sixteen years of age. Margaret, with my help, managed the household chores from then on until she married in 1931. We had a fabulous time watching Clarence grow. He was a wonderful little boy and brought into our family many joys. We had our hours of consternation too, as he was subject to all the children's diseases that came along. He had a real session with the measles and spent many days in Calgary General Hospital with mastoids, this being an aftermath of this child's disease. He was many weeks recovering. We also did all the cooking for the hay crews which came each year for a good six weeks every summer. Besides the immediate family, we had two hired men working all year around. We churned and made butter from approximately twelve to sixteen cows. As I look back over the years, I remember them as being very busy times, but apart from being busy there was many happy times too. We were very close to our cousins that lived just, "down the hill". We visited back and forth and we considered them a part of our family. Especially, Lottie and Claude, Nan and Jack, who each lived there for periods of time. I think Nan taught me everything I knew about sewing, knitting, crocheting and cooking. Those two cousins were well prepared for life in the country, as they were surely equipped when they arrived in Jumping Pound from Ireland.

Father passed away on the 27th day of April 1936, after a brief illness. He had a ruptured appendix and of course, in those days penicillin was unknown. It surely was a sad day for Clarence and myself. We were the last two members of the family at home at this time. He was just sixteen years old and still considered a minor.

The old home was left to me as long as I remained unmarried. That at least, was security for us at that time. Mr. McLaurin, our lawyer and one of the executors of Father's will, called me and Clarence into the Court House one day before Mr. Justice Tweedie. The good Judge wanted to see both Clarence and myself and to ask a few questions. He wanted to know if I had any plans to leave home, because if I did, there would have to be other arrangements made for Clarence. Needless to say, I had no plans to leave and certainly intended to stay in the old home as long as Clarence needed me there. It evidently satisfied His Honour, because I heard no more about it. I did stay until Clarence was able to establish a home of his own.

In the year 1938 I took a business course at Hepburn's Business College. Clarence spent the winter months at the Olds Agricultural College, so I thought it would be well for me to better my position by getting more education. I came home when he finished his year there and returned the next fall when he returned to College to complete his courses. I received my Secretarial Diploma in the summer of 1939. I had it framed but never hung it up on the wall. I thought I had worked real hard for that and hoped I would get a job without presenting it anywhere.

During the summer I got temporary work at Ingram's Shoe store. I hated it there. I still hate the smell of shoes when I go to buy a pair for myself.

Many of the girls didn't find work just then as jobs were hard to find. We all went back to the College to keep our short hand and typing in good standing. One day Mr. Hepburn called me in to tell me that a Mr. Mayhood had called the office and would like me to go and see him. Mr. Mayhood was an old friend of my brother Frank's wife Georgie, nee McDougall, and I suspect that Frank had told him that I was looking for work. I was thrilled about going to the old established law office of Short, Ross, Shaw and Mayhood for an interview. I got all prettied up, at least as pretty as possible and went to see Mr. Mayhood. The job was mine and I could start immediately.

The first few weeks I was really in a fog. I thought I would never find my way through that mass of legal documents and terms. However, Mr. Mayhood was a very patient and kind gentleman, and after about six months, things seemed to open up and I was really enjoying myself in my new surroundings. Mr. Mayhood had a large farm clientele. Estates, farm leases and transfers. I really felt at home and enjoyed meeting the people. I also felt fortunate in having such a wonderful man to work for. I was four years and about six months working for Mr. Mayhood and also, some work for the other members of the firm. Mr. Ross had been elected to parliament in Ottawa, representing Calgary East, at that time. He asked Mr. Mayhood if he could take me to Ottawa with him for the 1944 session. I think Mr. Mayhood really flattered me by saying he hated to loose me but thought it would be a fine experience for me, if I wanted to go. I did. Before I was able to go however, I had a bout with the mumps, which had been contracted from an English airman that had been out for the Christmas holidays at my sister Margaret's place. I thought at times during that session at my sister's place that I would never go anywhere if the mumps didn't subside. However, I did recover and went to Ottawa the latter part of January 1944.

Mr. and Mrs. Ross met the train in Ottawa after a three day trip down. They took wonderful care of me during my stay there and I wanted for nothing. I was placed on the pay-roll of the Secretarial Pool in the House of Commons and started to work for Mr. Ross immediately. I was called out to many other members too, but Mr. Ross had a lot of work to do and kept me fairly busy. He had a mailing list of 3,000 constituents to whom he sent news letters every month. That was a

In front of the library at House of Commons, Ottawa, 1944. L. to R. Mrs. George H. Ross, Mr. George H. Ross, M.P. Calgary East, Jean Ross and Annie Copithorne (Mrs. Idwal Jones).

job that kept both Mrs. Ross and myself busy a good part of my time. Mrs. Ross alway helped me with the folding and addressing of these news letters. I didn't realize at that time that one day I would come to live amongst some of the people that received those letters. I have never been able to find out whether they were read and appreciated or whether the most of them found their way into the waste paper basket.

Ottawa was the most beautiful city I had ever seen. I met many wonderful people there and still send Christmas letters and cards to some of them. They have since retired but it was a long and lasting friendship and helped to make my stay in Ottawa very pleasurable.

Mr. Ross had as an office partner, Mr. Jack Sissons. Most members shared office space with another member. Mr. Sissons was the member from Spirit River, Alberta, and a very fine man. He later became a well known and well loved Judge for the Northwest Territories. He wrote a book about his life called "Judge of the North." I bought it and added it to my library. I enjoyed reading it very much. He retired to Edmonton some years after and has since passed away.

Working in the House of Commons wasn't any picnic. When I arrived there Mr. Ross advised me not to leave my purse unattended or the office door unlocked if no one was in it. I soon discovered why. Everything that was left on your desk or anywhere else for that matter, disappeared very quickly. They never seemed to find out who was doing it but it seemed as if you just didn't trust anyone. It was to me a very strange state of affairs, because everyone that I knew or knew of were well paid and no one should have any need to steal.

When the House adjourned in August of that year, I was very happy to be on my way back to Alberta.

Mr. Ross again ran in the spring of 1945, for election, to represent Calgary East. However, he did not get elected and Calgary East was represented that term by a Conservative member. I might add here that Mr. Ross, his family and his Law Firm were Liberals of long standing. Mr. Joseph Shaw also spent a term in the House of Commons sitting as liberal member prior to Mr. Ross.

The next year or so were spent in the Law Office working for Mr. Ross. I still enjoyed that work. Every day was different and I was always meeting new people and lots of different people's problems. I gained a great respect for the Department of National Revenue. My advice to myself and friends was to always be true and keep complete records. It saves a lot of headaches if you do, as time marches on.

The year 1946 brought more changes in the family. My brother Clarence had met a lovely girl, Irene Robertson, and decided to get married. They were married in May of that year. Things were never quite the same for me after that event. They lived in the old home for a short while and then moved to where they built a permanent home of their own. When I arrived home on week ends there wasn't anyone there to clean up and cook for, or to visit with.

Always in the background was this man, Idwal Jones. We had been seeing one another occasionally during the years but now that seemed to have taken a more serious turn. We were married the 12th day of June 1947, and I left the business world to become a farmer's wife near De Winton, Alberta.

As I have written Idwal's history, in which our son Clarence and myself are frequently mentioned, I won't write further about our life together on the farm, except to say, that we were very, very happy and had our ups and downs just the same as most folks do.

I would like to mention here before I complete my story, that I was forever grateful to my father and mother, who came to this good country before there was much of anything here except hard work and loneliness. Father came to Calgary at the age of 27 years, in the spring of 1887, from County Cork, Ireland. He was the eldest member of a very large farm family. Mother, born Georgiana Sophia Wills, came a few years later from Wolf Island, near Kingston, Ontario. Father with Mother's help built a fine ranch with hard work, integrity and diligence. All this so that their children and grandchildren could have a better life.

IDWAL JONES — by Annie W. Jones

Idwal Jones was born, eldest son of Mr. and Mrs. James Jones, on the 23rd day of October 1904, at Wrexham, North Wales. He was the first born child of a family of eleven, being seven boys and four girls.

His brother, Iorwerth Jones, immigrated to Canada, in the year 1926. He was followed in the spring of 1928 by Idwal and a younger brother, Isaac. Idwal and Isaac went to work the first summer at Irricana for Norvill and Fred Davis. They were progressive farmers of that area at that time. Fred Davis was the member of parliament for that area at Ottawa during that period. When they were finished at Davis's they went to work for Dennis Howell at The Craigdhu Ranch. This was at the beginning of the depression in 1929. They stayed with Mr. Howell during the winter.

Isaac being the chief cook and bottle washer and Idwal doing the farm chores. It was during their stay at Dennis Howell's that Idwal trapped muskrats, weasles, badgers and coyotes in order to get more funds to bring out the rest of the family from Wales. His mother, Mary Jones, told me that Idwal raised $900.00 to help bring the rest of the family to Canada. That was quite an accomplishment in those days of unemployment and shortages of cash.

The three brothers, Idwal, Iowerth and Isaac then decided to find a home to bring the rest of the family to Canada. They purchased a corner lot in Forest Lawn, on the eastern outskirts of Calgary at that time. It was in 1929 they bought the home for the family for $1,-600.00 under an agreement for sale. They made a down payment of $400.00, and agreed to pay $25.00 per month until the principal and interest was paid off. In 1930 all the rest of the family were brought to Canada and to their new home in Forest Lawn. Times were very difficult in the early thirties and work hard to find. However, these boys were never without work. By this time Idwal, Iorwerth and Isaac were joined by brothers, Jim, Maldwyn and Emyr, to help maintain the family.

Iorwerth Jones was the first Jones boy to arrive in the hay crew at Jumping Pound. He worked one summer putting up hay for the C L Ranch, owned and operated by Richard Copithorne. This was in the year 1930. Idwal, Isaac and Jim came the following year. Idwal and Isaac were indulging in some reminiscences about their first days in the hay field on the C L Ranch. It seemed as if Isaac had never driven broncos before. He said he was very apprehensive about hitching up two horses, one quiet and one green broke, to a mower and then starting to cut hay. I guess it was quite a shocker for a young lad not too long out from Wales. He said, "and we had to change horses at noon and again at four o'clock in the afternoon." That meant that he had three different teams to drive in the day and each with one green broken horse and one that was gentle. In those days they made hay until seven o'clock in the evening.

Idwal worked about two weeks on the C L Ranch

James Jones family coming to Canada 1930. Front row: L. to R. Louisa, Mary, Esther, Mrs. Jones and Robert Peron in Mother's arms. Back row: L. to R. Eleanor, Emyr, James Jones, Maldwyn and James.

James Jones family 1938 and 20 below zero. First row: Mrs. Jones, Robert Peron, James Jones. Second row: Louisa, Eleanor, Mary, Esther. Third row: Emyr, Isaac, Maldwyn, James, Iorwerth and Idwal.

and was taken ill. He went home to recover and then came back to Jumping Pound tc work for the Lazy J Ranch, which was owned by John Copithorne at that time. He worked on this ranch for many years.

In about 1938 he left Jumping Pound and went to work at the Rolling Mills in Calgary.

He went in with his brother, Iorwerth and bought a quarter section of land in the Okotoks area in the early 1940's. He worked with him off and on farming until we bought the old Herb Currie farm, being the S.½ 20-21-29-W4th in 1947. We were married that year on the 12th day of June, and established our permanent home here.

The years that followed were busy ones for Idwal Jones. He still farmed with his brother and shared the machinery. Our farm seemed to have been in a hail belt for the next eight or ten years. We would have beautiful crops only to have them wiped out in about five minutes by savage hail storms. In 1951 and 1952 we had so much rain and hail that it was impossible even to bale what crop was left. The baler would bog down on the highest hill. We bought our feed in 1951 from Art Hall who had brought it in from Manitoba.

The farm seemed to be in jeopardy many days by fire. The C.P.R. tracks lay in the coulee on the west side of our farm. Many fires were started by the trains coming up the steep grade. They would puff and blow and out would come a shower of sparks and away would go a fire. Also, there was a danger when men were burning grass on the tracks, which they did in the spring of the year. However, the neighbors were always willing to come and help put them out. This surely made us appreciate the many good neighbors which we had.

One day Idwal had a little fire all by himself. He was hauling straw bales into the barn from the field east of the building. He decided to bring the tractor home to fill it with gas. He left the loaded stone boat on some grass land by the granaries. When he was filling the tractor he looked down and saw his stone boat and straw bales all on fire. He made a hurried call for help and ran down with a shovel. With the help of his women folk, his sister-in-law Helen, who came when we called her and myself, he managed to get it out before it burned up more than the stone boat and the straw bales. It is still a mystery how it got started. The only solution we had was the runners got so hot they started to burn the dry grass.

Our son, Clarence David, was born January 31st, 1952. He attended school in Okotoks except for two months spent at Pine Creek. He played most school sports and was active in the Students Union. In his senior year 1969-70 he received the Blue and White Award and the Catriona Gibson Memorial Scholarship. The Okotoks 4-H Beef Club and Foothills Sheep Club also, shared his interest at this time. Upon completion of High School, Clarence spent four years at the University of Alberta obtaining a B.Sc. in Agriculture. During this time he was active in Student activities and was President of the Agricultural Club in his final year. He returned to the home farm following graduation and is working for a change.

THE ED JONES FARM

The first known resident was Mr. Rider, a family man who lived here about 1890. George Rodyson, wife and boy came here in the early 1900's. Mr. Rodyson kept it four years, then moved to Calgary about 1904 or 1906. These were very wet years, as sometimes the wagons got bogged down. It was even hazardous sometimes to ride a horse. A caravan of U.S. immigrants came through in June, and had to camp in the school section.

Duncan Simpson, who lived on the Bryce place bought it and farmed it for ten years. He sold it to Tyson about ten years later, and he farmed it for three years. It was then sold to German Lebarmose and he later moved back to the U.S.A. Because of insufficient funds it was returned to Tyson, who with his son-in-law, Jim McNeil farmed here for four years. The land was then sold to Mr. Brown of Turner Valley, who built the brick house that is still being lived in today. Bricks for the house were made in the Sandstone Coulee Brick Plant, 2 miles southwest of the house. Earlier houses, north and south of the present site burned down.

Andy Christensen, about 1930 farmed and rented the land for four years. Mrs. Irving lived here for a short time until 1939. Mr. Brown put the place up for sale which was sold to Ed Jones in 1946. Ed Jones is still the present owner of the farm today located on S.W.¼ 21-21-29 W4. Mr. Jones of Calgary, was farming the Ed McLeod place east of Okotoks and later bought part of it.

Ed Jones married Helen Kennaugh of Carseland. They moved into the brick house. Helen taught school in several country schools including Melrose. Ed and Helen had two sons, Ronald who is working at Crossfield with Amoco and Robert of Calgary, who works for Cominco. Robert married Marilyn Poffenroth whose folks farmed in the De Winton area at one time. Rob and Marilyn have two sons, Darren and Wayne.

Helen and Ed Jones.

SPEARMAN CORBETT AND MINNIE (BAILEY) KENNEY — by Duncan Kenney and E. K. Leach

Spearman Corbett Kenney was born in Quebec City

in 1863 moving, with his parents, to Exeter, Ontario in 1870. There he married Minnie Bailey in 1884.

Three children; Dianah, Bill and Spearman Jr. (Pat) were born in Ontario. In 1890 the family came west to Pine Creek, N.W.T. They homesteaded three miles east of what is now De Winton. Their first home was built of logs which Mr. Kenney cut and hauled some fifty miles from the hills. Their first post office was Pine Creek but later they got their mail at Grierson P.O., N.W.T. and the children attended Melrose school two miles south of the homestead.

There were nine children born on the farm. Three little boys died in infancy.

Dinah, 1885-1969; Bill; 1888-1966; Spearman (Pat), 1889-1968; Sarah, 1893-1956; Duncan, 1898- ; Mark, 1902-1966; Kate, 1905- ; Norman, 1908-1966 and Ethel (twins); There are now only three members of the family living, Duncan, Kate and Ethel. Mother, 1866-1931; father, 1863-1934.

Dinah married Roy Wright and moved to Hart, Michigan. Bill and Pat moved to Rimbey in 1910. Bill married Hannah Binner, Pat married Eva Brawn. Sarah married Fred Goodkey.

Duncan came to Calgary in 1917. He worked at Crossfield and surrounding districts. He and Gladys Nutkins were married in 1923. They had six children; two boys and four girls. Their eldest daughter died in 1968. The rest of their family lives in Calgary. Duncan and Gladys are residents of the Bow Crest Nursing Home in Bowness and will celebrate their fifty-fifth wedding anniversary in September, 1978.

Mark and Jean McAllister married and lived in the De Winton area. The older children went to Melrose school until it was closed and then to Okotoks. The children were; Raymond, Glen, Gary, Shirley, Larry, June, Betty and Dwane.

Mark was a very good mechanic and kept the local cars in good running order far beyond their normal span.

Kate married Jim Brown and lives in Turner Valley.

Spearman Kenney's 71st birthday. Back row: Ted Brown, Kate Brown (holding Jessie), Sarah Goodkey (holding ?), Spearman Kenney, Dunc Kenney, wife Gladys, Chas. Urquhart, Dan Borthwick, Norman Kenney. Middle row: Ethel Kenney, Minnie Goodkey, Buster Brown, Georgie Goodkey, Front: Ethel Goodkey, Phyllis Brown, Nina Goodkey, ?,?,?,?, Mary McLucky.

Ethel married Axel Frederickson, lived at Turner Valley until her husband passed away and now lives at the Senior Citizens Home in Black Diamond.

Norman did not marry but stayed on the original farm all his life.

Mr. Kenney had quite a sense of humor and told many stories about himself. He used to drink too much and one time, when he was coming home from town, he met the minister who said, "Hello Mr. Kenney, drunk again?" The jovial reply was, "So am I!" Another time a local lady was complaining that she had only been paid ten cents a dozen for eggs. Mr. Kenney said it was hardly worth the wear and tear on the hens.

At the turn of the century the W. J. Andrews' home was moved from "The Rocks" to its present location, now the home of Marion and George Martin. Mr. Kenney helped in the moving. He had previously walled up the basement with field stone and mortar which, after all these years, is still in excellent condition. He had been a stone mason in his early days.

KENNY, MORGAN AND MAY — by May Kenny

Morgan and I have been roamers. We have lived in a number of places, but have never managed to complete a story for a local historical book before. The actual deadline for this one has come and gone, but fortunately time has been extended for procrastinators such as I.

Morgan's father Jim Kenny spent his early years in Ireland, and claimed to be Irish, although statistics show he was born in England. When I tell Morg he's a hotheaded Irishman (minus the red hair) he answers, "No, I'm a gentleman". Now, haul your hats ye Irishmen, for "shure" and he was only joking. Mr. Kenny came to Canada with his adoptive parents when he was six or seven. By the age of fourteen he had struck out on his own. Morgan's mother was a native of Ontario.

In 1908 Morg's parents moved to Stettler, Alberta, where his father operated a livery service, driving people to view their prospective homesteads. After a fire destroyed his equipment in 1909, they moved to a homestead near what is now Byemoor.

Here they raised their family. Morg had seven brothers — Pat and Jack now in Calgary; Jim who is in Stettler; Cleave in Delacour; and Ralph, Alton and Bob who are deceased. The only girl in the family died at birth.

My parents Ed and Lena Shultz were both born and raised in Michigan. I believe their ancestors were mostly Polish. At least I was a "bean pole" most of my life, but the more mature look has gained the preeminence. That goes for the boss too. Some people say it was the Peace River water, but Morg claims it was the moose meat.

My father and mother first came to Wimborne in 1909. In 1911 they filed on a homestead in the area, now known as Endiang. Father set out from Wimborne with ten dollars, but after paying a night's lodging he was almost broke. Travel was precarious, for the river was high and fording it was dangerous. His friend lost almost all his possessions downstream and owed his life to father's quick action. So my parents and four little ones started life on the homestead with only one dollar in cash, one cow and few other possessions. Within a short time the cow mysteriously disappeared. No wonder I didn't walk for two years, probably had rickets. Nevertheless, the wolf never gained entrance for father was an ingenious salesman. He even sold a cream separator to a farmer who had no cows.

I had two brothers, Elmer, recently deceased, and Jack who lives at Endiang. There were also five girls: Elsie Moen of Calgary; Bunny Boehlke of Endiang; Billie Boehlke of Calgary; Martha who died at birth and myself.

Morg and I are "Canucks" being born in Stettler and Wimborne respectively, one month apart and as far back as it takes to become a full-fledged Sr. Citizen.

Early in his youth Morgan rented land and tried farming but nature seemed to delight in devastating his crops. Nine out of twelve or thirteen crops were hailed out. Before we married, he began driving trucks and doing mechanical work.

When I decided to go to Normal School to train for teaching, times were indeed hard. Some of the family felt I shouldn't go, but Dad said, "If you want to attend Normal School I will sell my last cow to put you through". Mom made me promise I'd teach at least three years before I married. I kept my promise doubly well, teaching six years before and a good many afterwards.

Training was tough sledding. My sister Elsie gave me board and room. I walked miles to save carfare, and "runny" nylons and I were close friends.

When I graduated from Normal School teachers were "a dime a dozen". Hundreds of them were unable to get work. Perhaps it could be called luck — but the "pull" of a doting uncle who was a school trustee was responsible for a whole gunny sack of applications being left unread while I was given the position of teacher at Annasheim School at five hundred dollars annual salary. I received my first cheque (government grant) of fifty dollars at Christmas time. I was many years collecting those first few years' salary, but I didn't seem to mind.

Morg and I met at country dances. I well remember this bashful, handsome lad who always waited for a tag or a circle before he could muster up enough courage to dance. He always — but always, combed his hair, squared his shoulders, took a deep breath and then into a dance.

A number of years after we were married we decided to try farming again while I continued teaching. Well, I don't know whether bad luck dogged our footsteps or whether we weren't good "sticker-outers". Our first crop was harvested suddenly and very quickly — by hail — and no insurance. The second crop nearly dried out and we had an insurance premium to pay. In 1945 we raised the third crop. One night near harvest time we heard a very loud thump followed by a few seconds of deathlike silence. Then all fury let loose, and the hail claimed another crop. The strangest thing about the storm was that it jumped over several miles of other people's crops to strike another quarter of land which we had rented.

On December 15th, 1944, fire gutted our home and

what a bonfire it was! We had worked hard all the summer at interior decorating and raising and processing garden produce. The chickens were in jars, a beef hung on the north side of the house, the cellar was full of coal: Morg's coyote hides were in the attic, etc. We were basking in the satisfaction of being "well settled". The pantry was over-flowing with groceries for I had made purchases at numerous stores in order to obtain a quota of candy from each one for the candy bags at school. The Christmas gifts were wrapped, cards were addressed and stamped ready for the mail. I had finished the housecleaning and baked the Christmas cakes and puddings. Last, but not least, we had purchased a new (well, new to us, anyway) piano. All in all we had never been so well organized before — nor have we since! Foolish people we were, for the little insurance we carried only paid for the piano. Even our cash, which was pretty scarce in those days, had been in my purse lying on the dresser. Well, it was impossible to get a **decent** house so, after being hailed **out**, dried **out**, burned **out** and hailed **out** again we moved out to Byemoor where Morg worked in a garage. Would you believe there have been good crops on that farm ever since?

Nevertheless those were good years, for it was then that I discovered that Jesus, the Son of God, died for our sins. This has been a source of peace and joy ever since.

We then bought Morg's father's old farm and rented it to a relative. The first two years were so dry we didn't make tax money, but the third year there was a bumper crop. It was left to be straight combined and on September 4th it was quickly harvested — in the usual manner. We sold the farm. Again would you believe there have been good crops ever since.

Morg continued doing mechanical work in Byemoor, then Irricana, then Strathmore until we bought the White Rose Service Station business, at the De Winton corner, from Dan Gerlitz. Morg labored there for nearly ten years. When we started there our chosen daughter, Marlene, was three years old. Four years later our second chosen daughter, Ann, came to us. She was five years old then.

I tried to be a good helpmate for Morg, but service station work was not my cup of tea. I never could take people's money believe it or not. I'm sure I did nothing to encourage business, and constantly found myself

Morg and May Kenny's service station. De Winton.

Marg Kenny family: L. to R. Marlene, Ann, Morg and May.

back in the classroom as happy as if I were in my right mind. It wasn't easy, though Morg worked late so I answered all the night calls — usually someone wanting a package of cigarettes or a gallon of gas!!! Nevertheless, we progressed comparatively well until we moved from the service station living quarters to a house one mile west. Within nine months the service station had been broken into six times. The police didn't do very well so Morg began sleuthing himself. Then, with the police finally on the right track, although there were no arrests, the break-ins ceased as suddenly as they had begun. During this time I taught at Pine Creek, several years at Okotoks and part of a year at Black Diamond.

Now, I'll ramble a bit, recalling various incidents during my school career. Dot Gerlitz asked me if I remembered the candy hearts I decorated with scenes and names for Valentines Day. It's easier to recall such things as a bonfire that got away and ravaged a beautiful hay field.

I would like to see all the pupils I taught. Some are grandparents now!! One year I taught pupils whose parents I had taught. Then a few years later, I taught the younger brothers and sisters of these same kids. That really was interesting.

As well as grand kids, there surely were grandparents, too. At one school the parents conspired to bring "goodies" and visit us. Always, the "goodies" remained behind. At least once a week, a quart of cream arrived at school, having been carried on a Shetland pony — bareback at that. Hey, Morg, that proves, contrary to your arguments, that cream does not make one fat.

I always enjoyed putting on Christmas programs. One year at this time, I sent three boys to my house on an errand. When I arrived home that night I noticed that the dipped chocolates, which I had left spread out on the table to harden for the candy bags, had been thinned out considerably. I wondered if they would make it to the program that night and was quite worried when they did not arrive on time. However they came and managed to do their parts, but their

Mother couldn't understand why their tummy's were so upset.

The school parties were always fun especially the Quiz and Consequences. The people were always such good sports. After the hilarious consequences we would enjoy a sumptuous lunch and then we would dance.

One evening was a bit different. The parents were invited to hear "speeches" on subjects the students had chosed for themselves. Someone had found a magazine on which in bold letters were the words "Any damn fool can smoke". One pupil capitalized on that slogan and chose "smoking" as her topic. She got an "A" on her report card, convinced no one, and we lost a few good (smoking) friends.

One Friday, early in my teaching career, as I was hurrying home from school to help with the threshing, I had a flat tire — and no spare! Now What? Looking back, I saw nine or ten of my pupils galloping down the road. That day the pupils got an extra lesson — a real life lesson in Science. Using the log as a lever and a rock as the fulcrum, the children sat on one end while the other end lifted the car. I removed the tire, patched the tube and with more cheerful help, pumped up the tire and went merrily on my way.

I wonder if Marcel remembers the time the boys had to scrub the outhouses because they had written on them? After he had returned to the school he said, "She makes me so mad"! A voice right behind him said, "And you make me so mad, too". The general laugh eased the situation.

One day at school it was just like a movie. Suddenly a huge flame of fire appeared. In unison every child was on his feet and starting toward the door. Suddenly all remembered fire drill rules and stopped short. They looked so bewildered when no flame was to be seen. A pair of burned hands and a lighter was the only proof that there ever had been one.

School news was often hilarious. "My mommy's going to have a baby." "My mommy went to the doctor. She has to go on a diet 'cause she's too fat." "My Dad had to sleep on the chesterfield last night 'cause he came home drunk." "My Mom and Dad had a fight. Mom used too much electricity and Dad went pow, pow, pow. (Billy punching downward). Mom went pow, pow, pow. (Billy punching upward). Because "time was (suddenly) up" for news Billy finished his dramatic story at recess time to a few willing listeners.

One day my nose told me it was time to teach a health lesson on cleanliness. Next morning Charles' news was, " I told Mommy last night that I needed a bath, and she said, "Oh no, Charles. You'll catch a cold. You'll have to wait til spring." Of course, it was pretty cold in the land nearer the midnight sun.

Another day I taught the Grade One class a lesson on birds. In the course of the lesson I said, "When birds go south they migrate. Migrate is a hard word and I don't expect you to remember it." A few weeks later I asked, "Do any of you remember the word that means the birds have gone south for the winter?" Terry waved his hand enthusiastically, "Well, what is it Terry? "Hitchhiking!"

One evening a local organization used the

classroom for a social. They had a lot of orange drink left over so they left it for the pupils to drink — not realizing it was a metal container. Shortly after school commenced next day pupils began throwing up. Soon pupils were lying all over the room. I was throwing up, too, but not because I had drunk the juice — I just never was a good nurse! Fortunately there were among the pupils prospective nurses and doctors who helped, and that day we were more than fortunate as the district nurse arrived at the crucial time.

I could write a book on "school days", but space is limited, so I must stop. Anyhow, we worked hard, but had fun too. Our motto was "Work while you work and play while you play, for that is the way to be happy and gay."

When the White Rose Company decided to build a new modern service station, Morg moved his equipment to De Winton and operated a business there for a time.

One summer, along with friends, we toured the Peace River Country and fell in love with it. In 1958 we moved to Spirit River where we were both employed by the Spirit City School Board, I in a teaching capacity and Morg working at school bus maintenance. We spent a total of five years there, and although we really liked it, family ties drew us back to the south again, where we tried our hand at the grocery store business. Here again I was like a square peg in a round hole and spoiled Morg's business, I'm sure. Ann almost broke us drinking pop, eating chocolate bars and coloring the coloring books. We soon gave it up.

We tried city life, too. In Calgary Morg worked for Renfrew Motors and I, after substitute teaching for a while, joined the staff at St. Mathew's School. On Armistice Day an army truck jauntily pushed Morg into a light pole. From then on he felt the city was to much of a rat race for him. In a unique fashion, but then everyone is unique in some way, Morg started in the **middle** of things to start "quick-exit" proceedings. The middle of the month, the middle of the week, the middle of the day (Wed., 12 noon, April 15) Morg came home from work and said, "I've quit". And believe it or not, that very night (and not at home) but at my sister's house for a birthday supper, Morg received a phone call from a school trustee, offering him the job of shop foreman in the school bus garage at Delia. In June of 1976 he retired after ten years with the Starland board. I had retired from teaching several years previously, but have continued to work in the school doing substitute teaching, remedial teaching and teacher aide work.

Delia is a nice village and we're quite content here. Morg says he's too old to move again. Anyhow, I say we can't afford to!! I'm sure you'll agree there's more truth than fiction to that statement these days. We are within a short distance of our daughter Marlene. In 1966 she married Jim McGuire, and after a time in Calgary they and their son, Shawn, have taken up farming in the Craigmyle district. Their hobby is rodeoing. Shawn is expecting brother "Peter" any day now. He was thoroughly disappointed that "Peter" didn't arrive on his eighth birthday, May 8, which happens to be his Mom's birthday, too. Note" "**Miss Peter**" arrived on May 20, 1977, her name is Shana Dawne.

Our youngest daughter Ann married Wayne Justinen of Rocky Mountain House in 1968, choosing his parent's anniversary, May 2, as the date. They live in Carstairs and Wayne is an Air Traffic Controller (I.F.R.) at the Calgary International Airport. Their hobbies are flying and shooting. They have four beautiful youngsters, Trevor, Jodi, Corey and Brent.

We enjoy the occasional visits with friends from the various places we have lived. Morg is a poor traveller so we depend on our friends visiting us. From De Winton, Ed and Helen Jones have been faithful visitors and we enjoy them very much. For the first hour or so of their visit we ply them with questions. But maybe, just maybe, this summer we'll jump in our camper and make a tour of the De Winton and Okotoks areas.

CHARLES WILLIAM AND BERTHA (OESCH) KING — by Charlie King

I was born in the Holy Cross Hospital in Calgary, November 30, 1922, the first son of Maude and Bert King. I grew up on the home place doing most of the things boys love to do. Like riding the neighbor's cows and hitching up unbroke horses. I went to school at Pine Creek, walking most of the time but in winter I could ski part way.

I started to work for the Department of Highways April 1, 1942 and, in 1943, I took time off and joined the Army.

As I always had a few cattle, I got the brand my great-grandfather, T. H. Andrews had. I owned the NW¼-30-21-28-W4, in Davisburg. It was originally my grandmother Alice Shattuck's and then it belonged to my mother, Maude King. The Davisburg school sits on one corner of it.

I bought the NE¼ 30-21-29-W4 from my father-in-law, Irvin Oesch, it joined my other place, P.T. S.W. 31-21-29-W4. At one time it was a part of the VanTighem place. They now take shale out of it to make bricks.

On October 12, 1948, I married Bertha Louise Oesch, in St. Patrick's Church at Midnapore. Father Newman officiated. He had read the marriage vows for my mother and father, twenty-five years before. Our wedding dance was held in the old De Winton Hall which my Grandfather, Billy King, had helped to build.

Charles and Bertha King's wedding Oct. 12, 1948. L. to R. Tom King, Jack King, Charlie King, Bertha King, Theresa Hamilton, Lillian Oesch, Marg. Armstrong.

248

We also had our twenty-fifth wedding anniversary dance there.

Bertha was born in Shellbrooke, Saskatchewan and came to De Winton, Alberta in 1933, with her parents Irvin and Zena Oesch and her sister, Lillian. She went to Pine Creek School with me long before we ever thought of getting married.

We were blessed with three children; Lorne Charles, born November 3, 1949, married Lynne Charlotte Patience of Medicine Hat, Alberta, whose grandfather was an old timer of Calgary. They have two boys: Jason Lorne and Sean Cameron. Darryle Mervin, born August 24, 1952, married Lisa Harp. Charlene Louise, born January 29, 1956. They are all working and on their own. Bertha and I still live at De Winton.

MR. AND MRS. JOHN JAMES KORTH AND FAMILY — written by Ethel Korth

My parents, and five of my seven brothers and sisters, were residents of the De Winton area between 1919 and 1924.

My father, John Korth (better known as Jake) was born at Mankato, Minnesota in 1884. He was second youngest of the five children of Nicholas Korth and Katharina Beszlich both of German origin. When his only sister decided upon a religious vocation, he helped his blind mother in the house; and being the son of a tailor, his up-bringing in a city setting and convent school left him with much to be experienced while homesteading in Canada.

Dad emigrated to Canada with his parents and younger brother Lawrence in 1902. They settled in the Cudworth area of Saskatchewan where the boys operated the first store at Hoodoo. It wasn't all business as both young men played in the local band, and at a social function Jake met his future wife, a fun-loving lass, Grace Maude Tyndall.

My mother, Grace, was born at Fosston, Minnesota in 1891, the oldest daughter of Henry and Nellie (Reid) Tyndall. She accompanied her parents, four brothers and a sister to Canada in 1903 and they settled near Cudworth, Saskatchewan (see HENRY TYNDALL family).

Jake and Grace were married at the rural community of St. Benedict in January 1914. They endeavored to raise their three youngsters, Elizabeth, Henry, and Katherine by continuing to operate a country store at St. Benedict. Economic problems accompanying World War I made bartering an unprofitable necessity, and in January 1919 they moved to the De Winton area to farm.

They resided in the Melrose School District on the former Hedley holdings at T21 R29 S17 W4. Elizabeth (Beth), and Henry attended Melrose School when weather permitted. It was often a trying journey for Mother to drive them accompanied by her three younger children. Leona and James were born to the family while they resided on the De Winton farm and it is interesting to note that Jim visited the farm now owned by Mr. and Mrs. Tom Hebson on the fiftieth anniversary of his birth.

Uneconomical land area coupled with adverse weather necessitated Dad working out to supplement the family living. He worked at the Sandstone Brickyard in the early 1920s before becoming a sectionman with the Canadian Pacific Railway at De Winton.

My brothers and sisters have fond memories of their years at the farm. The cattle and horses are remembered by name, the berry picking picnics, the visits to Grandpa and Grandma Tyndall's farm, and the Sunday drives to church at Okotoks with a stop at Imler's for dinner on the way home. Mrs. Imler must have been an exceptional cook for the family still recall her delicious cooked parsnips, and for kids to like parsnips is something!

It was especially difficult for my mother to leave the farm in February 1924 when Dad was offered a better job with the C.P.R. at Woodhouse, Alberta. She had a special love for animals and growing things, and could appreciate the advantages of raising their children in the country.

During the ten-year stay at Woodhouse the family became complete with the arrival of Francis, Ethel and Margaret.

My father continued with the C.P.R. as section foreman. He served at Granum, Orion, Lundbreck and Foremost. The war years were again anxious ones with all three sons in the armed forces. Henry was in the 69th Transport Company of the Army Service Corps, Jim was with the tank corps of the Duke of Connaught's Own Rifles, and Francis served in the Royal Canadian Navy.

In July 1949 Dad and Mother retired to Lethbridge where they continued to enjoy such pastimes as gardening, woodworking, and quilting. They found much comfort in their family and much joy in their grandchildren and great-grandchildren. Dad died November 4, 1955 and Mom on June 21, 1970. All their family reside in Alberta. Elizabeth Irene (Mrs. Fred Wesley) lives on an acreage just out of Lethbridge. She and her husband (deceased) farmed for many years at New Dayton.

Henry Nicholas married Jean Turnbull of Lethbridge. They reside in Calgary where Henry is Bridge and Building Master with the C.P.R.

Katherine Viola (Kay) married Kenneth Avery of Tees, Alberta and she resides in Lethbridge where she is employed by Woolworth Co.

Leona Grace married Alex Wihnan of Lundbreck (deceased) and is now the wife of Rome Mueller of Warner. They farm in the Warner district.

James Peter married Grace Underdahl of Manyberries and they live in Calgary. Jim is in Sporting Goods wholesale business.

Francis (Frank) married Evyon Robinson of Etzikom and they live in Lethbridge were Frank is Detective Sergeant in the juvenile division of the Lethbridge City Police.

Ethel Ann and Margaret Marie also live in Lethbridge. Ethel is teacher/librarian at an elementary school in Coaldale and Margaret nurses at the Lethbridge Rehabilitation Hospital.

P.S. I was privileged to meet some acquaintances of my parents and grandparents when I taught at the Okotoks Elementary School 1951-52.

DAVE AND ELLA LEWIS — by Ella Lewis

Dave Lewis was born in Wales and came to Canada as a young man. He made his home with family friends on Vancouver Island, working at various farms. After several years he came to Cayley, Alberta, where he worked on ranches.

I was born in Ontario and after I finished High School, my father (N. D. Scott) moved the family to Cayley, Alberta. It was several years before Dave and I met. Some time after that he rented the C C Ranch, and we lived there for a year and a half after our marriage.

Dave bought a farm in the Buffalo Hills, north of Vulcan, where we lived for 22 years, through the good times of the late 1920's and the depressed years of the 1930's, and then during the war years. During this time Dave had been building a sheep flock, gradually acquiring some registered stock. After the war he wanted to specialize in pure-bred sheep, and also wanted to get nearer the market so bought the "Hislop farm," north of Okotoks, which constituted the E. ½-17-21-29-W.4th M.

After we had lived there for several years, Mr. Yauch, the district agriculturist, helped Dave start a 4-H sheep club in the area, with Dave as leader. Quite a number of the local boys and girls passed through the club, making a good showing in sheep husbandry — in fact, were outstanding at the Calgary shows.

Dave himself showed at many shows — Calgary,

Dave and Ella Lewis.

Edmonton, Red Deer, Lethbridge, the Royal in Toronto, once in Vancouver and in Salem, Oregon, winning a fair share of ribbons and trophies. In addition, breeding stock were sold in the U. S. A. as well as in Canada.

First row: L. to R.: Dave Lewis, Susan Banks, Sandra Banks, Mr. Yauch, Carol Aggett, Court Aggett. Second row: Not known, not known, Jackie Paul, Bill Macdonald, Larry Macdonald, Stewart Sinclair-Smith, Ralph Gough, Bob Hebson, Glen Norris. Third row: Not known, Cathy Sinclair-Smith, Dorothy Hebson, Marjorie Newman, Gail Paul, Julie Gough, Betty Bricker, Judy Newman, Karen Bricker, Peggy Aggett, Elaine Goddard, Marilyn Jones. Fourth row: Mrs. Sinclair-Smith, now known, not known, Dr. Banks, Donald Sandeman, Larry Kopas, Tom Hebson, not known, Allan Macdonald, Lawrence Norris, Jack Paul.

Over the years the sheep provided some amusing incidents. One I remember occured when Dave had me assisting him in treating a ram. I was holding the ram, leaning over with my arms around his neck, while Dave had gone for the medication. One of the other rams could not resist the target I presented, and before I knew it, he had up-ended me so that I landed on my back in front of the one I was holding. Dave arrived back just then, grabbed the culprit and up-ended him in retaliation.

Dave and I were involved to a certain extent in both church and community affairs over the years, Dave being an elder in the Okotoks United Church for some time.

After being badly burned in a flash fire in 1962, Dave bought a retirement home in Burnaby, B.C., but he could not give up his interest in the sheep, and we were on the farm when he died suddenly in 1964. After his death, I sold the farm and stock and went to Burnaby, where I have continued to make my home.

WILLIAM ROBERTSON AND CHARLOTTE ALICE (BELCHAMBERS) MACDONALD — by John Alistair Macdonald M.C.

My father was William Robertson Macdonald. He graduated from Edinborough University and went to Calcutta, India, on the staff of Dufton College and later became City Clerk of Calcutta. He married Charlotte Alice, youngest daughter of Robert Belchambers, Registrar of the High Court of Calcutta for over sixty years and a noted authority on the Laws of India. They came to Canada on a six month sick leave. Kamloops, B.C. being recommended. A stop over in Calgary resulted in the purchase of the R. C. Thomas' homestead at the confluence of the Bow River and Pine Creek.

We arrived in March or April 1901, my parents, three sisters; Nora, Alice, Marjorie, one brother; David, and I. I was born in Fifeshire, Scotland, the

Mr. and Mrs. W. R. Macdonald, 1902.

other children had all been born in India. A third son, Donald, was born in Alberta. My parents built a house and barns on the N.W.¼-4-33-39-W4, acquired additional lands adjoining and called their ranch "Strathpine". Our closest neighbours to the west were the Wolley-Dods, to the south-west, Mr. Joseph Moss, who sold his ranch and moved to the Arrowwood country. When the railroad was built, the town of Mossleigh was named after him. Mr. Moss sold to the Trouton Bros., who sold to Heaver and Sons about 1910. This land is still held by the Heaver family. Adjoining to the south and southeast was Neil Brodie (later owned by Alex Sangster), and, still farther east John Kenney.

The old Blackfoot Trail ran through Strathpine for about two miles. In addition to parties of Indians and large cattle drives from open range land to the east, the neighbours, from the east, who used the trail in passing and to visit Strathpine, were; Tom Andrews and his son, Jim, Harold Banister, Bill Moody, McMann, Bill Stewart and others. The remains of the old log shack built by a trapper named Cable stood just east of the point where the Cable Grade entered the Bow Valley. Cable was credited with the extermination of the beaver in the area. It was several years before the beaver again appeared in the beaver dam ponds.

In 1911, a Community Camp was arranged for at Strathpine and well attended by many De Winton families. Existing snapshots of the occasion bring to mind the names of some of those who attended and who helped to make it a happy memorial occasion. Some of those names, outside of the immediate family, are: George and Desdemona Gray, Mc Neills, Latimers, Ernest and Annie Reid, Heavers, Rogers Scotty Lorrimer etc.

My parents sold Strathpine to Frank Wonnacott in 1922 and moved to the U.S.A. They took up residence near Seattle, Washington, where they remained until their deaths, Mother in 1929 and Father in 1934.

Through the years my brother, Donald, was their mainstay. The only one of the family born at Strathpine. Following their passing he took up residence in England. He served in the Canadian Navy during WW 2. He died in England in the mid 1950's.

Nora, (Mrs. Arthur Wright), resided in Seattle for many years, where she died in 1929, leaving a family of twelve children. Most of them still survive and live in the U.S.A. The two eldest, Myrtle, (Mrs. John Coles) and Bob Wright live in Vancouver.

David, my elder brother, left Strathpine when quite young. He worked at various jobs, mostly in Victoria and Vancouver. During WW 1 he spent some time overseas with the Y.M.C.A. In his later years his main interest was in the organization of Co-operative Enterprises and Credit Unions. He died some years ago leaving a widow and four daughters, three of whom still live in B.C.

Alice, (Mrs. Godfrey Westover), lives with her husband on Vancouver Island. Most of their married life was spent in Vancouver. Two of their three daughters are living in the Sidney District of B.C. and the third one lives in Ottawa.

Marjorie, (Mrs. Herbert Boyden), is widowed, lives in Victoria with her eldest daughter who spent a number of years as a missionary teacher in various locations in East Asia. Robert, eldest son, lives in Edmonton. He was a "Pathfinder" pilot during WW 2 and was awarded the D.F.C.

I, John, was raised at Strathpine, married Eleanor Gray and we have three girls and one boy, thirteen grandchildren and three great-grandchildren. We reside at Jacques Lodges in Calgary.

MELVIN AND CORA (ANDREWS) MARTIN — by Russell Martin

Born in MacGregor, Manitoba in 1891, Mel Martin came to Alberta in 1902 with his parents. His father, James M. Martin, bought a farm where the international airport is now located. They soon became interested in dairying, and Mel told the story of peddling milk from door to door as a young boy. He would drive into the city with a team and wagon, with the milk in eight gallon cans, and a one quart dipper. The lady of the house would bring her container to the door and he would measure out the amount of milk she wanted.

In 1907 the family moved to Brandon and then on to Kenora where they operated a livery stable. In 1911 they returned to Alberta, to Morrin where the two oldest boys, Mel and Barsby each took up a homestead. The rest of the family lived in the town of Morrin. Then in 1913 the whole family moved to De Winton to the Davisburg district. S.W. 6-22-28 W of 4th.

On June 19th, 1918 Mel married Cora Andrews, the youngest daughter of pioneers Mr. and Mrs. W. J. Andrews. Cora was born on the homestead N.E.¼ 28-21-29 W of 4, on September 1, 1896. She attended Melrose School and then Central Collegiate Institute in Calgary for her high school education.

Mel and Cora built their home on the quarter south of the Martin home N.W. 31-21-28-W of 4.

Mel and Cora Martin, 1918.

In the fall of 1921 they moved to De Winton where Mel worked in the De Winton General Store, then owned by his brother-in-law H. M. Oneil. They stayed in De Winton for one year and then returned to the farm in Davisburg. Shortly after they returned they moved over to Cora's old home on the N.E. 21-21-29-W of 4, and there they stayed for the rest of their lives.

In 1928 Mel became secretary-treasurer of the Melrose School and he kept the position until the school was taken over by the Calgary Rural School Division.

The Martin home was a boarding place for a long line of teachers at Melrose, because it was so close to the school. One of the bedrooms was always known as "The teacher's room". The price for room and board was $20.00 per month.

Mel was also secretary-treasurer of the De Winton community hall on two occasions — from 1939 to 1940, and from 1941 to 1948. He helped build the United Church at De Winton in 1934, and Mel and Cora were long time supporters of that church. Mel was also an original member of the board of the Okotoks De Winton Rural Electrification Association and as such, was instrumental in getting the power distributed throughout the district in 1949 and 1950.

Mel and Cora had two sons Russell and George. They both attended Melrose School as their mother had done, and went to high school at De Winton. Russell stayed on the farm, and in 1947 married Marion Cameron of Okotoks. They had three children, Donovan born in 1948, Dorothy in 1952 and Ross in 1955.

George went to "Tech" in Calgary in 1948 and graduated as an apprentice mechanic in 1950. He completed his apprenticeship with General Supplies Ltd. and continued to work for them until 1962. He married Marion Downs in 1957, and in January, 1962, George, Marion and young son Douglas, who was six months old, returned to the farm. In 1966 a daughter Tammy was born.

In 1949 Mel bought the S.E.¼ 21-21-29-W of 4, from Mrs. Joe Hogge. Then in 1953 the N.W. ¼ and S.E. ¼ were cut in two by No. 2 Highway.

In the fall of 1954 the dairy barn was built and on April 16, 1955, the first shipment of milk went to Calgary. The Martins have been in the dairy business since that time.

Mel died on May 27, 1964. Cora continued to live in the old home until her death, February 23, 1975.

Donovan attended Melrose School for Grade I, then in 1955 the school was closed and the pupils sent by bus to Okotoks. He received his Bachelor of Education degree in 1970 from the University of Calgary and has been on the teaching staff at Red Deer Lake School since 1968.

Dorothy was a member of the first graduating class in the faculty of nursing, University of Calgary. She received her degree in 1974 and went to work at the Calgary General Hospital. On August 24, 1974 she married Greg Kakish who was enrolled in the Faculty of Education at the University of Calgary.

Ross is currently a second year apprentice with Quigley Electric in Okotoks.

George and Marion's two children, Douglas and Tammy are both attending school in Okotoks.

In the fall of 1973 the Martin farm was again bisected by roads leading to an interchange with No. 2 and No. 2A Highways. This project was not completed until the fall of 1975.

THE MAXWELLS — by Roy Maxwell.

My father and mother, Robert and Margaret Maxwell, and I (Roy), arrived in Calgary from Quebec on the 9th day of February, 1896. That spring, Dad rented a quarter section in the Davisburg district, and bought a few cows. That summer was one of the driest on record and the winter one of the coldest.

By the spring of 1897 Dad had had enough of Alberta and decided to head back east. He sold the cows and calves, loaded all their possessions and went to Calgary. There everything was put in the C.P.R. Station, tickets were bought, and we were to leave at midnight. We arrived at the station at 11:30 p.m., and the conductor told us there would be no train on account of a mud slide in the mountains. The train did not come for eleven days, and in the meantime Father had taken a job with the Eau Clair sawmills as fireman. He worked for the lumber company until freeze-up and then operated the Pacific Livery Barn for the winter.

In the spring of 1898, Dad bought a quarter of land southeast of De Winton and in the fall of 1899 I started to Melrose School where I finished my education. In 1916 I moved to what is now the Mossleigh district where I have resided ever since.

Mother passed away in 1931 and Father in 1942. A sister, Ethel, passed away in 1897, followed by a brother, Hugh Benjamin, in 1901, Arthur Edwin in 1923 and Frederick Raymond in 1971.

I still own the original home place southeast of De Winton. I have two children Margaret (Mrs. Clayton Daub), of Calgary, and Arthur, of Mossleigh, three grandchildren and five great-grandchildren.

THE McCONNELL FAMILY — by Catharine Reid

Theodore McConnell arrived in Calgary in 1909 at the height of the land boom. He had been born at Port Burwell, Ontario, and was always a Canadian citizen, although he had spent much of his life in business in New York and New Jersey. Now, nearly seventy and retired, he and his wife Lalia had come west on a trip and were so intrigued with the growth of the new country that they decided to try the real estate business, buy a house or two, and settle down.

Their daughter Elaine was with them, and attended school in Calgary. She was one of the first pupils in the tiny college which offered higher education for a few years before the first World War. It was closed in 1914, and years later re-opened and grew to become the present University of Calgary.

Their son Roy was attending Rutgers University in New Jersey to pursue a career in engineering. But somehow, thoughts kept coming through of the opportunities out West; the pleasant memories of childhood visits to his mother's family farm in the Annapolis Valley of Nova Scotia; and the experiences he had had living on a farm his parents had owned for a number of years in New Jersey.

The result was that he quit school, much against his parents' wishes, boarded a train for the West, and arrived at the Calgary station in February 1910, at the age of nineteen.

His father decided that if it were really what he wanted to do he'd better look for a farm for his renegade son. They located some land for sale five miles southeast of De Winton (S.E. 22, S.15, T.21, R.29, W.4th). It was owned at that time by a family named Bristow and Roy moved in with them for a few weeks to get acquainted with his new project. The Bristows held a sale in the spring and left, leaving Roy on his own.

During the next few years there were many hired men, one of whom was a childhood friend, Perry Fox, from Nova Scotia. Perry stayed for three years and then acquired his own farm at Olds.

Church services were held in the Melrose School, and were well attended. Lalia McConnell, Roy's mother, held Sunday School at the Davisburg School, and occasionally at the farm home. She and her husband made frequent visits to the farm, although their home was in Calgary.

In December 1915, Roy returned to New Jersey to marry Cressence Maier, the girl he had kept in touch with for five years. When he arrived with his bride, it was thirty below zero. There were no city conveniences such as she had known in the East, and it was a very long way from 5th Avenue, but she adapted quickly and in a few years, decided that she would never want to live in the East again.

Theodore McConnell died in 1918 and his wife, Lalia, died in 1935. Their daughter, Elaine, is still living in the old home in Calgary.

Roy McConnell died in 1966 after farming the original farm for fifty-five years. He sold it to Ed O'Connor and retired to Cremona shortly before his death. His wife, Cressence, is still living in Cremona.

Their only child, a daughter, Catharine, was born in 1925 and attended Melrose School from 1932-1938. She rode horseback to De Winton High School from 1938-

Roy and Cressence McConnell, Golden Wedding, Dec. 30, 1965.

1942 and later attended Olds College. She married Vair Reid of Cremona in 1946 and they have lived on the farm there ever since.

The Reids have four children: Dale, an electrical engineer working with Bell Telephone in Montreal; Doug, a veterinarian, presently practicing in Carstairs; Shirley, a high school teacher of French and English, now teaching in Okotoks, and Gerald, who is attending the University of Alberta, studying drama and Fine Arts.

JAMES AND CONSTANCE (TYSON) McNEILL — by Dorothy Scott

Jim McNeill was born in De Winton and his wife 'Daisy' Tyson came to the district with her parents, just one week before her 21st birthday in March, 1914. They were married November 10, 1915. For awhile after they were married, they took up residence on a homestead in the Blind Creek area, near Mossleigh. When it became necessary for John Tyson to leave the district, Jim and Daisy moved to the farm, N.E.¼-16-21-29-W4.

Daisy was a very outgoing person and joined in the community functions, however their stay on the farm lasted only three years. The few years following were spent at Banff, Lake Louise, Mission, B.C. and then back to Banff about 1933, where Daisy still lives. Jim died June 29, 1965, following surgery.

They had one daughter, Dorothy (Scott), born in Calgary in 1917, during their stay at Blind Creek. Daisy was in good health and riding her bicycle daily until her 76th year, when she suffered a fractured knee cap, from a fall and spent three months in hospital. She now lives next door to her daughter in Banff, but is in poor health.

Dorothy and Will Scott have two daughters; Joyce Althea and Norma Joan. Norma married Frank C.

Jensen and lives about two miles east of the weigh scales near De Winton. This land was part of the Heaver place, and Frank is busy raising 'Beefalo' cattle, so we have a full circle in one generation.

JOHN (JACK) MEEHAN — by A. Meehan

John Meehan homesteaded in the Melrose district in 1885, L.S.D. 15, NE¼-22-21-29-W4, four and one half miles southeast of De Winton. John Meehan was also an agriculture teacher at the Dunbow Agricultural School for Indian children. Many of these boys turned out to be very successful farmers. After some years Dr. Rouleau replaced him, as his own ranch required all of his time. He now had five quarters and 80 acres of land, 15 good horses and 100 head of cattle. The brand on the horses was four circles in a diamond shape on the right shoulder; the cattle brand was four circles on the right rib.

John Meehan married Elizabeth La Croix, a dressmaker from Calgary who came West from Sarnia, Ontario in 1890. They had seven children: R. H. (Dick), B.C.; Catherine (Katie) Impey, Winnipeg, Manitoba; George F., Calgary; Agnes, Calgary; Mary Hamilton, Black Diamond; Maizie Johnston, Calgary; and Ruth Mapey, Calgary. At the time of writing (1975), they are all living.

My father and John Greenfield built a brush plow in Mr. Greenfield's blacksmith shop. Many of the neighbors would borrow the plow to clear the land. It took eight horses to pull it.

John Meehan passed away in 1911, following a serious operation, and Mrs. Meehan continued to farm with the help of her children. In 1929 George took over the farm and worked it until 1949 when he moved to Calgary. During the first few years after George took over, Mrs. Meehan spent a part of each year in Winnipeg with her daughter Katie, returning to the

L. to R. Front row: Dalton Bristow, John Meehan, Robt. Maxwell, Frank McInenly. Back row: Bristow, Percy Tulford, John Greenfield, Bill Moodie.

Back Row, l. to r.: Jack Meehan, Bernard Meehan, Mary Meehan, (Mrs. George), Ruth Meehan, (Mrs. Dick), Dick Meehan, Jack Johnson. 3rd Row: George Meehan, Mary Meehan (Hamilton), Ruth (Meehan) Mapey, Katie (Meehan) Impey, John S. Hamilton, Maizie (Meehan) Johnston, Agnes Meehan. 2nd Row: Betty Hamilton with Joy on knee, Colina Meehan with Donalda, Mrs. Elizabeth Meehan, Theresa (Hamilton) Brown, with Larry on knee, Marie Meehan. 1st Row: Barbara Hamilton, Buddy Hamilton, Lana Brown, Patti Hamilton, Jim Mapey, 1953.

farm for about three months each summer. In 1951 she sold the farm and retired to Calgary where she passed away May 8, 1963. Both of the Meehans are buried in St. Mary's Cemetery, Calgary.

GEORGE & MARY MEEHAN
We took over the farming operations on the Meehan farm at DeWinton — N.E. 22-21-29 W4th in 1929. Mary and I stayed on the farm until 1949 and due to health reasons we moved to Calgary. We had three children, Marie, Jack and Bernard. Our first home in Calgary was at 608 - 15th Avenue S.E. which has now been taken over by the Calgary Exhibition. We are now residing at 81 Cumberland Drive N.W., Calgary.

TOM & MAMIE (McINENLY) MEEHAN — by Margaret Lucey
Michael Meehan of County Donegal, Ireland was born in the year 1840 and emigrated to Inverness, Quebec. He married and raised a family of eight children of whom Thomas was the fourth.

Thomas was born March 31, 1873. He came west to Calgary, Alberta in 1890 and homesteaded in 1901 in the Arrowwood district. At Cluny, Alberta he was married to Mamie McInenly in the year 1908. Thomas Meehan

Mamie Meehan.

Thomas Meehan.

255

was keenly interested in the U.F.A. and was a charter member. In 1927 Thomas had to give up farming because of ill health and moved his family to the De Winton district. He passed away December 25, 1929 at the Holy Cross Hospital, Calgary. Mamie died at home just a month later. They are both interred in St. Mary's Cemetery, Calgary.

Thomas and Mamie had five children:

Margaret (Mrs. Thomas Lucey) Okotoks, Alberta. They have three sons: William, Norman and Dan. Norman is married to Sharon Cruthers and Dan is married to Carell Burgess.

Harry, Innisfail, Alberta. Harry's wife Isabel passed away in 1972; they have one daughter Mrs. Marion Lavellee, Edson, Alberta. and one son, Joe at their farm at Innisfail, Alberta.

Joe, deceased July 9, 1969. Surviving is wife Marg, one daughter Patricia Ledene, Calgary and three sons; Thomas, James and Neil, all of Calgary.

Myrtle (Mrs. George Jackson) passed away June 30, 1971 and her husband George passed away September 14, 1975. Surviving are Georgina (Mrs. Robert Bellman) of Montreal and Ruth (Mrs. Ron Evans) of Winnipeg.

Harold, deceased May 1, 1974. Surviving are his wife Isabel, daughter Marilyn and son Fred of Calgary, Alberta.

HOWARD AND LAURA (ANDREWS) NORRIS — by Harold M. Norris

Howard G. Norris was born in the district of Milton, Ontario on March 3, 1891, the son of Mr. and Mrs. Charles Norris.

Howard was one of ten children, six boys and four girls. He lived and received his education in Milton until the age of nineteen.

In the year 1910 he decided to migrate west to join his brother John who had been in the west since 1907 and was working in the district of Okotoks, Alberta. Howard stopped in Winnipeg for six months, working for T. Eaton & Co. before continuing his journey west to join his brother John on a farm belonging to a Pete Idington of Okotoks.

During the year of 1912 Howard and John moved from Okotoks to the Davisburg district renting a section of land from the Shattuck family. They farmed here until 1914 when they moved a few miles south and rented a piece of land now known as the Herr farm, then leased by Frank Tucker. The following year Howard married a quiet lovely young girl, Laura Andrews, daughter of one of the older settlers in the Melrose district, William and Catherine Andrews.

In 1916 in partnership with his brother John, Howard moved with his young bride to the district of Mazzepa where they continued their farming operation.

It was in this year, Howard and Laura were blessed with the birth of a son, George Lawrence and repeated this blessed event in 1917 with another son, Charles Leslie. In the year of 1918 Howard and Laura and their two sons moved back to the Davisburg district to continue farming but without brother John, as their partnership was then dissolved.

On May 27, 1918 Howard and Laura received a prize package in the birth of twin boys, Gordon Stanley and Harold Maxwell. With four growing boys, Howard and Laura decided it was time they looked for a more permanent home, so they purchased the S½ 27-21-29 W4th. in the Melrose district not far from Laura's parents. It was 1919 before they had completed their home with the help of brother John and many good neighbors.

1920 proved to be another banner year for Howard and Laura. They were once again blessed with the birth of another son Howard Alvin.

The times were tough and with five boys to clothe and feed, Dad and Mother were forced to work many long hours, working the land with horses, milking cows, slopping pigs, feeding chickens and running after the sheep. Eighteen hours was a regular day and the sight of the old coal oil lantern being carried around the farm with tired hands became a natural thing for us boys.

Dad was a strict disciplinarian, demanding respect and good behaviour. He was not one to spare the rod and spoil the child. He always said that to see a child misbehaving or showing disrespect and not punish them was the same as telling them that these actions were right, and was better not to see them at all; however, I know that many times he turned his head and pretended not to see.

Mother was a gentle, hard working woman, never known to argue or purposely hurt anyone's feelings. She was content to have a good husband and a growing healthy family. She even did her best to please Uncle John, who lived with us off and on all his life. I will always remember Uncle John for the one that snitched on us boys when we swiped a jar of fruit out of the cellar and ate it on the step behind the house. However, as hard as Uncle John was to get along with, he did spend many hours helping Dad build the grain bins, helping with the harvest and breaking the many horses required for the field work. Uncle John was well known around the district, as he spent most of the summer months travelling Clyde and Percheron stallions to the different farms. He was also a carpenter by trade and built many of the barns in the surrounding districts which are still in use today.

Times were to continue to be rough, but by the late twenties, us boys were getting old enough to help with the chores and in the field. Dad taught us all at a very young age to drive horses, milk cows, weed the garden and the many other jobs around the farm. Mother used to spend many hours outside helping Dad, so we were also taught how to cook, churn butter, wash clothes, scrub floors, etc., many times under the watchful eye of Grandma Andrews, who used to stay with us on occasions.

I think our greatest love on the farm were the horses, we were always well supplied with saddle ponies, some we raised ourselves and others from the neighbors, who would give us a few dollars to break them to ride for use on their own farms. The highlight each year was the Okotoks fair where we had the opportunity of racing our ponies against the best in the district. I well remember the year Lawrence and Leslie, at the ages of twelve and eleven, ran first and second with their ponies, Bell and Laddie. The thrill of these races was to affect some of our lives years later.

Mr. Howard Norris with five boys, Howard, Lawrence, Gordon, Leslie and Harold, 1926.

All of us received our education at the little Melrose country school and later high school at De Winton three miles from home. We rode three miles every day on our ponies, as did many of the other kids from other districts.

Even with five boys, Dad and Mother longed for a little girl. In 1930 their prayers were answered when Catherine Violet was born. It must have been quite a life for her, with five older brothers jumping over each other to spoil her. However, with Dad's and Mother's strict guidance we were never allowed to do this and many a fight started when she was punished for doing something wrong.

The 1930's were to be even tougher than the previous years; eggs were selling at less than a cent each, hogs, beef and grain weren't much better. We were milking eighteen head of cows by hand, and a five gallon can of separated cream would bring in three and a half dollars. Early in the 1930's we four oldest boys quit school and started working for the neighbors around home and would send home a few dollars when we could to help Dad and Mother. I will never forget the time Leslie gave Mother five dollars. She was standing beside the stove and had a gum wrapper in her hand, she lifted the lid of the old coal stove intending on getting rid of the gum wrapper and threw the five dollars into the stove instead. Poor Mother cried real tears over this, as five dollars was a lot of money in those times and Leslie had worked hard to earn it.

My oldest brother, Lawrence, worked on numerous farms around the district: Goettlers, Bill Snodgrass, Gordon Dafoe, Alex Currie, etc. I think his most pleasant years were with Mr. Goettler and Bill Snodgrass, (I have a suspicion the reason for this was the pretty hired girls they used to have).

In the year 1941 Lawrence married a pretty young red-headed school teacher Margaret McLauchlan. They tried farming for a few years but even with the extra money Margaret earned teaching, hard times and bad luck, getting hailed out two years in a row, and a year of dry weather forced them to look elsewhere for a living.

In 1942, they were blessed with a son Glen and again in 1946 with a son Allan. At this time Lawrence and Margaret were living in De Winton. When the boys were quite young they moved to Okotoks where Margaret continued her teaching career in the Okotoks district, and Lawrence occupied the position of Manager of the Okotoks Seed Cleaning Plant.

Their boys went through school in Okotoks and then continued their education in college and university. Glen chose chemical engineering, and after finishing university, had spent some time in Montreal and Vancouver. He is married and has a son and a daughter. Allan received his college education in Lethbridge as a social co-ordinator and is now working in Calgary in this field. He is married also, and has one daughter.

"Leslie", the second boy, returned home in 1942 to help Dad and Mother on the farm. For a couple of years after he came home, Dad worked as a boiler man at the De Winton Airport, riding back and forth every day on one of his good saddle horses. Many times he had to let the horse lead him home during a blizzard in the winter months.

Leslie has remained a bachelor seemingly content with his herd of Black Angus cattle and his responsibility towards Dad and Mother.

As youngsters, Gordon and I were inseparable, playing hooky together, getting the strap in school together, running away from home together, etc. I guess of the boys, Gordon and I were the most trying for Dad and Mother. However, after quitting school we slowly grew apart, each going our separate ways.

"Gordon" met and married Ruth Campbell while working on her father's farm (Neil Campbell), south west of Okotoks. It was here their four children were born: Lorraine, Joan, Billie and Peggy. This was not to last however, as Neil sold the farm so Gordon, Ruth and family moved east of Calgary on one of Neil's acreages in the Ogden district.

Gordon worked at several jobs: Burn's Gravel, Premier Laundry and Firestone Tire. He was never really happy though and had never forgotten his love of horses, and with his young son, Billy, already an apprentice jockey, he decided to go into the thoroughbred racing business.

His son Billy was one of the top jockeys on the western circuit for many years and is now training, with the help of his Dad, at Calgary, Edmonton and Phoenix.

I, (Harold) like my brother, Leslie, remained a bachelor. At the start of the war I joined the airforce and was discharged in the fall of 1945. I worked on the farm for a short period with my brother, Gordon, and then joined my younger brother, Howard in the laundry and linen supply business in Calgary. During my years with this company, I purchased a small acreage in the Okotoks district and built up a thoroughbred breeding and racing stable. In 1973, after 21 years with Canadian Linen Supply, I retired to my farm in Okotoks and have continued my interest in thoroughbred racing.

Howard joined the airforce at the start of the war as a pilot. He served in England, Africa and for a time was stationed in India. After his discharge in 1945 he married one of the local belles from De Winton, Jane Wilson, daughter of Pete and Mabel Wilson. They moved to Calgary and after a year with Sherwin Williams Paint Co., Howard accepted a job with a laundry chain owned by Leo Smith. He served as Office Manager for one year and was then chosen by Leo to head a new company called Calgary Linen Supply. Howard was a born perfectionist and hated procrastination in anyone; I guess it was these traits, a lot of hard work and a lot of help from his wife, Jane, that made him such a success in business. Howard and Jane had two children, a girl Leslie Ann and a boy Hugh.

Tragedy struck too, early in Howard's life. He contracted a muscular disease and was forced to retire in July, 1973. Jane, Leslie Ann and Hugh were constant companions for the next year and a half, when he passed away on November 1, 1974.

Catherine, the only girl in the family, went through for a nurse and it was during her work in the hospitals she met the man she was to marry, Hartley Patton, the son of Mr. and Mrs. Patton of Drumheller. They were married in 1955 and were blessed with four children, Laurie, 1957; David, 1959; Lawrence, 1961 and Brent in 1963. Catherine has continued her career in nursing and along with her hard working husband, Hartley, they have a nice new home in Calgary and are raising a family they can be proud of.

Dad and Mother are still living in the home they built many years ago. The highlight of their recent years was the celebration of their Diamond Wedding Anniversary on June 16, 1975. The De Winton Ladies Church Group put on a lovely luncheon in the De Win-

ton Hall, where they met close to 250 of their old friends. They also received plaques, letters and telegrams from Queen Elizabeth, Prime Minister Trudeau, Mr. Robert Stanfield, Mr. John Diefenbaker, Mr. Joe Clark, Premier Peter Lougheed, Mr. Jack Horner and many other dignitaries too numerous to mention.

Mother and Dad still look forward to the visits from their children and grandchildren and their many friends in the districts.

LENT MORGAN ORTON — by Fay Dick

Lent Morgan Orton was born in Venango, Township, Erie County, Pennsylvania January 18, 1868. He worked in stone quarries, on railroads and farmed and ranched in various parts of the States before coming to Alberta to settle.

He married Laura Mosier in Spokane, Washington in 1906 and came to Canada where he bought a farm, N½ 29-21-29-W4, and farmed there until he passed away in 1953. His wife, Laura, predeceased him in 1932. They are buried in Moscow, Idaho.

THE PENNOCKS — by Les and Nan Pennock

We formerly lived at De Winton Service, at the junction of Okotoks turn off and No. 2 Highway. Although we can hardly be classed as Old Timers, we did live in the De Winton area for ten years (June 1948 to August 1958), and so we will try to add a little to this book of memoirs.

It was a new venture for us operating the Service Station; one we really enjoyed. People in the district were good to get along with; especially so as we were total strangers having previously lived at Elnora, on the C.N.R. line north of Trochu. My wife, 'Nan', and I 'Les', were kept busy as we had a grocery store along with the Service Station, selling pop, ice cream, etc.

Pennock's Service Station June, 1948.

Our daughter, 'Nina', started school at Melrose, a small school three-quarters of a mile east of the Service Station. Nina could not read at this time, but she could sell chocolate bars and pop over the counter as she knew the different bars by their wrappers.

In 1952, work started on the new four lane highway. Our station was in the way of the proposed highway, so we were in the thick of it. We had to secure new land and move over. This was an exciting time for

60th Wedding Anniversary, Howard and Laura Norris and Family, June 16th, 1975.

258

everyone. The new highway went through a lot of choice land, to a point just north of Aldersyde. This really made things inconvenient for many farmers. However, after many meetings with the government officials, settlements were finally made and things got back to normal. The government had two large camps for employees living quarters, supplies and machinery. Some local farmers worked on the highway with their tractors hauling packers over the new grades.

Some interesting projects took place during our ten years in the community. One such project of major importance was the successful drilling of oil wells on farms east of the Service Station, and they were fortunate in bringing in some high producing wells with a 34% sulfur content. Eventually this led to the building of a large processing plant at Okotoks.

Another project of equal importance was the coming of 'Hydro' with practically one hundred percent participation.

At the Service Station, we enjoyed long talks with many people who were really old timers. Hearing about their many experiences was always interesting. As far as our business went, it was a success, having a lot of local trade, and the summers brought in people from far away places.

We moved to Calgary, after selling the business, to live at 8224-4A Street South West. 'Nina', our daughter, is married to Richard Harder, from Caroline. They have a son and a daughter (Shawn and Charlene); both children now attend school. The family now lives in Calgary as well, after living in Caroline for five years.

Will Pennock centre and two sons Les and Richard 1957.

My Dad and Mother were retired and living in Longview, but they moved to the Service Station shortly after we bought it. They were a big help. Dad used to serve at the pumps and in the store during busy periods. Dad was a real Yorkshireman with a rich dialect. He sometimes had trouble understanding what people said to him. We used to say, "Well, they have the same problem understanding you."

All in all, it was an interesting and enjoyable episode in our lives. Writing this has brought back many happy memories of social and business contacts with the kindly folk in the De Winton district.

CLARENCE AND RUTH PEPPARD — by R. Peppard

When we were farming at Midnapore, in late 1934, we noticed a "Farm for Sale" ad. in "The Calgary Herald." The farm was at De Winton, Alberta and we went to see the owner in January. A week later we finally made an attempt to purchase this half section and moved from Midnapore early in April.

Money, for us, was spare and we built two large granaries and made them into three good sized living quarters and lived that way for fifteen years. We then bought a house in Turner Valley and moved it up to the farm to live in. We built other buildings between times. In 1936, Mr. Peppard decided he would like the quarter west of us and I wrote to Mr. Cockburn, who lived in Kashmir, India. I undertook the agreement and in 1944, after many ups and downs, we managed to buy both places.

In 1967, we decided to lease most of the half section and I sold the Cockburn Quarter. Mr. Peppard wished to remain on the farm and it was a pleasure to be free of the farm work. Living in the De Winton district was a happy time with very kindly neighbors.

Early in September of 1971 Mr. Peppard died suddenly, of a heart attack, and I sold the farm and live in Calgary. Our land was the E½ 28-21-29-W.4th and N.W.¼-28-21-29-W.4th.

EDITH (CURRIE) PINCHBECK

Mrs. John Currie (Edith's mother) often acted as a midwife for her neighbor ladies. After the babies were born her daughters came to care for the mother, baby and household until the mother was able to do so. Among those children whom Edith cared for were Les Marshall and Norman Hogge.

Edith married Robert Pinchbeck, an interior decorator and they lived in Kamloops, B.C. She was active in church and community affairs. She also did beautiful crochet and embroidery work.

She died in August, 1955 and her husband died in 1956.

ALEX SANGSTER — by Mrs. Alex (Mary) Sangster

George Sangster purchased a 1,200 acre ranch, with the buildings located on the E½ 26-21-29-W4M from Mr. Bryce Wright in about 1912-1913. This land is presently owned by Mr. Dave Hunt.

Alex Sangster stayed on the ranch owned by his father, George, until early 1915, when he left to join the army. Alex' brother, George "Kelly", Sangster came and lived on the farm, as well as a Russian couple who once managed the place. One of their neighbors were the Wm. Moodies. The ranch was sold in 1917 to Mr. Charlie Beeching.

Alex passed away at the age of 78 on December 8, 1973. His brother, George "Kelly", passed away at the age of 62, in the year of 1962.

JOHN AND PHOEBE (REDPATH) TYSON — by D. McNeill and D. Scott

On the last week of March, 1914, Mr. and Mrs. John Tyson and their three daughters, Constance Margaret (Daisy), Marjorie and Joan, arrived in De Winton. John purchased W½-15-21-29-W4 and NE¼-16-21-29-W4, from Mr. Simpson, in the Melrose district. However, my parents and two young sisters were not long there, as John had heart trouble and the altitude did not suit him. He returned to England to Westmorland, to sell three stores that he owned there. On his return to De Winton, he was advised by the doctor in Okotoks (possibly Dr. Ardiel), to seek a sea level location as soon as possible. He had also acquired a small farm from Ed Hayes on the Macleod Trail, and persuaded his cousin and her husband, Mr. and Mrs. Harry Usher, to come to Canada and run it. We had a sale of furniture and stock, and left the farm to live in B.C.

There were three daughters from this marriage; Daisy, (Mrs. Jim McNeill), born in 1893, who has one daughter, Dorothy (Mrs. William Scott), who lives at Banff, Marjorie, born 1904, married Leonard Israel at 16, was widowed and later married Tom Bate and has one daughter, Joan Elizabeth, (married to John Ferguson, the hockey player). Marjorie died in 1955. Joan, born 1913, died of spinal meningitis in 1926.

FRANK A. AND JOAN E. (CHRISTIE) WONNACOTT
— by Jean MacGougan
STRATHPINE FARM

Strathpine — a more beautiful spot is hard to find — was the home of the Wonnacott family from 1921 to 1944. The home buildings on the N.E.¼ of 4-22-29-W4 are on the old Dunbow Trail to Gleichen at the confluence of the Bow River and Pine Creek. Besides the Dunbow Trail, access was by "Cabell (Cable?) Grade" — a narrow dirt road, winding down to the valley floor. It was an isolated location, but very popular with fishermen and berry pickers. At one time this was the property of the late R. C. Thomas and I well remember a reunion of that family at our favorite picnic spot when one of the girls lost a diamond out of her ring. We children spent many hours on our knees, practically combing the grass and hoping, but all in vain.

Dad came to Calgary from a farm in Prince Edward Island in 1901 to work as a machinist at the Ogden Shops. He was always sports-minded and in those early days coached a hockey team and umpired baseball games. After working for McLeod Brothers for several years, he moved to Nanton in 1909 where he operated a men's clothing store for two years.

In 1910, while still in Nanton, he married Joan (Johanna) E. Christie who had come to Calgary in 1903 from Winchester, Ontario. Joan was a member of the first graduating class from Sleepy Hollow School, Calgary, and went on to Normal School in Regina. Her Professional First Class Certificate issued by the Alberta Department of Education is No. 50, dated 24 Nov. 1908. That year she taught in a rural school called Albert Park up on the hill above the irrigation canal, then at Alexandra Public School until her marriage.

When they moved back to Calgary, they bought a house on 9A Street in Sunnyside, opposite the east entrance to Riley Park, and Dad opended his own Men's Furnishing Store on 2nd St. East, between 9th and 10th Ave. This he sold when he joined the army. He went overseas as quartermaster sergeant with the 187th Battalion, transferring later to the machine gun section of the 31st Battalion. After serving with the Army

of Occupation in Germany, he returned to Canada in 1919 and received an honorable discharge. As a result of having been gassed and suffering from shell shock, he was no longer able to work indoors, so he turned to farming.

The move to Strathpine was a big decision which Mother accepted with only one stipulation — there had to be a water system to include a full bathroom installed in the house. How traumatic it must have been for a city girl to suddenly face the isolation and life as a farmer's wife. Melrose School was too far away for two greenhorns like Pat and me who didn't know one end of a horse from the other, so Mother taught us at home until we were ready for Grade 7 at which time we went to Calgary to our Grandmother's. By the time Fred was ready for school he was a farm boy with a pony and attended Melrose, as did Mary who was born after we went to the farm. They in turn stayed at our Grandmother's to attend High School.

I know that Mother's inexperience provided many a laugh at her expense, but soon with the advice and help of good neighbors she was baking bread, churning, selling eggs, etc. along with the best of them. In fact she sold eggs to a hatchery, with all the implications of R.O.P. chickens and weekly Government inspections. I believe that eventually she could do anything but milk a cow — and that she steadfastly refused to even try.

Hailstorms seemed to follow the river with the usual heartbreaking results, so within a few years the fields on the river flat were all sown to pasture grass and hay. The field nearest the original house was Kentucky Blue Grass — beautiful and level enough for us to have a tennis court at one corner — great fun until Dad started using it as a night fold for the ewes and lambs.

Perhaps the most unique feature of our farm was that there was never a motorized vehicle — all field work and transportation was with horses. Weeds were abhorred whether beside a building or in the middle of a grain field and since this was long before the days of chemical weed control, we all spent many hours pulling and hoeing weeds. The clean land must have contributed to the successful production of registered Crested Wheat Grass seed. Shades of the beautiful, neat farms of "The Island" were also very evident in the hundreds of trees and shrubs, obtained from Indian Head, that were planted as windbreaks, as well as the fine lawn, trees, flower beds and vegetable garden at the house.

Dad was a rabid, old-school Conservative who enjoyed nothing more that a good argument with a staunch liberal — friend of foe. He subscribed to and faithfully perused Hansard — no doubt for ammunition. An episode the family recalls with chuckles and delight occurred the day of a Federal election when the polling station was at Melrose School. Dad left on horseback without mentioning his plans, to drive with Mr. and Mrs. Heaver to the school. Upon his return, when Mother learned what he had done, he had no choice but to hitch a team to the democrat and Mother drove herself the long way around by Cabell Grade (no gates to open) to cast her vote. Need I say she was a loyal Liberal.

Wonnacott Home Circa 1930. Jean, Mrs. Joan, Pat, (Wonnacott), Mrs. Ward and three children.

Hailstorms were not the only disaster to strike. In 1927 (?) two cyclones passed through a few days apart, but we were lucky to lose only a granary and some large native trees. Every window on all sides of the house was smashed by hail, and on emerging from the cellar we found a hail-filled torrent of rain pouring down the hall to the back door. We scooped the hail into tubs with dustpans and since that old house never was very level and each addition was a step up from the original kitchen, we just kept sweeping to the back door and out. Poor Mother — what a sodden mess the place was.

In the spring of 1929 great ice jams sent the Bow River in flood over a small neck of land, raging down our little "spring" creek to the main channel. Some of the bank was undercut and before the water receded we had lost several small buildings, one of them the ice house. I can not forget standing beside Dad watching those blocks of clear ice bobbing along in the water, nor him saying he would never put up ice again. And he didn't. The only homemade ice cream we ever had from then on, was frozen with hail stones. The possibility of future spring floods was such a threat

that engineers were consulted and a great deal of time and money and hard work went into building breakwaters at strategic points upstream.

Times were tough, but the next few years were relatively peaceful until in 1931 fire broke out in the barn. No animals were lost, and the house was saved thanks to neighbors who arrived and kept the roof wetted down. When the barn and chicken house were replaced, a new site was chosen well away from the flood channel cut by the river in 1929.

Then in 1932 came the big flood. The Bow changed its course and within hours the bank was breaking away in great chunks. By the second day one end of the house was undermined and with a creaking and cracking of beams and ridge, away went the kitchen, pantry and store room. Within 24 hours the dining room and a bedroom were gone. With manpower, steel cables and heavy beams the rest of the house was anchored, and on June 3rd the living room, bathroom and two bedrooms, and what was left of the upstairs, was moved back from the river. During the summer this was moved to its present location and a large kitchen and porch added.

Over the years, Mother and Dad built up a small herd of registered Aberdeen Angus cattle, a flock of registerded Hampshire sheep and each spring bought a purebred Yorkshire boar at the Calgary Livestock Sale. Mother was a meticulous keeper of records, and all progeny were identified with metal ear tags issued from Ottawa. The years have proven their theory of producing and feeding good stock was correct, but sad to say they did not live to enjoy the benefits of increased demand and improved prices.

Strathpine was always a bird sanctuary and Dad served as district game warden for many years. Mother did considerable experimental work using hens to hatch pheasant, Hungarian and Chukkar Partridge eggs supplied by interested sportsmen. These tiny birds did well with their clucking mothers, but when

Frank Wonnacott home — another two rooms into the Bow — 1932.

released in the brush (on the hillside below the never completed railroad grade) they were easy prey for hawks and coyotes.

Dad died of a massive coronary while raking hay in August of 1944, just a few days after his 66th birthday.

Following an auction sale the property was sold, and Mother moved to Calgary. There she became an active member of Knox United Church and various Clubs, contributing freely of her time and talents. To the time of her sudden death at age 84 in 1969 she remained an intelligent, active, interested and interesting, kind friend, to all her associates.

MR. AND MRS. FRANK WOOD

Came from Missouri and rented the Orton place before 1929. Always paid his help in cash, he thought that cheques looked too much like a useless piece of paper.

They stayed only a few years and returned to the States. Mrs. Wood is still living in a nursing home (1977).

YOUNG FAMILY

Edwin H. Young and his wife Martha and two sons Thomas, age 12 and Gilbert, age 3, arrived at Calgary in October, 1900 from Dutton Elgin County, Ontario. a few miles from Lake Erie.

They were preceded to Alberta by Mrs. Young's brother D. P. McCall about 1894. Mr. McCall was a London Ontario University graduate who had been teaching in the High School at London before coming to Alberta. He then took on School Inspection work over a wide area of what was then Central Alberta for some years, until his appointment as Principal of Calgary High School. This position he held until leaving Calgary and going to Regina. Shortly after the Western Provinces were formed he became first Deputy Minister of Education, and some years later received a promotion of Superintendent of Education for Saskatchewan. He held this position until his retirement, about 1930, with an honorary appointment as Doctor of Laws.

He married a daughter of a pioneer Midnapore family, Miss Eva Brogden, shortly after coming to Alberta. They had three children.

Mr. Young and Thomas came west with a carload of settlers effects and livestock. They had a tedious trip of nine days enroute. The final incident right before the train pulled out for the west bound trip was that their valued collie dog killed a skunk. The "aroma" of this adventure came right along to Calgary. On the other hand, the train crew were treated to free hospitality of a couple barrels of good Ontario apples brought west by Mr. Young, which helped with the social atmosphere of a long tiresome trip.

Mrs. Young along with Gilbert preceded them to Calgary by passenger train. Zero degrees cold is almost unknown in South Ontario along Lake Erie, and the newcomers were given a brisk new experience by a 40 below zero cold snap soon after their arrival in November, but a quite open winter followed. The family found residence in Calgary for the winter, but moved to a homestead which later became known as Young's corner (S.W. 28-21-29 W4M),

The Young brothers completed their education at Melrose; Thomas having acquired most of his before arriving in Alberta. He later assisted his father with farm operations until the latter's death in 1929. Shortly afterwards, he moved to the McLelland farm, two miles south, which he had owned and also farmed since 1910. He was the local agent for Wawanesa Fire and Automobile Insurance Co. for twenty-two years preceding his death in 1956.

At age fifteen years, Gilbert whose health was rather delicate, became interested in the Poultry Fancy. The Poultry Fancy was then, and until the 1930's depression years, in its heyday. There were well supported and popular Standard Poultry Exhibitions winter and summer, which were featured at all leading centres. Giant hatcheries had not yet monopolized the industry. It was the day of the small home operated incubator and the good old broody hen. Owners took real pride in a quality small flock. Competition at leading Exhibitions such as Calgary was heavy, and business for those successful in winning coveted top awards in leading varieties was usually good with fancy prices quite the rule.

Gilbert in his early life on the home farm, which his dad was unhesitant in declaring, brought in as much profit, as all other combined farm operations. However, the depression years of the 30's spelled the end of the boom in the Poultry Fancy. Exhibits from the farm were first sent with Alberta Poultry Exhibit to the Royal Winter Fair in 1925 and were continued until 1960. With the Rose Comb White Leghorn variety, twenty best Display Diplomas have been won with about three hundred other awards at that great show over the years. Close to a total of three thousand prize ribbons have been won at Alberta and Eastern Shores, since the first exhibit at Calgary in 1913.

Prior to 1900, the Young place was inhabited by Arthur Griffin (bachelor) who was a missionary to the Indians for about eight or nine years.

One hundred and fifty acres of the Young's place was sold to Baptista in 1933 and then the remaining ten acres on the corner was sold in 1939 to Carsons who operated dog kennels. Mrs. Young died in December, 1936. Jack Hagerman bought from Baptista seven years later in 1943. Carson sold to Higman who later sold to Ruud.

Others Who Lived in the Melrose District but Sent No History

Boehlke; Gus and Billie, Reinhold and Bunnie. Bought the Wonnacott place in the late forties and sold to Assmus and Heichert in 1953.

Carson; James, Carson's Kennels, 1940s, SW¼ 28-21-29-W4.

Crockett, Mr. and Mrs. Chester, Betty and Kathleen, girls attended Melrose and De Winton High schools. Lived on several different places in the 1940s.

Gilmour; Agnes and son; Les, 1920 until about 1950. Agnes, later, Bowman, deceased 1978.

Hadden; Mr. and Mrs. A. J., Muriel and James. On Tyson place 1936-1942.

Halstead; Reverend Percy and Mrs., Percidel and Hedley attended school at Melrose and De Winton. 1931-1936.

Horning; Mr., SW¼ 32-21-29-W4 bought from Gooch in 1944. Son, Norman lived on the Macdonald place in Pine Creek.

Learmonth; Mr. and Mrs., twin daughters, Edith and Editha, Tyson place about 1917-1922.

Lemmerman; H., followed D. J. Simpson on NW¼ 15-21-29-W4.

Merkel; Mr. and Mrs. George, Alma, Esther, Albert, Norman; 1928-1932. NW¼ 22-21-29-W4.

Alex Patterson; also on Tyson place.

Ruud; Richard and Dagmar, Oliver (Mel), LeRoy, Doreen. SW¼ 28-21-29-W4 in 1950s.

Simpson; D. J., NW¼ 15-21-29-W4 around 1900.

Westerson; Carl and Pete with their families. 30-21-29-W4. Carl had the garage in De Winton in the late 1920's, later had a garage in Calgary, lives in Cochrane, Alberta.

Original buckboard built in 1850 by McLaughlin.

Norma Blackwood on horse (George Sutherland, Alex Blackwood)

Mr. and Mrs. Andrews in front of their home E½ 32-21-28-W4 in 1900.

Transportation

Mr. and Mrs. Rob Dalzell and Myrtle — 1906.

Mrs. J. Sheepy, Mr. and Mrs. Jack Dalzell, Stuart Dalzell, Mr. J. Sheepy driving, Annie and Rob Sheepy.

Mr. Latter heading for the homestead — 1913.

Harnan Singh Hari, 1913.

Going to Davisburg School — 1918 Teacher, Vera Andrews.

H. H. Harper setting off back to the hills with the sleighs — 1926.

Skiing in Davisburg — Jim Suitor December, 1927.

Sheila, Jean and Jack McNeill — 1928.

A pleasant spring ride!

Breaking horses: right George Samson, left Jack Meehan.

Putting up ice in the early 1930's. Ervie Miller in sleigh, Albert Elsdon in front of horses, Ike Morris beside him. Ben Bishop in front of the two men with backs to camera who are unknown.

Jenny, the Holden donkey with the Holden girls in the buggy.

Desmond and Arthur Holden ride to school on Jenny, the donkey.

L. to r. Mary Dick and Dolly Dalzell, 1967.

William Anderson and son Alex with four horse hitch on manure spreader.

LEATHER CHAPS

LEATHER RIDING SKIRT

SHEEP SKIN CHAPS

SWEDE SAW

POST MALL

BROAD AXE

BUCKSAW

RAIL AUGERS

JOINTER PLANE

RABBIT PLANE

WOODEN JACK PLANE

BLOCK PLANE

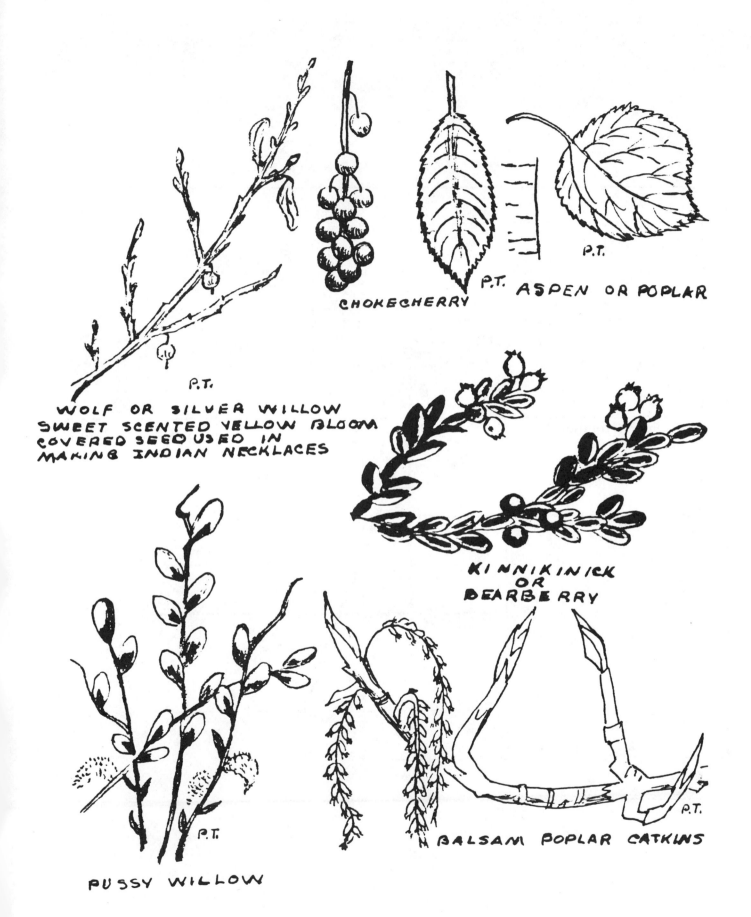

CHOKECHERRY

P.T. ASPEN OR POPLAR

WOLF OR SILVER WILLOW
SWEET SCENTED YELLOW BLOOM
COVERED SEED USED IN
MAKING INDIAN NECKLACES

KINNIKINICK
OR
BEARBERRY

PUSSY WILLOW

BALSAM POPLAR CATKINS

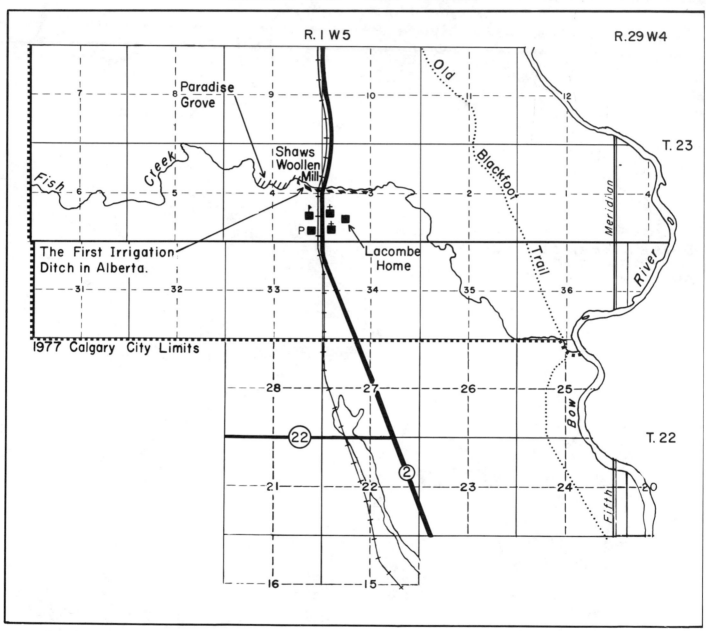

MIDNAPORE S.D. NO. 85

R. I W 5

R. 29 W 4

Paradise Grove

Shaws Woollen Mill

Fish

Creek

Old

Blackfoot

Trail

Meridian

River

T. 23

The First Irrigation Ditch in Alberta.

Lacombe Home

P

1977 Calgary City Limits

Bow

T. 22

Fifth

22

2

Midnapore School District

First Midnapore school where Grandfather Paling taught many years ago.

Midnapore Public School. Approximately 1936-37. Front row seated L. to R. Roddy Brown, Robert Fachini. 2nd Row: Bobby Hamilton, Dale Jeffery, Gordon Brown, Gwen Sanderson, Marjory Fachini, ? Rhinebolt, Stephanie ?. 3rd row: Bruce Hetherington, Olive Brown, Jim Hamilton ?. Back row: Bill Hetherington, Allan Brown, Stew Thomson, Valerie Lee, Irene Shaw, Lena Rhinebolt ?.

MIDNAPORE SCHOOL DISTRICT NO. 85

Midnapore was one of the earlier school divisions being next in line to Pine Creek. Very little information was gathered about the beginning of this district or, in fact, about its continuation.

It is known that Helen (Shaw) Millar taught pupils in Saint Paul's Church from 1887 until 1891 when; presumably, the first school was built. This school served till about 1916 or 1917 when the one that still stands on the hillside was built. One of the Shaw boys remembers that the school was too crowded for him to start when he reached school age and a larger one was needed.

In 1942, school space was once more at a premium and the Midnapore Hall was purchased, partitioned into two rooms and used for classes through 1969.

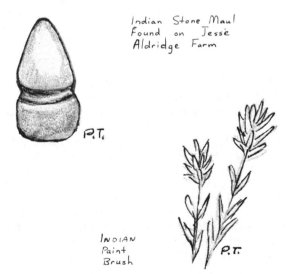

Indian Stone Maul Found on Jesse Aldridge Farm

P.T.

INDIAN Paint Brush

P.T.

TEACHERS AT MIDNAPORE

These may not be in order and we hope no one has been left out:

Helen Millar (Shaw) first teacher in Midnapore; Richard Paling; Two Buchanans; Miss Lousley; A. C. Russell; Mr. Barker; Mr. East; Mr. Martin; Mrs. Hoffman; Jack Howard; Jack Folkard; Roberta (Scott) Bottomley; Tom Sugden; Mrs. Scott; Mrs. Boos; Miss Thomas; Miss McLennan; Miss Fleming; Miss Sudre; Mrs. Kosling; Mrs. Wonnacott; Miss Dow; Miss Roberta Dawes; Audrey (Lynn) Irving.

Midnapore School Grades 1 to 6, 1946. Top row l. to r., ?, Ronny Denny (5), Billy Kindiak, Roger Cline, Austin Thompson (6), Rolfe Copithorne (4), Gerald Denny (4), Ron Whitney (4), Kevin Hoschka (4), Jim Hetherington (6), Second from top Row: Eleanor Shaw (4), Sharon Birney, Rosamond Sanderson (6), Allan White, Ian Copithorne (6), Floyd Thompson (4), Fred Farkas (4), Georgina Birney (4), Evelyn Goldsmith (4), Myrna Thompson (3), Third from Top Row: Marietta Thorne (4), Jean Birney (3), Patsy Gibson, Tressie Cline, Jean McInnes (4), Anita Thorne (3), Shirley Whitney (2), Elma Nicklesen (2), Laura White (4), Eileen Thompson (3), Beth McInnes (6), Bottom row: Eddie Mosier (2), ?, Gerald ?, Jack McInnes (4), ?, Larry McKevitt (4).

ST. PATRICK'S CHURCH — by M. M. Lee

(With indebtedness to Monsignor Anderson, Historian, Calgary Diocese, and many residents of the area).

When Calgary was born in 1875 Midnapore (Fish Creek) had one of the first Catholic families in the district, Mr. and Mrs. John Glenn, and three children. As other children were born, they were baptized in Calgary by Fathers Doucet and Scollen.

In 1885 John Glenn donated land for the construction of the Anglican church, at Midnapore. When the Catholics of the district wished to build a church, Patrick Glenn, (John Glenn's eldest son), donated the property beside the Anglican church.

To raise the money for the construction of the Catholic church the men of the district gave cash donations, and then donated their labour as well. Mrs. Victoria Whitney recalled how she and the other children offered their contribution, by singing and dancing at box socials. Quite often the bids at the social gatherings would go so high as twenty-five dollars per box, and on one occasion Joe Shannon bought four lunches at twenty-five dollars each. James Stevens, a Scottish stonemason, who owned a half-section of land north of McKevitt's, was hired to build the foundation, which he did from rocks and mortar.

Ed McKevitt, a young boy at the time, remembered carrying mortar in a lard pail to Mr. Stevens. Thomas Patton, a brother of Dan Patton, was the carpenter who built the church, with the help of the local men. In 1905 the church with a residence was finished, and it was named St. Patrick's.

When the churches at Midnapore were completed, Pat Burns, a Catholic, took it upon himself to tend to the painting of the two buildings, and he did this until his death. Every few years he would send out a work crew to paint the two churches. On one occasion, when the men had finished painting the Catholic church, the Anglican counterpart looked shabby, by comparison, so Pat sent his work crew over to paint the "heathens" church.

Father Lestanc said the first Mass at St. Patrick's. He had spent the previous night at the Pat Glenn home so that he could arrive early at the church. Father Lacombe was the first pastor, and he remained here until his death, in 1916. (In 1910, he had been instrumental in building the Lacombe Home, a home for orphan children and old folks). The Oblates to succeed Father Lacombe were Fathers Demeret, OMI, Cheveltier, OMI, and Remas, OMI.

In 1912, when the Calgary Diocese was formed, secular priests followed: Fathers Dougan, Smith,

Moriarty, Rouleau and F. A. Newman (1923-1948). Father Newman, the kind and witty priest, with a green thumb, landscaped the Catholic church yard and cemetery, and the orchard on the Lacombe Home property. Then, with the help of the boys of the Lacombe Home, and one of its senior citizens, Mr. Strong, he planted all the trees on these areas, and cared for them during his many years at Midnapore.

Before the construction of the church at Midnapore, a missionary priest from St. Mary's would pay monthly visits to the Catholic families south of Calgary. Sometimes, however, a priest would come from Cochrane, or Dunbow. When a priest was designated to say Mass at a certain home, his hosts would meet him at the CPR station, and lodge him for the night. The following morning the Catholic families in the area would come to that house to hear Mass. Later refreshments would be served, and the people would enjoy a great get-together, before dispersing for their homes. The priest who came most of the time was Father Lestanc, and he was followed by Father Dubois. Sometimes Father Jan or Father Lacombe came out from Calgary, and occasionally Father Rieu came from Dunbow.

Joe Pashak recalled how excited he and the other children were when they made the long trip, by wagon, to attend Mass at a pioneer home. When the Pashak family went to the George Hodgson home they would have to depart at six o'clock in the morning, in order to traverse the 16-20 miles, in time for services. and the trip to Mangans' was even longer.

Up until 1910, the children of the district went to St. Mary's for their First Holy Communion and Confirmation. With the construction of the Lacombe Home, in 1910, the children went there.

Mass used to be said at the homes of the following: James McKevitt, John Robinson, James Mangan, William King, Frank Pashak, George Hodgson, John Glenn, Patrick Glenn and Ed O'Rourke.

Some of the children who received their First Holy Communion and Confirmation at St. Mary's were: Ed, Anna, Nelly and Tom McKevitt (they had received their religious instruction from Mrs. O'Neil); Liza and Katie Robinson; Joe Mangan; Bert and Sanna King; Joe and Clyde Pashak; Elizabeth, Christina, Catherine, Victoria and Bertha Hodgson; and Russell and Eileen Evans, who had received their religious instructions from Father Chevellier, at Midnapore.

Some of the children who received their First Holy Communion and Confirmation at the Lacombe Home were: Joe, Albert, Jim, Patrick, Bernard and Katherine McKevitt; Edmund and Frances Glenn; Barton Evans; and William Kelly.

Bibliography: A Short History of the Catholic Church in Southern Alberta Report 1942-1943 — The Canadian Catholic Historical Association

EARLY HISTORY OF ST. PAUL'S ANGLICAN CHURCH FISH CREEK (MIDNAPORE) — by Jim Shaw

The little Church of St. Paul, Fish Creek, which stands in the Village of Midnapore, ten miles south of Calgary, is the oldest Church now standing in the Diocese of Calgary. It was erected during the in-

St. Paul's Anglican Church Midnapore.

cumbency of the Rev. E. Paske Smith, who was the first resident clergyman of the Anglican Church in Calgary, and who commenced his ministry there on Whit-Sunday, 1884.

Services were held in the houses of some of the farmers or ranchers in the district between then and August, 1885.

The Church was erected and opened for worship in September, 1885. The shell only of the building was at first put up, the lining of the interior being left until more funds were available for its completion. This was done about five years later when a garden party was held in the Church grounds, and a special train chartered to carry Calgary friends out to Midnapore for the occasion. Some of those who were present at the opening service were Mrs. S. W. Shaw and some members of her family, and Mrs. B. S. Lloyd.

In those days the numbers attending this Church were almost as large as those who worshipped in the Church of the Redeemer, Calgary, and the Rev. Paske Smith found it convenient to build a residence on land mid-way between the two places.

The first regular service was held on September 27th, 1885, and although the number present on that occasion is not recorded, the offertory amounted to $17.30.

The first service of Holy Communion recorded was January 10th, 1886, with seven communicants.

On May 9th, 1886, the regular service gave way to a funeral service when Kate McDonald Gibb, young wife of a Calgary citizen, was buried in the cemetery attached to the Church. This was the first interment to take place, followed in December by that of another young matron, the wife of H. L. Dundas, of Calgary.

The earliest recorded baptism in the district took place in Sept., 1884, when Laura Emily Maud Evans was baptized privately, the mother dying shortly afterwards. The next was that of John Edric Richard Lloyd on the 1st September, 1885, and then are recorded two baptisms on 18th April, 1886. The first to take place in the new Church, were those of Mary Ethel Eleanor Hermione Lloyd and Irene Julia Daphne Shaw. It is interesting to note that the mortal remains of the respective fathers and mothers of the last three named now rest in the churchyard at St. Paul's.

Three weddings are recorded as having taken place in dwellings in the district served by the Church prior to its erection, but the first to be solemnized in the Church was on the 27th April, 1887, when William Henry Goodwyn and Rosa Belle Watson were united in the bonds of holy matrimony.

The Rev. E. Paske Smith continued in charge of the Church until May, 1888.

On May 29th, 1887, the register shows that Cyprian Pinkham (Bishop designate of Saskatchewan) was present and preached, and on October 2nd of the same year, he made his first visit to the Church as Bishop of the Diocese.

Some insight into the travelling these early ministers did can be gained from a few entries made by the Rev. E. Paske Smith in an early mission register: On September 14, 1884 he baptized privately, Emily Maude Evans in someone's house; Some time later in January 1887 he baptized a child in Mr. Moore's house on the Bow River; On August 17, 1887, he baptized Henry Anderson at the freighter's camp on the Bow River; On August 26, 1887, he baptized a Gardner child at the old Gardner ranch — this child later grew into the very well known cattleman Clem Gardner; On December 12, 1887, he baptized the Indian Agent's son, Charles William Cornish, at the Sarcee Reserve; On March 11, 1888, we find him at the Blind Man River; On April 22, 1888 he was at Anthracite where he baptized seven children also officiated at a wedding.

On May 13th, 1888, the Bishop was again present and inducted the Rev. H. W. Gibbon Stocken as incumbent.

On one of these occasions, when one or two visiting clergy, in addition to the Bishop, had to be accommodated in the small chancel, additional chairs had to be provided, and Mr. Stocken brought a folding chair with carpet seat for his own use. When the clergy sat down to listen to the lesson which the Bishop commenced to read from the lectern, a crash was heard. The seat of the carpet chair had given way, and the reverend gentleman occupying it sat with its remains upon the floor! The congregation smiled, but the Bishop, whose back was toward the chancel, read on apparently unperturbed.

The first vestry of the Church, after Mr. Stocken was inducted, consisted of A. G. Wolley-Dod, Clergyman Warden; Arthur Winterbottom, People's Warden; other members of the vestry were F. C. Cornish, Mr. LeCrane, Mr. Collin Moore, Mr. C. White and Mr. S. W. Shaw.

About 1888-89 it was decided to build a shed to shelter the horses and buggies. A man by the name of MacMillan (his initials were not recorded) contracted to do the actual building for the sum of $20.00. The shed enclosed on three sides, was 60 feet long and 12 feet wide. The cost of the lumber including shingles for the roof was $63.59. These figures were taken from the ac-

tual bills presented to one of the vestry meetings, the minutes of which I was privileged to read.

Also in these minutes, I found that one time when the vestry was strapped for money, that Rev. Stocken's stipend from May 13th to September 30th amounted to $13.71, simply because that was all the money they had.

Attendance at the services were somewhat irregular in the early days, owing to the scattered condition of the settlement and the mode of locomotion, before the introduction of motor cars or of fast teams of horses. In the entries in the Register of Services often occurs the phrase — "No service — no congregation", or "No service — too cold", or "No service — too stormy". Once the entry occurs, "No service — ill in bed."

Among the visiting preachers of the '80's we come across the names of the Rev. Robert Inkster, a native of Saskatchewan, who for a short time was missionary to the Sarcee Indians; the Rev. J. W. Tims, of Gleichen; the Rev. A. W. F. Cooper, who succeeded the Rev. E. Paske Smith and became first Rector of Calgary; and Henry Allan Gray, Diocesan Lay Reader, who later became Bishop of Edmonton.

The Rev. H. W. G. Stocken continued in charge of the parish until the end of the year 1896, when he was appointed to St. John's Mission, Blackfoot Reserve, and Archdeacon Tims took charge until Easter, 1898.

In the year of 1897, a rather odd but significant incident took place in respect to the Church. The congregation, of course, was very scattered, and at this time Mr. S. W. Shaw was at odds with some of the members of the vestry and was not attending church where he normally played the organ for the services. Anyway, it so happened at that time that there were more active parishioners living near Pine Creek than there were at Midnapore, so they decided to move the building to Pine Creek without notifying Mr. S. W. Shaw who was one of the original subscribers to the building and also one of the trustees of the original Society who built the church. Naturally he was more than mildly perturbed, so he stopped them by placing the following notice on the door of the Church.

PUBLIC NOTICE

July 13th, 1896

It having been brought to the notice of the Trustees of the Midnapore Church of England and the original subscribers for the erection of the building on the S.W. corner of Sec. 3, Twp. 23, Rge. 1, West of the 5th Meridian at Fish Creek, to be used for religious and school purposes, that some evil disposed person is conspiring with or endeavoring to incite sundry people to commit a felony by secretly stealing the building. Warning is hereby given that any attempt to remove or steal this building will be followed by immediate prosecution of the offenders.

Signed on behalf of The Society **S. W. Shaw**
Signed on behalf of the Original Subscribers **William Henry Wood**

The people from Pine Creek actually started up the road to load up the building when one of their number arriving first saw the notice and went back and met the rest on the way. After talking it over they went

272

home again and that was the end of the Church moving episode.

The interior of the Church was completed during the summer of 1889, as on August 4th the service was held "in the school during repairs" and on November 3rd the "re-opening service" took place.

By this time a school had been built and the Church was no longer used as a school during the week.

On April 16th, 1898 the Rev. Eugene Perrin, who had come from England and opened a school for boys in Calgary, was inducted as the third incumbent of St. Paul's Church by the Bishop of Saskatchewan and Calgary. Mr. Perrin continued in charge until March 1900, when the Church appears to have been closed for four months. The next clergyman whose name appears on the register is the Rev. G. E. Gale, who conducted services regularly twice a month from August to December. In 1901 the Rev. G. H. Hogbin appears to have conducted eight services, and the Rev. W. Freemantle Webb, Secretary of Synod, one service.

The Church then appears to have been closed until June, 1904, when the following entry was made in the register: "Services were re-opened in St. Paul's Church, Fish Creek, by Rev. G. H. Hogbin, incumbent of St. Dunstan's with Fish Creek, Rural Dean of Calgary, on June 5th, 1904, after a good deal of enthusiasm had been aroused by a collection being taken in the district by Messrs. Wolley-Dod, Osborne, Brown and S. W. Shaw, for the purpose." Mr. Hogbin continued regular fortnightly services for five years with good average attendances. Since then a number of Church families have left the district and but few others have come to take their places.

When the Rev. G. H. Hogbin resigned in 1909 to take charge of Banff he was succeeded by the Rev. A. J. B. Dewdney (later Archdeacon) who continued fortnightly services to November, 1911, and was much appreciated by the congregation.

Following Archdeacon Dewdney, services were carried on first by the Rev. W. B. Church and then by the Rev. A. V. Grant, the latter afterwards succeeding Archdeacon Hogbin for a short time at Banff and then moving south to British Honduras.

The war was now in progress and a number of the clergy having joined the colours, a great shortage of ordained men made it necessary for those remaining to take on extra duties. Thus it came to pass that Archdeacon Tims, of the Sarcee Reserve, was asked once more to take charge of St. Paul's Parish. His incumbency commenced at Easter, 1916, and continued to 1943. He died in 1945.

The Parish originally included that of All Saints, Red Deer Lake and of St. Peter's Glenmore. During the incumbency of the Rev. A. V. Grant, All Saints, Red Deer Lake, was constituted a separate parish. Soon after Archdeacon Tims took over the work he found that it was impossible to get the Church people, living at the north end of the parish, and in what had become a suburb of Calgary, to attend any of the services of St. Paul's. A service had been held at Glenmore schoolhouse at intervals for many years past, and he re-commenced a fortnightly service there. The congregation was larger than at St. Paul's, but it had no official standing in the Diocese or right to send delegates to Synod until properly constituted as a parish by the election of wardens, etc. An application was then made to the Bishop, and the northern portion of St. Paul's Parish was cut off and separated as a new parish to be called "St. Peter's."

The Church is the proud possessor of a bell, thought to be the oldest in point of age of any bell in Canada. Its history will be found on another page. The Church also possesses a table and reredos, as well as a lectern, all of special interest as being the workmanship of Indian boys when they were students at St. Dunstan's Indian Industrial School, which was carried on by the government, but under the auspices of the Anglican Church, for a number of years. There are also two stained glass windows — one erected by the people of the district in memory of the men who went from the parish and "offered themselves willingly" and met death in the Great War. A tablet on the wall records their names. The other window is in memory of the father of Mr. F. L. Sanderson, the latter being for many years one of the Churchwardens.

In recent years stained glass windows were in-

50th Anniversary St. Pauls Church, Midnapore. Clery seated in front row. L. to R. Rev. Mr. Gibney, Rev. Mr. Herbert, Bishop Sherman, Arch Deacon Tims.

stalled in all the side windows of the Church by a donor who prefers to remain anonymous.

OLDEST CHURCH BELL IN ALBERTA — by Winnifred A. Tims
(By the courtesy of The Calgary Herald)

What is probably the oldest Church bell in Alberta, and possibly in Canada, hangs in the belfry of the little Anglican Church of St. Paul's, Midnapore, formerly called Fish Creek.

For nearly two centuries, perhaps, longer, it summoned the villagers of Thelveton (pronounced Thelton), Norfolk, England, to worship in their ancient Church of St. Andrew the Apostle — rang merrily at their weddings, and tolled at their passing with solemn knell.

About 1930 a new bell was installed in Thelveton Church, and the displaced bell given to the Church at Midnapore.

The tiny Church of St. Andrew the Apostle is one of the ancient Churches of England. Its first rector was appointed in 1308, which about fixes the time of its erection.

Repaired and Altered During Centuries

It has been repaired and altered several times during the centuries that have elapsed. The will of one John Perow, made in 1446, ordered that he should be buried in the adjoining Churchyard, and gave six shillings to repair the steeple and twelve pence to the High Altar.

Formerly two bells, said to have been cast in the reign of Henry the VIII, hung in the square steeple. Then, during the seventeenth century, one of them was sold to provide funds for much needed repairs.

When, in the early 18th century, the square steeple was pulled down and replaced by a small belfry, it seems reasonable to suppose that the remaining bell was again used.

Though of this we are not sure, it is a fact that the very bell which was then put up in the new belfry during the early seventeen hundreds is the same which now hangs in St. Paul's, Midnapore.

It was fitting that this old bell should go to one of the first-built Churches of the prairies rather than to one of the late erection. There it still carries on the work for which it was designed, and though far from its original homes, still calls the faithful to worship.

Much of this material was cut from a year book printed in 1933 and the balance from a tape I made when I had possession of all the old records of the church. I was a vestryman of the Church from my teen years until I was sixty-one. Nineteen of those years I was People's Warden and Secretary-Treasurer.

LACOMBE HOME MIDNAPORE — FOUNDATION

Father Lacombe — The Crees called him "The Man of the Beautiful Soul" and the Blackfoot called him "The Man of the Good Heart".

"Father Lacombe lived nearby in a small frame building as bare as the shack at Macleod in the eighties. Nothing of all the funds he had begged remained to him — nothing of all the gifts that had been showered upon him: for giving has been his special weakness". Reference: **Father Lacombe the Black-Robe Voyageur,** Katherine Hughes.

"Father Lacombe, deprived of one scheme of benevolence, immediately sought another. He was not inspired to throw all his energies into a Plan, which had been in his mind in a vague way for years . . . Very occasionally he had spoken of it, wistfully and timidly almost, as "my dream of an old missionary." He resolved to realize this now — and so provide a refuge for the orphans and homeless aged of Alberta.

Progress had made its own of the old hunting-ground of his Indians, and in its spectacular march the weak — as elsewhere — were thrust to the wall. Father Lacombe's heart called out to him to help these.

Everyone else in the West was intent upon the opportunities and necessities of development. Governments were absorbed in constructive legislation and public works. Young missionaries expended their energies in forming new missions for the in-pouring immigrants. Individuals were busy making fortunes or places for themselves. They had no time to seek those in danger of falling by the way: this mission remained for the Man-of-the-Good-Heart.

As soon as Father Lacombe realized that this was to be his next undertaking his mind became a glowing smelting-pot of plans about the Home. There must be found money to build and maintain the institution, a competent staff to conduct the Home, a suitable site in some pretty country place, where the children could learn to work the land — and a stream by which the old people would have a pleasant seat under the trees to dream or pray their last days away." Reference: **Father Lacombe The Black Robe Voyageur,** Katherine Hughes.

"In 1909, Father Lacombe opened the New Year with a series of collections for the Home. Lord Strathcona, on a trip to the West, gave Father Lacombe a cheque of $10,000. In 1910 after having collected $30,000 for the Home, he ordered the construction of a building costing twice that sum . . . The Home was officially opened on November 9, 1910 by Bishop Legal. It was named the Lacombe Home after Father Albert Lacombe." Reference: **Our Home,** Publication Volumes 1, 2 and 3.

The farm at Lacombe Home of 200 acres was donated by the Late Mr. P. Burns, (later head of P. Burns & Co. and in later years, Senator Burns), who

Lacombe Home 1912.

also gave $1100 for laundry equipment. He also furnished milking cows to the Home until such time as the Home could provide for itself, that is, from 1910-1927 and supplied the Home with meat and fish until his illness in 1935. Also — a horse, buggy and beautiful harness.

A second benefactor of noteworthy mention is C. J. Duggan who donated much in money to cover construction debts of the expanding Home. He donated $3000 towards kitchen equipment and also financed a new car and at his death, the contents of his last will weighed heavily in favor of the Home.

Dr. L. O. Beauchemin for 29 years was an active and generous benefactor.

Kiwanis Club — Mr. Mayland annually at Christmas, presents a $1.00 bill to each child at the Home. The Kiwanis Club supplies a gift for each child and all sorts of goodies. This continued for at least 20 years.

Knights of Columbus — The second Sunday after New Year's Day, the Knights take the children to a turkey dinner in Calgary where they also receive gifts and goodies and a picture show.

The Kiwanis and the Knights of Columbus along with the Sunshine Club give the children many a picnic either at Bowness Park, the Exhibition Grounds or on P. Burns Ranch. They have also supplied playground equipment. Reference: **Our Home**, Publication Volumes 1, 2 and 3.

The Lacombe Home was the realization of Albert Lacombe's "last beneficent dream" and it was here he expressed his wish that HIS HEART remain! He died December 12, 1916 at Midnapore where he had lived since the Home's opening November 9, 1910. He is buried at St. Albert. Reference: **Albert Lacombe**, Paul Emile Breton.

"The ranchers and farmers south of Calgary were visited by the Oblates from Calgary at their homes until churches and chapels were built in the small communities. It is likely that the Fish Creek area was also served from the Dunbow Industrial School.

John Glenn came to Fish Creek in 1873 and maintained a home and stopping off place for travellers until he died in 1886.

In 1885 he donated an acre of land to the Anglican Church on which they built their church about that time. There is no record that he also donated land to the Oblates, but since he was a Catholic, though not a fervent one, it is likely that he did so. There seems to be no other explanation for the two churches being placed side by side at Midnapore.

There is no Diocesan record of the building of St. Patrick's but Mr. Evans, a pioneer parishioner remembers that the church was opened in March, 1905. It was probably built by Rev. J. Lestanc, O.M.I. from Calgary.

Service of St. Patrick's must have been from St. Mary's in Calgary until the Lacombe Home was built in 1910. Thereafter the chaplains would have had the care of the surrounding Catholics.

In 1962 Midnapore was incorporated into the City of Calgary and St. Patrick's became a city parish.

Pastors: 1873-1910 — Oblates from Calgary and from Dunbow School; 1910-1916 — Rev. A. Lacombe, O.M.I., Rev. J. Chevallier, O.M.I.; 1916-1923 — Rev. J. F. Dougan, Rev. J. S. Smith, Rev. J. B. Moriarty, Rev. A. E. Rouleau from Calgary; 1923-1950 — Rev. A. Newman; 1950-1952 — Rev. F. J. Stefanski; 1952-1956 — Rev. J. M. McLaughlin; 1956-1960 — Rev. M. McGreevy; 1961-1962 — Rev. A. I. Hamilton; 1962-1969 — Rev. D. T. Sullivan; 1969-1970 — Rt. Rev. N. R. Anderson, P.D.; 1970-1972 — Rev. J. P. Kirley. Reference: **From the Buffalo to the Cross**, M.B. Venini Byrne.

MEMORIES OF MIDNAPORE — by Jean (Brogden) Ockley

One time a small granddaughter with a large curiosity, especially about "olden days" asked me about the lives and habits of dinosaurs. I had to admit I did not know anything about them and her astounded comment was "But, Grandma, you were here in the olden days." Many of these snippets of memories about early days at Midnapore are reports by others, even if I was here in fairly "olden days".

My father, Sam Brogden, told me the name had been suggested by a Captain Boynton who lived in the district and who had served in India with the British army. Whether the local terrain reminded him to that place, or whether he wanted to commemorate an event is not known now. The fairly large town of that name in India is northwest of Calcutta in Bengal province.

In recalling stories of early settlers in the area when old-timers got to spinning yarns there were names such as Glenn, even the notable Livingston family lived in the valley for a time and a man known as Jim Vocher. Actually the name was Votier and he was a member of quite a noted boat building family in Quebec, and a well educated man. The story is told of the then Governor-General, the Marquis of Lorne, being entertained in the Votier home and being quite amazed at the extent and quality of Mr. Votier's library. Just why he settled there is another question, never answered, probably never asked. In those days you did not probe into why people were here and non-committal if offered an unusual explanation.

There were stories of some of the unorthodox methods of augmenting the family income. One person had a cow with very motherly instincts. She insisted on having a calf . . . anybody's calf. So when she turned up at the home corral with a strange calf it was taken away from her and she was chased out on the range to repeat the process.

Of course, in very early days there were the Shaws, and Mr. and Mrs. Shaw were unique, and proud of it. I remember Mr. George Gamsby of the Priddis district, who had at one time freighted for the I. G. Baker Company, telling of seeing the Shaw family heading west from the end of steel. The Shaws had an enormous amount of settler's effects, including as has been told before, a complete woolen mill. Numerous wagons were needed to carry all this freight, and as many drivers, so members of the family were pressed into service, some of them astonishingly young for such responsible work. The whole retinue was strung out on the trail with Mr. Shaw leading the way on foot, supported by a long staff. Mr. Gamsby said, "He looked like Moses leading his people into the promised land."

It was noted that he wore a fur hat then, as he did in later years, as I have seen for myself, in summer as well as in winter. He was quoted as saying that what kept the cold out in winter would keep the heat out in summer, which seems logical.

Stories were told of the freighting and stagecoach days between Calgary and the United States, of the Red River carts whose soul piercing screech was heard for miles, and of the stagecoach driver who was a relative of Jesse James, presumably an honest one. I remember seeing covered wagons driven by American settlers heading for Canadian homesteads. I remember the long trip to Calgary with horses and democrat, and how cheering to see the half mile of poplar trees which had been planted by Sheriff King along his fence line, because we were almost in town then.

I remember the first Catholic sisters to come. They lived in a cottage on the east side of the road on the hill above the creek valley, which had at one time been occupied by some people called Murray. The time span between their arrival and the completion of the first section of the Lacombe Home is not clear in my mind, or the appearance of the children who were sheltered there. In the war years we would see a woman at the post office whose hands and head jerked uncontrollably. The story was that she had received word of her husband's death the day her baby was born and the double strain left her with this affliction. She found sanctuary at the home. I know a man whose mother died of 'flu' in 1918 and his father took his six children to the home where they were cared for and he did the farm work there in repayment. I also remember sisters from the home calling on people in the district asking for money or produce to help maintain the home.

My first teacher was Mr. A. C. Russell in the little old school near the station, and whose shabby interior held the accumulated dust of years. The new school on the hillside seemed like a palace, and was large enough for school concerts, and of course, dances.

Like the school, the hotel was there in my recollections. I believe Mr. and Mrs. Ed Johnson were the first proprietors, and as far as I know Mr. and Mrs. Monk were next. When Mr. Monk left the area, Mrs. Monk stayed on, but went back to her former name of Dowling. Her daughter, Vicki Dowling, with golden hair, blue eyes and a rosy complexion was the village belle and there seemed to be one or more of the "Dowling boys" around there. It was more or less unused for some time before it burned down.

The C.P.R. station was an important place for a number of years and a Mr. Kronk was agent there for some time. Freight and express seemed to move through there most days, money orders could be bought, or a ticket to Calgary for thirty-five cents. There was no grain elevator so at threshing time grain was loaded directly from wagon to boxcar. Seed grain came in in the spring and coal in the fall. Even cattle were handled in or out of the small stockyard there. North or south bound trains were all met to send or receive mail, except the mysterious Spokane Flyer, which was too fast and too important for that, although

it was whispered, but not actually believed, that it could be "flagged" if necessary.

There are a few of the things I recall. I am glad that, although Calgary has engulfed the area, the name still lasts. It is a little different to run of the mill names, just as those who lived there in the "olden days" were distinctive.

MIDNAPORE HALL — by A. McKevitt

The Midnapore Hall was built in 1928 with money collected from the district farmers and volunteer labour. I remember my brother helping to dig the basement with horses and a scraper. It was a great community effort and the majority of area residents did their bit to make it successful.

Operating as a community project, it continued until about 1934 when lack of finances began to cause trouble. As Mr. George Beatty of Midnapore had put extra money into it, he was carrying the mortgage and the hall board turned the building over to him. He con-

New Provincial Land Price Record Set Southwest of Midnapore

The ranch house on the George F. Beatty Stock farm, nine miles southwest o. which was sold recently for a record price of $130 per acre.

AGRICULTURAL ALBERTA

By Fred Kennedy

District Farm Sells For Record $130 Acre

George F. Beatty of Midnapore Receives $83,840 For Section of Land in Calgary Ranch District

What is believed to be a record price for land in the Calgary district was recorded recently when George F. Beatty of Midnapore sold his 640 acre stock farm to S. D. E. Hanker of Claresholm for $130 per acre or a total of $83,840.

The farm, one of the beauty spots of the Calgary district, is licated one mile west and one mile south of Midnapore or approximately 9 miles southwest of Calgary.

Mr. Henker will stock the farm with purebred Hereford cattle.

Mr. Beatty, who has farmed and ranched the place since 1918, said that he planned to take a long motor holiday before acquiring a small farm in the Calgary district. Prior to settling in the Midnapore district he farmed extensively in the Claresholm district.

He had raised both good quality grain and Hereford cattle on his Midnapore place for many years.

There are two George Beatty's in the Midnapore district. The other George Beatty is well known as a horseman and was an official at the Calgary Stampede for a number of years. He ranches west of the other George Beatty.

Mr. Beatty, who sold his stock farm to Mr. Henker said that folks are always getting them mixed up. "However", he said with a laugh, "I'm generally referred to as 'Old Man Beatty."

tinued to operate it as a hall but, as in the thirties, it was hard to raise money.

In 1942 it was decided that a new school was in order and the divisional trustee figured there was not enough time to build a new building and have it ready for classes in September. The hall was purchased, partitioned to make two rooms and was ready for school opening in the Fall.

From its inception as a school it continued in that capacity until 1969 when the pupils were bused to school in Calgary and, with the permission of the Calgary School Board, the community once again took charge of the building to use as an entertainment center and it is operating as such today.

RICHARD ALLEN — by his son Russell Allen

Richard Allen, was born in Ontario in 1869. Came to Alberta 1889 and got a job in a saw mill at Donald, B.C. for Col. Walker. Leaving there he went to work for R. G. Robinson on Chipman Ranch. There he met Eva Wright and they were married in 1896. He moved into Calgary and worked on building Robin Hood Mills. R. G. Robinson came to see, if he would go and work for a man called Jim Ryan on the 2 bar ranch north of Gleichen where he stayed until 1910. I heard him tell of taking a bunch of horses from Chipman ranch with Bert Henry to 2 bar ranch at Gleichen. From there he moved into Gleichen and worked at carpentry. There Ike and Austin were born. Ryan came to see if he would go back to ranch but he decided against that. He went to work for Dept. of Indian Affairs on Sarcee as a blacksmith but left Sarcee in 1918. Then he went back to Gleichen where he stayed a few years on a wheat farm. He left there and went to work for the 44 ranch west of Claresholm. As there was no school around there he moved into Claresholm and worked for Dept. of Agriculture at their school.

Later it was turned into an Old Folks home so he continued on until age 65. Moving to Turner Valley for a few years, he bought a place where he and Mrs. Allen lived the rest of their years.

MR. AND MRS. RICHARD ALLEN of Midnapore, who celebrated their golden wedding anniversary recently, are pictured above. Following their marriage in Calgary in 1897 they lived at Sarcee, Gleichen, Claresholm and Midnapore.

Their family were: Ike, Clarkston, Wash. U.S.A.; Austin, dead and buried at Midnapore; Cora Stange, Claresholm; Jack, died of polio; Russell, lives in Calgary; Dick, Mileston, Sask.

FRED B. AND MARGARET H. ARCHER

In 1914 a windmill behind the house a mile west of Midnapore bore the name 'JAVEM', made up of the names, Josephine Adolph Von Emaline Marie, the German owners. The acreage part of SW ½ 4-23-1-W5 was a chicken farm from which the upper windows of the house had a panoramic view of the surrounding country as far as Calgary on the north. When this acreage was purchased by Fred Archer in 1914 after the declaration of the First World War the story was that Adolph Von Marie had been hurriedly recalled to Germany and that the eight chicken houses, which had solid cement floors, were actually a cover for the cannon bases — the cannon to be turned on Calgary!

In 1906 Fred Archer, with his family, came to Calgary from Montreal as Office manager with the newly opened branch of the W. R. Brock Co. Wholesale dry goods. His hobby, even in the city, had been raising chickens and this acreage seemed an ideal location for raising prize poultry. The purchase included a small country store up the hill, which Mrs. Archers' parents, Mr. and Mrs. John Jackson, took over from Mr. Frizzle.

The two older Archer children, Jack and Muriel, walked a mile to the village school which, at that time, was east of the railway tracks and later became the site of Wm. Shaw's first home and work shop.

One incident which stands out in memory. One morning a mock battle was staged by the militia at Fish Creek. Naturally the school children, en masse "went to see" at noon hour but failed to return to school on time. Punishment was meted out by the teacher, Mr. A. C. Russell, but still it was a worthwhile experience.

After two years, the Archers returned to Calgary where Fred resumed his former position.

Completing his education, Jack became a clergyman in the Anglican Church and, after appointments in Olds and Hanna, went to the Mission Field in British Guiana where he died in 1934. Muriel became a teacher and received her B.A. degree from Queen's University. Her last teaching position was at Midnapore in 1931-33. She then worked as a seed analyst with the Federal Department of Agriculture, till her marriage to Fred Ratcliff in 1938. Douglas, the youngest Archer, was a chemist in the oil industry, spending 20 years in South America, before his retirement in Calgary and later in B.C.

See John and Margaret Morton story.

GEORGE AND ALICE BEATTY — by George Beatty Jr.

My father, George Beatty Sr., his wife, Alice and three children, Jack, Edna and George Jr., arrived in Calgary from Londonderry, Nova Scotia, in 1910. Dad was an architect with Alliance Investments Co. during the big building boom in 1912 until after W.W.I My sister, Edna married an Australian, George M. Beatty (no relation), a dentist in 1914 and lived in Sydney, Australia until her death in 1955. Jack served overseas in W.W.I from 1914-1918 when he returned and worked as a carpenter with Dad.

In 1922 the family bought the Bill Reinhardt place in the Red Deer Lake district where they took up farming. Dad died in 1926 and Mother lived there until her death in 1948. Jack also served overseas in W.W.II and, upon his discharge in 1945, resumed farming. In 1946 he married Gwaldys Mahood from Jasper and they have two children: Anna and Donald. Anna married Ray Stanton and they have three children; Billy, Michael and Beverley and presently reside in the Raven district, west of Innisfail. Donald married Sharleen Trudeau, an Edmonton girl, and they have one son, David, who lives in Vancouver.

In 1964 Jack sold the farm at Red Deer Lake and bought a place north of Didsbury where he resided until his death ln 1971.

In 1926 I bought some land from Dan Patton in the Red Deer Lake district and started farming on my own. In 1927 I married Florence Thiessen and we have three children: Bill, Edna and Betty. In 1936 I sold the farm and we moved to Cochrane but when Jack went overseas we moved back to Red Deer Lake to look after his farm for him. In 1946 I bought Mrs. Billy Reinhardt's place where I farmed and did carpenter work in the district. In 1958 I sold out and bought the Jack Schroder place west of Olds. Bill married Vi Gerlitz from Westoe district, Edna married Bud Gardner from the Raven district, they have seven children and all live at Sundre. Bill now owns part of the farm and operates all of it. Flo and I are enjoying semi-retirement on the farm.

NATE AND EILEEN (EVANS) BEEBE

Nate and Eileen were both born and raised in the Forestburg, Alberta area. They were married in 1936 and have three children, Vernon, Mona and Marjorie.

They farmed in the Forestburg area and Nate also worked as a coal miner in the local mines until moving to the Millarville area in 1945 where he worked in the oil fields.

In 1953 they bought a lot in Midnapore which was the old original ball diamond. They moved their house from Millarville on to it and it is still their present home.

Nate has been employed at the Holy Cross Hospital as a steam engineer since moving to Midnapore in 1953.

In 1962 he helped organize and manage the Midnapore Royal baseball team which won the city championship in 1963.

PERCY JAMES AND GERTRUDE (LLOYD) BIDDELL

Sara Gertrude Lloyd was born August 6, 1881, to Mr. and Mrs. Ben Lloyd in London, England and came with them to Calgary in 1884. They homesteaded southwest of Calgary, their land abutting on what is known as Lloyd Lake on the map. Gertie attended Red Deer Lake School for a number of years and then remained home until her marriage. Of a quiet and unassuming disposition, few people realized how responsible and dependable she had become as the second eldest in a family of eight children. During childhood a real love of Nature developed — also a love of the farm and all that it engendered. In November, 1908, after marrying Percy James Biddell they went to live in Cowley where 'Jim' had a livery stable business in partnership with John Kemmis. As Justice of the Peace and General Overseer, he was kept busy. Jim came out from England in 1890 and led a very colorful life, working and roaming the ranges, all the way to Mexico. He later depicted his many experiences in water colors and etchings. Jim and Gertie lived in Cowley until 1918 during which time they had four children: —

A daughter born in 1909 (deceased at birth).

Elizabeth (Betty) born in 1911, married Ian Sanderson of the Midnapore district. They farmed there until 1973 and are presently farming south east of Olds. They have two sons, Lorn and Leonard.

John (Jack) born in 1912, married Vivian Roper of Bittern Lake. They have two boys; Garry and Kenneth, and are living in Edmonton where Jack has run a service station for many years.

Brian born in 1914, farmed in the Red Deer Lake area, married Pat Seffern (deceased 1973), presently farming in the Sundre district.

In 1918 Jim and Gertie left Cowley and spent some time with the Ben Lloyds where their fifth child, Daphne, was born in 1919. Daphne married Donald Fraser and they have three children; Marjorie (Mrs. Ray Ward) has two sons and lives at Therhild, Donald and his wife, Lise, have a daughter, Sara, and live in Edmonton. Barbara, the youngest, still lives at home.

After being moved around to various places, as Brand Inspector for the Alberta Government, in 1920, Jim was transferred to Winnipeg to help curb the cattle rustling. As this was, supposedly, a temporary move, Gertie rented the Station House in Midnapore, (now in Heritage Park), and the family moved there to be close to school. They lived there for thirteen years and then moved to Edmonton where Jim was Brand Inspector and, part-time, Grazing Inspector. They passed away in Edmonton, Gertie, in 1947, aged 66 and Jim, in 1967, aged 93.

WALTER KENNETH BIRNEY — by Jean (Birney) Tucker

Born in Calgary in 1910, he lived there until the death of his father (Fred) in 1914. His mother remarried, Ernest Morris, and they moved to the Gladys Ridge area in 1916. Later, they moved to the Rocky Mountain House area, in 1922. In 1925 they moved to Montana and Dad worked there, in a dairy, until he returned to the Red Deer Lake area in 1927. In 1937, Dad came to Midnapore where he worked for the

Shaw Brothers (Maltman and Hugh). He married Ruth Shaw (deceased 1975) and they had eleven children; Mrs. Leona (Harold) Hogge, Mrs. Sharon (Mike) Campbell, Mrs. Georgina (Frank) Cranstone, Mrs. Jean (Bert) Tucker, Mrs. Donna (Don) Fraser, Fred, Glen, Gordon, Mrs. Dorothy (Adrian) Maertz, Mrs. Gloria (Lloyd) Want, and Judy, who still lives at home with Dad. He has nineteen grandchildren.

Today, Dad enjoys good health and works for the William Roper Hull Home. He has resided in his present home in Midnapore for the past seventeen years.

BOW VALLEY RANCH 1912-1915 — by Hugh Macklin

It was a beautiful spring morning in late April, 1912 that I first saw Bow Valley Ranch. It lay in the valley of Fish Creek, almost where it joined the Bow River. It consisted of a large area of deeded land, extending from Pine Creek, in the south, to the stockyards in East Calgary and bounded, in the east, by the Bow River and on the west by the Macleod Trail. It was bisected by only one trail, as the road allowances had been bought out years before. This trail was from Midnapore and connected up with the Blackfoot Trail just east of the buildings. The land was mostly in grass, good hard prairie wool, very little was cultivated Several sections were kept for hay, half of which were cut each year. Some five or six hundred tons were put up every year. The Bow Valley Ranch originated as a Government Farm in 1879, for the purpose of raising cattle to supply the Sarcee Indian Reserve with beef as, by this time, the buffalo had disappeared from the prairies and the Indians were in danger of starvation. It was eventually purchased by W. R. Hull who built the beautiful house still standing and in very good con-

dition. The Pat Burns' Company were the next owners of the property until, recently, when part of it was purchased as a Provincial Park. All of that part north of Fish Creek is now covered with houses and soon some of land south of Fish Creek will be also.

When I first saw it that spring morning, from a high bank, just north of the buildings, Calgary seemed a long way off, in fact, it had not extended south of the Elbow River. The ranch lay, a vast expanse of good grass land, undisturbed and secluded.

I had come down from Calgary after spending the winter in Guelph Agricultural College, taking a course in Agriculture, to see Mr. Norman Willans who was cattle buyer, at that time, for the area south to the border. I had a slight acquaintance with him and I was looking for a job. He told me he could give me a job in about a month's time, in the meantime, I could help him on his buying trips. He drove a California cart, one of the team he could ride so that he could ride out into the fields to look over the cattle. Eventually I was taken on as a ranch hand, my work consisted of the handling of cattle, fencing, haying, at that time of year, and feeding cattle in the winter months. We had basket racks which were large, 10'x20' with sides about four feet up connected to the bottom by willow stakes and wire. Half way along was a gap, closed by wires when loading, which could be unhooked, when unloading, and the hay forked out while the team walked around the feed ground. The Bow Valley Ranch was used mainly for a holding ground for the plant in Calgary. All cattle brought to the west and south of Calgary were brought there to be weighed and paid for. In the fall there were many hundreds of head available for slaughter, mostly three year olds, at the

The William Roper Hull House, Bow Valley Ranch. Note: Whale bones (ribs) on Verandah.

Calgary plant. Whenever cattle were required for slaughter, word would come out and we would bring in whatever number was required. There were a few automobiles but no trucks in those days and all stock was moved on foot. As they were wild range animals it was often difficult to get them into the Burn's stock yards. A person, on foot, would "spook" them more than anything else and it often took some hard riding to hold the band together. Some of the large ranchers would bring in as many as five hundred head, mostly by foot, but some from the far south would come in by rail to Midnapore where he would unload them and bring them on to the ranch. After riding on the train they were usually pretty wild and excited and would take off, regardless of fences, and it took some good hard riding before we got them all rounded up.

Mr. Burns would occasionally come out to the ranch, he had one of the few cars in Calgary at that time, it was quite large and he had a driver. Mr. Pat Burns was always very immaculate, he wore a business suit, small hat, a butterfly collar and bow tie. He was fairly short, rather stout, had white hair and a crisp, white moustache. Sometimes he would ask for a horse so that he could ride out and look at the cattle. I occasionally went with him to where the cattle were. He had a phenomenal memory and could tell where many of the cattle came from though he had many thousands of head on his many ranches. He never stayed at the ranch house over night but, his young son, Michael, and his governess used to come through the summer months. His nephews and nieces also stayed there during the summer holidays but, otherwise, it was seldom used.

The Chinese cook, Charlie Yuen, kept it in beautiful condition. Charlie was very different from most Chinese, he was about six feet tall and slender, spoke quite good English, took care of a fairly large vegetable garden, milked the cow, did the cooking and, in a pinch, if we needed extra hands to handle the cattle, he would saddle a horse and come out to help us. He had come up from California, worked on C.P.R. construction through the mountains as a blaster, worked for W. R. Hull, before being employed by Burn's, and stayed there until he retired, returning to China to end his days.

Prior to the 1912 Stampede, which was the first Stampede ever held in Calgary, the bucking horse bunch was pastured out on the ranch, a snaky looking bunch, of all colours and descriptions.

During my stay on the ranch one of the railways began construction on a line, down through the Bow Valley, and some of it came through the ranch property. It was never completed but the grades constructed are still in evidence yet all the work was done with horses and mules, with slips and fresnoes, no mechanical machinery was used.

Burns had many ranches at that time and thousands of head of cattle. Most of the ranches were quite large; the Milk River Ranch, on the border, the Circle, near Stettler, Waldron Ranch, near Lundbreck, Quirk Ranch, near Millarville, these were a few.

The Bow Valley Ranch is rapidly being covered with streets and residences and soon the remainder will be blotted out by modern, up to date homes — an era finished and a new one started.

GEORGE BRADSHAW — by A. McKevitt

From information I can gather, the Bradshaws were originally from England and came to the Midnapore district about 1920. They built a cabin and lived on the McArthur quarter with Ed. McKevitt and milked cows for a couple of years before moving on to eighty acres purchased from my Uncle Barney; S 80-NE¼-25-22-2-W5.

People of the district would remember George driving an iron wheeled farm wagon to Midnapore to put milk on the train every day. One morning, coming down Midnapore hill, the front end of the wagon box came out and milk cans began to slide out, hitting the horses and gaining speed. When George slipped on the wagon floor he fell out. The team ran away stopping at the Lacombe Home hill.

As time went on prices were not very good and it was hard to buy feed and grain for cows on eighty acres. In 1931 they decided to sell and go back to England.

THOMAS AND EDITH (MARRIOTT) BROWN.

Tom Brown was born in Leicester, England in 1894. He came to Canada with his sister and arrived at Granum, Alberta in 1910 at the age of fifteen. At sixteen he was made section foremen for the C.P.R. at Granum.

In June, 1915 he joined the 130th M.R. from which he transferred and went overseas with the 50th battalion, Calgary. In 1916 he was wounded at the Somme and sent back to England. There, in 1919, he married Edith Marriott of Aefreton, Derbyshire. They returned to Canada and settled at Aldersyde, Alberta where he was again made foreman for C.P.R. He was transferred from there to Blackie and then to Midnapore in 1935 where he stayed until his death in 1951.

Mrs. Brown, aged 82, as well as sons, Allan, Gordon and Rod and a daughter, Ruth, still reside in Midnapore. A second daughter Olive, resides on a farm at Peace River.

BROGDEN AT MIDNAPORE — by Jean (Brogden) Ockley

James Brogden came to Calgary from Galt, Ontario, in 1883, working or walking his way from the end of steel somewhere west of Medicine Hat. Early in his stay in Calgary he filed on a homestead, N.W.¼ Section 10-22-1-W5, and preempted the adjoining south quarter. He worked in Calgary and at one job, in Col. Walker's sawmill, he lost all the fingers on his left hand. Workmen's Compensation had not been established in those days. Having been a Mason in Galt he was interested in getting a lodge started in Calgary and was among those who did establish the Bow River Lodge.

In 1889 his only living son, Samuel Stirling, and his sister Lil came to Calgary. She was a teacher and got employment in Calgary and "Sam" was a carpenter and worked on several projects around town, including the original courthouse (now demolished) and the A. E. Cross brewery. When carpentry was not available he freighted lumber out of the Knee Hill Valley area and brought back coal.

In 1890 Mrs. Brogden and the two younger girls, Eva and Mabel, came to Calgary. The girls had had their high school education in Ontario and went to Normal School in Regina, that being the only teacher training facility in the N.W.T. Eva at one time taught in Midnapore School and Mabel at Tongue Creek before working in Calgary. Lil married a local barrister, J. A. Bangs; Eva married a school inspector, D. P. McColl; and Mabel married N. M. Burnett who was in the plumbing and sheet metal business.

Mrs. Brogden was an active person who took an interest in her neighbours, and stories are told of her visits to local brides, helping deliver babies, and one old-timer told the writer some years ago . . . "I will always remember. There was a large number of us children and not much money. Mrs. Brogden helped us . . ." Probably she did not have much money either, but the help she could give was remembered with gratitude many years later. She had been living with her daughter, Mrs. McColl, in Saskatchewan and died there in 1918. Mr. Brogden spent the last years of his life with his daughter, Mrs. Bangs, in California and died there at the age of 94.

Sam Brogden met his wife at the home of Mr. and Mrs. John Owen at Pine Creek. They were married in 1901 and lived on the land homesteaded by James Brogden. Mrs. Sam Brogden had been a nurse and for about two years before her marriage had been in charge of the old and quite primitive hospital in Macleod.

Their children were Jean, a baby which died soon after birth, Stirling and Harry. All started their education at Midnapore School.

Jean Brogden married Walter J. Ockley of Priddis, and the family moved there in 1933, where they farmed and operated a small sawmill. Mrs. Brogden died after a lengthy illness and S. S. Brogden died suddenly some years later.

Stirling married Gladys Runge of the Priddis district. They had two sons, William and Arnold, who still live there. Harry married Annie Given, also of the Priddis district. She died very suddenly, leaving one son. Harry later moved to Hawaii with a Calgary building contractor, and is still there, as is his son.

RAY AND JOAN (McKEVITT) BURSTON

Ray Burston was born in Bredenbury, Saskatchewan. He came to Alberta in 1946. He worked in the northern area of the province for two years. He then came to Midnapore and worked for Burns at the Bow Valley Ranch from 1948 to 1950. He married Joan McKevitt, daughter of Edward McKevitt in 1951. Joan worked as assistant post mistress, for six years before she was married, at the Midnapore Post Office. She was born in the Red Deer Lake district and raised in Midnapore. They moved from Midnapore in 1965 and lived at Shepard, Alberta for ten years. They are now residing in the Ogden area of Calgary. They have three children; all married, two living in Calgary and the other in Langdon, Alberta. They have two grandchildren.

DEWITT CHARLES AND JEAN (RUSSELL) BUTZ

Dewey is the son of John and Ellen Butz, former owners and operators of the B bar and D cabins in Midnapore. Dewey was born in 1925 in Mayerthorpe, Alberta the youngest of the family having three older sisters, Beatrice, Roxie and Jeri. The family moved to Calgary in 1928 and lived on the North Hill. Dewey attended King George and Western Canada High schools. In 1946 he married Jean Russell of the Ogden district whom he met at Western High.

Jean was born in Vulcan but came to Calgary as a baby with her parents, Alfred and Mary Russell.

L. to R. Terry, Dale, John, Kim and father, Dewey Butz.

Dewey and Jean lived in Calgary until moving to Midnapore, with their three small sons, Terrance, Dale and John, July 1, 1951. He bought a long frame building on the present sight of the Midnapore Texaco Service, from Fred and Floyd Watkins, turned it into a garage business called Midnapore Motors. The property was sold in 1956. Dewey, a master mechanic, worked over the years for Banff Trail Service, the Ammonia plant, Standard Auto Parts, International Harvester and Shaw Construction, Midnapore as well as his own business. After selling the garage with living quarters above he moved to a house on Bannister Road, with his family, by now grown to six sons having added Kim, Robin, and Richard and a tiny baby daughter, Janice, very much welcomed by Mother, Dad and brothers. In the new quarters they quickly added two more daughters, Julia and Christina.

In March, 1967 Dewey went into real estate, working for Metro Realty and is still with the same company, now calling itself Buxton Realty.

The children are now grown; Terry, 29, is employed by Alberta Government Telephones in Red Deer and with his wife, Amy, and seven year old son, Kelly, lives on a farm near Lacombe. Dale, 28, Calgary, works for Leo's Lumber. John, 26, Midnapore, works for Electric Motor Maintenance. Kim, 25, Vancouver, works for Add Print, owned by his aunt and uncle, Jeri and Tom Konkin. Rob, 23, his wife, Sharlene and year old son, Damon, have a home in Midnapore where Rob is employed, as a plumber, by Keith Construction. Ricky, 22, Calgary works for Riverton Construction, Midnapore. Janice, 21, married to Lyle Brown, works for Lucerne foods and lives in Queensland Downs, Calgary. Julie is married to Will Halford, they have a home in Queensland Downs where they live with their five month old son, Bradley. Tina, 18, is still at home.

JOHN WILLIAM AND ELLEN (SWAN) BUTZ

John William Butz was born in Overbrook, Kansas, April 16, 1894. His parents came to Canada and settled on a homestead in the Vermilion, Alberta area. John joined them in 1910. He served overseas with the 151 Battalion from 1916 until his discharge in 1919. He won the Military Medal and Bar, for bravery in the field.

In July, 1919, he married Ellen Swan who was born in Wakefield, Michigan, October 24, 1898. Ellen came to Canada with her parents in 1909 and homesteaded in the Islay area.

After farming for a few years in the Dewberry and Mayerthorpe areas they moved to the Brule mines. In 1928 they moved to Calgary with their four children where John barbered for a number of years.

In 1946 John, Ellen and daughter, Jeri (Dunham) operated a restaurant in Canmore. In 1948 they sold the restaurant and started the motel and trailer court, (known as the B-D), in Midnapore.

John, a jack-of-all-trades, kept building and adding to the motel until ill health forced him to sell. He passed away in 1964 and is survived by his wife, Ellen, Calgary, one son, Dewey, Midnapore and three daughters; Jeri (Mrs. Tom Konkin), Vancouver, Roxie (Mrs. Hugh Taylor), Bowness, Beatrice (Mrs. Jack McCloskie), Calgary.

JACK CAMERON — by Sheila Bateman

The first time Jack Cameron came out west from Ontario was in 1939. He went to Craigmyle, Alberta to help with the harvest. He returned east, entered the army and served for four years. When he returned to Ontario he went into a small trucking business for a while. The west, however, he had never forgotten and in 1948 he left Ontario for Innisfail, Alberta and worked for George Thompson in the gravel hauling business. In 1949 he went to work for Shaw Construction of Midnapore. Jack drove a truck and ran a dragline. In the winter, rather than working in the shop, he took to the road and drove transport trucks on long distance hauls to the east and the States.

Jack worked in the construction business for fifteen years and then ventured out on his own trucking business, hauling gravel.

I've been told that, when Jack was a youngster, you could always find him where there was some horses. Well, things have not changed, when he is not driving truck he is driving horses. He drives in the Stampede Parade every year and had the honour of taking Miss Grey Cup in the 1975 Grey Cup Parade held in Calgary.

He now lives in a new home near Academy Siding

where he has room to enjoy his horses and a country kind of life.

THE COPITHORNE FAMILY

E½, Sec 20, T. 22, R.1, W5th.

We arrived in Midnapore on the 6th day of April, 1946. It was Easter Sunday. Prior to coming to Midnapore we had lived in Grand Valley, about sixteen miles north west of Cochrane.

The biggest attraction on this property to us were the many beautiful trees and shrubs that had been planted prior to our arrival. There were spruce trees that were at least fifty feet high. Lilacs, honeysuckle, and maple trees. What a lot of work for the ones who planted them! A lot of credit and many thanks should be given them for the pleasure they gave to the people who came after them. We added more shrubs as the years passed. Rolfe and his Dad were the two that seemed to have the green thumb.

There are three sons, Claude William (Bill), married Peggy Philip, Calgary. Bill is employed by A.G.T. He and Peggy have two sons, Shaun and Mark. They live south of Red Deer Lake on an acreage.

Charles Ian, (Ian) married Eileen Ward from Calgary. They have two sons, Cody and Dallas. Ian and Eileen farm west of Rimbey, Alta. Before moving to Rimbey Ian was employed with Mannix Construction in Calgary.

Rolfe Albert, (Rolfe) married Dagmar Von Oppen from Berlin. They have a son Dale and a daughter Sherry. Rolfe is employed by Mannix Construction. He lives in Priddis.

Ian and Rolfe were both quite involved in the Cadets while attending school. The boys went to Midnapore to school and then to Western Canada. There was no busing at that time, so, "Mum" had the pleasure of making two trips a day to Calgary to bring them back and forth. Rolfe also spent some time in the Reserve Army.

We spent many hours renovating the original house. A great deal of the building had been done with square nails (hand made). It has had many face liftings over the years. The old log stable was taken down several years ago. The logs at the bottom had rotted away.

There has been many changes in the last few years. I believe we were among the first to sub-divide in that area. The first two being in 1956. The first subdivisions were sold to Mr. Diamond, Mr. Hawkins, Mr. Butz, and Mr. Allan.

Charlie, better known by his family as (Pappy) passed away in 1964. He was fond of music, dancing, woodwork. His grandchildren were his big hobby.

I eventually sold a couple more parcels, and sold the balance to Mr. Southern. He has built one of the finest stables in Canada I believe. He has many fine horses and has horse shows.

I have many happy memories of the thirty years we lived there and still feel just a little bit home sick as I drive by.

There were two of the most violent hail storms that I can ever remember during our time there. One storm on a Wednesday afternoon, there were still hail stones along the ditches the following Tuesday. It was in July. The force of the wind, rain and hail swept the fences, and all the hay, right across the field and into the ditch along the east road. Another storm, prior to that one, broke windows, shingles, and actually left indentations in the siding on the house. The leaves were all stripped off of the trees. Then there were the years that a lot of us spent looking to see if there wasn't a sign of a rain cloud. The fall of 1950 the land was so soaked, a lot of us had a problem getting the machinery on the land. Some of us just got a portion of the harvest. That spring we had a plague of mice. People living here at that time will remember seeing them by the thousands. So you see we did have a variety of conditions.

I have a small holding in the Priddis area and reside there now. I like this area very much. I have a beautiful view of the mountains, I am surrounded by trees and have a creek at the end of the property. Will have hard surface right at my door in the near future. Clean fresh air, friendly neighbors, and last but not least "my family". What more could any one ask for?

THOMAS AND HARRIET (SOMERVILLE) COPP

Thomas (T.R.) Copp was born in Ontario and in 1886 came west and worked for Colonel Walker for a year then, in 1887, he took up a homestead on SW ¼ 32-21-1-W5 next to his brother, David, who was on the SE ¼ of the same section. Later on he acquired a considerable amount of land in the district including NE ¼ 21-22-1-W5 which has always been called "the Copp Place".

Harriet Somerville, daughter of James and Anne, became the wife of T.R. in 1889 and they settled down to win their fortune. Prices for land must have been very low in those years for he paid only $500.00 for his place at Midnapore. The first crop was frozen and T.R. pawned his gold watch to buy seed for the second year. He recalls swimming his horse across Pine Creek to get the mail. Looking at the size of Pine Creek today, one would have a hard time visualizing water deep enough for a horse to swim in it.

Two sons born to the union died of pneumonia about 1900. There was also three girls; Dorothy (Boucher), lives in Calgary, Annie, deceased, Olive, deceased. Mrs. Copp died in 1956 and T.R. in about 1958.

KEN DENOON FAMILY

My wife, two sons and myself bought 40 acres on Anderson Road in 1949. With the help of two Indian boys and a cabinet maker, we built a log home with a coal stove and fireplace. It was the first home we ever owned. Mr. and Mrs. Boucher and family moved next door to us. They purchased the Jim Watts place, formerly the Layton property. The Mahaffeys built, a few years before us, to the west. Ron Brown bought the Dose place on Fish Creek now owned by Fred Mannix. Mr. and Mrs. Tom Pickford and children built on the corner of Anderson Road and 24th Street.

We were the City Slickers because the Old Timers had lived there many years; namely, Harry Anderson, for whom, I believe, Anderson Road was named. The roads were terrible — in fact I wore out a car jack the first year getting out of mud holes mainly on 14th Street. We City Slickers made an agreement that the first time we got snowed in we would have a party in one of the homes. This happened in the month of June, 1953. We happened to hear Harry Anderson, on the telephone, telling one of his friends about the predicament of the newcomers. He was laughing and made the remark about our modern homes that we couldn't get enough water to wash our teeth. This was exactly right as the power was off for a week; no water, no heat. The old pumps and coal furnaces looked awfully good to all of us newcomers at that time.

These were great days and the original neighbours took pity on us newcomers and everyone helped each other. It was great to enjoy the benefits of the country.

GEORGE DILTS — by A. McKevitt

George came to Midnapore about 1910. He spent most of his life working for Hugh Shaw on the farm and on the threshing outfits. When the Shaws took haying contracts for P. Burns, one dry year, they went to the Peace River country to put up hay and ship it home to Midnapore. George of course had to be along as the key man. He was a big man and a good worker.

He passed away in 1941 and is buried in St. Paul's Anglican Cemetery in Midnapore.

MR. AND MRS. SYD EADON

Mr. and Mrs. Eadon came to Midnapore District in January, 1931, from Bearspaw after working for Mr. Landale. They bought a farm from Jack Snell and the Soldier Settlement Board, NW¼ 28-22-1-W5, where they farmed, kept a few cattle, a lot of chickens and sold chickens and eggs in Calgary. One thing Mrs. Eadon remembers is a bad dust storm about 1936. She and her husband had gone to one of the Thiessens to buy some pigs and while they were there this storm came up. They made for home as they had left when the weather was fine and they had left all the windows open. Needless to say the house was full of dust.

About 1965 Mr. Eadon was bothered with a heart condition and had to rent his land out but continued to live on the place until 1973 when they moved to Calgary, sorry to have to leave Midnapore and a lot of friends. Mr. Eadon passed away in 1976.

THOMAS EARDLEY — by A. McKevitt

I was told that Tom Eardley came to Red Deer Lake about 1913 and worked for Pete Cleland. The story was that he was not a top hand but Mrs. Cleland wanted to keep him on because he had such nice table manners. He stayed with them until he joined the Armed Forces in the First World War of 1914-1918. I understand he was taken prisoner of war and while a prisoner he learned to knit and even after his return he never lost the knack.

He was married overseas and on his return bought E½ 35-22-2-W5 and farmed there until about 1928 when he went back to England for a trip. His wife talked him into remaining in England so he rented his place to Allister Massie.

REPORT ON THE F.M. RANCH 1952-1977 — by Margaret Mannix

Back in June of 1952, a little girl dreamed by day and night of having a horse in her own back yard. The morning of her eighth birthday, she discovered that her dream had become a reality, for there stood a beautiful twelve-year-old 15.2 hand Bay Thoroughbred gelding — "Hotfoot".

Well, since there were five in our family, one horse could hardly be expected to accommodate us all, and living in the city was not the ideal place for a five-horse stable — our back yard was not nearly large enough and added to this, we were sure our neighbours might have some objections.

Immediately we started looking for a place in the country, for the horses, as well as a week-end and holiday retreat for us. Luck was with us and we found an adorable little house situated on 10 acres of land with Fish Creek running past our front door and just nine miles past the City Limits. A small stable already existed and the horses, by then we had acquired five more — were moved out. We were told that this cottage was originally a Boy Scout camp consisting of one room. Each previous owner had added to the house and improved the property, so when we took over, we had a good sized living room, two bedrooms, two bathrooms and a kitchen. Moving the bare essentials, we decided to try living in the country — at least for the summer months!

December found us still here. No one wanted to go back to town, and we began in earnest to make this area our permanent home. Thank you "Hotfoot"!

To the west and north of us, we were bordered by the Sarcee Indian Reserve — but across the road and to the East lay the Shannon Estate, consisting of approximately two sections. That Spring, we acquired 720 of these acres which included the farm house, a large cattle barn and what was known as the old Burns land picnic ground. Plans were quickly drawn up, a site decided upon, and in September, construction began on our new home. We had outgrown the cottage — the children were growing up and needing their own rooms — a large Great Dane dog and another little smart 57-variety type having been added to our menagerie. George and Betty Reid with their two young daughters moved into the farm house, the horses were moved over to the big barn, Hereford cattle were put into the fields, chickens into the hen house, geese in the farm yard, and George was the good manager of what became known as the FM Ranch for the next twelve years. The three girls rode the horses to school at Midnapore that first year, but moved back to the city schools the next year. The two boys attended school in Calgary, Father commuted to and from his office and Mother seemed to be "on the road" many hours every day. With no deliveries of any kind, there were children to get to and from school, groceries to lug home, cleaning to be taken in and picked up, etc., etc. A station wagon was the answer. It never went to town or returned empty. Pony Club became a reality in Calgary and every Saturday A.M. the children rode their horses six miles to the Chinook Polo Grounds for their lesson, then of course six miles back after two hours of instruction in the ring. The cattle began producing and each child picked out his or her own calf and joined the 4-H Club. We never had the question asked "What can I do?" Thank you "Hotfoot"!

June 5, 1954 as the children and I left the cottage with the last load to be moved to the new home, our older son, Fred, looked back at the little house and said, "Mummie, don't ever sell this place. I want to live here when I get married." He was eleven years of age at the time and fifteen years later, he and his bride moved in. Gradually a large part of the Shannon Estate became part of the F.M. Ranch. Then the 160 acres on the South side of the Creek which belonged to the Marshall family was also added.

In 1956 Mr. George McMahon acquired 160 acres adjoining the F.M. Ranch to the East and built a lovely home known as The Moyie. Jammed in between the Moyie and the F.M. Ranch lay ten acres of property owned by Mr. Sellers and on it there was a log house and a log stable built originally I believe by Mr. Norman Willens about 1929. Now, with no road access to his property, this was most inconvenient for Mr. Sellers, Mr. McMahon and for us, so Mr. Sellers traded his ten acres for ten acres of our north fields, which he later sold to Mr. Ross Calder. We then renovated the old log buildings and still use them today for part of our horse operations.

In 1967, Mr. McMahon moved to the Bahamas and the Moyie stood vacant for two years until we purchased the 160 acres and our son moved in. A house needs a family.

Meanwhile, the little Creek cottage has been constantly occupied, either by our sons, our daughter, or by friends, and everyone has adored and taken good care of it.

For several years, the Fish Creek branch of Pony Club met here for their weekly instruction under the expert direction of Mr. and Mrs. Ray Ellard. Many of their rallies, cross-country competitions and breakfast rides have taken place on this property. Pony Club members as well as our neighbours and friends have always been welcome to enjoy the riding trails and the many jumps which have been erected.

They too say, "Thank you Hotfoot"!

The Alberta Light Horse Association organizes a series of psuedo hunts each year and the F.M. Ranch has always been one of the locations for this interesting event. One year we had 175 horses and riders show up. Three groups were formed — the fast riders and good jumpers going off first. Ten minutes later the less experienced riders and their mounts followed. Trailing came the very young and even some grandparents who did not have to jump at all since each obstacle is erected in a location where one can ride around it.

We have made good use of the land by developing a purebred herd of Hereford cattle. A stable of Thoroughbred horses is now in operation, the fields have been continuously farmed on an economical basis, and the wooded Creek area has been cared for by removing dead trees and cleaning up after trespassers.

Now, after 25 years of happy country living, the city has caught up to us. New developments to the North and East are springing up and the Provincial Government has decided they want 350 of our Creek acres for Fish Creek Park. A caveat has been placed on this much of our land, which includes our home, our stables. Expropriation! Progress? But we still say "Thank you, Hotfoot"!

GIUSEPPE (JOE) AND MARIO FACHINI

Giuseppe (Joe) Fachini came from Italy about 1912; and worked at different jobs from a base near Midnapore. He grew a lot of vegetables and his garden just south of Fish Creek along the Macleod Trail became a landmark. He also was adept at weaving small willows into comfortable chairs and sturdy tables. He was fond of birds and fashioned many birdhouses and fed the birds regularly.

When Mario arrived from Italy at age twelve, and arrived at the C.P.R. station in Calgary, he wondered why everyone was staring at him and finally realized it was because he was smoking a large Italian cigar.

Following Mario's arrival, they went to a bush camp near Golden, B.C. where Mario worked as a flunkey and his dad cut trees. When they returned they settled on a small acreage NE¼ 30-22-1-W5 and they used to come and help pick potatoes at Mr. McKevitt's place.

It was in about 1925 that they moved to Fish Creek and bought a small acreage from Mrs. Helen Shaw and started a service station. Joe was a familiar figure with his grey beard and piercing eyes. They were a popular pair and ran the station for many years.

Mario later married and had four children. Both Mario and Joe have passed away.

DANIEL AND JEMIMA (SHIELDS) FRASER — by Ken Fraser

Dating back to 1916, my parents, brother, Colin, and I moved to the Shannon Ranch, west of Midnapore. We came from the John A. Turner place in Glenmore. We kids were real small. We brought a few horses and cows and some hens with us, later, we had several hundred sheep on shares. All the work and travel was done by horses. The winters were quite severe and buildings poor. Fuel, food, clothes and money were real scarce. There were many good horsemen in those days such as Trevor Willans, Osborne Brown, Harry Bamford.

The Shannon place was nearly all grassland and pasture. There was 1120 acres which we rented for several years at $1.00 per acre per year. The summers were beautiful, a bit on the dry side I guess. Fish Creek ran below the house. It was so pretty, lots of birds, a beaver dam and bushels of saskatoons.

We started to school about 1918 with Indian ponies from the reserve. It was about three and a half miles and we had to ford the creek as there was no bridge until about 1921. Some of the families going to that school at the time were: Shaws, Sandersons, Lees, Biddells, Brogdens, Moons, Balls, Greens, and Sheepys. The teachers I remember were Mr. Folkard, a fine teacher, also Miss Hofman, Mr. Yeart and Mr. Barker. (These names may not be spelled correctly.) I remember there were flocks of bluebirds that would fly ahead of us from post to post. The Sarcee Indian Agency was half a mile west of us and we had many good friends there that came often to visit. Archdeacon Tims was the preacher there and we went to their church frequently. One family that we liked and remember was Oscar Otter and his wife, Daisy.

Sometimes our sheep would stray into the Indians' crop and this was bad for relations. We had good friends at the Agency some of whom were; Gordons, Allens and Miss Hircum. She and her friends came to tea often with my mother. When she moved she sold us her buggy. It was a real good buggy and saw many years of service for us. Mother would drive to Midnapore and trade homemade butter for groceries and coal oil for the lamps. The store was owned by Mrs. Shaw and I think the name of the operator was Mr. Grant. At any rate, they were very kind to us.

One of the things I remember about the Shannon place were the wild geese flying north, their wings shining in the sun, they were a beautiful sight and the flocks seemed endless. Ours was the only road and the McKevitts and many of the other farmers used to pass through our yard going and coming from Calgary. We liked to see them all and it was not a happy time when, for financial reasons, we had to leave the "Shannon" in 1923. My sister, Mary, was born about this time and got her schooling in Dry Creek, a small school near our new home at Balzac. Mary is a fine, happy person who likes nearly everyone. She is a good housekeeper and a great help to us.

I should mention Johnnie Hamilton who was a fine horseman, he had a big, beautiful palamino horse "Goldie", always well groomed and in wonderful condition. He was a delight to watch as he travelled with his singlefoot gait. Johnnie owned the Sparrow Ranch, west of Midnapore as well as a garage in Calgary. He had been a stage coach driver.

The best horse we ever owned was "Dandy", she came from McKevitt's at Red Deer Lake. She had run in the Millarville races for the McKevitts and we got her from Johnnie Hamilton in a trade. She could chase horses, drive cattle and do anything better than any other horse we ever had.

When we left the "Shannon" we rented a quarter in Glenmore owned by Joe Hone, one mile south of the Chinook race track. We had good crops and gardens at Hone's and rode our ponies to a two room school at Glenmore where Miss Martin was the teacher. Hays, Andersons, Johnstones, Wordens, and Bamfords were our neighbours there. In the spring of 1925 the Hone place was sold and my father went to work for Mr. H. G. Woolley who had two places across from us. He was a fine man to work for. The first year my father had a fine young man working with him. He was Jeff Jeffery who now lives with his family west of Midnapore. The following year Colin left school and went to work for Mr. Woolley and I stooked for him in the fall. The crops were good for the five years we were there and the threshing was done by the Shaws.

Mr. Woolley was a reckless car driver and seemed to play Russian Roulette with the street cars. One time he left his pipe on the seat of the car, garage and everything went up in smoke.

We were able to buy a Model T Ford while we were working for Mr. Woolley and, on May 24, 1926, we drove to Banff. It was just the most beautiful place I had ever seen. The roads were gravel and the old car boiled a lot.

We attended St. Peter's church while we lived at Glenmore and Spencleys and Mills were great church supporters. Mrs. Dewdney taught us Sunday school at her place and I'm sure helped us a lot.

In the spring of 1930 Mr. Woolley sold his farms to Mr. Steadman and we found a new home west and north of Balzac. It was quite a trek, we came 25 miles with horses and wagons. The country was bare and treeless and we were quite homesick. The land was good and many of the farmers hauled prairie wool to the hay market in those days. We have seen dust storms, blizzards, hail-storms but have harvested many beautiful crops and have always had feed for our stock even in the bad years.

The war broke out in 1939 and Colin went overseas with the Loyal Edmonton Regiment. They left me to work the farm. Colin made it home alright but many of the boys with him were not so lucky.

We rented three quarters until we were able to buy it outright in 1945 and later acquired another quarter in 1952. All the work was done with horses until 1940 when we got a tractor and some better machinery.

A very sad thing happened to us in 1953 when our father was killed in a farm accident with a bull. It was a terrible blow to us all. My mother never seemed to get over it and passed away November 5, 1956. My father was a strong and healthy man all his life and a good farmer and stockman.

We have milked cows and shipped milk to Calgary nearly all our lives up to 1972. This was in no small way, one of the reasons for our financial success. The hauling was a hard job but at the last, the hauling was done with a tank truck. Girletz, Bushfield, Young and Perry are some of our good neighbours at Balzac. We thank God for health all our lives and the many blessings and pray for His strength and blessing in the time to come.

MR. AND MRS. WILLIAM GIER — by L. Beck

They were both born in Grand Valley, Ontario and married there in 1884. They had six children, four grandchildren and seven great-grandchildren. Their ancestors were of English and Scotch descent. William Gier and his brother raised and exhibited Shorthorn cattle.

In 1901 Mr. Gier with his wife and children moved to a ranch at Okotoks. He raised and exhibited and sold light harness and saddle horses and Clydesdales. In 1912 they sold and lived in Calgary until buying the Thompson place at Midnapore in 1917. They had chickens and a few cows and sold the produce from them. They sold the place about 1927 (to Thomsons I believe) and lived the rest of their lives in Calgary.

All their lives they were steady churchgoers, belonging to the Church of Christ Disciples, when there was one near enough. They celebrated their sixty fifth wedding anniversary in 1949. Joanna Jane Gier died, at ninety-two, in 1949 and William was ninety when he died in 1951.

Regarding the 'Midnapore Musical Society Concert' in 1918; I can't remember my mother telling me much about it. She was the Miss Gier of the Duet and Quartet. I believe it was short lived. The only other name that means anything to me is Miss Tims and, I believe, she was the daughter of Archdeacon Tims of the Anglican Church.

JOHN AND ADELAIDE (BELCOURT) GLENN, Sources: Tom Ward and Frances Marshall

"Live within your means and save a beet for a rainy day". This was the motto of John Glenn, the first settler in the Fish Creek valley.

John Glenn was born in 1834 in Mayo County, Galway, Ireland. As a young man, he left his native hearth to seek his fortune in England. Homesick, he returned to Ireland with the intention of visiting his home but, when within a few miles of his father's farm, changed his mind and re-crossed the Irish Sea to Liverpool, England. From there, at the age of 16 years, he emigrated to New York, U.S.A.

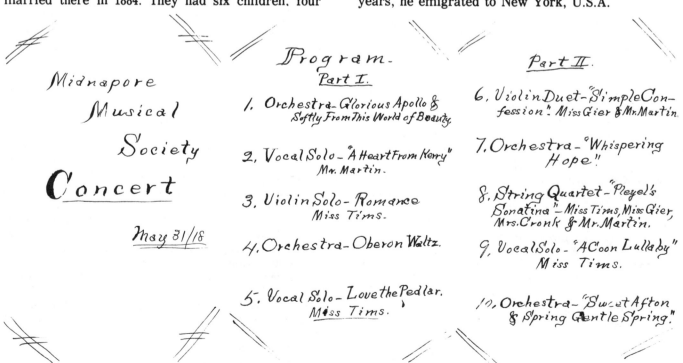

Midnapore Musical Society Concert
May 31/18

Program.
Part I.

1. Orchestra – Glorious Apollo & Softly From This World of Beauty.

2. Vocal Solo – "A Heart From Kerry" Mr. Martin.

3. Violin Solo – Romance Miss Tims.

4. Orchestra – Oberon Waltz.

5. Vocal Solo – Love the Pedlar. Miss Tims.

Part II.

6. Violin Duet – "Simple Confession". Miss Gier & Mr. Martin.

7. Orchestra – "Whispering Hope".

8. String Quartet – "Pleyel's Sonatina" – Miss Tims, Miss Gier, Mrs. Cronk & Mr. Martin.

9. Vocal Solo – "A Coon Lullaby" Miss Tims.

10. Orchestra – "Sweet Afton & Spring Gentle Spring".

Travelling west, he obtained employment of a ranch near Waco, Texas. In 1861 he was drafted into the Confederate Army. Opposed to slavery, he deserted and joined the Northern Federal Army, serving under General William Tecumseh Sherman until the end of the American Civil War in 1865.

Following the war he journeyed around the central and western states, working in mines and, in 1867, moved on to British Columbia and then panned for gold in Barkerville along with James Voiture and Sam Livingstone, men who were, in later years, to become his neighbours in the Calgary district.

When searching for gold, struggling over the Yellowhead Pass, he met the Sanford Flemming expedition heading for Kamloops in their survey for a suitable right of way for the C.P.R. In Grant's book, "Ocean to Ocean", there is a description of this encounter; "Two miles from the "red Pyramid" that looked so kindly and touched a chord in our hearts, the sound of a bell was heard. Jack said it must be the bell horse for another pack train but in a few minutes a solitary traveller, walking beside his two laden horses, emerged from the woods ahead. He turned out to be John Glenn — a miner on his way to prospect for gold on hitherto untried mountains and sand bars. He was a speciman of Anglo-Saxon self reliant individualism, more striking than that pictured by Quinet of the American Settler, without priest or captain at his head, going out in the deep woods or virgin lands of the new continent to find- and found- a home. John Glenn calculated that there was as good gold in the mountains as had yet come out of them and that he might strike a new bar or gulch that would "panout" as richly as "William Creels" in the Cariboo; so putting blankets and bacon, flour, and frying pan, shining pick-axe and shovel, on his horses and, sticking revolver and knife in his waist, off he started from Kamloops to seek "fresh fields and pastures new". Nothing to him was lack of company or of newspapers; short days and approach of winter; seas of mountains and grassless valleys, equally inhospitable; risk of sickness and certainty of storms; slow and exhausting travel through marsh and muskeg, across raging mountain torrents and miles of fallen timber; lonely days and lonely nights: — if he found gold he would be repaid. Prospecting was his business and he went about it in a sim-

ple, matter-of-course, style as if he were doing business 'on change'. John Glenn was, to us, a typical man, the modern missionary, the martyr for gold, the advance guard of the army of material progress and, who will deny or make light of his virtue, his faith, such as it was? His self-reliance surely, was sublime. Compared to his, how small the daring and pluck of even John Milton and Cheadle? God save thee, John Glenn! and give thee thy reward."

John also carried a letter from the Hudson's Bay Company agent at Kamloops telling the Flemming party that their personal baggage had arrived from Toronto via San Francisco and was waiting for them.

After years of solitary wandering the forty year old bachelor decided, in 1873, that it was time to settle down so married Adelaide Belcourt of Lac Ste. Anne in a ceremony performed in the mission (built by Father Lacombe at St. Albert, twenty years previously) by Reverend Father Leduc.

With two horses and a mule, they started south to find suitable land on which to settle. Impressed by the fertile soil in the broad valley where Fish Creek flows into the Bow, the newlyweds decided this was the spot for their future home. They built a log cabin complete with sod roof, stone fire place and chimney. Here, in 1873-74, they wintered and thus became the first settlers in the Calgary (Midnapore) area. Later he said; "I like the climate better than any I have found between the Atlantic and the Pacific; The Rio Grande and the Peace, over all of which territory I have travelled. There is everything in the country a settler can desire."

Sons, Pat and William Glenn, continue the story.

They, our parents, stayed there till the spring of 1874. At that time an uncle of Mother's was going north from Montana. Mother, not being well, Father decided to send her home to her parents at Lac Ste. Anne and he continued on to Sun River, Montana, headquarters for the I.G. Baker company. There he bought a wagon and one mule, giving him a team of two horses and two mules; he took a full load of trade goods; tea, flour, sugar and tobacco, to trade with Indians; taking furs, buffalo hides and pemican in pay. He arrived back at Lac Ste. Anne in June, having disposed of all trade goods. Patrick Glenn was born on June 3, 1874. They now proceeded south again, stopping at Fish Creek for a few days, they continued on to Sun River, where he sold all his furs, etc.

They bought another team of four horses and harness and a wagon. With two full wagon loads of all kinds of provisions, they started back toward Fish Creek, where they intended to trade off all their goods to the Indians. Somewhere, south of Lethbridge, they met a group of N.W.M.P. under the command of Colonel Macleod, October, 1874, and guided them into, what was soon to be, Fort Macleod. There they sold all of their provisions to Colonel Macleod.

Mother stayed with Mrs. Macleod and Father helped to build the Fort as well as all the stone chimneys and fireplaces. In the spring of 1875 they went back south, this time to Fort Benton, and bought two full loads of goods, including stove, windows, hardware, all for a new, permanent home they were intending to build. At that time there was no Macleod

John Glenn, 1880. Adelaide Belcourt Glenn, 1880.

Trail. The only road used to be farther west, in the hills, via the old Mission and Morley, where the MacDougalls had a trading post and mission. On July 3, 1875, Johnny Glenn was born at Sheep Creek. Three days later they arrived at the old Mission on the Elbow River. This is where Mother first met Mrs. Sam Livingstone. Livingstones had built their cabin there in 1874. After several days of rest, they continued down the Elbow to where Calgary was later established and on down to Fish Creek. This would be about mid July, 1875. In September, Mother went back to the old Mission and stayed with Mrs. Livingstone. Later, when the Livingstones located at Fish Creek, Father helped them built their first home.

Each of the next three years, he made one, and sometimes two, trips to Fort Benton. In these years he had a crew of men. In charge of Mr. Bearer, a French half-breed, they erected a large dwelling, barn and other buildings (completed about 1878 or 79) which became an established stopping place; meals 50 cents and everyone carried his own bed. At this time he started raising cattle and broke some of the virgin sod to grow grain. The land was not irrigated except for natural flooding but the soil was fertile and the crops flourished. Three years later the farm consisted of nine, partially fenced, acres sown to oats and barley, a hay meadow and a vegetable garden.

John Glenn did not remain there. In 1879 Edgar Dewdney, Commissioner of Indian Affairs in the North West Territories, sent Thomas Wright to select a suitable site for an Indian Supply Farm, in the Morleyville area. While in the Calgary district, on other business, Dewdney, after inspecting the Glenn holdings, considered Fish Creek Valley ideal for the project and sent for Wright to join him there.

In his report for 1879 the Commissioner, wrote; "after spending a couple of days looking for a location, I found at the mouth of Fish Creek, at its junction with the Bow River, a beautiful site for a farm.

A man, of the name of Glenn, had a small crop of barley and oats — 4½ acres of each — partially fenced and with enough rails to complete it, two small cabins — one large enough to stable four horses — the other about the same size and which will make a good storehouse, with large root house adjoining, and a small stock of hay.

I thought it necessary to get rid of him before making up my mind to locate there, and as soon as Mr. Wright returned from Morleyville I took him down to see the place and get his idea of it, as well as to put a value on the improvements that had been made by Glenn. Mr. Wright was enchanted with the place. The barley he considered the finest piece of grain he had ever seen grown. It was about three feet high and as level as a billiard table, and he estimated there would be fifty bushels to the acre. The oats were also very fine, the cabins he estimated at $50.00 each and the crops he thought would turn out — barley 9,600 lbs.; oats 6,800 lbs.

I saw Glenn and asked him what he would take for the improvements. He valued the whole thing at $350.00.

I endeavored to induce him to throw in a milch cow and calf but he refused, and I closed giving him $360.00

for his improvements and the cow and calf. The Department took possession on August 1, 1879."

Thus Glenn's first property became Indian Supply Farm Number 24.

Having sold the farm, John Glenn moved "up the creek" to settle on land legally described as SW¼-3-23-1-W5. Here he set up his farmstead near the south banks of Fish Creek about a stone's throw east of the Macleod Trail.

The Marquis of Lorne, then Governor General of Canada, wrote in his book, "Memoirs and Travels of the Marquis of Lorne" — John Glenn, not being accustomed to royalty and nobility, said to the Marquis "I don't know what they call you but you shall be called 'mister' here and he states that from then on he was known, in the Territories, as Mr. Lorne.

After moving to what would be his last home in 1879, John Glenn started, if he did not complete, the construction of his historic irrigation system, nineteen years before the Alberta Irrigation Company started their first project near Lethbridge. Glenn erected an earth and rock dam about one half mile west of the Macleod Trail and with 2" x 4"'s, sixteen feet long, diverted the water from the creek into a ditch which carried the water to irrigate his fields east of the Trail.

A sketch of general details in connection with the irrigation ditch constructed by the Glenn Estate, approved and certified by the chief Inspector of Survey, J. S. Dennis, on October 3, 1895, shows the dam to be 80' long; constructed of gravel and boulders, in the shape of an equilateral triangle 6' at the base; the head gate was two feet wide, manually activated, the fluming under the Calgary Macleod Railroad right of way was 5'6" wide 2' high, constructed of 2" x 4"'s, 49' long; and the 14' bridge across the ditch was made from 3" planking nailed to five, 3" x 8" stringers.

The system was built without the benefit of legal status; the first Irrigation Act didn't come into force until 1893, some fourteen years later. When the railroad (now C.P.R.) was built from Calgary to Fort Macleod in 1891, this company recognized the prior right established by Glenn, by installing a box culvert under its grade, 650' south of its bridge on Fish Creek. This culvert was relocated September, 1958 when an iron pin nearly 20" long and ¾" thick, was found at the east end. The pin, hand made, with a carefully belevelled head and a chiselled point, likely served some engineering purpose, either to fix the elevation or the location of the culvert. It should be added this pin provides the only available artifact of the John Glenn irrigation project.

The area actually irrigated by Glenn has been variously given as from 20 to 40 acres, while the Government report published in 1895 states 130 acres could have been irrigated. The irrigation works served to supply water for his nearest neighbour, Samuel William Shaw, who arrived from England in 1883 and settled west of the Macleod Trail on Fish Creek, next to Glenn's farm. The supply ditch cut through the Shaw quarter and for a number of years about 6 acres of land was irrigated from the Glenn project. Therefore it was also the first neighbour irrigation system built and used on the Canadian prairies. The project also supplied water for the woollen mills operated by the Shaws.

According to eye witness, the diversion works were partly washed out by a heavy flood in 1885 when the course of the creek was changed. Despite this, the system continued to operate; the Shaws continued to use the water until 1902 when the diversion works were completely destroyed and were never rebuilt.

From affidavits in support of application for homestead (No. 100149 dated August 10, 1885), we learn that John Glenn had fenced 200 acres, was farming 90 acres, had built a house 26' x 20' with an addition of 28' x 15', of logs and outbuildings, including a stable 80' x 40' and a store house 20' x 20'. His patent (title of land) was issued by the Department of the Interior on January 3, 1886 and sent to him on March 31 of the same year.

His interests extended beyond farming, as evidenced by his lively participation in community affairs. He possessed a high degree of business ability and according to one neighbour also possessed the spirit of prophecy. He was one of 30 pioneers who attended the first sale of lots in section 15, in what was to become the City of Calgary. Later, a report published in the Calgary Herald Mining and Ranch review, March 26, 1884 listed that Glenn had three buildings under construction, one 25' x 45', one 25' x 68' and one 120' x 48'. The 1887 Town of Calgary Tax Roll revealed that the real value of the John Glenn estate was $2,600.00. He had erected the largest livery stable (Frontier) and two of the largest business buildings. In 1884 he donated two acres of land to the Anglican Church who, with the aid of Queen Anne's Bounty (which went to raise churches in the far-flung corners of the Empire), built St. Paul's Anglican Church, Midnapore. His name is to be found on subscription lists supporting any worthy cause.

Adelaide and John were blessed with six children, Patrick, John, Alfred, William, Edward and Maggie. As there were no schools in the area, Patrick and John were educated at St. Boniface school in Winnipeg. Margaret (Maggie died while a young girl and the three younger boys went to James Shortt school and later, St. Mary's school in Calgary. Patrick was the only one of the six to marry. His wife was Philomena Hodgson, daughter of George Hodgson, Indian Agent at Sarcee Indian reserve.

Family of Patrick and Philomene Glenn, 1912. Clockwise from Edmund Patrick; Matilda Lucy, Dorothy Violet, Kathleen Cecilia, Mary Frances.

Patrick and Philomena had five children; Dorothy (Darling) now of Seattle, Washington, who had three daughters and a son who died in infancy; Kathleen (Ships) deceased, no children; Matilda (Stage), deceased, no children; Frances Marshall, Calgary, two boys and three girls; Edmund Patrick, deceased.

Very little about Adelaide Glenn has been recorded for posterity. It is safe to say that she complemented her husband by looking after the home in a manner associated with the responsibilities of a pioneer woman. In addition to her household duties and attending to the comfort of their many guests, she

Patrick and Philomene Glenn, 1897.

mothered six children in ten years. Frances (Glenn) Marshall remembers her grandmother driving to Calgary for supplies; how she went swimming with her grandchildren and how she derived special pleasure from berry picking and going fishing. She also told how her grandmother delivered all but one of the McKevitt children and that she was called to be mid-wife for Mrs. James Lougheed. She also took unusual interest in the well-being of her grandchildren and was "Granny" to all and sundry children that came to the home.

Regrettably, the story of John Glenn has an unfortunate ending. In late December, 1885, shortly after the Riel Rebellion, he and one of his drivers had a difference of opinion which resulted in a fist fight. The story was related by an old time resident of Midnapore. "His driver was a man named Bill Smith and an argument arose between the two men over some matter concerning the horses and the men engaged in a fight. Glenn was badly beaten and left unconscious on the side of the road near Calgary. A passer-by found him and took him home. He never fully recovered and died of pneumonia early in 1886.

He was an astute business man, a good neighbour and interested in the progress of development in the city of Calgary as well as the farmland to the south.

Following the death of her husband, Adelaide and the boys continued for some time on the farm. Patrick had married and moved to Vancouver where his wife died in 1908. Adelaide went to Vancouver to stay with the young family in 1912. The two younger children; Frances and Edmund returned to the Midnapore area, where Frances stayed at the Lacombe Home. Later, one of her sons, a carpenter, built Adelaide a house on 18th Avenue, near St. Mary's Cathedral in Calgary. The house still stands. After a full and satisfying life, Adelaide died of pneumonia in her 88th year.

REMINISCENCES OF JOHN GORDON

Rev. John Milloy was 80 years of age when he retired from the ministry of the Presbyterian Church and began a new life as a rancher in Southern Alberta. That was in 1901 and he lived an active life, in good health, until his final illness and death in September, 1907.

Rev. John Milloy (1827-1907).

Several years later I used to ride past his former property (E½ 32-22-2-W5) on my way to school in Midnapore. The old house and other buildings were on the northern quarter, not far west of the village, and they were of special interest to me because John Milloy was my grandfather.

Mr. Milloy was born in Argyleshire, Scotland, educated there, at Glasgow University and, after coming to Canada in 1852, at the University of Toronto where he graduated in Divinity from Knox College in 1856. He served congregations in Ontario and in Quebec's Eastern Townships, serving in his last charge — at Crinan, near London, Ontario — for 30 years. It was from here that he moved to Midnapore. After my grandfather's death my grandmother moved back East, to Ottawa, where she died in 1915.

This information comes from notes which I found in the effects of my aunt, Jane Isabella Milloy, who died in Winnipeg in 1948 at the age of 86. She noted that my grandfather "thought Alberta the finest country in the world."

There were nine children in the Milloy family, the first, a girl, dying at the age of three. The others were three boys and five girls, my Aunt Jane being the eldest and my mother, Henrietta C. Milloy, the youngest. In between were Arch, who became a dentist in Vancouver; Ann, who taught school in Alberta for many years; Kate and Hannah, who both died before the family moved West; Jim, who farmed in B.C. and later in Northern Alberta; Jack, who was in business in Regina for many years.

It was while the Milloys lived at Midnapore that Mother met and married my father, William Gordon, who was employed by the Department of Indian Affairs at the Sarcee Reserve. My father then went to the Blackfoot Agency at Gleichen for five years, returning to the Sarcee as Indian Agent from 1917 to 1921. During this latter period I attended Midnapore public school, riding the four (?) miles from the agency on my half-Clydesdale mare, Biddie. One winter the teacher (Mrs. Hoffman) boarded me in her rooms behind the school during the coldest months.

In 1921 my father was transferred to Manitoba where he was Indian Agent at Norway House and then at the Sioux Reserves at Griswold and Pipestone until his retirement. He lived in Winnipeg until his death in

Mr. and Mrs. William Gordon and son, Jack, with Arch Deacon Timms at the Sarcee Agency (around 1920).

1964 at the age of 91. My mother predeceased him by about eight years.

All of the Milloys of my mother's generation are now dead but, at last word, I still had cousins at Abbotsford, B.C., and Lavoy, Alberta.

My own adult life has been spent in Winnipeg, where I graduated from the University of Manitoba then worked for 19 years at The Winnipeg Tribune, where I was latterly Managing Editor, and six years with The Winnipeg Free Press as an editorial writer and Features Editor. I left newspaper work in 1958 to become Assistant to the President of the University of Manitoba and Executive Director of the Alumni Association. I retired in 1976. My wife, the former Marguerite Guertin, and I have two sons and six grandchildren. Our elder son, John, is with the United Nations in Geneva, where he is director of U.N. volunteer programs, and our younger son, Tony, operates his own audio-visual business in Toronto.

* * *

I remember three teachers at the Midnapore school. Mrs. Hoffman was tall, very proper and strict — at least, that's how she appeared to a small boy. She was actually very kind to me. The other two were, as I recall, Engishmen whose names I do not remember. Both were stern disciplinarians and punishments for any infraction of the rules were immediate and painful.

Looking back, it seems most of the pupils were Shaws. There was Oliver and Myrtle and the twins, Helen and Exilda, and there may have been more. There was Mabel Scott, now Sanderson, whose parents I also remember well. In their home, just to the west of my grandfather's old place, one found warmth and friendship — and good food.

Two frequent visitors at the Sarcee Agency were Clem Gardiner (he was my boyhood hero — Canada's champion steer roper and owner of what seemed to me to be the tallest horse in the world) and Johnny Hamilton. I can remember Johnny riding his horse across the infield at the Calgary Stampede (the first year of its revival, I think) and the announcer noting that the combined ages of horse and rider totalled more than 100 years.

My playmates at the Agency were Teddy Allen, son of the blacksmith, Dick Allen, and Hodge Lee, grandson of George Hodgeson, the interpreter. The Hodgesons had an old Edison gramophone that played cylindrical records. Two, I remember, were: "Yaka Hula Hicka Doola" and "In the Blue Ridge Mountains of Virgina, on the Trail of the Lonesome Pine." Sometimes I played with the Fraser boys who lived near the reserve. They were Scottish with broad accents and were not interested in books, as I was. They were more interested, they said, "in the beasts." One warm summer day, the Foster boys and I made an expedition to "Snake Hill" and massacred 50 garter snakes (I suppose the hill has long since been levelled and is now somewhere in the middle of a Calgary housing development).

The trail I rode to school was replaced years ago by more modern roads. We had to ford Fish Creek and Biddie liked to frustrate me by balking in mid-stream. More than once I had to slip down into the creek and tug and brow-beat her across. On one occasion Johnny Hamilton arrived at the critical moment and lured her across with a handful of oats from his saddle bag. When I rode Biddie bareback I would occasionally slide off her wide beam. I would then have to lead her to the nearest fence, which I used as a ladder to climb back on.

On Sundays we would bundle into the old Ford touring car, with its cloth top and "isinglass curtains", drive north across the Reserve and down "corkscrew hill", over the bridge below Sarcee army camp, over the wide-open spaces of South-West Calgary, into the city to attend Knox Church. There were few houses in those days beyond the brows of the north and south hills. Mount Royal was near the edge of town.

My family's Calgary friends included the Gows (Dr. Gow brought me into the world), the MacLeans (Wendell MacLean, druggist, whose daughter became a well-known pianist), the Lintons (James Linton, stationery) and Mrs. Grevett who, as I recall, was one of the West's first Women's Libbers.

I must have felt, like my grandfather, that Alberta was a wonderful place, for I can still remember the heartbreak when we had to move away. I think I said "goodbye" with tears in my eyes to every wire gate and fence post on the way to Calgary to catch the train to the East.

FRANCIS VIVIAN AND META (LOGAN) GOUGH

Francis Vivian Gough was born in Okotoks in April, 1897, the son of Francis Joseph and Evelyn Flora (Shaw) Gough, old-timers of the Okotoks district. He received his schooling in Okotoks and Midnapore. In the spring of 1918 he joined the Royal Air Force and was discharged later the same year.

He worked in industrial factories in eastern Canada for some time prior to being married, in 1921, to Meta Logan of Belfast, Ireland. Their family of five girls and four boys are mostly around Calgary and vicinity.

Vivian ran the store in Midnapore, known as the Midnapore Supply Company, for a while before working for Parrish and Heimbecker, loading grain at the rear of the store into boxcars, in 1923.

The present elevator in Midnapore was built and operated by Parrish and Heimbecker before being sold to the Alberta Wheat Pool. Vivian ran the elevator from the time it was built until his retirement in 1963. He was also the secretary of the Red Deer Lake Credit Union from its inception until 1971 when his eyesight failed enough that he could not carry on. He is still a director of the Credit Union and continues to live in Midnapore.

HALFORD'S HISTORY — 'Ghosted' by Bill Dardis

The name of George Halford appeared on the Midnapore horizon in the deep years of the Depression — in July of 1930, to be more exact.

That summer, George hitched the star of his future to the Ray Barkley dairy farm, and for a year and a half struggled with the sometimes-mysterious world of the dairy business.

Money wasn't in great supply when, after that year and a half, George decided to leave Ray Barkley and throw in his lot with Albert McKevitt at the "home place." George's "wage" settlement with Ray Barkley consisted of four pigs and eight bags of chop. (No unions in those days, says George.) He fed the pigs for five months, then promptly sold them for $4.50 each. (Ah . . . the work of big business — even in the Depression years!)

During the time George worked for him, Albert McKevitt had a sale and moved to what was then known as the Copp place. About the same time, George went haying for Malt Shaw at Midnapore, and continued working for Malt off and on for about four years. He also put in stints at the farms of the late Bob and Johnny Hamilton, Richie Hope, and spent two seasons with Allister Massie. In the meantime, Albert McKevitt operated Shaw's old store and post office, where George "wintered" and ran the skating rink.

Hard cash being the rare commodity it was during those Depression years, George still managed to amass the considerable "fortune" of $28 at the bank by 1936-37. The lure of the Exhibition proved strong that summer, and George withdrew $14 from the bank as he and employer Allister Massie laid plans to take in the Fair. (Allister wasn't without his own "fortune": $3.60 from the sale of a can of cream, and a dollar he had in his pocket.)

Sufficiently fortified (or, as George more colorfully puts it, "with a skinful") after a stop at the beer parlor, he and Allister headed for the racetrack.

Lady Luck proved a cruel companion all afternoon — until the Quinella race, on which George and Allister planted their last two dollars — and came up with a payoff of better than $28. Their fortunes (and their self-confidence) thus restored, the happy gamblers repaired to the Empire Hotel to share the wealth. Time slid by quickly for the celebrating bettors and their friends, and it is rumored that when the two "spirited" gentlemen arrived at the Massey home about midnight, Mrs. Massie was hard pressed to find any humor in the situation.

Allister Massie, however, recovered his wife's good graces the next Saturday by taking her and the children to the last day of the Fair — after pressing George into service to look after the farm and borrowing $10 from him to boot to finance the trip. ("Those were the days," recalls George.)

George spent the years 1938-40 with Malt Shaw, and in the fall of 1940, on Thanksgiving, went to work with Bob Worden at Trotter and Morton, in the Red Deer and Penhold areas.

He worked there for about four years, making weekend trips to Midnapore, where he stayed with the Albert McKevitts. It was in the course of those weekend visits that George "met his Waterloo" in the person of the pretty blonde who lived next door to McKevitts. George married Kay Gough, daughter of Midnapore elevator man and Reeve, Vivian Gough, in June, 1944.

George, not being of Kay's Catholic faith but looking at the ten strapping children born over the years of their happy union, is convinced that he listened to at least some of the pre-marriage instructions given (in this case by Father Pat O'Byrne) to all couples before a Catholic wedding! Nearly all grown and on their own now, Kay and George's brood includes Bobby, Johnny,

Billy, Kathleen (Sis), Freddie, Jerry, Phyllis, Brian, Ronney, and Jayme.

Active as a baseball coach for many years, George's teams were four-time champions of the Continental Baseball League, and on one occasion captured the City championship as well.

George has owned his own plumbing firm since 1952, and still lives in Midnapore.

JOHN HALIFAX — by Robert Worden

John Halifax was a bachelor who owned the farm which is now the north half of Canyon Meadows including Canyon Meadows golf course, Roper Hull boys' home and bordering Anderson Road on the north. He came from Ceylon in the early 1900's. He had owned a tea plantation there.

When the city of Calgary annexed the property north of Mr. Halifax they should have called the road Halifax instead of Anderson Road. The Halifax property extended nearly the whole length of Anderson Road west of the Macleod Trail, Mr. Halifax lived there long before the Anderson family came to the area.

He did not farm this land but rented it out to various other farmers. W. Worden, John Nicholson and others farmed it for many years. Mr. Halifax lived in a one room shack on the property and spent most of his time playing solitaire, until his death in the 1940's.

The place was later sold to Mr. Bond of Bond and Wright, cattle breeders from Irricana, Alberta.

THE H. G. HALL FAMILY

The Hall family moved to Midnapore from Calgary, May 12, 1951. At that time the family consisted of Harry, Mabel and son, Bob. Trudi was born May 13, 1951. Bill, April 1, 1953. Bonnie, April 12, 1960. Hi-Lites: Harry; Helped start Scouts and Cubs in Midnapore in 1954. Was first Group Committee chairman and subsequently acted as Cub Master, Scout Master and Group Secretary Treasurer. In 1960 he became a member of Calgary Headquarter Staff, remaining active till 1976. He received the Medal of Merit and Silver Acorn for exceptional service to Scouting. He had a total of 45 years as an adult leader. He was a member of Midnapore Community Association and held offices of Vice-President, Secretary-Treasurer and President, at different times. He was a member of St. Paul's Anglican Church and served as Vestry man, Rector's Warden and Treasurer, during that time. He was employed as Technichal Writer by Canadair Flextrac and worked for the same company from 1945 till his retirement in 1976, . Mabel; Was the first Brownie leader when Guides and Brownies started in 1962 under the sponsorship of St. Paul's Anglican Church and, for eight years was a member of the Ladies' Auxiliary to Midnapore Scouts and Cubs. She was a member of St. Paul's Anglican church and its Altar Guild. She worked at Mary Mont Convent when it was operating in Midnapore. Was a member of Good Neighbours club and spent five years as its president. Worked at Eaton's, South Centre from its opening in August, 1974 till November of 1976. Bob; Attended school in Midnapore, graduated from Henry Wise-Wood High School, Calgary in 1968. Took a welding course at S.A.I.T. and won the award for top student in his class

Moved to New Westminster in 1973 where he operates his own business in sales and repairs of lawn mowers and gas driven engines. Trudi; After taking early schooling at Midnapore, graduated from Lord Beaverbrook High School, Calgary as one of its first graduates in 1969. Went to University of Calgary for three years where she majored in fine arts. Like most teen-age girls, she did her stint of baby-sitting for our neighbours. She was active in Guides, Brownies and Church. She moved to Vancouver in 1972 where she was employed by a non-licensed pharmacist. Married in 1973, has one daughter and is now employed by the City of Vancouver in Social Services. Bill; Also a graduate of Midnapore school system and Lord Beaverbrook in 1971. Worked many years as sound and lighting technician with various theatre groups in Calgary. Principal hobby is photography. Resides in Calgary where he is foreman in a paint warehouse. Bonnie; Though she started her education in Midnapore she became an early victim of the "System" and finished elementary and Junior High in Calgary at Andrew Davidson and C. O. Nickle schools. Took five years baton twirling classes, is an accomplished roller-skater. Now living in Victoria with her parents where she is employed as a dance instructor. Pot▸ Pourri: First neighbours, the Dewey Butz family. Lived side by side at two locations for over twenty-five years. In 1955 the Butz, Zoback and Hall families purchased lots in the Burns sub-division and built homes on lots 3, 4, and 5, Block 2. We remember the school and community concerts and the fun we all had, including the occasional mix-ups in the Butz and Halford children. The "flood" in 1963 when the only mode of transportation was by boat, believe it or not. The Scout and Cub chuck-wagon races which we won more than once. The Hughes, the Lows and the friendships of our SMALL COMMUNITY.

ARRIVAL OF HAMILTONS IN SOUTHERN ALBERTA

It might be said that Robert, George and James Hamilton took the long scenic route when moving from their place of birth, Woodstock New Brunswick, to Southern Alberta.

Filled with the spirit of adventure, in 1861, they sailed around Cape Horn to San Francisco. The trip around the Cape in a sailing vessel in those days promised to be adventuresome, the area having a history of shipwrecks during violent storms. Adventure was also anticipated when they reached their destination, for this was the time of the California Gold Rush. In later years the brothers were joined by their younger brother, Johnny, who travelled overland from New Brunswick.

A promise of new adventure in the Cariboo Area of British Columbia lured the brothers from California in the 1870's. Johnny and James secured positions of drivers with Bernard's Express Stagecoaches which travelled 385 miles between Yale and Barkersville. This trail was considered an engineering marvel of the day, and was described by Sir Fredric Butler in his book "Far Out": "As a narrow ledge cut out of the rock, smooth as a table ledge, holding in mid air the heavy coach and its six horse team, no fence, no parapet breaks the sheer descent into the horrendous chasm where 600 feet below the river roars in unseen tumult and above the rugged mountain topples black against the sky." The stage carried large consignments of gold from Barkersville. This was placed in leather pouches and chained under the driver's seat to the floor boards. Robbery was always a danger but no such incident ever occured while Johnny or Jim were driving the coaches. Jim later was responsible for the herds of Bernard's horses, most of which were brought from Oregon and pastured near Kamloops which is still known as the Hamilton Range. George and Robert ranched in the Kamloops area during this period of time.

Upon the completion in 1886 of the Trans Canada railway in British Columbia, Johnny brought two carloads of horses to Calgary. He felt the area offered new challenges and decided to move here. His brothers George and Robert soon followed Johnny to Calgary and settled on land which now forms part of Manchester and Highfield Districts of Calgary. Jim returned to California where he married and spent the rest of his life. He had two daughters, Linda and Minerva, the latter coming to Calgary when she had grown and where she⋅ met and married George Crooks. They lived in Calgary for a number of years.

Shortly after the railway was completed to Calgary, another brother, Sam, came from Woodstock New Brunswick and filed on a quarter section in the Red Deer Lake District. His son, George, followed four years later and filed on a quarter section nearby.

A sister, Minnie Wheeler, came to Calgary from her home in New Brunswick a short time after the railway was completed to Calgary. She kept house for her brother George and taught school in the little Central School in Calgary. She later married a Calgary lawyer named Parlow and they had a daughter, Cathleen, who became a world famous violinist.

BOB & EDNA HAMILTON AND FAMILY — by Connie (Hamilton) Fleuter

In the fall of 1925 Bob Hamilton purchased the "Poplar Grove" farm from Mr. H. W. Morgan situated ½ mile west of the Vader farm, where he had been living with the Hamilton family. In December, 1925, he was married in Calgary to Edna Carrington and they moved to their farm at Midnapore where they enjoyed farm and community life. The Ladies' Community Club was of special interest with Mrs. Dan Patton as president for many years. The members met in their homes, most of which had large living rooms and kitchens that they filled to capacity, and especially when the roads were bad the men obliged by taking their wives by buggy or car. (Actually they wouldn't have missed the opportunity to gather and exchange the news of the day.) Now, in 1977, the ladies are still meeting once a month in their homes in Calgary, having retired from the farms and still holding on to the old friendships. Other activities included a Ladies Riding Club organized by Mabel Hanson of Red Deer Lake. Also there was the five-table bridge parties, with delicious lunches, looked forward to each winter.

Bob was a Charter Member of the Red Deer Lake

Curling Club and a member of the Southern Alberta Pioneer & Old Timers' Association.

In 1929 Robert Colvin Hamilton was born followed in 1931 by his sister Constance Ruth. The farm was a good life for the children, sharing their fun with their cousins and the neighbor kids. They all had their birthday parties which were great fun. In the winter they skated on the creek and sleighed on the side hill. But their biggest interest was riding. They rode four and a half miles to school, and on weekends went riding with their friends.

In the spring of 1949 Bob sold their home quarter and moved back to the Vader Place (E½ 16, SE¼ 21-22-1-W5. He also purchased the Tom Phillips place NE¼ 19 & NW¼ 20-21-2-W5, at Millarville, which he used for summer grazing, and to put up hay. Bobbie attended the Olds School of Agriculture for two years, and Connie finished her High School in Calgary and attended Mount Royal College for a Secretarial Course.

In June 1954 Bob became seriously ill. He and Edna moved to their home in Calgary, and he passed away June 25, 1955. His funeral was largely attended by his family and many friends. Bobbie is now employed by the University of Alberta with the Botanic Garden. He makes his home in Edmonton and often spends weekends in Calgary where his mother still resides.

Connie, now Mrs. Arthur Fleuter, lives on a farm at Charlie Lake, B.C., with her husband and has two sons, Douglas and Michael.

We all remember the "Good Old Days", back when — we cleaned the stove pipes and with a rope and a sack cleaned the brick chimney: we cleaned the carpet on the clothes line with a baseball bat: we had eight tons of coal roar in to the basement for the winter fuel, and dusted a plate rail with thirty ornaments. And when we left the grocery list at the Humfrey's Store — if we were late we picked the groceries up from their veranda, and if it rained when away we would get stuck in the mud on the way home. We especially remember our favorite hired men who were like part of the family, and the only thieves were the coyotes and the chicken hawks. And the excitement to see a car turn the corner, knowing that "There was company coming up the road". We loved the company — the relatives, the neighbors, the teacher, the Minister, etc. And then there were the very happy times when the sad irons were retired, the hand powered washer was ditched, fly spray was invented, and the cream turned to butter! And we all remember our farm animals and our gardens as being a pride and joy.

FRED HAMILTON

Born in 1891, Fred was a strong active child who enjoyed riding, swimming and all the other activities young people of the day who lived on a farm enjoyed. During the second year of school, Fred was stricken with polio which left him paralysed. He was never able to return to school, so his mother assumed the role of teacher and taught him to read which gave him a great deal of pleasure for the rest of his life. Fred often recalled the persistence his father showed in massaging his legs each night, which no doubt was a factor in his being able to stand and eventually walk with the aid of crutches. As a child and adolescent, Fred could not participate in many of the activities of others his age. However he liked to be where the action was and his brothers and sisters would see to it that he was with them and their friends. This sometimes meant transporting Fred around on a small sled or wagon.

After Fred's mother died in 1915, he lived with Mr. and Mrs. Bill Worden until moving to the Vader Place in 1922 with Bob, Clara and Johnny. Fred and the family were always very grateful to the Wordens for the kind care given during these years.

During the summer months while living in the Vader Place, Fred undertook to look after the chickens and managed to feed them and gather the eggs which was quite a feat while walking on crutches. After Johnny married in 1927, Fred continued to make his home with Johnny and Annie until the house burned in 1929. For the next three years Fred made his home with Bob and Edna on their farm,

In 1932 Fred moved to the Old Folks Home in Calgary where he resided until his death in 1967. After moving to Calgary, Fred acquired a wheel chair which enabled him to become independently mobile. He became a familiar sight on Calgary Streets, travelling to the Fair Grounds for livestock shows and the Stampede; to Central Park on many summer days; to church and along 17th Avenue on shopping errands for his friends at the Home who were confined indoors.

Fred's infliction never caused him to lose interest in life and he will be remembered by many for the cheerful attitude he had towards life.

JOHNNY HAMILTON SENIOR

When Johnny Hamilton arrived from Kamloops, B.C. in 1886, with several carloads of horses, it was necessary to find extensive amounts of pasture for them. His first land acquisition was the purchase of approximately two sections and the leasing of several sections of land in the Red Deer Lake district. This land extended east and west, from where Walter Thiessen now lives, to the Priddis turn-off and, north and south from where Highway 22 is now located, to Pine Creek. After disposing of this property he purchased, from Angus Sparrow, two and one half sections, known as the Sparrow Ranch and Dowker place. A large lease in the Godsal Valley went with this property. He disposed of this property in 1920 and purchased three quarters of a section of land two and one half miles south of Midnapore, known as the Vader place. (SE¼ 21 and and E½ 15-22-1-W5. Other property in the district which Johnny owned at one time or another was a half section one mile west of Midnapore which was later known as the Meyers' half section and a half section immediately north of Anderson Road which was purchased from Mr. Lorn Sanderson about 1912.

Many will remember Johnny driving along the roads between Calgary and his ranches. When he met a team of horses which he fancied, he would stop the driver and offer to buy the horses on the spot. He was often successful and the fact that he always paid for his purchases with cash (of which he always carried large sums) often influenced the owners to sell at Johnny's offered price.

Johnny often visited his ranches but maintained a home in Calgary, where he had many interests. Shortly after he arrived in Calgary, he purchased the first livery stable which was known as the Alberta Stable and was located on Ninth Avenue between First and Second Streets, West. Later he bought another stable between Centre and First Streets South East which was known as the Bain's Stable. In 1908, Johnny and Ike Ruttle built another stable on Sixth Avenue between Second and Third Streets South East. This was called the Elk Livery and operated until 1914. William Parslow and Johnny formed a livestock commission agency called Parslow and Hamilton. They sold this operation in 1918 to William's son, Verne, and George Denoon.

As Johnny never married, he had no family of his own but many people in need benefitted from Johnny's generosity. During the last few months before his death in 1933, Johnny lived with his nephew, Bob, and his family.

JOHN (Johnny) HAMILTON

Johnny moved to the Vader Place in 1922 with his two brothers Fred and Bob and his sister Clara Roughton and her daughter June. In 1927 he married the neighbour girl, Annie Sheepy, and they continued to live on the same farm until the house burned to the ground in October 1929.

After the house burned, Johnny and Annie purchased the NW¼ Sec 15; Twp 22; R1; W5M which was directly across the road from the Vader Place. This quarter had been owned by a Miss Cameron who was a sister of Mrs. John McInness. On this land they built a set of farm buildings and moved there in 1930. In later years Johnny also farmed the SW¼ of the same section which Annie had inherited from her mother's estate. In addition to farming these two quarters, Johnny continued to farm the Vader Place jointly with his brother Bob until he moved to Calgary in 1949.

During the Depression Years, the proximity of the farm to the railway tracks resulted in regular daily guests coming for a meal. Money was scarce but food was plentiful and none were ever turned away hungry.

In earlier years, roads in the district were not conducive to motor vehicle travel during much of the year. Johnny spent many hours, day and night, pulling cars from ditches, snowbanks and mudholes. He never accepted remuneration for these services and always considered it as a way of extending a helping hand to his fellow man. It was usually possible to travel by car from our farm to Calgary but often times the road was impassable beyond. Therefore families living beyond would pull their cars with a team of horses to our place, leave their team in the barn and proceed to Calgary in their cars.

Recalling road conditions, we remember when roads were not passable to cars, the mail route driver would drive his vehicle to our farm and Johnny would lend him a saddle horse to enable him to complete his route. The postal workers of those days were more concerned in performing their duties than what a union leader could obtain for them in the way of wages, hours of work, etc.

Annie (Sheepy) and John Hamilton, 1960's.

Johnny's and Annie's two sons Jim and Jack rode to Midnapore for Elementary and Junior High Schooling. Always looked forward to with excitement were the Christmas Concerts and summer picnics, the latter being held on Fish Creek at Shaws or Hoschkas.

Social gatherings in the winter evenings and Sunday visiting with friends and relatives are fondly remembered.

Johnny was always a sports enthusiast and played hockey with the Midnapore team in his earlier years and curled at Red Deer Lake in the later years. After moving to Calgary, Johnny continued to be an enthusiastic curler and took up the game of golf for summer recreation.

After moving to Calgary, Johnny worked with the Department of Public Works until his retirement in 1967. He died in Calgary after a brief illness on September 23, 1973.

Annie still lives a very active life in Calgary. Also living in Calgary are the two sons and their families: Jim and Clara (nee Wilson) and their children Alan and Cathy Doudican; Jack and Betty (nee Stanton) and their children Brian, Robert and Heather.

ROBERT HAMILTON SENIOR

One of Robert's neighbours, while living on his farm on the outskirts of Calgary, was Matilda Colvin who was the widow of Jim Colvin. Jim and Matilda had been married in 1883 in Winnipeg after which they travelled to Calgary, by railraod, to the end of the line which, at that time, was at Moose Jaw. They proceeded on from there by ox-cart. Mr. Colvin had come to Calgary earlier and worked at the J. King General Store and, later joined the N.W.M.P. Mrs. Colvin had two children; Harry and Ethel, born in 1884 and 1885 respectively. Ethel, Mrs. Jim Morrison, is in her ninety second year and living in her home at Lethbridge.

In 1888 Robert married Matilda. They moved to a ranch on Sheep Creek, four and a half miles west of

Okotoks. R. C. Thomas recalled: "It was not until 1890 when Bob Hamilton, a homesteader from Gladys Ridge, imported a few bushels of Kansas Red Turkey wheat, by covered wagon, from Kansas City, that wheat farming was considered more than a foolish gamble for this country." Kansas Red was a fall wheat and when Bob sowed the seed, in July 1890, his neighbours chuckled to themselves. When the crop yielded sixty bushels to the acre, worth $1.00 per bushel, the neighbours changed their attitude!! Fall wheat continued to be grown, with success, in Alberta until after the turn of the century when Marquis spring wheat was introduced.

Robert and Matilda had five children: Fred, Lulu, Clara, Bob and John. After Robert passed away, in 1903, Mrs. Hamilton moved her family to the town of Okotoks where they resided until 1908 when they moved to Calgary. The death of their mother, in 1915, resulted in the family union being broken.

By 1922 Lulu had married Jappy Rogers and was living in Bottrel. Fred was living with Mr. and Mrs. Bill Worden on their farm which was located where the Braeside district of Calgary is now. Bob and Johnny were in the Conrich district where they had been farming together for two years. Clara, who was widowed, and her young daughter, June Roughton, kept house for Bob and John in the summer and lived in Calgary in the winter.

The family's Uncle Johnny Hamilton had recently purchased land in the Midnapore district which was referred to as the Vader place being SE¼ 21 and E½ 16-22-1-W5. He invited John, Bob, Fred, Clara and June to make their home together on his new farm. The invitation was accepted and the family was reunited.

They were soon to become integrated in the community and were going to dances, houseparties and skating parties on Fish Creek. They had inherited a love for horses and enjoyed riding to visit their neighbors. Bob and Johnny were on a hockey team which competed with teams from Calgary to Kew, the latter proving quite a social event as the wives and sweethearts travelled along in a big box sleigh and, after the game, all spent the night at the homes of the host team. The ladies were always in comfortable beds but, as Bob was later to recall, he was bunked with two other men, in one bed, with him on the outside and a big man in the middle. When the latter rolled over he took all the blankets with him and resulted in a very chilly night for Bob.

Clara was an excellent cook and homemaker as is attested to by many friends and relatives who came to visit. She played the piano and sang with others who gathered around the piano, one being her friend from Calgary, Edna Carrinton (Mrs. Bob Hamilton). Uncle Johnny sat in the shadows of the lamp-lit room and voiced his approval of his favourite songs. June was an active child and a delight to them all.

Bob and Johnny worked the land and broke many horses some of which they worked and rode and others which were sold.

The family unit stayed intact until December, 1925 when Bob married and moved to a neighbouring quarter. Johnny married in January, 1927 at which time Clara and June moved to Calgary.

WALTER AND EVA (TOWNER) HEMENS

I was born in Somerset, England in 1891 and came to Priddis from Costa Rica in 1912 where I worked for Studdy on the Old George Ethel Place, 33-22-3-W5. Our neighbours were, H. C. Wallis, Billy Patterson and J. Baxter Keith, who was on the Pomery homestead, after they went to Pirmez Creek. Studdy and Walter Ockley bought a threshing outfit in 1913 and I worked with them. I left for the First War and served from 1916-1919. On my return, the Priddis District presented me with gold cuff links.

I worked for Frank Hopkins and Peter Massie until 1929 and then rented Pie Hone's from Chet Wallace of Vulcan (20-23-3-W5) for three years.

In 1935, while living at Chilliwack B.C., I married Eva Towner, youngest daughter of Ernie and Mrs. Towner, of Midnapore. We returned to Midnapore in 1936 and our son, Stanley was born in 1937. He is now in the Air Force.

In 1945 we moved to Calgary and I worked for the Union Milk Company, the Co-op Milk Company and the Provincial Government until 1953 when we moved to Vancouver Island. I was attached to the Canadian Corps of Commissionaires, for 17 years, until retiring.

SECTION 29-22-1-W5th.
STANLEY D. HENKER

My parents, Mr. and Mrs. Richard Henker, came from North Dakota to Granum, Alberta in 1902 where they homesteaded, farmed and ranched for many years. In 1930 my father started in the registered Hereford business, and in 1941 a bull he raised topped the Calgary Bull Sale. After my father's death, I carried on with a portion of the registered Herefords.

In 1945 I purchased a ranch at Pincher Creek, Alberta, from the honorable J. J. Bowlen. It was a real good ranch with exceptionally good prairie grass, good farm land, with an abundance of water. The chinook winds would melt the snow in winter, but constant west winds from the Crowsnest Pass, year around, made me decide to sell and move father north.

In 1951 I purchased the George Beatty Farm west of Midnapore and continued raising registered Herefords with much success. We raised champions with both Polled and Horned Herefords in major shows such as Calgary and the Toronto Royal.

In 1960 our son Blair had the Grand Champion steer at the Calgary 4-H Show and Sale, and in 1961 the Grand Champion steer at Calgary fat stock show and sale.

We have the distinction of selling the first Polled Hereford bull to England from the province of Alberta. He was the Junior Canadian Champion at the National Show and was bred and raised here at Midnapore. We have sold all the registered cattle and a portion of the farm, but still feel the Midnapore area is the best place to live.

CHARLES AND WILMA (GRAVELY) HUGHES

Charles Hughes was born in London, England in 1903 and he and his family immigrated to Lockwood, Saskatchewan in 1912.

After homesteading in Saskatchewan for eight years, the family moved to Calgary in 1920 where

Charlie took up the trade of automotive mechanic, a trade he followed for the rest of his life.

In 1930 Charlie married Wilma Gravely of Gadsby, Alberta and they had two children; Garry and Vivian. In 1937 Charlie and Wilma moved to Okotoks where Charlie worked for Waldron Motors and Sheperd Motors, Turner Valley.

In 1941 Charlie joined the army and served in the R.C.E.M.E. branch until his discharge in 1945. After his discharge, Charlie and Wilma moved to Midnapore where Charlie worked for Shaw Construction and various automotive dealers in Calgary.

In 1971 Charlie passed away after a brief illness. His wife, Wilma, now lives, with her son, in Carstairs and her daughter, Vivian, now lives in Cranbrook, B.C.

ED HUTCHISON — by A. McKevitt

Ed came to the Midnapore district about 1912 and worked for different outfits in the area. For years he worked for Shaws doing many different jobs but mostly as a separator man with the threshing outfit. Known as an honest man, he would not accept payment until he had done an honest day's work for it. If he had repairs to make he would not go to bed until the machine was ready to go for the morning.

As far as I know he was a bachelor and he passed away about 1964.

HAMMOND WILFRED AND MADGE (CHAPMAN) JARDINE — by Bud Jardine.

I, Bud, was born, twins with a girl, that's a pretty bad start. Apart from that about the only thing of note that I accomplished was to last out two world wars as well as some seventeen years in the active militia making twenty seven and one half years service. I started as a very awkward private and finished with the rank of Major, (still awkward), four service medals and the efficiency decoration. After that I just about blundered from one meal to another and tried to keep out of trouble.

I met Madge soon after returning from overseas when I arranged for room and board at her parents' home. This was about 1921. After a somewhat stormy start we finally started 'going steady' as the saying goes and we were married in 1927.

We had a family of four boys, the first one died at birth. Wilfred Donald was born in 1930, Douglas Raymond, 1932 and Roy Vernon, 1933 (deceased 1974).

I believe I am correct when I say that we purchased the first lot in the new subdivision (Midnapore). I know that we were first to establish location being even ahead of the surveyors who, when they did arrive, ran a line from the boundary across in front of where the house now stands and I had guessed right on. The boys were especially helpful in helping me to roof our house where I would have found it most difficult to crawl around with a stiff leg. Madge and I moved into the house within a month of its inception and, after a winter of occupying two rooms and a path, so to speak, we finished the building as funds became available and, while it was not too comfortable at first, it was ours and later became quite cosy.

The first person to call on us was a, not too tall chap who, when I looked at him, I felt that he smiled much more than he showed dislike. He was none other than Johnny Butz. After his brief welcome and, noting that the corner of my proposed house had ruined a perfectly good baseball diamond and was plumb across the main (used to be) trail between Calgary and Fort Macleod; he said he was still glad to know me and offered me water until I was able to have my well drilled.

While I was hurriedly putting some wind proof siding on the house — it was getting late in the season, around the end of October — another very nice chap stopped his car and made himself acquainted. He was Nate Beebe and, after finding who to contact in Calgary, lost no time in becoming the second settler. Of course he brought his house with him and could live quite comfortably while getting a foundation to set it on. The next, I believe were Listers, they also brought their house with them. After that the place filled up too fast to remember.

Improving our house was a hobby with me and I spent my spare time in improving it. I still had lots to do, thoughts of Midnapore are always with me, happy and sad.

Madge was a good wife and mother. She loved her boys and her home. When she passed on, she left three sons, three grandsons and two granddaughters. I miss her terribly. This bit of information is forwarded with much emotion. Madge passed away in 1972 at the age of 72 years after we had been married 44 years. I'll always remember Midnapore with a great deal of nostalgia, hard times and mostly good times.

DALE JEFFERY

I was born in Calgary, April 29, 1929 and have lived all my life on the home farm. I attended Midnapore Schools, seven years in the old school, west of the elevators, and three years in, what is now, the Community Hall. I also attended Olds School of Agriculture 1946-1947.

We used to go to town once a week to get groceries at Humfrey's Store which was at the edge of town, now 66th Avenue and Macleod Trail, it seemed a long way then.

Our first tractor was an Advance Rumely. It was a real experience learning to drive that!!

I married a girl from Scotland, Hazel White, in 1962. We have two daughters; Heather and Susan.

Dale Jeffery learning to ride.

R. M. (JEFF) JEFFERY W½-32-22-1-W5

I came to Canada from Birkenhead, England in March, 1921 and, after working on farms in Ontario that summer, ($15.00 a month and board half a day off every other Sunday), I came west on a harvest excursion, ($15.00 return from Toronto to any point on the prairies), as far as Moose Jaw and, from there got a job at Elbow, Saskatchewan where I stayed for 18 months, then a summer in the Fraser Valley at Dewdney and a winter in Vancouver and, in the spring of 1924, came to Calgary and worked for Norman Willans, Hugh Macklin and various other farmers in the Glenmore, Midnapore, Red Deer Lake and Millarville areas. In 1928 I bought land from Tom Scott, married Nena Harrison, whom I met in 1924, and we had one son, Dale. Each fall I toured the district in a bundle rack, threshing with Billy Durant, Pattons, McKevitts, Malt Shaw and Murray Scott, to mention a few of the outfits. Though it was hard work and long hours it was a great way of getting to know the district and the people in it. Many of the people I met in those days have been my friends ever since although a lot of them have 'gone down the "Sunset Trail" and others have moved to different parts of the country.

Soon after I started on my own, in 1928, we ran into the depression years but, around this district, most farmers had a few pigs and chickens, a milk cow or two and a good garden so, although cash was almost non-existent, we generally managed to eat very well and for amusement we had card parties, surprise parties, at which everybody would converge on a certain house, without warning, taking their own refreshments, clearing the furniture out of the biggest room in the house and have a dance. A lot of the boys could get 'real music' out of a 25¢ mouth-organ so an orchestra was no problem.

Next came the war, in 1939, and most of the able bodied boys joined up and hard times were back again. A few years after the successful conclusion of the war Calgary started to boom and has been growing and expanding, almost beyond belief, ever since, and in a few short years from now, our farm, along with many others, will be submerged under rows of houses, high rises and shopping centres.

EDWARD AND MANDELLA JOHNSON — by Ruth "Johnson" Hamilton

Edward Johnson was born in the year 1858 in Hampshire, England. At the age of 14 years he went to work in one of the largest breaking and sales stables in the south of England. He worked there for two years and then shipped as a deck hand on board the full sail rig ship Belvedere owned by Goodhall and Perkins from San Francisco. The ship was bound for Valparaiso, Chile. He worked for the Chilean Government breaking remounts for their army and then one year for the Governor of Juan Fernandez (Robinson Crusoe's Island). When the war between Chile and Peru broke out, he was put on transport duty, shipping horses to the front. After the war he travelled north through Peru, Mexico, Acapulco and San Francisco. He also went to the Sandwich Island and Honolulu, then to Victoria, B.C.

In 1879 he worked at Ashcroft, B.C. for the Douglas Lake Cattle Co. Ed was known as "Wild Horse Johnson". He came through the Crows Nest Pass riding for Oscar Rush. They took 150 head of horses and broke them at Fort McLeod for seventy dollars per head.

When he first came to Okotoks, there was only a store run by Hybert Brown. In the fall of that year 1887, he and Charlie Priddis went into partnership on a homestead at Priddis (named after Charlie Priddis).

The next year Ed and Charles Berry contracted with J. Bean of the Elbow River (herd ranch) to go to British Columbia and corral five hundred head of wild horses and bring them to Calgary. After his return from B.C., he tended bar at the Old Grand Central Hotel in Calgary for H. McLeod.

In the spring of 1888 while working at the Grand Central Hotel, he met and married Mandella Minthorne who came from Oakwood, Ontario. An orphan at the age of eleven years, she travelled alone to Broadview, Saskatchewan where she stayed with a married sister until she came to Calgary. She was seventeen years old when she married Ed and moved to the homestead at Priddis. The house and out buildings were made of log as were most builldings in those days.

At one time Ed was employed as a stage-coach driver by the B.C. Express, which was run by Wheeler Mickle. The route was the old Caribou Trail, one hundred and ten miles of winding treacherous roads.

He worked on the Oxley Ranch for a while and in 1891 took charge of the Glenbow Horse Ranch which was owned by Leslie Hill.

While Ed was away working at these jobs, his wife Mandella, stayed on the homestead at Priddis, looking after the chores, one of which was bucking up wood to keep the stoves going. During this time she had four children, Eva, Nettie, Sam and Bill. Only on one occasion do I recall her tales of hardships and loneliness. Pioneer wives accepted it as their duty and seldom were heard complaining.

In 1903 the Johnson family left the homestead and

Edward and Mandella Johnson.

Midnapore Hotel (Dominion House) 1905. Man in wagon , standing l. to r. Bill (Tip), Ed and Mandella Johnson. Sam on horse.

moved to Midnapore, where Ed built the Dominion Hotel. He and his wife Mandella ran this place until 1911, when he sold out and bought the Royal Hotel in Okotoks.

In 1913 he moved to the old Creighton Ranch west of Okotoks. He leased this ranch from a man by the name of Stacks who was from England. They ran the ranch for five years and then moved to a farm at Idasley on the southern outskirts of Calgary at that time. (Now part of the country is all a part of the City of Calgary.) From there they moved to Calgary and lived on 15th Avenue just north of the Stampede grounds.

Mandella Johnson was a great tribute to the memory of the women of the early west. Her days consisted of back breaking work (every chore in those days was done the hard way). Her children, of which she had twelve, were her life. She was a gentle, kind woman, loved by her family and neighbours.

By 1931 the family had all gone their own way so Ed and Mandella moved back to Midnapore to the C.P.R. Station house. Here life was a lot easier for them both. Never a day went by, but what some relative or friends would stop to visit or to take them to town. They were made most welcome and were always served tea, as Mrs. Johnson, as well as being a most gracious lady was a very good cook.

They lived in the old Station house quietly and happily until 1949 when Ed passed away at the age of ninety-three years to be followed by his wife Mandella in 1952. The old Station house they lived in has been moved and is now a part of the old west at Heritage Park in Calgary.

Of their 12 children, nine grew to maturity, Eva, Sam, Bill (Tip) and Edythe are now deceased. Those remaining are Nettie at Vancouver, Claude at Victoria, Dolly at Vernon, B.C., Marjorie at Armstrong, B.C., and Maurice at Montreal.

JOSEPH JUTRAS

Joseph Jutras came from Drumheller to work at the Lacombe Home. He later worked for P. Burns Ranches at Midnapore. He joined the army as soon as World War II was declared and was among the first to be sent overseas. He remained overseas during the war and returned when peace was declared. He took over his father's farm at Drumheller. While overseas he married a Scottish girl. They were blessed with five children. Joe passed away suddenly in July, 1976 with a heart attack.

EDWARD KUNDER — by J. McKevitt

Edward (Eddie) Kunder was born in Ontario in 1902 and came west to live at Acme, with an aunt and uncle, Mary (Dalzell) McLellan and her husband, when he was orphaned, at the age of 14. When the McLellans moved into Calgary, he went to work in the Red Deer Lake district.

Eddie was a cousin of the Dalzells and Sheepys but I didn't know him until about 1937 at which time he was operating a grader for the government on No. 22 Highway, west from Midnapore to Turner Valley. He remained with that job until he joined the army and went overseas. On his return from the war, he worked for the City but ended up in the Belcher Hospital where he had a leg amputated as a result of a war injury. He died in hospital about 1964.

He leaves one daughter, Jean, (Mrs. W. Mills) of Bluffton, Alberta. Jean lived with us from the age of five years until she was married in 1949.

GEORGE FRANCIS AND ELIZABETH ROSE (HODGSON) LEE — by Ted Lee

George Francis Lee and Elizabeth Rose Hodgson were married in Ontario in 1913. They farmed in Trent River, Ontario for a few years but both longed to go west. Elizabeth was born and raised in the west and George had ranched for several years in the Millarville district around the turn of the century. By 1917 their minds were made up and they sold the farm in Ontario and moved west to Midnapore, Alberta to the S½ 5-23-1-W5.

George and Elizabeth had five children; John Francis (Hodge) and George Edward (Ted) were born at Trent River and Philip Henry, Mary Madeline and William Thomas (Dogie) were born in Calgary. Elizabeth passed away in 1952 and George in 1965. Both are buried in Saint Patrick's cemetery in Midnapore.

Hodge married Jeannette Therrien in 1939. At the time he was employed by the Bell Telephone Company in Montreal and, shortly after, joined the Navy where he remained until the end of World War 2. He then returned to work for the Bell Telephone Company until his retirement in 1970. Hodge and Jeannette now live in Ottawa, Ontario. They have four children; Robert, Richard, Denise and Raymond.

Ted married Marjorie Mary (Marge) Fachini in 1949. They acquired a few acres of land from the George Lee Sr. farm where they built their home and presently live. They had nine children; Patricia, Jeannette, Marguerite, Elizabeth, Edward, Judith, Michael, Thomas and Richard.

Philip married Hazel Runge in 1949. After living in Midnapore for a number of years they moved to a farm at Pigeon Lake, Alberta. They had five children; Raymond, Brian, Myrna, Lorne and Dale.

Mary Madeline taught school for quite a few years but left to take care of George Lee Sr. for the last few years of his life. She is now retired and lives in Calgary.

Dogie married Muriel Carrie in 1951. After living in Calgary for several years they bought a farm in Bluffton, Alberta where they now live. Dogie and Muriel have four children; Catherine, Brenda, Janice and Yvonne.

JOSH LITTLETON — by Albert McKevitt

Just a note about Josh Littleton. He bought out Jim Stephen I think about 1910 or '11. Mr. Littleton had a good crop and it got snowed under, September 18, 1911 and the snow never went off till spring.

Emil Hoschka was looking after a bunch of cattle for P. Burns on the Joe Shannon place and he would move them around the district, buy the crops and let the cattle clean up the grain. That is what happened to Mr. Littleton's first crop.

I don't think he farmed too long, he used to rent the farm and live in Calgary where I think he sold real estate.

EDWARD MASSE

Edward Masse, born in Calgary on September 5th, 1915, is the son of Joseph and Adrienne Masse. When still an infant, his parents moved to Mossleigh area, where they farmed until 1927. They then moved to

a farm at Ensign. When Edward finished his schooling, he worked with his father on the farm. In 1933 he started working for Burns ranches at Bow Valley, Midnapore.

During his years with Burns he was a ranch hand, cowboy, did farm work, truck driver and cat-skinner. In 1941 he married Evelyn Hoschka. He has two sons and one daughter and eight grandchildren. In 1954 he and his family moved to Midnapore and he began work with Standard General as a welder. Land that he farmed while with Burns is the same land that in later years he worked on with Standard General to create the Lakes of Bonaventure, Bonavista and Midnapore.

THE MAYHEW NURSERY 1949-1970

In the fall of 1949 my parents, Alma and Carl Larsen, were able to realize their dream to own their own home and business. Father had purchased the Mayhew nursery from Mr. Wm. Mayhew and we planned to move from Calgary to the "country" in the spring.

Father came into the nursery business with a landscape gardener's working knowledge of this area's hardy trees, plants and shrubs. Much of this he had learned from nursery men such as Mr. Mayhew, Mr. George Horn and others. The skills he had learned while farming his family's farm in Denmark were to prove a valuable asset. He had come to Canada from Denmark in 1929 and his fiancee, Alma, arrived in Calgary in 1930. It was difficult to be a "New Canadian" in the thirties. Jobs were scarce and it wasn't till 1933 they felt they could afford to be married and I didn't fit into the budget until 1942.

The nursery and house were located on 21 acres of land stretching between the old and new No. 2 highways, with the railway crossing at north and south points. The house is of historical note having belonged to John Glenn. At that time it had been situated well east of the nursery location. By the time we came to live in it, it had had several additions and renovations and it wasn't until we began inflicting more changes on it that we found it had originally been a squared-log house of very solid construction.

Moving day was March 15, and it seemed an auspicious day to move as we were enjoying a very warm chinook. However, as March chinooks often prove to be, this one was fickle and changed, over night, into a blizzard. By the next morning we were snowed in. The house was cold and little had been unpacked. The excitement of moving had disappeared and the atmosphere was heavy, especially in the kitchen. This was due, in part, to the aggravations of moving but mainly to an un-cooperative wood stove that Mother could not cajole nor coerce into giving up smoking and into giving enough heat to perk the morning coffee. Fortunately, the Mayhews had moved just down the road. It took a visit from these good neighbours, who knew the idiosyncrasies of the stove, before Mother and the stove came to terms.

From the first spring we knew that all springs at the nursery would be hectic. The yard seemed to be always full of activity and inside the phone and the door seemed to ring and bang incessantly. Mother learned to cook and bake, take cash, sort out orders and bills and answer the phone as if all at once.

As the city of Calgary grew, so did the nursery. Eventually the shovel and wheel-barrow method of selling was abandoned and a sales lot established to provide easy access to an increased variety of pre-dug and pre-potted stock. By the 1960's, most of the nursery stock sold had been grown in the nursery rather than imported. This had been accomplished through improved methods of propagation, land management and marketing. Horticultural experts provided Father with much help and technical advice for which he was grateful as it reduced the time spent learning through trial and error.

By 1970, Nu West Homes was eager to include the nursery in their Canyon Meadows development. My parents were ready to retire and, in due course, the property was sold. After 21 busy years, they left the nursery in the fall of 1970 to move to their new home in the De Winton area.

During these years I had completed my education and, in 1964, had married Butch Shaw. Of our children, only Sam, born in 1966, will have memories of the nursery. John Carl was just a new baby in 1970 and Mary Frances didn't arrive until 1972. However, I can still take them over to Canyon Meadows and show them the two lovely Chinese Elms, planted by Mr. Mayhew, that mark the site where the house stood. And I know too that there is a lot of the Mayhew nursery stock growing in Calgary and district gardens. It is a rare shopping trip for my parents that someone doesn't recognize them as "the folks from the nursery" and tell them how much the trees and shrubs have grown that they bought years ago.

WILLIAM AND EDITH (LARTER) MAYHEW — by Christine Logan

William "Billy" Mayhew came to Canada with his wife Edith, and two and a half year old daughter, Ina,

from Norfolk, England in 1912. He first became gardener and chauffeur for W. R. Hull, living in the old "Coach House" which now stands in Heritage Park, used originally as a stable then later as a garage, the upper level being the living quarters. A second daughter, Christine, was born during the five years he worked there. Then he moved to look after the garden of Pat Burns who owned the lovely sandstone home a short distance from the Hull estate. Here he remained from 1915 till shortly after the death of Pat Burns in February, 1937 when he moved to the Midnapore area. He moved a log-constructed house from across the MacLeod Trail to a small acreage and developed his own nursery business.

Probably his greatest satisfaction during his years working for Pat Burns was in directing the planting and caring for the Poplar trees on both sides of the MacLeod Trail, a memorial to Pat. To the sorrow of many of the old timers these trees have mostly been removed to accommodate the widened highway.

In 1950 when he found the work getting too much for him to continue in the nursery business, he sold to Carl Larsen.

Not wanting to leave the country he enjoyed so much and the many friends around him, he moved a house from down on Fish Creek to the south of his property and resided there with his wife until the fall of 1964 when they moved to the Hillhurst district of Calgary where they stayed until their deaths. Edith in 1975 and William in 1976.

Mr. Mayhew was one of the original members of the Calgary Horticultutral Society, both he and his wife showing plants, flowers, vegetables and entering the Burn's gardens in competition over many years and then, in his later years, acting as show judge.

THE McINNES FAMILY, listed in chronological order, and all born in Priceville, Grey County, Ontario, to parents of Scottish origin, born on the Island of Iona in the Hebrides. They came directly from there by sailing vessel to Canada and settled on a farm in Grey County, Ontario.

Hugh: Born 1852 Priceville, Ontario. Died at Midnapore, Alberta May 14, 1908. He remained a bachelor.

Charles: Born approximately 1853 Priceville, Ontario. Died at Calgary around 1891. Married to Katherine McArthur, Paisley, Ontario. There were no children.

Malcom: Born 1857 Priceville, Ontario. Died at Calgary 1943. Married to Kate McArthur of Paisley, Ontario a first cousin of his brother Charles wife.

Children: Hugh: Born at Calgary 1889, Died 1959; **Charles Malcom:** Born 1891 at Calgary, Died 1971 at Bristol, England; **Peter Earl:** Born at Calgary 1894, Died 1975 Reno, Nevada; **Archie:** Born 1901, Died 1973, California; **John:** Born 1864, Died at Calgary 1946, Married to Margaret Fletcher Cameron of Priceville, Ontario who died at Calgary 1933.

Children: all born at Priceville, Ontario. Christine: born October 11, 1896 died at Calgary September 30, 1961. Margaret Iona: Born May 15, 1899. Jean Cameron: Born September 1900, died at Toronto, Ontario 1969.

Margaret McInnis, Charles McInnis (son), John McInnis.

Charles Duncan: Born December 22, 1903 died July 24, 1951.

Margaret McInnes Shannon: Married to Joseph Shannon, Born August 24, 1866, Died at Calgary 1950, No Children.

In 1883 the three older McInnes brothers came from Ontario to North West Territories, later named Alberta in 1905, to Fort Calgary and secured themselves Homesteads within a mile of each other, and the hamlet which was to be known as Midnapore.

Hugh's homestead adjoined the Shaws and was named Grass Valley Ranch. The brand he registered was "HI". Hugh, a bachelor all his life, built his log cabin and, having a natural instinct for gardening, planted Spruce trees around his dwelling which became a landmark in the community. The 160 acres was beautiful property with a spring on it, perfect for grazing of cattle and horses. Some of the acreage was planted with grain, and the frontier farmer began a new way of life in a new world. As the years passed he acquired more land and at his death owned 480 acres.

Charles secured his homestead a mile away with water on the property. He soon married and brought his bride, Kate, from Paisley, Ontario, to carry on farming, having built a log cabin. There were no children of this marriage. Charles died very young, about 1895. His widow returned to Paisley, Ontario and rented her property but returned each year to see how the tennants were progressing. Her ties in the west were close because she had her McInnes brothers-in-law and two brothers in Calgary.

Malcom had his homestead opposite Hugh's property, on what is known as the Macleod Trail. He was a very adventurous man, coming west in 1875 to Vancouver via San Francisco by train and boat. He took up the cattle business for three years and in 1879 went placer mining for gold in British Columbia until 1883 when he snowshoed through the mountains to Calgary, meeting his brothers to homestead. Later on he went into partnership in the cattle business with Pat Burns, under the name of McInnes and Burns. He married a first cousin of his sister-in-law also Kate McArthur of Paisley, Ontario and a sister of a well known settler in the Red Deer District, Peter McArthur. They had five

sons, four survived. Their eldest son met a tragic death falling from his horse at an early age. Shortly after that the family moved to Calgary where Malcom established himself in the lumber business but retained his property at Midnapore which he rented. Malcom's grandsons all live in Calgary at the present time.

John as a lad of seventeen, many years younger than his brothers, born in 1864, came west where his brothers were establishing themselves. With other farmers and ranchers he was conscripted to aid in the Riel Rebellion where he drove a transport wagon and was present when the murders, by Riel, of Father Delaney and Dunlop were discovered.

He had left his aging father, a widower in Priceville, Ontario to go west at that time. It was understood that he would return to the west after his father's death. This he did in 1905, twenty-two years after his first trip, with his wife, Margaret Fletcher Cameron, and their four children, three girls and a boy, and came to join his brother, Hugh, at Midnapore as had been arranged by the two brothers many years before.

By now there were many changes from 1883. The bachelor brother had meanwhile built a frame house, painted white with red roof, large enough to house comfortably this family of six. The old log cabin became a place for supplies. He had added to his homestead acreage and now owned 480 acres.

This was a new beginning for John, now 41, who had always lived with his father, continuing to do so after his marriage. It was also a new world for his wife, now 39, coming into an already established home of her brother-in-law, so many years older, whom she scarcely knew, with her four lively children, one already school age, and into a land so utterly different from what she had left.

Hugh, on his part, had to make staggering adjustments, but he and his sister-in-law were friends from the start, and the children, who had never known an uncle before, loved him from the start and he them, especially the boy, the youngest child.

This new life for everyone, was alas, only to last exactly three years for beloved Hugh died in May 1908 from a massive coronary. His death was a shock and grief to all for many miles around.

From that time, the property, known as Grass Valley Ranch, became John's, and the only place in the community where a McInnes lived. He and his wife threw themselves into the life of the community and were loved and thought of as good neighbors. John always seemed to feel that in throwing himself into the community he was doing so for the older brothers who were no longer there.

One of his early assignments was secretary of the school board of the little log school at Midnapore. The many teachers who came over the years, usually from Ontario or England, and strange to the country, looked upon the McInnes home as a special harbour where they were helped to understand this new way of life in Alberta.

He had a very happy and rewarding association with the Lacombe Home, built in 1910, remembering Father Lacombe as the beloved Padre of the Rebellion

Jordison Bros. — Auctioneers, Calgary

Jordison Bros. Auctioneers, Calgary.
Telephones 524 & 885. P.O. Box 1172.

Sold on account of M.McInnis Esqr in re estate of H.McInnis (deceased)
Calgary, August 29. 1907

LOT No.	NAME OF ARTICLE	NAME OF PURCHASER	FOLIO	Dollars	Cents
	Pots & pans	J.McInnis	2317	1	00
	6 chairs	Cash	2318	1	00
	Pots & pans	Cash	c		25
	Arm chair crockery	Johnson	2320	2	50
	Harness	J.McInnis	2317	13	00
	do	Breckenridge	2321	13	00
	do	J.McInnis	2317	1	00
	Bob sleighs	do	2317	5	00
	Job lot tools	do	2317	2	00
	do	do	2317		75
	Collars	do	2317	1	00
	Rain wagon	do	2317	42	00
	Buggy	McCarthy	2322	19	00
	Stock saddle	M.McInnis	2323	5	00
	Single Harness	J.McInnis	2317	7	00
	Saws	Bennett	2324		50
	Augur	Bramner	2325		35
	Brace & bits	Johnson	2320	1	00
	Scales	do	2320	5	50
	Gang plough	McInnis	2317	8	00
		carried forward:-		128	85

Jordison Bros. Auctioneers, Calgary.
Telephones 524 & 885. P.O. Box 1172.

Sold on account of _____
Calgary, _____ 190_

LOT No.	NAME OF ARTICLE	NAME OF PURCHASER	FOLIO	Dollars	Cents
	brought forward			128	85
	Drag harrows	J.Robinson	2326	12	50
	Fanning mill	do	2326	10	00
	Chaff cutter	McIntosh	2327	2	00
	Mower	J.McInnis	2317	19	00
	Grindstone	Ford	2328		75
	Trees	do	2328	1	25
	3 guns	Cardiff	2329	1	75
	Job lot	McClelland	2318		25
	13 head stock	Ford	2328	172	25
	Milk cow	M.McInnis	2323	26	00
	36 head cows	Ford	2328	666	00
7	3 yr bay filly	D.Patton	2330	98	00
6	8 " " Mare & Foal	Breckenridge	2321	149	00
5	7 " bn mare	do	"	90	00
23	5 " by gelding	do	"	182	00
11	3 " " filly	Adams	24_	152	50
10	4 " " "	Breckenridge	2321	140	00
1	1 " " gelding	J.McInnis	2317	50	00
24	3 " " "	Hamilton	2332	120	00
		carried forward:-		2133	10

Jordison Bros. Auctioneers, Calgary.
Telephones 524 & 885. P.O. Box 1172.

Sold on account of _____
Calgary, _____ 190_

LOT No.	NAME OF ARTICLE	NAME OF PURCHASER	FOLIO	Dollars	Cents
	brought forward:-			2133	10
21	2 yr bay filly	D.Patton	2330	197	00
22	" " " "				
25	3 " bn gelding	Parslow	2333	135	00
20	2 " by "	Hamilton	2332	100	00
15	6 " " mare	Breckenridge	2321	142	50
16	3 " " filly	Dodds	2334	200	00
19	7 " bn mare	Ford	2328	300	00
12	" " " "	do	"	300	00
14	6 " by " & foal	Breckenridge	2321	150	00
27	4 " " gelding	do			
28	5 " " "	do	"	315	00
2	Yearling gelding	Hamilton	2332	45	00
3	" "	do	"	45	00
4	" "	Johnson	23 20	50	00
18	4 yr bay mare & foal	Cardiff	2329	197	50
13	Brown work horse	J.McInnis	2317	91	00
	Mare "Maud" & twins	Littleton	2335	105	00
17	2 yr grey gelding	Hamilton	2332	42	00
	Black saddle horse	M.McInnis	2323	35	00
		carried forward, -		4583	60

Jordison Bros. Auctioneers, Calgary.
Telephones 524 & 885. P.O. Box 1172.

Sold on account of _____
Calgary, _____ 190_

LOT No.	NAME OF ARTICLE	NAME OF PURCHASER	FOLIO	Dollars	Cents
	brought forward:-			4583	60
	Kitchen cabinet	McClelland	2318	2	00
"	Range	J.McInnis	2317	9	00
	Heater	do	2317	10	00
	Sideboard	McClelland	2318	13	50
		Total:-		4618	00
		less one cow		18	60
				4599	60

Jordison Bros. Auctioneers

---

days in 1883. The sisters in Charge always turned to him for advice and counsel in the farming activities of the home.

He was Chairman of the Board of Managers of St. Andrews Presbyterian Church at Pine Creek. He was a life member of the Southern Alberta Pioneers. Also a member of the Old Timers Association, The United Farmers of Alberta, the Alberta Wheat Pool. He was the local Justice of the Peace from 1910-1935.

He was one of the community responsible for getting the telephone into the district of Midnapore and Red Deer Lake District in 1912, making a house to house canvas in his buggy.

Everyone who visited the McInnes home was delighted by the hospitality showered on them. Many of the young people, now grown old, remember with joy the times they gathered around the piano with John leading in song, with his glorious tenor voice.

Many of the men who were hired to work came back for visits years after they left, knowing they were coming to share their joys and sorrows with good friends. This was especially so among many of the men who returned from the 1914-1918 war.

The four children of John McInnes grew up in the community and attended school at the little log house and went on to do high school elsewhere.

Christine, known in those days as Ina, went to Toronto for 2 years where she lived with her mother's only sister and attended a very well known Collegiate, returning to take her last 2 years at Calgary Collegiate, then on to Normal School. After some years of experience teaching in country schools she came to teach in the Calgary Schools until her death in 1961.

Margaret second daughter, went from Midnapore school to Toronto to a girls Private School until she matriculated to University of Toronto from where she graduated and became a Social Worker in Toronto. She came back, on her annual holiday, to her parents at Midnapore, thus keeping in touch with her friends in the Community.

Jean, third daughter, went to High School at Calgary, then on to the same school Margaret had attended, planning to get her Ontario matriculation

Joe and Maggie Shannon. Chris and Jean McInnes, 1917.

enabling her to enter University of Toronto to study medicine. She was only in school a few months when she was stricken with rheumatoid arthritis. She was never able to get to University, nor to have permanent employment of any kind due to her health. She remained in Toronto with Margaret where they shared a beautiful home with their Aunt. She returned to Calgary in 1941 to live with Christine enabling her to see more of her father in his last years. The arthritis slowly became worse, in spite of getting all available treatment on this continent. After Christine's death in 1961, she returned to Toronto to live with Margaret until her death in 1969. She had the devotion of everyone who knew her.

Charles Duncan attended school at Midnapore and went to Western Canada College at Calgary for high school period. He returned to his parents, now the only one of the family at home, taking over much of the responsibilty and work. Two years after his mother's death in 1933, he married Margaret Dunbar of Calgary. Shortly afterwards his father retired to Calgary to live until his death in his eighty-second year.

Charlie and Margaret carried on the farm, raising Shorthorn cattle under the Herd name; Marinvale Shorthorns; and dairying. They were one of the original members to ship milk to Alpha Milk Company via milk train. They raised three children Elizabeth, and twins, Jean and Jack. The children attended the school at Midnapore, as the previous family had done, going on to High School at Calgary. Charlie died suddenly from a heart attack in July 1951 aged 47. Margaret continued living on the farm, managing it and teaching school in Calgary until her early death age 47, November 1961.

Elizabeth met and married Mickel Barca of Taber and lives in Calgary. She has one daughter Bonnie.

Jean married Robert McLerie of Grandview, Manitoba. They have two daughters, Heather and Margaret, and two sons, Cameron and Duncan, and farm at Dickson, Alta.

Jack the only son of Charlie and Margaret remained on at the family farm, Grass Valley Ranch, carrying on the work as his father and grandfather had done before him. He married Elaine Scott of Hanna, Alberta. In 1973 Jack and Elaine sold the property which had been in the McInnes hands since 1883, almost a century ago and moved with their two small children Charles Darren and Joanne, to Olds, Alberta where they purchased a farm.

Thus ends the saga of the McInnes four generations in this old, old community of Midnapore.

MR. AND MRS. JOSEPH SHANNON

Mrs. Margaret Shannon was the sister of the four McInnes brothers. She came to the west in the late eighties as a young unmarried woman to keep house for her bachelor brother Hugh whose homestead was at Midnapore.

She met Joseph Shannon, always known as Joe who was a well known friend of her brothers and married him in the early nineties, going to live on his Ranch on Fish Creek. There were no children by this marriage.

Joseph Shannon was born at Weston, Ontario of parents of Irish decent. He went as a very young man to the west in 1882 and secured a homestead on the Fish Creek, his property adjoining the Sarcee Reserve. He was an enterprising rancher and enjoyed great prosperity. His property, which was 160 acres grew in size to 1100 acres when he sold it in 1911. By this time he became afflicated with rheumatism, requiring a warmer climate to live in, and they went to California and built a beautiful home in the town of Pomana.

The Shannon home on Fish Creek was called "The Diamond Ranch" and the brand used on their horses and cattle was registered double diamond. He had a very happy understanding with the Sarcee Indians, many of whom were in his employ over the years. His friendship with the officials of the Sarcee Agency was that of a good and understanding neighbor. His genial disposition, endeared him to everyone in the community and the ranchers for miles around. This was especially so of the many English Remittance men who introduced Polo into that area and from whom he learned the game and played with them, being an expert horseman.

The Shannons delightful home on Fish Creek was a shelter for many cowboys especially the young Englishmen who loved to visit this high spirited Canadian whom they called Joe and his hospitable wife who often sensed their loneliness so far from home.

Being a childless couple, they were the special Aunt and Uncle, dear to all the nieces and nephews who paid them a visit in their school holidays.

The Shannons sold their home in California and returned to Calgary in the early twenties and purchased a home in the Mount Royal district. Mr. Shannon died in Calgary in 1935.

Mrs. Shannon died in the late nineteen fifties in Calgary, being the last to die of the McInnes pioneer family.

DON AND DOROTHY McKAY — by Dorothy McKay

Don and I moved into Midnapore in June of 1955 from Turner Valley where Don had worked on the pipe line. My folks also lived at the Valley. We had 3 daughters at this time. Margaret was 10, Jean 9, Louise 6. Margaret and Jean had started their schooling in the Valley. Louise started in Midnapore they finished their education in Calgary. At least Margaret and Louise did. Dan was working at Calgary Steel Tank when we moved. He painted propane tanks, a job he did until his health was affected, at which time he quit and started working for Barry Smolkin on a pig farm in Hubalta in 1963. We had the four daughters by this time, Isabelle was born January 1957.

We moved from the cabins at Fish Creek to a house owned by John Butz Sr. and stayed there for nearly 14 years where our oldest 3 daughters finished school and got married. Margaret married Donald J. Daves from West of Priddis in October 1964. They now are at Leslieville on a farm and have 3 daughters of their own Dianna, 11, Debrah, 8 and Donna, 3.

Jean married the following year in Aug. 1965 to John McEathron from the Big Rock area. They now live at Vulcan and have 2 daughters and 2 sons, Dannie, 9 and Darcie, 8, Dean 5 and Dwayne 2. John has a truck.

Louise married the next year in Aug. 1966 to Leslie Daves a brother of Donald's, also from west of Priddis. They live at Vulcan where they have an Esso bulk station and a trucking business, they have 2 children, Truna 5, and Kenneth 3. Isabelle grew up in Midnapore and went to school there and Calgary. She married Allan Mall from Kathryn, March 1966. Don left the pig farm to work for Berry Smoling cooking feathers. We left Midnapore in Oct. 1974, bought our own home in Airdrie. We miss our friends in Midnapore but do not regret the move to Airdrie. We enjoy a visit from our 8 children and 9 grandchildren very much.

ENOCH MEYERS — by L. Beck

Enoch was born on his father's farm at Elmwood, Ontario in 1890. His family had come from Germany in 1854. He came to Alberta in 1920 and bought 320 acres (E½ 32-22-1-W5), one mile west of Midnapore which was jointly owned by Anderson and J. Hamilton. The price paid was $38.00 per acre.

Until 1925 he spent part of his time farming at Edenwald, Saskatchewan. On January 1, 1925 he married Mamie Arzetta Gier who was the daughter of his neighbour, William Gier. She was born in Grand Valley, Ontario and came west with her family in 1901. Enoch and Mamie had one daughter, Lorena, born in 1926. In 1945 they sold ' the farm to Douglas Sanderson and moved to Malton, Ontario where Mrs. Meyers died in 1967. Mr. Meyers sold and lived in Calgary, Waterloo, Ontario, and Port Credit, Ontario before buying a one hundred acre farm, in 1969, at the edge of Elmwood, Ontario, where he now lives by himself. His daughter now lives at Inglewood, Ontario.

ANNIE (DOWLING) MOORE, MONK—by Geraldine Percival, Countess of Egmont

My grandmother, Annie Moore, was born in Montreal and was the second eldest daughter of James and Margaret Moore. She married Henry Dowling, born in England in 1852. He immigrated to New York with his parents and as a young man he went to Montreal where he met my grandmother. They were married in January, 1882. Their first son was James Patrick, born February 14; 1883, John Henry was born July 9, 1885 and in 1886, John and Annie with their two sons and Annie's parents, Mr. and Mrs. James Moore, left Montreal and settled at Priddis, Alberta. James and John worked their homestead. John and Annie had seven children, five born in Priddis: Elizabeth, my mother, 1887; married Douglas Gerald Moodie (son of Inspector Moodie of R.N.W.M.P.); Margaret (Bab), 1888, married James Kavanaugh; Charlie, 1890, married Annie Thiessen; Victoria Ellen, 1891, and Tommie, 1893. They were all raised at Priddis and even the young children helped with the chores of milking and feeding cattle.

In September of 1893 (Goggie), my grandmother and her husband, John, were in Calgary to pick up their winter supplies when Grandpa collapsed on what is now eighth avenue. He was taken to Holy Cross Hospital where he was left and Grandmother returned to Priddis with their supplies. The following morning she was on her way back to Calgary, when she got to the hospital they told her that her husband had passed away the night before. She went back to Priddis and stayed there with her family of seven small children and her parents. Her father passed away in 1897 and her mother in 1900.

Goggie, a nickname I gave my grandmother, left Priddis in 1904 to live in Calgary where the children finished school. In 1912, she married Fred Monk, a butcher who had come from Atlantic City. They bought the hotel at Midnapore where they stayed for about six years. Goggie sold the hotel to a Tom Stone and bought a small house and some land across the C.P.R. tracks from the hotel. Later she sold out and moved a few miles north of Fish Creek. In.1932, my husband, (Fred Percival, Earl of Egmont), bought the land that Goggie and Aunt Vickie lived on. My uncle Charlie and Aunt Annie had land on the north of us. Goggie sold what land she had left in 1946, she and my Auntie Vickie moved into Calgary where she passed away in 1949. Aunt Vickie, who had stayed with Goggie passed away in 1971.

THE MOON FAMILY — by Roy Moon

In 1903 Tom Moon and his son, Willard, sold a farm in Wisconsin, U.S.A. and moved to Alberta where they settled on S½-28-22-1-W5, a farm in the Midnapore district, which Tom had purchased the year before. Tom brought his wife, Mary, and youngest daughter, Rose,

Mrs. Charles (Annette), Marshall and Mrs. Willard (Nora) Moon about, 1935.

three other children were married and away from home. Willard brought his wife, Nora, and three children, Blanche, Fred and Roy. Two daughters, Vera and Ethel, were born later in Canada.

When they came they brought all the farm machinery they needed along with work horses and some cattle and milk cows, also pigs. They brought asparagus roots and many other plants for the gardens. These were loaded into boxcars and shipped to Midnapore Siding which was two and a half miles from the farm. They also brought a carpenter who was a relative of Mary Moon, to build the houses. A house and other buildings was built on each quarter of land.

It was quite a shock to them, when they arrived in March, to find it still winter. It was spring when they left Wisconsin.

After some years, Rose married and moved to Coronation to live. Several years later, Tom became ill and he and Mary moved to Coronation to live with their daughter.

The buildings on the east quarter were moved to the west quarter and Willard farmed the half section.

Blanche married Reg. Sheepy. They farmed in the Midnapore district for some years and then moved to Calgary where Reg. went into the trucking business. Blanche died in 1975. They have one son, Cecil.

Fred married Marjorie Marshall and worked in the motor car business in Calgary. He worked for the Calgary Motor Products until he retired to Bragg Creek where he had built a house. He died in 1972. There were two children, Barbara (Atherton) and Willard.

Vera married Dave Jowett and lived in Calgary where Dave had an Electrical shop. Dave died in 1952. They have two daughters and Vera still lives in Calgary.

Ethel married Bill Lee and they still live near Millarville where they ran a service station for many years.

Roy still farms the same land that they settled on at the start.

JOHN AND MARGARET G. MORTON

John and Margaret Morton were the next tenants of 'Poultry Farm Javem'. John was born in Kilmarnock, Scotland and, after eleven years with the Bank of Scotland in London, emigrated to Canada. A transfer from the Canada Permanent Loan Co. in Winnipeg took him to Calgary where he married Margaret Ratcliff, a nurse from Peterborough, Ont., in the spring of 1914. They too spent a couple of years in this location before John returned to his former firm and was moved to Victoria and then back to Winnipeg.

On resigning his position about 1919 the Mortons returned to Midnapore. They purchased the old hotel site from Mrs. Monk, at the corner of 146th Street and Banister Rd. While building on this location they operated a small store and gas pump on 5th Street south of the 146th Avenue and west of the C.P.R. They moved to their comfortable home with adjoining store and also operated the Post Office and rural mail route, west to Priddis, Millarville and Kew. Following Jack's death in 1926 Margaret's brother, Fred, came west from Bowmanville, Ontario to form a partnership in the business. They operated in the same location till Fred purchased the Union Oil (later the B.A. and then Gulf) Service Station at the corner of Shaw Road and 149th Avenue South East, from 'Pop' Ward, in 1937. The store and Post office were then moved to this location where Margaret continued their operation till 1949 when she retired and returned to Ontario to be nearer her family.

See Ratcliff story.

ROBERT AND ELIZABETH HOPE (Beattie) NICHOLSON — by R. Nicholson

I came to the Midnapore district in 1936 and I married Elizabeth Hope Beattie from Scotland, in 1938. We have two daughters, Elizabeth Marion, who is a Lt. Com. in the Navy in Halifax and Rena Frances, in Calgary.

We farmed the Halifax place for eleven years. Our brand was 5R on the left shoulder. I came to Canada from Scotland in 1927.

The Nicholson Family.

MR. AND MRS. W. G. PARRISH

Mr. and Mrs. Parrish moved from Calgary in the early forties and Mr. Parrish took care of the grounds of St. Patrick's Church in Midnapore for many years.

They had three sons; Henry and Terence in Calgary and Gerald in Summerland, B.C. Two daughters; Mrs. K. Allan and Mrs. Ed. McKevitt still reside in Midnapore.

Mr. Parrish passed away in Midnapore in 1964 at the age of ninety-three and Mrs. Parrish in 1976 at the age of ninety-eight. Both are buried in St. Patrick's Cemetery, Midnapore. A daughter, Mrs. E. Hoschka, predeceased them in 1969. She is also buried in Midnapore.

As a young man Mr. Parrish was in the Grenadier Guards during the Boer War as a private detective to Lord Roberts. He received three medals and seven bars for battle engagements

FRED J. AND MURIEL V. RATCLIFF

Fred married Muriel Archer in the fall of 1938. They had two children, John and Margaret.

Fred managed the service station and rural mail route from 1937-1944 when he took over the store. He was appointed Postmaster and still had to dispatch the rural route mail, from the Midnapore Post Office, for the independent courier. The service station was rented to D. L. Lukenbill. During this time, Fred was active with the Boy Scout Group Committee, who presented him with a life membership in the Association. He donated the old service station to be moved and used as a Scout Hall.

When ill health forced Fred's retirement, in 1958, the family moved to Calgary where Fred died in 1960.

See Morton and Archer stories.

ROUSSEAU — by Theresa Michaniuk

Mr. Elphege Rousseau was born in St. Hughes, Quebec, the year 1894. At a young age he left home to homestead in the Northern part of Manitoba called Machanak. He then came to Carstairs in 1914, where he worked for Mr. and Mrs. Munro and for other farmers around that area. Father met our beloved mother, Germaine Dugal who had been raised by her Aunt and Uncle, Mr. and Mrs. Roy who had come West from Scott, Quebec, in 1914.

Mother went to school in Carstairs for a short time and met our dear father in the fall of 1917. They married the following Spring, and resided in Midnapore in Turnbull's house across the road from Mr. and Mrs. Hugh Wylie. For a small family income, Father hauled hay with a team of horses, in different parts of nothern and southern Alberta.

In 1920, the first born was a boy who was given the name Camille. They were still living in Midnapore. A few years later, due to mother's poor health, they were advised to move further West to a lower altitude. So they went to New Westminster, British Columbia. Father then took on a series of jobs, one of which was a lumberjack in a nearby camp. Three years later in 1923, I was born. They called me Theresa.

Because British Columbia no longer agreed with my father, we moved to Springbank, Alberta in the fall of 1924 where he had made an agreement of exchange for a small section of land at $12.00 an acre. Seeing as the complete section was still all bush, enough space had to be cleared to build a small house and a barn to provide for our winter needs. A small lovely Spring only one quarter of a mile from the house, provided us with fresh clean water.

As the years increased, another female had been added to the family, this was in 1931 and she was named Denise and yet another in 1938 called Annette. So each year father would clear more land, a little at a time, and before too long the house had to be added onto as the family grew steadily. In 1932, I had, what the Doctors then diagnosed as Polio. Only thirty years later, after going to the Mayo Clinic in Rochester, Minnesota, it was diagnosed as spinal meningitis.

After discovering a large two-storey building with three bedrooms in it, on seventeenth Avenue in S.E. Calgary, father bought it, but at the same time he also kept the Springbank farm which he visited occasionally. Finally in July of 1942 another addition to the family; another brother was born, he was named Elphege, after his father, of course. In 1948 father opened the O.K. Feed Lot in East Calgary which was, at that time, across from the Alberta Distillery and father worked it till 1962.

Camille, the oldest was given the Springbank farm when he married Velma Vertock in 1944. He still resides there with his wife and five children.

As for myself, I have resided at the same residence since 1956 in S.E. Calgary with my husband, Mike Michaniuk and three children who are no longer at home.

Denise, the second oldest girl also married in Calgary to Benjamin Nadon, and resides in Dawson Creek, B.C. since 1958 with five of her nine children.

Annette, the third and last girl married in Calgary to Daniel Danis and lives in the Lake Bonavista area with their five children.

Elphege, the youngest, married Kay Million. They lived in Hartnell till 1973 then moved. They bought another farm East of Westaskiwin, Alberta where they still live with their three children.

Father was involved in real estate, in and around Calgary, up until he took sick and died shortly after in 1964.

Father and mother were regular members of the Ste. Famille Church in Calgary. He was also a member of St. John Baptist organization and helped to build the new Church of Ste. Famille. He never saw its completion, but his was the first funeral service to be held there in 1964.

Mother lived in the house on seventeenth Avenue, S.E. across from the Calgary Stampede Grounds until she took sick and died of Cancer, February 25, 1969. Her funeral service was also held at Ste. Famille Catholic Church. They were both laid to rest in St. Mary's Cementry.

FRANK LORN AND ISOBEL MARY (HODGSON) SANDERSON — by Ian and Ross Sanderson

Lorn was born in Cawnpore, India in 1871, son of Colonel Henry B. Sanderson, British Army in India, and Minnie (Pigou) Sanderson. He married Isabel Mary Hodgson in 1901 in Kingsworthy, England and they sailed for Canada soon after to stay with her brother, Matthew Hodgson, at Sheep Creek. Charles had come to Canada and the Millarville district before 1900 and his glowing accounts of this country had decided then to start their married life in Canada. Lorn purchased a half section of land, north of the Halifax place, which is just north of Fish Creek, west of the present highway and south of the old polo grounds in the area now known as Southwood sub-

Lorn and Mary Sanderson 1901.

division. They build their first house here and called it Auldhame and settled down to ranching. Years later Auldhame was purchased by the Earl of Egmont, moved across the highway, added on to and became his home. The building was later destroyed by fire.

Lorn helped to establish the polo club, probably called the Fish Creek Polo Club, becoming its first secretary. He was People's Warden of Saint Paul's Anglican Church, Midnapore for many years and also school trustee for the Midnapore School.

After selling out in 1909, to Johnnie Hamilton, Lorn and Mary with their three sons, returned to England and farming in Kent. However, the west was calling them and they returned to Alberta in 1912, built the present Sanderson house on the south side of Fish Creek on a beautiful thirty acres which included part of Fish Creek, two miles west of Midnapore, Pt. 5-23-1-W5. There they raised polo ponies and other half-bred horses.

Lorn passed away in 1928 after several years of ill health but his widow, Mary, continued to live in Midnapore until moving to Calgary in 1940. She had many friends in the district, amongst the old families, and many interests in sport. She was always an ardent hockey fan and another of her main interests was the Millarville Racing and Sports Association in which she maintained her membership until she died. She was an active member of Saint Paul's Church, Midnapore, working with the Women's Auxiliary for many years. Mary passed away in 1960 and, with her passing, another link with a past era was broken, a graciousness of living, a hospitality extended in a correct and courtly manner, a certain Old World touch. These things characterized Mary Sanderson.

Lorn and Mary had three sons who all farmed in the Midnapore district. Douglas Henry was born in 1902, was educated at Bishop Pinkham Boy's School, Calgary and Western Canada Boy's School, Calgary which later became Western Canada College. He married Mabel Eleanor Scott in 1929 and they had two daughters, Gwendolyn Mary, born in 1930 and, passed away in 1950 and Rosamond Anne, born in 1936. Douglas lived with his family in the old Sanderson house. He was a director in the Millarville Racing and Sports Association until he was made Honorary President during his later years. He became Peoples' Warden of Saint Paul's Anglican Church in Midnapore from 1928 for many years, later becoming Rector's Warden until 1964. Douglas passed away in 1969 after a long illness.

Ian Lorn was born in 1907, married Elizabeth Marjorie Mary Biddell in 1933. They had two sons; Brian Lorn born in 1934 and Lenard James born in 1941 and they are currently farming at High River and the Didsbury district.

Malcolm Ross was born in 1909, married Joyce Hodgson in 1940. They had two daughers; Gillian Mary, born 1941 and Jennifer Thelma, born 1947.

THOMAS AND ELIZABETH (MacBAIN) SCOTT — by Mabel Sanderson

My father, Thomas Scott, was born and raised in Galt, Ontario, a son of Mr. and Mrs. William Scott, formerly of Dunfries, Scotland.

Upon reaching manhood, he had a great urge to come to Western Canada and travelled, via the Great Lakes, eventually arriving at Winnipeg. He was strongly advised not to go further west and so returned to Galt. After that he went to Michigan and, after working for a time, was joined by his brother, John Scott, and they set out for Pike's Peak, Colorado. I understand that John tried very hard to have my father go with him to Kansas but Dad felt his destiny lay in The North West Territories and they parted. My father reached Calgary in 1883.

He hauled freight for the C.P.R. through the Kicking Horse Pass during the time the railway was being built. When the Riel Rebellion started in 1885, he joined the Alberta Mounted Rifles and served until the rebellion ended. He was given a quarter section of land in what is now the Hillhurst District of Calgary for his service. He also received a medal which I have in my keeping. Later he sold the land and homesteaded SW¼ 32-22-1-W5 in the Midnapore area, receiving the patent in 1888. He added the NE¼ 32-22-W5, purchased from Jim Fisk.

After the Rebellion, he joined the C.P.R. as pumpman at Cochrane, travelling as far as Kananaskis.

In 1898, he married Elizabeth MacBain, she had come to the Cochrane District to stay with her sister, Mrs. John McNeil. They resided on the Spring Coulee Ranch at Mitford which he had homesteaded. They leased more land and raised Clydesdale horses. A son, Murray, was born there.

My father enjoyed living in the Cochrane area very much. He was very musical and played the violin for the local dances. When more homesteaders arrived the leased land had to be given up and my parents decided to move to the half section in the Midnapore area in 1906. They traded the ranch for another quarter, NW¼-7-22-1-W5, which later sold to Ernest Towner. I was born two years later.

My parents continued to farm, with the aid of Murray. One section was sold to Roy Jeffery in 1928. My father died in 1934 and later Mother sold all but a small acreage to Roy Jeffery. She continued living there with Murray until she died in 1950.

Murray married Roberta Bottomley in 1940 and continued to farm until he passed away in 1974.

I married Douglas Sanderson in 1929 and we farmed in the area. We had two daughters, Gwen and Rosamond. They both attended school in Midnapore and Calgary. Gwen passed away suddenly in 1950. At the time she was attending the Holy Cross School of Nursing in Calgary. Douglas passed away in 1969 and Rosamond and I continue to live in the old Sanderson home which is north of, and across the road from, my father's homestead.

LEN SHAW — by Myrtle Shaw

Len was born in Ontario and came west with his parents, two sisters and a brother, when just a child. He spent most of his life in Alberta. When a young lad he hauled water for Jack Patterson's threshing outfit at Okotoks. He was a great lover of horses and always had a saddle horse. He rode in many small stampedes. Len came to work for my dad, the late Hugh Shaw, in 1936 and we were married in 1940. His riding days

came to an end when he broke his ankle in several places while trying out bucking horses at the Midnapore Stampede Grounds. For many years we took care of Paradise Grove Park at Midnapore. Len also worked for P. Burns Ranches, the Lacombe Home and Pacific Cartage. Although we never had any children of our own, our home was a home away from home for any who chose to come by. As the years pass along I must thank them all for the joys they brought us. Many a haircut Len used to give to the young boys of Midnapore among whom I remember Larry McKevitt, the Gough boys and Kennaird Lynn. A few will remember getting their ears nicked. Len came to an untimely death in 1952 while working for a road construction crew near Balzac. He was buried in St. Paul's Cemetery at Midnapore.

SAMUEL WILLIAM AND HELEN MARIA (YORK) SHAW AND FAMILY — by J. Shaw

The Shaw family came to what at that time was known as Fish Creek in the year 1883 from Rochester in Kent, England. They landed in Montreal in early April and were met there by Oliver York, Mrs. Shaw's brother, who was then in Montreal as an Engineer working on the building of the C.P.R. The Shaw family's intended destination was the Peace River country.

They were a family of eleven plus two men who had come with the family to help them in this momentous move. One of these helpers having been Dick Lloyd who took up land at what we today call Red Deer Lake but which on the map is called Lloyd Lake. The other helper was a family relative who returned to England once the family was established at what is now known as Midnapore.

The brave man who came with all these responsibilities was Samuel William Shaw and his wife, Helen Maria, nee York. Their family consisted of Helen who later became Mrs. Malcolm Millar of Millarville. Louise who married R. C. Thomas who at the time of their marriage was a rancher on the Bow River, south of Calgary, where the Kerslakes later made their home. Another daughter, Evelyn, married Frank Gough of Okotoks who farmed in that area until his death. Elfie married Walter Phillips of Kew where they ranched. Hugh Kinnaird Hunter Shaw, the oldest

Samuel William Shaw.   Helen Maria Shaw.

Samuel William Shaw original house, 1883.

Original house with two storey addition of S. W. Shaw.

of the boys, married Augusta Kai and lived where No. 22 Highway meets No. 2 Highway better known as Macleod Trail. Kinnaird, another boy, died when he was twenty-four years old after working in the family woollen mill most of his life. Another son, John, died in England. Maltman William Stephen married Maud Miller and York Shaw married Victoria Graham. These young women had come to Calgary in 1904 from Belfast, Ireland. Irene, the only one of the family born in Canada, married Dick Goodall who took his bride to a homestead in the Coronation area. Irene was the first child baptised in St. Paul's Church, Midnapore.

When this family left England they brought just about everything with them that was movable. Their family furniture which, by the way, included a grand piano, many cases of books (technical, scientific, and all the old classics), all the machinery for the setting up of their woollen mill, a complete set of dental equipment, all the necessary equipment and materials for a chemist shop, photographic equipment, cobblers tools, and, like the auctioneers say, "Items too numerous to mention".

They came from Montreal to Winnipeg on the C.P.R. where they left their woollen mill equipment and everything they were not able to load onto two covered wagons. Only themselves, their clothes, and personal items.

While in Winnipeg they purchased two wagons, the necessary oxen, and the food they were going to need until their caravan reached the Peace River. They spent two weeks in Winnipeg and then set out on a work train to go as far as the steel was laid.

When they got to the end of the steel they slid all their belongings out of the box car, on a ramp made of poles, onto the bald headed prairie which must have been a very desolate sight. They camped there for the night to rest, sort, and load all their belongings. They had not travelled very far when they had to reload and find their belongings as they found themselves in a whirlwind which scattered everything all over the prairie. Their livestock had to be rounded up and many of their belongings reloaded.

They eventually reached the Bow River Ferry crossing in East Calgary and had to wait for several days for their turn to cross on the ferry as there was a back log of C.P.R. equipment waiting to be ferried across the river. In the meantime, Mr. Shaw walked across on the ferry and went to the R.C.M.P. post to inquire of the whereabouts of one John Glenn whom he had read about in an English newspaper. Mr. Glenn had been out to Vancouver among other places and his scalp was much sought after by the Indians because he had long blond curls. The R.C.M.P. told Mr. Shaw that Mr. Glenn was homesteading south of Calgary, on Fish Creek, so he walked out to visit him and during the visit was talked into settling across the Macleod Trail from him. So that is where the Shaw family later set up their woollen mill and farmed. Part of the original homestead is owned by J. M. Shaw; and pre-emption is now owned by another Samuel William Shaw. The property is now the location of the Shaw-Nee Slopes Golf Course.

Hugh Shaw arrived Fish Creek with his family, the late S. W. and Helen Shaw, in 1883. Hugh married Augusta Kai, daughter of David and Catherine Kai, of the Red Deer Lake district on February 16, 1906.

Mr. and Mrs. Hugh Shaw.

Augusta passed away July 6, 1931. Hugh passed away January 12, 1960. They had four daughters Helen and Exilda (twins), and Myrtle and Ruth. The twins were a rare event at that time. People came from near and far to see them, even the Sarcee Indians. Joe Shannon wanted to trade Augusta some horses for one of her girls. Helen married Cecil Lynn and they had one son. Exilda married Albert McKevitt and they have three sons and three daughters. Ruth married Walter K. Birney and they had three sons and eight daughters. Myrtle married Leonard Shaw. They had no family. Exilda said she was too busy raising "Hell!" Augusta cooked for the threshing crew and in the hay fields in the cook car for many years. She also ran the Midnapore Supply store for Mrs. Shaw. The first special event in Hugh's life was the Riel Rebellion. He took a message on horse back to warn the troops that the Indians were coming. As he was only a boy he was not suspected of anything. He mined coal at the Fish Creek coal mine for some years and then hauled the coal to Calgary and the Lacombe Home. He spent a few years in California before settling down. Seeing the prairie sod being broken and grain farming taking over, the family invested in two large steam threshing outfits. Hugh threshed at Cluny, Claresholm, High River and Midnapore for many years. He drove eight horses on a grader, building roads for the municipality, to work off taxes. In 1919 he foresaw a shortage of feed for the cattle so he and Sandy Massie went to Grourad on Lesser Slave Lake to put up hay. They baled it and shipped it by rail to Midnapore. All the work was done by horses they had shipped up there. To do this Hugh sold Augusta's driving team which did not make him very popular. Hugh and Maltman had a contract to cut and stack hay for Burn's Ranches at Bow Valley for many years. Many good times were had by Exilda and Myrtle raking the hay. They used to race to

the cook car at meal times causing quite a confusion. They also helped their father to farm, with horses, the land where Canyon Meadows Estates now are and also on the Shaw-Nee Slopes Golf Course. Hugh owned the picnic grounds on Fish Creek known as "Paradise Grove" which he ran until he died. He was one of the organizers of the Midnapore Stampede in 1933. There was a thirty mile horse race held and started at the Stampede Grounds which proved very successful. Hugh was always an active participant in the Stampede Parade. He was a very active member of the Southern Alberta Pioneers and Descendants. The family are still members of the association.

Hugh Shaw, one of Midnapore's first residents, 1934.

Maltman William Stephen Shaw with his older brother, Hugh, as boys, hauled logs, to build the woollen mill, from the old Cow Camp Site about four miles west of Priddis. Maltman spent all his youth working in the woollen mill and was the engineer in charge of the steam boilers as well as responsible for the dyeing of the wool. The farming operation increased in demand and the woollen mill was sold to Bucham & Murray's who had used a lot of material

Mr. and Mrs. Maltman Shaw.

311

Woollen Mill built 1884-5.

from the mill in their tailoring business in Calgary. During the first World War Bucham and Murray's went broke and were not able to meet their payments and the mill was closed down. The family were not able to reopen it at that time as the new owners had changed over from the manufacture of blankets to tweeds. It lay idle for some years and burnt to the ground shortly after the end of the war.

Maltman and Maud Shaw had eight children. Their first daughter, Edith, died at an early age. Frances Evelyn Maud completed her high school education at Crescent Heights High School in Calgary, trained as a nurse at the Calgary General Hospital where she worked as a supervisor for two years. Then she worked as an X-ray technician for twenty-five years. She worked at the Col. Belcher during the second World War years, at a downtown office and also spent most Saturdays and Sundays doing X-ray work for the Junior Red Cross Hospital. She is now married and lives just north of Priddis with her husband, Everett Russell Borgal, raising Charolois cattle. Samuel William Shaw also attended the Midnapore School. He studied at the Southern Alberta Institute of Technology and, on completion there, took a job with McGregor Construction building telephone lines. He left McGregor Construction and took on the servicing of the Springbank and Stockland Mutual Telephone Companies. This business was sold to Walter Mosier who looked after these two services until taken over by the Alberta Government Telephones. Bill Shaw, as he is better known, then started a road construction company known as Shaw Construction Company Limited which he operated until he started Shaw-Nee Slopes Golf Course. His hope was, and still is, to preserve the lovely land that was originally homesteaded by his grandfather. Bill says he would hate to see it cluttered with houses and I, too, hope it never will be. Bill enjoys his business and has become an avid golfer. He married Alice Anderson, a Calgary girl. They have three daughters and one son all living at Midnapore with their families, but instead of being a farm family they are a golf course family on the old family farm.

James Miller Shaw, second son of Maltman, is married and lives on part of the farm. He was a farmer all his life until his retirement in 1974.

Mary Victoria, like all the Maltman Shaw family, attended school in Midnapore and Calgary. She trained in the Calgary General Hospital graduating in. 1934. She, like many of our good Canadian nurses, went to the U.S.A. to work where salaries were better than in Canada. She met and married Bruce Hunt and has two daughters and three grandchildren.

Annie York after attending school in Midnapore, took a hairdressing course. She worked in Waterton Lakes during the summer months and in Calgary during the winter. She married Donald Lineham of Okotoks and has lived in Midnapore for the last thirty years. The Lineham's have two daughters and one son plus three grandchildren.

Caroline, on completion of her high school, worked for a few years in the Dominion Seed Branch. She then took a course as a Pathological Technician and worked in the Lab at the Calgary General Hospital. She then moved to Washington where she continued in the same work. She met and married George Klavano, in Pullman, where he was studying to be a veterinarian. They came to Calgary on completion of his studies where he was associated with Dr. William Nagge and Brian Edge in the Animal Clinic. The Klavanos later moved to Sherwood Park and Dr. Klavano is on the staff on the Provincial Department of Agriculture. They have one daughter and two sons.

Irene Daphne Julia has lived in Midnapore since her marriage to Allen Brown who is a partner in Trotter and Morton Plumbing. Irene spent several years in the Wrens' during the Second World War, and Allen as a pilot in the R.C.A.F. Allen had a very illustrious career in the Air Force having won the Distinguished Flying Cross. They have four children and one grandson.

York Shaw, like all of Samuel and Helen's family, spent his youth working in the woollen mill but moved to Calgary where he had a coal and wood business, a garage business and also the Blue Label Bottling Company, which made soft drinks. He had one son by his first marriage, Oliver York, who worked with his father in York Shaw Building Moving Business. York's three sons, by the second marriage, also joined the business of moving buildings. They have successfully moved everything from grain elevators and hotels to garages. The business is still owned and operated by the family in Calgary. York Shaw and his wife also had two daughters, one of which died in her youth. He boasted fifteen grandchildren when he died.

Mrs. Millar, nee Helen Shaw, worked in the mill and family business. She taught school in St. Paul's Anglican Church at Midnapore which constituted the first school in the area. The family had a store on Stephen Avenue which is now called Eighth Avenue and First Street West. Helen had been apprenticed to a tailor in England and not only did she do tailoring for the store but did much of the family tailoring. Helen told a delightful story about filling an Indian Chief's hat with potatoes while he was having dinner with the family at Midnapore. A few days later the Elbow River was swollen in Flood and she had to walk over the C.P.R. trestle to cross the Elbow. Her arms were full of woollen goods she was taking into the store in Calgary. She met the same Indian Chief coming towards her on the trestle and expressed her terrible fear that he might push her off into the swollen river.

Louise, who married R. C. Thomas, moved from their Bow River Ranch into Calgary where they set up a livery stable which grew into a machinery agency, then Alberta Ice Co., the Royal and Wales Hotel. They had two sons and two daughters and six grandchildren.

Evelyn, who married Frank Gough in Okotoks, had three sons and three daughters. The oldest son Vivian spent most of his life in Midnapore, as a boy, living with his grandmother, and for many years he ran the Wheat Pool elevator in Midnapore. Vivian still resides in Midnapore where he raised a large family of ten children.

The pioneer Midnapore Shaw boys, namely Hugh and Maltman, did a great deal of custom work in the early days. Maltman, who had his Steam Engineer papers, masterminded undertakings of great magnitude.

Mr. and Mrs. S. W. Shaw were married in a small village just outside the city of London called Watford in 1861. They came to Canada in 1883 from a house in Rochester, Kent which is now a historical site.

The Shaw's kept very busy as you can well imagine. In addition to the farming operation, the woollen mill, and the Calgary store, they had a store in Midnapore and Mr. Shaw was the postmaster. He also had a chemist shop, was a fine musician and spoke five languages. He was organist for St. Paul's Church from the time the church was built in 1885 until shortly before his death. The only exception during these years was a two week period during which the church had no organist. This was the result of the Bishop telling Mr. Shaw that he could not smoke his pipe in church. He replied that if he could not smoke his pipe, he would not play the organ; and he did not! However, as there was no other organist available, the Bishop was obliged to withdraw his statement. Church service was always held at three o'clock in the afternoon and the congregation all gathered at Mrs. Shaw's for afternoon tea after the service. Mr. Shaw died in 1919. Mrs. Shaw lived to be ninety-seven years of age and passed away in 1941. Following her husband's death, she continued to rule the family. She once told Prime Minister Bennett that if he would forget about bringing in all his trainloads of colonists that she could do a better job of populating the country then he. She boasted twenty-nine grandchildren and sixty-nine great-grandchildren when she died.

ALBERT GEORGE AND MABEL E. (SCOTT) SMITH — by M. Smith

Mr. Albert George Smith (Bert) was born in Fort Quippe, Saskatchewan in 1901 and moved to Calgary, as a young lad, in 1909, where he received his education.

In 1927 he married Mabel E. Scott, daughter of Thos. R. and I. M. Scott, who had come to Calgary from Ottawa in 1905.

For much of their married life they lived in Calgary and owned and operated the United Engines and Threshers Ltd. and Alberta Hart Parr Ltd.

In 1947 they bought land in Fish Creek district and

Original Store and Post Office in Midnapore.

later sold this and bought land on 24th Street and 146th Avenue west and have lived there since.

Bert and Mabel have three children in their family, Lola Jean, wife of E. A. Warren, Peachland, B.C., Glenn Cameron, married Audrey Wark of Calgary and Christopher Allan, married Eva Harasyn of Calgary.

Bert passed away in 1968 and Mabel has kept her residence in the district.

REXFORD AND CATHERINE (McLEOD) SMITH

Rexford Smith came from Swan River, Manitoba in 1927 with two brothers, George and Dick, lived in Calgary and did some building.

He moved and started a lumber and lathe mill at Priddis, Alberta. In 1935 he married Catherine McLeod of Calgary. They had two sons, Hugh and Donald and a daughter, Gwen.

In 1946, Rex started a lumber yard in Midnapore and he still has some lumber and works around Midnapore as a handy man when someone wants alterations done. His brother, George, moved to Nanaimo, B.C. and Dick still works around Kendall's sawmill at Millarville.

JIMMIE STEPHEN — by Albert McKevitt

Jimmie Stephen homesteaded NE¼ 36-22-2-W5, homesteaded No. 6565. It is not known just when he came but his name appears on the 1895 map.

One story that was told to me took place about 1908. Mr. Stephen was driving with a team and sleigh, to Calgary, where met some friends and got into the 'giggle juice', the weather was pretty cold and, on the way home, he got badly frostbitten. He got as far as the Midnapore Hotel which, at the time, was owned by Ed. Johnson. I was told that my dad got a message to come to the hotel and drive Mr. Stephen to have the frostbite damage repaired.

My older brother, Bernard, says Mr. Stephen sold out to Josh Littleton in 1910 and moved to the Innisfail district.

MR. AND MRS. HERBERT STOBO — by Doug Stobo

Mr. and Mrs. Herbert (Bert) Stobo came west from Ontario in the year 1904 where they settled on a farm ½ mile south of Midnapore. In 1910 they had the misfortune to lose their home in a fire after which the family moved to the Red Deer Lake district, four miles west of Midnapore.

The older children, who were born in Red Deer Lake, attended school there. In the one United Church at Red Deer Lake, Mrs. Stobo played the organ for the Sunday services.

The family left Red Deer Lake in 1919 after selling the farm to Dr. Hackney, and moved to Calgary where Mr. Stobo worked for the Union Dairy for many years.

The four boys joined up at the beginning of W.W. 2 and served in different divisions of the services. The eldest son, Robert Mervin, passed away in Calgary in 1962. He had two sons, Jack of Calgary and Bob, who lives at Hythe, Alberta. John Ray, (Jack) and his wife, Eileen, have lived for many years in Ontario and they have one son and three daughters who also live in Ontario. The rest of the family now live in B.C.: Douglas Herbert and wife, Edna, in Victoria, have one daughter, Marjorie, (Mrs. John DeWitt) of Courtenay, B.C. Lester and wife, Margaret, in Nanaimo, have six children; five of whom are living in and around Calgary and one son, Bobby, in Nanaimo. Mrs. E. (Bus) Stoddart, (Marion), in Victoria has one daughter, Mrs. I. Aecheli, in Vernon. Mrs. C. Hawkins (Mildred), a widow living in Vancouver, has one son, Pat, also in Vancouver. Mrs. Frank Tucker (Betty), Nimkish, V.I., has two sons: Ronald and Bradley. Mrs. Dawn Dove (Gwen), Comox, has a family of four; Doug and Coleen, Calgary and Mrs. D. Chaisson (Debbie) and John at Comox.

Mrs. Stobo passed away in Calgary in 1940 and Mr. Stobo continued to live in Calgary until he passed away in 1949.

I always remember the time Mervin, Marion and I were going to Red Deer Lake school in horse and buggy and the mare we were driving ran away and we couldn't stop her. I think it was Albert and Charlie McKevitt saw we were having trouble and came racing on their saddle horses, one on each side, and caught her and got us out of trouble. "Thanks Albert!"

WALTER SWAN FAMILY

Walter Swan family moved to Midnapore in 1946 when Marilyn was two years old, from Priddis where he had been engaged in Coal Mining with his father, Hanny Swan.

Moving into the Post Office and store building turned into apartment on corner of Bannister Rd. and 146 Ave. S.E. The other apt. was occupied by Mr. Marton. Later they bought the property for a home. The home place was sold to Dr. Carter, a Veterinarian in 1972.

Barry and Brent were born and also raised there. Walter was employed with Shaw Construction Co. as well as various other construction Companies around the district. For a while he was water well drilling around Midnapore and vicinity.

After Marilyn finished High School and University of Calgary she taught in the Hebrew School. She married Jerry Crawford, son of Mr. and Mrs. Jessee Crawford of Calgary, later moving to Ontario.

Barry, after graduation took his training for a Chartered Accountant and is presently employed with an Oil Co. He is married to Maura Kadustki, daughter of Mr. and Mrs. Peter Kadustki of Scarboro, Ontario and they have a year old daughter, Jennifer.

Brent, after a European tour is back in University of Calgary. He lives with his mother in S.E. Calgary who is employed by the Red Cross of Canada. In 1977 after a serious industrial accident, Walter retired and lives in S.W. Calgary.

T. M. SWENSEN

Thomas Marshall Swensen came up from Brooklyn, New York through Winnipeg, Manitoba with his parents, Juell and Petra, October 1910.

For ten dollars they had bought a quarter section of land, three miles north of the Gregory ferry on the Red Deer River. All requirements were completed. So that three years later it was proved up and the title received.

In 1915 we put up the first building in Patrica,

Alberta. This was a board and rooming house. In 1916 and on we bought and built in Duchess, Alberta.

Juell Swensen died 1st January 1921. Petra married the late Jack Anderson in 1924. There were four children from the two unions: Thomas Marshall, Stanley, and Helen Swensen, and Jack Anderson Jr. In the second world war Thomas served in the medical corp, Stanley in the R.A.F., and Jack in the navy.

After the war I was shunted into the Holy Cross Hospital as an orderly. In 1955 I went to work in the Colonel Belcher Hospital. John Butz had left there by then. I retired from there in 1973.

In 1955 I bought a roughed-in house without basement from Johnny Glembeck. The address became 1109 changing to 15211 Bannister Road, Midnapore. This road had been the old No. 2 highway.

One night arriving home from work at midnight, I turned the T.V. on and started to relax. A murder mystery was on. The murderer was chasing a woman witness. Jumping into the laundry chute she grabbed its top moulding to slow her descent. At this point the pursuer was making a great attempt to seize her by her wrists. Then the electric power failed, the lights went out and the T.V. picture disappeared. Needless to say this frightened me out of my wits. The cause of this was that the driver of a north bound tractor trailer on highway No. 2 fell asleep at the wheel. Out of control, it ran off the road, up over the 154th Avenue intersection, knocking over power poles, breaking the power lines then rolling over on its back. Over an hour later the dead driver was released from the cab.

My mother (the late Mrs. Petra Anderson) lived with me for a while in the early sixties.

On the 28th of April 1965, Fedora (Doll), a nursing aide working at the Col. Belcher Hospital, and I were married. From then on work began in earnest of improving the house from a out-of-door facilities type of bachelor quarters to a modern bungalow.

During July, 1965 upon returning from holidays we encountered blocked roads. We were compelled to go around so as to come in from the back way. There had been a flash flood. The run-off had come down so fast from the hills to the west that it had plugged the drain ditch along the track. The water raised up and ran over the C.P.R. railroad washing out over two miles of track. The R.C.M.P. evacuated tenants from the Wheel Inn cabins at Midnapore by boat. It flooded the Calgary Stampede midway. Four feet of filthy water was deposited in our basement. A city crew used a two inch power pump to remove the water but were only able to lower it to a depth of eighteen inches.

My wife's father (H. E. Dunning) died at White Rock, B.C. in 1971. At that time Mrs. H. E. Dunning came to live with us. She died 1972.

In 1974 a year after retiring we moved away from Midnapore and the advancing city, to Scandia, Alberta. Scandia is another friendly community similar to Midnapore which we were loathe to leave.

THE THOMPSONS — by Kenneth Floyd Thompson

My grandfather, William James Thompson, born in Ontario in 1899, and my grandmother, Delia Calhoun, born on Grindstone Island, New York in 1890, arrived in Calgary soon after their marriage in Clayton, New

Delia and William James Thompson with son, William Henry.

York, October 29, 1909. They made their home here for the next three years during which time my father, William Henry, was born June 25, 1910. My grandparents moved to Port Alberni, B.C. for a short time, returning in 1915 to work on the Highland Ranch, Nanton. In 1919 they moved to the Gregory place, NE¼ 28-22-2-W5. From 1921 to 1923 they lived on a quarter section across Highway 22 from the Eckersley place and, from there they moved to the Hamilton place, SE¼ 9-22-2-W5, which they rented for the next ten years, before retiring to Ogden. While on the Hamilton place, my uncle, Kenneth George, was born, June 3, 1924. Grandfather Thompson passed away in 1940 at the age of 85 and Grandmother Thompson lived in the Ogden area until her death, in 1965, at the age of 75.

My father, Bill, attended the Red Deer Lake school. On October 29, 1934 he married my mother, Winnifred Francis, who was attending Red Deer Lake school while living with her sister, Mrs. Ralph Goodwin. My father worked for a short time for McBees and

VanWyk's sawmills. In 1936 he went into general trucking and he and my mother moved to Midnapore area. Around 1940 Dad went to work for Shaw Construction, Midnapore. Then, in 1961, Dad went to Burnco, as an independant trucker. He stayed with Burnco until his death in 1976 at the age of 65. In 1973 he left the Midnapore area and moved to the Millican area of Calgary. My mother is now residing in the Acadia area of Calgary.

Mother and Father had seven children: William Austin born 1935. Austin attended the Midnapore school and later worked for Shaw Construction during the time he lived in the Midnapore area. After his marriage, in 1959, to Bette (Kopas, Marshall), who had three children; Linda, Terry and Richard, from a previous marriage, the family moved to the Fairview district of Calgary. Austin and Bette have one daughter, Wanda Ann 1964. Kenneth Floyd born in 1937, attended school in Midnapore and Calgary. In 1952 I went to work for Finley's race horse farm which was located in, what is now, the Braeside district of Calgary. In 1953 I moved to the Jack Beatty farm, south of the Red Deer Lake store, then, in 1955, I joined the R.C.A.F. After my discharge, I worked, for a short time, for Shaw Construction, Midnapore. In July 1960 I married Norma Alexander of Calgary and moved into the city. We have three children; Bradley Douglas, 1967, Dianne Michelle, 1968 and Alexandria Margaret, 1970. Florence Eileen, born in 1938, attended school in Midnapore and Calgary and is a 1959 graduate of the Medicine Hat Hospital School of Nursing. After her marriage, November 1959, to William Scott Massie, of Red Deer Lake district, they moved to High River. In 1964 they moved to Red Deer Lake area where they did custom farming until 1975 when they moved to their own farm in the Caroline district. Eileen and Scott have one daughter, Pamela Rae, 1961 and a son, Reginald Scott, 1964.

Myrna Viola, born 1940, attended school in Midnapore and worked for Alberta Government Telephones in Calgary until her marriage to William Henry (Red) Turner in October, 1958. They lived in the Midnapore district until moving to Calgary in 1961. Myrna and Red have two daughters; Deborah Marie, 1959 and Lisa Marie, 1968 and one son, William Henry, 1960.

Bruce Reginald (Reg), born 1942, attended Midnapore school. In the late 1950's he went to work for Shaw and McRae Paving where he worked until his death in December, 1963.

Ralph Charles, born 1943, attended Midnapore school and worked for Renton Construction until shortly before his marriage to Diane Tilten in May, 1965.

After their marriage Ralph worked for the Midnapore Feed Mill and farmed. During this time they lived in the Midnapore district. In 1975 they moved to the Sundre area where they have their own farm. They have five children; Beverly Evonne, 1965, William Trevor, 1967, Teresa Lynne, 1969, Tracey Michelle, 1971 and Brenda Dawn, 1977.

Sylvia Barbara, born 1947, attended Midnapore school. After leaving school she resided in Calgary and Edmonton. In December, 1974 she married Steve Faulkner of Calgary. They reside in Calgary and have two sons; David Daniel Thomas, 1976 and Russel William Thomas 1977.

JAMES STEWART AND VIRA JOSEPHINE (MAWHINNEY) THOMSON — by S. D. Thomson

James Stewart Thomson was born at Kilfinnan, Argylshire, Scotland March 31, 1884. Immigrated to Canada in 1906 and settled in the Nemiscam, Alberta area for five years and then moved to Foremost where he farmed for fourteen years.

Vira Josephine, daughter of David Mawhinney was one of a family of two sons and four daughters. She graduated from the Toronto Conservatory of Music and was engaged in teaching piano and also played all the musical scores for the silent movies in the Grand Theatre on 1st Street West in Calgary.

James and Vira were married in 1918 and had one son, Stewart Duncan, born August 3, 1923.

The family moved to Golden, B.C. in 1926 with the intention of establishing a fox ranch there but moved to Midnapore, Alberta in 1927 and settled there on fourteen acres approximately ¾ miles west of Midnapore. The fox ranch business was carried on there for twenty-three years. They retired in 1950 and Father carried on with his hobby of raising thoroughbred race horses.

I, Stewart, attended Midnapore public school from 1929 till 1941 and finished grade twelve at Western Canada high school in Calgary. Served with No. 7 Bombing Reconnaissance Squadron, Pacific Command with the R.C.A.F. as wireless Air Gunner from 1942 to the end of the war. Married Gladys Smith of Beausejour, Manitoba in 1945. We have five chidren; Terrence James, Cathleen Annette, Kenneth David, Linda Margaret, Kimberly Ileen. Following discharge I engaged in fox and mink ranching on forty acres in the Glenmore district where Woolco shopping Centre stands. Moved to Cloverdale, B.C. in 1952 and continued mink ranching till 1973.

Father died October 14, 1954 and Mother, April 30, 1951 at the age of 59.

Thomson fox ranch in Midnapore area, taken approximately 1930.

VADER, CHARLES — by Jean Ockley

Charlie Vader and his wife, Libby, I remember as a small child quite distinctly, but I do not recall hearing where they had originated. Trivialities remain when they were impressed on a young mind and I can remember Mrs. Vader coming to call on my mother, and when tea was suggested she took a small packet of green tea out of her bag and asked my mother to use it.

They had no children of their own, but for some years a niece, Mary Frances (Frankie) Pomeroy, later Mrs. Charles F. Harris, lived with them. She died in October, 1977.

Mrs. Vader died when I was quite a small child. Here again, I remember my grandmother doing the neighbourly thing by going over to help "lay out" this friend, which was, I suppose, commonly done in those early days.

Mr. Vader later married Miss Miriam Murray (?) who had come from Scotland with a niece who later became Mrs. George Anderson. I can remember Mr. and Mrs. Vader as dependable supporters of Pine Creek Church.

There had been a brother of Charlie Vader, but he died before my time and I have only hazy memories of references to him.

EVERT VAN GINKLE — by Albert McKevitt

I have known Van Ginkle since the 1920's. He worked around the Red Deer Lake district for quite a few years. Last time I remember him in the district he was working for Peter Massie.

In the 1930's, when prices were so low, he stayed at Hugh Shaw's and was buying and butchering pigs and cattle and selling them to butcher shops.

He joined the Army and, during time overseas, he married a Scotch girl and returned to live in the Manchester district in Calgary. Some people would remember "Van" as he worked at the Co-op on the Macleod Trail, in charge of the plants. He has since sold his place in Manchester and gone, with his wife, to retire in Ontario.

MR. AND MRS. NORMAN WILLANS — by May Bowman

Norman Willans, born 1870 at Rochdale, Lancashire, England, came to Canada with his elder brother, Bernard, in 1886. Both attended Guelph Agricultural College taking a two year course in agriculture.

In 1890 Norman came west and found work in the Millarville district where he later met and married, in 1898, Alice Maud Deane-Freeman. She had come from Ireland as a child in 1887 with her family, to the homestead "Monea" on Sheep Creek. The marriage was one of the earliest performed at Christ Church, Millarville, shortly after that lovely little log church was built. The bride and groom took up residence a few miles west on Norman's homestead, known as Anchordown. Here they ranched till 1901 when the family moved to Calgary and Norman started buying cattle for P. Burns and Co. Ltd. which he continued to do for the next twenty-three years. A man of great integrity — "his word was as good as his bond".

In 1910 the Willans family took up residence in the Midnapore district when Norman was appointed manager of the well known Bow Valley ranch, ten thousand acres owned by P. Burns, and also continued as cattle buyer for the Company. Here the family remained until 1918 when they purchased a half section NE¼ 6 and NW¼ 5-22-3-W5, several miles west of Midnapore, from Addison Hone. This ranch was known as "BeeBow" where Norman set up a farming operation and continued to buy cattle for Burns for four more years until forced to give up on account of failing vision. The east quarter was sold in 1926 and the family moved to the North Hill in Calgary. When Norman's eyesight improved following surgery, he set about building a log home on the west quarter and the family moved back to their country property in 1932, residing at "Cosy Cabin" until 1949 when they retired to High River. Both passed away in 1950.

Mr. and Mrs. Norman Willans, 1940.

OF THE FAMILY

Trevor was born in 1900, died 1939 as a result of an untimely and tragic accident at the Calgary Horse Show.

Dorothy married to Arthur Smith, resides in High River, Alberta. Elizabeth, widow of Bruce Whiteford, makes her home in Red Deer, Alberta. Two Deane-Freeman nieces were brought up in the Willans' home; Barbara Read of Vancouver, B.C. and May Bowman of High River.

The Willans will be long remembered for their open door and wonderful hospitality. Their 50th wedding anniversary on June 28, 1948 was a joyous occasion when so many friends and relatives gathered in the cosy log home to bring their greetings and good wishes to one of the finest Pioneer couples.

WILLIAM AND ANNIE (BAMFORD) WORDEN — by R. Worden

Mr. William Worden was born in the village of Walton-LeDale, near Preston, Lancashire, England, April 27, 1884. There he spent his early years in the Market Business. It was here that he met his future wife, Anne Bamford, whose family was also in the business. In 1909 Mr. Worden moved to Belleville, Ont., where he worked for a farmer, receiving fifteen dollars a month, for work done from four in the morning to eight at night, from a man who expected too much work from his men. He left to work at the Rolling Mills in Belleville and, after a few months of this, decided to come out West with the Bamford boys. The year was 1910.

Upon his arrival in Calgary he went to work for Archdeacon Dewdney at Glenmore, where the Rocky View Hospital now stands. While residing there, he received a job with G. E. Wallace making roads for the City of Calgary. At that time there was only two houses in Elbow Park.

He stayed with the City for a year whereupon he went to work for the Herald Wester Printing Company, in the lithograph department. Here he helped to make the book for the first Calgary Stampede. The cover of this book was a Mounted Policeman and on the back were "The Big Four" men, Burns, Cross, Maclean, and Lane. In memory of these four men the Big Four Building at the Stampede Grounds was built.

During this time he married Annie Bamford who had come from England with her family. They wed on June 4, 1911, in St. Paul's Church in Midnapore. A few years later they left the city and worked for Mr. Ova Wolley-Dod, the place presently owned by the Maclins at Millarville. After a year they moved to the Littleton place where they started in the dairy business, staying there for a number of years. They then rented the

R. to L. Mrs. Worden, Mr. Worden, Barney McKevitt, Bill Worden, friends from Ontario. Harold and Bob Worden (front) at Bow Valley Ranch Bridge about 1925.

Halifax place on Anderson Road, which is now Canyon Meadows, and remained there for nine years.

Then the depression came! Wheat went from $2.50 a bushel to 80¢. Wanting a farm of their own before things got worse, the Wordens bought the Brogden place which is now the Farkas farm. During that time they shipped many a head of Holstein cattle to Los Angeles and China. They stayed on this farm until 1939 and then bought the present place, Pt. SW 27-22-1-W5. During these early years of William and Annie's married life, they had three sons, Bill, Harold and Bob.

Bill married Minnie Butlin from the Balzac area. After working on the farm for a few years they moved to Calgary. Following his retirement from the Fire Department Bill and his wife moved to Sicamous, B.C. They have three sons.

Harold, the farmer of the family, worked for Jim Shaw for a few years but when the Second World War broke out he joined the Army and spent several years down east. After leaving the Army Harold came back to the farm and carried on the family tradition of gardening.

Bob drove the mail route from Midnapore to Millarville for two years before joining the firm of Trotter and Morton Mechanical Contractors where he worked for thirty-five years, retiring, for health reasons, as Vice President of the firm. In 1944, at Saint Paul's Church in Midnapore, Bob married Gwen Stanton of the Westoe District. They have three daughters and a son. Except for the first year of their marriage, Bob and Gwen have lived at Midnapore, just north of the Market Garden.

Mrs. William Worden passed away in June 1950 and Mr. Worden has resided at the Lacombe Home in Midnapore since 1973. Despite his 92 years, Mr. Worden took a great interest in life, listening to news broadcasts, all sports events and was especially interested in the problems of the younger generation. Until his passing in January of 1977, he was able to get out once a week to visit his family and friends in Midnapore.

THIRTY MILE HORSE RACE MARATHON — by Alma E. Hogge

On May 24, 1946 at Paradise Grove, Midnapore, Alberta a thirty mile cross country race was held with 46 horses starting out. All horses were examined by veterinarians and were pronounced sound just before the race. Five of these horses died or had to be destroyed after the race.

The race was sponsored by the Western Light Horse Association, and was the first and last of its kind to be held in Canada. This was due to strong feelings about the death of the horses. Some felt the race was alright but there was human error regarding the care of the horses. Also too fast a pace was set at the start of the race. At the 17 mile post a horse called Cavalier, owned by Clem Gardiner, was leading. At the last mile a horse called Skipper, owned by Floyd Haynes of High River, came on fast. Skipper won the race, time one hour, forty-one minutes, eighteen and two-fifth seconds, with Cavalier one second behind. Seven horses in this race broke the world record of one hour and forty-nine minutes set in the State of Texas.

From the hills of Midnapore 30,000 people watched the race, only 10,000 of them having paid to get in, as the entrance to Paradise Grove couldn't handle the crowd. Cars were lined up on the road as far as Calgary. Thousands had to be turned away.

A Gymkhana was held on the same day but the 30 mile stock saddle race was the first event, post time 1:30 P.M. with the 46 horses and riders competing for $1,050.00 in prizes, money and trophies.

First Prize — $500.00 and trophy.

2nd Prize — $250.00.

3rd Prize — $100.00.

4th Prize — $50.00.

5th, 6th, 7th, 8th, 9th, and 10th prizes of $25.00 each. A handsome wrist watch was donated by Harry Jacques, jeweller, to the rider of the horse finishing in the best condition among the first ten. Riley & McCormick donated a silver mounted engraved belt to the winner of the 30 mile race.

THE MIDNAPORE STAMPEDE — by Kennaird Lynn

The Midnapore Old Timer's Stampede, as it was called, was held in a natural grandstand in the Fish Creek valley, approximately three-quarters of a mile west of the Fish Creek bridge, on the No. 2 highway south of Calgary, on land owned by Hugh K. Shaw. As near as I can figure out from the ledger that I have with the minutes of the committee meetings, the first Stampede was held July 5, 1933. The following are some of the motions made that year.

Moved that the stampede be held on July 5; carried.

Moved that Walter Birney be chairman of the stampede board; carried.

Moved that all the arrangements for the dance to follow the stampede be left to Walter Birney; carried.

Moved that Bob Carry and Gerald Webster be the committee to look after the stampede events; carried.

Moved that Harold Banister be appointed chairman of horse and foot race committee; carried.

Moved that R. A. Johnston be appointed official announcer; carried.

Moved that George Lee be clerk of the sports committee with power to appoint assistants; carried.

Moved that Ed. Johnson and Hugh Shaw be appointed as the committee to arrange for advertisement posters, tickets and arrange for gate admission and, that everyone pay admission, including contestants, who will be refunded their money when they pay their entrance fees; carried.

Moved that procuring of the bucking horses be left to Slim Lynn and Bob Carry; carried.

Moved that Walter Birney be appointed to look after procuring the calves for roping and the steers for riding; carried.

Meeting held May 11, 1933;

Moved that the open horse race be omitted and replaced by a district horse race, open to district horses that have not ever raced on the circuit. Purse to be $30.00; carried.

Moved that Walter Birney's tender of providing 25 cows and 25 calves, 15 head of dry stock for $25.00 be accepted and that damage to any animal be paid for at market price; carried.

For the 1934 Stampede the first meeting was held on May 27, 1934. At that meeting it was moved that George Beatty, H. H. Harper, Bob Hamilton, H. C. Hervey, H. S. Parker, Albert McKevitt and Fred Marshall be added to the committee; carried. They elected new officers at the same meeting as follows: Hugh Shaw, president; Walter Birney, Vice president; George Lee, secretary; Hugh Shaw, treasurer; Bob Carry, manager and H. C. Hervey, assistant secretary.

Walter Birney supplied the cattle for the stampede to be held June 20, 1934 and the horses were supplied by the Sarcee Indians. The Shaw girls were given the concession booth for the stampede and dance so long as they provide a cash register. They didn't think the judges and pick-up men were worth much in those days as they got $3.00 and $5.00 respectively and ground help got $2.00. This stampede lost money as the ledger has a notation as follows: Unpaid accounts of the 1933 Stampede are to be paid as soon as the stampede board has the money. Monies owing: Walter Birney — $11.75; Slim Lynn — $10.00; Hugh Shaw — $3.00.

At the first committee meeting held right after the June 20, 1934 stampede, the committee decided to hold another stampede on August 9, 1934.

In an effort to make more money, they raffled off a sorrel horse, an association saddle and bridle, built by

ADMISSION TICKET - 50¢

MIDNAPORE STAMPEDE

Wednesday, Afternoon, Aug. 29, 1934.

A brand new Association Saddle and Bridle (on exhibition at Riley & McCormick's, 136 7th Ave. E.), and horse (a complete outfit) will be presented to the person holding lucky ticket number.

Tickets must be purchased not later than August 27th.

Presentation will be made on the grounds.

N°. 684

Prize and the winning ticket at the 1934 Midnapore Stampede.

Riley and McCormick. This was won by Grace (Barklay) Latter. She still has the saddle, bridle and winning ticket. She told me she sold the saddle but, in later years, bought it back again and it is still being used by her family.

Prize monies and entry fees were far less than they are today. The following is a breakdown of entry fees and prizes for events in the second stampede held August 19, 1934. Calf roping; fee, $2.00, prize, $10.00: Saddle bronc; $2.00 and $10.00: Bareback bronc; $1.00 and $10.00: Stake race; $2.00 and $5.00: Steer riding; $1.00 and $10.00: Wild cow milking; $1.00 and $5.00: Saddle horse race; $2.00 and $15.00. Chuck wagon race; $2.00 and $15.00: Kid pony race; free and $5.00: Best bucking horse got $6.00 for saddle bronc and $4.00 for bareback.

All prize monies were split on a 50%, 30%, 20% basis with entry fees added to the prize monies in the calf roping, saddle bronc, bareback bronc, steer riding and chuck wagon races. The stake races and saddle horse race were run in the same manner. Charlie Birney supplied the cows and calves with four men for $40.00. The bucking horses were supplied by the Sarcee Indians for $60.00.

I have been told by Albert McKevitt that the horses were so wild that some of them didn't know what a fence or a corral was. They would run right through them. Two saddled horses got out and the committee got permission to shoot them in order to recover the saddles but this was not necessary. One of the saddles was found later by one of George Lee's boys, on their property. Most of the corrals and infield fences were built out of poplar rails. The chutes and chute gates were built out of plank supplied by the VanWyck brothers of Priddis. My dad, Slim Lynn, built the calf chutes and decorating chutes out of discarded fish boxes he got from Pat Burn's packing plant.

I am unable to tell you who all the various contestants were or who won the different events but I would say that such early riders as Pete Knight, Sykes Robinson, the Watrin brothers, Frank Sharp, Jack Hill, Clem Gardner, Jappy Rogers and Dave Crowchild were a few who were in there trying their luck. Eddie Bowlen, Don Thompson, Joe Fisher, Norman Edge and Bill Mounkes are a few that I found out were there.

Eddie Bowlen can't remember for sure which stampede it was but he was in the wild cow milking contest. He tells me they gave the cows a good start from the far end of the arena. When the ropers went after them the cattle were really moving. By the time they caught up with them they had run into the fence at the south end of the arena, breaking it down, all but the top rail. Eddie managed to catch a cow before she got out but no other ropers were as successful.

While Eddie was busy milking his cow the rest of the ropers were looking for a way out of the arena without having much luck. As there was a lot of brush surrounding the south end they never would have had much luck out there either. When Eddie turned his cow loose, most of the other ropers went after it. Ed can't remember who else caught her but she was roped two more times and first, second and third money was won on the same cow. This was against the rules but, with no other cattle in the arena, the judges had to let it go.

Don Thompson, from Black Diamond, was quite lucky at that stampede as he won the calf roping and the bareback bronc events. The judges were Percy Bennett and Charlie Mickle. He won the bareback on a fast moving, pinto horse and in the calf roping was mounted on a standard-bred-thoroughbred cross that he broke during the early summer. He said he considered himself quite lucky as this was the first time he had ever roped with his lariat tied hard and fast to the saddle horn and they were big calves, weighing 300-350 lbs. His winnings for the day were; $15.00 for the bareback and $20.00 for the calf roping.

Bill Mounkes won the roping in 1933 on a horse that Jappy brought to Midnapore for him to use. Norman Edge won the bronc riding that year. He can't remember what the prize money was but he does remember he won a pair of chaps, donated by the Earl of Egmont. He rode one of the horses that got out of the arena and it was his saddle that was found on Lee's property. The only damage was a broken cantle. Norman also told me that two Americans, Bob Crosby and Ike Rude were in Calgary awaiting the Calgary Stampede and the committee asked them to act as judges which job they graciously accepted.

Joe Fisher tells me that in the 1933 stampede they never had any pick-up men; just a rope stretched across the arena, you could grab and get off the stock or just jump off. He rode in the 1933 stampede after Norman Edge had been turned out. He thought it was quite comical when he saw Norman's horse leaving the arena with the saddle on. The same thing happened to him. Joe never did get his saddle back but he heard, some years later, that a skeleton of a horse and a saddle were found in the Bragg Creek area, but never did go to see if he could identify it as his.

The stampede was never held after August, 1934 but, in later years, the track was used, by the Calgary Motorcycle club and races were held on the 24th of May for several years. In 1946, the Western Riders held a 30 mile horse race and gymkhana on the grounds. Houses now encircle the top perimeter of the grounds and the rodeo arena and race track are all covered in small timber and brush. Although it is possible the stampede had to abandon for financial reasons, everyone I ever talked to said they always put on a good show. The committee members and contestants, named and un-named, should be thought of as "Pioneers of the West."

William Hamilton on Fish Creek trail. Joe Fachini's garden on left about, 1917.

Bill Hamilton's outfit cutting brush with horses in early 1920.

Clint Patton and tractor with brush cutter, 1940.

Cutting firewood: left to right William Thiessen, Ted Allwarden, Walter Thiessen, Roy Thiessen.

Tom Hooley and John Hartwick around the turn of the century.

Mrs. DeMings and Mom Brinton, 1917.

Victor, Clara, Ed, Dan Poffenroth, sawing wood 1927.

BALD EAGLE
DARK BROWN,
white head
-tail.

GOSHAWK RARE
GREY BLUE UNDER PARTS
BROAD WHITE EYE STRIPE

COOPER'S HAWK
BIRD OF THE WOODS
GREY BLUE UNDER PARTS,
BROAD WHITE EYE STRIPE

SPARROW HAWK
SMALLEST FALCON
REDDISH BROWN BACK, TAIL
AND CROWN

LARGE SOARING HAWK
RED TAILED
LIGHT UNDER PARTS

HORNED OWL

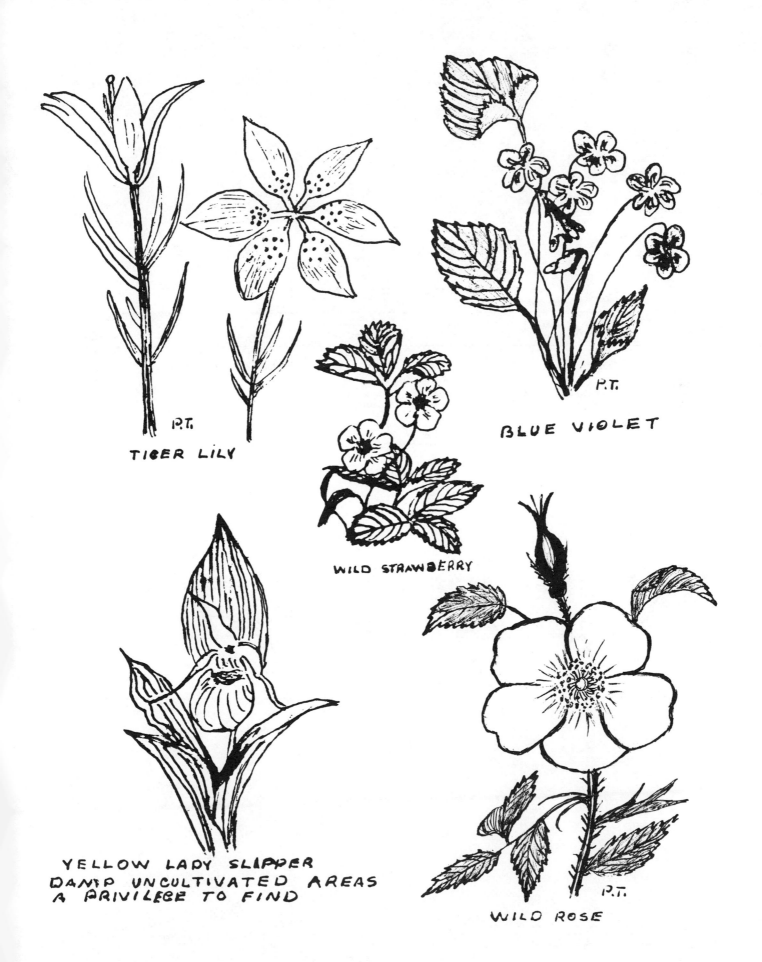

TIGER LILY

P.T.

BLUE VIOLET

P.T.

WILD STRAWBERRY

YELLOW LADY SLIPPER
DAMP UNCULTIVATED AREAS
A PRIVILEGE TO FIND

WILD ROSE

P.T.

323

PANIMA S.D. NO. 581

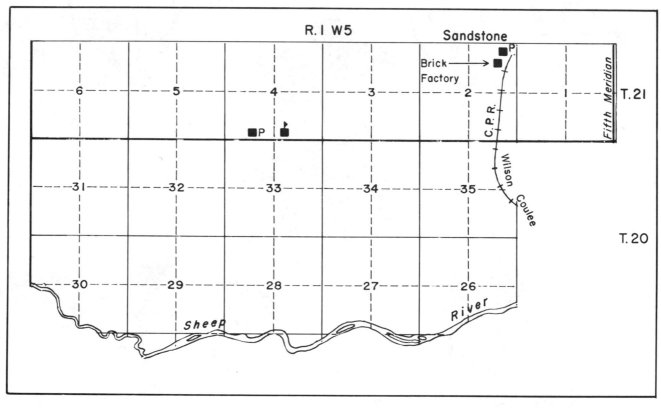

Panima School District

PANIMA SCHOOL NO. 581

We have no record of Panima School as to just when it was started and how the business was carried on. When such names as Donald Gray show up on the records of Stormount School when it was being organized it shows that Panima residents were interested in getting that school going so Panima must have come somewhat later. There was one point in the history of the two schools when the Stormount pupils had to attend Panima because they had no teacher.

Anyone that lived in the district will remember the dances held in the Panima school house and when the old school house became too run down for further use, how a new one was built and how the dances carried on and what great family fun they were. There will be those who still recall 'Blind Mac' at the piano and Connie Ford and his parents and so many others that supplied the music and often played until dawn.

Pupils will remember the learning process being supervised by one or more of these teachers. They are not in order of time but we hope that none are omitted. Hazel Tillotson, Miss Constantine, Nellie Duncan, Ethel Hemus, Miss Quinton, Margaret Lynch, Margaret Windle, Clayton Hicks, Margaret Scott, Allan Christie, Mr. Austin, (Pincher Creek), Miss DeLong, Robert Standish, Catherine Morrow, Nesta Woodhouse, Douglas Pakenham as well as substitute teachers; Olive Hilton, Serena Otterbein, Jean McIntyre, (Tucker). Throughout the years these dedicated people guided young pupils through their courses of learning and, looking back, I'm sure they were all appreciated.

Children from Sandstone also attended school at Panima and some of the pupils from that location were; Hirst; Clifford, Eileen, Gilbert and Eva. Moerton; Lily. Sleno; Eugene, Noreen, Wilfred, Eva. Linton; Walter, George, Roland, Harry. Hare; Dorothy, Frank, Keith, Marshall. Varty; Viola. Pegler; Winnie, Ruby, Frances. Bereski; Nick. Kimmel; Walter, Harold.

Pupils from the Panima district proper included: Eugene Goettler; George, Eileen, Ginger, Frank. Ed. Goettler; Clare, Nina, Kay, Bernice. G. Lumsden; Margaret. Ivan Cressman; Mervin, Earl, Gertrude. Betts: May. Harry Petersen; Margaret, Jim, Ralph, Donald. William Haynes; Roy, Laura, Bill, Albert (?). Zean Howery; Ed, Dale. Lyle Cressman; Iola, Neil, Lyle, Nina. Jake Whymer; Eugene. Isaac Kaplan; Louie, Ben, Shepherd, Jacob, Sydney, Mary, Moses. Kiam Kaplan; Dave, Sam, Annie, Jake, Shepherd, Rachael. Heitman; Eleanor, Alfred, Alice. Boggs: Lucille, Stan, Oliver, Merlin, Richard. Olson; Donald,

Panima School: 1st row. l. to r. Wilfred Sleno, Mervin Cressman, Eva Sleno, Nina Goettler, George Goettler, Frank Hare. Back: Winnie Pegler, Annie Kaplan, Sam Kaplan, Kay Goettler, Margaret Peterson, Earl Cressman, Dorothy Hare, Harold Kimmel, Jim Peterson, Gertrude Cressman, Walter Kimmel.

Merton. Rimmer; Celia, Theresa. Votaw; Robert, Alfred. Vanderploeg; Leonard, Annie. McMillan; Tommy. Bailly; ?. Littlejohn family. Holms; Christine, Grace. Cole; Freddie, Harold. Swarbrick; Norma, Glen. Thomas; Gwynydd, Dorothy. Graham; Katie. Johnson; Hazel. Rogers; Jappy, Paddy, Marjorie. Moore; Edna, Bertha. Moore; Frank, Earl. Blain; Mark. Deane family. Gray; Annie. Duncan; Nellie, Luella. McNab; John, Danny. McKinnin; Mildred, Jean. Hemus; Gladys, Ethel, Humphrey. In lieu of having pictures we have included these names. Perhaps some will recall school day memories.

Sources for this material; Ruby Cole, Mrs. Pegler and Douglas Pakenham.

MEMORIES OF PANIMA — by Ethel (Hemus) Rhine

My father, Harry Hemus, lived at Panima, on the farm just west of Macdonald's. My sister, Gladys, and myself attended school there and Humphrey began school there. The teacher was Miss DeLong, an excellent teacher. My youngest sister was born there in 1909 and died in 1941.

When we attended Panima school other pupils were: Jappy and Paddy Rodgers, also Margery Rodgers, Edna and Bertha Moore, (who lived somewhere north of the Goettler farm where Rawhide Moore lived). His sons, Frank and Earl were pupils also some of the Blains. The Deane children, who lived on the Arnold or Kaplan place, opposite the school. Donald Gray's daughter, Annie, who died at an early age, oh yes, and Nellie and Luella Duncan. There were quite a few pupils.

When I taught there at one time, I had only eight pupils; Dorothy and Gwynydd Thomas, Tommy McMillan, Robert Votaw, Hazel Johnson (Tooker), John and Danny McNab, Who was the eighth?

About 1909 there was a bachelor named Charlie West living on the corner of NW¼ 2-21-1-W5.

MEMORIES OF PANIMA SCHOOL No. 581 — by Ruby Cole

Class memories of Panima School began for me in 1923 when Miss Margaret Windle was our teacher. Our school then was on old one room building with a high ceiling and stove pipes that went all along the room to a bracket chimney at the other end. All the heat used to go up from the big stove we had for heat. This stove

Panima School.

had a tin guard all around it to protect the children from being burned. It stood at the back of the room, to one side of the entrance, and here we would keep our overshoes warm, ready for going home. Our lunches would freeze on the long horseback ride to school and we would thaw them out at the stove.

We usually had Phys.-Ed. first thing on the cold mornings, this meant arm exercises, leg exercises, bending, and a march, several times around the room, by then we were warmed up and ready to start our studies, mainly the three "Rs" reading, (W)riting and (a)rithmetic with some history, hygiene, geography, grammar, spelling and art. One teacher taught all grades, one to nine inclusive, with an approximate attendance of twenty to twenty-five students. Our big event of the school year was the annual Christmas concert when the parents, relatives and friends of the district all came, with horses and sleighs, at twenty degrees below zero F., to the big "Do". Santa always managed to know the right night and had candy bags and gifts for all the children. Our second big event was the school picnic, when school was out for the summer holidays, two whole months, July and August.

By 1926 our school building had seen better days and a new school building of one room, two cloak rooms and a full size basement, was built. It had a coal burning furnace in the basement and a room to play, in foul weather. The old school was sold to Kiam Kaplan and is now on the Dick Connop farm being used as a work shop.

One afternoon, in June of 1931, when the students were writing final exams, on a terribly hot and humid day, up came a dry thunder storm, about three o'clock. The lightning was very close and scared everyone. Our teacher that year was Miss Nesta Woodhouse and she was afraid it had struck the school but after looking around and finding the pupils were all safe went back to work. Some of the senior students were writing their grammar exam and some of them made the high mark of nineteen out of one hundred! At three thirty we were dismissed for home time and we all went to get our horses from the little paddock beside the school where they were kept and one horse had been struck down by lightning. It belonged to May Betts who lived on the A. J. Voss farm (SE¼-34-20-1-W5).

Another incident in memory of Panima School days was one warm, chinooky morning in February, all the students were present at school and all was serene until about eleven o'clock when the wind changed and blew in a great blizzard from the north, drifts were piled high and roads blocked by mid-afternoon. Everyone was kept inside the school until men from the Goettler farms, with horses and sleighs and blankets, came to pick us up. They let all the horses loose from the paddock to find their way home through the storm and they stayed alongside of the sleighs. The students and teacher were taken to the closest farm homes until the next day when the storm had abated.

My school days at Panima ended in June of 1932 when Nesta Woodhouse was still the teacher. She also was teaching in 1933 and that was the year that we decided to get the piano. Nesta was all for it and she directed our play titled "That's one on Bill" with five young men and five young women in the cast, namely;

Nesta Woodhouse, Clare Goettler, Nina Goettler, Viola Varty, Ruby Pegler. Earle Brinton, Harold (Lefty) Cole, George Gale, Hughie Gough and Bob Baxter.

Nesta chose a comic play and we had a lot of fun at practices even though it was sometimes hard to get together during the winter evenings. Hugh Gough rode horseback to practices and had to open and close nine gates on his route across country. He almost met with a serious accident of one trip when his horse floundered through the big drifts of snow. Myself, I walked almost a mile with a lantern or a flashlight in my hand, from Sandstone to the Cole farm, to catch a ride with Lefty Cole and Earle Brinton, (who was then the hired man on Cole's dairy farm). We would travel with the horses and sleigh over to Ed. Goettler's and pick up Nesta, Clare and Nina then proceed through another farmer's field, taking the best route through the deep snow. On one trip we had two dogs following along with us and when we came through George Lumsden's yard, about ten at night, the dogs jumped into his pig pen and there was a little excitement until we could get them out again.

However, January, 1933 saw our play well rewarded with a packed house. Then, later, we went through the play again and put it on in Aldersyde. That night we closed it off and had our celebration.

Those were the depression days when people had very little of material things. They had faith and trust in their fellow man, they needed each other and money was not master, the latch was off and a welcome mat at the door.

ON PANIMA SCHOOL by Margaret (Windle) Gallagher

Panima School was situated on the road, west out of Okotoks on the north side of Sheep Creek about six miles from Okotoks. It was situated on a good ranching and farming country and the families were all good citizens of Alberta. I taught there in 1926-27 and boarded with a very fine lady, Mrs. East. She had a son Harvey and her granddaughter, Bernice Ewing, who attended Panima school.

The families there at the time as I remember were two families of Goettlers, two of Cressmans, two of Kaplans, Slenos and Votaws and, I am sure, others. Memory fails over a matter of fifty years.

There was a very sad accident when I taught there. The children nearly all rode horses as distances to the school were some miles. One evening Alfred Votaw's horse fell and stepped on his chest and he died that night. He was a very nice boy about ten years old and the community was saddened by his death.

This was a very friendly community and I enjoyed my stay there very much. In 1928 I went to the North Turner Valley school district and in 1929 I married Jack Gallagher and have lived in Black Diamond ever since.

MEMORIES OF PANIMA SCHOOL — by Nesta (Woodhouse) Trevenan

In June of 1931 I signed a contract to teach Panima School, about eight miles west of Okotoks. This was a rural school, including grades one to nine. There were about twenty-five children. The building was com-

paratively new; it had been built a year or two before. There was a complete cement basement with a furnace. The east side was mostly windows and the whole building was attractive, sunlit and airy.

For three years I boarded at the home of Mr. and Mrs. Harry Barker. They lived west of "Hillside Farm" (owned by Tom McMillan Sr.) about three and a half miles from the school. When the Barkers moved away, I boarded at Ed Goettlers, east of the school.

In June of 1935 I left the school. I married Billie Trevenan of Calgary and, in those depression days, any female teacher who married was not allowed to continue teaching.

Some of the Panima pupils that I remember are George Goettler and his sister, Eileen, and brothers, Eugene (Ginger), and Frank, the children of Margaret (Hamilton) and Eugene Goettler. Their cousins, Clare, Nina, Katherine and Bernice, children of Katherine (Kitsy Lumsden) and Ed Goettler. Clare and Nina had finished their elementary education before I went to Panima.

Close by the school lived the Harry Petersons and their children, Margaret, James and Ralph. There were two other families of cousins who were pupils; Mary, Moses, Sidney and Jacob Kaplan who were cousins of Rachel Kaplan and her two brothers. I remember when Mary was about ten she looked like the picture of Christ, as a boy, in the temple. She had a beautiful smile.

Then there was Alfred Heitman and his pretty sister, Alice. Alice had a beautiful voice and helped make any entertainment or Christmas Concert enjoyable.

I remember Dorothy Hare and her brothers, Frank and Keith.

Ruby and Frances Pegler were pupils then. Frances also had a beautiful voice. About that time she wanted to be an actress and was very pleased that the most famous actress then was a little girl called Shirley Temple.

Another pupil, Margaret Lumsden, cousin of the Goettlers, a quiet, smiling girl, sketched lifelike horses.

May Betts lost her horse one June afternoon. A bolt

Panima Picnic 1943. L. to R. Kay Goettler, Margaret Peterson, Clare Goettler, Bella Wilson, Ruby Pegler, Tom Stordy, Frances Pegler.

of lightning struck the animal in the field beside the school.

Ruby Pegler and Viola Varty, another of the senior girls, took part in a couple of community plays we put on in the school. With the proceeds we bought a school piano.

Most of the children rode to school on horseback. Those who lived nearby walked. George, Eileen and Ginger rode on sturdy Shetland ponies.

By now most rural schools have vanished. The academic reasons for larger school divisions seemed sound but, as is often the case, many, barely recognized but valuable, factors of the earlier education process were lost. In smaller groups there is less discrimination; to make up a team, baseball, hockey, you use what children are available, boys and girls, younger and older, everyone plays.

Nostalgia gives a roseate hue, perhaps, but I think the personal relationships were closer. Perhaps I should say, "there was more caring."

THE SANDSTONE VILLAGE AND ITS BRICK INDUSTRY — by Ruby Cole

The village of Sandstone, Alberta, was located about four (4) miles northwest of Okotoks, NE¼-2-21-1-W5, on the main line of the Canadian Pacific Railway. At one time it was the site of four brick yards. The largest one being in the village of Sandstone.

As far as is known, this property was homesteaded by Alex McLeod in the late 1800's and the brick industry began in the early 1900's, by a man named Watson (Gravity Watson). He was an engineer for the City of Calgary. The first bricks bearing the imprint of 'WATSON'.

In 1906, Alberta Portland Cement Company took over the Watson plant. Their bricks bore the imprint 'A.P.C. Co.'

Another change in 1909 saw a new owner. The Canada Cement Company. Their imprint was "C.C. Co.", and, on some bricks, just a small "c.c." The cottage school on Gladys Ridge, built in 1918, had chimney bricks bearing this marking.

The shale for the making of bricks was hauled in dump carts by horses from the pits and all work was done by pick and shovel.

The Canada Cement Company also shipped rock out of Sandstone to the Calgary Cement plant for the making of cement, until the Exshaw plant started up.

The year 1912, saw the peak of the brick industry, with Sandstone Yard turning out twelve million bricks during the working period from March until November. The bricks sold for an average of eighteen dollars per thousand, and were manufactured for approximately ten dollars per thousand, including the wages. Some of the bricks manufactured in that year went into the building of the Okotoks High School, up on the hill.

The industry was thriving with a population of approximately one hundred people, from England, Ireland, Scotland and Europe. Many lived in one room shacks and tents as there were only five company houses. The superintendent of the company lived in a large brick house. Another large building, (at first built for a kiln), was remodelled to a boarding house, with kitchen, dining-room, wash rooms and reading room. The sleeping quarters were upstairs. This building was also used for entertainments.

The village had its own post office, railway station and general store. A family doctor attended from

The thriving village of Sandstone in 1912.

One of the round kilns and two of the men with their pokers for tending the fires.

The industry had to close down that year, and the natural gas was removed.

In 1919, the industry started up again and, back to coal for the kilns. Coal was very expensive as a fuel and had to be hauled in. Other brick industries using a natural gas, became stiff opposition. In 1923, there was discontent among the workers and they went on strike for higher wages. The superintendent put through a phone call to the head office in Montreal and the word came back to close down the industry. This finalized the brick industry and the Canada Cement Company finished up the firing of the kilns, then brought in a demolition crew to take down and move away the factory.

Some of the last bricks manufactured in 1923, and bearing the small c.c. imprint, were used in the first

Wheel barrows used for loading bricks into the cars. The men protected their hands with inner tire tubes cut into pads for the hands and thumbs.

Okotoks and also a visiting clergyman. The milk was delivered from a neighbouring farm dairy. The children of the village took their education at Panima School west of the village, most of them travelling on horse back. There were two passenger trains in the morning and two in the evening. The fare to Okotoks was twenty-five cents return. The C.P.R. had a two spare track, siding, with a spur line running into the factory, for the loading of bricks and building rock.

In 1913, natural gas was piped in from Bow Island. 1914, saw the world at war and many of the men from Sandstone answered the call to the Mother Country.

Removal of natural gas pipe line from Sandstone, 1914.

part of the present High River Hospital. In 1925, the property was sold to Percy Pegler who farmed the land until 1951, when it was sold to Rube Lynch, then to a Mr. Mooney, who sold it to Mr. Lorne Dennis.

In April of 1958, the little railway station was dismantled and removed to Cressday, south of Manyberries, Alberta, to be used as a bunkhouse. The tall brick chimney and the superintendent's brick house still stand as a land mark of a once thriving industrial site. The present owner is Mr. John G. Thompson.

THE CRESSMAN FAMILY — by Nellie Cressman

Ivan Cressman and Miss Mary Wambold were married Nov. 25th, 1914. They moved from Mazeppa to the farm west and north of Okotoks in 1925 with their three children. Mervin, born Jan. 10, 1916; Earl born Sept. 22, 1918 and Gertrude born July 10, 1920. They farmed and milked cows. Mary was very well known for the cheese she made and sold throughout the district. The family had a very short life together as Gertrude died at the age of nine. Ivan died in 1936 — followed by his wife in 1954.

Mervin and Earl continued to farm the family farm, then in 1945, Earl purchased a quarter three miles west. In 1963, Mervin sold out at Okotoks and moved to Rimbey where he died in 1969.

Earl married Nellie Wathen on July 26, 1947 and they had two children — Lois, born in 1950 and Larry, born 1954. In 1964 Earl sold the farm west of Okotoks and bought a farm one mile southeast of Okotoks. We sold that farm to Keith Construction in July, 1975, Earl died in October, 1975. I moved to an acreage north of Okotoks.

Lois married Joe Whiteside Nov. 22, 1969 and lives in Okotoks. They have three children, one girl and two boys.

Larry married Linda Ivie in March, 1975 and they have one boy. They moved to Gadsby in 1976 where they are farming and raising purebred Herefords.

EDMUND CUFFLING

Edmund Cuffling homesteaded SE¼-6-21-1-W5 No. 40388 and pre-sale SW¼-21-1-W5 No. 1904. The homestead is listed prior to 1892. He was a bachelor and raised both cattle and horses. He was an avid cricket player. Following a stroke, suffered in 1905, he moved to Okotoks where he resided until his death in 1910.

THE GIER RANCH — (taken from information submitted by L. H. Gier)

William Gier bought the Ranch from Charles Mackie in 1900. He moved his family and effects to the Ranch in 1901. There were six children in the family, four girls and two boys. The two eldest girls — Mamie and Winna — were past school age. Ray and I (Laurence) attended Stormount school in 1901 and 1902 until Panima school was built in 1902 or 1903. I finished school in 1905 as I had to work full time on the Ranch.

When Father first bought the Ranch, it consisted of one section of land, twenty-five horses and fifty cattle. By 1905 its size had increased to two and one half sections (1600 acres) one hundred horses and two hundred and fifty head of cattle.

In the winter of 1906-1907, the cold winter, I hauled hay from morning to night from the meadow one and a half miles south. In January of that year it was 55 degrees below zero for one whole week.

In 1908 I left the Ranch to work in the CPR machine shop in Calgary — where I lived until 1967.

The Ranch was sold to a man named Shaw in 1910.

The enrolment at Panima ranged from twenty-five to thirty-five pupils. I can just remember three teachers — Miss Mead, Mrs. Seaman and Kate Creighton. Her parents farmed off the Black Diamond road west of Big Rock.

Names I can recall of people living in the Panima area are: Donald Gray, wife and three children (attended school); Dick Henderson, wife and six children (four attended school); Mr. Allan, wife, no children. (Allans usually boarded school teacher); Renicks — five children, all school age; "Rawhide" Moore, had two boys — Frank and Earl — school age; "Long" Moore four children — mostly girls; "As well" Thompson, five children all school age (one boy, four girls); Stocton, two boys of school age; Duncan, one girl and one boy, Larry, who was a chum of mine for years as we both lived in Calgary. Larry still lives in Calgary; Jack Cuffling — bachelor; Tom Cannon — Bachelor; The Notons — an English couple; Jonathan Cuffling, had three boys, Tommy, Harry and Monty (Tom and Harry now live in Calgary); Robert Turner, The Alexanders and MacMillans all lived in the area.

Laurence H. Gier who submitted the information for this history was born in Ontario in 1889.

The Gier Ranch is now known to many as the Widney Ranch.

HISTORY OF THE GOETTLER FAMILY TO 1976. by Margaret Goettler.

The Ontario Government opened up land, called the Huron Tract, in 1829. To this area came the Seeback family, Pioneers of the Huron Tract, they cleared brush and trees to make a home and livelihood for their family. In our treasures we have a picture of the Seeback Family, nine boys and one girl, Eva. This picture was taken in 1929 when a Cairn was built to honour the Seeback family, by the Sebringville town council, and surrounding residents. The district which they pioneered and built their homes was finally named Sebringville, Ontario. As more and more families came into this area from Europe and the British Isles, the Seebacks built a hotel, in 1896, where these new people stayed until they chose their respective farmlands.

Not many miles away was a town called Stratford and to this town came a Doctor Edward Hillebrand who had a practice there. He married Eva Seeback and they had a daughter, Mary, who married Anthony Goettler in 1874. Many of the homes built at that time are still in use today. A T.V. program recently showed a home that, now, houses a bank in Stratford and another, now, a small hotel in Sebringville in which Jeanette MacDonald and Nelson Eddy stayed while performing in Stratford. Their idea was to get a quiet hotel, away from Stratford.

After running a flour mill for fifteen years, the Goettlers left for Virden Manitoba where Eugene Goettler was born. A younger son, George, was also born there, he died of pneumonia after they arrived in Okotoks. Seventeen years of farming in the Virden district was ended when they moved to Wauchope, Saskatchewan where they took up homesteads. Wauchope was the name of a Scottish Estate under the reign of Mary Queen of Scots.

In Wauchope, baseball was very important and the Goettler boys played on the best teams. The family also had their own orchestra, playing at dances and other social events: Anthony on violin, Ed on violin, Karl, harp, Mary, piano, Maggie, organ, Caroline, flute, Carl and Gene were also excellent square dance callers.

After six years in Wauchope they came, in 1911, and looked at land in Leduc and Okotoks, finally decided to buy land five and a half miles north-west of Okotoks, mostly brush but near Calgary and a good market. They moved up here in 1912, bringing good horses, some cattle and machinery. The bush was cut and the land ploughed, they picked willow roots for years. Eugene cleared all the fields with his brother, Ed.

The district and school was called Panima. It was the Indian name for "Valley below the hill where they made pemican." Saskatoons grew here and were mixed with meat from the buffalo.

Eugene and I, Margaret Hamilton, were married January 5, 1920 and settled on this farm with Eugene's parents. Ed. Goettler settled close by and had four daughters; Clare (joined an order of nuns and has been in the Precious Blood Monastery in Calgary and Ontario at present in Vancouver.) Kay, Nina and Bernice are all married and live in Calgary.

Our family of three boys, George, Ginger and Frank, settled on the farm and Eileen, married and lived in the Oil Fields.

In 1939 Eugene Goettler and William Hamilton started a chuckwagon outfit, bought and trained horses for it. They were in it for some four years and in 1939 made the world record for speed.

Eugene died in September, 1970 and boys, Frank and Ginger carried on the farm for some time.

George sold his farm and now lives in High River. Frank and his wife, Betty, and sons, Geno and Guy have a dairy of 34 cows, also two herds of Hereford beef cattle.

Eugene was councillor for roads on the Foothills council for 37 years.

Ginger and his wife, Geraldine, live in Calgary. Eileen (Hoffner) is widowed and also lives in Calgary. I make my home in the old house on the farm.

L. to R. Ginger Goettler, Barry Hoffner, and Frank Goettler, 1959.

GEORGE AND ISABEL (WILSON) GOETTLER

George Goettler and Isabel Wilson were married on April 7, 1945 in St. James Catholic Church in Okotoks. We lived for a few years on his family farm, west of

Eugene Goettler.

Okotoks. While there we had two children, Paul and Jane. In 1948 we moved to a farm across Sheep River, five and a quarter miles east and south of Black Diamond, where we lived for twenty-two years. Rosemary, Raymond and Marie were born while we were on that farm.

In 1971 we sold our farm and moved to High River where George is busy at cabinet making and carpenter work.

We have three married children now; Paul is married to Sue Sokulski, they live in Edmonton; Jane is married to Don Kirk of De Winton, they live in Okotoks and have a small son, Jeffrey, born January 10, 1978; Rosemary is married to Barton Brocklebank, they live on the family farm north west of High River and have a small daughter, Lee, born April 12, 1977. Raymond and Marie are at home attending high school.

DONALD AND ANNIE (McRAE) GRAY

Donald a young man of good humour, was born in Ontario in 1861 and came west to Calgary in 1880. After working for the Department of Indian Affairs for some time, he decided to take up a homestead S½ 4-21-1-W5 where he made his home for the next 30 years.

Annie McRae, also from Ontario, became his bride in 1888, after living in Okotoks for a year. Together they ran the Panima post office until it closed in 1903.

As well as raising cattle and horses, he was a blacksmith and helped out many of his neighbours in that capacity.

The farm was sold in 1920 and the Grays moved to B.C. where Mrs. Gray died in 1929. Following the death of his wife, Donald lived with a daughter, Isabel Hanson until his own passing in 1943. They are both buried in the Okotoks cemetery.

Three children blessed this marriage; William Bain, 1889-1953; Isabel (Hanson) 1891, Okotoks; Annie, 1894-1909.

THOMAS G. AND KATE ELIZABETH (DAFT) HARE — by Dorothy (Hare) Harland

My father, Thomas G. Hare, was born in Durham, England, May, 1887. He came over from England, with his parents, at the age of six weeks. They lived in Ohio before settling in the Airdrie district where they farmed. He and his brother had land at Half Moon Bay on the Northern B.C. Coast. He also worked in the coal mines, at Kicking Horse Pass, before he was married, and in the mines at East Coulee, after he was married.

My mother, Kate Elizabeth Hare, was born in Leicestershire, England, July 1884. Her father was a saddler and supplied the gentry with harness and riding equipment. She came from a large family and one sister, Ada, still lives in the same place. Mother left England in 1914 and lived with a sister, Mrs. Constance Bailey, at Airdrie before she moved to Calgary and worked for Mayor Costello and his wife.

My parents were married at the Key Ranch, Airdrie, April 6, 1916 and they drove a McLaughlin car while he lived there.

Father worked for the Ogden Shops in Calgary before we moved to the Sandstone Valley, west of Okotoks. I, Dorothy, was the oldest and I was in grade

three or four when we moved. I had two brothers, Frank and Keith, my youngest brother, Marshall, was born on the farm in June, 1927. We all attended Panima School.

After two years on the original farm at Sandstone, known as the Bishop farm, my parents rented the adjoining farm from the Serviss Family and rented their own land to the Linton family. A year later they were back on their own place as the Bill Varty family had taken over the Serviss farm.

Dad earned the title "The Potato King" with his twenty-five acres of potatoes which he sold for twenty-five cents a hundred pounds. One fall, when pigs were hard to sell, Mother made English pork pies, headcheese and sausage, a skill learned from her parents, and sold them, door to door, in Okotoks. Her customers liked them so well that they asked her to go into business. Mother decided it would be too much work for her, by now the cold weather had arrived and the snow was deep and, she had a young family to care for. Her home made soap won first prize at the U.F.A. Fair.

I learned to make bread on the farm. Father had learned before he was married and taught Mother the art and when Mother was ill and I had to stay home and help with the work, he taught me too.

We moved to Maryland in 1936 where I met my husband, Ernest Harland, (deceased 1966) and we were married, in Calgary. We have four children and eight grandchildren. Dorothy (Mrs. Darryl Daniels) graduate nurse, lives on the farm at Rolling Hills, Alberta, has four children; Debbie, Donna, Michael and Gregg. Robert, graduated cum laude from Colorado University, married Tamara Hamilton, has two children; Nancy and Robert Junior, lives in Boulder, Colorado and works, as a Public Chartered Accountant, in Denver. Barbara (Mrs. Jim Douglas), has two children; Robert and Kerriann, all living in Calgary. John, married to Janice Rice, lives in Broomfield, Colorado and is assitant manager in an automotive centre.

My oldest brother, Frank, lives in Calgary with his wife, Joyce (Weston) and four daughters; Brenda, Charlene, Gayla and Deanna and son, Craig.

Keith works in Banff, for the C.P.R. but lives in Canmore with his wife, Georgina (Raper) and three children; Lori, Cheryl and Tommy.

Marshall lives in Calgary with his wife, Margaret (Brownridge) and two children; Neal and Catherine.

I have worked for the Crippled Childrens' Hospital in Calgary for the past twenty-three years and presently reside in Calgary.

My parents celebrated their Golden Wedding Anniversary April 6, 1966, at Jacques Lodge in Calgary. Mother returned to England, for a family reunion, after being away almost fifty years. Father died April 9, 1971 and Mother, December 26, 1974.

THE DICK HENDERSON FAMILY — by Blanche (Henderson) Swanson

Dick Henderson, my father, came west in about 1900 with his eldest son, Harry and several other men. They worked for different farmers in the Okotoks and Midnapore areas. In 1902 he returned to Essex County,

Ontario and brought his wife, Eliza and the remaining six children west in March of that year. They travelled by train and the two youngest children, Blanche (born 1897) and Hope (born 1900) took sick with either measles or scarlet fever. The train was cold and drafty and both girls were very ill when they reached Okotoks. Hope, the baby, died and Blanche lost her hearing as a result of the sickness.

The family homesteaded a half-section west and north of Okotoks — property now owned by Dick Connop and Bud Imler.

Libbie (born Jan., 1890), Bill (born April, 1892), May Belle (born 1894) and Blanche attended Panima school. Harry, (born 1885) and Kenneth (born 1887) were working at home or elsewhere.

Our closest neighbors were the Kirks who lived just east of us — other names I recall are Thompsons, Grays, Moores, Renicks, Stocktons, Giers and Wests. I remember Charlie West, a very kind hearted man, decided to put up a swing for the students at Panima school. Some of the neighbors disapproved because he did the work on a Sunday, but the kids didn't mind a bit and got a lot of enjoyment from that swing!

My first pet was a baby badger that followed me around the farm like a pup would.

I remember my father telling us about his first and last horseback ride. He had never learned to ride and when he was working for a farmer between 1900 and 1902, the farmer asked him to ride four miles to the neighbors on some errand. He slid around on the horses back so much that he wore holes in the seat of his trousers.

Then there was the time Kenneth thought he would quieten the buckskin horse Grandfather had bought for Libbie. After riding for a while he went to the house for something. He tied the horse to Mother's hand-operated washing machine, which was sitting outside. When Kenneth returned he found the horse had run away, dragging the washing machine. He had quite a job catching the horse and a bigger job re-assembling that precious washing machine.

I remember trips to Okotoks in the summer with the team and wagon. We'd stop along Sandstone Hill and fill up on the saskatoons that grew in great abundance there.

The family moved to a farm southeast of Okotoks in about 1904 or 1905 (now the Hartley farm).

Harry married Mamie Cameron, an Okotoks girl. They had six girls and two boys and lived mostly in the Okotoks and Turner Valley areas.

Kenneth married Lydia Greenfield from north of Okotoks, had two boys and one girl. They lived in Washington State, U.S.A.

Libbie married Harry Fyfe. They had one boy and one girl. They farmed for some time in the Okotoks area — west of Big Rock.

Bill married Edith Iler of Kingsville, Ontario. They had four boys and two girls and lived in Okotoks, Black Diamond and Devon areas. Bill also spent two years in Egypt working for an oil company.

May Belle died of the Spanish flu and was buried on New Year's Day, 1919.

Blanche married Sandy (Alexander) Swanson, had three boys and one girl and farmed in the Lacombe area. After her husband's death in 1943, Blanche and her family moved to a farm at Bentley, Alberta. Blanche's daughter, Betty, married Ernest Cole of Okotoks and they farm west of Okotoks.

Blanche is the only living member in her generation of the Dick Henderson family. She moved from her farm at Bentley to an apartment in Calgary where she now lives.

FRED AND MARIA HOLMES — by K. Hemus

Fred and Maria Holmes moved to the Panima district, from Millarville, in the spring of 1922. They farmed on the Fred Johnson place for two years. There were four children; Fred, Christine, Grace and Kathleen. The older three attended Panima School. Christine and Grace rode their pony "Sandy" to school. Clayton Hicks was their teacher. Fred Junior attended Panima School for two years, his teacher was Mr. Austin referred to, by the pupils, as "the Sheik of Pincher Creek". Fred recalls playing quite a bit of "shinny" with a rubber ball and a board, slanted like a hockey stick. Other pupils they recall were; Hirsts, Peglers, Slenos, Mortens, Swarbricks, Kaplans and MacMillans.

Grace recalls one winter when the four Holmes children contracted scarlet fever. In those days it meant ten days in bed and six week quarantine for the family. She said at the end of ten days the skin started to flake off and they would stand and shake their nighties and watch the flakes fall to the floor. Quite a novelty for them!! At the end of the six weeks their dad had to get sulphur and burn it in the house for twenty-four hours. It meant no one could sleep in the house for one night so, he set up a stove in the loft of the barn, took blankets and pillows and they slept in the hay — that was an enjoyable event for the kids.

Mrs. Holmes remembers driving her buggy into Okotoks for groceries and she talks of the busy time in the fall cooking for threshers.

In 1923 the Holmes family moved to Okotoks. Christine died in 1933 and Mr. Holmes in 1948.

Grace, now Mrs. Wally Wittkopf, lives in Edmonton and Kay, now Mrs. Cliff Hemus, lives in Victoria. Fred and his wife live in Kimberley, B.C.

Mrs. Holmes lived in Okotoks until 1975 when she moved to Victoria to live with her daughter, Kay "Granny", as she is known, had eight grandchildren and twenty-one great-grandchildren. She is ninety years old and keeps well and very active.

THE IMLERS — by Bud Imler

Pioneering in the Okotoks-De Winton district takes the Imler name back to some of the earliest settlers in this area. Bud Imler's grandfather came to the Okotoks district by covered wagon in 1890 where he settled with his family to take up homesteading and carpenter work. Some of the first Okotoks buildings were built by the Imlers. Bud Imler's father pioneered in the Okotoks-De Winton area, breaking up land and threshing with the steam engine. The Bud Imlers moved to the De Winton area in 1949, better known as the Panima district, on land previously owned by the Kaplans. This move still had to carry the pioneer spirit because of the lack of telephone, electricity and gravel roads. The roads were badly blocked with snow in the winter of 49-50 so a number of times we had to rely on our neighbors, the Jim Rowans, and the black team and cutter to provide us with transportation. However this is only a memory now; with the Bud Imlers still at this residence and carrying on with the farming.

HELGE AND ALMA (MILLER) JENSEN — by Margaret Harvey

Helge Jensen was born in Jutland, Denmark in June of 1914. In 1927, his father, Thomas, sailed for Canada, established a farm near Markerville, Alberta and settled down to wait for his family. A year later they arrived, his wife, Meta, and seven of their eleven children.

Helge worked for various neighbours, learning the language and the many skills of farming, that he still uses today. In 1938, he rented his first land in the Markerville area. He married Alma Miller of Rockyford, in the Fall of 1939. Two years later his first daughter was born in Innisfail.

He moved to the Okotoks District in 1943 and rented the Tooker Place for four years, two more of his children were born there. Then, in 1947, he bought a half section of land from Tommy MacMillan, a well established rancher, and his last three children were born there.

There wasn't a building on the place so we lived in a "cook car" until a house was moved in. Every building, with the exception of the house, he constructed himself. Brush was cleared, stumps torn out and, gradually, the land took shape. Every fall he ran a threshing crew and was often away from home. It was then that Mother milked ten cows by hand and hauled water from the creek for a hundred pigs. She raised a large garden, preserved fruit and vegetables and cooked huge meals for the threshing crew. Gradually, trees, flowers and lawn were planted, new buildings replaced the old and the farm stands today as a reminder of the very hard work of two exceptional people.

They have six children; Shirley Ann, born 1941, married Ervan Poffenroth, Raymond Frank, born 1944, a pipeline superintendent, Margaret Jean, born 1945, married Wilfred Harvey, Wayne Douglas, born 1950, married Karen Knupp, Patricia Gaye, born 1957, second year nursing student, Thomas Brian, born 1958, employed with L and M Construction.

THE JOHNSTONE FAMILY — by Hazel Tooker

Fred Johnstone bought the farm five miles west of Okotoks and along the north bank of Sheep Creek. Our mother, my sister, Sarah, and I, (Hazel), lived on the farm with Fred. We came to Alberta from Ingersoll, Ontario. Sarah died in 1914 and Mother died in 1919.

I attended Panima school — travelling the two and one-half miles on foot or by horseback. I can remember Mr. Imler helping me past the Arnold farm where there were several cranky dogs. The school I attended was the old, original Panima school house which now serves as a garage on the Connop farm.

John Campbell and I were married in 1921 and lived on the Campbell farm. We had one daughter, Della, who is married, has two sons and lives in Brantford, Ontario.

After John's death, I left the Campbell farm and moved back with my brother, Fred, again.

Times have certainly changed as I can remember buying a pretty box of talcum powder when I was a young girl. Knowing my brother highly disapproved of such things, I hid the box of talcum under the oat bundles. However, on my return from school one day I found Jim Cole and his son, Fred, had come for oat bundles and my brother had discovered the box of powder. I can't remember what the punishment was, but I never got the talcum back!

In 1913, Layton Tooker came from St. Paul, Minneapolis to work on the Shaw ranch (originally the Gier Ranch): Layton was a city boy and often rode to town on horseback. My brother Fred used to remark "That Englishman better learn to ride or he'll break his neck!"

Layton and I were married in 1938. We have one son, Jim, who is now married, has one boy and one girl and lives in Cranbrook, B.C.

Fred died in 1942. Layton and I farmed the place and sold it to J. B. Cross in 1965. We now reside in Hillcrest Manor on the hill in Okotoks.

CHARLES AND MARIE (SHEIERMAN) KIMMEL — by Mrs. W. Kimmel

Charles Kimmel was an immigrant from Russia who moved to Calgary in 1903 when he was three years old. He met and married Marie Scheierman who was born in Calgary of German immigrant parents, in 1919.

They lived in Calgary until 1926 when they moved to a farm in Acme with their three sons, Walter, Harold and Wilfred. They stayed at the farm for one year and then moved to the Panima District. The two eldest boys, Walter and Harold, attended Panima School even after the family moved to the Sandstone Valley, riding "Cap", a bay pony with a blaze face, the four and a half miles to and from school. They stayed in the Valley until 1929 when the family moved back to Calgary to enable Charles to join his brother-in-law in the cattle buying business.

In 1933 they took advantage of the "back to the land" scheme and homesteaded a quarter section 25 miles west of Wetaskiwin, Alberta, living in tents until a cabin could be built.

Walter left the farm after five years to return to Calgary to work and joined the Royal Canadian Corps

Charles and Marie Kimmel with children, Walter and Wilfred. At Panima.

334

of Signals in 1942 in which he served for four years in England and on the Continent. He was decorated with the Croix-de Guerre with Bronze Star and mentioned in dispatches for bravery in France in 1944. He married Joan Stavorinus, an English war bride, in 1945 and she joined him in Wetaskiwin in 1946. They lived in Prince George, B.C. and Whitehorse, Yukon with their four children, Gail, Gary, Lorne and Laurel and owned and operated Kim's Meat and Grocery Market until they returned to England in 1957, with the two youngest children, Lorne and Laurel, to open the Aurora Hotel in Gillingham, Kent where they still reside.

Their eldest daughter, Gail, is married with one daughter, Laurel, and lives in Powell River, B.C. with her husband, Hans Gloslee.

Gary is a member of the Royal Canadian Mounted Police and is stationed in Kamloops, B.C. with his wife, Evelyn, and daughter, Sheri, and son, Jamie.

Lorne is also a constable with the Royal Canadian Mounted Police, unmarried, and stationed in Bassano, Alberta.

Laurel, the youngest, and now eighteen, is a medical secretary in the local hospital in England.

Since leaving the farm in 1948, Harold, who married in 1944, resides and works in Calgary. He has three children, two girls and a boy.

Wilfred, the youngest, married in 1947 and had a family of six boys and a girl. He passed away in 1968 after several years of blindness from diabetes. All his family still reside and work in Calgary.

Kim (Walter), doesn't remember too much about the community life except that it revolved around the school with the Christmas Concert being the highlight of the year. All the family entertainment came from visiting neighbours where adults played cards and the children played the usual games of Ludo, etc. He particularly remembers a bachelor neighbour, Mr. Stordy, who enjoyed visiting them but sometimes overstayed his welcome and then his Dad would say, "well good-night Mr. Stordy; blow out the light when you leave!"

Kim remembers that they had about eight horses and quite a big herd of dairy cows, a few of which were purebred Holsteins — quite a rarity at that time.

He also hurt his foot quite badly, hopping off the binder while watching his dad cutting oats. He slipped and jammed his foot in the drive chain and stopped the binder and team of four horses. He remembers breaking his wrist when he fell off a pile of boards in the school yard and had to be taken to Okotoks to have it set.

THE ALLAN J. MACDONALD FAMILY — by Edna Macdonald

Allan was born Jan. 15, 1913 at Loma, twelve miles east of Blackie, Alberta, the son of William and Agnes Macdonald. He attended West Arrowwood School and later S.A.I.T.

I, Edna, was the youngest living child of Andrew Gillanders and Mary McKeage of the Gladys Ridge. My family moved to Calgary when I was ten years old. I attended Stanley ones Public School Crescent

Heights High School and Calgary Normal School. I taught for eight years in rural schools near Blackie, Countess, Herronton and finally in Carseland.

Teaching salaries, for me from 1935 to 1943, varied from $500 to $1300 a year. I have had as few as four pupils to over forty. Board and room ranged from $20 to $25 a month. I substituted in Okotoks in the sixties when wages were somewhat better.

Allan and I were married in Calgary in 1943. We worked for Roy Widney Sr., for thirteen months. Our son, Bill, was born there. Then we returned to Blackie and rented the Albert Swartz farm for a year. We were completely hailed out.

In January, 1946, we purchased the Voss farm for $42 an acre. This consisted of the E½-34-20-1-W5 and S.W.¼-35-20-1-W5. (In a year or so Mr. Knowles of Okotoks, dropped in one day to see if we were interested in selling the farm. I said "No, but when we can get $80 an acre, we will sell." and we both laughed heartily at that ridiculously high price.)

That first winter on the Voss farm was a cold one. The house was a large two-storey affair heated by several tin wood-burners but there was no furnace. The well was in the basement with a cistern pump in the kitchen.

Larry was born March 21, 1947. Spring had come early and the grass was green. We may have had a few snow storms after that but nothing too serious. However, 1948 was a different story. The roads between our place and Okotoks had eight foot drifts in spots. We all drove horses and sleighs through the fields to get to Okotoks. Finally Bud Imler cleared the roads with a "cat", pushing the snow crosswise. As late as the 24th of May there still were banks of snow in the fields.

Colleen was born Feb. 1, 1951. Miss Quinn, the grade one teacher told me she was very pleased when Colleen finally arrived because Bill, who was in Grade

Macdonalds' Production Line. Billy milking, Larry and Colleen Macdonald looking on.

one, had given a progress report each morning in his oral news report. Jane was born Sept. 30, 1952 and last but not least, Marion arrived May 26, 1956.

Electricity came our way in 1949 and in 1950 I received $500 as my inheritance from my father's estate. So I blew it all on pink bathroom fixtures. This was indeed a luxury I enjoyed with five youngsters to raise. Many a black Aberdeen Angus calf who arrived in a blizzard or on a terribly cold night owed its existence to the life-giving warmth of a bath in that pink tub.

We thought we were busy raising kids and paying for our place but really, those were happy days. We had good neighbors — Goettlers, Millers, and Coles, Rowans, Tookers, Jensens, Imlers and Widneys. There were a couple of bachelors who called regularly Tom Stordy and Duncan MacMillan. Dunc has a way with words and we still get many good laughs out of his stories of the early days as well as his native Scotland.

We had a mixed farm, cattle, horses, sheep, chickens and milk cows. Allan grew mostly oats, barley and rye. We grew a big garden and milked a few cows. The kids all helped with chores. The boys helped with the field work when they had time and I drove the truck for harvest when they weren't there.

One episode remains etched on my memory. It was late September and we were combining. The weather forecast was for rain and Allan was hurrying to finish this one field so he could turn the cattle in for pasture. He and one of the boys came in with a truck full of grain to unload around 9 p.m. I went out to help Allan to unload and to take the truck back for the next load.

The night was pitch dark and the wind was blowing a near hurricane. We had to hold up a sheet of plywood to keep the grain from being blown out of the hopper before it was augered into the bin. Finally we got it unloaded and Allan drove the truck back out to the combine. He jumped on the combine and drove off up the field. After he reached the far end and headed back down the field I started the truck and followed him. I thought the truck didn't seem to have much get-up-and-go but decided the wind was holding us back. Anyway, when I reached the far end of the field and turned to come up behind the combine, I saw Allan in the lights of the combine, jump off and come racing toward me yelling and waving. I stopped the truck and got out to try and hear what he was saying. Then I saw the red glow coming from under the truck. I hadn't released the emergency brake and it had caught fire. He rolled under the truck and pounded the fire out with his mittened hands.

In his haste he had left the combine running so he shouted at me to pull the lever that would stop the cylinder. There were two levers side by side — one to operate the cylinder and one to unload the grain hopper.

You've guessed it. I pulled the wrong one and shot the combined grain out into a pile in the field. Allan finally got things back on an even keel and started down the field just as the rain hit with all its fury. We called it a night! Our marriage was a little shaky for a few days after that but I certainly was the one who went out the next day and gathered up that miserable pile of grain before the cows could be let in.

Bill attended N.A.I.T. where he took Gas Technology. He worked for Gulf Oils for six years. Now he and his wife, Penny Munn, farm at Delburne. They have three children — Scott, 8; Bonnie, 6; and Lana, 2.

Larry received his Bachelor of Science Degree in Geology from the U of A. He works for Pan Can Oils in Calgary. He and his wife Gloria Bruchal, have built a home on forty acres they bought from us. They have one girl, Erin, age three.

Colleen attended U of A for three years and received her diploma in physiotherapy. She worked in Saskatchewan for five years and last year she went back to University at Saskatoon to get her Bachelor of Science in Rehabilitative Medicine.

Jane has her Bachelor of Science degree as a Speech Therapist. She worked in the town of High River and at present is working in the city of Red Deer.

Marion attended U of C for a year where she studied Physical Training. Then she worked at landscaping and in a sports store in Calgary to earn money for a trip to Australia. This past year she has returned to U of C where she is just completing her second year of Physical Training.

Allan and I sold the home quarter of the Voss place and built a new home just across the road from Goettler's farm, in 1973. We still farm ½ section and run a few head of cattle. We plan on staying here as long as we are physically able. There is no place like the farm to live out one's years.

CHARLES MICHIE

Charlie Michie had homestead No. 39030, pre-sale No. 1829 and CPR Grant No. 1423 which consisted of the north half 6-21-1-W5 and NE¼-5-21-1-W5. Nothing is known of him other than a listing on an early survey map and the fact that this name appears on early hotel registers in Calgary.

LESTER A. AND MARJORIE (KIMMEL) MILLER — by Marjorie Miller

Lester Miller was born at Suffield, Alberta on December 9, 1914 and in December 1939 he married me, Marjorie Kimmel, of Carstairs.

After being hailed out for five successive years at Didsbury we decided it was time for a move so we purchased the E ½-28-20-1-W5 from Ken Doze. We moved to this farm west of Okotoks in December 1950.

In 1961 we sold the farm and bought a farm to the north E ½-33-20-1-W5, where we still live. Our place is known to old timers of the district as the "old Arnold" or the "Tom Stordy" place.

PERCY AND LIZZIE (COX) PEGLER — by Lizzie Pegler

Percy Pegler immigrated to Canada in 1911 from Gloucestershire, England. He came to Alberta and found work on a farm at Innisfail for two months. Then he went to Aldersyde to help with the threshing. When that was finished, he went to Sandstone and found a job cooking for thirteen men. In the spring of 1912, he started working in the brick yard for the Canada Cement Company at Sandstone.

Lizzie Cox immigrated to Canada from Gloucestershire, England in 1913, and was married to Percy Pegler the same year. We were married in St. Peter's Anglican Church in Okotoks. We lived at Sandstone until the brickyard closed down in 1914. Because of the war, a lot of the men enlisted, the rest had to find work elsewhere. Percy found work again on a farm, this time in the De Winton area. The next move for us was to Gleichen, Alberta.

In 1919, the brickyard started up again so in 1920 we moved back to Sandstone and Percy again worked in the factory until it closed down permanently, in 1923. The factory was dismantled and in 1925, Percy bought the land and farmed it until 1951, when he sold it to Mr. Rube Lynch and we moved to Okotoks to live.

Percy was janitor at the lower school, for eight years and he enjoyed the young children. He passed away in August, 1973. The new Elementary School is named in his honour.

Mr. and Mrs. Percy Pegler and three daughters, Winnifred, Ruby and Frances.

60th Wedding Anniversary, Percy and Lizzie Pegler, July 1st, 1973.

We had three daughters who were all born in Sandstone, and took their education at Panima School. This meant a three and one half mile ride on horseback.

They all live in the Okotoks district and are Winnie (Mrs. Thomas Hebson), Ruby (Mrs. Harold Cole), and Frances (Mrs. Alvie Tillotson). There are also four grandchildren and six great-grandchildren.

HARRY AND SYLVIA PETERSON — by Margaret Batycki

Harry and Sylvia Peterson came from the Gladys District in 1925 to the Cuffling place, now part of the Widney ranch. In 1929 they moved to the Donald Grey place on which the Panima school was located. They lived there until 1948 when they moved to Didsbury and finally, in the 1960's they moved to Calgary where they celebrated their 58th Wedding Anniversary. Both passed away in the Fall of 1973 at the ages of 83 and 85.

Their four children; Margaret, Jim, Ralph and Donald, all attended Panima School.

Margaret married Philip Batycki, who was well known in the De Winton and Okotoks districts. For many years they operated a shoe repair shop in South Calgary. They had three children; Robert, Ronald and Donna, all of whom are married. Philip passed away suddenly in April, 1969 and Margaret now resides in Big Valley, Alberta.

Jim married Eula Bert, spent most of his life farming, has no children.

Ralph served with the Canadian Airforce during WW2, went into the dry cleaning business where he did very well. Now resides in Victoria. Is married to Iris Bagnell and has one son, Richard.

Donald married Jackie Hilderbrandt of Winnipeg, has two sons, Douglas and John. Donald spent from age 23 to this last year in the Air Force, serving at Penhold, Winnipeg and now, Edmonton. He was on the Air Force search squadron, looking for lost planes for many years.

DANIEL AND MINNIE RHINE — by E. Hemus

Daniel was born, January 22, 1867, in Nashville, Illinois and Minnie was born, November 29, 1872. They were married in Nashville in December, 1887. There were four children; Jessie Leona, born June 28, 1889, married August John Voss in 1910 in Tekoa, Washington, and moved to Alberta where the Voss Brothers, Gus, Charlie and Ed built grain elevators. Gus retired in Calgary, deceased 1946 or 47, three children, Merle, Weldon and Hardin, all living in the States. Leona died in Calgary in 1974 and is buried in Spokane. The second daughter, Winnie Sybil, born November 30, 1892 had three children; Robert and Alfred (both deceased) and Harold, living in the States. Merle Lillian, born March 27, 1895, passed away in Wallace, Idaho in 1916. Lewis, born April 12, 1887, married Ethel Hemus in 1919, farmed near Okotoks, worked in Turner Valley, now lives in Innisfail. Has two children; Ronald and Florence. Ronald married Kathleen Ede of Nanton, after returning from war and is now principal of a school in Edmonton, has three children, David, Van and Louanne. Florence (Mrs. Dave Kerber) has three children, Terry, Susan and Jody, all of Okotoks.

To digress a little, Alfred and Robert attended Panima School. Miss Windle, now Mrs. J. Gallagher, was teacher and Alfred, then about eight years old, was very fond of her. He never left the school without saying a special "good-bye." One day she chastised him for something and he felt so badly that he couldn't say his good-bye so he got on his horse and, on passing the door, threw a note in, to express his sorrow and his good-bye. Alfred was killed at age ten, riding his horse. The horse put his foot in a badger hole and fell, the saddle horn punctured Alfred's lung and he died on the way to the hospital.

Minnie died in 1944 and Daniel died in 1946, both are buried in Spokane.

JIM AND FLO (MOORHOUSE) ROWAN — by Lorraine (McLean) Rowan; Assisted by Stan and Barb Rowan, June Kirkham, Bob and Frank Rowan.

The Rowans are very proud of their heritage and rightfully so. James Leonard Rowan's great grandfather, in 1790, received a "King's Grant", a strip of land one mile wide and two miles long, on the Ottawa River where the City of Pembroke, Ontario is now located. Jim's wife, Flo Moorhouse, was one of six children born to pioneer Robert Franklin Langford Moorhouse and wife Mary Louisa Whiting. Frank and brother Oscar owned two ranches; one at Carseland and the other, the "Bug" ranch, settled in 1888 situated between Calgary and Chestermere Lake became the most famous. Land at that time and in that area sold for twenty dollars a half section and cattle with the bug brand roamed the area. Flo's mother, Mary Louisa Whiting, had relatives that dated back to the United Empire Loyalists, so it is understandable why the Rowans have such pride in their pioneer forefathers.

Jim wandered westward from his home in Ontario and during the First World War saw action in England, France and Belgium with the Scottish 51st Highlanders of Winnipeg. After the war, Mr. Rowan ventured even further west and began work for Imperial Oil around 1920. His job took him from Ft. Norman to Jumping Pound to Turner Valley where he was well respected and well known as a quiet man who was fair to his men and was a hard working driller.

It was during this time that Jim met a small well refined lady, Florence Aileen Moorhouse, a registered nurse who had graduated from the Calgary General Hospital (in 1923); nursed in High River four years, attended college in California, and became the first female X-ray technician in the Calgary General Hospital where she was now employed. Her patients remember Flo as a very sensitive well liked girl who showed the good up-bringing of her venerable parents.

Florence and Jim were married in February of 1929. Their eldest son, James Stanley Langford, travelled with Mr. and Mrs. Rowan as Jim's job took him from Calgary to Turner Valley. Mrs. Rowan was another example of the pioneer women who were left behind during the thirties while her husband sought work with Imperial Oil in Nova Scotia. Dust and grasshoppers roamed the surrounding area and jobs were welcome wherever they could be had. After two years away from his family Jim returned home still

Florence and Jim Rowan at Banff.

with Imperial Oil and settled again in the Turner Valley area. It was then in 1932 that Jim and Flo gave birth to the second member of the family and eldest daughter, June Alberta.

Hillside Ranch, five miles straight west of Okotoks on the north side of the road, formerly owned by Tom Macmillan Sr. was purchased in July of 1940. Grandfather Moorhouse, having sold the Bug Ranch in 1912, now offered his bug brand to his son-in-law, Jim Rowan. Since the section was all grassland, the brand would become very useful.

It was at this time that the Rowans met a man who would play a very significant role in their family. Jack MacKenzie who had been the foreman on Tom Macmillan's section was riding over to see the new owners of the place, the Rowans. On his way, his horse, having one too many, slipped and Jack suffered a broken leg. So that year of 1942, Dunc McMillan, no relation and still a confirmed bachelor even at eighty, came to the Macmillan Ranch as foreman. Later he became a very close friend of Jim and Flo Rowan and chief babysitter of Hillside Ranch for Robert Franklin was born in 1940, Mary Jo in 1943 and Frank Warren in 1947.

The pasture of Hillside Ranch was rented to the Macmillans under the watchful eye of Dunc who previously travelled a government Clydesdale stud. Hardy Salter, a well known horse breeder of the time, grazed and raised the finest purebred Percheron horses on this site. From his stud, Glen Laet, a beautiful mare, Star Laet, won awards at the Toronto Royal, in the United States and world wide. Constant humorous rivalry existed between the owners of these two breeds of horses as to which member of the equine family could pull the most, which temperament was

Mr. and Mrs. Moorhouse with grandchildren, Stan, Bob and June Rowan.

better and whose foot was biggest. It was when Mr. Rowan quit the oil fields in 1944 that he purchased, from Roy Widney Sr., Pinky and Dixie as brood mares and work horses; and what an impressive team they were!

It was then that Jim and Flo stamped their bug brand on Hereford cattle and Jim, with son Stan, began to break land. It was the Rowans, Widneys and MacDonalds that formed the harvest crew. Its at this time that Dunc tells of how the crew would come in from the field dusty and dirty and how Mrs. Rowan always made sure there was a clean linen table cloth on the table and plenty of good food to eat.

The old 1934 Massey Harris tractor with continental motor made the mixed farming a little easier where barley, oats, cattle, horses and chickens became a way of life.

The house having been severely hit by lightning was somewhat a chilly place for Flo and her family so the Rowans moved to Okotoks and Jim commuted to the farm daily.

When Mrs. Rowan took fatally ill and passed away in 1956, Mary, their youngest daughter, lived with Doctors Janet and Morris Gibson while the two youngest sons, Bob and Frank lived with their father on the farm. However, Jim also turned ill and was forced to sell the farm in 1961 to John and Pat Legge, now of Boulder, Colorado. Jim Rowan died in November of 1965.

However, the children of this fine family still live on; Stan, June and Bob of Calgary, Mary of Toronto and Frank of De Winton. Oh yes, and one life member of the family adopted by the offspring, their excellent babysitter, Dunc McMillan.

ALONZO SERVISS — by A. Muriel McCord

My grandfather, Alonzo Serviss, and his son, Cyrus, came west from Brockville, Ontario, in 1898 or '99, with the intention of farming. However, when they saw the clay and the quantities of pure water available on their land (three springs on one quarter section), they immediately lost interest in farming. In the east they had been bricklayers by trade, and had worked in brick yards, so that is where their interests lay.

Alonzo Serviss.   Cyrus E. Serviss, 1899.

The C.P.R. laid a spur line into the brick yard and they shipped bricks all around Alberta. Several buildings still standing in Calgary, (among them, the Underwood Block), were built with Grandpa's bricks. In Okotoks, the United Church and several homes on the main street were built by my Grandfather, utilizing his bricks.

I must disgress here to tell of an incident which is amusing, to me anyway. My father was working in Detroit and mailed my mother's engagement ring to her. To avoid paying duty, he rolled it inside a newspaper. The day the paper arrived in Okotoks, Grandpa picked up the mail but forgot to take it home after work. The paper lay out on top of the church wall all night, Mother's diamond and all.

My mother, Agnes Serviss, and my grandmother, came to join Grandpa and Uncle Cy, about a year later, bringing Grandpa's mother with them. Mother taught school at Panima School that first year, but she decided the salary of $200.00 per year was quite unsatisfactory, and returned to Brockville, to take a business course. When she came back to Okotoks, she worked in Mahon's store, as bookkeeper, until she left for Detroit to marry my father, in 1907.

Grandma's brother, John Shields, came out to help

with the brick yard. He and Aunt Grace, later lived in Okotoks where they raised two daughters. Mildred, married Pat Windal and lived at the Oilfields and are now living at Red Deer. Evelyn, was a school teacher. She married Fred Cameron, Royalite Manager. They live in Calgary and celebrated their 50th wedding anniversary in November, 1975.

James, (Jimmie) Hughes was another worker from the east. He stayed with my grandparents even after the brick yard closed. His brother, Pete, worked for the Town of Okotoks and raised a family there.

Some of the neighbors whose names I remember are; Stockton, and later Bishop, on the same farm, Gough, Laycock, Duncan, Biddle. The latter were an English couple who, with their daughter, Eileen, lived on the farm previously owned by the Thompsons.

Uncle Cy married Elizabeth, "Lizzie" Thompson. By 1909 or '10, larger brickyards were operating at Sandstone, so, my uncle and his wife left Okotoks and went farming at Bulwark. Grandpa then contented himself with farming too, and the brickyard was demolished.

My parents, Jack and Agnes Cowan, came to the farm when Grandpa found it too difficult to carry on alone, in December 1921.

My brothers, Arnold and Donald, my sister, Eileen, and I, all attended Okotoks School. Father bought a pony from Mary Hayes and Grandpa built us a two wheeled cart to drive. A far cry from the modern school vans today! Maybe our classmates will remember the run away, every day after school, until 'Molly' finally settled down to the harness.

Farming was not my father's forte as he was a tool and die maker by trade. He moved the family to Calgary in 1926, and my grandparents went with them. My parents and grandparents have all passed away, all of them reached their eighties or nineties. We of the younger generation, are now growing old, with grandchildren of our own.

Perhaps I should mention that my grandparents first came west at the persuasion of Grandma's sister and brother-in-law, Mr. and Mrs. Robert Shields, of Davisburg.

THOMAS STORDY

Born in Carlyle, Cumberland, England to a family that were quite well to do. He was of Quaker religion. Settled on land around the Coronation district with a partner Larkin Collins. Tom farmed and Larkin had a business in Calgary. After several years of being dried out, Tom gave up and came to the Okotoks district to farm. He purchased the E½ 33-20-1-W5 from Victor Arnold.

In the early years Tom farmed with horses and later he purchased a tractor. He grew grain and also raised hogs. He liked cats and always had quite a number in the house for company. He always had a dog, quite often a female, so he usually had pups to give away.

Tom was a great visitor and, in his younger years, he would walk three or four miles to a neighbour, and often rode a horse to the Millarville Fair. This was one event that he always planned on attending as he enjoyed visiting with the people. He contributed to the Millarville Fair and most of the other causes in the neighborhood. Later he had a car but if the conditions didn't allow him to use it, he would go visiting with the tractor.

He lived across the road from the Panima school so was interested in the activities that went on there. Most of the teachers didn't have cars so he offered them rides to the bus or other places.

As he grew older, he developed asthma and it was necessary for him to have the neighbours work his land, grind grain for the hogs and do various other jobs for him. He finally rented his land and went to live in the hotel in Okotoks.

In 1959 he sailed to England but was very ill with asthma attacks. He spent Christmas with his sister in England but was there less than a year when he passed away in 1960. J. B. Cross purchased this parcel of land.

THE VANDERPLOEG FAMILY — as told by Leonard Vanderploeg

My father, Carl, came to Canada, from Holland, in 1911, first to the Okotoks and later, the Black Diamond, area where he worked in the creamery for 18 months. In December of 1913 he went back to Holland and married Jennie Liersma. They returned to the Black Diamond district where they worked on a dairy farm, milking up to 75 cows and also working in the creamery.

In 1927, my parents, with four children, moved to the Panima School District to farm SE¼ and NE¼-34-20-1-W5 which belonged to Mr. August John Voss. We rented it for one year and that year we had the promise of a very rewarding crop, oats stubbled in on 25 acres of willow back-setting and wheat, on breaking, all coming along so bountifully until — the hail season hit!! Hail storms hit three times in 1927 and one storm, accompanied by a cyclone, struck and completely demolished two granaries and left us with memories never to be forgotten. These storms missed our crop on NW¼-3-21-1-W5 but, early snow fell and flattened the whole crop in the field. It delayed harvesting and the crop had to be cut one way, when possible, then, more moisture and a delay in threshing until winter settled in and the crop lay under the snow for months to come.

My sister, Annie, and I attended Panima School and our teacher for the spring of 1927 was Clayton Hicks of Okotoks and, for the spring of 1928, Miss Margaret Scott of Calgary. We left the Voss farm in 1928 and moved to Brant, Alberta where we farmed for twenty years.

Mother and Father had five children; I, Leonard, was born in 1914, Annie in 1916, Juka in 1921, Elizabeth in 1924 and Simon in 1931. My father passed away on October 23, 1948 and Mother is a resident of Medicine Tree Manor in High River.

In 1942 I married Kathleen Jordan of Prince Albert, Saskatchewan and we farmed at Brant until 1945 when we purchased NW¼ and SE¼-2-19-26-W4, near Blackie and here we farmed for 26 years as well as milking cows and raising pigs.

We have five children; Ann (Gourley), a trained nurse, has three daughters, lives with her husband, in Cochrane, Alberta. Kathy (Perryman), lives on our home quarter, has five children. Johnny, a tradesman in High River, married with two boys. Len, single, is assistant Pastor at Queen's Park Full Gospel Church in Calgary after graduating from Eastern Bible College in 1975. Ralph married Joan Yauck of Calgary and is a tradesman in that city. Andrew lives at home.

We retired from farming in 1975, due to ill health, and presently reside in High River.

WIDNEY (ROY JESSE AND FAMILY)

The Widney Ranch, originally the "Old Gier Ranch", was acquired by Roy Jesse Widney, Sr., in 1936. The ranch was owned by Livingstone and he traded it to Mr. Widney for a farm at Trochu.

Roy Widney, Sr., was born in Dry Run, Pennsylvania in 1886. At age nineteen he moved to Bakersfield, California, where he became an oilfield driller. In 1911 he came to Alberta in search of the much publicised C.P.R. land. Unable to obtain any land he headed for the just discovered Turner Valley oilfield and was one of the pioneer oilmen of that area, drilling the second producing well, "The Old Southern Alberta".

In 1919 he married Irene Elizabeth Wilkinson of Leamington. Ontario and moved to Langley Prairie, B.C. to further oil exploration. There, three children were born; Archie (Bud), Daniel Roy of Ardrossan and Norma Irene (Mrs. Harry Alger), who now resides on the "Old Hunt Estates".

In 1945, Archie (Bud) came to the Ranch and is still residing there with his wife, Geraldine Claire (formerly Watchorn of Turner Valley.) Three children were born of this marriage: Lynn Elizabeth (Logace) of Camrose; Lee Louise (Vosburg) of Edmonton and Roy Jesse Jr., who married Dianna Graham of Quesnel, B.C. and is now operating the Widney Ranch.

This is the third generation of Widneys on this place. The ranch home is on Section 6-21-1W5.

To my recollection, the neighbors of the present ranch were L. W. Barrett of Aldersyde, Ike and Kean Kaplan, Mr. and Mrs. G. Kelson, Thomas MacMillan, the Jim Rowans, Art Hall on the original Turner Ranch, Sinclair-Smith, to the west — Alf. Heitzman, the Roberts and Shiermans and to the north — John Gerlitz. Through the years the ranch acquired the Kaplan and old Harry Barker place — also known as the Bob MacIlbride place, also land from Tom and Albert Sandeman and the old original water quarter. The original tenant of the ranch was Oscar Olson of Carseland and a couple who were employed by Roy Widney, Sr. was Annie and Mel Wilford of Okotoks.

Under some of the stormy conditions of the '40s and '50s some of the winter nights might have been long and lonely had it not been for our friendly councillor, Gene Goettler. Another fond recollection of this era was our faithful school bus driver, Fred Pryce, who managed to transport our children through adverse conditions to Okotoks school for some fourteen years.

Others who lived in the Panima district but Sent No History and are Not Mentioned in the School Lists.
Jim Beattie; Sid Bird; Boggs, Lucille. Davis; Stan Edwards; Bob Eccelles; Grenek; Heater; Kneofli; Huckvale; Lomas; Larson; Mason; McMillan; McKinnon; Nagel; Nicholson; Miller; McLeod; Stordy; Thompson; Westlake, Bill and Maude; West, Charlie; Ruzicki; Rimmer; Also Howard Appletoft; Lena Parnell (Tims); Lucy; Frank Michuich; Frank Strow and Alf Woods.
From Sandstone: Bereski; Bishop, carried the mail; Blades; Dick Bradley; Eccles; Pete Hughes; Frank Hamlin; A. W. Pegler, brother of Percy; George Strange; Leo Moerton; Harry Peachy; Snazel; Jim Thomas; Lindenburger, about 1900.

Old Houses

Forest Herr house.

Bill Stewart's home in Davisburg, 1900.

Jack McInnes homestead, Late 1890's. Charlie Marshall on horse, McInnes family in doorway.

John Currie house, 1901.

John Meehan's ranch; l. to r. Jack McInenly, Frank Percy, Dan McInenly, John Meehan.

The farm house as it looked when Mr. and Mrs. J. Hambling moved to Red Deer Lake April 23, 1936.

Wonacott log house.

Log house on the Peter McArthur place — Thiessen family.

Archie Bremner's original homestead April, 1915.

Upright log wall in Anderson house.

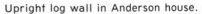

F. Barker farm house on the home place.

Stopping House on Macleod Trail. The old Anderson house.

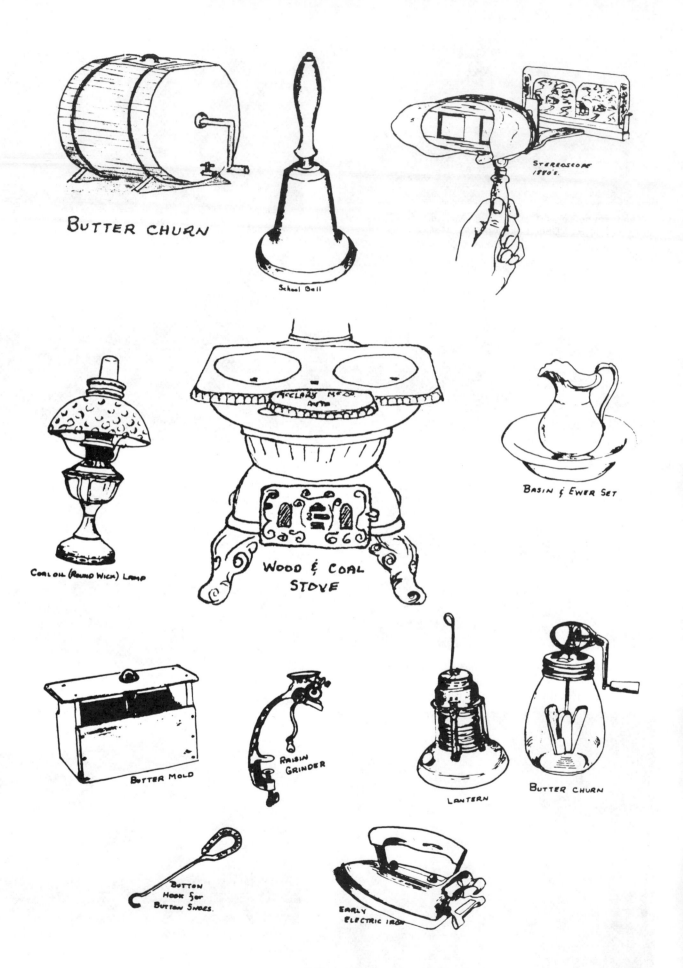

BUTTER CHURN

School Bell

Stereoscope 1880's.

Coal Oil (Round Wick) Lamp

Wood & Coal Stove

Basin & Ewer Set

Butter Mold

Raisin Grinder

Lantern

Butter Churn

Button Hook for Button Shoes.

Early Electric Iron

"GOPHER" (RICHARDSONS' GROUND SQUIRREL)

SKUNK

RED FOX

WHITE TAILED DEER

MOOSE

DISTRESS HORN CURRIE PRE 1896

"GRAYLING"

RAINBOW TROUT

345

PINE CREEK S.D. NO. 84

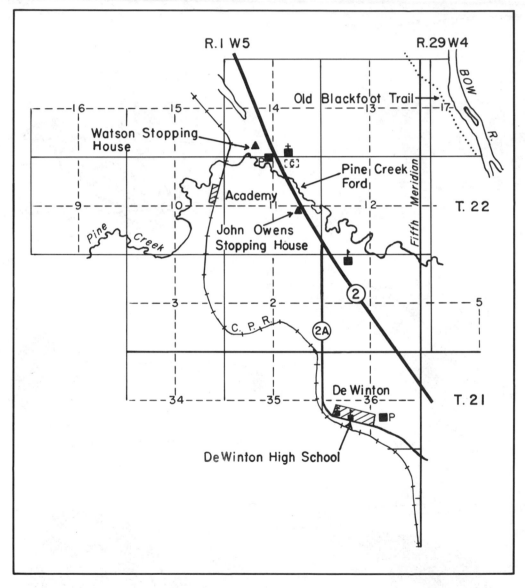

Pine Creek School District

PINE CREEK SCHOOL DISTRICT NO. 84 — by R. Lynch

The first recorded meeting of Pine School District was held in the school house located on the S.E. corner, S. 16, Tp. 22, R. 1, W5. The minutes of the meeting were as follows: ''Jan. 30th, 1897

The meeting was called to order at 2 p.m. Mr. Wolley-Dod stated that he had been asked by the parents of some of the children who had lately come to reside in the district to call this meeting for the purpose of ascertaining whether there were sufficient

children in the district to warrant the re-opening of the school, and had posted the usual notices calling such meeting. It was proposed and carried that Mr. Wolley-Dod be chairman of the meeting and Mr. Hooley be sec'ty. After some discussion it was decided to re-open the school and to leave the period for which it was to be opened to the trustees when elected.

The following names were then proposed as trustees in the order named, and as only three names were submitted they were declared duly elected: Mr. Wolley-Dod, Mr. Brogden and Mr. Douglas.

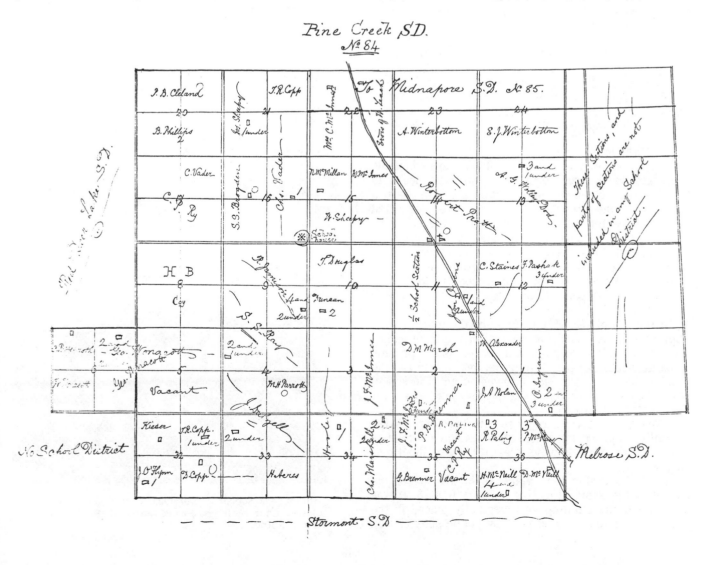

The meeting was then closed.

Mr. Richard Paling was elected auditor. A. G. Wolley-Dod, Chairman.''

"Jan. 30th, 1897

The trustees then met at the same time and place and by unanimous consent suspended clause 78 in order to transact business with as little delay as possible. Mr. Brogden was elected chairman and Mr. Wolley-Dod Secretary-Treasurer.

The secretary was instructed to write to the Department of Education, asking for the necessary forms and papers, to procure an assessment roll and a seal for the district.

It was decided to open the school for eight months commencing April 12th.

The secretary was instructed to advertise in both papers for a teacher at a sum not to exceed $40 per month and also for tenders for the necessary repairs on buildings, viz. , new foundations, fixing doors, windows, and outhouses. Mr. Paling was appointed assessor. S. S. Brogden, Chairman
A.G. Wolley-Dod, Sec.''

At this time the Department of Education was located at Regina, N.W.T.

"May 3, 1897

The trustees sat as a court of revision on the above date. There were two appeals, one from Mr. Duke who claimed he was not a resident, and the other from Mr. Cleland who claimed that he had been overassessed for one cow and that $75 had been put upon the buildings, more than in former years, and that the buildings had not been altered during that time.

The former was struck off the roll, and the latter allowed the claim. S. S. Brogden, Chairman
A. G. Wolley-Dod, Sec.''

"June 30th, 1897

A meeting was held on the above date when the secretary was instructed to obtain two more desks, to have the well cleaned, and to obtain a bell, a chair, a blackboard, and a few books of reference as suggested by the inspector. The well had been ordered to be cleaned and the pump repaired at the previous meeting and the secretary reported progress.

The inspector complained of the roof, but as it was watertight it was considered unneccessary to meddle with it. S. S. Brogden, Chairman
A. G. Wolley-Dod, Sec.''

In the fall of 1897, Miss Macklin (the teacher) had applied to be released for the rest of the term as she was most anxious to go east at once. As the parents were agreeable to Mr. Paling being engaged for the rest of the term, she was allowed to go. The school would be closed as soon as the weather got too bad for the children to attend.

"The trustees were requested to consider the advisability of procuring a coal stove, in place of the box stove, as there was always great difficulty about getting wood.''

Some discussion took place as to the site of the school at the annual meeting January 6, 1898. It was stated that the building was originally placed in the centre of the district and built by public subscription

and did not really belong to the present trustees, who had only possession by the sanction of the trustees of the building. The latter appeared to be quite willing to allow the school to be held there as the building was not used for any other purpose. The secretary-treasurer was voted $40 for his services to the end of the year and also allowed 5% for collected taxes.

The school tax rate was struck at two mills in 1900.

At the annual meeting January 24th, 1901,
"After considerable discussion it was unanimously decided not to tax buildings and improvements in the future, but only land and stock. This was moved by Mr. Owens and seconded by Mr. Dalzell.''

The year 1902 was one of plans and activity regarding a new school. The original boundaries were

Pine Creek School 1902 or 1903. L. to R. Tom Kelly, Bill McInnes, Chas McInnes, Frank Marshall, Earle Marshall, Francis McInnes.

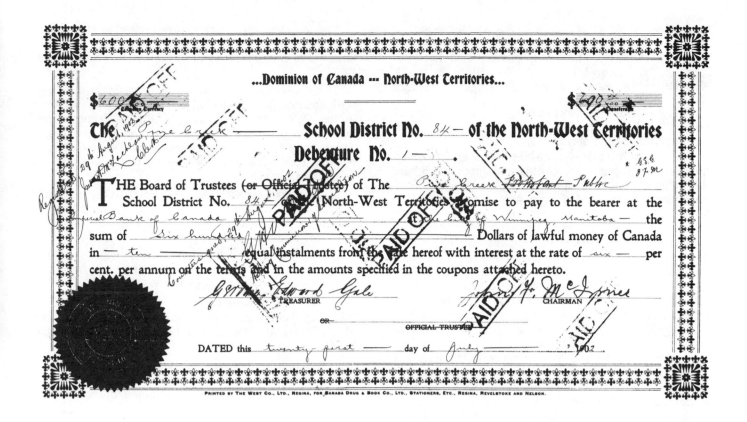

Coupon No. 20... Debenture No. 1....
The Board of Trustees (or Official Trustee) of the Pine Creek Public School District No. 84 of the North-West Territories will pay to the bearer at the bank of Canada at Winnipeg Man on the twenty-first day of July 1913 the sum of $3.00 dollars, being the first payment with the total interest at

changed by process of a committee petitioning the Council of Public Instruction. Actually the district then would not extend so far to the west and north as it did originally. It was felt if the school was located south of Pine Creek it would prove to be a more central location. At the time, the children of the Hugh McNeill's and O. Ingram's were attending classes at Melrose School for it was closer, but were also paying school taxes to Pine Creek School District, which were later refunded to them.

As the board was unable to obtain a satisfactory title to the new site chosen for a school at SW corner, Sec. 12, Tp. 22, R. 1, W5, it was decided to locate the school building on an acre of ground situated on NW corner, Sec. 1 Tp. 22, R. 1, W5, "and immediately south of site heretofore chosen."

The Toronto Loan Co. was asked to furnish debentures to build the new school in the amount of $600.00 at 6% per annum for ten years and to furnish the form free of charge to the district.

The contract for building the school was given to Mr. Minue of Okotoks whose tender was $692.00. It was proposed that Mr. Minue come to DeWinton to sign the contract.

In the meantime, Mr. Paling's offer (August 22, 1902) of the use of the west wing of his residence as a temporary schoolroom was accepted (located near NW corner NW ¼, Sec. 36, Tp. 21, R. 1, W5). "The secretary (Rev. Gale) was asked to communicate with Messrs. McArthur and Brogden, the trustees of the old school building, asking permission to hand over the said building to the present trustees of the school district in order that they might sell the same and devote the funds to the school district."

It is understood that the building remained vacant for a number of years and was finally sold to Chas. Vader who used it for a cow barn.

The annual meeting of ratepayers was held in the new school house on Wednesday, January 14th, 1903. The taxation rate was to be 3½c per acre for that year. A motion was made that one-half of the government grant earned by the district on the basis of the inspector's reports be expended on books for the school library.

At a meeting of the school board November 24th, 1906 "Moved by Chas. Vader, seconded by J. F. McInnes, that tenders be called for a shed twelve feet wide by twenty-four feet long, seven feet high, to be covered with shiplap with shingled roof and two doors." This would be the barn that served at that school for years, then was moved over to the next school yard when another school was built in 1930.

At the same meeting, the motion was made to re-engage the present teacher for the year 1907 at a salary of six hundred dollars per annum, provided she agreed to open the school at half past nine during the winter months and took no more than one hour at noon. This would be Miss M. Cardiff, who must have been agreeable, for she stayed until the end of 1907.

At the March 30th, 1911 meeting it was moved by Robt. Dalzell, seconded by Chas. Marshall, that the following names be added to the assessment roll as owners of lots in the De Winton survey: Peter Murray — Lots 17-20, Block 1; T. E. Streeter — Lots 14-15,

Block 2 and Lots 11-16, Block 1; E. A. McDougall — Lots 9-10, Block 1; W. R. McDonald — Lots 5-6, Block 2; Frank Pashak — Lots 5-6, Block 3 and Lots 1-2, Block 2; Nick Kurylyk — Lots 3-4, Block 2; W. V. Mencke — 1½ acres; Alonzo DeMings — ½ acre Block 5.

This DeWinton survey, making it a subdivision of SW¼, 36-21-1-5, at the time owned by Hugh McNeill, was registered on February 28th, 1907.

The school interior meanwhile had been freshened up with a paint job — the ceiling and upper walls pale blue, lower part of walls a light brown. More blackboards were added plus new maps and extra desks. Most school supplies were ordered from Christies School Supplies in Brandon, Manitoba.

Miss Margaret Teskey was engaged as teacher for 1914 at $720.00 per annum. She noted daily weather conditions, news items or local happenings in the daily register, as well as the children's roll call.

In 1915 the tax rate was still 6½c as was decided in 1911. The DeWinton lot owners were required to pay the magnificent sum of 25c on lots less than one acre and 50c on lots of one acre or more.

As there was never a teacherage with the school, it was customary for the teachers to board with families in the community who had available space and were within walking distance of the school

In 1917 Mr. J. H. Evans was elected Secretary-Treasurer tax collector, assessor, and was also to look after school supplies, at the same salary ($60.00). This position he continued to hold until the end of the local school board.

Pine Creek School about 1917: back: Earl Brinton, Victor Poffenroth, Della Bryan, Georgie Warrack, Marjorie Marshall, Jack Warrack, Alex Hislop, Front: Wenty Brinton, Violet Poffenroth, Dolly Warrack, Violet Hislop, Lucy Brinton.

"It was moved by Chas. Marshall, seconded by F. Tindal, that the stove belonging to the school be donated to the Community Hall at DeWinton. Carried." The above notation is from the annual meeting of ratepayers, January 11, 1919, which was the year the new hall was built. School taxes jumped to 9c per acre.

The 1920's saw the beginning of the local school fair — a day set aside in September to show the work of pupils from Melrose, Stormont, Alexandra, and Pine Creek schools. The board usually contributed $20.00 toward the fair's expenses. De Winton High would later join them.

The ladies of the district were invited to attend the ratepayers meetings, which resulted in Mrs. S. Sutherland being elected to office as chairwoman for 1926.

Tom Dalzell started his trucking business, hauling milk and cream, etc., to Calgary and bringing supplies to the DeWinton Store, and he always dropped the local village children off at school in the morning. They would find their own way home. Other children walked, rode horseback, or drove a buggy in summer or sleigh in winter.

High School fees for Ena Bailley at Central High School in Calgary for the term September to December 1926 amounted to $12.00 and were paid by the local school board.

School was closed for three or four weeks during the fall of 1927 due to the epidemic of infantile paralysis and sleeping sickness.

Grade nine was included for the 1929-30 term. The following year high school classes were held in the Minto House at DeWinton while the school was being built.

It was found necessary to build a new school at Pine Creek so the trustees applied to the Utility Commissioners for permission to sell debentures in the amount of $3,000.00.

The contract to build the school was awarded to John M. Ladner, Calgary, July 14, 1930 — the building to be completed by August 25, 1930 — for the sum of $3,118.00.

It was located in SW corner, 12-22-1-5, and the barn from the former school was moved there. The old school was demolished —only the cement foundations remain. About that time, highway No. 2 was re-routed and by-passed DeWinton. The teacher's salary was $800.00, then later $840.00.

About 1935 the board paid $4.00 for having the walls washed and the floor scrubbed and oiled. Re-setting some fence posts, stretching 80 yards of wire, and hanging a small gate was $3.50.

Several unsuccessful attempts to find water were made — quicksand was thought to be the reason for failure. Arrangements had to be made to have water brought to the school.

A piano was purchased in 1938 for $85.00.

For years the school district had land included in the Stockland M.D. No. 191 and the Sheep Creek M.D. No. 190. During 1938 the School District was under the Calgary School Division No. 41.

Eventually Pine Creek, along with other local schools, became part of the Foothills School Division. Most of the one-room schools were closed and the pupils bused to Okotoks. Pine Creek, however, remained open with Grades 1-6 being taught. Mrs. Mary Poffenroth was the teacher when its doors finally closed on June 30, 1961.

The school building was sold to Mr. and Mrs. A. Strachan and moved to their adjoining property in November 1974, where it rests against a background of trees, the large windows facing west. The wobbly old barn of 1906 vintage stands alone in the school yard.

Pine Creek School. Back row: Albert Van Tighem, Tom King, Jack Evans, Margaret Welsh, teacher, Jean Van Tighem, Melvina Fox, Doreen Minor, Vera Fox. Centre row: Robert Van Tighem, Ronald Martin, Robert Martin, Vera Evans, Shirley Jamison, Audrey Jamison, Lorena Fox, Alice Evans, Sheila Marshall. Front row: Bernard Van Tighem, Lloyd Fox, Andrew Wilson, Jimmie Marshall, David Evans. 1941-42.

Pine Creek School — 1954. Standing — Left to right: Teacher, Mrs. Margaret Norris, Bonnie Poffenroth, Jacqueline Harmatta, Josephine Van Tighem, Myrna Marshall, Alice Van Tighem, Glen Norris, Ronald Graham, Wayne Vold, Brian Horsfield, Brian Myers, Jack Altenhoven, Raymond Gorrall, Henry Altenhoven. Seated at desks (in front of teacher) Rita Gorrall, Nancy Altenhoven, Jeannine Harmatta, Kathleen Marshall, Kathy Harmatta. Seated (back row) Donna Anderson, Allan Norris, Frances Gorrall. Seated (second row) Raymond Van Tighem, Lynne Horsfield. Seated (third row) Dennis Poffenroth, Keith Graham, Lorne Jamison. Seated (fourth row) Lee Jamison, Norma Myers, Linda Knupp.

PINE CREEK S.D. No. 84
TEACHERS
1897 — Miss Macklin (to Nov. 15) Mr. Paling finished the year.
1899 — Miss Robinson
1900 — Miss Williams
1902 — Patrick Monaghan
1902 — Miss Fyfe ($40.00 per month)
1903 — James Weir (Sept.-Dec.)
1904 — Alice M. Gillis (Jan.-Sept.)
1904 — Beenie A. Matheson (Oct.-Dec.)
1905 — Beenie A. Matheson (Jan.-June)
1906-7 — Mayme Cardiff ($650.00 per year)
1908-9 — Miss Margaret Stevenson
1911 — Miss Grace B. Davis (Mrs. G. B. Latimer)
1912 — Miss E. Stubbs ($660.00)
1913 — Miss Margaret M. Johnson
1914-15 — Miss Margaret Teskey ($720.00) (Mrs. Johnson)
1916 — Miss E. Bruce
1919-20 — Miss E. Lowrie (Aug.-June)
1920-21 — Marie C. Cameron
1921-22 — Lola V. Grant
1922-23 — Jessie E. Moodie (Aug.-Mar.)
1923 — M. A. McIsaac (Apr.-June)
1923-24 — Mrs. Ethel Gier
1924-25 — Vera E. Marshall
1925-26 — Muriel Davidson (school started Sept. 8th)
1926-27 — Rhoda M. Rouse
1927-29 — Mrs. Blanche Heaton
1929 — Mary W. Daggett (Sept.-Dec.) (Mrs. M. Wild)
1930-39 — G. M. Thomas (Jan.) (Mrs. Kelson)
1939-40 — Mona Ward
1940-41 — Mona Ward
1941-42 — Margaret Welsh
1942-43 — Elinor M. Blake
1943-44 — Lorraine Bourque
1944-45 — Lorraine Bourque
1945-46 — Audrey Lynn
1946-47 — Mrs. Chadney
1947-48 — Elinor Blake
1948-49 — Miss Pierce
1949-50 — M. Garner
1950-51 — May Kenny
1951-53 — E. Eroshinsky
1953-59 — Margaret Norris
1959-61 — Mary Poffenroth

CHAIRMEN
1897 - S. S. Brogden; 1902 - J. F. McInnes; 1904 - Frank Pashak; 1905 - P. M. Kelly; 1914 - J. H. Evans; 1917 - A. T. Dalzell; 1918 - Chas. Marshall; 1920 - A. H. Bryan; 1922 - W. C. Standish; 1923 - H. Graham; 1924 - A. Anderson; 1926 - Mrs. S. Sutherland; 1927 - S. Jamison; 1935 - W. B. King;

SECRETARY-TREASURERS
1897 - Arthur Wolley-Dod; 1902 - Duncan J. Rose; 1902 - Rev. Gervaise Edward Gale; 1904 - Owen King; 1910 - W. G. King; 1917 on - J. H. Evans

AUDITORS
1897 - Mr. R. Paling; 1898 - W. Phillips; 1899 - A. Pratt; 1900 - R. Pratt; 1901 - James Brogden; 1902 - D. J. Rose; 1911 - Geo C. S. Paterson; 1912 - W. R. Macdonald.

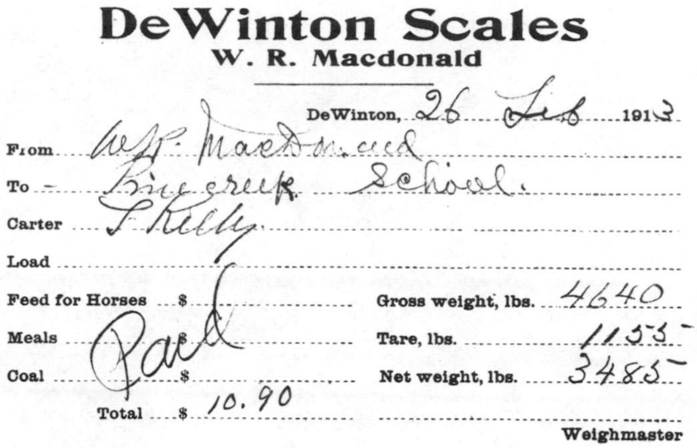

DeWinton Scales
W. R. Macdonald

DeWinton, 26 Feb 1913

From _W. R. Macdonald_
To — _Pine Creek School._
Carter _S. Kelly_
Load
Feed for Horses $
Meals $ _Paid_
Coal $

Gross weight, lbs. _4640_
Tare, lbs. _1155_
Net weight, lbs. _3485_

Total $ _10.90_

Weighmaster

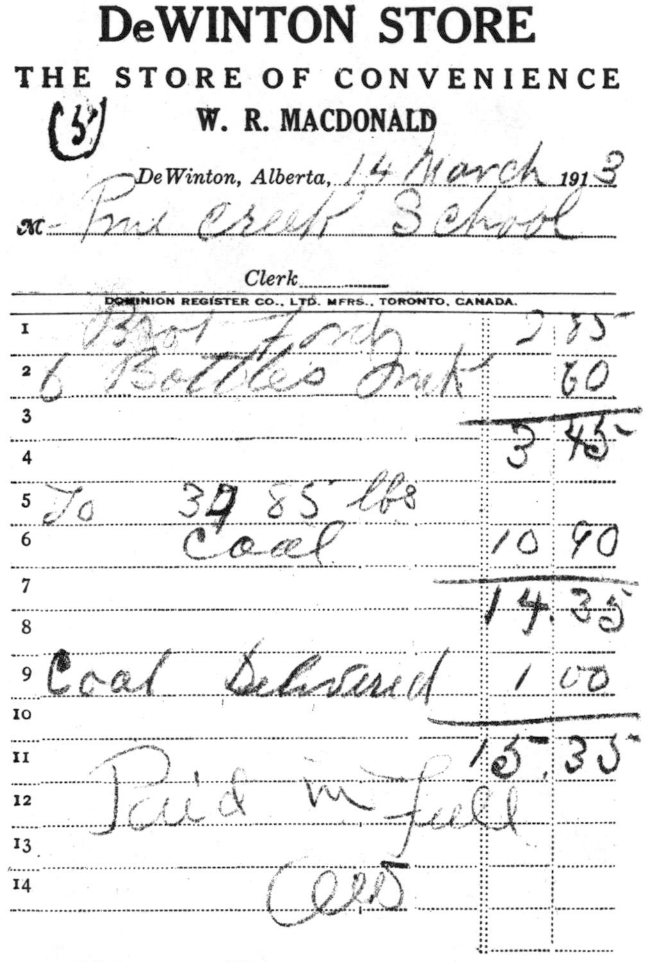

DeWINTON STORE
THE STORE OF CONVENIENCE
W. R. MACDONALD

DeWinton, Alberta, _14 March_ 1913

M _Pine Creek School_

Clerk _____

DOMINION REGISTER CO., LTD. MFRS., TORONTO, CANADA.

1	Boot Jack	2.85
2	6 Bottles Ink	60
3		
4		3.45
5	To 3785 lbs	
6	Coal	10.90
7		14.35
8		
9	Coal delivered	1.00
10		
11		15.35
12	Paid in full	
13		
14		

№ 9

TRUSTEES (usually elected for 3-year term)
1897 - A. Wolley-Dod; 1897 - S. S. Brogden; 1897 - T. Douglas; 1898 - G. Wonacott; 1899 - S. S. Brogden; 1900 - A. G. Wolley-Dod; 1901 - J. F. McInnes; 1902 - D. J. Rose; 1903 - C. Vader; 1903 - F. Pashak; 1904 - A. P. Bremner; 1905 - P. M. Kelly; 1906 - Chas. Vader; 1907 - Geo. H. Dunfield; 1908 - P. M. Kelly; 1909 - R. Dalzell; 1910 - Chas. Marshall; 1911 - Wm. Anderson; 1913 - J. H. Evans; 1914 - Chas. Marshall; 1915 - T. Dalzell; 1916

Pine Creek S. D. No. 84

Attendance for the Month of May 1914

PUPIL'S REGISTER No.	AGE	STANDARD	NAMES OF PUPILS	Total
1	14	VIII.	Vera Marshall	19
2	15	VIII.	June Marshall	19
3	14	VIII.	Eleanor Gray	18
4	13	VII.	Bert King	19
5	11	VI.	Leslie Marshall	19
6	9	IV.	Marjorie Marshall	18
7	15	IV.	Byron Crowell	
8	11	IV.	Harry Gammond	15
9	14	IV.	Orton Crowell	4.5
10	12	IV-V.	Barton Evans	17
11	11	II.	Eugene Crowell	7
12	8	II.	Kenneth Pollard	18
13	9	I.	Earle Crowell	7
14	6	I.	Harry Pollard	18

TOTAL DAILY ATTENDANCE: 13, 11, 12½, 12, 10, 13, 13, 10, 11, 10, 9, 7, 10, 9, 8, 10, 9, 10 — 198.5

Weather notes (by day): Warm. Sunny. / Cold north wind. / Cold. Cloudy. / Warm. Sunny. / Cloudy A.M. Dalgells funeral. / Arbor Day. / Sunny — Windy (Flowers in to seed) / Warm. Cloudy P.M. / Warm. Sunny. / Warm. Windy. (Oil at Black Diamond P.M.) / Cloudy. / Warm. Sunny. / Cloudy. / Rain. / Sunny A.M. Rain P.M. / Sunny A.M. Cloudy P.M. / Victoria Day. / Sunny. Warm. / Windy. Dusty. / Sunny. Warm. / Sunny. Warm.

Aggregate attendance for the month... 13

I hereby certify that the above record of attendance is correct in every particular.

...... Margaret Teskey ......
Teacher.

No. of teaching days school was open during the month. 19

Aggregate days' attendance for the month. 198.5

Average attendance for the month... 10.44

Percentage of attendance for the month. 80.30

- J. H. Evans; 1917 - Chas. Marshall; 1918 - T. Dalzell; 1919 - A. H. Bryan; 1919 - F. Tindal; 1920 - H. Pakenham; 1920 - H. Graham; 1921 - W. C. Standish; 1922 - A. Anderson; 1923 - A. H. Bryan; 1924 - Mrs. Sutherland; 1925 - Stuart Jamison; 1926 - Geo. Anderson; 1927 - R. Collins; 1928 - S. Jamison; 1929 - H. Harper; 1931 - Geo. Anderson; 1933 - John McNeill; 1933 - A. Van Tighem; 1934 - W. B. King; 1935 - E. Bremner; 1936 - A. Van Tighem; 1937 - W. B. King; 1937 - C. L. Marshall; 1938 - E. Bremner; 1939 - C. L. Marshall.

MISS MARGARET TESKEY (JOHNSON) — by R. Lynch

Miss Teskey and her family came from Ontario to Calgary in 1910, and later moved to the Okotoks district. She took her teacher training in Ontario, but was required to attend normal school at Calgary in order to teach in Alberta. While there she was in great demand as a substitute teacher because of her previous training. She recalled the Okotoks blood donor clinics being held in the hotel dining room during W.W. I.

In 1914 Miss Teskey was engaged as teacher at Pine Creek School at $720.00 per annum and also taught in 1915. While teaching there she boarded with the Tindal family down on Pine Creek and with Bryans, southeast of Bremners. She became very good friends of the Pollards, who built the greenhouses near DeWinton.

The Marshall children looked after the fire and the sweeping. On arriving at school one morning she discovered the key had been lost in the snow so everyone had to climb through a window to classes. Of course, that would be the day the inspector arrived and had to make his entrance by the same route. He commended the teacher for her efforts and was amazed to think she could climb in and out of the window too!

One Monday morning in the spring she rode out from Calgary on a horse that was to be delivered in the district. At this time the number of automobiles on the old Macleod Trail was increasing due possibly to the discovery of oil at Black Diamond. On the way home to Tindals from school she had to lead the horse because many of the people in cars were yelling and whooping over the good news.

She sometimes brought a rifle to school — probably in gopher season — and would allow the older boys to fire it under her supervision. She could not recall having any discipline problems and thought she had a very good group of students.

Miss Teskey (Mrs. Johnson) has retired from teaching and lives in Okotoks. (1976)

MEMORIES OF PINE CREEK SCHOOL 1926-1927 — by Rhoda M. Rouse

September 1926 found me established as teacher at Pine Creek School. I understand the building was erected in 1902 and was Number 84, in order of erection in what was then Northwest Territories.

After school closed in June 1927, one or two small twisters went through the area, one damaging the roof of the school and one doing some damage to the Evans' home on Pine Creek west of the school. A more recent school building was erected about 1931 east of the original school, and only in recent months, after many years of disuse, has been moved farther east by one of the newer residents for use as a workshop.

Pine Creek School served the village of De Winton, where the fall school Fair was held, and a fairly large area to the north. The Brinton family came from De Winton, while from the north and west, there came the Grahams, Poffenroths, Winnifred Turnbull, Jean and Ruth Anderson, and the other family of Anderson cousins — William, Robert, Murray, Jack and Ivy — who lived in the old Pratt place. From the old Pine Creek Stopping House down at the creek came the

Miss Margaret Teskey looking for gophers at Pine Creek School barn, 1914.

Pine Creek School 1925-26, Miss Davidson teacher. L. to R. Travis Brinton, Goldie Brinton, Wentworth Brinton, Lucy Brinton, Norman Graham, Paul Brinton, Robert Anderson Holding "Molly".

Pine Creek School possibly 1926-27. L. to R. back row: Paul Brinton, Winnie Turnbull, Alf Poffenroth, Wentworth Brinton, Norman Graham. Next row: Robert Anderson, Amelia Youngman, (top of head not known) Travis Brinton?, Goldie Brinton, Grace Murray. 3rd row: Jean Anderson, Jean Alverson, Alice Standish, Jack Anderson, Murray Anderson, Harry Youngman. Front row: Ruth Anderson, Betty Bailey, Ivy Anderson, Betty Alverson, Rees Alverson, David Jamison, John Harper, Gordon Graham, Martin Poffenroth.

Standish family, and Grace Murray came from the Sutherlands, where I also boarded.

The school was heated by the popular pot-bellied stove in the middle of the room. Drinking water hauled in cream cans by the Poffenroth family who drove from west of the school. It was dispensed by the usual public "dipper".

Transportation from Calgary was mostly by car. The train went through Academy, then swung east to De Winton, where it was still over two miles from the school. Mr. Sutherland and Lallie were in town during the week at business and school, so Monday mornings and Friday afternoons, either my brother would bring the Sutherlands out and return with me, or George Sutherland would take me in, and return with his father and sister.

However at some time in the late fall or early winter, I became aware that the Model Bakery made a daily trip with a truckload of bread to Turner Valley. By being out at the school gate after school, I could ride in to town Friday, or any day during the week I wished to come in. As the driver passed our house in southwest Calgary I was back at school in plenty of time in the morning.

This arrangement led to an amusing incident. On Valentine's Day we had the usual Valentine Box, and among others, I received one from "The Modly"! Am quite sure I know the guilty party! At least he had a sense of humor.

I remember one day arriving home in Calgary much too early. Something had happened to the spring of my watch, causing it to gain time very rapidly. Since there was no clock in the school I sent one of the boys out to the road to hail a car to get the correct time. The bright youth saw a chance of early dismissal, and advised me that it was much later than it actually was. So school was out and I was home much too early.

Another event of interest at the school was the passing of the Duke of Windsor and his younger brother, the Duke of Kent, on their way home from the ranch west of High River.

Mr. and Mrs. Bremner and Jean lived across the road west of Sutherland's where I stayed. As Sutherlands had no phone I sometimes walked over to Bremners to phone home. Some years later I understand that Mrs. Bremner, at about 70 years, learned to drive a Model T Ford and thought nothing of the fifteen mile drive on gravel roads to Calgary and return.

We had many pleasant excursions down to Pine Creek in our noon hours. Once, at least, we tried skating, and had many picnics in spring and summer.

The land on the edge of the trees east of the school sloped northeast toward the creek bank. It was quite swampy in the area, and here in June grew the most beautiful longstemmed dark purple violets. For years after, it was an annual June pilgrimage of mine to find the gorgeous wood violets. In the same area, Sanna King, a Normal School classmate of mine had a summer cabin. I believe her father owned that land at the time.

Many more interesting items of a more personal nature could be related. For example, the time the family answered a letter I had written and sent home to the parents. They were not aware of the fact I knew the circumstances, but as they were leaving the district, we let the matter drop.

And so this era is part of the history to be compiled in "De Winton District Diary — Sodbusting to Subdivision". May success crown the effort of those interested in preserving the history of the area.

PINE CREEK SCHOOL — 1930-39 — by Mrs. G. Kelson (nee Gwynydd Thomas)

The rural school of yesterday has become more or less of a legend, and the present generation will have no memories of them. Looking back a good many years, I recall my first six months of teaching at Pine Creek, which were in the original school. In the summer of 1930, a new school was built. It was east of the old one in a very sheltered place with trees on the east and north side and a lovely view of the foothills and mountains to the west.

There was a nice big yard, ideal for sports and the school ponies kept the grass down in the spring and fall, but were stabled on the cold days.

The new school boasted of a full sized basement and a cloak room for the boys and one for the girls. It was heated by a gas furnace so we never arrived at a cold school, and the basement was ideal for playing games in at recess during the bad weather in winter. We were all thrilled at having such a modern school and took pride in keeping it clean and tidy.

Many of the boys and girls rode to school, but the ones from De Winton came with Mr. T. Dalzell in his truck, and he so often came for them at night if the weather was bad. They all loved and respected him, and he taught them so many things such as kindness to others, punctuality and obedience.

Besides the school work there were many other goals to work for, namely the School Fair, Christmas concerts, Musical Festivals, ball games with neighbouring schools, and at the end of the year, a school picnic. The School Fair was held at De Winton in September. The schools taking part were Melrose, Stormont, Alexandra and Pine Creek.

Pine Creek School 1930-31. Teacher Miss Thomas. Back row L. to R.: Jack Anderson, Kitty Harper, Isabel Wilson, Martin Poffenroth, Gwynydd Thomas, Russell Wilson, Gordon Graham, John Harper. Middle row: Ellen Graham, Marion Dalzell, Helen Brinton, Ruth Anderson, Madelyn Martin, John Wilson, Ivy Anderson. Front row: Jack King, Jane Wilson, Harold Poffenroth, Charlie King, Eleanor Jamison, Tom King, Jack McNeill.

Pine Creek School, 1950. Standing: Peter Van Tighem, Virginia Graham, Mrs. Kenny. Back: Margaret Evans, Josie Van Tighem, Pat Paul, Jacqueline Harmatta, Myrna Marshall. Middle: Harvey Marshall, Robert Poffenroth, Ron Graham, Jeannine Harmatta, Bonnie Poffenroth. Front: Kathleen Phillips, Doreen Marshall, Kathy Harmatta, Kathleen Marshall, Glen Norris, Alice Van Tighem.

In the spring, each pupil was given vegetable and flower seeds to grow, and they showed the results of their work. They also had classes for school work, cooking, sewing and livestock. There wasn't a boy or girl who didn't go home with a good many prizes. Here I pay tribute to Mr. Russell Evans who was the Secretary Treasurer. A short time after the fair, he visited each school and gave each boy or girl their prize money that they had won. This was always a day to be remembered.

The boys and girls through various ways, raised enough money to buy a piano for the school. The parents were wonderful the way they helped with anything pertaining to the school. It is sad to think that so many of them have passed away, but always such a pleasure to meet those who are still left, and talk over old times at De Winton and Pine Creek.

Our Christmas Tree and Concert was held at the De Winton Hall. Pine Creek, Stormont, Melrose and the De Winton High School all contributed a half hour programme. It was always such a happy occasion.

The boys and girls of Pine Creek were always a pleasure to teach. They came to school to learn, and always gave of their best. The nine years I spent with them were happy years. They have all made good citizens, and have led useful lives.

Another thing that added so much to my nine years at Pine Creek was being privileged to stay with the Sutherland family. It was just another home to me.

Pine Creek School continued for a good many years, before the pupils were bused to larger schools. It is sad to think that there are no longer rural schools which served the communities so well.

PINE CREEK CHURCH AT SE¼-14-22-1-W5 —
Researched and written by I. Blackwood

The first meeting of the Presbyterian Church at Pine Creek was held at the home of Mr. Robb in July 1883 and was conducted by Mr. Angus Robertson who was then a missionary in Calgary. The services in 1883 were held once a month and in 1884 every two weeks. In 1885 Mr. Herdman conducted the services occasionally. During the spring and summer of 1886 Mr. Robertson was in charge, having oversight of Sheep Creek, High River and Pine Creek. Rev. Johnstone was appointed in June of 1889 and retired in October 1889. Rev. Munro was appointed in October 1889 and stayed until March 31, 1892.

Money for the church was raised through box socials and parlour socials.

On December 26, 1889 the congregations of Pine Creek and Red Deer Lake met at John Owens' new store. After a devotional service, Rev. R. A. Munro stated that the meeting had been called for the purpose of procuring a site in order that a church might be erected, and he stated reasons why Pine Creek Crossing would be the most central place for the church. Mr. John Owens and Mr. R. Pratt each offered a site. Mr. Pratt's site was accepted after a vote was taken. The accepted offer was to consist of land fronting the Macleod Trail to the extent of 100 feet and going back to the extent of 150 feet.

Mr. John Owens, Mr. Hugh Ingram, A. Pratt, A. Bremner, Joseph Moss, and D. McArthur were

First Pine Creek Minister, Rev. Munro.

appointed managers. The elders were: Mr. D. McArthur, Mr. A. J. Wilkin and Mr. James Grierson.

At an informal meeting in February 1890, the adherents of Red Deer Lake and Pine Creek Presbyterian Churches agreed to quarry stone and convey it to the site of the new church and to apply to Winnipeg for a grant of $200. They decided to advertise for tenders for a frame and brick church, the advertisement to be put in the **Calgary Herald Tribune**. The nine tenders were opened at the home of Mr. Pratt on June 9th and it was agreed to accept the lowest tender providing the contractor of same was a "likely man." The contract was given to Mr. D. J. McLachlan. A social evening was planned to raise funds for the church.

It was agreed to call the new church St. Andrew's at Rev. Munro's request and to open it on October 5, 1890 with Rev. J. C. Herdman and Rev. A. J. Matheson taking part. The collection on opening day was $60.00.

At the annual meeting held in January 1905, it was decided to confer with the congregations of Melrose and Davisburg regarding the building of a manse.

As early as 1906 the church board was approaching the Ladies Aid for a loan of $25 to help pay the minister's salary. Through the years the ladies' club has come to the aid of the church when it was in financial difficulties.

It is of interest to note that in March 1907 a basket

Pine Creek Church early 1920's.

social was held when repairs to the church were needed and $183.50 was realized.

Early organists of the church were Mrs. Philips, Miss Eleanor Gray and Miss Jean Bremner.

In the early years of the church, a program was held after each annual meeting. This consisted of instrumental music, vocal music, and recitations, followed by tea. To quote one secretary: "After which we retired, imbued with the sentiment that it is good for brethren to dwell together in unity."

St. Andrew's Presbyterian Church at Pine Creek was struck by lightning and destroyed by fire on Wednesday afternoon, July 19, 1933. Some of the contents, such as the pulpit, pews and organ were saved.

Services were held in Pine Creek School until the fall term started. Church services were then held in the De Winton Community Hall until the new church opened on January 6, 1935 with Rev. Warwick Kelloway, pastor of Knox Church, Calgary, as the speaker and Rev. Percy Halstead as the preacher.

PINE CREEK CEMETERY—by Ruth Hamilton

The hardships, joys and tragedies of the occupants of the first covered wagons to reach this part of Alberta have been told and retold through the years but the most heartbreaking event must have been when one of their members died and had to be buried in a grave by the side of the trail. Especially so for the parents of children who knew that, after the burial, they would never again see the place where their child had been laid to rest. It is with small wonder then, when they finally found the land they had searched for, and settled into a community, they set aside a small piece of ground as a last resting place for their loved ones.

And so it was, when Edward and Christina Robb's little girl, Edna, died in 1889, that Mr. Robb donated a piece of land on their own farm, on the north side of beautiful Pine Creek Valley, as a public burial ground for the surrounding area. Little Edna Robb was the first one buried in the quiet country cemetery.

There were quite a number of early settlers and children buried before 1900. A few of the names to see on the old headstones are: Edna Robb, 1889, John Currie, 1891, Oliver Ingram, 1892, Ida Hamilton, 1893, George Shortt, 1893, James Somerville, 1890, his wife, Anne, 1893. Also A. Kirkpatrick, Catherine McArthur, Edna Cathleen and Ruby L. McArthur and John Calvin Currie.

Many plots contain more than three graves from one family. Charles Marshall and his wife, Annette, are buried along with five of their children; Ernest, Harold, Hazel, Frank and Vera. Roland and Mary Ness and their two sons, Newton and Herbert and many more.

On June 22, 1900 Pine Creek became a registered cemetery. A certificate of title was made out in the names of William Anderson, Robert Pratt and Robert Jamison and reads as follows:

All that portion of north east quarter of 11-22-1-W5.

Commencing at the north east corner of said quarter section, thence southerly along the eastern boundary of the said quarter section, four chains and one foot. Thence westerly and parallel to the north boundary of the said quarter section, five chains and three feet. Thence northerly and parallel to the east boundary of the said quarter section, four chains and one foot to the north boundary of the said quarter section, thence easterly along said north boundary five chains and three feet, more or less, to the place of the beginning. Two acres, more or less. P.O. Address: Pine Creek, N.W.T.

The first written record to be found for the cemetery was in June, 1900 and was in the form of a receipt as follows:

Price for deed—8.95
four books twenty five cents—.25
for fixing fence, R. Pratt—3.00
Total—$12.20
Balance on hand forty ($40.00) dollars.

It is interesting to note that an entry in 1929 still showed a balance of forty dollars on the books.

Some record of the early care of the cemetery is still available but, through the years, a number of books and documents have been misplaced and, to date, have not been located.

It is quite possible that Robert Pratt was the first person to keep a record of the cemetery. From him it is believed that George Pratt Anderson took over as his signature is found under two or three entries. George Anderson died in 1942 and Stuart Jamison cared for the books until 1952; Tom Dalzell 1952-1961; Les Norris, 1962-1967 and Mrs. Bill Hamilton, 1968 to the present time.

One note of interest is the fact that in 1900, a plot large enough to accomodate three adults (14' x 14') sold for $5.00. In 1968 it was increased to $10.00 per lot and, in 1974 to $20.00, and so it stands today. A very modest cost indeed when compared to the cost of cemetery plots in neighbouring towns and cities. The cemetery is still active and every year or so it sees the sale of a plot or two.

It had been the policy of the people in the district to hold a work bee once a year to keep the cemetery looking neat and in good repair. It wasn't all work by any means as the women would take lunch and coffee and at noon tables were set up for the food and blankets spread on the ground for the workers to sit on while eating and spinning yarns. Mostly the talk was of remembered times about the very people whose graves they were tidying up that day.

As the years went by, interest in the cemetery began to wane and it wasn't long before it was a tangle of grass, weeds and buckbrush, a disgrace to the community. In 1968, Mrs. Hamilton was asked to form a committee and, in March a meeting was held in the De Winton United Church basement which resulted in the appointment of a board of directors. President; Mrs. Bill Hamilton; Secretary Treasurer; Mrs. Les Marshall, and Directors; John Hamilton, W. S. McInnes, Lloyd Fraser and Steve Chernow. By April the new directors had the cemetery resurveyed. John Hamilton made and donated new cement markers for the plot corners, new maps were made and brought up to date. Trees were cut and trash removed, the parking area was graded up and gravelled. The ground was sprayed twice for weeds and once for buckbrush and the grass was mowed and hauled away. By 1970 the grounds were very nice, the grass green and one corner, which had been boggy, dried up and returned to prairie grass. The scent of wild sage and mint was wonderful.

John Hamilton and Bill McInnes were dedicated workers. With donated funds, the committee bought a second hand lawn mower and John and Bill saw to it that the grass was mowed at least once and, sometimes, twice during the summer. John passed away in 1974 and Steve helped with the mowing for a while but neither Bill nor Steve is any longer able to do the work and now it is up to the directors to find volunteers to help with the work each year, a job that is becoming increasingly difficult.

Each year; from the north, the city of Calgary gobbles up more acres of land for development and, in so doing, comes closer and closer to the resting place of those early citizens. While, on the west, the Macleod Trail, that once boasted of bull trains, horses and buggies and wagons, is an asphalt strip on which an endless agony of cars; trucks; busses and trailers zooms by, the passengers too unobservant to notice the little grave yard near by.

What does the future hold for the little country cemetery that holds, within its bosom, the mortal remains of the early settlers whose untiring work and sacrifice made this district of Pine Creek such a wonderful and privileged place to live? Does anyone know? Will anyone pause long enough to care?

GRAIN HANDLING AT ACADEMY SIDING

The siding, just south of where the rails cross Pine Creek, was left to accommodate the overload of cars when trains were negotiating the steep grade northwest of De Winton. This was its only use until 1928 when Pitchford and Wooding, grain dealers from Calgary, and owners of Crown Feed, decided that it would make a handy place to load grain. Two bins were built by an open platform on the west side of the tracks and, with the use of a boxcar, it meant that three kinds of grain could be handled. Bill Robbins was the first man to run the operation. In 1930 Ken Lockett took over but the large elevator companies had their eyes on it and, in 1931 Midland had an elevator moved in from Brockett and the Voss brothers were hired to finish construction for an operable unit. There was an office in the structure and the first two men hired to run the elevator, Jack Hislop and then Gordon Young,

Academy Elevator 1940. Hugh Graham at front.

Culvert under C.P.R. tracks near Academy Siding. Tom Dalzell on horse, Matt Parks standing.

lived in the office. When a Mr. Neufeld became the agent, a house was moved in from Hussar for his convenience. Hugh Graham, John Nordstrum, David Jamison, Gerry Mooney and Ralph Stinn were the other agents that worked there before it was closed to grain deliveries in April, 1965 and used only for storage as a holding station. In September, 1971 it was demolished. U.G.G. had owned it from 1954 on.

It was a small elevator, 15,000 or 20,000 bushels and when the annex was built in 1936 it added room for another 20,000. It served a large district and handled a huge quantity of grain. Now the district that it served is pretty well subdivided and very little grain finds its way to an elevator.

THE GEORGE ANDERSON FAMILY — by Ivy Kolafa

Our farm was located on 14-22-1-W5 and SW¼-13-22-1-W5.

To the best of my knowledge this place was purchased by Sandy Watson who came from Winnipeg in 1885. The house was built in 1886. A few years later it was taken over by my two great uncles, Andrew and Robert Pratt.

In 1901 my grandparents, William and Margaret Anderson, their daughter Margaret and their two sons,

"Sunday Best" George and Jessie Anderson with Ivy, Jack, Murray, Rob and Bill. About 1921.

Alex and George (my father) came to Canada from Fifeshire, Scotland. My father married Jessie Murray, who came out from Durrisdeer, Scotland in 1912. I was born and raised at Pine Creek with my four older brothers.

Bill was killed in action at Caen, July 25, 1944, at the age of 30. He lived all of his life in the Pine Creek district and worked for a number of the neighbors, including Gordon Heaver and Les Marshall. Bill never married but he left a host of friends to mourn his loss.

Bob passed away April 25, 1952 at Bashaw, Alberta, leaving his wife, the former Jessie McKay of Okotoks, and four daughters — Barbara Valley, now in Red Deer, twin girls, Ivy Cowan of High Level and Brenda Tickler of Calgary, and Kathryn Kennedy of Edmonton. Jessie later became Mrs. Tom Patton and now (1975) lives in Calgary.

Murray passed away May 9, 1955, leaving his wife, the former Jessie Fielding of Hanna, one son George (now an auctioneer at Lloydminster, Saskatchewan) and one daughter, Donna Marie Sevik of Hussar. Jessie later married Ralph McElroy of Hussar, where they still live.

Jack married Ann Harder of Didsbury. They have two sons, George and Ron, both in Calgary, and one daughter, Cheryl Kohut, also in Calgary. Jack still lives in Calgary.

I lived on the farm until my marriage to Albert Kolafa of Rosetown, Saskatchewan. We lived in Calgary until his transfer with the Government to Red Deer in 1959 and have resided here since. We raised two sons, Jack and Bill.

Jack was married in 1967 to Barbara Bill of Red Deer, has five children and is employed by CFCN in Calgary as a photographer.

Bill was married in 1972 to Nancy Dann of Winnipeg; he is employed by Standard Aero Engines as an aircraft technician.

Our Dad passed away at Pine Creek on August 6, 1942, and Mother on April 1, 1957. They are both buried in Pine Creek Cemetery.

The farm was sold in 1956 to Isadore Koschitzky.

WILLIAM ANDERSON S12-22-1-15 and SW¼-13-22-1-5 — by J. Lowe

The family of William and Margaret (Pratt) Anderson came to the Pine Creek district in 1901 from Kingskettle, Fifeshire, Scotland. They brought with them their daughter Margaret (who later married William Douglas and farmed in the Horseshoe Canyon region near Drumheller) and sons Alex and George.

Mrs. Anderson's two brothers, Andrew (1847-1900) and Robert Pratt (1846-1929) had arrived in this area from Scotland in 1883. Blacksmithing and farming — later lived in what had been a stopping house built in 1886.

Mr. Anderson took up a homestead near the Horseshoe Canyon at Drumheller in 1907 and also a farm adjoining the Macleod Trail at Pine Creek. Mrs. Anderson passed away in 1931. His two sons continued to farm this land following his death in 1937.

George passed away in 1942, his wife Jessie in 1957. They had five children. The eldest son Bill was killed at Caen, France, July 25, 1944.

Mr. and Mrs. Wm. Anderson.

Alex farmed on the south side of the creek from 1923 (W½ 11-22-1-5) — a mixed farming operation which included the growing of certified seed grain. He retired with his wife Margaret to Calgary in April 1949. She passed away August 10, 1959 and her husband December 13, 1965. They had two daughters.

Since this retirement the property has been farmed by their son-in-law and daughter, Lionel and Ruth Lynch. They have three children; Sharon and twins Kathleen and Brian. Brian is married to Corinne Poffenroth and lives in the district.

Their other daughter Jean lives in Calgary with her husband Robert Lowe.

Mr. and Mrs. Alex Anderson early 1940's.

MR. AND MRS. WILLIAM ANDERSON

The Andersons bought the De Winton store in 1919 when prices were high and on the rise however, soon after they came into possession prices began to slump and they lost money. They came from England and were used to people having shopping bags and if a dozen oranges were ordered they were put loose on the counter to be carried away however possible. Jim Harrison rode in on horseback one day and all his groceries were laid out on the counter and he had to scrounge around to find a sack to carry them in. I guess it soon became the custom for everyone to bring their own shopping bags.

They had a son serving in the Royal Navy and when he came to visit on leave, he gave all the children very generous amounts of candy for their money. His parents didn't appreciate that but the children sure did.

The business was sold to Oneil and Andrews in 1920.

FRANCIS CHARLES AND AUGUSTA MARY (DUKE) AUSTIN — by Monica Wilson.

My Grandparents left the De Winton area prior to World War One and I remember my mother telling me about a Gaskell boy, Clair, I believe, coming to say good-bye to her and my grandmother chasing him away with a broom.

My grandfather, Francis Charles Austin, came west from Quebec City at the time of the Riel Rebellion, falling in love with the country, he decided to homestead. My grandmother Augusta Mary Duke, came from Chichester, England, to visit her mother in Calgary. She was 34 or 35 at the time. My grandparents were married in 1897 and my mother was born in 1898, in a log cabin, as their home was not finished. (I marvel at the fortitude of the early pioneers, like my Grandmother, who were totally unused to, and unprepared for, life on the "Frontier").

They had four live children; Laura Monica Comley-Combe, 1898, has two daughters; Henry Reginald, 1899-1964, two sons and one daughter; Alfred Knight, 1900-1955; Doris Enid Miller, 1902-1954, one son and one daughter.

Grandfather died in 1927, a truly kind and gentle man. Unfortunately, I was not old enough to remember him. Granny Austin died in 1948. She was an exceedingly strong willed woman, who, regardless of her eccentricities, commanded respect from all who knew her well.

Mother often spoke with horror of the fire they had on the farm, when all their horses were burned to death. She would shudder when she recalled it. Fora-Dora, must have been her favorite horse as it is one whose name I remember. Grandfather and my mother had a great love for horses. Mother said she was the first white child christened in the Anglican Church near them. My grandmother played the organ in that church and never missed a Sunday, regardless of the weather, (or so I was led to believe). One Sunday morning, a terrible winter day, Uncle Alf, a few months old, fell out of the sleigh. By the time the other children were able to attract their mother's attention, they had gone some distance. The baby was found safe and sound in a snowbank. My mother also speaks of the frequent trips her mother made to England, with the two girls, leaving Grandfather and the boys behind. One winter the boys spent with cousins in Ottawa. Uncle Alf told me about that. How they missed the farm, and how unhappy they were in the formal, servant oriented, world of the Capital.

Mother always regretted her haphazard education, between tutoring at home, the country school and school in England. She would love to have had a stable childhood on their farm. She spoke with joy of the large slough, ice skating, the Indians coming to help with the harvest, and their fascination with the white children, the young friends and relatives who came West to work for the summer, their favorite treat, (snow and strawberry jam), horseback riding, the cat having kittens in my grandmother's best hat, (and my grandmother's fury), my grandfather's loving kindness, overnight visits to neighbouring farms and towns!

JAMES AND JOCK BEATTIE — by Jim Beattie

My father, Jock, and I came to De Winton in 1949 from Chilliwack, B.C. We lived with Mrs. Jean Kellock and her son, Jim, on their farm E½ 9-22-1-W5. I went to Pine Creek school and then to De Winton High school. Some of the fondest memories I recall from those days are: Riding horseback to school daily with the Marshall and Poffenroth children. It seemed like a daily adventure riding to school and, some days we felt more adventuresome than others and didn't make it, seeking the hills instead.

In 1952 I moved in with Mr. Walter Turnbull while my father went to work in the oilfields around Sylvan Lake, Alberta. I left the De Winton area in 1954 and joined my father in Sylvan Lake and continued my education in Red Deer.

Within two years we had moved back to Calgary and occasionally took to dancing in the De Winton Hall where everyone had a good time.

My father remarried and eventually moved to Prince Albert, Saskatchewan where they ran a florist shop until his death in June 1965.

I remained in Calgary, joining the Calgary Police Service in 1958 where I am still employed. I married Patricia Ferguson from Stavely and have three lovely children. We occasionally drive through the De Winton area and visit friends. It still seems like a home area to me as I still maintain close friendship with persons I met there as a youngster.

THE A. W. BENSTEAD FAMILY — by Mrs. W. C. (Ethel) Philips

Arthur William Benstead and his wife, Sirsa, moved to the De Winton district in 1917 when Dad gave up his job at A. M. Terrill Greenhouses, where he had worked as a gardener for many years.

In De Winton he started working for Harry Cushing at the greenhouse and on the acreage as a gardener and grower. These greenhouses were owned by W. H. Cushing of Calgary, owner of the lumber mills. Harry was a nephew of W. H. Cushing.

Dad had gone to De Winton ahead of the family to get the house ready. Mother and we children, Bill, Ethel (Dona), Irene and Henry, followed a short time

later and we were met at the station by Dad. We arrived on the "Spokane Flyer" on a very cold, blustery night. We older children could not understand why no street lights. When we asked Dad which way to our house, he pointed to a tall chimney which was the smoke stack to the greenhouses. It seemed miles away.

We attended Pine Creek School which was two miles from our home. It was located on the main highway, just above the coulee where the Standish family lived. All that remains today is the foundation that is barely visible as it is overgrown with weeds and grass. We went to the Pine Creek church and Sunday School on the other side of the coulee, near the Pine Creek Cemetery. The church was three miles from home and we were picked up on Sunday by a man with a horse and buggy.

As I was only seven or eight at the time, I do not recall much of our life there. Some of my memories are pleasant ones, like the day Bill came home from town and told Mother and Dad the war was over; the community picnics, held in the field behind the Tom Dalzell farmhouse.

One Valentine's Day, Mother and Dad took us all to a box social in the community hall. Mother had decorated boxes for my sister Irene and I, mine was bid on and bought by Dick Meehan. In the summer, Dad and Mr. Cushing would hitch Nell, our horse, to the dray and we would go picking saskatoons in the hills, where the highway now goes through. The school concerts were always exciting as we would perform for our parents and friends. One I recall, in particular, was in the spring and it really poured rain. Bill had to be there early to have the door open and he walked the two miles, carrying a lantern. He got soaked to the skin. Two of the teachers I remember were Miss Laurie and Miss Campbell.

We stayed at De Winton for about three and a half years and then returned to Calgary. Dad passed away in 1956 and Mother in 1972. Bill passed away in 1966, leaving a wife and three sons, Arthur, Frank and David, also five grandchildren. Ethel (Dona), Mrs. W. C. Philips, has two daughters, Margaret and Elsie, and two grandchildren. She and her husband live in Victoria B.C., Irene (Poffenroth), lives in Calgary, has four sons, Peter, Robert, Kenneth and Kevin and seven grandchildren. Henry, lives at Airdrie. Elsie (Mrs. H. M. Bailes) of Red Deer, has five children, Brian, Irene, Brenda, Bill and Carol, also ten grandchildren. Elsie was born while we lived at De Winton.

THE STORY OF THE BREMNER FAMILY

Archibald Patterson Bremner (Archie) - born Renfrew, Ontario May 23rd, 1850. His wife Grace Ann Cardiff - born Renfrew, Ontario November 12th, 1865. Their family:

Ebenezer Buchanan (Eben) - born De Winton, Alberta. September 25, 1889;

Ethel Agnes - born De Winton, Alberta. January 20, 1893;

Ada Jane (Jean) - born De Winton, Alberta. September 25, 1895;

Ethel married Louis Osman Murray, December 18, 1916. Their family:

Mr. and Mrs. A. P. Bremner with grand children; Edith, John and Wallace Murray. About 1930.

Edith Louise, born May 9, 1918, John Bremner, born May 11, 1923, Wallace Landels, born June 9, 1925, Keith Osman, born January 22, 1931.

Archie and his brother George came west to Winnipeg in 1882 and homesteaded near there. The next year they decided to come farther west. During that trek they saw their first mirage - an illusion caused by atmospheric conditions. It was like many teams and wagons, and they expected to meet them very soon, but it wasn't 'till noon the next day that they met; each had been travelling toward the other all that time, with only time for sleeping.

The railroad was being built, so they joined the crew building the grade. They left them later when the sidings of Shepard and Langdon were being built. Dad came on into the little town of Calgary August 1883, therefore being ahead of the railroad.

His first job was working for Angus Sparrow at his livery stable. During that time he drove the first commercial traveller, a young Irishman named Dowler, to Fort Macleod, staying at stopping houses along the way. At Fort Macleod the hotel had a sign that read, "Ft. Macleod Hotel by Old Kamoose." When told that Kamoose meant "horse thief," he was aghast and was all for moving on. However, he got some very large orders, and was delighted.

Dad homesteaded in the Pine Creek area (later De Winton), along with Charlie Marshall and Jack McInnes. Their first winter they lived together in Mr. McInnes' cabin. He was the cook. Mr. Marshall looked after the cow and milked her, and Dad looked after the horses.

The next year they all joined the Transport Division of the Riel Rebellion, taking supplies to the troops. Their very good friend, Bob Fitzsimmons, was cook for their outfit, and when stopping by a lake or stream, Bob would wade into the water up to his arm-pits to get clean water for their meal before the horses got it all muddied up. Many years later Bob went to live with a nephew who was ranching in the Drumheller area, and eventually died there.

The transport men were unarmed and they held an indignation meeting to discuss the situation, so Mr. McInnes and Dad were appointed to talk to General Middleton about it. Jack McInnes had a wire in his hand and was carelessly hitting his boot with it.

General Middleton said, "Who is this man? Is he a dynamiter?" They were issued guns and ammunition and felt safer in case of a surprise attack from the Indians. However, they never had to use them.

Dad sometimes spoke of General Middleton, General Strange and such places as Frenchman's Butte, Frog Lake, Victorie, Batoche, Ft. Pitt, which was a Hudson's Bay Co. Trading Post, 150 miles east of Ft. Edmonton and 35 miles southeast of Frog Lake, a wild, lonely and very beautiful country. He spoke of the massacre of the priests, and of Gowanlock and Delaney. Mr. Delaney was a farming instructor about forty and Mr. Gowanlock was twenty-eight.

They returned to Calgary after the rebellion and that fall, 1885, Dad decided to go east to his home town, Renfrew, Ontario. When he got off the train, the first girl he saw was Grace Ann Cardiff, whom he later married. They were married January 27th, 1886, at the home of his sister, Mrs. Robert Craig. Mother's mother was very opposed to the marriage.

Dad came back west in March with a car load of "Settlers' Effects" and Mother came in June. On the same train, also from Renfrew, were Rev. and Mrs. Charles McKillop, on their way to Lethbridge where they were to spend the rest of their lives.

My mother recalled her fifteen mile drive out from the little town of Calgary to her future homestead in a wagon, over the lovely prairie, which had such an abundance of wild flowers - so many varieties. She said she never saw it so lovely again, after the cattle came and the farmers plowed the land. Mother was privileged to be here in time to see the last of the Great Bull Trains, bringing in supplies for the I. G. Baker store in Calgary, from Fort Benton. The wheel marks of those great Bull Trains were visible for many, many years, and, I believe still are in some places.

Mother and Dad's home was made of logs. My brother, Eben, was born there and later, when they built a new home, the original one was used as a stable. They had great difficulties in getting water, and dug several wells. When the railroad came, it passed through the barn-yard, and the buildings had to be moved. The logs for the house came from the Millarville area, west of our place. It must have been quite a project, entailing many trips, getting them down on the running gear of wagons.

My sister Ethel and I were born in the house that replaced the first one. Many years later it was boarded over, for extra warmth - it was getting old! It still stands on our old place, fifteen miles south of downtown Calgary and one mile from DeWinton.

Women didn't go to town for the birth of their babies in those days. My mother's very good friend, Mrs. Harper, a trained nurse who had married a rancher, and lived in the Millarville district, came and stayed for the birth of each child. Dr. Lafferty came for the "baby matinee."

In the 1890's times were very hard on farms. My father grew a lot of potatoes intending to sell them in Calgary, but he couldn't get anyone to even come and dig them for free, if they would supply their own sacks. Finally he hauled them out and spread them on the fields for fertilizer.

He took his family and nine teams of horses to the Crow's Nest Pass to join in the building of the railroad grade. He would drive one team himself, hiring teamsters for the other teams. It would have been a good living, but fate, in the form of distemper, took his horses — all nine teams and all but one died. She survived, and later when we returned to the farm we brought her with us, a well-loved horse.

At Moyie, south of Cranbrook, after his horses died, he built a small hotel where miners roomed and boarded, so that was our living. Later when times were better in Alberta, we returned to the farm.

A half-section of land joining ours on the north was for sale by Billie Sharples, who went to Vancouver. Dad acquired it, giving us a good farm. Through good times and bad, hail, drought, cut-worms and frost, we managed to survive.

Eben and Ethel had started to school in Moyie, and when we got back to the farm, they went to school at Mr. Vader's place near Sheepy's. Later they went to Melrose school, driving a little Indian racing pony on a cart. When other youngsters came galloping up behind them, away would go "Joe," and Ethel would have to slide down in the bottom of the cart to avoid going out the back. Later our Pine Creek school was built. Before it was finished, school was held in Mr. and Mrs. Paling's kitchen. They had started a small store in their home. Then they moved to the village of De Winton, and started the first De Winton store. They later moved to Lashburn, Saskatchewan, having traded their store to Mr. Frank Pashak for cattle which they drove over land to Lashburn. It took them about six weeks! Later Mr. Pashak moved to Calgary and started the Mission Grocery.

Mr. and Mrs. Paling were our closest neighbours; lovely people, who came from England, where he had been a schoolmaster, to farm in Canada. For some time he rode to Midnapore, about seven miles, to teach school there.

Until he got more land broken, Dad rented a field from his good friend, Alex McIntosh, and I recall Mother driving a team on a roller and I rode along.

Time marched on, and many changes came. We enjoyed a good community life, and had many good friends and neighbours. Mother was active in church and community work, being president of the W.M.S. of Pine Creek Church, the Red Cross, and the U.F.W.A. During the first World War, the Red Cross members met weekly at De Winton, knitting and sewing for the men overseas.

The 24th of May was usually celebrated with a picnic. Sports of all kinds for all ages, followed by a scrumptious lunch, to which all families had contributed, and a good time was had. There was the Okotoks Fair to which we always went, and I recall one year that Mother's baking powder biscuits took first prize, and Eben's pony also took a prize. We were so pleased and proud!

To go away back, when Mother first came there was a Watson family that had a Stopping House. One of their daughters, Elizabeth, became Mrs. Charles Knight. She was Mother's dearest friend and my sister and I often spent our Easter holidays with her.

Usually on Sundays the young men of the district rode into the yards of the married people and stayed for a meal — or two! It was called "riding the grub line." Hospitality reigned, all were welcome, and great and lasting friendships were made.

We had many "hobos" come to the door for a handout. We were between the railroad and the trail therefore we got them from both sides and Mother always fed them. Sgt. Thomas of the Mounties always came to our place for dinner when in our area. He told us that when he saw stones on fence posts he always knocked them off, because in hobo's sign language that meant good eats. Sgt. Thomas was stationed at High River. We always enjoyed his visits. Like all the Mounted Police, he had a good horse, and both man and beast were well cared for.

Dad always had good horses, Clydes for the farm work, and always a good team for our democrat. We always had ponies to ride.

EBEN BREMNER — by Eben Bremner

I was born September 25th, 1889, in Calgary and was raised on a homestead at Pine Creek (now De Winton, since the railroad went through). I grew up there on the SE¼-2-22-1-W5, and attended school at both the old Pine Creek and the Melrose School. I worked on the old place until I was 21, and then left for a few years.

I had teams working for the city and also hauled sand from Mission Hill. Fred Lowe, a real estate man used hydraulic water pressure, washing the clay from the sand and flooded the flat known now as Roxboro, and made it a residential district. The sand was hauled to large building sites on 8th Ave., Canada Life Building was one of them. I had two four horse teams and dump wagons, and a very good man to work with me.

In 1914, I bought a car and ran a taxi service for a time. In 1915 and 1916 I ran a large threshing machine for Tony Beggs, east of Queenstown. It was a large 40-80 gas tractor and a thirty-six inch separator. We had a sixty day run in 1915, the year of bumper crops, and in 1916 there were lighter crops and we had only 30 days.

In the winter of 1916 I moved to Gleichen and ran the repair shop for the Ford dealer, Mr. McKee. In 1919, I got a farm lease on the Blackfoot Reserve, southwest of Cluny, on the south of the Bow River, and farmed there till 1923, when I returned to the home place. After selling my lease on the reserve, I rented the Tyson section, in the Melrose District and farmed it along with the home place. When we sold the homestead in 1947, I sold my stock and equipment and moved to High River, where I operated a service station and bulk oil business for 5½ years. During this time I bought a half section farm, two miles east of Cheadle, which I operated.

In 1957, my first wife, Cynthia, passed on and in July of 1958, I married Rhoda Stormes from St. Thomas, Ontario. She was a widow with two sons. We stayed at Cheadle till 1963, when, due to poor health, we sold out and moved to the Crescent Heights District of Calgary, where we still live on 7th Ave. N.E. Our oldest son, Dan, is a diesel mechanic and welder, and lives at Salmo, B.C. The second boy, Charles (Chuck) has his own saddlery here in the city and lives in the small Standish house at the top of Pine Creek Coulee.

I am an associate Director for the Calgary Stampede and in charge of getting teams for parade work, which is a job I have been doing for the last eleven years.

EARLE PERCY AND MARGARET LAVINIA (CAVERELY) BRINTON — by Helen Christie

Earle was born in Nova Scotia in 1884, married Margaret Caverely in 1907 and moved to De Winton from Whitney, Ontario in 1910. There were two children at this time, Earle born in 1908 and Lucy born in 1910. Five other children were born in De Winton, Wentworth in 1911, Paul, 1912, Goldie, 1914, Travis, 1916 and Helen, 1921.

Earle was the C.P.R. station agent from 1910 to 1933. The family lived in the station until the house was built. The house was made from the existing implement shed left by Mr. Pashak. First a kitchen was added to the rear and then a second story was added.

All the children went to Pine Creek School and we took part in the community activities. Mother used to bake huge batches of bread for the store. We always had a big garden. My brothers were typical and got into lots of mischief.

After a twenty-three year stay, we moved to Cayley and remained there for seven years, then to Didsbury for ten years. Dad retired to Calgary in 1950 and resided there until his death in 1957. He was a member of the King Hiram Lodge in Didsbury and the Al Azar Shrine in Calgary.

Mother was born in 1888 and passed away in Calgary in 1966.

Earle married Mary Gange, and they had two chosen children, Bruce and Margaret. Earle passed away in 1951, Mary has remarried and lives in Red Deer. Lucy (Mrs. Clifford Ingram) lives in Calgary, had four children, Peggy, Pat, Clifford and Barbara, all married and living in Calgary. Wenty married Lillian Houlden and they had four boys, Earle, Ronnie, Howard and Charles. They are all married. Wenty passed away in 1955 and Lil lives in Vulcan. Paul married Belle Brookman who lives in Calgary, no children by this marriage. Travis married Freda Faulkerth who lives in Calgary, no children from this marriage. Goldie married Archie Cameron who lives in Salem Oregon, no children. Helen married Jack Christie who lives in Cayley, has four children, Doug and JoAnne both married and Debbie and Bill at home.

CHARLIE AND MRS. (HEY) BROWN

Miss Hey was a teacher at Alexandra school about 1912 and boarded with the W. J. Turnbull family. While there she met Charlie Brown, a bachelor who had worked around the area since his arrival in 1910. They were married about 1914 and lived on several different places including NE¼ 3-22-1-W5 and NE¼ 18-22-1-W5.

Miss Hey had a pronounced English Accent and called herself Miss 'Ey, and some of her pupils have been known to write about their teacher, Miss Aye.

It is not known just when they left the district but both are deceased, Mrs. Brown in 1938 and Charlie about 1966.

The Brinton House in De Winton 1914.

JACK AND GLORIA (CLARK) BROWN — by Jack Brown

Gloria and I were married in the fall of 1952, following our graduation from the University of Alberta. Gloria, who was a graduate of the University Hospital in nursing, was from Meadow Lake, Saskatchewan where her family had been involved in the fish and cattle business. I was raised on a farm at Acme, Alberta where poultry production was one of our major pursuits. It was only natural that we were interested in agriculture of one form or another. Integrated and mass production of poultry intrigued us, inasmuch, as the amount which had to be invested in land was minimal.

In the spring of 1953 we purchased from a Mr. Mowers, who had previously purchased from Mr. Standish, a 20 acre parcel in the SE¼ 11-22-1-W5. This subdivision of property was probably one of the first in the district and understandably was viewed with mixed emotions by many of the long time residents.

Nan and Ralph Graham had recently built to the north of us and Keith and Delnor Horsfield to the south. Vern and Muriel Myers acquired the parcel of land between ourselves and the Graham's and built their home at the same time as we did, in the spring of 1953. It was something of a miracle that the Myers home was ever finished without someone being seriously injured or killed for Vern, or C. V., as he was known, was not mechanically minded and was always in trouble of one kind or another. His tractor was either in the basement from having driven too close or his car had rolled down the hill into the slough at the bottom because he forgot to put on the brake.

Bill and Pat Naylor built across the highway, just north of Pine Creek school, a few months later. One of the Naylor boys, Milton, worked for us after school and on weekends for a couple of years until he finished school and then on a full time basis until 1973. Milt was a good carpenter and helped in the construction of most of the buildings.

By the year 1959 most of our construction had been completed and Pinecrest Poultry Farm was in full operation.

Our daughter, Laurel, was born in the fall of 1953 and attended Pine Creek school in 1959-1960. The school was closed in 1960 and her education was completed at Okotoks and the University of Calgary. A teacher, she is now married and living in Calgary.

Brad was born in 1955 and Hal in 1958. Both boys attended Okotoks school and later Lord Beaverbrook in Calgary. Brad is presently in his fourth year at the University of Alberta in Edmonton and Hal in his second at the University of Calgary. At this writing Pinecrest Poultry Farm is still in operation.

PAT, MARY AND ELI BROWN

Pat and his wife, Mary, and his older, bachelor brother, Eli, were Indians belonging to one of Alberta's northern tribes. For some reason they left the tribe and came down to the De Winton area where they worked for various farmers. Eli was adept at luring coyotes and they made pocket money trapping and shooting. On moving into De Winton, they built a small cabin of poplar logs, on the hillside, south of the C.P.R.

tracks and lived there for a good many years. They were well known in the countryside and tanned hides for some of the district residents. They left the area in the late nineteen forties and are all deceased.

HOWARD AND MARY (BRUCE) BRYAN

The Bryan family came to the Pine Creek district in 1914. There were three children; Della, Howard and Harold. They lived on NW¼ 36-21-1-W5. Mr. Bryan was a great promoter of sport for the young men and put on boxing matches to raise money for the baseball team, which was his real love. He umpired baseball games (hard ball) when Cayley, Turner Valley, Millarville, Kew, Davisburg all had teams. He was popular with all the boys.

One year a neighbour had pigs running loose and they were doing damage to Bryan's crop, when he was asked to restrain them he said shoot them if they come on your place.'' Shortly after, the pigs returned and some were shot. The neighbour took the case to court and Bryan was sent to Lethbridge jail. All of the other neighbours drew up a petition and managed to have him released after he served only a few days.

Mr. Bryan was also a good carpenter and worked over much of the district in this capacity. He was instrumental in helping get the community hall built in 1918.

The children attended Pine Creek school and Mrs. Bryan was active in the social life of the area. In 1924 Mr. Bryan passed away and the family moved to the States.

CHARLES EDMUND AND FLORENCE MARGUERITE (WRIGHT) BURGE — by David Burge

Charles was born at Beckenham, Kent, England in 1889. He apprenticed as a brick-layer in England before coming to Canada in 1907, to his Uncle Rod McKenzie's ranch in Cardston. He worked on his uncle's ranch and on various farms in the Okotoks area and, as a brick-layer, throughout the United States until 1923.

Florence was born in Armstrong, B.C. in 1898 and moved, with her family, to Springbank, Alberta in 1910 and later to Calgary. She attended high school and Normal School in Calgary, taught at Big Rock, near Okotoks, east of Cayley and at Mount Royal College, in Calgary until 1923.

They were married in 1923 and moved to Chicago where they remained until 1932 when they returned to Alberta to live in Nanton, until 1940. In 1940 they moved to Calgary and finally, in 1955, they moved to De Winton where they lived out the remainder of their lives, Charles died in 1970 and Florence in 1972.

They were good neighbours and took an active part in the community, loved to play cards and were often playing partners of Dalzells, Chernows and Grahams. They kept a beautiful garden and were generous with its produce. Florence tutored some of the children that needed extra attention.

Charles and Florence left two boys; David Edwin who attended high school and Mount Royal College in Caglary. Was in the U.S. Air Force from 1945-1947 and moved to California to attend University of California in Berkeley. Graduated in 1949 and has lived in California ever since, with the exception of four years at Oregon State College 1954-1958. Married, with three children, all living in Santa Clara, California, he is president of Wescan Incorporated, a small manufacturer of specialized instruments for chemical analysis. William Roderick, the other son, attended high school and Southern Alberta Institute of Technology in Calgary, graduating in 1950. He worked in Toronto for a year before returning to Calgary where he lived until 1964. Moved to Chula Vista, California where he now lives with his wife and two children. He is department manager at the U.S. Naval Air Station in San Diego.

JESSIE CAROTHERS

I, Jessie Carothers, daughter of Tom and Dollie Dalzell married Keith Carothers in August of 1940. Keith served overseas in World War II for two and a half years. We had two children, Ron and Dale. We moved to Calgary in October of 1949. Keith worked for the Canadian Western Natural Gas Co. and was killed in a pipe line accident on October 17th, 1964. Ron now lives in Inuvik, N.W.T. Dale is married to Jim Barbaro and lives in Calgary. I moved to Okotoks in April of 1969 and in July of 1971 moved to Black Diamond where I am still living at the time of writing — July 1974.

JAMES COPEC

Jim was born in Missouri and raised in a strict Catholic family. Following his elementary education, which included religious training and serving as an altar boy, he entered classes to train for the priesthood. Before his initial training was complete he had managed to get himself into a couple of scrapes which resulted in his leaving, not only the school but his home district as well. Somewhere along the way he was married but little is known of that time in his life. He arrived in Alberta sometime in the late thirties and went to work in logging camps and sawmills. He lived as a bachelor and seldom mentioned his previous life.

After a stint in a sawmill near Turner Valley, he arrived in Calgary looking for work on threshing outfits and ended up on the Marshall crew in the fall of 1943. When the season was over he wanted to stay on in the district and worked for a number of farmers, doing odd jobs, chores and carpenter work. Through the years he worked for Gordon Dafoe, Henry Poffenroth, Alex Anderson and several others. Finally he settled down to live in Scottie's shack on the edge of De Winton.

One night, April 13, 1964, he had settled in for the night and the shack caught fire. Jim met a tragic death for he was unable to make his way out. He was buried in High River cemetery.

HARRY AND SARAH CUSHING — by Ina Blackwood

Harry and Sarah Cushing and their son, Gordon, came to De Winton from Calgary. Mr. Cushing operated a greenhouse just west of the village and Mrs. Cushing taught piano lessons. Many of her pupils came from as far away as Davisburg, driving themselves to De Winton with the horse and buggy, on

Mr. and Mrs. Harry Cushing and Gordon.

Saturday. She was known for many miles around as she played for most of the dances. For several years she was the pianist for the Country Club dances.

They moved back to Calgary in the nineteen twenties and, for a time, Mrs. Cushing was organist at Trinity Methodist Church. After her death in 1959, Mr. Cushing moved to Ottawa, to be with his son and his family. He died there in 1970.

Gordon worked in Calgary for the Read Stock Exchange and the Calgary Brewery. He became interested in the Labor Union and, when he was made Executive-Vice-President, he, and his young family, moved to Ottawa in 1949. At the time of his death, in 1965, he was Assistant Deputy Minister of Labor in the Federal Government.

Gordon married a Calgary girl, Grace LeDrew, in 1937 and they had three children

JAMES ALFRED DALEY

"Alf" Daley was born near Arnprior, Ontario and came west to the Estevan-Primate district of Saskatchewan. In the early thirties he had the General Store at Shepard and, unable to collect many of his accounts, was forced to go out to work for district farmers. In 1932 he came to work for Les Marshall and in the ensuing years he worked for many of the farmers in the De Winton district including; Alex Anderson, Henry Poffenroth and Vera Gillespie.

During the second world war he worked in Kingston in the locomotive works and the munition factory. After the war he returned to the area making his home with the Les Marshalls. He worked for the Empire Hotel in Calgary for a number of years but had to retire because of severe arthritis. He returned to the Marshall farm until he recovered the use of his hands and then went to work for the Government Experimental Farm at Brooks, Alberta. About 1962 he once more returned to the De Winton area and stayed a good part of the time at the Marshall farm. In about 1964 he went to live in Vancouver, B.C. where he passed away in 1968.

JAMES AND CLAUDE (BONY) DALZELL

James (Jim) Dalzell, brother of Jack, Tom and Bob Dalzell came west and settled in the Carbon area of Alberta early in the century. While working in the district, he met and married Claude Bony in 1907 who had come, with her parents and family, in 1902. Jim and Claude remained in the Carbon area until about 1919 when they moved to locate in De Winton. For the first while they lived in the Anglican church manse. Jim opened a garage in the hamlet which he operated, with the help of brother, Tom. Shortly the garage was bought by Artie Maxwell and Jim went to work on the road. He purchased the NW¼ 25-21-1-W5 and continued to work for the Department of Highways until his retirement.

Jim took an active part in the social life of the area and was a popular emcee at the local dances as well as for the Okotoks Country Club. One corner of his property became a baseball diamond and many an exciting ball game was played there. One of his hobbies was making watch chains out of horsehair, a popular item of men's apparel in the 1920's.

Mr. and Mrs. Jim Dalzell and Marion.

A daughter, Marion, was born in 1921 and attended Pine Creek school. She married Clinton Rye of Okotoks and they had two daughters; Donna (Nelson), Seattle, three children; Joan (Cramer), Falher, Alberta, one daughter. Marion passed away in 1961.

Claude, still living, aged 94, is a resident of the Southwood Nursing home in Calgary. During her stay in the De Winton area she was active in the womens' clubs and the United Church. Now, in 1977, she still tells of how kind Mrs. E. P. Brinton was to her when Marion was ill and the family was quarantined. Apparently Mrs. Brinton showed up every day with something special for the child patient or perhaps just to pass on some local news. She always stayed far enough away from the house to prevent getting the infection but managed to keep in close contact. Her concern must have been greatly appreciated in order to remain so long in Claude's memory.

Jim passed away in 1956 and is buried in Pine Creek cemetery.

Jim, Tom, Rob and Jack Dalzell.

ROBERT AND ANNIE (CURRIE) DALZELL — by Myrtle (Dalzell) Gilday

Robert Dalzell and Annie Currie were married at De Winton, N.W.T. March 25, 1902.

Robert Dalzell came from Stratford, Ontario in the early 1890s. His brother Jack had come west earlier.

Annie Currie came west with her mother, Mrs. John Currie, and several of her brothers and sisters. Her father and brother, Herb, had come out the year before. Mrs. Currie and the children came on the first passenger train west on the new C.P.R., and settled in Davisburg for one year. They then moved to the farm, three miles south of De Winton, that was the "Currie Place" for around 80 years.

When Robert and Annie were married they moved to a farm on Pine Creek, known as the Owens' farm. They lived in the house on the east side of the road. In the house on the west side of the road, just the width of the road allowance between them, lived Rev. James Shortt and his mother, when Rev. Shortt was the minister of Pine Creek Church.

Annie and Robert's three children were born at this house on the Macleod Trail. They were Myrtle, Bertha and Colin. Myrtle started school at Pine Creek.

They left De Winton for their new homestead on 27-27-11-W4th, nineteen miles south of Stanmore, Alberta, and arrived there Christmas Day, 1911. They farmed there until 1933 when they moved to a farm one mile east and one and one-half miles north of Lacombe, Alberta.

Annie Dalzell died in December 1939 and Robert

sold the farm a few years later. He moved into Lacombe where he lived until his death in 1963.

Myrtle married Harold Gilday, three of their children were born on a farm, three miles north of Sunnynook, Alberta. During the next several years they lived in and around Lacombe, then moved to Calgary and finally to Yahk, B.C., where Harold passed away in 1964. Myrtle is now living in Cranbrook, B.C.

There were four children, Robert of Cranbrook, Irene (Chalmers) of Lacombe, Marguerite (Kerbes), near Stettler, Mick, with the Calgary Fire Department.

Bertha married Verne Mabbott, they had one daughter Eva (Mullins) widowed and living in Red Deer, Alberta. Bertha passed away in 1948.

Colin married Thelma McKeage, there were four children; Stanley of Nanaimo, B.C., Patricia (Barnes), Orilla, Ontario. Dixie, deceased 1961, and Linda (May), Calgary.

THOMAS AND DOLLIE (DOUGLAS) DALZELL — by Jessie Carothers

Thomas Dalzell was born in Ontario in 1882 and lived at Drumbo until coming west in 1905. He married Dollie Douglas in June of 1908. After spending some time in the Carbon country, they moved to Calgary where he drove for the Pacific Cartage Co. In 1911 they moved to the Douglas place on Pine Creek where they lived until the summer of 1918 when they moved to the Turnbull place. In the spring of 1919 they moved to the McNeill place in De Winton, living there until 1926 when they bought the place where Walter Linn now lives from Jim Dalzell. Tom drove the De Winton Express and hauled milk and express for twenty-one years.

Tom passed away August 21st, 1964 at the age of 82 years. Dollie passed away August 29th, 1970 at the age of 84 years. They are both buried in Pine Creek cemetery.

Tom and Dollie Dalzell.

ALONZO AND SUSAN DeMINGS

The DeMings family came from Nova Scotia and bought the Paling house from Frank Pashak in late 1911. They made it into a type of stopping house and called it "Minto House" after their home in Nova Scotia. Mr. DeMings was Portuguese and well schooled in the life of fishing and must have found in the foothills a vastly different kind of life style.

Alonzo took over the post office in 1912 and ran it until 1926. His daughter, Myrtle, acted as postmaster for much of the time, as they also had the mail carrying contract and were responsible for supplying someone to do that job as well. Alonzo had a little wooden van type of enclosure with side windows and a windshield that he put on wheels in the summer and on sleighs in the winter. There was a small coal burning stove in it for the cold weather and he carried the mail to Gladys Ridge three times a week. His round trip was 44 miles and he was not always able to make it in one day. Fringers was his usual overnight stop when that was necessary. In 1912 and for some time after, he was a partner with W. R. Macdonald in the De Winton Store.

The restaurant part of the operation provided opportunity for some of the local girls to work in the community. One of these was Hazel Stewart. After Myrtle was married and had small children it was also a place for girls to help out and two of these girls were Dorothy Wakeford and Maizie Meehan.

Mrs. DeMings was a kindly gentle woman and much admired by all that passed her way. She worked hard at the house and provided good meals for all travellers. She passed away in 1921. Alonzo stayed on in the community but his son-in-law, Steve Williams, carried the mail. He died in 1930 and is buried in Pine Creek cemetery.

His son, Fielding, a bachelor had lived with them off and on through the years. In about 1932 an older son, Arthur, came, with his family, to live in the house. There were two boys Max and Murray, who attended High School and played ball on the local baseball team. There was also a sister, now Mrs. Nabors of Calgary. Max (deceased) and Murray lives in Edmonton.

SAMUEL AND CAROLINE DESJARDINE

Sam and Carrie purchased the old Brinton house when they arrived in the district from Water Valley and proceeded to remove the top storey. They also purchased the old Ness farm house and used the lumber to help construct a new home on the eastern outskirts of the hamlet, now owned by Tom and Marilyn Bell. This was in the late '30's. There were two children; Emmylou (Harmatta) and Lawrence. Larry attended De Winton high school and served in the Navy in WW2, later moved to Winnipeg where he passed away a number of years ago.

The DesJardines were great community supporters and Sam acted as caretaker for the community hall for several years. Avid card players, they attended all the card parties and also played at local house parties as well as in their own home.

They moved to Vancouver in the '50's and Sam passed away some years ago but Carrie is still living in that city.

ROY AND LOUISE DONKEN

In 1925 when the gas company was putting in a line towards Wylie's, Roy Donken took a job hauling pipe. He and his wife, Louise, lived on the hill above the section house. After a three foot snowfall, the mud was so bad that the roads were impassable and Roy ended up doing odd jobs around the community. They left the area early in the 1930's.

THOMAS DOUGLAS — by Jessie Carothers

Thomas Douglas and Ann Charlton were married in England on March 9, 1866. They left Newcastle-on-Tyne, England for Canada in 1870 settling at Weston, Ontario where they lived until coming west. Tom Douglas came west to Calgary in 1881 and after working as a foreman on a government farm near Midnapore for awhile took up a homestead on Pine Creek in the De Winton area. He had a house built and returned to Ontario in 1885. In 1886 he brought his family west to their homestead on Pine Creek — N½ 10-22-1-W5, where they lived until 1919 when they moved to Calgary.

Mr. T. Douglas.   Mrs. T. Douglas.

They had a family of eight, four girls and four boys. Nellie (Mrs. Klugg) did not come west. Elizabeth married Joseph Harkley and Isabella married Tom McIvor. Pete worked in B.C. for several years before coming back to De Winton and later Calgary. Tom married Margaret Robinson of Midnapore and moved to Carbon where he farmed until 1920 and then moved to Soda Creek, B.C. Will married Margaret Anderson of De Winton where they farmed for a few years before moving to the Horseshoe Canyon west of Drumheller. Jack married Lillian Guitard and farmed the Douglas homestead on Pine Creek and then moved to Maycroft, Alberta. Dorothy (Dollie) married Tom Dalzell in 1908 and in the spring of 1911 they moved to the homestead on Pine Creek where they lived until 1918.

Tom Douglas passed away on November 10, 1920 at the age of 82. Mrs. Douglas passed away on January 21, 1930 at 86 years of age. They are both buried in Pine Creek cemetery.

Mr. and Mrs. Douglas and family were among the original homesteaders in the Pine Creek area, and surviving them were many grandchildren and great-grandchildren.

LeROY DOWLING AND FAMILY—from notes by Florence (Pashak) and Raymond.

Mr. and Mrs. Dowling with their four oldest children arrived in Alberta from Kansas in 1904. They travelled by covered wagon and spent their first few months living in a tent in Calgary. After looking over the prospects, Mr. Dowling decided on the Nanton-Vulcan area and took up a homestead in 1905. During their homesteading years there three more children were born, Florence, Helen and Raymond. In the early 1920's they lived on the Tom Douglas place and Helen and Raymond attended Pine Creek school from

The Douglas House. Mrs. Douglas left, Mrs. Tom Dalzell (Dollie) and Jessie Dalzell centre. Albertine Harkley right.

November, 1922 until the end of June, 1924. Between the years at Nanton-Vulcan the SE¼ 18-22-2-W5 was purchased and the older children went to Priddis school for some time.

Following this they moved to the Olds district and Mrs. Dowling passed away in 1931. Mr. Dowling passed away in 1948 after going to the Peace River country with the three older boys, where they took up homesteads.

Harley served in WWI and after leaving the Peace River settled in Pentiction B.C. Raymond resides in California and the rest of the family have all passed away.

HUGH GEORGE AND ELIZABETH KEYES (BROWN) DUNFIELD

In 1906 the NE¼ 36-21-1-W5 was purchased from P. McKay by H. G. Dunfield from Renfrew, Ontario and by 1911 Dunfield's address was Hand Hills, he had sold to Patrick Kelly. Dunfields lived in the original house but when the Kellys arrived they tore the old structure down and used the lumber for other building.

There were two sons, Leslie and Irwin, both attended Pine Creek school. The family took an active part in the life of the community and were missed when they left.

Leslie married Muriel (?) and they had three children, Eunice, Earle and Olive as well as three grandchildren. They farmed in the Delia district from 1920-1951 when, due to Leslie's health, they moved to Calgary where he passed away in 1956. Irwin married Edythe (Dowler) a primary school teacher who passed away in 1967. Irwin still lives in the Delia area. Hugh lived to the age of 93 and Elizabeth to 88. Both are buried in Delia.

RICHARD DUNN — by George Dunn

My father, Richard (Dick) Dunn, actually was not an oldtimer in De Winton as he arrived from Saskatchewan in February, 1931. He started driving the mail route on April 1 of that year. I don't recall how many years he worked at this job.

He came to B.C. about four years prior to passing away in 1965 in his eighty-fourth year. He was predeceased by my mother in 1956.

I attended De Winton High School and after spending several years in Calgary, moved to Vancouver where, along with my son, I have operated my own business for a number of years.

FRANK AND KATE EMERY

Frank Emery lived on what was later the VanTighem place. He was a bachelor and had a Mrs. Bailly as his housekeeper. There were two Bailly girls, Ena and Betty, who attended Pine Creek school from 1924-1929. Frank married and Mrs. Bailly and the girls left.

Frank and his wife used to visit with the George Anderson family and on one occasion while the Emerys were at the Anderson house, Murray and Rob Anderson slipped away and put a flock of pullets through the window into the Emery's bedroom. Caused quite a commotion!

They left the district, probably in the early '30s,

lived for a while on NE¼ 12-21-29-W4, in the Allan district and then moved to land at Big Rock. After disposing of this land he worked for the town of Okotoks and passed away one day while at work.

THE EVANSES

Three generations have lived on the S½ 10-22-1W5. On August 1st, 1905, the Evans family moved to Midnapore from a homestead in the Priddis area.

The family consisted of Mr. and Mrs. J. H. Evans (Emma Filgiano of Hamilton) and three children, Eileen, Russell and Barton. Five years later the family moved to the S½ 10-22-1W5. The children attended school at Midnapore, Pine Creek and Calgary. Mrs. Evans passed away in 1922 (four years before insulin could have helped her). Mr. Evans was active on the Pine Creek School Board for many years. He died in an accident in 1945 at the age of 76. Eileen went to Vancouver to take her nursing training and married Cyril Gaunt, an engineer. The Gaunts went to England to visit his ailing father prior to World War II. Unfortunately Eileen's husband died just as war commenced so she stayed and nursed in London for the duration. In 1946 Eileen returned to Vancouver. She passed away in 1967.

Mrs. Evans, Russell, Eileen, Barton, J. H. Evans, on the farm.

Russell went overseas in World War I. He was wounded in 1916 and transferred to army headquarters in England where he remained until the War ended. Upon returning to Canada he farmed on SE¼-1-22-2W5 and NE¼ 36-21-2W5. He devoted his life to helping the young people in the community through working with Alexandra School, De Winton High School, the local School fairs and many other youth activities. He also took a very active part in St. Patrick's Church, Midnapore. He retired from farming in 1968 and is at present residing at the Lacombe Home, Midnapore.

Barton farmed with his father until he married Jessie Hunt of Priddis in 1928. They farmed on the Ghost Pine near Three Hills for six years before returning to the Pine Creek place where they still live. They had five children, Jack, Vera, David, Alice and Margaret Rose, who passed away in 1953 at the age of nine.

The Priddis homestead was used for summer pasture until it was sold in 1965. The cattle brand used by the Evans family is PTI.

All the children took their schooling up to Grade 9 at Pine Creek School. Jack, Vera and David attended High School in De Winton. Vera finished her education at Lacombe Home School, Midnapore. Alice finished her education at St. Mary's in Calgary.

Vera went to Vancouver to take her nursing training. She and her husband Greg Curtis still live in Vancouver. They have no family and Vera is still nursing.

David and Elinor have three children and at present reside in Calgary.

Alice and her husband, Bill Chauncey, have a family of eight children. They live at St. Albert, Alberta. Jack lived at home where he farmed until he married Shirley Best in 1956 and they moved to W½ 15-22-1W5. Jack and Shirley have four children Lorna, Margaret, John and Joan, and they attend school at Red Deer Lake and Calgary. In 1967 Jack and family moved back to S½ 10-22-1W5.

JAMES AND ANNE GILCHRIST EVERSON

In 1930 when the Midland and Pacific elevator in De Winton was in need of a new man, Jim Everson was sent to run it. Jim came, originally, from South Dakota and his wife, Anne, from North Carolina. They had lived in Alberta for some time before taking up residence in De Winton. They had one daughter, Hazel, who became a registered nurse and, later, married Tony McKinlay of Calgary.

Jim was a former baseball player and used to umpire the local games here. He was a popular man and much in demand to play the cornet at De Winton dances. He and Anne were avid card players and attended all the card parties around as well as playing at neighbours' homes. Anne soon became known for her excellent cooking and beautiful handwork, her ready help whenever it was needed. They opened their home to make a convenient boarding place for the high school teacher on different occasions.

The Eversons retired to Calgary in 1954 and Jim passed away in Sept. 1966. Anne continued to live in her own home until illness forced her to enter Sarcee Auxiliary Nursing Home where she still resides.

Hazel had three children: Sharon, now Mrs. Beddome, mother to two; Patrick, father of six, lives in Calgary and Raymond, Ph.D. in economics, father of two, lives in Winnipeg. Hazel passed away in April 1965.

GEORGE AND KATHRYN FOX — by Lloyd Fox

George and Kathryn Fox and family left De Winton in 1951. They originally moved from Cluny, Alberta, in 1937 and rented a quarter section of land approximately ten miles southwest of the town of De Winton. The land on which they first settled was owned by Mr. Alfred Boyce of Calgary. The oldest six children attended Alexandra School, which was four and a half miles northwest of their home. Summer and winter this daily trek was made, to and fro, by horseback, or occasionally, by foot. Other schools attended by the Fox children were Pine Creek and De Winton High School.

In the early spring of 1940, the Fox family moved to a half section of land, located one mile due north of De Winton. This property was rented by them and was owned by Mrs. Soley of Calgary. This was the family home for eleven years until they moved to Calgary.

In 1956, Mr. and Mrs. Fox decided to move to Salem, Oregon, U.S.A. By this time however, some of the older children were already grown up and had jobs and homes of their own, so, only the younger children moved south with their parents.

Mr. Fox passed away in 1964 in Salem. Mrs. Fox has since married Mr. A. Meidinger and they reside in Lodi, California. Mr. and Mrs. Fox and their fourteen children were probably one of the largest families ever to make their home in the De Winton area.

During the war years, Harold, the eldest son, worked for the federal government at E. F. T. S. (Elementary Flying Training School), located approximately nine miles east of De Winton.

Don Fox, presently living in the De Winton area, is a grandson to George Fox. His father, Reinhold, is George's son by a previous marriage. There were five children from this marriage; George, deceased; Reinhold, Edmonton; Esther, Vancouver; and Freda, Vancouver. The first Mrs. Fox was a victim of the flu epidemic that followed World War I.

Members of the Fox family have taken up residence in various parts of Canada, the United States and Europe. Harold, father of two in Lethbridge, Alberta; Leonard (deceased), father of five, lived in High River; Melvina (Hill), mother of three, Kelowna, B.C.; Vera (Freisen), mother of three, San Diego, California; Lloyd, father of two, Calgary, Alberta; Lorena (Ashlyn), mother of four, Salem, Oregon; Merwin, father of two, Calgary; Audrey (Nameth), mother of two, Calgary; Kenneth, father of two, Grande Prairie, Alberta; Leslie, father of three, High River, Alberta; Alfred, father of four, Lodi, Califonia; Larry, father of two, West Germany; Norman, father of three, Lodi, California; Glen, Reading, England.

IDA AND ALFRED GOOCH

Ida and Alf Gooch, brother and sister, were the children of an affluent, socially prominent family in

James and Anne Everson, Sharon, Raymond, Hazel, (Everson) and Patrick McKinlay.

England. Both were well educated and knowledgeable. Early in the 1890's they came to the De Winton area where Alf homesteaded SW¼ 28-21-1-W5. He was on the board of trustees of the Stormount school district from 1908-1910 and served as chairman of the board for this period.

When the Arrowwood district opened up for homesteads, John McNeill took up a homestead there which he later traded to Alf Gooch for his Stormount area farm. After a few years on his newly acquired place, Alf decided that the De Winton district was more to his liking and returned to purchase SW¼ 32-21-29-W4 where he remained until selling to Mr. Horning in 1944.

He lived in the Minto house in De Winton for awhile and then moved to Okotoks where he passed away in February, 1959.

In the days when all farming was done with horses Alf had his horses stolen just when spring work was about to begin. He was so upset by the ordeal that he suffered a mild stroke which left him unable to think things out clearly or to remember anything for very long. He became a familiar sight walking from his farm to the store with a basket over his arm, reminding himself all the way of what he had to purchase when he arrived.

When the cyclone went through the district in 1927, Alf had his horses tied in the barn, the wind lifted the shell of the building and carried it away leaving the horses still tied in the stalls.

Ida was a pleasant young woman, an accomplished rider and possessed a wry sense of humour. She was most unfortunate in losing her hearing due to a bout with scarlet fever. For the first years she kept house for Alf but when he went to Arrowwood she bought twelve lots in De Winton including the building that Mr. Willet had erected and lived there from then on. She was an excellent needlewoman and managed to contrive a short coat, a pair of one finger mitts and a hat with generous earflaps, all from a long coonskin coat owned by Mr. W. Hamilton Sr. This job was done for Sam Hamilton and he wore the outfit for a good many winters.

Ida was assistant postmaster to Bob Smith for quite a number of years. She passed away in May, 1961. Both Ida and Alf are buried in Okotoks.

GORDON A. AND RUBY (HART) GRAHAM — by Virginia Wright

Gordon, second son of Hugh and Mary Graham, was born in the district, attended Pine Creek School and worked on the farm as well as carrying the rural mail. Ruby, came to the district with her parents in the early thirties, attended De Winton High School. Following their marriage they lived on the "Old Morgan Place," W½-34-21-1-W5. Their eldest daughter Virginia was still a baby when the old house burned down. Fortunately there were no injuries but the house was a total loss. All that remained was the chimney, a small square of bricks, three storeys high. The old cook house from the Anglesey oil well was purchased and moved on to the property as a dwelling.

There were two boys, Ronald and Keith, born during their stay on the farm. They later moved into De Winton where Sue-Ellen was born and another daughter, Maureen arrived after they left the district.

The three eldest children attended Pine Creek School until its closure when they were bused to Okotoks.

Ron, Sue-Ellen, Keith and Maureen all reside in Calgary and I, Virginia, have spent my married life in British Columbia. Mother passed away in 1961 and Dad, at this time, is in Okotoks.

HUGH AND MARY (McNEILL) GRAHAM — by Norman Graham

Hugh W. Graham was born in Earltown, Nova Scotia, went to Vancouver as a young man and joined the Vancouver Police Force. It was here he met and married Mary McNeill. In 1918 they came to live near DeWinton. Their eldest son, Hugh Norman, was then about two years old and later there was a second son, Gordon A. and a daughter, Mary Ellen (deceased 1951). They first lived on NE¼ 3-22-1-W5 where they built a house. After several years they moved to the E½ 21-1-W5 and lived in the old Hooley house still retaining their quarter.

About 1925, when Ellen was still quite a small child, she developed scarlet fever and Hugh also came down with it, a very serious thing at his age. The neighbours were all very helpful and brought groceries and looked after the place until he was up and around. Dad had another misfortune, after we moved up to the Hooley place, he cut his foot, quite seriously, with an axe, and again, the neighbours lent helping hands.

Mother used to raise hatching eggs for the hatcheries and was successful at it. Using an old type, coal oil burning, brooder didn't make it an easy task and there was always the danger of fire. We always had a big garden and kept a few milk cows.

Dad was the Elevator Agent at Academy for quite a

Hugh and Mary Graham with grandchild — 1944.

few years and used to walk back and forth to work on the track. This prompted one small boy, when asked what ran on the railroad, to say, "the train and Mr. Graham."

We children all went to Pine Creek School and I went to De Winton High School. We rode saddle horses and, sometimes, walked. There seemed to be always quite a good number of pupils going to school and we found lots to do. I remember when Ellen was going to Pine Creek, the snow got so deep that Dad and Stuart Jamison had to go and dig through drifts for the saddle horses to get through.

My parents were especially fond of cards and played a lot of 500 with the neighbours. Tom and Dolly Dalzell were close friends with common interest. They took part in community affairs and Dad served on the Pine Creek School Board.

Dad passed away sudddenly at home in 1958. Mother moved to Calgary where she lived until her death in 1976.

I, Norman, married Lilian Hart, live in Calgary, have four children, Bill, Lawrence, Joan (Richardson) and Danny, one son, David died in childhood, and six grandchildren.

Gordon married Ruby Hart (deceased) and has five children and nine grandchildren.

Ellen was married to Emil Befus.

RALPH AND NAN (RODIE) GRAHAM — by Nan Graham
Blocks 3 and 4 Plan 7744 G.N. Pine Creek E½ 11-22-1-W5

We bought two, north-west parcels of the Clarke Standish place where Pine Creek and the Macleod Trail cross, one of the earlier sub-divisions of land, to small holdings, in the De Winton area. Commuting from city employment, (Ralph was a sales executive and I was a registered nurse) we worked evenings and week-ends to build a hobby farm, raising hay, horses and cattle. With Ralph's hobby of woodworking and carpentry, we built up a very convenient place.

We were both enthusiastic supporters of community activities and were involved in Fall Suppers, dances, concerts, hall cleaning and decorating bees, even cemetery care and landscaping. As we often stated, "one meets the good people, old timers and new-comers alike, at such gatherings.

I organized a Pony Club, officially recognized as the Pine Creek Branch, in 1955. It was inspected by Colonel Michael Gutewski, then as now, in charge of rider development for Canadian Olympic Teams. I taught riding, Western and English saddle, care of tack and horse, organized trail rides and show events, that are high-lights in local memories. I also raised and exhibited horses and ponies at Calgary, Edmonton, Saskatoon and the Royal Winter Fair at Toronto. As well as Pony Club activities I was a member and director of the Alberta Light Horse Association and was named Horse-Woman of the year and made an Honorary Life Member, in 1955. I worked on many horse show committees and became an associate director of the Calgary Exhibition and Stampede. My present involvement in the horse show world is judging horse shows as a registered horse show judge in the Canadian Horse Show Association and the American Horse Show Association.

On our property was an original, log stopping house, Post Office and store, one of five such cabins between Fort Macleod and Calgary. An original daily store account book (1890-1892), rescued from between the cabin walls by Clarke Standish, acquired, preserved and bound and still in my possession, is still much prized by descendants of the customers whose names and purchases are recorded therein.

Both of us inherited an understanding of pioneer history for Ralph's folks were among the first of Cypress Hills Settlers and his Grandmother was the first nurse at Assiniboia, (Medicine Hat), attending victims of typhoid attacks in N.W.M.P. and early settlers. My father's relatives (Tom Rodie) were also here in pre-province times later moving to the Okanogan, where I was born.

Ralph was a keen collector of Early Canadiana, he had a fine collection, gathered through the years.

Due to Ralph's problem, we moved to Calgary in 1970 where Ralph died four years later. I still reside in Calgary and nurse at the Calgary Exhibition and Stampede Park.

LUKE GREY
A bachelor, steam engineer, built a shack on the hillside south of the C.P.R. tracks. An ardent admirer of Heaver's 'hired girls'. Returned to the States, still single, in the early '20s.

HERBERT C. HAINES
Herb. Haines, as a young man, worked at various farms in the De Winton district during the years 1910-12. One in particular was Archie Bremner's.

He was remembered as an excellent piano player and was in great demand to play for dances held in "Pashak's Hall", located over the De Winton store.

From De Winton he went to Vancouver where he was employed in the office of the C.P.R. Express. He and his wife, Isabelle, and family, Bill, Gertrude and Angus made their home on Kingsway, near New Westminster.

HUGH AND ELLA HAMILTON — by Ella Hamilton
In September of 1933 we arrived in De Winton where Hugh was to be the new station agent. We were told that the station was from the old Northern Alberta Railroad and we could well believe it was true, although we don't know it as a fact. It was an old, cold barracks and the wind blew right through it. However, we spent six happy years there. When we arrived the family consisted of Hugh Jr., Margaret and Shirley, our youngest son, Jim, was born during our stay there.

The children went to Pine Creek School and when I get together with the girls, we often talk of the De Winton days. How Tom Dalzell took them to school in his truck and they walked home, winter and summer. Miss Thomas was the Pine Creek teacher and when Margaret was in high school the teacher was Miss Barroll. Hugh Jr. was on the ball team and I belonged to the Community Club and the Ladies' Aid. Hugh Sr., Lily Hart and Lent Orton played for the dances and Hugh put on a play one year. We used to enjoy the annual picnic and wonder if they still have them.

Hugh and Ella Hamilton, Golden Wedding Anniversary.

Douglas Harkness.

After leaving De Winton, we spent time at various other points and finally settled in Calgary. We operated a coin wash for a number of years and after Hugh passed away I took an apartment and still reside in Calgary. Hugh Jr. was drowned in a tragic accident at Lake Louise, in 1946. Margaret (Reesor), lives in Ottawa, has two children, Kathy and David. Shirley (Fulmer), has two daughters, lives in Tripoli, Libya, and Jim lives in Vancouver, has one daughter.

HON. D. S. HARKNESS — by D. Harkness

I bought S.E.¼ 2-22-1-W5, the Archie Bremner homestead, in 1947 and spent that fall fixing up the two old houses and putting pig pens in the barns. In December I hired a man and his wife and put in thirty sows, in pig. The man left the next summer and I hired Ray Glasco who remained with me until 1956 or '57. During this period we ran some fifty sows and sold large numbers of weiner pigs as well as finishing up several hundred a year as market pigs. We had a crop in every year, chiefly barley and oats to feed the pigs. Considerable quantities of barley and oats were also purchased from farmers in the district and from the De Winton elevators.

After I joined the Federal Conservative Cabinet in 1957, several people were on the farm working it on shares for me. Finally I had such an arrangement with Ralph Stinn, the elevator agent at De Winton, for several years and lasting until his son, David, was killed in a highway accident, early in 1976. During this period the farm was seeded to grass.

During the period from 1947-1957, my wife and I lived on the farm a good deal of the time, when Parliament was not sitting. We have not lived there since.

FRANK AND EMMYLOU (DesJARDINE) HARMATTA

Frank and Emmylou, with their tiny daughter, Jacqueline, arrived in De Winton in the late 1930's and settled into the Orton house, presently owned by Ivan Dick. Frank bought the bulk oil business from Pete Goerlitz as well as some land which he farmed, across the road from the old Shell service station. Three more daughters were born to them. Kathy, Jeannine and Cherie. All four girls attended Pine Creek school. The family remained as active members of the community until the 1950s when they moved to Vancouver where they still reside. All of the girls are married and there are several grandchildren.

HENRY H. AND CONSTANCE R. (PRATT) HARPER — by Catherine MacKenzie

Henry Harness Harper was born in 1887, in Bristol, England and came to Canada, to homestead west of Turner Valley, in 1912. Due to the war, this land was sold and he joined "The Highlanders", and transferred to the Signalers where he became a Lieutenant. In April of 1916, he married Constance Pratt in Okotoks.

Constance R. Pratt was born in 1888, came to Canada in 1912 to live with her brother, Harold Pratt, who at that time was farming south of Okotoks. She worked as a nurse for Dr. Ardiel.

A son, John, was born in England. Following the war, there was a short farming stay at Sundre, and at the Halifax place (now the Canyon Meadows area of Calgary). From there we moved four miles south and a mile west of Midnapore on Pine Creek, purchasing

Harper family: Henry Harness and Constance R. (Pratt) Harper April 22, 1916.

Barbara Harper with the pony she rode when she won the cup for best girl rider under fifteen at the Calgary Summer Show.

the farm from the Douglas Estate in 1924. The buildings were log and situated in the valley by the creek. Only forty acres were broken at this time. In 1929, new buildings were built on top of the hill, but due to the depression setting in, the house diminished in size, and it took many years to shingle the barn.

Forty acres were cut off the south-east side of the half section by the C.P. Railroad. By the railway was the Midland and Pacific Elevator. It replaced a large board granary owned by Crown Feed. A road ran through the farm, leased by the elevator company, for the surrounding farmers to haul their grain. It was closed one day a year for ownership rights. It was a busy road with four horse teams hauling grain tanks in the fall. Later, the horses were replaced by trucks. Many Indians used this road travelling to the Stampede.

I can remember the day the Pine Creek Church burned down after being struck by lightning. The men went to put the fire out, and I watched from the up-stairs window.

Water was a problem in the dry years. The creek was dry, and holes were dug in the creek bed, but they quickly dried up. Cattle were thin and feed was scarce. Our chief income was from cream and eggs. Pigs, sheep and calves were also raised.

There were two other children — Catherine, born in Okotoks, and Barbara, born in Calgary. We all went to Pine Creek School, and De Winton High School, using the usual modes of transportation, riding, buggy and sometimes cutter.

John married Jean Blackie of Priddis, and now is operating a dairy farm at Rocky Mountain House. Catherine, (Kitty) married Alexander MacKenzie of Scotland, and now is nursing at the Turner Valley Municipal Hospital. Barbara married Mason Ramsay of Nova Scotia. She died in July, 1972.

In 1949, Mr. and Mrs. Harper retired to a 1½ section farm in the Dalemead area, and the farm was sold to Louis Lakatos. Due to poor health, this land was sold a year later and the Harpers retired to Brentwood Bay, Vancouver Island. Here Mr. Harper worked as a com-missionaire until his 82nd birthday. He died in December 1972 at the age of 82. Constance died August, 1972, at the age of 84.

Through the years on the farm, they used the same brand, which is registered and now used by their son, John. The brand shown elsewhere in the book.

DAVID WILLIAM AND SUSANNAH LILIAN (MOSS) HART — by L. Graham

My father, Dave Hart, was the section foreman for the C.P.R. coming to De Winton from Pincher Station in 1932. Our family consisted of my parents, one sister, Ruby, and myself. Ruby attended De Winton High School, married Gordon Graham, younger son of Hugh and Mary Graham, and they lived in the district for some years before moving to Turner Valley. I married Gordon's older brother, Norman, and we moved to Calgary where we have lived ever since.

My parents left De Winton, to reside in Calgary, in the fall of 1947. Mother died in December, 1950 and Dad is still living in Calgary.

ULYSSES GRANT AND ANNIE (REID) HARTWICK — by Fred Hartwick

Father was born in Michigan in 1869, and was married to Annie Reid in 1891.

In the fall of 1893, father arrived in Olds, Alberta, and purchased land northwest of the town. The following summer, his wife and oldest son, John, came west to their new home. They drove seven miles to their log house, which Father and Uncle Will Reid had built. A second son, Frederick Grant, was born on November 19, at home.

In 1896, they moved to the DeWinton district, where a third son, Newton, was born on March 11, 1898. Mother and Father worked on two different farms; first for John Owens, and then for Henry Hooley, until they rented a farm, south of Midnapore in 1902. Mother died in 1904, and is buried in Pine Creek Cemetery. In 1905, we moved back to Olds, where my brother, Newton, died. That fall, we moved east of Brant, where Father took a homestead.

Mr. and Mrs. Grant Hartwick and sons, John, Fred and Newton, about 1900.

ULYSSES GRANT AND MARGARET (DALZELL) HARTWICK

In 1909, November 9, Father remarried to Miss Margaret Dalzell. In 1910, he sold the homestead and farmed rented land for three years, after which, he purchased land near High River in 1912. This is where I farmed until 10 years ago, when we retired to High River.

I, Fred, took over the home place in 1919, and Father bought a quarter section, a mile east of this farm. In 1943, he sold this land and bought two lots in DeWinton, where he built a small house and retired.

Father died in June, 1951, and Mrs. Hartwick in 1961. Both are buried in the Pine Creek Cemetery.

Mr. and Mrs. Hartwick were both very active in community work, and in the church and Sunday School. The student minister boarded at their home, also some of the school teachers. Many acts of kindness were performed, of which no one but those concerned, were aware.

Fred Hartwick and Alice Watt were married on June 12, 1923, and raised a family of five children; Grant A., Marion A. (Kinnear), Gwendolyn I. (Miller), Jean E. (Morrison) and Norman.

ISABEL (DOUGLAS) HAZLETT — by I. Hazlett

In 1910-11, at the age of seven, I attended Pine Creek School. The nearest school was many miles away from where my folks lived in the Horseshoe Canyon district near what is now the city of Drumheller. The only immediate solution was to live with grandparents, Mr. and Mrs. William Anderson, and attend Pine Creek School.

Our teacher's name was Miss Davis. Some of the pupils' names that I remember were; June, Vera, Leslie and Marjorie Marshall, Kathleen and Willy Kelly, Ida McInnes, Sadie and Hugh McNeill, Doris Watson, Bert King, Barton Evans, Jean Bremner, and Myrtle Dalzell. I liked to chum with Marjorie Marshall.

I had less than a mile to walk along the Macleod Trail while some of the others rode horseback or drove in a buggy, or a sleigh in winter.

Most of our writing was done on a slate instead of paper as it is today. At noon and recess we enjoyed games such as "Hide and Seek."

The school was heated with a big wood and coal heater at the back of the room. Water was carried to school by some of the older pupils.

During the year our teacher, Miss Davis, was married and became Mrs. Latimer. I remember we gave her a gift of silver-wear and Leslie Marshall had the honor of making the presentation. Miss Stubbs replaced Miss Davis as our teacher.

My year at Pine Creek School was a memorable experience. Besides the privilege of living with my grandparents I made many friends.

ALEXANDER AND JEAN (GRANT) HISLOP — by Bill Hislop

Alex Hislop was born in the village of Maxton, East End, Scotland, in 1881 and Jean Grant Hislop was born in the town of Rosemarkey, County Inverness, Scotland, in 1884.

Alex came to Calgary from Scotland in 1906, with his boyhood friend, Jock McRae. Jean Grant came in 1907 and they were married the same year.

McRae and Hislop worked for a contractor, building houses in Calgary, in 1906 and in 1907, McRae went to homestead in Hemaruka, Alberta. Hislop went to work for A. M. Terrill's as a gardener, having apprenticed for this in Scotland. He worked for Terrills

Alex Hislop Sr. family about 1918.

both in Calgary and Medicine Hat. In 1910 he went to work for the C.P.R. in the Bridge and Building Department, constructing aqueducts in the Lethbridge area. When the depression came, in 1912, he returned to Calgary and worked as a gardener for Dr. McKid Sr., later going out to his farm in Davisburg, to build the house and farm buildings.

He continued in the contracting of farm buildings in the Davisburg District. With Jim Dalzell and volunteer labor, he built the De Winton Hall in 1918.

The Hislop family lived in the De Winton area all through these years. In 1923, we moved to Okotoks but Dad continued contracting in the farm areas till 1927 when he went back to the C.P.R. Bridge and Building Department and stayed through 1928 and 1929, constructing the buildings at the Lake O'Hara Resort Centre in the Banff Park Area. Following this, he went with Tom Visser Construction and, during the depression years, built the Okotoks Arena and the J. H. McNeil hardware store. When Tom Visser died in 1935, Alex Hislop Jr. took over his business in Oilfield Contracting and Hislop Sr. stayed with the business till 1939.

They purchased a farm north of Okotoks where they lived till 1947, then they built a house in Okotoks and stayed there until retiring to Calgary in 1950.

Jean Hislop died in 1951 and Alex, in 1954. They had five children, Alex Jr. presently living in Sicamous, B.C., Violet, born in Medicine Hat, deceased 1928, Jeanette, living in Port Alberni, B.C., Arnold, born in De Winton, living in Kaleden, B.C., and Bill, born in De Winton and living in Calgary.

CHARLES HENRY HOOLEY

Mr. Hooley arrived from England about 1887 and acquired the W½ 34-21-1-W5 and the W½ 3-22-1-W5 and proceeded to make arrangements to have a set of buildings put up. It is not known exactly when the family took up residence but sometime in the early 1890's. A full retinue of servants accompanied the family and a regular English manor type of operation began. There was a gardener as well as stable boys, groom and household help. A second dwelling was built and occupied by locally hired families. The first of these families is believed to be Grant Hartwick and it was during his time of employment there that they undertook to dig a well. One noon hour, when they had reached the depth of about ninety feet, and the men had gone into the house for dinner, water burst into the well at about the half-way mark of the excavation. All of the tools had been left in the bottom and the water was boiling out of the top of the well when the men returned to work. This has been a flowing well in wet years ever since. A windmill was erected and the wind power was used to grind grain, one of the few of that type of grinder ever used in this country.

A three storey frame house, with beautifully landscaped grounds became the centre for neighbourhood gatherings and friends from England were also much in evidence. Trees were planted around the house and flowers flourished in great abundance, it was a real show place.

His wife and two sons as well as a brother, Walter, made up the family. Walter stayed with the family for a few years and then moved to the Millarville district where he married Norah Polkinghorne, in 1912. His body was found in the Bow River in the fall of 1913. His widow and infant son returned to England some time later. In 1906 the barn burned down, seemingly caused by children playing with matches. Fortunately no one was injured. In 1910 the farm was rented to Greigs for the year and Hooleys went to Vancouver.

The Hooleys had a sale and sold the farm W½ 34-21-1-W5 to Mr. E. Morgan who bought it for his son, Percy, to farm. This was in 1911 and it is believed that the Hooley family returned to their home in England.

GEORGE AND ALICE (STANDISH) IRVING — by Alice Irving

George grew up in the Vulcan district and is the son the late Austin Irving, who spent his younger years in the Davisburg district. George's grandfather, John A. Irving, and family came west in the 1880's, and bought the farm now occupied by Larry and Evelyn Herr.

George and I were married in 1940, after spending the first summer at Vulcan, moved to De Winton, and rented Mother and Dad's farm as a going concern. We carried on with the dairy business until the spring of 1945.

We took over the White Rose service station at the De Winton turn-off and operated it until fall. Dad had a sale in the fall of 1945, disposed of cattle and machinery, and we returned to the farm and rented the land.

While we lived at De Winton, our three daughters were born. Jean was born in 1943 and took her first two years of schooling at Pine Creek. She completed her education at Sundre, and married Joe Hart in 1966. They have one daughter and live at Hinton.

Shirley was born in 1946 and was educated at Sundre. She married Marvin Kubik in 1968, and they live in Olds with their two children. Betty was born in 1947, educated at Sundre. She married Ronald Rose in 1967, and they and their three children live at Sundre.

In 1951, Dad sold the farm, and we moved to a place of our own at Sundre, where we farmed till 1973. We sold out in the fall and spent the first winter touring the Southern States. We returned to retire to a home in Olds.

There are so many things I remember when I was growing up in the De Winton district, a few of them being:

The Mounties patrolling the country on horseback, wearing their red coats; Mr. and Mrs. Jack Dalzell driving to church with the horse and buggy; Mr. Jack Davis with his steam threshing outfit; Tom Dalzell taking Mrs. Dalzell to Calgary with him and forgetting to bring her home; Vera Marshall taking us down to skate when she was our teacher; Mrs. Archie Bremner driving her Model T touring car; Mrs. Gier living in a tent, winter and summer, while she taught at Pine Creek School for two years; the 1927 hailstorms and cyclones; the hockey games and skating on the Poffenroth slough; Pine Creek Church burning down after being struck by lighning, and the good times we had with our school mates, ones that are still here and others that have passed away.

ROBERT AND MARY CATHERINE (HENDERSON) JAMISON

Robert Jamison was born in Ireland and came to

Robert and Mary Jamison about 1879.

Canada as a young man. In about 1879 he married Mary Catherine Henderson whose parents owned the Rosemount Hotel in Rosemount, Ontario. Mary was sixteen at the time of her marriage. Following the birth of their first three children, they set out for the west and travelled for three months, across Canada to Vancouver and back to the De Winton area where they took up land, NW¼ 9-22-1-W5 which was C.P.R. grant No. 567.

The story is told that Robert looked down from his hill and saw Mr. Douglas ploughing with a "riding plough" and remarked "my, my, riding and ploughing, what is the world coming to?" He is also credited with being the first one to have one of his boys drive a team and democrat while he sat with his legs dangling out the back and broadcast his seed grain.

Through the years their family grew to eleven children, one of whom died in infancy, Mary (Ross) died in 1970, Elizabeth (Kearney) died 1974, Belle (Mrs. J. McInnes) died early in the century, Sarah (Dalzell) died 1963, Robert of Kitscotty, died 1969, Maria (Currie) died 1957, Stuart, 1886-1952, married Margaret Wylie, four children surviving, Willie, married M. Bristow, died in the 1930's, Clara, (Sunderland), died 1973, left one daughter, Lenore (Wilson), David, the youngest, killed overseas in 1915 at the age of 21.

After leaving the farm, Mrs. Jamison lived in Calgary and through the years a number of the young girls from this district boarded with her when they were attending school in the city. She was loved by all and sadly missed when she passed away in 1929.

The family was raised in the district and many of them married local residents and lived out their lives here. Their home was a haven for young bachelors when the girls were growing up. When Robert opened the door one day to have a young man tell him he was in search of a heifer that had strayed away he said, "the heifer you are looking for is just behind the door." It was, no doubt, an embarrassing moment for the fellow, but he is purported to have married "the same heifer" a short time afterward.

The farm was sold to Dr. Lindsay in 1912.

STUART AND MARGARET BAIRD (WYLIE) JAMISON — by E. Hill

Robert and Mary Ann (Henderson) Jamison came across Canada from Ontario in 1884, to settle in the Pine Creek area. It was here that same year that Stuart Jamison was born. He attended the old Pine Creek School and, in later years, worked on farms in the district. He worked for 'Daddy' Grey and also for Frank Pashak, in the store. In 1914 he joined the army and served overseas until being honorably discharged, because of injuries, in 1918.

In 1919, he married Margaret Baird Wylie, who had come from Scotland several years before. They homesteaded a farm just ½ a mile south of where he was born. They lived there until Stuart's death in 1952, where they were active community workers through the years.

Stuart was Government Weed Inspector in the De Winton, Okotoks and Turner Valley areas for several years before his death.

They were both staunch supporters of the church and worked hard for it. Stuart served on the church board for many years. All community affairs were of interest to them and they were always in evidence when there was work to be done.

Maggie was a professional seamstress and had taken her training in Scotland and she sewed for everyone in the district. She made the stage curtains for the old hall, as well as a very nice Santa Claus suit for use at the Christmas Concerts.

Mr. and Mrs. Jamison had five children: David, Sylvia, Eleanor, Shirley and Audrey. David farmed with his father and later served in active duty with the Royal Canadian Air Force from 1941 to 1944. He spent time as a prisoner of war in 1943-44. On his return to De Winton, he married Fern Orton and settled on the farm for several years. They now live in Calgary and have three sons. The other children: Sylvia, died in infancy; Eleanor Hill resides in Calgary and has two children; Shirley Noble who lives in Langley, B.C. and has four children; and Audrey Smith who lives in Calgary.

Stuart Jamison family: l. to r. Shirley, Eleanor, Maggie, Stuart, Audrey, David.

GEORGE AND JEAN (ANDERSON) KELLOCK

George Kellock had expansive interests in the Coleman coalmines and the family had resided in Coleman for quite a number of years when he decided to buy the E½ and NW¼ 9-22-1-W5 from Dr. Lindsay. It was to be a home for his daughter Agnes and her husband Mr. Pratt. The young couple did not live there long, for Agnes died at the birth of her first child and the place was run by a series of hired help.

A landing runway had been built for light aircraft and Mr. Kellock often flew up to keep in touch with farm progress. He also had several granaries built from cement blocks, not very satisfactory.

Mr. Kellock died from a heart seizure about 1940 and the farm was rented for a while when Mrs. Kellock and her son, Jim, moved in. Mrs. Kellock was a tiny woman who had been raised in a large family in Scotland. She never relinquished her childhood fears of poverty and was very careful in the handling of money. She enjoyed playing cards and often had neighbours in to make up a table to pass the cold winter nights. She was good company and had a sharp wit. Jim, his wife, Ellen and their son, George, spent a good deal of time at the farm. In about 1953 Mrs. Kellock moved into a house in Calgary where she passed away in the 1960's.

Jim predeceased his mother and George Junior is the only one left.

Hugh Brown lived on the place from 1953-1955 and then it was sold to Dr. Duffin.

THE KELLY FAMILY — by Tom Kelly

In the spring of 1903 Dad and Mom, Mr. and Mrs. Pat. Kelly, arrived in De Winton from Dominion City, Manitoba. Dad had been out earlier and bought a half section of land about one mile northeast of De Winton. At that time, De Winton was not much of a town, a post office, store and blacksmith shop. It has never been a very large town, and has really not grown much since the early days.

Dad raised horses and cattle, also did some farming. I remember we used to haul grain to Calgary by team and wagon when I was still quite young. I often made a trip every day. I remember when coming home once, I met one of the first automobiles - not much to look at by today's standards. My horses did not like it a bit. They took off across the prairie and it took some time to get them under control. Imagine today with the millions of cars, a horse would not even look at them.

Dad farmed until 1913 when he rented the farm and bought a house in Calgary. He figured on retiring but one year was enough of that, and he returned to the farm. After a short illness he passed away in 1916 at age fifty-nine years.

There were seven children in the family when we

The Kelly Family in the late 1880's. Mr. Patrick Kelly with Margaret, Mrs. Kelly, a cousin and Janie Kelly, J. I. Kelly seated in front.

arrived in De Winton and around 1908 another son was born which made a family of eight.

"Doc", the oldest, took up dentistry. He practised in the old Herald building in Calgary for over fifty years. He passed away in Ottawa at the age of eighty-three in 1969.

Janie, my oldest sister, was educated in a convent in Calgary as a teacher. She married Joe Van Tighem, a bank manager at Strathmore. She passed away in Calgary in 1946.

Margaret, my second sister, went to Pine Creek school for a while and finished her education in Calgary. She was a nurse in the Holy Cross Hospital for a while and later joined an order of Sisters. She spent most of her life in Seattle and passed away in 1975 at the age of eighty-five.

Marie, my third sister, went to Pine Creek School at the same time as I did. She finished her education in Calgary and worked in the Bank of Montreal. She moved to Vancouver in 1928 and still resides there.

Kathleen, my youngest sister, went to Pine Creek School for a while and finished her education in Calgary. She married Frank O'Brien and moved to Vancouver in 1928. Later she moved to Seattle where she still resides.

Bill, my second brother, got most of his education in Calgary. He joined the Army in 1917 and after his return, went into the moving picture business. After more than fifty years in the business, he retired and now lives in Calgary.

Wilfred, the youngest of the family, went to school in Calgary and later worked for the Dominion Livestock Department. He retired about three years ago and now resides in Calgary.

That leaves me to be accounted for. I received most of my education in Pine Creek School. I remember every day two of us would go down to Pine Creek and get a pail of drinking water. We used to have a stick we would push through the handle of the pail and then, with one child on each side, we would pack it up to the school. Of course, we would take as much time as possible, and therefore received many a "bawling out" from the teacher. By the way, my mother used to board and room the teacher for years.

After Dad's death, I took over the farm for three years, had three complete crop failures and was really starved out. I ended up in the restaurant business, and also worked for a catering company in the north country for several years. I retired in 1972 and now reside in Calgary.

On Christmas Day in 1903, we had our dinner out on the veranda and took a picture of it to send back to Ontario.

Mother passed away in Vancouver in 1933.

OWEN KING

Owen was a bachelor brother of W. G. King and settled on W½ 12-22-1-W5 which he purchased from D. J. Rose through Canada Permanent Loan Co. in 1902.

He was Secretary of Pine Creek school district from 1906 until his death in 1909 when his brother, Bill, took over for him. Frank Pashak was executor of his estate.

This was the period just following the Boer War and

Owen King.

Owen had a horse which he called Kronje after the Dutch general of that name. Both horse and master were on the lean side and were referred to as the 'two bags of bones'!

WILLIAM KING FAMILY

Father, Billy King, died 1930; son, William Bertram, born 1900; daughter Sanna Isobelle, born 1902, died 1976.

My dad, Billy King, my sister, Sanna and myself came west to Alberta from Teeswater, Ontario in June of 1906. We came by train, bringing with us our cows and horses. We settled on a farm by Pine Creek, 12-22-1-W5 and 7-22-29-W4. My father helped to start and build the De Winton Hall. There was many good times held in it. We all travelled to dances with a horse and buggy in those days.

Mr. King and Sanna.

I got married in 1921 to Maude Adelia Shattuck. She was the daughter of Charles and Alice Shattuck of Davisburg, old timers of the district. We were married in St. Patrick's Church, Midnapore. We took over on the farm and raised three sons; Charles William, 1922; John Clayton, 1924; (died 1977); Thomas James, 1926. They all went to school at Pine Creek; and then on to make their own way of life.

Maude passed away in 1953, I carried on with the

farm and as a livestock dealer and lived in Calgary during this last stage of farming.

I married Christina Flynn in 1957. Chris had been a friend of my sister, they taught school together in Calgary. She was principal of Sacred Heart School until retiring.

We sold the farm in 1958, to J. F. Burns, and moved to North Vancouver, B.C. which is still home to us. We come back, mostly to weddings of grandchildren, of which there have been quite a few, and visit friends in the area.

My sister, Sanna, taught school in Calgary and then down by Turin. She married Paul Geldrich and made her home in Turin where they raised sugar beets.

JACK AND LOIS (DICK) KNUPP — by Lois Knupp

I, Lois, was born at DeWinton, and attended Stormont School for nine years. Then to DeWinton High School for one year and to the Olds School of Agriculture for a year. After finishing school, I went to work in High River, where I met and married Jack Knupp.

Jack was born and raised at High River and attended Zepher School. We lived two years on a farm near High River, then we moved back to DeWinton and made our home in the United Church Manse for eighteen years.

Jack started working with the City of Calgary in 1950, and retired in 1974.

In 1968, we bought and moved to my Grandmother's place which is west of DeWinton. We have five children; Larry, Linda, Karen, Ricky, and Melody. The four oldest children are married and we have six grandchildren.

MR. AND MRS. JAMES LA CREN

Mr. and Mrs. James (Jimmy) LaCren from Wimborne, Dorset, England, first show up on the Pine Creek tax roll in 1897 as the owners of W½-12-22-1-W5. They must have stayed only a short time for by 1899 the roll shows the farm in the possession of Campbell Staines. The LaCrens had no children and little is known of their life in the area.

It is said that, when they were trying to sell their place, Jimmy was having difficulty finding selling points to promote and his wife prompted him, "the fruit, Jimmy, the fruit," she referred to the abundance of saskatoons on the land.

N. J. LINDSAY M.D.

Dr. Lindsay bought the W½ 3-22-1-W5 from C. H. Hooley in 1911 and the following year purchased E½ and NW¼ 9-22-1-W5 from Mrs. R. Jamison. He owned the place until 1931 when it was sold to George Kellock from Coleman, Alberta. The farm was rented out most of the time and the tenants included Jim Ross, whose two sons, Gregor and Jack, were born there.

Neville Lindsay, now a Calgary lawyer, spent some time on the farm while his father was the owner.

WALTER LINN — by W. Linn

I arrived in De Winton, April the 1st, 1927, to work for Eben Bremner, a De Winton farmer. In the days of the horse, farm help was taken on around the 1st of April as the horses had to be put in working condition after the long winter idleness, harness to check and maybe repaired, farm implements to make ready, etc. .

Eben was a top horseman, one of the best. All work had to be done right, and on time. Horses had to be well groomed and well fed. All horses had to be groomed before going to work and the last thing at night. A well groomed horse will rest better. To take a horse out to work ungroomed was an unforgivable sin. I was raised to this sort of horse care at home, so to me it was part of a day's work. I did not have to shave every day but the horses had to be groomed. Eben was strict, but a fair and just man, this made him a good man to work for. Eben was well liked in the community and everyone knew how he felt about his horses and how they were handled.

One night when Eben was at the De Winton store (the store was open late on Wednesday and Saturday nights) someone asked him, "What kind of a man have you this year?" Eben smilingly replied, "Well, if the horses take a notion to go he would be about as much good as a big knot on the end of the lines, but the main thing is he knows what to do and how to do it and he is willing, that makes up for his size".

By Eben saying a good word for me, that was all that was needed by the rest of the community. I was accepted and made welcome. The De Winton people were all very friendly, they treated me as if I had been around for years. Oh, yes! in case I forget, my size, I stood all of 5 foot 3 inches and weighed 95 pounds at 20 years of age. Eben always said, and will still say, that I only weighed 95 pounds fresh in out of the rain, soaking wet. He always said I should have been a jockey. By the way, I did not hear of Eben's remarks for a long time after he made them.

I went to Calgary and took a barber course, I worked at it when work could be found, as in 1928 and 1929 work was hard to find. I think the world was getting us prepared for the hungry 30's yet to come and they did. I had a barber shop in De Winton for a while, it was located in the old MINTO HOUSE owned by Mr. De Mings.

1927 was the year of the cyclone. My father and my younger brother Orville maintained the gravel highway from Okotoks to the Calgary city limits on the Macleod Trail. Their camp was about a half mile east of De Winton on a little pie-shaped piece of land owned by Jim Dalzell. Jim lived across the highway to the south, it is now the home of Mrs. Eileen Vold. One day I was at my father's camp which consisted of a tent and make-shift barn. The barn was big enough for the four horses, a car roof and just the earth for a floor, it was just for summer use and to keep the horses away from the flies and the rain. A younger brother about 14 years of age and a nephew about 6 years of age were visiting from Cochrane for a few days, it started to rain and get windy so we went into the tent, the storm got worse and the tent blew away. This I did not think too much of because I had seen tents blow away before. So I took the boys into the barn, the roar the storm made, I had never heard anything like it before, just as we got into the barn and the door closed the wall started to bend in. I knew it was going to go so I

Jim Dalzell's out buildings after cyclone July 1927 at De Winton.

Jim Dalzell's house after cyclone, 1927 July at De Winton.

called to my brother to lay down as it's going to go. I had my nephew with me, I layed down and took him with me thinking my brother would do the same. It happened so fast I had no time to look, then away went the barn. When I looked around my brother was not in sight, the storm was getting worse, starting to hail. I took my nephew and we made our way to an old house that sat close to where the tent was. I went to the north end of the old house taking my nephew with me.

We stood close to the house wondering what was going to happen next, then a board came off the roof of the old house striking me on the shoulder, not real hard but enough to tell me that we were not safe there. In my mind was a bush to the north, just on the top of the small hill we were on. When I left the shelter of the old house and got back into the wind it felt as if I was in water too deep to touch bottom. My feet were leaving the ground. I had no idea of a cyclone, in my mind it was just a strong wind, a bad storm and it was blowing me away so I lay down with my nephew under me so the wind could not hit me as well as to shield him the best I could. We crawled in the direction of the bush, how far I had no idea, even a few yards would seem a mile.

Then I saw the mattress from the tent coming, it was just floating along a few inches off the ground. I got it and put the young lad under it. I could not get very far under or the other end would lift, I could get my shoulder and side covered but not my back, it had to take whatever came. By laying on my side I could reach along the mattress and hold it down as the wind was easing off. Soon the storm was over and Jim

Dalzell came over to see if he could help. Mrs. Jim Dalzell took my nephew while Jim and I looked for my brother. We found him laying unconscious with the boards from the barn all around. Jim picked him up and got him down to the highway as a car came along. We stopped him, he was from Black Diamond, he took my brother and I to the Calgary General Hospital. As we neared Midnapore we met my father, we stopped and told him what had happened. He could hardly believe it as the road was dry where he was, we went on to the hospital. The nurse called the house doctor. He saw my back and said, "Looks like you have the wrong man in bed, look after this man". I was given dry clothes and put to bed. My father and mother came to the hospital that night, my father had to drive his team back to his camp and mother had to come from Cochrane. When they visited us on Sunday I was released. My brother was unconscious for two days, we were both badly beaten by the hail stones, some the size of golf balls or hens' eggs. When we returned to De Winton I had my father drop me off at the home of Tom Dalzell. I had some things there, Mr. and Mrs. Tom Dalzell had made me welcome the year before and told me to consider their place my home any time I wished. When my father came back for me Mrs. Dalzell said, "You had better leave him here, he is in no condition to go to your camp or back to Cochrane". I stayed there and Mrs. Dalzell cared for me until I was able to go back to work. For about a week after the cyclone we had hail storms every night, this was strange as you never had hail after sundown, the old rule did not apply this year, the storms would start just as darkness set in, we would board the windows up each evening, then the second twister came. It came from the west, it passed about a mile north of De Winton, it crossed the path of the first one at the farm of Gordon Heaver, he had them both. His son Victor is still living on the home place.

One day Eben Bremner stopped to see how I was and if I thought I could help him work down the field that had been hailed and hit by the second twister. He told me that if I saw a storm clouding up I was to unhitch and head for the barn, (if the storm came I would be safer there than in the field) if it does not come so what, we just lose a little time and we have lots of that. I don't want to see you get in another storm. I would like to explain for the reader who has never worked horses or had them in a hail storm, that the best thing you can do if the storm is bad is to separate them and let them go. To do that with a 9 horse team which I was driving, would have been too much for me if the storm struck, so Eben was right when he said, "don't wait for it to strike". I went to Eben's, there were no more storms.

I continued making my home at Tom Dalzells. Tom operated a commercial truck, I often helped him and ran it when he wanted time off. In later years when Tom Dalzell passed away Mrs. Dalzell could not cope with the work around the home place, Mr. Ralph Stinn often helped her when water got in the basement. I was with the thoroughbreds on the race track at the time, Mrs. Dalzell wrote me telling of her troubles so my wife Ada and I came home to help her, it was my opportunity to care for her and try to repay some of the kindness she had shown me over many years. I am not ashamed to say I loved her very much, she was a wonderful person. Their daughter Jessie is well liked and, like her parents, is always willing to help where and when she can. When Mrs. Dalzell passed away it marked 43 years that I had made this my home. I still live in the Tom Dalzell place, there is no one in the village today who lived here when I came in 1927.

Eben Bremner now lives in Calgary, he has been in charge of the pioneer section of the Calgary Stampede Parade for some time. Last year he asked me if I could drive a team for him in the Calgary Centennial Grey Cup Parade, this I did, it was freezing cold and snowed heavily throughout the parade. I drove a team for him in the 1976 Stampede Parade and in a small parade each morning throughout the 10 days of the Stampede. Just a little over 49 years since I first worked for Eben.

In closing I wish to thank the Tom Dalzell family and all the wonderful people of the De Winton community who in 1927 made me welcome and gave me the opportunity to became 'a De Winton person'.

WILLIAM ATHELSTANE LORIMER

"Scotty" came to Alberta early in the century, worked with Charles (Buckskin Charlie) Wilkinson for some years and then moved into the De Winton town area and worked for various farmers as well as being a barber to the men and boys of the community. Later on, he worked as a clerk in the general store for Mr. Macdonald and stayed to assist others that followed in the store. The last one he worked for was Barsby Martin.

He was a well educated man, graduate of Oxford, his father worked for Lord Strathmore, father of the Queen Mother, Elizabeth. Scotty did not fit into the family social life and was sent to Canada.

When he first lived in De Winton he lived in a shack that was behind the store but before he had been there very long Barsby had the shack moved to the point of land where the road and the railroad meet. There Scotty lived for the rest of his life.

When W.W.2 broke out Scotty worked as a guard at the E.F.T.S. at the De Winton airport. In the summer of 1941 Scotty became ill and Lent Orton and Pete Wilson gave blood transfusions for him, he rallied for a short time but in the fall he passed away. He is buried in Calgary.

William A. Lorimer.

MR. AND MRS. RUBE LYNCH — by Mayme Lynch

We moved to the Midnapore District in the spring of 1937 from Elnora. We got the place from Mr. Murphy who was renting it from Burn's Ranches. He leased it to Rube, cash rent, for two years and then Rube leased it directly from Burn's Ranches. The first year we had only two hundred and fifty acres but later rented the whole five hundred and fifty acres.

Mr. and Mrs. Kerslake had owned the place previously but it had either been sold or reverted to Burn's.

The first spring the wind and dust were terrible, you couldn't see from the house to the barn, and we had very little money. I thought our chance for a crop that year was pretty slim. We filled the barn with good milk cows and sold the cream and fed the milk to calves and pigs. Rube never missed a sale on Saturdays at McLeans. Our cows averaged $17.00 a head and they were good milkers. I raised a lot of chickens and sold eggs and fryers in Calgary. We had a wonderful crop that year and everything went well for us the rest of the fourteen years we lived there.

Of course the first thing Rube bought that first fall was a new car. I thought our 1928 Chevrolet was good enough but, like all men he liked new cars.

Marjorie and Lester Miller came and stayed a year with us and that helped. Marjorie Miller is my sister. That was in 1941. They then moved back up to Carbon, Alberta where they had some land. They moved back in 1950 and bought 320 acres west of Okotoks where they live now.

We rented for five years and made enough to buy the place, it was over 700 acres, and we paid cash. We also bought the Kerslake quarter which joined ours.

Rube was a real cattle buyer and dealer and it seemed everything we touched turned into money. I am almost sure the people today couldn't believe it but, as we paid cash for the land, they sold it for $16.00 per acre. They had asked $17.00 but as we paid all cash they came down to $16.00. In 1951, we sold to Art Dawes for a good price.

We had a good sale so we retired and bought a house in Calgary in which I still live and that is twenty-five years ago. Rube had fifteen years of retirement. He enjoyed fishing and hunting.

We bought our home in Calgary on a Thursday and the following Saturday, we went to Okotoks and bought the Pegler place. It was just a quarter section but we bought all the stock, chickens and farm machinery and moved out there in the spring. Lester helped Rube put the crop in and, that fall, we took a trip to California. After we got back, Rube bought the quarter that joined us on the south and, in the summer, we sold to Gerry Mooney and moved back to Calgary.

Those were wonderful years and times. Rube passed away ten years ago and I am in the same house in Calgary.

JOHN ALISTER AND G. ELEANOR (GRAY) MACDONALD — by J. and E. Macdonald

John was raised, as a child, at Strathpine which consisted of 4-22-29-W5 and N½-S.W.¼-3-22-29-W4. He took public schooling in Victoria, B.C. and was one of the original students of the Claresholm School of

Agriculture, starting in 1913 and graduating in 1915. That fall he enlisted and went overseas with the 50th Bn. and served with this unit until it returned to Calgary in June, 1919.

Eleanor Gray was raised at "The Grange", S.W.¼-5-22-29-W4 and attended Pine Creek School and Crescent Heights High School in Calgary.

Following demobilization, John purchased the George Gray home quarter through the Soldier Settlement Board and rented the other three quarters that comprised the farm. On the 31st of July, that year, he married Eleanor Gray, a young lady to whom he had been engaged for two years. Vera Marshall was the bridesmaid. In 1928 he was employed with the Soldier Settlement Board as a field supervisor, rented the farm and moved away.

What started out as a one year absence from the farm lengthened out to twenty-five years, including four years (1940-44) in the army. In 1946-47, circumstances made it advisable to sell the farm and break connection with the De Winton district, worn thin by the long absence.

The two oldest children, Mona and Jim, went to Pine Creek School and, in the late thirties attended De Winton High School. The two younger daughters were born at Hanna, Alberta.

Mr. and Mrs. J. A. Macdonald, 50th Wedding Anniversary, 1969.

In 1969 the four children surprised their parents with a Fiftieth Wedding Anniversary party, inviting friends from far and near to join the celebration. Vera Marshall, the bridesmaid of long ago, was able to attend.

The four children; Mona (Hyde), Calgary, James D., Grand Cayman, B.W.I., Charlotte (Behncke), Calgary and Mary (Rutledge), Ottawa have presented their parents with thirteen grandchildren and they, in turn have produced three great-grandchildren.

John and Eleanor presently reside in Jacque's Lodges, Calgary.

CHARLES AND ANNETTE (REPSUMER) MARSHALL — by Marjorie Moon

Charles Marshall was born in 1860 in the Gillingham District of Wisconsin. He left Wisconsin as a youth and worked his way west at various jobs, mostly in lumber camps. He was an excellent axeman having learned the art at an early age in his native Wisconsin. His last place of work in the U.S.A. was Missoula, Montana.

In 1883, he came to the North West Territories, by team and wagon, with his friend, John McInnes. Together with a friend, Archie Bremner, whom they met in Calgary, they settled on adjoining land, near what is now De Winton. They all spent the first winter together in a small log cabin on the McInnes quarter.

When the North West Rebellion broke out, all three were employed by the Government Transport Division, hauling supplies to the army.

In the fall of that year they returned to their land. Charlie filed on his homestead NE ¼-34-21-1-W5, and later on the SE ¼-34-21-1-W5. During the years of proving on his homestead, he worked for John Glenn at his place in Midnapore. The men worked together and each completed a log house, hauling the logs from the Millarville district. The land was broken with a walking plow and it was a slow process. Two wells were dug and stayed in use until 1901.

After getting the homestead into shape, Charlie returned to visit friends and relatives in Wisconsin, in the fall of 1893. On January 1, 1894, he married Annette Repsumer and they both returned to the farm where

Annette (Repsummer) Marshall, 1894.

Charles Marshall, 1894.

cattle, not always his own. Morris Robb, son of Ed Robb, then in his teens was hired to haul feed to the cattle. He took a load from the home place every day and fed the cattle, using horses and rack or a sleigh in season. This was quite a chore and it took a husky man to accomplish. When the South African War broke out Morris joined up and went to fight. The quarter was sold and the cattle dispersed.

It was during this time that a young man from the district was hired to help with the chores. Frank was

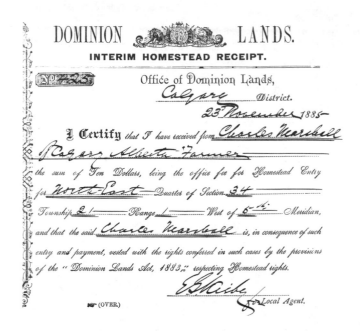

they spent the rest of their lives, except for a few years Annette spent in Calgary nursing home, before her death in 1966, at the age of 98. Charlie died in April, 1940 at the age of 80. Both are buried in Pine Creek Cemetery.

They were known throughout the community as "Mom and Pop" Marshall.

Annette was not a young girl when she was married and that probably stood her in good stead as the change in her way of life was extreme. Indians were very much in evidence and often stopped looking for food etc. One of her earliest experiences with Indians was to look up from her kitchen table, where she was kneading dough for bread to see an Indian looking in from the outside. It gave her quite a start. The Indians played a part in the development of the district as they were hired from time to time to fence, stook, thresh etc. They seldom stayed for any length of time but some of them did good work and, at a time when help was scarce, they were needed. It was the time of home births with only the neighbours to help and Mom was called upon in the capacity of mid-wife several times. She, in turn, had help from others in the neighbourhood. When Les was ill as a small child, Edith Currie, (later Pinchbeck) came to help nurse him, Mom was fortunate in having the Bremners, McInesses, Robbs and Owens as fairly close neighbours.

In the last half of the 1890's Pop bought a quarter down near the river, NW¼ 5-22-28-W4, where he kept

about three years old and for some reason this young lad had been asked to stay with Frank for a short while. Pop used to load his own shot-gun shells at the time and the lad found a partially loaded shell, (just the powder and the wad, no shot), loaded it into the gun and took it upstairs. He discharged the gun and the wad caught fire, struck Frank in the leg and set his clothes on fire. Fortunately he was dressed in the fashion and had a long dress on. The wad made a permanent scar on his leg, had there been shot in the shell it would have mangled it.

Before the turn of the century there were four children; Benjamin Franklin 1894, Earle Austin 1896, June Alberta 1898, Vera Eva 1899. A larger house was necessary and a two story log home was constructed in 1895. It was sided on the outside and lathed and plastered on the inside. John Dewar did the plastering and Malcolm Dewar built the stairway and some of the inside woodwork. The old log cabin was used as a kitchen until a lean-to was added to the main house in 1911. This building was done by Bill Davis.

In 1901 Bricker and Snyder were hired to drill a well and it is interesting to note that the drill bit was fastened to wooden rods rather than cable or rope. They lost their tools at 70 feet and had to move to a new location where they hit solid rock at 187 feet but there was ample good water and the well was in steady use until 1972, when Sanderson, of Black Diamond drilled a new well. He found water at the same level.

Plowing with a walking plow was still in progress and in 1913 it was decided that pigs might be a good investment so a pig barn for 8 sows was built. Feed was grown on the place and the venture was quite successful. In 1919 pure bred Hereford cattle were acquired.

During these years five more children had arrived, Charles Leslie 1902, Marjorie Virginia 1904, Hazel 1906, (died at 6 weeks), Harold Bernard 1910, (died in 1922), and Ernest Harvey 1914, (died in 1915). The older children were in school, attending classes at the

old Paling home until the Pine Creek School was opened in about 1903.

Pine Creek was in the electoral District of Victoria, women didn't have the vote, the men voted by calling out the name of their choices of candidate and the D.R.O. recorded it.

By the time 1915 had rolled around Frank was old enough to be doing the plowing and broke the last 20 acres, still with a walking plow, that year. In 1917, the first tractor was brought to the place and Frank and Earle both went out to break land for the neighbors. 160 acres for T. Copp in 1917, 250 acres for Burns in 1918, 60 acres for Warracks in 1917 and various fields for McIntosh, Pearson, the Godsell Valley and other neighbors in the next few years.

A Mr. Kinneburgh, from Calgary, was travelling the country with a team and dray selling for the Karn Piano Company of Woodstock Ontario. His procedure was to arrive at a farm house in the early evening, too late to return to Calgary, and ask to leave an instument at the home for a trial period. It was in this way that we got an organ in 1911. Pop traded oats for it. It is still in use in the old home. Ethel Bremner was the first one to play it and her playing was great entertainment and much appreciated. A piano was acquired in the same way, several years later.

In 1917, Mr. Renard travelled around the country taking subscriptions for the proposed telephone line. I remember when the phone was installed, about 1918, I was rather timid about using it.

By 1917, Vera had gained her teaching certificate and was teaching in the rural schools, Standard, Cayley, Alexandra and Pine Creek were some of the schools she taught. She was a successful teacher but about 1926 she took a business course and went to work in Calgary. Frank and Earle had been to Garbutt's Business College and returned to the farm and in late 1918, Earle was called into the army and served with the Medical Corps during the 'flu epidemic.

One of the first motorcycles in the area was purchased in 1916, it was an Indian, it was a novelty and rather limited transportation. Les managed to sustain a serious injury to his heel while riding postern on it. He caught his foot in the spokes. The cycle was sold and a second hand Model T of 1918 vintage was purchased. This was power and mobility, you could take your friends along. A trip to Cayley to bring Vera home for a weekend was a real adventure. This car served its purpose until 1920 when a new 490 Chevrolet, sedan, replaced it.

From the early 1890s through the early 1900s a great many changes had taken place. Churches, Anglican and Presbyterian; schools, dance halls and a pool hall had all made their appearance. The ladies had formed a Missionary Society, the bachelors had a club and there was a theatrical society that put on plays in the hall. House parties had been the standard entertainment up to this point but now things were taking a new course and public dances and card parties came into style.

In 1916 we had acquired a threshing machine, pulled with horses and Frank and Earle threshed all over the country. That first year they threshed till after Christmas. Until this time most crops were threshed from the stack but this was threshing from the stook. The men were fed at the farm homes and it was a very busy time. When the crew arrived at a farm house there was usually some outside help brought in for the wife. I can remember Ethel Bremner being at our home and how much we children enjoyed having her. It was not too long before June was able to fill the job and it was no longer necessary to have extra help.

Sport had been developing in the district too and there was some interest in hockey. It was completely unorganized and the activity took place on a slough at the Evans' place. Gene Goettler was responsible for getting some of the boys interested but this sport never grew to be very popular. Baseball (hard ball), was a different story and and a good team was made up. They used to play on our hill across from where the gun club stands now. They rode to the games on horseback and it was usual to see most of the team at the Marshall table after the games. The team travelled around to play at such places as Kew, Calgary, Dunbow, Davisburg and the Oilfields. It was a good grade of ball and drew lots of spectators.

Turkey shoots were quite in vogue and my brothers brought home their share of the birds. My father brought back a 30:30 rifle when he visited his home in 1908 and it was much sought after to use in competition. Bill Davis was one man that was an expert shot and he won a lot of the time. The shoots were sometimes sponsored by De Mings and sometimes by Ed Johnson of the Dominion Hotel at Midnapore. Along with the turkey shoots, the pool hall was a gathering place for the men and boys, as were the boxing matches supervised by Mr. Bryan.

Les and I had been the ones that looked after the chores but now we were into the twenties and June, who had been the mainstay in the house, was married to Fred Cole and moved to her new home, we had added a cook car to the threshing outfit and I was elected to cook on it. The men were mostly local ones and, with all the work, I enjoyed the experience. A few years later Frank was also married and went to Seattle for a short while. He married Frances Glenn (granddaughter of John) and when they returned from Seattle with their small daughter, Patricia, it was decided to divide the assets of the farm and Frank and Earle moved to a farm in the Shepard area. Les was left to run the home place with Pop. This was in 1926 and the 490 Chev. went to Shepard and Pop bought a Dodge from Will Johnson for Les to use.

The Dodge didn't last long. On Christmas Eve, 1928, while returning from Okotoks with Bill and Sam Hamilton, Dick Meehan and Jim Turnbull, they came upon a bread truck parked in the middle of the road and, as it was just over the brow of the hill, they were unable to see it in time to pull off of the road and hit the back fender. Sam saw the truck first and leaned over from the back seat to try and pull the emergency brake. He was not successful and the impact sent him into the windshield. Both Sam and Dick were quite badly cut and ended up in the hospital in Calgary. Jim, apparently in shock, just wandered off but turned up at home later. Bill, hurt his shoulder and the wooden steering wheel broke when it came in contact with Les's ribs. After being taken to Dr. Ardiel, in Okotoks

by a passing motorist, Sam and Dick were sent to Calgary and Bill accompanied them. Les was taken to Okotoks by Laura Pope (now Head) and her escort but was able to go back home without further treatment. The driver of the truck ran and hid in the brush when he realized that he had left the truck in such a bad spot. He had stopped to see if he could assist a couple that were stranded at the side of the road. A truck that had been working for the Anglesey Oil Well was stored in Dick Meehan's garage. It was owned by the Diamond Drilling Company of California and a call to that company okayed the sale of the truck for $200.00 The boys spent the rest of the winter transferring the body of the car, which was not badly hurt, onto the frame of the truck and they were mobile again. Pop never did learn to drive.

There was a series of young boys from the neighbourhood that came to work for periods of time and in 1927, Pop agreed to take on a young Irishman, Bob McDonald, fresh over from Belfast. He was not a great help but he certainly provided much amusement.

By 1928 I was married to Fred Moon and left to live in Calgary, Les and my parents were alone. With the help of part-time 'hired men' he carried on the farm work, continuing to run a threshing outfit, milking a few cows and raising grain and hay. In 1929 he bought his own new car an Essex. Things went well for a few years but in 1932, Pop became ill and required an operation from which he never completely recovered. He was partially paralysed and was crippled for the rest of his life. During his stay in hospital Mom also became ill and had to undergo surgery. Marjorie Dalzell came to help in the house and made things much easier. When Pop was finally able to come home, Tom Dalzell very kindly offered to bring him home as he had a heated car, unusual at that time, and the weather was extremely bad. Mom's brother Stanton came over from Creston to help care for Pop and stayed for several months until Mom and Les were able to take the job on themselves.

Les was married to Jean MacRae of Calgary, in 1934 and in 1936 they moved down to the Graham place and Mom and Pop were at the home place with Alf Daley to keep an eye on them and help Pop get around a bit. Pop passed away in 1940 and Les and his family moved back to the old home. Mom stayed on with them but as she grew older she became very forgetful and, after surgery in 1953, she entered a nursing home in Calgary where she passed away at the age of 98,

Frank (deceased 1976) and Frances have five children; Patricia (Laycock), living at Chestermere Lake. Has seven children. Colleen (Glenn) living in Edmonton, has three children. Carol (Gosling), Calgary, has four children, Loretta (Melen) Rocky Mountain House, three children, Rod, Chestermere Lake, two children and Brett, Bruce and Craig, all at home.

Shirley (Roberts) three boys and nine grandchildren.

Glenn, Calgary, five children and four grandchildren.

Merla (Laycock), Calgary, three children.

Charles (Chuck), Singapore, six children and four grandchildren.

Earle married Beatrice Kinlock (deceased), retired and living in Calgary.

June (Cole) lives on the farm near Okotoks, has three children and seven grandchildren.

Vera, lived out her last years in Calgary.

Leslie, on the home place, six children and seventeen grandchildren.

Marjorie (Moon), lives at Bragg Creek, has two children, Barbara (Atherton), of Penhold, one son, and Willard of Edmonton has four children.

C. LESLIE AND JEAN (MACRAE) MARSHALL — by Jean Marshall

We were married in the middle of the "Great Depression" and my first memories of the district are of the warm and friendly neighbours. The community was a much more closely knit unit in those days. Everyone was struggling to "make ends meet" but there was always time for a friendly visit. Mr. and Mrs. Marshall Sr. were still on the farm when I came to stay but Les had been running it for a number of years. Mr. Marshall was not able to get around due to complications following a serious operation. I remember the visits paid him by his old friend, Archie Bremner. John McNeill used to come faithfully and shave him and cut his hair. There was always time to be of help to the one who needed it. Hugh Graham was also very good to "Pop" and spent many hours visiting with him.

After our second child was born we moved to the Graham quarter N.E. ¼-3-22-1-W5. In 1936 we were situated with summer fallow on three sides of us and the wind blew continuously. The house was not wind proof and the dust that came through the walls coated everything. The dishes were not put into the cupboard but rather left upside down on the table for the dust gathered everywhere. Before going to bed, the bedding had to be taken out to shake. Even ones teeth got gritty with the dirt. That same year the army worms came and destroyed crops and gardens in a wide swathe across the countryside. I can remember we dug a shallow ditch along the south side of the house and filled it with dry straw, sprinkled coal oil on it and set it on fire to try to get rid of some of the worms. They crawled over anything that was in their path and, in this instance, our house happened to be just there. They crawled in through cracks in the walls and one way or another found their way into house. They lasted for about four days and we were pleased to see the last of them. Fortunately we have never had them again. That winter was a bad one for cold and snow and I was not off the place from November till March. My first outing was a visit to the Hugh Grahams. That night was a joy.

Two more of our children were born while we lived on the Graham place but seven months after Doreen was born "Pop" became ill and died. That was in April of 1940 and we moved back onto the home place where we have been ever since.

During our stay at the Graham Place Hugh was the elevator agent at the Academy Elevator and used to stop in each night on his way home from work. He would sit and rock Harvey in the rocking chair while I got the supper ready. He used to tell us of helping Mrs. Stanfield, of Stanfield underwear, by holding her wool while she wound it into skeins. In those long ago times she used to knit underwear by hand. All the children watched for him coming each night and missed him on the week-ends.

Being so close to the railroad track in the thirties was quite an experience. Trains went on the average of one every hour. They were always well loaded with men "riding the rods." Hardly a day went by that someone didn't come to the door looking for food. So many different types came and it was interesting to talk to them about their adventures. I remember one in particular that came from the Peace River country where he had a farm. Things got so bad that he had to get out and try to get some cash somehow to keep going. He had a beautiful collie dog with him. Said he was so fond of it that he could not leave it with anyone else. When we gave the man his supper he was about to give the dog a goodly portion of it and was so grateful when we gave the dog its own meal. Sometimes very young boys would show up on our doorstep and it made one wonder just what led to their being out on the road. One man that came acted rather strangely and as Les had just left to go up to the home place, I called him back. The fellow was odd looking and was wearing an old World War I army great coat that came down to his ankles. When he took his cap off we could see a great scab covering half of the top of his head. After he left, I took all the dishes he had used and boiled them, then I burned the towel and face cloth he used, even foolishly, burned the soap he washed with. He walked down the track towards Academy and Hugh Graham saw him coming. He stopped to ask for more help at the elevator and Hugh was suspicious enough about him to call the "Mounties". We found that he had escaped from Essondale near Vancouver and was being hunted all over the province. I guess we were lucky that he was on good behaviour while he was in our house.

Tom Brown of Midnapore was the section foreman for the C.P.R. and often stopped in to visit at the noon hour. One year he had potatoes planted in part of the garden plot and often brought young Gordon with him when he came to look after them. Our children thought it was great when this happened for they didn't see too many other children.

It was during our stay there that the Queen came to Canada to visit. Her train was to pass on the track right in front of the house and there was much excitement. People went into Calgary in every sort of conveyance that could be imagined. Lack of licence plates were excused for the occasion and many an old car that had not been on the road for months made its way into the city for the big event. When someone asked Scotty Lorimer if he were going in to see the queen he said "No, she knows where I live and she can come and see me if she wants to." Scotty's father used to work as a gardener, for the queen's father and he remembered seeing her when she was just a young girl.

Through these years Shirley Temple was the rising child star of the motion pictures and Aberhart was promoting his Social Credit politics in Alberta. All eyes were on Alberta politics and all ears were tuned to the rantings of the 'mad paper hanger' in Germany. Both of these were to have an impact on our way of life. There was a third happening about this time that made history and that was the arrival of the Dionne quintuplets. They became the focal point of interest in a country beset with poverty and uncertainty.

The winds blew and the cattle prices slumped. Seed was blown out of the ground and it was necessary to reseed. The Prairie Farmers Assistance Act came into being and was helpful to a small degree. Hailstorms and drought followed each other and depression was more than the state of the economy. Throughout this time people gathered together for moral support and the community became a unit fighting a common enemy. Dances (.50¢ for men and the ladies brought lunch), concerts, plays, talent shows, card parties and afternoon meetings for the women were the general ways of finding diversion from the grim realities.

Earle, Wenty, Paul and Travis Brinton, Bill and Rob Anderson, Norman Graham all served as 'Hired men' on our farm. One after the other as they left school and were ready to go out to work. There were no jobs available in industry and they at least were able to survive as farm hands. Toward the end of the '30's the government would pay a farmer $5.00 a month to take on a man as well as give the man an equal amount of cash plus a mackinaw jacket and a pair of boots. It was under this scheme that Alf Daley first came to work for us. We gave him the $5.00 that we received from the government as we felt he was worth much more than we could give him.

After milking, separating and delivering, one was lucky to get $2.95 for a can of high-test, sweet cream. Cash was very scarce and I well remember the day I acquired a copper bottomed boiler. Something I had wanted for a long time and I was delighted with it. Anti-freeze was not yet in use and water had to be heated for car radiators. The first job for my new boiler was to heat water to get the car going, the temperature was more than —30 degrees F., it was the day of "Pops" funeral . . . The water was duly poured into the radiator, the car started, the boiler set down on the ground. As the car went ahead my precious boiler was crushed under the wheels. What desolation!! and "no! I never got another one."

When we moved back to the home place we transported our belongings on a hay rack. The slough beside the railroad track was so deep that the water was lapping at the floor of the rack. I don't think those fields have ever been so wet since.

The daily 1 o'clock Texaco news cast had become a run down on the progress of the Ethiopian War instead of fifteen minutes of local and national news. Young men were thinking about going to join the forces when, horror of horrors, the Second World War was upon us. Young fellows and girls from all around the country side were joining up and going off to war. Young women were off to jobs for the war effort as well. Help was in short supply and farmers were asked to produce for the good of the nation. It was a busy, anxious time for everyone. We had become accustomed to making do with whatever materials were available so giving for the war effort was not the ordeal it might have been for an affluent society. Many meatless dishes had

been invented, flour sacks were used for all sorts of things, dry cereals were put up in fancy print sacks that made clothing for small children.

There were two more children born to us after we returned to the home place, the youngest arrived on V.E. day. That was the time that Bob Smith organized a celebration in De Winton, complete with bon-fire, and burning Hitler in Effigy. I can't recall Bob joining in any other gatherings during my time in the district.

Our personal war effort didn't consist of much more than knitting a few articles, sending some 'comfort packages', gathering scrap metal, buying Victory bonds and producing food. I remember Mr. H. Harper and Mr. Gordon Heaver selling bonds around the district. The children bought their war savings stamps to fill up certificates to the value of either $5.00 or $10.00. I believe the stamps were 10¢ each. Rationing was in full force and ration stamps for gasoline, sugar, jam and butter plus other commodities had to be doled out when purchases were made. Gasoline stamps, during threshing time, were the cause of much bother and many a deal was made between farmers then.

A couple of weeks before Pop's death we lost a treasured neighbour, Mrs. Isabella Hamilton, a truly 'gentle woman'. Our children loved to visit her and she was sorely missed by the whole community. At the same time of the loss of these old-time residents a new citizen made her appearance, as a close neighbour, she was Virginia Graham, daughter of Gordon and Ruby (Hart) Graham and grand-daughter of Hugh and Mary (McNeill) Graham. Thus a fourth generation of the McNeill family began in the area.

Throughout these years, Barsby Martin had the local store. He kept it open till ten o'clock on Wednesday and Saturday evenings and it was a gathering place for all the men and young fellows of the neighbourhood. Had it not been for Barsby's generous credit, many a family would have starved and Barsby would have become a rich man. What a blow to the community when the store burned down in 1944 and how fortunate for the community that the Martins didn't close their business but opened a store in the old Minto House until they were able to build a new place of business.

New Year's Eve was always a time for the neighbours to gather at our home. And, after the New Year was six or seven hours old, it was not unheard of to finish off the festivities with a breakfast of bacon and eggs at Hamilton's. Quite simple entertainment compared with the sumptuous affairs that are held today.

When the roads in the district were high graded in 1948 travelling was almost impossible. I remember Hugh Graham taking me, by team and democrat, over to the highway to catch the bus for Calgary. It was all the horses could do to pull that light load with gumbo up, almost, to the axle.

It was about this time when the roads in our district were high graded that we also got a new road councillor who decided that the method being used to take the drainage water was all wrong and proceeded to have a number of the culverts in the area changed. The disastrous results are still evident. Roads and ditches were washed out and travel was quite restricted for some time. Also about this time we had a very wet spring and the ground literally turned to liquid mud and ran through the land, cutting great gouges and ditches. Any one who had a caterpillar was in demand to fill the ditches and make it possible to take farm machinery over the fields again. The Huck boys did a lot of that type of work in our part of the district.

When the weather modification idea was put into operation, we had one of the 'furnaces' in our yard. The idea was to burn the chemicals provided and the theory was that the smoke would carry the residue up and seed the clouds to make the moisture come down as rain rather than hail. Some say that the system worked. We had the apparatus for about three or four years.

Our children all attended Pine Creek and De Winton High School except for Kathleen (Kelly) who took her high school in Okotoks and Myrna finished her high school in Okotoks.

Sheila (Davis) lives in Calgary has four children; Joanne, Michael, Leslie and Billie. Jim is married to Anne Hanlan of Ottawa, served ten years with the R.C.N. is in the Real Estate business in Calgary, has three children; Brian, Wayne and Linda. Harvey married Elaine Teare of Calgary, works for Imperial Oil in Calgary has two children; Blaine and Lisa. Doreen (Powell) lives in Calgary, has two children; Bradley and Ryan. Myrna (Orr) lives in New Jersey, U.S.A., has three children; Craig, Shaun and Jeannine. Kathleen (Nobert) lives in Vulcan, has three children; John, Faron and Darren.

We still live in the old house and Les not only sleeps in the same room in which he was born but also in the same bed. The country has been good to us and, although the city keeps creeping closer each year, we would not want to live anywhere else.

BARSBY AND AGNES (GRAY) MARTIN — by Ann (Martin) Robinson

Barsby Martin was born in the small Manitoba town of MacGregor in 1894. In 1906 he came with his

Back, l. to r.: Agnes and Barsby Martin, Martha Gray, Mrs. and Mr. H. Alverson, Earl Brinton, Middle: Ruth Kerr, Betty and Rees Alverson. Front: Madelyn Martin, Jack Alverson.

family to the Nose Creek District, north of Calgary. His father, James, operated a dairy farm on the land which is now McColl International Airport. The three older Martin children, Melvin, Barsby and Sadie, attended Nose Creek School, where they were taught by Maude Riley. Riley Park in Calgary is named after her husband.

The family moved back to Manitoba, spent some time at Kenora, Ontario, returning in 1913 to the Davisburg district. Three quarters of land were purchased with Barsby farming the one on which Albert Herr now lives. The younger Martin children, Lila, Clarence and Ena attended Davisburg School, where they were taught by a young teacher, Agnes Gray, who was to marry Barsby in 1919 and share his life for the next forty-eight years.

Agnes Gray was born in Virden, Manitoba in 1895. In 1904 she arrived in the Carbon district of Alberta, where she lived until going to Calgary to attend high school. After graduating from Central High, she attended Normal School and then set out to teach. She taught first at Melrose and then Davisburg.

Agnes and Barsby Martin.

After their marriage, Bars and Aggie spent three years on the farm. In 1921 the store in De Winton was for sale and Bars, who had always had a love for stores, bought it. For the next forty years he operated the store, adding an insurance business and the Post Office in later years. His original De Winton store was a two storey building located across the road from Ivan Dick's home. It had a veranda running across the front with a hitching rail off to the side. It stayed open every Wednesday and Saturday night until ten p.m. and became a gathering place for many farmers of the district. At any time you could find men shaking five dice in a leather cup for pop and chocolate bars. The Martin family, which by 1936 had increased to five children, lived upstairs.

After the war started and an airport had been built east of De Winton, Barsby went to work at the airport driving a fire truck. Aggie stayed home to look after the children and mind the store. One February morning in 1944, the store and house were destroyed by fire. For the next two years the family lived in the De Winton High School, and the store was operated out of a vacant building which, at one time, was the De Winton Hotel (Minto House). During this time, a large vacant garage, inhabited only by bats, was converted into a store. The next year a house was built on the back, and once again the store and family were located under one roof.

Barsby and Aggie lived here until 1956 when they retired to Calgary. Barsby Martin died in 1967 and Agnes Martin in 1968.

Of the Martin children, Lynn (Madeline) married Jim Teeling, also of De Winton, and they live in Red Deer. They have three sons. Bob Martin is in London, Ontario and has five children. Ron Martin married Karen McAlpine, is living in Red Deer and has four sons. Carol married Alex Nistor, is living in Three Hills and has one daughter. Ann married Joe Robinson, is living in Calgary and has one daughter.

W. H. (HARRY) AND MARGARET A. (ANDERSON) MATTHEWS — by Florence Cozart

Our family were not "old timers" to the De Winton district. My father, W. H. (Harry) Matthews, followed Mr. Hugh Hamilton as C.P.R. station agent and we moved there in August, 1939. Our stay was short lived but we all enjoyed it. Mother finally realized one of her pet dreams while there. For years she had fretted about the small size of the rooms that comprised the living quarters in the stations and longed to knock out a wall in order to provide more space. This was finally agreed on by the "powers-that-be" at C.P.R. head office and the wall between the living room and dining room came out. What a difference it made!! It was thoroughly appreciated by the whole family. In January, 1941, Fate stepped in and Dad passed away suddenly, his death occuring on my sister, Helen's twenty-first birthday. We moved to Calgary at that time and Mother passed away in 1947. Helen (Mrs. Robert Thomson) still resides in Calgary. I, Florence, married Hugh Cozart and we live at Bruce, Alberta.

McINNES FAMILY — by W.S. McInnes

John Francis McInnes was born of Scottish parents in Lanark County, Ontario. He left Ontario at an early age, crossing over into the States, then travelling west to Montana. At this time railway construction and tie making were the sources of a man's making a living. Somewhere along the line he met up with Charles Marshall and, as they both had ideas of heading into what was then the Northwest Territories, in the spring of 1883 they left Montana and headed north. The only means of transportation was by a team of horses and, I suppose, the covered wagon. Crossing rivers was a constant risk, as at that time of year the spring runoff caused all creeks and rivers to be running high.

On arriving where De Winton is now located and on looking over the country, north and east, they thought that was the best place to take up land. So they filed on

homesteads one mile north and one mile west of De Winton. At that time this property was known as situated one mile south of Pine Creek.

Shortly after they had established cabins and barns, they decided to join up with the government forces who were being organized to take part in the Northwest Rebellion, as there was Indian trouble east of Edmonton. A neighbor, Mr. Archie Bremner, was also in the group. When this government work was over they returned to the homesteads and the hard work of making a living was under way.

About this time the Robert Jamison family had settled on Pine Creek, a short distance west of the present railroad. They were of Irish descent and came west from Alliston, Ontario. John F. McInnes married Isabella Jamison about 1891. They raised a family of three girls and three boys. The three boys were Charles Edward, Henry Francis, and William Stuart. The girls were Effie Elizabeth, Ida May, and Edna Alberta. The mother died in 1904 and Edna was adopted by her aunt, Maria Currie, when less than a year old.

John McInnes family. l. to r.: Willie, Mrs. (Belle Jamison), Charlie, Ida, Francis, Mr. and Effie.

Stormont and Pine Creek schools were used as the places of education. Edna attended Melrose School and later taught school at different places. She lost her life in the Red Deer River near Buffalo in 1923.

In 1913 the farm was sold to Mr. H. Poffenroth and the family moved to Vancouver. John F. McInnes died in 1943 in Calgary, and Charlie, who had enlisted in the First World War, was reported missing in June of 1916. Two members of the family are still living (1975), Ida M. McInnes, now residing in Toronto, and William S. McInnes, who has been residing in Calgary since 1944.

W. S. McInnes married Madeline M. Hallworth of Lethbridge in 1938 and they have one daughter, Marilyn, who grew up in Calgary and took her nursing training at the General Hospital. Later Marilyn married and shortly after, her husband took a position with Price Waterhouse & Company in Australia. There are now two grandchildren and they are returning to Canada, which of course will be the highlight of 1975.

PETER McKAY

Peter McKay was a bachelor and first shows up on

the Pine Creek tax roll in the 1890's. He was a bachelor and a very popular fellow. He homesteaded the NE¼ 36-21-1-W5 prior to 1892, homestead No. 34986. His home was a two storey frame house on the hillside. When the Bremner family returned from B.C. they stayed with Peter while their own house was being put back into shape after standing empty for so long. In 1906 H. G. Dunfield shows up as the owner of the same quarter. After selling the property Peter went to Calgary. He owned a plot in the Pine Creek cemtery but it is not known whether he was buried there or not.

BENJAMIN FRANKLIN McLAUGHLIN

"Benny", a young bachelor, came to the De Winton district in the late 1890's and worked for various farmers. Always popular in the community, he worked toward having a place for himself and, finally, in 1903 he acquired the NE¼ 3-22-1-W5 where he settled down to farm on his own. After some years of fending for himself, he decided that it was time he got married and put an advertisement in a country paper announcing that he was looking for a woman to share his life.

Mr. and Mrs. Ben McLaughlin.

It was not too long before he went off to Calgary and returned with a mate, all ready to join the community activities. The lonely life and lack of social involvement soon led the young lady to realize that the country life was not for her and she left to return to her former home. Ben remained on the place until 1910 and it was sold to Mrs. Frank Austin. In 1918 it was sold to Hugh Graham.

MR. AND MRS. DANIEL McNAB — by Linda Fritz

Daniel McNab was born in Scotland in 1887. He was raised at Clydebank near Glasgow and, as a young man, married Margaret Hunter. It was their associa-

tion with the Begg family at Clydebank that brought the McNab family to the De Winton area.

The Beggs, owners of Begg Distillers, sent their son, John, a remittance man, to Canada in 1906 in hopes he would settle to a quieter, more reserved life. They bought him a ranch, near the Dunbow School, where the Highwood and Bow rivers meet. His ranch was knowm as Dunbow Ranch and was later sold to Bill McEwan in 1914.

Daniel's wife and her father operated a bar in Glasgow for Begg Distillers and, in the spring of 1910, John Begg arranged for the McNab brothers, Daniel, Sandy, Andrew and Jimmy, to come over to the Begg ranch (Dunbow). Sandy went to the mines in Nordegg, Jimmy returned to Scotland (to return to Canada in 1913), and Andrew left for Chicago. Daniel stayed on the Dunbow Ranch and arranged for his wife and three sons to join him.

Margaret and three boys, Danny 4, George 2, and Johnnie, a babe in arms, left Scotland in September of 1910. They crossed the Atlantic Ocean on what turned out to be the last trip of the 'Levethian!' They were caught at sea in a bad storm which detoured their journey around the Azores. After forty-two days on the water they were forced to dock at New York for extensive repairs to the propellers of the Levethian. Because of quarantine, the passengers were forced to stay on board for the two or three days it took to repair

Mrs. Dan (Margaret McNab), John, Danny and George about 1911.

the storm damages. They sailed to Halifax and then travelled across Canada on the C.P.R.

Life on the Dunbow, for Margaret was certainly a different experience for her. "The Big Cattle Dip" was located on the Dunbow Ranch and all the cattle were treated there for lice or other diseases. The ranch also bordered on the Indian school and buildings and many times Margaret was afraid they would be attacked. The Indians frequently came to the door to request sugar, flour, tobacco, coffee, etc. and would sit on the hill in front of the door until she gave them what they wanted. She soon learned they did not want to harm her family. She became a very close friend to Mrs. Johnny Whitney, (One Spot, late of the Sarcee Reserve), a teacher at the school.

In the early spring of 1912, Daniel took the mail route from De Winton to Gladys Ridge and moved his family, (including a new son, Alex), to a small house, on a few acres, at Pine Canyon. He delivered the mail, by saddle pony or democrat, every Tuesday, Thursday and Saturday. Occasionally, if the weather made it too difficult to travel, he made the trip on foot.

From Pine Canyon, in 1914, they moved to De Winton where they rented the Bill Grierson place. Their son, Jimmy, was born here and Daniel still rode the mail route. In January of 1915, he arrived home, after delivering the mail in a raging blizzard, both feet frozen, to find that his wife, Margaret, had died at home, giving birth to their daughter Margaret. He was left alone with six young children to raise!

The children were placed in the Salvation Army Home but this was an unhappy situation for them and after a few months they were taken to Don McBride's (formerly of Gladys Ridge). They were split up when Daniel joined the Canadian Expeditionary Force in the fall of 1915. Danny stayed with the McBrides, George, went to the Curries, Johnnie, to the Bremners, in De Winton, and Alex and Jimmy, to the Steiners at Vulcan. Margaret was adopted by the Bishops.

Daniel was sent immediately overseas. He was the victim of Fos Gene gas, the first time it was ever used, at Vimy Ridge, in France and was hospitalised for several months in England.

When the war ended in 1919, Daniel returned home, gathered his family together and took a homestead in the Ballyhamage district. This land, NW¼-24-21-2-W5, is presently farmed by George. He later purchased another quarter bordering this land which was turned over to Alex. Alex sold this quarter in the late '50s and is now in Calgary and the land is subdivided into acreages.

Daniel remarried in 1925 and retired to Calgary in the late 1950s. During the Second World War he was a Commissionaire at the De Winton Airport. He died in Calgary in June of 1960 at the age of 73. He had cancer of the lungs.

Son, Johnny, now lives at Drumheller, Danny, died at a very young age, while working for Mr. Ness, Jimmy, passed away in 1972 and his widow still lives on a farm near George. Margaret, lives in Calgary.

DUNCAN McNEILL

Duncan McNeil was born in Colonsay, Scotland, about 1836 and came to Canada in the late 1850's. During the American Civil War he went, along with several thousand other Canadians, to fight for Lincoln's Army. Following his discharge, he was given a quarter section of land, in South Dakota, and the sum of eight hundred dollars ($800.00). He lived on his land and worked for other people around the country. When he returned from one of his working trips to find his home completely domolished, by a cyclone, he decided to join his brother, Hugh, in Alberta, North West Territories. The date of his arrival is not known exactly but, probably, about 1895. He purchased the S.E.-¼-36-21-1-W5, for the sum of three dollars per acre.

He spent a good deal of his time, during the latter part of his life, at the home of his brother, Hugh. One morning, he told his niece, Mary, that he had a strange dream and that a "Mountie" had come and taken him away. It was very soon after that he passed, quietly away. He left the quarter section to his nephew, Jim McNeill. Duncan is buried in Pine Creek Cemetery.

HUGH AND SARAH (McGILLVRAY) McNEILL — by Jean Pakenham

Hugh McNeill was born in Colonsay, Scotland in 1846. His wife, Sarah McGillvray, was born in Paisley, Ontario in 1862. In 1887 they came from Ontario to Calgary with their two oldest children, John, born in 1885 and Jim, born in 1887. They lived in Calgary until 1891. Two daughters were born while they were in Calgary, Lena, in 1889 and Mary, in 1891. In 1891 they moved to farm at De Winton, living on the hill above De Winton station and two more children were born there. Hugh, "Peck", was born in 1896 and Sadie was born in 1897.

Around 1894 a post office was opened in their home and for years Hugh drove the mail to Grierson Post Office, east of De Winton then on to Morris Stewart's home, known as Davisburg Post Office. His route also included the Indian Industrial School. He had an excellent relationship with the school staff and at times would drive one or more of them from De Winton to the school. In 1898, he extended his route to include Gladys Post Office, adding an extra ten miles to his travel. As the country became more settled he began

The Luxury of Furs. Mary, Hugh, Sarah, Jim and Sadie McNeill. About 1904.

to deliver twice a week and also carried mail for Dinton, Glenview and Mossleigh. These trips had many hazzards and thrills, bad roads, culverts washed out, unexpected blizzards etc. In the spring of 1897 his son, John, swam the Highwood River on horseback to get letters to their destination.

Through the years, his daughter, Lena, ran the Post Office and John, Jim, and Mary often helped on the mail route. One trip, when roads were so bad, Mary accompanied him to open the gates to cut across fields. She opened twenty-one gates to get there. One blizzard almost proved too much for him and he collapsed but his faithful horse took him on to the Indian School where willing hands cared for him and his horses.

About 1911 they gave up the mail route and post office, sold the farm to son, John, and with the exception of John and Jim, the family moved to Vancouver.

The Hugh McNeill and Archie Bremner families about 1912.

Hugh passed away in 1921 and Sarah in 1918.

John married Alison Scott and they had three children, two girls and a boy.

Jim married Constance "Daisy" Tyson and had one daughter.

Lena married M. Stewart, a Vancouver policeman, and had five children, two boys and three girls. After her first husband died she married F. Henbest and had one daughter. She passed away in Vancouver in 1968.

Mary also married a Vancouver policeman, Hugh Graham, and they returned to De Winton to farm. They had two boys and one girl. She passed away in Calgary in 1975.

Hugh, "Peck", served in World War I and married an English girl. They had one daughter. He was killed in an industrial accident in Vancouver in 1935.

Sadie married N. Shore of Vancouver, they had no family. In the early '60s they moved to White Rock B.C. where Sadie passed away in 1972.

JOHN AND ALISON (SCOTT) McNEILL — by Jean Pakenham

My Dad, John McNeill, was born at Ellerslie near Paisley, Ontario on March 12, 1885. He came to Calgary with his parents and brother Jim, in 1887. In 1891, the family moved to De Winton to the house on the hill above the station. They farmed and ran the post office. He attended school at Pine Creek, Melrose and Stormount. Also helped deliver the mail to Gladys Ridge and in 1897 when the wooden bridge over the Highwood was washed out, Dad swam a horse across, carrying the mail sack with letters only — 'he was twelve years old!'

In 1912 Dad went to homestead at Blind Creek near Mossleigh. After three years he turned the homestead over to brother Jim and came back to help his father farm, also to go to school in Calgary to obtain his steam engineer papers. He later bought his father's farm. In 1916 he married Alison Scott, a school teacher from Scotland who was teaching at Stormount School.

Dad was an excellent rider and rode in many of the early round ups. He also was good with a gun, which helped keep meat on the table during the depression years. For several years he went to the Arrowwood area to run a steam engine at threshing time for a Mr. Kennedy.

In 1919 he bought a farm, five miles west of De Winton, from Alf Gooch. We rented the house in De Winton to Tom Dalzell and moved. I remember our good neighbors there; Jacobs, Goerlitz, Harrison. My sister, Sheila, and I rode horseback three miles to Stormount School.

Around 1925 Dad developed signs of Multiple Sclerosis and from then on he did not enjoy good health but was able to carry on with his work for several years.

In 1926 Tom Dalzell moved to a house in town and Harry Youngman moved to our De Winton home. In 1927 the big house burned down and another one was built. When Youngmans left Dick Meehan rented the house and had the mail route.

In 1930 we moved back to De Winton so my sister and I could attend De Winton High School which had just opened.

Dad served on the school board and was often called for jury duty. Mother and Dad loved to dance and the whole family went to the dances as there were no baby sitters then. They were also ardent card players and my memories of our home was that it was always blessed with company, both young and old.

In 1943 they sold the farm to Charlie Nemeth and, again, moved to the west place.

They only stayed three years as Dad's health was so poor that he could not work. The land was rented to Victor Poffenroth and only by the kindness of Victor and Clara Poffenroth and Dan and Elsie Poffenroth, were they able to get groceries, mail, etc. Doug and I came home weekends to help with the garden and other chores. In 1947 he sold the farm to Victor Poffenroth and moved back to De Winton where they rented a house from Bob Smith.

In 1949 they retired to White Rock, B.C. where they lived for twelve years, enjoying the climate and living by the sea. In 1950 Dad was forced from a wheelchair to become a bed patient and Mother nursed him for years. Her only break was when I went, for a month each year, to nurse him and give her a holiday.

In 1961 they flew back to Calgary, Dad on a stretcher, and they lived in a house on the north hill owned by a friend of mine, Mrs. Nan Jensen. After nine months there Dad went to Blunt's Nursing Home where he stayed for eight months. From there he went to Sarcee Auxiliary Hospital where he spent the last ten years of his life. Although he was paralysed he enjoyed life, loved T.V., and was ever grateful for the visits of family and friends and the care of the wonderful staff at Sarcee Hospital. Not once did he complain.

He was a member of the Southern Alberta Old Timers Association for many years as well as the Multiple Sclerosis Society. He passed away August 20, 1973, after twenty-three years of being paralysed in bed.

My mother, Alison Scott, was born in Lanark, Scotland in October 1890 and came to Canada in 1911 on the same ship as Maggie (Wylie) Jamison and Jessie (Murray) Anderson.

Although she had been to university in Scotland, she was required to attend Normal School in Calgary before she could teach in Alberta. Her first school was at Dog Pound, (west of Carstairs). She then taught at Stormount School, west of De Winton, and boarded with Mr. and Mrs. Jack Dalzell and also with Mr. and Mrs. Rollie Ness.

She took a great interest in community affairs and helped to organize several house parties in the district, one in particular, the farewell party for Percy Morgan when he left for the First World War. She was a member of most of the organizations in the area and served on the executive panels of many of them; a very good neighbor and friend.

Mr. and Mrs. John McNeill, 50th Wedding Anniversary, married April 16th, 1916.

She lived with Eleanor and Alf Hill for two years after Dad went into the Sarcee and then moved to the Elbow Valley Lodges where she stayed for eight years. In 1974 she moved to Cedars Villa Nursing Home and it was there she passed away August 8, 1975.

Mother suffered ill health for the last several years of her life and she was also a patient in the Sarcee Hospital in 1966 when she and Dad celebrated their fiftieth wedding anniversary. Over two hundred friends and relatives attended and paid their respects at their Anniversary Tea. They both said it was the best day of their lives.

Dad and Mother are both at rest in the Pine Creek Cemetery.

My sister, Sheila was born in 1916 and worked for several years for the Porteous Brothers in the Koffee Kounter in Calgary. In 1943 she was married in Seattle, Washington, to Jimmie Rubbelke (formerly of Queenstown, Alberta). She worked as a dental nurse for many years in Seattle and passed away in 1972. They had no children.

I, Jean, was born in July 1918 and was married August 20, 1940, to Doug Pakenham, a teacher at that time in Panima School, west of Okotoks.

During my growing years I attended school at Stormount and De Winton High School, worked for a number of different neighbors, cooked on a cook car for Harrisons and played baseball with the De Winton girl's team.

After our marriage we lived in several towns, including Herronton, Brant, Blackie, Okotoks, Banff and Exshaw where we now reside, and Doug is now in his forty-first year of teaching. We have one son, Wayne, born June 27, 1942 and presently living in Calgary.

My brother, Jack was born August 14, 1925 and joined the R.C.A.F. in 1943. He went Overseas in April, 1944 and returned in July, 1946. He went to school at Pine Creek. In March of 1949 he married Thelma Sverdahl of Delia and they have three children; Ken, born in 1949, Judy, born in 1950 and Blake, born in 1959.

Jack has worked in the Oil Industry since returning from Overseas and they have lived in Calgary, Edmonton and Regina. Presently, they live in the Haysboro district in Calgary.

Although we have been gone for many years, our memories are dear and our roots are deep in our home — De Winton!

RICHARD (DICK) MEEHAN
Meehan's Garage, De Winton, Alberta. Fall 1927 to Spring 1931.

Richard H. Meehan was born March 25th, 1899, from pioneer parents, John and Elizabeth Meehan. He attended Melrose School and Claresholm Agriculture College.

Dick operated the Meehan farm from his early years until 1927. He then opened his own garage in De Winton. From 1928 until the spring of 1931 he also ran the Rural Mail Route from De Winton to Gladys Ridge Post Office.

In 1931 he joined the Canadian Bakery's staff as a mechanic on their trucks, cars and machines.

He was employed by Freeman — Wilson from 1932 to 1962 as a full time mechanic, with three cer-

L. to r. Sam Hamilton, Maizie Meehan — 1930 holding Marie, Dick and George Meehan, Wenty Brinton, Pete Murray, (seated) Herman Alverson.

tificates; mechanics, electric hands, body and fender with the exception of three years. He was in the army during the second world war where he served with the R.C.E.M.E. as an instructor.

On his retirement he moved to Boswell, B.C. where he and his wife Ruth, built their home overlooking the beautiful Kootenay Lake. They lived there until their deaths, Ruth passed away December 26, 1975 and Richard on February 26, 1976.

GERRY AND WILMA (LEGGAT) MOONEY — by Wilma Mooney

Gerry and Wilma moved to Sandstone in 1953 with their three daughters; Lynn, Barbara and Sandra.

In 1955 we moved to Acadamy and Gerry ran the elevator and farmed. We had many good times in "Mooney's Meadow". In the fall of 1960 we moved to High River but still keep in contact with De Winton.

Our three daughters are married and we have three granddaughters and a grandson.

E. PERCIVAL MORGAN

In 1911, Mr. E. Morgan purchased the W½ 34-21-1-W5 from C. H. Hooley and, his daughter, Anne and son, Percy set up housekeeping and undertook to run the farm. The first crop was put in by Earle Marshall and was snowed down and had to be cut one way. Percy had acquired a binder and cut the crop himself and, at one point, had a runaway that caused considerable damage to the machine but did no damage to himself.

Percy was a typical English gentleman and, along with a group of other young English lads, took an interest in social events of the surrounding area. Felix Schroeder was one of his companions and, together they managed to have quite a time. One of their favorite pastimes was duck hunting which can be the means of getting one's feet well soaked. It got to be a standard joke of Felix to say that he must pay Percy a visit as he had no more socks. Percy had borrowed them all after getting his own wet while duck hunting.

A motorcycle was his usual mode of travel although he had a nice team of high spirited horses as well. He as a rather reckless young man and managed to upset the motorcycle many times while turning corners. He also was adept at overturning his buggy by driving right up to a corner and then suddenly pulling on the line for the horses to turn. He never seemed to get injuries from his many mishaps.

The year that the Morgans came, Anne, and one of her friends from England, decided they would like to see a threshing outfit at close range and stationed themselves under the stack at a machine being run by Eben Bremner on the Marshall farm. One of the threshing crew, a Scot by the name of Tavish McTavish let his sense of humour get the better of him and sent several bundles tumbling down on top of the young ladies. It was a long-bearded barley and must have been most uncomfortable for the girls.

It was during these years that the De Winton Theatrical Society was in operation and Percy took an active part in their affairs, appearing in some of the plays and attending social functions sponsored by the society.

Shortly after World War I broke out, Percy left to join the Forces. He saw active service overseas and was killed in action.

A gala farewell party was held for him before he left to join up. It was arranged by some of the young people of the district with Alison (Scott) McNeill and Mary (Dalzell) Dick as the chief organizers. It was well attended by the neighbours of the area and talked about for years afterward.

Before leaving, Percy had packed away all the family possessions, linen, dishes, etc. along with his tuxedo and other personal belongings, and made arrangements to rent the farm. All these things were destroyed in a fire that demolished the house in 1940.

JOSEPH MOSS — by Josephine (Moss) McKeage

My father, Joseph H. S. Moss, was a member of a Survey Party, which left Winnipeg by Red River carts and horses in the spring of 1879 to survey the 5th Meridian. Also in the party was Charles McGrath, a great friend of Dad's. Charlie McGrath became a Member of Parliament eventually for Southern Alberta.

My father worked at the freighting of supplies from Benton, Montana during the Louis Riel Rebellion and eventually filed on land on the edge of Pine Creek hill where it empties into the Bow River. Dad had an unfortunate incident involving a Blackfoot Indian man who had been ransacking Dad's cabin on more than one occasion. When Father came home at noon and caught the culprit the Indian wanted to shake hands, which was refused. The Indian followed Dad back to the bush where Dad had been chopping wood, and after stalking Dad for some time, finally found the chance to spring on Dad and stab him in the back. Father was able to reach a neighbour's and receive help, and later recovered from a close call with death.

My mother, Elizabeth Shortt, had come West with a younger married sister, Mary (Mrs. John Bell), in March 1886, and was called into duty to nurse my father when he was recovering from the stabbing assault by the Indian. My parents were married two years later, September 5th, 1888. They ranched at Pine Creek, but were crowded out for pasture for cattle and horses and sold out to Troughton Brothers in May 1901.

They trekked all their horses, cattle, chickens and household goods to Mossleigh in June 1901. There was no Mossleigh in those days, in fact our nearest neighbours were McHugh's Beef Camp nine miles away.

My parents had a family of five. George was the oldest; Florence an infant who died. Next was Josephine (myself) - Lil was next and another infant Joseph, also died. The last was Mary, the only one not born at De Winton.

Mr. and Mrs. J. H. Moss, Josie, Lil and George.

We rode ponies to Melrose School and can remember taking turns with other pupils in carrying a pail of drinking water from Grierson's well. The Kenny family, Ethel, Laura and Cora Andrews, Roy and Fred Maxwell, Edith, Edward, Wellington, Mabel and Etta Currie were among the pupils I remember best.

I was eight and one-half years old when we left that district and quite capable of riding herd on the cattle when moving to the Arrowwood country. Our neighbours at De Winton were Neil Brodie, the Ingraham brothers, Whalens and Kennys among others. We got our mail at De Winton and if I remember correctly, Mrs. McNeill ran the Post Office. There were John, Jim, Lena, Mary and Hugh McNeill. We visited Bremners quite often - Eben, Ethel and Jean.

Santa Claus came around as usual, and we apparently were satisfied with what the stockings were filled with. The stockings were the long black woollen kind which the ribbon candy stuck to.

The first generation are all gone, and unfortunately too many of the second generation are too, making the job of gathering the history of the early days not as thorough as one would wish.

Our parents are buried in Pine Creek Cemetery. Mother died in April 1911, Father three years later in 1913. Our brother George died in July, 1955 and buried at Kamloops, B.C. My sisters and I live in Calgary.

PETER HUTTON AND GRACE MARGARET BROWN (FOWLIS) MURRAY — by Grace Skelding

Pete Murray was born in Fifeshire, Scotland in 1881. He became a blacksmith and in 1910 enlisted and went to the Boer War as a farrier. In 1912 he settled at De Winton, where he built a home and blacksmith shop and became De Winton's first "Village Smithy".

His childhood sweetheart, Grace Margaret Brown Fowlis, came out from St. Andrews, Fifeshire, Scotland and they were married in 1913.

l. to r. Bill Grierson, ?, Frank McHugh holding Grace Murray, Mrs. Pete Murray, 1918.

Pete Murray and daughter, Grace, 1920's.

During the 'flu epidemic of 1918 my mother worked tirelessly, nursing and helping all the stricken neighbors she could manage. She became quite run down with the exertion and in December she became ill herself and passed away on Christmas Day, leaving a small daughter, Grace Isabel.

Before his marriage Pete's home was a gathering place for most of the young men of the neighborhood. He was popular with all the local residents, and spent a good deal of time fishing and many a farmer would come in with repairs only to find a sign on the door "gone fishing". He grew a large garden, vegetables as well as flowers and was most generous with the produce, his sweet peas were said to be the best in the district.

In 1931 he sold out and moved to Calgary, then to Rosedale and East Coulee, where he was a blacksmith for the mines.

In November, 1956, he suffered a coronary and was in the Belcher Hospital, Calgary, till his passing February 1, 1957.

MARY (GALVIN) O'CONNOR — by Deborah Crandel.

Mary Galvin was a young girl from Ontario who arrived in De Winton early in the century. She helped Mrs. Pashak and worked in the store for Mr. Pashak. She was a popular girl and took part in the plays that were put on in Streeter's Hall. An excellent shot, she won a turkey at one of the many turkey shoots that were held in those years. She was also a very good rider.

During her stay in De Winton she became ill and had to go to Rochester, Mayo Clinic for an operation. During her convalescence, she got in touch with the Pashak family and was asked to come back to their home. She went to Calgary when the Pashaks moved there and was hired to work in their Calgary store in the Mission District. Later she worked for Alderman Samis then volunteered to nurse in the Soldier's Hospital in east Calgary, during the war. There she met her husband, Hugh O'Connor. For some time after their marriage they farmed on Veteran's land, near Coronation. It was here her husband died and she returned to Calgary and became an accredited nurse's aide.

When my mother Catherine Pashak became ill, Mary nursed her for three months with twenty-four hour service.

IRVIN GRANDVILLE AND ZENA (GORRELL) OESCH — by Irvin Oesch

I was born in Boyd County, Nebraska, March 6, 1900. My parents brought me to Canada with a wagon train in 1917, and we settled on a homestead in Saskatchewan. As time went on I got my own homestead near Spiritwood, Saskatchewan. After making a trip to Alberta in 1919 and with it getting harder to make a go of farming in Saskatchewan, I decided to come to Alberta in the spring of 1933. I came with my brother-in-law, George Gorrell.

I married Zena Jeanette Gorrell, in Shellbrook, on November 8, 1928. She had come from the States, with her folks in 1919. They came by wagon train, trailing their sixty horses. Zena was born in Hutchinson, Kansas, July 23, 1909.

In the summer of 1933, Zena and our two girls came out to join me.

I joined the Royal Canadian Engineers in the fall of 1939. I was overseas for five years, coming home in the spring of 1945.

We have three children; Bertha (King), Lillian (Davis), and David. Bertha and Charlie have three children; Lorne, Darryle and Charlene. They live at De Winton. Lillian and Ray have two children, Lyle and Donna Ray; they live in Calgary. David married Annette Haase, and they live in Calgary with their three boys, Wesley, Jeffery and Darin.

ASHBEL ERNEST ORTON — by Fay Dick and Lent Orton

Ashbel Ernest Orton, brother of Lent Orton, was born in Erie County, Pennsylvania on May 14, 1873. He lived in various parts of the United States before moving to Rumsey, Alberta in 1908 where he lived for two years before the town was built up and railroad came through. He was the town blacksmith and the citizens built a blacksmith shop for him. In 1923 he moved to Spokane, Washington and worked in lumber camps as blacksmith in Idaho before returning to De Winton as blacksmith in 1932.

His first wife passed away in 1914. They had four children: Ashbel, Georgia, Mary and Millicent. Children of his second marriage were: Lent, Fern and Fay.

Mr. Orton passed away in 1944 and is buried in Rumsey.

LENT AND LORNA (IRVING) ORTON — by Lent Orton

I was born in Rumsey, Alberta, August 22, 1920. In 1923 I went to Spokane where I lived until returning to De Winton in 1932. I was interested in the banjo and, in 1936, began playing for dances, an activity which I enjoyed for 34 years.

I attended Pine Creek and De Winton High schools.

During WW2 I served in the Navy and was on convoy duty on the Corvette La Malbaie for two years.

Lent, Lorna and Donna Orton, 1962.

Following the war, I returned to De Winton and went to work for the Alberta Department of Highways as a maintenance man, grader man, mechanic and, for the last ten years, until retirement, in 1975, as assistant shop superintendent.

In 1946 I married Lorna Edythe Irving and we lived in Scotty Lorimer's shack for the first year and then moved to Okotoks. We have one daughter, Donna, born May 10, 1949. She is a trained nurse, married to George Willcock from Turner Valley, and presently living at Fort St. John, B.C. They have one son Jody Allan, born on Fathers' Day, June 16, 1974.

JOHN AND LUCY (KENNEDY) OWENS

The exact year of John Owen's arrival is not known but he was one of the very first men to settle in the district. He came from Ontario with two nephews, William and Samuel Owens, and acquired a number of N.W.H. Board grants including N½ and SE¼ 20-21-1-W5 No. 34 and No. 122, NE¼ and 80 Acres NW¼ 16-21-2-W5, No. 10, W½ 12-21-2-W5, time sale No. 4322 as well as squatting on land in Pine Creek coulee. He later homesteaded E½ 11-22-1-W5 homestead No. 36380 and No. 65953. The nephews were expected to carry out the homesteading duties and also care for stock. When a stopping house and store was erected on the Pine Creek property, the boys kept store. It is said that John Owens worked every day of the year with the exception of New Year's when he went into Calgary to visit with friends and order supplies. He is also credited with inventing the wire gates still in use today and they were dubbed the John Owen's patent gates.

David Fulton was a long time employee of Owens and was hired to transport horses, usually driven over the old Leather Trail, to and from such places as Vernon B.C., Kamloops and Jasper. There was a brisk business in horse trading in those days.

John married Lucy Kennedy, a school teacher, and there were two sons, Alexander and Fred. Allie was a construction engineer in 1914 when the Government elevators were built. Mrs. Owens was the church organist for some time. They left the district early in the century and Herb Haines, Bob Dalzell and Frank Tindal were renters before the place was sold to Clark Standish in 1920.

There is a William Owens buried in Pine Creek Cemetery in 1899 at the age of 21 years, we were not able to verify a connection.

During the time Owens had the store and stopping house they kept a daily journal of expenses which has been repaired, plasticized, leather bound and is in the possession of a Calgary resident. The journal contains much information about the residents of the area during those years and the prices of merchandise make today's prices seem like highway robbery. When S. and F. Hamilton traded 61 pounds of butter on July 9, 1892, they received $9.15 and proceeded to spend it as follows: 1 sack flour — $3.50; 14 pounds ham — $2.50; nails — $0.25; 1 hat — $1.00; 1 pail — $0.30; 12 pounds sugar — $1.00. Clothing prices were equally low and, on August 12, 1892, Wm. Pearce bought 1 suit of clothes for $6.00; 1 pr. shoes — $4.50; 1 shirt — $0.85; 1 tie — $0.30 and 1 hat — $2.75. It almost makes one wish they could go back to the "good old days" doesn't it?

Demolishing the old Stopping House at Pine Creek. Winter of 1949-1950.

The remains of the store and stopping house are buried far beneath the surface of the Macleod Trail at the bottom of Pine Creek coulee. Much of the history of the early times is buried with them. They saw the great bull teams come from Fort Benton carrying goods to Calgary and further north. Many a pioneer family stopped overnight or for several days on their trek to find a new home. The post office made it a place for neighbours to gather and exchange news but those who used it as a meeting place are no longer around to tell us of the history that was made there.

HARRY AND JESSIE (HARKLEY) PAKENHAM — by Jean Pakenham

Harry Pakenham was born in Peterborough, Ontario, December 1890. He came to Calgary in 1910. In June of 1912, he was married to Jessie Harkley, granddaughter of Tom and Annie Douglas. They moved to the Douglas Place, on Pine Creek, in January, 1919.

They resided there for two years, one of which, Harry served on the Pine Creek School Board. He was

50th Wedding Anniversary, Harry and Jessie Pakenham, June 15th, 1912-1962.

also instrumental in putting on a talent show to help pay for the De Winton Hall which was just newly built. He recalls some who contributed talent as, Mrs. Bessie Heaver and Lallie Sutherland, singing and the Bremner sisters, whistling. He broke twenty-five acres and planted wheat for the first time and had a bumper crop which was hauled to Calgary.

In 1921 the family moved to Carseland where Harry was manager of the Prairie Lumber Co. They moved back to Calgary in 1929 and to B.C. in 1936. From 1936 to 1963 they lived in several B.C. towns where Harry was office manager and accountant for lumber firms. In 1963 they retired to Calgary.

They have three children; Patricia, (Mrs. Cliff Farr) of Airdrie, has one daughter, Donna; Douglas, married to Jean McNeill of De Winton, has one son, Wayne, teaches school at Exshaw; Clayton, married to Ethel Langdon of Creston B.C., has two sons, Jim and Terry.

Jessie and Harry still reside in Calgary and will celebrate their sixty-fourth wedding anniversary in June, 1976, still enjoying fairly good health.

THE RICHARD PALING FAMILY — by Gladys Green

This family arrived at De Winton, Alberta, from London, England, on Easter Sunday 1889. The group consisted of Richard Paling and his second wife Marina Laura, with their son Fred Leonard, and the children of Fanny Chaplin, Richard's first wife; Bertram, Ernest, Caroline and May Chaplin. Richard and Cyril Paling were born at De Winton.

Their first home and store was in a log house one mile north of De Winton N.W.¼-36-21-1-W5. Later they built a larger store in De Winton. I can remember that store when we visited there. We, the Hope children, remember sleeping in the upstairs while visiting them. We also remember the old house, near the store. The old iron pump was of special interest to us.

Richard Paling, in the 1890's, taught in the old school at Midnapore and in the first Pine Creek School on the corner of the C. Vader place S.E.¼-16-22-1-W5. He was, by profession, a school teacher in London. His daughter, Caroline, (later Mrs. Joseph Hope), had been a pupil teacher in England. She did not teach school in Alberta. We remember her saying that she was afraid to go to those lonely school houses. The Paling children attended Pine Creek School. In 1905, the Palings sold the store to Frank Pashak and moved to Lloydminster, Saskatchewan. They later homesteaded along the Battle River, south east of Lashburn, Saskatchewan.

Ernest Paling had moved to Lloydminster in 1903 where he ran a livery barn and had teams for hauling mail and freighting. He helped to haul freight for the Barr Colonists from Battleford to their new settlement. The story of the Barr Colonists is a most interesting one. Ernest also homesteaded at Lashburn before going to World War I. He had also served in the Boer War. His nephew, David Paling, Castlegar, B.C., has in possession the following medals that were awarded to Ernest.

A silver medal of the Boer War marked:—

Mr. and Mrs. Richard Paling.

"Johannesburg, Orange Free State, Cape Colony — by Queen Victoria Regina et Imperialtrix"

Another :— "Boer War, Pte. E. J. Paling T.H.E. Canada N.R."

A gold watch with the following inscription:— "Presented to E. J. Paling by his friends of Pine Creek on his return from South Africa." January 19, 1901."

A silver medal:— "The Great War for Civilization 1914-1918, 928 Pte. E. J. Paling, King Edward Horse" and a final one:— 1914-18 928 King Edward Horse, E. J. Paling.

When Ernest returned from the war he took land at Taylor Flats in B.C. along the Peace River near where the big railway and highway bridges now span that mighty river. Ernest and his war bride, Mabel, arrived, by boat, travelling along the Peace River to Taylor Flats.

He died at Fort Saint John, B.C., October 8, 1946. He and Mabel had retired there and Mabel died a few years before Ernest. Both are buried at Fort Saint John.

Uncle Fred Paling retired to Lashburn, Saskatchewan in 1955 where he lived until his passing in 1975 at the age of 88.

Uncle Richard Paling and his wife, Madge, retired to Lashburn in 1965, where they still live.

Cyril Paling farmed at Lashburn from 1905 to 1927 (22 years), at which time he moved to Edmonton, Alberta where he was a stationary engineer. On December 8, 1923, he married Ethel Mary Fraser.

They had two children; Mary (Mrs. Gilbert Yaeck), of Edmonton and David Alexander of Castlegar, B.C.

May Chaplin married Neil Brodie at De Winton and her story is included with his.

Caroline Chaplin married Joseph Hope of Red Deer Lake at the Anglican Church in Midnapore on December 12, 1893. Canon Stocken was the clergyman and Mrs. Wolley-Dod was the organist. It was one of the coldest days of the winter and Mrs. Wolley-Dod said her hands were so cold she had trouble playing the hymns.

Grandfather, Richard Paling, died on the farm at Lashburn on September 29, 1915. Grandmother Paling, Marina Laura, died at Lashburn, where she had retired, on September 27, 1934. They are both buried in Lashburn cemetery.

FRANK AND CATHERINE (MALONEY) PASHAK
— by Joe Pashak

Frank Pashak was born in Hamilton, Ontario and Catherine Maloney was born in Renfrew, they met in Minnesota, U.S.A. and were married in 1894. In 1899 my father came to Calgary, North West Territories, for his health. He bought the Robb farm north of De Winton and my mother and three children, Joe, Clyde and Deborah, followed in the fall.

Dad started to build his house, hauling the lumber from a mill west of Priddis, run, I believe, by the Mills Brothers. The house is still standing. When the house was finished, we all moved out. I didn't like it as there was no store among the trees on the farm.

We soon met the Marshalls, McNeills, McInnes's and Pratts and were made to feel at home. The people of the west were very friendly and helped one another. We farmed, had good crops always, had a small herd

Mr. and Mrs. Pashak and Deborah, about 1903 or 4.

of cattle, milked ten cows and fed fifty pigs each year. It was a lot of work but we were happy.

After farming for three years, we bought the store at De Winton as the farm work was too hard on my dad. He was not well and the children were too small to do much but chores. It was about 1904 when we went to De Winton, the store was doing very well then. We built a new store and lived in the old building. We later sold the old store building to Alonzo De Mings and he called it 'The Minto House,' named for his old home place in Minto, Nova Scotia. They ran it as kind of a stopping house.

We had the store and the machinery agencies for Massey Harris implements and Port Huron threshing machines, the coal business and kept the livery barn. We bought our coal from Lethbridge, known as Galt coal. Farmers left their horses in the livery barn when they went to Calgary on the morning train and returned for them at about seven in the evening. We also had the dance hall over the store where we had dances and shows until the people of the district built a very nice hall which served De Winton till it burned down in the early 1970s.

For sport and fun in the summer there were picnics, fishing in the Bow River, baseball games etc., in the winter, great dances, shows, sleigh rides, skating on the sloughs; at that time there was a lot of water around the country. I think, to us, at De Winton that everything was enjoyable, not much money but no one needed it that badly, we raised our own food and there were no cars and no drinking, "can you believe that?"

The McNeills had the post office in their home across the track, on the north side of the hill. A great Scotch family, three boys and three girls. Mrs. McNeill was a great gardener, as I remember. It was about this time that Pete Murray came to De Winton and opened a blacksmith shop. He was a great fellow to fish and hunt and all the boys and men in the district were over at his place a lot of the time. He married a girl from Scotland and then he had to tend to business and did not hunt so much.

At this time, the Anglican church and manse were across from Bremner's corner, it was later moved to De Winton and Reverend Streeter was the minister.

There was no school at De Winton at that time and we attended school in the Paling home across the road from Bremners. Our teacher was Miss Cardiff from Ontario, a relation of Mrs. Bremner. A year later, 1903, I think, the Pine Creek School was built and we old timers think more about that than of De Winton. They used to have school concerts and I remember going to meetings there. There were box socials and political meetings. I think that Eben Bremner was the oldest pupil going at that time. On the 1903 roll there were; Marshalls, Kellys, Palings, McInnes's, McNeill's, Bremners, Pomeroys, Airds and Pashaks. There were twenty-eight pupils in 1903 and the teacher was James Weir. Other neighbors that I remember are, Gray, Dunfield, Woolford, Brinton, Jamison and King.

I remember well Marshalls baling hay that they hauled to De Winton and sold by the car load. We had the weigh scales that the farmers used as there was no elevator then.

"First Twins Born in De Winton. Gerald and Gertrude Pashak, 1910.

When we sold the store in 1910, we moved to Calgary and W. R. Macdonald became the owner.

During our stay in De Winton the family grew to seven, Francis, Leonard, Gerald and Gertrude (twins), were all born there. Harvey and Margaret were born in Calgary.

In 1902 we sold oats at 20¢ a bushel, barley at 40¢ and wheat at 80¢, after hauling it to Calgary in wagons. Pork was $6.00 per hundred and cattle $30.00 per head. Men worked for farmers for $30.00 a month and board.

Walter Poffenroth, Harold Marshall, Alf Poffenroth and Harvey Pashak, 1921.

Frank Pashak died in 1917 and Catherine in 1938. They are buried in Calgary.

Joe and his wife, Sadie, are retired and live in Calgary. They have a boy and three girls; Clyde is a widower, resides in Calgary and has one boy and three girls; Deborah (Crandel), no children, lives in Calgary; Francis (deceased 1964) two boys and one girl, his widow, (Florence Dowling), lives in Calgary; Leonard and his wife Julia, both retired and in Calgary, two boys and three girls; Gerald and his wife Ada, retired, one boy and one girl. Gertrude, the twin, drowned in the Elbow River in 1915; Harvey and his wife, Ann, two boys and four girls (Harvey works for the School Board); Margaret (Webb) deceased 1974, leaves her husband, Al and three boys and one girl in Renton, Washington.

There are twenty-nine grandchildren and fifty great-grandchildren.

FRANCIS AND FLORENCE (DOWLING) PASHAK

For about two years during the latter part of the 1920's Frank and Florence Pashak lived in the "greenhouse" in De Winton with their two tiny children, the youngest, just a small baby. Two things stood out in Florence's mind concerning that period. First was a severe storm that blew snow inside the house and piled it in impassable drifts outside. She had been left alone with the children and was out of coal and nearly out of food. It got so bitterly cold that she even took the carpet from the floor to wrap around herself and the children to try to keep warm. When morning came she recalls Pete Murray, the village blacksmith, struggling down the road from De Winton with a sack of coal and some groceries. She was forever grateful to him for his concern. The second incident involved working out in the yard where she lost her engagement ring. They searched for it all the time they remained at the place but never found it. She felt that a chicken had probably picked it up and swallowed it.

Things were not working out in the money making field so they returned to Calgary where Frank went into the sales business and spent a good many years travelling around Alberta with different companies. The oldest boy, Frank, and his wife were killed in a tragic automobile accident quite a number of years ago, a second son, Larry, lives in Edmonton and their daughter, Delores (Michaud) lives in Calgary. Frank passed away in 1964 and Florence in 1977.

In the summer months Helen Dowling, a sister to Florence, stayed with them and helped with the children. Helen passed away in 1975.

SONG SPARROW

BROWN SPOT ON STREAKED BREAST

ARTHUR AND ELIZABETH PAXTON

Lived in the Willet house in 1919, Arthur clerked in the store for Mr. Anderson. There were two daughters. They stayed only a year and the property was sold to Miss Ida Gooch.

Back of the Post office De Winton, Paxton family.

ALFRED FREDERICK AND CHRISTINA (HOUSTON) POFFENROTH — by A. and C. Poffenroth

I, Alf, was born on the farm at De Winton (SW¼ 2-22-1-W5), in the big house, with Doctor Ardiel attending my birth and lived on the farm all of my life until 1972 when we bought a home in Okotoks.

I attended Pine Creek School and, like many country children, drove to school with a horse and buggy. "Nigger", our horse, would always try to go through the small foot gate instead of the one made wide enough for the buggy. This caused a lot of trouble and we often had to walk home. Nigger was also fond of lunches and if any child left a lunch where Nigger could get at it everything would be gone. The only thing he wouldn't eat was oranges.

In 1938 I married Christina Houston of Calgary and we raised four children; Bonnie Jean attended Pine Creek and De Winton and Okotoks High Schools, took a business course in Calgary and presently works for the Vancouver Cancer Clinic. David Alfred attended Saskatoon and Edmonton Schools for the Deaf and is employed by Calgary Tent and Awning. Barry Frederick took his first grade at Pine Creek with Mrs. Lawrence Norris and then attended school in Okotoks as the bus stopped at our gate. He is married to Carol Kerr of Okotoks, has two sons, Kerry Christopher (4 years) and Tyler Lee (1 Year), they live in Calgary and Barry is with the Calgary Fire Department. Our youngest, Grant Henry, took all his education in Okotoks and is now working in the construction business.

We had good neighbours on the farm and have a lot of pleasant memories. We always enjoyed the De Winton Community Picnics, more food (the best) than you could eat served at 1 o'clock, sports all day long then supper and home to milk the cows (we always had a dairy farm), get ready and return to the dance, even though we had to be up early to milk again. It was a good life!

Now we take an active part in the community affairs in Okotoks and Alf is employed by the Department of Highways.

HENRY AND CATHERINE (KAISER) POFFENROTH

Henry Poffenroth was born in 1885, and with his parents immigrated to Colfax, Washington, in 1888. From there they came to Alberta in 1894 and homesteaded at Bashaw. Leaving there, the family acquired C.P.R. lands, six miles west of De Winton, where they farmed until about 1900, when they moved to Calgary and operated a dairy farm on 11th Avenue South West, near the present Colonel Belcher Hospital. In 1905, the growth of the city forced them to move the dairy to North West Calgary on the site of the present Confederation Park. Shortly thereafter, Henry married Catherine Kaiser and they operated the dairy, which was one of the first dairies in Calgary to deliver milk to the hotels and private homes. In 1912, during the land boom, Henry and Catherine sold the dairy and purchased the homestead of Jack McInnes at De Winton (SW 2-22-1-W5M, SE 3-22-1-W5M, NW 35-21-1-W5M). There they continued dairying and were prominent in the breeding of Holstein cattle. Part of the farm is still owned and operated by a son, Walter.

Henry and Catherine had five children. Victor, who left the farm about 1924 and followed a career as a first aid attendant in the Merchant Marines, Armed Forces and in construction work. He worked mostly in British Columbia which included construction of the Alaska Highway and the Rogers Pass. He died in Vancouver in 1966.

Violet moved to Calgary and worked there until she married Robert Overand of Okotoks, moving to Turner Valley at the height of the oil discovery. Still in the oil

Henry and Catherine Poffenroth, 50th Wedding Anniversary, Dec. 17th, 1955.

Henry Poffenroth Jr. family; l. to r. Henry, Walter, Violet, Martin, Catherine, Alfred, Victor.

industry, they moved to Trinidad and then to San Francisco where Rod served in the U.S. Marine Corps. They returned to Calgary in 1971, where they now reside.

Walter married Janet MacBeth of Calgary and they live on the farm at De Winton.

Alfred married Christina Houston of Calgary and they reside in the Town of Okotoks.

Martin married Della Lehman of Calgary, leaving the farm in 1940 and serving in the Armed Forces. Since then, Martin has worked in the auto body and insurance appraisal businesses, and is now manager of an insurance appraisal centre, residing in Calgary.

Henry C. Poffenroth.

HENRY C. AND MARY (KROM) POFFENROTH

Henry C. Poffenroth arrived here from Saratov, Russia in 1912, after serving his time in the Russian Army.

He made his home in the De Winton area about ¾ mile north of the hamlet of De Winton, which was located on the NW¼-36-21-1-W5M.

He married Mary Krom, daughter of Adam Krom of De Winton on August 6, 1916. They had one son Harold. He married Bernice Goettler. They had three sons Dennis, Brian and Garry, and one daughter Gail.

Dennis the eldest son, is married and is living in Chatham, New Brunswick. They have four girls.

Brian was the second son, and is living in Calgary.

Gail is married and is living in Shamrock, Saskatchewan. She has one girl.

Garry the youngest boy is living in Calgary.

Henry C. Poffenroth cleared his own land of trees and broke it up with hired help from the De Winton area and lived here until his death in April, 1955.

WALTER CARL AND JANET (MacBETH) POFFENROTH

Walter Carl Poffenroth was born in Calgary, and lived with his parents on the family farm at De Winton. In 1932, he married Janet MacBeth of Calgary, and in 1936 they moved to Turner Valley where he worked in the oilfields on drilling crews until 1945, returning to De Winton to take over the family farm with his brother, Alfred, when their father, Henry, retired. Walter and Alfred continued in the dairy business and built up their father's foundation herd of Holsteins, winning in 1956 the Provincial Award for the highest producing grade herd on test in Alberta. In 1962, they sold the dairy herd, and continued farming together until 1972 when Alfred moved to Okotoks. Walter still farms and lives on the old family farm.

Walter Poffenroth family, l. to r. Barbara, Robert, Janet, Walter, 1967.

Walter and Janet have two children, Barbara and Robert. Barbara, a registered nurse, is married to Keith Groves of Champion and they have four boys, Maury, Richard, David and Corey. Robert is practicing law in Calgary.

ANDREW AND ROBERT PRATT — by R. Lynch

The Pratt brothers, Andrew (1847-1900) and Robert (1846-1929), came to Alberta in 1883 from Kingskettle, Fifeshire, Scotland. They homesteaded in the Pine Creek district — Andrew on N.E.¼ 14-22-1-W5 while Robert settled for S.E.¼ 14-22-1-W5. They also acquired S.W.¼ 13-22-1-W5.

L. to R. John Owens, Bobby Pratt and Archie Bremner.

They were blacksmiths by trade and worked that in with farming. By 1899 they had bought W½ 14-22-1-W5 from Lafferty-Moore, the owner at the time. It was on this half section that the stopping house, built in 1886 was located — on the west side of the Macleod Trail at the top of the hill north of Pine Creek. Barns, blacksmith shop and the well were on the east side of the road as was the original log shack.

They were active in church and school affairs. Robert's offer of the site for the proposed Presbyterian Church was accepted at a congregational meeting held Sunday, December 19, 1889 at John Owen's store. The church, built in 1890, was also located on the east side of the "Trail".

After the death of Andrew in 1900, Robert returned to Scotland and brought the William Andersons (his sister Margaret) and family back to the farm.

Before local grain elevators appeared it was customary to sack grain for sale and haul it by team and wagon to the Robin Hood Mills or the government grain elevators in Calgary. The sacks were long, narrow and made of heavy cotton and would probably hold about three bushels of oats and usually had the owners name printed on one side.

The W½ 11-22-1-W5 (school land) was bought after the turn of the century. At one time a cattle dipping tank was developed by the creek and was used by the neighboring farmers to control a general outbreak of mange.

Uncle Bobby did not drive a car so his usual mode of transportation was by horse and buggy. During the twenties he would drive Queenie, the buckskin, to De Winton to pick up the mail.

EDWARD AND CHRISTINA ROBB

The Robbs came to the Pine Creek district in 1882 and settled on the E½ 12-22-1-W5 which place they later homesteaded. They were a kindly couple and well

Isabelle and Morris Robb, about 1888.

regarded in the area. Their name last appears on the tax roll in 1899. There were four children: Maurice (Morris?), Watson, Isabelle and Edna who died at the age of three years and is buried in Pine Creek cemetery.

When the tiny child died there was no cemetery in the area and Mr. Robb donated acreage for the purpose. Hers was the first grave and her marker stands in the north east corner surrounded by an ironwork fence made by the Pratt brothers, local blacksmiths of that era.

Maurice went to the Boer War and was badly wounded, apparently never able to walk again. No more information about the family was submitted.

REGINALD AND BLANCHE (MOON) SHEEPY

Reg and Blanche were both members of old time families in the area. They were married in the twenties and lived on SW¼ 15-22-1-W5. They had only one child; Cecil, who attended Pine Creek school from about 1931-36 and is now living in Calgary. Blanche and Reg are both deceased.

GRACE ISABEL (MURRAY) SKELDING — by G. Skelding

I was born at De Winton, August, 1914. My school days were spent at De Winton (Pine Creek, Melrose, De Winton High) and in Calgary, (Haultain, St. Mary's and East Calgary High). I trained for a nurse at the Calgary General Hospital, graduating in 1938. In 1940, I was married to Elbert Arthur Skelding and we resided at the farm south of Fort Macleod until Elbert's death in 1974. We had four children, three boys, Murray, George and Edgar and one daughter, Linda.

CLORNE SMITH

Orphaned while still a young lad, Clorne made his way from his home in Tennessee north to Wisconsin where, in 1894, he heard about the fine open country in Alberta, Canada and set out to find out about it for himself. He had gained the nickname "Tennessee" from his birthplace and it stuck with him most of his life. His worldly goods consisted mostly of his personal clothing and some quilts and spreads that his mother had made. The spreads were beautifully handwoven from hand dyed cotton, mostly a dark blue and white. Very lovely.

The only thing he knew how to do was work on the land and he spent the next years of his life working around the local farms. He was a good "hand" but when work was not available and he stayed at a farm home and got room and board, he insisted on paying with the spreads. He greatly admired Mr. Tom Douglas and when the Douglas family left to go to the Drumheller district, Tennessee was not far behind and he homesteaded up there. He finally settled in Calgary where he lived for a good many years but we have no record of his life there.

ROBERT VOSS SMITH — by Mrs. Una Rodger

Robert Voss Smith was born in Perthshire, Scotland, coming to Canada in the early 1900's.

He had worked at the Robin Hood Mills and been overseas in World War I. He was a Private with the 1st Depot Battalion, Alberta Regiment, joining up in 1918 and being discharged on July 19th, 1919, and then he came to the De Winton area to settle.

Bob had been a Mason with the Okotoks Chapter also a member of the Royal Canadian Legion No. 1, Calgary.

Bob treasured his privacy and consequently very little is known of his early life. A chosen few were invited into the "Inner Sanctum" of his home to enjoy his warm hospitality. He had many interests; well drilling, apiarist, watchmaker, taking great pride in restoring old clocks and watches. He was Postmaster of De Winton for many years and there are many episodes that the inhabitants of the De Winton area

Bob Smith, De Winton Postmaster 1926-1957.

remember with mirth about "Postie Smith". Bob's fantastic driving was one of these and everyone kept off the route between Bob's garage and the station at train time. One Saturday he was a little late getting back from Calgary and the train was leaving the station as he approached De Winton; the old chev. took on the challenge for the race to Okotoks to retrieve the mail bags; a Greyhound Bus got in the way and so Bob and Gyp, his Collie dog returned without the mail, only one car door handle and in a very foul mood. "Pete took the mail off the train", he was informed. "Why in hell didn't someone stop me" Bob roared! "When we heard you coming everyone got off the road . . . who wanted to be killed", was the reply.

People sometimes gathered in the post office lobby while the mail was being sorted and it was education to hear the running commentary between the Postmaster and the Mailman, Dickie Dunn.

Under Bob's gruff exterior was a kind man, having time for children, animals, and was very generous to his friends.

When Bob decided to retire he had Jack Cram take him into the Bow Valley Lodge in Calgary where he enjoyed city life. No one was informed of his departure and concerned neighbours who missed seeing him for a few days looked through a window and saw a form on the bed. News spread like wild fire and a crowd quickly gathered while the police broke into the house. A dummy had been placed in the bed, perhaps to deter would be vandals from entering the building. This incident gave the townsfolk something to discuss for a long time.

Bob passed away in Calgary on March 16, 1976, as he had lived, few knowing he had gone until after the event. He is survived by a sister, Mrs. Elizabeth Taylor in Musselburgh, Scotland.

WILLIAM ORANGE SOMERVILLE

Mr. Somerville filed for homestead No. 41343, SW¼ 24-21-1-W5, sometime before 1892 it is not known whether he proved it up. He was the first postmaster in De Winton being appointed April 1, 1894. He left the district the following year and went to seek his fortune in the Klondike gold fields. He died in the Yukon Territories in 1898. He was the second son of James and Anne (Findlay) Somerville.

JAMES SOMERVILLE FAMILY

James Somerville and his wife Anne, nee Findlay, came from Litchfield, Quebec, arriving in the Calgary area in the spring of 1889. Their two younger daughters, Frances Grace and Harriet, accompanied them. One son, William Orange had come earlier and their eldest son, Thomas, and his wife were already established in Calgary.

William homesteaded near De Winton. In addition to farming he worked for the Post Office department. Starting late in 1893 he undertook to transport the mail from the railway station in De Winton to Pine Creek. During the years 1894 to the end of 1897 he carried the mail on other routes, namely between De Winton and Dunbow, De Winton and Grierson and De Winton and Rosebud.

The De Winton place became the Somerville fami-

James Somerville —
about 1865.

ly home. The father, James, was not well, having come to Western Canada for his health and he died in 1890. Anne, his wife, passed away three years later. Of the daughters, Frances Grace was a teacher and taught on the Blackfoot and Sarcee Reserves and privately, so spent little time at the De Winton home. On December 19, 1905, she married Thomas Jameson of Millarville. Harriet, the younger daughter, kept house for her brother until her marriage in 1895 to Thomas Richard B. Copp.

William responded to the lure of gold and left for the Klondike in 1898. The family never heard from him again and enquiries proved fruitless. Eventually it became accepted that William Orange Somerville was one of the many casualties of the Klondike gold rush.

There was a fifth member of the Somerville family who had come west — an older daughter Elizabeth. She was the wife of George Creighton of Grand Valley but died a comparatively short time after settling in the area.

In addition, James and Anne Somerville had lost two sons, Ernest and Jack, who as young men were drowned in the Ottawa River. A little girl, Anne, died in infancy.

WILLIAM CLARK AND ELIZABETH (HUNTER) STANDISH — by Elizabeth MacLeod and Alice Irving

Dad was born on June 30, 1881, near Port Elgin, Bruce County, Ontario. In 1886, when he was 5 years old, the family came west to Alberta. They settled on a farm east of Glenmore School, on the south side of Calgary. It was here that Dad took his schooling.

After apprenticing three years in Calgary as a blacksmith, he went to Priddis where his parents were living, and set up his own shop.

In 1902, he married Elizabeth Hunter, who had come to teach the Priddis School the year before. She was born in Edinburgh, Scotland, and came to Calgary in 1884 at the age of 3 years, with her mother and brother. Her father had come through to Calgary with the railroad in 1883. She received her education in Calgary and then went on to Normal School in Regina, N.W.T. While in Priddis, their first child, (Mike) William, was born in 1904.

In 1907, they moved out to a homestead three miles east of Priddis, where they farmed, and Dad also continued on with his blacksmith work. He raised and sold

a lot of horses especially during the war years, 1914-1918. He disposed of the horses while they were still a good price and raised more cattle. While on this farm, there were three more children born; Elizabeth, 1909, George, 1911, and Alice, 1916.

In 1920, the farm was sold to Dad's brother, and we moved to the De Winton area. Dad had bought the John Owens place on Pine Creek, E½-11-22-1 W5th, where he went into the dairy business.

Mr. Owens had settled on this land before there was a survey. When the survey went through, this land turned out to be a school section. In those days, squatter's rights were recognized, so he was able to retain the land. Mr. Owens operated a stopping house as well as a store. The stagecoach road to Fort Macleod went through the land, and the same road is now the No. 2 Highway. The log barn was built in the 1880's, and was built with a large door in the front for the coach teams to enter.

When Dad started dairying, he shipped milk to Pallesen's Dairy in Calgary, and then to Union Milk Company. At first the milk was hauled to De Winton, in summer by car and in winter, by team and sleigh. From there, it went to Calgary by train. On Sunday, the milk had to be at the station early as the "Spokane Express" picked it up around 7 a.m. This was the only train that travelled on Sunday. Finally we got truck service. The O.K. Express from Okotoks hauled the milk for a while. One driver we remember was Murray Scott from Midnapore. After a few years, Tom Dalzell took over the milk run, and he must have hauled it for nearly twenty years. Only once in all that time did he fail to get the milk to Calgary. He was caught in a blizzard and ran off the road.

Dad and Mother carried on with the dairy business until 1940 when George and Alice Irving rented the farm, and they moved to Burton, B.C. where they lived till 1949 and then came back to the farm.

In 1951, they sold the farm, retaining five acres in the north-west corner where they built a small house, and lived in retirement. Dad spent his time gardening and working in his shop. During this time he was asked by Mr. Norman Luxton to make a pair of oxen shoes

Clark and Elizabeth Standish taken in early sixties.

408

for the Luxton Museum at Banff. Dad was the only blacksmith he could find that had any knowledge of ox shoeing. These shoes are now on display in the Glenbow Foundation.

Dad had worked at several places around Priddis when he finished school. During that time, he worked for John Ware at Millarville. He told us several tales about this wonderful gentleman.

In March 1966, Dad passed away at the age of 84. Mother lived in their little home for another year, and then went to reside in the Medicine Tree Manor in High River. For the last few years, she was at the Twilight Rest Home in High River. She passed away in High River Hospital May 7, 1975 at the age of 93, and was laid to rest in Pine Creek Cemetery beside Dad.

William (Mike) went to farm in the Priddis area, married Gertrude Thompson of the Westoe District in 1933. They had a family of ten children, including two sets of twin boys. In 1968 he moved to a farm at Bassano where he still resides.

Elizabeth attended school at Pine Creek. She married Wilson A. McLeod in 1938 and had a family of five children. They farmed at Mountain Hill for eight years and then moved to Pincher Creek where Wilson was Police Magistrate. He passed away in 1965 and Elizabeth still resides in Pincher Creek.

George attended school in Pine Creek. Upon completing his schooling, he went to work in the area for Eben Bremner, Charlie Taylor and Freemans. He went to work for Royalite Oil Company in Turner Valley and married Emma Peat of Millarville in 1938. They had a family of seven children. The Royalite Oil Company became B.A. Oil and now is Gulf Oil. George took a mechanic's course and was transferred to Kamloops, B.C. He is now retired and still living in Kamloops.

Alice attended school at Pine Creek and De Winton High School. She married George Irving of Vulcan in 1940 and they have a family of three. They resided on her parent's farm till 1951 when they moved to a farm at Sundre. They sold their farm in 1973 and are now retired in Olds.

SUTHERLAND, DONALD M. AND SARAH

The Sutherlands moved to the De Winton area in 1921. They rented the farm from Mrs. Lillian Soley, daughter of the late well-known lawyer, P. J. Nolan, with the understanding that they could not buy it, as the big white house had been built for his bride and had sentimental value. Mr. Sutherland was employed as building inspector for the city of Calgary and only came out weekends and holidays. His son George farmed the land.

Lallie Sutherland attended classes in the Pine Creek School. When she began working in Calgary, she stayed with her father while Mrs. Sutherland kept house for George. This arrangement carried on till George's marriage to Audrey Banister of Okotoks, when Mrs. Sutherland moved into the city with Mr. Sutherland and Lallie.

It was on this farm that George, on his own initiative and ambition, encouraged by his father, practised the many athletic events that eventually brought him recognition and won him the Dominion Decathlon championship (the best in 10 events). Known as the "Veteran Athlete", he still held this honor till the time of his death in 1951 at the age of forty-eight. He had competed in the Calgary Highland Games the year before and won in his special events. George represented Canada at three British Empire Games and was chosen for a fourth which he was not able to attend, but he was issued the official outfit. He figured he was the only one who could boast of owning four B. E. Games blazers. (See picture of them modeled by George and his three children). He was always proud to have DE WINTON printed on his sport tops, but when wins were reported in city papers he was said to be from Calgary.

George and Audrey's two oldest children were born while they lived at De Winton. Audrey Ann is married to Albert Herr — they have three sons and one daughter and live north of Okotoks. Donald George is the survivor of twin boys, born prematurely; his brother Harold lived just three days. Donald lives on a farm in Davisburg. Robert Bruce was born after his parents moved to Davisburg. He is now a major in the armed forces and stationed at Trenton, Ont., is married and has one daughter.

Lallie Sutherland married M. V. Morgan (Dai), an officer in the R. A. F. stationed at De Winton E.F.T.S. during World War II. She joined Dai in Wales in 1945. He died in 1974. Mrs. Sutherland left Calgary to live

Modeling four years of British Empire Games blazers. l. to r. Bruce, Donald, Anne and George Sutherland.

George Sutherland — hammer-throw, 1930's.

with Lallie and Dai in the late forties and remained there till her death in 1956 at the age of 84.

After Mr. Sutherland's retirement, he lived with George and his family at Davisburg, and outlived his son by two years, dying at the age of 81 in 1953.

Audrey Sutherland married Gustav Bolin in 1961 and they reside in Calgary.

THE FRANK TINDAL FAMILY — by Agnes Wight

Like many others of that time, our mother and father came from Scotland to make their home in Canada. Dad took a homestead in the Leslieville area, but was burned out, abandoned it and came to Calgary. My mother came to Quebec through a relative of Roland Ness, and later came to Calgary and worked for E. D. Adams and John A. Turner.

Dad got a job with Pacific Cartage and one of his fellow workers was Tom Dalzell. Always with farming in mind, he later rented the John Owens farm (the old Standish place). This farm had been rented to Bob Dalzell (Tom's brother), who was moving to the Youngstown area.

Mother and Dad were married January 1st, 1912 and moved onto this farm. They had very little by way of cash or goods. Mr. Bob Dalzell left them some machinery and some colts to break, and this is how they got their first crops in. Later they moved to the Kelly place (Van Tighem) where Dad raised Aberdeen Angus cattle and Clydesdale horses. They sold out and moved from De Winton in 1924, later living in Cochrane and Calgary.

Mother and Dad are both deceased as is our older brother, Bill, who leaves a wife, Marion, two daughters and a son farming at Huxley. Frank and Peter both live and work in Calgary, as does Jean. Belle (Mrs. Gordon Hall), lives in Cochrane and Agnes (Mrs. Gene Wight), lives in Black Diamond.

MR. AND MRS. HARRY USHER

Mr. John Tyson acquired a farm from Ed. Hayes and asked his cousin and her husband, Mr. and Mrs. Harry Usher, to come from England and operate it for him. Soon after they arrived in 1914, Mr. Usher decided that he would rather keep store than farm and bought the store from Mr. Macdonald. He ran the store until 1919 when it was sold to an Englishman, Mr. Bill Anderson, and Ushers raised Hereford cattle on the Mencke place for a year or two. It is not known where they went from there. They had one son, Chris. They were active in the De Winton Theatrical Society.

ADIEL AND MARIA (CAUNEPEEL) VANTIGHEM — by Mrs. R. VanTighem

Adiel VanTighem was born May, 1892 in Melebeke, Belgium. He immigrated to Canada in 1909 with only two suitcases. Adiel worked on the Kelly farm, SE¼-1-22-1-W5, at De Winton for his room and board for a year. This included helping haul grain to Calgary with a four horse team. He went to Montana for a year, working at different ranches. One year was spent at Winnipeg in college, improving his English and taking agriculture. In Calgary in 1914, Adiel joined the Army and after training for only a few months, was shipped to fight overseas. During the war he was wounded several times but his most serious injury occurred during the final days of the war when he was gassed, resulting in the loss of one lung. This injury caused him a lot of trouble and plagued him for the rest of his life.

After returning from the war, Adiel went to Strathmore where he rented the farm from his brother, Joe. In 1922 he made a trip back to Belgium visiting friends and meeting Maria Caunepeel. After returning home and writing letters back and forth he persuaded Maria to come to Canada to be married in October, 1924. The four oldest children were born at Strathmore. In 1930, Adiel bought 680 acres at De Winton, moving onto the farm in February, 1931. At this time there was no highway, just a road from Calgary, south, that went past the Pine Creek School and through the hamlet of DeWinton. At that time the farm consisted of a fifty year old farm house, creaking old barn, and many, many acres of bushland. The fire in the house would have to be stoked four or five times during the night and rounds made to see that the children were all covered. Mom recalls the time a sack of potatoes, standing behind the pot bellied stove, was partially frozen during one night. After re-stoking the stove, when the house was warm, the potatoes warmed up also and the water started coming out of the frozen sack, resulting in quite a mess.

In 1938 a new house was built consisting of five bedrooms, livingroom, diningroom, kitchen, a modern bathroom and a complete basement with a partitioned off, coal and wood bin with a handy chute to the outside. This house was one of the first in the area to boast modern plumbing.

The two older children started school together in 1933 at Pine Creek School, Miss Gwen Thomas was the teacher. At that time none of the oldest children could speak English so school was quite an experience, learning the language, besides other basic skills taught in the one roomed school house. School also meant walking across the field in all kinds of weather, sometimes getting a ride with someone going past the school with a horse drawn wagon or, occasionally riding horses. As there was no water at the school, families took turns hauling the water in five gallon cream cans.

During the winter when things weren't so busy, the land was cleared of the brush. Anything that could be used for fence posts was put into one pile, kindling wood was stacked in another pile to be cut in the fall and used for fuel the following winter. The brush, small branches and refuse was stacked to be burned. Every Saturday, the week's supply of wood was taken from the cut and stacked pile and placed on the wagon, taken to the house and put down the chute to the basement. The grain was hauled to De Winton with a four horse team and wagon as were pigs to be put on the train for Calgary. During these early years, horses were used for all the work around the farm and in the fields. Albert drove six horses in the field at the age of nine.

The first tractor was purchased in 1936. Russell Evans was the first person in the district to own a tractor with a mounted stacker. This was used for field work in exchange for stacking Russell's hay. During the war years, when help was not available, school was missed many days to help with the threshing, the whole family pitching in and doing all the work themselves.

Adiel always milked cows and the first registered Holstein cow was bought from the C.P.R. farm at Strathmore in 1930. From then on he gradually built up a purebred Holstein herd, milking as many as forty cows. First cream was shipped by taking it, by wagon, to the station at De Winton, once even in 54 below zero weather. He started to ship milk to Model Dairy in 1935, later to Pallesen Dairy and, finally, to Palm Dairies Ltd. By 1945 there was a pressing need for better milking facilities as the thirty cows were still being milked by hand. Nothing could be built at this time as there was a great shortage of building materials etc., with the war just over. Therefore, ten lots of land were purchased at 902-38th Ave. N.W.

Van Tighem family 1949. l. to r. front row; Alice, Adiel, Raymond, (on knee), Maria, Josie. Middle: Marcel, Jacqueline, back; Robert, Louise, Bernard, Jeanne, Albert.

Calgary, where there were two barns and a house. Besides this, a section of grazing land was leased from the City of Calgary. In 1946, the dairy herd was moved to North Calgary, where the first milking machines were used. Louise, Jean, Albert and Robert looked after the milking and chores at this farm, the boys hauling all the feed from home, the milk to the dairy and both attending S.A.I.T., taking Agricultural Mechanics. In 1950, power was installed at the De Winton farm, the dairy herd was taken back home and a new steel quonset barn was built with all the modern milking equipment and a milk house built on to accommodate cooling the milk and storing the necessary equipment. Next, the rickety old red barn was demolished and a new red barn was built by Albert, Robert, Bernie and Pop with a cement floor, eight stanchions, horse stalls and a chicken house on the opposite side. In 1952, the cows were put on the Government Record of Performance Plan Program and were tested every month by a government inspector, coming to stay one day, testing cows for morning and night milkings. Thus the poorer cattle were culled and a better herd built up. Although it took several years to see results, Adiel went on to breed one of the better registered Holstein herds in Alberta.

Sunday meant going to Mass at St. Patrick's Church in Midnapore, with the whole family participating. On Sunday afternoons, in the winter, the family, friends and sometimes a few neighbours, would play hockey or skate on the frozen spring behind the house. Some Sunday afternoons in the warmer weather meant a few hours of relaxation before the week's chores started again.

In 1958, Mom and Pop retired to Calgary. Pop still continued to be active on the farm which was, by now, rented to Robert who was continuing to dairy farm. After several years Pop's health started to fail and from then on he made many trips back and forth to the hospital. In 1974, Adiel and Maria celebrated their fiftieth wedding anniversary with all their children together for the first time in many years. They have thirty-five grandchildren and one great-grandchild. Adiel passed away in June, 1975 but Maria is still very active and well and resides at 5011-Stanley Road S. W. in Calgary. Ten children;

1. Louise, married Bill Praeker, farms at Strathmore, (seven children, Josephine, Anne, Herman, Ronald, Theresa, Kathy and Randall).

2. Jeanne, married Cliff Berthot, lives in Big Valley, (one son, Robert).

3. Albert, married Shirley McKevitt, farms at Shepard, (five girls, Maria, Carla, Laurie, Julie, Annette).

4. Robert, married Marian Stunell, farms at Okotoks, (four children, Dale, Beverley, Glenn and Wayne).

5. Bernard, married Bunny Haggen, lives in Olds, (three children, Rickey, Kim, Bonnie).

6. Jackie, married Don Cruickshank, lives in Revelstoke B. C., (four sons, Allen, Dean, Jerry and Darrell).

7. Marcel, married Allaine Fairhead, lives at Shepard, (four children, Tyler, Tammi, Tanya, Tyson).

8. Alice, married Bill Malin, lives in Calgary, (four children, Gary, Valerie, Sandra, Robert).

9. Josephine, married Edward Gauthier, lives in Campbell River B. C., (two children, Shane, Cheryl).

10. Raymond, married Jackie Vollmin, lives in Calgary, (one son, Travis).

The VanTighem farm was on the SE¼-1-22-1-W5.

VAN TIGHEM, ROBERT

Robert, born in 1930, was the fourth child of Adiel and Maria Van Tighem. At the age of seven was given two cows to milk by hand. By the age of eight years was helping to milk all the cows before going to school in the morning and after returning home at night. Spent two years in Strathmore living with an aunt. Went to De Winton High School. In 1946 the dairy herd was moved to north west Calgary so he was sent up to the other farm to look after the farm there. In 1948 and 1949 went to Southern Alberta Technology of Art taking a two year agricultural mechanics course. In 1950 a new barn was built so the cows were moved back to De Winton. By this time the three oldest were married so I took over the milking for Dad until 1955. I then rented a farm at Glenmore Dam from Bud Robbins where I started shipping milk on my own to Palm Dairies. After one year, I moved back home as by this time Dad was willing to rent the farm to me. After many years of dairying, I was able to buy part of the farm from Dad with Marcel (Pete) buying the other forty acres. In 1958 Dad and Mom moved to Calgary but Dad still came out for a couple of years to truck the milk to the dairy until we had to switch to bulk milk pick-ups. In 1959 I married Marian Stunell who was a stenographer for Palm Dairies. During these years I had accumulated a good milking herd by continuing on the Record of Performance testing plan that Dad had started. In 1960 I bought a bull calf for breeding purposes and he gave me many good offspring so I was later able to sell him to the B.C. Artificial Insemination Unit.

As my children became old enough, they all joined the Foothills 4H Dairy Club. In 1973 my daughter, Beverly, won all the honors in the Foothills Club and then went on to win the Grand Champion award at the Calgary Exhibition & Stampede. The following year this same heifer went to the Alberta Provincial 4H finals in Red Deer to be reserve grand champion for Alberta 4H in 1974.

As the land beside mine was gradually being subdivided, the forty acres south of the airport road was the first to be sold. In 1975 the rest of the original farm on SE 1-21-1-W5 and S½ 6-22-29-W4 was sold and I retired from dairy farming. I now live on half section south west of Okotoks where I only milk a couple of cows. Four children — Dale, Beverley, Glenn and Wayne.

THE HARRY VOLD FAMILY

The Vold family moved to De Winton in 1953 to the Jim Dalzell place located on the NE 25-21-1-W5M.

Three of the children Wayne, Dona and Doug were born in Ponoka, a year later Darce was born at De Winton.

Wayne was in grade two when we moved. He went to Pine Creek School with Margaret Norris being the teacher. A year or two later Dona started school. Wayne and Dona, the Gerlitz and Kenny kids rode horseback to school during the summer months.

The school buses took over and it seemed to end an era of Christmas concerts, horses, sleigh rides, but also had many advantages such as basketball and hockey games, musicals, sewing and domestic science.

We have been in the rodeo and cattle business all our lives and in 1965 Wayne took over the family rodeo and continued producing rodeos in Canada and parts of the United States. It still is a family business with all of us working at it.

Wayne has combined a singing career with this and has his own television show out of Calgary. He has three children Shane 13, Cody 11 and Lisa aged 8.

Dona went to college in the U.S.A. where she got her degree in Home Economics. She married Bill Larsen, a rancher from Alzada, Montana and has a little girl Tami who is 5 years old.

Doug has gone on in the rodeo game, riding saddle broncs in Canada and the United States. At the Canadian Finals in Edmonton the past two years he has finished well up in the top ten. Doug is also known as a top notch pick up man. Currently he has a share in a Western Store in Edmonton. They claim he can sell ice to the Eskimos!

Darce is still living in De Winton and for the past five years has been employed by the Calgary School Board. In the summer and vacation times she times rodeos in the United States and Canada.

Although our family is wide spread, we certainly do enjoy getting together as often as possible at the home place. No matter where or how far our travels lead us, De Winton will always be our home.

JOHN AND GEORGINA WARRACK — by Georgina Seville and Annabelle Raymond

The Warrack family arrived in the De Winton district and took up residence on the "Morgan Place" which was the W½-34-21-1-W5.

The Warracks had arrived in America in 1911 and lived in Spokane for a year before coming to Canada — Calgary in July, 1912 because of a building boom. Our father had a cement contracting business but when the war broke out in 1914, the building business ceased and in September 1914 we went farming west of Midnapore to "White's Place," a large log house which had been owned by the Wilkins. In 1915 we moved to the "Hemingway Place" and in 1916 to the "Morgan Place" where we stayed until 1924, moving to the Strathmore district that year.

Our father John Warrack died in 1944 and our mother Georgina, in 1960. Tom, the youngest of the family, was killed in a plane accident in the Arctic in 1948. Annabelle, Georgie, Bill and Dolly live in Calgary, Alice in Edmonton, Margaret at Redland, Jack at Cheadle, and Aleck at Langdon.

SAUNDERS WATSON

Early in the 1880s, Saunders (Sandy) Watson came with his family to the Pine Creek district, and was associated with John Owens at his stopping house but in 1886 a new stopping house was erected at the north end of Pine Creek coulee on the west side of the trail. The Watson family took over the running of the establishment. Sandy was the first Postmaster of Pine Creek 1887-1889 then John Owens took over the job, after Sandy resigned.

Eliza married Charles Knight in 1888 and lived in the Priddis district for some time, there were no children. Margaret (Peggy), married Dr. Maxwell Ingles, Coroner of Winnipeg, Manitoba. They had two children; Harry M.B. of Vancouver and Marjorie (Coste) of Toronto, Ontario. Harriet married Alfred Nelson, a lad who had been living around the district, they moved to Fort Steele, B.C. where Alfred was a gold assayer. There were no children. George had two sons and lived in the Lloydminster area, is deceased. Harry married Annie Olson of the Millarville Priddis area, both deceased, they had two children; Georgina (Georgie) and Cecil (Baby) and they lived on the Hooley place when Georgie was of school age. Caroline married a Haines, a bank manager in Fort Saskatchewan, they had two daughters and they all moved to Vancouver to live.

MR. AND MRS. H. R. WILLET

Mr. Willet was a cabinet maker and bought four acres in De Winton in 1914 where he built a house and shop which later became the post office. They had one daughter and they spent 1914 Christmas with the Turnbull family.

Mr. Willet built a lean-to on the J. W. Turnbull house and is also credited with making a desk for John Dalzell, apparently of excellent craftsmanship. Others in the area were disappointed when they were unable to have similar pieces made for themselves.

After the family left in 1919 they received their mail through A. Paxton, the next owner of the property. Nothing further is known about them.

DAN AND CORA WILLFORD — by Jessie Beckton

In 1898 Dan and Cora Willford left Jackson County, Nebraska in a covered wagon with five girls and two boys. They settled in De Winton, Alberta where Mrs. Willford had the first boarding house and Mr. Willford was section foreman for the C.P.R. He had worked building the C.P.R. as it came through.

A sixth girl was born soon after and, later, a son was born at Okotoks. Mr. Willford is still remembered by some of the men in the district as having taken them for rides on the hand-car. This seemed to be a special treat at the annual picnic.

All the girls married and settled in southern Alberta for many years. Two boys settled in Nelson, B.C. where they married and one boy settled in Sheridan, Wyoming where he married.

Of the original possessions with which they left Nebraska there are two chairs still in use by a granddaughter in Lindale, Alberta.

Mr. Willford passed away at Nelson, B.C. in 1936 at the age of 89 and Mrs. Willford passed away at High River, Alberta in 1947 at the age of 86.

STEVE AND MYRTLE (DeMINGS) WILLIAMS

After serving in WW1 and being seriously wounded, resulting in having a steel plate placed in his head, Steve Williams came to the De Winton area to haul buffalo bones from the old jumps in Davisburg. He made his headquarters at DeMings "Minto House". At the time, DeMings had the post office and Steve carried the mail for a period of time.

Myrtle was the daughter of Mr. and Mrs. Alonzo DeMings and worked in both the stopping house and

May Willford's wedding, 1903.

the post office. She was a great promoter of lotteries of all kinds and, I am told, even ran a turkey shoot or two.

Steve and Myrtle were married a short while after he came to the town and had five children, one of whom died in infancy. The others were; Stevie, Philip, Louise and Dorothy. Little is known of them after they left the district but Phillip served in WW2. Steve Sr. (deceased) and the last anyone in the area heard, Myrtle was residing in Victoria, B.C.

While they were in the area, Steve had a pool hall in the back of the small house they lived in, next to Tom Dalzell's home. It was a popular gathering place for the men of the district.

PETER AND MABEL WILSON — by Jane Norris

Peter Wilson (Pete) came to Canada from Scotland in 1908 in charge of a shipment of Ayrshire cattle. He spent one year working for the Ness family in Quebec and came West in 1909. For two years he travelled in Alberta with Clyde horses and later worked for Bobby Pratt on the Anderson place and then for Tindals and Dalzells on the Standish place.

Following his marriage to Mabel Currie, daughter of early pioneers, Mr. and Mrs. John Currie, they went to Stoppington, Alberta to homestead. They moved back to the De Winton district in 1923, living on the Todd place. For a brief while Pete worked for the Regal Gas Plant in the Manchester district. In 1927 he returned to De Winton where he bought grain as an elevator agent for eighteen years. In 1946 he moved to the Millarville area to farm and in 1958 he retired to Okotoks where he lived 'till his death in 1966. His wife, Mabel, passed away in 1967.

Pete and Mabel had five children, four still living.

Russel Wilson.

Russell, the eldest, died in 1960 at the age of forty-one. Isabel married George Goettler and they live in High River. There are five Goettler children, Paul, an electrical engineer at Brooks; Jane, R.N., working as a Public Health nurse in Calgary; Rosemary (Mrs. Dwayne Noble) living in High River; Raymond and Marie are still attending school in High River.

John Wilson is married to Janet Watson - they have a home in Okotoks. There are three married children; Chris (Mrs. Brian Sills); Jim married Irene Sills, and Georgina (Mrs. Brent Laidlaw).

Jane Wilson married Howard Norris in 1946 and they have two children. Leslie is a medical stenographer and lives with her mother in Calgary. Hugh married Joan Sutherland and is employed with Canadian Wildlife Service.

Andrew, the youngest of the Wilson family, married Shirley Rose. They live in Calgary and their two girls, Carol and Barbara, are both attending school.

MR. AND MRS. YOUNGMAN — by Harry Youngman

Although our stay in De Winton was so brief, I retain many memories — fond and otherwise. So I will attempt, with the help of Amelia and Mother, to make it as brief as possible.

Mom and Dad were married in 1914 in Calgary, 3 children Amelia 1914, Harry, 1917, and Wesley 1922. Dad had opened a Meat Market, as this was his trade. In 1925 they decided to become farmers and moved to De Winton, occupying the Graham farm. In 1926 we moved back to Calgary, and Dad again became a butcher. In 1927 they decided that farm life wasn't too bad after all, so back to De Winton — this time right in town on McNeill's property.

The house was a 2 storey log building, and the barn and sheds the same. I imagine it must have been one of the oldest in the district. I know many times I would have cherished the history of it. At this time, Dad had the mail run to Gladys Ridge. It seemed inevitable however, that our family was not destined to become farmers, what with the cyclone of 1927, which spread havoc in the area. The strange thing about it was, the narrow path it cut across the country. The sky turned dark almost suddenly. Mother had gone with Dad on the mail run and the kids were home alone. When the storm hit, I ran into the pantry and must have prayed. It would be difficult to describe the velocity and sounds of a cyclone, I know there were three scared youngsters waiting for their parents. They didn't even ask if a cyclone had hit the place, it was very evident.

Following this, in 1928, Amelia and I were returning from school (Pine Creek) and as we rounded the curve west of town, we noticed smoke in the area of our farm. As we approached nearer, we saw that the house had been levelled. Apparently the fire started by an overheated incubator on the back part of the log building.

Very little was saved — Dad was on the mail run, and Mom was alone with Wes. I remember them, and a few of the neighbours, standing around the smoldering ruins.

At this time, as some of the old timers should recall, we had a distinguished visitor in De Winton,

Lord Anglesey, who had his private railway coach parked on the sidetracks, just below our home. He had witnessed the fire and was one of the first to offer help. Mom shed a few tears, as this gentleman gave her a $100 bill, which was quite a sum in those days.

It didn't take long for the townspeople and neighboring areas to hold a social at the community hall. Food — clothing — shelter was provided in abundance, thanks also to the Red Cross. These are things you never forget.

Our next home was to be on the Cushing Farm, a short distance west of town, and adjacent to Old Man Gooch's hut beside the track.

Amelia had now gone to Calgary for her Grade 9, but shortly after decided to get a job in Eaton's in 1929.

I recall one weekend, her coming home. Mom had baked a lemon pie and set it out back to cool, and Rags, our St. Bernard ate it. Mom was so mad, she got a rope and was going to hang a 125 pound dog. Imagine! I think Rags thought Mom was playing.

I guess children are relieved of the responsibility of finances. I know that my parents were not well off. Later, a small house was built on the same site and once again a move. Had it not been for the generosity of Mr. Martin and others, I think our stay in De Winton would have been much shorter.

Eventually, or finally, a farm auction (7 cows — pigs and chickens, some machinery) and back to the City. I remember that day well. One of the neighbors bid 50¢ on a sleigh that I had hammered together, I don't think it was worth firewood.

Dad went back to his trade as a butcher and in 1931 opened a shop in the City Hall Market. I think it was our destiny to follow in his footsteps.

Amelia married Nick Kozak in 1937, 2 children — Roger and Ruth. Harry married Evelyn Field in 1939, 1 child, Lynn. Evelyn is a cousin of Ruby Field, married to the late Jimmie McNab, of the area. Wes passed away in 1940.

Dad retired in 1957 and used to help me out in my shop until he died in 1961.

Eventually I tired of the meat business, and obtained a job with the C.N.I.B. Mom remains in fairly good health at 81, has very poor eyesight, but still very sharp.

Others Who Lived in the Pine Creek District but sent no History

Aggett: Court and Margaret (Overand), daughters: Marlene and Carol, a third daughter, Peggy, born after they left. Lived on Jack Macdonald Place in the late '30s and early '40s. Presently reside in Calgary.

Allan: Dyce, bachelor friend of Stuart Jamison. Worked for farmers in the district. Later went to Vulcan, married, had two daughters and was Mayor for several terms. His widow lives in the Vulcan Nursing home.

Alverson: Mr. and Mrs. Herman, children; Betty, Jean, Rees and John. Midland and Pacific elevator agent before Jim Everson.

Annear: Ed; widower, WW1 veteran, (deceased).

Bailly; Housekeeper for Frank Emery, daughters; Ena and Betty. 1924-29.

Bergh: Robert and Margaret, children; Beth, Bob and Jimmie. P & H elevator agent.

Birkett: Deceased, wife, Edna, lived in High River for some years. Was the C.P.R. agent. No family but always supplied the children at the Christmas concert with dixie cups of ice cream. Much appreciated by the children.

Bjornsen: Louis and Louise, son, Hughie, worked for Henry Poffenroth about the time of WW1. Louis was a musician and played the violin at the dances.

Carey: Lived on E ½ 34-21-1-W5 1909-1911.

Coulson: C.P.R. agent, sons; Ken and Bob, went to De Winton high school.

Crowell: Sons; Eugene, Byron, Earle and Orton. Lived on the Kelly place before WW1.

Dawes: Mr. and Mrs. Arthur, children; Roberta (Stephens), Andrew and Marylou, lived on the Kerslake place.

Duncan: Mrs. and Mrs. J., daughters; Bella, Bessie and Joey. S½ 10-22-1-W5. Came about 1900, sold to Evans.

Ecklin: Robin, worked for Eb. Grant, had the first Triangle service station at junction of Macleod Trail and Airport road. Married Muriel Grant. Has Elkana Ranch at Bragg Creek.

Erickson: Gus, Section foreman for C.P.R. after Gammond till 1932.

Frier: Frank, English, bachelor, carried mail for McNeills, worked with the Theatrical Society, before WW1.

Gale: Later Canon Gale. Gervais, wife and sons; Frank (Calgary), De Winton (deceased) and others; Gervais was first Anglican church minister also secretary of the Pine Creek school board. 1900.

Geinger: Art Grainger and his mother Alice, bought the Jack Macdonald place.

Gammond: son, Harry attended Pine Creek school in 1914, C.P.R. section foreman before Erickson.

Gopp: Billy; first resident on 30-21-29-W4 (the gore). 1880s.

Gorrall: Charles and Dora (deceased), children; Mary, Raymond, Rita, Frances, Wanda. Charlie lives in Okotoks.

Greig: Wife and three children; lived on W ½ 34-21-1-W5 before WW1.

Jensen: Henry and John, orphan brothers, worked at many of the local farms before WW1. Both went overseas, Henry was killed in action and John returned to the area.

Jensen: Mr. and Mrs. and granddaughter, Doreen Minor, lived at the greenhouses. Doreen went to Pine Creek school. Sold to Fred Dick.

Kerslake: Ed and Harriet, children; Bert, Cliff, Eva. NW ¼ 13-22-1-W5.

Kievit: Dutch people worked at the greenhouses, children Sybrand, Siva and Ronald attended Pine Creek school 1924-25.

Matthews: Lived on several places including NW ¼ 36-21-1-W5 before WW1.

Murrin: Joe, wife and family lived on the Bremner place.

Naylor: Bill and Pat, Midnapore, sons; Chuck, Wayne, Milton, Randy and Mark. One of the first small holdings just north of Pine Creek school. Randy is a

United Church minister and served the Cochrane charge and is now in Africa doing mission work.

Nemeth: Charles (deceased) wife, Katie, Calgary, children: Steve, Albert (deceased). Hermina (Hill) Calgary. Katie still owns SW¼ 36-21-1-W5.

Parrott: Matthew (Matt) SE ¼ 4-22-1-W5 before 1890, house moved to W ½ 34-21-1-W5.

Myers: Vern and Muriel (Dingle), children; Brian, lives in the district, Norma and Ricky.

Phillips: Jack (deceased) and Mary, daughter, Kathleen, attended Pine Creek school, Susan born after they left the district. P & H elevator agent.

Pollard: Built the greenhouses in De Winton about 1912. Sons; Kenneth and Harry went to Pine Creek school.

Richardson: one of the first station agents, before 1900. Bachelor but married during his stay at De Winton.

Saunders: Photographer before WW1.

Saunders: Ross, wife and children; Elinor and Mildred. Elevator agent 1923-25.

Street: Charles, NE ¼ 32- and NW ¼ 33-21-1-W5 before 1892.

Staines: Campbell, homesteaded W ½ 12-22-1-W5 before 1892.

Teeling: Jim (deceased) and Ilah, sons; Jim, Garth and Dennis. Station agent in the 1940's.

Vance: One of the first section foreman for C.P.R. before 1900.

Warner: Lived on the Jack Macdonald place. Children; Jim (deceased), Grace (Grant) and Lucille.

Whelan: J., wife and several children. Son, Eddie was killed overseas before he reached the age of 17. Lived on SE ¼ 18-21-1-W5 before 1892, also on a number of other places in the area.

Winterbottom: A., S ½ 23-22-1-W5 before 1890.

Winterbottom: E. J., S ½ 24-22-1-W5 before 1890.

Hallman: Arthur and Rhoda, ran a turkey farm and raised chinchillas. W80 of SW ¼ 15-22-1-W5.

Harper: Brother of H. H., lived at the Hooleys and taught Stormount school in 1913.

Lakatos: Louis and his wife and brother Bert (Pete). Plasterers, lived on N ½ 10-22-1-W5.

Martman: two sons, Benjamin and Clarence, lived on SW ¼ 9-22-1-W5 in the 1930s.

Horvat: wife and daughter, section foreman for the C.P.R. 1940s.

Horsfield: Keith (deceased) and Del; children; Brian, Lynne, Janet. Vicky and Holly. One of the first families in the Standish subdivision.

EXPERIENCE OF A SMALL BOY — by Eben Bremner

In the summer of 1897, my father, Archie Bremner, took some teams through to the Crow's Nest Pass on the construction of the Crow's Nest Railroad. He worked on construction and freighted supplies for the different camps and I was just a kid. We drove through from De Winton. Dad had a covered wagon fixed up and Mother and my two sisters and he rode in the wagon pulled by a four horse team. I had the extra horses trailing behind, I was riding my pony. It took us three days to get to Fort Macleod. We camped there overnight and got up in the morning and our horses were gone with the exception of Dad's saddle horse and my pony which were tethered. So, Dad had to make arrangements for Mother and the girls to stay. We had a tent and a covered wagon and they were left while Dad and I went to hunt for the horses.

We started out backtracking, going in to the different homesteads and ranches along the road, to see if they had seen anything of these horses. They were all work horses with manes and tails trimmed and so forth, so were different to the range horses they were used to seeing. We rode to each house and finally located them just near Okotoks. It took us three days riding at that time and, of course, when we had located them, we had to stay overnight at a ranch before starting back with them. It took us another three days going back. Then, of course, we pulled on and started for Crow's Nest and got out there, having made around about twenty-five miles a day. When we got there Dad had to fix up living quarters for us and find work for his teams. We got as far as Moyee and Dad built a hotel there and still had his teams working, freighting ore from the mine at Eugene Mountain, with two six horse teams, two wagons with each team. When we were going back up we freighted back supplies for the mines, taking about two ton loads, with the weight of the wagons, which was a good load for six horses going up. Coming back down we had, I think, about six yards of ore on each wagon. They were very heavy wagons with plank boxes with brakes on each one. The ore was freighted down this way until they put in a bucket cable line and brought it down that way. I was about eight years old by that time, and there was the odd time, when one of the teamsters had been drunk and had a big head, Dad would put me on one of the wagons and have me take one of the 'six ups' to the mine. Of course one of the men was with me at all times and the horses were well broke and knew what they were doing, possibly a little better than I did at that time.

After the freighting was through at the mine Dad sold his horses and we returned to the homestead at De Winton. That was the winter of 1899 and 1900 and we spent some of that winter with Peter McKay a bachelor neighbour, while our home was repaired and Dad purchased another ½ section of land in 1902. And that is kind of the history of that trip, out of the Crow's Nest and on to Moyee, on the construction of the Crow's Nest Railroad.

LITTLE REMEMBRANCES — by Harry Youngman

The morning our teacher opened her desk drawer and found a live snake in it. Wonder who done it.

The day Gordon Cushing got dunked in Pine Creek.

Winnie Turnbull's beautiful horse.

The first gopher us city kids ever caught. Drowned him out, then felt sorry for it, so we took it in the house, dried him out, then let him go.

The Sweet Williams on the Cushing Farm, seemed like acres of them.

My first quill pen. I was trying to stick it in the ceiling in school, it stuck for a second or so, then came down and stuck in Bill Standish's head. He looked like an Indian.

Murray Anderson's sure cure for Warts — caustic stick — I've still got the scar.

Dad and Amelia going to Calgary in a Model T touring car, to pick up a live pig. She didn't exactly enjoy the trip home in the back seat, holding down an excited passenger.

Les Marshall's new 1926 Dodge?

The night they went to Okotoks and racked it up. Were his passengers — Brinton — Poffenroth — Hamilton?

Amelia's first experience in driving was a 1928 Chev. owned by Big Henry Poffenroth. She didn't stay on the road long — ended up in the ditch, going the wrong way.

The day Mr. Ness drove into town with his new 1928 Model A. First one we had seen.

How we idolized George Sutherland.

Miss Davidson and Mrs. Heaton, school teachers at Pine Creek School.

I believe Dave Jamison's sister married a cousin of ours — Alf Hill.

I REMEMBER — by Jean Pakenham

I think the first thing I remember is learning to ride a horse at about the same time I learned to walk, then to milk a cow when I was five years old. Both of which led to work on the farm; from that time on you worked! You learned to break horses, brand, butcher calves, stook, pitch hay and manure. The one thing that went along with the work was NO MONEY.

The only money you saw was the money you earned climbing trees to gather magpie eggs, crow and hawk eggs and feet; also snaring and trapping gophers for the tails. All these were kept in big Eddy match boxes and gradually smelled to high heaven before being assessed.

I remember Mrs. Goerlitz, our neighbour, coming to visit Mother with her gift of homemade sauerkraut, which Mother loved. When they visited they often slipped into Mrs. Goerlitz's Mother tongue, which my Mother had learned in University in Scotland. I suspect now it was so we couldn't understand what they didn't want us to hear.

I remember the butcher, Mr. Cook, who called at all the farms in his big touring car. The back had curtains which had to be lifted up to show the beef, pork, sausage, hamburger, liver, etc., along with a big round of Canadian cheese.

I remember heating stones in the oven all day in the winter to put in the straw in the bottom of the sleigh to go to the dances and Christmas concerts in De Winton. Coming home was cold! The dances and concerts were "super".

The year 1927 was one to remember. It was the polio year and I was one of the victims but I'm thankful I was one of the lucky ones. Have often wondered if it was Dr. Ardiel's order of half-a-cup of castor-oil every second day that helped me. It was also the year of the cyclone and we took shelter in a shed at Pine Creek Church and watched it. Although Dad and Mother knew what it was they didn't mention the word till it was over.

The next year, having had my appendix out, my sister and I had to go to school in a cutter. We had a real run-away one day and only the fact that Danny Gerlitz, who was on horseback, was able to overtake and stop our horse, am I able to write this today.

My dad seemed to be the barber for the countryside in those early years and he would go on horseback to cut the hair of the old men who could not come to him. "Oh yes! he barbered us too, shingled right up to the back!!"

The school fairs were the big event of the school year. Everyone learned to cook, bake, sew, and darn by hand, grow vegetables and groom calves. The competition was strong but so was the comradeship. So often the weather was foul. The ones with the most points went to Claresholm Agricultural School for a week. I remember the year Dave Jamison and I won. We were like two frightened field mice who had never been away from home. Another annual event was the Community picnic and dance. Those were the days when an ice cream cone and a bottle of pop was a real treat.

I especially remember the dances because I loved to dance so much. The ones at De Winton with Len Davis's orchestra, Tom Dalzell calling the square dances and Stuart Dalzell step dancing. The Panima School House dances with Maudie Hutchinson on piano and Roy Haynes on violin. They went on till four A.M. and you went home and changed your clothes and went for the cows. There were also the Country Club dances in Okotoks. You had to be members to go but I often went as a guest of my good friend, Jessie Dalzell. Mrs. Cushing played the piano and of course Tom Dalzell called the Quadrilles. The barn dances at Davisburg were fun too.

I am sure everyone remembers their school days. When I started Stormont, I had to be lifted onto the big horse we rode and my sister and I both rode in the saddle. In later years we each had a horse. Then the High School in De Winton, I remember the day Lawrence Norris, George Dunn and I got expelled and I was to go home. You had to have permission from the school board to get back and my dad was chairman of the board. I sat on the steps all day and finally, the kind-hearted teacher let me back in with a firm warning. I never laughed out loud in school again.

We went to church, Sunday school and choir practice. How fortunate we were to have Mrs. Heaver to help us with choir.

I remember the threshing days when I cooked on a threshing outfit for John Harrison and Pete Goerlitz. It was hard work. The bosses went home at night to sleep, leaving strict orders with the men not to go to the cook car after supper. However, when men offered to do dishes if I would heat water for them to shave they were quickly let in. I remember how kind they were to me although many were strangers. Especially the day I put a cup of sugar in the stew instead of in the applesauce! They never said a word! (and neither did I). I guess they realized I was only fifteen years old and there were seventeen men to cook for.

Our Sunday entertainment was ball games. I remember them well and the frantic rush it was on the days of the double headers when you had to rush home and milk the cows and get back for the evening game. The day in May of 1939 of course stands out in my memory as that was the day my husband, Doug, broke his leg and spent seven weeks in hospital.

One year Hugh (Scottie) Hamilton, directed a play. We practised and rehearsed for weeks and one night, about five days before the concert Hughie Hamilton, who had an important part, shaved all of his hair off. I think his dad nearly had a stroke and I know the rest of us had hysterics every time we looked at him.

I remember spending many happy times with my good friend, Alice Standish. Although we milked "a thousand cows", I loved to go over there as they had a gramophone and lots of Western records and always a bowl of maple buds.

After I was out of school I worked for several people. Many times for Aggie and Barsby Martin and probably Bob and Ron remember the odd smack they got on their bottoms. I also worked for Alex Currie and; although Rita and I worked hard, we had fun as the Norris family were on the next farm and there were always good friends around. I helped one year at Mr. and Mrs. Peppard's and I remember their kindness to me. When Mrs. Jim Wilson broke her leg I worked for Jim and I rode ten miles home on Saturday night for my day off and back again on Sunday night. The nights were dark and the coyotes kept me company. I also worked for Mr. and Mrs. Ness and believe me I learned how to make bread as Mary Ness was known province wide for all the prizes she won at the Stampede Fair.

My second home was Tom and Dollie Dalzells and every Sunday when Tom came home with the truck I watched eagerly because if the white towel went out it meant he had brought home a gallon of ice cream and I was invited. I often helped Dollie when she cooked for road and power crews and Jessie and I were, and still are, as close as sisters.

Who could forget the war years? Watching your friends and relatives leave and the brave parents who let them go . . . the telegrams and the awaited telegrams regarding prisoners of war. And the happy reunion dances as each one came home, including my brother Jack.

I remember many things but most of all I remember my friends, who, today I thank God, are still my friends. Many are gone but "Oh yes — I remember."

MEMOIRS OF THE NORTH — From J. F. McInnes to A. P. Bremner

I suppose, you have heard of that Louis Riel
and the troubles he raised near to Ft. Qu'Appelle
he opened the door to bloodshed, I'm told
by raising an army of warriors bold.
To fight for his rights, it was his intent
to make Sir John long live to repent
the day he withheld, from the Breeds, every one
the land scrip entitled to father and son.

So he then sent a courier off to the north
in search of old Big Bear, Chief of the Cree
he asked him to put on his war paint and come forth
and many white scalps he surely would see.
So the Indian arose with a war cry like thunder
their object in raising was plunder and murder
they killed all the whites, at the old Frog Lake Mission

and in the Hudson's Bay Co., there rests some suspicion.

But — soon General Strange, came on to the scene
the man who is true to his country and queen
he buried the remains of the dead as you know
and he swore, to the devils no quarter he'd show.
So we marched to the coulee, beyond Frenchman Butte —
where we scarcely expected to receive a salute —
but the sharp crack of rifles, just in advance
caused our men for to shout, our horses to prance.

We unlimbered a gun, a nine pounder in size
which caused the red men for to open their eyes
when a hailstorm of bullets burst forth from a shell
and sent many, bold braves, to where I can't tell.
Then we kept the ball rolling, three hours and a quarter
and never was time, that seemed any shorter
till three of our men fell, two of them, sons of France
one shot through the breast, as if pierced by a lance.

Then we retreated to Pitt, where we had to await
fresh orders from Middleton, a man we all hate
for he was afraid that his feet would get wet
if he followed Big Bear any further you bet.
But seventy men Major Steele had to take
and Corral Big Bear, somewhere near Coon Lake
that Middleton, might with his gattling gun
Show the boys from Toronto, some real English fun.

And last but not least, I will draw your attention
to an outfit of thieves who's names I won't mention
but suffice it to say, that they came from Quebec
and the hemp it is growing to put round their neck.
They fed us on hard tack, Corned Beef, and Bacon
and the rest of the stores Captain Wright must have taken
But I think, my dear friends, that I now will conclude
by saying farewell, to the government dude.

IMPRESSIONS OF A CYCLONE — by Mrs. Jim Dalzell

The day of the cyclone, we were both at home and my husband was putting up a screen door. A great cloud came up and I told him he had better come in. Instead of coming in, he went to put his tools away. As the wind started he came for the house, I was at the door, waiting for him, and it was all we both could do to push the door shut after him. As we got it latched the wind hit and broke the latch, blowing the door open again, it blew mud in from the slough and coated the walls with mud. I said that we must get down to the basement. I had Marion, our little daughter, in my arms and was urging Jim to come. As I was standing there a puff of wind hit him and knocked him against me and knocked me head first into the cellar. I cut a bad gash in my head. I put the child down on her feet, I didn't have time to think, it was just instinct. All she could say was Oh, my poor kitty". I told her that her kitty would be alright and that we would find it after the storm was over. She kept fussing about her kitty, she was only a little thing, just able to talk, about two and half years old. When the storm was over we came up out of the cellar and you never saw such a rubble. I had a cupboard made, in our new house, like a pantry, with an opening into the dining room so that I could just pass things through. Of course I had left my dishes rather open to the wind and I just had one big plate of my big set left and one cup and saucer, and as long as I kept house, I kept that plate. I had some little geese with a hen. I stopped to put the geese in but the storm was too close and it started to hail. I managed to pick up one little gosling and brought it in with me. It was the only one we had left. The wind picked up an old stove that had been in a shack, by the well, a big, heavy old range, and carried it, it must have been two city blocks, and set it down, upright, with the lids still in place. That must be hard to believe but it's true. There were three little boys staying in a tent with their father just across the road. When the wind hit, the oldest one, Walter Linn, picked up the youngest one and told the middle one to run for the house, an old abandoned house, probably the original Somerville house, but the child never made it, the wind picked him up. The people in De Winton had seen the storm hit our place and Pete Murray, the blacksmith, a big strong man, came running down to see how we had survived. When he found that the small boy was missing he began to search through the buck brush and soon found him, put him on his shoulders and came trotting to the house with him. He laid him on the kitchen floor and asked me if I had any brandy. I said that I had, if the wind hadn't taken it. "Sure enough the bottle was standing on the shelf, where I had left it, just waiting for me." "We managed to get a few swallows of brandy down his throat and he revived." The doctor said later, that if it had not been for the brandy, he would never come out of it. I said "Blessed brandy, I'll never be without it in the house again!"

Shortly after, a couple, strangers to the country, drove into the yard to see if they could be of help. Somebody said "if you will take this boy to the hospital it would help." They took a quilt and a pillow and put him in the back seat and took him to Okotoks. They came back the next day and brought me my quilt and pillow. They got him in there safe and the doctor said that if it hadn't been for the brandy he never would have made it. We never found out who the people were and I have wondered so many times who those good people were for they risked their car and they risked everything when they pulled in over all those broken down poles and wires.

We had a mare and a little colt and we had three horses loose in the pasture and they came running up to the gate. The old mare knew that there was a storm coming, she would look at the sky and then she would look at her colt and 'nose' it and she was very nervous. After the storm had passed she always remembered it. If there was a storm coming she got jumpy and stood watching. I'm sure she remembered. They say that animals can't think but "you bet they can think".

The wind sucked the pump and pipe out of the well and bent it over. Our buildings were scattered all over the country side. There was debris scattered for miles.

We had just moved into our brand new house the day before and it took a long while to repair it after the storm.

There was an old shack right down by the road that had been converted into a garage and it had two old trucks in it. The wind took the walls from the building and left the trucks sitting on the floor and there they stayed for some years, covered with mud and junk. This all happened in 1927.

Haying

Joe McConkey, Siesta time.

Stacking on the Andrews' farm (about 1903). Frank Matthews (hired man), W. J. Andrews, Hugh Andrews, Laura, Cora.

Putting up hay 1904 on Riches farm.

Labor saving in the 1919's. Putting hay in barn with sling. Suitor farm 1919.

Ted Allwarden in foreground hauling hay for Mr. Peter Massie in background.

Making hay on the Bryce Farm.

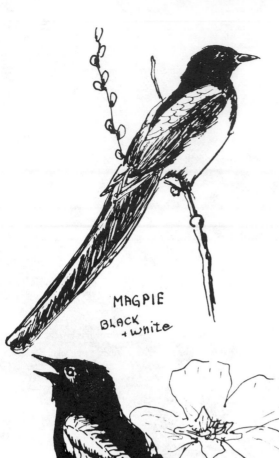

MAGPIE

BLACK
+ White

CROW
glossy black.

ROSE BREASTED
GROSBEAK

ROSE
CHEST
BLACK - WHITE

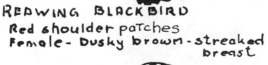

REDWING BLACKBIRD
Red shoulder patches
Female - Dusky brown-streaked
breast

COWBIRD
Sparrowlike
bill.
Seal brown
head

YELLOW HEADED BLACKBIRD
yellow head - white wing patch
female - pale yellow throat.

PAINTED LADY

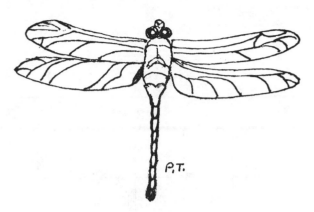

DRAGON FLY

SALAMANDER
LIVES IN SHADE OF ROCKS
SHALLOW WATER
SPENDS WINTER IN BURROWS

SWALLOW TAIL

GARTER SNAKE
HARMLESS

LEOPARD FROG
ROUND OR OVAL DARK SPOTS
WHITE UNDER THIGHS
BACK GREY-BROWN OR GREEN

RED DEER LAKE S.D. NO. 128

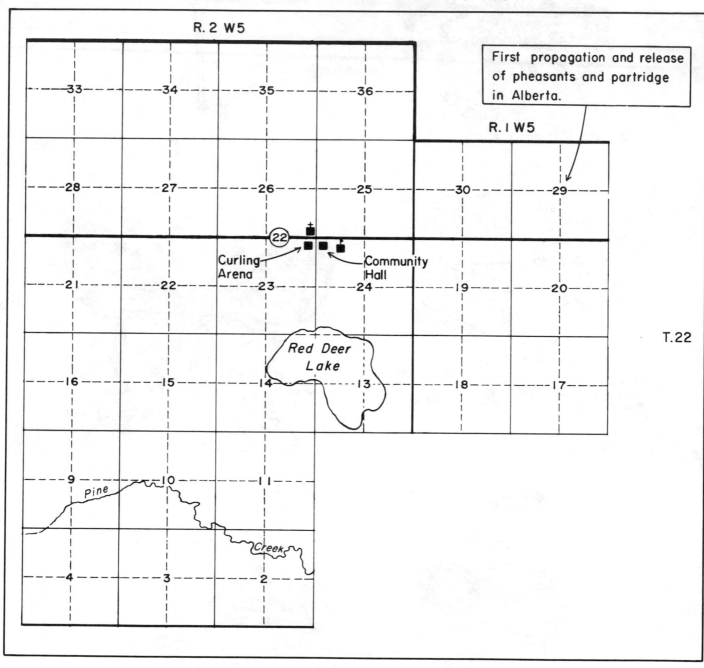

Red Deer Lake School District

RED DEER LAKE SCHOOL NO. 128

The first school was in 1887 when Maggie McArthur (cousin of Duncan McArthur) held classes in Jerome's log home, NW¼ 12-22-2-W5. In the Fall of 1888 classes were held in the Ben Lloyd vacated log home on the SE corner SE ¼ 24-2-W5. The first board, Dave Hall, Ben Lloyd and Alfred Wilkin opened a frame school in 1889 on land provided by Frank Faeiry on the SW corner, NW ¼ 24-22-2-W5.

In 1901 a second school was built on the NW corner, NW¼ 24-22-2-W5 on land provided by Ben Lloyd. The 1889 school is still on the farm of Richie Hope. The 1901 school burned down in 1938 and was replaced with the building now used as a teacherage. In this year the school was awarded the Dr. Gunn Cup for collecting the most crow and magpie eggs and gopher tails.

The first teachers were: Maggie McArthur, Ed Holbrook, McQueen and Bertha Hawkey.

Families sending pupils to the early school included: Lloyd; Ralph, Hermione, Gertrude, Bertie, Edric, Ronald. McArthur; Norman, Jessie, Gordon. Bell; Elizabeth. Hall, Henderson, Hudson and Wilkin families were also represented.

RED DEER LAKE SCHOOL NO. 128 — Thanks to Bob Worden

Our earliest records show that a meeting was held December 30, 1899 for the purpose of having trustees Duncan McArthur and G. W. Reinhardt sign a request for Mr. Harris to become teacher and he apparently accepted the offer. The first annual meeting, held at 2 p.m., January 13, 1900 drew the huge crowd of nine persons. It was decided that 5% interest should be charged on all outstanding taxes ninety days after notice of assessment. The treasurer was instructed to borrow $40.00 from the bank to pay the balance due on Mr. Harris' salary and it was also decided that the secretary should inquire about having a well bored, for the school, by the government. In February of the same year the trustees put out a tender for someone to assess the school lands but when the March meeting rolled around they had only one tender, sent in by Mr. Hope, for $10.00. This was deemed too high a price and Mr. Harris was asked to tender for the job.

By June, 1900 tenders for a school fence were put out with the specifications that it be 70 posts, 12' apart, 2' in the ground, 6" tops, 4 ½' above ground, two gate posts with 9" tops, 3' in the ground, well braced, cor-

ner posts, one strand of barbed wire to be supplied. Old posts were to be piled in the school yard for later use. Mr. George Reinhardt got the contract for $25.00. In July Mr. Stephens was to make a stone foundation for the school and two vents, screened against gophers, were to be imbedded at a cost of 25¢ each, the total price for the job to be $40.00. In December Mr. McKevitt's offer to supply firewood at $3.65 per cord was accepted, Mr. Harris was paid $52.50 in cash, leaving an outstanding balance of $40.00 on his salary but he was rehired. By January it was decided that it would be better to burn coal than wood and the windows were to be repaired and storm windows purchased.

A meeting was held in March of 1901 to protest the forming of a new school district to the south. In April the new assessment added 10 head of cattle at the difference of $220.00 to the total and the rate was set at 4 mills. At the same meeting Mr. B. Phillips was to pay, in advance, the sum of $1.00 per month tuition fees for his children and a new axe was to be purchased. The next month pupils' tuition was to be $1.00 per month for those with no school district and 50¢ for the Phillips children until they leave Pine Creek S. D. Mr. Harris was to receive half of the tuition fees and his salary to be adjusted accordingly. March, Phillips children sent home after ten days notice of unpaid 50¢ fees.

June 1901 brought a letter proposing the removal of sections 7 and 12 from the district and adding 17 and 20 and it was proposed to intervene.

In December, 1901 Mr. Harris was asked to continue at $40.00 per month and winter holidays were set; January 1-20 and summer holidays to be four weeks starting July 14.

January 18, 1902, it was decided to dig a well 4' square, to borrow $20.00 to pay insurance. On April 14, 880 acres were assessed at 3¼ mills for a total of $483.60 and in September it was agreed that the school could be used for church services, second and fourth Sundays for Reverend Gale, Anglican, first and third for Presbyterian.

March, 1903 Mr. Harris resigned and Mr. Boyer contracted to teach for $480.00 for the rest of the year. In May fever was rampant in the area and the school was closed. There was much discussion as to whether the district would get the full grant and whether the teacher should get full salary. In May a new assess-

Old Red Deer Lake school, ½ mile south of existing school. 1908. Ella Thiessen, Kate Robinson, Anna McKevitt, Ed Eckersley, Clifford, Eckersley, Gladys Hope, Harvey Harrison, Kate McKellar (teacher), Agnes Robinson, Tom McKevitt, Bernard McKevitt, Front: Roy Thiessen, Minnie Hope, Jim McKevitt, Nul Lylad, Bill Thiessen, Nellie McKevitt.

ment of 3¢ per acre on 15,024 acres was made to bring in $450.58 and the secretary was to borrow $50.00 from the Union Bank to pay advance on teacher's salary. December saw them borrow $160.00 from the Imperial bank to pay the balance of the salary.

Through 1904-1906 the assessment dropped from 3½¢ per acre to 3¼ to 3. In 1907 Miss Kate McKellar accepted the teaching appointment for $630.00 per annum to be paid each quarter.

January 1910 Mr. A. Eckersley became secretary at the sum of $350.00 a year. In September, 1910 they considered borrowing $1,000.00 for the construction of a new school on NW corner of NW ¼ 24-22-2-W5, the indenture was to be at no more than ten installments at 8%. In October they accepted the debenture of Miss O'Hara of Winnipeg for $1,004.00 at 6% and the next month the old land was transferred to B. Lloyd in

Red Deer Lake School, 1917. Teacher, Laura Davis. Florence Thiessen, Chas. McKevitt, James McKevitt, Catherine Watkins, Ellen Watkins, Charlie Birney, Catherine McKevitt, Hazel Waddell, Holly Hervy, Floyd Watkins, Peter Massie, Norman Waddell, Pat McKevitt, Alister Massie, Minnie Hope, Jessie Thiessen, Walter Thiessen, Clint Patton, Albert McKevitt, Merle Birney, Douglas Scholefield, Richard Hope, Joe Patton.

return for the new site. H. Hervey took the contract to build concrete foundations, 22' x 32' x 1', to take seven yards of material and cost $60.00. Contract for the building went to Bull and Eckersley, $11.00 per M. and $1.30 per M. for studs, $8.00 for building the chimney.

In 1911 assessment rose to 5¢ per acre; 1912, 5½¢; 1914, 7¢; 1919, 8¢. Teacher's salary had risen to $1200.00-$1300.00 per year by 1921. In 1923 one acre was added to the school grounds for pony pasture. In 1926 the secretary was to inquire the inspector's views concerning a new district to be formed to the west. 1927, due to losing the row of sections to the west there was a smaller attendance and salary had to be cut to $1100.00. 1928, mill rate set at 9 mills.

By 1934, $750.00 was the offered salary but due to the denial of the department to hire a teacher at less than minimum wages it was agreed to pay $840.00 but have the teacher do the caretaking. In 1937 a noiseless, Remington typewriter was to be purchased as well as some books to cost about $21.45. The children were asked to do janitor work and light the fire for 15¢ each time.

On Friday night, February 4, 1938 tragedy struck and the school burned to the ground and a new place of operation had to be found immediately. The church was acquired for this purpose and $1,000.00 in insurance was taken out as a gesture of appreciation. It was proposed to borrow $600.00 by debenture to help finance a new school and, in July, Beaver Lumber submitted a tender of $1410.00 which was accepted.

Red Deer Lake new School, 1938.

1938 also saw us nominating a trustee to attend and represent this district as subdivision No. 3 of Calgary Division No. 41. We remained in the Calgary Division until 1954 when we switched to the Foothills Division where we are today.

1955 brought the union of Ballyhamage, Alexandra, Fish Creek, Priddis, Westoe and Red Deer Lake schools and a 5568 square foot school was constructed on the same location. A further, masonry, addition was built in 1963 having 14,149 square footage and in 1974 a second masonry addition of 12,275 square feet was added making a total of 31,992 square feet. Our gymnasium is 4800 square feet. Today we have a total of eighteen teachers and about 346 pupils in our fifteen room school.

Teachers: Mr. Harris 1900-1904; Miss Brown 1904 (8 mos.); Mr. Draimore 1904 (3 mos.); Mr. Spence 1905-1907 $52.50 per month; Miss Kate McKellar 1907-1910 $630.00 year; Mr. Lattery 1910-1912

Red Deer Lake School Children 1939. Back row: Grace Barkley, Fred Barkley, Roy Goodwin, Margie McKevitt, Hazel Massie, Patty Hervey, Miss Jameson, Jean Hambling, Edric Lloyd, Francis Lloyd, Nell Lloyd, Jean Kunder. Front row: seated Lawrence McConkey, Dale Brown, Jim McKevitt, Ronald Goodwin, Gerald McConkey, Jack Hervey.

$720.00 year; Miss Raymond 1912 $720.00; No mention of teachers from 1912-1920, Ina McInnis taught part of that time also a Miss Ryan: 1920-1921 Miss Laura Davis $1200.00 year; Miss E. B. Watts 1921-1923; Miss Mary Jerrolds 1923-1925; Miss McPherson 1925-1926 $1100.00 year; Mrs. Skene 1926-1928 $1200.00; Miss Olive Patton 1928-1929 $1000.00 year; Miss Ruth Ruttan 1929-1932 $1000.00 year; Miss Ida Herbert 1932-1934 $840.00 with grade 9 added; Robert Peattie 1934-1935 $840.00 year with caretaking; Miss Jessie Patterson 1936-1938 $840.00; Miss Patricia Jameson 1938; Miss Sheilagh Jameson.

Trustees: Duncan McArthur 1899-1902; G. W. Reinhardt 1899-1900; James Stephens 1900-1903; Rogers 1900—; Joe Hope 1901-1903; B. J. Lloyd 1902-1905; Duncan McArthur 1903-1905; Thomas Patton 1907-1914; Shortt 1909—; Nicholas Harrison 1908-1911; Wm. Thiessen 1910-1915; James McKevitt 1915-1917; Mr. Woods 1916-1919; W. G. Birney 1916-1919; Sam Waddell 1919-1923; Dan Patton 1920-1925; H. C. A. Hervey 1920-1925; Edric Lloyd 1924-1925; Dec. 19, 1925 all trustees resigned; W. G. Birney 1926-1931; Peter Massie 1926-1930; W. G. Reinhardt 1926-1929; J. P. Wilson 1930-1932; Sam Waddell 1931-1939; H. C. A. Hervey 1933-1939; Tom Eardley 1932-1934; Chris Bamford 1935-1937; Ralph Lloyd 1938-1941; Joe McKevitt 1940-1941; R. D. Goodwin 1940-1948; Walter Thiessen 1942-1949; Alister Massie 1942-1945.

Secretaries: Mrs. S. J. Reinhardt 1899-1909; Albert Eckersley 1909-1941; Mr. Eckersley retired January, 1941. Note of Bob Worden; "It has been a pleasure reading Mr. Eckersley's minutes while collecting this information. His writing is precise and clear in every way. He served his community well for many years."

RED DEER LAKE SCHOOL NEWS

The Massie name has been continuously on the Red Deer Lake School roll since 1914. Peter Massie, son of Mr. and Mrs. John Massie was the first to start and since then children, grandchildren and great-grandchildren of the original Peter Massie Sr. family have been attending.

FOOTHILLS FIELD MISSIONS

Through the kind co-operation of Jack McInnes we are able to share with you some of the history of the Foothills Field of the Presbyterian Church. This field covered Glenmore, Priddis, Sheep Creek and Red Deer Lake and, for this history, we are concerned with the Red Deer Lake station.

Dating back to 1897 we find a missionary by the name of H. R. Grant taking charge of services. Services were held at Red Deer Lake on alternate Sundays at 11 a.m. and the recommendation that the missionary board at either Red Deer Lake or Priddis was made because Glenmore and Sheep Creek were farther removed from the bulk of the population. It was further recommended that the missionary outfit himself with either harness or saddle and that Hutchins and Riley of Calgary would 'give him every satisfaction and liberal terms.'

The families listed as adherents, at that time, were; Mr. McArthur, Peter McArthur (bachelor), Mr. Hamilton, Mr. Rogers, Mr. Lloyd (Anglican), Mrs. Reinhardt (Anglican), Mrs. Philips (Anglican), Mr. Hope (Anglican), Mrs. Wilkins, Mr. Stevens, and the Members were; Mr. and Mrs. Duncan McArthur and Mrs. Rogers.

By July of 1898 the missionary had been replaced by Calvin A. McRae and his reports were more concerned with the number in attendance and the amount of the collection. Through the summer months and until the end of November services were held every Sabbath; on the second and fourth week they were held at 11 a.m. and the first, third and fifth weeks at 7:30 p.m. The largest congregation was at a song service when

31 attended and the smallest was five. It is surely a sign of the 'bad times' economically when we read that the total offerings for the season amounted to only $45.50 and we note that this amount 'met their indebtedness without the necessity of collection by subscription.'

'The English Church also held services here and though there are more Episcopalians than Presbyterians, the former have been extremely kind and take great interest in our services.'

A report submitted on October 10, 1899 shows that William Simon had been the missionary in charge and, 'owing to prolonged season of wet weather and the impossible condition of many of the trails, the average attendance at the various points was greatly reduced. The largest attendance was 35 and the least five. The Sacrament of the Lord's Supper was dispensed by Reverend G. Scott of Okotoks, the offering received at this service was devoted to Home Missions and amounted (from the four charges) to $16.00.

A period from October 1899 to October 1902 is missing from the records and then we find the Reverend D. McKeen in charge of only three points; Red Deer Lake, Priddis and Glenmore. A student missionary, Mr. Beverage had, by subscription, obtained the promise of the three points to contribute the sum of $425.00 yearly.

When Communion was dipensed on August 2, 1903, the following were received by certificate; Mr. James Stephen, from the Established Church in Edzell, Scotland, Miss Mary Wilkins, from Knox Church in Calgary, Mr. and Mrs. Thomas Patton, from the Presbyterian Church, Edgar, U.S.A. and Mrs. MacDougall from a Presbyterian Church in Canada. Mr. James Stephen was received on profession of faith.

On March 2$, 1904, Mr. and Mrs. Peter Cleland were received into membership and Mrs. James Stephen was 'removed by death'. In January of that year the missionary had dispensed Communion in their home and the Communicants were; Mr. and Mrs. James Stephen and Mrs. D. McK. Reid. In October Mr. Ben Phillips was granted a certificate of disjunction.

In October of 1903 the Foothills Mission was raised, by petition and subscription of the people, to the status of an Augmented Congregation, by the Presbytery of Calgary. Reverend James Shortt of Davisburg was appointed Moderator of Session. No settlement was effected at that time and Reverend D. McK. Reid was asked to remain in charge.

On April 30, 1904, Mr. Reid severed his connection with the congregation and at that time the roll of membership stood as follows; Miss Mary Wilkin, Mr. and Mrs. Thomas Patton, Mrs. MacDougall, Mr. and Mrs. Peter Cleland. The following had been removed by certificate of disjunction; Mr. Duncan McArthur, Mr. Gordon McArthur and Miss Jessie McArthur and Mrs. Jen Phillips. Mrs. J. Stephen 'removed by death!' From December 1902 until the end of April, 1904, a total of eighteen months, a total of $287.00 was raised, by Red Deer Lake, towards the minister's stipend.

In May of 1904, Mr. Fred W. Kerr, Arts student in Manitoba College, very ably supplied the charge until it was taken over by Charles O. Main, June 12, 1904.

'Until the close of September a small Sunday School was maintained at Red Deer Lake, but for several reasons and with great regret it had to be discontinued. Efforts were made, however, to have parents give their children regular instruction at home and Sunday School papers were regularly distributed.' On November 13 a special Thanksgiving Service was held at all three points. In Red Deer Lake and Priddis the buildings were beautifully decorated with oats, barley, hay, moss, flowers and vegetables. The motto, 'God Giveth the Increase' was displayed. The text of the sermon was Ephesians 5:20, 'Giving thanks always for all things unto God.' The total collection from all three charges was $13.60. 'It was thus disposed among the schemes of the Church; Augmentation $5.00, Home Missions $8.60.

Communion Service on October 8, 1904 had seen the names of Mr. E. Paul Holmes and Mr. Clarence Patton also Miss Lily Patton, added to the list of members.

In September Reverend J. S. Shortt of Pine Creek occupied the pulpit in exchange and on Christmas Day, Dr. J. C. Herdman, Superintendent of Home Missions, was the welcome preacher at all three places. The infant daughter, (Margaret) of William Henry and Hepzibah Lucy King of Sheep Creek was baptized at Red Deer Lake by Dr. J. C. Herdman.

'January first, 1905, with the consent of all the managers, the three services were discontinued during the short days and rough winter weather, and ' at a meeting of the Calgary Presbytery on February 9th and 10th, I was released from the charge of the "Foothills" and left February 14th, regretting the severance of a pleasant relation' signed; Charles O. Main.

The next Missionary to be employed was the Reverend H. McKellar and he was to serve from July 1905 to December 12, 1911, a very popular and respected gentleman. By this date there were services held on a weekly basis at Red Deer Lake. Owing to a prevalence of diphtheria or what some believed to be tonsilitis, together with a snow storm and the bad state of the road, there was one service missed. The attendance at Red Deer Lake has been good but, due to the number of church families leaving for other parts, the attendance of Priddis and Glenmore has become very poor. The children's service held at Red Deer Lake in September realized $3.15 which was forwarded to the Reverend Dr. Warden.

The missionary visited every family in the charge, the distances between each one makes it difficult to successfully overtake the work of this widely extended field. The majority of the people settled in these parts belong to the English Church, more are German families of the Lutheran Faith. New members welcomed included; Mr. and Mrs. Joseph Shannon and Mr. Peter McArthur. By July, 1914 Mr. and Mrs. Stobe, Mr. and Mrs. and Miss Harrison had joined our ranks.

In August of 1907 the Reverend Mr. Harcourt from India gave three excellent addresses on Foreign Missions, one at each of the charges. The total collection for that day was $20.00 which was sent to Reverend Dr. Somerville, Treasurer, Toronto.

By April, 1908 Mr. and Mrs. Ruttan and Miss Annie Thiessen and Mr. Levet(?) had become members. The order of services had been changed by order of the Presbytery and consent of the Mission Stations. Red Deer Lake was to have services on the first, third and fifth Sundays. These services were well attended, not only by our own members but by brethren of other denominations. Red Deer Lake contributed to the aid of the Fernie Relief Fund, $22.20 and $15.50 to Reverend H. R. Grant, Presbyterian Minister to Fernie, to assist himself and family in their great loss caused by the late disastrous Fire.

September of 1908 saw Mrs. Birney, Mrs. and Miss Mulloy and Miss Lena McDonald added to the membership.

1909 will be remembered as a great year for Red Deer Lake Presbyterian Church for the people, of their own accord, built a comfortable and beautiful church which was opened, free of debt, on May 2, 1909 with the Reverend A. Mahaffey B.D. Convener of the Presbytery's Home Missions conducting the dedicatory service and Reverend James Shortt, Associate Pastor of Knox Church Calgary preaching at an Evening Service the same day. Large and representative congregations greeted these brethren both morning and evening. The day was fine and the building committee consisting of; Messrs. D. Patton, P. McArthur, J. Shannon, G. Hamilton and P. Cleland and Wm. Gordon, deserve great credit for the efficient manner in which they carried out the work committed to their trust at much expense of money, time and work voluntarily given. The people also responded liberally and heartily to the appeal made for assistance. Reverend J. A. Clark, Senior Pastor of Knox Church Calgary preached the Communion Ser-

vice on May 9th and there was a fine congregation present representing different branches of the Church. The ordinance of Baptism was also administered. The Reverend A. D. Archibald, B.A. of Ponoka, Convener of the Synod's Sabbath School Committee visited the Mission Field on June 6, 1909 and urged the organization of Sabbath School at each of the three charges. Mr. Wm. Gordon kindly consented to be superintendent. The services in the new church are very well attended also the Sabbath School, by young and old. Mr. and Mrs. Stobe had their child baptized in their home on Thursday, July 15, 1909. Before the end of the year there was a shed constructed and a fence built around the church grounds, a stone foundation put under the church and all this was completed free of debt. The proper title of the acre of ground given freely by Mr. D. Patton and partner was secured and trustees appointed.

The beginning of 1910 Mr. and Mrs. Gordon joined by certificate and Ralph, Hazel and Frank Patton, by profession of faith. The 21st day saw the Pastor, Reverend H. McKellar, leave for Vancouver where he spent nearly three months for a change, by permission of the Presbytery. During his absence the services were conducted by brethren sent by Reverend Mr. Mahaffey, Convener of the Presbytery's Home Mission Committee, every second Sunday at Red Deer Lake. The Pastor resumed his duties April 24th, 1910, and on May 24th three new elders were elected ordained, Messrs. Gordon, McArthur and Hamilton. The Ordination service was held September 25, on a Communion Sunday when Reverend Mr. Kennedy from Bank View Church in Calgary preached the sermon. Messrs. Robert Pratt and Angus McIntosh of the Pine Creek Session were approved by the Presbytery to

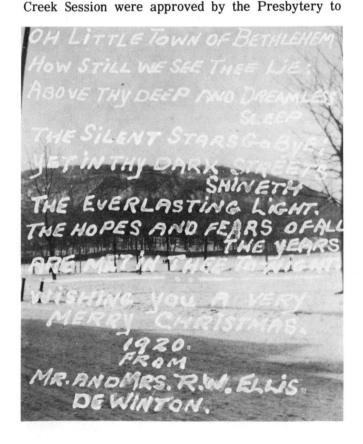

Red Deer Lake United Church, 1920.

assist in the ordination of the elders. Mrs. George Wonacott became a member, and Miss Emma Thiessen also joined us.

The notes from May 24, 1910 to January 22, 1911 show that times must have been improving for Red Deer Lake made quite a large contribution, it included $10.00 from Children's Day, $20.00 in aid of the Foreign Mission Fund, $3.00 for the Synod Fund, $12.84 for Church Papers plus $300.00 towards the Missionary's stipend. In March, 1910 Mrs. Birney Senior passed away, she was highly respected by the whole community.

The concluding paragraphs, of the notes show this list of members; Mr. and Mrs. Gordon, Mr. Peter McArthur, Mr. and Mrs. G. Hamilton, Mr. and Mrs. Peter Cleland, Mr. and Mrs. Dan Patton, Frank Patton, Miss Wilkins, Mr. and Mrs. Stobe, Mrs. George Wonacott, Hartwell R., George A., Grace I., Ruth A. Wonacott. The following had left the church; Mr. and Mrs. J. Shannon, Miss K. McKellar, Mr. Hugh McKellar, all left with certificates; Miss Hazel Patton, 'removed by death', Mr. and Mrs. T. B. Patton, Clarence and Ralph moved to Glenmore, Mr. and Mrs. McKay left for other parts.

The Red Deer Lake Station has suffered a serious loss financially and otherwise owing to the departure from our midst of Mr. and Mrs. Joseph Shannon who have been loyal supporters of our cause here for many years past. Also by the removal of Mr. and Mrs. McKay who have attended our services. The three districts comprising the Foothills Mission Field, Red Deer Lake, Priddis and Glenmore are undergoing changes owing to so many of the early pioneer settlers selling out and moving to other parts. The purchasers are as a rule not connected with our branch of the church but I am thankful to be able to record that a missionary enjoyed the good will of the people connected with other churches, a goodly number of whom attended our services more or less regularly. Reverend H. McKellar.

There are no more notes until a short entry made in September 5, 1917 when a union meeting of Davisburg, Melrose, Pine Creek and Red Deer Lake, in Pine Creek Church, for the purpose of extending a call to a minister for this charge. It was moved by Mr. Pratt and seconded by Jno. Massie that we extend a call to Reverend R. E. Clark.

Moved by Mr. Blackwood and seconded by D. Patton in view of there being difficulty in filling the call until Mr. Clark is duly received into the Presbyterian Church of Canada, that he be duly authorized to fill this pulpit until such time as he can be ordained here.

RED DEER LAKE HALL — from notes of Walter Birney

The Red Deer Lake hall was opened in 1904 and was first built with a kitchen, for a sit down supper, and a gallery at the west end where people could sit and play cards.

"I had always been fond of dancing, from the time I was fifteen years of age and called the quadrilles from the age of twenty. I was asked by the committee in charge to emcee the opening dance. There was a good turn out for that occasion and we continued to have good dances until the first world war broke out. I was in charge of running the dances."

When it was built it was not on a firm foundation, the stringers were laid on blocks and as the years passed the blocks began to rot and the building to sag. It gradually got so that it could not be used for dances and, during the war, it got so that it was no longer usable as a community hall. After the war was over, we got together, as a community, and jacked up and levelled the hall, put substantial supports under the sills, shingled the roof and so carried on until 1934 when we cut off the lean-to kitchen part and extended our hall that extra 14' for dancing space, and put in a No. 1 grade fir floor. When it was completed badminton was played, twice weekly, and we held community dances twice monthly. All in all we got a great deal of pleasure from our hall. In my own candid opinion, there is no community hall anywhere that served its purpose for community affairs as did the Red Deer Lake hall.

While the hall is no longer used for dancing, it still serves the community as a meeting place for continuing education classes.

RED DEER LAKE CURLING RINK — from notes of Walter Birney

Curling has been one of my favorite sports from the time I threw my first rock. I was a member of the Priddis Curling Club from 1908 till 1914 and, in 1908-9 and 1911-12, I curled, with George Lee as skip, at the Calgary Bonspiel. The first year we won the Visitors' cup and the next time the Tuckett Trophy. In my opinion, no game in sport, for old and young combined, is equal to curling.

In the winter of 1947-8, a few of us got together to see if we could not raise money whereby a curling rink could be built to serve our community. After discussing this matter at some length, it was decided that we organize for that purpose and I was appointed president. With the idea in mind that we should each pay $25.00 towards this project and that we would collect the rest by contribution, a committee was set up with Mr. R. D. Goodwin as chairman of the building committee. Mr. Goodwin and myself looked over some of

Supreme Champions, Red Deer Lake, 1950, l. to r. George, Flo, Betty (Beattie), Steve Bruketa.

Red Deer Lake curling rink under construction.

the more modern curling rinks and decided we would erect one of a quonset type. As chairman of the collecting committee, I immediately got busy on the job, contacting many of the Calgary business firms who responded very generously and, by May 31 I had collected the sum of $1,252.00 and building operations commenced as soon as the crops were in. By December we had the rink closed in so that we could make ice and, the first week in January, 1949 we were curling. Each year, from that date, until 1955, improvements have been added to the rink. Completing the interior, purchase of matched rocks etc. made the rink more satisfactory. Curling in the rink came to an end in 1966 and for a few years the rink was used as a recreation center for the children. The property was sold in the early '70s, demolished in 1976 and now nothing is left but memories.

MR. AND MRS. EDWARD ALLWARDEN — submitted by Jessie Fleischman

Ted came to the Red Deer Lake district about 1930 and made his home with Mr. and Mrs. Thiessen. From there he worked out as a farm hand for several years. He also worked with a team of horses and a fresno to help rebuild highway No. 22.

About 1933 or 34 he went into partnership with Jim McKevitt (Sr.) to open a store at Red Deer Lake — which is the original store that Mr. and Mrs. W. J. Norrie own today. At that time the store was called "Corn Centre" and Ted and Jim were known as "Eb" and "Zeb".

Ted bought his first truck at this time to haul provisions for the store and started a trucking business in the community as well.

When Jim McKevitt was married in 1935 he bought out Ted's share in the store and Ted built up his trucking business until he owned two 3 ton trucks and hired another driver.

During the harvest season he would shovel and haul grain from one farmer who was threshing and during the night would empty the bin for another farmer so he could continue with the harvest.

In 1941 Ted bought a farm from Mr. Manly Ruttan — one mile north of the Red Deer Lake School.

In June of 1942 Ted and I (Jessie Parker) were married and settled down to mixed farming.

We had three children, Marion (Hawes) born 1943,

Terrence 1946 and Nancy (Hornby) in 1951. All three children were active in 4H Clubs in the district.

Marion trained at the General Hospital for a nurse and in 1966 was married to Michael Hawes and they now live on the ranch West of Calgary. They have two children Kevin and Debbie.

Terry got his B.A. at U. of C. and worked for three years as a land man with Hudson Bay Oil and Gas. He now resides in Calgary and is busy in the real estate business.

Nancy finished high school and worked for a year with the Royal Bank before marrying. She spent two years in Nigeria in West Africa before returning to Calgary where she now resides and is employed by Alberta Gas Trunk Line.

Ted was a great community minded person and served on the school board, the Red Deer Lake Hall board, on the C.C. Curling Club. He was a vestryman at St. Paul's, Midnapore, and superintendent of the Sunday School there for five years. He was also a member of the Rockyview Hospital Board and served on the Agricultural Service Board until his death in 1960.

I carried on with the farm with the help of our three children and our good neighbor Mr. Roy Hambling until 1966 when I was married again to William Fleischman of High River. In 1967 we moved to Calgary.

The Allwarden Family — l. to r. Nancy, Jessie, Marion, Terry, and Ted — 1954.

THE BAMFORD FAMILY — by Mac Bamford

The Bamford family came to Canada in 1910 from Preston, England, where they had been engaged in the market garden business. After a brief stay in Belleville, Ontario, they came west and settled south of Calgary in the Glenmore district. My grandparents, William and Ann Bamford, worked for Archdeacon and Mrs. Dewdney who lived where the hospitals of Glenmore Park and Rocky View now stand. Their eldest son, Bill, and his wife soon moved back to Belleville.

My aunt Annie married William Worden, a long time friend of the family and they worked for Mr. Wolley-Dod before renting the Halifax place, south of where the Corral Drive-in Theatre is now located. They later moved to the Red Deer Lake district where they farmed before buying the property they later developed into their market garden.

Uncle Dick worked around the country and later went to work for the city. He married the former May Mills and they lived in Calgary.

Uncle Harry also worked around the area and then spent several years working for Doctor McKid. He married Elsie Longdon. They bought property and built a house along 14th Street, now part of Eagle Ridge. They were noted gardeners and Uncle Harry worked for the city as maintenance man at Glenmore Dam. In the early sixties they moved to the Red Deer Lake district where they continued gardening, specializing in gladiolas. Aunt Elsie passed away about twelve years ago but Uncle Harry continued to grow his beautiful flowers.

My parents, Chris and Mary, better known as Polly, and their infant son, Mac, (myself) went to work for Osborne Brown in, what is now, Bayview. He was a great horseman and raised some beautiful pacers and polo ponies.

When my parents decided to farm for themselves, we moved to a place, south and east of where South Centre is now located. Osborne Brown gave Dad a team of horses and a wagon along with one of his favorite old pacing horses. One night some horse thieves came and tried to get him out of his box stall. Somehow he got away, got caught in a wire fence and bled to death.

A few years later we moved to the Gadsby district where Dad farmed and hauled coal from the mine to the station. Times were very hard. I can remember walking over four miles to school through great snowdrifts. When we got there we sat around a big, potbellied stove. We usually got dried out just in time to start home again.

Four years later we again moved to the Glenmore district and, in the next few years, lived at several different places including one, just north of the Balgreggin Farm, where my wife grew up, beside the Indian Reserve. Her parents, Ward and Ida Barkley, bought this farm in 1925 and developed it into the Glen-Bar Dairy Farm which they operated for forty-two years. This area is now Oakridge. We also lived a short time on the Milton Williams farm, now Palliser, before moving to the McCorkill place, handy to where the K Mart is today. I attended school at Glenmore and Midnapore. Glenmore School was located where the Y.M.C.A. stands, on Heritage Drive. My parents attended the little church of Saint Peters, then located where Phil's Pancake House now stands. I can remember, as a small boy, attending the Sunday School Picnics held on Brown's Island in the 'Backwater', just south west of where Heritage Park is today. This was a beautiful area and is now covered by the waters of Glenmore Lake.

When I was fifteen, I quit school and went to work for Doctor Hays so I could earn some money to help my parents buy a farm of their own. I helped the Hays boys, Tom and Harry, to break the show cattle to lead, we also broke several horses. We had our own little stampedes. This is where I also learned to milk cows.

In 1928 Dad bought the farm at Red Deer Lake, on 25-22-2-W5, from Dan Patton. We hauled the lumber from Calgary by team and wagon and we built the house which is across from Norrie's store. I worked for Peter Massie for a couple of years to bring in some extra money and then I did some custom work, breaking land about the country. I also had a threshing machine and did custom threshing. By this time Dad had built a small herd of Ayrshire cows and we shipped milk to Calgary. Bert Ollive hauled our milk. In the early forties Dad sold the dairy cattle.

Mother and Dad raised four children. Besides myself, there is Richard, (Dick) who worked for Maclin Motors for twenty-five years. He was an officer in the army during the war years, and is now living in Longview, Washington. Our sister, Nancy (Dolly), married Walter Thiessen, also of Red Deer Lake. Cyril served with the R.C.A.F. during the war and upon his return he married and settled in the east; now living in London, Ontario. In 1946 I married Helen Barkley who was teaching at Westoe School. We built a small house on the home place and a short time later I bought the Walter Hemens place, which joined our farm to the north, and we moved our house across the field to where it now stands.

Helen's father was a dairyman so when I got her I got her little Heifer calf the beginning of our present Holstein herd. We have been dairying ever since, shipping fluid milk to the city.

Dad died in 1958 at the age of 76 and Mother passed away in 1975 at the age of 89. Both they and my grandparents are buried in the little cemetery in Midnapore by the little Anglican Church they attended.

Helen and I have five children who all help us with the dairying and farming operation. Bruce married Mary Shaw and they live at Midnapore with their two children, Christopher and Elizabeth. Carol married Gary Potter and they have their own home here on the farm and have a little girl, Lisa. Bob and Cathy attend school at Bishop Grandin and Brent is busy full time helping me with the farming. All of our children have been very active and reaped many benefits from 4-H in 1966, Carol had the champion Shorthorn steer at the Royal Winter Fair in Toronto and, last year, Bob's dairy heifer was Grand Champion at the 4-H show in Calgary. We are grateful that they had the opportunity to grow up in a district such as Red Deer Lake.

RAYMOND ORVAL AND LAWNA (BRAY) BARKLEY — by R. O. Barkley

I was at one of my neighbours, Mrs. Arthur Thom,

where I used to work on weekends, when her brother, M. D. Carlyle, from Calgary, was there visiting. While visiting with him, he gave me an invitation to come out to Alberta, his home, anytime and he would give me a job on his farm. This was in the month of May, 1917. I told him if Father got his harvest done early and there was still a harvest excursion train going west I just may do that. In those years there were two excursion trains from the Maritime Provinces to Winnipeg, for the fare of $10.00; and from Winnipeg to any place in Manitoba, Saskatchewan, Alberta or British Columbia, the fare was half a cent per mile. The second excursion train that year was on August 2 and Bruce, my brother, and I decided to come out and see Alberta.

We arrived on a Saturday around 5 p.m. We still had enough money to get a lunch. We got in touch with a man who worked, delivering milk, for the Carlyle Dairy (Union Milk Company). We went home with him, riding four miles in the back of a 1915, Model T Ford Coupe. It was raining heavily. We had a nice, over night visit with Mr. and Mrs. Clark Thom, I had gone to school in Ontario with some of the Thom children, Nettie and Lyle, and went over to the M. D. Carlyle's farm on Sunday to get acquainted with the Carlyle family. There we met Mr. and Mrs. Robert Brown. Bruce went home with Mr. Brown, an early pioneer who lived at Conrich, about ten miles away. Bruce had a job harvesting and steady work as long as he wanted it as Mr. Brown raised beef cattle and horses. He kept from fifty to eighty head of brood mares and his own stallions, and sold horses to young homesteaders. No tractors around in those days!! Horses played an important part.

I myself, had a steady job, harvesting with M. D. Carlyle, we started threshing a few days after I arrived and got in thirty-six or thirty-seven days of threshing. On the odd rainy day, I would help dig potatoes or build fences around the straw stacks and build granaries to store the winter feed in. The threshing machine was a big one, twelve bundle teams and twenty-nine men of a crew which filled a large dinner table. They sold a lot of their grain directly to grain buyers and it was hauled and loaded on the railroad cars. Strong and Dowler, Cummings Grain Company and other grain buyers, paid cash to the farmers just as soon as the grain was weighed at the Government Elevator scales in South Calgary. We had five teams hauling grain. Some grain was stored in bins on the farm. When more storage space was needed they made open bins of posts, lumber and barbed wire and shipped grain through the winter.

Later on, I had a job feeding beef cattle and milking cows. Come spring we seeded several hundred acres of oats, barley and wheat. The going wages in the fall of 1917 were from $2.00 to $2.50 per day for an eleven hour day of threshing.

Bruce returned to Ontario in November of 1917. I worked at Carlyle's until April 1, 1919 and from there I went to work on a dairy farm at Airdrie. I worked on the dairy farm from April 1, 1919 to March 1921 when I rented a farm from the owner, Mr. Louis Petrie, of Calgary. The farm consisted of four hundred and eighty acres of which about one hundred and fifty acres was under cultivation; the balance was hay and pasture. We cropped the hundred and fifty acres all to oats had a nice crop which we were ready to cut when along came a rough hailstorm, on August 17, and destroyed it 100%. That left me with no crop or green feed for the dairy cattle so we had to buy all our hay and grain the first year. We carried on and rented the farm for six years.

I was married on January 12, 1926 to Lawna Bray of Strathmore, Alberta. Our son, Freddie, was born at Airdrie, Alberta and in March of 1927 the farm was sold. In April, 1927, I moved fourteen miles south to a quarter section dairy farm on Nose Creek. I worked out helping other farmers harvesting; with Tally Cleveland, Delacour, in 1928, I worked for O'neil Brothers at Winnifred, Alberta and, in 1929, I worked for Bennet and White Construction Company in Calgary for several months working on the south half of the Hudson's Bay Company Store on First Street West and Eighth Avenue. Our daughter, Grace, was born at Nose Creek. We operated that dairy farm for three years.

We then moved, on April 1, 1930, to a quarter section farm that was purchased from James McKevitt of Midnapore, Alberta, the piece of land being the SW¼ 31-22-1-W5. As depression years started about the same time, we had to rebuild our roads for the milk and feed trucks to use, also had to improve the dairy barn and build a new one, to accommodate our milk cows, which were very expensive. Using second hand lumber, we managed to pass City Inspection as a milk producer and we enjoyed delivering our few cans of milk daily with our Model T Ford truck, over muddy roads in the summer and snow banks in the winter. We never missed a day shipping milk!

The milk prices in those days were very low along with the livestock prices. Choice steers selling at 2½¢ to 3¢ and the odd few at 3½¢ per pound; cows from 1¢ to 2½¢ per pound; for choice, week old Holstein heifer calves, from 25¢ to 35¢ and bull calves, 15¢ to 20¢ each, at MacLean's Auction Market. Fat hogs, delivered to the packers, live weight, selling at 2½¢ to 3½¢ per pound and brood sows, with litters of six to twelve piglets, selling from $12.00 to $15.00, for the family. Eggs as low as 4¢ cash or 5¢ in trade, per dozen. We grew several hundred bushels of potatoes and some carrots for a few years. These we sold in Calgary, when we could, for 1¢ to 2¢ a pound and, sometimes, traded them for groceries.

With our first crop here, two hundred and thirty-two bushels of oats went on the ground, had no granary, cut some of the forty-two acre crop for feed. Bought our grain for the stock and chickens. Cleaned up a few more acres as the years went by and cleared the brush from several more acres. Got under cultivation about eighty-five acres.

As we have seen many different parcels of land that have changed hands over the last twenty-five years still, many of the sons of former owners are still farming the land today just as the case in my family. I retired from farming in 1972 and my son, Freddie, and his wife, Edith, are now farming this very land.

Our son, Freddie, married Edith Morrison of Midnapore and they have a family of four children; Darlene (Mrs. Kenneth Downing), has a family of five three boys and two girls, lives at Big Valley, Alberta. Daryl married Marian Stewart of Priddis, has one son and lives in the Midnapore district. Cheryl (Mrs. Ian Traquair), has two sons, lives in the Midnapore district. Wayne is attending Junior High School in Calgary.

Our daughter, Grace, married Roy Latter of the Red Deer Lake district and they have a family of four girls and one boy, lives on the farm that Roy's father purchased, from the C.P.R. Land Company, in the early days.

HARVEY RICHARD AND EDITH OLIVE (MAPLE) BARLOW by Jean (Barlow) Read

Harvey R. Barlow was born at Whitefield, Lancashire, England on November 3, 1874. He emigrated to Calgary in December, 1902. He worked for Jack Halifax and Joe Shannon at Midnapore and, later, for Jocelyn Littleton at Red Deer Lake. Then he rented the latter's farm known as Pillaton.

On June 26, 1912, at the Pro-Cathedral of the Redeemer in Calgary, he married Edith Olive Maple who was born at Harbledown, Kent. Miss Maple was on her way to New Zealand and had stopped to work for the Edwards of Red Deer Lake.

About 1917 the Barlows moved from Pillaton to the Scully Place, later the Hayes Dairy in southwest Calgary, where they were employed by the Crown Feed and Produce Company.

In 1919 they lived on the P. M. Hodder place (NE ¼ 22-21-2-W5) which they later bought, while they built on their own quarter N¼ 15-21-2-W5, using logs and lumber from the old Hemmingway place near Red Deer Lake.

Harvey R. and Mrs. Barlow — 1939.

Their children attended Ballyhamage school.

The Barlows retired in 1948. They had three children: Jean (Mrs. Leslie J. Read), Calgary; John J. who married Betty Munn of Cremona; Marjorie (Mrs. W. L. Wood) Calgary.

Jean has four children and ten grandchildren. Jack has four children and four grandchildren. Marjorie has one son and four grandchildren. Jack and Betty lost their eldest son, Richard by drowning at Water Valley, July 30, 1967. He was trying to save his sister who now lives at Cremona.

Dad passed away in 1959 and Mother in 1972.

Among the many friends I so well remember from Red Deer Lake I can clearly recall "Auntie" Mckevitt. She gave me my first baby spoon and high chair.

I forgot to mention that I was brought into the world by a nurse from the Red Deer Lake area named Mrs. Reinhardt.

WALTER G. AND EMMA (KAI) BIRNEY — by Merle Griffiths and Walter (Bud) Birney

Walter was born at Guelph, Ontario, October 5, 1881, son of William and Ellen Birney, and came, with his family, in 1890 to Keith, west of Calgary. The last two years at Keith he herded horses for Mr. Ross, one of Calgary's first photographers, in the summer. The family moved to Glenmore, then, in 1898, his father bought a ranch in the Priddis district, just west of Red Deer Lake.

At age nineteen, he joined the South African Constabulary (a corps used as soldiers during the Boer War and, later, as Mounted Police at the end of the war.) Arriving in Cape Town, South Africa, April, 1901, troops later received remounts, the horses were a small breed called Basuto Ponies'. On line duty the troop transport consisted of ox wagons and mules with Kaffir drivers and lead boys. Eight to ten oxen were used in the 'span', during rainy season on the veldt more oxen were used. On a trip for supplies he became ill with Enteric Fever and was taken to hospital at Heidelberg, being big and strong, he recovered, and joined his troops at Pretoria. They were sent from there to do police duty at an outpost near the Rhodesian border, to see no trouble arose between the Boer prisoners, returning from Bermuda and Ceylon, and the Kaffirs of the district. Riding on patrol duty always accompanied by another trooper, he learned enough of the Boer language to be able to talk to them. Returning home in April, 1903, he stayed with his parents and brother, Harry, ranching and doing a little farming.

In 1906 he married Emma Kai of Red Deer Lake who came, with her parents and part of her family, from Nebraska in 1904. In 1910 he erected buildings on his own property, NE¼ 28-22-2-W5. Being a very dry year in the south he shipped his threshing outfit (steam-engine) to Olds and threshed there that fall. Other years he threshed in the Brant and Ensign districts.

In 1918 he purchased all of 23-22-2-W5 and SW¼ 34-22-2-W5, known as the John Robinson Place, selling the quarter section to Arthur Gregory for cash. By now there were five Birney children and a nephew, Cecil Birney, in our family. Losing our house and all its con-

Walter Birney.

tents in a fire, the money from the sale was used to buy clothing for all the family, also bedding, furniture etc. for a large ten room house we moved into. That year he was elected to the Rural Council of Stockland, later the Municipal Districts of Turner Valley, and Highwood merged and became Foothills. After serving as councillor and Reeve for thirty-seven years he became the longest sitting Councillor, of any one Council, in the Province of Alberta, at that time. He also served as Secretary-Treasurer of Red Deer Lake Church and on the Rural Hospital Board.

Dealing in the cattle business, he bought mostly from the ranchers in the foothill country, he sold through the Company of Parslow and Denoon. We all liked riding and trailing cattle, getting pretty dusty at times. As more main roads became gravelled, droving cattle was soon past history. Dad always liked the hills, making many friends during this period.

All of our family loved dancing, Dad always called the square dances, a talent he developed at an early age, and usually would emcee the dances at Red Deer Lake. We all went to dances at Midnapore and Priddis, sometimes going to Kew and Bragg Creek, always ready for a good hoe-down. Mother was always used to young people and would encourage us to have our friends come and stay. We had a large house, open to everyone, we would clear out the dining-room furniture and dance to gramophone records. Mother belonged to the Women's Institute and enjoyed the charitable work and friendly get togethers.

In early 1948 some of the neighbours got together to try and raise money to build a curling rink. Dad was enthused about this, he curled at Priddis with the George Lee rink. They appointed a Collections Committee and a Building Committee and, after the harvest was over, the men got busy and with real community spirit, had the rink built and were curling in January, 1949.

The Southern Alberta Pioneers and Old Timers Association, an organization in which Dad was very active, decided, at an executive meeting, that an effort should be made to erect a suitable building as a memorial tribute to the pioneers of Southern Alberta. A committee was set up, with Dad as Chairman, and the members went to work to try and raise money

from oil companies, business firms and private individuals. Don McKay was Mayor of Calgary at the time and he co-operated in every way. A site was chosen, overlooking the Elbow River and known as Lindsay Park. The city of Calgary donated this land and, finally, in 1954, the go-ahead was given and, on June 8, 1955, The Memorial Building was opened by Lieutenant Governor J. J. Bowlen.

In January, 1954 our mother passed away, Dad sold the place to Mr. Finlay and, in partnership with his son, Bud, held a sale in 1955 with Harry Hays and Archie Boyce the auctioneers. After moving to Calgary he still longed for the open spaces and bought a ranch at Youngstown and had Tom Gilchrist of Millarville running it. Later he sold it to Tom and had a small house built for himself on the ranch and spent his summers there and winters in Victoria, always returning home in time to attend the Spring Bull Sale and meet some of his old pals. He died, suddenly, at Creston, B.C. on March 12, 1960 and was buried in Calgary on March 17, exactly fifty years, to the day, from when his Mother was buried.

Of the six children born to our parents, two survive; Mrs. John (Merle) Griffiths and Walter (Bud) Birney, a moving consultant with Madison Moving. John died in infancy in 1919. Pearl (Brown), Deceased 1945, had three children; Shirley (deceased in infancy), Leonard (deceased 1956), and Cheryl (Meikle) who has four children. Viola Jacobson (deceased 1959), had three children; Ronald, married with two children, Myrna (Martisko) and Dale. Charlie ranched in the Millarville area before moving to Calgary, (deceased 1969) left two children; Beverley (Czipoth) who has three children and Audrey (Egan) who has four children. All families live in Calgary.

STEVE AND VICTORIA BRUKETA — by Mary Bruketa

Steve and Victoria Bruketa were both born in Yugoslavia. In 1924 Mr. Bruketa came to Canada looking for work, leaving his wife and infant son, Steve Jr., behind in the old country, as was the custom at the time. He was employed by the C.P.R. as a section foreman at Tilley, Alberta.

In the fall of 1933 he went back to the old country and brought his wife and child back to Canada with him. He continued to work for the C.P.R. full time until the spring of 1939. During this time a daughter was born in 1937.

The family moved to the Red Deer Lake district in April of 1939 at which time Mr. Bruketa purchased the E½-22-22-2-W5. In the five years that followed, Mr. Bruketa continued to work for the railroad and left his wife and son on the farm to look after it; he came to be with them on week-ends. In 1944 he left the railroad and moved to the farm and continued to work there with his family. In subsequent years other parcels of land were acquired.

In the fall of 1950, Steve Jr. married the former Mary Balzina of Nelson, B.C. They had three children, two sons and a daughter.

In 1957, Victoria Bruketa became ill with cancer and that prompted them to move to Calgary in the fall of 1958. She lost the battle with cancer and passed

Steve and Victoria Bruketa, 1950.

away in the spring of 1960. Mr. Bruketa Sr. still resides in Calgary.

Steve Jr. has been purchasing the farm from his father over the years and continues to operate it with the help of his family. They have experienced many changes through the years. They went from farming with horses to tractors, from using threshing machines to combines, from coal-oil lamps to electricity, from burning coal and wood to propane and eventually to natural gas, and we mustn't forget the telephone that made its appearance during the same time. Indoor plumbing too was welcomed by all. All of the foregoing conveniences are taken for granted by most people today but they were real events for us as they came about, one at a time.

DAVID AND MARTHA (SHORTT) CARTER—by J. (Moss) McKeague

David Carter came from near Granton, Ontario and was a cattle rancher on Fish Creek, near Priddis, Alberta. Homesteaded NE ¼ 26-22-2-W5 and, in 1892, married Martha Shortt, second daughter of George Scott Shortt and his wife, Mary.

The Carters ranched on Fish Creek until the early 1900's, moving to Calgary where David carried on in the real estate business and was an Alderman.

He died, very suddenly, about 1904, of a heart attack, while finishing building a house at Mossleigh. His wife, Martha, and three children; Alfred, Gwendoline and Harold, lived in Calgary for many years. Harold died of spinal menengitis when a very young man and Gwendoline (Mitchell) died at the birth of her first child. Alfred served in WW1 as an aviator pilot in the Airforce and is at present living in Vancouver, B.C.

Martha lived the latter years of her life in Victoria and Vancouver and passed away in November, 1943. She is buried in Calgary.

PETER B. AND MARY E. (HADSKIS) CLELAND — by Carrie Forrest

Peter was born in Woodstock, Ontario on February 2, 1848. He took his training as a carriage maker. He was a veteran of the North West Rebellion and came west with the C.P.R. as a time keeper, arriving in Calgary in 1883. From here he decided to go ranching and settled on a ranch 3½ miles SW of Midnapore. The trees that are around the home buildings were planted by him as a wind break.

He was married to Mary E. Hadskis of Winnipeg, Manitoba, at the Church of the Redeemer, in Calgary, by the late Reverend E. Paske Smith. He helped build the Red Deer Lake Church which the family attended until his retirement in 1916 when they moved to Calgary. He also was agent for Galt Coal in the district.

Mary was active in the Red Cross during the First World War in Midnapore and Calgary. Mary passed away on January 7, 1926 and Peter on October 17, 1933.

They are survived by two daughters; Mrs. John C. (Carrie) Forrest and Mrs. George (Jessie) Green. Four grandchildren and six great-grandchildren.

The ranch is now known as Spruce Meadows owned by Mr. Ron Southern.

ROSA AND ARNIE ESTELL — by Rosa Estell

My husband, Arnie, myself, and our five daughters, moved to the Red Deer Lake district in 1926. We rented the E ½ 18-22-2-W5 and lived there about two and a half years. We farmed some of the land, had a few cattle, pigs and sheep. Like most people in those days, we milked cows so had our own milk, cream and eggs and we grew a big garden.

Arnie had a threshing machine and used to thresh for a lot of farmers in the district. He also had a grinder and would go from farm to farm and chop grain for pig and cattle feed. In the winter time he ran a trap line trapping coyotes, weasels and badgers.

We had good neighbours in those days. Some of our close neighbours were; Pearsons, Waddells, Reinharts and McConkeys.

Our girls, Recha, Evelyn, Ila, Pollyanna and Irene, all went to Red Deer Lake School. In summer they either rode horseback or walked and, in winter time, they drove a team and sleigh. Some of the teachers who taught them were; Mrs. Ida Skene, Miss Jerrold and Miss Patton.

In the spring of 1929 we moved to the Priddis District where we lived until my husband passed away in 1958.

The girls are all married and live close by except Recha who went to the States to work and married a farmer. They are wheat farmers and live close to Waterville, Washington.

I now make my home in Turner Valley with my daughter, Evelyn. I have 8 grandchildren, 22 great-grandchildren and one great-great-grandchild. I will be 86 on my next birthday, April, 1977, and enjoy very good health. I still enjoy my garden and get a great deal of pleasure from it.

GEORGE AND MARY KATHERINE FARKAS by John A. Farkas

George Farkas was born in Kosicka-Bela

Czechoslovakia in 1901. He emigrated to Canada in 1928 leaving behind a young wife, Mary Katherine, and a two year old son, John Allan.

He worked in the Calgary area at various jobs for approximately three years. Loving this land, he formed a partnership to go farming with two other young men who had also left their wives and families in Czechoslovakia. The three of them bought a section of land, 22-22-2-W5, west of Red Deer Lake. They farmed with horses, later acquiring a Hart Parr tractor.

Grain was hauled to Midnapore elevator in a wagon box pulled by a four horse team. One day they delivered some grain to the elevator the only problem was that it happened to be Sunday. They had to leave the wagon there and come back with the team. They probably lost track of time as all three of them took turns at cooking and housekeeping.

Father had an ancient double barreled shot gun and, as game was more plentiful then, he occasionally got the odd prairie chicken or deer. He would melt the pellets and form a slug for the shell. I am in possession of this old relic now.

By 1935 my father had saved enough money so that he could book passage for Mother and me to come to Canada. In 1936 my father decided to go on his own so he bought a half section in the Ballyhamage district, 22-21-2-W5. With two hired men he worked hard all winter cutting trees. I remember picking roots with him after the land was plowed.

The old Ballyhamage school was on the S.W. corner of our farm then. At that time he also bought a model A Ford, quarter ton truck from Pete Watkins, canvas top, plexiglass curtains and all. Father and Pete happened to be in Calgary that day when a terrible blizzard came up. It took them two days to get

home. The drifts were so big that in places they had to detour through farmers' fields to get home.

In 1939 my father bought a farm in the Red Deer Lake, Midnapore area, 16-22-1-W5. Diligently he broke and improved the land, always striving to have a more viable unit. I farmed the land with him until 1971 when he and my mother retired and moved to Calgary. They had belonged to St. Patrick's church in Midnapore. Mother passed away February 6, 1977. My brother Fred David was born in 1938 and is a geologist in Calgary, married Shirley Ann Scotvold of Hythe, Alberta. They have a son Ryan Thomas.

My wife, formerly Wilma Jean Rost of Innisfail, and I took over the farming operation from my father and still farm the place. We have two daughters and two sons. Cathy Ann (now married), Lori Jean, Don George and Allan John. We also have a granddaughter, Cindy Ann.

THE J. R. GODLONTON FAMILY — by W. G. Godlonton

Our family consisted of three sons and one daughter — Jim, Leslie, Bill, and Florence. My sister, Mrs. A. H. Walsh, lives in the Madden district, on the farm where she and her husband (deceased) settled in 1924. My brothers, Jim and Les, have both passed away. Jim's widow, now Mrs. Charles Patching, lives in Lethbridge, and Leslie's widow, Doris, lives in Calgary. The children of both families are living in various parts of Alberta, I believe.

My wife and I live in Lethbridge, as do our three married children. I have been employed by the McIntyre Ranching Company as foreman and manager for the last twenty years, and up until late in 1972 we lived on the ranch at Magrath.

My father Jim purchased a three-quarter section farm from a Mr. Towner in the Red Deer Lake area in 1913, and we moved on to the place in August of that year. We were engaged in a mixed farming operation. Cattle and horse brands appear elsewhere.

The property extended from the east end of Red Deer Lake east to a farm rented by Charlie Brown, and I understand, later purchased by a Mr. Bottomley who operated there for many years.

All but my eldest brother Jim attended the Alexandra School. I made my start there under a teacher named Miss Hay, who later became Mrs. Charlie Brown.

Conditions that made a lasting impression on my very young mind were three in particular. First, the declaration of the First World War, and the many young fellows that used to visit with us, joining the Army and going to the battles in France. Secondly, the wet year of 1915, when my father was Councillor, and it seemed to me that the entire population was stuck in the many mud holes on the poorly-developed roads which my father was supposed to keep in repair. I can remember the entire Wonacott flat being flooded by Pine Creek. This impressed me very much, as we had to cross Pine Creek to get to Alexandra School.

Finally, during this time the Model T Ford touring car was introduced. These snorting, rattling contraptions, controlled by very incompetent operators, created something of a transportation

George and Mary Farkas with sons John and Fred.

hazard, not only to themselves, but more so to citizens still dependent on horses for their travel requirements.

My father sold the farm to a Mr. George A. Pearson in June 1918 and we moved to Calgary for the remainder of that summer. During the fall Dad purchased another mixed farm in the Bottrell district.

In the fall of 1924 I started to work for Gordon and Mrs. Heaver and made my home with these fine people off and on for about six years; as a matter of fact, I feel that I have been accepted in their home, as an adopted member, ever since.

During my permanent residence in the De Winton district, I made many fine and lasting friends. We had many good times, although on looking back, it would be quite dull compared to today's standards. The big excitement was to ride to De Winton and sit around Barsby Martin's store, telling each other what good men we were! On occasion, activities at Pete Murray's residence, Steve William's pool hall, or the De Winton Hall supplied us with many interesting and entertaining conversations and, no doubt, valuable history for our grandchildren.

RALPH DAVIS AND EDITH (FRANCIS) GOODWIN — by R. Goodwin

Ralph Davis Goodwin was born in 1897 at Revere, Massachusetts. He came to Calgary with his parents, Edgar and Ida, and his two brothers in 1907.

In 1919, Markus Goodwin, his uncle, purchased 22-2-W5, Edward's place. Also, in the spring of 1920, Edgar and Ida and son, Ralph, moved onto the section.

During 1914, Ralph joined the army in Calgary and went overseas to serve with the Canadian Engineers. In 1915 he was wounded and returned to Canada in 1919.

While digging a place for vegetables, in 1920, he unearthed a bottle of Hudson Bay Brandy. This being prohibition time, he presumed that it had been put there for medicinal purposes! After the contents had been put to good use, he informed Sandy Massie and, I am sure it must have made him 'feel good'.

In 1921, Ida Goodwin died, at the age of 52.

In 1922, Ralph purchased SW¼ 23-22-2-W5, through the Soldier Settlement Board, from the Massie Brothers. He built a home on the quarter in 1923.

On June 12, 1926, he married Edith Francis, known as Pixie, who was born in Winnipeg in 1903. Pixie's father was from Wales and her mother from Newfoundland.

R.D., as he was known, worked off the farm many times. This included being the road foreman for the Municipal District for several years, working with horses and scraper. Also, in 1931, he contracted to place culverts on 22 Highway from Lees' store to Macleod Trail and, from Midnapore to De Winton on the Macleod Trail. Fred Watkins was a partner in this work. He built a number of teacherages and schools for the Rural School Divisions.

He was foreman of construction when the Red Deer Lake Curling Rink was built and an active member of the club while the rink was in operation.

Ralph and Pixie still live on the place and the family celebrated their fiftieth wedding anniversary this June 12, 1976.

R. D. Goodwin family, 1974. Back; R. D., Bruce, Art, Ray. F. Ron, Pixie.

Ralph and Pixie's family are as follows; Raymond, born in 1927, married Betty Fehr, children are, Diana, Dale, Sandra. Ronald, born 1930, married Kathy Morgan, children are, Beverly, Brent, Michael. Arthur, born in 1935, married Valerie Johnson, children are, Jimmy, Marlene, Carol Ann. Second marriage, Doreen Paulik, children are, Cherry, Joleen, Karen, Rodney. Bruce, born in 1944, married Mary Pryke, child is Cheryl.

THE NICHOLAS HARRISON FAMILY — by Nena Jeffery

I arrived in Calgary, the year 1905 with my parents, and brother, Harvey, from England. My father bought a farm, near Red Deer Lake, from Mr. Alf Rogers (in later years the Huck Family owned it). Mother made good friends among the neighbours. I remember visits from the Brogdens, Lloyds, Hopes, Clelands, Miss Wilkins, Pitchfords and many others. Father used to tell how helpful the men were with advice in farming methods that were so different from the ones in England where he had farmed previously.

The Nicholas Harrison family on their Red Deer Lake farm, 1909.

Harvey rode his pony 'Punch' to the Red Deer Lake School; I think that pony knew that his new master was a 'green Englishman' as he bucked him off regularly until one day Edric Lloyd rode by and offered to give him a working over. After that he behaved himself.

The Christmas School Concert was one of the highlights of a young child's life. In those days I was too young to go to school but I can still remember, after so many years, the thrill of being driven, on a cold winter's night, in a sleigh, the crisp air and the sound of the sleigh runners crunching in the snow.

Father drove us all in to Calgary to see the 1912 Stampede, quite a drive with a team! I never heard what time we arrived home that night but I do remember the story of another trip Father made to town. He had left in the morning with the eggs and butter, etc. which were to be sold and groceries brought home. Night time came and passed and no sign of him so, Mother, who had become very anxious, walked over to ask Mr. Reinhardt for help. He hitched up his team and drove her home and was going to drive to Calgary to look for Father but when they drove into the yard there was Father. His team had been taken from the Livery Barn by mistake by a Springbank farmer's new hired man and had to be returned before Dad could come home. No phones in those days!!

My father was one of the men who hauled lumber, from a Priddis mill, to build the Red Deer Lake Church and our family were among the earliest members.

My parents sold the farm in 1912 and returned to England where my father died. In 1919, Mother, Harvey and I returned to Canada and settled in the Midnapore district where I met and married R. M. (Jeff) Jeffery and have lived here ever since.

Mother died in Calgary in 1962 and Harvey in 1974. They were both members of Saint Paul's Anglican Church in Midnapore for years.

P. C. BARNARD AND PENUEL (HOLCOMBE) HERVEY

P. C. Barnard Hervey, a lieutenant in the 3rd Welsh Guards, immigrated to Canada in 1883 where he procured a job Sept. 8th with the Grand Trunk Railway as baggageman and Assistant Divisional Superintendent at the noble salary of fifty cents a day.

Penuel Holcombe set sail from Liverpool on the S. S. Aurania May 17, 1884 arriving in New York May 25. She proceeded to Palmerston, Ontario, where on June 4th, she and P. C. B. Hervey were married.

The following year the eldest son, Harcourt, was born. They moved to Stratford, where their son, Gerald Essex was born in 1891.

In 1890 P.C.B. came to Calgary as representative of Sir James Ross in construction of the C and E Railway from Calgary to Edmonton. Mrs. Hervey and the two boys came to join P.C.B. in Calgary in 1893, where they resided until moving out to the Arthur Peake, Lone Spruce Ranch in 1896, which they purchased and renamed Abercorn Ranch. It was here that their third son Vyv was born in 1899.

Mrs Hervey and the three boys lived on the ranch whilst P.C.B. was away on construction. In 1897 and 1898 he was in charge of engineering supplies for location work on the Crowsnest Railway.

P.C.B. also worked on the Calgary and Springbank irrigation companies. In 1900 he assisted William Pearce in the subdivision of townships between Lacombe and North Battleford. The following year he became chief engineer for the western section of the C.P.R. irrigation ditch.

In 1907, Mr. and Mrs. Hervey moved to Calgary where they resided until Mrs. Hervey's death in 1934. Then P.C.B. spent his summers at the ranch and his winters in Montreal with Gerald and Vyv.

About 1912, P.C.B. became Commissioner of National Parks for Western Canada retiring in 1918. After retiring, he took a great interest in his garden, workshop and politics at all levels. P.C.B. Hervey died in 1945 at the age of 86.

Gerald attended school at Red Deer Lake and Calgary. He joined the staff of the Bank of Montreal taking leave of absence to go overseas in World War I. He became a fighter pilot in the Royal Naval Airservice winning the D.F.C. After the war, Gerald was a member of the Forestry Patrol stationed at Morley and High River. He later went back to the bank taking leave of absence once again to serve his country during World War II with the rank of Wing Commander. Gerald returned to the bank after the war and is now living in retirement with his wife in Point Claire Quebec. He has one son.

V. H. Hervey was also educated at Red Deer Lake and Calgary. He enlisted and went overseas in World War I at the age of seventeen. He transferred to the

Mrs. Harrison — on her 85th birthday, 1953.

Airforce and was shot down in flames over England. He was badly burnt but recovered fully. Vyv also served in World War II as a Wing Commander. After the wars he worked for various motor companies moving to Montreal where he lived until his death. He has one daughter and is survived by his widow.

COLONEL H. C. A. HERVEY

Harcourt Charles Antrobus Hervey moved to the Red Deer Lake district as a boy of eleven. He took on the responsibilities of the ranch with his mother and the kind tutorship of Dave Carter, their neighbor, while his father, P. C. B., was away working on the surveys and irrigation. He attended Red Deer Lake School having previously gone to school in Calgary.

As a youth, Harcourt became an excellent shot. He used to go hunting with Dave Carter and Walter McKay. Harcourt won many medals and trophies for target shooting with the Priddis Rifle Association and the Elbow River Rifle Association.

In 1901, Harcourt joined the Canadian Mounted Rifles as a private having a most successful military career in which he was a winner of many competitions for both shooting and tent pegging. He served in both World Wars and his military career is to be treated elsewhere in this book. When not serving his country as a soldier, Harcourt ranched and later farmed.

In 1907, he and Hermione Lloyd were married. She was the daughter of the Benjamin Lloyds and was the first white girl born in the district. She and Irenie Shaw were the first two babies baptized at St. Paul's Church in Midnapore. Hermione received her education at Red Deer Lake School.

The Hervey property consisted of Harcourt's homestead S.E.¼ 34-22-2-W5, P. C. B.'s homestead N.E.¼ 34-22-2-W5 and the Peake quarter N.W.¼ 34-22-2-W5 all of which is still in the family. Harcourt and Herm raised grade beef cattle mostly of Shorthorn and Hereford breeding, and heavy and light horses.

Harcourt took a great interest in the community. He was for many years a school trustee, the weed inspector and was instrumental in getting the district electrified and in establishing the Curling Club. Harcourt died at the age of sixty-five in 1950.

Herm carried on the operation of the farm with the help of her youngest son, Jack. She was always a very hospitable person and loved having visitors. She was especially fond of the young people of the district who seemed to return her affection.

In later years Herm spent the summers on the farm with Betty and Jack and the winters in Calgary with Penny. Finally she was only able to take short visits to the country which she loved dearly. Herm died on her ninetieth birthday November 2, 1975.

Harcourt and Hermione had four children — Harcourt Halcombe Charles Benjamin (Holly), Elizabeth Penuel (Penny), Hermione Patricia (Patty) and Donald John (Jack).

Holly joined the R.C.M.P. and is now retired and living in Edmonton. He supervises tours of Government House and the Legislature having worked for the A.L.C.B. after his retirement from the R.C.M.P. He married Elsie Bowyer and they have three daughters.

Penny married Gordon Ridge now retired from the

Holly Hervey, R.C.M.P. Calgary Stampede infield official mountie 1940's.

R.C.M.P. They have no children and reside in Calgary. Penny is very active in the Alberta Thoroughbred Association and raises registered Persian cats.

Patty married George Ingram, eldest son of Alex and Blanche Ingram formerly of the Red Deer Lake District. They have two sons and a daughter and live in Calgary where Patty teaches music.

Jack married Elizabeth Ena (Betty) Waldron. They live on and operate the family farm. Betty is prominent in church and community work. Jack is a partner in an implement dealership in High River. They raise beef cattle, grain and hay. Betty also has Pinto saddle stock. Jack and Betty cross-country ski, curl and ski-doo for recreation.

They have two sons and a daughter. Ken works for his dad in the implement business. Garry works and helps out at home. Karen is a Red Deer Lake schoolgirl.

HILTON BROTHERS DAIRY FARM — by Edna Hudson

In March, 1941, William and George Hilton, better known as Bill, and Geordy, with their wives, rented a farm on Fish Creek known to all as the Shannon Place or Burnsland Picnic Grounds. They moved into the district from West Calgary where their parents had a dairy farm since 1918.

Their parents, Mr. and Mrs. James Hilton came to Canada from Scotland in 1912, and settled in the Rosscarrock District. They shipped milk to the Union Milk Company and later owned their own milk company known as the Rosscarrock Dairy. Shortly before Mr. Hilton's death in June, 1938, they sold their dairy business to Pallesen's Dairy in Hillhurst.

Geordy Hilton and his wife, Edna, had four children; Bob, Anne, George and Edward. Bob and his wife, Jan, live in Wetaskiwin and have their own construction company, R. H. Hilton and Associates. Anne and her husband, Dennis Hehr, live on a ranch, west of Priddis. George and Wendy live in Vancouver where George is employed by Farmers' and Merchants' Trust Company. Edward lives with his mother in Calgary.

Bill and his wife, Hazel, had three children; Gary, Jimmy and Beverley. Gary and Annette live in Surrey, B.C. where Gary is employed by B.C. Hydro. Jimmy and Sandy live in Williams Lake, B.C. and Jim is employed by the Department of Forests. Beverley and Don Brooks reside in Calgary.

In March, 1948, the Hilton Brothers, Geordy and Bill, bought the Sandy Massie farm, E½-36-22-2-W5, in the Red Deer Lake District. They continued milking cows and shipping milk to Palm Dairies at the rate of approximately one half million pounds a year. In 1961 they built the first loafing barn and installed the first pipe-line milker in that area.

In 1963, Geordy Hilton died, very suddenly, of a heart attack, which ended the Hilton Bros. operation. Bill continued with the operation until 1968 when he retired and moved, with his wife, Hazel, to Surrey, B.C.

Geordy's wife, Edna, lives in Calgary where she married George Hudson in 1972.

JOSEPH AND CAROLINE (CHAPLIN PALING) HOPE — by Gladys Green

Joseph Hope sailed from Maryport, Cumberland, England in 1879 and arrived at Winnipeg, Manitoba, by way of Minneapolis, Saint Paul, U.S.A. He worked as a labourer in and around Winnipeg. I remember him speaking of Rat Portage so possibly he worked for the new C.P. Railway at one time. He had intended to homestead near Winnipeg but became discouraged because there were so many boats stranded away from the rivers, proving that there had been serious floods at one time. Before coming to Calgary he was employed driving supply wagons from Swift Current to Battleford during the Riel Rebellion. He told us that there was a crowd of men who left Winnipeg supposedly to work for the C.P.R. building crews in the Rocky Mountains. He said many of them left the train at various places all along the line — he jumped off at Calgary. This happened in 1885.

In December, 1886, he homesteaded SW¼-14-22-2-W5 at the south west corner of Red Deer Lake, seventeen miles south west of Calgary. Here he lived and proved up on the land. He bought the quarter to the east of this in 1900 with $400.00 sent from Aunt Jennie as well as money earned by digging wells for other people.

He was married on December 12, 1893, to Caroline Chaplin Paling of De Winton, by Canon Stocken, at Midnapore Anglican Church. Mrs. Wolley-Dod of De Winton was organist. Miss Paling had arrived in De Winton on Easter Monday, 1899, with her parents Richard and Marina. They homesteaded one mile north of De Winton where they also operated a store. They later built a larger store in De Winton. Mr. Pal-

ing taught school at Midnapore and Pine Creek. Caroline had also studied to become a teacher in her native England but did not care to teach in the lonely Alberta schools.

After their marriage in 1893, Mr. and Mrs. Hope resided and worked on their farm until their deaths — Joseph on October 13, 1935 and Caroline on May 16, 1936. Both are buried in the family plot in the Anglican Church Yard at Midnapore.

During their earlier years on the farm they encountered the usual problems of the pioneer families. Long distance to town, lack of hospital and doctors, and constantly, the lack of money. I can remember Dad working as foreman of a sewer gang in Calgary when the sewer lines were installed in downtown Calgary. While he was in Calgary he belonged to the first Firemans' Bucket Brigade.

Caroline (Paling) and Joseph Hope with Leonard Francis, 1897-98.

There were six children in our family:— Leonard Francis, who died of spinal meningitis when he was 2½ years old, and before I was born. He was ill for only a week and is buried at Midnapore. I, Gladys was next, then Hilda, Minnie, Richard and last, Gerald, who died in an accident at the age of 18 years and is also laid to rest at Midnapore.

We lost our first home to fire when I was about six years old. It was replaced by a three roomed house, built by Neil Brodie, and later added to when the new Red Deer Lake school was built and we had Eben Bremner, of Pine Creek, move the old school up beside our small home. This became our permanent home where we grew up.

We all attended Red Deer Lake School. Our nearest neighbours to walk to school with were the Watkins family. They came from Oregon and lived a mile north of our place.

We all had our chores on the farm and we learned to milk early. "Daisy" was a quiet old cow and we all learned to milk her. Mother made thousands of pounds of butter in her lifetime and sold it to customers in Calgary. Many of them lived in the "Parkhill" district. We also raised chickens so she sold eggs as well. There was always a large garden from which we sold vegetables. Mother made a weekly trip to Calgary with her produce and the evening before the trip was always a busy one. Vegetables had to be picked and washed and tied, chickens were killed, plucked and prepared for delivery. In the fall potatoes were picked and put into pits for a while. Later on they were sacked and a double wagonbox load was taken to Calgary to be sold to customers or to John Irwin's grocery store.

All the work was done with horses until the boys were old enough to buy a tractor and run it. On Sunday no unnecessary work was done. We attended the Anglican Church at Midnapore and the Presbyterian Church at Red Deer Lake. I was christened in the Anglican Church at Millarville and, as it is about fifteen miles away from our farm, I often wondered why. My parents belonged to the Southern Alberta Old Timers' Association and my sisters and I also belong. There is a link with the past in the events that are held in the Old Timers' Lodge.

Since grade eight was the highest grade taught at Red Deer Lake it was necessary to go to Calgary for high school. On Monday mornings we arose at four o'clock, Hilda fed, harnessed and hooked up the team to the democrat while Mother and I had breakfast and prepared for the trip to Calgary. It was fifteen miles to the south end loop of the Manchester, Tuxedo Park, street car line. I remember the "Spokane Flier" travelling along beside the highway. It was a through train from Spokane to Calgary. I trained as a teacher and was a member of the second last class able to take only a four month Normal course in order to get a second class teaching certificate. Mother changed her market day from Saturday to Friday in order to bring me home on week-ends. When Minnie's turn came to go to high school she trained to become a stenographer and while attending school worked for her room and board. One of the places that she worked was for the Jenkins of the Jenkins' Groceteria.

Hilda stayed on the farm and helped Dad through the war years. As was usual in war time Dad was unable to hire help. I can remember, while in Calgary, going to see train loads of young men leaving the C.P.R. station. Many of them did not return. These were the young men that might have been hired to help with the farm work. Hilda later married Ted Payne. They had three daughters and one son. Mabel (Murray) lives in Delburne, has two boys. Ernest Payne married Gloria Reimer, he is a trucker and they live on his parents' farm. Margaret (Heer, Doble), lives at Rainier, has four boys and two girls. Doreen (Raho), trained as a Nurses' Aid, lives at Stettler and has four girls.

Richard finished grade eight and then went to work on the farm. He eventually took over the farm, where he still lives, and became a successful, thrifty farmer. He never married.

Minnie married Harold Nelson while she was working in Calgary. Later she and Harold moved to California with Harold's father. They have no children. Over the years they almost always visited my parents once a year.

Ted Green and I were married in 1919. Ted was a water well driller for almost fifty years. He covered a large part of Central Alberta in his work. We celebrated our fiftieth Wedding Anniversary on April 4, 1970, with family and friends of Calgary, Edmonton and our surrounding district. We had five children. Ernest, our baby died at the age of ten months. Herbert, a bachelor, served in the Armed Services in

Hilda, Minnie and Gladys Hope about 1905.

World War 2, lives in Lousana and farms east of the town. Gordon, married Gladys Lee, they have three girls and live and farm four miles east of Lousana. Dorothy (McWhan) lives at Lousana, has seven children. Lois (Craig), lives at Fairview in the Peace River country, has three children.

As we grew up on the farm there were many things that we did that would seem far removed from ordinary life today. Water had to be hauled and heated for the washing. Ironing was done with "sad irons" heated on the kitchen range. Cows were milked by hand and the cream raised in "creamers" and then skimmed off the top. I remember our first cream separator was a "Sharples". One time when Minnie was changing a full pail for an empty one, her hair caught in the whirling bowl. Mother had to cut all of her hair off before she could be released and she had a sore head for a long time. Butter was made in a huge wooden churn usually about three times a week, making as much as thirty-five pounds to a churning. Another distasteful chore was cleaning and trimming the coal-oil lamps.

The first telephone that I remember was installed in the Red Deer Lake School. It was put in the school for the use of the community. I don't remember the year.

I can remember Canon Gale coming from De Winton to preach in our Anglican church at Red Deer Lake. We had a friendship with the Gale family that has lasted through the years.

Dad hauled coal from Midnapore for the "Home Comfort" range that stood in the kitchen. There was a small coal mine at Priddis and some of our coal was brought from there and sometimes Mother brought some home in the back of the democrat.

There are two beautiful spruce trees growing where Mother had a little flower garden. The largest one, taken from the patch of willows on the farm, was planted by Richard, Gerald and I, in memory of our little Ernie. Later when we lost Gerald, Richard and my children and I planted the other one, a memorial to him. I hope all of our children will notice those trees for there may come a time when they do not belong to the farm. We all hope that any future owners of our home will come to love and appreciate it as we have done.

JOSEPH AND ANNA (EICHLER) HUCK

Joseph Huck of Calhan, Colorado and Anna Eichler of Ludington, Michigan were married in Calgary in the summer of 1912. They moved to the Red Deer Lake district in 1924, along with their seven children, five sons and two daughters. Here, they rented the Bruketa place until 1929 when Mr. Huck purchased the Estelle farm, across the lake, to which he moved his family. Joe Huck farmed the "Home Place", as it was called by the family, until his demise in 1966. He was predeceased by his wife, Anna, in 1949. A son, Lyle, passed away in 1969 and a granddaughter, Anne Louise Wilkins, in 1957.

It may be of some interest to the readers and to those who knew Mr. and Mrs. Huck as to how it came about that Joe Huck first came to Alberta in 1909.

Joseph Huck was born in Washburn, Illinois, one of eight children, where his parents, Joseph and Angelina, farmed. His father later moved the family to Calhan, Colorado, just south of Denver, and continued farming. Joe Huck's father bought the very first "Hart Parr" tractor which the five sons learned to operate and repair expertly. It was in the spring of 1909 that Joe Huck and his brothers read in the Denver paper that Hart Parr tractors were being shipped to Alberta, Canada and that experienced operators and expert repairmen were much needed. So it followed that all five brothers packed, came to Alberta and were hired, at five dollars a day, which was considered an unbelievably good wage in those days. They would work, summers, in Canada, going back home to Calhan for the winter months. The brothers all liked Canada, especially Joe, who found the Calgary area much like his home in Colorado.

The older brothers married and eventually settled down around Denver. Joe, however, along with his brother, Edward, and Ed's wife, Cora, came back up to Calgary in the spring of 1912 and rented farmland in the Carseland area. It was that summer of 1912 that Joe brought his fiancee, Anna Eichler, from Michigan to Calgary and they were married. Ed Huck and his wife moved back to Colorado in the fall of 1912 but Joe and Anna stayed and eventually became Canadian citizens.

While renting land and farming it in the Carseland, Mossleigh and Beiseker districts, from 1912 to 1924, Joe also broke virgin prairie sod with a '110' Case steam tractor, later changing to a Rumely Oil Pull.

The Hucks moved from Mossleigh to the Red Deer Lake area in 1924 and rented the Bruketa place. Although happy and liking the people in the Red Deer Lake district, they were still farming rented land. Hearing that there was farmland available in the Grande Prairie area and at a reasonable price, Mr. and Mrs. Huck motored up north in 1928 to look the land over. They returned fully prepared to move the family up there. However, that fall the Estelle farm, across the lake, came up for sale, Mr. Huck made an offer to purchase, it was accepted. So it was, in the spring of 1929, they packed up their belongings, and by now, seven children moved to their new place. It was a joyous occasion, for now, after seventeen years of marriage, Joe and Anna were finally realizing a dream, to own their own farm.

Shortly after this move and to supplement the farm income they started raising foxes, a venture that involved the whole family. Along with the farming in the summer and the year round work of raising the foxes, leisure time was an unknown luxury.

By now, the depression had really set in, crops were poor and money was scarce. The farm and the foxes still did not produce enough income to feed and clothe a family of nine and also meet the payments for the land. So it was that Joe Huck, with his knowledge of operating machinery, took a position of building roads for the municipality. This he did from 1932 until 1939. Building roads was summer work, so was farming, this meant that the farming fell to the older boys. Mrs. Huck, besides doing the housework spent innumerable hours caring for the foxes. Thus it was, that Anna Huck, deservedly, and with much pride, wore a fox fur stole and matching muff, that her husband had made up for her, as a gift, one Christmas. Later, the two daughters, Pauline and Alberta, were to receive the same type of gifts before the family gave up fox farming.

Though the depression years were rough and tough on most everyone, they were not entirely without the happy times. There was badminton, dances and Whist drives at the Red Deer Lake hall. There were picnics in the summer along with ball games. A hockey team in winter when the Red Deer Lake team played teams from neighbouring districts. To this day, the Huck family laughs hilariously about the time, the always joking, always jovial, Albert McKevitt, a grown man, attended a Whist drive with the greatest case of measles you ever saw, much to the consternation of the mothers who had taken their children, too young to leave at home. Then, there was the weekly trip to town for supplies at Williams Brothers which, at that time, was a genuinely 'General Store', selling everything; meat, groceries, hardware, dry goods, etc. The wives would place their orders while the men visited, talking farming, politics and any other subject that brought laughter. The kids could hardly wait to get home from school on Thursdays, which was grocery day, for there was always a sack of candy, thrown in free by Williams Brothers, a personal touch unheard of today.

The seven Huck children all attended Red Deer Lake school and Midnapore high school. The transportation to school was horse and buggy in the summer and horse and sleigh in the winter. The oldest boy was the driver and was responsible for the safety of the younger ones.

As the children grew up, Sundays, the Huck place would be bursting at the seams with neighbouring boys and girls. Mom was always prepared to put another leaf in the old dining room table for the extras who stayed for dinner, even though this sometimes entailed two settings.

Pauline and Alberta are both graduate nurses of the Vegreville Hospital. Pauline, the first married, continued hospital nursing for many years. Alberta, after graduating, became a stewardess for Trans Canada Air Lines until her marriage.

When the second world war broke out in 1939, Lyle, the eldest son, joined the Army. Joseph Junior (Tad),

Orville and Lee joined the R.C.A.F., Robert, the last one to leave home, joined the R.C.N. in 1942.

With all the children grown and gone, the farm paid for, Anna and Joe had time, at long last to enjoy many things they had foregone through the hard years. There were trips to Michigan and to Colorado, visiting relatives. There were sight seeing trips to Banff when relatives came up to visit them. Mom, who was an excellent seamstress, had been kept busy through the years sewing clothes for the family, now she had time to go back to her beloved crocheting. Before her marriage, she had written a column, for a Milwaukee paper, on crocheting and many of the family still treasure her work.

When the war ended in 1945, the children, nearly all married now, came back to settle in Calgary. The "Home Place" once again became a gathering place for children and grandchildren. Every Sunday the house was alive with merriment. The daughters and the boys' wives, kept up, to some extent, the family gatherings after Mom's untimely death in 1949.

What was alway known as Hucks' farm, is now broken up into small acreages, the land is there but the landscape, now dotted with houses, will never be the same.

"Remember when", is a common phrase as the family laughingly reminisces about the childhood days. Memories and photographs are dearly treasured with much love and gratitude to our parents, Mom and Dad.

Joe and Anna Huck never once regretted settling in Canada and farming in the Red Deer Lake area. It was their home for many years!

ALEX AND BLANCHE (GLOVER) INGRAM — by Keith Ingram

Alex Ingram was born in the town of Keith, Banffshire, Scotland in 1884. Fifth in a family of ten, he spent his early years on the family farm. In 1909, he immigrated to New York and drove crane in a stone yard for his uncle. However, this inside job didn't provide any companionship with his beloved Clydesdale horses. In 1910 he came west to Calgary and started a cartage business which he operated until 1936. A favorite practice for Alex was to buy a bronc at a weekly auction sale, break it over the week-end, work it on the streets all week and return it to the sale the next week as a broke horse at a handsome profit. One of Alex's earliest jobs was hauling dirt for the Centre Street Bridge construction project. Another big job, in later years, was hauling materials for the Glenmore Dam. In 1929, in step with the times, he augmented his horse "fleet" with a Ford truck, which, incidentally, is still in good working order.

In 1915, he married Blanche Glover who immigrated, with her family, from New Brunswick to Calgary, in 1908.

In 1936, Alex, Blanche and their three sons, George, Keith and Allan, moved to the Red Deer Lake District after buying W½-35-22-2-W5 from Dr. Hackney who had purchased it from Bert Stobo in 1918.

Alex was keenly interested in breeding and showing Clydesdale horses. In 1915 he followed the major show circuit of Western Canada and triumphed at all nine shows with his four and six horse teams. He was a regular exhibitor at the Calgary Exhibition and Stampede and at the Royal Winter Fair in Toronto. Alex also judged shows on numerous occasions, the probable highlight being the invitation in 1955 to judge at his hometown, in the heartland of the Clydesdale horse, in Scotland.

In the days of horsepower, the farming was done with up to twelve horses in one hitch. A sight to behold, but quite a chore to assemble and dis-assemble. After the appearance of our first tractor the horses gradually diminished to only a few show pieces. Today, a few sets of work harness, some heavy horse-shoes and a few weathered single-trees are about the only nostalgic remembrances of the historic horse era.

A registered herd of Aberdeen Angus cattle was started in 1940 from three bred calves and a bull calf, purchased from the CPR herd at Coaldale, Alberta. From this nucleus the herd grew and supplied the foundation stock to many breeders in Western Canada. The herd is still in production on the farm which is operated by Keith and his family.

THE KAI FAMILY — by their Grandchildren

Mr. and Mrs. David Kai came to the Red Deer Lake District from Millard, Nebraska with their family in 1903. They had seven children, two sons, Charles and Henry and five daughters; Emma and Augusta, who came with them, Elizabeth and Dora who remained in Nebraska, Kathrina, her husband, William Thiessen, and their eldest five children; Emma, Anna, William, John and Ella, came to the Red Deer Lake District the previous year, 1902.

Mr. and Mrs. Kai settled on SE¼-30-22-1-W5, which was known as the Henderson Place. Charles, his wife, Elizabeth and two children returned to Nebraska the same year. Henry married Josephine Duncan of Pine Creek and they had two children, Grace and John he lived in Calgary until his death in 1909. Emma married Walter Birney and they had six children; Charles, Merle, Bud, Pearl and Viola, another baby passed away in infancy. Augusta married Hugh Shaw and had four daughters; Helen and Exhilda, (twins), Myrtle and Ruth.

Mr. and Mrs. Kai moved from the Henderson Place to the old Schroeder Place which is SE of the intersec-

Mr. Kai and grandson, Roy.

tion of Highway 22 and the Macleod Trail, from there they moved to a small parcel of land from Dan Patton's, west of Patton's house, with access to the north-south road allowance. They were building a new house on the place when Mrs. Kai died in 1912. She is buried in Pine Creek Cemetery. Mr. Kai stayed with his married daughters for a while then he went back to Nebraska in 1923 and died there in 1925.

WILLIAM FREDERICK AND WINNIFRED LATTER — by Roy Latter

William Frederick Latter was born in Croydon, England in 1884 and, at the age of twenty-five, he came to Canada, via New York and Chicago, where he worked at the Studebaker plant for a year. Then the call of "go west young man to the land of opportunity" hit him and he headed for Brandon, Manitoba. (Where no one ever harvested less than fifty bushels of wheat per acre.) Things were pretty well settled up here so he moved on to Edmonton where, in 1910, he took up a homestead sixty miles north at Tawatinaw. He built a cabin and got things settled a bit and then sent back to Croydon for the girl he left behind to come out. In the spring of 1913 Winnifred arrived in Edmonton, fresh from the big city, to start married life on the homestead.

Their experiences in those first years would have sent most women back to Mother. All their supplies were hauled from Edmonton by wagon, drawn by oxen. The country around Tawatinaw, at that time, was covered in large trees tamarack and spruce, and the land was wet and boggy. Once when they were camping out, a bear slit the tent, in which they were sleeping, from top to bottom. One day when Winnifred was out riding she was surrounded by a pack of wolves. The two dogs kept running under the horse for protection and, although she carried a gun, she was too scared to use it. The wolves followed them the three miles back to the cabin. Every fall during hunting season they would hang a lantern on the gable of the house and many a lost hunter would turn up guided by the light. They once had a man stay with them three days before he left and one week later the mounties arrived on his trail. It seems he had committed a murder in Montreal and had been running ever since. The folks always claimed that he was a gentleman, well mannered and well educated. The cabin was a stopping place for game wardens, mounties, hunters and the like, as they were the only English people there at the time.

In 1916 their first son was born and they called him Clifford. In 1917 they moved out and went to Champion, Alberta where they farmed the Bob Tyler place for three years. These were hard years, the prices were high, but hail and grasshoppers took their toll. They paid seventy five dollars a ton for hay the cattle wouldn't eat. The grasshoppers, when they came, turned the country into a moving mass of green. Dad would throw out a wagon load of poison while Mother drove the team. When the wagon was empty the horses could hardly pull the wagon back; the ground was so slippery with dead grasshoppers. The 'hoppers never went around anything, up telephone poles and down the other side, over buildings, barns, corrals, everything turned green, eating everything as they went. They left no garden, no crop and no grass behind them. In the third year their second son, Roy, was born. This, I guess, was the straw that broke the camel's back for we packed up and left for Calgary.

Things went along very well for a spell and both boys received their education here. Then, when the depression was at its worst, the fall of '31 saw Dad out of a job just like thousands of others. For a year or so he worked wherever he could — for a while on Glenmore Dam. Then, in the spring of 1933, we went back farming and took over the S½ 35-22-2-W5, south west of Midnapore.

There was no road in at that time, just a wagon trail through the neighbour's land. For three years, we stayed home if it rained, and, whenever we went to town in the winter we either cleared most of the snow off with a V-plow drawn by horses or we shovelled our way out and in. When we went visiting we could mostly walk the one, or three miles, depending on which neighbour we were visiting. The first year the family stayed out on the farm and Dad was working in town; he would come out at night and leave before daylight in the morning. We heard later that the neighbours thought that we were bootleggers because everyone came and went under the cover of darkness. We thought this was quite funny because neither Dad nor Mom smoked nor drank!

At that time rabbits were plentiful and Cliff and I used to shoot them and sell them for fox meat. This kept us in pocket money for a year or two until the

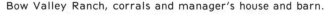

Bow Valley Ranch, corrals and manager's house and barn.

Fred and Winnifred Latter and sons at old Midnapore Bridge, 1930.

depression eased up a bit. Summers we used to play ball and we had a pretty good league going locally. Red Deer Lake, Westoe, Priddis, Millarville, Midnapore and De Winton all played and, on odd years, Glenmore, Okotoks and Turner Valley played too. These ball games were the focal point of the community and if we got fewer than forty spectators, it was a poor turnout. This was quite good as we were all farmers and had to get our chores done and have supper and then be at the game by 6:30 p.m. on Wednesdays and 2:00 p.m. on Sundays.

In the winter we played hockey for Millarville and played against teams from Turner Valley, Kew and Westoe. Dances were held in the local schools; Alexandra, Ballyhamage and Fordville. Music for these dances was supplied by Gerry Berry and his accordion, with his wife on the piano. The McNab boys, and Harold Anderson and the Jack Pine Knots used to play at the Fordville school. To these dances everyone went, Dad, Mom and all the kids. When the kids were played out they went to sleep on the benches until 3 o'clock, when the folks went home. We travelled by saddle horse, sleigh and car and I can remember Mrs. Cannon, Helen, Dave and Neville coming across country one night on snow shoes. Soon the school dances shut down and we would go to Red Deer Lake, Priddis and De Winton to dance. By this time we were dancing to three and four piece orchestras and the halls were packed.

In 1939 the war broke out and a lot of the boys joined up and went overseas. Cliff joined the airforce and, in 1942, married Bernice Eckersley and they had one daughter, Joan, now married to Jim Lisoway, living in Calgary. In 1945 Cliff came back from the war and moved to a warmer climate on the west coast. During this time I remained on the farm with the folks.

In 1948 I married Grace Barkley from Red Deer Lake and, in 1949, my folks retired to Calgary. On September 28, 1950 Frances Winnifred passed away in Calgary at the age of sixty two and, the following February 11, 1951 Fred Latter passed away at the age of sixty six. They had lived and worked hard all their lives and they were part of the pioneer stock that opened up the country.

Grace and I still have the farm and we have raised our family here. Four girls and a boy; Peggy married to Herb Elhorn with one son, Colin, in Edmonton. Judy married to Earl Shermerhorn with a girl and a boy, Shelley and Dan, living in Calgary. Kathy working in Edmonton and Colleen and Dean working in Calgary.

It used to be twenty miles to the city limits, now it's just six. My how things have changed!

THE LLOYDS

Benjamin Simmonds Lloyd and Jane Elizabeth Eld were married February twenty-seventh 1879 in London England. In 1884 they set sail for Canada with their three children Harry, Gertrude and Ralph. On May the twentieth after a long tedious journey, they arrived at their destination in what is now known as the Red Deer Lake district, where they joined Ben's brother, Richard, who had come out the year before.

Three weeks later, Edric was born in a little log shack with a sod roof. This little one-roomed shack was to be the Lloyd home for several years. Hermione was also born there. At the time of her birth, there was a heavy rainstorm which lasted for several days. The roof leaked and the only dry spot was occupied by a trunk on which Mrs. Lloyd sat nursing the new baby and trying to keep the other children dry. That was pioneering! Over the years three more children Ronald, Bert and Joel arrived to join the happy family.

The Lloyd brothers had planned on supplying the C.P.R. with charcoal but discovered the available wood was unsuitable for charcoal burning commercially so they turned to ranching instead. Ben was a good horseman and many good horses, both heavy and light, wore the BL brand on the left shoulder. The Lloyd cattle brand was BL on the left ribs.

Times were hard, my mother (Hermione) remembered having to stay in bed many times when it was cold because there were not enough clothes to keep all the children warm. Mrs. Lloyd knitted all the stockings and socks as well as mitts for everyone in the family. Yard goods were bought by the bolt from which Mrs. Lloyd made the clothing.

There were many prairie fires which kept the brush burnt and the settlers busy fighting fire to save their homes and livestock. There were no fences and very little cultivated land.

During the Rebellion of 1885, and for some time after, my grandmother used to carry a loaded revolver in her apron pocket for protection. However, the Indians remained on friendly terms with the settlers. They used to lay their arms on the ground when they came to visit to show that they came in friendship.

When the children started school, Mr. Lloyd would hitch Old Maud up to a stone boat, head her in the direction of the house where Mrs. Lloyd would tuck the children up and head the old mare towards the school where the children would turn her around and send her home. After school, the faithful mare would bring them home.

The Lloyd household was known for its hospitality. They baked bread every day and my grandmother, being a religious woman, twice on Saturdays. At first there was no fresh fruit, except the wild berries which were quite plentiful as a rule. Eventually, Ontario apples began to appear, they were shipped in barrels. People planted big gardens which did not always thrive due to many hazards including hail, rodents, cattle and drought.

The Lloyd property included the S.W. ½ sec. 24-22-2-W5, the N.W.¼ Sec 24-22-2-W5 acquired by Mrs. Lloyd from Frank Fairy and the quarter section now owned and occupied by Mrs. McConkey. The N.E.¼ sec 24-22-2-W5 was owned by Richard although all the Lloyds lived there for many years after moving from the sod-roofed shack into the newly built house before Ronald was born.

Harry went to the South African War. Sometime after his return he went to England to see his uncle, Charlie Lloyd. In November 1908 Harry died in England of diptheria.

Ronald became a civil engineer. He rode the range, became a ditch rider for the Irrigation Development. He went to Magrath where he was in charge of irrigation for the C.P.R.. In 1913 he married Gladys Stallard and they have two sons Maurice and Charles. Later when the Alberta Government took over the the C.P.R., Ronald kept on with his work in irrigation receiving many promotions. He is survived by his widow who lives in Coaldale.

Bert worked at home until the outbreak of World War I when he went overseas with the C.M.RS. He served with the Lord Strathcona's Horse, was transferred to the Airforce, and served in Egypt until he was invalided back to England where he died October twelfth 1918.

Joel worked at home until he married Bertha Young and went into the Land Department with Lott and Company where he worked for many years before going into business on his own. There are two daughters Barbara and Isabel. Joel died September 25, 1945.

The other children will be discussed elsewhere.

In 1908 or 1909, a new house was built on Ben's land at the east end of the Poplar Bush. This house is still in use. The property was known as Seighford Ranch.

The land on which the Red Deer Lake Hall stands was a gift from Ben to the community. The school is also on land once owned by the Lloyds.

During World War I, Mrs. Lloyd did a great deal of work for the Red Cross. In later years she continued to knit for them. It was seldom that she was without her knitting needles.

When Ralph returned from the War, he operated the farm for his father who was in poor health. Ben died November twenty-fourth 1921 after a long illness. Ralph farmed the place in conjunction with his mother until her death March twenty-fifth 1941 at the age of eighty-three. For many years previously she had made her home with the Biddells, visiting her other children for short periods but always going back to Gertie's.

J. E. R. LLOYD

John Edric Richard Lloyd, fourth child of Ben and Jane Lloyd, was born June 12, 1884 just three weeks after the arrival in Calgary of the family from London, England. He was the first white baby born in the district.

Ben Lloyd, his father, homesteaded south-west of Calgary on the north-east side of Lloyd Lake, presently known as Red Deer Lake. A sod-roofed log cabin was called home.

Education at that time, consisted of a one room school with teachers of varied credentials and talents. Self-education became a major part of learning.

After leaving the school occupations were varied — cutting and hauling wood for charcoal and firewood and logs for building, and routine ranch chores. Edric later worked as a mange inspector for the government. This meant long hours in the saddle, going from herd to herd checking animals and O.K.ing dipping vats. The territory was quite extensive reaching south and east of Calgary.

September the eighteenth 1912, J. E. R. married Dorothy Grey, eldest daughter of Sir Henry and Lady Grey, Enville Hall, Worcestershire. They made their home on the west side of Red Deer Lake on the old John Bell property. There is one daughter married in Montana. She has two sons and two daughters.

Edric raised beef cattle of Shorthorn and Hereford breeding along with the usual farm and ranch milk cows, pigs and poultry. He was known for his purebred Shires and Clydes, and he also raised good half-bred saddle stock.

After some years, Edric moved to Calgary, where, in 1947 he married Mary W. O. Scott who survives. During this time he was associated with Webbs Seeds and Crown Feed. He was also employed as an estate appraiser and in oil leasing properties. At one time Edric served several terms as school trustee at Red Deer Lake.

Although Edric resided in Calgary for many years, it was not until shortly before his death in 1970 that he sold that farm which Brian Biddell, his nephew, had been operating for him.

R. E. A. AND HELEN (SWINBURNE) LLOYD

Ralph Ernest Alwyne Lloyd was born in London, England on December 10, 1882. He was the third child of Mr. and Mrs. Benjamin Simmonds Lloyd. Early in 1884 he travelled with his parents, his older brother and his sister, and arrived in the Midnapore district on May 20 of that year.

Ralph received his school education in the local one room country school. At the age of 18 he joined the Militia and took military training.

Upon the outbreak of World War 1, he went

overseas to the Front with the "Canadian Mounted Rifles", where the C.M.R.'s were attached to the Lord Strathcona Horse. After the end of World War 1, without serious mishap, he returned to his parents at Seighford Ranch, Midnapore, with the rank of Major, conferred on him by the "Canadian Light Horse". Later he received the rank of Lieut. Col. with the "Fifteenth Canadian Light Horse".

In 1921 he married Helen Swinburne, a specialist teacher in art, who was born and educated in Edinburgh, Scotland; the daughter of a Scottish mother and an Icelandic father, and a graduate of the Edinburgh College of Art.

Sadness filled their hearts when their first born child, Benjamin passed away before he reached the age of one year.

Francis, their second son, now resides in Calgary and is employed by the Calgary School Board. He has two daughters, Kathleen (Mrs. Stanley Maksymiw) and Elaine. His wife Anne came to Canada from Lancashire, England.

Eleanor (Nell) is married to Dean Oltean, a Saskatchewan grain farmer. Her paintings in oils have found their way to private and public collections in a number of countries.

Edric has two sons, Randolph and Christopher, and a daughter, Jennifer. He resides in Spokane, Washington and is a professional engineer.

Ralph Lloyd, rancher, with Mr. and Mrs. Tony Pretty Young Man. Sarcee Indians, 1930's.

Ralph, Helen, their family, Helen's mother Mrs. Sveinbjornsson and her brother Dr. Thordure Swinburne spent many years at Seighford Ranch, where Ralph engaged in mixed farming. As busy as life became, both he and his wife found limited time to devote to their interests in the arts. Helen continued to paint; she found great joy in the many wild prairie flowers which she depicted in water colour. Ralph also liked to dabble in paint when time permitted. They both enjoyed writing poems, which were published in the local newspapers from time to time.

World War 11 broke out. Ralph was keen to enlist, but his health was failing and he felt unable. He suffered a painful illness, without hope, but he bore it bravely, like a good soldier. In 1943 he passed away,

and was buried in the cemetery of the Midnapore Anglican Church.

Helen has resided in Calgary for over twenty-eight years. In spite of being confined to a wheelchair, and suffering from failing eyesight, she does her best to continue to paint and write. At the age of eighty she compiled her poems and published a little book entitled "Cloth of Gold and Other Poems".

As a tribute to all good friends and neighbours of the Red Deer Lake and Midnapore districts she writes:

I came to Midnapore, a bride,
In nineteen twenty-one.
I walked upon the prairie wide,
A stranger to Alberta sun.
Still within my heart I hold
Memories fond and dear.
Kindness never is forgotten,
It grows within the heart each year.

RICHARD LLOYD

Richard Lloyd left England for Canada with the Samuel Shaw family. They arrived at the end of steel in what is now known as Swift Current. From there, they travelled by ox-cart to Midnapore arriving some time in 1883. Richard went on a bit further to what is now the Red Deer Lake district. For a while Dick, as he was usually called, worked on the survey. In 1884 he persuaded his brother Ben and family to join him.

The Richard Lloyd homestead, the N.E. ¼ of section 24-22-2-W5, later pre-empted the quarter now owned by Norman Waddell. All the Lloyds lived as one family in a two-storey log house they built on Dick's homestead. Water was scarce and was drawn by a pail on a rope and a windlass from a dug well. A good number of years later, Dick had a well drilled a short distance away which turned out to be an artesian well.

In 1908 or '09 Dick went to England where he married Rose Brooks. At this time the Ben Lloyds moved into their new home across the creek.

Rose and Dick had no children but brought up Douglas Scholefield, Dick's great nephew, whose Mother had died when he was a small child.

In 1924, Rose and Dick sold out moving back to England where Dick outlived Rose, dying in his hundreth year.

Douglas attended Red Deer Lake School, then Champion College in Regina coming back to the Priddis district where he married Leona Storey. There are two children from this marriage. A number of years after Leona's passing Douglas married Margaret Ames. They have eight children and reside in Calgary.

ALLISTER AND ETHEL MASSIE

Alex Massie married Jessie Scott in 1908. She had come to Spokane, Washington, U.S.A. in 1903. She had also lived a while in Portland, Oregon. Alex lived in Spokane and Allister was born there in 1910 then, sometime in 1911, they came to Calgary and the Massie brothers had a cement business. They did most of the cement work done in the Mission part of Calgary.

Allister, his mother and dad went for a trip to Scotland and they were going to come back on the

Titanic. They had their tickets but the mother refused to go on the ship as she said it was going to sink. They took the next ship out.

While they lived in Spokane the grandfather, Peter Massie, died and was buried there. Allister's mother died when his sister, Jessie, was born in 1914 and Grandmother Massie and her sister, Aunt Gena, looked after the children until his father married Julia Robinson, when Allister was seven years old. Both Grandmother Massie and Allister are buried in Union Cemetery, Calgary as well as his father, uncles and aunts and stepmother. Allister died of a heart attack in August, 1957 and left his wife, Ethel, (whom he married in 1934) and four sons; Peter Allister, Donald Alexander, William Scott and Kenneth Edwin.

Peter is living in Red Deer, Alberta. He worked for Goodyear for twenty-four years and is now selling real estate. Don is working with Seismic services, Scott is farming at Caroline, Alberta and Ken is with White Ram concrete. Allister's widow is living in Didsbury, Alberta.

GEORGINA MASSIE

Georgina was born March 21, 1879 in Aberdeenshire, Scotland, coming to Spokane, Washington in 1910 and with the rest of the family to Calgary in 1912.

Georgina never married and kept house for her brother William.

With no transportation of her own she never minded walking to visit relatives and neighbors even in later years of her life.

She was an active member of Westbourne Baptist Church in Calgary.

Georgina passed away in December, 1949.

MR. AND MRS. JOHN MASSIE

Mr. and Mrs. John Massie and their two sons, Peter and Jack, moved to the Midnapore district in 1913. They farmed the McArthur place and, in 1914, farmed the Riddell place. Peter and Jack attended Red Deer Lake School from 1914 to 1920.

In 1920 the John Massies moved to Vulcan. Mr. Massie passed away in 1956 at the age of 78 and Mrs. Massie in January, 1969, she was 86.

Peter and his wife, Isabel, live in Calgary. Their daughter, Anne (Mrs. Laverne Harder) has two children; Tim and Janice.

Jack and Lydia live in the Madden district and have four daughters and one son. Phyllis (Mrs. Melvin Farquharson), Calgary; two daughters, Terry (Mrs. Brian Wilson), Madden and Jean (Mrs. Keith Cochrane), son Barry, daughter, Judy, Crossfield. Doris (Mrs. Don Wyman), Calgary, one daughter, Cathy Anne. Joyce (Mrs. Harry Roth), Madden, son, Ken, and daughter, Debbie. Dale is married to Beth Rosenberger from Balzac, lives in Calgary and has two daughters, Kim and Shannon.

PETER MASSIE — by Wm. K. Massie

My father, Peter, was born in Aberdeenshire, Scotland, July 9, 1876. He came from Bonnie Scotland with his parents Mr. and Mrs. Peter Massie Sr. and brother Bill, and sister Georgina, to join his older

Mr. and Mrs. Peter Massie Sr. and Family — 1895. l. to r. Georgina, Peter, Rebecca, Alice, Alex (back row) John, Mrs. Massie, Jim, Peter Sr., Bill.

sister, Mrs. Rebecca McKay and brothers Sandy, Jack and Jim in Spokane, Washington in 1910. They formed a cement business known as Massie Bros.

In 1912, they came to Calgary with their contracting equipment which consisted of horses, dump wagons, wheelbarrows and shovels. They continued in the contracting business laying sidewalks in the Roxboro district when it was being developed as a country suburb of the city.

The brothers rented the MacArthur Place to winter their horses (S.W. 31-22-1-5) and soon after my father, his parents and sister Georgina, moved to the Gregg Place, a parcel of (S.W. 30-22-1-5). His parents, Peter Massie Sr. died in 1914 and his mother in 1919.

My father married Emma Dickinson in 1917. She was born in Otley, Yorkshire, England in 1890, arriving in Calgary 1911 with her sister Sadie, Mrs. Joe Standish. My mother worked for several pioneer families

Peter Massie family: L. to R. at back Bill and Peter. Front row, L. to R. Flora, Nell, Hazel, Margaret, Mrs. Emma Massie.

449

in the Priddis district before returning to England for a short time. She came back to Canada and shortly after met and married Peter. The day they were getting married they started to walk to Midnapore to take the train to Calgary and on the way one of the McKevitt boys gave them a ride in their democrat to their destination.

They had two children Flora and I before moving to the Priddis district in 1920 where we lived for a year before returning to the Patton Place (S.W. 30-22-1-5) in the Red Deer Lake district which he rented and later bought where Margaret, Nel and Hazel were born.

He lived on this place until retiring. During this time he bought the Cuffling Place — three quarters in the Ballyhamage area and Elliot Place (N.W. ¼ 19-22-2-5). He also rented the Allan Ruttan Place (W ¼ 20-22-1-5) for many years.

He often walked the fifteen miles to Calgary, with his faithful dog, driving cattle to the stockyards.

This was the beginning of his cattle ranching and feed lot operation. He also raised sheep and purebred Herefords for many years. He devoted his life to hard work and contributed much to the community.

In 1936 my mother passed away at the age of forty-six which was a great loss not only to her family but to the community as well. She had faithfully attended the Red Deer Lake Church where she played the organ.

Dad married Lillian Pearl Hargreaves of Innisfail in 1942 and retired in 1947, moving to Calgary. His interest continued in farming and livestock until shortly before his death in 1966 at the age of eighty-nine.

FLORA GEORGINA (MASSIE) ANDERSON — by Mrs. V. Anderson

Flora Georgina, born December 22, 1917, the eldest daughter of Peter and Emma Massie.

The formative years of my life was spent in the Red Deer Lake district, where I attended the little, brown, one roomed school. I think much can be said in praise of the country school and its teachers. One of my teachers had an enrollment of forty-five children and she taught grades one to nine with pupils in every grade. We had already gleaned a wealth of knowledge by the time we reached the ninth grade! The strap was always handy and most everyone was introduced to it sooner or later.

When Mother died in March, 1936, from a siege with pneumonia, I did not return to Western Canada High, but spent the next few years at home. After Dad remarried in 1942, I took a business course in Calgary. It was while I was employed as a tele-typist with C.P. Telegraph that I met Vair Anderson. We were married in December, 1944 and, for the next year and a half, we lived in Millarville where Vair was the principal of the Sheep Creek School.

Returning to the Calgary district, we lived the next sixteen years on Anderson Road where our two sons were born, Bruce in 1947 and Byron in 1952.

Our next move was to the Priddis district, that beautiful foothills country was to be our home for the next eleven years.

Both our sons are married and now live in Clearwater, B.C. where Bruce has a medical practice and Byron is employed as an electrician.

My husband and I moved out to this picturesque, North Thompson Valley, too, in 1974.

WILLIAM KENNETH MASSIE

I was born in Calgary, August 1919, the second child of Peter and Emma Massie. I am still living on the same quarter section where I was born, except for one year when the family lived at the "Hilliker Place" in Priddis in 1920. I attended Red Deer Lake School, finishing grade eight at the age of thirteen. This was the beginning of the livestock business for me.

I worked with my dad until his retirement in 1947. He was a hard worker and expected the same of his family. I questioned this when I was younger but in later years appreciated it.

My father bought cattle throughout the district and surrounding area. Consequently, my sister Flora, aged ten, and myself, aged eight, spent many hours trailing cattle home and to the stockyards in Calgary.

We had a variety of experiences. I remember one time when Dad bought a carload of hogs (150) at Lethbridge and had them shipped to Midnapore. He took Flora and me by car to Midnapore and left us to chase the hogs home. We got along fine until they saw the straw stacks in Shaw's field. In fifteen minutes, every straw stack had pigs around it, while others were headed back to the boxcar. Carrie Shaw and Brian Bidell saw our troubles and came to our rescue! They helped us gather them back into one bunch and we were on our way again.

Another time, I trailed forty cows with their calves from Calgary to south of Turner Valley. It took three days and I was paid ten dollars. There were many times the neighbors asked me in for tea — especially Mrs. Harrison who lived on Anderson Road east of 24th Street.

In 1941, I married Helen McCuaig, born in Kerrobert, Saskatchewan, daughter of Jack and Belle McCuaig. In 1935, her family moved to Sundre Alberta and Helen finished her grade school in Rockwood. She came to Calgary in 1938 to attend Western Canada High and Garbutts Business College.

We have five children. The eldest daughter Sharon, now Mrs. Dale Argetsinger, of Portland, Oregon, attended Western Canada High and later received her R.N. degree at Calgary General Hospital and her B.Sc. at Portland State University. She has continued working in Public Health.

Carol, now Mrs. Art Kurtz of Calgary, attended Henry Wise Wood. They have two sons, Michael and Mark. They have a business in Claresholm.

William Jr. (Bill), now married to Cheryl Cutler, attended Henry Wise Wood, Mount Royal College and Colorado State University where he received his B.Sc. in Agriculture. He is in business with me making the third generation on the same farm.

Gail, now Mrs. Danny Finley of DeWinton, attended Lord Beaverbrook. They have one son, Danny Jr. and have a business in Nanton.

Our youngest son David, is still at home and is attending Red Deer Lake School.

All our children attended Red Deer Lake School and were active in the 4-H Beef Club.

We showed at the Calgary Fat Stock Show and each

had the honor to win the D.E. Black Shield and other championships throughout the years.

We purchased the Patton Quarter (S.E. 30-22-1-5) and later sold it to R. M. Sanderson. Also we purchased the McKevitt quarter (N.W. 30-22-1-5) and recently, a 2700 acre ranch west of Claresholm.

MARGARET (MASSIE) STEELE

Margaret Walker, born June 21, 1921, the middle child of Emma and Peter Massie in their family of five. A most enviable position for I usually was able to take part in the activities of the older set as well as the younger!

Growing up on the family farm, we had fun times especially on a hot summer day when Mother would hitch up the team to the wagon and off we would go to the old swimming hole at the Burnside Picnic Grounds which was operated by my Uncle Jim Massie. We would pick up any of the neighbours that cared to join us. I loved the water.

School was a horse of a different color. As a rule we got off to a bad start. Each day as we, my two younger sisters and I, climbed aboard old Buster we hoped this ride would be an uneventful one but, as we took off down the road, the first car that passed invariably we found ourselves in a heap on the ground. Buster, quite content with his success, would be munching away on his favorite tid-bit. To add to this insult we would arrive at our destination only to be tortured by over-sized red ants that were deposited down our backs by those inevitable rogues. Then came those 'BOOKS'!!!

In 1938 my Dad hired a quiet, red headed man by the name of Morwood 'Red' Steele. June, 1941 found Morwood and I standing, happily, before the altar. My father's wedding gift was the little house on five acres of land, the NW corner of SW¼ 32-22-1-W5. Morwood was in partnership with my father and brother for several years then, for twenty-two years, he worked for Dom Tar Packaging.

We moved to Calgary in 1970 and in 1976 he took an early retirement from Dom Tar and is now employed in the No. 8 Co-op Complex, close to our home.

We were blessed with three sons; Ronald, Barry and Wayne. The early years of their childhood were dark and difficult due to some physical problems but we are grateful to Our Loving Heavenly Father, who stood with us, strengthening us and sparing them to reach manhood. We were also thankful for kind and understanding neighbours. Ron is happily employed at Advance Industries. Barry is married, has two daughters, operates his own construction company and lives on a small farm in the Gladys Ridge district. Wayne lives in Calgary and is employed with Air Canada.

NEL (MASSIE) SARCHET

I was born, the fourth child of Emma and Peter Massie, and lived on the family ranch until 1941 when I left to work in Calgary.

I married Hal Sarchet of Spokane, Washington in 1947, reared two children; Zella (Sarchet) Ramsey, Seattle and Brian Sarchet, Spokane, Washington, (unmarried).

I have the dubious distinction of having no grandchildren!!

HAZEL (MASSIE) McINTOSH

I was born on a cold February day at Grace Hospital, Calgary, the youngest child of Peter and Emma Massie.

I met my husband, Alex McIntosh, when he came to work for my father, as a ranch hand, in November, 1946. We were married July 16, 1947 and returned to his home province of Ontario. We took up residence in Brantford 'The Telephone City' and this is where we raised our family; Pearl, born in December, 1948 and Fred, September, 1951. Pearl has been employed at the 'W. Ross McDonald School' (formerly 'Ontario School for the Blind'), for the last eight years. Fred has been employed at 'Fisher Control' in Woodstock since finishing his schooling at Mohawk College. He married a Brantford girl, Bonnie Jarvie, November 10, 1973 and their son, Jeff, is eighteen months old. (March, 1977).

For the past eighteen years I have worked at the Brantford General Hospital as a registered Nursing Assistant.

WILLIAM T. MASSIE

William was born January 9, 1875 in Fintray, Aberdeenshire, Scotland, coming to Spokane, Washington in 1910. He came to Calgary in 1912 and worked with his brothers in the cement business. He bought (N.W.¼ 31-22-1-5) and lived there for a number of years and then on the Ruttan place which his brother, Peter, had rented. He operated a threshing outfit for many years in the Red Deer Lake District until shortly before his death in August, 1941. He never married.

DUNCAN McARTHUR FAMILY Sources; Mrs. M. McGuinness, Mrs. McCrimmon, Rankin, Mrs. P. D. (Stella Weston) McArthur.

Duncan McArthur came to the Red Deer Lake district in the late 1880's. He homesteaded SW¼-30-22-1-W5, homestead No. 54049, land that is half a mile north and east of the Red Deer Lake store. He and his wife had four children; Jessie about 1889, Gordon, Norman

An evening at the McArthur home at Red Deer Lake; 1910. Gordon McArthur, Mrs. J. Shannon, Dan Patton, Mrs. Dan Patton, Joe Shannon and James McKevitt. At the time of this picture house owned by Duncan McArthur, later by Dan Patton and now by Mr. Massie.

Norman McArthur, Kate McCrimmon, P. D. McArthur (Pete).

and another child who died in infancy. His brother, Peter, lived on a quarter section north of Duncan's homestead.

About the turn of the century, Duncan, Jessie, and Gordon moved to a farm at Graburn, Saskatchewan while Norman stayed with his uncle, Pete, and attended Red Deer Lake school. Dan Patton bought the original McArthur homestead at Red Deer Lake.

Later, Duncan and family made their home in Edmonton where Norman attended the University of Alberta and, when World War II broke out, he joined the Princess Patricia regiment, went overseas and was killed in action. Gordon married Maude Tracy (?), from Coronation, Alberta and they made their home in Edmonton where he worked for the city. They had three daughters; Catherine, Margaret and Dorothy (who died suddenly at about 15 years of age.)

In 1916, Jessie married Robert Talbot Hollies, son of a pioneer North West Mounted Police officer from Fort MacLeod, Alberta. Talbot Hollies also served in the Canadian army with Jessie's brother, Norman. They had one son, Dr. Norman Hollies, who presently resides with his wife, Shelagh, and five sons in Washington, D.C.

JOSEPH AND AMY (LAWRENCE) McCONKEY — by A. L. McConkey

Joseph McConkey was born in Eureka, Kansas, U.S.A. He came to Canada in 1906 with his brother, Claude, who later returned to the States. Joe remained

in Canada and with another cowboy looked after cattle on a ranch near High River. The owner lived in U.S.A. It was a bad winter and the loss of cattle was great. They had to travel, in deep snow, four miles every day for hay and lost only one steer. It fell through rotten boards into a cellar.

He made forms for cement for McGregor Lake, also broke land near Hanna with eight-horse teams. He hauled water pipe for fruit orchards up steep hillsides in B.C.

He took up a homestead in Tawatinaw, near Rochester, Alberta, in 1914 and left it in 1916 for Calgary. He got work on a threshing outfit at Mr. Ben Lloyd's and liked the country so he stayed and looked after Colonel Harvey's ranch while he went to the first World War. He also looked after Mr. Edric Lloyd's place while he went to England.

On one threshing crew, the cook was Chinese. The pigs used to rub themselves on the cook-car. One night some of the boys thought to play a prank on the cook. They rocked the cook-car, the cook thought it was the pigs and picked up a kettle of hot water and poured it out the window on what he thought was the pigs. The men didn't try a trick like that again.

Joe bought a farm west of Edric Lloyd and later sold it to Mr. Sanderson. Then he bought S.W. ¼-19-22-1-W5 from Mrs. Ben Lloyd, where he lived until his death in 1964. He married Amy Lawrence of Shropshire, England, in 1936. They had four sons; Lawrence and John still live on the farm, Norman, in Calgary and Gerald, in Red Deer. There are two granddaughters.

McKELLAR, KATHERINE (KATE) M.

Each son and daughter of the McKevitts will agree that even a brief summary would be incomplete without at least a mention of one whose worthy influence touched each and every member of the family — Miss Kate McKellar. As a pioneer educator (graduate of Queen's University, Kingston, Ontario — honors Math.) at Red Deer Lake School between 1906 and 1910 she taught all Grade I to VIII, and also Grade IX and University subjects at night. She instilled not only knowledge of the "three R's", but ideals of patriotism, community spirit and some awareness of the size and ways of the world. She maintained her keen, friendly interest in the welfare of each person in the McKevitt family until her untimely death in 1956.

Whenever a new baby was born — if it was a boy — the mother received a bouquet of roses. If a girl, some other quite lovely flowers that "Mac" perhaps did not admire quite so much! It is reported that she was the only lady to ride side-saddle around the country in those days.

Her father, the Reverend Hugh McKellar, D.D., Presbyterian Minister, held services and preached at Red Deer Lake Church located on part of the SE ¼ 26-22-2-W5, which was built by the entire community in 19 . Kate McKellar also accompanied her father on his circuit into the west and south, preaching to the homesteaders.

ALBERT AND EXILDA (SHAW) McKEVITT — by Marcelle McKevitt

Albert McKevitt married Exilda (Sid) Shaw,

daughter of Hugh Shaw of Midnapore, Alberta on December 4, 1929. They have six children; Sheila, Hugh, Larry, Alberta, Audrey and Edwin; seventeen grandchildren and one great-grandchild.

Sheila married Don Bateman and they have six children. Hugh married Maureen Allan of Midnapore and they have five girls and one grandchild. Larry married Marcelle Stringer of Calgary and they have one girl. For many years Hugh, Larry and Don all worked for Shaw Construction. They travelled all over Alberta, into the mountains and parts of B.C. Since 1964, both Hugh and Don have worked for Burnco Ind., Calgary and Larry has worked for Western Co-operative Fertilizers, Calgary.

Alberta married Ken MacMillan and they now live on a farm at Okotoks. Audrey married Jack Whitley and they have two children. They live in Calgary where Jack works for West Canadian Color. Edwin married Linda Webb of Midnapore. They have three children and live at Fort McMurray Alta. where they have their own trucking firm.

Albert McKevitt was born on November 4, 1905 at Midnapore, Alberta, the fourth youngest in a family of eleven children. When he was young he farmed with his dad and his brother, Joe, on the home place: N½ of NE¼ of 25-22-2-W5. They farmed, milked cows and, being Irish, grew a lot of potatoes — some of which they sold. He remembers hauling coal from the Derouche mine at Longview for Hugh Shaw's steam threshing outfit. Some of the places that come to mind, just west of High River, were Shorty McLaughlin's, Jack Brady's and Red McClay's which was known as the Bar S Ranch. He enjoyed driving horses and broke quite a few for Sandy Massie back then. In 1935 Albert gave up farming and moved to Shaw's old store. "In

Front: Hugh, Mr. and Mrs. Albert McKevitt, Sheila. Back: Alberta, Edwin, Audrey and Larry, 1960.

the 30's" he says with a laugh, "when farm prices were very poor, I made a lot of friends trading radios for horses, cows and pigs. Anything to make $10.00". Later he went into the trucking business and continued to do so for many years.

Albert and Sid still live at Midnapore where he takes an active part in community affairs. Since two hip operations, a few years ago, for arthritis, he is once more challenging anyone on the dance floor and, last year, at Stampede time, we found him driving a team in the Old Timers' section of the parade, which he has done for the last 18 or 20 years. He has served over the years and been associated with the Red Deer Lake Credit Union; Boy Scouts Association of America; Midnapore Community Association and is an Honourable member of the Old Timers' Association.

Reflections of the past —

We grew a lot of spuds and one day in the fall of 1926 (it was wet that fall) I had carried 65 bags of potatoes out of the root cellar on the home place and had loaded them on the wagon for town. Destination was the Old Palace Cafe in Calgary and was across the street from where the Calgary Tower is now located. Anyway, I was going along just east of the Sarcee reserve when my wagon dropped through the frost and right down to the axles. There was only one thing to do and that was unload. An Indian came along (I think his name was George Crane) and said he would help me to unload and carry the sacks past the mud hole. We finally pulled my wagon out backwards, drove around the hole, loaded up all those spuds and I was on my way. Lucky, I had some money in my pocket to pay him. Fifty years is a long time ago, but I think if I went back there, I could find the exact spot that happened and, who knows, maybe even my footprints along the fence line."

"One of our neighbors was a Mr. Watson who lived on the Littleton Place. Mr. Watson made a living milking cows and many people might remember him because he also was a collector for the Massey Harris people. Well, this night my two brothers, Pat and Charley, decided to play a little trick on poor old Watson. They knew he would be going to the barn after supper and waited until he did so. Then, they tied a piece of wire across his gate, where he would pass, and hid in the grass and waited. Finally he arrived, carrying the milk pails and a lantern. Of course Mr. Watson, the milk pails and the lantern landed in a heap and the air was blue for quite some time. The boys had quite a laugh over that. Charley wasn't laughing one other time though — This night, he and a friend of his ran around a Mr. Bradshaw's barn with torches and scared all the cows. Bradshaw took after them, chasing them all over his quarter section. Charley hid in under a box spring near the house where the cream and milk were kept. Mr. Bradshaw, who was by this time tuckered out, came and sat right on a plank over top of this box spring and proceeded to light his pipe. To put it mildly, he was not very pleased with the boys and was talking to himself, e.g. "If I ever catch those buggers I'm going to wring their necks, etc. etc.". He never did find out, that while he was sitting on that box spring and talking to himself about what he would do when he "caught up to those two scoundrels", one of them was, in fact, huddled directly below him and all he had to do was lift up the plank and his greatest wish would have been fulfilled."

"When we were young boys we made our own fun. One game we played was where four boys pretended to be a team of horses. The horses were supposed to jump over this partially broken fence and this one day, I guess, the horses stampeded, anyway, the driver, who was Richie Hope, got his hands tangled in the fence. Richie ended up at the schoolhouse where the teacher had to do a repair job with the first aid equipment. Today the teacher would have probably sent him to the school nurse — how times have changed."

"Noon hours passed slowly so some of us boys used to go behind the Presbyterian Church, which was next to the school, and make cigarettes from the dry bark off fence posts. This went on for some time until one day Mr. Massie saw us through his field glasses and being a concerned parishioner, reported us to the teacher. That was the end of our noon hour freedom for some time."

Running races was a form of entertainment at many gatherings in the summer time and as Albert was a good runner when he was younger he usually entered. There were also fun races like the "Cherry Race." This is the way it went — You stood at the starting line with a cherry balanced on the flat side of a knife and had to go a certain distance without dropping the cherry. "I remember a cherry race at Millarville in 1921" he says. "The first time I tried this race the cherry just didn't want to stay on that knife. The second time I put a little dirt on the cherry and it clung all the way but it wasn't really stable. Now the third time, that cherry got a gentle little squeeze onto the knife with my thumb and it rode really good all the way to the finish line." The soda biscuit race was another fun race. The idea was to run to your partner, eat a soda cracker and whistle. The first to whistle won. Peter Massie was Albert's partner once at Millarville and would you believe that when Albert reached Peter, that soda biscuit had been licked clean of salt and sufficiently damped so that he ate it and whistled like a bird. I should mention that Albert won the race but it was also a win for Peter who had made money betting on Albert.

Around 1926 Albert and Sid (later his wife) and couple of other girls organized a dance party. Allister Massie, Pat and a couple more lads were supposed to meet them at Cooper Hall, west of Calgary. Due to a misunderstanding the boys ended up at De Winton and Albert and his girls and six bottles of Concord wine, which was all they could afford in those days, had a great time at Cooper Hall. Shortly after this he took to making dandelion wine but put screw caps on instead of corks and the whole batch exploded one night in the cellar.

One night at Red Deer Lake Dance Hall the dry squad were looking for a bootlegger and instead found a few of the boys out having a little refreshment. The police promptly loaded up six or seven of them and took them to Calgary where they appeared in court the next morning. Walt Birney known as "Tinribs" was the last to appear before the magistrate who asked

"Why are you here?" "I guess I'm just here for the ride!" Walt answered and they had to let him go because they had forgotten to book him.

"In 1938 I was driving a 1928 Chev and one day I took Father Newman to Calgary in it. A lot of people knew Father Newman as he was the priest at Midnapore for St. Patrick's Church and the Lacombe Home for about 25 years. Well getting back to my trip to Calgary, we were going down the Cemetery hill when one hind wheel came off and passed us. Father Newman asked "What was that bump Albert?" "Don't worry Father" I said, "It's just one of our wheels!" Of course we didn't go far on three wheels. Father Newman thought it would be safer to continue on his way by streetcar and did so. I jacked up the car, got the wheel partly on and slowly went down to Attridge and Millar on 11th Ave. and was welcomed in. They ground the shaft, put new threads and a new nut on. Father Newman must have said a few words for me as the cost was only 80¢ and I was a perfect stranger to them."

JAMES FRANCIS AND JULIA (KIELY) McKEVITT — by Mary Horler, Daughter of Anna McKevitt, Granddaughter of James Francis McKevitt

The pioneer father of this family was born at Carrickmacross, County Monaghan, Ireland, in 1863, and emigrated to Canada early in 1883. After a brief stay in Toronto, he heeded the "call of the West" and came to Alberta. During 1884-1885, he worked on a survey crew for the Canadian Pacific Railway through the Banff to Field, B.C. portion of the Rocky Mountains. At that time the C.P.R. construction crews were averaging 2 to 2.5 miles a day of tracklaying, passing through towns like the now deserted Silver City, then a lively mining town located near the present station of Castle, and on to Laggan, now known as Lake Louise. Work got slower as winter came and on December 22nd, orders came to quit work, one-half mile from the summit of the Great Divide. In the spring of 1884, the survey crews were working again, with headquarters at Lake Louise. The "big hill" was conquered and after many runaway engines and wrecks, the company decided that the best engines, with air brakes on the wheels, would be needed and dispatched them to Lake Louise from Winnipeg. Even then, the utmost care was taken, including building safety switches on grades, to Field.

James McKevitt left to return to Calgary, which had been a sleepy Mounted Police Post but now, with the railroad, was starting to become an industrial and

Contract No. 8685   INTERIM RECEIPT.
LAND DEPARTMENT.
CANADIAN PACIFIC RAILWAY COMPANY.
L. A. HAMILTON,
LAND COMMISSIONER
Winnipeg, Dec 10th 1897
Received from Jas. McKevitt
the sum of Thirty five 95/100 Dollars
as first payment on N½ of N¼ of Section 25 Township 22 Range 2 W 5 Mer.,
80 acres at $3⁰⁰ per acre, this being an interim receipt, subject to the conditions
of the Company and pending completion of Agreement for the purchase of said land.
$35 95   Recd 4/12/97   L.A. Hamilton
LAND COMMISSIONER

454

mercantile centre of the western plains. We can recall his many stories of the railroading experience. There was no tunnel then to the Cave of the Cave and Basin as it is known today. This was cut through the rock later for convenience. Then, the entrance to the cave was through the small hole at the top and a ladder. Many went down the ladder to bathe in the hot sulphur pool. It is told that when the cave was first discovered the ceiling was covered with stalactites which were broken off one by one and carried away as souvenirs.

His work on the railway made him eligible for a land grant and he took up a homestead on a high point of land facing the mountains, four miles due west of Midnapore, and what was then 13 miles from Calgary. In 1890, he married Julia Agatha Kiely, also from Ireland. She was born in 1870 at Lismire, County Cork, and came to Canada at age 18 to work in the household of Justice Charles B. Roleau, the first judge of the Supreme Court of the Northwest Territories in Calgary.

The McKevitts raised 8 sons and 3 daughters on their mixed farm. It is difficult for people today to understand the many hardships and privations of those early days but there was adventure and pleasure too, and they brought with them their old country standards and traditions. Their home became a centre of hospitality in the new community and there are still some "old timers" who can recall the warm welcome

extended to all who came that way. They attended church at St. Patrick's at Midnapore after 1903 — before which time services were held in various of the pioneer homes.

The children were named: Edward Francis, Anna Elizabeth (Mrs. Joe English), Mary Ellen (Mrs. Emil Hoschka), Thomas, Bernard, Joseph, James, Albert, Charles, Patrick, and Catherine May (Mrs. Paul Lambright). The family now numbers upward of 260

At James McKevitt's home at Red Deer Lake, 1910. Back: Dan Patton, Rev. Hugh McKellar, Albert Eckersley, Pete McArthur, Barney McKevitt Sr., Kate McKellar, Ed Eckersley, Ed McKevitt. Middle: James McKevitt, Mrs. Dan Patton, Nell McKevitt, Clifford Eckersley, Mrs. Eckersley, Harry Levesque. Front: Joe McKevitt, Joe Patton, Jim, Albert, Bernard, and Tom McKevitt.

13 McKevitts and I. McKellar — 1913. Tom, Kate McKellar, Ed, Bernard, Nell, Mrs. McKevitt, Anna, Joe, Mr. McKevitt, Jim. Front: Catherine, Charlie, Pat and Albert.

members. Four of the above have passed away: Ed, Nellie, Joe and Pat. Anna English lives at Calgary; Tom at Lloydminster, Alberta; Bernard, Edmonton; Jim, Brentwood Bay, B.C.; Albert, Midnapore; Charlie, Lloydminster, Saskatchewan; and Catherine at Tampa, Florida, U.S.A.

Several of the sons can recall working at the Father Lacombe Home — a refuge for orphans and old folks, where the large garden and farm always needed workers. Father Albert Lacombe, famous pioneer missionary priest, died at the Lacombe Home in November, 1916.

The Indians were not happy about the steel rails going through their hunting grounds. Their habit was to come in little bands from their camps by the creek — squaws and children often, wandering up to the homestead begging for tea, tobacco and food or to have their lard pails filled with milk. There is one story about Mrs. McKevitt turning away a squaw one day after it had become almost a daily occurrence for her to appear at the door. On her way down the road the squaw grabbed small son Tom, put him under her blanket and was hurriedly moving away. There was an Irish lady in full pursuit immediately, too angry to be frightened. Needless to say, the squaw was given what she asked for that day!

Aside from whole families visiting other families, the only social functions were school Christmas concerts and dances, which everyone attended.

There was never any lack of hard physical exercise: clearing the land with an axe, chopping wood, carrying water from the well and filling the troughs for the animals, to name a few jobs. It was a requirement of the land grant that a certain amount of land had to be cleared, then roots and stones picked and a specific number of acres brought under cultivation each year. James McKevitt told of sowing, reaping, stacking hay and hauling it to Calgary to exchange for a sack of flour. He also knew at first hand the backbreaking effort involved in seeding, cultivating, digging and sacking potatoes to be traded for staples for his large family.

To summarize the present activities of this family is a challenge. Among the descendants of this pioneer couple we now find farmers, truckers, nurses, teachers, construction workers, geologists, ranchers, business men, secretaries, welders, architect and pilot. Contrary to the current trends which show people steadily gravitating to the cities, a great many of the McKevitt offspring still prefer the country life — to till the soil and to be on their own. They have found this to be the good life.

Interesting Notes: A neighbor, Dan Patton, introduced the first Chinese ring-neck Pheasant and Hungarian Partridge to the Red Deer Lake area.

CHARLES McKEVITT

Charlie finished school at Red Deer Lake and then worked at the Lacombe Home before moving to Lashburn, Sask. He married Hilda Ratzloff and they had three children. Pat, Darlene and Dwayne. Charlie's wife passed away in 1957 and he is now retired and living in Lloydminster, Sask.

PATRICK McKEVITT

Pat also finished his schooling at Red Deer Lake and then went to Campion College in Regina, Sask. He then went to Lloydminster where he worked for his brother, Tom, for a couple of years before purchasing his own land. He married Leona Christie and they had four children. Patsy, Maureen, Tom and Gerard. Pat passed away on May 15, 1963. His wife, Leona, still lives at Lloydminster.

CATHERINE LAMBRIGHT (McKEVITT)

Kay finished her schooling at Sacred Heart Convent in Calgary and then went to Norman Wells as a stenographer. There she met and married Paul Lambright in 1946 and had four children. Michael, Julia, Valerie, and Paula. For some time they lived in South America. Paul passed away May 21, 1971 at Coral Gables, Florida where they had lived for many years. Catherine now lives in Tampa, Florida.

BERNARD McKEVITT

Barney was a good horseman and worked for Massie Bros. west of Midnapore when they used to show the Clyde horses. Later he worked at Bow Valley Ranch for P. Burns and also farmed with Mr. Worden on the farm south of Anderson Rd. known as the Halifax place which is now part of Canyon Meadows. He moved to Lloydminster, Sask. where he married and they had four girls. He is now retired and living in Edmonton. His wife, Irene, passed away in April 1976.

JAMES McKEVITT, JR.

After coming out of school at Red Deer Lake he worked as Chauffeur at the Old Lacombe Home and at P. B. Ranches before going farming in the Red Deer Lake district and then operating Red Deer Lake Store known as "Corn Centre". He sold to Bill Norrie and moved to Brentwood Bay, B.C. and worked for B.C. Electric then took up real estate and is now semi-retired and still lives in Brentwood.

MARY ELLEN HOSCHKA (NELL McKEVITT)

She was born in Calgary in 1896 and attended school at Red Deer Lake. She met and married Emil Hoschka in 1918, who worked for some time at the P. Burns (Reid) Ranch at Olds. They later acquired land of their own east of Olds, where they farmed for many years. They had six children — Margaret, Catherine, Andrew, Jean, Theresa and Patrick. She died in 1953 at Calgary and Emil Hoschka died at Olds in 1965.

TOM McKEVITT

When Tom finished school at Red Deer Lake he went to work for John Robinson of the Red Deer Lake district, then to the Father Lacombe Home at Midnapore. He was working there when Father Lacombe died in 1916. From there he went to work for P. Burns Ranch at Olds, known as the Reid Ranch and then entered the army. In 1921 he freighted across country and took up land at Lloydminster, Sask. and is still there, retired, and living in Lloydminster, Alta. His wife, Annie, passed away in March 1966.

EDWARD McKEVITT

Ed was born in Calgary in 1892 and lived and worked around Red Deer Lake. He married Doreen Parish of Calgary, April 7, 1920 and they had three girls: Sheila, Joan and Shirley.

Ed farmed a number of years on the SW¼ of 31-22-1-W5. He sold in 1928 and went to work for Burns Ranches, living on the MacInnes place south of Midnapore. For years he helped plant and take care of the trees on Highway 2. For a few years before retiring he worked at the Lacombe Home. Ed passed away in 1972. His wife, Doreen, is now living at Midnapore.

Ed and Doreen McKevitt 50th Wedding Anniversary.

ANNA ELIZABETH ENGLISH (McKEVITT)

Anna was born in Calgary in 1893. She attended Red Deer Lake School and St. Mary's Girls' School in Calgary, while boarding at the Sacred Heart Convent. She became a teacher and taught all grades at Alexandra School and also west of Crossfield where she met, and later married, Joseph English in 1916. He was also a teacher at Airdrie, Alta. They moved to Calgary about 1918 and had seven children — Mary, Anna, John, Joseph, Catherine, Ellen and William. Mr. English died in Dec. 1975. Anna English still resides in her home in Calgary.

MR. JOSEPH MICHAEL PATRICK AND HELEN (BIRNEY) McKEVITT — by Margaret, Jim and Delores

He was born on July 24, 1900 and grew up on his father's farm situated three miles west of Midnapore and 1 mile south. He attended Red Deer Lake School.

He married Helen Birney, daughter of F. Birney, in Feb. 24th, 1927 and lived on the farm he bought from his father on January 7, 1927 for $4,800.00 and had to make payment of $200.00, plus interest, a year until paid for. NW¼ 36-22-2-W5. He grew a lot of potatoes and garden vegetables, which he had the Sarcee Indians, mostly the women, help pick up in the fall. These were taken to Calgary stores and cafes, some were traded for groceries. They also milked a few cows and made butter. He also did custom work, as cleaning grain and would trade for cattle or pigs. These animals he would dress out and sell to the Holy Cross Hospital which he supplied in meat.

They had three children, Margaret K. (Mrs. Harold Mills) Married with eight children. James F. married Dorothy Lunn with two children and living on a farm in Black Diamond and A. Dolores (Mrs. D. Mark) living in Langley, B.C. married with two children.

As youngsters we would go with Dad to deliver his goods to the stores and the cafes. The best treat we would get was pie a la mode at the Royal Cafe, Calgary, while dad would take the vegetables to the cellar.

Dad broke most of his land himself but later on he had Clint Patton and also the Massies do some for him. He had a threshing outfit and did custom threshing. He had the bunkhouse for the men and the cook car to feed the men. Mother did most of the cooking.

Helen and Joe McKevitt — 1965.

Dad was active in a number of things. He served on the Red Deer Lake School District No. 128 as a trustee a director on the Telephone Company as a director for the Red Deer Lake Credit Union and with the Curling Club. He was also on the Red Deer Lake Hall committee. In the second world war they had a dance once a month to raise money for cigarettes to send to the boys overseas. Dad also was an active member of the Southern Alberta Old Timers Association. He sold the farm in 1972 and moved to Okotoks in the spring of 1973 to retire and passed away in December of the same year. Mother had passed away in June 1969.

RUDY MULDER AND FAMILY — 1948-19??

It was as early as 1930 when I first helped Dawson Turner from the Priddis area together with my two older brothers, Erick and Bert, to chase 26 purebred Clydesdale horses, young and unbroken, along what is now Highway 22, through the district that is now known as Red Deer Lake. Arriving at the stockyards we loaded them in the boxcar in the dark and saw them pull out to go to Toronto where the horse market was better than here.

We were 20 hours in the saddle before we came home (which was just a bit N.W. of Millarville, and little did we realize that one of us was to make a permanent home in the district we had passed through — specifically on the S½ 26-22-2 W-5. In 1932 I drove four horses on a wagon to haul a load of seed oats from the very same place — we came in from the west and went through a lot of bush before coming to the house.

Jim Massie was living on the place then. A lot of changes would take place before we settled there; the Brown family resided there after Massie moved and in 1936 the John Hambling family bought the entire section 26. Mr. Hambling was a farmer from Three Hills (see page 371 — **As the Years Go By**, a history of the Three Hills rural community from 1916 to 1928) and after the dry years he decided to move to this Parkland area of Alberta. At the time the Hamblings moved in only a little over 100 acres were cultivated and the buildings were in a forlorn state. However, the Hamblings put their sights to the future and gambled on the fertility of the soil which was Mr. Hamblings' main interest in life. He got Clint Patton to brush as much as he could afford to get done in a year and as the years went by all, except 20 acres, was cleared by 1939.

Some of the finest crops were produced on this land, even Thatcher Wheat, a product one did not dare mention 12 years before unless one wanted to be considered a green, greenhorn, because it was impossible to grow anything which did not ripen before the middle of August, as frost was always expected then. However, after the land became more and more cleared the frost struck somewhat later.

Jack Hambling was also the first to add artificial fertilizer to his crops in the district which led to the early 117 Massie Harris Combine. What a scientific piece of machinery, then as now, compared to the space ship. A special man from Massie Harris had to run "the Thing" while it was hauled around by a tractor. The same fall during a wet spell that machine was replaced by a self propelled 21 Massie Harris combine. It had two canvas tables delivering the grain to the middle where it went up through the combine for processing. Unique to this very efficient machine were its 82 grease fittings which had to be serviced three times daily. To find each one was like looking for a wild steer in three sections of heavy brush.

Grain from these combines had to be transferred to the bin by heavy metal scoops and staying power. It was not unusual when the land was new to expect 18,000 bushels from this section in one year's harvest.

The Hamblings planted various government sponsored trees around the buildings, which are today in 1976 a source of pleasure for their daughter, Selina and her whole family. It was a happy atmosphere that the Hamblings lived in, humble as it may have been, yet they brought unvoiced and unpretentious happiness to many of their surrounding neighbours, which was also reflected in the equal recognition of the Department of Agriculture for his achievements.

The Hambling Family — 1939. Standing l. to r. Elsie Hambling, Selina, Roy, and Jean. Sitting John Hambling Sr.

His son, Roy, was very much a part in the success story of his father over these years. The Hamblings also had two daughters, Selina and Jean. The youngest, Jean, chose a nursing career with good success and later married Ken Watson. They live in Calgary and have four children.

Selina chose a teaching career and her first assignment in 1937 was Sheep Creek School, just two miles west of Millarville. She had ten grades in a one room school; however this career came to an early and abrupt end in 1940 when I became the fortunate one to become her husband. From this union we raised two daughters in Millarville on the old Polkinghorn place north-west of the town (see page 180 **Our Foothills**).

In 1947 Jack Hambling became bothered with a heart ailment and decided to retire. He divided the section into two parts — the east and west halves. He made an annuity agreement with his son for the east half and with his daughter Selina and myself for the west.

This was a great opportunity for us to start a new life. We sold our Millarville place with much regret as we both loved it and still do. But at the same time we became so absorbed in our new way of life that no time was left to look back. We added more and more trees each year so today when they have grown to an appreciated height, we enjoy them to no end. The Hamblings lived happily retired in Calgary, but Jack, the farmer, felt uncomfortable without land, so in 1951 he purchased the Andy Kirsten section — 30-22-2-W5 — and gave us an opportunity to go in the cattle business on a share basis together with the extra 300 acres of cropland.

When land prices started to rise to the point of tripling the original value in six years, the Kirsten place was sold to J. W. Gregg and three associated businessman. And we still continued to manage that place to about 1972 when we decided to retire also. However, our retirement came only on a gradual scale, and we hope this scale will only diminish as our ability warrants its lifespan. Today we have the very best 100 acres of our half section where the original house still is our home.

Little did Jack and Elsie Hambling realize that their lifework and ambition should live on, not only, but grow to the extent it is today; an example of that saying that "one does not have to become famous before one is famous". Both in their own way molded in their children that what society is all about and what is so little adhered to by today's standards.

Jack Hambling died in 1968 at age 84; Elsie followed in 1974 also at 84. They left a heritage much respected by all who knew them.

Roy Hambling married Ann English in 1940 and they built on the north-east corner of the half section that would become theirs in 1948. The result from this wedlock were four boys and one girl who today are also absorbed in society from farming to different sectors in industry. In the following years Roy was to become successful and well respected not only in his farming methods but as a supplier of seed grain on which many farmers from a large area became dependent.

When we moved here in 1948 early in the spring, it had to be the worst spring for snow. Our auction sale in Millarville had to be postponed three times and finally it was dug out by the municipal bulldozers before we finally held it. Then a blizzard hit again and closed the then gravelled highway 22 just south of our place. We had to detour through the fields of the Thiessens, and further east through the fields of Massie and the old Parker place, now the Spruce Meadows show place of Canadian equestrian fame. No bulldozer could easily clear this mess, and as shown in the photos, they had to eventually push the snow sideways with the newest dozer, a D7, from the municipality of Foothills, assisted by the provincial government dozers. They could be seen piling snow over fences and bushes and climbing 15 feet to get rid of it.

We had good times that followed our arrival and also bad times. Crops were at times abundant; there were days when I combined 3,000 bushels in one day and was assisted by Tom Gillham who farmed the Ruttan's place just east of us. He would haul grain to the bins all day as well as milk his 30 odd cows morning and night. What a change in farming methods in a short period.

In 1951 we had about 600 acres seeded, the most I ever had and would ever have again, when a hail storm in July and repeated in August, cleaned us out so we did not have the benefit of one straw or one kernel of grain that year — no insurance, but 36 windows broken in our buildings alone, and the house roof threaded to pieces. We had to tighten our belts many notches but our spirit and imagination were to roam free.

The next year, 1952, it was so wet that on our home place we only could seed five acres down, but had a bit better luck on the Kirsten place where we had to put two tractors on the disker to till and seed in one operation. These were the testing years which makes a family in agriculture proud and happy when they with their own ingenuity can overcome and look back upon such days and enter them in their diary of memories under the "miscellaneous with credit to experience". It was in these years that our third daughter and youngest son were born on this place, and together we had a life unequalled and envied by many.

All four children had their first education in the Red Deer Lake School, the first two in the one room school, the other two in the enlarging new school. How little did the rural population of Alberta realize that during the next fifteen years, education would become a showplace for the architect and a booming business for construction firms, but the quality of education, the basic essence of education, would become darker and darker to the extent that today in 1976 we come to realize that for many decades to come we and our children will suffer from this oversight.

Red Deer Lake always was a unique community, sometimes difficult to fathom, and yet one that has found its place in our society with dignity and esteem, perhaps more so by value than by character. Walter Birney, my neighbour to the west was so active in the community that his name and the community's were synonymous. Besides having served for 40 odd years in municipal affairs, he was also looked upon as the organizer of most community projects. His connections were from many districts surrounding us and his love for curling established a rink entirely of donations and later artificial ice was installed. Many events took place in that two sheet rink, and for years it was the main attraction of the entire community. We also had such events as badminton, dances, and once a month for 3 years we even had documentary film shows very much enjoyed by everyone until television replaced it in 1956.

The Col. Hervey family also with their connections with the Loyd's were instrumental in the welfare of the entire community. If one wishes to distinguish between the two above mentioned families in an unbiased and inexperienced version, one can not say it better than it would be the difference between quantity and quality.

Now in our retired and declining years, we overlook the community in comfort and think back on how grateful we are to realize that during our short stay here we were so well received and treated by our neighbours in general. One wonders if that is how the pioneers must have felt when they first came to settle here many years ago.

Summing it all up I still can not come up with the answer to the often repeated question of who, why and when did the official name of Loyd Lake become changed to Red Deer Lake; perhaps between the mysterious question and the answer lies the true identity of this community's character, which to me resembles the centre of a three pronged "star" — the first point reaching to the north-east where it was dependent upon the community of Midnapore which symbolized the central post office of all the communities south-west of Calgary and which was so cruelly wrenched away from us all and changed our identity when the city of Calgary extended its boundary one mile to the south of it. This first point also takes in the city of Calgary which was a life line for Red Deer Lake in the early years as it is now. The second point reached south-east where it encompassed a large sweep of country, and took in such communities as Ballyhamage, Alexandra and the whole of the watershed of Pine Creek from its source down to where it crosses Highway No. 2 and borders the De Winton district there. Then the third point reaches west where it was very actively involved in the social activities of the Westoe district and also the Priddis district. Its economic and municipal level of government was centred in the village of Millarville, 20 miles southwest where the Stockland municipal district of No. 191 was established for many years with W. H. King as secretary-treasurer and in 1940 was transferred to Turner Valley with Percy Wray as secretary-treasurer. Though all the councillors were still the same as before the name changed to Turner Valley municipal district No. 32. In 1953 the municipalities were grouped in larger blocks and we became part of the Municipality of Foothills No. 31 with administrative activities under Leonard VanTighen as secretary. The administration was centered at High River.

Our greatest pride has always been in the success and our participation in the two communities where we have spent all our lives. Our personal pride lays in the golden memories that we have had in bringing up our four children who now are scattered throughout the domain, yet have an eternal link with these two districts. Our oldest daughter, Connie, graduating from the University of Alberta in Edmonton with a B.Ed., married John D. Prentice, also a graduate from Edmonton in agriculture and together now own a large modern hog operation south-west of Edmonton (3 miles north of Calmar). They have two daughters and a son to carry on the tradition. Joan, the second daughter graduated from Edmonton with a B.Ed. and after teaching one year at Okotoks High School, she travelled around the world for a year and a half before taking a position with Alberta Vocational Centre where she had sabbatical leave last year to study at the University of Calgary and was successful in obtaining her Masters Degree with the completion of her thesis. She is now writing curriculum with the Adult Education program of the Alberta government. She lives in Calgary in her self-styled modern way of life, but always, at any opportunity, comes home to the farm where her heart-felt-pleasure is centred in horses.

The third daughter, Bonnie, after graduating from Henry Wise Wood School in grade 12, decided to travel to Australia with her friend Judy Widdows (now Priest) of Priddis and in that interval of a year she decided to marry Robert Brown, also a traveller from Toronto and they have settled in Toronto after first travelling around the world. Robert is now employed with the post office in Toronto where they have settled with their two children, one girl and one boy who are their pride and glory.

Douglas, our youngest son, graduated from Lord Beaverbrook with grade 12, and by working at different jobs, he also went to Australia and after a years absence came home. However, after a short homecoming of 6 months decided to go back to Australia, where at present he still is trying to sort things out in his young career. We are confident that time will help him to find himself in the reflection of his fellow men.

And as I started to say in our family story in the Millarville **Our Foothills** history book, how little the A. Mulder sons realized when they came here, how permanent the home of Canada would be for their four sons in 1925. How grateful and perplexed both my wife and I are when we look into our autumn years and see the years change. Even if it may seem confusing to some yet no calamity can darken our faith in the future as we have been rewarded from the past. We started with an I.O.U. and we received a "Paid in Advance" for our future.

W. J. (BILL) NORRIE

Born in Arrowriver, Manitoba in 1913. He lived and worked at Crandall and Isabella and arrived in Calgary, Alberta in April, 1936, in a spring snow storm.

Travelling the rods, he and three friends, Sam Harvey, Alex Miller and Bill Yeardye took off to B.C. They were turned back at Golden by R.C.M.P. They jumped off at Cochrane and walked back to the Palace of Eats on Ninth Avenue East in Calgary.

Bill arrived in Midnapore and stopped at Albert McKevitt's store where he located work south of Midnapore at Dan Patton's farm. He also worked for Ian Sanderson and A. Ruttan breaking sod for the summer.

He moved to Priddis district and worked at the Ovan's farm (now Bob Seaman's) and on the W. H. King ranch, for the winter.

In April, 1937 his brother, George, arrived from Manitoba to work at Sandy Massie's and then went to Dr. McKie's to milk cows for the winter. Bill worked for Peter Massie feeding steers. He worked for W. G. Birney, R. D. Goodwin and Ted Allwarden until he joined the Calgary Highlanders in 1940. After overseas

1937 Bill Norrie, Alex Waddell, George Norrie.

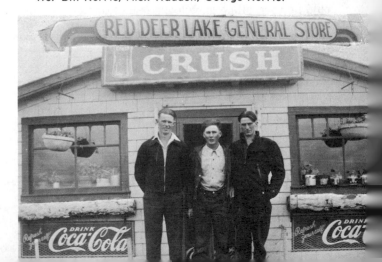

Aerial view of Red Deer Lake store.

duty he returned to Calgary in October, 1945 and started trucking. When Jim McKevitt retired in 1949 he sold his store to Bill.

Bill married Lois Morgan of Springbank and they have three sons; John, married to Debbie Haight, George, married to Karen Brown, Midnapore, Jim, at home and one daughter, Marilyn, attending school in Calgary. His brother, Gordon, drove one of his trucks for a while before moving to High River. His trucks, driven by sons, Jim and George, still travel the roads.

MR. AND MRS. H. G. PARKER — by A. E. Parker

My husband, Warrie Parker, our two children, Jessie age 2 years and 9 months and Winston 1 year and 10 months — and I, arrived at the old Stobo farm at 7 p.m. in May 1919 to find our furniture unloaded on the grass in front of the house and it was drizzling. The addition to the house was not completed and the two carpenters were occupying the largest bedroom. What a welcome! However, we had to make the best we could and I learned fast. I didn't know farm machinery at all and thus was not much help outside for a while, but was mowing, raking that same year and before long I was helping milk the cows too.

Shortly after arriving on the farm I went to Calgary with our neighbor, Mr. Woods, taking Winston with me and leaving Jessie with her Dad. He decided to go to Kierans to buy a saddle horse and left Jessie in care of our helper — a man named Willis. When he went to get the milk cows in he put Jessie in her crib — and checked to see if she was O.K. on his return and found the crib empty. He wrote a note saying he was out hunting Jessie and so when we all met we organized a search. Our neighbors — the Herveys, whom we had

not yet met, saw a white child running backwards and forwards on the Reserve and Col. Hervey went out to investigate and found Jessie. He thought she might be a child of ours so put her in front of him on his horse and was riding towards our place when my husband met them and it was very soon that I was caught up and advised — What a relief!

We worked long hours and hard — raised horses — Thoroughbred, ½ breds and Clydes — Shorthorns, old English sheep dogs, pigs and chicks. Geoffrey was born in April 1921. We had to fetch our mail from Midnapore — no store at Red Deer Lake for a long time.

My sister Jessie Churchill, arrived in 1920 and stayed with us for 3 years, and without any previous experience — she soon learned to ride and drive and rode horses in the shows and put rings in the bulls — but never took to milking — wise no doubt.

Mrs. A. E. Parker and Jessie.

461

H. G. Parker.

We had many good Thoroughbred stallions standing for service, among them 'By George' sire of one Derby winner. We showed Thoroughbreds, ½ breds and Clydes for a while and continued with the light horses classes until after all 3 children had left home and were married. We left Red Deer Lake in 1935 and moved to the Commander Kingscote Ranch, now known as the Sandy Cross Ranch.

Whilst in Red Deer Lake district our children attended the one-room school, Winston and Jessie later attending the school at Midnapore — riding 5 miles each way on horseback. Jessie and Winston later

Winston, Jessie and Geoffrey Parker April 1941.

finished in Calgary. Geoffrey went on to school at Westoe and Olds Agricultural College. Later both Winston and Geoffrey flew with the R.C.A.F., overseas, in World War 2.

We had many unexpected experiences through the weather — one morning waking up to find the wind had blown our shed on to the top of the greenfeed stacks.

We worked hard — and long hours — particularly with saddle horses and jumpers, and had many visitors every weekend — mostly looking at the horses — and made many friends in consequence.

Our land was situated near three very good neighbours, the Harcourt Hervey family to our west, Tom Eardley to the east and Jim Massie to the south. Good neighbours become your friends and were wonderful to have in those days. On the north side was the Sarcee Indian Reserve from where we often bought cordwood and willow fence posts. One family — the Otto Oscars — often visited us and sometimes, Mrs. Oscar helped me with the housework. They were a fine family and I was proud to call them my friends.

My husband passed away in October 1946 and I am now residing with my daughter in Calgary at ninety-one years of age.

DAN PATTON FAMILY

Mr. and Mrs. Dan Patton were married in Winterset, Iowa, in 1891, and came to Calgary in 1902. They stayed a short time at the Blue Rock Hotel, located at the corner of 4th Street and 25th Avenue S.W., Calgary. Tragedy struck their family while staying there in the form of scarlet fever which took the lives of three of their sons before they were able to settle on their farm at Midnapore. Their other sons, Frank, Joe and Clint grew up in the district.

Dan and Burd Patton, with the help of their boys, broke and farmed approximately three sections of land between Midnapore and Red Deer Lake. They raised sheep which were enclosed by one of the first Page woven-wire fences in the area. They also had one of the earliest Ford cars and gasoline tractors (1910).

The Pattons donated the site (1909) and were involved in the construction of the Red Deer Lake Presbyterian (United) Church which is still being used. They also gave gasoline mantle lamps to the Church. The Minister was the Rev. Dr. Hugh McKellar

Dan and Burd Patton.

whose daughter, Miss Kate McKellar, taught in the Red Deer Lake School. The Pattons often boarded the teacher in the early days.

Dan became well known as a bird conservationist. The largest variety of migratory birds (exclusive of waterfowl) was recorded at their place. As early as 1908 he released 70 pair of Hungarian partridge. This was the introduction of Hungarian partridge into Alberta from Michigan. Later quail, Chukar partridge and pheasants were released. Chickadees and other small birds were protected on the farm, making a full time hobby for Dan.

Beaver were taken from Fish Creek and sent to the Banff Zoo, Calgary and Banff Museums.

Dan and Burd spent many leisure hours travelling by team and wagon, camping and fishing along the Highwood and Sheep Rivers.

Burd found a hobby of her own hooking rugs and sewing patchwork quilts. She made nearly 200 rugs from rags which she cut, dyed and hooked in her own designs. In 1941, The Duke of Windsor was given one of her rugs with the well-known E. P. Ranch as the motif. Many quilts were given away to charities and friends. In addition, she was an active community club member and a helpful neighbour. Confinement to a wheelchair in her later years was faced with the same courage she showed throughout her life.

Burd and Dan retired to Calgary in 1951, just prior to celebrating their 60th wedding anniversary. Dan passed away in 1953 and Burd in 1955.

Friends and strangers alike were always welcome at the Patton farm where farmers, fishermen, hunters, conservationists and photographers would meet.

Their three sons, Frank, Joe and Clint reside in Calgary.

Frank, the eldest son, attended Red Deer Lake School. He farmed the home place and broke much of the surrounding land. Frank married Hazel Davis and shortly after they moved to Calgary, where Frank operated his own garage business and after retirement took up photography. They had three children, Kay, Anna and Franklin.

Joe left the farm to take up mechanical work, qualified as a pilot and later enlisted during World War II, serving five years with the R.C.A.F., discharged as Flight Lieutenant and was awarded the Air Force Cross. Joe married Germaine Lemoine and they had one daughter, Joan. Joe recently retired from Field Aviation and spends his leisure time fishing.

Clint resided at home for many years being involved with custom farming. He married Annette McLean who passed away within two years leaving one daughter, Patty. Clint later married Helen Beebe. They have two daughters, Ethel and Carol. Clint has been actively associated with motor mechanics for many years.

The house the family lived in for more than thirty years still stands a mile and a half east of Red Deer Lake School.

THOMAS B. AND ELLA C. PATTON — by Clarence R. Patton Red Deer Lake District

The Pattons arrived in Red Deer Lake District in 1903 by cattle train from Nebraska, U.S.A. Thomas and Ella brought their six children with them: Clarence (deceased), Blanche (deceased), Lily (in Bowcrest Nursing Home, Calgary), Mark (deceased), Ralph (living with his wife Florence in his Glenmore District homestead at 96th Ave. and 14th St. S.W. Calgary) and Hazel (deceased). Ralph Patton (now 82 years of age) can remember being hidden in the hay on the train with brother Mark as they crossed the border into Canada.

The Pattons settled on a half section (N½ Sec. 19-22-1W5) where a farming and large market gardening operation was begun. The farm was sold in 1910 to Samuel Waddell and the Pattons moved to Glenmore District.

Thomas Patton supervised and helped construct the first Presbyterian church in the area, which building still stands beside Highway 22 across from the Red Deer Lake School. He was also responsible for building Red Deer Lake's first community center (dance hall) which I believe is still standing. He was involved in the construction of St. Patrick's Roman Catholic Church at Midnapore. Over the years Thomas Patton and his sons built many homes and barns in the Midnapore and Red Deer Lake Districts. Some of the homes are still in use; such as the Dan Patton, Alex Waddell and Eckersley residences.

Thomas Patton was an oil painter of some repute and his landscape paintings found ready customers across Canada and the United States.

J. R. ROBINSON

John Robinson came to the Midnapore District in 1882 from Montana. His homestead was one and a half miles west of Midnapore, it is known as the George Lee farm today. Sometime after this the family moved to a farm, one mile west of Red Deer Lake which is better known as the Birney Farm.

John and Mary had eleven children; Maggie, married Tom Douglas and had three children. Jenny, married Tom Ramsay and had seven children. Johnny, married Lena and had three children. George, moved to the United States and has not been heard from since. Lize (Elizabeth) married Jim Massie and had six children. Julia, married A. W. 'Sandy' Massie and had two children. Catherine, married Charles Robertson and had two children. Agnes married Norris MacMillan and had one child. Tommy, died as a young child. Joe, married Margaret (Peggy) Rennie and had one child. Margaret married Bill Souter and had five children.

Mary Robinson passed away in 1910. John retired from farming in 1916 and built a home in Midnapore. He resided here until his death in September, 1916, at which time he was 82. His home in Midnapore is still standing, 1977. The home mentioned is known as the Old Midnapore Post Office and is owned by Mr. Ratcliff.

THE RUTTAN FAMILY — by M. C. Ruttan

My father, J. A. Ruttan, was born on the 24th of February, 1846, on a farm near Adolphustown on the Bay of Quinte, Ontario, of United Empire Loyalist stock. As a young man he moved to Essex County, Ontario where he married Lucinda Clark. After some years, he and his family of two boys, Allan and Manley and one girl, Marie moved to Manitoba where a third son, Earle, was born. They farmed there for some years before moving to Claresholm in 1904 and, a few years later, to Calgary where Earle and Marie went to school.

Marie became a teacher and her first school was at Priddis where Albert Eckersley was Secretary. She later taught in Calgary. Earle became a musician and he and his family now live in Vancouver, B.C.

Allan and I farmed in different places. While living in Calgary my father bought a farm, E½-31-22-1-W5, about 1907, more or less for a hobby. He drove to Calgary for week-ends with a horse and buggy. He also bought the quarter section directly north, known as the White Quarter. Part of this land will become a part of the proposed Fish Creek Park. For several years the beavers had a dam on Fish Creek on which my father had a boat. One fall the beavers suddenly moved away and the following spring the creek had changed its course and the dam was left high and dry. How did the beavers know? My father later sold this quarter to Clarence Peppard who farmed with mules.

My father died in December, 1926 and my mother on October 24, 1943.

*   *   *

My wife and I were married February 6, 1917. She was Hazel Spence of Fordwick, Ontario. In 1914 she came to Calgary and taught school there until we were married.

In the spring of 1918, we moved from the Hanna District to the farm which we had bought from my father. A few years later, my brother, Allan, bought a farm a mile south of ours.

During the summer of 1918 we had a house built by a carpenter, Dave Blow, of Calgary. It was constructed with a carload of lumber bought through Eaton's Catalogue. A year or two later I built a barn with lumber that Walter Birney delivered from a mill near Priddis.

In 1933 we sold the farm to Ian Sanderson and moved to the Jas. McKevitt place. We also bought the George Beatty quarter that, at one time, belonged to Joe Shannon, a real old timer. There we had Charlie Stockford build a house. Philip Sampson, whose family came from England, worked for us for several years and later rented the farm until he joined the Air Force. We then sold the farm to Ted Allwarden, reserving sixty acres where we lived until we sold to Norman Pegler and moved to Calgary in 1944. We still reside at 331-22 Avenue S.W. in Calgary.

Looking back, we think we had the best district, with the nicest neighbours you would find anywhere. We lived about half way between a nice old church, near Red Deer Lake, and a very old Anglican Church, in Midnapore, with a Catholic church near it.

Local trustees were better for the district and less expensive. Without radios and T.V. we had our own good times with house parties, card parties, picnics, skating and dances. Dances were held in the Midnapore school house and the Red Deer Lake hall. At one dance, at the hall, the police came and took about six men to Calgary. They were looking for a bootlegger

(not of our district) and a book could be written on that episode.

Pheasant and partridge were started, some on our farm. One cock pheasant stayed with our hens for a few years and often fought with the rooster but would not go into the hen house.

Horses did the work and raised colts that sold for money. Crops were generally good. One year fall wheat would not ripen and another the same field had fifty bushels per acre of spring wheat. Most farmers prospered, one so well that when he was told that "you can't take it with you" replied "then I won't go!"

I remember, about 1912, an old trail that must have started back in the Priddis country and angled through the McKevitt, McArthur, Ruttan, Scott, Lee, or Malloy, and Shaw farms and then on to Midnapore.

DOUGLAS E. STUART SCHOLEFIELD

I was born in Victoria B.C. in 1908 and came to the Midnapore district in 1911 to live with my grandfather's brother and his wife, Mr. and Mrs. Benjamin Lloyd. The next year I was transferred to his other brother and his wife, Mr. and Mrs. Richard Lloyd. This all happened because my parents separated and my mother died.

I was raised here until I was fourteen and went to Red Deer Lake school through grade eight. Then I went to work on the farms around for about two or three years. When my granduncle sold the farm I went to Campion College in Regina for two and a half years. I met Pat McKevitt there, one of my old school-mates. At college I won the medal for boxing, had to win all fights. My thanks to the late W. W. Stewart for teaching me how to box and my sparring partner, John Smith, who worked at the time, for Ralph Lloyd. As money got scarce college had to be abandoned and Joe Huck sent me a ticket to return, which I agreed to work out. I later worked for Walter Birney until 1929 when I went to Atlee to run a combine and to Crossfield to thresh and stayed with my cousins, the Jim Scholefields. In 1927 I worked for Guyn Brothers of Acme before I went back to Birneys.

There was always lots of work but, as the "Hungry Thirties" hit, money was as scarce as hen's teeth, so I went to work at Priddis. I stayed with Mike Standish and went to work on the road, threshed with Ed Winthrop in 1933 and stack threshed with Joe Standish till nearly winter. I bought an old Tudhope car, with the engine and chassis, and pulled it around with horses for a couple of years sawing wood and grinding grain, between working in sawmills. One was Larrat's and another, VanWicks.

In 1934, as liquor was expensive, I thought of manufacturing some but the Mounties stepped in and confiscated it and gave me a three months holiday in Lethbridge. When that was finished the Watkins Brothers took me in until I found work again.

In 1936 Leona Benson, who was living at Dick Story's, and I got married. We have two children; Patricia, married and living in Saudi Arabia in the oil patch and Stephen who owns a truck and trailer and lives in Regina.

In 1939 I worked for Pete Watkins drilling water

wells around the Red Deer Lake and Midnapore districts.

From 1940 to 1950 I had a truck and hauled wood to two school districts, No. 41 and No. 38, working from Morley to the Crow's Nest and hauled mine props to Drumheller and brought coal back.

In 1950 Leona died of cancer and I went to Springbank and stayed at Jim Bellway's and worked for different truck owners as mine was sold.

I have not been back to Midnapore since working for Ted Huck cutting brush in 1951.

I remarried in 1957 to Marguerite Ames and we have eight children; Bob, married to Glenda Marr; Mary Jane, married to Jacques Davis; Mona; Joe; Leona; Sharon; Davina and Walter.

GEORGE SCOTT AND MARY (SHEILDS) SHORTT — by Josie (Moss) McKeage

George Scott Shortt was born June 12, 1829 near Dalkeith, Edinburghshire, Scotland and moved to Canada, with a brother, Adam, in 1852. A miller by trade he started a mill in Bruce County, Ontario, their home was in Walkerton, Ontario. On leaving Ontario they came west and settled on a farm near Red Deer Lake, Alberta, North West Territories. He died May 9, 1893.

He was married on January 10, 1859 at Glencoe, Ontario to Mary Sheilds. They had eight children: Adam, Margaret, Martha, Elizabeth, Mary, Agnes Isabelle, George S. and James Sinclair. Their family all married and lived out their lives in different parts of Canada.

Rev. George and Mary Shortt.

At Red Deer Lake, besides themselves, were their daughter, Mary, her husband, John Bell and children Beth and Jim. Also their son, George S. Junior, who married Jeanette Isabella Campbell on December 17, 1902. They had seven sons: John, James, George, Morris, William, Douglas and Donald. They also had a ranch near Red Deer Lake.

Margaret Shortt married Conrad Clerihue and lived in B.C.

Adam Shortt married Elizabeth Smith and lived in Ontario.

Martha married David Carter and lived at Fish Creek.

Elizabeth married Joseph H. S. Moss and lived at Pine Creek until moving to Mossleigh in 1901.

Agnes Isabelle married Alex Aird and lived at Sheep Creek, Alberta.

James Sinclair married Christine McLeod and they lived their last years in London, Ontario.

George Scott Shortt and wife, Mary, are buried in Pine Creek Cemetery. Their son, James, was ordained as a Presbyterian minister and preached in many localities in Alberta before going to London, Ontario. Their son, George S. Junior, ranched near Red Deer Lake before moving to Calgary to reside. His sons, James and Morris, still reside in Calgary.

A number of other grandchildren of George and Mary Shortt still reside in Alberta. Winnie (Aird) Lehody, Lethbridge; Alice (Aird) Beckett, Edmonton; Mary (Moss) Ballard, Lillian (Moss) Stinson, Train, and Josie (Moss) McKeage, Calgary.

These pioneers and their survivors lived and made history which will never be experienced again. Not to mention those of us lucky enough to see Ed Aldrun and Neil Armstrong walk on the moon.

CHARLES (CHARLIE) STOCKFORD — as told to Walter Turnbull

I arrived in Nova Scotia March 15, 1910 and in Calgary March 20, 1910. Two days later I went to Dalroy to farm which was really pioneering in those days. I dug wells and built new fences. On Dominion Day, steam power arrived so I started breaking land with a steam engine which pulled a 14 bottom plow and did this until freeze-up. Next spring I went to Carseland and helped fence 354 sections. While there I met all the McHughes and the Bartches. That fall I went back to Dalroy and threshed all winter. I then came to the Midnapore district and have spent my life in this and the Millarville districts. I went in for carpentering and built for the Millars and Jappy Rogers at Millarville and built the Millarville store. I also did some major repairs on the Ranchman's Hall, west of Millarville, in 1920.

After the 1927 Millarville races a dance was held in the Ranchman's Hall which lasted until 6 a.m. and, by morning, even two Mounties joined in playing Crown and Anchor, on the doorstep.

I also built houses for Ross Sanderson, Ruttans, Johnnie Hamilton and the Red Deer Lake store. I also built log barns and, for a few winters, I put up ice, worked in the Turner Valley Oilfields and looked after cattle.

I served with the 31st C.E.F. in the First World

War. I was gassed in Passchendale, Belgium and have suffered ill effected from it all of my life. I returned from overseas and reached Calgary on Christmas Eve, 1918 and was discharged on Valentine's Day, 1919.

I will be 86 on May 6, 1977. I have had a happy life and for many years have enjoyed making knick-knacks some of which, I am told, are worth money as collectors' items.

THE WILLIAM THIESSEN FAMILY — by The Thiessen Family

Red Deer Lake (Lloyd Lake on the official map).

We came from Nebraska in March, 1902, to Calgary and stayed at the Blue Rock Hotel which was located on the corner of 4th Street and 25th Avenue S.W., just north of the Elbow River. It was run by Mr. Mullon, generally known as 'Irish'.

A car load of machinery and household effects was moved out to where our house was being built on the NE¼-23-22-2-W5, about 200 yards west of the NE corner and south of the east-west road allowance which is now Highway 22. The land was bought from Ben Phillips for six dollars an acre, he had bought it from the C.P.R. a short time before, for three dollars an acre. He had started a house and this house was completed for Grandfather Thiessen who came up with us. We stayed there for a short time and moved to the log house on the Pete McArthur place, this was a mile east and a mile north of the new house. From this place we moved to the Billy Reinhardt place on the east side of Red Deer Lake. It was the part of the north half 14-22-2 not covered by the lake, so we were closer to Grandpa Thiessen.

Grandpa moved back to the States in 1909 and we went back to the N½-23 and occupied his house. Dad and Mother carried on farming this land until they passed away. Mother passed away August 9, 1937 at 70 years of age and Dad passed away September 3, 1944 at 77 years of age.

There were ten children in the family; Emma, Anna, Henry, William, John, Ella, Roy, Jessie, Florence and Walter.

Emma married Ley Harris, a land surveyer, now retired, in 1914. They had three children; Dorothy, Herbert and John who are all married and have families of their own.

Anna married Charles Gillespie in 1912. He was a mail carrier from Calgary to Priddis to Kew. Charles passed away in 1915. Anna's second husband, Charlie Dowling, was a plumber and later was in partnership with his brother, Tommy Dowling, in the Calgary Tent and Awning. They were married in 1922 and Charlie passed away in 1964. They had no children.

William and John started farming in the Red Deer Lake District on Jimmy Steven's place, north of McKevitts. In the spring of 1926 they shipped stock and equipment to Lloydminster where they had purchased land in Big Gully district, east of Lloydminster, and continued farming operations there. William, better known as Bill, married Margaret Jerrold in 1926, a school teacher who was teaching school at Langdon. They had one child who died in infancy and they were foster parents to Roma Boch, (now Mrs. Ken Ranger).

John married Mary Jerrold in 1925. She taught

W. Thiessen Family — Front Row l to r — Florence, W. Thiessen, Walter, Mrs. Thiessen, John. Back Row: Jessie, Roy, Ella, William, Anna and Emma.

school at Red Deer Lake for two years. They had three children; Florence, Gordon and Grace all married with families. John passed away November 1966.

Ella married Ed. Larson in 1923, a farmer in the Lloydminster District. Ella passed away in 1929 and had no children.

Roy married Miriam Beebe in 1938, they have two boys; Alan and Neil, both are married with families.

Jessie married Charles Stanton in 1924, they had two boys; Vernon, born in 1925 and died in 1933, Johnnie born in 1931 and died in 1932. They spent a good deal of time fur farming in Bragg Creek and Red Deer Lake area.

Florence married George Beatty in 1927, a farmer in the Red Deer Lake district. They have since moved to a farm west of Olds. They have three children; William, Edna and Betty, all married. Bill farms with his father and has no family. The girls both have children.

The youngest of the family, Walter, married Mary (Dollie) Bamford in 1934, they have three children; Fred, Mary and Jeanette, all married. Fred and Mary have families of their own.

All the original Thiessen family attended Red Deer Lake School. The school was ½ mile south of the present school and located in SW corner of NW¼-24-22-2-W5. The land was donated by the Lloyd family. Edric Lloyd was at the opening of the present school and said he started school in 1889. Emma and Anna were the oldest of the family and they started school in 1902, soon after they arrived in the District of Alberta. It was not a Province until 1905. The Ontario school books were used and the teacher, Frank Harris, was also from Ontario. As they became of age the rest of the family also attended this school, or the present one. Walter, the youngest, of course followed suit. Not only he but all his family went to this school. His daughter's children, whose great-grandmother was a Lloyd, also attended Red Deer Lake School so they really have played quite a part in the school activities through the years.

After the death of our father, the half section was divided between Roy and Walter. Roy farmed the NE¼ and Walter, the NW¼. Roy has since sold his quarter and taken up carpenter work, he was also in the motel business.

Through the years we have seen many changes. The first years were hard and it took a lot of effort to gain a footing. Grandpa Thiessen told about planting ten bushels of big potatoes in the spring and all he could find in the fall was seven bushels of little potatoes. The year 1902 was the last in a series of four wet years. We had to roast the wood in the oven before we could burn it. There were good features too, every one was in the same boat and all were out to help each other to the best of their ability and resources.

The school, in the early days, was used as a community centre. It was used for church services by both the Anglican and Presbyterian ministers. And, of course, the Christmas Concerts were always held in the school.

ERNEST AND CHRISSIE TOWNER by Tiny Hemens

Ernest and Chrissie Towner and their three daughters came out to Calgary in 1906. They settled on a farm on the Macleod Trail and the girls attended Glenmore school. They also farmed at Pine Creek and Dalroy before retiring to Red Deer Lake in 1928.

Gladys married Ralph Hankins of Calgary, had two sons; Dr. Gerald Hankins of Calgary and Murray of Ottawa. Elsie (Todd) married Phil Brown of Vanderhoof, B.C. and had two daughters; Mrs. Christie Douglas and Mrs. Gwen Lawrence, living in Mission, B.C. Eva (Tiny) married Walter Hemens of Priddis. They have a son, Stan, in the forces, and three grandchildren. Eva and Walter are retired and living in Sidney, B.C. Eva is the only remaining sister.

One thing remembered by Albert McKevitt about Ernie Towner when he was in the Red Deer Lake district was visiting Mr. Towner one day. Mr. Towner kept a lot of chickens and said to Albert; "It's a funny thing about these Leghorn chickens, they won't eat that Garnet wheat, I have to buy Marquis wheat for them."

SAMUEL JOHN AND ROSETTA (DISNEY) WADDELL — by Norman Waddell

Samuel Waddell was born in Claremont, Ontario, in 1882 where he resided until he married Rosetta Disney in 1902, just prior to moving west to Chestermere Lake in 1903. A short time later he moved to the Springbank area where he farmed until moving to Midnapore in 1910. Samuel was a member of the Red Deer Lake United Church, also served on the school board for a number of years. He was an active member of the community until his death in 1959. He was predeceased by his wife in 1953.

They had three children, the eldest being, their only daughter, Hazel, who married Jack Cullen, resided at Springbank for a time before moving to Olds where she resided until she passed away in 1974. They had four children; Arthur, Noreen, Ernest and Marshall and they are, at present, all living in Olds. Noreen (Mrs. Willard Durant) has two boys, Douglas and Brent and one girl, Tracy. Marshall married Beverly and has three boys, Garry, Glen and Kevin. Ernest and Marshall are still single.

Norman, the second child, married Alison Wylie, together they bought a quarter section of the Dick Lloyd place. He presently lives there with his son, Alvin, daughter-in-law, Karen (Cutting) and their three children, Roger, Roma, and Betty. His daughter, Ione, married Alexander (Sandy) Geals. They reside in Canmore with their two children, Kathy and Ricky.

Alex, the youngest, is still living on the home place with his wife, Doris, and their three children, Gordon, Ronald and Shirley, none of whom are married yet.

In reminiscing through the past for this story, one thing sticks in my mind. It is the story about my father and the car salesman who came to try and sell Father a car. Father told him that he had a nice Grey Dort. The salesman went to the next place and was telling them about this car, which, in the end, turned out to be a team of grey horses.

HAROLD WARD — by Bob Worden

Harold 'Pop' Ward farmed in the Red Deer Lake area on the farm known as the Sculley farm. Later he was on the Harrison farm and, presently, the Huck farm, 18-22-1W5, which is sub-divided. About 1925 Pop married Nellie Templeton, a Scotch girl, sister to Andy Templeton.

In 1927 or '28 Pop moved to Midnapore and started a service station, selling Union Oil products. About the same time he contracted the Rural Mail Route known as RR No. 1, Midnapore. This route had been run by Joe Waugh for the four prior years.

For many years, when the roads were bad, due to rains or heavy snow storms, he had to use a team of horses to take the mail. It took two days to cover the route from Midnapore to Priddis, then to Millarville and on to Kew, back over the divide by the Sparrow Ranch to Midnapore. This was travelled twice a week and then, later on, three times a week. Pop would borrow the horses from Mr. Roy Jeffreys.

When Pop first opened the service station things were not too prosperous, if anyone asked him "how is Business?" he would say that he was very busy with I.W.W. (Information, wind and water), but Pop built up a very large business from all his friends that he made on the mail route, from surrounding neighbours and from the Blackie District from where he had come. The commercial travellers were also among his customers as he had a special on oil changes, they would come in the evening, have their oil changed and a fill of gas and for 25¢ more they would receive an extra quart of oil to carry with them.

Pop was also a very talented piano player, he would play any tune the first time he heard it on the radio even if it had been the day before. The first two children, Dorothy and Jack, were also very talented, Dorothy, at the age of four years, could sing any one of Harry Lauder's songs, Scotch accent and all, perfectly. With Pop at the piano, she also danced any of the Scottish dances. She later won a music festival in Vancouver. Jack's talents were a little different, at the age of two years he would go around to all the customers at the service station with his penny bank which was a miniature Union Triton Motor Oil can, given free to promote the new oil in quart cans, and ask them to put 25¢ in it.

During the depression years Pop also had a job of going around collecting back taxes in the Blackie District. He had a saying that if the farmers had three loaves of bread in the house he took two of them.

In 1936 he sold the service station to Fred Ratcliff and it is now the Gulf Station in Midnapore. Fred also took over the mail route and the Ward family moved to Union Bay on Vancouver Island along with Don Carnagie who drove the mail for Pop for many years.

Dorothy married the son of the Fletcher's Music family in Nanaimo, B.C. Jack was hauling coal from a mine up in the mountains to Union Bay and loading into barges the last time I visited with them.

Pop passed away several years ago, Mrs. Ward remained and still lives on Vancouver Island.

As I had the honor of working with Pop Ward on week ends and later drove the mail and worked at the service station for Mr. Ratcliff for two years I know the hardships that prevailed on the mail route due to weather and road problems.

SANFORD R. AND ENETH (EDWARDS) WATKINS — by S. R. Watkins

Sanford R. (Pete) Watkins came to the Red Deer Lake district at the age of one year, in the year 1913, with his father Albert J. Watkins and his mother, Lydia. There were five older children, Fred, Della, Ellen, Catherine and Floyd.

Al Watkins and his identical twin brother, Alfred, were born in Fresno, California. Their parents were born in Ireland and had emigrated to California in the early 1800's. Al was a blacksmith and in his younger days had mined gold and driven stage on the Oregon Trail. In 1898, Al married Lydia Koopman, at Boise, Idaho, where he owned and ran a blacksmith shop. A few years later they moved to Pine Valley, Oregon, where they started another blacksmith shop.

Lydia's father and family had come to Pine Valley, in 1883, by wagon train, from Kansas. They homesteaded in the Valley where many of their descendents still live.

In 1912 Al Watkins and his father-in-law, Fritz Koopman, came to the Red Deer Lake district and purchased the north 220 acres of 15-22-2-W5 from Mr. Hamilton. Al stayed and built a house for his family and then brought them to live in the district in the Fall of 1913.

When Sanford was a small boy the Watkins' next door neighbours were the Massie Brothers who owned a steam threshing machine. Young Sanford was fascinated with the operation of the machine and would follow Peter Massie around like a shadow. The men nicknamed him "Young Pete" and he has kept the name, Pete, ever since.

Al farmed and ran a blacksmith shop until he passed away in 1930. The Watkins boys did custom threshing and breaking for a few years. Fred and Floyd built and operated a Service Station and repair shop in Midnapore. They sold and Fred moved to Bragg Creek to run his saw mill and Floyd built Watkins' Machine Shop which he still operates.

Pete stayed on the farm with his mother. He farmed and drilled water wells as well as custom threshing. In the spring of 1940, Lydia Watkins passed away after a lengthy illness.

On October 3, 1940 Pete married Eneth Edwards. Enie and her older sister, Jean, came to Priddis in November, 1928. They were accompanied from England by their mother, Mrs. Winifred B. Edwards, widow of the late Capt. C. T. Edwards, Valparaiso, Chili. After a short stay they moved to Calgary where Mrs. Edwards worked for the Hudson's Bay Store. In the spring of 1930 they moved to the Stettler district where both girls received their education. Jean returned to Calgary and married Joe DeSutter of DeSutter Auto Body. They are now retired and live in the Canmore, district. In 1938 Enie came to the Red Deer Lake district to visit her cousins, Philip and Peggy Sampson. At the time Mr. Sampson operated M. C. Ruttan's farm. She met Major J. H. Beatty and his mother and went to work for them.

Mrs. Edwards came to the Red Deer Lake district in 1955, she resided, for a number of years on the Watkins farm. In 1967 she moved to Calgary where she passed away April 5th, 1975.

Fred Watkins now resides at High River. He has one son and five grandchildren. Della (Deweese) is widowed and lives at Creston, B.C. Ellen (deceased 1951) married Charlie Gulick, Pine Valley, Oregon. They had five children. Catherine married Edward Lacombe, has two children living and four grandchildren, lives at Grand Forks, B.C. Floyd and his wife, Ruth, have four children and five grandchildren.

Pete and Enie still reside on part of the home farm, they have three children and three grandchildren. All reside in the district. Pete still farms and drills water wells with his son, Ted. They also operate a repair, machine and black smith service.

ALFRED JOHN WILKIN 1837-1900 — by R. H. King and Arthur Patterson

A. J. Wilkin came to the Midnapore-Pine Creek area with his wife, Lucy Emma, (nee Rix) and their four children in 1884. Both Mr. and Mrs. Wilkin were born in Tunbridge Wells, Kent, England, however, they had spent the last fourteen years in Japan where he was engaged with an English importing company, dealing mainly in the silk and tea trades. Needless to say they and their children were completely unaccustomed to the type of climate and rigors of pioneering in the Canadian west.

At that time the main line of the C.P. Railroad was still under constuction but trains were reaching Calgary from the east, the rails having reached and crossed the Elbow River in August of the previous year.

Little is known as to their "landing" and how circumstances lent themselves to accomodating the "newcomers from the Orient", however it is known that the Shaw family had established their place at what was soon to become Midnapore and it is believed that the Lloyd family had settled near the east end of Red Deer Lake before the arrival of the Wilkins. At any rate the Wilkin family, father, mother and four children, Lucy, Margaret, Frank and Mary, ranging in

Wedding Group — Marriage of Lucy Wilkin to Willie King, October 17, 1900. l. to r.: Rev. R. M. Webb — Peploe, Mrs. Webb — Peploe, Margaret Wilkin, Mary Wilkin, Mrs. Wilkin, Lucy, Wm. H. King, C. C. McDonald, E. D. Adams, H. Shand, F. Marsack, Mrs. Marsack, R. K. Bennett, B. Middleton.

age from twelve to eight years, arrived accompanied by two loyal and devoted Japanese servants. Since a home and shelter were essential as soon as possible, the land was obtained and a substantial house built at "Trewlands" on the SE ¼ 12-22-2-W5. The new Wilkin establishment was named after the old family home in Tunbridge Wells, England.

It is not known and it is difficult to guess what motivated Mr. Wilkin to bring his wife and small children to this sparsely settled country. However, the fact remains that with friendly help and wonderful neighbourliness of the few other settlers in the area the family survived and carried on their farm-ranch operation for a considerable number of years.

In or about 1894 Mr. Wilkin accepted employment again in Japan and returned to Yokahama, taking youngest daughter, Mary, with him. His wife and daughters, Lucy and Margaret, remained to manage the ranch with the help of one or more hired men.

In 1898, A. J. Wilkin was stricken with a tropical illness and returned to England for treatment. He died in 1900 and was buried at Tunbridge Wells near his childhood home.

His wife, Lucy Emma, and daughter, Mary, continued living at Trewlands near Pine Creek until Mrs. Wilkin's death there in 1913.

The eldest daughter, Lucy, was married in October 1900 to William H. King of Millarville where they ranched until her death in 1926. They had five children, the first of which was drowned, as an infant, in an accident when her parents were crossing the north fork of Sheep Creek near Millarville.

Margaret Wilkin was married in 1901 to David "Frank" Patterson but died when her first daughter, Fanny, was born in the fall of 1902. Upon Margaret's death her sister, Mary, undertook the care of the infant daughter and raised and educated her until she launched out on an adventurous life teaching at such frontier posts as Grenfel Bay in Labrador and later at Indian schools at Island Lake in northern Manitoba and Port Simpson B.C.

Frank, the only son, was sent to eastern Canada for education and later became a graduate of McGill

University following which he proceeded to Rossland B.C., then a busy gold mining camp. After several years working in the mines he was employed by the C.P.R. surveying and locating engineering. In this work he advanced quite successfully and over the next few years "located" a number of the branch lines in Western Canada including the famous Kettle Valley railroad in southern B.C. It is probable that his employment with the C.P.R. as a locating engineer was prompted by his efforts, while on vacation at the ranch at Pine Creek, to have the Calgary- DeWinton railroad which was just being located, routed up the Pine Creek valley to avoid the excessively steep grades where the line was eventually constructed. Because he was unsuccessful at persuading the "powers that were" to rearrange their plans, we still hear the long freight trains chugging slowly up a steep grade that could have been avoided.

In 1914 Frank joined the army and became a Lieut. Colonel in the Royal Canadian Engineers.

MARY KATHERINE WILKIN

Mary was the youngest of the Wilkin children brought to western Canada by their parents in 1884. Approximately ten years later, when her father returned to Japan, she accompanied him and remained there until 1898. Shortly before the turn of the century Mary rejoined her mother and sister at Trewlands.

After her mother's death in 1913 she and her young niece, Fanny, moved into Mary's newly constructed house about half a mile to the north. The Trewlands place was eventually sold but Mary retained her portion, complete with buildings, and made it home for herself and Fanny. Here she kept numerous horses, cattle, sheep and chickens which she dearly loved and cared for as members of her family. A particularly close member of the family was Moses, a most devoted pup, who followed Mary wherever she went usually yapping at the horses' heads as she drove her sorrel team, Skagway and Robin, on numerous trips to Calgary or to visit some neighbour.

Mary was extremely kind and generous with the most charming voice you have ever heard. She cared

469

only for the comfort and welfare of others. She loved the simple things around her, for instance, while looking at wild flowers in the pasture, she eyed a rose which was pink and white with fully double blossoms. She noted that this was quite unusual so she transplanted it to her garden and propagated it to the point where there are now many of these "Mary Wilkin Double Wild Roses" in the community. From Mary there was never any outward show of emotion, even in times of stress or tragedy such as deaths in the family the departure of Fanny to boarding school and later, to teaching in distant places and finally, Fanny's tragic death in 1938.

Mary lived on at her place near the south shore of Red Deer Lake, only retiring to the comforts of city life during the winters of the last few years before her death in 1957.

FREDERICK D. AND OLIVE H. WILLIAMSON — by A. D. Williamson

Fred Williamson immigrated from England in his early twenties to the prairies at Lousana, Alberta, in the early 1900's. There he took out a homestead, broke up the land and built a house. On October 14, 1914 he married Olive H. Knights of Lousana, at Pine Lake.

He would recall the early days of the first Calgary Stampede and the Pat Burns cattle drives. Other adventures led him to running a livery stable, a lumber yard and buying fur pelts from the Indians in the winter time.

In 1920 he sold his homestead and moved to Calgary. There he worked in the real estate and stock exchange business for a number of years. By this time he had a family of four sons and one daughter. A love of farming once more drew him to Okotoks in the 1930's, where he bought a half section of land one mile north of town. (NW½ 33-20-29-W4) In 1938 he sold this farm to D. Wedderburn and moved to Armstrong, B.C. to again take up ranching and farming. After a few years the farm was turned over to the three eldest sons and for a short time he lived in Vancouver, only to return to farming again in the Shuswap area of Salmon Arm B.C.

A restless urge once more returned him to Calgary in 1949 for a short time, and then to purchase a quarter section of land from Roy Thiessen, west of Midnapore at Red Deer Lake, where he farmed until 1955. (NE¼ 23-22-2-W5).

Returning to B.C. he retired at Penticton until his passing in 1958. Olive Williamson resided in Penticton and later at Armstong B.C. where she passed away in 1975.

FRANCES LUCY (PATTERSON) WOOD 1902-1938 — by R. H. King and Arthur Patterson

Fanny, as she is fondly remembered by her family and friends, was a fine and determined person whose main ambition, during the mature years of her life, appears to have been the education and help of the native people of the country. A review of her life and endeavors bespeaks a tribute to her parents and her aunt, Mary.

She received her education at boarding schools of St. Hilda's and Mount Royal College in Calgary and later graduated from the Provincial Normal School to become a teacher.

The first few years of teaching were spent at rural schools in Alberta after which she enlisted, for two years, with the Grenfel Expedition at a remote bay on the coast of Labrador where Dr. Grenfel had instituted a school and hospital for the native people. She later spent two years each at the Indian schools of Island Lake, in a remote part of northern Manitoba, and at Port Simpson. B.C. Fanny then came back to Alberta to marry Herbert Wood in 1937 but, unfortunately, their married life was cut short by her death in 1938. Herb. and Fanny had one child, Dorothy Elaine, who is now married to Keith Sweeney and they have three boys. The Sweeneys live on the very land where her mother spent her childhood with her great-aunt, Mary.

THE WOODFORD STORY — by T. O. Woodford

H. G. Woodford arrived in the Red Deer Lake district in May 1912, with his wife and family of four boys and three girls. They lived on a farm that was known as the Edwards' place for two years and then moved to the George Hamilton place on Pine Creek early in 1914.

There were two other boys by Mr. Woodford's former marriage: E. E. (Ted) and J. G. (Jack) who had come to Canada in 1904 and had spent some time in Manitoba and B.C. before coming to Alberta. They were all together for a time but at the outbreak of the first world war (1914-1918), both Ted and Jack joined the army and went overseas. Jack became an invalid and came home in the spring of 1918. He died some months later. Ted came home in 1919 with an English war bride. They had a farm at Priddis and farmed there until 1945 when they sold and went to White Rock, B.C. Nellie, Mrs. Woodford died in 1965 while on a trip to England and Ted returned to White Rock, B.C.

The rest of the family stayed on the Hamilton places for several years before moving onto some C.P.R. land farther west on Pine Creek and eventually as we grew up we left home and went our various ways.

There are only three members of our family living at this time of writing. Miss P. K. (Kate) Woodford, of Calgary, F. G. (Frank) Woodford of Fort St. James, B.C. and I.T.O. (Tom) Woodford of Turner Valley, Alberta.

Father died in 1916. The youngest daughter Olive, died in 1936. Bob the youngest boy and only member of the family born in Canada died in 1955. Mother died in 1961. Jerry the eldest son of the second family died February 24, 1973. George the second son died March 10th, 1973. Julia the second daughter died March 21st, 1973. Ted the eldest son of the first family died Sept. 22nd, 1973.

There is a more detailed account of the Woodford family in a book "Our Foothills" published by Millarville, Kew, Priddis and Bragg Creek Historical Society.

CONCERNING THE SECTION OF LAND 26-22-2-W5 — as told to Ann Hambling by Bernard McKevitt.

In 1912 Rev. Hugh McKellar, a Presbyterian minister built the Red Deer Lake Church in the south east corner of 26-22-2-W5. As the years passed many denominations worshipped there. Today there are regular Sunday United Church services held and is usually filled to capacity. A former school building has also been moved onto the property and with a good deal of renovating and work on the part of the church members and the community it is now used for church and community meetings, elections and Sunday school classes.

In 1912 the Massie brothers, Peter, Sandy, Jack, Jim and Bill arrived in the district. They came to Calgary first from Spokane, Washington. They worked in Calgary paving the streets before they moved to the Red Deer Lake district. They moved onto the Pete McArthur place the ¼ section on the east side of the road running north of the now Red Deer Lake Store. Jack Massie moved onto the Riddel place which was 26-22-2-W5, one mile west of the McArthur place. Jack Massie and his wife had two boys Jack and Peter. They put their crop in with four 4-horse teams. Jack Massie and Charlie Robertson were on the gang plows. Bill Massie on the harrows, and John Wallsen on the seed drill. Bernard McKevitt did the milking, hauled the grain to the field to the seed drills.

In the fall of 1915 Massie's bought a big steam thresher and threshed all around the district. They ended the season around Christmas time at the Pete Cleland place where Sheila and Stewart Sexsmith now live. Bernard earned about $35.00 a month. During the winter he hauled water even when it was well below zero.

In 1917 Massie's had a big auction sale, selling all their construction and paving equipment, horses, harness and some cattle. They then went in for registered Clydesdale horses. They bought an outstanding stallion called Bonnie Woodside paying $3,-200.00 for him.

The Massie's neighbors to the north were Mr. Bert Stobo who came from Manitoba. He had the half section which is now known as the Ingram place. Another family joining the Stobo ranch was Mr. and Mrs. George Wood which was later called the Yardley place. Mrs. Wood came there as a bride and Mrs. McKevitt hitched up a team and drove over to visit her and was her first neighbor to visit. Mrs. Wood died in 1918.

Tom McKevitt left Red Deer Lake District in 1916. He went to the Reed Ranch owned by Pat Burns up in the Olds District. He stayed there six years then on April 1, 1922 he left by hay wagon and travelled to Lloydminster taking 2 weeks to get there.

In 1921 he and Jack Massie went to Vulcan and Peter Massie went to Priddis. In 1910 Hugh and Malt Shaw broke some land around the district.

Others Who Lived in the Red Deer Lake District but sent no History

Bell, John: NW¼ 14-22-2-W5 about 1895.

Elliot, Bob: Lived on S½ 35-21-2-W5 from about 1910 to 1932. Moved to Priddis area.

Frank Faiery: NW¼ 24-22-2-W5 settled around 1882, sold to Lloyds.

Wilfred Garnot: SW¼ 13-22-2-W5 appears on 1895 map.

W. Hunt: SW¼ 12-22-2-W5, appears on 1895 map.

W. W. D. Jerram: NW¼ 12-22-2-W5, appears on 1895 map.

Reinhardt, G.W.: NE¼ 22-22-2-W5, also Sarah Jane; NE¼ 13-22-2-W5 early settlers.

R. Robinson: SW¼ 34-22-2-W5 before 1887.

Templeton; Andy: S½ 35-21-2-W5, present Latter place.

RED DEER LAKE PICNICS

One of the big events which was held every summer to which we all looked forward to and thoroughly enjoyed was the community picnic. We would gather at Dan Patton's place the night before, each family bringing milk, cream or eggs, (bachelors supplied salt and sugar) and Mrs. Patton would superintend the making of gallons of ice cream. Next day we would hitch up our democrats or wagons, as the case might be, and converge on a given point, arriving there about 11:00 a.m. While the women prepared the tea and coffee, we menfolk would arrange a program of sports for the children. What a time we had! What pleasure it was getting the children all lined up in their different categories and ages and they would all give their best, knowing that a prize awaited the winners at the other end.

I might add here just a word in regard to the culinary art that was displayed by the various families. I think that each one tried to outdo the other and the result was that we always sat down to a bountiful feast and how we enjoyed it! Everyone joined in the festivities and all ages took part in the fun and games. What wonderful family affairs they were.

RED DEER LAKE LADIES' RIDING CLUB — by Lawna Barkley and Hazel McKague

After moving from Nose Creek to Midnapore in 1930 I became acquainted with Mrs. Nena Jeffery and we were both interested in and enjoyed horseback riding and we often went for a ride together. Then I became acquainted with Mrs. Dora Hanson, who lived at Priddis, and we did a lot of riding in the west country, to Van Wykes and that part of the country. In the middle thirties other ladies of the Red Deer Lake district became interested in riding; Mrs. Hazel McKeague, Florence McKevitt, Audrey Giroux, Pat Graham, Tiny Towner (now Hemens), Flo Beatty, Nellie Robins, Ida

Red Deer Lake Ladies Riding Club 1932. L. to R.: Nena Jefferies, Dora Hansen, Pat Graham, Florence McKevitt, Lawna Barkley, Irene Jackson.

Herbert (now Anderberg), who was the teacher in the school and whom we taught to ride, Audrey McNain, Irene Jackson (now Neil) and others.

We often took canned spaghetti and our tea can and rode up Fish Creek for our supper. On a Sunday, when the weather was nice, we would have a paper chase. Two ladies were given a ten minute head start and made a trail of newspaper bits, west over the Sarcee Reserve, and the rest would try to catch them. The leaders were supposed to have our gallon honey pail boiling for tea when the rest arrived. There were up to twenty-six on some of those rides.

Some holidays were spent at Mrs. Tomlinson's or Mrs. Hanson's, west of Priddis and south of Black Diamond. We packed our food and blankets and for three or four days we would sleep in straw stacks or garages and make our meals outside. Mrs. Tomlinson and daughters often went to Bragg Creek with us. We would have a swim if near water.

We took a complete chuckwagon, with four black horses, all over twenty years old, to the Stampede Parade one year but did not enter for competition. We called it the Red Deer Lake Ladies' Riding Club. This was a very happy part of our lives.

THE WALKER BAR-B-QUE

Mr. Walker, an insurance agent from Calgary owned land at the south end of Red Deer Lake and, in June of 1920 or 1921, he issued a blanket invitation to the residents of the countryside to attend a sports day and bar-b-que, as well as a small rodeo. There was a tremendous response to the invitation and every district was well represented. Cooks had been hired to come out the day before and start the bar-b-que. A deep ditch was dug and fuel burned to create a base of embers to cook a whole steer. The steer was impaled on a pipe about 20' in length with a handle for turning it on the end. The meat was served well, medium or rare cooked and bread, butter and boiled beans rounded out the menu.

The small rodeo got away to a good start but, fearing the horses would injure some of the bystanders, it was called off before many of the would-be performers had a chance to compete. Forest Herr and Sam Hamilton were two of the competitors.

About 5:30 p.m. a hail storm came up and everyone had to rush to get away before the roads became impassable. Many of the cars that had cloth tops had them ripped to pieces with the hail stones. Horses stampeded and people were desperate to find any shelter. The Godlonton boys who were working for Mr. Pearson at the time, had come on saddle horses and rode to the Pearson barn opening the door just in time for the Marshall car to drive inside. What had started out to be an enjoyable outing had turned into Bedlam and some of the guests were unable to make it back home that night.

It was an outing well remembered by those who were in attendance and an event that had not been matched in the ensuing years.

THE MASSIES — by Albert McKevitt

My brother Bernard hauled water for the Massies at one time. They had a steam threshing outfit and Bernard told me one year he got in 53 days harvesting, hauling water. To save time, if he was hauling a long way, he would sometimes hook up his team after supper (he always drove four so he was able to make good time) go down the road and put his hose over a farmer's fence and fill his tanks from the farmer's water tank. I imagine this was long after the farmer was in bed.

Around 1916 there was an election for or against prohibition. The Massies had to go to Midnapore to vote. I should have mentioned that there were five brothers, Jack, Alex, Peter, James and William. They found out William was voting different from the other four brothers and he had to walk that three miles to vote as the rest would not let him ride in the wagon. I can't remember who was voting for or who against. As time went on William lived west of Midnapore and did custom farming with a tractor and threshing outfit. Back in 1928 when United Engines were selling Hart Parr tractors, Alex, or Sandy as he was called, bought horses and shipped them east for some years. I used to break horses for Sandy and I chased a lot of cattle for Peter as he was quite a cattle dealer. When they separated Jack went running a farm east of Carstairs until retiring to Crossfield where he passed away. Jim left Midnapore district and took his dairy farm to Chilliwack, B.C. until he sold to his boys and returned to retire in Calgary where he passed away.

MEMORIES OF MY LIFE AT RED DEER LAKE WITH MY FAMILY 1936-1947 — by Jean Watson

It was a cool, rainy day, April 23, 1936 when I moved from Calgary, with my parents, Mr. and Mrs. J. G. Hambling, to our, newly purchased, farm, 26-22-2-W5. Since coming to Canada, from England, my father had worked at many things from feeding cattle, in the winter, for P. Burns and Company, putting up hay, building railway at Rush Lake, Saskatchewan, and digging basements, in Calgary, with a fresno and horses. At the time, when Calgary was a growing, thriving town, he had twelve teams of horses working for him. Having been brought up on a farm in Suffolk, England his first love was always farming. After marrying my mother in England (1914), he spent two more years in Calgary before taking up farming in Three Hills, Alberta. Leaving there, in 1928, he returned to England with his family, now numbering three children; my brother, Roy, sister, Selina and myself, Jean. Although he originally planned to stay in England, jobs were scarce and farm land not readily available so, we all came back to Canada in 1930 and my father drove a truck, during the depression years, hauling anything and everything in order to make a living. In April of 1936 he was able to get back to farming again when we moved to Red Deer Lake.

At that time there was only 100 acres of cleared land, the rest was brush, mostly willow, with a few poplar. He and my brother, Roy, worked very hard to clear more land in the next few years. Roy and Clint Patton invented a 'brush cutter' which helped immensely as a labour saving device but, after the cutting, there was brush to be burned and roots to be picked off of the land, piled up and burned. This provided excellent crop land, some of which is still being farmed today. My father was also interested in cattle and Roy still has the registered brand. My mother loved flowers and, in the ensuing years, had a wonderful and colorful garden every year with daisies, tiger lilies, scarlet lichens and monk's hood, to name a few of the flowers. As well many trees; fir, maple and poplar, were planted around the perimeter of the farm and still survive.

Some memories of those days are very clear in my mind — going to a one room school with grades, one to nine, altogether — playing Coyote and Dog (remember that one?) — the two years that Jean Patterson stayed with us while teaching there — the excitement of getting ready for the Christmas Concert, starting in November, — Mother helping out, for several years, as the accompanist for the musical numbers — when 8:00 pm arrived on the 'Great Day' and Santa Claus came with a present for each student, then lunch — staying for the dance until 2:00 am!! — the year when Miss Campbell was teaching and one of the boys brought a, very highly perfumed, goat to school to 'help out' with a Christmas Concert practise in the Community Hall!! — the night the school burned down, February 5, 1938, and classes were resumed in the church on February 14 and continued there until the summer holidays — skating on Red Deer Lake in 1940 in January, when there had been a heavy frost with little snow. (my mother kept a factual diary from the time we moved to the farm until her death in 1975) — walking to school in the spring to the accompaniment of an enthusiastic meadow-lark — playing baseball with the children from Westoe and Priddis — the wonderful school picnics, held on June 30 on Fish Creek, 'Burnside' (now a part of the Mannix Holdings) with races, baseball and home-made ice cream. Everyone in the family went to these picnics and really had fun — Hallowe'en Parties at school, with costumes, ducking for apples and apples on a string were two of the games we played and our mothers were invited to tea on that day — playing badminton in the Red Deer Lake Hall — the dances that were held every other Friday night at Red Deer Lake, starting at 9:00 pm and going till 2:00 am — having wonderful teachers, Miss Patterson from 1936 to 1938 followed by Miss Pat Jameson and Dorothy Campbell — the times that my mother played the organ in the little white church on the corner of our section, when Anglican services were held there. These occurred only when there were five Sundays in a month and our service was held on the fifth Sunday in the, otherwise, United Church.

All in all, they were very happy times and will always be fondly remembered,.

Due to a heart condition my father had to give up active farming ln 1947 and moved to Calgary. However, work and production on the land was continued by my brother, Roy, and his wife, Ann, and also by my sister, Selina, and her husband, Rudy Mulder. My father's interest in farming continued until his death in 1968, after having 20 years of retirement, during which time he always kept in touch with everything pertaining to agriculture.

Farm Work

Minneapolis tractor owned by Johnson Bros., later owned by Forckel and Sons. L. to R. Bob Forckel, unknown, Bob Currie, rest unknown.

"Old Betsy" one of the first gas tractors. Joel Lloyd, 1916.

First stook threshing outfit in the district. Brought in by rail and hired local boys. 1908.

Will Johnson threshing outfit on the move.

Eben Bremner's outfit threshing at Poffenroths 1939. Eben and Irvine Oesch on racks.

Bremner's 1939 threshing crew; standing l. to r: ?, Joe Carothers, Leonard Fox, Ivan Dick, David Jamison, Eben Bremner, Irvine Oesch, ?, seated; Joe Meehan, Bill Scott.

The Shaw outfit threshing. This crew consisted of a cook and bull cook, a water wagon man, a coal man, four spike pitchers, an engineer, and thirteen bundle racks and drivers.

SHORT EARED OWL
BRIGHT BUFFY BROWN
DARK BACK
PALE BREAST
DARK FACIAL DISK
WHITE BORDER

P.T.

P.T.

SAW WHET OWL
SMALL BLACK BILL
NO EAR TUFTS
YELLOW EYES
RUFOUS STREAKED
UNDER PARTS

RING NECKED
PHEASANT

RUFFED GROUSE

PRAIRIE CHICKEN
Grayish brown-white

CANADA
GOOSE
Black head & neck
BROWN ABOVE
GRAY below.

HUNGARIAN PARTRIDGE
brownish color
chestnut horseshoe
on lower breast

MALLARD DUCK
Green neck-white ring
Lower neck-chestnut.

476

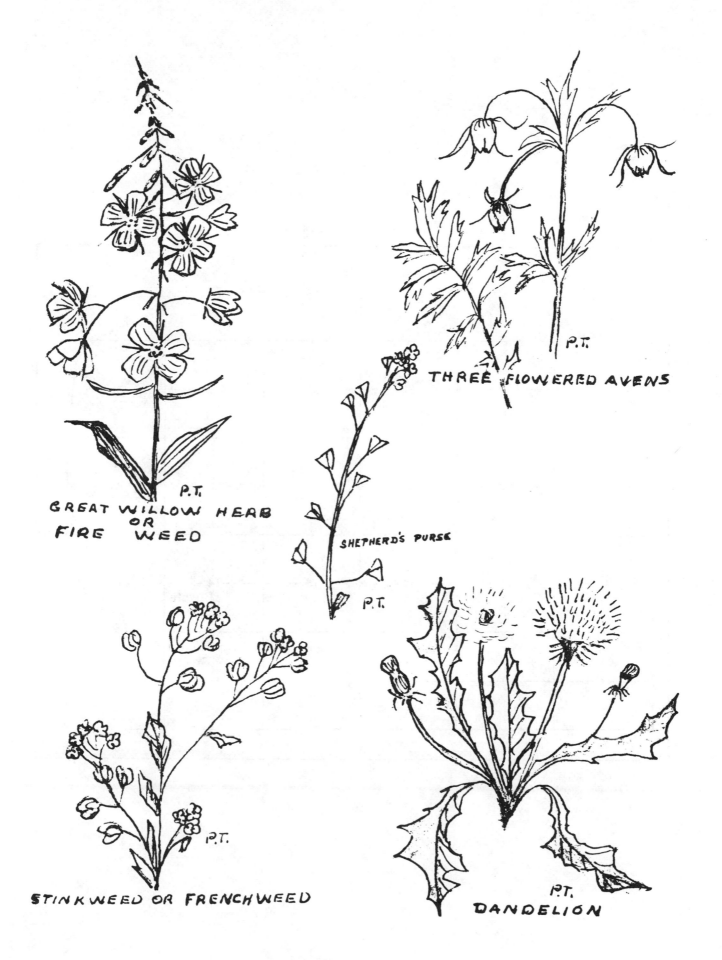

THREE FLOWERED AVENS

P.T.

GREAT WILLOW HERB
OR
FIRE WEED

P.T.

SHEPHERD'S PURSE

P.T.

STINKWEED OR FRENCHWEED

P.T.

DANDELION

P.T.

477

STORMOUNT S.D. NO. 183

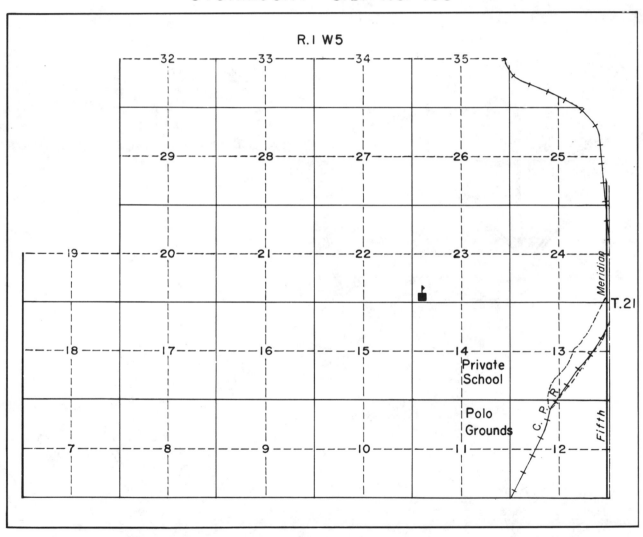

Stormount School District

STORMOUNT SCHOOL — Dot Gerlitz

No matter where our forefathers settled, their first community projects were the building of schools, in the hope that their children would have an easier life. As the areas became populated, schools soon sprang up around the countryside with about one to each township and so it was with Stormount.

In our research into the history of the Stormount School, the earliest date on the records was 1884, with the school district being registered as No. 183 N.W.T. with a population of one hundred at that time. The early settlers were mostly Scottish and the name Stormount is believed to have originated in Scotland.

The first official records of the school are dated October 2, 1897, when there was a sale of land at the Stormount School House comprising part of the S.E. ¼ Sec. 2, sold to the school trustees for the sum of $21.00. Mr. Donald Gray served as secretary-treasurer, with Mr. Charles West, chairing the meetings, during this period — Mr. Gray's salary was $40.00 per year.

The schoolhouse was not opened till April, 1899; after a stone wall was constructed under it for a foundation. Prior to this there were not enough children in the district for the school to be eligible for the government grant; as an average of six children had to attend school continuously to keep it open.

Miss Roxana (Roxy) Alexander was one of the first teachers hired at a salary of $40.00 per month and she lived in a little house near the school which belonged to the MacMillans. In 1901 a shed was built by the ratepayers volunteer labour at a cost of $25.00 and the following year a stable for the children's horses

Some of the teachers who taught in the early years were Miss V. Kerslake, Miss Christina McNaughton, Miss Morrison, Miss Bruce, Miss Ross, John Moffatt, Miss M. Bredin, Mr. Harper — 1913, Miss Allison Scott

Stormount School No. 183.

— 1914-1915, and Mr. Griffith. Their salaries varied from $40.00 to $60.00 per month and an extra dollar allowed per month for doing janitorial duties. Children carried water to the school in lard pails as there was no well till 1909. At this time permission was granted by Mr. James Muir to put a spring box on his land for the water supply for the school.

The schools were kept open, weather permitting, the availability of teachers and the amount of money derived from the collection of taxes from the ratepayers. The Stormount School District was assessed at 2½¢ per acre in 1901 varying to 7¢ per acre in 1920.

There is a small gap in the teachers at different periods, but Miss Andrews taught in the early years and in 1910 the children had to attend Panima School until a teacher could be hired. Mr. Percy Frye taught in 1912 followed by Miss Leitch.

During the years 1913 and 1914 repairs were made to the school and on "Arbor Day" in "14" the ratepayers gathered to plough a fireguard and plot for a garden, also to plant trees and erect a fence. In 1915 a drinking fountain was purchased.

Mrs. A. Benson was hired in 1917 followed by Mrs. C. W. Drake. Miss Margaret Hamilton, a daughter of one of the local pioneers, was engaged for teaching duties from August 15, 1918 to the end of December 1918, subsequently was engaged at a salary of $840.00 per year for one year from August 18, 1918. Margaret enjoyed her teaching days at Stormount and was a great favorite with all the pupils entrusted to her care. She taught Grades 1-9 and some of her first pupils were Amelia Goerlitz, Mark Blaine, Lydia Goerlitz, Harold Cole, Mary Hoffman, Amelia and Jessie Kromm and Elizabeth Goerlitz. The greatest number of pupils she had was thirty. Margaret boarded at the home of her parents while teaching and either walked or rode horseback to school, often racing on horseback for some fun. Each day she carried a bag of kindling to start the stove. She received $10.00 for her janitorial duties which included: sweeping the school, cleaning the stove pipes and blackboards. The rural schoolteacher had to be adept at many things besides teaching the three "R's". In the early days the teachers had to spend two years in a rural school and obtain a good report from the inspector before getting a position in a city school. During Margarets' time, the inspector had occasion to visit the school (this was done twice yearly) and he commented on the beautiful singing of the students. Mrs. Frank Jacobs was responsible for the musical talents of the local children, spending many hours with them, cultivating their singing or playing. There was an old organ in the school and it was put to good use. Great planning and effort was put into preparation of the annual Christmas concerts. Margaret remembers the excitement of the children as the time drew near. The night before the girls had their hair put into rags, so they could look their best. In 1918, during the war, it was moved by the school trustees that the teacher be given the authority to prohibit any other language than English being used on school premises. Margaret ignored this demand as she had enough to do coping with the children and their desire to speak proper English, to ban them from conversing in their native tongues during noon hour and recess. In 1919, Miss Hamilton requested a supply of kindergarten articles for use by the younger students — total cost not to exceed $5.00! The school had a very good library which provided many delightful hours of reading. Margaret used to feel sorry for the children that walked to school through Mr. Roland Ness' pasture. He had Ayrshire cows and they often gave chase to the children, who would flee across the pasture, losing their lunch buckets (usually Rogers Golden Syrup pails) en route and arriving at the school in tears. In 1919, Margaret Hamilton resigned and the board gave her a commendable Testimonial regarding her qualifications as a teacher. She married Eugene Goettler and has raised her family in the Panima District.

Miss Lena Dalzell was hired in 1919 and taught until 1922, and at the same time Mr. R. Ness leased one acre of land to the school for the pasturing of the students horses. Lena boarded with her sister and brother-in-law, Mary and Fred Dick, and she walked to and from school. She also did the janitorial duties; so it was early to rise and late home each day. A big pot-bellied stove was used to warm up frozen lunches and frozen pupils and teachers alike. Often the toques, coats and mitts were left on for some time before it was warm enough to remove them. The school board held their meetings in the school also. Miss Dalzell, now Mrs. Mongomery is at present in the Medicine Tree Manor in High River and is fondly remembered by her former pupils.

Mrs. Ethel Rhine recalls her teaching days at Stormount from September, 1921 till December, 1924, as a time of great pleasure. She had so much personal contact with the pupils and also with their parents. The pupils were a great bunch, there were no disciplinary problems. The teacher and pupils alike were good friends. At one point she allowed the boys to dig a cave in the hillside near the school and they often spent the whole noon hour in it. There was a sign on the door they built, which read "No girls allowed", which annoyed the girls to no end. One day as she sat at her desk she saw a envelope addressed to her. It was a formal invitation from the boys, inviting her for lunch in the cave with them and had this P.S. at the bottom. "Please bring your own lunch." She went and more or less crawled into the dug-out where they ate their lunch. One boy rose (Leslie McIntosh - she thinks) and

made a little speech, to which she replied thanking them for their hospitality. This is just an example of how the children occupied their time: the building of the dug-out and leaving the girls alone would no longer be permitted. They held their Christmas concerts in the school and at the De Winton Hall and thanks to pupils and parents they were always very good. After Mrs. Rhine had knocked off the rough edges of the songs, Mrs. Frank Jacobs completed them and accompanied the children on the piano. Mrs. Jacobs taught Katie and Jessie Kromm to sing "Whispering Hope" in harmony and it was excellent. All the parents were willing to do their share in making costumes etc. Mrs. Rhine rode or drove three miles to school and on some days thought she would freeze. The Jacobs and Goerlitz children came about the same distance. The first thing they did on an extremely cold day was to take a drink of ice-cold water, which they believed drove the heat to the outside of the body. On the other hand, to see them do this made Mrs. Rhine colder than ever, so she had a cup of tea or coffee. One early spring morning, Jessie Kromm and Mrs. Rhine happened to meet on the way to school. They rode along together, Mrs. Rhine on a tall horse and Jessie on a little pony. They were galloping along when Jessie's pony slipped on a piece of ice and threw her under Mrs. Rhine's horses feet. Mrs. Rhine was really frightened but knew enough not to pull her horse up, as it was always good at missing badger holes, etc. if you gave him his head — like the "Ancient Mariner". She was afraid to look behind her, but both Jessie and the pony were okay, and they continued on together. Some years later Jessie Kromm became Mrs. Rhine's sister-in-law.

The families were very friendly and Mrs. Rhine spent many pleasant evenings with them. One of the saddest events was the death of Newton Ness, a dear little boy, who died from diphtheria.

When Mrs. Rhine recalls her pupils, she wonders at the fact that a school containing so many different backgrounds and religions could get along so well. There were United Church members, Anglicans, Seventh Day Adventists, Christian Scientists and together they all helped her in the performance of her duties. She had several German families who spoke German at home and had to learn English at school. One of her former pupils Reinhold Kromm often has a laugh with her over her efforts to make him say "WOLF" instead of "WOOL-OF". She also recalls Amelia (Millie) Goerlitz getting into mischief one day at school. It was in Millie's first grade and her knowledge of English was very scant. Millie was made to stand in the corner and each time Mrs. Rhine asked her if she was sorry she tearfully replied "No" — thinking she was being asked if she would repeat her misbehavior. This same question was asked several times with the same reply. Finally Mrs. Rhine's thinking something was amiss, asked one of the older family members if Millie understood what she was being asked. The teacher felt very badly when she found out Millie thought she was being asked if she would misbehave again and she had replied "no".

Some of the teachers who followed were Miss Jenny Hardbattle, Miss Milligan, Miss Kemis and Miss

Stormount School 1928. Back row: Herb Ness, Elmer Gerlitz, Mary Johnstone, Sheila McNeill, Pauline Kromm. Middle: Fred Kromm, Grace Johnstone, Jean McNeill, Campbell McIntosh. Front: Fred Johnstone, Ivan Dick, Albert Kromm, Esther Kromm.

Back row: Alice Brown, Betty Dafoe, Doris Poffenroth, Lois Dick, Jack Dafoe, Wally Krom, John Hamilton. Middle row: Violet Brown, Alan Dick, Robert Poffenroth, Nick Chernow, Harold Schaber, front: Herbie Krom, Delbert Brown. Stormount School about 1938.

Stormount School, 1954. Standing L. to R. Bobby Wooten, April Singh Hari, Darleen Poffenroth, Peter Chernow, Marion Schmaus, Mary Poffenroth, Dale Singh Hari: Sitting — Yvonne Friedley, Bob Ness, Billy Hamilton, Sam Hamilton, Teacher — Mr. Paul Kuntz, Barbara Hamilton, Dianne Schmaus, Isabella Hamilton.

Preston (an English exchange teacher who had trouble maintaining discipline and on one occasion had Danny Goerlitz, one of her pupils, take one of the rowdier boys outside and give him a licking). There was Blanche Serviss, Miss Grace Donnison, Beatrice MacRae, Helen Ebson, Frank Jacobs, Mr. Holt, Madeline Lee, Mrs. Samuels (nee Miss Deedles), Edna Burton, Verna Patterson, Florence Anderson, Mrs. McArthur, Miss Shirley Crowdis, Miss Bobbie Lee, Mr. Kunz and Miss Anderson (1942-1943). Also Miss Harriett Crossman, now Mrs. Harriett Copithorne from the Elbow River Ranch who taught school when the district had the great snowstorm in June, 1951. In 1954 the school was closed and the children were bussed to Okotoks.

Some of the early trustees of the school were Donald Gray, Charles West, John Dalzell, Harry Watson, Frank Austin, Charles Knight, W. B. McNeill, Angus McIntosh, John Dewar, H. V. Mencke, Hugh Fraser, D. J. Moore, Sam Hamilton, Wm. Robertson, James Urquart, Alf Gooch, C. E. Booth, E. A. Reid, F. S. Jacobs, R. Ness and many more. Early homesteaders are now gone and the names and dates of early folks who lived and taught in the district may be a bit conflicting; however I have done the best I could possibly do. Most teachers boarded with the folks in the community and often a spare bedroom was kept solely for "the teachers' room".

In the spring of 1927 or 1928 the Marquis of Anglesey from Wales, whose father owned coal mines in Britain, presented the Stormount School with a steel flag pole. The Marquis had met an oil promoter by the name of Flemming, who had drilled an oil well on the R. Ness farm. This well took two years to drill and was called the Anglesey Number 1 and went down 3,000 feet. It was the first rotating rig in Canada and the first to be powered by electricity. The steel for the flag pole was made from a piece of the oil well casing and presented to the school complete with flag and set in cement. After the ceremony, the children got a half day off from school, thus an occasion to remember!

In 1928 a new barn was built at the school and south of the school was where the girls' toilet was located. The boys' toilet was joined on solidly to the school so there was no chance for an upset on Halloween. A well wasn't drilled for the school until around 1930.

Some of the older boys recall playing hockey at the noon hour with some Indian children whose parents were clearing brush on the Schaber land. They played on a slough south west of the school. Their hockey sticks consisted of willow sticks and their skates were moccasins and a good time was had by all.

Miss Harriett Crossman was the last teacher to live in the teacherage. In 1957 George Haynes purchased this building and moved it onto his land converting it into a house for hired help. Mr. and Mrs. Al Kneeshaw purchased the schoolhouse in 1958 and moved it onto their land, making a cozy home out of the original schoolhouse.

Many lady teachers came from the city, inexperienced girls, and after a year or two of teaching in the rural areas would leave as mature women of the world, benefitting from their sojourn in the country. Some stayed on as wives to the district farmers. Not all the country teachers were women — young men also taught and were introduced into the way of country folk. They look back with pride on the day they started on their own in some remote rural school. The teacher not only taught the three "Rs'" to their pupils but coached softball teams, directed plays, gave advise on many community undertakings and above all played a great part in shaping our heritage.

JOSEPH and MARGARET BLAIN as told to Dot Gerlitz by May Maxwell

Mr. and Mrs. Joseph Blain immigrated from Griswold, Iowa, in the spring of 1907, accompanied by their six children, three boys and three girls. They brought with them six horses, four cows, chickens, two dogs and the necessary farm implements.

They rented a farm two miles south of Okotoks, on the old Bemus place, near the cemetery and stayed there for two years. In 1909, they moved to the Morrison place, which was one and a half miles further west and here they stayed for four years. They then moved to the Thompson place (now belonging to the Cole family) and they stayed there until 1917, farming one section there and one section at the Pascal place.

Mr. Blain farmed and ran a dairy business there, keeping around 25 or 30 milk cows at all times. The price of a quart of milk in those days was 5¢. In 1917 they moved to farm at Sandstone, which Mr. Blain purchased, and here he raised cattle and was engaged in the dairying business. The land he bought was E½ Sec. 12 T21 R1 W5 and the land he rented was W½ Sec. 12 T21 R1 W5. The cattle that he raised were put out to pasture, grass fed and when fattened they were driven to market along the Macleod Trail, accompanied by riders on horseback. The Blain family stayed here for 10 years till 1927, when they moved to the Mencke Place, two miles south of DeWinton, where they stayed till selling out in 1937.

While the family was living in the Sandstone district, they were very interested in the Sandstone brickyard, where the manufacture of bricks was carried out. It was in operation in 1910 until 1915, with between 50 and 60 employees, living in huts and tents. Irvine Hurst was the manager and he later owned the Canadian Cement Co.

Their children are as follows;

May, who married Roy Maxwell, with two children.

Margaret, in Calgary with three children.

Arthur, a bachelor, farming at Mossleigh.

Alex, in Camrillo, California, married to Margaret McCallum, with two boys.

John, moved to California in 1927, where he ran a dairy farm in Sacramento until he passed away in 1967.

Ina, Mrs. A. Leiper, with two boys and one girl. Lives in Calgary in the Cedars Villa Nursing Home.

Christine, married to Carl Parker. Went first to California, then to Oregon. She has now returned to Calgary and is in the Crossbow Nursing Home.

Mark, left the home district in 1936 for the Oilfields and in 1946 he went to Leduc. He married Hilda Farley and they live at Devon, Alberta, where he is engaged in the oil business. They have two sons and one daughter.

GEORGE BREMNER

George was a brother to A. P. Bremner and came to settle on a C.P.R. quarter, which he later bought, in about 1895. He was a widower with six sons but Jim is the only one we have any mention of. George lived alone in a shack on SE¼ 35-21-1-W5 and Jim stayed with the Archie Bremners from the time he was twelve years old. George attended all the local dances and was, self appointed, judge of who was the 'Belle of the Ball'. He died in 1912 and is buried in the East.

ROSCOE AND ALETHA BROWN FAMILY — by Aletha Bakstad

We moved to the De Winton District from Spring Coulee in 1935 and bought our land from Mr. Joe Blain. This was NE½-13-21-1-W5 and we sold some of it to Mr. Singh Hari. We had five children when we came, four girls and a boy. Muriel was 14 at the time, Joyce, 9, Alice, 7, Violet, 5, and Delbert, 1½. During the six years we lived there the children went to Stormount School.

We didn't have very good luck through this period; I was ill and nearly lost my life, it took two years for me to recuperate. Rock, my husband, had spinal meningitis and spent 54 days in the hospital. The youngest daughter, Violet, had tonsil and appendix operations, Alice had Rheumatic Fever, was in the hospital in Calgary and recovered well. All the children had Scarlet Fever. One year we were hailed out, had no crop at all. The hail killed all my turkeys which really didn't matter as we had no grain to feed them. We bought 200 sheep which promptly became ill and lost all of their lambs. They weren't getting enough milk. The sheep also lost all their wool, some kind of a fever they had.

Rock's health wasn't good so after selling out to Mr. Bill Heater in 1942 we went to Meadow Lake, Saskatchewan, where my folks lived. This was a better move for us and we stayed there for fifteen years before we moved to Haney, B.C. where we stayed for another fifteen years. It was here that my husband died from a heart attack in 1968. Two years later I

Rock and Aletha Brown, 1942.

married Carol Bakstad and moved to Wildwood, Alberta where I now live.

All of my children are married, Muriel and Violet live in Meadow Lake, Saskatchewan and the other three live in Alberta.

THE CHERNOWS

Antony Chernow and his son, Steve, arrived in the De Winton area in the spring of 1927 and took up residence one-half mile south of De Winton. A daughter, Florrie, also lived with them for a while. In 1930 Steve married Annie Malyk and, in the next eight years they had three sons. Nick, born 1931, married Myrna Schmaus, they had four children; Wayne, 1956, now with the R.C.A.F.; Glen, 1959; Kevin, 1963 and Kimberley, 1971. Nick lives in Nakusp, B.C. and Myrna in Calgary. Alfred, born 1936, married Jeanette Tapper in 1960, has one son, Darren, they live in Calgary. Peter, born 1938, became an American citizen in 1970 has his own clothing and hairstyling business (A Man's World) in San Diego, California.

The boys got their education at Stormount school and took an active part in the community before going off on their own.

Annie and Steve were card players and took interest in the development of the community. They continued to farm until 1970 when they sold their place and moved into Calgary. They still take part in some of the community affairs and keep in touch with their old neighbours.

Steve is on the Pine Creek Cemetery board.

Antony left the district in 1935 to live in Calgary and passed away in April 4, 1964. Florrie has also passed away.

Darren Chernow is a member of the Thornhill Swim Club and has won many swimming championships.

HAROLD EDGAR COLE — by Ruby Cole

Harold was the youngest son of James and Mabel Cole. He was born in Plymouth, England and emigrated with the family to Chicago, U.S.A. in 1906. There his father and mother ran a butcher shop. In 1913 the family moved to Calgary, Alberta and settled in the Twin Bridges district west of Calgary. Here they started their dairying business. Harold rode horseback to the Elbow River country school four miles away. In 1918 the family moved to the Sandstone district, northwest of Okotoks, Alta. (N.W.¼ 2-21-1-W5).

Harold attended the Panima and later the Stormont country schools. Here he grew up and worked with the family, clearing brush, breaking sod and milking cows. He was an ardent curler and was greatly interested in hockey and the World Series Baseball.

When his father retired from farming, he took partnership with his brother Frederick Walter and the farm carried on under F.W. & H. E. Cole (Cole Brothers).

In 1955, Harold had an added interest and on Oct. 13th of that year, saw the foundation of a new home on the S.W.¼ 2-21-1-W5. On May 26th, 1956 in St. Barnabas Church, High River, Alta. he married Ruby May Pegler of Okotoks. With this union the secret of the once missing milk cans on a Hallowe'en night was

Mr. and Mrs. Harold E. Cole, May 26, 1956.

Cole Family front row: L. to R. Harold, Jim (Father), Mabel (Mother), Fred. Back Row: May and Lil.

revealed. Harold had married one of the culprits whom his father had paid ten cents to find the cans which were missing from the Sandstone C.P.R. station platform.

Harold continued working on the family farm until his sudden death on October 25th, 1963 at the age of 59 years.

My mother and I live here in our little home which holds so many happy memories of a short seven and a half years of married life.

JAMES AND MABEL (TURNER) COLE & FAMILY

James (Jim) Cole emigrated from Plymouth, England in Nov. 1905 to Chicago, Ill., to start a new butchering business. He returned in April, 1906 for his wife, Mabel Elizabeth (nee Turner) and four children: Lillian, May, Frederick Walter and Harold Edgar. The family remained in Chicago until 1913 and then, because of increasing gangster activity in those days prior to prohibition, Jim and Mabel decided to move their family west. (Fred could recall a shooting taking place on the street in front of their Chicago home.) Mabel had a married sister living near Calgary so that is where they headed. Jim rented a farm in the Twin Bridges area west of Calgary and lived there until 1918. (Mabel didn't like the idea of moving to the farm at first so she ran a boarding house on 4th Ave. in Calgary for about two years before going to the farm.)

Jim bought a farm (N.W.¼ 2-21-1-W5) from "Windy" Moore. The family moved to this farm, located northwest of Okotoks on April 1st, 1918. Fred recalled riding horseback and driving the cattle to the new farm on Easter Sunday, 1918.

The family — now the third and fourth generations — have been in the dairy business ever since and this is probably one of the oldest family dairy farms in Alberta. Over the years more land was purchased and the farm grew to include W½ 2-2-21-1-W5, E½ 2-2-10-21-W5, approximately 70 acres on the SE¼ 2-21-1-W5 (now owned by Jack Blight) and the S½ 2-11-21-1-W5 (This was purchased from the Canada Cement Co.)

Jim Cole died in Oct. 1953 and his wife passed away in Jan. 1958.

Lillian Cole returned to England to care for her ailing Grandmother and married Ernest Robinson, a British Navy man. Lil died in 1972 and is survived by her husband, one daughter, Honor and two granddaughters, Mary and Margaret, all living in England.

May Cole married Bert Blight and lived in Calgary until her death in 1948. She is survived by her husband and three sons: Jack of Calgary, Jim of Victoria, B.C. and Dick of Red Deer, also five granddaughters, two grandsons and four great-grandchildren. She was predeceased by one son, Rex.

Fred (born Aug. 1899) married June Alberta Marshall (born June 1898). (Marshall history to be found elsewhere in this book) They have three sons, Frederick Charles (Freddie), Ernest James and Edward George (Ted). Fred farmed on the home place until his sudden death on March 22nd, 1976. June and two of her sons (Freddie and Ernest) still live on the farm. Fred and June celebrated their 50th wedding anniversary in Jan. 1973, with a gathering of family and friends in the old De Winton hall.

Fred (Sr.) loved to talk of old times — travelling by horseback or team and sleigh to country dances; card parties and friendly get-togethers with sing-songs around the piano. (Lil played the piano and Fred had a very fine voice and loved to sing.) Bert and May Blight, their family and many old country friends spent summer Sundays at the farm enjoying what they called the "Devon and Cornwall" picnics.

Fred recalled his father going to a spring meeting of the U.F.A. in De Winton in about 1919. The main topic of discussion was placing a ban on the road. Jim felt roads were built to use and was disgusted with the idea of a ban, expressed his opinion and didn't return to any more U.F.A. meetings.

Harold used to maintain some of the local roads for the Municipality in the '30's. The family owned a rubber-tired tractor, (McCormick Deering W30) a novelty in those days. This was used to pull a "float" weighted with two lengths of railroad track to drag the roads.

Freddie, born Aug. 1923, married Lucille Ellis of Okotoks in 1950 and they have two children: Lorraine, who married Greg Darling, has one daughter and lives in Victoria, B.C.; Tim, who lives at home and is apprenticing as a plumber. Freddie spent three years in the airforce during World War II and was based in Toronto and Trenton, both of Ontario, and Claresholm, Alta. He is presently farming with his brother, Ernest.

Ernest (born June, 1925) married Betty Swanson of Bentley, Alta. and has two sons and a daughter; Richard is employed, at the present time, by the Town of Okotoks; Annette and Billy attend school in Okotoks.

Freddie and Ernest took their schooling at Panima and Stormont country schools and the old De Winton High School.

Ted was born on Jan. 30th, 1936 and attended school at Stormont and Okotoks. He married Linda Pitt of Calgary and has two sons, Bradley and Jeffrey. Ted is employed by Shell, Canada Ltd. He and his family live in the Acadia district, Calgary.

The family farm and dairy business have seen several changes — from hand milking to machines and a new pipe-line set up. At first the milk was hauled in cans down Sandstone hill to the CPR station by team and wagon, then by truck. "Scottie" Rogers of Okotoks, who worked on the Pegler farm at one time, recalls one day that Fred Sr. was late for the train. In his haste, Fred rounded the corner on the hill too fast with the team and sleigh swung around on the icy track and cans of milk went flying, rolled down the hill, spilling milk all over. No milk reached the train that day! Later milk was hauled to De Winton CPR station and then to the Okotoks station. In the early fifties, the Okotoks Transport, then owned by Bob Grisdale, picked the cans of milk up at the farm and hauled it to Union Dairy in Calgary. In the early '60s we were forced to install a bulk tank and the milk is picked up every second day by a tank truck.

Fred (Sr.) could recall many changes that have taken place over the years and we regret not writing this sooner when we would have had his vivid memories as a source of information.

MILTON CONNELL

Milton Connell was an early settler in the Stormount area, arriving in the 1880's. He homesteaded the NE¼-26-21-1-W5. He remained a bachelor and came to an untimely end in a shooting accident while duck hunting on what was known as the Connell slough, on his own property. This land is subdivided into several parcels. His original shack was purchased by Ben McLaughlin and moved to NE¼-3-22-1-W5. It is still in existence as a part of the Ivie residence.

ROBERT GORDON DAFOE AND FAMILY

Gordon Dafoe was born in Welwyn, N.W.T. (later Saskatchewan) on June 26, 1896, the second son of John and Margaret Dafoe. He moved with his family to Calgary, Alberta early in 1897 — living in a house on the site where the old Naglers Store was later located. He received his education in Calgary and spent his summers on the 2 BAR ranch, north-east of Gleichen, which was managed by his father.

He served with the Strathcona Horse overseas during the first World War and on his return home, farmed with his brother, Sam, at Gleichen.

In 1925 he married Georgina McMillan of Gleichen who had moved there with her family from Kilgore, Idaho in 1906.

Gordon and Jean farmed in the Shouldice area for five years during which time their son, Jack and daughter, Betty were born.

In the spring of 1930 they moved to the DeWinton area where they farmed the Simpson homestead one mile south of Melrose School, which their children later attended. In 1936 they moved to their present home N.W.¼-14-21-W5 (the old Dewar homestead).

Jack and Betty completed elementary school at Stormount School.

Betty was a 1950 graduate of the Calgary General Hospital School of Nursing and presently is living in Okotoks with her husband, Ted Weaver and their family.

Jack and his wife Eva are continuing the family farm.

JACK DAVIS

Jack Davis came from Ireland about 1913 and settled on bottom land along the Sheep River, in or around the Panima district. He operated a big steam threshing outfit which he used to do custom threshing for the farmers in the area. He was on this farm two years and then moved to the half section farm in the Stormount district that was to be his home for the rest of his days. This farm was across the road from Sam Hamilton's homestead, NW¼ 26-21-1-W5.

Jack was a bachelor when he came to De Winton, but hired a lady to keep house for him, whom he later married. He was the first man to occupy this land and it was heavily wooded. He broke most of this land with eight horses and a walking plow. Later he hired Andy Giffin with his tractor to complete the job.

With the help of his wife, Jack operated a mixed farm where they grew grain and raised hogs, milked cows and shipped cream. Jack worked very hard as did most men in those days and his health started to fail. In 1935 he took his own life. They had no children, so his wife rented the farm to Jack Goettler and she returned to England where her family lived. In 1938 the farm was sold to Con Poffenroth.

JOHN AND SARAH (McMILLAN) DEWAR — by Belle Culley

John and Sarah Dewar came to Calgary from Glengarry, Ontario, in 1889 and made their home on 17th Avenue, off of 1st St. southeast on the north side of the avenue. Sarah's mother and her brother, John were then on the farm where John and Sarah later lived, and presently owned by the Dafoe family. Their first daughter, Jessie, was born in Alexandria, Glengarry, Ontario, the only one of the children to be born in the east. Seven more were born in Alberta. All of them, with the exception of Hugh, who was born in Calgary, were born on the farm. They lived in two different houses on the farm; one up on the hill and

John and Sarah Dewar.

later, in the larger house, below the hill, where a creek ran by.

John plastered a number of homes around De Winton, among them, the Charlie Marshall home. One day, when John was away plastering some home, Sarah saw Pat Burns and his men ride by. A short time later a nasty blizzard blew up, Sarah put a lamp in the window, the men saw it and came to the house where they were fed and bedded down on the floor. The next morning after breakfast, they fed and watered their horses and one horse put his foot through Sarah's copper boiler. Copper boilers were very precious in those days but the rider didn't compensate.

John was a piper and Scottish dancer, he played in parades in Calgary and Edmonton. He played in Edmonton when some Earl from England arrived and was given royal treatment, fireworks and all.

As the family was growing up in the larger house below the hill, Holts were their neighbors to the south, Tuckers were on the same farm at one time; Frasers were to the west; Austins, to the northwest, (later, the R. Ness home); Stormont School was directly north. John served on the Stormont School Board for many years.

Jessie, the first born, lived on the farm until she was 16 years old, then went to Edmonton to attend business college. She lived with her Aunt and Uncle, the Malcolm Dewars. After becoming a stenographer, she went to work in the Land Titles Office in Edmonton. She had quite an experience when she, and a group of friends got on a raft on the Saskatchewan River. A storm blew up and they lost all their food and whatever else goes on a raft. No lives lost. She met and married a young English gentleman, Cecil Edwards, just out from England. They first lived in Glenbow, west of Calgary, and ran the Post Office and General Store until they bought a farm at Delia, where they lived until they sold out and moved to New Westminster. It was here that they both passed away, Cecil, at the age of 90 years and Jessie at 86. They celebrated their sixtieth wedding anniversary in Calgary in 1970. Their family is all living.

Hugh, the second child went to high school in Butte, Montana, after finishing at Stormont. He spent some time at home after finishing school before he went to Scotfield to homestead. He met and married Jessie Anderson and they had four of a family. In 1923 they left the homestead, because of drought, and moved to Burnaby, B.C. where Hugh still resides. Jessie passed away in 1970. They had four children, Evelyn, George deceased at 42, Pearl and Jack. Hugh remarried at the age of 80 and he and his wife are very happy, enjoying bridge and dances.

Katie, was third, she also attended school in Butte after leaving Stormont. She lived with her Aunt Bella, her mother's sister. One time, after returning from Montana, she saw a previous admirer riding towards her home, but she was not anxious to see him so she ran upstairs, climbed down a ladder that had been left where they were building a new addition, and ran across the plowed field to the Holt home. The admirer never did catch up with her. After her folks moved to Calgary, she attended Bankview Presbyterian Church, where she met William (Bill) Cunningham and they were married in 1918. They had two sons, David and William (Bill Jr.). They bought a home on 13th Ave. S.W. in Calgary. With the exception of four years in Regina, they lived there until Katie became ill and passed away in the Glamorgan Nursing Home. Bill, her husband, kept the house for sometime after but finally sold and moved to the Granada Apartments, where he is now living with his nice wife Leala Berger Cunningham. Their son Bill lives in Calgary and David in Saskatoon.

Alexander (Alex), the fourth child attended Stormont School until the family moved to Edmonton for two years, then back to the farm for two years and then they all moved to Calgary. He joined the 49th Battalion, (later the 10th), and went overseas to fight in the first World War. Alex was 19 when he went overseas, he came home shellshocked and eventually had to have a leg amputated. While in England, he met a pretty nurse and married her. He had to come home ahead of her as she had to wait for papers allowing her to come to Canada. They have six children, all living. Alex died in 1962, his widow still lives in Calgary with her daughter, Violet.

While Miss Alexander was teaching at Stormont school she thought that she would like to learn to shoot. Alex Dewar put up a target for her. She had never fired a gun and when she took aim and fired, Alex, standing to one side of the target, fell to the ground. She thought that she had killed him!

Roy, sometimes called Rory, was the fifth child. After his schooling he became a stenographer and bookkeeper and ran his own 'Steno Office' after he returned from the war. He joined the 50th Battalion when he was 18 years old and went overseas came home seriously wounded, had a series of operations. His mother said that if she had her life to live over again she would have no sons because one just raised sons to go to war and be killed or wounded. Roy married Lulu Peters and they had two children, Roddy and Vivian. Rod was lost at sea, when the ship he was on was torpedoed near the Cape of South Africa. Roy passed away in Vancouver at the age of 56 and his wife, Lulu and daughter, Vivian live in Vancouver.

Myles was the sixth, was born on the farm and was quite a mischief and tease. His mother once said that he would grow up to be bad or grow up to be great. He did all right. He spent most of his working time, forty-five years, with the Y.M.C.A. He started in Calgary and served in Toronto. He was with the Armed Forces for five years, 1940-1945, in Ontario, Newfoundland, England, Belgium, Holland, and France. On returning from the forces, he served in Hamilton and in Saint John, New Brunswick, as General Secretary, Y.M.C.A., during the raising of funds for, and the building of, a new Y.M.C.A. He ended his career as Executive Secretary of the Etobicoke Y.M.-Y.W.C.A. when he was honoured, on retiring, with a book of letters. In 1925, Myles married a Calgary girl, Rene Bateson, who was an excellent swimmer and diver and also a piano teacher. They have three children, Mylene, Dahlia and John, nine grandchildren. They live in Etobicoke, Ontario.

Bella, (now Belle), the 7th child, was born on her Dad's birthday, "some birthday present!" Belle said they must have felt like throwing her back in, her being the 7th. No matter, they were all loved. She remembers having to attend school when only 5 years old because there were not enough pupils to keep the school open. It must have been very dull as she was not taught anything. She remembers being invited by the Fraser girls, Isabelle and Mildred, to go with them to their home after school, and she did, her folks didn't know where she was and were all out looking for her. Her brother, Roy, found her and gave her a rough ride home on the back of his pony. Not much punishment from her parents, I guess they were glad to see her. She met her husband, Willard Culley, while still going to school. He became a druggist. They had four children; Lois, now living in Santa Barbara, California, Raymond, in Lethbridge, Donald, killed in an accident in 1944, and Robert, now with IBM in Calgary. Husband, Willard, went overseas with the 8th Field Ambulance as a pharmacist. He became ill with malaria while in Italy and at one time, they thought he was dead and he was put in the morgue. He came to, hearing a priest giving the last rites to another soldier and demanded to be taken out of there in pretty strong language . . . cannot repeat. After the war he became manager of Government Stores in Banff and his wife, Belle, became the Weather Lady (meteorologist), for 19 years. He died in the Belcher Hospital in Calgary from war disabilities, in 1961. Belle, now retired, lives in Calgary. Son, Raymond, at 18 was on the Summerside Corvette during the war.

James, (Jim), the youngest of the family, lives in Calgary now after many years in Vancouver. He married Bethel Scott, daughter of Mr. and Mrs. Percy Scott of Calgary. They have a girl and a boy. Carol (Mrs. Tom Jones) has a son; Brent, lives in Calgary; Brent, a childless widower, lives in Vancouver. Jim worked in the Gas Company until he joined the Pay Corps during the war, at that time they lived in Calgary. He was an accountant and his wife Bethel, worked for Dr. Duncan Sr. while they lived in Calgary.

A dance and party was held at the John Dewar home; about 1906 or '07 Jessie Dewar and John McNeill were quite chummy and someone gave Bella a large ladle and told her to present it to the couple. At the time, she had no idea why, but later learned that it meant they were spooning. She was only 4 years old at the time. During one square dance, at the same party, she remembers her mother being 'Birdie in the centre' and she thought how pretty her Mom was.

John Dewar lost 13 head of cattle during the blizzard of 1907. Bella remembers her Dad having two lovely black horses and a new black democrat (high class in those days). She remembers scratching the lovely back of the front seat with a pin when she had been put down for a sleep on the way back from the Exhibition in Calgary. Doesn't remember being punished for same, her Dad was a big man and she should have been afraid of a spank.

Alex spent some time helping brother Hugh, on his homestead and also helped his father at home until the farm was sold to a man by the name of Stuckey. This was not a very satisfactory deal as John never managed to get all his money, it was a very distressing time for all concerned.

When the Dewars left the farm in 1912, they bought a home on 14th Street S.W. where they lived out the rest of their years. John died in 1930 and Sarah in 1945.

FREDERICK PERCIVAL AND MARY (DALZELL) DICK — by Lois Knupp

Fred Dick came to DeWinton in 1915 as an agent for "Home Comfort" stoves. He came from New Brunswick and stayed at the Latimer place and following his marriage to Mary Dalzell in 1918, made the Latimer place their home.

Fred was on the Stormont School Board for many

Fred and Mary Dick — 50th Anniversary.

years and put in many a day helping to build the old DeWinton Hall. He was also, a director of the Panima Mutual Telephone Company for most of the time it was in existence.

Mary belonged to the Ladies Red Cross and the Ladies Aid Groups. She was noted for the huge flocks of turkeys and chickens she used to raise. Their home was always open, and was a frequent stopping place for their many friends. They had three children; Ivan, DeWinton, Lois Knupp, DeWinton, and Alan of Calgary.

They lived on the Latimer place for twenty years and then sold it to the Singhs. They moved to a quarter north of them, which they had bought some years before. They lived there until 1955, when they sold and moved to the "Old Cushing Place" at DeWinton.

They celebrated their fiftieth wedding anniversary in the DeWinton Hall in 1968, with an open house for their many friends.

They retired to Calgary in 1970 and Fred died in 1971. Mary now, in 1976, resides at the Southwood Nursing Home in Calgary.

HUGH AND EMMA LOUISE (LLOYD) FRASER —
by Lloyd and Bernice Fraser

Hugh Fraser was born August 3, 1871 at Dunvegan, Glengarry County, Ontario. Emma Louise Lloyd was born in London, England, on January 7, 1867. She married Hugh Fraser on November 20, 1889, in Calgary, North West Territories.

Hugh was engaged in the dray business in Calgary and three children were born during that time. In 1893, the Fraser family moved to Section 22-Twp.2-R1-W5th which was just west of Stormont School, where there were some buildings and a spring. Later this was part of the Ness place. They later moved to S.W.16-21-1-W5 and finally to S.E.¼-16-21-1-W5. They raised Clydesdale and Hackney horses, Shorthorn cattle, chickens and milk cows. A trip to Calgary, with horses and democrat, would require rising at four in the morning, so eggs and butter would keep cool. The return trip would perhaps be at seven in the evening with staples for a growing family.

They had a five-roomed log house, and eight children were born in this homestead home. In 1912, the last one, John Stanley, was born with Dr. Murray from Okotoks in attendance. Ten children walked over the big hill to attend Stormont School. The big hill belonged to the Big Bend Cattle Company and later was the Schaber farm.

In 1912, Dan and Hugh left to go homesteading at Youngstown. Hugh was drowned while riding his horse on July 20, 1915, across the swollen Berry Creek near Scotfield, Alberta. He is buried in Pine Creek Cemetery near De Winton.

In 1917, the Frasers moved to Vancouver, leaving Gilbert to do the farming. Gilbert was called into the army, so his father would spend his winters at the coast, and return in the spring to help with the farming. In 1927, Dave Kromm bought their half section.

March 17, 1947, Hugh passed away at the age of 86. Emma Louise passed away April 14, 1955, at the age of 88. Both are buried in Forest Lawn Cemetery, Burnaby, B.C.

Emma Louise Fraser and Hugh Fraser — 80 Years old, with grandson and name sake, Hugh Fraser.

The children of Hugh and Emma Louise Fraser are as follows; Isabella, born 1890, in Calgary, N.W.T., passed away in infancy. Daniel William, born March 12, 1891, married Elizabeth Adelia Young, died in Calgary, October 1975.

Hugh, born March 28, 1893, in Calgary; drowned July 20, 1915, and is buried in Pine Creek.

Gilbert, born June 16, 1895, at De Winton and now lives in Calgary. Isabel Margaret, born April 2, 1897. She married Dick Hansen (deceased), living at Crescent Beach, B.C.

Mildred May, born May 3, 1899, married Robin C. Henderson (deceased). She died February 20, 1976.

Alexander E., born December 11, 1900, married Ethel Alberta Herr (deceased). He died in March, 1975.

Alfred John, born March 28, 1902, married Claire Sirr, living at Didsbury, Alta.

Gordon James, born February 7, 1904, married Anne Rapier, lives at Burnaby, B.C.

Lloyd, born February 17, 1906, married Bernice Wright, lives on R. R. No. 2 Okotoks.

Norman Malcolm, born June 17, 1908, married Edna Merry, died May 24, 1956 in Burnaby, B.C.

John Stanley, born November 28, 1912, married Barbara Larsen, died July 20, 1962 in Burnaby, B.C.

LLOYD AND BERNICE (WRIGHT) FRASER — by Bernice Fraser

On April 28, 1932, Lloyd Fraser and Bernice Wright were married in Calgary. Lloyd farmed his father's farm nine miles north-east of Calgary. On April 7, 1933 their son, Douglas Lloyd was born in Calgary. In the spring of 1934, Lloyd put the crop in on his father's farm and in June we moved to 10-21-1-W5, the west half, which was the McNeil farm at De Winton.

We moved in a twenty-four foot cook car belonging to Lloyd's father and pulled by six horses. We travelled on the east side of the Macleod Trail, through Midnapore, and took the back trails west, arriving at the McNeil farm at dark. The Macleod Trail was gravel and all the side roads were dirt at that time. It was reported to us later when we passed a farm north west of here, the people said, "There goes two who will never make it!"

Our cook car had two rooms, one ply of boards, and was covered with tar paper. Later we were able to afford pale blue building paper to line the inside and that was a slight improvement. It was very hot in summer and could get very cold in winter. We had a Home Comfort stove and with plenty of Willow wood it would heat up in a short while. Night time in winter was another story. Wood has no staying power and we certainly couldn't afford coal. We lived in the cook car until 1938.

We owned a Model T 1926, Ford half-ton truck. In the winter of 1933 Lloyd worked in Swift's feed lot for fifteen dollars a week, which enabled us to buy two horses and two cows.

Shortly after we arrived on the place, H. B. McNeil had a farm auction sale. He had some good Shorthorn Cattle and we were able to purchase three of the cows. The price of these cows ranged between twelve and eighteen dollars. Forty years later in 1974, we sold the major portion of our cows and some were descendants of the above three.

Lloyd spent his winters cutting brush with an axe and burning what was not suitable for fire-wood or for use as fenceposts. In summer he broke land, worked it and picked roots. There weren't any dull moments and it was work and more work, but when you are young, healthy, and happy, with plenty of ambition, you don't really mind.

There was a creek running through this place and it was a joy to have, but unfortunately, it was not always reliable. In dry years it was reduced to a trickle and in winter it would freeze up, so then you either had to haul water or melt snow. We dug several holes, with Lloyd in the hole and me pulling the dirt up with a pulley. All we ever got was seepage, but even that was better than the other system. In about 1944, we were able to afford a drilled well.

It didn't matter how hard you worked, there was barely enough money for the necessities of life. In 1937, Lloyd saw a little wagon in McNeil's Hardware in Okotoks for $4.95. He wished to purchase it for our son's fourth birthday but he just didn't have any money. The hardware man trusted him to pay later, so there was a happy father and little boy. Thank goodness for all the people who trusted us!

In 1938, Mrs. H. B. McNeil passed away in Chesley, Ontario. She owned the major portion of this farm and left it to her brother, Archie McNeil, and he immediately put it up for sale. Harold Victor Reeves of Okotoks bought it for $17.50 per acre. Reeves agreed to rent us the place and also helped us to purchase a tractor. Up to this time we farmed with horses.

In March, 1938, our daughter, Evelyn Louise, was born. Reeves built a two room house, and later in the year we were able to move into it. It was heaven after living in a cook car for four years!

Our last child, Margaret May, was born on December 16, 1940. Stormont School was in the Calgary School District and all three or our children rode horses and, like their father, were able to obtain their grade eight there. The division between the Calgary and Foothills School Divisions was our south fence. When Douglas was ready for high school in 1947, they allowed him to ride the bus, providing there was room. Luckily there was space for him all through his high school and also for Evelyn for one year. Somewhere along the way, Stormont was taken into the Foothills Division, the dirt roads were gravelled, and in 1954, the school bus came right past our gate. The children no longer had to walk three miles to the closest corner.

Lloyd purchased a threshing machine in 1941 so we were able to thresh our own grain and do some custom threshing. For the master and his wife the hours were usually from four in the morning to eleven at night. There was the milking, separating, feeding the horses, and breakfast on the table by six in the morning. The men were in the field by seven in the morning, and worked till seven at night. With our own family that made fourteen people for meals. The men worked hard so this required huge quantities of food for lunches and three meals a day. I kept Doug home from school the odd day to help bring in water, and do other odd jobs because it was very hard for me to keep up with everything. Usually about half of our crew stayed through the full run, and the other half was on the move. This meant that Lloyd was taking a man into Calgary after supper, and searching the beer parlors for another one to bring out. With all the trouble with men, horses, wagons and the threshing machine, at the end of harvest you were ready for twenty four hours of sleep. Wages for help in the early forties were very low. In 1950 we stopped using men, teams and wagons, because it was no longer economical to do it that way. Wages, by then, were eight dollars a day. For a number of years we threshed with a "Farmhand" but, change was inevitable, so in 1954 we went the combine route. Men still worked long hours with the combine but you certainly got the work done a lot cheaper. In some cases women had an easier life but some had to learn to run the machines, and work right along with their husbands.

We raised cows, pigs, chickens, turkeys and for about fifteen years we shipped broiler hatching eggs. Prices for produce in the thirties and forties and beyond were a disaster. In 1933 I had thirty roasting chickens and I got fifteen dollars for all thirty! One time we had two bins of wheat that we couldn't sell. Lloyd was going to burn the stubble, so he ploughed a fire guard around the bins, the fire jumped the guard, straw by straw, and then it had the bins on fire. Lloyd came dashing home for sacks and cream cans of water. He kept hollering at me to work harder because the roof was on fire. Finally I said; "Let it burn, it isn't worth saving!" Lloyd saved the bin by throwing dirt on the roof. He sold the wheat for the magnificent sum of sixty cents a bushel. I thought we would never get the farm paid off, but eventually from a homestead environment, things did gradually get better.

Here it is 1976, and after forty two years on the same farm we are at the end of the road.

THE CLIFFORD R. FRIEDLEY FAMILY — by Marguerite P. Friedley

The Friedleys were not old timers of the Stormount district; as Clifford and his wife Marguerite, with their daughter, Yvonne, didn't move there until October, 1944, but they farmed there for twelve years. They moved back to the Delia district after this period, which was their original farm. The following is the history of the family, who either stayed or visited Clifford and family, and were known to most people in the community.

Their mother, Emma Sarah, resided with Clifford and family for over five years. She was born on May 11, 1886, at Day, Ontario and lived on Manitoulin Island before coming west in 1912, marrying Philip Friedley at Delia in 1914. There were nine children born in this family, namely, Ralph Clifford, Roy Wilfred, William John, Harold Clayton, Phyllis Elizabeth, Daisy Louise, Raymond Garfield, Elmer Morris and Vera Lorraine. They attended Delia School and in 1928, Philip passed away, and Emma in 1965.

Clifford married Marguerite Lomas on December 3, 1941 at the Drumheller Baptist Church. Three children were born; Yvonne Celine, Kenneth Ralph, and Donald Raymond. Clifford farmed in partnership with his brothers at Delia. In the summer of 1944 he purchased a farm from Harold Reeves (The Fred Huckvale land) in the DeWinton district. Roy and Grandma Friedley also moved there till the other four Friedley brothers returned from the forces. Yvonne, born in 1943 started school at Stormont and her teacher was Harriet Crossman. She also attended Okotoks school. She is now Mrs. John Lowry, living in Drumheller, her husband is owner of the "Big Country Plumbing Co." They have three children; Jim, Cathy, and Stephen. Kenneth was born 1946 and also attended the same school as his sister. Ken lives in the town of Delia and farms. Donald was born 1953 and attended school in Delia. He is married to Loree Sutherland of Edmonton and he owns his own farm and also is an air spray pilot.

Roy never married, and he now farms in partnership with his brother Clifford.

William and Harold joined the Canadian Ordinance Corps, third division in 1941, returning in 1945. They stayed with us at DeWinton for that winter and then returned to the farm at Delia. They farmed in partnership until Harold died at his home in December 1966. William married Joan Sterling in 1951 and they have two sons, Phillip and Kevin.

Phyllis married John Birkhiem and they spent most of their married life in British Columbia as he worked for the C.P.R. Phyllis passed away at Vancouver in 1960. They had three children; Gordon, Victor and Shirley.

Daisy married William Killian and she lives at St. Albert. He passed away in 1975. They had three children; Thomas, Judy, and Linda.

Raymond joined the Royal Canadian Engineers fifth division in 1941. He served in the United Kingdom, Central Mediterranean, and Continental Europe. Raymond returned in 1945 and worked on the DeWinton farm with his brothers for two summers. He then went to work for Imperial Oil at Leduc. On June 20th, 1951 he married Martha McMinnis, and they were both killed two days later at a railway crossing near the Calgary Municipal Airport.

Elmer married Pauline Grauman in 1943. He served with the R.C.A.F. and now lives on his farm in the Delia district. They have five children; Joan, Judy, Gordon, Garry, and Douglas.

Vera married Abraham Schartner and they had four children; Robert, Reginald, Richard, and Deborah, all of Aldergrove, B.C.

In the spring of 1956 we sold our farm to my parents, Mr. and Mrs. Frank Lomas, who had already purchased the Harry Swarbrick farm. They lived there for some time before selling out to Jim Cross. They moved to Calgary and then to Drumheller where Mrs. Lomas passed away in 1964, and Frank passed away in 1969.

We met many nice people in the community and enjoyed the Christmas concerts at Stormount School and also fellowship at the Gospel Church in Okotoks. While Stormount School was open we boarded the student teachers, who were sent out from the University of Calgary every fall and spring, for seven years. We still reside on the same farm we moved to when we left DeWinton.

JACK AND IDA GOETTLER

In 1935 Jack and Ida Goettler with their two children, Merle and Jackie, moved on to the Jack Davis place NW¼ 26-21-1-W5. They came from Mortlach, Saskatchewan where they had suffered through seven years of drought and blowing soil. Things finally got so bad they loaded all their belongings, "livestock and machinery" included, on the freight train and shipped them to De Winton. They came early in the Spring and, with the help of neighbours, moved everything from De Winton to the farm in one day. It was quite late when they finished and the neighbours were going to leave for home, but Ida insisted they stay for supper. The stove had been set up and the table. From out of the jumble of packing boxes, barrels, etc., she produced a most delicious meal in about twenty minutes. Everything came from jars, and all from Ida's own garden in Saskatchewan. She was soon to become famous in the district for her good cooking, needle work, gardening, and poultry raising.

Merle and Jackie attended Stormount school. Jack raised some hogs, milked a few cows, and grew grain. They were good neighbours and much respected in the district. In the spring of 1938 they moved to a farm in Didsbury.

ADAM AND MARY GOERLITZ — by Dot Gerlitz

This story is a tribute to our parents, Adam and Mary Goerlitz and to all the brave and courageous people of the early years — their way of life was hard, but has left us a better place in which to live.

Adam and Mary Goerlitz (the former Mary

Elizabeth Kaiser) emigrated to Canada from the province of Saratov, on the Volga river in Russia in 1898. They were accompanied by their eldest daughter, Mary, and subsequently their family consisted of nine children, the rest being born after they filed on the homestead farm, three miles west of De Winton located at N.E. 28, 21, R1, W5. They left Russia after the Bolshevic Revolution, arriving in Canada with no worldly goods but with the true pioneer spirit and desire to succeed.

In their early years they carried on with mixed farming and gradually cleared their land of the brush in order to sow their crops. All the brush was cleared with axes and good strong backs. Indians were hired to help with this work, with the bucks sharpening the axes and often the squaws wielding them. The original farmhouse was built of logs which were chinked together with cow manure and clay stamped by the horses. This had to be done frequently to keep the cabin warm. The family were all raised in this log cabin and attended Stormount School for their education. In 1919, they suffered through a bad winter; hay was $60.00 a ton and they had to dig straw and sticks from the thatched roof of the barn to feed the animals.

Once a week a trip was taken to Calgary in the horse and buggy to trade sour cream for groceries at Shuler's Grocery located on 6th Avenue and 4th Street East. It took about six hours with a good team to make the trip.

Saturdays were days spent in the pursuit of their Seventh Day beliefs. They took turns holding their services at the different homesteads. So early Saturday morning, after chores, the family climbed into the democrat and left for the day. They took basket lunches with them which included their favorite German dishes — cabbage rolls and cabbage bread. The Goerlitz family usually drove through John and Jess Harrison's yard on the Sabbath and had a little visit with them on their way to the church services. The day was spent listening to sermons and singing hymns.

In later years, when cars were beginning to replace the horse and buggy, Mr. Goerlitz, accomplished the great feat of driving a Gray Dort car. He could do this providing his sons drove to the road allowance and put the car in high gear for him. Off he would go, all the way to Shuler's Grocery, where he turned off the key to stop the car! Coming home it was the same procedure, someone would start him off again in high gear. As he neared home the family who were on the look out for him sped to the gate to let him through. In he drove to the safety of home where he turned off the key. His son, Danny remembers getting out of the car on Pine Creek hill and racing for rocks to put behind the wheels, so the car wouldn't roll back down the hill. It took a real pioneer to trade horses for a seat behind the wheel of a car.

Their family consisted of Mary, who married Conrad Schneidmiller. They had two children, both

Back Row: standing: Elizabeth, Mary, Peter, Frank, Elmer, Danny, Lydia. Seated: Rose, Mrs. Goerlitz, Mr. Adam Goerlitz, Amelia, 1920's.

boys, one Ivan, who died at the early age of three, and Clarence, who is married and has two children living in Calgary.

The eldest son Frank married Charlotte Simmonds of Pollockville, Alberta. They have a family of five. After farming for many years at Acme, they have retired to Kelowna, British Columbia.

Peter, the second son, married Clara Charlesworth of Blairmore. Prior to this he farmed and was a partner with John Harrison during the early thirties. They did custom threshing and harvesting operations. One of Peter's favorite expressions was "Never say whoa in a tight spot", and he put this adage to use when hauling grain with sleigh and horses, when the snow was sparse. He worked many years as a bulk fuel dealer in and around Calgary, finally retiring to a well earned rest in the city. Peter passed away in February, 1976.

Lydia, the next child, likes to recall the days of trekking to Stormount School with her brothers and sisters. Sometimes they walked bare-foot through the fields, or rode two or three per horse providing the horse was not pulling a plow. Lydia worked hard at home and the majority of her chores were done outdoors, where she worked alongside her brothers in the barn and in the fields. She married H. C. (Bert) Rushmer and farmed with him for many years at Rosetown, Saskatchewan. They had four children, three boys and one girl. Their daughter Ramona, who had been working as a hair-dresser in the town of

Golden Wedding of Lydia (Goerlitz) and Bert Rushmer.

Okotoks, had a tragic accident on her way back to Rosetown for Christmas, and died on Christmas day, 1948. The three boys are married, Ivan and Wayne making their homes in Kelowna, and Norman in Calgary. Norman is now retired from the armed forces. Bert and Lydia moved to Okotoks in 1950 where they were both active in community affairs and made many friends. Lydia pursued her hair dressing career and was kept very busy with this. In 1975, they sold their home in Okotoks and retired to Kelowna, B.C., where they are enjoying their retirement. They celebrated their golden wedding anniversary in Kelowna in 1976. Lydia will always be remembered for her excellent angel food cakes and her brown bread — delicious!

Elizabeth, the next girl, received her advanced education at the Seventh Day Adventist College at Lacombe, Alberta and taught at several country schools before marrying Ted Bechthold of Beiseker. They had one daughter Doreen. Elizabeth was the victim of a fatal car accident at Beiseker in 1942.

We have included a few excerpts taken from the March 11, 1929 issue of The Western Farmer when an article about Elizabeth and her struggles to obtain an education were written by Mrs. Frank Jacobs of De Winton.

"We hear a lot in these days of the success achieved by older people. Here is a story that should be an inspiration to those girls and boys who are wondering how they are going to complete their high school studies and then go on to college and perhaps to university. The subject of this article had to overcome difficulties unknown to many of us. Elizabeth's parents, not too well acquainted with the country, were not in a position to give her much advice. She had to rely largely on her own effort, and yet she succeeded. Surely there is a challenge here for all of us."

"Elizabeth, though fond of school did not get ahead very fast. Of course there was the long distance to school, helping to milk the twelve cows, chores till time to rush to school, and chores at night till ready to fall asleep. The family at home spoke German which did not help Elizabeth with her studies in English literature, history and composition, so when she tried for her entrance exam at age fifteen, she failed to pass. She discussed it with the neighbors, who told her that little girls could often wash dishes or care for children in city families and go to school at the same time. Through a friend of her sister Lydia, she heard of a Doctor's family that had children, and wanted a girl to help. Elizabeth went to Calgary to live with them and found a happy home with educated English speaking people, which was the turning point in her life."

"Every spare moment was devoted to helping the Doctor's wife in any way possible and at the same time she forged ahead at school."

"Two years later Elizabeth went to Lacombe College with that years tuition paid for by her father. The following year was another critical point in her education, due to lack of funds. During that summer she went out alone with an old horse and buggy, driving throughout the countryside selling $300.00 worth of books for an Alberta book company. These funds enabled Elizabeth and her sister Millie to complete the following year at college. The following summer she sold $2,500.00 worth of books in the short time of six weeks, which made it possible for her to finish college and gain her Normal certificate in June, 1928."

"Elizabeth excelled in painting and drawing and had proven herself a natural salesman. She is now well on the road to success and forgotten are all the times when she was tempted to give up her ideals."

Amelia (Millie) the next daughter, after graduating from Crescent Heights High School, attended Canadian Union College at Lacombe. Her sister, Elizabeth sponsored her by canvassing Alberta farm homes to sell a book entitled "Home Physician and Guide to Health". This looked after the tuition. Sad but true, Millie did not conform to all the rules and regulations of the college; such as "length of skirts", "make-up", "meatless diets", "dates with the fellows" and so after two years she returned to Calgary to pursue her first love "Hair Dressing."

Millie was a mischevious child and recalls the day when she and her sister Rose were banished to the dark cellar for misbehaving when their parents were in Calgary. In spite of the fact that they were placed back to back and their pigtails tied together, they enjoyed their punishment as they emptied many jars of delicious home preserved fruit — thus ended punishment in the cellar.

She married A. C. (Sandy) Luft, who owned and directed Leyden's Funeral Homes. Millie owned and operated Millie's Hairstyling Shops for forty years. Millie and Sandy were both active in softball and bowling, and participated in the Provincial Finals for both sports. Millie was very active in ladies clubs in Calgary.

They have two sons, Barry, who is a teacher counsellor at Lord Beaverbrook High School, and Murray, who teaches sociology. Murray has spent several years in Bolivia in "the Mission Field". Both boys also excelled in sports and are very musical. Barry, married Lynn Harbough of Spokane, Washington, and they have two girls, much to the delight of Grandma and Grandpa.

Millie and Sandy are now retired and spend most of their spare time golfing at the Earl Grey Golf Club.

Rose, the youngest daughter, after completing her education at Stormount School, spent her time working on the farm until her parents retired to Calgary. In her early years she took piano lessons from Mrs. Frank Jacobs, one of their close neighbors. After moving to Calgary she married Vernon Rhoads. In the early years of their marriage they moved to Kent, Washington, U.S.A. They were blessed with a daughter Janice and a son Bob, but unfortunately, Vernon was a heart victim at an early age, leaving Rose to care for her young family. She became a member of the working world to provide an education for her children. Rose is now married to Howard Rose, and they are both retired. She is an organist in her Seventh Day Adventist Church where she is kept very active. Her daughter Janice is married to Knut Jensen, who is with the I.B.M. in Eugene, Oregon. Her son Bob served his country overseas working in the military hospital.

Danny, the next son, was ready to take over the homestead and further acquired lands when his parents were ready to retire to a well earned rest in Calgary in 1930. He married Dorothy McCulloch and they have three children: Sandra, Doug and John. They still have the original farm and enjoy the activities of the community.

Elmer, the youngest and the bachelor of the family, farmed for many years on some of the original homestead. He sold a quarter section of the original homestead in 1966, and retired to Vernon, British Columbia. He is kept busy raising grapes as a hobby and enjoys the mild climate of Vernon.

Mr. and Mrs. Goerlitz retired to Calgary, in the mid-thirties where they spent several happy years amongst their many German friends and relatives of Saratov connections. Mr. Goerlitz passed away suddenly in October, 1950 at the age of 82. Mrs. Goerlitz died in March, 1959 at the age of 88.

Mr. and Mrs. Goerlitz remained loyal to their Seventh Day Adventist faith throughout their life. They were real pioneers who toiled hard and enjoyed the true friendships and simpler things of life.

FRANK AND CHARLOTTE GOERLITZ

Frank Adam Goerlitz, the eldest son of Mr. and Mrs. A. H. Goerlitz helped at home in those early days brushing and breaking land.

About 1920, the Marshalls and Goerlitz' had the first stook threshing outfits in the district. Frank and Peter had a good run of 48 days the first year.

In 1925, Frank left the old home to make a start for himself buying land at Acme, 60 miles northeast of Calgary. In 1929 he married Charlotte Simmonds of the Berry Creek district south of Hanna.

Their five children all received their high school education at Canadian Union College, Lacombe, and their university in U.S.A. The two eldest daughters Dolores and Alice became nurses and the youngest girl, Rose, is a teacher. Garnet, the eldest son is in construction in Calgary and Sherwin the youngest, has his masters in Educational Media from Lorna Lindu University.

In 1965, after 40 years of farming at Acme, Frank and Charlotte sold out and retired at Westbank near Kelowna, B.C. and the Okanagan Lake, where they have a small ranch, keeping a few cattle and with a hobby of rejuvenating antique machinery.

They have 12 grandsons and two granddaughters.

THE HAMILTON FAMILY

The small town of Huntington, in the Province of Quebec, was no different than most other towns in the year 1881. Many of the young men were caught up in the fever and excitement of going out west where, they believed, the opportunities to make good were without limits. The William Hamilton Family, who originally came from County Cavin, Ireland, in 1840, to settle in Huntington, were no different than the rest. With a family of four boys and five girls it was inevitable that some of them would venture "out west".

FRANK HAMILTON — 1883

Frank Hamilton came to the De Winton district in 1883 and went into partnership with his brother Sam.

Frank Hamilton, with sons, William, Raymond and Stewart. 1895.

He married a girl from around Calgary named Sarah McDougal. They had four children Billy, Stewart and Raymond. A daughter Ida died at 1½ years and is buried in Pine Creek Cemetery.

In 1894 the partnership was dissolved and Frank and his family moved to Calgary. He became very active in the real estate business. Later he moved to Vancouver where he continued selling real estate.

SAMUEL "SAM" HAMILTON — 1881-1915

The first to come west was Samuel who arrived in Calgary in 1881. After looking around he decided to homestead on the NE¼ 27, 21, 1 W5. One mile west and one mile south of De Winton and was the first settler in this area.

Sam raised Clyde horses on his homestead which were well known for their superior quality and dispositions. Most of the families that came later to homestead bought their first work teams or driving horses from Sam. His brother Frank joined him in 1883 and together they increased their holdings until they had a good-sized farm. The partnership was dissolved in 1894.

In 1885 Sam built a log house with the help of his neighbour to the north, Charlie Marshall, Sam's brother William, and a carpenter. The logs for the house were hauled from the Priddis district and stock piled until they had enough to complete the building. Some of the logs were two feet thick and very heavy.

About this time he was joined by his sister Martha

Mrs. Wm. Munro (nee Martha Hamilton).

Hamilton who stayed with him for a few years. She later worked at the stopping house at Pine Creek. From there she went to Calgary where she and her sister, Mary Hamilton, ran a boarding house. She married Billy Munro and moved to Springbank where they ran a successful dairy farm.

Sam lived on the farm until 1914 when he became very ill and was taken to the hospital. He died in June 1915 at the age of 52 years. He never married.

SAMUEL HENRY AND MARY (MEEHAN) HAMILTON — by Theresa Brown

Their land location is NE¼ 22-21-1-W5 and SE¼ 27-21-1-W5. This land was first owned by an uncle, Samuel Hamilton, in the early 1800's.

Samuel H. Hamilton and Mary (Meehan) Hamilton on wedding day.

In 1925 Samuel Henry Hamilton was married to Mary Adeline Meehan, daughter of John and Elizabeth (LaCroix) Meehan, who farmed east of De Winton. Sam and Mary had two children, Theresa Elizabeth and John Samuel. They farmed the land until Sam became ill and passed away in December 1942. They were active in the community and the children attended Stormont School. Sam was interested in rodeo and was an outrider in the chuckwagon races.

Following Sam's death Mary moved to Calgary and with her sister Agnes, operated dress shops in Calgary and Claresholm finally retiring to Black Diamond, where she resides with her daughter.

Theresa married Menno Brown in 1949. Menno served in the armed forces for 30 years and retired to

Black Diamond in 1969 where they still live. They have five children; Helena Mary (Mrs. Gerry O'Niell), presently living at Sedalia, Alberta, and mother of two children, Theresa Ann and Calvin John; Lawrence William, married to Donna Mensinger and living in Calgary; Terrance Menno, Murray Wayne and Penny Bernice, all living at home.

John married Lillian Mill Breen and is still living on the home place. They have seven children one of whom attended Stormont School. Barbara (Mrs. Archie Bell), of Colgate, Saskatchewan, with one child Angie Grace; Patti Lynne (Mrs. Gerry Knight) of Calgary with two children, Diana Lynn and Jason Dwayne; John Richard, married to Jacqueline Dearle, with two children, Buck William and Heath Richard, living on the home place; Marsha Joy (Mrs. Tom Crowe), living near Priddis, Alberta; Cameron Samuel, Linda Elizabeth and Helen Bernice all living at home.

WILLIAM AND ISABELLA (BABINGTON) HAMILTON — by R. Hamilton

William Hamilton came west to Calgary in 1882 working his way building bridges ahead of the steel. In 1883 he was a volunter in Red River Rebellion and was put to work hauling coal from the Drumheller mines to the army camps. After the rebellion he worked for a while on a farm east of Calgary, then returned to Calgary where he worked for a man who operated a wheelwright shop. After he left there he opened up a business of his own on 9th Avenue. Along with his wheelwright work he did a thriving business dealing in cattle, horses, wagons, buggies, etc.

In 1895, May 10th he was married to Isabella Babington, a Scotch lass from a small town named Killwinning near Glasgow. She had come from Scotland to Calgary and was working at the Alberta Hotel when Billy Hamilton met her.

Around 1897 there was a big mining boom at Trail, B.C. He sold his house and shop and together with his wife and daughter moved to Trail where he bought a hotel. In a year's time the ore seams started to run out and the mining business faltered and rather than move on, Billy and his family moved back to Calgary and became active again in the wheelwright business where he had a shop on 7th Avenue. He moved his wife

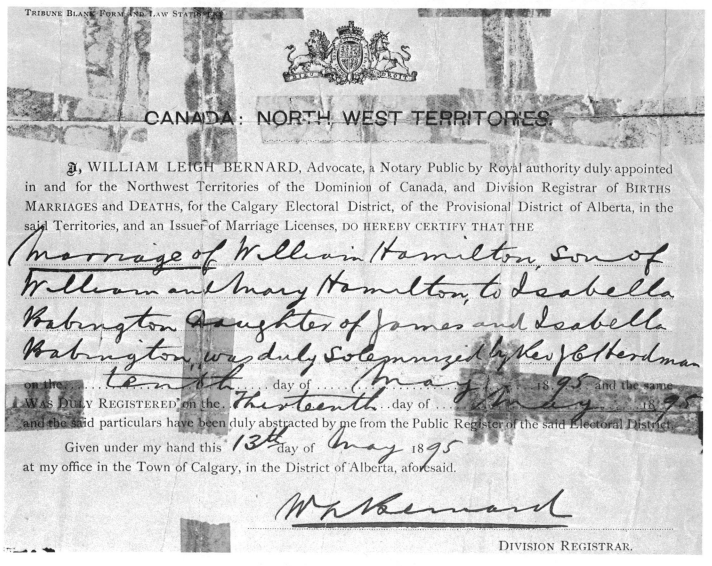

Isabella Babington, wife of William Hamilton Sr.

William Hamilton Sr.

WILLIAM JAMES AND RUTH (JOHNSON) HAMILTON — by R. Hamilton

William James Hamilton was born in Calgary, September 6, 1900. Son of William and Isabella Hamilton.

In 1916 he moved to the homestead at De Winton with his father. His mother and the rest of the family came out in 1917.

The Hamilton farm was always a place of great activity. Bill and his brother Sam loved to ride broncs and on the weekends it was nothing to see the young men of the neighborhood at the Hamilton place where they would run in the unbroken horses and try their luck. Most of them stayed for supper before going home. Bill's mother was a most gracious lady and no-one ever stopped at her house without having a cup of tea, a meal or spending the night.

The early cattle and horse buyers in the district always made the Hamilton farm one of their stopping places when they were trailing their stock to market. The animals were put into corrals and fed, the men came in for supper and stayed the night. In the morning, after an early breakfast, they would be on their way again.

Everyone worked long hard hours, but Sundays were set aside for fun and relaxation. Lots of hilarious tales have been told about events that happened in the "early days".

Around 1930 Bill joined the local ball team aptly named the Sod Busters. For quite a few years the team kept the district and surrounding area entertained with real good baseball and there was lots of fun among the fans, who never missed a game.

and family into a house at 223 — 2nd Avenue West.

A few years later Billy got a homestead and preemption ten miles west of Crossfield. His wife and children stayed there in the summer, Billy coming out on the weekends with supplies. In the winter he had a man look after the place. He later rented a farm in the Rocky View area which he operated for a few years along with his Calgary business.

In 1916 Billy bought the homestead at De Winton from his brother Sam's estate. It had been rented for two years to a man named Whelan. He and his eldest son Bill looked after it the first year and in 1917 he sold his business in Calgary and he and his wife and four children moved to De Winton.

Billy Hamilton, in 1927, died at the Hamilton homestead in the log house he helped build. He was 66 years old. His wife Isabella died in 1940. Both are buried in the old Pine Creek Cemetery. Four children; Margaret, married Eugene Goettler, Cecilla, died at 16 years, Bill, married Ruth Johnson, Samuel, married Mary Meehan.

Bill Hamilton Sr. and wife Ruth, 1939.

Billy and Sam Hamilton, sons of Ruth and Bill, still ranch the homestead.

Bill, and his brother Sam, raised some good light horses and were becoming interested in the Chuckwagon Races that were held every year in Calgary. In 1936 their brother-in-law, E. Goettler, entered a wagon with the boys. The first outfit was driven by Eben Bremner. The outriders were, Sam Hamilton, Alf Poffenroth, George Tosh and Speck Gale. All local boys. The outfit was trained at the Bremner place and they ended the week by becoming the world's champions. They won the Championship again in 1939 tying the world's record and setting two new ones from 1 min. 14 sec. to 1 min. 10 sec. The driver was Sam Johnson. Outriders were: Bill Hamilton, John McNab, Billy Haynes and Ernie Irving.

About a month before the races the Hamilton farm was a hectic place. The driver and outriders would come to stay and everyday the outfit was hitched up and out they would go to practice the figure eight around the barrels, in the summerfallow, until noon and then again in the evenings. This, along with spring seeding, branding, fencing, etc. and the wife cooking for the wagon crew and hired men and doing the gardening really kept things on the go. But no matter how busy things were, those years are looked back upon as real good times and lots of fun.

In 1939, Bill was married to Ruth Johnson, daughter of Sam Johnson, who was one of the great horsemen of his time. They still live in the old log house built by Bill's father and uncle in 1885.

They have three children. William James Jr. is married to Pat Sparrow. They have a daughter Marci. Samuel Hunter is married to Sharon Bolt. One daughter Isabella Miller who has three children; Billie-Ruth, Bobbi-June and Tyler Reid.

The boys, Billy and Sam, make the fourth generation of Hamiltons' who make a living by farming the original homestead. Together with their Dad they still raise Hereford Cattle and some good quarter horses. Sam trains rope horses and ropes at the Stampedes. Isabella lives on a acreage on the farm and is active in the Girls Rodeo Association, and was Canadian All-Around Champion Cowgirl three times. The children also are active in Rodeo with Billie-Ruth winning the Canadian Junior Championship in 1975 and Tyler the Boys Steer Riding at the Calgary Stampede.

HARNAN SINGH AND KHEM KOUR HARI — by John Singh Hari

Harnan Singh came to Canada in 1909 after arriving by ship in San Francisco. He served as a Sergeant in

1921, Harnun and Ojuguar Singh Hari.

the Indian Army and then decided to try his luck in a new land. He came with little but a strong back and determination. He first got a place at Kingsland-Turner Siding district on which he raised pigs for many years. Later he acquired most of the land in the Kingsland area. He developed farms at De Winton and the surrounding district. He was acquainted with a lot of the cowboys in the Calgary District. He gave a great deal to the church and to charitable organizations and was respected for his deeds.

He had one son, Ojuguar, who was born in India and came to Canada in 1919.

Harnan and his wife, Khem Kour, lived with Ojuguar and his wife, Sujan, at one of the farms near De Winton, 23-21-1-W5, for a number of years before returning to his native India where he did much good for his village. Both of the Senior Haris passed away in India.

OJUGUAR SINGH AND SUJAN KOUR HARI — by John Singh Hari

Ojuguar was born in India and came to join his father in Canada in 1919. He and his wife, Sujan Kour, moved to the 23-21-1-W5 in 1933. They had six sons and four daughters. Three of the daughters live in India and April Kour (Bairina) lives in Toronto. She took her B. Ed. in English at Calgary U. of C. Charles was killed in an accident in 1948. Harchet lives in Vancouver, Harnet at Tongue Creek, Alberta, Paul at De Winton, Dale and John in Calgary. All of the children but Harchet and Charles attended Stormount School.

Ojuguar passed away in Calgary in 1976. Sujan still remains on the farm.

WILLIAM AND PAULINE (KOCH) HEATER — by A. G. Heater

William Heater was born on a homestead, south east of Medicine Hat, Alberta, in the area, called Gros Ventre District. He spent his youth near "The Hat" and at the age of twenty-six, he married Pauline Koch, from Hilda, Alberta. He and Pauline then resided in the Schuler District for six years and, in 1937, moved onto the farm, in the Okotoks, De Winton District, where they have been ever since.

At times, it was really hard going as the land had to be cleared and broke before any crops could be grown. The land was good, though, and soon they were in a position to buy three quarters of land, two miles south of De Winton.

Bill and Pauline had three sons when they arrived in the De Winton area; William, the oldest, is now a Chartered Accountant, in public practice, in Calgary. Elmer, the second son is with Horne and Pitfield in Calgary. Reuben, the third son, is a Chemical Lab. Technician with Imperial Oil Ltd. in Calgary. Fifteen years later, Alan their youngest son, was born and he is currently enrolled in the Chartered Accounting program.

It was on January 1, 1972, that William passed away, leaving Pauline to look after the farm by herself but, as she was in no shape to run the farm, all the livestock and most of the machinery was sold at an auction, the following spring.

Pauline remarried on January 31, 1974, to John

Bischke and continues to live on the farmland, south of De Winton.

DAVID AND JANET HOLT — by Garfield Holt

David and Janet Holt with their family, of two boys and a girl, moved from Ontario to Alberta in the spring of 1903, landing in Calgary, on the first of April, in the middle of a snowstorm. They continued to Okotoks where David had a job with G. W. Mahon, owner of a machine shop and general store. The job was secured before we left the East. David worked for him for about two years and then started his own business, selling and repairing pumps and windmills. His shop was just east of Patterson's Livery Stable. He bought a quarter of land from D. J. 'Windy' Moore. It was located about three miles north of Okotoks and bordered John Dewer on the east.

In 1908, David and Oliver started to look for a new location. They went to Wetaskiwin where a real estate agent took them out to New Norway where they bought a half section. David operated the farm until 1918 when he and his wife moved to Canoe, B.C. In 1939, Mother passed away and Dad came back to Alberta and lived with his son, Garfield, and wife, for three years and then retired to a home in Wetaskiwin where he passed away in 1951, at the age of 93.

Oliver took over the farm in 1918 and operated it until he retired in 1946 and his oldest boy took over. They had two boys. Oliver passed away in 1972 and his wife in 1975.

Garfield, David's other son, was married in 1918 and moved to a farm half a mile south of the home place. There are four boys and one girl in our family. One of the boys is on our home place.

Ida, David's daughter, married Harry Newstead in 1917 and they lived in New Norway district. They had six girls and two boys. Harry passed away several years ago and Ida and one of her boys are still on the farm. Ida is now 79 years old.

Garfield now resides in Camrose, Alberta.

THE JACOBS FAMILY AT DeWINTON

Frank S. Jacobs and his wife Eva (Brownie) moved to DeWinton in the spring of 1917 to the old Booth homestead 4½ miles southwest of DeWinton.

Frank Jacobs had just been "fired" from his position as Professor of Animal Husbandry and Manager of the farm at the Manitoba College of Agriculture — now the University of Manitoba. He had lost his position because, as farm manager, he had refused to buy a herd of cattle riddled with tuberculosis which belonged to Manitoba's Minister of Agriculture. The Minister's plan was to sell the herd to the College, then have them tested — and condemned and slaughtered so that the College and not himself would pick up the tab for the loss of the cattle. This Mr. Jacobs refused to do, and the Minister, who signed all the College-staff cheques, refused to sign Jacobs' salary cheque, so he was forced to resign.

Before teaching at the College in Manitoba, Mr. Jacobs had for many years been the editor of the Farm and Ranch Review in Calgary, and before that, of the Farmers' Advocate in Winnipeg. He was a graduate of the Guelph Agricultural College and in his youth was a noted athlete, starring in many team sports, but his speciality was the 100-yard dash.

Brownie Jacobs, before her marriage, had been a school teacher in London, and had degrees in both voice and piano from the Toronto Conservatory of Music.

Because of the suddenness of his departure from Manitoba, Mr. Jacobs had not put together adequate capital to start farming, so he entered into a number of share deals in order to stock his farm with purebred livestock — Shorthorn cattle and Clydesdale horses. These deals turned out to be most unprofitable to Jacobs, particularly after the price collapse of 1919.

To help out with farming income, Brownie used to teach music, both voice and piano. For many years, she drove every Saturday to DeWinton in a buggy to conduct classes there, and she also taught music at home. Several local girls, particularly the Goerletz and Kromm girls, who had lovely voices and a keen interest in music, used to help Mrs. Jacobs with her house work in exchange for music lessons.

Brownie used to help out with Christmas concert programs and for a number of years she held an annual Hallowe'en Party at the farm. At one such party, several teen-age boys exchanged the wheels on her buggy as a prank. The next morning Mrs. Jacobs drove to DeWinton to teach her music classes with the back wheels of the buggy on the left side and the front wheels on the right, much to the amusement of some of the pranksters, but to the shame of a couple who, as soon as possible, put things right again for her.

Brownie Jacobs was also a writer, in fact, was the first president of the Calgary Women's Press Club. For many years, she wrote for farm periodicals and was an active member of the Canadian Women's Press Club. Her membership in this organization entitlted her to railway passes and she frequently travelled to Eastern Canada, usually taking two of her young children with her.

Frank Jacobs was active in local affairs, acting as Secretary-Treasurer of the Stormount School District for most of the time he lived at DeWinton. In 1929 he was appointed to the Dominion Tariff Board, position he held for just over a year, until the election of the R. B. Bennett Government in 1930. For two years, while the Jacobs' family was living in Ottawa, Jim Wilson and his wife Lulu, rented the Jacobs farm. Frank Jacobs died of a sudden heart attack, July 2, 1936 and the farm was run by his son Frank, for a couple of years, with the assistance of Jim Ross and his sons Gregor and Jack. During this time, Frank also taught school.

In 1938 the farm was leased to Tom Coyle and his son Doug for a period of three years, after which it was turned back to the Booth estate for a small cash settlement.

After her husband's death, Mrs. Jacobs moved to Hamilton in Ontario and conducted a radio program for children there. She returned to Alberta in the spring of 1943, became suddenly quite ill and died of cancer in September. Mr. and Mrs. Jacobs are buried in Pine Creek Cemetery.

There were six Jacobs children — five girls and one boy. Most of the girls left the farm after completing grade eight in order to attend high school. Ruth, the eldest, moved to Ottawa when she was 13 to live with her grandmother, Sarah Williams, Later she attended the University of Western Ontario and obtained a B.A. degree and subsequently a degree in Library Science from Columbia University in New York. Ruth worked in libraries across North America and then in England and spent a number of years teaching library science in South Africa at the University of Rondebosch. There she met and married Leonard Wertheimer. When the racists troubles became acute in South Africa, the Wertheimers moved to Toronto and are still living there. Ruth, now in retirement, is active in a number of civic affairs and in 1976 served a term as president of the Association of Woman Electors.

Mabel (Laele) completed her high-schooling in Calgary, moved with the family to Ottawa for more schooling, returned to Calgary and worked as a secretary for a number of years there for United Dairy. She married Allan Haszard and the Haszards had two children, Julie and Margaret. Laele died of cancer in 1949. Both daughters are married and now live in Vancouver.

Shirley, the third daughter, worked a number of years as a nurse at the Scottish Private Nursing Home in Calgary. Later she lived with family on the DeWinton farm for a few years and married Raymond Hoeght of Hussar. The Hoeghts have four children, three boys and a girl. The two eldest boys, both of whom are university graduates, now operate a craft camp in Ontario. The other two children live in Calgary.

Kathy (Frances) remained in Ontario after the family moved west in 1930. She lived with her grandmother in London while completing her highschool and normal school training. She taught school in London for a number of years and later worked with Dr. Shupe of Vitamin E fame while her husband, William Girling, was overseas during World War II. William Girling is an artist and naturalist and in recent years has conducted out door nature education programs for the London schoolboard. Kathy has acted as a teacher-librarian in London schools for many years. The Girlings have two children, a son and a daughter.

Marjorie (Mardie) completed her highschool at Crescent Heights in Calgary, attended business college and for many years worked as a secretary for Campbell and Griffin Ltd. During this time she was active in professional women's affairs. She married Harry Faunt of Calgary. The Faunts have three children and six grandchildren. After her family had grown, Mardie worked for many years as a secretary with the Calgary School Board, retiring in 1977.

Frank, the only boy in the family, taught school in Alberta for twelve years, including a year and a half at Stormount, in the late 30's. He obtained two degrees from the University of Alberta, in education and agriculture, became a high school principal and later a teacher of vocational agriculture, first at Medicine Hat and then at Red Deer. He later moved to Salmon Arm B.C. to teach agriculture.

In 1953 he was appointed editor of Canadian Cattlemen Magazine, a position he held for 21 years. Retiring in 1974, Frank continued to write part time for the magazine and also did consulting work with the Sibbald Group, the agricultural arm of Haskins and Sells Management Consultants, a world-wide organization. As an editor, and later as a consultant, Frank travelled over much of the world — Latin America, Oceana, Africa and Europe.

He started ranching in the Sundre area in 1966 but sold out his land there and acquired a farm and feed lot northeast of Edmonton at Newbrook in April 1976. Through the years Frank received many awards and honors and in 1975 was admitted to Alberta Agriculture Hall of Fame.

He married Rachel Wear in 1946. They have five children, four boys and a girl — all of whom live in Calgary.

JOSEPH AND GRACE BELL (DAVIS) LATIMER

Joe Latimer and his father purchased the whole of 25-21-1-W5, in the Stormount district, when they first arrived from Tennessee in about 1909. They proceeded to farm with mules, animals not often seen in the area, and also to travel around selling Home Comfort stoves. Their wagon was also pulled by mules and they became a familiar sight. Their approach to selling was to throw a stove from the wagon to the ground, declaring that they were indestructable. Another approach was to have gatherings much like a picnic in style and demonstrate the merits of the stove. There were a good many of these stoves sold throughout the country and some of them are still in use today. In 1915, Fred Dick, newly come from New Brunswick, joined the sales team and worked with them for quite a time.

In 1911, Joe married the local Pine Creek school ma'am, Grace Bell Davis, and they settled down on his father's farm for several years, later moving to Okotoks. Mr. Latimer Sr. had returned to Tennessee and Joe and his wife made their final move, to Calgary, in about 1919.

There were seven children; Ermine (Stevenson), Bottrel, Alberta; Myron, Madden, Alberta; Glen, Oregon, U.S.A., Dale, Washington, U.S.A.; Warren, Los Angeles, California; Lloyd, (deceased); Joyce (Forster), Black Diamond Alberta. Mrs. Latimer passed away in 1927 and Joe, in 1959.

JANET (FISHER) MacMILLAN (MRS. MYLES) — by B. Culley

Janet was the mother of Mrs. Sarah Dewar. She married Myles MacMillan in Glengarry, Ontario. She was a Protestant and Myles was a Catholic. The children were brought up in the Presbyterian Church. When Myles died, Janet came west with her son, John, and homesteaded on the farm where Dafoes now live, NW¼-14-21-1-W5.

John Dewar, her son-in-law, later bought that farm and Janet lived with her son, John, in Edmonton. Her sister, Sarah, also lived there. After leaving Edmonton, Janet lived with John and Sarah Dewar in Calgary part of the time and with another daughter, Mary (Eberley), on a farm near Okotoks, the rest of the time.

Mary and James Eberley had two daughters, Etta and Jessie. Etta married Reverend William Morrison of Okotoks, but Jessie never married. That family have all died.

Janet MacMillan died while staying with Mary and Jim Eberley about 1912.

Other children in the MacMillan family were; Bella (Mrs. Rod MacDonald), lived in "The States", Alex, died before his mother came west, Millie, (Mrs. MacLean), lived in Edmonton, had two sons, George and Alex.

CATHERINE (DEWAR) MacRAE — by Laura Paterson

The glowing accounts of "Life out West" with its great opportunities was well advertized in newspapers in the eastern provinces and it was this incentive which brought Catherine to the Stormount district. She was widowed when her husband, Kenneth died, April 29, 1887 and was left with four children to support: Annie, Roderick, Donald and Katy. Her ambition was to file on land for her boys.

They came to the home of her brother, John, who had arrived from Kirkhill Glengarry County, Ontario in 1889 and taken out a homestead on NW¼ 14-21-1-W5 in 1890.

During the time spent at her brother's home, her youngest daughter, Katy, became ill and needed constant care. She passed away in 1894. My grandmother's dream was not to come true for, in nursing Katy, her own health failed and she, with her daughter, Annie, moved to Calgary where she hoped to resume her nursing profession. (Letters of recommendation from an Ottawa doctor testifying to her nursing capabilities, are treasured by us today.) However this plan, also, was not to be for her health did not improve and she passed away just five months after Katy. Both are buried in Pine Creek cemetery.

After the death of her mother, Annie, was employed by the Calgary Telephone office and, in 1896, married James A. Hornby, well known in Calgary's political life and as a construction contractor and later, fire insurance adjuster for E. A. Lilly Co. They raised a family of eight children: Alice (Sipes), Malcolm, Marian (Campbell), all deceased, Isabel (Lovatt), Vancouver, Rosamond (Tebo), Laura (Paterson), Esther (Kwiat) and Robert all of Calgary. Annie died in Calgary, December 26, 1927, aged 53.

Rod and Don went their separate ways. Rod continued to work for farmers in the Stormount district, one of them was a bachelor by the name of Milton Connell, and, after two years, went to join his uncle, Malcolm Dewar, at his homestead, near Edmonton. The "lean years" were developing by then so, in 1898, Rod decided to return to Glensanfield, Ontario. He enlisted for the Boer War and served in Africa until the war was ended. Letters written to Annie were evidence of the poor conditions and terrible suffering they encountered, and he came back with a rheumatic condition for which he received a small pension when discharged. Rod married Jennie Harper in Ottawa in 1903 and they came west to Calgary on their honeymoon and remained there for the rest of their lives. Rod did manage to file on a homestead but was unable to keep it. They had a family of seven; Kenneth, deceased in infancy, Ian A. deceased 1972 who served many years with the Calgary Police Force; Rhoda (Kopas), Calgary; twins, Roderick, deceased in infancy and Crawford (now Collin Creagh) of Vancouver; Reginald, retired in Calgary after a career in the Canadian Air Force; Jean (Marshall) at De Winton. Rod passed away in 1948.

Donald, after working in the district for a while, went to the States and served in the Spanish American War. He sailed to Manila on the Sardinia in 1899. His service was short as he contracted malaria in March, 1900 and spent three weeks in hospital. He served on the south firing line where most of his mates were captured. Later he acted as Quarter Master for the U.S. Army in Manila. His intention was to join Rod in Africa but the war ended so his plans were changed. He elected to follow the "Gold Dust Trail" and mined in the Klondike, Yukon, and California before making his home there. From his letters to Annie, his health was poor, his malaria had flared up again and he died in California in 1915. Donald had remained a bachelor.

MELVIN FRANCIS AND ADA (STEADMAN) McBEE

Mack was born in Springfield, Oregon in 1889. In 1921, he came to the De Winton district and was manager for the Big Bend Land & Cattle Co. of N½ and SW¼ 14-21-1W5.

Mack married Ada Steadman who came from Surrey, England. Their son Wallace attended Stormont School.

The barn on the Big Bend place was a huge building and one of the great land marks in this area. The first summer they were there, Mack and his wife Ada, and one helper painted the barn, he mixed all his own paint and that paint job lasted until the barn was torn down by the present owners in the early 1960's.

The next summer was spent breaking land on the west section.

In 1924 he moved to Lake Louise and worked for Brewster's stables. In 1925 he moved back to the De Winton district and settled on the Ernie Reid Place, now owned by Jim Cross. Mack bought a big steam engine and he and Gilbert Fraser did custom threshing for many local farmers. He was a genius at running seperators and was much in demand by his neighbours. He was separator man for years for Bill Hamilton.

In September of 1928 he moved to the S½ 24-21-2-W5. He, his wife and son, Wallace, cleared the land and while Mack went out doing carpenter work, Mrs. McBee and Wallace picked rocks and roots, etc. (Ada McBee worked harder helping to improve their land than any man. At threshing time she forked bundles along with the men in the fields, leaving for the house in time to prepare meals for the crew. She milked cows, worked land, hayed, grew a huge garden and had a good flock of turkey and chickens. The role of a pioneer wife surely was not an easy one.)

Mack did carpenter work for the Oil Wells and local people. No job was too big or too small, from farm repairing to building houses. The Ken Burns and the Befus houses are two still remaining in this district built by Mack.

In 1931 Mack, his brother, Loris, and Clifford Cane started a saw mill south west of Priddis which they operated for a few years with local help.

Melvin (Mac) McBee.

Every chance Mack got he would go hunting or fishing. He was a crack shot and it was common knowledge that he never lost his direction even in the thickest woods.

On the 13th day of May 1942 Ada McBee passed away and Mack moved back to the States the next year. He lived there for 2 years and then moved to B.C. Mack died in 1956 at the age of 67 years.

Wallace McBee and wife Joan still live on the home farm. They have five children.

WALLACE AND JOAN (SMITH) McBEE

Wallace was the son of Ada and Melvin (Mack) McBee. He married Joan Smith of Crossfield in December, 1941. He lived at Priddis for eight months and then moved to his dad's farm S¼ 24-21-2-W5 which he purchased in 1945.

Wallace and Joan have five children; Helen Ada, born 1942, married Ross Agnew, has two children and lives at Chestermere Lake. Edward Wallace, born 1943, married Evelyn Bruce, had four children and lives at Millarville. Florence Ann, born 1945, married Don VandereVilde, had three children, lives at Dalemead, Alberta. Caroline Frances, born 1947, married Dick Polowanuik, had two children. Linda Mary Joan, born 1951, married Otto Wichert, lives at Cache Creek, B.C.

ANGUS CAMPBELL AND CHRISTINE (INA) McINTOSH — by Leslie McIntosh

My father, Angus Campbell McIntosh, came to Calgary in 1890 from Moose Creek, Storemount County, Ontario. His father, Hugh, had come from Inverness, I believe, with fluent Gaelic as a second tongue. His mother was Jessie Campbell, but I am not sure if she was Canadian born.

He worked on the building of the C.P.R. mainline south and spent one or two winters cutting ties for the C.P.R. in the mountains west of Banff, directly across from Castle Mountain, now Mount Eisenhower.

He homesteaded SE¼-24-21-1-W5, later acquiring NW¼-13-21-1-W5 and S½ and NW¼ of 25-21-1-W5, C.P.R. land I believe, at something like $3.00 per acre. (Cheaper than homesteading if you could find the three dollars.)

He went in for pure Clydesdale horses and at one time had a reputation for good draft horses. The

"Laird of Bersallach" was a grand champion at the Calgary Horse Show for two or three seasons.

Somewhere around 1920 he purchased the "Godsell" valley — - 1,200 acres of beautiful country about six miles further west, a heck of a long way in those horseback days — as pasture for his horses and for the Galloway beef cattle that R.A. (Dick) Wallace of High River had introduced to the area. About 1918 or 1919 he was a candidate for M.L.A. in the Alberta House, losing by 150 or so votes. Always active in community affairs, he was president of the High River Liberal Association (in their more conservative days), chairman of the building committee of the De Winton Community Hall, etc.

His great friend was Bobby Pratt of Pine Creek who lived with his sister and her family, the Andersons, directly across the Macleod Trail from the old Pine Creek Church. Bobby's advice to new landowners was: "Leave the right side of the sod up!" In other words, ranch, rather than farm. Other good friends were Archie Bremner (a real old-timer) and later, Professor Frank S. Jacobs of De Winton and Malcolm McGougan of Okotoks.

He died of a stroke in 1928 at the age of 64 in Calgary.

My mother, Christine (Ina) McNaughton, came to Alberta from Maxville, Ontario, having there attended the church at which the Canadian author Ralph Connor first preached. She lived and taught school, first in Cochrane, then Lacombe, and later at De Winton, perhaps Stormont. She married my father in 1910.

She was always community-minded, ready to talk politics at the drop of a hat, and was active in the work of the Pine Creek Church.

The first teacher I encountered at Stormont was Margaret Hamilton, sister of Bill and Sam, later to become Mrs. Gene Goettler. Then Miss Lena Dalzell, a very conscientious and capable teacher. Next, Mrs. Rhine, who also leaves fond memories with me. Then Miss Milligan who boarded at Ness's. About this time I graduated from Grade IX and left for high school in Okotoks.

As I recall from my days at Stormont, there were always from 11 to 15 or 16 pupils and never less than eight grades. Times change! Now teachers have forty pupils in one grade!

People I recall as schoolmates are: Mark Blaine, Marshall, Newton and Herbie Ness, Danny Gerlitz and his sisters, Rose, Amelia and Elizabeth, Katie, Jessie and Reinhold Kromm, Glen Swarbrick, Harold Cole, Lyle Cressman and his sisters, Bob and Isabel Todd (nephew and niece of the Hamiltons), Sheila and Jean McNeill. Also close friends but not schoolmates were the Brintons: Earl, Wenty, Paul, Travis, Goldie and Lucy.

I recall the deaths of the youngest Marshall boy, Harold, Glen Swarbrick and Newton Ness, all quite young.

The Christmas combined concert at De Winton Community Hall was always a big deal. Vera Marshall, teacher at Pine Creek, was a most imaginative and productive teacher and as a result there was always an excellent production of some kind out of that school. Stormont usually produced some

excellent girls' singing group. Santa always showed and there were many firm believers, including me.

I should mention that the Hopes lived as close neighbors for some years on NE¼-13-21-1-W5, farming the remainder, N½ and SW¼ of section 24. (Our home was on SE¼-24.)

HUGH BETHUSALUM McNEIL — by Bernice Fraser

Hugh Bethusalum McNeil homesteaded W½ 10-21-1-W5 in 1887. In 1906 he returned to Chesley and married his cousin Jenny McNeil. Mrs. McNeil was approximately 42 years old when she married. She came from a nice home in the east and tried to keep things nice in her homestead home, but life was very hard. They got their water from a creek in summer and melted snow in the winter. Wood was a big problem as it had to be cut with an axe and hauled home and chopped up. Few people could afford coal in the early days. Her brother visited her several times and each time he tried to get her to return with him to the east, because he felt the west was too hard on her.

They had Shorthorn cattle and horses and she raised chickens and turkeys and gradually got very attached to her home in the west.

The winter of 1934, Mrs. McNeil suffered a stroke and Eugene Goettler took her to the General Hospital in Calgary. She got out of hospital in June and came to the farm for a short period of time, and then her brother came and took her back east to Chesley. She died in 1938.

Mr. McNeil, known as "Darby", to all his neighbors, farmed a few acres in his younger years. Later, when he wasn't able to put up feed for his cattle and horses, the stock suffered as in those days it was the survival of the fittest.

Mr. McNeil passed away in 1940.

MR. AND MRS. W. V. MENCKE

The 1892 Department of the Interior map shows W. V. Mencke owning the W½ 24-21-1-W5 and the notes on Stormount school district show his purchase of "NE¼ 24-21-1-W5, comprising 158 acres, more or less, for $86.00 of which $12.30 has been paid on April 9, 1898, leaving a balance of $73.70." He acted as secty. treas. of Stormount school district from 1901 through 1905 and had been chairman for a short time just previously. In 1911 his name shows up as paying taxes on 1½ acres in the Pine Creek school district.

An adopted daughter, Margaret, was with them until they had a child of their own and Margaret went to live with another family. Mr. Mencke died in 1916 and Mrs. Mencke returned to Ontario where she taught school.

ALBERT J. AND KATHLEEN M. MILLS — by K. Mills

Mr. Albert J. Mills and Kathleen M. Mills moved to DeWinton area September, 1955, having bought the property in 1954. Location, Pt.W 29-21-29-W4. Thirty acres of the Frank Harmatta farm which had been bisected by the Macleod Trail. With sons, Michael and Paul, they set up small farming.

Mr. Mills, born in Calgary in 1918, took his education at Hillhurst, Stanley-Jones, Crescent Heights and

Commercial Schools. Very active in all sports, excelled in soccer-football, a sport that his father, coming from Scotland, also excelled in. Robert Mills was one of the city's original stone masons, building many of the sandstone buildings in Calgary.

Mrs. Mills, born in Devon, England, immigrated with her parents and brother, to Canada, in 1924. Settling at Craigmyle where the family farm still exists. Many are the memories of the "Dirty Thirties", blown out crops, herding cattle on roadsides for feed. Riding ten miles to school came in handy as practise in training horses later on. High school education was taken in Winnipeg at Rupert's Land Ladies' College, then, five years working for The United Grain Growers Company where she met Albert, who recently retired after being employed by the company for forty-six years.

Married in June, 1940, they previously lived west of Calgary on the Bragg Creek Road and 40St., now Richmond Road, in the sub-division of Holmpatrick. There they farmed on small holdings as did a number of other young couples. The husbands driving into Calgary to work. All owned old Model T's or Chevrolet coupes. None earning more that $100.00 a month. Buying their homes, paying for coal and coal oil for light; no luxuries here! As the city expanded, taking in the sub-division, high taxes forced many to sell. Mr. Mills gave up being Municipal Councillor for this area, moving to DeWinton where they had many friends. Developers only wished to buy land so, the Mills moved their buildings to their new acreage where farming continued. Mrs. Mills continued to raise registered Morgan horses which they showed with great success. Mrs. Mills, greatly interested in 4-H Movement, acted as leader of the DeWinton 4-H Horse Club for nine years.

Mr. Mills continued to commute to Calgary to the Grain Company. His main hobbies were gardening and acting as Secretary-Treasurer of the B.P.O.E. No. 31, Okotoks.

Son, Michael, educated at Okotoks, Mount Royal College, Olds Agricultural College, later taking first course at S.A.I.T. of Ambulance Paramedic in Alberta. Paul, eight years younger, also graduated from Okotoks High School to become employed as a driver of produce for MacDonald Consolidated Company, Subsidiary of Safeway Canada. Is interested in all sports.

CONRAD "CON" MINGELCAMP

Con came from Pluce County, Washington and settled on what was then known as the Big Bend Land and Cattle Company farm in the Stormount area W½ and NE¼ 14-21-1-W5. He was married and had two little girls. A year or so later he was joined by his younger brother Joe.

Joe hauled pipes for the natural gas lines that went through by Wylie's place from Turner Valley. The pipes were shipped to De Winton by freight, then loaded on wagons and hauled to the site by Con's six big bay Belgian cross work horses.

Con's main source of income was hogs. The little pigs were locked up with the sows until weaning time and then were turned out to pasture where they grew to maturity. They were then rounded up and herded by foot to the stockyards at De Winton. Joe would drive ahead with the team and sleigh and Con, with the help of some of the neighbour lads, would bring up the rear. One such drive consisting of 200 head of hogs was herded to De Winton in this way with Gilbert Fraser and Bill Hamilton helping to keep the herd together and on the move.

Con is remembered by the old-timers of the district as the only man they had ever seen who could chew snoose, eat an apple, and drink coffee at the same time. While they were on the Big Bend a son was born to Con and his wife and they named him "Little Joe".

Con's brother Joe was only here two years or so, when he was killed on the Macleod Trail. He was changing a tire on his car when he was struck by a passing vehicle. He was just a young man in his early twenties.

Con never really got over his brother's death. He left the Big Bend in 1920 or 1921 and moved to a place on or around the old Sandeman place near Black Diamond. He had sold all his pigs except 10 black gilts which he took with him. The next spring he had one hundred little pigs, an average of ten pigs per sow.

However, he only stayed on that farm for two or three years, then he and his family moved back to Washington.

HERBERT AND FLORENCE (MATTHEWS) NESS — by Florence Cozart

Herbert was born on the Lakeview farm in the Stormount district in 1918, third son of Rowland and Mary Ness. He lived all of his life on the same farm and, with his brothers Marshall and Newton, attended the little, one room, country school, Stormount, which taught grades from one to nine.

In 1946 Herb married Florence Matthews who had lived at the C.P.R. station house in De Winton for a few years. Herb's parents retired to Vancouver leaving the farm in the capable hands of Herb and Florence. They continued with the Ayrshire cattle and continued to show them at the Calgary Exhibition. In fact, the Ness cattle were exhibited in Calgary for forty-three consecutive years. Unfortunately fate took a hand and Herb developed a serious heart condition. He struggled hard to overcome it and made a trip to Rochester, Minn, in hope that medical science had progressed to the point where something could be done to help him. One of the highlights in the life of Florence and Herb was the community benefit dance that was put on for him and the money donated by their friends from the De Winton, Okotoks and Springbank districts helped make the trip possible. Money itself was greatly appreciated but the boost they got was in having friends who would do such a wonderful thing. They will never be forgotten. The doctors in Rochester were unable to do anything to help him and, in 1956, he passed away at the young age of thirty-eight.

Florence and her two sons, Bob and David, were unable to stay on the farm and it was sold, as a going concern, to Roy and Olga Price-Jones of Calgary. The Nesses moved to Calgary and Bob still resides there. David has recently moved to Red Deer with his wife and small daughter.

Florence remarried some time ago and she and her

husband, Hugh Cozart, lived north-west of Calgary for several years before moving to Oxbow, Saskatchewan. Recently they moved to Bruce, Alberta where they plan to spend their later years raising and enjoying horses which have been and are their livelihood.

ROWLAND AND MARY (MOORE) NESS — by Marshall Ness and Florence Cozart

Rowland Ness came west from Howick, Quebec about 1908 and settled on what is now Lakeview Farm. He brought the first pure bred Ayrshire cattle to Alberta and continued raising purebred cattle, horses and poultry which he exhibited all over Canada. He was one of the original directors of the Calgary Exhibition and Stampede.

Rowland Ness married Mary Moore, daughter of Mr. and Mrs. James Moore, in 1911. James Moore homesteaded the farm where the Cole family now live, a quarter of 20-21-1-W5. The Moore family came to the area in 1900 when Mary was eleven years old.

Mr. and Mrs. James Moore, Bertha and Edna, children unknown. About 1918.

Rowland built two big barns, one to accommodate horses and the other for the purebred dairy herd that he continued to have until his retirement in 1945 when they moved to Vancouver. The Lakeview Ayrshires became well known in the prairie provinces as Rowland took his best animals on the show circuit throughout Manitoba, Saskatchewan and Alberta. In earlier years he also showed horses.

They suffered the usual hardships of pioneer families trying to make a living from the land and many a time it seemed utter foolishness to keep a herd of purebred cattle and pay registration fees when cattle were worth so little. However, they shipped cream and boarded the Stormount school teachers and, somehow, were able to make progress. All three of their boys attended Stormount school.

One of the landmarks of the Stormount district was located on their land. In 1928 an oil company (the Anglesey) moved in a rig and drilled for black gold. Apparently it was quite unsuccessful and when their money ran out they abandoned the well.

Mary Ness was noted for her prize winning baking all across Canada. She won the gold medal for bread at the Royal Winter Fair and lesser prizes at the Calgary

Herb Ness, Mr. and Mrs. R. Ness, Mr. and Mrs. Marshall Ness, 1938.

Exhibition, Millarville and Okotoks fairs. For a number of years she was a judge of baking at Millarville. She took an active part in the community and was a member of the Missionary Society, Red Cross and Community Club.

In the forties, Mrs. Ness decided she had had enough of the cold old house and they built a snug little bungalow complete with bathroom and power provided by their own thirty-two volt plant.

In the fall of 1945 they decided it was time to take life a little easier and retired to Vancouver, leaving their son, Herb, and his wife, Florence, to run the farm. They moved back to Calgary where Rowland died in 1948. Mrs. Ness spent her last years in a Calgary nursing home and died January 15, 1974, just one day after her eighty-fifth birthday.

They had a family of three boys, Marshall, married Jean McKay of Okotoks, has three children and lives in Creston, B.C., Newton, (deceased in childhood) and Herbert, (deceased 1956), married Florence Matthews of De Winton, leaves two sons, Robert and David.

Rowland and Mary are buried in Pine Creek cemetery along with their two sons.

CONRAD AND MATILDA (GIRLETZ) POFFENROTH — by Tillie Poffenroth

Conrad and Matilda (Tillie) Poffenroth bought the Davis place, one mile west of De Winton as the crow flies. The family consisted of four children, ages at the time were: Alfred (Alf) fourteen years, Doris, eleven years, Robert (Rob, Bob) six years, and David (Dave), two years. We moved from Calgary, March 12, 1938 on a cold, wet Saturday. The three youngest ones attended Stormont School and De Winton High School. The family attended the Okotoks Evangelical Free Church. We were all happy and did well on the farm.

Alf got married and moved to a farm east of Red Deer. He has seven children, all well and happy.

Doris took nurses training and went to Australia for a little over a year. She was married there and one daughter was born there, and one daughter was born in Calgary. She came home when her Dad took sick. She lives in Calgary and is still nursing.

Bob farmed with his Dad on the home place and

later bought a farm three miles west. He has four children, three boys and one girl.

Con was ill and passed away November, 10, 1955.

Bob and Dave farmed the home place until 1958 when Bob moved and Dave farmed alone. I kept house for him until he got married in August, 1965, and then I moved to Calgary.

In 1972, Bob and Dave both sold out and moved south, Bob, to Nanton, and Dave to Blackie.

Dave has four children, one girl and three boys. When he moved from De Winton he was the same age as his Dad was when we moved to De Winton, and he moved March 12, the same day we came to the farm.

My family now consists of one daughter and one son-in-law, three sons and three daughters-in-law, seventeen grandchildren. One granddaughter married and two will be married this year (1976).

THE PORTEOUS BROTHERS — Clifford and Lyman

After several years in the restaurant business in Calgary, Cliff and Lyman bought the old Booth place at De Winton, a half section of land located on N. 21, 21, 1, W5. They set up a dairy farm here milking approximately 15 cows, with a hired man to do the milking. They shipped the cream and also raised pigs. George Lundseth looked after the cattle and the ponies which Cliff raised. Peter Goerlitz was hired to fence this farm and put up a mile of fence in one day, charging 10¢ per hole for the job — all manual labour — a far cry from today's post pounder attached to the tractor. They kept this farm for three years, selling it in 1948 when they purchased the Arthur Geinger farm located on sec. 5, 22, 29, W4. They kept this farm for three years.

In 1950 Lyman and Grace Porteous bought the Jim Dalzell farm and they lived there till 1953, when they sold to the Harry Vold family. They purchased 40 acres across from the old Jim Dalzell farm and built a new home there. Lyman and Grace sold out to Addie Wilson. They retired to Summerland, B.C. to enjoy the mild climate there.

Clifford and Anne bought a farm at High River before moving to Summerland, B.C. They have since returned to Calgary where they are enjoying their retirement.

HAROLD VICTOR AND MARGARET DUNLOP (MURDOCH) REEVES — by George Reeves and Frances Allin

Our father was born April 20, 1887, at Ryde on the Isle of Wight, England. He attended public school at Horndean Hants and then went to Royal Naval College at Greenwich. While at the college he was a contestant and winner of several events at Queen Victoria's Diamond Jubilee in 1898. He was also in the Guard of Honour at Queen Victoria's funeral in 1901.

He came to Canada in 1904 and settled and worked for a French family at Neepawa, Manitoba. After a few years, he homesteaded with a friend at Wolfe, Saskatchewan where they built a sod house and broke land. Harold owned one of the first tractors west of Winnipeg. The winters were so cold that their blankets used to freeze to the walls. During the winter months he used to work as a furnace man and shoe-shine boy in

Prince Albert. With the chance of another job, he gave up the homestead and worked with a team and fresno on the C.N. Railway through the Riding Mountains. He eventually ventured to Calgary in 1914 where he met our mother, Margaret Dunlop Murdoch, at a Bible class and they were married June 24, 1915.

While in Calgary he worked for the Union Milk Company but in 1916 he was asked to run a ranch in Kamloops which he did, for two years, returning to his job with Union Milk in Calgary in 1918. It was at this time that he met Dr. Taylor who had a farm near Okotoks and asked Dad to run it for him. Mother and Dad moved to the Taylor farm where they stayed for three years. Their son, George was born before the move and daughter, Frances, was born during their stay. They returned to Calgary and Dad once again resumed his job with Union Milk until 1929 when they returned to Okotoks.

In 1936 they bought a quarter of land at De Winton and another quarter about 1940. It was at this time that they moved to De Winton and farmed there N½ 11-21-1-W5 for four years when he sold the farm and returned to Calgary and bought several houses and built some.

In 1953, due to deteriorating eyesight, he sold all his houses and moved into an apartment and became a member of the C.N.I.B. where he was actively involved as long as his health permitted. He especially enjoyed bowling and excelled at it.

Margaret and Harold Reeves.

Mother was born June 15, 1888, at Annbrook in Ayrshire, Scotland. Her young years were hard as her mother passed away while she was quite young. She came to Canada in 1912 and worked as domestic help in Calgary, returned to Scotland for a brief period and then returned to Calgary.

Mother was a hard worker and supported Dad completely during their life together. During the last ten years of her life, her health began to fail but, due to her faith and devotion, she kept going and her main concern was looking after Dad.

In 1975 Dad's health began to fail and he passed away October 16, 1975. He was a true pioneer, worked hard to build this country and never asked for something for nothing. Following his death, Mother became seriously ill and passed away November 7, 1975, three weeks after Dad.

Mother loved flowers and had a gift of adding graciousness and beauty to whatever she did. Her strong belief, which she kept within herself, was felt by anyone who was with her. She was a beautiful person!

JOHN AND AMELIA SCHABER

John Schaber was born on May 2, 1902 at Harvey, North Dakota, U.S.A. Amelia was born on December 13, 1904 in Russia.

John came with his family as a young child to the Rosebud-Carbon area. He met Amelia Kromm and they were married on June 12, 1923. John and Amelia farmed in the Rosebud area until 1927, when they moved to the De Winton area where they farmed on section 15, township 21, range 1, west of the 5th.

They had three children, Gladys, Harold and Marjorie. Gladys married Leslie Hodel and they reside in Portland, Oregon, U.S.A. Harold lives in Calgary and married Mavis Indergaard. Marjorie married Norman Atkins and they reside in Leduc, Alberta. They have twelve grandchildren.

Allan Schaber, Harold's eldest son is fulfilling his grandparents greatest desire of becoming a Doctor of Medicine.

They retired in the fall of 1963 and moved to Calgary, Alberta. They sold their home in 1976 and moved to Bow Valley Lodge in Calgary.

John Schaber passed away on January 31, 1977 at the age of 74.

MELVIN AND RUTH SCHMAUS — by R. Schmaus

We moved to Alberta from Saskatchewan in the fall of 1936 and lived on the farm 17-21-1-W5, owned by Dr. W. G. Hunt and located eight miles west of De Winton. We raised four girls who made pretty good farm hands.

The oldest, Vivian, started school at Panima in 1940 staying there until the school was closed when she changed to Stormont. After finishing public school she attended high school at De Winton. Myrna, the second daughter, also followed this pattern of schooling. They rode horseback summer and winter, every day. In 1946, Marian's turn came to start school, it was to Stormont that she went and continued there until 1956 when all of the small country schools were closed down. From then on she had the luxury of leaving the horse in the barn, catching the school bus at the gate and receiving her high school education in Okotoks. Diane, the youngest, also started to Stormont but switched to Okotoks and continued her education there, graduating from Okotoks High School.

In 1950, Mel and Ruth purchased the farm and continued to live there until 1967. The years saw many changes and progress in the district. Most of the roads were gravelled easing the problem of becoming stranded on the roads. This happened many times in the early years.

The farm was sold to Harry Alger in 1967 and the family retired to Victoria, B.C.

Vivian married and had four children; Geary, Mitchel, Jody and Tracey. She is now residing in Calgary. Myrna married and had five children; Wayne, Glen, Kevin, Stacy and Kimberley, now living in Calgary. Marian married and lives on a ranch at Turner Valley and has two boys, Harley and Joel. Diane married in 1969 and has one son, Dean, and is now living on a ranch at Biggar, Saskatchewan.

We are blessed with twelve grandchildren all living in Alberta except one, Wayne Chernow, who is stationed in Vancouver, B.C. and is with the Armed Forces.

MEMORIES OF JOHN S. SNELL — by John S. Snell

I arrived at Midnapore from England in 1909, then at De Winton in 1910. Worked for Hapermann and Patrick, surveyors, on running gas lines from Bow Island to Calgary. Cold weather all winter, camping out in tents. Worked with Fred Dick at Latimer's farm

1937. Melvin Schmaus and daughters Vivian and Myrna.

and then got a job with Heaver and Sons Ranch where I stayed till 1913.

I remember well many people around the districts of Midnapore and De Winton; Andrews, McNeills, Shattucks, Turnbulls, Grays, G. Sutherland, Marshalls, Roly Ness, Earl Brinton, the station agent, Frank Frier, Rev. Streeter and his wife — all the concerts, plays and dances we used to have in the Community Hall, which all the neighbours had helped to build in the evenings. Many good dances and box socials were held there. Orchestras — Charlie Shattuck (violin), Will Turnbull (piano), Kay and Bob Rodgers on instruments. Sometimes John Snell would play a few notes.

Vic Heaver and I went to the 1912 Stampede together, stayed three days at the Alexander Hotel, which I think was built that year.

Worked for Frank Austin in 1909. He sold out to Roly Ness. Our neighbours there were Ernie Reid, Charley Booth, The Fraser and Dewar families. West of Frasers was open range. Other names west of De Winton were Kromms, Kroms, Gerlitz, Girletz, Koch and Kaiser, Wonacott, old Col. Clifford, Jack Dalzell and Hugh Wylie. Closer to De Winton was Sam Hamilton, (a bachelor). I worked with Fred and Guy Dick on a farm owned by a man called Latimer, who was the President, I think, of Home Comfort Ranges. Many of these stoves could be found in homes across Canada.

Other families in the district were Moody, MacDonald, (down on the Bow), Kennys and McBrides (both very large families), the Currie families, Dunc. McIntosh, also another McIntosh who lived beside Hedleys. Frank Pashak ran the store then, and the De Mings had a Stopping House. Also there was a bachelor, Charlie Brown, who used to bring a young school ma'am, Miss Hay, to the dances.

Young men who worked in the district were Stuart Jamison and Dyce Allen, a young Scotsman, who later became the mayor of Vulcan. Frank Frier worked for McNeills, I think.

I moved into Calgary at the end of 1913. Joined the 12th C.M.R.'s January 4th, 1915 — married on February 25th, 1915 — left for England October, 1915. I was Instructor in Machine Gun at Shorncliffe, took my commission and left for France early in 1916, to Machine Gun Squadron, Canadian Cavalry Bdge. (Strathcona's F. G. Horse and Royal Canadian Dragoons).

After the war, I returned to Canada. Served in the W.W. 2 with the Veterans' Guard from January 5th, 1940 to June 1946.

HARRY AND ADA SWARBRICK

Mr. and Mrs. Swarbrick moved to the Voss place in 1919 and in 1922 bought N½ 11-21-1-W5.

They had two children; Glen, attended school at Stormount and went to Agricultural College at Claresholm where he became ill, developed pneumonia and died, very suddenly, about 1927. Norma, married John Adams, who had been living, with his brother, on the Big Bend property and later moved to the McIntosh place.

Harry and Ada retired to Vancouver where they both passed away. They sold the farm to Frank Lomas. Mr. Lomas, later, sold to J. B. Cross.

Norma is widowed and lives in Sundre, Alberta.

JAMES VERT — by Mrs. T. W. Hebson

James (Scotty) Vert came from Portabella, Scotland, about the turn of the century. He worked in the De Winton District for Mr. Mencke until he purchased a piece of land from the C.P.R. The railroad ran through this land, situated partly along the Sandstone Coullee about half-way between Okotoks and De Winton. This comprised approximately 97 acres and was surveyed as SE¼-13-21-1-W5.

'Scotty', as he was known to his friends and neighbours, was a bachelor and lived in a two room shack. He raised cattle, milked cows and had several horses and some poultry. He was very fond of dogs and usually kept an Airdale. During the years, up to 1923, when the Sandstone brickyard was running, he was usually their milkman and sold vegetables to the people of the village. He also enjoyed playing the violin and was known to play for dances.

Scotty never owned a car, he went by horse and buggy to Sandstone during the brickyard days, to get his mail and groceries and to deliver his produce. At times he would drive on down to Okotoks to deliver his cream and eggs to the Okotoks Creamery, taking his trusty dog with him to guard his horse and buggy while he did his shopping.

He was the Game Warden for several years.

His favorite singer was Harry Lauder. He was very fond of oatmeal Porridge, the kind that takes half an hour to cook. He would make a big pot of it in the morning have a large bowl full for breakfast and have enough left over to slice cold and fry in butter for dinner or supper.

By 1942, Scotty's health began to fail and he was taken to a Calgary Hospital. He returned to his farm for a short while and then entered the Old Folks' Home in Gleichen. He died about 1945 in his late '60's. He had no relatives in Canada. An auction sale was held to dispose of his belongings and the land went to the Municipality. It has been sold and resold several times since and has now been divided into three parcels of land of approximately 32 acres each with separate owners and buildings on each. Thus another piece of land goes from sod-busting to sub-division.

WALTER AND MAE (CROCKETT) WRIGHT — by M. Wright

Walter Wright was born, of Scottish descent, in Armstrong, B.C., in 1895. He moved, with his parents, to the Springbank district in 1906. His parents were among the early settlers of the Springbank area. His mother, having been a teacher, taught him the first two school grades at home, then followed Public school in Springbank and High School at Calgary Collegiate Institute from which he graduated.

During his high school years, and after, he was very active in sports. He played hockey, lacrosse, baseball, tennis and took part in track and field events, at which he won a number of medals. He played rugby with the Calgary Canucks and the Calgary Tigers. His real love is rugby (football).

He married Mae Crockett who came to Calgary with her parents in 1910. She was born in Nova Scotia. She also received her high school education at C.C.I. She played hockey at high school (a girls' team) and also played with a city team later.

After they married they farmed at Nanton for a number of years, coming back to Calgary during the depression years. Walter took up carpentry and contracting. They purchased an acreage in the De Winton district in 1942, built a home and Walter commuted to Calgary for a number of years. He also did considerable building in and around De Winton until retiring.

Walter and Mae have two sons and five grandchildren. Donald, an Electronic Process Engineer, lives in Vancouver with his wife, Marian and their three children, Stuart, Diane and Colin. Walter, a Petroleum Engineer, lives in Calgary with his wife Sheila and their two sons, Doug and Bruce. An older son, Gordie, died at the age of ten years in 1969.

Walter and Mae celebrated their fiftieth wedding anniversary on January 2, 1976.

MR. AND MRS. JAMES WILSON

Jim came from Scotland to the De Winton area before 1920 and worked for Angus McIntosh. Some years later he married a local widow, Mrs. Oneil, nee Hope, who had a daughter named Hope.

Around 1936 he and Mrs. Wilson moved to the Godsal Valley, two sections of beautiful country, west of Adam Krom's. Here they raised cattle etc.

In 1940 they decided to move to White Rock, B.C. and held an auction sale to dispose of their livestock and household goods. The auctioneer was R. J. Johnson, an extremely witty man and said to be the best farm auctioneer in the whole country.

Jim and Mrs. Wilson died within a year of each other at White Rock.

Others who Lived in the Stormount District but had no History

Adams: Jack and Ray, bachelor brothers, lived on the Angus McIntosh place for a number of years. Jack later married Norma Swarbrick and they lived on NW¼ 11-21-1-W5. There were two children; Mae and James. They moved to the Sundre area where Jack passed away. Norma resides in Olds.

Booth: Charles, came from the United States about 1907 or 08 and settled on N ½ 21-21-1-W5. One of his sisters came to keep house for him. He remained a bachelor, sold the place to Frank S. Jacobs in 1917.

Coyle: Mr. and Mrs. Tom and son, Doug, rented N½ 21-21-1-W5 from Jacobs from 1938-41 and then returned east.

Goddard: Eric and Nina (O'Neil), daughters, Ilah and Elaine, attended Stormount school. Bought N ½ 11-1-21-W5 through the D.V.A.

Hope: Mr. and Mrs. and son, Don, daughter, Lulu (Oneil) lived on E½ 24-21-1-W5 in the 1920s.

Lomas: Mrs. and Mrs. Frank, bought the H. Swarbrick place . . . Lived on it off and on and moved to Delia in 1956.

Reid: Mr. and Mrs. Ernest, Ernie came from England about 1906 and settled on a section and a quarter in the Stormount district; N ½ 16-21-1-W5, S ½ 21-21-1-W5 and NE ¼ 20-21-1-W5. He married one of the Booth girls. After several trips back to England to look after business interests they decided to stay here. When they passed away the land was left to Mrs. Jack Harrison, a sister of Mrs. Reid, and she, in turn, sold it to J. B. Cross.

Ross: James and Ruth (Wonacott) rented and farmed several different places in the district. Ruth died when their two boys, Gregor and Jack, were very young and Jim raised them alone. He later bought SW¼ 13-21-1-W5 and NW¼ 12-21-1-W5. The land was left to the boys. Gregor (deceased) sold his quarter to W. Falconer and Jack still owns the north one.

Stuckey: Mr. and Mrs. Charles. Bought from John Dewar about 1912.

BRANDING TIME — by R. Hamilton

Years ago when the boss poked his head in the door and yelled "branding time tomorrow, if the weather holds" everyone would get into a flap. Two men were sent to Okotoks for veterinary supplies and refreshments for the helpers along with a threat on their lives if they delayed at the Willington Hotel on the corner.

Others brought in wood from the woodlots and piled it beside a big old iron wheel which was used for a fire bed to heat the branding irons.

There was one man, sometimes two, who did nothing but heel the calves. The roper got his calf by using what they called the corral loop, which consisted of one swing and a back handed throw. He then dragged the calf to the fire where the wrestlers were waiting to stretch the calf. Then the vet and the branding man took over. If everything went well you could do a calf in five minutes, and on to the next until all were finished and back with the mothers. It was hard, dusty, noisy work but there was also a lot of fun and hilarity connected with it.

Say what you will, the busiest member of the branding crew was the cook. Never was the little woman warned ahead of time, so when they yelled "branding tomorrow", it was a flurry of baking bread, pies, peeling vegetables, roasting meat, along with sterilizing the instruments. In all my life as a rancher's wife, I have never helped at the branding corrals. My job was strictly to feed the crew.

The funniest branding bee I remember at our ranch took place in the fall of 1951. We had a dandy crew.

Branding L. to R. Robert, Charles and John Forckel about 1916.

Branding scene L. to R.: Norman Hogge, John Wedderburn, Lorne Hogge, Lawrie Wedderburn, Barry Cope (back to camera), Greg Wedderburn (standing at back).

Charlie Munro from Spring Bank (a cousin of Bill's) and Jimmy McNab, who lived seven miles west of us were both masters at corral roping, came to help. The wrestlers were Johnny Hamilton, Jimmy Carothers, Wilf Fleming and Bill Hamilton.

They started branding in the morning and after dinner ran out of vaccine. Instead of one man going for more supplies, the whole crew went and it was late afternoon before they returned and quite apparent that they had been doing more than getting vet supplies.

So the operation started up again. Either Jimmy or Charlie roped a six hundred pound heifer and the rope tightened too much and she choked. I was working at the sink, and the door flew open and there stood Wilf Fleming yelling for the butcher knives and saws. I asked "what for" and he just hollered, "they had to butcher a heifer to save her life." They had her dressed and hung in twenty minutes as Jimmy and Bill Hamilton were topnotch butchers.

After that, they went back to branding and a bunch of horses came into the yard to drink. Jimmy McNab roped a three year old that had never had a hand laid on him. Johnny Hamilton took a run and jump and landed on the horses' back. That son of Satan bucked all over the yard and was heading for the gate and the wide open space beyond, when Charlie Munro started yelling, "hang on Johnny, I'll save you." He swung a wide loop and it settled under Johnny's arm pits and jerked him off the horse and he landed on the hard ground. Johnny said Charlie would have made a hell of a pick up man at the Calgary Stampede. All the cowboys would be cripples.

After that episode a large bunch of hogs wandered into the yard. One was a big Yorkshire sow. Jimmy Carothers jumped on her back and started fanning the air with his hat. After a few squealing turns around the yard, she headed for a four stranded barbed wire fence with old Jimmy bellowing for help. Jim McNab roped him just as the sow hit the fence.

So, back to the branding and by the time they finished, it was dark. Needless to say, while all this was going on, back in the kitchen was an irate cook. Anyone who has been told to hold the vittles "grub" knows how hard it is to keep a meal hot and still tasty for three hours.

About twelve years ago, the branding operations changed considerably. The summer pasture (the old Barrett Place) was sold and our new lease about 25 miles away now makes it necessary to brand all the calves in the spring before they are sent to pasture. Instead of fall branding bees with big husky calves, we now brand in the latter part of May. The calves are small and easier to handle.

Also the crews have changed. Our son Sam does all the heeling and son Billy takes his turn at everything. With the boys are John and Dave Neish, Leonard Johnson, Danny Gittens, Huey Vang, Tom Crowe, and Bud Hamilton as wranglers. Don Kopas is the branding man with Ginger Goettler as the head vaccinating man. Sharon Hamilton looks after the vaccine and syringes as well as helps round up the cattle along with our daughter Isabella Miller. Sharon and Pat Hamilton help me with the food. Sandy Neish helped for a number of years, but he passed away two years ago. He was the best branding vet in the country. Bill's job now is to open the gate and shut gates along with the help of Trish Jones.

In about two weeks time the same crew will go from place to place branding for neighbouring ranchers. It's a good thing it lasts no longer as the ranchers are most generous when it comes to refreshing the boys. At the end of two weeks they are more than happy to settle down to everyday ranch work.

A lot of people turn up just to watch and bring their wives, kids or girlfriends. It's a good day for young country folk to get together and have a lot of fun.

I also made a change. Now all the meals are cold, "buffet style." The men can come and eat whenever they want, there are no hot meals to spoil on the back of the stove, and most important of all, they are served by a smiling happy cook.

HIRED HANDS — by B. Fraser

During threshing one year, a fellow stopped his team in the middle of the field one afternoon and just walked off towards Calgary and we never saw him again. He must have been really fed up because he had two days wages coming.

During the early 1940's the Government had harvest excursions from the east for a fare of ten dollars. Hopefully a man would earn some money plus his fare back east. We got a young man, a student, seventeen years old, from Montreal. He told us that his parents were in the restaurant business. We fixed him up with a team and rack and sent him to the field. The sheaves he would get on the rack would immediately fall back off again, so he got exactly nowhere. The other teamsters were mad because he was not getting to the machine in time for his turn, and it was putting more work on them. We sent our twelve year old son to help and show him how it should be done, but it was just too tough for him. Seeing as he had told us that his parents were in the restaurant business, my husband thought he might be a help to me. It was a lovely day so I set him to peeling potatoes outside. He had never peeled potatoes before so he was surrounded by peelings for about two feet in all directions. I told him if he had been in the house he would have faced a big clean up job. I tried him at many jobs but he didn't succeed at any of them, except eating. We felt he hadn't even earned his grub, but my husband gave him his fare back to Montreal and enough money to eat on the way. For several harvest seasons we had a fellow and each year he was going to visit his sister in Cranbrook. Each year he would blow his wages in the usual manner. One year he had about four hundred dollars and that was a lot of money in those days. After harvest he took only about one hundred dollars and headed for Calgary to buy a suit, and a ticket to Cranbrook. In a couple of days he returned in a taxi over muddy and gumbo roads, as they were not gravelled in those days. The taxi driver charged him twenty-five dollars. My husband wanted to pay him off but he just wanted enough to sober up, then he was still going to visit his sister. He returned three times in a taxi, and finally had all his money used up. He was killed in an accident in a lumber truck, near Cochrane, and we are sure he never did get to visit his sister.

Another old chap was with us for over three years, and he was a real plugger, with never an idle moment. He usually did what he wanted and not what you wanted him to do. He only did things when he thought that it was his idea. One September day we had our first snow storm and he decided to take our truck and go to Okotoks to buy some winter underwear. He didn't have a driver's license and left here at ten in the morning. When he hadn't returned by afternoon, I was very concerned. I phoned around to see if anyone had seen our truck. One garage man had pulled him out of the ditch and he asked them not to say anything to us about it. Finally, at five o'clock, he came home and he wasn't in great shape. I bawled him out and he quit immediately.

Our children used to like pancakes for supper on Saturday night so every once in a while we would have them. After about three pancakes this fellow left the table and said he was walking to Okotoks. My husband drove him to Okotoks and left him there until the bar closed. After a few beers in him he started telling everyone about just having pancakes for supper in a loud voice so everybody could hear him. Needless to say when the story came back to me from several sources, I was probably more provoked about the pancakes than he was.

HIRED HELP - - by R. Hamilton

One thing I remember most vividly about our early years on the ranch were the men we hired to help with the work. In those days the hours were long, the men rising at a quarter to five and working through until after dark. Harnessing horses, feeding beef, milking cows, etc. in the light of an old coal oil lantern, must have been a chore that required exceptional eye sight and patience. The lantern, even one with a bright shiny glass threw a light of only a dozen feet or so.

The men, mostly young people from farms themselves, acted and were treated as one of the family and were included in all community activities, such as Church picnics dances, ball games, etc.

Scottie Strachan was the first one I remember. He came from near Glasgow, Scotland and was a real good worker. Scottie had a most irksome habit of contradicting everything you said. He also liked to eavesdrop on the ladies conversations.

I remember one day a neighbour, Mrs. Ness came to visit and had supper with us. After the dishes were done and the men had gone upstairs to bed we settled in the front room to visit until her son Herbie came to pick her up. Our house, like many in those days had a stove pipe hole in the front room ceiling which led into the bedroom upstairs. I remember we were discussing the age of one of our friends and disagreed as to the number of years we thought her to be. Suddenly the old floor boards in the room above started to creak and a face showed itself in the chimney hole, a Scotch brogue shouted "she's forty-two". Mrs. Ness was still laughing when she left for home.

Joe Desourcie was the next one I remember well. He was seventeen years old and came from Stony Plain. Joe had two great passions in life. One was to wear the brightest colored shirts he could find, the other was to be a cowboy.

His desire to learn to ride was a great joy to the other young men around, who took a diabolical delight in "helping" him achieve his ambition. They mounted him on some of the rankest horses on the place and would stand there shouting good humored insults until he bit the dust.

One rainy day the men were hanging around the barn restless and bored, as it had rained for days. The corral was a foot deep in muck and mire and standing in the corner, wet and dejected looking, was a young three year old the men were breaking. This, they told Joe was just the kind of weather to ride broncs. On went the halter and saddle and Joe was boosted aboard, the horse bucked like a demon and Joe's head kept getting closer and closer to the muck. By sheer force and determination Joe clawed his way back on the horse and rode him to a standstill. The thought of landing in that sea of stinking mire made a rider out of Joe. His nickname from then on was cowboy Joe. When he left to go back to Stony Plain he had a brand new outfit from hat to boots, even a lariat rope. He was going to show everyone in Stony Plain what a real cowboy was.

Breezie came next. He drove into our yard with a team and hay rack looking for threshing work. He was hired on the spot and stayed with us for three years.

Breezie and the boss got along well and he was a good worker, but for three years he and I had a running battle.

I remember when our three young children got the measles. Breezie declared he had had all the childhood diseases and that people made too much fuss over them. All you need to do if you get the measles said Breezie is put on a pair of dark glasses. You don't even have to quit work.

About a week or so later I looked out my kitchen window and couldn't believe my eyes. My husband, Bill, was coming to the house with the team and stone-boat and stretched out on the stone-boat was Breezie, deathly sick. We got him to bed and called Dr. Ardiel from Okotoks. Breezie had been working summer-fallow and was almost as black as the land. Doctor Ardiel came into the kitchen after attending to Breezie and said "Ruth, don't you own a bath tub?' I assured him I did and he said, "Give that man a boiling bath; he has the measles and if they don't kill him the dirt will". Breezie was very sick for weeks. During his time with us he came down (along with the kids) with mumps and chicken pox.

In the spring I had so much to do with a new baby to look after that Bill told Breezie to help me plant the potatoes, the garden being my responsibility. We set to work. I dug the hole, Breezie plopped in the potato, I filled in the hole. Finally I looked at Breezie and said "don't you think you should be doing the hard part?" He gave a silly grin and said what beautiful lips I had. I was so angry I took a swipe at him with the shovel, he dropped the pail of potatoes and ran. I finished planting the garden myself.

When Breezie left he was headed north on a one-eyed Pinto horse.

My brothers Leonard, Ralph and Gordon worked here off and on. Leonard and Ralph were in their teens but they worked hard. Len said to work for Bill Hamilton you had to be able to survive on liniment and porridge. Gordon and his wife Helen were here the spring of 48. That was the worst spring I can remember. The snow was so deep no one with cars could get to town. My son Sam was a tiny baby and had to have special milk. The druggist in Okotoks would send it by train to DeWinton and either Gordon or Bill would meet the train with the horses and sleigh. On the way back they picked up groceries for the neighbours who were snow bound. The young calves were especially hard hit and the men had every building on the place full of calves, even the hen house. We ended up calling Gordon Dr. Johnson as all he did day and night was calve out cows and doctor calves.

Gordon left to work in the oilfields.

Some of the young men working for us joined the armed forces during the war. Johnny Wilson was only eighteen when he joined; he had worked here a year and was a local boy from De Winton. He now lives in Okotoks. Stan Edwards who came originally from England was here two years and left to join the army. He now lives in High River. Joe Meehan another local boy joined up from here. Joe has since passed away. Andy Waldner joined the air force. Now has a farm in Saskatchewan. Tom White was a veteran from the first world war and had been with us awhile. When the second war was declared, he got his call within five days. I remember Tom best as a story teller. He had a wonderful education and was a master at describing places he had been and things he had seen. Tom has since passed away also. They were all wonderful boys and the best part of all, they all came back from the war. How proud we are of them.

So many names and faces come to mind, Wilf Fleming, the most kind hearted man in the world, also a veteran. I never had an empty wood box or water bucket while he was with us and a day was never too long when times were busy. My three kids loved him and they cried when he left.

Then came James Aloysuis Rylie, a real worker, the only trouble was he could tell tales as fast as he could work. He said he was an orphan. He worked here a year and a half then went to B.C. We received a letter asking us to send his saddle and gear to him. It turned out he had a Dad and Mother and two brothers and his name was not Rylie. None of that mattered as Jim was a great favorite of ours and the kids would listen to his tales for hours.

Then came Claude. He was so mean he couldn't pass the dog without kicking it. He never smiled, complained constantly and chewed a packet of tums every day to settle his stomach.

There was Art and Jim Krotch, now farming north of Calgary. Joe and Jim Carothers, a couple of brothers from DeWinton worked here a year or two and then moved north to a farm of their own.

Raymond and Earl, a couple of teenagers — good kids if you were prepared for the unexpected. There was never a dull moment with them around.

Charlie Gorrell was the last man to work for us and he was with us eight years. Charlie was a man who worked all his life at jobs that were back-breaking. He could tell you tales of terrible hardships while working on freighting outfits crossing the lakes in Northern Saskatchewan. During his life, Charlie has done almost every kind of work. Ranching, farming, fishing, road work, logging, etc.

Charlie is now retired and lives in Okotoks but he

still has a cabin here on the ranch that he comes back to every once in awhile.

Now our family has grown up and we no longer require extra help. The boys, Sam and Bill run the ranch, but Bill and I still live in the old house. What a wonderful surprise it is when you answer a knock on your door and there stands one of the 'boys'. Sometimes alone,

but more often with a wife and family, We talk late into the night about the old days and remembering is so good.

The hired man played a very vital role in the development of this area and without them the pioneers would have found the job of "settlin in" an almost impossible undertaking.

FARM WORK

Charlie Marshall stooking 1925.

Marshall's — 1923. Back Row: Gerald Blight, Tom Kelly, George Sutherland, Front Row: Frank Marshall, Mike Standish, Fred Moon, Bill Hamilton, Jim Harrison.

1927, threshing on Gordon Giffin farm after snow fall. Sold wheat for feed.

William Bruce and Chlorsalda Balderson and family — 1928, Nash.

Alex Anderson binding barley around 1917.

Threshing in the snow at Hogge's. Hauled the sheaves in to threshing machine on sleighs. 1928 or 29.

W. H. Jenkins in oat field 1937.

Ernie LaBerge, Vic Goss and Bill Herr 1930.

Philip Sampson, Roy Hambling and Pete Watkins swathing downed grain early 1945.

Putting up silage on Riches farm.

DOWNY WOODPECKER

BLACKBIRD

HOUSE WREN

YELLOW EYE
PURPLE TINGE TO
FEATHERS

BLACK BARS ON WHITE OUTER
TAIL.

BROWN - CARRIES TAIL
ALMOST VERTICAL

BARN SWALLOW

Fox Sparrow

CHESTNUT FOREHEAD + THROAT-BUFF UNDERSIDES
BLUE-BLACK ON TOP

BRIGHT RED TAIL

KILDEER

P.T.

MOURNING DOVE
SEED AND FRUIT EATERS

DOUBLE BREAST BAND
ORANGE-BROWN RUMP-TAIL
BROWN BACK

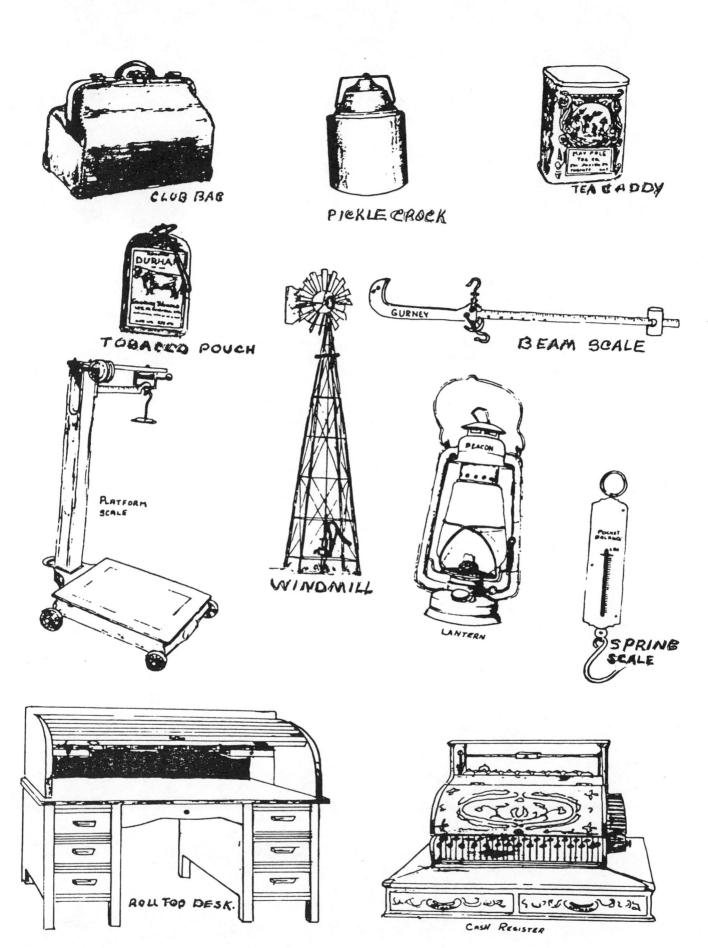

CLUB BAG

PICKLE CROCK

TEA CADDY

TOBACCO POUCH

WINDMILL

GURNEY BEAM SCALE

PLATFORM SCALE

LANTERN

SPRING SCALE

ROLL TOP DESK.

CASH REGISTER

GOVERNMENT OF THE NORTH-WEST TERRITORIES OF CANADA

DEPARTMENT OF AGRICULTURE

REF.

ADDRESS YOUR REPLY TO
THE DEPUTY COMMISSIONER
DEPARTMENT OF AGRICULTURE
REGINA

DO NOT WRITE ABOUT MORE THAN
ONE SUBJECT IN ANY LETTER

REGINA 28th April, 1899.

Sir,

Referring to your letter of March the 8th and to previous correspondence on the subject of your brands, I beg to say that it has been found possible to give you the brands asked for, and I therefore enclose certificates of the same. While regretting the delay,I would say that the matter would have received attention sooner had you replied to the Department's circular of the 9th of June last.

Yours obediently,

Charles Peterson

Deputy Commissioner.

H.McInnes, Esq.,

Calgary,

Alta.

*Please Return to
Jack McInnes
Box 627
Olds, Alberta
Tom 1v0*

Brands in Alberta

Cattle brands in Alberta are now registered in six positions: the shoulder, rib and hip, on the right or left side of the animal. Except in the cases of a few registered old-time brands, quarter circles must have points away from other characters ZO ZO, and half diamonds must have points toward the other characters ZO ZO. It is also usual to depict the letter "G" as reversed Ɔ to distinguish it from the regular "C". Horses have additional brand positions; jaw, neck, hoof and inside leg brands.

All brands must be renewed by their owners every four years. If they lapse, the brand is open for registry again. In other cases, a brand may be passed down through the years with the ranch to whom it has always belonged. Today there are approximately 50 thousand brands registered in the province alone. You can judge from this how important a brand book is for identifying cattle, on the range, or in the stockyards.

Stories are still told of ranchers who receive cheques for cattle they never even knew they had! This comes about when a calf running with a cow on the range is picked up at roundup time and, according to the unwritten law of the cattleman, is branded with the same brand as the cow. Later the calf is shipped to market and the cheque for its sale sent to the registered brand owner.

Many an old brand runs today as it did almost a hundred years ago — but as ever, the language of brands is a living language — changing, growing, developing. No wonder the brand book is the cattleman's bible — a printed history and a daily working tool!

GOVERNMENT OF THE NORTH-WEST TERRITORIES OF CANADA

OFFICE OF THE RECORDER OF BRANDS

Extract from Record of Brands, LA₁ F.15. No.3086

DESCRIPTION OF BRAND,

HI

RECORDED FOR *horses: on left thigh*

ALLOTTED TO *Hugh McInnis Calgary Alta*

DATE OF ALLOTMENT, *February 28th, 1899.*

I, *Chas W. Peterson* , Recorder of Brands, hereby certify that the above is a true and correct extract from the Record of Brands kept by me under the authority of The Brand Ordinance

Regina, *21st Apre 1899*

Chas W. Peterson
Recorder of Brands.

GOVERNMENT OF THE NORTH-WEST TERRITORIES OF CANADA

OFFICE OF THE RECORDER OF BRANDS

Extract from Record of Brands, LA₁ F.15. No.3086

DESCRIPTION OF BRAND,

HI

RECORDED FOR *Cattle: on left ribs*

ALLOTTED TO *Hugh McInnis Calgary Alta*

DATE OF ALLOTMENT, *February 28th 1898*

I, *Chas W. Peterson* , Recorder of Brands, hereby certify that the above is a true and correct extract from the Record of Brands kept by me under the authority of The Brand Ordinance

Regina, *Apre 21st 1899*

Chas W. Peterson
Recorder of Brands.

ALEX STEWART 15 l.r.	FR. + A.M. AUSTIN BIF w.a.	A. VAN TIGHEM JU r. sh	R.M. JEFFERY JZ l.h.	JOHN R. HAMBLING 5VV rt.r.
JESSIE ALLWARDEN 3A l.r.	ALLAN BALDERSON AB l.h.	F.C. AUSTIN BIF w.a.	C.W. LANG CWL l.r.	P. BURNS RANCHES VL l.r.
P. BURNS RANCHES 4T r.sh+l.h.	P. BURNS RANCHES 6 l.r.	F.W. + J.S. ROWAN l.r.	JOHNSON BROS. A5 l.sh.	ROGER BLACKWOOD TL l.h.
S.M. MARTIN UL l.h.	STEVE MAGYAR MS l.sh.	ANDREW MAGYAR 31 l.r.	GEORGE IRVING T7 l.h.	CECIL IRVING T7 l.r.
JOHN BOLTON HC l.r.	JOHN DALZELL B3L rt.r.	D. SUITOR C7X w.a.	E. QUINN IQ l. rump	McHUGH BROS H2 l.r.
HEAVER BROS. H8Y w.a.	Wm. ANDREWS IT rt.h.	THOMAS H. ANDREWS 19 l.r.	A.P. BREMNER IL l.r.	THOS. + CHAS. NASH JN l.h.
ROYAL N.W.M. POLICE MP l.sh.	R.O. CHILDREN RC rt.h.	Wm. FORAN ↓V— l.r.	ROBERT MAXWELL 6U l.h.	JAMES TURNBULL 6R— l.r.
VICTOR POFFENROTH CQ rt.th.	FREDERICK HYDE FV rt.sh.	W.K. BIRNEY 9L rt.r.	VICTOR POFFENROTH CQ rt.h.	JAS. HARRISON 77 rt.r.
GEORGE POFFENRATH 5U l.h.	JOHN HARRISON P4 rt.r.	HENRY + WALTER POFFENROTH 9KT l.r.	B.L. HAYES C6H w.a.	J. McINNES 60 rt.r.

GEORGE BREMNER — 1/4 — rt. h.
RUSSEL EVANS — 29 — rt. r.
MRS. MARY EBERLEY — IZ — l. r.
FRED GORDANIER — 77 — rt. r.
ROBERT DALZELL — CJ — rt. r.

JOSEPH MOSS — FJ — rt. h.
JACK McINNES — XO — rt. r.
THOMAS ROWLES — D3B — w. a.
HENRY & KATIE SHIERMAN — 2V — rt. h.
JOE HOGGE — VIV — l. r.

IORWERTH (ED) JONES — A — l. h.
BERT WONACOTT — DV — rt. h.
MRS. T. ROWLES — DIC — w. a.
ADAM + KATHERINE SHIERMAN — 2→ — rt. h.
ALFRED H. WATHEN — +6 — rt. r.

ROBERT HAMILTON — ⊙ — l. h.
EBEN BREMNER — DX — l. h.
THOMAS PRIEST — KF- — l. r.
RUDY MULDER — F — rt. h.
CONRAD GIRLETZ — 44 — rt. h.

MRS. ROBERT HAMILTON — NFI — w. a.
HILTON BROS. — HB — rt. r.
JOHN GREENFIELD — rt. s.
DAVID WYLIE — DV — rt. h.
R. MULDER — 7K — rt. r.

GEORGE RICHES — IZ — rt. h.
WALTER THIESSEN — -O4 — rt. r.
JOHN GREENFIELD — rt. s.
EUGENE MAGYAR — 13 — l. and r. ribs
ALEX S. BLACKWOOD — LX — l. h.

J.A. IRVING — JAI — l. sh.
LESTER MILLER — OT — rt. r.
ALAN WARD — A7 — l. h.
GORDON DAFOE — rt. r.
C.H. HOOLEY — CH — l. r.

A. FORCKEL and SONS — MX — l. r.
ULYSSES G. HARTWICK — L3F — w. a.
WALLACE STARKE — S N — rt. h.
JOHN-CHARLES + JACK McINNES — XO — rt. h.
GORDON DAFOE — H — rt. r.

EDWIN IRVING — Y4 — rt. h.
OLIVE SHATTUCK LABERGE — L2 — l. sh.
W.W. STARKE — WWS — rt. h.
ALEX CURRIE — LOY — w. a.
ALAN MACDONALD — AM — l. r.

R.D. GOODWIN — RD — rt. r.
CLIFFORD CALL — IZ — rt. r.
WALLACE STARKE — T P — l.h. - rt.h.
JOHN CURRIE — 91 — l. h.
CHARLES SHATTUCK — L2 — rt. h.

JACK EVANS — HU — rt. r.
JAMES SUITOR — C7X — l. r.
R.J. YOUNG — YY — l. h.
HERBERT CURRIE — NIU — w. a.
CHAS. MARSHALL — BY4 — l. r.

BARTON EVANS — PTI — w. a.
W.J. HAMILTON — H7 — l. r.
MISS OLIVE ALDRIDGE — WA — l. h.
E.J. CURRIE — VO — l. h.
JOHN (JACK) MEEHAN — -E6 — rt. r.

JOHN. H. EVANS — PTI — w. a.
MRS. MERCEDES McMULLIN — rt. r.
FRANK BARKER — FOO — l. h.
WELLINGTON CURRIE — OU — rt. h.
MORRIS STEWART — MS — l. r.

PETER MASSIB — 9M l.h.	JAS. S. INGRAM — EP rt.r	OTTO SALLENBACH — OS rt.r	ALBERT HERR Sr. — HER rt.sh	LORNE HOGGE — VIV l.h.
PETER MASSIB — MP l.h.	J.E. INGRAM — XW l.r	HAROLD BISWANGER — –U7 l.r	CLIFFORD HERR — RD l.r	MARSHALL BALLARD — –JV rt.r
ALEX WADDELL — WAW l.r	J.E. INGRAM — 9BU w.a.	WILLIAM CHARLES COULTRY — Ⓒ rt.sh	ROBERT HERR — R/H l.r	COPE BROTHERS — ƎV l.h.
THOMAS SCOTT — 14 rt.sh	WALTER K. BIRNEY — ƆB rt.r	HAROLD COULTRY — Ⓒ rt.sh	WILLIAM HERR — HER l.r	DALE JEFFERY — ᴙ l.h.
WM. HAMILTON — NH rt.r	P.R. CLELAND — PCl w.a.	NORMAN HOGGE — ᗡU rt.h	MRS. W. HERR — ᴙH l.r	DAN PATTON — K4U l.r
RON GIRLETZ — ƎE r.h.	JENKINS BROTHERS — JB rt.r	JAMES ALEXANDER HOGGE — 11 rt.r	LAWRENCE HERR — LH l.sh	FRED LATTER — R/G l.h.
IDWAL JONES — CX l.r	J.H. JENKINS — XJ l.h.	WALTER RENARD — K6 l.r	MARGUERITE DIXON — –MH rt.r	GEORGE FARKAS — ƆF rt.r
FRANK L. SANDERSON — 96 l.h.	ALEX ALLAN — 66 rt.h	MELVIN CHRISTENSEN — –40 l.r	JOHN HAMILTON Sr. — 111 l.h.	JOSEPH SHEEPY — ICU rt.r
DAN GERLITZ — 69 l.r	W.H. JOHNSON — JO l.r	ALEX H. BLACKWOOD — OIL l.r	WILLIAM GRIERSON — 3KY l.r	FOREST HERR — I l.h.
RON GIRLETZ — 44 rt.h	FRANK COYLE — CX h.	SARA IRVING FLETT — 7Y rt.sh	GEORGE LEE — H rt.n	ALBERT HERR — I rt.h
J.S. McKEVITT — K7 l.h.	JOHN D. WEDDERBURN — UY rt.r	HENRY TYNDALL — KY l.r	ALEX FRASER — ᴎH l.h.	GORDON HERR — H–7 rt.r
S. BRUKETA — ᗡK l.s.	PAT McCARTHY — PMS rt.r	STEPHEN (STENO) BANISTER — T1 rt.r	EVA BEATTIE — EVA l.r	GORDON HERR — H–ᒐ l.r
WALTER WILDE — VW / ᴧII rt.sh	HERB STEPHENSON — DU rt.r	GROTTO RANCHES — 37 r.rib	STELLA NELUBOWICH — H3 rt.r	DAVID HUNT — H/X r.r

J.E.R. LLOYD 7H l.r.	A.W. MASSIE LJ l.h.	R. LLOYD B8V w.a.	E. DRAPER rt.sh	A.J.T. PEACH l.h.
GORDON VIRTUE V9 l.sh.	FRANK S. JACOBS UK l.r.	WALLACE McBEE M-F rt.r.	C.M. BAMFORD 4B l.h.	SANDERSON BROS. 76 l.h.
RAYMOND BARKLEY D-1 rt.h.	COLE BROS. 3V l.h.	S. FEADON OV l.h.	J. McKEVITT M rt.h.	W.K. MASSIE MP l.h.
W.K. MASSIE M l.h.	SHER. A. HUGHES S/I l.h.	D.A. HUGHES H l.r.	PAUL A. RUSCAK P-R rt.r.	F.M. HOLDEN MH rt.r.
ROY F. LATTER B/S rt.h.	OKOTOKS & DIST. FEEDER ASS. l.r. + rt.	CHAS. H. COPITHORNE CO l.h.	GEORGE W. GOETTLER U7 rt.r.	ROY J. WIDNEY RW l.h.
W. HEMENS -H l.sh.	MISS. MARGARET C. MORRIS MC l.h.	JOSEPH A. HUCK IU l.r.	R. VANTIGHEM JU rt.sh.	Mrs. M.J. McHugh JW l.r.
an Davis + l.sh.	Walter Turnbull D l.r.	Wm. N. Graburn W l.sh.	H.J. Carroll 86 l.r.	Joeseph & Kenneth Bryce KJ rt.sh
PRATT BROS. PS l.r.	Wm. HAMILTON NH rt.r.	Wm. ANDERSON & Son 06 l.r.	Alex Anderson P.S l.r.	David J. Neish D-N rt.r.

Tattoo Marks For Fur-Bearing Animals	J.S. Thomson PAL rt. ear.	Mrs. J.S. Huck DSD rt. ear.

We have made a sincere effort to trace all the brands for our districts. We are sorry if there are any errors or omissions. We sincerely hope this list of Brands will be of interest to all.

The Brand Committee

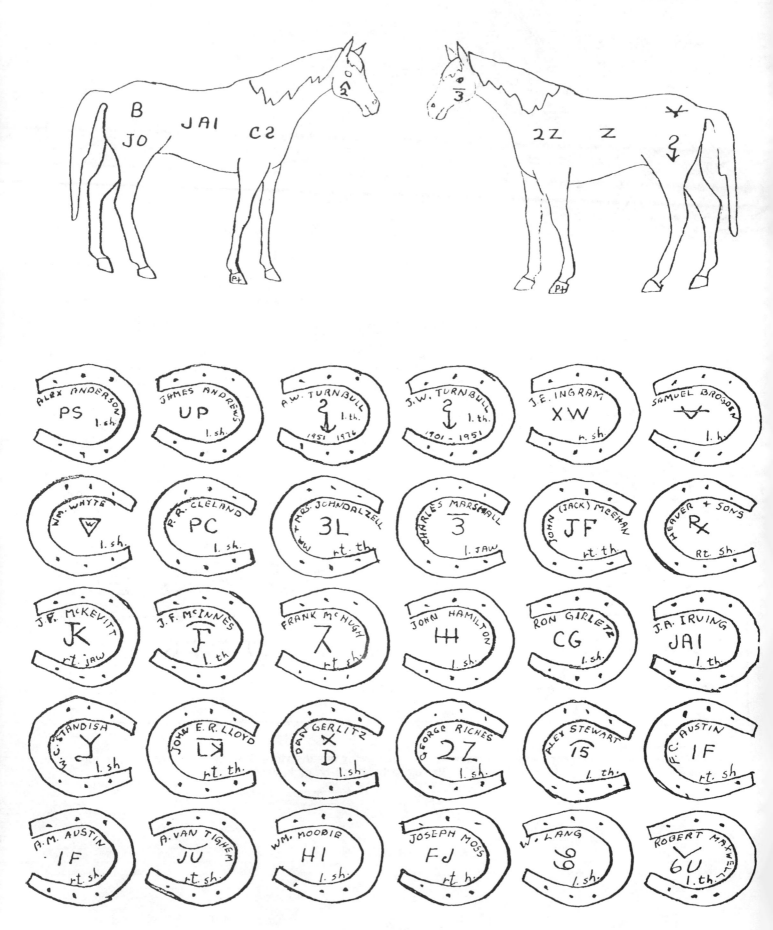

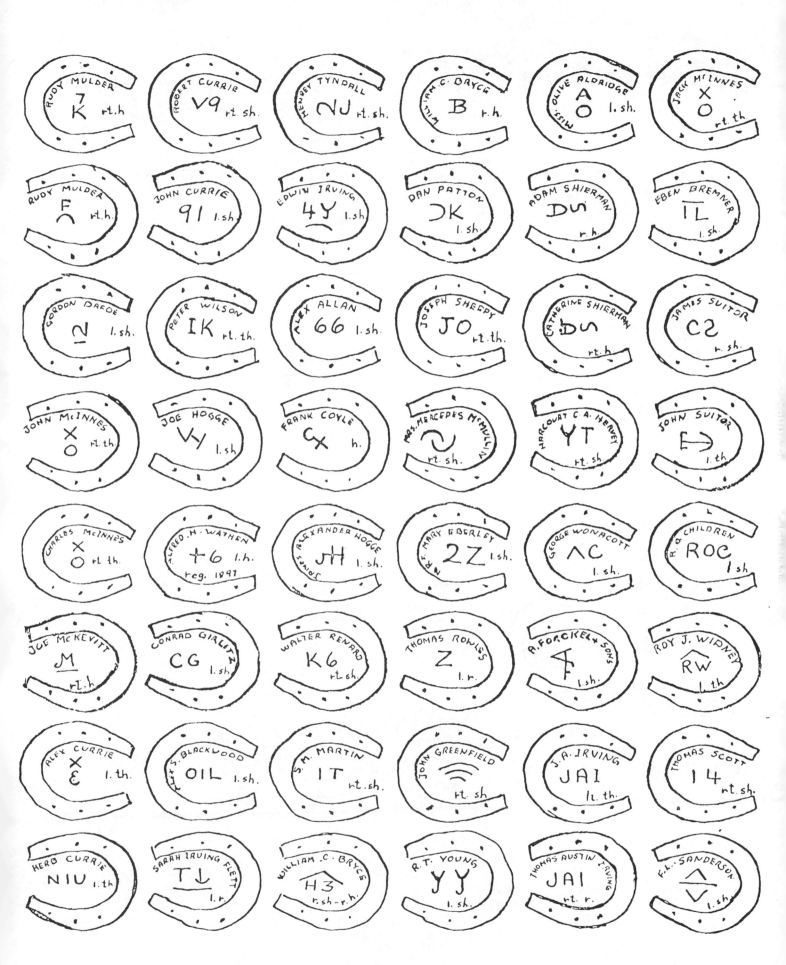

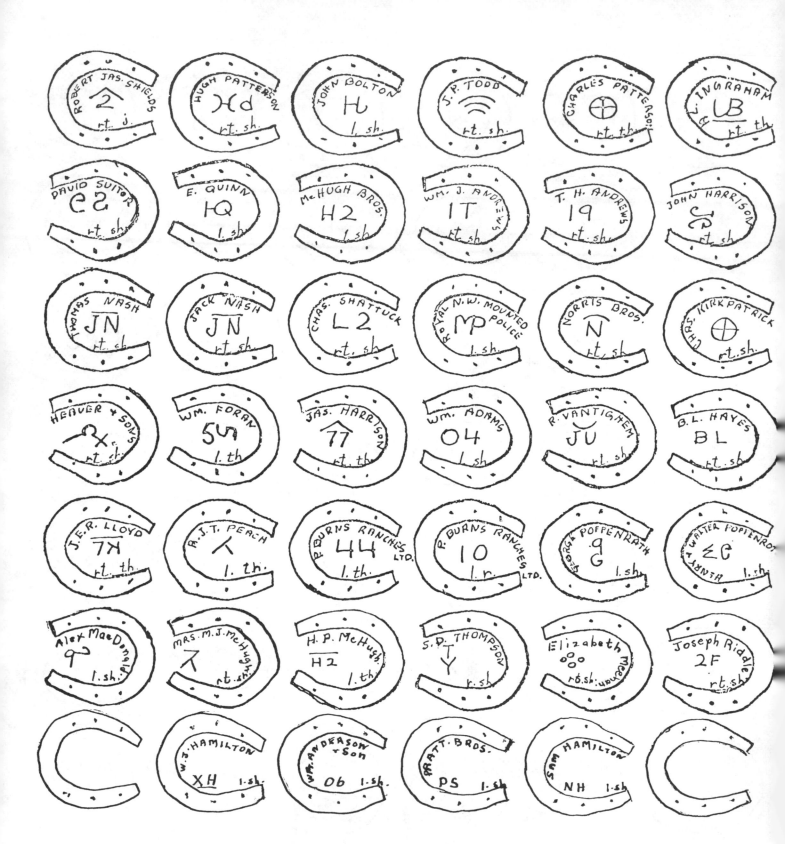

Brand Abbreviations

rt.	right	t.	thigh
l.	left	h.	hip
w.a.	whole animal	r.	rib
sh.	shoulder	n.	neck
		j.	jaw

524

Stories of General Interest

THE BLACKFOOT TRAIL — by I. Blackwood

This was used as the link between the reserves at Gleichen and Morley, crossing the Highwood close to its confluence with the Bow River. To the east it followed the south branch of the Bow for many miles. After crossing the Highwood, it followed along the valley, going directly west for five or six miles, before turning north to follow the Bow into Calgary. St. Joseph's Industrial School at Dunbow was built at the Crossing. There was also an Indian burial ground adjacent to the school. After the settlers came, they followed the old trail to Calgary with their herds of cattle to be sold, and also to do their trading. Even after the advent of the motor car, it was still used to some extent, even if it meant fording Fish Creek behind the Father Lacombe Home at Midnapore. It wound its way past the government elevators in east Calgary and on by the stockyards, but I do not know where it continued on to Morley.

At the time of writing (1975) plans are being made to restore the Indian burial grounds at Dunbow.

OUR EARLY ROADS — by Harold Biswanger

The early roads of this country consisted of Indian trails and bull trails of the early pioneers and freighters. The settlers' trails for the most part, went from farm to farm and headed towards a town or to a main trail to the cities. This gradually changed as the land became more settled and the land, being broken up, the trails were cut off.

The wagon traffic was forced to use surveyed road allowances. When there were sloughs, coulees and hills, you could use farmers' fields to get around these obstacles. Many times during the winter and spring break-up, you went through the farm fields, as they were not being used this time of year, and the snow was too deep in the road, or mud made it impossible to get through. Slowly, as the farms were being fenced, a lot of this had to be stopped, or gates would have to be left in the fences. The farmers and the local improvement districts or municipal districts started to construct graded roads on main road allowances. Eventually all road allowances were graded up to have a ditch on either side. This was done at first with the slip, which was a large metal scoop with two handles out behind and pulled with a team of horses or mules. It filled in sloughs and small dips in the road.

The fresno was also used. It was much larger than the slip and had two skids on the bottom to run on, with one handle out at the back. It was pulled with four horses or mules. Both machines were lifted by the handles till the front dug in and then it would flip over and empty. These were used mainly for putting in culverts.

A plough was used to loosen the earth for these machines to work. Another implement was the road drag, which consisted of three large pieces of metal on edge set at an angle and fastened together and pulled with a four horse team. The driver walked behind or stood on a plank at the back.

Later on came the graders, drawn by eight or ten horses or mules, until tractors became more popular. As time progressed, the elevating grader was introduced. These machines were pulled along in the ditches with a caterpillar tractor digging up the earth and dumping it on top of the road, which was then smoothed out with the grader. This method didn't cut down bad hills or fill in depressions, so they went around many steep hills in to the farm property.

During the lean years of the '30's, a lot of the roads were maintained by the farmers, and they were allowed a reduction in their taxes. In some cases in Alberta, they were paid in "script" or "Aberhart alfalfa", which was Social Credit money, which could be cashed for food or supplies only in certain stores, such as Nagler's in Calgary.

Macleod Trail (No. 2 Hwy.) Feb. 1930. In the distance Anderson buildings and Pine Creek Church. The buildings close are the Standish place. The shed on the back of the house on right was the original John Owens homestead shack.

Road building with elevating grader in the 1930's.

March 1948, looking east to Red Deer Lake Community on Highway 22. M.D. No. 31 new D7 with Ed Smith at controls. Red Deer Lake Church in the background left and Roy Thiessen's new house, right.

Washed out road near Aldridge farm. Harold Biswanger, Olive Aldridge and Harry Barker (at right).

Gradually, the roads were being built up by larger and better machines like caterpillars, and pulling buckets which scraped up the earth. They could haul it great distances and dump it. With this method, they could cut down steep hills and fill in all the low places, making the roads a lot more level and straight. Some of the elevating graders which were pulled by "cats", as they were called, were used only on the flat lands. The motorized grader graded the roads, and ditches were built.

In the spring, the mud was impossible, and with the horse and buggy and wagon giving way to the car and truck, it was necessary to gravel the roads. This was largely the farmers' responsibility so with wagons and some small trucks, they went to the nearest river or gravel pit and shovelled on the gravel, hauled it to the roads and spread it out. In later years, it was loaded for them by machines, and in some cases, payment was in the form of reduced taxes.

Gradually, the M.D. took over all road work, with full-time help and better machines. Crushed gravel was used instead of pit run, which had a lot of large rocks in it, which we see coming to the surface sometimes today. They are also back sloping most all ditches back in to the farm fields to stop drifting in winter time. One man in particular who was a great gravel shoveller into the wagons was a man by the name of Carl Olsen. He could shovel gravel with a number ten scoop, when others used a number eight scoop. He also shovelled faster, and received double pay for his efforts. He later ranched in the Turner Valley district.

EARLY HISTORY ALONG MACLEOD TRAIL

The Lethbridge Herald is adding to Alberta lore by encouraging writing of early history. One of the recent subjects has been the "Macleod Trail" written by Freda Smith Mudiman. The writer gives a very complete history of this historic north-south trail, which was originally a part of the trail from Mexico to the Mackenzie. The story of the trail extends back to prehistoric times when ancestors of the Plains Indians crossed from Asia to America, pushing steadily southward. It is the past century which has seen the greatest changes on this trail. All Indian trails follow lines of least resistance, but on the Macleod Trail there were mountain streams that reached great heights in flood time. Fragments of the interesting story are copied from the Lethbridge Herald.

"Along this trail 100 years ago" said the writer, "there might be seen herds of buffalo, antelope, elk, the odd bear, abundance of wild fowl, and in the streams beaver and mountain trout.

"First traffic on the Macleod trail was strictly pedestrian for it is little more than 200 years ago that horses appeared in southern Alberta. It is possible that the first white man to use this trail was David Thompson who was on the Highwood in 1797, and then went south to Missouri. Few white traders followed him because the land below the Bow was Blackfoot territory and the Blackfoot Indians were the terror of the plains. But missionaries went up and down Macleod Trail quite unmolested leaving records of fierce storms, chinooks, prairie fires and blizzards.

"In the late 1860's white traders from Montana did move on to the plains. They first dealt solely in trade, calico and tea for furs; but the second added a bit of whiskey but eventually settled down as solid citizens. The third type of traders were footloose brigands fresh from the American Civil War to whom lives or property rights meant little. These were traders of whiskey for fur, and to protect themselves against drink-crazed Indians, they banded together in palisaded forts. Amongst these were Whoop-Up, Side Out, Stand Off and Robber's Roost. The one who made their head-quarters along the Highwood were the Spitzie Cavalry, and no doubt the trail echoed to their rebel yells."

The trade goods and whiskey kegs came up from Montana by ox team. So creaking ox carts now were seen on the Macleod trail. A typical wagon train would have three teams of 20 oxen each, with each team hauling three wagons. The wagons were heavily loaded with flour, sugar, tea, coffee, calico and liquor.

Red River Carts

In 1870 ten Red River carts came down the trail from Edmonton to Fort Benton, making the round trip in two months. Ox teams were on all the trails from the Rio Grande to the Bow. In 1872 Fred Kanoose guided up the Macleod Trail but the party was attacked by Indians for three days.

But there came a new sound on Macleod Trail, the creak of saddle and jingle of spurs. Trim North West Mounted Police rode up the Macleod Trail in the fall of 1874 to apprehend whiskey traders at Pine Creek. Then in 1875 a group of police went up the trail and on to Red Deer on a military mission. The I. G. Baker Company erected buildings at Fort Calgary and brought up enough goods to start a store. Some time later a ferry operated on the Bow, with charges of $1.00 a wagon. In 1876 the Baker Co. sent a big shipment of furs over Macleod Trail to Benton, then by water to St. Louis, the fur centre of that day.

Lots of Travel

Now there was much travel up and down the trail between police posts. The police had a contract to deliver mail every two weeks to the forts, making the trip in light canvas-covered wagons. The mail came and went by Benton, and U.S. stamps were used. In fact the U.S. flag flew for years over Fort Whoop-Up till police came.

Stock Moving Up

The first domestic stock travelling the trail was a small herd going to MacDougall at Morley. But soon the trail saw some really large herds on the move. Amongst those early ranches were the Oxley ranch west of Stavely, the Cochrane ranch and so on.

In 1881 the governor-general Lord Lorne, travelled the Macleod trail, witnessing a buffalo hunt on the way, and enjoying fresh vegetables from the garden of John Glenn on Fish Creek.

The Stage Coach

In the eighties came further influx of people to establish ranches and homes. Many travelled in prairie schooners, known as Conestoga wagons. They were capacious and broadwheeled. Another new vehicle on Macleod Trail at this time was the stagecoach. The Concord coaches lumbered peacefully along the trail. Fare from Calgary to Macleod was $15, with baggage extra. Soon the mail also travelled by coach. After the C.P.R. reached Calgary, the mail service was more regular. Canadian stamps were used and Southern Alberta felt it was a part of Canada. Freight was still by oxcart, still 2 cents a pound.

Going south from Calgary the stagecoach left Calgary early in the morning to reach Sheep Creek by noon. If the water was high on the creeks the passengers climbed to the roof of the coach. Drivers were very expert in fording. Mosquito Creek was the extent of one day's journey and coaches from north and south met there at the Trollinger stopping place. It was a log building with dirt floor, and men usually rolled up in their own blankets on the floor. Four horses were usually enough but six were used in bad weather. The noon stop on the second day was at Willow Creek and Macleod was reached by night.

The Greatest Ride

What was probably the greatest ride ever made over the Macleod Trail was when word came of the outbreak of the North West Rebellion. Sergeant Horner on his horse, Caesar, rode from Macleod to Calgary between sun-up and sun-down.

In 1890-91 the railway from Calgary to Macleod went through. A prairie fire had blackened the surveyors' stakes marking the trail, so the workmen used pieces of buffalo bone to mark the Macleod Trail.

After the Calgary-Macleod railway was completed, the stagecoaches were taken to Macleod for runs east and west to Lethbridge and Pincher Creek.

Today only faint traces remain of the original Macleod Trail but its course is paralleled by a modern highway, a railway line, an air route, all of which wind northward in the lee of the Rockies, as did the Old North Trail from Mexico to the Mackenzie.

THE C.N.R. GRADE — by E. Leach

Here and there in the Davisburg-Pine Creek district and elsewhere between Calgary and south of High River, one finds what appears to be a disused railway. Really it is the railroad that never materialized.

The ditches and grades cut up the landscape, disfiguring it and spoiling many a fine view. Nature, however, has healed some of the wounds with the growth of grass, wild flowers, buckbrush, willows and small poplars. Many people never question why or when this disfigurement took place.

The C.N.R., then a private company, had purchased the right of way for a line from Calgary to Fort Macleod to provide farming folk with better marketing facilities and lessen the long haul to the C.P.R. line.

Construction began previous to W.W. I, using horses, scrapers, fresnoes, and man power. Tractors were not in common use at that time, which seems difficult for us to believe.

As was customary, the Canadian government subsidized the C.N.R. with huge grants of money. Investors in Britain and other countries made available large sums of money, expecting to make small fortunes in this comparatively new country.

When W.W. I broke out in 1914 the project was set aside. After the end of the war in 1918 improved roads, farmer-owned trucks and cars lessened the previous long distances and there appeared to be no longer a need for this second railroad. Of course, too, there was a shortage of investment money which is always a factor, and the whole thing became a dream gone wrong.

THE WEST OF THE '80's — by Mrs. E. Leach. Taken, by permission, from the 1942, Christmas Edition of the "Gremlin".

To many of you the word "De Winton" means only desolation, for you think this place is almost the end of the world. If you could travel back some sixty or so years you might rightly think this was a long way from civilization. This country was devoted primarily to ranching. The name was derived from one of the early ranchers Sir Francis De Winton Aide-De-Camp to the Marquis of Lorne. The present day stampedes try to show, to a certain extent, the skill of the early ranching days when cowboys rode bucking bronchos and were skillful with the lariat. It was then a part of their very existence for saddle horses had to be broken, cattle and horses had to be rounded up and branded. A top cow-puncher was a necessity on any ranch.

The big ranches soon gave way to the farming element and many of the large lease lands and open ranges were settled by homesteaders. It was a common saying that the Dominion Government made a bet, "of one hundred and sixty acres of land against ten dollars and three years residence on the land," that the homesteader would starve to death. Very few starved but the living was often pretty slim for there just wasn't any money in the country. There was, however, plenty of initiative, courage and hard work with just enough stick-to-it-iveness so that very few lost their bets.

Most of the pioneers of this immediate district came from the County of Megantic in the Province of Quebec with a few adventurous souls from Merry Old England and Bonny Scotland to add a bit of spice to living. They threw in their lot together, mingling work and play, fully determined to make the best of everything.

There weren't any roads in the early eighties. The prairie trails, which were soon worn, were fine in dry weather, but when the rains came, they rapidly developed into a sea of mud. Creeks and rivers had to be forded and many a time the horses had to swim. Those of you who complain about being bounced around a bit in the bus should have travelled in the old days when heavy work horses and the wagons were the means of transportation. Calgary was the nearest town and at that time, it was not much bigger than De Winton is now. Trips there were, more or less, semi-annual affairs, supplies being bought to last six months or so. The farmer's wife had a rather lonesome time of it for transportation was poor and there was always a lot of work to be done. When sickness came, however, there was always time to help each other. No one was ever too busy to take home the family washing or to bake a big batch of bread. The women had their quilting bees; the men exchanged work at threshing time. They held their little country fairs which later grew to exhibitions.

Soon a school was needed and the Davisburg School was built. It bears the proud number of 79 which means that it was the seventy-ninth school, not only in Alberta but, in the whole of the North West Territories, of which Alberta was only a small part.

The next big enterprise was a church. If you look across the fields you will see a small, white church on the hill, weather beaten it is true but where services are still held. It was built away back in about

1889, all the money being donated by the settlers. The work of hauling the lumber from Calgary was done voluntarily and most of the labour was done locally. These early pioneers not only built the church but they attended services regularly. It was not a case of someone going to represent the family — oh no! everyone went, rain or shine. Many of them sleep in the little cemetery behind the Church which they helped to build. Those of us who pass that way cannot but say, in our hearts, "Well done good and faithful servants."

In the old days when a load of coal was needed it did not come to the door in a truck. Friend Farmer hitched his team to the sleigh and travelled some thirty miles south-west to the Black Diamond mine which is in the vicinity of the now world famous Turner Valley Oil Fields. Often he would have to wait a day or two to get a load of fuel and then had the long trek back home again. The coal was soft and dirty, but it created lots of heat in spite of the soot that soon filled the stove pipes.

It was not until 1911 that the rural telephone was put through this district. Not many of us would like to be without it now.

This country is famous for its fine grain fields, some of the finest wheat in the world is grown right beside this airport. Good horses and cattle are raised, to say nothing of "Bacon for Britain". All of these find ready sale, with the exception of wheat. When the war is won we will again have our European market.

Alberta has always been known for its sunshine and fine bracing air. When the Dominion Government planned a chain of Air Training Schools it fittingly chose a stretch of land in Alberta, from north to south, this No. 31 E.F.T.S. at De Winton being a part of the great scheme. Those of you who are inclined to feel sorry for yourselves because you are stationed here please bear in mind what this country once was and how far it has advanced in the short space of sixty years. Note: The land referred to was purchased from two fine Old Timers, Mr. William Stewart and Mr. James McAndrews. They arrived in the very early '80's.

FROM THE NOTES OF REVEREND DYKE, 1884

Being provided with a span of ponies and a buckboard, we started on a journey to see the country around Calgary. We made no selection of farms and farmers but visited them indiscriminately.

The first stopping place was just beyond Fish Creek at Mr. McInnes'. There are four brothers, all bachelors, who settled here a year ago, they have 1300 acres of land, two comfortable houses, barns and stables. They have 27 acres in oats, potatoes and general crops. Besides this they have 40 acres broken and intend breaking more so as to have at least 100 acres under crop next year. Leaving the genial bachelors in serious contemplation of matrimony, we drove several miles across the prairie and were disappointed when we found three houses, in a row, empty — their occupants being away in the distant valleys making hay while the sun shines. But, continuing our journey, we found Mr. Lloyd and his assistant building

a large stack of hay on his farm near Red Deer Lake with all the care of a newly arrived Englishman, who likes to see his western hay stack as neat and trim as those well built, well raked, heavily thatched hay stacks in England. Going from the stack yard to the house, the chattering voices of children assured us that this was not a bachelor's domicile. We found Mrs. Lloyd and her three sturdy children very pleasant and anxious for us to stay for tea but, being desirous to visit as many places as possible, we hastened on to the next settlers.

Just as the clouds of evening were settling down upon the hilltops, and casting their long shadows across the valleys, we drove up to the farm of George and William Wonacott who came to 7-22-1-W5, only last September. They have built a very good log house and barn with a large, well fenced, corral, along the north end of which they have planted a row of poplar trees which seem to be doing well. They have six acres of oats, a small patch of wheat and a good garden with potatoes that your correspondent thought, at first sight, to be turnips. They were so large and smooth and, when cooked, were as dry and mealy as any we have ever eaten. The recent hail storm was very slight here, did no damage at all. They have thirty acres broken and intend going into stock quite largely in the spring. At present they are busy putting 100 tons of hay into stacks. Passing from here, we called at Mr. Ray's farm. He had eight acres of oats which have been slightly hurt by the hail storm but which will yield, even now, a larger crop per acre than is raised in some of the eastern provinces. He has eleven head of beautiful cattle, seven of which are good cows, supplying a large quantity of butter for the Calgary market and special customers every week. He had a good flock of hens and ten acres of land broken besides that on which the crop stands. Our next stopping place was at the mouth of High River at Begg's Dale, the loveliest, wildest, most romantic scenery we have gazed upon for a long time. The high bluffs look down upon the fertile valley, at the bottom of which, High River rushes, gabbling, into the bosom of the Bow. Mr. Begg Junior, entertained us to tea and made us feel at home, with true bachelor hospitality. Mr. Begg Senior was absent, bringing in a large flock of sheep. A shower of rain and the lateness of the afternoon prevented us from calling at the Industrial School but, we have promised ourselves another visit to this charming spot when we will make ourselves more fully acquainted with that public building.

Leaving Sheep Creek, we made a few visits at Pine Creek. Messrs. Robb, Moss, Owens, Lacren, Pratt and Smith are among the principal settlers on this creek. The recent hail storm has done some damage to the barley and oats. The storm seems to have gone in streaks, doing slight damage in some farms and serious on others. Even though settlers who have suffered most, and there are but two or three whose crops have been seriously damaged, are not at all disheartened but are full of faith in the country's growth and future prosperity.

This trip was taken in September of 1884 and the Mr. Ray referred to would be Samuel Stanley Ray who lived on SW¼ 9-22-1-W5, C.P.R. Grant No. 1735.

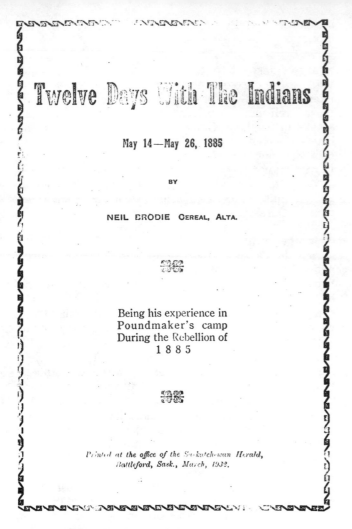

Twelve Days With The Indians

May 14—May 26, 1885

BY

NEIL BRODIE CEREAL, ALTA.

Being his experience in
Poundmaker's camp
During the Rebellion of
1885

*Printed at the office of the Saskatchewan Herald,
Battleford, Sask., March, 1932.*

Twelve Days With The Indians

By Neil Brodie, Cereal, Alta.

Being his experience in Poundmaker's Camp During the Rebellion of 1885.

On Thursday, May 14th, 1885, about 10 a.m., I and twenty others who were freighting supplies with twenty-one yoke of oxen for Col. Otter's column from Swift Current to Battleford, were about twelve miles south of Battleford in the Eagle Hills, where there were small bluffs of poplar, when Poundmaker's warriors surrounded us We ran our oxen into a circle with the wagons outside and with ten rifles held back the Indians. Suddenly a halfbreed rode out, with his hands high over his head, signalling for a parley. Frank Cox, one of the few who kept all his wits, agreed to go out and talk if I would protect him I drew a bead on the halfbreed's breast and Frank, walking out under my rifle, made terms of surrender. We were to leave all; they to escort us as near to Battleford as they could risk their own lives.

There were about three hundred well-armed Indians and halfbreeds; besides a great many more with shot guns, war clubs, tomahawks and knives; perhaps,

eight hundred altogether. Now, these Indians and halfbreeds, through Jobin and Sayers, accepted these conditions. We started with an escort of about twenty horsemen, we hanging on to the stirrup straps as we ran. We ran for about a mile when another small band of Indians, about twenty in number, rode us down and demanded that we return to camp or die here. Our escort said he could not keep his promise. However, he kept them from shooting us.

We went back to the Indian camp and they held a council to decide what to do with us The chief, minor chiefs and principal warriors, perhaps thirty, sat down in a circle. The speaker rose and gave his opinion which was not hard to understand although we could not speak their language If the speaker wanted to kill us, he would dance around with his rifle in the hollow of his arm and speak loud and fast. If he was willing to spare our lives, he would leave his rifle on the ground and walk around the cir-

cle and talk quietly. Finally they agreed to keep us alive if none of us tried to run away if we did, then the blood-thirsty had the privilege of killing the rest

We, of course, accepted the terms Then Chief Poundmaker, with an interpreter, had a talk with us He said our lives were safe and advised us to thank God. Asked if there was anything we wanted, I asked that he give us an interpreter to camp with us so that we might know what was wanted. He consented and gave us a nice quiet man, who was good company and gave us good advice, as how to get on with the Indians. When an Indian visited us and expressed a wish to kill the prisoners, this man let us know his wish. We all requested that our clothes be returned. They took my bed, coat and vest, and I gave them my money, thirty-four dollars. I did not like parting with my cash (Scotch). In fact, I refused to give it up, although they threatened me with a loaded rifle and saying "Shunia", but on the advice of Jobin not to vex the Indians, I gave up my money.

Shortly after this the whole camp started moving south-east. A minor chief selected me to drive his oxen. His wife and I

occupied the front seat; just behind me was my guard, armed with a three and a half foot cutter bar of a mowing machine, all the sections removed but five. It was now about three o'clock when all the outriders doubled back and ordered us to drive to a deep ravine that we had just passed through. We were travelling in five columns, covering about one quarter section each way when we came to a halt The armed sharpshooters passed forward. With them was Charles Bremner, riding a bay pony with a rifle across his saddle-bow. When they came back they told me that they had killed a redcoat, N. W. M. P. [Elliott]. I did not see the shooting but heard it. Elliott did not even wound an Indian He was shot in the back of the head. They buried him by carrying soil from a badger mound close by. Again we moved south-east, my boss scouting about four hundred yards in front of me. I was driving the lead team on the left hand column. We camped about 5 30 o'clock.

My host killed a calf for supper. His wife, her sisters and mother, prepared supper of peeled potatoes, boiled meat, bannocks, hard tack, tea, milk and sugar. We

(2)

sat on our heels, tailor fashion in the teepee around the food. I ate my hostess' rights and she says that I had plenty to eat This ended the first day. I was driving for another Indian next day, moving in the same direction. Again my hostess was good to me. This has been my experience with very few exceptions, that the women were good. On passing a creek I let my guard know that I was going to get a drink I let the oxen go by themselves. When I had a drink, I ran to catch the team, passing a dear old squaw, who caught me by the wrist and rubbed my hand all over her head Here was sympathy for me without a word being spoken. I smiled in return for her kindness

A few hours before our capture we were joined by eight horse teamsters These made a dash for liberty, three of our party going with them Two got clear away, outriding the Indians The third one and a horse teamster, riding his team with the neck-yoke on, were overtaken by bullets from the enemies' rifles and decided to surrender. They were robbed of their watches, knives and trinkets; two hours later the springs and wheels were decorating the Indians hair "Me

grandfather's watch", said Paddy. Another horse teamster, a young Frenchman, jumped off his horse, which was blind, and took shelter in a bluff of poplars until the evening, expecting the Indians to be away. He was caught and asking what they intended doing with him, was told that he would be taken to the ravine where the other prisoners were. Ravine being translated as "hole" gave this poor fellow a bad fright. He certainly was glad to see us alive, and told me so.

The third night was very cold, there being about one quarter of an inch of ice on the water in a slough close to our camp We were sleeping on the ground between two wagons which had a canvas thrown over them. We had but one double blanket to six men. Two of the men thought they would be warmer in one of the wagons but when they got in they could not be seen. We had a guard all around, but about every hour some Indian who did not trust them, counted us to see if we were all there. I was asleep and awakened with a tremendous hubbub An Indian was standing with one foot on each side of me (close to my heart) with a candle in one hand and a knife in the other, counting

(4)

with his butcher knive for a pointer. Two men short; so they were pleased, for now they could start the killing. About this time I raised my head off my pillow (which was very likely my boots as I made a practice of using them for a pillow), when the interpreter called, "Lie down, the Indian thinks you are going to run away" Our good interpreter maintained that none had left but could not account for the missing men. This kept up for about twenty minutes when the men were found and all was peace again. Just here I might say it was a relief to be taken by the Indians to drive their chariots, for then I got away from the oft repeated question, "How long have we to live?" My answer was, "Perhaps five minutes; perhaps we might live to be old men". Then again by moving from place to place I had a good chance to see the Indians at home

We camped there waiting for news from Riel, who was fighting Gen. Middleton, at Batoche. Poundmaker's runners were expected to bring good news but brought word that Riel had lost the battle and was taken prisoner, and that Dumont had been wounded and was on his way to the States. Then the Indians and halfbreeds put away their arms and, after a couple of councils, decided to take the prisoners to Battleford and ask for terms.

We were taken in four or five wagons. Just as we were ready to start Strike-him-on-the-back struck each of us on the shoulders with a quirt. This was on the 22nd. On the 26th Poundmaker and his warriors surrendered without terms. Very few who read this will realize that we had made one trip of over two hundred miles and were on our second of over one hundred when we were caught.

Poundmaker, head chief of the big camp, which included seven reserves, was a very fine looking Indian. Tall, with very long hair hanging in two braids in front. Dressed in blanket shaps, moccasins, cow hide waistcoat covered with rows of round headed brass tacks; sometimes carrying his Pukamakin

Another Indian that I remember very well, Jacob by name, who came to our lodge and enquired of our welfare, and gave us some clothes to replace those taken from us. Then there was the Indian they called "General Gordon"; a real dandy who could speak many languages, was an

Indian this time, next time a halfbreed. He told me that he had killed one poor devil. He was in shackles when we left the Indian camp. He was hung for killing Bernard Tremond. His sweetheart made him a nice pair of moccasins for his last journey. So said W. B. Cameron, of Big Bear fame There were very few wounded that I saw. Their doctor and I had dinner together one day after attending to the wounded which he did very well. The others were just Indians, except one old buck, about seventy-two years old, dressed in a short, dirty white cotton shirt and moccasins - nothing more—carrying a bow and sheaf of arrows. He came in among us, searching our pockets for money and trinkets, straddling over the heads of those who were sitting. One resented this and gave him a "skelp". He just smiled and passed.

The squaws came often to have a look at the prisoners. They did not say much; just sat on the ground, nursing their "papooses", who were nude as a rule I think they pitied us, more than they rejoiced in our misfortune. One old squaw, who was poor and alone, (she had all her world's goods on the travois of a fat spotted dog) let me know that she was sorry for me One young squaw asked me to open a two pound can of Armour's beef for her. I placed it on a board and with a common axe cut it in two with one sharp blow. Then I was a "hero" and had to repeat the trick for others.

Father Cochin, who died in 1927, gave us his tent for two nights. Instructor Jefferson had a long talk with me, for the benefit of the Indians, who wanted to know what was thought of the war by the government at Regina and were disappointed that they did not make a greater impression. "They thought that they were making a small earthquake", said Jefferson.

The first night with the Indians we were given a tent and some blankets When these were divided I got none and, not being good at pushing for the best place, I was relegated to the door of the tent. Every little while some Indian came to have a look at us. One of them, seeing me without blanket, coat or vest, returned with a very rare article, a rabbit skin blanket, under which I went sound asleep and forgot all my troubles.

On being released we were taken to Col. Otter for an examination. Then he had guides ap-

pointed to find us sleeping quarters but did not even mention supper; we had no dinner that day. Our sleeping quarters were on the east end of the plateau. On the way there our guides, members of the Queen's Own, asked us a great number of questions and we were quite willing to talk, after nine days of very little talking. It was by this time quite dark and with so much talk we failed to hear the challenge of the sentry, who called out the main guard, thinking we were Indians. The officer's command to "HALT" would make the deaf hear. Then when he learned who we were and why we were there, he asked more questions; in fact, the whole guard questioned us some more. Tuesday, Angus Kennedy, of the Montreal Witness. also questioned me. He was then a young man with golden hair; the last picture I saw of him his hair appeared to be grey.

On the 26th, Gen. Middleton sat on a chair (north of the Battle River) facing west; at about fifteen feet sat P. Hourie on a chair, facing east. The Indians sat on the ground to the south I stood about fifteen feet north of the general, inside the soldiers' lines.

The first question or statement was, "Poundmaker, you are ac-cused of high treason. What have you to say?" Then after a dispute or talk between Hourie and Poundmaker, the interpreter made the statement, "There is no such a word as high treason in in the Cree language." I never saw that recorded, so take note of the substitute, "You are accused of throwing sticks at the Queen and trying to knock her bonnet off". Sir Fred just nodded and asked more questions. Finally he asked for all murderers and leaders. The soldiers arrested about one dozen, including the Indian who whacked us on the back. The Indians returned all our oxen but two; these we found two days later, tied in a bluff very hungry. Some of the freight stolen from us was returned. This I took to the storehouse in the fort.

Although the Indians could not speak English, it was wonderful how they could make us understand. They are pastmasters of the sign language. I am satisfied that I had many friends among the Indians when we left. The only one I ever met since, gave me his hand with a smile. We were offered some rare presents to gain our favor One was an ivory covered prayer book which I did not accept but traded hats with Nitchie and wore his hat which pleased him very much.

At Swift Current our train of twenty-one yoke of oxen was divided into two companies with a leader to each. Donald McLean led the first and Frank Cox the other. I was the last on the line and had charge of the food for eleven teams and their drivers. There were stations at certain places along the trail. Some officers in charge had very small hearts. With these we had to quarrel to get a few lumps of sugar for our tea; others had their hearts in the right place and gave us sugar, tea, biscuits, corned beef and hard tack, besides hay for the oxen, saying "Yes, of course; the government provides it and you shall have it."

We were not armed on the first trip, so when about fifteen miles from Battleford we camped and waited for an escort that our leaders had sent for by a company of scouts who passed us the day before. A squad of twenty Mounted Police came for us. When about eight miles from town we camped, putting the wagons in a ring for protection, the men and teams inside.

I was put on guard on the west side, the police supplying me with a heavy revolver. About eleven o'clock we located a scout of Poundmaker's taking stock of us. He was not molested. Everything became quiet about one o'clock; horses quit stamping, oxen lay down; men went to sleep; officers walked around softly; I was lying under a wagon with head and shoulders outside the the ring, the revolver under my hand, when I heard, "Are you asleep?" "No, sir " That was the truth or I could not have answered.

Before starting for second load we asked for an escort through the hills. Colonel Otter sent a mounted policeman with orders for us to move on in fifteen minutes or we would be put under arrest and our teams taken from us and given others to drive We weakened and obeyed orders But Otter was wrong; he had not driven the Indians out of the hills nor frightened them one little bit, as we afterwards found out.

On November 16th, 1885, I was driving four yoke of oxen with four loads of fifty-two bushels of wheat each, on my way to Regina. When just west of the N. W. M. P. barracks I was stopped by a policeman who told me to turn to the right and keep outside the stakes with a red flag on them. Going around the stakes was all "turtleback"; no road at all. If these oxen had not been well trained to go by the voice alone I would have had a big job. We got to the main road; then two miles and we were in Regina. The first salute I got was, "Riel is dead". He was being hung while I was going around the stakes.

On May 23rd, 1885, southwest of the barracks in Battleford, I met two men carrying a fish that they had caught in the Battle River that day. They had a pole through its gills and on their shoulders, and then its tail trailed on the ground. It must have been over five feet. Sorry I have not the names of these men. Perhaps they are alive and remember the incident.

NEIL BRODIE,
Cereal, Alta.

SOME OF THE MINISTERS OF THE DISTRICT CHURCHES THROUGH THE YEARS

From available records it would appear that Pine Creek had the first missionary minister when Angus Robertson held services in Robb's store. (Owen's?) This was in 1883 and he filled the position until Reverend Herdman began to take an occasional service in 1885. Reverend John Stone preached for a few months in 1889 and Reverend Munro came full time from 1889 to 1892. While Munro was at Pine Creek J. A. Matheson was at Davisburg and stayed till 1894.

Ministers were not too easily come by in those days and Mission students were used from 1894 through to 1898. A Mr. Walker in 1896 and A. F. Smith in 1898. Davisburg had been fortunate to have J. A. Helyer replaced in 1896 by Reverend Walker and, by 1898, Reverend Hugh Geant was preaching in the school house at Red Deer Lake. He was followed by Reverend

Woodside, 1900 and Maine in 1902, Reid in 1903 and Reverend Hugh McKellar in 1904. McKellar started his service in the school but when the Red Deer Lake church was built in 1904 he continued at the charge till 1913.

Reverend William Simons was at Pine Creek from 1902 to 1905, replaced by Reverend James Shortt from 1905-1907 with R. W. Collins overlapping, 1906-1909. Reverend Simons had started his work in the area by preaching at Melrose school in 1901. From 1909-1911, Pine Creek had Reverend Whiting; Reverend Campbell 1915-1917 and Reverend Clarke, 1918.

In 1917 Melrose, Davisburg and Pine Creek united as a three point charge and Reverend Clarke continued to preach through 1919. Reverend Ellis 1920, 1921, Reverend Trefry 1921-1922, Reverend Hattie 1922-23, Reverend Barrett arrived in 1923 and remained until July, 1931 when he was succeeded by Reverend Halstead who, with his wife and two children Hedley and Percidel, lived in the manse at Melrose from 1931-1936. There had been much talk of moving the manse to De Winton and this was finally accomplished in 1936 shortly after Reverend Horricks came to the charge. The Horricks family lived in the manse until 1940 and was the last ministerial family to live there. In 1941 Reverend Wilkinson took the charge but lived in Calgary and was followed by George Peacock, 1944-1946, who also lived out of the area. Reverend Harden was the last regular minister to take the charge, 1946-1947, and he made his home in "Scotty's shack" during his term. Students of the ministry were the next church workers and from 1950-1953 a young student spent the summer months working in the charge. These included; Mr. Ross, Ross Creighton, Mr. Wonfor, Bernice Moore, Mr. Ross again, Ken Murray. Reverend Howey, from Okotoks, took services for a few months in 1952-1953 and then we were able to put in a call for a full time minister once more. Bert Loree was the first 1953-1958 and he preached at the different points of the charge on alternate Sundays. By this time Okotoks had become the central point in the charge and Melrose had ceased to have services some years before. Red Deer Lake was included in the Charge and Davisburg also ceased to have its own service and joined the De Winton congregation. St. Andrew's United Church continues to operate in De Winton in conjunction with Okotoks but Red Deer Lake dropped out of the charge and joined the Calgary Presbytery in the 1970's.

Since joining with Okotoks the minister has lived in the Okotoks manse. The men serving for the last twenty years have been; Reverend Holter 1959-1963; Reverend Jenner, 1964-1968; Reverend Myles, 1969-1972; Reverend Gardner, 1972-1976; Reverend Millard, August 1976 —.

I REMEMBER FROM A VANTAGE POINT OF EIGHTY PLUS YEARS

The Bremner sisters, Ida Jane and Ethel, whistling duets at local entertainments.

Willie McInnes having an ear torn off in a run away horse race.

Joe Moss unintentionally leaving his wife behind in Calgary.

Seeing the CPR tracks moved to the south side of Midnapore slough when it was so wet in 1902.

John Dewar playing his bagpipes.

Will Turnbull and Alex Anderson playing the violin for dances.

Bachelors buying their bread in Calgary, in quantity, and burying it in snow banks to keep it fresh.

Jack Davis declaring at a school meeting that "three and two were six when I went to school, By Juggers".

Pete Murray shoeing horses.

Sid Aird teasing Mary McNeill's lamb.

The two Anderson boys, Murray and Rob, putting a skunk under the Pine Creek Presbyterian church just before Sunday service.

Draining Midnapore slough into Pine Creek, about 1904, the marks are still visible on the north side of Pine Creek Coulee, on the east side of the road.

Reverend Streeter and Frank Frier being instrumental in getting the hall built and working with the Theatrical Society.

Lena McNeill running the postoffice at DeWinton.

Earl Brinton making a house, by degrees, out of the machine shed in De Winton.

George Cable almost eliminating the beavers in his area by trapping.

Missing friends lost in WW1.

The "full dress" Balls, held in Streeter Hall.

Both Mr. Worden and Mr. Riches being badly injured by dairy bulls.

Filing a claim to pan for gold on Blackwood's creek.

Christmas concerts in the hall above Pashak's store.

Jim McNeill hiring the Streeter Hall for dancing after the close of a Christmas concert.

Stuart Jamison driving Daddy Gray's little buggy.

Mary Galvin shooting in competition with the men and winning.

Having two bachelors for Christmas dinner during prohibition and the hi-jinks that came after.

Hugh McNeill's home being popular with the boys when he had several daughters at home.

Robert Jamison having many male callers at his home when his girls were single.

Alec Blackwood being Justice of the Peace.

Cliff Suitor getting a new coupe in a strange way.

George Bremner picking out the "Belle of the Ball" at every dance.

Box socials when some boxes brought bidding that almost led to blows.

The 'flu epidemic of 1918. So many friends were taken.

Bobby Pratt at the Pine Creek church.

The Belgian "army type" foreman when they put the natural gas line in.

Watching Halley's comet, wonder if I will see it the next time? It's due in 1986 I think.

Alex Blackwood swinging across the rafters in the DeWinton Hall dressed in a flannelette nightshirt.

Huge herds of cattle being herded along the Macleod Trail to Calgary.

Indians pitching their tents in our yard when they came to help.

Watching my father helping to fight prairie fires with our neighbors and being terrified that he would get hurt.

Seeing feed for starving cattle being dropped from aircraft.

The Bow River in flood, changing its course and taking parts of buildings with it.

Hearing my father tell of the early settlers coming in Red River carts, usually in groups.

The monthly visits from the Mounties to see that all was well.

Leaving before dawn for the 1912 Calgary Stampede and getting back long after dark.

Going in to the Sherman rink in Calgary in 1918 to see the Habitants hockey team play an exhibition game. Their goal keeper, Joe Hall I believe, got the 'flu. and died. The rest of the tour was cancelled.

Lord Anglesey's private car, side tracked at De Winton, when the oil well was being drilled.

Flying ants driving us from the hay field.

Trying to cut "down grain" with a baulky team.

The first disc plows.

When gramaphones were taken to schools and dance halls for entertainment.

Watching Mother skim cream from the creamers with a perforated metal scoop.

Having to reseed twice during the 1936 season. Such hard, dry wind. Hailstones wiping out a ripe crop in a few minutes. A year's work voided.

Screeching of slate pencils on our slates. It hurt the eardrums.

The 1927 cyclone taking Heaver's garage and leaving the car sitting.

Crows flying in massive numbers, took hours for them to pass, and returning to their starting point in the evening.

Figuring that a bachelor was going to marry if he put up a clothesline and an out house.

The large assemblies of song birds, especially meadow larks.

How friendly the blue birds were.

Seeing a man, prodding the cattle under the fluid in the dip tank, fall into it himself. Now that was a mess!

Breaking the ice on the water pails (in the house) in the morning.

Shovelling grain, into, and coal, out of, box cars.

Putting up ice on the river.

Living through the introduction of riding plows, seeders, phonographs, telephones, radios, tractors, automobiles, cream separators, natural gas, electricity, insect and crop sprays, AI and embryo transplants, aircraft and household appliances—such a long way to come!

NOTES FROM THE OKOTOKS ADVANCE 1908

De Winton January 26, 1908.

G. W. Gray returned from the Coast Thursday.

F. Pashak is home again from hospital. He is much improved in health though his head bothers him a good deal.

The dance held in the hall last Friday night was better attended than the one two weeks ago but the usual crowd was not present.

The skating rink is almost completed.

The appearance of De Winton is much improved since the English Church and parsonage have been moved in.

Reverend and Mrs. Whiting entertained a few of their friends on Monday evening.

Frank Frier is carrying the mail instead of the other 'Frank' as stated last week.

Davisburg October 6, 190?.

Willie McBride who is ill with rheumatic fever, is recovering.

The Okotoks Review.

VOL. 2 NO 15.   OKOTOKS, ALBERTA, THURSDAY JULY 27th 1905 $1.00 PER YEAR.

School Picnic at Panima.

Very Interesting Function

Miss Medd a Popular and Successful Teacher— Various Other Topics of General Interest Contained in these Columns.

The closing exercises of the Panima school were held in the school house on Friday afternoon July 21s A large number of the parents of the district were present and listened to the following programme by the scholars:

Selection by the school
    The flag we love
Recitation - Willie Henderson
The Bee Song - Five girls
Recitation - Bessie Rennie
Instrumental - Mr. Souder
Recitation - Frank Moore
Song - Mr. Vote
Recitation - Annie Gray
The Blacksmith Song.
Recitation - Ray Grist
Selection on Gramaphone
Recitation - May Henderson
Talk to Pupils - Rev. Carscallen
Recitation - Eddie Rennie
So Very Early in the Morning
    Song by five girls
Recitation - Libbie Henderson
Song - Mr. Vote
Recitation - Harry Stockton
Dialogue - Playing School
Instrumental - Mr. Souder
Recitation - Winna Grist
Gramaphone Selection
Recitation - Earl Moore
The Wind song - Five Girls
Recitation - Miss Medd

Song by the school.

The programme was of an exceptionally high order for such an occasion and reflects great credit on the teacher, Miss Medd, as well as on the pupils taking part. Without exception the children acquitted themselves well. A vote of thanks was tendered Miss Medd by those present for the afternoon's entertainment. At the conclusion of the programme lunch was served on the lawn by the scholars. About six o'clock the gathering dispersed all voting it a splendid success, and hoping that this might be only the first of many such functions.

Stock Owners Take Notice

I will be prepared to winter feed a number of cattle next winter on my ranche east of town. Stock owners can either write or interview me on my ranch. I will also deliver in town hay by the load or ton. Drop a card to 27j 27   J. CHILDREN, Okotoks

Any person coming across cattle branded IV on left hip and 9D on left hip will confer a favor by communicating with Donald Stewart, Davisburg.

The social advertised to take place at the home of Mrs Andrew Melrose, on Friday last was postponed owing to the accident which occurred to her little daughter. It will be held on the evening of Thursday, August 17. Everybody welcome.

Do you relish homemade bread? If so you can obtain same from Mrs. Edwards of the finest quality Read her advt on 4th page.

Mr. Edwards is engaged in constructing a comfortable home on the ranche of Mr Lee, lately purchased from Mr. Brice in the Davisburg District.

Wedding.

On Wednesday evening July 26 a very pretty home wedding took place at Pleasant View, the home of the bride's parents, Mr and Mrs John Children, in which Miss Cora Belle Children was united in marriage to Mr. Melvin George Folger. The bride was beautifully attired in ivory silk and carried a shower bouquet of sweet peas and was ably assisted by her sister Lillian Pearl, as bridesmaid, she was attired in white silk organdie and also carried a bouquet of sweet peas. The groom was assisted by a brother of the bride, Raymond O. Children. The house was prettily decorated and after the ceremony the wedding party partook of a sumptuous dinner. Rev. H. Locke Kempton officiated.

Came to my premises about six weeks ago one blue gray cayuse gelding, branded L on left shoulder Owner may have same upon proving property and paying expenses.

G. P. Smith.

Well Digging

The undersigned is prepared to receive orders for well digging in all its branches. Rock work a specialty. Orders left at this office will receive prompt attention. DAVID YOUNG

The Dominion government has brought down resolutions making the Premier's salary $12,000 and the sessional indemnity $2,500 to members and Senators. The leader of the Opposition will get $7,000 and ex-Ministers will get $7,500. The salaries of judges have been materially increased.

DISTRICT POST OFFICES OF THE AREA
DAVISBURG:

Located 32-21-28-W4 and having four Postmasters dating from the appointment of T. H. Andrews, July 1, 1888 and serving until November 13, 1894, followed by John Nash who served from February 1, 1895 to June 12, 1896. On the first day of January, 1897 Mrs. M. Stewart took the position and remained until December 30, 1905 and, at her retirement, C. K. Patterson took over and stayed from January 4, 1906 until the postoffice closed, September 30, 1916.

De WINTON:

The De Winton Post Office, located in the Electoral District of Macleod and located on 36-21-1-W5, was officially opened on April 1, 1894, when William O. Somerville was appointed Postmaster. He continued in that position until 1895 when he resigned because of non-residence in the district. Hugh McNeill was appointed Postmaster on August 1, 1895 and served until July 13, 1911 when he resigned and Alonzo DeMings took over on March 3, 1912 continuing until March 3, 1926 when he also resigned. July 2, 1926 saw Robert (Bob) Smith embark on what was to be a thirty-one year career as Postmaster, retiring on April 30, 1957. The local store keeper, Barsby Martin, was acting Postmaster from May 1, 1957 and appointed officially in 1959 on April 10. Barsby resigned August 8, 1965 and Mrs. Cornelia Irvine became acting Postmaster. She was officially instated October 6, 1965 and remains the Postmaster at the present time, 1977.

DUNBOW:

Located 26-21-28-W4 with Robert A. Begg as Postmaster, appointed July 1, 1885 and continuing until June 30, 1898 when the Post Office was closed.

GRIERSON:

Located on the side of a hill, near a spring, on what was later the Mel Martin place and then moved closer to the Macleod Trail. James Grierson was the first Postmaster from July 7, 1890 until June 29, 1892. From July 1, 1893 until March 12, 1898, John Currie was Postmaster and had the Post Office in his home. April 1, 1896, the name of the Postoffice was changed to Rosebud and then changed back to Grierson, December 1, 1898. The last postmaster was J. A. Grierson who started May 1, 1898 and stayed till October 8, 1908. The Post Office was closed April 10, 1909.

HARRISBORO:

Located 35-21-29-W4 where Thomas Harris was Postmaster from June 1, 1890 until the Post Office closed May 31, 1895.

MIDNAPORE:

This post office was established February 1, 1884 with F. W. Shaw as Postmaster. He remained till May 8, 1919. The location was 4-23-1-W5 and, later, 34-22-1-W5. Harold Hamilton followed Mr. Shaw but served only from February 7, 1920 till W. J. Bloye Ball took over, June 6, 1920 and continued till June 1, 1922. John Morton was next serving from July 29, 1922 until February 26, 1926 when Mrs. Morton began her stint, April 28, 1926 and continued till July 15, 1944. Frederick James Ratcliff acted from October 16, 1944 to July 3, 1958 and Muriel Ratcliff was acting Postmaster from July 3, 1958 to April 1, 1959 when Hammond Wilfred Jardine became acting Postmaster. He was appointed

Postmaster May 4, 1960 and stayed until October 2, 1966. Del Alton Stanley Johnson was in office from October 10, 1966 till May 31, 1968, followed on June 1, 1968, by Mrs. Margaret Mary Strauss. In 1977 she is still there.

PANIMA:

Panima Post Office, located 4-21-1-W5, opened with Donald Gray as Postmaster, March 1, 1894 and closed March 28, 1903. Mr. Gray was the only Postmaster.

PINE CREEK:

Pine Creek Post Office in the Electoral District of Macleod and located 11-22-1-W5 was officially opened on April 4, 1887, with Saunders Watson as Postmaster. He continued in that position until 1889 when he resigned because of non-residence. On June 1, 1889, John Owens became Postmaster and remained until the Post Office closed, May 13, 1896.

SANDSTONE:

On March 1, 1907, Sandstone Post Office, located on 2-21-1-W5, was opened with George W. Dollar as Postmaster and he served until August 4, 1908. On September 29, 1909 Miss Alice Prendergast was appointed and stayed until sometime in 1910. She was followed by Frank C. Tuffin who started his duties October 1, 1910 and stayed till March 14, 1912. Robert Eccles served from April 1, 1912 until December of 1912. Mrs. A. E. Hamlin held the position from March 11, 1913 until April 14, 1914. Henry Bishop took over July 1, 1914 and stayed until February 27, 1917. The last Postmaster was E. Hirst who served from March 31, 1917 until July 9, 1924. The Post Office was closed August 30, 1924.

THE GAS PIPELINES WALKERS

When the first natural gas pipeline was put through from Bow Island to Calgary in 1912 it was compulsory

George Thom, Gas line walker 1916-1943.

Bob Noonan walking the gas line, 1940's.

to have the line patrolled. The first man to have the job was known to the Pine Creek school children simply as "Gassy". He used to arrive at the school yard at noon hour on the day he walked the line and found time to play with the pupils and was quite a favorite person with them. The next man to take the job was George Thom who started in 1916. From 1916-27 he walked from Claresholm to Calgary and, in 1927 shifted to the walk from Calgary to Turner Valley. During his years on the job he stayed, on Tuesday night, with the Sutherlands. He continued until 1943 when he was replaced by one or two men who did not stay long with the job. One of them was only able to do the task for one week. In 1945 Bob Noonan took over and stayed until 1954. Both George Thom and Bob Noonan were handicapped by the loss of an arm. Bob stayed with the Eben Bremners on the night that he spent in the district, and during his time on the job was never known to miss a day of work.

The purpose of the men was to locate leaks, ex-

Gas line digger for natural gas 1925. L. to R. Pete Murray, engineer   , Travis Brinton, Andy Harkley, Wenty Brinton behind, Goldie and Lucy Brinton.

Hauling pipe for the Bow Island to the Calgary Gas Line. Maltman Shaw standing by front wheel of engine.

amine river crossings and exposed pipes and fittings and blow drips. In later years, when they had charts and telephone lines, it was the responsibility of the walker to replace charts and check telephone lines.

Line walking was discontinued about 1955 when the vegetation survey system to locate gas leaks was introduced. The men who walked the lines provided a vital service but it was found that the visual inspection of vegetation was more efficient.

OIL AND GAS WELLS IN THE DISTRICT

Lack of interest and co-operation detracts significantly from the information available on this subject. Aside from some first hand knowledge concerning the first well to be drilled in the district, we have only rather dry statistics on the subject.

Anglesey Well on Ness farm, 1927.

The district was well behind Turner Valley in getting started in the search for oil. Lord Anglesey came over from England, had his private parlor car side tracked at De Winton in 1927 and proceeded to organize the drilling of Anglesey (Lakeside) well located on LSD1-22-21-1-W5, on the farm of Rowland Ness. It was immediately dubbed "De Winton's Dream". There was great excitement in the area and a number of the local boys were hired to work. A road into the site was the first priority and Bill Hamilton and Les Marshall were hired with their teams and small graders to work on the construction of a passable road. The going was so bad and the rock so hard that a man was brought in to dynamite the road bed. The men and teams went

across the road behind the Stormont school barn but, even at that distance some of the dirt and rock travelled to where they were. No one was injured but it was quite a blast. Mr. Visser and his crew were hired to build the derrick and, on July 14, 1927 the well was spudded in. It was classed as a new field wild cat well, no cores were cut and, after going to a depth of 4500' the well was abandoned on September 25, of the same year. There went a community dream!! Seven years later a speculation promoter came into the district and set out to reopen the well. He collected a lot of financial support, built a new derrick, some new quarters for the crew and, in general, put on quite a show. There was never any more drilling done and the gentleman in question left the country in a bit of a rush.

The next effort was in 1929 on LSD7-16-21-28-W4 when Twin Dome No.1 was spudded in on August 8, and was also classed as a new field wild cat. There were no cores cut and no drill stem tests run and, after reaching a depth of 1255' the well was abandoned on December 20, 1929.

It was nine years later when the next well was started, December 20, 1938 located on LSD7-16-21-28-W4. This one was named Anglo-Canadian Twin Dome No.1. There were a number of cores cut but no drill stem tests done and, on April 5, 1939, at a depth of 7152', also a new field wildcat, was abandoned.

Twin Dome No. 2 oil waste burned off around 1938.

THIS INDENTURE made this   day of
December, A.D., 1913

WE, the Undersigned being the Lessors under
certain Agreements dated the   day of   * A.D.
expressed to be made between us and John Niven Oldham
of the City of Calgary in the Province of Alberta, Barrister-at-
Law, as Trustee for a Company to be incorporated according to the
laws of the Province of Alberta, whereby we undertook, covenanted
and agreed with the said John Niven Oldham to lease to him and
also granted to him an Option to purchase as Trustee foresaid the
rights, premises and lands described in the said Agreements and
upon the terms, covenants and conditions set forth therein.

AND WHEREAS it has been covenanted and agreed
between us and the said John Niven Oldham, as Trustee foresaid,
that a further agreement shall be entered into as follows:-

NOW THEREFORE IT IS MUTUALLY COVENANTED AND
AGREED that in consideration of the sum of One (1) Dollar paid
to us by the said John Niven Oldham, as Trustee foresaid, that
as the Company is to acquire certain rights, lands and premises
under the said Agreements and to drill for oil on any of the lands
therein described that in the event of the Company exercising
the Option to purchase contained in and set forth in Clauses 5,
of the said Agreements of any one portion of the lands acquired
by it, thereunder, the Company shall purchase all of the lands
described in the said Agreements between us and the said John
Niven Oldham as Trustee foresaid, and it is further covenanted
and agreed that the Company shall retain in its Treasury out of
its Authorized Capital shares equal in value to the sum of Six
hundred and forty thousand (640,000) dollars until the Company

exercises the Option to purchase in pursuance of said Clauses
5, of the said Agreements as aforesaid, and the method of
payment of the purchase price by the said Company has been
completed and agreed upon between the said Company and each of
us.

IN WITNESS WHEREOF the parties hereto have hereunto set their hands and seals on the day and year first above
written.

SIGNED SEALED AND DELIVERED	(sgd)	Donald R. McDonald	(seal)
in the presence of	(sgd)	A. N. Allan	(seal)
	(sgd)	Alec S. Balckwood	(seal)
	(sgd)	A. Forckel	(seal)
	(sgd)	Alice Forckel	(seal)
	(sgd)	R. J. Shields	(seal)
	(sgd)	S. W. Haslam	(seal)
	(sgd)	G. T. Wasson	(seal)
	(sgd)	Frank Barker	(seal)
	(sgd)	C.K.K. Patterson	(seal)
	(sgd)	William U. Bryce	(seal)
	(sgd)	Duncan McIntosh	(seal)
	(sgd)	T. H. McConnell	(seal)
	(sgd)	W. R. MacDonald	(seal)
	(sgd)	Alice MacDonald	(seal)
	(sgd)	W. V. Mencke	(seal)
	(sgd)	Robt. Maxwell	(seal)
	(sgd)	Chas. A. Hughes	(seal)
	(sgd)	Harry Usher	(seal)
	(sgd)	Geo. N. Hedley	(seal)
	(sgd)	John Currie	(seal)
	(sgd)	J. B. Cassady	(seal)
	(sgd)	E. A. Hayes	(seal)
	(sgd)	Mrs. A. E. Hayes	(seal)
	(sgd)	S. C. Kenney	(seal)

DATED   1914

BETWEEN: THE LESSORS

-and-

JOHN NIVEN OLDHAM as Trustee

SUBSIDIARY AGREEMENT

HANNAH STIRTON & FISHER

Royalite De Winton No.2 on LSD13-24-21-1-W5 was spudded in on May 5, 1947, classed as a development well, it was drilled to a depth of 10401' and five drill stem tests were run. There was no production and it was abandoned on November 4, 1947.

October 12, 1950 saw Okotoks Shell McKid No.1 get underway but, here again, the new field wildcat, classed, well did not go into production, after 10501' it also was abandoned on May 16, 1951. It was located on LSD1-19-21-28-W4.

Okotoks Shell Shattuck No.1 was next. It began activity on March 31, 1952 under the development class. Total depth was 8513' and there was no production so, it too, was abandoned, June 24, 1952.

The first success was to appear in the Okotoks Shell Herr No.1 well which was begun on August 19, 1951, under development classification. After a considerable number of core cuts and drill stem tests, at a depth of 9185', the well went into production and is a flowing gas well. It was completed June 19, 1959 and is located on LSD12-19-21-28-W4.

LSD7-17-21-28-W4 became the site for Okotoks Shell Shattuck "A" No.1. This is also under development classification, was drilled to a depth of 8493' and capped. Activity stopped, with no production, April 14, 1953. Began December 2, 1952.

A depth of 8765' drilled on LSD11-6-21-28-W4 by Devon Palmer and others, with no drill stem tests run,

Shell Crown No. 1 LSD 6-12-21-29-W4th.

Hudson's Bay Co. well on N.E.¼ 8-22-1-W5.

A class, outpost, well was drilled on LSD10-34-21-29-W4 starting January 8, 1965, drilled 8749', no drill stem tests run, abandoned February 13, 1965. Texas Gulf Sulphur Okotoks was in charge.

Texas Gulf and Others Okotoks spudded in on LSD10-18-21-28-W4 on June 21, 1967 drilled 8750' and completed a flowing gas well on October 31, 1967.

Trenholm Barker Well at night.

brought forth a flowing gas well. Started December 10, 1958 and completed June 1, 1959.

July 14, 1952, Okotoks Shell — Blackwood and Norris No.1 was spudded in on LSD10-13-21-29-W4 and, after a depth of 8790' went into gas production. It was completed July 21, 1959.

Hudson's Bay Twin Dome No.1 under new field wild cat classification began on LSD16-8-22-1-W5 December 31, 1955 and was abandoned May 31, 1956 after reaching 9537'.

Onion-Kcy-HB Twin Dome, under the Union Oil Company, tried a new field wild cat on LSD16-33-21-1-W5 but without success. Starting June 9, 1958 and drilling to 8124' it was abandoned July 23, 1958.

Devon Palmer and others Okotoks produced a flowing gas well on LSD10-25-21-29-W4 starting September 16, 1959, drilling 8621' and completing March 7, 1960. Ran no drill stem tests.

Texas Gulf and Others, Okotoks drilled a development classification well on LSD11-7-21-28-W4 starting January 13, 1964, drilling 8750' and finished August 10, 1964. No drill stem tests run.

Mesa Alcon, under an outpost classification, began drilling on LSD6-5-22-28-W4 on December 27, 1967 and, after drilling 8410', abandoned on February 5, 1968.

A depth of 8650' was drilled by Texas Gulf Sulphur on LSD10-2-22-29-W4 starting June 4, 1971, completed December 15, 1971 and abandoned October 17, 1974.

Some of the farms concerned with these activities were, non producing; Shattuck, Magyar, HFT Enterprizes, Manalta Holdings, Hughes, Bryce and Quenitz. Producing; Petts, Herr, Jobson, Hunt, Biswanger and Zeus Farms.

ALLAN MUTUAL TELEPHONE COMPANY — by Maurice B. Ardiel

During the early thirties the Alberta Government Telephone Company was experiencing trouble in operating the rural telephone services at a profit and came up with a proposal whereby the farmers would form rural mutual telephone companies and pay A.G.T. a nominal monthly rental fee for service to the Government exchange.

The first meeting to discuss such proposed services in the Okotoks district was held in the Elk's Hall, October 27, 1934. Edward W. Gould was appointed Chairman with Willis R. Barker, Secretary and Mr. Monroe of A.G.T. in attendance. The seventeen rural circuits were divided into six groups each to form a separate company.

An organizational meeting was held January 24, 1935 which resulted in the formation of Allan Mutual Telephone Company Limited. This company would take over circuits 7, 12 and 13 in group 5. Charles F. Forckel was elected President, Charles W. Johnson Vice-President, Willis R. Barker Secretary-Treasurer and George Riches, Jimmy Coombe and Gerald Gough Directors.

By-laws were drawn up and some of the highlights of some of these by-laws which appear quite humorous by today's standards are as follows: One of the objects of the company was to create a reserved fund for the line maintenance, etc., not to exceed the sum of $300. Each shareholder agrees to donate two days each year for work on line construction and maintenance. The capital of the company is divided into 40 shares at $24 each for a total of $960. Each subscriber to supply his own batteries for his phone, to be bought from the company. No person shall be allowed to use the phone for more than 5 minutes at a time except for long distance calls. Common conversation shall not be permitted when the use of the line is required for business messages. No subscriber shall allow the use of their telephone free of charge to any person not a subscriber except it be a member of his family, a partner in business, an employee or a guest who is actually staying with the family. The charge to any person not included in the above shall be ten cents, when the message is transmitted to central and five cents for other calls. Such money received by the subscriber shall be paid to the secretary with the monthly accounts. No person shall be allowed to take down the receiver for the purpose of listening to a conversation not intended for him or her.

Between January 24, 1935 and the first annual meeting of the Allan Mutual Telephone Company on January 7, 1936, the executive of the Allan Mutual held no less than ten meetings. The highlights of such meetings being as follows:

There would be a maximum of 40 shares sold to subscribers at a value of $24 each, and the monthly rental would be $1.75 per month for the first year. Twenty-three applications were received for shares in the company. The Allan Mutual paid A.G.T. $484.50 for the lines taken over, poles and wire being $274.50 plus 28 phones at $7.50, such amount was payable at $121 in cash and the balance in two payments on March 1, 1936 and March 1, 1937 respectively. The cost of material for installing ten new phones was $21.90, varying from a minimum of 40 cents for one subscriber to a maximum of $4.70 for another.

Mrs. Wilbur Anderson, chief telephone operator in Okotoks, was asked to collect the monthly rental fees and agreed to do so at no charge for the first year. The monthly rental fee per subscriber to A.G.T. was 60 cents. On June 10, 1935 payment of the following accounts was approved. Scov Lumber Co. — 45 cents. J. H. McNeil Hardware — 10 cents. W. R. Barker supplies — $3.95. J. H. Forckel supplies — $1.36. It would appear that inflation was unheard of in 1935.

Lineman wages were set at 30 cents an hour and he was to supply his own transportation. The secretary's salary was set at $5.00 a month. On September 2, 1935 the monthly rental per subscriber was reduced from $1.75 to $1.40.

W. H. Jenkins was appointed auditor of the company at a fee of $2.50 and he acted as auditor of the company until his retirement in 1961. He was succeeded by Herb Stephenson who was auditor until the dissolution of the company.

At the first annual meeting held on January 2, 1936, each subscriber agreed to donate two days' work to line maintenance each year. At the second annual meeting held January 21, 1937, M. MacGougan was appointed secretary of the company to replace W. R. Barker at $50.00 per year to include the collection of the accounts. He passed away in 1937 and William Fisher was appointed as secretary-treasurer and acted as such until he retired in May of 1948. He was succeeded by M. B. Ardiel at $3.00 per subscriber per year, who filled this position until the Allan Mutual disbanded and wound up its affairs in October of 1972.

In June of 1939 the monthly phone rental charge was reduced to $1.25 from $1.50 and batteries in the future would be supplied free of charge to subscribers when needed by the company but only one replacement every two years. In January 1940 the monthly phone rental was reduced to $1.00 and there were 42 subscribers. $400 was invested in War Bonds at this time. The lineman's pay in 1943 was increased from 30 cents an hour to 50 cents an hour. Herb Jenkins Jr. was the company's lineman for many years, retiring in 1947. He was replaced by Walter Mosier at 10 cents a mile and 90 cents an hour. Walter remained as lineman until 1970 when he was forced to retire due to ill health, having served the company well for twenty-three years.

On June 1, 1956, the agreement between the A.G.T. and the C.P.R. whereby the C.P.R. be given free phone service in return for free passage for A.G.T. officials on C.P.R. lines was terminated and the C.P.R. station at De Winton was charged for phone service for the first time.

The subscribed capital of the company was increased to $30,000 divided into 100 shares at $300 each. During 1963 the company had been converted to dial telephones. The company borrowed $8,000 from the A.G.T. revolving fund to finance the change, and the upgrading of telephone lines, at 4½% interest repayable in twenty years. Considerable line upgrading was necessary as dial telephones were much more sensitive than the original crank telephones which would operate under quite adverse conditions. During the regime of the old crank telephone it was not unusual to hook downed lines to the barbed wire fences and get through.

In 1964 there were 72 shareholders in the company and two non-shareholders. Over the years several new lines had to be added. Monthly rental rates ranged from a low of $1.00 during the earlier years to $3.25 for shareholders; non-shareholders were usually charged $1.00 extra. The secretary's salary was increased by $1.00 per subscriber per year to $5.00, the first increase in the past fifteen years. On April 3, 1965, W. E. Mosier's wages were increased to $2.00 an hour and ten cents a mile.

In 1967 the A.G.T. proposed to take over the Mutual Telephone Companies in the area by 1977 or 1978 and install underground lines.

On April 16, 1968 the secretary's salary was again increased to $6.00 per subscriber a year and the lineman's wages increased to $3.00 an hour and ten cents a mile.

In 1969 the share capital of the company was again

Lella (Pope) Anderson. The Okotoks switchboard.

increased to $36,000 consisting of 120 shares at $300 each. A new line was installed making a total of nine lines.

On December 6, 1970 the A.G.T. took over the Allan Mutual and the board of directors started to wind up the affairs of the company. This take over was advanced three years to provide service to dozens of acreages on new sub-divisions in the area.

On April 15, 1971 an auction sale of all poles and wire was held. $1,968 was realized in the sale of copper wire. Poles and other wire, etc., realized an amount of $2,784.00.

The final meeting of the board of directors was held on October 25, 1972 and a bank balance of $13,672.50 was divided among the ninety-seven bona fide shareholders at $140.95 each. Of these ninety-seven, twenty-seven were original shareholders who joined the company at its inception in 1935.

In summing up tribute should be made to the various presidents, vice-presidents and directors who guided the destiny of the Allan Mutual Telephone Company through thirty-five years of providing cheap telephone service to the rural area, namely: Charles Forckel, Johnny Forckel, Charlie Johnson, J. H. Jenkins, Willis Barker, W. H. Jenkins, George Riches, Jimmy Coombe, Doug Ward, Wally Currie, Dave Wedderburn, John Wedderburn, Herb Jenkins, Forest Herr, William Cope, Walter Wilde, Gerald Gough, Doug Herr, Jim Dalzell, Idwal Jones, Robert Miller, Tom Dalzell, Fred Dick, Ralph Stinn.

Also non-members of the company who contributed to the company in no small measure in its successful operation over the years include: Mrs. Lella Anderson, Malcolm MacGougan, Walter Mosier, William Fisher, M. B. Ardiel.

So we write a finish to another colorful era in our Alberta Heritage.

THE DAVISBURG MUTUAL TELEPHONE COMPANY LIMITED

The Davisburg Mutual Telephone Company Limited was incorporated on April 7, 1936. It was described as that portion of the physical plant known as rural circuits 2, 3 and 16 at Okotoks. This included all poles, insulators, anchors and other attachments, and twenty-eight telephone sets. It was bought from Alberta Government Telephones for the sum of $573.70. The Davisburg Mutual Telephone Company Limited served an area included within townships 21 and 22, ranges 28 and 29 west of the 4th meridian.

The directors elected at the first annual meeting held on January 12, 1937 were as follows: F. Davis, S. M. Martin, A. Blackwood and H. R. Call. F. Davis served as the first president and H. R. Call was the first secretary holding this office until 1940. Ruth Peppard was secretary of the Mutual from 1940 to 1946 and then George Sutherland took over from 1946 to 1951. Una Rodger was the fourth secretary who remained in office for seventeen years from 1951 to 1968. Virginia Jacobson then became secretary which position she held until the Company closed its books in 1971.

Others elected as presidents through the years included Jim Davenport, Howard Norris, Clarence Peppard, Jack Morasch, Norman Cushon and Russell Martin.

Some who served as directors were Wm. Herr, Chester Leach; Jim Quinn, Ted Campbell, Roy McConnell, Cliff Herr, Jim Suitor, George Meehan, Dave Hunt, Wm. (Scotty) Rodger, Chuck Groeneveld, Alfred Henriksen and Steve Magyar.

The forty-three miles of telephone lines required considerable upkeep. Much of this was done by the subscribers themselves, in order to keep costs down. However, there were linemen who were paid to keep the phones working. They included Fred Maxwell, Jim Davenport and Olaf Jacobson. In 1951 Walter Mosier became head lineman, who was assisted by his son Ed, Wm. (Scotty) Rodger, Martin Davis and Eugene Magyar. By the mid-sixties there were usually eighteen to twenty subscribers on one line. There were no such things as secrets on the party line, as there usually were people who spent their pastime "rubbering in" and the secrets exposed usually came back to the original teller in an exaggerated state. One long ring for emergency sent every subscriber running to the phone, as it signalled a fire or some other situation requiring the aid of all the residents of the district.

In 1967 the old phones were removed and dial phones were installed with only four subscribers on one line. With increasing population due to the subdivisions, there was a greater need for more phones. The Mutual was unable to provide this service, so in April, 1970 the Davisburg Mutual Telephone Company Limited revoked its license and registered area and made an integrated agreement with Alberta Government Telephones to take over this area. This was finalized June 30, 1971 and underground wiring was installed at this time. The telephone poles and wires were all removed making quite a change of appearance to the countryside. Thus ended the era of the Davisburg Mutual Telephone Company Limited.

PANIMA MUTUAL TELEPHONE COMPANY —
from Secretarial notes

As the economy of the country slid ever faster down hill, so the economy of the Alberta Government Telephone Company slid until, in 1936, it became evident, that in order to have phone service, it would be necessary to form a District Mutual Company.

An organizational meeting was called on May 3, 1936 and a company was formed with Ed. Geottler chairman and F. S. Jacobs as secretary. The following slate of officers was installed; President, Ed. Geottler, Secretary, Fred Cole, and directors; F. S. Smith, F. S. Jacobs and R. Ness. Vice-President Harold Thomas.

It was decided to incorporate the company with forty-five shares at $28.00 per share and set the monthly rate at $1.75.

Mr. Munro, from the A.G.T. was helpful with his cost estimates. Using lines 9, 10 and 11 as models he estimated the cost at $400.00 for poles and wire and $150.00 for twenty phones. This made a total of $550.00 or share value of $27.50. This was to be payable at one quarter cash and the balance in two annual payments. With thirty subscribers the total would be $625.00 with

share value set at $21.00. Mr. Munro also outlined a method for reorganization.

Mr. F. S. Smith moved that a company be formed, called Panima Mutual Telephone Company Limited, to be effective from May 1, 1936. This motion was seconded by Mr. Duncan and carried. Thus the company came into being.

Meetings held in May, September and December of 1936 got the rules of the Company pretty well established and the first annual meeting was held in January of 1937.

Through the years of operation from 1936 to 1973, there were very few changes made in the executive positions of the Company. There were the usual problems of unpaid bills, unsatisfactory service etc. but, by and large, the operation was a success.

Prices of work and materials varied greatly through the years and, while a Secretary was worth forty dollars per year, the lineman was paid only by the hours worked and, by the mile, for traveling. A jack pine pole was worth 75¢ this was in 1938. By 1948, the lineman was getting 60¢ an hour plus 10¢ a mile and the following year wages were raised to the full $1.00 per hour plus 10¢ a mile and the helper was paid 75¢ per hour. In 1956, poles were worth $5.95 for a 20' and $8.25 for a 25'. By 1968, the secretary was paid $6.00 per year per subscriber and the lineman got $3.00 per hour plus 10¢ per mile. Poles were $5.50 for a 16' and $9.90 for a 25' and, by the time the company was phased out of existence in 1973 there was a net balance of $5,087.25 to be equally distributed to the 57 bona fide shareholders at a value of $89.25 each.

Twice, in the life of the company, a member of the executive died while in office. Mrs. K. I. Goettler while secretary treasurer in 1949 and in 1966 Mr. F. Sinclair-Smith, who had served as president for the past fifteen years.

The monthly rate for a phone changed from time to time. After starting out at $1.75 per month, the rate was lowered to $1.50 which was the lowest rate ever charged. As the years went on and the war and the depression were past, the rates went gradually upward until they reached $4.00 which seems to be the highest rate charged.

There were only about four different linemen during the existence of the company. R. C. Brown, Merv. Cressman and Walter Mosier are three that are mentioned. Walter Mosier took over in 1952 and continued until the company was dissolved. Thomas E. Roberts was the secretary treasurer from 1951 to 1956 when M. B. Ardiel took the position and held it until 1973.

A sinking fund was established in 1940 with the sum of $200.00 and, in 1941, $100.00 of this money was used to purchase War Saving Certificates, then at a special meeting in February 1941, the secretary was authorized to buy 5, $40.00 War Saving Certificates. There were times when money from the special funds was drawn on but when a storm, in June of 1951, flattened miles of line and broke most of the poles, it was decided to cash in bonds and take the money from the savings account to be used to get the lines back into shape. Again, in 1962, there was a severe storm and the farmers were asked to aid in repairing the lines. There was need to replace 751 poles and miles of wire. It was necessary to borrow $3,000.00 from the bank. The sum total of the bank accounts at that time was only $2,-407.57.

In January of 1963, it was decided to convert to the dial system. Mr. Spooner from A.G.T. at Edmonton outlined a system of financing the change-over. Total assets of the company were $10,000.00, this divided by the 50 shareholders made each share value $200.00. Mr. Spooner figured that the value of the shares should double in twenty years. $200.00 per shareholder would be applied to the installation and any further cost was to be borne by the subscriber. The loan would be repaid over a period of 20 years at $6.31 per thousand per month. A cost plus basis with Mr. Mosier was worked out and the job was to be completed by May, 1963.

Ed Goettler served as president of the company from 1936 to 1950, F. Sinclair-Smith, from 1951 till his death in 1966, George Bull, from 1966 to 1968 and finally Gordon Dafoe from 1969 till the final meeting. Secretaries included Fred Cole, Mrs. I. K. Goettler, Clare Goettler, Frances Imler, T. E. Roberts, and finally, M. B. Ardiel from 1957 until the last meeting. Other members of the executive through the years were; Harold Thomas, Bill Hamilton, Lloyd Fraser, A. S. Widney, A. J. McDonald, Mel. Schmaus, W. Parker, R. Ness and F. S. Jacobs.

STOCKLAND MUTUAL TELEPHONE COMPANY — by R. Stanton

The first rural telephone line from Calgary to Millarville was installed by the Alberta Provincial Telephones about 1909. It followed the Priddis Trail across the Sarcee Reserve. Henry Ford and J. W. Hyneman (now deceased) both of the Priddis District are considered responsible for getting some of the first rural lines in Alberta. This line provided service for some of the people in the Priddis and Millarville areas. The subscribers were asked to provide the poles or pay pin space rental charges which amounted to 10¢ per pair of wires per pole per annum. The subscriber was responsible for the cost of installation from the trunk line to his residence, less the cost of telephone instruments which were provided by A.G.T. In case of a break in the line, the subscriber was asked to assist in repairing. This line ceased to operate during the First World War.

Rural telephone service, from Midnapore west to the Harry Birney homestead, started in 1912. John McInnis (now deceased) of Midnapore canvassed the Midnapore and Red Deer Lake districts for funds to provide rural telephone service for the two districts. I am assuming the same sort of deal with the Provincial Government operated on a pin space rental basis, only on a much larger scale as a greater number of people were serviced. This service was installed in the area in 1912, Albert McKevitt states. When he attended the Red Deer Lake School, he remembers the telephone crew used the Red Deer Lake Hall for a living quarters and had bunks along one side of the hall. The hall kitchen was used for a cook house. In 1921 the A.G.T. erected a new line from the east to service three toll telephones in the Post Offices at Priddis, Millarville and Kew. The toll charges were 15¢ per call.

When economic conditions forced the A.G.T. to abandon most rural lines or give the rural people the alternative of organizing the Mutual Telephone Company, the latter was chosen. However, during the 30's if a subscriber was in arrears up to $10.00, he was given a 10% discount. If he allowed arrears to go over $10.00, his services were disconnected. The Stockland Mutual Telephone Company was organized in 1936 and included the following districts: Midnapore, Red Deer Lake, DeWinton, Pine Creek, Ballyhamage, Alexandra, Priddis, Millarville and Kew.

The first officers of the Stockland board were: President, Walter Birney (now deceased), Vice-President, Col. Hervey (now deceased). Albert Eckersley (now deceased) was elected secretary and treasurer. Maintenance W. Shaw's wages were 35¢ per hour.

Directors were as follows (please note that the following directors were not all serving at the same time, but served during the period that the company was giving service). Mr. Mayhew (deceased), Jim Shaw, Wm. Warden (deceased), Bob Warden, Vic Heaver Sr. (deceased), R. G. Evans, Arthur Patterson, Sid Eadon (deceased), Stan Henker, Joe McKevitt (now deceased), R. D. Goodwin, E. Allwarden (now deceased), Rudy Mulder and W. Massie. Priddis: Francis Borgal (Shaw), C. R. Hopper, George Johnson and Vivian Shaw (now deceased). Millarville and Kew: W. Lee, W. Jackson (now deceased), Roy Sims, D. E. Robinson, A. Laycraft and John Jackson. (Please pardon if I have omitted any people).

Each subscriber was asked to purchase a share of $26.00 per share. Most bought shares. Non-shareholders paid 25¢ per month more. The $26.00 share was used to cover operating cost and not for purchasing the system. The pin space charges paid for the cost of renting the trunk lines which amounted to approximately $300.00 per year. In 1960 the share value increased to $40.00. In 1964 the value increased to $200.00. The value of this share was applied to the cost of installation but had to be paid before installation commenced.

When Mr. Birney sold his farm in 1955, Mr. Jim Shaw was appointed president and continued until he received individual line service. After Jim Shaw's retirement, Mr. Vic Heaver was appointed president with W. Massie as Vice-President and continued until the company was taken over by the A.G.T.

Mr. Albert Eckersley was secretary and treasurer of the company for a great number of years and retired after selling the farm and moving to Calgary. He was a most wonderful asset to the company.

E. Allwarden was appointed as secretary and treasurer in 1958, but owing to ill health resigned. A special meeting was called and the writer of this article was elected as Secretary-Treasurer. I continued until the company was taken over by the A.G.T. In 1959 the company had 159 subscribers and finished up with over 300. During that time the company engaged Mr. Walter Mosier as maintenance man. He was real good man on the job and knew his work 100%.

In 1936 the service wasn't too good, as there were 12 to 14 subscribers on each circuit. However, communication was very good, as every one listened in instead of reading the newspaper, you got it all over the telephone. One subscriber was a truck driver and owner. He would get very impatient and in a very loud voice would say "Please get off the phone and go do your dishes." He claimed that it always worked. Later on after considerable regrouping, each circuit had 10 subscribers.

I am sure we all appreciate very much the improved services provided by the A.G.T. On behalf of the Ex-Stockland Mutual Telephone Company, we wish to thank the A.G.T. for their very helpful co-operation. The underground 4 party line service of 2 subscribers on the negative and 2 on the positive side has made the rural people very happy.

In conclusion, I would like to thank all the executives and directors along with the subscribers for their wonderful co-operation during my term of office and a very special thanks to Vi Stanton (my daughter-in-law) for being my assistant secretary.

OKOTOKS, DeWINTON RURAL ELECTRIC CO-OP
by George Riches

How the Okotoks, DeWinton Rural Electric Co-op came into existence. When the DeWinton Air Force Base was closed, the power lines from Okotoks east two miles, then north to the air field remained, but it was reported that the Dominion Government intended to scrap them.

Mr. John Forckel and some of his neighbors decided they should investigate the possibility of acquiring the line to service the community with power. Calgary Power was contacted and they advised the steps the community should follow to purchase the line.

John Forckel and Vera Gillespie should get much credit for bringing this prospect to completion, as they put in many hours of their time gathering all the information they could find to make this venture a reality.

On the evening of January 22, 1948, Mr. and Mrs. John Forckel called a meeting at their place. Those present were Mr. and Mrs. Wilde, P. Sallenbach, Cliff Herr, Doug and Rusha Herr, Mrs. Vera Gillespie, C. Duncan, W. Lang, George and Pearl Riches, L. Hogge, B. Hyde, and J. Davenport.

Mr. Forckel was elected chairman at the meeting and he nominated Vera Gillespie as secretary. Mrs. Gillespie made a motion that we form a Rural Electrification Association Ltd. this was seconded by Doug Herr.

Mr. Bruce Hyde made a motion that we name the association the Okotoks DeWinton Rural Electrification Association Ltd.

A lengthy discussion on the size of the proposed area was held at this meeting, one suggestion was the area from the Sheep River to the Highwood River, to the Bow River and west to the C.P.R. tracks.

As there was no one present from the DeWinton area west it was only possible to estimate the number of members we may have. We estimated a possible 80 members. It was decided at the meeting that we should elect a provisional board of directors to canvas the area and find who all would be interested in joining for the power.

This provisional board of directors was made up of

Bruce Hyde, John Forckel, George Riches, Lorne Hogge, James Davenport, and it was felt there should be two more directors from the DeWinton area. At a meeting held shortly after this date at the home of Mr. and Mrs. Mel Martin, with 35 present, Mr. Mel Martin and Ted Heaver were elected directors to canvas the area of Melrose north and west. This was the beginning of one of the largest Co-op's as it extended north to Red Deer Lake and south to the Sheep River.

The first annual meeting was held at the DeWinton Hall, September 4, 1948. Most of the members were present, as the area was much larger than originally planned, it was decided that the board of directors should be twelve. This board was made up of: From Okotoks: J. Forckel, D. Herr, W. Wilde, G. Riches, L. Hogge From Midnapore: Col. Hervey From DeWinton: T. Heaver, J. Davenport, M. Martin, H. Shierman, W. Poffenroth, B. Hyde.

At the board meeting following the annual meeting, Mr. J. Forckel was elected chairman, Col. Hervey was elected Vice-chairman. Mrs. Gillespie was elected Secretary-treasurer, and Mrs. D. Herr as assistant secretary. These were the chartered board members, and there were 121 chartered Co-op members. When all was finalized the board was reduced to five members, with Mrs. D. Herr as secretary.

Much credit must be given to Mr. Fred Gale of Calgary Power, at that time head of Farm Electric Dept. and later John Butler head of F.E.S.L. also Mr. Fitzpatrick, head of Co-op's in Alberta for their assistance to our Co-op in general and legal advice. Mrs. McKeage, Secretary of Gladys Ridge R.E.A. attended our meeting August 21, 1949 and gave us valuable advice from their experiences doing things certain ways to get best results.

There was much organizing and planning that took place before our Co-op was running smoothly. If I remember correctly the power was turned on in February 1950, there were many interruptions in the early times of our association, but as we look back it was not so bad.

On June 19, 1968 the 20th annual meeting was held at the DeWinton Hall, at this time Mrs. D. Herr resigned as secretary, as she served for twenty years. Mr. M. B. Ardiel then agreed to be secretary, and held the position until the association transferred the ownership to Calgary Power, with a membership at that time of approximately 500.

ALBERTA WHEAL POOL

History of Alberta Wheat Pool's operations at Okotoks, Midnapore and De Winton. No Alberta Wheat Pool elevators have ever been located at Academy.

Okotoks

— 40,000 bushel elevator built in 1927 by Voss Brothers

— 29,000 bushel wartime balloon annex built in 1939 by K. R. McNeill

— 37,000 bushel cribbed annex built in 1941 by F. W. McDougall

— handlings: total, 2,019,811 bushels; high, 239,574 bushels in 1969-70; low, 52,589 bushels in 1961-62.

Elevator Managers who have operated the Pool's

Okotoks elevator are listed below with their dates of service.

H. F. Lewis, November 16, 1928 to May 31, 1935; P. Zipse, May 31, 1935 to March 31, 1938; A. Murray, March 31, 1935 to June 30, 1969; W. S. Wylie, June 26, 1969 to August 30, 1971; R. G. Laidlaw, August 30, 1971 to present.

Midnapore

— 27,500 bushel elevator — built in 1926 — acquired from Parrish and Heimbecker in 1929.

— coal shed also acquired with elevator from Parrish and Heimbecker in 1929 and sold to R. H. Field in June 1959

— 33,000 bushel cribbed annex built in 1941 by Voss Brothers

— handlings: total, 2,220,973 bushels; high, 310,370 bushels in 1969-70; low, 94,520 bushels in 1958-59.

Elevator Managers who have operated the Pool's Midnapore (Calgary) elevator are listed below with their dates of service.

F. V. Gough, August 1, 1929 to October 31, 1962; F. J. Crossie, November 1, 1962 to March 29, 1976; M. D. Kober, May 3, 1976 to present.

De Winton

— 40,000 bushel elevator built in 1929 by Voss Brothers

— elevator dismantled in 1936 — rebuilt at High River, Alberta

— no handling figures available.

Elevator Managers who have operated the Pool's De Winton elevator are listed below with their dates of service.

J. R. Wood, September 18, 1929 to May 1, 1933; E. Edey, May 1, 1933 to August 1, 1933; C. A. Craig, August 1, 1933 to November 30, 1933; Elevator Closed, November 30, 1933 to August 1, 1934; E. Edey, August 1, 1934 to January 24, 1935; Closed, January 24, 1935 to October 7, 1935; G. C. McLeod, October 7, 1935 to November 30, 1935; Closed, November 30, 1935 to May 2, 1935; G. C. McLeod, May 2, 1936 to May 20, 1936; Elevator Closed, May 20, 1936.

List of delegates who served in these areas:

DELEGATES & DIRECTORS IN OKOTOKS AREA
Delegates

W. S. Morrison	High River	1929-34
W. R. Barker	Okotoks	1935-39
W. S. Morrison	High River	1940-62
K. B. Christofferson	Brant	1963-74
E. F. Seney	Blackie	1975

DELEGATES & DIRECTORS IN MIDNAPORE, DE WINTON AND ACADEMY AREA
Delegates

J. O. Anderson	Blackie	1925
C. S. Kiddoo	Glenview	1926
J. O. Anderson	Blackie	1927-28
W. S. Morrison	High River	1929-34
W. R. Barker	Okotoks	1935-39
W. S. Morrison	High River	1940-55
F. Noel	Okotoks	1956-63
A. G. Bricker	Calgary	1964-67
J. A. Brander	Langdon	1968-73
H. J. Stewart	Dalemead	1974-75

Directors (Apply to all four areas)

O. L. McPherson	Vulcan	1926-27
J. J. Strang	Claresholm	1927-36
G. G. Coote	Nanton	1936-53
H. I. Montgomery	Nanton	1953 (Died in office)
R. C. Bell	Carstairs	1953-60
O. K. Rosenberger	Balzac	1960 (Died in office)
N. Jacobsen	Arrowwood	1975

PROSPERITY CERTIFICATES (SCRIP) — by Reta Reynolds

In July of 1936, thirty workmen engaged in grading and leveling the Edmonton highway at Beverley, a few miles east of Edmonton, were to have the distinction at the end of that particular week of receiving the first taxable Prosperity Certificates issued by the Province of Alberta under Premier William Aberhart. These were to be a cure for unemployment.

These workmen were to be given scrip in $1.00 and $5.00 denominations, and since they were men previously unemployed, they probably went in hot haste to the local storekeepers to use them in exchange for goods. The certificates were negotiable and could be passed from hand to hand. At the end of two years, the Government was to redeem them for $1.00 on the dollar certificates and $5.00 on the five dollar certificates, in the meantime having collected that much by the weekly issuance of stamps.

According to the original Act, denominations of twenty-five cents were to be issued too, but little information is available on these.

The scrip, which was about the size and color of a Canadian dollar bill, had 104 spaces on the back on which to place the stamps. Each space was dated, the date being the Wednesday of each week. Thus, each certificate required a one-cent stamp to be affixed every week for two years. The additional $4.00 being to cover the costs of administration.

THE GOVERNMENT OF THE PROVINCE OF ALBERTA
PROSPERITY CERTIFICATE
DATE OF ISSUE AUGUST 5, 1936   A 6899

THE PROVINCIAL TREASURER WILL PAY TO THE BEARER THE SUM OF ONE DOLLAR ON THE EXPIRATION OF TWO YEARS FROM DATE OF ISSUE HEREOF UPON PRESENTATION HEREOF PROVIDED THERE ARE THEN ATTACHED TO THE BACK HEREOF ONE HUNDRED AND FOUR ONE CENT CERTIFICATE STAMPS

ONE DOLLAR

William Aberhart PREMIER   PROVINCIAL TREASURER

WESTERN PRINTING & LITHOGRAPHING CO. LTD. CALGARY

ALBERTA 1 CENT	ALBERTA 1 CENT	ALBERTA 1 CENT	ALBERTA 1 CENT	ALBERTA 1 CENT	ALBERTA 1 CENT	SEPT. 23, 1936	SEPT. 30, 1936	OCT. 7, 1936	OCT. 14, 1936	OCT. 21, 1936	OCT. 28, 1936	NOV. 4, 1936	NOV. 11, 1936	NOV. 18, 1936
NOV. 25, 1936	DEC. 2, 1936	DEC. 9, 1936	DEC. 16, 1936	DEC. 23, 1936	DEC. 30, 1936	JAN. 6, 1937	JAN. 13, 1937	JAN. 20, 1937	JAN. 27, 1937	FEB. 3, 1937	FEB. 10, 1937	FEB. 17, 1937	FEB. 24, 1937	MAR. 3, 1937
MAR. 10, 1937	MAR. 17, 1937	MAR. 24, 1937	MAR. 31, 1937	APRIL 7, 1937	APRIL 14, 1937	APRIL 21, 1937	APRIL 28, 1937	MAY 5, 1937	MAY 12, 1937	MAY 19, 1937	MAY 26, 1937	JUNE 2, 1937	JUNE 9, 1937	JUNE 16, 1937
JUNE 23, 1937	JUNE 30, 1937	JULY 7, 1937	JULY 14, 1937	JULY 21, 1937	JULY 28, 1937	AUG. 4, 1937	AUG. 11, 1937	AUG. 18, 1937	AUG. 25, 1937	SEPT. 1, 1937	SEPT. 8, 1937	SEPT. 15, 1937	SEPT. 22, 1937	SEPT. 29, 1937
OCT. 6, 1937	OCT. 13, 1937	OCT. 20, 1937	OCT. 27, 1937	NOV. 3, 1937	NOV. 10, 1937	NOV. 17, 1937	NOV. 24, 1937	DEC. 1, 1937	DEC. 8, 1937	DEC. 15, 1937	DEC. 22, 1937	DEC. 29, 1937	JAN. 5, 1938	JAN. 12, 1938
JAN. 19, 1938	JAN. 26, 1938	FEB. 2, 1938	FEB. 9, 1938	FEB. 16, 1938	FEB. 23, 1938	MAR. 2, 1938	MAR. 9, 1938	MAR. 16, 1938	MAR. 23, 1938	MAR. 30, 1938	APRIL 6, 1938	APRIL 13, 1938	APRIL 20, 1938	APRIL 27, 1938
MAY 4, 1938	MAY 11, 1938	MAY 18, 1938	MAY 25, 1938	JUNE 1, 1938	JUNE 8, 1938	JUNE 15, 1938	JUNE 22, 1938	JUNE 29, 1938	JULY 6, 1938	JULY 13, 1938	JULY 20, 1938	JULY 27, 1938	AUG. 3, 1938	

According to Mr. Aberhart, it was a loan of Alberta credit — many of the people were unable to think of it in these terms, however, business and professional men of any standing and successful farmers who had built up sound enterprises through years of hard work and good judgement, gloomily forecasted disaster.

Wholesalers refused to co-operate from the start, and would not take them from the retailers. As a result, the retailers had to send them to the Treasury to have them redeemed. A good deal of the certificates were bought up by tourists as souvenirs. Cabinet Ministers promised to take them as part payment of wages, but they never did.

The Alberta Government Telephones agreed to accept them in payment of former subscribers' accounts, in payment of capital notes due by mutual telephone companies, and in payment of individual notes signed by former A.G.T. subscribers to obtain connections with rural mutual companies. However, A.G.T. would not accept them for current accounts due by subscribers, switching fees due by mutual telephone companies, or as the first payment (25 per cent) due by new rural mutual companies on the purchase of a plant. This first payment had to be in cash, but subsequent payments in scrip were acceptable.

The Boards of Trade and the Chambers of Commerce in the larger cities wrote letters of protest to Mr. Aberhart, pointing out that it was discriminatory; that it would circulate mainly in the hands of wage-earners and retail merchants. These classes would therefore have to pay the tax and that wholesalers and manufacturers could not accept its use because of their commitments outside the Province requiring good money. The above mentioned bodies posted hand bills in various places warning the retailers against the use of scrip. However, all of these pleas were ignored, and the Act was put into operation in the summer of 1936.

The real author of the taxable scrip plan was W. A. Fallow, then Minister of Public Works. Mr. Fallow modeled it closely on an experiment by the Austrian municipality of Woergl which had some striking initial success until the Austrian National Bank decided to interfere.

Those who co-operated in the scheme, tried to keep them in circulation as long as possible, re-issuing them in their communities and having them circulate there. However, the prosperity certificates which were issued in the summer of 1936 were abandoned in August 1936, the probable cause being lack of co-operation on all levels.

According to one M.L.A. in office in 1938, Mr. G. L. MacLachlan, the chief reasons for the certificates being unsuccessful were: (1) The government did not take the prosperity certificates for any government revenue. (2) The lack of facilities for clearing these in various districts.

Mr. MacLachlan's version of the whole idea was to reverse the usual procedure of collecting taxes and then paying them out for services rendered, and collecting them by the use of the stamps on the prosperity ,certificates. The hope was, by so doing purchasing power would be increased by paying out the money first, and collecting it back in gradual stages.

According to the Prosperity Certificates Act, the aggregate amount of certificates of the different denominations was not to exceed $2,000,000.00. There was $359,800.00 worth of scrip issued and by September of 1938, there was still about $19,500.00 that had not been turned in for redemption.

Although the prosperity certificates idea was not successful in Alberta, it was certainly instrumental in having so many roads built as a basis for the good road network that winds throughout the Province today.

SHIN PLASTER

The Shin Plaster was a nickname for a twenty-five cent piece of paper money. The paper twenty-five cent piece was first introduced in the U.S.A. shortly before 1870 when the silver coins were becoming scarce, because the Canadians were using a lot of the U.S. coins at this time as the British did all the Canadian minting and we did not have enough coins. To add to the shortage Canadians were melting down the silver coin for the silver.

The nickname Shin Plaster came from the American soldiers, who were issued new high leather boots which had very stiff leather in them. The leather rubbed on their shins, so at this time having nothing else to pad the boots they put layers of paper twenty-five cents in the boots to stop the chaffing of the shins and this is how the name was derived.

The Canadians started printing their own paper twenty-five cent pieces and the nickname crossed the border.

The Shin Plasters were printed in three issues in Canada 1870, 1900 and 1923. The Bank of Canada recalled all the Shin Plasters in 1935 and after this time it was no longer legal tender and any that remained in people's possessions became collectors items.

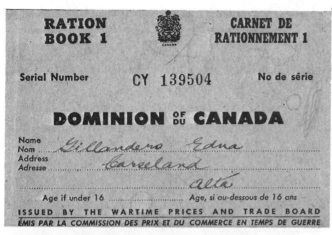

RATION BOOK 1 / CARNET DE RATIONNEMENT 1

Serial Number   CY 139504   No de série

DOMINION OF DU CANADA

Name / Nom ...... Gillanders Edna
Address / Adresse ...... Carseland
...... Alta.

Age if under 16 ...... Age, si au-dessous de 16 ans

ISSUED BY THE WARTIME PRICES AND TRADE BOARD
ÉMIS PAR LA COMMISSION DES PRIX ET DU COMMERCE EN TEMPS DE GUERRE

LETTERS / NUMBERS   Prefix and Serial Number
LETTRES / NUMÉROS   No de Série (avec lettres)

CY 29884

Name / Nom ...... Riches   Pearl Jane
Last Name—Nom de famille   First Name—Prénum

Street Address or R.R. No.
No et rue ou R.R. No.
City or Town / Ville ou Village: Okotoks
Province / Province: Alberta   Telephone Number / Numéro de Téléphone

RATION BOOK 6 / CARNET DE RATIONNEMENT 6
RB-215   CANADA

RATION BOOK 2 / CARNET DE RATIONNEMENT 2
RB-50   CANADA

Name / Nom ...... Gillanders Edna
Street Address or R.R. No. / No et rue ou R.R. No.
City or Town / Ville ou village: Carseland
Prefix and Serial Number: CY - 139504   No de Série (avec lettres)
Age if under 16 ...... Age, si moins de 16 ans

ISSUED BY THE RATION ADMINISTRATION W.P.T.B.
ÉMIS PAR LE SERVICE DU RATIONNEMENT C.P.C.T.G.

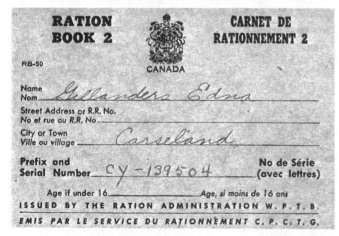

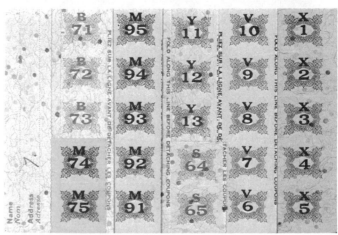

This coupon when detached by supplier permits delivery of
1943/1944   ONE UNIT OF GRADED GASOLINE
G. R. COTTRELLE, Oil Controller.

This coupon when detached by supplier permits delivery of
1943/1944   ONE UNIT OF GRADED GASOLINE
G. R. COTTRELLE, Oil Controller.

This coupon when detached by supplier permits delivery of
1943/1944   ONE UNIT OF GRADED GASOLINE
G. R. COTTRELLE, Oil Controller.

This coupon when detached by supplier permits delivery of
1943/1944   ONE UNIT OF GRADED GASOLINE
G. R. COTTRELLE, Oil Controller.

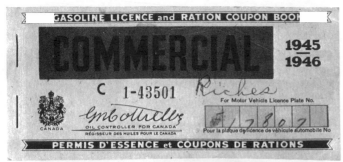

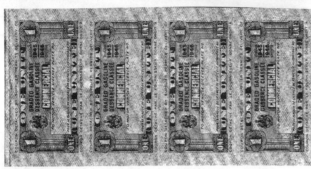

UPLAND GAME BIRDS OF THE AREA

The general area between Calgary and Okotoks was the first in Alberta to host the Ring-necked pheasant and Gray (Hungarian) partridge. Dan Patton, in association with three others, including Austin Winters and Fred Green, introduced the Ring-necked pheasant (Phasianus colchicus) into the Midnapore district in 1908. Approximately twenty-five crates of young chicks were imported from China and raised on Dan's homestead located in Sec. 29-22-1-W5. Initially the young hens were exceptionally prolific, laying as many as twenty-one eggs, or twice the usual setting. This necessitated enlisting domestic hens to incubate the eggs and raise many of the chicks, which proved amazingly successful. Other shipments of chicks were imported in 1912, 1913 and 1919 by this same group. The entire venture was oft criticized by Dan's brother Thomas and nephew Ralph, as these aliens frequently feasted on the relatives' market gardens, especially the new peas and strawberries.

Dan Patton and associates also imported the Gray partridge (Perdix perdix) from Hungary in the same year. This planting of seventy pair was augmented with another ninety-five pair in the following year. They propagated so rapidly that a hunting season was permitted in 1913.

In 1930 they introduced the Chukar partridge (Alectoris chukar). The Alberta climate proved too severe for this native of southern Eurasia as this attempt and several others which followed in many areas of Alberta, were all unsuccessful.

ERA OF HEAVY HORSES — by Ruth Hamilton

WHERE THE CHILDREN USED TO PLAY

The old farm home is mother's yet and mine
And filled it is with plenty and to spare
But we are lonely here in life's decline
Though fortune smiles around us everywhere.
We look across the Gold
Of the harvests, as of old.
The corn, the fragrant clover and the hay
But most we turn our gaze
As with eyes of other days
To the pastures where the children used to play.

Our sloping pasture lands are filled with herds
The barn and granary bins are bulging o'er
The groves, a paradise of singing birds
The woodland brook leaps laughing by the door
Yet lonely, lonely still,
Let us prosper as we will
Our old hearts seem so empty everywhere.
We can only through the mist
See the faces we have kissed
In the pastures where the children used to play.

HEAVY HORSES

Nothing can get me reminiscing like this favorite old poem from Riley's farm rhymes. One needs only to shut their eyes to see the bright rose and purple of day break and to hear again the chorus of singing birds heralding in a new day. In the pasture new foals ran and bucked, accompanied by the delightful shrieks of children who chased after them.

From every field you could hear the farmer shouting to his horses as he started his plowing for the day. In the early days, they used three horses on a sulky plow, five or six on a gang plow and eight on a three bottom plow. As the day wore on the fields got smaller and smaller, row upon row of long black humps of fragrant black earth turned over embracing the warmth of the early spring sun.

But what of the big beautiful horses that pulled the plow? Where did they come from? A man's most valuable possession in those days (sometimes even above his wife) were his horses. He depended on them for nearly everything, transportation, working the land, harvesting, hauling the winter fuel supply from the woodlots, etc.

Nearly every farmer kept a few good mares and about June or July someone would travel through the area with a stallion. For a fee of about fifteen dollars your mare was assured of an offspring. Most pastures the following spring could boast a few new foals walking on wobbly new legs through the lush green grass.

I have tried to trace some of the men who led these beautiful big horses through this area, but most of the early pioneers are gone and it's only from some of the remaining ones that I have managed to get the following information.

Around 1900 Frank Hamilton travelled the Midnapore — Priddis — Red Deer lake area. Unlike most of the other men who either rode or led their horses, Frank drove a lovely bay standardbred on a cart. Good driving horses were as essential to the farmer as were his work horses. He and his brother Sam raised Clyde horses on the homestead, but they never travelled a stallion. Mares were brought to the place. The name of his beautiful Standard Bred stallion has been forgotten over the years.

The name that comes up next is Andy Rowles. He travelled a black Percheron for Harry Connel, who lived in the Gladys Ridge area. Later he travelled a big Clyde named Sandy Madura owned by The De Winton Horse Breeders Association. Andy always made it to the Charlie Marshall farm for dinner. From some of the older farmers in the area it is said the Madura left a lot of bad tempered offspring but good horses once they were broken.

The name Frank Tindal is mentioned, but I could get no information on him.

Both Howard and John Norris led stallions about this time. John led Royal Splendor. His route was west of the De Winton area. Howard Norris led a Harry Connel horse, a Percheron through the Davisburg area. The Norris's had a stallion of their own and raised some of the best Percherons in the area, but they did not travel this horse. Howard Norris is a great horseman and it was a known fact that if you bought a Norris horse you got a good one. Mr. Norris still lives on the farm east of De Winton and in his mid eighties I'll bet the sight of a good horse still gives him much pleasure.

John Norris holding Royal Splendor, 1925.

Next comes to mind a man named Harry Lusk. He travelled a big Clyde named Nicomen Chief owned by Bill Moodie, also one named Enterprising. Later he traveled Burgys Last owned by Andy Dollar. Of these men I could find out little of their route and where they made their overnight stops.

About 1926 or 27 Duncan McCallum travelled a big Clyde owned by Bob Allen. This horse was the holder of the famous name of British Footprint and left some grand colts, many of them future champions. McCallum is a first cousin of Dunc McMillan, who still lives in this area. His route was to Wylies' and White's, and around the Stormount area. I believe he made his headquarters at White's. He only stayed in Canada two years and then went back to his

Nicomen's Chief — owned by Will Moodie, 1922.

native Scotland. Dunc McMillan went back to Scotland this summer for a visit (His first since he came to Canada as a young man) and he stayed with his cousin Duncan McCallum who travelled British Footprint in our area so many years ago.

Next came a man whom I knew personally and had great respect for, Alex Crawford. Two of his horses were Garnet Sensation and Cragie Ensign.

Alex walked every mile he and his horse travelled. We could see him coming down the road from the north and what a welcome visitor he was. The men nearly always had a cool beer down in the spring cribbing on the day Alex arrived and when he had attended to his horse with feed, water and a brisk grooming, he would sit on the edge of the water trough with his barefeet dangling in the cooling water, a pair of clean socks slung over his shoulder ready to put on when his feet felt rested from the long walk. In his hand a cool beer and a look of complete contentment on his face. We always had an especially good supper for Alex for he had walked many miles that day, but the best part of all was the news he brought of the neighbours. I'll always remember how we sat at the table and talked and talked, while the dishes waited to be washed. In the morning he was up at dawn to look after his horse, had breakfast and was on his way with the sun barely up.

One morning I will never forget. In those days you

Alex Crawford with one of his Clyde stallions in the early 30's.

could actually get wooden apple and orange boxes and we always used them for kindling the morning fire. I remember taking out the nails and setting them on top of our old Home Comfort stove. One of them rolled off into one of the pancakes cooking on the griddle.

Anyway, when Alex was eating his bacon and hot cakes he bit into the nail. I had a young girl helping me that summer and Alex held the nail aloft and said "Oh Suzzie" it's getting pretty bad when you have to nail your pancakes together.

Later Alex stayed at Sam Hamilton's for a year or so. Sam was very sick with heart trouble and he and Alex were good friends. Sam found great pleasure in Alex's visits.

Alex quit walking his stallions and hired a young man named Mel Brown to make his rounds with a stallion named BeauJest. He stayed at our place also but only for a couple of years.

Bill Hamilton travelled a Belgian stallion named Duke DeFarceur. His route was east of De Winton to Herr's — Ernie Miller's and back to Stormount area. He was a beautiful red roan and to my knowledge was the only Belgian travelled in this area.

Ralph Johnson holding Bill Hamilton's Belgian stallion, Duke de Farceur; weight 2230 lb.

Speck Gale holding Belgian stallion (Monarch). He lived with the Goettler family for twelve years and was killed in 1934 on Goettler's threshing outfit.

The Hamilton Brothers, Bill and Sam owned their own stallion and raised purebred Belgians. Many of them winning championships at the Calgary Exhibition.

These men and their horses played a very vital role in the development of our area and should be recorded in our history.

DR. A. E. ARDIEL — by M. B. Ardiel

Dr. A. E. Ardiel was born in London, Ontario in 1877. He served overseas in the South African War in 1900 and after returning home, attended Western University in London, Ontario, graduating as a Physician and Surgeon in 1905.

In 1908 he came out west to Okotoks, Alberta, and purchased the medical practice and house of Dr. Delong and started his career as a General Medical Practitioner.

In 1908 he returned to London, Ontario, and married Gertrude Armitage and brought her west to live in Okotoks in the two storey brick house in which he had his office. They had three children, Leonard, Kathleen and Maurice.

Dr. Ardiel served Okotoks and district, ministering to their medical needs for 43 years, until his death in January of 1950.

In the early days he travelled by horse and buggy in the summer and by sleigh in winter, in an area as far east as the Blackie area, south as far as Aldersyde, north as far as Midnapore and west as far as the Foothills. He was predeceased by his wife in 1943 and by his son Leonard, who was killed overseas in the second World War, in 1944. Kathleen passed away in 1975. Maurice still resides in the Old Family Brick House, in Okotoks, where he was born.

Dr. A. E. Ardiel.

DR. W. M. GIBSON & DR. J. GIBSON

The Gibson family arrived in Okotoks in June, 1955 taking up residence in Elma Street. The district had had a succession of doctors since the death of Dr. Ardiel but had no doctor at that time. They practised from their house for a few months, for no office space was available but eventually they bought the Skye Glen School House which was lying disused in the country. The town put on a "work bee" and the old wooden school house was hauled in on skids, set-up on foundations, and once alterations and decorations were completed, became a comfortable little medical centre, seeing much service for the next 15 years. They both held the degrees of Bachelor in Medicine and Surgery of Glasgow University, Scotland, graduating in September 1939; Janet spent most of the war years as a house surgeon and physician in British hospitals, marrying her husband in 1941 when he was a captain, Royal Army Medical Corps.

Catriona was born during the war and was a little girl of 11 when the Gibsons arrived in Okotoks after 10 years of general practice in Hull, Yorkshire, England'

Life in a small foothills town was very different from city life in England and so was the practice of medicine, but for the Gibsons the next 14 years were to be the most fulfilling of their medical careers. They felt they had arrived in Okotoks at the end of an era, for the town's population was under 700, the streets were unpaved, and as an English visitor said, "It looked as if Buffalo Bill would ride up the street any minute." Both held privileges in High River Hospital. Catriona attended Okotoks High School, winning the graduating class award, and after taking a degree in political science at the University of Alberta, Edmonton, moved to Queen's University, Ontario, taking her law degree with distinction and becoming a member of the Alberta Bar. She was the first woman lawyer to be appointed by a major Calgary Oil Company as their legal counsel. However she was asked to join Osgoode Hall Law School in Toronto where she was Assistant to the Dean and received a scholarship to take the degree of Master of Law. In 1969, when 26 years old, she was killed in a car accident.

In 1970 the Gibsons bought the "MY WIGWAM" Restaurant and converted it into the Sheep River Clinic, but it never really lost its original name, one resident always having to make his appointments with "The Chief Medicine Man". The Gibsons had many experiences; Janet got to one emergency on a farm by standing behind the driver of a tractor, the only vehicle that could move through the Spring "run-off", and Morris and a colleague did a housecall in midwinter to the top of Plateau Mountain where the crew of an oil well had a bad accident.

Morris's first baby in the slums of Glasgow was a difficult delivery — he didn't quite know what he was doing. His last was difficult for another reason — it was carried out in the back of a very small car stopped by a blizzard at DeWinton and there was barely room to move inside.

Both were active in the community, 10 years as a school trustee for Morris, while his wife was President of the Parent Teachers Association and the Okotoks Red Cross.

In 1971 they moved to Calgary where Morris was appointed Professor and Head, the Division of Family Medicine at Calgary University Medical School, no longer a country doctor but enjoying the challenge of training young people for a career in medicine.

THE OKOTOKS AGRICULTURAL SOCIETY by Effie Leach

Thanks to the Glenbow Foundation for making available the records from which we gleaned the following information. Our appreciation to Sheilagh Jameson for supplying the proper files.

The earliest records show that the Sheep Creek Agricultural Society which was the forerunner of the Okotoks Agricultural Society, met in 1892 with the address of Dewdney, Alberta.

As this area had recently been settled, probably in the early or mid eighties, it was an enterprising and commendable undertaking to have a 'Fair' which seemed to have been held in October, 1892. Judges had been appointed for cattle, horses, sheep, dogs, pigs, poultry, blacksmithing, grain, vegetables, butter, cheese, bread, and 'Ladies Work'. Apparently this was all honorary as later a vote of thanks was given to the judges for their kindness in acting. The secretary was instructed to do so publicly through the press. Previously, in the May meeting, the secretary read a list of special prizes offered by different Calgary merchants which was accepted with a vote if thanks for their kindness. These 1892 records show that the secretary had earlier corresponded with the Fish Creek and Davisburg Agricultural Societies asking them to amalgamate with them for the year.

In January, 1893 another meeting, another election of officers, when it was decided to hold an annual show at Dewdney. Directors were appointed and assigned to look after the various competitions. There was some discussion as to the possibility of starting a creamery to be within one mile of Dewdney. The secretary was instructed to send a notice to the two local papers (could this be Calgary papers?) and the Toronto Globe suggesting that Dewdney would be a suitable place for a competent man to start a creamery. It was also decided to select a piece of land for an Exhibition Ground. No record of results!

In 1894 a committee was appointed to look for grounds suitable for making a race track for the fall fair to be held October 3, 1894. Plans were made to rent the 'Gopher House' and grounds for the fall fair and again appointments were made for members to look after the various exhibits.

The February, 1895 meeting shows that the secretary was awarded $25.00 for his 1894 year's work!

In 1896, among other things, it was agreed that the prize list for Grade class (presumably cattle) be made the same as the Davisburg Society list of 1896.

April, 1897 records are now headed as Okotoks (not Dewdney) the name having been officially changed. It was moved and seconded that; "We members of the Sheep Creek Agricultural Society express our willingness to enter into negotiations with the Davisburg and Fish Creek Societies with a view to amalgamating the three."

There is not any record on the archives of the decision made. The name was later changed from Sheep Creek to Okotoks Agricultural Society.

All these earlier records show the financial affairs were always in good shape. There was never a deficit-always some money in the bank. The expenditures were according to funds available. Most work was volunteer and people did not seem to be out for 'the Almighty Dollar'. We pay tribute to these fine people and could easily learn a good lesson from them.

Evidently the Okotoks Fair prospered for some years, the surrounding areas competing and making the day a real holiday for the whole family. Then there was a recession.

There is no record of the price paid for the Exhibition Grounds but one statemnt shows they were valued at $370.00. One year the pasture was rented at $10.00 for the season.

In 1933 the grounds were rented out for $15.00 with the stipulation there would not be any interference if a fair should be held. It was in this year that George Hoadley, Minister of Agriculture, announced that grants would not be made that year but that a judge would be supplied should there be a plowing match held.

1938 shows a membership of only twenty members at $1.00 per year. A plowing match was arranged for 1938 and also 1939. Coffee urns and tables were available from the Masonic Lodge while the Ladies' Aid loaned the dishes. In this year there was a reorganization with the view of having an Agricultural Fair. Prizes offered were small but people seemed to be again interested.

In 1949, eleven years later, a plowing match was held June 15 with approximately six hundred present. Prizes were a bit better. The women helped and the Ladies' Auxiliary was asked to appoint members to be at the entrance to the grounds to collect contributions! Elmer Piper supplied the use of his new garage for a free dance and also paid for the orchestra.

At this time there was a total of ninety-seven paid up members with addresses of Aldersyde, Calgary, De Winton and Okotoks.

1950 shows that a garden competition was to be held in the fall and there was some discussion as to a home cooking competition.

1951 membership dropped drastically to thirty-one. There had been heavy rains, five hail storms and consequently many events had to be cancelled.

1953 shows a coyote drive in which seventy or more animals were destroyed.

We must not let this go to press without remembering kindly the many, many years Mr. Ed Hayes had a prominent part in guiding the Okotoks Agricultural Society. Our grateful thanks to him for his many years of faithful service.

OKOTOKS COUNTRY CLUB — by J. Herbert Jenkins

In 1915 the residents of the Allan district held house parties and this was the beginning of the Okotoks Country Club.

When the Club was going from house to house for their meetings, whist was played mostly and sometimes ended up with a little dancing. The music for these dances was supplied by Mr. A. N. Allan, with his violin, Mr. J. P. Todd and Roy McConnell, with their violins and everyone who could play some instrument. Lots of young people learned to dance and no one was left sitting just one happy family.

As the dance parties were getting overcrowded the first hall was rented over the Richie and Allan Hardware which was located on the corner where the Royal Bank is now.

On April 1, 1919, at the Orange Hall, Okotoks, the annual meeting took place. The President, Mr. Henry Johnson, took the chair and called the meeting to order. The secretary was asked to read the minutes, after it was moved by Mr. Charles Forckel and seconded by Mr. W. Johnson the same be accepted as read. Miss Laura Riches was to audit the books.

Miss Margaret Teskey, representing the recreation Club, put before the club that the two Clubs unite as one. After much discussion it was decided not to join. Then later it was rescinded, still keeping within the limit of 40 members.

The election of officers took place next. Mr. Charles Forckel was president and Mr. W. H. Jenkins as secretary-treasurer. The committee was appointed next. Mr. W. Johnson, Mrs. Allan, Mrs. W. H. Jenkins, Miss T. Allan and Mr. W. Lang. It was moved by W. Johnson and seconded by Mrs. C. Imler that a dollar per meeting be paid to the Orange Hall. Mrs. J. H. Jenkins moved and seconded by Mr. W. Johnson to hold a whist drive which was a complete success. The winners: Women's 1st Mrs. C. Imler, 2nd Miss M. Teskey. Men's 1st, Mr. Ayr, 2nd, Mr. Jack Wilson. The membership fees were a dollar for the gents and fifty cents for the ladies.

Each member had the privilege to invite a guest at anytime. The names to be given to the entertainment committee and an invite sent by mail. The fee of one dollar and fifty cents per couple was collected at the door by the secretary after the invite was presented. In this way it was never overcrowded.

A dance was held at the Orange Hall April 16, 1920. Mrs. Trainers music was $45, Mr. Dann Supper $25, Advertising $6, Tickets $3, Light $2, Hall Rent $10, Total $91, Receipts $72, Deficit of $19.

The reason for the deficit being muddy roads.

The club then moved to the Victoria Hall and then to the Lineham Hall in 1922, this hall was over the W. J. Thomsons Hardware and Tin Smith Shop. Mr. M. B. Ardiel has his building there now, many changes took place in this hall.

A lunch committee was formed and they were responsible to have so many couples bring cakes and sandwiches to the dances.

The single girls had their night, also the bachelors had their night. Many picnics were held, several at Mr. J. P. Todd's farm where the Forest Herrs now live. The Forckel Place, Fish Creek and Bowness park were some other picnic sites. Very good picnics they were too.

In order to become a member you made an application signed by two members, and then the club voted on the application by ballot. The club used a ballot box, white ball, elect and black ball, reject. The dues were now $6 for men and $3 for ladies.

Country Club Picnic, Todd's place.

The highlight was the Annual Banquet, Box Socials and Hardtime Dances. The old time music was played by Mrs. H. Cushing and others, Mr. Dean Twist, Mr. Niel Dorsey, Mr. Lyle Ulman, Mrs. May Lock and Mr. Len Orton.

Quite a few romances began at the Country Club. One was Bob and Tina Grisdale. Bob was working at the Wilson and Robertson Garage, located where the Royal Bank is now. Bob would let the cars out after the dance and collect the money. There was no anti freeze in those days just water in the radiators.

The club then moved to the Masonic Hall and took on more members. Mr. Charles Forckel was still president. He was instrumental in organizing the club and was president for twenty-three years. He passed away in 1943. His brother, Mr. John Forckel, was then president and Mr. W. H. Jenkins was secretary treasurer.

Later the club moved to the Elks Hall. Mr. Albert Herr was the last president and his grandfather Mr. Harry Lock was secretary until the club ended in 1961-1962.

OKOTOKS COUNTRY CLUB FINANCIAL STATEMENT 1926

Receipts		Expenditure	
Gross receipts	$588.43	Gross Expenditure	$527.50
Dues	$300.00	Coffee and Sugar	$ 16.00
Rent	$154.00	Music	$155.50
Collection	$ 79.50	Stamps and	
Box Social	$ 40.55	Stationery	$ 6.65
Interest	$ 1.30	Rent	$160.00
Balance on hand		Light	$ 33.66
from 1925	$ 13.08	Gas	$ 12.60
		Janitor	$ 38.50
		Insurance	$ 10.34
		Piano tuning	$ 12.00
		Business tax	$ 9.00
		Incidentals	$ 72.25

Receipts:	$588.43
Expenditures:	$527.50
Balance on hand:	$ 60.93

ASSETS AND LIABILITIES

Assets		Liabilities	
Furniture, light and		Rent due	$ 96.25
gas fixture, etc.	$150.00	Excess of Assets	
Piano	$200	over Liabilities	$349.68
Rent due	$ 35.00	Total	$445.93
Total	$385.00		
Cash in Bank	$ 60.93		
Total	$445.93		

THE GOLD WATCH — A COINCIDENCE — by Hugh Macklin

This incident occurred while I was working for the P. Burns Co. on the Bow Valley Ranch. We were moving several hundred head of cattle down the Macleod Trail from the Bow Valley to Billy Henry's at High River. The Macleod Trail was a dirt road in those days with never a car on it. Big herds were moved by two men taking 40 or 50 of the leaders and pushing them along ahead of the main bunch allowing the rest to stay out behind for a considerable distance, which prevented them from bunching up and crowding each other and getting over heated. Two men usually were on the tail end to see that none broke back. The Macleod Trail then went through De Winton which was a very small hamlet a few houses and a Post Office.

I was on the tail end of the herd and as we came up to the Post Office I saw a small bunch of people outside. One of them came up to me and inquired had I seen somebody running. I said "I had not". He explained that he lived about a quarter mile up the road and had seen a man jump out of the window of his house, going to investigate he found a Gold Waltham watch was missing. Waltham watches were very expensive those days and so reliable that they were used by most railway men.

Continuing on our way, after going about three miles I noticed the sun glistening on something by the side of the road, partly covered by road dust, I got off my horse and kicked the dust away and discovered a Gold Watch. It was undamaged as it had a Hunter cover over the face and the glass was not broken. After going a few more miles I told the lead men to go ahead into Okotoks and get their dinner while I stayed on the tail end to keep the cattle from straying back. While sitting by the road side I could see, coming from the direction of Okotoks, a Mountie on a horse, when he got up to me I asked him if he was on the De Winton case and he said he was, so I showed him the watch which I had picked up. He gave me a receipt besides a very suspicious look and said he would show it to the De Winton postmaster. Some days later on my way back from delivering the cattle I called in at the De Winton post office to inquire if the watch I had found was his, he said it was not. I heard from the the police that the watch had never been claimed, but as I had lost the receipt in the meantime I was unable to claim it. A peculiar and interesting coincidence but not one from which I benefitted.

PROHIBITION DAYS — by Albert McKevitt

This article I know to be true for it was told me by a man whose name I will not mention but whom I know to be a truthful man.

He had been through the first world war and was used to taking chances and had lots of nerve. During the war they would get tired of eating canned beef, otherwise known as bully beef, and sometimes would take off at night and raid some farmer's chicken house then pick a spot where they killed and fried the chickens. They were used to being careful and watching out for themselves.

When he returned from the war he was working for the C.P.R. as a crew foreman on the tracks. Going to work one morning he noticed some cases of whiskey in the right of way ditch so he stopped the work crew and they loaded up two or three cases and took them home. He dug a hole in the dirt floor of his basement and buried two cases of the whiskey and covered it over and placed furniture over it. The C.P.R. police suspected him and came and made an inspection of his house including the attic and basement but failed to find the loot. He had to be very careful not to let his wife and children know about his find for his wife didn't approve of drinking.

If I remember rightly, the whiskey got into the ditch when a couple of fellows hid in the baggage car in Calgary and when they got to the Aldersyde area they threw out a number of cases of whiskey. They were a disappointed lot for when they went to gather them up they were several cases short.

Another story told me concerned a man who used to do blacksmithing and lived on the Macleod Trail near Pine Creek. One day he saw a car stop and someone got out and put a large parcel under a culvert, got into the car and drove away. The gentleman in question took time to go and investigate and discovered a case of whiskey had been cached there. He returned to his shop and got a wheelbarrow with some straw in it, loaded the whiskey, covered it with straw and wheeled it across to his home. Mounties passing by at the time did not take the time to stop and question him about what he had in the wheelbarrow. From stories I hear about prohibition times, I guess the Mounties were kept pretty busy most of the time.

The blacksmith was not a drinking man but liked to keep a treat on hand for his customers while they were waiting for their teams.

***

I think prohibition came into being about 1916, during the first world war, when I was about eight years old. Why? I do not know but maybe people were spending money on booze that could have been put to better use such as clothes, blankets, socks and especially war savings bonds.

One special event that I remember well was about five brothers. They were of Scottish descent and, with an election coming up, they got into some fiery arguments about alcoholic beverages, whether they should be put on the shelf until the war was over or whether they should be able to drink some and give advice on how to win the war. As these arguments progressed it was discovered that four of the brothers were going to cast their ballots for the same side and the fifth brother was in opposition. They had to travel a good distance, about four miles, in order to vote and the four that were in accord took the team and wagon and left the dissenting one behind and he had to walk the four miles. I don't recall which side won in the election.

THE MOCK WEDDING

Myrtle (DeMings) Williams used to have contests periodically to guess the number of beans in a jar or the number of sunflower seeds in a flower head etc. One contest was to guess the weight of an enormous fruit cake she had baked, the prize to be the cake. Stuart Dalzell was the lucky person and, when Mrs. Dalzell worried about how she was to use up so much cake, a party was organized and part of the entertainment was to be a mock wedding. Most of the young people in the neighbourhood were involved in the preparations for the event. Jack Warrack was the preacher, Stuart Dalzell, the groom, (the only time he was ever married), Miss Ida Clare (Les Marshall) the bridesmaid and Miss Lena Gainster (Bill Hamilton) the bride.

It was a bitterly cold night, about —20 degrees and the cars in those days, 1922, had gravity feed. Earle Marshall was driving the bride and bridesmaid, they were dressed in all their finery, silk stockings and dresses, and the feed line on the car froze up. They nearly froze while waiting for someone to go back and get some hot water to thaw out the line. In the meantime the preacher had arrived all dressed in Percy Morgan's tuxedo (long tails) and he had to be hidden in the pantry to wait for the rest of the wedding party so he put in a cold and anxious time till the others showed up.

The 'ladies' had false hair and Bill, who had rather large hands for a young lady, had to keep them covered under a fancy shawl. Mrs. Dalzell made quite a fuss over the two strange young ladies and had them shown in to the bedroom to remove their wraps. When Mary Dalzell heard them introduced with those outrageous names she knew at once there was something odd going on but didn't recognize the boys right away, however she went along with the masquerade. There were several tables of cards in progress and the 'girls' were taken around and introduced to all the guests. Their make-up must have been very good because these people were all close neighbours and none of them realized who the girls were.

Following the ceremony, the bride and bridesmaid circulated among the guests and caused quite a furor by making up to the gentlemen who were playing cards, most of whom had their wives or girl friends with them. One lady in particular became highly indignant when the bridesmaid sat on the arm of her husband's chair and put an arm around his shoulder and patted him on the cheek.

During all this time the 'girls' had kept their hats on and the guests were wondering if this was a new fashion in the city. As the evening wore on their heads became too warm for comfort and they had to remove their hats and the attached hair. There was great merriment as well as great embarrassment (among the jealous young ladies).

After this experience there was no danger of these two men ever deciding that women's clothing was the thing to wear.

DAGGETT'S PARLIAMENT SEAT

One Saturday evening in 1921, some of the fellows decided that Miss Gooch's outhouse would look much better sitting on the north side of the Macleod Trail and proceeded to place it there. Quite an uproar resulted and Joe Miller, the A.P. policeman in Okotoks, was called to settle things and have the building returned. When he was seen arriving onlookers congregated to watch and listen to the proceedings. No one was about to admit to taking part in the prank or to point the finger at anyone else. Joe had to return to Okotoks having accomplished nothing. The building sat by the side of the road for some time and, one Sunday afternoon when a group of men were riding steers at Jim McNeill's farm (the Tyson place), Daisy McNeill told them that she had a great idea. There was an election coming up in a few days and E. A. Daggett was one of the candidates. Daisy promised to supply the paint and a brush if the boys would paint "Daggett's Parliament Seat" on the outhouse and move directly in front of the hall where the polling booth was to be. This deed was carried out with dispatch and when election day dawned the outhouse was displaying its sign for all to see.

Mr. Daggett visited the polling station that day and is said to have had a good laugh but not so the Deputy Returning Officer. He had groomed his horses, polished their harness, shined his buggy and driven into town in fine style. When he saw the sign he turned his team around and drove back home. A new man had to be found to do his job before the polling station could be opened.

It was never officially established just who was responsible for the act but it was Mr. W. J. Hamilton Sr. and Harry Cushing that moved the edifice back to its site behind Miss Gooch's house.

George Hoadley, U.F.A., won the election.

VISITORS FROM ENGLAND

In far off England, early in the century, before the outbreak of WW1, three daring and adventuresome young English ladies decided to brave the wilds of the colonies and visit the Canadian west. One of the three had a brother, Percy Morgan living near De Winton W½ 34-21-1-W5 and they set out to be his houseguests and perhaps to find husbands. They were Miss Morgan, Miss Seego and Lady Gray.

When they arrived they were eager to see everything in the strange land. One of the first things they did was to go to visit a threshing crew at work in a nearby field. It was a steam run engine and a large machine busy threshing very dusty grain. The girls insisted they wanted to see inside the machine as it worked. The boss, Eben Bremner, rather reluctantly opened the side door on the machine and the girls were instantly covered with dirty black dust and chaff. They were good sports though and continued to inspect the inside of the machine as it ground out the grain.

One of the girls had vowed that she would marry the first man that she saw on a horse and she did but the union didn't last and she moved down to Montana with a neighbor of theirs. The second one married Shirley Matthews, lived in the district for a while and they disappeared. The third one, Miss Morgan, returned to her home in England and remained single for the rest of her life.

SPORTS — BILL "SCOTTY" RODGER

Until coming to Canada, Bill took an active part in the track and field division of the Highland Games in Scotland. Later, when living in the Calgary area, he was still competing in the Calgary and Edmonton Highland Games, but in a lesser degree with George Sutherland. He won the Aggregate at Edmonton in 1940. While in the Canadian Armed Forces, Bill won the shot put in Italy in 1944 and in Holland in 1945.

He was part of the tug-o-war team for the De Winton — Okotoks area which won the Highland Society Cup for three consecutive years. This cup has been returned to the society.

CANADIAN PONY CLUB ASSOCIATION PINE CREEK BRANCH — by Nan Graham

The Pine Creek Branch of Canadian Pony Club Association was organized in the early fifties and officially recognized and inspected by Colonel Michael Gutowski of Toronto, then as now, in charge of rider-development for Canadian Olympic Teams. Members rode both Western and flat saddles. A number of young riders had been members of the Alberta Light Horse Association (junior division) and, as this membership appeared to be transferring to the, newly formed, Calgary Pony Club Branch, it was decided to form a branch for the De Winton area. Nan Graham was named first Pony Club Commissioner and was assisted by Mrs. Kay Dunford, Mrs. Kay Mills, Mrs. Shirley Van Loewen, Miss Edith Rodie, Tom and Ingrid Hewitt and Mrs. Ann (Neilson) Scott.

The first meetings were held at Nan and Ralph Graham's place on Pine Creek and Macleod Trail Junction. Later, due to change of local members, meetings were changed to Ab. and Kay Mills, Tom and Marilyn Bell's arena, and to Jerry D'Arcy's arena. Members transferred to the 4H Horse Clubs in the late sixties.

During the winter months they joined with the Calgary Branch at Christ Church for theory lessons

Keith Horsfield taking a picture of the first trail ride by the Pine Creek Pony Club. Destination Mooney's Meadow; Lionel Lynch driving team. Nan Graham in checked shirt at other side of team.

and attended, as a group, the rallies at Graham Ranches, Millarville and Mac Glen Ranch at Priddis, the Okotoks Horse Show and their own horse shows and play days, where musical tires, on horseback, were played with the same keen competition as played, with chairs, on foot, at the De Winton Community Hall on party nights.

Early achievement nights were members' own organization, including the toasts and entertainment. Plays, written by the group, were staged on the mezzanine balcony, over the living room at Graham's, genuinely entertaining parents and friends.

The highlight was the Sunday Trail Ride when riders and friends enjoyed many (then open) trails. The camp-fire meals of the "Chuckwagon Queens", rotating committee of four or five mothers, faced with the serving of one hundred to one hundred and twenty-five people, were fantastic in organization and taste. Many lessons in picketing, tying and general horsemanship were given on these rides, both practical and in theory.

Many members are still riding for pleasure, some teaching the second generation. Many carried on their horsemanship in top competition — Barbara (Mooney) Kumlin, as a jockey on her racing Quarter Horse, Norma (Myers) Chornaka, as a jump rider on the Canadian Team along with Barbara (Simpson) Kerr, from Kay Dunford's school, Isabella (Hamilton) Miller, champion in Canadian Girl's Rodeo Association events and who, successfully, passed horsemanship tests for the Calgary Stampede Queen Contest along with Dixie (Girletz) Simpson, Anne (Neilson) Scott, Kelly (Marshall) Nobert and Cheryl (Going) Hall. The Vold boys, Wayne and Doug, followed rodeo riding competition, successfully, "must have learnt to read a horse." Johnny Alcock rides race track 'pony horse', picking up run-away thoroughbreds on the race track and easing flighty colts into the starting gate. Doug Gertlitz followed the Pony Chuckwagon Circuit with his Dad. Many are either teaching their own children or chauffeuring them to new Pony Clubs and are heard to repeat, at gatherings or reunions, the worn phrase — "not as much fun as we had in the old days."

SPORT ORIGIN OF PONY CHUCKWAGONS

Although chuckwagon races at the Calgary Stampede were initiated as more of a stunt act then anything else they soon became one of the most exciting events of the annual rodeo.

Some 20 years after the formation of these races, a few farmers in the Foothills district began toying with a cut-down version of the Calgary chuckwagons. They used horses that could be no higher then 48 inches at the withers, and a 650 pound chuckwagon. Both harness and wagon had to be specially made.

Danny Gerlitz, who like many other farmers in the district, had driven horses all his life, became interested in this miniature chuckwagon racing and started what would prove to be a summer hobby for many years to come, back in 1951.

The pony wagons originally didn't play many shows, but wherever they did go, they proved to be an instant hit.

To gain more interest in pony wagons by both spectators and prospective drivers a Pony Wagon Association was formed in 1956. Danny Gerlitz became the association's first president and held that position for many years to follow. The late Dick Cosgrave was the association's Honorary President. There were only 17 members, and 10 chuckwagons, involved at that time as it took many years to get people to build outfits.

The wagons began to gain acclaim; something they hadn't known for 10 years previous, and in 1957 they were invited to the Royal Winter Fair in Toronto.

Because they could race in a much smaller area then the big wagons, towns in Alberta began to hire the ponies for their rodeos. The biggest show in Alberta was in High River at the Little Britches, and the wagons toured about 8 other sites during the summer. Pony chuckwagon fever spread to Saskatchewan, and they boasted the biggest show of them all, in Saskatoon at Pion-Era Days. Some 20 outfits ran there.

The wagons continued to gain acclaim and travelled to Vancouver, Spokane, and Colorado Springs.

Well, that little group of 17 members just had to grow. By 1967 they had 90 members and last year (1977) the association had grown to 400 members with

Trip to Armstrong, B.C. 1950. Wagons were dismantled and loaded on boards above the ponies. Quite a chore! Now replaced with modern horse trailers.

150 chuckwagons and an equal number of chariots. Pony wagons were now racing in B.C. and as far east as Ontario. The biggest show now had an entry of 70 wagons.

The original founders of the Pony Chuckwagon Association had no idea that what they started would grow into what it is today.

SPORT BASEBALL

The first hardball team in De Winton was formed in 1918 or 1919 and the first few games were played on the site of the new De Winton Community Hall. This area proved to be too rough for ball games, so the team moved and staked out a new diamond at the Les Marshall farm. Some of the original players were: Gene Goettler, Fred Cole, Harold (Lefty) Cole, Carlton Impy, Bill Hamilton, Gerald Gough, Lloyd, Alec and Alf Fraser, Fred Moon and a fellow by the name of Wakeford. Three men who had played pro ball in the states were working on the section at the time, so they played along too. Two of these players were Crowdis and Munro. There were four teams: Okotoks, Kew, Dunbow School and De Winton.

In 1930 the Sod Busters were formed with Earl, Travis and Paul Brinton, Alex Blackwood, Jim Turnbull, Dwight Barrett, George Sutherland, Bill Hamilton, Gordon, Harold and Howard Norris, Doug Pakenham, Wally and Alf Poffenroth, Max and Murray Demings and Stan Hutchinson. Danny Gerlitz played a few games with this team before going into the services.

The games were played at Jim Dalzell's place before the war. The teams were Millarville, Red Deer Lake, Midnapore and Westoe.

In 1945 after the war a new ball club was formed.

Sod Busters baseball team early 1930's. L. to R. back row: Trav. Brinton, George Sutherland, Paul Brinton, next row: Jim Turnbull, Max Demings, Wenty Brinton, Front row: Murray Demings, Bill Hamilton, Dan Gerlitz.

559

De Winton Boys Ball Team. L. to R. Doug Pakenham, Jim Peterson, Gordon Graham, Harold Norris, Ivan Dick, Hugh Hamilton, Lent Orton, Leslie Gilmour, Howard Norris, Gordon Norris, Leslie Norris, David Jamison, Norman Graham, Jack McNeill. (Mascot) 1937-38.

De Winton Girls Baseball Team 1939. L. to R. back: Eleanor Jamison, Margaret Hamilton, Marion Dalzell, Howard Norris, K. Harper, Anna Carothers, Jean McNeill. Front: Janie Wilson, Chrissy Carothers, Barbara Carothers.

De Winton Ball Club, June 1941. Back row: L. to R. Charlie King (pitcher), Vic Heaver (rover), Jack King (first), Les Gilmour (pitcher), Howard Norris (third — short), Russell Martin (extra), Leonard Fox (field — 2nd), Herb Ness (field), Danny Gerlitz (pitcher), Ted Heaver (catcher).

De Winton Ball Team — about, 1940. Back row l. to r.: Howard Norris, Donnie Anderson, Russell Martin, Fred Cole, Gordon Graham, Vic Heaver, Charlie King. Front: Ted Heaver, Tommy King, Gordon Norris, Danny Gerlitz, Lent Orton, Jack King, Herbie Ness.

The games were played in the slough across from the present Shell Service Station on the No. 2 highway. The teams were Millarville, Red Deer Lake, Midnapore, Okotoks, Turner Valley and De Winton. Games were scheduled for Wednesday evenings and Sunday afternoons and all work stopped for the ball games. There was great rivalry between the teams and always a good gathering of fans to cheer their teams onto victory.

The players on the De Winton team were Charlie, Jack and Tom King, Danny Gerlitz, Les Gilmour, Howard and Harold Norris, Herbie Ness, Lent Orton, Russell Martin, Ted and Vic Heaver, Red Schneidmiller, Lenard and Harold Fox, Freddie Cole, Gene Befus, Hughie Hamilton, Donnie Anderson, Harold Poffenroth, Wally and Alf Poffenroth.

Jim Everson was called on to do the umpiring at the games at De Winton, George Halford at Midnapore and Ritchie Stanton at Red Deer Lake.

The De Winton Team wore sweaters carrying the Purity 99 emblem for one year and White Rose sweaters later on.

In a 1945 game at the De Winton airport, after the game Danny Gerlitz made all the team do a route march with bats as guns, there was a great deal of hilarity over this episode.

They later played a team from Sarcee. Attempts were made to start the youngsters playing ball at De Winton, but those interested played in Okotoks because they were attending school there.

Wednesdays and Sundays were great family days as everyone went along only to enjoy these outings.

RODEO

Red Deer Lake Championship Ball Team — 1938. Back Row: Walter Birney (coach), Ted Huck, Roy Latter, Elmer Gilbert, Richie Hope, Ted Allwarden, Joe Huck (coach), Centre Row: Lee Huck, Cliff Latter, Walt Thiessen, Orville Huck. Front Row: Bob Huck, Glen Brown, Shorty Brown, Anderson.

Red Deer Lake Baseball Team, 1948. Front: Roy Latter, Albert Goerlitz, Richie Stanton Jr., Robert Worden, Fred and Walter Thiessen, back: Jim McKevitt, Fred Barkley, Dave Cannon, Jim Mangan, Bert Bradley.

Black Diamond about 1946. Johnny Hamilton riding.

Goettler, Hamilton, Bremner Chuckwagon Outfit; 1934 Championship. Driver — Eben Bremner, holding lead team — Bill Haynes, riders — John McNab, Sam Hamilton, and Speck Gale.

Johnny Hamilton of De Winton and his "Hurry Up" wagon, winner at first chuckwagon race in Edmonton.

Sam Johnson driving year 1939. This was the year the Goettler, Hamilton wagon won the world's Championship. The wheel came back up and they finished the race in record time.

Goettler-Hamilton wagon 1939. Driver Sam Johnson. L. to R. Sam Hamilton, Ernie Irving, Billy Haynes, Eugene Goettler, Bill Hamilton, John McNab. They won the race.

Pine Creek Pony Club entry in Calgary Horse Show, 1955. Won $700.00. Dan Gerlitz driving.

Canada Kid, Lee Faris, who worked for Frank McHugh when he won many championships at Calgary.

Isabella Hamilton Miller, Canadian Cowgirl champion three times.

ALL-ROUND CHAMPION of the ninth annual Little Britches Rodeo was Buddy Hamilton of DeWinton. It marked the third time in his junior rodeo career that Buddy has achieved this honor. He won his first Little Britches championship in 1964 at the age of 13 and repeated again last year.

(Garon photo)

L. to R. Pat McHugh wild cow milking champion. Wayne Vold Can. Am. Bronc champion.

564

RECIPES

GOPHER STEW, 1936

Skin, clean and wash the gophers, cut into pieces and soak in salt water for about fifteen or twenty minutes. Roll pieces in seasoned flour and brown in frying pan with enough bacon grease to keep it free from sticking. When brown place in boiling water and boil until tender and the meat comes freely from the bones. Add more water during cooking if necessary and add about 1½ tsps. salt during the last hour of cooking. About ½ hour before cooking is complete, add a few vegetables to flavor the stock. Carrot, onion, celery are good ones to use. Also add some seasonings such as cloves, peppercorns, bay leaves, thyme, poultry seasoning or any combination of these.

Skim: any fat from the stock and remove gopher meat. Discard the bones and dice the meat, return to the stock which has been thickened with flour. If the animals are inclined to be tough, 1 tablespoon of vinegar may be added to the cooking water.

Gopher Fricasse

Follow the recipe for stewed gopher but omit browning the meat before boiling. When tender, remove from stock, dip in flour and brown. Remove meat to a hot platter. Make a brown gravy with the stock, pour over the meat or serve separately.

TO COOK A RABBIT, 1897

When nicely dressed lay it in a pan and cover with cold water, add ½ cup salt and soak overnight; in the morning drain off water and cover the rabbit inside and out with dry cornmeal, and let it stand till time to cook for dinner; then rinse, cut up and parboil in slightly salted water until tender; take out, roll in cornmeal and fry a nice brown; an onion sliced and laid over it while parboiling is an improvement for those who like the flavor.

Farmer's Pudding, 1880

Heat one quart of milk to boiling, then stir in, slowly, one cup Maizena (corn meal). Mix with this about six good apples, pared and sliced, and add two tablespoons of sugar, one of butter, a little nutmeg and allspice. Pour the whole into a deep dish and bake until done, which will be about forty minutes.

How to Cook a Steak, 1884

Now, if you only knew how to cook a steak to make it good, that would do, but it always makes me sick to see a woman cook a steak. She invariably puts her frying pan on the stove, and puts in a hunk of grease about as big as my fist; and when it is hot enough to begin to crackle, she puts in her beef, and never thinks of covering it. The smoke and steam from it goes to the very ceiling. After she cooks it in this way until it begins to look like an old rubber shoe sole, she calls it done. When you go to eat it there is no more taste to it than a chip. Now, if you want a good steak, have a clear, hot fire, set your clean, empty pan on it, cover it up, then pound your steak, and when you pan is very hot, lay in your steak and cover quickly. As soon as it has cooked enough to let go its hold on the pan, turn over and cover quickly; turn again as at first, and continue to do so about every two minutes until you have turned it about six or eight times. Have a hot, buttered dish ready for it and lay it in; add a sprinkling of

pepper, salt and sugar, and cover tightly. Now, if you wish a gravy, put a bit of butter in your pan. When hot, rub in a pinch of flour, add a small teacup full of boiling water, let it boil a few minutes, then put it in a gravy boat instead of putting it over your beef, to draw out the juice. Now try this plan just once, and you will see that you women know nothing about cooking a good steak.

Homemade Soap, 1880

1 lb. can of potash
5½ lbs. strained grease
½ cups ammonia
½ lb. package borax

Dissolve the potash in 3 pints of cold water and when cold stir in melted grease and then ammonia and, lastly, the borax, stirring constantly. Pour into a pasteboard box.

Baking Powder, 1890

Cream of tartar, 6 oz.; bicarbonate of soda, 2-2/3 oz.; flour, 4½ oz. This is the recipe for one of the best brands made.

SHORT CUTS SAVE TIME ON IRONING AND VARIOUS METHODS FOR HANDLING CLOTHES

If one has the strength to wash and iron the same day the work is done quicker and easier. One can watch the prints and as soon as they are half dry they should be brought in and rolled up until the wash is finished. Then if the irons are hot the lines can be watched and as each article gets to the proper degree of dryness, it can be ironed at once and hung up to finish drying on the clothes rack or house line.

This saves two handlings of the clothes, the sprinkling and rolling, and the unrolling and shaking, belonging to the overnight method.

Most women, however, find themselves too tired at the end of the washing to attempt the ironing the same day, and are compelled to put the last operation off, even though a third of the labor could be saved by doing it at once. For them the following suggestions will be of value:

SPRINKLING METHOD

Here is a shortcut in sprinkling. Have a boiler on a box in the yard if it is fair weather, or in the house during the winter, and also a dish of water. As the dry clothes are taken from the line in small armfuls, place each article in the boiler separately and sprinkle as required. Place the tans in first, then the darker clothes, the prints, and finally the whites. The clothes will not dry out partially if the lid is placed on the boiler when all the clothes are in, and the method does away with the necessity for rolling each piece and saves a lot of handling. At the same time one should have available a clothes basket for the reception of all those things that are not to be ironed.

Underwear can be folded, as can also towels and pillow cases, and if desired these can be given a quick ironing without sprinkling. Such articles in every day use do very well if ironed on the top-folded side only, and then placed on the top-folded side only, and then placed on the top shelf of the stove to complete the drying.

A line behind the stove is handy to put the stockings on; so often the heavy woollen ones are not quite dry.

PAD IS NEEDED

The best and quickest work is done on a large, steady table, and this should be padded. The pad should be at least half an inch thick with an old sheet or blanket folded. There should be at least four thicknesses of these, as less than this number will slow down the ironing process. If this pad is left folded and put away on a shelf, it takes but a moment to get the ironing table ready.

In ironing children's garments do the sleeves first. Iron the front and then double it back from the elbow and iron the other side of the cuff. The top of the sleeve back is done when the back of the dress is done. The collar follows the sleeve, then turn the dress over and iron the back as flat as possible. Whichever side has the neck opening is done next. The iron is slipped inside the garment to iron the side opposite the neck opening. The two halves of the opening are then done, and a good finish is the result.

In ironing a dress work from the shoulders down to the waist following with the wrong side of the hem on the other side of the dress-slip the iron in without lifting the garment. Then place the front side of the skirt on this and finish this part. By using this method for both front and back the inside and out can be finished, also the hem and the plaits, with no extra placing or arranging on the table. The garment has but five placings on the table, the fronts of each sleeve, the collar, the back of the dress and then the front. Often the entire dress can be ironed in about three minutes by this method.

With blouses, if the left hand is used to gently stretch the goods away from the iron as one works, the task is accomplished much quicker. Full skirts and frills are quickest done away from one, that is, with the top of the frill next to the ironer and the iron pushed away.

Tucks and hems are best ironed on the wrong side first, then on the right. Cuffs should be ironed inside and then outside.

Pillow cases are best handled by placing the back of the hem on the table first, iron to edge of table, fold bottom of the pillow case up to the hem, iron again, fold again and iron, and then for the first time, turn over. Two minutes are all that are required for this.

Iron the collars of men's shirts first, then the fronts of the sleeves and the reverse side of the cuffs. Now lay the garment flat and pull into shape, then slip the iron inside and do the inside of the yoke and a part of the back. Next comes the front opening, pockets and front of shirt. To iron the front of the shirt, turn up the tails over the front and first the wrong side of the front one and on top of this the right side of the back one. This results in the complete ironing of the shirt in one position in front of the ironer all the time.

Hang each garment as ironed on a line as high up as possible in order to catch the heat of the room. They should be hung singly.

Tablecloths should be folded in four and turned and folded until all sides are ironed. Handkerchiefs can be done a dozen at a time. Place them, one on top of another, full size, and with a hot iron commence with the top one. When it is finished you will find the one beneath only needs the hem done and folding. Fold with the left hand while ironing with the right. It is best to have two piles, one for men's handkerchiefs and one for smaller ones.

Sheets can be pressed by simply putting them under the ironing sheet.

For the best results the hottest of irons should be used. A steady coal fire and at least six irons will save time and give much better results.

Plan for an ice supply if possible. Ice houses cost little to construct and they may be filled when there is nothing else to do. A supply of ice will mean money in the pocket if you have dairy cows and will be appreciated by the family next summer.

MENU SHOULD INCLUDE RAW FRUIT AND VEGETABLES

Prunes, raisins and dates should be included now and then in the menu — so should nuts of all kinds.

Raw cabbage is one of the best of winter foods. Used in salads with chopped apples and nuts the family will relish it.

Carrots and onions can be grated and added raw to salads, celery, lettuce and radishes added as often as one can get them.

Cooked fruits should appear twice a day in jams, sauces and preserves. The old-fashioned baked apple and unsweetened applesauce are splendid standbys.

Use all the vegetables the family will eat, if possible cooked without water.

The busy housewife will soon get in the way of checking things up — Has everyone had raw fruit? Have they had a raw vegetable? If we cannot get a raw vegetable each, make it two raw fruits and two cooked vegetables. Then she can plan for cooked fruits, puddings, pies, preserves, canned fruits and applesauce; she will always use up plenty of milk, a quart for each child and more in cooking.

She should not stint on eggs, butter or cream once a day, and she should add fish twice a week — fresh, frozen, canned or salted; a chicken now and then and as much variety in her meals as her locality offers.

Then to all this she should add tomatoes three times a week in some form or other, stewed or in soup or in beans or on toast, as tomatoes are said to be a neutralizer for certain things. Especially in Spring should one have tomatoes.

Home-made pickles, catsups and relishes are needed with the meat and potato diet of outdoor workers. Such things should contain only weakened vinegar and diluted spices. A little is enough. Settle these few things in your mind and then feed them to the family along with the same old things they like and always want: meat, potatoes, pies and cakes.

Glossary

GLOSSARY OF PIONEER TERMS AND EXPRESSIONS — compiled by Harold Biswanger and David Jenkins

Pioneer words, tools and equipment used on farms and ranches, many in slang form but will soon be lost to modern day language.

A, B, and C batteries — batteries used on early battery-operated radios.

achitt — a large platter used to put meat on.

adz — was used to trim logs to square timbers.

Aladdin lamp — a kerosene lamp with tall glass chimney. It had a mantle with a clear white light.

almanac — calendar or table showing the days, weeks and months.

am scray — beat it or get lost.

anti I over — children's game played with a ball being thrown over a building or hedge.

anvil — used to straighten, bend or cut iron on, in a blacksmith shop.

apple barrel — wooden barrel for storing apples.

apple peeler — mechanical device with hand crank used to peel and core apples.

artesian well — a well that flows like a spring.

ass over biscuit barrel — term used for clumsiness.

awl — tool used to make a hole in leather used by shoemakers and harness makers

babiche — rawhide, not smoked but merely dried and cut into strips.

backfire — a fire set in the path of an oncoming fire, an internal combustion engine misfiring.

backhouse — out door privy or toilet where discarded catalogues were used.

bald-faced — a horse having white on its face, sometimes over one or both eyes.

bald-headed — a horse with a white face in front between the eyes.

ball and musket — early style gun, loaded with ball and powder, a ram rod was used to pack the powder before the ball was inserted, fired with a flint-lock.

balky — word pertaining to a horse refusing to go ahead.

Banana Belt — southern Alberta where the Chinooks blow.

bannock — oatmeal, flour and water made into a flat bread and cooked on a pan, grill or top of stove.

barber pole — a candy spiral striped pole denoting a barber shop.

barn dance — a dance held to christen a new barn, usually held in the loft.

barn-raising — a number of neighbors getting together to build a barn for a neighbor.

bay — light reddish colored horse with black mane and tail.

beau — a girl's boyfriend.

bed-warmer — long-handled pan, with a lid, which you put live coals in, then moved over the bed to warm it.

bee — neighbors getting together to do some kind of work.

beef ring — farmers take turns butchering a beef and sharing it with each other.

Bennett buggy — old car made into a buggy or wagon and pulled with horses, used during the 30's.

bevel shoe — hoof-correction shoe.

bill — a fifteen-inch piece of metal two inches wide sharpened on one edge with a handle on one end, used to cut brush or fire wood.

bite the dust — a horseman thrown from a horse and hitting the dirt or dust.

blacksnake — long, thin whip used by cowboys to herd cattle.

black strap molasses — thick, black molasses.

blacksmith weld — a powder put on white-hot metal and hammered to make it bond. Powder comprised of steel filings and soda.

blacksmith apron — leather apron used by blacksmiths to stop wear on clothing.

blaze — white strip on face of a horse, or to mark a trail through bush.

blinker — part of a horses bridle so he could only see straight ahead.

block house — military strong hold above ground used to shoot from.

bloomers — woman's loose trousers gathered in at the knee, undergarment.

boot jack — metal or wood frame to assist in taking off riding boots.

bowler — a hard, round top hat usually black, small brim, referred to as a derby.

Box Social — a dance, and partners are decided by auctioning off box lunches.

breachy — an animal that is hard to keep confined in pasture.

breeches — loose pants worn by boys, laced at the shin and the stockings were pulled over, made of corduroy.

breast drill — hand drill with a pad on top to fit the breast to push on.

broad axe — a wide-faced one-edged axe.

bronc — an unbroken or wild horse.

bronco buster — a person who breaks a horse to the saddle or harness.

brush axe — axe used to cut brush, with hook on end.

broom tail — scrubby, wild mountain horse.

buck — name for a male Indian, or one dollar bill.

buck board — a light four wheeled buggy that had slats for springs.

buck saw — bow-back saw or a hard wood, vertical ends with a turn buckle tightener at top.

buck skin — a light yellow horse with darker mane and tail.

buck sweep — hay sweep pushed by horses to bring in the hay to the stacker.

buck wheat farmer — a farmer not properly working his land, or a lazy farmer.

buffalo chips — dried buffalo or cattle dung used for fuel.

buffalo wallow — a depression in the land where the buffalo used to wallow in.

bug bag — a sleeping bag.

buggy blanket — a light rug used to protect the knees and legs from the cold or dust.

bulk cheese container and cutter — a large round glass case with a cutting knife used to cut whole cheese in the grocery stores.

Bull Durham — fine-cut tobacco in a small bag with a draw string on it.

bull trails — early trails used by oxen teams in the pioneer days.

bull trains — freight wagons pulled by oxen.

bull wheel — large wheel on binders with lugs on it. It was used to power the binder.

bun fight — a game played by children using horse manure.

bundle carrier — a place where the sheaves were placed and later dumped into piles to make a stook.

buzz box — coil box used for ignition on model T Fords. It used to buzz when switched on.

bustle — a frame fastened to a woman's waist to make a dress stick out farther at the back.

button hook — long piece of heavy wire with a hook on the end, used to button up high button shoes for women.

button boots — women's boots that came above the ankle and buttoned with a button hook.

cackle berries — hen's eggs.

carpet beater — heavy wire, shaped in a long hoop one inside the other about 3 feet long and 1 foot wide, fastened to a handle, carpet was hung over a clothes line then beat with the beater to get the dust out of it.

cayuse — an Indian pony.

cellar — a hole dug out under a house.

celluloid collar — hard, stiff material, like plastic, shaped like a collar and buttoned to the top of the shirt for a man's collar.

Chautauqua — a touring variety show usually held in a large tent.

chaps — leather or sheep skin leggings used to protect cowboys legs in bush country.

chemise — an undergarment worn by women.

chimley — slang for chimney.

chinking — filling in the space between the logs on a log cabin.

chivaree — surprise party given to newly weds.

cistern — under ground container for storing water.

cloud 9 — living in a dream world.

club coupe — 2 door car with small seats that folded out of the side, used by salesmen to carry samples.

coal oil — kerosene used for lamps and heaters.

coal scuttle — pail with square wide spout to put coal into heater or stove.

commode — a piece of furniture that held a wash basin, water pitcher and chamber.

corduroy road — logs laid across on the road in swampy areas to hold up the traffic.

corn binder — slang word for International trucks.

coulee — a deep valley cutting back into a hill or mountain.

coupe — 2 door car without a back seat.

cow bell — a square bell around a cows neck so you could find them in the bush.

cow catcher — sloping V-shaped frame in front of a train engine, used to push buffalo or cattle off the track.

cow waddies — cow punchers or cowboys.

C.P.R. strawberries — prunes used for dessert on railway gang cook cars.

cradle scythe — scythe with a cradle or frame on backside to hold grain in bunches so it could be tied in sheaves.

crank phone — a telephone that had to be cranked to call the operator, or crank a combination of rings to call a neighbor.

cream separator — machine used to separate cream from the milk by centrifugal force.

cream skimmer — long handled, very shallow ladle for skimming cream off the milk.

creamer — tall narrow pail with glass window at bottom and a tap at the bottom, used to separate milk from cream by settling.

creepins-up — all the time you have lived.

crupper — part of a harness that goes under the tail of a horse.

crystal set — early type of radio using a crystal and ear phones.

cuff behind the ear — something that should be done to children more often these days.

curling tongs — used to curl women's hair and heated by kerosene lamp.

cut nail — tapered square nail.

cutter — a one-horse sleigh.

cupola — small wooden or metal frame on barn roof with a ventilator in it to vent the barn, sometimes with weathervane on top.

dashboard — short wall in front of driver on a buggy to keep mud and rocks off the driver or passenger.

dead furrow — when plowing in lands you start in the middle of the field and work both ways.

dead man — an anchor buried in the ground to take a pull on.

dead weight — the heavy weight of anything inert.

Delco Plant — used to generate electric power on farms where there was no hydro.

democrat — four-wheeled buggy pulled by two horses.

De Winton round steak — baloney. (bologna)

dime store — beer parlor or pub.

dinner bell — bell used to call workers in at meal time.

dinner horn — cow's horn with both ends out, blow into small end to make sound.

Dirty Thirties — term used during the 1930's because of the hardships and the dust storms.

Divide — water shed where rivers run east or west in the mountains.

dogies — cows or cattle usually smaller ones.

donkey engine — stationary engine.

double-tree — part of a wagon fastened to the tongue to keep the work load even for the horses.

dove tail — a method of cutting the ends of logs to build log buildings to make them fit tight together, also used in making furniture drawers.

drawers — long leg underwear.

dray — wagon used to carry freight in towns in the early days.

dry rot — decay of seasoned wood causing it to crumble to a dry powder.

dug well — wells that were dug by hand and then cribbed with wood or a metal culvert.

dumb waiter — a shelf on a pulley that lowered to the cellar or basement to keep the food cold.

dust bowl — area of the prairies where the dust blew badly during the 30's.

dust devil — a small whirling column of dust, funnel-shaped, often seen in the fields during dry weather.

dust kitty — dust in a fluffy form, gathers under beds and furniture.

end gate — removable end of a wagon or truck box.

evener — made of metal or wood and fastened to the tongue to keep the wagon load even for the horses.

Factor — man in charge of an early trading post.

fag — a cigarette.

fan tail — a slang word for horse or a breed of pigeon.

feet as long as a sleigh track — big feet.

farrier — a man who shoes horses.

file a claim — to file on a homestead or register it, file for a mineral right claim.

Finn — five dollar bill.

fish eyes — old-fashioned tapioca.

flap jacks — pancakes.

flapper — young girl in the late 20's, used make-up, short hair, etc.

flat iron — used to iron clothes and heated on top of the stove, some had permanent handles the others had movable handles to take off the cool ones and put on the hot ones.

flunky — a person doing odd jobs.

fly sticker — a long two inch wide sticky strip of paper which hung from the ceiling to catch flies.

foot rail — brass rail in old saloons.

foot warmer — one-furrow plough, feet sliding and stumbling around on freshly-turned sod made the feet warm walking all day, also hot stones put in early buggys in winter to keep feet warm.

forge — used in a blacksmith shop to heat metal.

four eyes — a person with eye glasses.

fresno — used in road construction for moving dirt and pulled by four horses.

funny money — money used during the 30's by the Social Credit Government.

galoshes — high over shoes with water proof canvas on the top with buckles in front.

gang plow — a plow with two mouldboards and pulled with horses.

gee and haw — terms applied to horses for turning right or left.

goose grease — grease rendered from a goose used for medical purposes and softening leather.

gramophone — early type of record player. It was wound up by a hand crank.

grass belly — animal fed on grass giving it a large stomach.

green broke — a horse that was partly broke.

green horn — a newcomer to the west who did not know the ways of the west.

grindstone — a large flat round piece of sandstone set in a frame to sharpen axes, scythes, mower knives etc, operated by foot pedals and later by a small pump engine.

grist — grain to be ground for feed.

grist mill — a place where you took grain to be ground for feed.

grub hoe — single cross blade for hoeing ground or for digging small hole to plant trees.

grubstake — enough food to take for a special time or project.

gunny sack — a burlap sack made from jute and used to hold grain, potatoes, etc.

hames — made of hardwood or metal, some with brass knobs on top, fastened around a horse collar which the tugs were fastened to, in order to pull a load.

hand car — small four-wheeled platform pumped by hand to run on railway tracks used by railway workers.

hand shoes — mitts.

hat pin — long metal pin about 8 inches long often with an ornament on the end, it was pushed through the hat into the hair to hold a woman's hat on.

hay burner — a horse.

hay knife — long blade with large notches sharpened with two handles at right angles to each other, used to cut hay in loose hay stacks.

hay seed — a farmer.

hay sling — rope and hardwood slats which hay was stacked on and then pulled up into the loft of a barn by horses.

head land — grass strip around crop land for the tractor to go on for the first round around the field so no crop would be tramped down.

header or barge — box-like frame attached to binder for holding heads of short crops of grain.

helping Henry — a frame with two idlers and a drive pulley put under early cars back wheels to drive buzz saw to cut wood.

hen fruit — chicken eggs.

hick — slang for a backwoods country boy.

high tail it — means to go in a hurry somewhere.

his nibs — referring to the husband or man of the house.

hit the hay — go to bed.

hit the sack — go to bed.

hitch — a horse hook up.

hitch in his gid along — lame leg.

hobbles — tying the front legs of a horse together leaving enough slack so the horse could move about to graze but having it tight enough so it could not run away.

hog scalding — when preparing a hog for butchering you scald it to make the hair come off easily.

hogsback — sharp ridge on top of long hills.

Home Comfort stove — early heavily-made stove which was square in shape and could take very rough handling without hurting it.

homestead — a 160 acres of land given to a settler to break and build a house on in a specified amount of time.

homesteader — one who occupied a homestead.

horse buns — horse manure.

horse collars — a padded collar around a horse's neck which took the pull of the harness when pulling a load.

ice box — ancestor to the fridge. Ice was placed in the box in the top and cool air was circulated down through the rest of the box.

ice house — an insulated building where ice was stored in saw dust.

ice saw — a saw used to cut ice out of lakes and rivers.

ice tongs — large metal tongs to carry large blocks of ice.

Indian giver — a person who gives a gift then takes it back.

Indian list — to interdict; an administrative order prohibiting certain people from consuming alcohol in public.

ink well — small ink bottle placed in top of school desks for students to write with.

Irish grapes — potatoes.

isinglass — mineral that divides into thin transparent layers, used to make side curtains in early buggies, also windows in early stoves and heaters.

Jack of all trades — one who is handy at most all trades.

jack pot — a scrape, fix or corner which you have gotten yourself into.

jag of hay — a loose load of hay on a hay rack.

jalopy — an old automobile in poor condition.

jerk necking — leading a team behind a wagon to save an extra driver.

jerky — strips of dried meat.

jerry built — a building poorly put together, often shoddy.

Jim Dandy — a small hand-operated rope maker.

juice the cows — to milk the cows.

kalsomine — a cheap water-type paint used often in early pioneer homes.

kicking chains or kickers — put on milk cows to stop them from kicking you when you milk her.

kick the bucket — term used when you die.

kine — cattle.

kindling — small pieces of wood used to start a fire.

klinker — a hard material left after burning dirty coal.

knickerbockers — short loose-fitting trousers gathered in around just below the knees.

knuckle buster — crescent wrench.

lantern — a glass-enclosed kerosene burning lamp with a long loop handle for hanging it out doors.

lariat — a rope with a honda or running loop at one end used by cowboys to catch animals.

lean-to — addition to a building with slanted roof; or a single building with half-gable roof.

lick — a natural salt or mineral lick used by wild animals.

linch pin — used to prevent wheel from coming off, cotter pin or key.

livery barn — a place to put up horses in towns.

loft — place to store hay in top half of a barn under the roof.

lye soap — early forms of home-made soap.

magic lantern — an early type of slide projector.

Manitoba back breaker — ½ bushel scoop for scooping grain instead of shovelling, with handle at back and large loop handle on top.

marcelled — curling women's hair into waves with a hot curling iron.

martingale — horse harness restraint across the chest.

Massey Harris — cheap loud ticking pocket watch, or early farm machinery.

Mater — mother.

maverick — a stray or unbranded animal.

Mexican drag line — hand shovel.

mill stone — used for grinding flour, powered by water wheel or large wind mill.

monkey wrench — a square end wrench with adjustment on the handle.

muley cow — a cow born without horns.

moon shine — illegal whiskey made in home stills.

mother — vinegar starter.

muff — hand warmer.

muffler — wrap or scarf worn around the neck.

mule skinner — a person who drives mule teams.

mulligan stew — a stew of vegetables and meat, often used during hard times.

Murphies — Irish name for potatoes.

muskeg — a swampy stretch of peat moss often sparsely treed with stunted spruce.

musket — hand fire arm carried by soldiers.

mustache cup — cup with part of top covered to keep mustache out of the cup.

muzzle loading — loading fire arms by putting gun powder in through open front end and ramming it down.

navy bean — for making home made pork and beans.

never slip — a wrench for putting in corks in horse shoes.

nib — used on straight pens to dip in ink to write with.

nigger-head — hard round top rocks just below the surface of field that implements get caught on; or a mound of soil and grass surrounded by bog or muskeg.

Nitchee — slang name for an Indian.

nose bag — to put oats in and tied over horse's head to feed it when away from home.

nose net or basket — to protect horse's nose from flies, made from screen or sacking.

nincompoop — silly fool, or simpleton, a brainless person.

oil cloth — a table covering made of specially prepared cloth coated with oil paint, sometimes with a pattern printed on it.

old codger — an old person.

open range — unfenced grass land.

ornery — term applied to an animal or one that has a stubborn disposition.

out to pasture — a saying applied to the retired farmer or rancher.

Palliser Triangle — a triangular area with a base along the U.S. border; northern point at Saskatoon, angling southeast to the Qu'apple Valley, and southwest from Saskatoon to Pincher Creek. Explored in 1857 by Captain John Palliser and he recorded that sustained agriculture would be a precarious industry. This area contains approximately 800,000 acres.

pantaloons — trousers.

pantry — a small room just off the kitchen where food and dishes were kept.

papoose — native word for North American Indian child.

parlor — sitting room used only for company.

paste irons — branding irons with small grove in them where you put an acid in to make the brand on the animal.

Pater — father.

pemmican — cake of pounded venison or other meat smoked, mixed with fat, first used by American Indians.

petticoat — a woman's undergarment.

picket — to tether a horse or cow on a long chain or rope and allow it to graze without wandering too far.

pip — slang for any mild human ailment.

plate rail — a moulded board fastened to the wall about six feet above the floor to set fancy plates on it on their edge.

player piano — played mechanically by pumping air through holes in special paper rolls using foot pedals.

plus fours — loose knickerbockers reaching well below the knees, worn by golfers.

pocket door — doors that slid between the wall between two rooms.

poke — a frame around a cow's neck to keep her inside a fence, or a cowboys or miners money or gold in a small sack.

Pom Pom Pull Away — childrens game.

Pony Express — a pony relay system for carrying mail across the country in the 1800's.

post and beam construction — square timbers to frame a barn and sheeted vertically, mostly used in the east.

post drill — hand-operated drill mounted on a post used in a blacksmith shop.

post vice — vice fastened to a bench with a leg that

went to the floor so you could hammer on it and it was solid.

pot-bellied heater — a Waterbury heater with a round fire box.

pot hole — a depression left in the land after a prairie fire; a hole in the road.

powder horn — a flask, cow horn, used to carry gun powder in for old muzzle-loading guns.

prairie fires — fires that spread across the open grassland.

prairie wool — a type of wild native grass which was cut every second year, very rich hay.

pre-emption — land adjoining a homestead for sale to the homesteader.

prohibition — a period of time during the 20's when no alcoholic beverages could be sold.

proving up — fulfilling the requirements to obtain a homestead.

pulling mane or tail — to shorten a tail or mane without cutting it.

punk — rotten trees and lumber.

push binder — like a regular binder but the tongue was out the back and the horses pushed it.

putees — bandage-like wrapped around the top of the boot and lower leg; used by army during W. W. I.

quack — a person who pretends to have medical knowledge and cures.

Quebec heater — early 1900 heater used in parlors.

quill — the hollow stem of larger tail feathers of birds used for pens, usually from goose quills.

quilting bee — a number of women getting together to sew thick material or wadding together between two layers of material to make a quilt.

rack — antlers on a deer, elk, moose etc.

radiant heater — gas mantel heater usually set into a false fireplace.

rag bag — large bag which had old clothing in, or pieces of cloth in to repair other clothing.

rail auger — a large hand-twist auger to bore holes in poles to make rail gates.

ram — a machine for raising water by the energy of the water itself combined with the pressure of air caused by the movement.

ramrod — a metal rod used to ram home the charge and shot of a muzzle-loading gun; a man in charge of a crew of men and called a foreman.

range — unfenced grassland or the kitchen stove with a large oven and a water reservoir and a warming oven at the top.

rasher — a serving of bacon.

ration — food and gas allowances covered by coupons during World War II.

razor strap — a long two-inch wide leatherstrip hanging on a hook by a washstand or sink used to sharpen a straight razor on. Also used to spank children's bottoms.

red flannels — underwear made in one piece, made of red flannelette or wool.

Red Light — children's game.

remuda — extra collection of horses kept in a roped-in area on a roundup.

reservoir — water container at right end of coal stove to heat water in.

remittance man — men of wealthy families usually from England who were not much good (black sheep) sent out here and paid an allowance to stay here; some made good.

riding drag — to ride at the rear of a herd of cattle.

roadster — a two door coupe with a rumble seat.

root house — a place to store vegetables underground.

round up — gathering up horses or cattle.

rubbering — to listen in on someone else's telephone conversation on a party line.

rum runner — person who attempts to smuggle prohibited liquor into a country, or a vessel being used for the same.

rumble seat — open seat in the rear of the car on coupes where the trunk is now.

Run Sheep Run — children's game.

running board — step on the out side of an early car to help you get in and out because the cars were higher then.

running gear — the wheels and tongue under a wagon attached together with a reach.

runt — small pig or other animal of a litter.

rut — depression left in the surface of the ground by continuous traffic in the same track; a person doing the same thing over and over.

sacked — to be dismissed or fired.

sad iron — heavy boat-shaped, flat-bottomed iron heated on stove to iron clothes.

sand point — to drive in the sand in a well to get water from the well with screen to stop the sand from entering the cylinder.

saw bones — a surgeon or doctor.

saw buck — ten dollars.

Scotchman's glue — oatmeal porridge.

script — a type of currency issued by the Social Credit Gov't in Alberta in the mid-thirties.

scub board — corrugated glass or metal, set in wood frame to rub wet clothes over to get them clean.

scuffler — horse-drawn garden cultivator.

scythe — a long metal blade with long, curved handle to cut grain or weeds.

self commencer — hand crank to start an engine.

separator — machine used to separate the cream from the milk; large machine used to separate the grain from the straw.

setting hens — hens used to sit on eggs to hatch them.

shafted — someone put something over on you, or gypped you.

shafts — two poles fastened to a buggy to which a horse is harnessed between to pull the buggy.

shaganappi — thongs made of rawhide.

shay — one-horse carriage.

sheaf — a bundle of hay or grain tied together in the middle with the butts at the bottom.

shin plaster — twenty-five cents in paper money.

shindig — a community dance.

shingled — a method of cutting women's hair in layers.

shingles — soda crackers.

shod — to shoe a horse with iron shoes.

shoe horn — ivory or metal device with hollowed blade used for easing your heel into the shoe.

shoe last — metal frame to repair shoes on.

shoe tree — adjustable frame to go into a shoe to keep it in shape or stop it from shrinking.

shocks — eight or ten sheaves of grain stacked together with butts to the ground.

sickle — short-curved metal blade with short handle to cut grain or weeds.

side board — dining room furniture that held your good china and silver ware.

single tree — cross bar made of wood or iron to which one horse was hitched to pull a wagon or buggy.

sink pump — water pump mounted on counter by sink with shallow well under house or a cistern in basement.

skinner — a person who drove many horses or mules hitched to a wagon.

Sky Pilot — a minister or priest or one who preached the gospel.

skunk juice or gas — gas purchased from early Turner Valley gas wells; had terrible smell.

slicks — an animal with no brand.

slicker — long oil-skin rain coat worn by cowboys.

slip — horse-drawn machine to move dirt.

slop the hogs — feeding the hogs the left overs from the kitchen.

slop pail — pail used to hold table scraps usually kept under the kitchen sink.

slough — a large depression in the land that holds water.

smudge pot — smouldering fire in a container to drive away frost or mosquitoes.

snubbing post — a post in the middle of a corral which a horse was tied to.

soap hole — low-lying area which caught water and held it and made the land sour.

sod buster — a farmer who broke the prairie sod with a plow.

sod house — a house or dwelling that was made of blocks of sod for early pioneers.

soup's on — expression used for calling you to dinner.

sour dough — fermented dough used to make bread, usually kept some dough back to start next batch of bread.

sparking — courting your lover.

spats — cloth gaiter covering ankle and top of shoe, used for dress.

spectacles — eyeglasses.

spittoon — the round metal or enamelled receptacle in a hotel lobby, at which tobacco chewers aimed.

squeaker — baby turkeys or coming close to an accident.

stays — corset worn by women.

steel lugs — metal lugs attached to a smooth wheel used on early tractors or other machines that were ground driven.

stereoscope — optical instrument for showing a single object in two views taken in slightly different angles.

stitching horse — a vice like device that you sat on to hold leather for sewing or cutting leather, controlled with a foot lever.

stile — steps or slats to climb over a fence.

stone boat — two short skids with planks nailed on top used to haul stones or pulled with horses.

stook — eight or ten sheaves of grain with butts on the

ground leaning into each other at the top, put like this to dry for threshing.

straight pen — a pen holder with a removable nib used with ink to write with.

straight razor — high grade steel honed to a fine edge and folded into a handle used to shave the face with.

straw boss — second foreman, an assistant on a farm or ranch.

street paving blocks — blocks of wood about eight inches long and four inches wide and four inches thick soaked in tar and laid out on streets to walk or drive on.

stubble jumper — a farmer.

sty — a place where pigs were raised.

sulky — a light two-wheeled carriage to carry one person.

sulky plow — a one-bottom plow mounted on three wheels and pulled by three horses.

sweat box — a long tub about 6 feet long 3 feet wide wooden sides, one foot high made of wood, metal bottom to make concrete in with shovels.

Swede saw — one and two-handled, was used to cut cut trees or logs, has course cutting teeth.

talking iron — a hand gun.

tea caddy — a metal container to keep or store tea.

tea cosy — a cloth cover for a teapot to help hold in the heat.

tender foot — someone new to the west.

three finger glove — used for hunters and army men so you could use the trigger finger to fire a gun.

thunder pot — chamber pot.

tin lizzy — slang for Model T Ford.

tin ticker — cheap watch.

tongs — large pliers like tool with long handles used in blacksmithing to hold hot metal.

tongue — a pole fastened to a wagon with a horse on either side and fastened to the horses.

tongue and groove — boards with a tongue on one edge and a groove on the other edge to make a tight wall or floor.

travois — two poles fastened together at one end to form a frame and tied part way down with two cross poles, top end was fastened over a horse's back and he dragged it along.

trip hammer — used in a blacksmith shop to shape heated metal and plow shares.

trip the light fantastic — to dance.

tug chain — chain fastened to harness tug to adjust length on a single tree.

twister — a large twister type whirl wind.

veranda — a porch on a house with roof.

varmint — rascal, mischievious boy, or objectionable animal.

vamoose — an expression meaning to go away or get lost.

vent — to cancel a brand on an animal by burning a bar through it or repeating the same brand over or under the first brand.

waddies — a cowboy.

wagoner — driver of a wagon, man in charge of a team.

wagonette — four-wheeled open carriage with two seats facing each other behind the coachman's seat.

wagon bunk — cross beam which wagon box sat on so the wheels could turn either way.

wagon tongue spring — to hold up weight of wagon tongue.

walking on a cloud — a person in dream land, or in love.

walking plow — a plow pulled by one or two horses and the driver walked behind.

wall flower — a girl who sat out the dances.

wallop — a short blow.

wannigans — felt boots for winter wear.

water glass — a solution in which eggs were preserved.

water jacket — method of heating water in coal stove or oil stove to circulate to the water tank and taps.

water wheel — a large wheel with cups fastened to it; water drops in cups and the weight turns the wheel.

wattle — a method of identifying cattle by cutting a piece of skin on the neck and letting it hang down.

weathervane — wind direction device on a barn roof.

whipper snapper — a small agile youth.

whipple trees — a cross bar on back of wagon tongue to fasten single trees to harness horses to.

white wash — solution of lime and water to disinfect and whiten inside of buildings.

whoa — word used to stop a horse.

whoop and a holler — a short distance away.

wind charger — a wind powered generator to produce electricity.

wind mill — large fan on top of a tower which the wind turned to pump water.

windy — slang for window; or talking a lot or bragging.

Winnipeg couch — a bed by night and couch by day got its name from ordering it from the Winnipeg catalogue.

witching — searching for underground water streams, usually by the use of forked willow branch.

wood splitter — a flywheel with an axe head welded to it and turned with a belt and pulley from an engine.

wooden pump rods — pump rods made of wood with metal ends to fasten together to lift water in a well.

wooden well pipe — pipe for water well made of hollowed out wood.

wrangler — a person who tends to horses used at a round-up.

yoke — a frame that fitted over an oxen's neck to fasten harness to, or over a person's neck to carry two pails of water, a piece of hard wood with metal ends and a ring to fasten two horses together and a center ring to put tongue in to pull a wagon, or hold back wagon on a hill.

33 x 3½ — early Model T tire size.

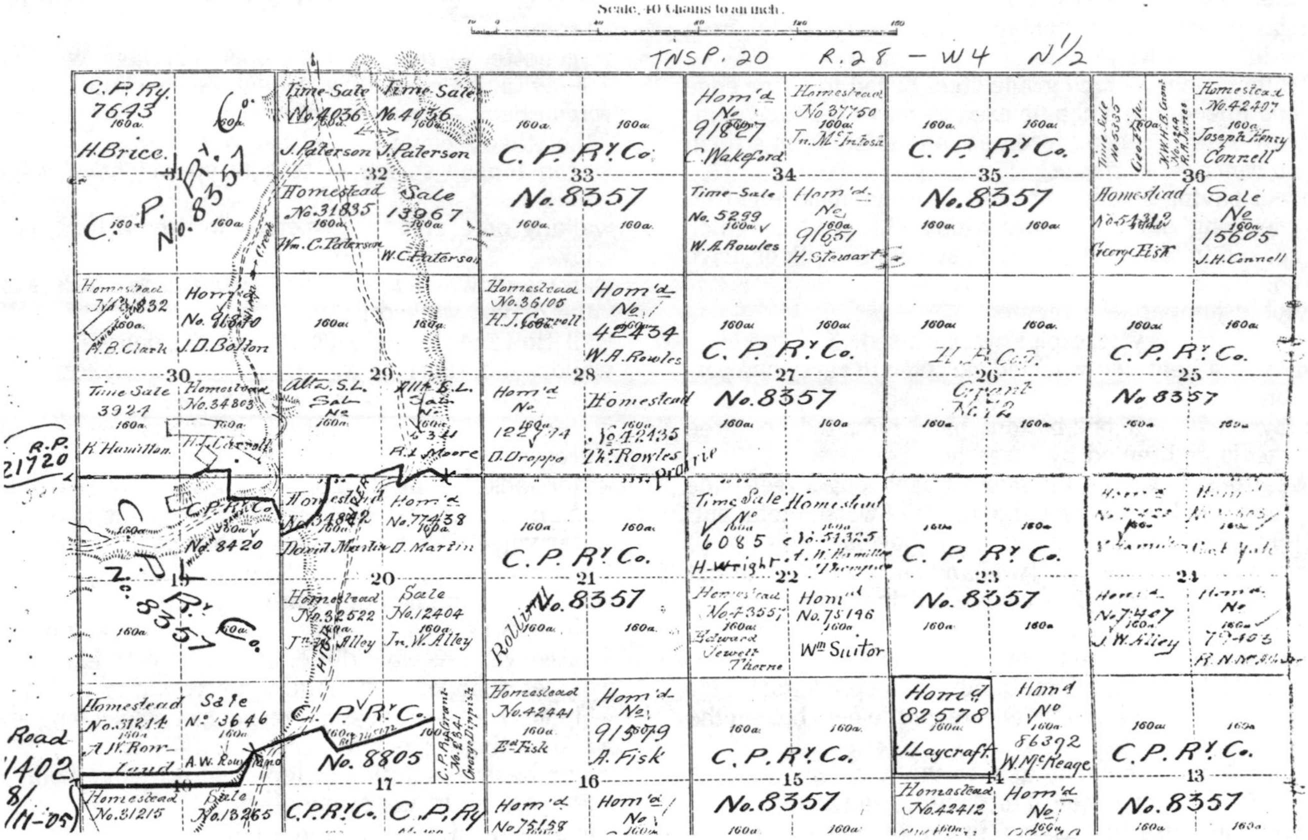

OLD MAPS

Scale, 40 Chains to an inch.

TNSP. 20   R.28 — W4   N½

C.P.Ry. 7643 160a. H.Brice.	Time-Sale No.4036 160a. J.Paterson	Time-Sale No.4036 J.Paterson	C.P.Ry.Co. No.8357 160a.	Hom'd No.91827 160a. C.Wakeford	Homestead No.37750 160a. Tn.McIntosh
C.P.Ry. No.8357 160a.	Homestead No.31835 160a. Wm.C.Paterson	Sale 13967 W.C.Paterson		Time-Sale No.5299 160a. W.A.Rowles	Hom'd No.91651 H.Stewart

(Township grid map, sections numbered 13–36, various homestead, time-sale, and C.P.Ry.Co. No.8357 / No.8805 designations)

TOWNSHIP 22   R.29   W. 4TH

(Second township map with river/creek features, sections including No.107, No.11161, No.8212, Homestead entries)

DEPARTMENT OF THE INTERIOR
TOPOGRAPHICAL SURVEYS BRANCH
Ottawa, 16th June 1891
Approved and confirmed
E.Deville

EXPLANATION OF COLORS:
Woods... Green   Scrub... red green   Water... blue

Compiled from surveys by
R.C.McPhillips ...... D.L.S. 1883
T.F.Hewson 1883
T.B.Greene 1887
C.F.Miles 1887

Contents
Land in S......
Roads ......
Water ......
Total Area ......

574

ALBERTA.
Scale, 40 Chains to an inch.
TOWNSHIP 21
R.29 W. 4TH
C.P.R'Co. No. 8810
C.P. R'y Co. No. 8385
C.P.R'y Co. No. 8386
C.P.R'y No 7872
Homestead No. 35350 Jn. Smith
Hom'd No. 68818 E.J. Wheler
Homestead No. 34319 H.B. Ingram
Homestead No. 34098 W.O. Ingram
Hom'd No. 86426 D. McIntosh
Homestead No. 35319 J.A. Turner
Homestead No. 35348 Bryce Wright
NO. 34106
OLIVER INGRAM
GEORGE DAVIDSON
NO 102843
H.G. Weaver
H.H. McKenzie
Homestead No. 39124 H.P. Griffith
Homestead No. 31408 W.J. Andrews
Can. Pac. Railway
Grant No. 2836.
Peter Turner Baker
N.W. H. B'd Grant No. 1 Thos S.C. Lee
H.B. Co'y Grant No. 81
C.P.R'y Co. No. 8407
Homestead No. 37895 Arthur R. Griffin
Homestead No. 55323 Wm. James Andrews
Lent M. Orton
Homestead No. 38134 J. Currie
Homestead No. 34164 Jas. Grierson
C.P.R'y Co. No. 8385
C.P.R'y Grant No. 2333 Bryce Wright
Homestead No. 45586 Joseph Hogge
Homestead No. 37775 John Meehan
Military Homestead No. 4478 Alex'r S. Blackwood
Homestead No. 41709 Hy. Currie
Time Sale No. 4414 J. Stevenson
Homestead No. 34117 Jas. Alex'r Hogge
Homestead No. 37776 Fk. Percy
Homestead No. 39460 H. Greenfield
Homestead No. 42452 W. Greenfield
Homestead No. 36371 Adelia E. Crockett
Homestead No. 36113 Thomas Banbury
Can. P.R. Grant No. 4346
Military Homestead No. 4582 Jas. E. Kennedy
Homestead No. 34120 Geo. Allingham
C.P.R'y Grant No. 3617 W.F. Worden
Pre-emption Sale No. 1624 Adelia Ellen Crockett
Hom'd No. 67978 D.J. Simpson
Homestead No. 34137 John Greenfield
H.B. Co'y Grant No. 81
C.P.R'y Co. No. 8085
Military Homestead No. 5374 Edwin A. Hayes
Homestead No. 35875 R.J. Shields and R.J. Shields
Homestead No. 34143 R.J. Shields
Homestead No. 36115 J. McDonald
Homestead No. 37279 Donald McDonald
Alta Sch'l Lands Sale Nos 549-550
Hom'd No. 73448
Homestead No. 42460 Israel A. Blair
Homestead No. 34121 Jn. Sissons
Sale No 15606 B.L. Hayes
Homestead No. 40960 Bayard J. Hayes
C.P.R'y Co. No. 8385
Road No. 10445 Field Book No 7297
TOWNSHIP 21 R. 29 W. 4TH
CAL. & ED. RY.

TOWNSHIP 21 R.29 W. 4TH

Compiled from surveys by

R.C. McPhillips, D.L.S.	1883
Thos. Drummond, D.T.S.	1882
Thos. R. Rowson, D.L.S.	1883
C.F. Miles	1889
C.A. Bigger	1886
T.D. Green	1887

DEPARTMENT OF THE INTERIOR

TOPOGRAPHICAL SURVEYS BRANCH

Ottawa, 16th Mar. 1892

Approved and confirmed

E. Deville

Surveyor-General.

Contents

Land in Sects.	19740.30	Acres
Roads	413.23	"
Water		"
Total Area	20153.53	"

EXPLANATION OF COLORS:

Woods: ...... Green. Scrub, or Prairie and Woods: Dotted green. Water .... Blue.

Marshes: Yellow with small strokes of black. Hills or Slopes: ... Etching or Grey Shade.

ALBERTA.
Scale, 40 Chains to an inch.

TNSP. 20
R. 29
W 4
N ½

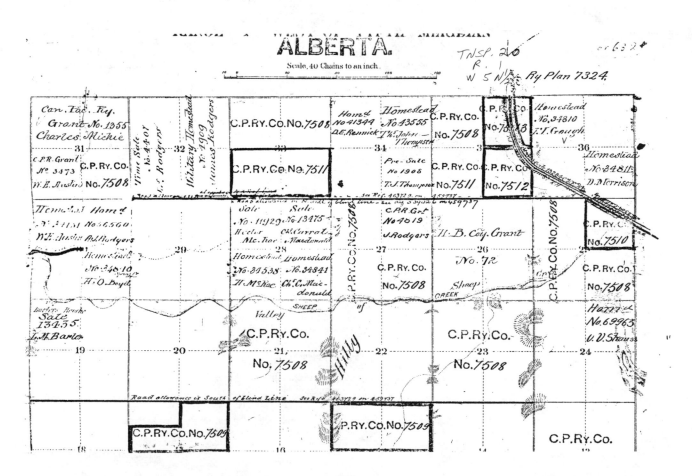

ALBERTA.
Scale, 40 Chains to an inch.

TNSP. 20
R. 1
W 5 N ½ Ry Plan 7324.

Township survey map — Plan No. 654½, Field Book No. 5004, TNSP. 21, R. 28, W 5 - S ½

Top row (Sections 31–36):
- C. P. Ry Co. No. 8558 — 31
- N° 55312 — T. H. Andrews
- N. 86557 — J. McKenzie Andrews — 32
- C. P. R. No. 4407 — T. H. Andrews and Jos. M. Andrews
- N° 5836 — 33
- No. 36875 — W. K. Newbolt
- C. P. Ry Co. No. 8558 — 35
- C. P. Ry Co. No. 8363 — 156.00 a / 149.15 a
- C. P. Ry Co. No. 9402 — 36
- C. P. Ry Co. No. 9402

- Trail 543
- C.P.Ry Co. No. 8362 — Can Pac Ry Grant No. 3028 — Thos. H. Andrews — 31
- Homestead No. 34104 — T. H. Andrews — 32
- Homestead No. 34107 — Jas. McK. Andrews
- C.P.R. Gt No. 4832 — J.M.K. Andrews
- C. P. Ry Co No. 8084 — 33
- Homestead No. 34110 — Alex Stewart / Sale No. 14750 — W. K. Newbolt

River

Second row (Sections 25–30):
- Homestead No. 34.111 — Christina C. Marshall — Time Sale No. 5300 — C.E. Shattuck
- Fib. Sch. L. Sale N° 540 — T. H. Andrews — 29
- Sale N° 539 — Hilda School Lands — J. McK. Andrews
- Homestead No. 34109 — Wm. Stewart — 28 — Homestead No. 34069 — M. Stewart
- C. P. Ry Co. No. 8548 — 27 — Can Pac Ry Grant No. from the Dept. of the Interior O.in C. 655 — C. P. Ry Co. No. 8361
- H. B. Coy Hon. Sec. Grant No. 95 — No. 34114 — Alex Begg — 26
- C.P.R. Grant No. 2157 — 25
- C. P. Ry Co. No. 9402

- Homestead No. 63445 — C. E. Shattuck — Sale No. 13147 — Parker McKenzie
- Alta Sch. Lds Sale N° 538 — T.H. Andrews
- Hom'd No 2 No. 91643 — W. Stewart — Homestead No. 55814 — Morris Stewart — C. P. Ry Co. No. 8362
- C.P. Ry Co. No. 8358 — 26 — J. B. Coy Grant No. 95
- 80.00 a — A. & L. W. Begg

Third row (Sections 19–24):
- C.P.R. Grant No. 4642 — J. Ab. Irving — 19
- Homestead No. 34551 — Jr. Stanffer — 20 — Hom'd No. 11 52979 — D. McBride
- C. P. R. Grant No. 1895 — 21
- Homestead No. 16734 — Land Suitor
- C.P.R. Grant No. 2158 — 23 — A. & L. W. Begg — 159 a
- Mil. Mary Hom'd N° 4550 — E.M. Begg — 24 — Mil. Homestead

- C. P. Ry Co. No. 8558 — Homestead No. 46097 — H. M. Stark — Hom'd No 66638 — A.V. Cuffe — John Thompson
- Homestead No. 46717 — John Suitor — 64.36 a

Fourth row (Sections 13–18):
- Sale No. 12603 — J. H. Vanwart — 18 — Homestead No. 37573 — J. H. Vanwart
- C.P.R Grant No. 1450 — 17 — Samuel S. Rogers
- Time Sale 4135 — 157.28 a — C. M. Thompson — 21.62 a
- C.P.H. Grant — 90.16 a — 30.09 a — 53.69 a — 113.53 a — 16 — Homesteads No. 34864 — Wm. Thompson — William Thorburn
- No. 1971 — 15 — Jas Quirin
- Time Sale No. 4711 — E. M. Begg — 14 — Sale No. 13687 — T. S. Ford
- C. P. Ry Co. No. 8358 — 13

- Military Homestead No. 5041 — John Ccrow Vanwart

Fifth row (Sections 7–12):
- C. P. Ry Co. No. 8805 — 7 — C. P. Ry Co. No. 8358
- Hudson Bay Coy Grant No. 96
- C.P.R. Grant No. 8696 — John Thompson — 8 — HIGH — 55.84 a
- C. P. Ry Co. No. 8358 — 9
- Military Hom'd No. 4551 — B. S. Holcroft — Military Homestead No. 4599 — Edward C. Quenn — 10
- 147.64 a — 11 — 149.28 a
- N.W.H.B. No. 17029 — F. H. Janes — Curtis State Line, Blizzard Lake

Bottom row (Sections 1–6):
- Hom d.1 No. 52113 — H. Brice — Time Sale No. 3666 — J. Brice — 6
- C. P. R. Co. No. 8359 — 158.79 a / 158.25 a — 29.34 a — 93.00 a / 84.30 a / 111.93 a
- Sale No. 13738 — David Thorburn — Hom'd No. 79366 — O. Thorburn — 5
- Homestead No. 34099 — 138.09 a — 14976 a — G. C. Strachan Paterson — Hom'd No. V 77482 — H. H. Wilson
- C. P. Ry Co. No. 8806 — 3
- N.W.H.B. No. 74192 — F. H. Janes — Homestead No. 41705 — Stanley H. Janes — 2 — Hom'd No. 82633 — E. A. Adams — Hom'd No. 79408 — E. O. Adams
- C. P. Ry Co. No. 8358 — 1
- Road 165

- Homestead No. 34.959 — J. Brice — Hom'd No. 55821 — J. Brice

DOM. HIGH LANDS LITHOGRAPHIC OFFICE.

Dominion Lands Office
Ottawa

24th April 1885
Approved and confirmed.
E Deville

This line Surveyed by Thos. Drummond.

Plan No. 654½
Field Book No. 5004

TNSP. 21
R. 28
W 5 - S ½

Contents:
Land in Sections	22567.32	Acres
Roads	432.84	"
Water	712.75	"

TNSP. 22
R. 28
W. 4 N ½

C. P. R.ᵧ Co No. 8366 31	Horn'd Nº 91502 C. Green / Horn'd Nº 91501 H. Green 32 / Hom'd Nº 35096 N. ANDERSON / Time-Sale No.5500 H. Green	C. P. R.ᵧ Co. No.9404 33	Hom'd Nº 108156 G.W. Akin / Hom'd Nº 103774 S. Soli 34 / Hom'd Nº 103557 L.F. Akins O. RAKINS
C.P.R.ᵧ Co. No. 10794 / Hom'd Nº 91574 J. Jinks 30 / Horn'd Nº 86356 J. Ness	C. P. R.ᵧ Co. Nº 10690 29	Hom'd Nº 103561 J.R. Wood / Horn'd Nº 103562 J.R. Wood 28 / Hom'd Nº 539349 C.L. Merritt / Horn'd Nº 99783 T. Russell	C. P. R.ᵧ Co. No. 9404 27
C. P. R.ᵧ Co. No. 9404 19	Horn'd No. 91575 D. Jerry the younger / Horn'd Nº 103776 T.N. Pattrick 20 / Horn'd No. 91568 J. Smith / Horn'd Nº 100697 F.H. Leavers	C. P. R.ᵧ Co. No.9404 21	Horn'd Nº 103563 T.P. Cullen / Hom'd Nº 107392 G. Crozier 22 / Horn Nº 103564 S.G. Sherlock / Hom Nº 108165 O.T. MELLAND
Horn'd 70666 G.F. Powna / C. P. R.ᵧ Co. Nº 10794 18 / Horn'd No. 91620 W.I. Banister	C. P. R.ᵧ Co. No. 9404 17	N.W.H.B. A1362 A2668 Charles R. Brown / Horn'd Nº 89482 C.R. Brown 16 / A2869 N.W.H.B. A1363 C.R. Brown	Can. Pac. Ry Grant No. 1111 15
C. P. R.ᵧ Co. No. 8366	H. B. Coy. Grant 8 95	Can. Pac. Ry. Grant No 1111 9	Sale No. 1810 10 Can. Agr. Coal and Colonization Coy
Time-Sale No. 4702 H. Banister / Homestead No. 59769 6 Ho... B...nister	Homestead No. 34414 R.E. Bannister / Horn'd Nº 89475 A.E. Banister	Can. Pac. Railway Grant No. 3173 The Can. Pac. Railway Company 5	Homestead Sale Nº 34802 / Homestead Time-Sale No. 34115 No. 5571 B.T. Ban... 4 RIVER

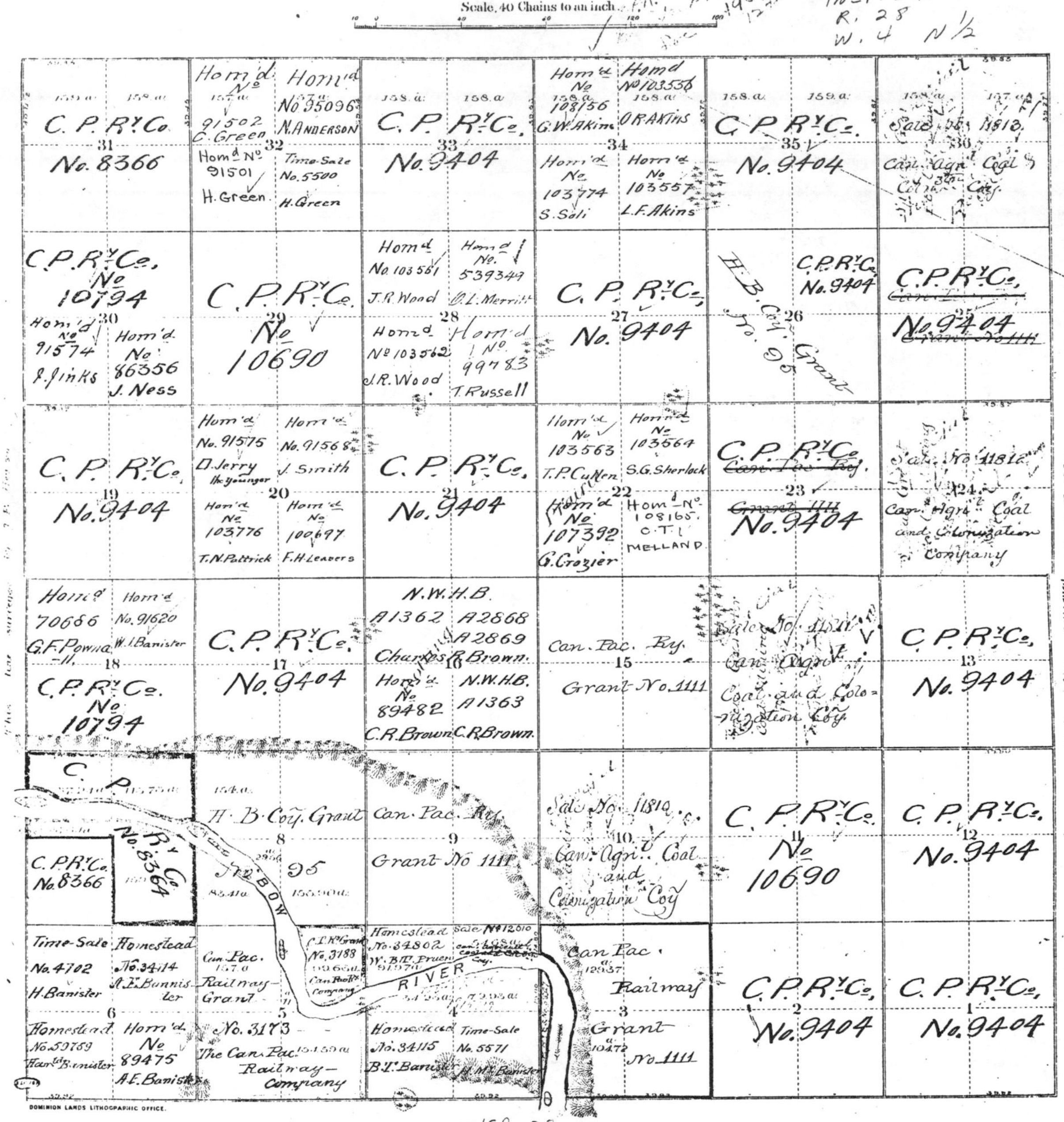

Dominion Lands Office
Ottawa

24th April 1885

TNSP. 22
R. 28
W 4 S ½

Contents:

Land in Sections .... 22720.62 Acres
Roads .... 15828 "

DOMINION LANDS LITHOGRAPHIC OFFICE.

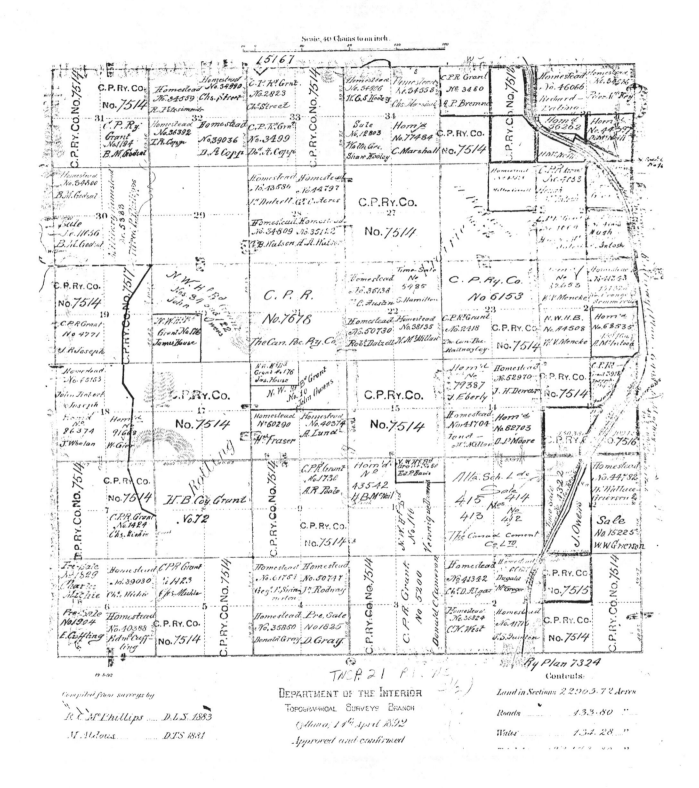

Scale, 40 Chains to an inch.

15167

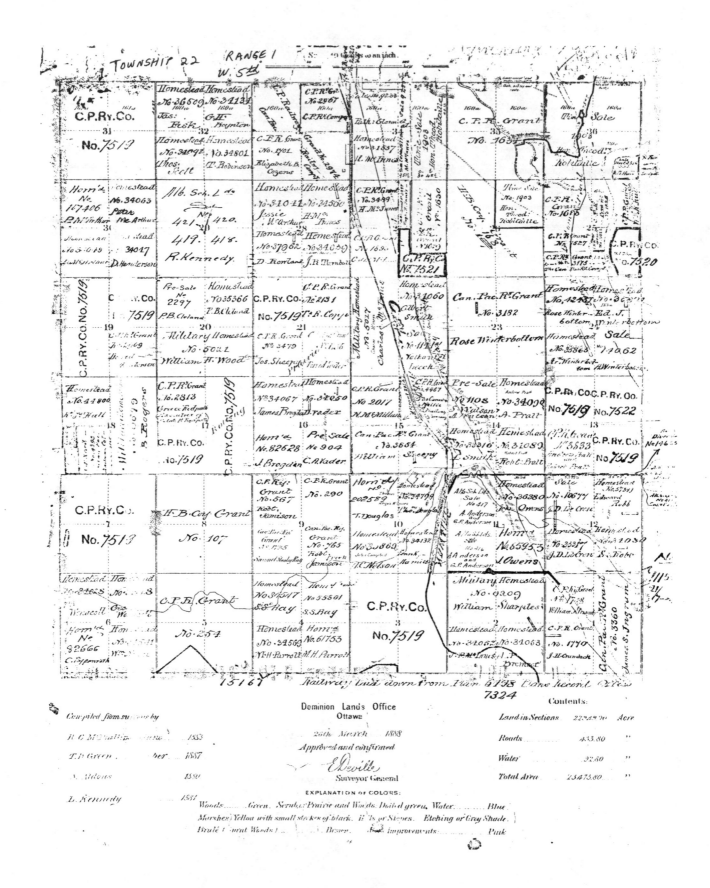

Compiled from surveys by

R. C. M?Phaillie 1883

T. D. Green 1887

?. Adams 1880

L. Kennedy 1881

Dominion Lands Office
Ottawa

26th March   1888

Approved and confirmed

E. Deville
Surveyor General

Contents:

Land in Sections	22342.20 Acres
Roads	433.80 "
Water	92.80 "
Total Area	23473.80 "

EXPLANATION OF COLORS:

Woods .... Green. Scrub or Prairie and Woods. Dotted green. Water .... Blue
Marshes Yellow with small stokes of black. Hills or Slopes. Etching or Grey Shade.
Brulé (Burnt Woods) .... Brown. Improvements .... Pink

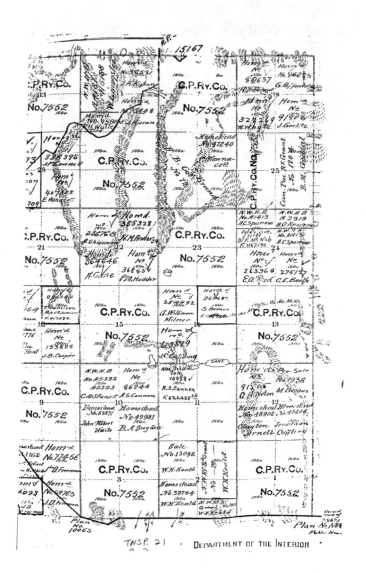

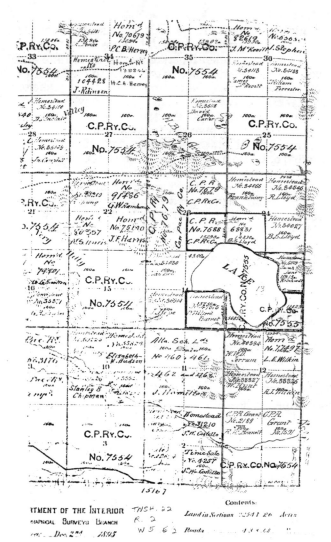

EPILOGUE

Within the pages of this book the history of the De Winton area comes to life. All those who have so willingly and conscientiously given of their time and expertise, delved into the past to unearth the histories of our pioneers, must be commended. It is a task not undertaken lightly — this historical epic which is for the most part factual, at the same time entertaining, for dullness has no place in today's readership.

Gamblers all, these pioneers who formed and chiselled out Alberta from raw wilderness. The first to arrive were the fur traders; then came the Canadian Pacific railway, carved by human sweat onto the face of a continent; bringing adventure of every sort but mostly farmers looking for free land.

Many years were to pass before a new breed of gambler made his appearance; a man with a drill who pushed his bit down into primeval wells filled with oil and brought unforeseen prosperity to Alberta, De Winton and surrounding area caught up in the inevitable boom.

You will find many accounts of how, at the turn of the century, land in western Canada was opened for homesteading. How land-hungry immigrants arrived in droves from Britain, Europe and the United States. The railroad tooted and steamed its way through unfenced prairie that stretched far as eye could see, sprinkling settlers at every whistle stop along the way.

With your mind's eye, follow that roughly clad man on the dusty street of an early Alberta village. He has a lean, get-it-done look about him. In any setting he would be tagged as a man of the land . . . an Alberta farmer who came west to build a new life with other freedom loving people. As with the farmer of today; there walked the spirit of independence and determination which forged the province out of a rugged inhospitable land.

Women and children in the homestead era were of necessity made of strong stuff. These were the days of flour sacks and lard pails; a waste not want not society. There were no promises of a rose garden. None was expected, but there is nothing more certain than home was where peace and contentment lay; a security around the old kitchen stove for the most part lacking in today's culture.

Not all immigrants were farmers. The sparse settlements that dotted the pioneer prairie revolved around the General store. It was at once a social center and post office; quite often the only building in town. The shelves lining the walls were filled with a conglomeration of staples such as flour, sugar, tea, coffee, syrup and the inevitable beans. But tucked here and there, without regard for orderly display, were horse harnesses, coal oil for lamps, bolts of dress goods and an assortment of sturdy boots.

This intrepid merchant was as much a part of the Alberta agricultural revolution as the grain binder. As binders gave way to a self-propelled combine, so the all-purpose General store gave way to the modern supermarket.

No one can deny the handsomeness and prosperity of the De Winton country. In any direction, your eye takes in the wealth of golden grainfields and poplar bluffs, pastures where cattle, horses and sheep munch away peaceable, slaking their thirst at nearby sloughs. It is indeed the promised land.

Westward, like toes on a giant's foot, the foothills rise to the Majestic mountains; playground for natives and tourists alike. We are rather complacent about it all. Not often do we take time out to give thanks for the good life and consider how it all came about. We mourn the lack of heroes in our past, envying other nations who tend to deify their heroes, not realizing they are after all, mostly myths. We keep poking around for a supposed identity; groping for a role. Unaware that we are fulfilling to the best of our ability the dreams of our forefathers.

This book was compiled to remember, and pay tribute to the pioneers of De Winton and area. The years go by; past history easily forgotten. Perhaps it would be fitting to end with a quote from Alfred Lord Tennyson:

"Love thou thy land; with love far-brought
From out the storied Past, and used
Within the Present, but transfused
Thro' future time by power of thought."

" BYGONE DAYS "

Five Generations. See Victor Poffenroth story by Hilda Poffenroth.

PRINTED IN CANADA